MW00813141

West's Law School Advisory Board

JESSE H. CHOPER
Professor of Law and Dean Emeritus,
University of California, Berkeley

JOSHUA DRESSLER
Professor of Law, Michael E. Moritz College of Law,
The Ohio State University

YALE KAMISAR
Professor of Law, University of San Diego
Professor of Law Emeritus, University of Michigan

MARY KAY KANE
Professor of Law, Chancellor and Dean Emeritus,
University of California,
Hastings College of the Law

LARRY D. KRAMER
Dean and Professor of Law, Stanford Law School

JONATHAN R. MACEY
Professor of Law, Yale Law School

ARTHUR R. MILLER
University Professor, New York University
Formerly Bruce Bromley Professor of Law, Harvard University

GRANT S. NELSON
Professor of Law, Pepperdine University
Professor of Law Emeritus, University of California, Los Angeles

A. BENJAMIN SPENCER
Professor of Law,
Washington & Lee University School of Law

JAMES J. WHITE
Professor of Law, University of Michigan

PUBLIC SECTOR EMPLOYMENT
CASES AND MATERIALS

Second Edition

■ ■ ■

By
Martin H. Malin
Professor of Law and Director, Institute for Law and the Workplace
Chicago–Kent College of Law/Illinois Institute of Technology
Ann C. Hodges
Professor of Law
University of Richmond School of Law
Joseph E. Slater
Eugene N. Balk Professor of Law and Values
University of Toledo College of Law

for
THE LABOR LAW GROUP

AMERICAN CASEBOOK SERIES®

WEST®
A Thomson Reuters business

Mat #41043295

Thomson Reuters created this publication to provide you with accurate and authoritative information concerning the subject matter covered. However, this publication was not necessarily prepared by persons licensed to practice law in a particular jurisdiction. Thomson Reuters does not render legal or other professional advice, and this publication is not a substitute for the advice of an attorney. If you require legal or other expert advice, you should seek the services of a competent attorney or other professional.

American Casebook Series is a trademark registered in the U.S. Patent and Trademark Office.

© 2004 THE LABOR LAW GROUP
© 2011 THE LABOR LAW GROUP

ISBN: 978–0–314–26599–9

To: Joyce Willenborg, my wife and best friend,
and our children Martha Malin and Catherine Malin

M.H.M.

To: my husband Stan Meyer and our children Debbie and
Chuck Hubler, Elizabeth and Keith Buchholz, and Lisa Meyer

A.C.H.

To: my wife Krista Schneider and our wonderful son Isaac Slater

J.E.S.

FOREWORD

The Labor Law Group had its origins in the desire of scholars to produce quality casebooks for instruction in labor and employment law. Over the course of its existence, the hallmarks of the group have been collaborative efforts among scholars, informed by skilled practitioners, under a cooperative non-profit trust in which royalties from past work finance future meetings and projects.

At the 1946 meeting of the Association of American Law Schools, Professor W. Willard Wirtz delivered a compelling paper criticizing the labor law course books then available. His remarks so impressed those present that the "Labor Law Roundtable" of the Association organized a general conference on the teaching of labor law to be held in Ann Arbor in 1947. The late Professor Robert E. Mathews served as coordinator for the Ann Arbor meeting and several conferees agreed to exchange proposals for sections of a new course book that would facilitate training exemplary practitioners of labor law. Beginning in 1948, a preliminary mimeographed version was used in seventeen schools; each user supplied comments and suggestions for change. In 1953, a hard-cover version was published under the title *Labor Relations and the Law*. The thirty-one "cooperating editors" were so convinced of the value of multi-campus collaboration that they gave up any individual claims to royalties. Instead, those royalties were paid to a trust fund to be used to develop and "provide the best possible materials" for training students in labor law and labor relations. The Declaration of Trust memorializing this agreement was executed November 4, 1953, and remains the Group's charter.

The founding committee's hope that the initial collaboration would bear fruit has been fulfilled. Under Professor Mathews' continuing chairmanship, the Group's members produced *Readings on Labor Law* in 1955 and *The Employment Relation and the Law* in 1957, edited by Robert Mathews and Benjamin Aaron. A second edition of *Labor Relations and the Law* appeared in 1960, with Benjamin Aaron and Donald H. Wollett as co-chairmen, and a third edition was published in 1965, with Jerre Williams at the helm.

In June of 1969, the Group, now chaired by William P. Murphy, sponsored a conference to reexamine the labor law curriculum. The meeting, held at the University of Colorado, was attended by practitioners and by full-time teachers including nonmembers as well as members of the Group. In meetings that followed the conference, the Group decided to reshape its work substantially. It restructured itself into ten task forces, each assigned a unit of no more than two hundred pages on a discrete topic such as employment discrimination or union-member relations. An individual teacher could then choose two or three of these units as the material around which to build a particular course. This multi-unit approach dominated the Group's work throughout much of the 1970s under Professor Murphy and his successor as chairman, Herbert L. Sherman, Jr.

As the 1970's progressed and teachers refined their views about what topics to include and how to address them, some units were dropped from the series while others increased in scope and length. Under Professor Sherman's chairmanship, the Group planned a new series of six enlarged books to cover the full range of topics taught by labor and employment law teachers. Professor James E. Jones, Jr., was elected chairman in 1978 and shepherded to completion the promised set of six full-size, independent casebooks. The Group continued to reevaluate its work and eventually decided that it was time to convene another conference of law teachers.

In 1984, the Group, now chaired by Robert Covington, sponsored another general conference to discuss developments in the substance and teaching of labor and employment law, this time at Park City, Utah. Those discussions and a subsequent working session led to the conclusion that the Group should devote principal attention to three new conventional length course books, one devoted to employment discrimination, one to union-management relations, and one to the individual employment relationship. In addition, work was planned on more abbreviated course books to serve as successors to the Group's earlier works covering public employment bargaining and labor arbitration.

In 1989, with Alvin Goldman as Chair, the Group met in Breckenridge, Colorado, to assess its most recent effort and develop plans for the future. In addition to outlining new course book projects, the Group discussed ways to assist teachers of labor and employment law in their efforts to expand conceptual horizons and perspectives. In pursuit of the latter goals it co-sponsored, in 1992, a conference held at the University of Toronto Faculty of Law at which legal and nonlegal specialists examined alternative models of corporate governance and their impact on workers.

When Robert J. Rabin became Chair in 1996, the Group and a number of invited guests met in Tucson, Arizona, to celebrate the imminent fiftieth anniversary of the Group. The topics of discussion included the impact of the global economy and of changing forms of representation on the teaching of labor and employment law, and the impact of new technologies of electronic publishing on the preparation of teaching materials. The Group honored three of its members who had been present at the creation of the Group, Willard Wirtz, Ben Aaron, and Clyde Summers. The Group next met in Scottsdale, Arizona in December, 1999, to discuss the production of materials that would more effectively bring emerging issues of labor and employment law into the classroom. Among the issues discussed were integration of international and comparative materials into the labor and employment curriculum and the pedagogical uses of the World Wide Web.

Laura J. Cooper became Chair of the Group in July, 2001. In June, 2003, the Group met in Alton, Ontario, Canada. The focus there was on labor law on the edge, looking at doctrinal synergies between workplace law and other legal and social-science disciplines, and workers on the edge, exploring the legal issues of highly-compensated technology workers, vulnerable immigrant employees, and unionized manufacturing employees threatened by foreign competition. The Group also heard a report from its study of the status of the teaching of labor and employment law in the nation's law schools and discussed the implications of the study for the Group's future projects. Members of the Group began work on a case book on international labor law at this meeting. During Professor Cooper's term the Group also finished its popular reader *Labor Law Stories* which examines the stories behind many of the most important American labor law cases.

In July 2005, Kenneth G. Dau–Schmidt became the Chair of the Labor Law Group. Shortly after his election, the Group held a meeting in Chicago with nationally recognized practitioners to discuss how best to teach students about the practice of labor law in the new global economy of the information age. The outline that resulted from this meeting served as the basis for *Labor Law in the Contemporary Workplace*. Since the Chicago meeting, the Group has met again three times to discuss and work on new editions of its books and new projects: June 2006 in Saratoga Springs, New York; June 2007 in St. Charles, Illinois; and June 2010 in Lake Arrowhead, California. Other Group projects that grew out of or benefited from these meetings include *International Labor Law: Cases and Materials on Workers' Rights in the Global Economy* and *A Concise Hornbook on Employment Law*. The Group has also hosted: a November 2007 symposium on the problems of low-wage workers, the proceedings of which were published in the *Minnesota Law Review*; a February 2009 symposium on the American Law Institute's Proposed Restatement of Employment Law, the proceedings of which were published in the *Employee Rights and Employment Policy Journal*; and a November 2010 symposium on labor and employment law policies under the Obama administration, the proceedings of which will be published in the *Indiana Law Journal*.

At any one time, roughly twenty-five to thirty persons are actively engaged in the Group's work; this has proven a practical size, given problems of communication and logistics. Coordination and editorial review of the projects are the responsibility of the executive committee, whose members are the successor trustees of the Group. Governance is by consensus; votes are taken only to elect trustees and to determine whom to invite to join the Group. Since 1953, more than eighty persons have worked on Group projects; in keeping with the original agreement, none has ever received anything more than reimbursement of expenses.

The Labor Law Group currently has eight books in print. In addition to this volume, West has published: *Principles of Employment Law* by Rafael Gely, Ann C. Hodges, Peggie R. Smith, and Susan J. Stabile; *Labor Law in the Contemporary Workplace,* by Kenneth G. Dau–Schmidt, Martin H. Malin, Roberto L. Corrada, Christopher David Ruiz Cameron and Catherine L. Fisk; *International Labor Law: Cases and Materials on Workers' Rights in the Global Economy,* by James Atleson, Lance Compa, Kerry Rittich, Calvin William Sharpe and Marley S. Weiss; *Employment Discrimination Law: Cases and Materials on Equality in the Workplace* (Eighth Edition), by Dianne

Avery, Maria L. Ontiveros, Roberto L. Corrada, Michael L. Selmi and Melissa Hart; *ADR in the Workplace* (Second Edition), by Laura J. Cooper, Dennis R. Nolan and Richard A. Bales; and *Legal Protection for the Individual Employee* (Fourth Edition), by Matthew W. Finkin, Kenneth G. Dau–Schmidt, and Robert N. Covington. Foundation Press has published the Group's eighth book, *Labor Law Stories*, edited by Laura J. Cooper and Catherine L. Fisk.

THE EXECUTIVE COMMITTEE

PREFACE

Since 1971, when the Labor Law Group first published a casebook on public sector labor law under the authorship of Donald Wollett and Don Sears, the field has changed dramatically. The skepticism which characterized early legislative and judicial attitudes toward collective bargaining in the public sector has been replaced by general acceptance. Union organization in the public sector, in contrast to the private sector, has continued to grow. In 2009, for the first time in history, a majority of union members in the United States were employed by a unit of government. Debates over whether the public sector is different from the private sector have become more nuanced, focusing on the inevitably political context of public sector bargaining and its implications for the structure and processes of bargaining and dispute resolution. And while private sector labor law continues to provide a model for the public sector, there has been a good deal of experimentation, at both federal and state levels, with different ways of structuring the bargaining relationship. Perhaps the most notable experimentation since publication of the prior edition of this book has been the requirement in several states that employers recognize exclusive bargaining representatives on the basis of authorization cards signed by a majority of the members of the bargaining unit, without the need for a representation election.

Succeeding editions of the original casebook, *Collective Bargaining in Public Employment*, with continued authorship by Donald Wollett along with Joseph Grodin, Reginald Alleyne and, later, June Weisberger, sought to bring developments up to date through modifications within the same basic format. Ten years after the last edition of that book, it became apparent that a brand new volume was required. This new book, *Public Sector Employment,* first published in 2004, authored by Joseph Grodin, June Weisberger and Martin Malin as a successor to *Collective Bargaining in Public Employment,* extended coverage to include the individual employee-employer relationship in the public sector, including constitutional rights of public employees and civil service and tenure systems. This edition continues the evolution of the book with expanded coverage of constitutional rights of public employees and civil service and tenure systems. The new edition further develops legislation governing the public sector workplace, including special Fair Labor Standards Act rules and whistleblower protection. It also covers Tenth and Eleventh Amendment limitations on federal regulation of state and local government employment relationships. Accordingly, the book should be useful for courses on public sector employment even in the minority of jurisdictions that have no public employee bargaining statutes.

The new edition updates the material from the first edition. Developments since the first edition have included the debate over the compatibility of collective bargaining for public employees with national security, including the litigation over regulations issued by the Departments of Defense and Homeland Security that greatly restricted the scope of bargaining; the move by a number of states to requiring card check recognition; and significant constitutional decisions such as *Garcetti v. Ceballos*, 547 U.S. 410, 126 S.Ct. 1951, 164 L.Ed.2d 689 (2006) and *Engquist v. Oregon Department of Agriculture*, 553 U.S. 591, 128 S.Ct. 2146, 170 L.Ed.2d 975 (2008). References to statutes and regulations are current as of at least July 2010. We have retained the emphasis upon state law but, we have included substantial references to developments regarding federal employee labor relations. We continue to contrast public sector employment with the private sector, and to raise questions concerning the degree to which the private sector model should apply when government is the employer.

It remains the case that there is no one body of public sector labor law. Indeed, one of the attractions of courses on public sector employment is that the different jurisdictions truly serve as laboratories for different approaches to the issues and allow for comparisons across jurisdictions. We have included material from a wide array of states, but we assume that professors and students will want to supplement the materials in this casebook with materials from their own jurisdictions. A convenient source of information about the law in different jurisdictions is the Association of Labor Relations Agencies (ALRA). ALRA's membership consists of the national, state, provincial and local labor relations agencies in the United States and Canada. Its website, www.alra.org, contains links to the websites of its member agencies which, in turn, contain links to statutes, regulations and decisions of their jurisdictions.

A few notes about the editing of cases and readings. We have edited out most footnotes, but retained those we believe to be particularly significant or pedagogically useful. In those cases, we retained the original footnote numbers. We have used asterisks instead of ellipses to indicate where we have deleted material in the editing process but also edited out lengthy string citations and pinpoint citations without indicating this with asterisks. Where cases quoted material and used ellipses, we replaced the ellipses with asterisks. We have added parallel citations and otherwise standardized type face and citation style.

We gratefully acknowledge the efforts of many others who helped make this book a reality. We thank Cass Casper (Chicago–Kent College of Law), Paul Falabella, Joseph Laws and Joyce Yoon (University of Richmond) and Kelly Walsh and Sarah Corney (University of Toledo) who provided crucial research assistance and Meredith Fleming (University of Richmond) who provided editorial assistance. We deeply appreciate the invaluable administrative and secretarial support from Sharon Wyatt–Jordan at Chicago–Kent and technical assistance from Lucy Moss of the Chicago–Kent College of Law Library. We thank the following professionals for very helpful comments during the revision process: Martin W. Baumgaertner, R. Douglas Collins, Peter Davis, William Herbert, and Daniel Nielsen. We acknowledge helpful comments on drafts of various chapters from our colleagues in The Labor Law Group. We appreciate financial support from the Labor Law Group, the Hunton & Williams Summer Research Fund at the University of Richmond, and the Marshall–Ewell Research Fund at Chicago–Kent College of Law. Most of all, we express our gratitude to those who came before us on *Collective Bargaining in Public Employment* and the first edition of *Public Sector Employment*: Donald Wollett, Don Sears, Reginald Alleyne, Joseph Grodin and June Weisberger.

MARTIN H. MALIN
CHICAGO, ILLINOIS

ANN C. HODGES
RICHMOND, VIRGINIA

JOSEPH E. SLATER
TOLEDO, OHIO

August 2010

THE LABOR LAW GROUP

Executive Committee

Kenneth G. Dau–Schmidt
Chair
Indiana University—Bloomington

Richard A. Bales
Northern Kentucky University

Lance Compa
Cornell University

Laura Cooper
University of Minnesota

Marion G. Crain
Washington University—St. Louis

Catherine L. Fisk
University of California—Irvine

Martin H. Malin
Illinois Institute of Technology, Chicago–Kent College of Law

---

Dennis Nolan
University of South Carolina

Peggie Smith
Washington University—St. Louis

The Labor Law Group

Editorial Policy Committee

Richard A. Bales
Northern Kentucky University

Lance Compa
Cornell University

Laura Cooper
University of Minnesota

Kenneth G. Dau–Schmidt
Indiana University—Bloomington

Joel W. Friedman
Tulane University

Rafael Gely
University of Missouri

Melissa Hart
Colorado University

Ann Hodges
University of Richmond

Alan Hyde
Rutgers University

Michael Selmi
George Washington University

Peggie Smith
Washington University—St. Louis

Lea S. VanderVelde
University of Iowa

The Labor Law Group

Currently Participating Members

Steven D. Anderman
University of Essex

James Atleson
State University of New York, Buffalo

Dianne Avery
State University of New York, Buffalo

Richard A. Bales
Northern Kentucky University

Stephen Befort
University of Minnesota

Robert Belton
Vanderbilt University

Dr. Roger Blanpain
Institut voor Arbeidsrecht

Christopher David Ruiz Cameron
Southwestern Law School, Los Angeles

Lance Compa
Cornell University

Laura Cooper
University of Minnesota

Robert L. Corrada
University of Denver

Robert N. Covington
Vanderbilt University

Marion G. Crain
Washington University—St. Louis

Kenneth G. Dau-Schmidt
Indiana University—Bloomington

Cynthia Estlund
New York University

Matthew Finkin
University of Illinois

Catherine L. Fisk
University of California—Irvine

Joel W. Friedman
Tulane University

Ruben J. Garcia
California Western School of Law

Rafael Gely
University of Missouri

✈ Melissa Hart
Colorado University

Ann Hodges
University of Richmond

Alan Hyde
Rutgers University

Brian A. Langille
University of Toronto

Pauline T. Kim
Washington University B St. Louis

Tom Kohler
Boston College

Orly Lobel
University of San Diego

Deborah Malamud
New York University

✈ Martin H. Malin
Illinois Institute of Technology, Chicago–Kent College of Law

Mordehai Mironi
University of Haifa

Robert B. Moberly
University of Arkansas

Dennis R. Nolan
University of South Carolina

Maria L. Ontiveros
University of San Francisco

Kerry Rittich
University of Toronto

Michael Selmi
George Washington University

Calvin W. Sharpe
Case Western Reserve University

Joseph E. Slater
University of Toledo

Sara Slinn
York University

Peggie R. Smith
Washington University—St. Louis

Susan Stabile
University of St. Thomas

Katherine V. W. Stone
University of California—Los Angeles

Lea S. VanderVelde
University of Iowa

Marley Weiss
University of Maryland

Michael Wishnie
New York University

Noah Zatz
University of California—Los Angeles

Affiliated Practitioners

David A. Rosenfeld
Weinberg, Roger & Rosenfeld, Alameda, CA

Eugene Scalia
Gibson Dunn, Washington, DC

Other Members

Harry W. Arthurs
York University (Emeritus)

Alfred W. Blumrosen
Rutgers University (Emeritus)

John E. Dunsford
St. Louis University

Julius G. Getman
University of Texas (Emeritus)

Alvin L. Goldman
University of Kentucky (Emeritus)

Joseph R. Grodin
University of California—Hastings (Emeritus)

James E. Jones, Jr.
University of Wisconsin—Madison (Emeritus)

Charles J. Morris
Southern Methodist University (Emeritus)

Cornelius J. Peck
University of Washington (Emeritus)

Robert J. Rabin
Syracuse University

George Schatzki
Arizona State University (Emeritus)

Herbert L. Sherman, Jr.
University of Pittsburgh (Emeritus)

Eileen Silverstein
University of Connecticut (Emeritus)

Clyde Summers
University of Pennsylvania (Emeritus)

June Weisberger
University of WisconsinBMadison (Emeritus)

Donald H. Wollett
University of the Pacific (Emeritus)

Founding Trustees

The Late Robert E. Matthews

The Late Bertram Willcox

The Late W. Willard Wirtz

Acknowledgements and Permissions

The authors gratefully acknowledge the following permissions to reprint copyrighted materials:

Chapter 4.

Joseph E. Slater, *The Court Does Not Know What a Labor Union Is: How State Structures and Judicial (Mis)constructions Deformed Public Labor Law*, 79 Oregon Law Review 981 (2000), reprinted with permission of the author and of the Oregon Law Review.

Richard B. Freeman, *Through Public Sector Eyes: Employee Attitudes Toward Public Sector Labor Relations in the U.S., in Public Sector Employment in a Time of Transition* (Dale Belman et al., eds. IRRA 1996) pp. 59–83, reprinted with permission of the Industrial Relations Research Association

Clyde Summers, *Bargaining in the Governtnent's Business: Principles and Politics*, 18 University of Toledo Law Review 265 (1987), reprinted with permission of the author and of the University of Toledo Law Review.

George Nesterczuk, with Donald Devine and Robert Moffit, *Taking Charge of Federal Personnel*, Heritage Foundation Backgrounder #1404 (2001) reprinted with permission of the author and of the Heritage Foundation.

Joseph E. Slater, *Homeland Security vs. Workers Rights? What the Federal Government Should Learn from History and Experience, and Why*, 6 University of Pennsylvania Journal of Labor and Employment Law 295 (2004), reprinted with permission of the author and of the University of Pennsylvania Journal of Labor and Employment Law.

Ann C. Hodges, *Lessons from the Laboratory: The Polar Opposites on the Public Sector Labor Law Spectrum*, 18 Cornell Journal of Law and Public Policy 735, 749–55 (2009), reprinted with permission of the author.

Chapter 6.

Clyde Summers, *Bargaining in the Government's Business: Principles and Politics*, 18 University of Toledo Law Review 265 (1987), reprinted with permission of the author and of the University of Toledo Law Review.

Eli Rock, *The Appropriate Unit Question in the Public Service: The Problem of Proliferation*, 67 Michigan Law Review 1001 (1969), reprinted with permission of the Michigan Law Review.

Peggie R. Smith, *The Publicization of Home-Based Care Work in State Labor Law*, 92 Minnesota Law Review 1390 (2008), reprinted with the permission of the author and of the Minnesota Law Review.

Chapter 8.

June Miller Weisberger, *The Appropriate Scope of Bargaining in the Public Sector: The Continuing Controversy and the Wisconsin Experience*, 1997 Wisconsin Law Review 685, Copyright 1977 by the Board of Regents of the University of Wisconsin System, reprinted with permission of the author and of the Wisconsin Law Review.

Donald H. Wollett, *The Bargaining Process in the Public Sector: What is Bargainable?*, 51 Oregon Law Review 177 (1971), reprinted with permission of the author and the Oregon Law Review.

Martin H. Malin, *The Paradox of Public Sector Labor Law*, 84 Indiana Law Journal 1369 (2009), reprinted with permission of the author.

Ann C. Hodges, *The Interplay of Civil Service Law and Collective Bargaining in Public Sector Employee Discipline Cases*, 32 Boston College Law Review 95 (1990), reprinted with permission of the author.

Chapter 9.

Martin H. Malin, *Public Employees' Right to Strike: Law and Experience*, 26 University of Michigan Journal of Law Reform 313 (1993), reprinted with permission of the author and of the University of Michigan Journal of Law Reform.

Chapter 10.

George Taylor, *Public Employment: Strikes or Procedures?*, 20 Industrial & Labor Relations Review 617 (1967), reprinted with permission of the Industrial & Labor Relations Review.

Deborah Kolb, *The Mediators* (M.I.T. Press 1983), reprinted with permission of the author and of M.I.T. Press.

Joseph R. Grodin & Joyce M. Najita, Judicial Response to Arbitration, in *Public Sector Bargaining* (Benjamin Aaron et al., eds, 2d ed. IRRA, BNA 1988), reprinted with permission of the Industrial Relations Research Association.

Chapter 11.

Ann C. Hodges, *The Steelworker Trilogy in the Public Sector*, 66 Chicago–Kent Law Review 631 (1992), reprinted with permission of the author and the Chicago–Kent Law Review.

SUMMARY OF CONTENTS

TABLE OF CONTENTS

Table of Cases

The principal cases are in bold type. Cases cited or discussed in the text are in roman type. References are to pages. Cases cited in principal cases and within other quoted materials are not included.

PUBLIC SECTOR EMPLOYMENT
CASES AND MATERIALS

Second Edition

CHAPTER 1

INTRODUCTION

■ ■ ■

This casebook examines legal rules and related policy issues in public sector employment. Government employers and their employees are a significant part of overall employment in the U.S. In 2009, governments at various levels employed more than 22 million people, which was 17 percent of all U.S. employment. Local governments alone had more than 14.5 million employees.[1] Thus, attorneys who practice labor and employment law are likely to encounter public sector issues, and they should be aware of special rules and concerns in this area.

Public employment, the laws governing such employment, and policy debates involving such laws have a long history. Government bodies in the U.S. have always had employees, and some public workers had organized unions as early as the 1830s. In the nineteenth century, government was smaller, and unionized public workers were often members of mostly private sector unions, for example members of skilled trade unions working in naval yards. Still, government employees often lobbied for laws covering their employment. Public workers in Philadelphia won the ten-hour day after a protest in 1835. In 1840, President Martin Van Buren signed an executive order establishing the ten-hour day on federal works' projects. In 1861, Congress passed laws providing that the hours and wages for the employees of the Navy would be comparable to those for similar jobs in private industry.[2]

The first known formal agreement between a municipal agency and a union was signed by the Chicago Electricity Department in 1905. Early public sector unions also worked to pass civil service statutes, as their members generally did better in the absence of the political patronage "machines" that the merit system was designed to undercut.[3] The second decade of the twentieth century saw an increase in public sector unionism that was cut short by the Boston police strike of 1919 (discussed further in Chapter 4, section A). The growth of public sector unions really took off

1. Donald J. Boyd, *State/Local Employment Up Slightly Since Start of Recession, But Cuts Are Now Underway*, The Nelson A. Rockefeller Institute of Government (Aug. 20, 2009).

2. Joseph Slater, *Public Workers: Government Employee Unions, the Law, and the State, 1900–62* 16 (2004).

3. *Id.* at 17.

beginning in the 1960s, as states finally started enacting laws providing for collective bargaining rights for public employees.

The laws governing public sector employment differ from those governing the private sector in three significant ways, and this book will address all three. First, some laws and legal doctrines which are very important in the public sector simply do not apply to the private sector: *e.g.*, civil service laws, and Constitutional rules. Second, labor law—rules governing the relations of unions and employers—is especially important due to the high union density in the public sector. Notably, public sector labor law can differ from private sector labor law in some important respects, and public sector laws themselves vary considerably among different jurisdictions. Third, some employment laws have special rules that apply only to the public sector and not to the private sector: *e.g.*, Fair Labor Standard Act (FLSA) rules permitting the award of compensatory time for overtime work.

This book discusses each of these areas. For example, civil service rules often set both basic entrance requirements for jobs and require some form of "just cause" for discharge. These rules have a long history. The Pendleton Act of 1883, passed in response to an assassination attempt on President Garfield by a man allegedly disappointed by not receiving a patronage job, attempted to decrease the role of political spoils and increase the role of merit in federal employment. It created civil service exams, barred dismissals of covered employees for political reasons, and created a Civil Service Commission to enforce these rules. State governments followed suit in the twentieth century, and today most public employers are covered by civil service rules that incorporate these same principles and procedures. This book describes the law and policy of civil service laws, and other laws unique to the public sector, such as teacher tenure laws.

Public employment also involves Constitutional law. The government acting as an employer is state action and, since the 1960s, courts have held that public employment generally cannot be conditioned on relinquishing a Constitutional right. Thus, public employees have certain rights under the First Amendment, Fourth Amendment, and other parts of the Constitution *vis-a-vis* their employers. But public employers have certain rights as *employers* toward their employees that the government does not have toward citizens at large. This book shows how courts balance these rights in crafting constitutional law doctrines in public employment.

Labor law is central because unions are very active in the public sector. In 2009, more public employees (7.9 million) belonged to a union than did private sector employees (7.4 million), despite there being five times more workers in the private sector. The union density rate in the public sector as a whole was 37.4%, with union density in local government at 43.3% (reflecting, among other things, the especially high unionization rates of police, firefighters, and teachers). Those density rates refer to percentage of eligible employees who are actually union members. Including employees who are not union members but who are covered by union contracts (see Chapter 12 for an explanation of that), the overall unionization rate in the public sector in 2009 was 41.1%, and the rate in local government employment was 46.8%.[4] Thus lawyers involved in government or labor relations are almost certain to encounter public sector labor law.

This book highlights the many significant variations of public sector labor law. While private sector labor law is set by one of two federal statutes, public sector law is mostly state and local law, and it varies dramatically among states and sometimes even within states. A majority of states give most of their public employees the right to bargain collectively through unions, but some states only give that right to a few specific types of public employees, and some states do not give any statutory authorization for public sector collective bargaining at all. Some states allow some public sector unions to strike; most do not. The states that allow collective bargaining but not strikes have adopted a wide range of procedures to resolve bargaining impasses. Public sector labor laws also differ among each other and diverge from private sector labor law on the issue of what topics unions may negotiate and on a number of other points.

All these differences reflect important and interesting policy choices, which the book also discusses. Most broadly, to what extent should labor and employment law rules from the private sector simply be extended to the public sector, and to what extent is government employment sufficiently different to justify different rules? From the point of view of the employee, public and private employment may often look very similar. From the point of view of the employer, and arguably the public, they can look quite distinct in some regards. The law has treated the two sectors differently in some ways for a considerable amount of time. For example, public employees have long enjoyed civil service protections and private employees have not. On the other hand, private employees won collective bargaining rights long before public employees did, and even today private employees have more rights under labor laws than do government workers. Can public sector collective bargaining have an anti-democratic effect, by giving unions the power to determine certain conditions of public employment that should rightly be left to public officials? Or does bargaining improve morale and the quality of the workforce by giving employees a voice, and better pay and working conditions? These debates, as old as the Boston police strike, continue on into the twenty-first century, as debates over bargaining rights for employees of the Department of Homeland Security and the Transportation Safety Administration (discussed in Chapter 4) demonstrate.

This edition of the book has expanded its coverage in all these areas from the previous edition. It describes civil service and teacher tenure

4. Bureau of Labor Statistics, *Union Members Summary*, USDL–10–0069 (Jan. 22, 2010).

laws in much more detail. It includes new sections on, among other things, the special FLSA rules for the public sector, Eleventh Amendment immunity for states from suits under certain employment laws, and union activity in states without collective bargaining laws. There are more materials on federal employment, including the Merit Service Protections Board and debates over labor and employment rights at the Department of Homeland Security, and more materials on Constitutional law in public employment. All previously existing sections of the book have been expanded and updated.

The book starts with the Constitutional rights which apply to all public employees. It then moves to statutory employment law rights, including a type of constitutional immunity states have from certain employment law suits, special FLSA rules, civil service laws, teacher tenure laws, and whistleblower protections. Next, the book focuses on public sector labor law: the right to form unions; the right to bargain; what topics are negotiable; how impasses are resolved (including but not limited to strikes and interest arbitration); the administration of the collective bargaining agreement; and rights of individual union members. A section also examines union activity in the absence of statutory protection. Throughout, the book covers both legal rules and the policy arguments for and against various approaches. Because the law of public sector employment is controversial, it is often being significantly revised in response to policy and political concerns. Students considering entering this field need to know not just what the law is, but also why it may change, and what it may become.

Chapter 2

Constitutional Rights of Public Employees

■ ■ ■

Because the actions of public employers are by definition governmental actions, public employees enjoy a measure of protection under federal and state constitutions which is generally not available to private employees. Under the U.S. Constitution, those protections expanded in the 1960s with the demise of the "privilege-right" distinction. In the 1970s, independent state constitutional jurisprudence took root and began to blossom. This chapter examines these developments.

A. THE DEMISE OF THE "PRIVILEGE–RIGHT" DISTINCTION

One important difference between public and private employment is that when a public employer takes some action with respect to its employees, that action is a state action. Thus, the "state action" requirement for application of federal (and most state) constitutional protection is obviously satisfied.

Before the 1960s, however, the legal consequences of this obvious proposition were severely limited. Courts held that because public employment is a "privilege" rather than a "right," public employees may be required to relinquish their constitutional rights as citizens in order to obtain or maintain employment. As Justice Holmes put it when he was on the Supreme Judicial Court of Massachusetts, in an opinion rejecting a police officer's claim of interference with his free speech rights, "[t]he petitioner may have a constitutional right to talk politics but he has no constitutional right to be a policeman." *McAuliffe v. New Bedford*, 155 Mass. 216, 29 N.E. 517 (1892). That proposition was called into question in the cases which follow.

GARRITY v. NEW JERSEY

United States Supreme Court, 1967.
385 U.S. 493, 87 S.Ct. 616, 17 L.Ed.2d 562.

[A New Jersey statute provided for dismissal of "any person holding * * * any elective or appointive office, position or employment" who "refuses to testify upon matters relating to the office, position or employment in any criminal proceeding wherein he is a defendant or is called as a witness on behalf of the prosecution, upon the ground that his answer may tend to incriminate him or compel him to be a witness against himself * * *." Appellants, police officers accused of fixing traffic tickets, made incriminating statements after being warned that invocation of the privilege against self incrimination would lead to dismissal, and these statements were subsequently used to convict them of conspiracy to obstruct administration of the traffic laws. The officers appealed, contending that their statements were unconstitutionally coerced.]

DOUGLAS, J. delivered the opinion of the Court.

* * *

The choice given petitioners was either to forfeit their jobs or to incriminate themselves. The option to lose their means of a livelihood or to pay the penalty of self-incrimination is the antithesis of free choice to speak out or to remain silent. That practice, like interrogation practices we reviewed in *Miranda v. State of Arizona*, 384 U.S. 436, 86 S.Ct. 1602, 16 L.Ed.2d 694 (1966), is "likely to exert such pressure upon an individual as to disable him from making a free and rational choice." We think the statements were infected by the coercion inherent in this scheme of questioning and cannot be sustained as voluntary under our prior decisions.

* * *

Mr. Justice Holmes in *McAuliffe v. New Bedford*, 155 Mass. 216, 29 N.E. 517 (1892), stated a dictum on which New Jersey heavily relies: "The petitioner may have a constitutional right to talk politics, but he has no constitutional right to be a policeman. There are few employments for hire in which the servant does not agree to suspend his constitutional right of free speech as well as of idleness by the implied terms of his contract. The servant cannot complain, as he takes the employment on the terms which are offered him. On the same principle the city may impose any reasonable condition upon holding offices within its control."

The question in this case, however, is not cognizable in those terms. Our question is whether a State, contrary to the requirement of the Fourteenth Amendment, can use the threat of discharge to secure incriminatory evidence against an employee. We held in *Slochower v. Board of Education*, 350 U.S. 551, 76 S.Ct. 637, 100 L.Ed. 692 (1956), that a public school teacher could not be discharged merely because he had invoked the Fifth Amendment privilege against self-incrimination when questioned by a congressional committee: "The privilege against self-incrimination would be reduced to a hollow mockery if its exercise could be taken as equivalent either to a confession of guilt or a conclusive presumption of perjury. * * * The privilege [against self-incrimination] serves to protect the innocent who otherwise might be ensnared by ambiguous circumstances."

We conclude that policemen, like teachers and lawyers, are not relegated to a watered-down version of constitutional rights. There are rights of constitutional stature whose exercise a State may not condition by the exaction of a price. Engaging in interstate commerce is one. Resort to the federal courts in diversity of citizenship cases is another. Assertion of a First Amendment right is still another. The imposition of a burden on the exercise of a Twenty-fourth Amendment right is also banned. We now hold that the protection of the individual under the Fourteenth Amendment against coerced statements prohibits use in subsequent criminal proceedings of statements obtained under threat of removal from office, and that it extends to all, whether they are policemen or other members of our body politic.

Reversed.

NOTES

1. What distinction did the Court make between *McAuliffe* and *Garrity*?

2. See also *Uniformed Sanitation Men Association v. Commissioner of Sanitation*, 392 U.S. 280, 88 S.Ct. 1917, 20 L.Ed.2d 1089 (1968) (holding unconstitutional discharge of city employees for refusal to sign waivers of immunity before grand jury or for invoking their constitutional privilege against self-incrimination before investigation commissioner, who had advised them that their answers could be used against them in subsequent proceedings).

3. Do the Court's decisions interfere with the ability of the employer to investigate possible employee misconduct? See *Lefkowitz v. Turley*, 414 U.S. 70, 84–85, 94 S.Ct. 316, 325–26, 38 L.Ed.2d 274, 285–86 (1973) where the court stated:

> Although due regard for the Fifth Amendment forbids the State to compel incriminating answers from its employees and contractors that may be used against them in criminal proceedings, the Constitution permits that very testimony to be compelled if neither it nor its fruits are available for such use. *Kastigar v. United States*, supra. * * * Also, given adequate immunity, the State may plainly insist that employees either answer questions under oath about the performance of their job or suffer the loss of employment. But the State may not insist that appellees waive their Fifth Amendment privilege against self-incrimination and consent to the use of the fruits of the interrogation in any later proceedings brought against them. Rather, the State must recognize what our cases hold: that answers elicited upon the threat of the loss of employment are compelled and inadmissible in evidence.

4. *Keyishian v. Board of Regents*, 385 U.S. 589, 87 S.Ct. 675, 17 L.Ed.2d 629 (1967), decided in the same term as *Garrity*, held unconstitutional, under the First Amendment, a New York regulation which required every college teacher to certify that he was not a Communist. The regulation also required any teacher who had ever been a Communist communicate that fact to the President of the State University. Acknowledging that a similar requirement had been upheld by the Court in *Adler v. Board of Education,* 342 U.S. 485, 72 S.Ct. 380, 96 L.Ed. 517 (1952), the Court, in an opinion by Justice Brennan, declared: "Constitutional doctrine which has emerged since that decision has rejected its [premise] that public employment, including academic employment, may be conditioned upon the surrender of constitutional rights which could not be abridged by direct government action."

5. Does it follow from the Court's rejection of the "privilege" argument in *Garrity* and *Keyishian* that public employers may not impose upon their employees any restrictions they could not impose upon citizens generally? Or does the existence of an employment relationship and the obligations of government to provide efficient and adequate public services justify some restrictions upon what, for citizens generally, would be protected constitutional rights?

B. FREEDOM OF SPEECH

The year after *Keyishian*, in *Pickering v. Board of Education*, 391 U.S. 563, 88 S.Ct. 1731, 20 L.Ed.2d 811 (1968), the Court held that the First Amendment precluded dismissal of a public school teacher for writing a letter to a newspaper criticizing the school board's handling of a revenue measure and its allocation of funds between educational and athletic programs. The Court acknowledged, however:

> [T]he State has interests as an employer in regulating the speech of its employees that differ significantly from those it possesses in connection with regulation of the citizenry in general. The problem in any case is to arrive at a balance between the interests of the teacher, as a citizen, in commenting upon matters of public concern and the interests of the State, as an employer, in promoting the efficiency of the public services it performs through its employees * * *. [T]he question whether a school system requires additional funds is a matter of legitimate public concern on which the judgment of the school administration, including the School Board, cannot, in a society which leaves such a question to popular vote, be taken as conclusive. On such a question free and open debate is vital to informed decision-making by the electorate. Teachers are, as a class, the members of a community most likely to have informed and definite opinions as to how funds allotted to the operation of the schools should be spent. Accordingly, it is essential that they be able to speak out freely on such questions without fear of retaliatory dismissal. [Pickering's statements were] critical of the ultimate employer but [had not been shown] to have in any way either impeded the teacher's proper performance of his daily duties in the classroom or to have interfered

with the regular operation of the schools generally. In these circumstances we conclude that the interest of the school administrator in limiting teachers' opportunities to contribute to a public debate is not significantly greater than its interest in limiting a similar contribution by any member of the general public.

CONNICK v. MYERS

United States Supreme Court, 1983.
461 U.S. 138, 103 S.Ct. 1684, 75 L.Ed.2d 708.

WHITE, J. delivered the opinion of the Court.

In *Pickering v. Board of Education* [391 U.S. 563, 88 S.Ct. 1731, 20 L.Ed.2d 811 (1968)], we stated that a public employee does not relinquish First Amendment rights to comment on matters of public interest by virtue of government employment. We also recognized that the State's interests as an employer in regulating the speech of its employees "differ significantly from those it possesses in connection with regulation of the speech of the citizenry in general." The problem, we thought, was arriving "at a balance between the interests of the [employee], as a citizen, in commenting upon matters of public concern and the interest of the State, as an employer, in promoting the efficiency of the public services it performs through its employees." We return to this problem today and consider whether the First and Fourteenth Amendments prevent the discharge of a state employee for circulating a questionnaire concerning internal office affairs.

The respondent, Sheila Myers, was employed as an Assistant District Attorney in New Orleans for five and a half years. She served at the pleasure of petitioner Harry Connick, the District Attorney for Orleans Parish. During this period Myers competently performed her responsibilities of trying criminal cases. In the early part of October 1980, Myers was informed that she would be transferred to prosecute cases in a different section of the criminal court. Myers was strongly opposed to the proposed transfer [in part because of her concern that the transfer would create a conflict of interest because of her participation in a counseling program for convicted defendants] and expressed her concern to several of her supervisors, including Connick. Despite her objections, on October 6 Myers was notified that she was being transferred. Myers * * * spoke with Dennis Waldron, one of the first assistant district attorneys, expressing her reluctance to accept the transfer. A number of other office matters were discussed and Myers later testified that, in response to Waldron's suggestion that her concerns were not shared by others in the office, she informed him that she would do some research on the matter.

That night Myers prepared a questionnaire soliciting the views of her fellow staff members concerning office transfer policy, office morale, the need for a grievance committee, the level of confidence in supervisors, and whether employees felt pressured to work in political campaigns. [See Appendix A following majority opinion]. Early the following morning,

Myers typed and copied the questionnaire. She also met with Connick who urged her to accept the transfer. She said she would "consider" it. Connick then left the office. Myers then distributed the questionnaire to 15 assistant district attorneys. Shortly after noon, Dennis Waldron learned that Myers was distributing the survey. He immediately phoned Connick and informed him that Myers was creating a "mini-insurrection" within the office. Connick returned to the office and told Myers that she was being terminated because of her refusal to accept the transfer. She was also told that her distribution of the questionnaire was considered an act of insubordination. Connick particularly objected to the question which inquired whether employees "had confidence in and would rely on the word" of various superiors in the office, and to a question concerning pressure to work in political campaigns which he felt would be damaging if discovered by the press.

Myers filed suit under 42 U.S.C. § 1983, contending that her employment was wrongfully terminated because she had exercised her constitutionally-protected right of free speech. The District Court agreed, ordered Myers reinstated, and awarded backpay, damages, and attorney's fees. The District Court found that although Connick informed Myers that she was being fired because of her refusal to accept a transfer, the facts showed that the questionnaire was the real reason for her termination. The court then proceeded to hold that Myers' questionnaire involved matters of public concern and that the state had not "clearly demonstrated" that the survey "substantially interfered" with the operations of the District Attorney's office. Connick appealed to the United States Court of Appeals for the Fifth Circuit, which affirmed on the basis of the District Court's opinion. Connick then sought review in this Court by way of certiorari, which we granted.

For at least 15 years, it has been settled that a state cannot condition public employment on a basis that infringes the employee's constitutionally protected interest in freedom of expression. *Pickering v. Board of Education*, 391 U.S. 563, 88 S.Ct. 1731, 20 L.Ed.2d 811 (1968); *Perry v. Sindermann*, 408 U.S. 593, 92 S.Ct. 2694, 33 L.Ed.2d 570 (1972); *Branti v. Finkel*, 445 U.S. 507, 100 S.Ct. 1287, 63 L.Ed.2d 574 (1980). Our task, as we defined it in *Pickering*, is to seek "a balance between the interests of the [employee], as a citizen, in commenting upon matters of public concern and the interest of the State, as an employer, in promoting the efficiency of the public services it performs through its employees." The District Court, and thus the Court of Appeals as well, misapplied our decision in *Pickering* and consequently, in our view, erred in striking the balance for respondent.

The District Court got off on the wrong foot in this case by initially finding that, "[t]aken as a whole, the issues presented in the questionnaire relate to the effective functioning of the District Attorney's Office and are matters of public importance and concern." Connick contends at the outset that no balancing of interests is required in this case because Myers' questionnaire concerned only internal office matters and that such speech is not upon a matter of "public concern," as the term was us *Pickering*. Although we do not agree that Myers' communication in case was wholly without First Amendment protection, there is much force to Connick's submission. The repeated emphasis in *Pickering* on the right of a public employee "as a citizen, in commenting upon matters of public concern," was not accidental. This language, reiterated in all of *Pickering's* progeny, reflects both the historical evolvement of the rights of public employees, and the common sense realization that government offices could not function if every employment decision became a constitutional matter.

For most of this century, the unchallenged dogma was that a public employee had no right to object to conditions placed upon the terms of employment—including those which restricted the exercise of constitutional rights. The classic formulation of this position was Justice Holmes, who, when sitting on the Supreme Judicial Court of Massachusetts, observed: "A policeman may have a constitutional right to talk politics, but he has no constitutional right to be a policeman." For many years, Holmes' epigram expressed this Court's law. * * * The Court cast new light on the matter in a series of cases arising from the widespread efforts in the 1950s and early 1960s to require public employees, particularly teachers, to swear oaths of loyalty to the state and reveal the groups with which they associated. In *Wieman v. Updegraff*, 344 U.S. 183, 73 S.Ct. 215, 97 L.Ed. 216 (1952), the Court held that a State could not require its employees to establish their loyalty by extracting an oath denying past affiliation with Communists. In *Cafeteria Workers v. McElroy*, 367 U.S. 886, 81 S.Ct. 1743, 6 L.Ed.2d 1230 (1961), the Court recognized that the government could not deny employment because of previous membership in a particular party. By the time *Sherbert v. Verner*, 374 U.S. 398, 83 S.Ct. 1790, 10 L.Ed.2d 965 (1963), was decided, it was already "too late in the day to doubt that the liberties of religion and expression may be infringed by the denial of or placing of conditions upon a benefit or privilege." It was therefore no surprise when in, *Keyishian v. Board of Regents,* 385 U.S. 589, 87 S.Ct. 675, 17 L.Ed.2d 629 (1967), the Court invalidated New York statutes barring employment on the basis of membership in "subversive" organizations, observing that the theory that public employment which may be denied altogether may be subjected to any conditions, regardless of how unreasonable, had been uniformly rejected.

In all of these cases, the precedents in which *Pickering* is rooted, the invalidated statutes and actions sought to suppress the rights of public employees to participate in public affairs. The issue was whether government employees could be prevented or "chilled" by the fear of discharge from joining political parties and other associations that certain public officials might find "subversive." The explanation for the Constitution's special concern with threats to the right of citizens to participate in political affairs is no mystery. The First Amendment "was fashioned to assure unfettered interchange of ideas for the bringing about of political and social changes desired by the people." *Roth v. United States*, 354 U.S. 476, 77 S.Ct. 1304, 1 L.Ed.2d 1498 (1957); *New York Times Co. v. Sullivan*, 376 U.S. 254, 84 S.Ct. 710, 11 L.Ed.2d 686 (1964). "[S]peech concerning public affairs is more than self-expression; it is the essence of self-government." *Garrison v. Louisiana*, 379 U.S. 64, 85 S.Ct. 209, 13 L.Ed.2d 125 (1964). Accordingly, the Court has frequently reaffirmed that speech on public issues occupies the "highest rung of the hierarchy of First Amendment values," and is entitled to special protection. *NAACP v. Claiborne Hardware Co.*, 458 U.S. 856, 102 S.Ct. 3409, 73 L.Ed.2d 1215 (1982); *Carey v. Brown*, 447 U.S. 455, 100 S.Ct. 2286, 65 L.Ed.2d 263 (1980).

Pickering v. Board of Education, supra, followed from this understanding of the First Amendment. In *Pickering*, the Court held impermissible under the First Amendment the dismissal of a high school teacher for openly criticizing the Board of Education on its allocation of school funds between athletics and education and its methods of informing taxpayers about the need for additional revenue. *Pickering's* subject was "a matter of legitimate public concern" upon which "free and open debate is vital to informed decision-making by the electorate."

Our cases following *Pickering* also involved safeguarding speech on matters of public concern. The controversy in *Perry v. Sindermann*, 408 U.S. 593, 92 S.Ct. 2694, 33 L.Ed.2d 570 (1972), arose from the failure to rehire a teacher in the state college system who had testified before committees of the Texas legislature and had become involved in public disagreement over whether the college should be elevated to four-year status—a change opposed by the Regents. In *Mt. Healthy City Board of Ed. v. Doyle*, 429 U.S. 274, 97 S.Ct. 568, 50 L.Ed.2d 471 (1977), a public school teacher was not rehired because, allegedly, he had relayed to a radio station the substance of a memorandum relating to teacher dress and appearance that the school principal had circulated to various teachers. The memorandum was apparently prompted by the view of some in the administration that there was a relationship between teacher appearance and public support for bond issues, and indeed, the radio station promptly announced the adoption of the dress code as a news item. Most recently, in *Givhan v. Western Line Consolidated School District*, 439 U.S. 410, 99 S.Ct. 693, 58 L.Ed.2d 619 (1979), we held that First Amendment protection applies when a public employee arranges to communicate privately with his employer rather than to express his views publicly. Although the subject-matter of Mrs. Givhan's statements were not the issue before the Court, it is clear that her statements concerning the school district's allegedly racially discriminatory policies involved a matter of public concern.

Pickering, its antecedents and progeny, lead us to conclude that if Myers' questionnaire cannot be fairly characterized as constituting speech on a matter of public concern, it is unnecessary for us to scrutinize the reasons for her discharge. When employee expression cannot be fairly considered as relating to any matter of political, social, or other concern to the community, government officials should enjoy wide latitude ir ing their offices, without intrusive oversight by the judiciary in t of the First Amendment. Perhaps the government employer's dis the worker may not be fair, but ordinary dismissals from gove service which violate no fixed tenure or applicable statute or regulation are not subject to judicial review even if the reasons for the dismissal are alleged to be mistaken or unreasonable.

We do not suggest, however, that Myers' speech, even if not touching upon a matter of public concern, is totally beyond the protection of the First Amendment. "The First Amendment does not protect speech and assembly only to the extent that it can be characterized as political. 'Great secular causes, with smaller ones, are guarded.' " *United Mine Workers v. Illinois State Bar Association,* 389 U.S. 217, 88 S.Ct. 353, 19 L.Ed.2d 426 (1967), quoting *Thomas v. Collins*, 323 U.S. 516, 65 S.Ct. 315, 89 L.Ed. 430 (1945). We in no sense suggest that speech on private matters falls into one of the narrow and well-defined classes of expression which carries so little social value, such as obscenity, that the state can prohibit and punish such expression by all persons in its jurisdiction. For example, an employee's false criticism of his employer on grounds not of public concern may be cause for his discharge but would be entitled to the same protection in a libel action accorded an identical statement made by a man on the street. We hold only that when a public employee speaks not as a citizen upon matters of public concern, but instead as an employee upon matters only of personal interest, absent the most unusual circumstances, a federal court is not the appropriate forum in which to review the wisdom of a personnel decision taken by a public agency allegedly in reaction to the employee's behavior. Our responsibility is to ensure that citizens are not deprived of fundamental rights by virtue of working for the government; this does not require a grant of immunity for employee grievances not afforded by the First Amendment to those who do not work for the state.

Whether an employee's speech addresses a matter of public concern must be determined by the content, form, and context of a given statement, as revealed by the whole record. In this case, with but one exception, the questions posed by Myers to her coworkers do not fall under the rubric of matters of "public concern." We view the questions pertaining to the confidence and trust that Myers' coworkers possess in various supervisors, the level of office morale, and the need for a grievance committee as mere extensions of Myers' dispute over her transfer to another section of the criminal court. Unlike the dissent, we do not believe these questions are of public import in evaluating the performance of the District Attorney as an elected official. Myers did not seek to inform the public that the District Attorney's office was not discharging its governmental responsibilities in the investigation and prosecution of criminal cases. Nor did Myers seek to bring to light actual or potential wrongdoing or breach of public trust on the part of Connick and others. Indeed, the questionnaire, if released to the public, would convey no information at all other than the fact that a single employee is upset with the status quo. While discipline and morale in the workplace are related to an agency's efficient performance of its duties, the focus of Myers' questions is not to evaluate the performance of the office but rather to gather ammunition for another round of controversy with her superiors. These questions reflect one employee's dissatisfaction with a transfer and an attempt to turn that displeasure into a cause celebre.

To presume that all matters which transpire within a government office are of public concern would mean that virtually every remark—and certainly every criticism directed at a public official—would plant the seed of a constitutional case. While as a matter of good judgment, public officials should be receptive to constructive criticism offered by their employees, the First Amendment does not require a public office to be run as a roundtable for employee complaints over internal office affairs. One question in Myers' questionnaire, however, does touch upon a matter of public concern. Question 11 inquires if assistant district attorneys "ever feel pressured to work in political campaigns on behalf of office supported candidates." We have recently noted that official pressure upon employees to work for political candidates not of the worker's own choice constitutes a coercion of belief in violation of fundamental constitutional rights. *Branti v. Finkel*, 445 U.S. 507, 100 S.Ct. 1287, 63 L.Ed.2d 574 (1980); *Elrod v. Burns*, 427 U.S. 347, 96 S.Ct. 2673, 49 L.Ed.2d 547 (1976). In addition, there is a demonstrated interest in this country that government service should depend upon meritorious performance rather than political service. *CSC v. Letter Carriers,* 413 U.S. 548, 93 S.Ct. 2880, 37 L.Ed.2d 796 (1973); *United Public Workers v. Mitchell*, 330 U.S. 75, 67 S.Ct. 556, 91 L.Ed. 754 (1947). Given this history, we believe it apparent that the issue of whether assistant district attorneys are pressured to work in political campaigns is a matter of interest to the community upon which it is essential that public employees be able to speak out freely without fear of retaliatory dismissal.

Because one of the questions in Myers' survey touched upon a matter of public concern, and contributed to her discharge we must determine whether Connick was justified in discharging Myers. Here the District Court again erred in imposing an unduly onerous burden on the state to justify Myers' discharge. The District Court viewed the issue of whether Myers' speech was upon a matter of "public concern" as a threshold inquiry, after which it became the government's burden to "clearly demonstrate" that the speech involved "substantially interfered" with official responsibilities. Yet *Pickering* unmistakably states, and respondent agrees that the state's burden in justifying a particular discharge varies depending upon the nature of the employee's expression. Although such particularized balancing is difficult, the courts must reach the most appropriate possible balance of the competing interests.

The *Pickering* balance requires full consideration of the government's interest in the effective and efficient fulfillment of its responsibilities to the public. * * * This includes the prerogative to remove employees whose conduct hinders efficient operation and to do so with dispatch. * * * We agree with the District Court that there is no demonstration here that the questionnaire impeded Myers' ability to perform her responsibilities. The District Court was also correct to recognize that "it is important to the efficient and successful operation of the District Attorney's office for Assistants to maintain close working relationships with their superiors." Connick's judgment, and apparently also that of his first assistant Dennis Waldron, who characterized Myers' actions as causing a "mini-insurrection," was that Myers' questionnaire was an act of insubordination which interfered with working relationships. When close working relationships are essential to fulfilling public responsibilities, a wide degree of deference to the employer's judgment is appropriate. Furthermore, we do not see the necessity for an employer to allow events to unfold to the extent that the disruption of the office and the destruction of working relationships is manifest before taking action. We caution that a stronger showing may be necessary if the employee's speech more substantially involved matters of public concern.

The District Court rejected Connick's position because "unlike a statement of fact which might be deemed critical of one's superiors, [Myers'] questionnaire was not a statement of fact, but the presentation and solicitation of ideas and opinions," which are entitled to greater constitutional protection because "under the First Amendment there is no such thing as a false idea." This approach, while perhaps relevant in weighing the value of Myers' speech, bears no logical relationship to the issue of whether the questionnaire undermined office relationships. Questions, no less than forcefully stated opinions and facts, carry messages and it requires no unusual insight to conclude that the purpose, if not the likely result, of the questionnaire is to seek to precipitate a vote of no confidence in Connick and his supervisors. Thus, Question 10, which asked whether or not the Assistants had confidence in and relied on the word of five named supervisors, is a statement that carries the clear potential for undermining office relations.

Also relevant is the manner, time, and place in which the questionnaire was distributed. As noted in *Givhan v. Western Line Consolidated School Dist., supra* "Private expression * * * may in some situations bring additional factors to the *Pickering* calculus. When a government employee personally confronts his immediate superior, the employing agency's institutional efficiency may be threatened not only by the content of the employee's message but also by the manner, time, and place in which it is delivered." Here the questionnaire was prepared, and distributed at the office; the manner of distribution required not only Myers to leave her work but for others to do the same in order that the questionnaire be completed. Although some latitude in when official work is performed is to be allowed when professional employees are involved, and Myers did not violate announced office policy the fact that Myers, unlike Pickering, exercised her rights to speech at the office supports Connick's fears that the functioning of his office was endangered.

Finally, the context in which the dispute arose is also significant. This is not a case where an employee, out of purely academic interest, circulated a questionnaire so as to obtain useful research. Myers acknowledges that it is no coincidence that the questionnaire followed upon the heels of the transfer notice. When employee speech concerning office policy arises from an employment dispute concerning the very application of that policy to the speaker, additional weight must be given to the supervisor's view that the employee has threatened the authority of the employer to run the office. Although we accept the District Court's factual finding that Myers' reluctance to accede to the transfer order was not a sufficient cause in itself for her dismissal, and thus does not constitute a sufficient defense under *Mt. Healthy* this does not render irrelevant the fact that the questionnaire emerged after a persistent dispute between Myers and Connick and his deputies over office transfer policy.

Myers' questionnaire touched upon matters of public concern in only a most limited sense; her survey, in our view, is most accurately characterized as an employee grievance concerning internal office policy. The limited First Amendment interest involved here does not require that Connick tolerate action which he reasonably believed would disrupt the office, undermine his authority, and destroy close working relationships. Myers' discharge therefore did not offend the First Amendment. We reiterate, however, the caveat we expressed in *Pickering*: "Because of the enormous variety of fact situations in which critical statements by * * * public employees may be thought by their superiors * * * to furnish grounds for dismissal, we do not deem it either appropriate or feasible to lay down a general standard against which all such statements may be judged."

Our holding today is grounded in our long-standing recognition that the First Amendment's primary aim is the full protection of speech upon issues of public concern, as well as the practical realities involved in the administration of a government office. Although today the balance is struck for the government, this is no defeat for the First Amendment. For it would indeed be a Pyrrhic victory for the great principles of free expression if the Amendment's safeguarding of a public employee's right, as a citizen, to participate in discussions concerning public affairs were confused with the attempt to constitutionalize the employee grievance that we see presented here. The judgment of the Court of Appeals is Reversed.

APPENDIX A (Questionnaire distributed by respondent on October 7, 1980)

Please take a few minutes to answer the following questions. You can freely express your opinion WITH ANONYMITY GUARANTEED.

* * *

1. How long have you been in the Office?
2. Were you moved as a result of the recent transfers?

3. Were the transfers as they effected [sic] you discussed with you superior prior to the notice of them being posted?

4. Do you think as a matter of policy, they should have been?

5. From your experience, do you feel office procedure regarding transfers has been fair?

6. Do you believe there is a rumor mill active in the office?

7. If so, how do you think it effects [sic] overall working performance of A.D.A. personnel?

8. If so, how do you think it effects [sic] office morale?

9. Do you generally first learn of office changes and developments through rumor?

10. Do you have confidence in and would you rely on the word of:

[naming four employees including Dennis Waldron]

11. Do you ever feel pressured to work in political campaigns on behalf of office supported candidates?

12. Do you feel a grievance committee would be a worthwhile addition to the office structure?

13. How would you rate office morale?

14. Please feel free to express any comments or feelings you have.

THANK YOU FOR YOUR COOPERATION IN THIS SURVEY.

BRENNAN, J., joined by MARSHALL, BLACKMUN, and STEVENS, JJ., dissenting:

Sheila Myers was discharged for circulating a questionnaire to her fellow Assistant District Attorneys seeking information about the effect of petitioner's personnel policies on employee morale and the overall work performance of the District Attorney's Office. The Court concludes that her dismissal does not violate the First Amendment, primarily because the questionnaire addresses matters that, in the Court's view, are not of public concern. It is hornbook law, however, that speech about "the manner in which government is operated or should be operated" is an essential part of the communications necessary for self-governance the protection of which was a central purpose of the First Amendment. *Mills v. Alabama*, 384 U.S. 214, 86 S.Ct. 1434, 16 L.Ed.2d 484 (1966). Because the questionnaire addressed such matters and its distribution did not adversely affect the operations of the District Attorney's Office or interfere with Myers' working relationship with her fellow employees, I dissent.

* * *

The court's decision today is flawed in three respects. First, the Court distorts the balancing analysis required under *Pickering* by suggesting that one factor, the context in which a statement is made, is to be weighed twice—first in determining whether an employee's speech addresses a matter of public concern and then in deciding whether the statement adversely affected the government's interest as an employer. Second, in concluding that the effect of respondent's personnel policies on employee morale and the work performance of the District Attorney's Office is not a matter of public concern, the Court impermissibly narrows the class of subjects on which public employees may speak out without fear of retaliatory dismissal. Third, the Court misapplies the *Pickering* balancing test in holding that Myers could constitutionally be dismissed for circulating a questionnaire addressed to at least one subject that was "a matter of interest to the community," in the absence of evidence that her conduct disrupted the efficient functioning of the District Attorney's Office.

* * *

The Court seeks to distinguish *Givhan* on the ground that speech protesting racial discrimination is "inherently of public concern." [The reference is to a footnote in the majority opinion, ed.] In so doing, it suggests that there are two classes of speech of public concern: statements "of public import" because of their content, form and context, and statements that, by virtue of their subject matter, are "inherently of public concern." In my view, however, whether a particular statement by a public employee is addressed to a subject of public concern does not depend on where it was said or why. The First Amendment affords special protection to speech that may inform public debate about how our society is to be governed—regardless of whether it actually becomes the subject of a public controversy. * * * [The dissent's discussion of prior case law is omitted].

The Court's decision today inevitably will deter public employees from making critical statements about the manner in which government agencies are operated for fear that doing so will provoke their dismissal. As a result, the public will be deprived of valuable information with which to evaluate the performance of elected officials. Because protecting the dissemination of such information is an essential function of the First Amendment, I dissent.

NOTES

1. What led the majority to determine that Myers' speech was not a matter of public concern? What persuaded the dissent that it was?

2. In *Givhan v. Western Line Consolidated School District*, 439 U.S. 410, 99 S.Ct. 693, 58 L.Ed.2d 619 (1979), referred to in the principal case, the Court applied the *Pickering* principle to a teacher's dismissal for statements criticizing the school's allegedly discriminatory policies in a series of *private* encounters with a school principal. The Court held that the teacher's speech did not lose its First Amendment protection merely because it was uttered privately to the employer instead of to the public at large. How did Givhan's speech differ from that of Myers?

3. A clerical employee in a county constable's office, upon learning of the attempted assassination of President Reagan in 1981, was heard to remark "If they go for him again, I hope they get him." Can she be fired for that speech,

without violating the First Amendment? Does her speech relate to a m public concern? What interests does her employer have in restric speech? Does the balance favor allowing or prohibiting her discha *Rankin v. McPherson* 483 U.S. 378, 107 S.Ct. 2891, 97 L.Ed.2d 315 (1987).

4. In *United States v. National Treasury Employees Union,* 513 U.S. 454, 115 S.Ct. 1003, 130 L.Ed.2d 964 (1995), the Court struck down a statutory ban on federal officers and employees receiving honoraria for an appearance, speech, or article. Challengers included a mail handler who gave a lecture on the Quaker religion, an aerospace engineer who lectured on black history, a microbiologist who reviewed dance performances, and a tax examiner who wrote articles about the environment. Proclaiming that *Pickering* rather than *Connick* controlled, the Court said, "Respondents' expressive activities in this case fall within the protected category of citizen comments on matters of public concern rather than employee comments on matters related to personal status in the workplace. The speeches and articles for which they received compensation were made outside the workplace, and involved content largely unrelated to their government employment." Do you agree that all of this speech relates to matters of public concern? Under the rationale of this case, is a police officer who spends his off duty hours making and selling sexually explicit videos of himself in a police uniform protected from termination for this activity by the First Amendment? *See City of San Diego v. Roe,* 543 U.S. 77, 125 S.Ct. 521, 160 L.Ed.2d 410 (2004). (Held: No). While the Court found that the speech did not relate to a matter of public concern, it also stated that the speech was job-related and harmful to the employer. If the officer avoided any connection to law enforcement, would the result have been different? Should a police officer or teacher who publicly supports a racist organization during off-duty hours be entitled to First Amendment protection from disciplinary action by the employer? What if the employee instead is a clerk in the city's utilities department? See Helen Norton, Constraining Public Employee Speech: Government's Control of Its Workers' Speech to Protect Its Own Expression, 59 *Duke Law Journal* 1 (2009).

5. Although most statutory employment laws exclude independent contractors from their protection, the government cannot terminate contracts to retaliate against government contractors for speech protected by the First Amendment. *See Board of County Commissioners v. Umbehr*, 518 U.S. 668, 116 S.Ct. 2361, 135 L.Ed.2d 843 (1996) (applying the *Pickering* balancing test).

GARCETTI v. CEBALLOS

Supreme Court of the United States, 2006.
547 U.S. 410, 126 S.Ct. 1951, 164 L.Ed.2d 689.

KENNEDY, J. delivered the opinion of the Court [joined by ROBERTS, C.J., and SCALIA, THOMAS, and ALITO, JJ. STEVENS, J. wrote a dissent which was joined by SOUTER and BREYER, JJ. SOUTER, J. wrote a dissent joined by STEVENS and GINSBURG, JJ. BREYER, J. also wrote a separate dissent.]

It is well settled that "a State cannot condition public employment on a basis that infringes the employee's constitutionally protected interest in freedom of expression." *Connick v. Myers*, 461 U. S. 138, 142 (1983). The question presented by the instant case is whether the First Amendment protects a government employee from discipline based on speech made pursuant to the employee's official duties.

* * * Ceballos was a calendar deputy and in this capacity he exercised certain supervisory responsibilities over other lawyers. In February 2000, a defense attorney contacted Ceballos about a pending criminal case. The defense attorney said there were inaccuracies in an affidavit used to obtain a critical search warrant. The attorney informed Ceballos that he had filed a motion to traverse, or challenge, the warrant, but he also wanted Ceballos to review the case. According to Ceballos, it was not unusual for defense attorneys to ask calendar deputies to investigate aspects of pending cases.

After examining the affidavit and visiting the location it described, Ceballos determined the affidavit contained serious misrepresentations. * * *

Ceballos spoke on the telephone to the warrant affiant, a deputy sheriff from the Los Angeles County Sheriff's Department, but he did not receive a satisfactory explanation for the perceived inaccuracies. He relayed his findings to his supervisors, * * * and followed up by preparing a disposition memorandum. The memo explained Ceballos' concerns and recommended dismissal of the case. * * *

Despite Ceballos' concerns, [his supervisor] decided to proceed with the prosecution, pending disposition of the defense motion to traverse. The trial court held a hearing on the motion. Ceballos was called by the defense and recounted his observations about the affidavit, but the trial court rejected the challenge to the warrant.

Ceballos claims that in the aftermath of these events he was subjected to a series of retaliatory employment actions. The actions included reassignment from his calendar deputy position to a trial deputy position, transfer to another courthouse, and denial of a promotion. Ceballos initiated an employment grievance, but the grievance was denied based on a finding that he had not suffered any retaliation. Unsatisfied, Ceballos sued in the United States District Court for the Central District of California, alleg[ing] petitioners violated the First and Fourteenth Amendments by retaliating against him based on his memo of March 2.

* * * Petitioners moved for summary judgment, and the District Court granted their motion. Noting that Ceballos wrote his memo pursuant to his employment duties, the court concluded he was not entitled to First Amendment protection for the memo's contents. * * *

The Court of Appeals for the Ninth Circuit reversed, holding that "Ceballos's allegations of wrongdoing in the memorandum constitute protected speech under the First Amendment." * * *

We granted certiorari, and we now reverse.

* * *

Pickering and the cases decided in its wake identify two inquiries to guide interpretation of the constitutional protections accorded to public employee speech. The first requires determining whether the employee spoke as a citizen on a matter of public concern. If the answer is no, the employee has no First Amendment cause of action based on his or her employer's reaction to the speech. If the answer is yes, then the possibility of a First Amendment claim arises. The question becomes whether the relevant government entity had an adequate justification for treating the employee differently from any other member of the general public. This consideration reflects the importance of the relationship between the speaker's expressions and employment. A government entity has broader discretion to restrict speech when it acts in its role as employer, but the restrictions it imposes must be directed at speech that has some potential to affect the entity's operations.

To be sure, conducting these inquiries sometimes has proved difficult. This is the necessary product of "the enormous variety of fact situations in which critical statements by teachers and other public employees may be thought by their superiors * * * to furnish grounds for dismissal." *Pickering*, 391 U.S. at 569. The Court's overarching objectives, though, are evident.

When a citizen enters government service, the citizen by necessity must accept certain limitations on his or her freedom. * * * Government employers, like private employers, need a significant degree of control over their employees' words and actions; without it, there would be little chance for the efficient provision of public services. * * * Public employees, moreover, often occupy trusted positions in society. When they speak out, they can express views that contravene governmental policies or impair the proper performance of governmental functions.

At the same time, the Court has recognized that a citizen who works for the government is nonetheless a citizen. The First Amendment limits the ability of a public employer to leverage the employment relationship to restrict, incidentally or intentionally, the liberties employees enjoy in their capacities as private citizens. So long as employees are speaking as citizens about matters of public concern, they must face only those speech restrictions that are necessary for their employers to operate efficiently and effectively.

The Court's employee-speech jurisprudence protects, of course, the constitutional rights of public employees. Yet the First Amendment interests at stake extend beyond the individual speaker. The Court has acknowledged the importance of promoting the public's interest in receiving the well-informed views of government employees engaging in civic discussion. *Pickering* again provides an instructive example. The Court characterized its holding as rejecting the attempt of school administrators to "limi[t] teachers' opportunities to contribute to public debate." 391 U. S., at 573. It also noted that teachers are "the members of a community most likely to have informed and definite opinions" about school expenditures.

Id., at 572. The Court's approach acknowledged the necessity for informed, vibrant dialogue in a democratic society. It suggested, in addition, that widespread costs may arise when dialogue is repressed. * * *

The Court's decisions, then, have sought both to promote the individual and societal interests that are served when employees speak as citizens on matters of public concern and to respect the needs of government employers attempting to perform their important public functions. Underlying our cases has been the premise that while the First Amendment invests public employees with certain rights, it does not empower them to "constitutionalize the employee grievance." *Connick*, 461 U. S., at 154.

With these principles in mind we turn to the instant case. Respondent Ceballos believed the affidavit used to obtain a search warrant contained serious misrepresentations. He conveyed his opinion and recommendation in a memo to his supervisor. That Ceballos expressed his views inside his office, rather than publicly, is not dispositive. Employees in some cases may receive First Amendment protection for expressions made at work. See, e.g., *Givhan v. Western Line Consol. School Dist.*, 439 U. S. 410, 414 (1979). Many citizens do much of their talking inside their respective workplaces, and it would not serve the goal of treating public employees like "any member of the general public," *Pickering*, 391 U. S., at 573, to hold that all speech within the office is automatically exposed to restriction.

The memo concerned the subject matter of Ceballos' employment, but this, too, is nondispositive. The First Amendment protects some expressions related to the speaker's job. See, e.g., ibid.; *Givhan*, supra, at 414. As the Court noted in *Pickering*: "Teachers are, as a class, the members of a community most likely to have informed and definite opinions as to how funds allotted to the operation of the schools should be spent. Accordingly, it is essential that they be able to speak out freely on such questions without fear of retaliatory dismissal." 391 U. S., at 572. The same is true of many other categories of public employees.

The controlling factor in Ceballos' case is that his expressions were made pursuant to his duties as a calendar deputy. * * * That consideration—the fact that Ceballos spoke as a prosecutor fulfilling a responsibility to advise his supervisor about how best to proceed with a pending case—distinguishes Ceballos' case from those in which the First Amendment provides protection against discipline. We hold that when public employees make statements pursuant to their official duties, the employees are not speaking as citizens for First Amendment purposes, and the Constitution does not insulate their communications from employer discipline. * * * Restricting speech that owes its existence to a public employee's professional responsibilities does not infringe any liberties the employee might have enjoyed as a private citizen. It simply reflects the exercise of employer control over what the employer itself has commissioned or created. * * *

Ceballos did not act as a citizen when he went about conducting his daily professional activities, such as supervising attorneys, investigating charges, and preparing filings. In the same way he did not speak as a citizen by writing a memo that addressed the proper disposition of a pending criminal case. When he went to work and performed the tasks he was paid to perform, Ceballos acted as a government employee. The fact that his duties sometimes required him to speak or write does not mean his supervisors were prohibited from evaluating his performance.

* * * Our holding likewise is supported by the emphasis of our precedents on affording government employers sufficient discretion to manage their operations. Employers have heightened interests in controlling speech made by an employee in his or her professional capacity. Official communications have official consequences, creating a need for substantive consistency and clarity. Supervisors must ensure that their employees' official communications are accurate, demonstrate sound judgment, and promote the employer's mission. Ceballos' memo is illustrative. It demanded the attention of his supervisors and led to a heated meeting with employees from the sheriff's department. If Ceballos' superiors thought his memo was inflammatory or misguided, they had the authority to take proper corrective action.

Ceballos' proposed contrary rule, adopted by the Court of Appeals, would commit state and federal courts to a new, permanent, and intrusive role, mandating judicial oversight of communications between and among government employees and their superiors in the course of official business. This displacement of managerial discretion by judicial supervision finds no support in our precedents. When an employee speaks as a citizen addressing a matter of public concern, the First Amendment requires a delicate balancing of the competing interests surrounding the speech and its consequences. When, however, the employee is simply performing his or her job duties, there is no warrant for a similar degree of scrutiny. To hold otherwise would be to demand permanent judicial intervention in the conduct of governmental operations to a degree inconsistent with sound principles of federalism and the separation of powers.

* * * [T]he parties in this case do not dispute that Ceballos wrote his disposition memo pursuant to his employment duties. We thus have no occasion to articulate a comprehensive framework for defining the scope of an employee's duties in cases where there is room for serious debate. We reject, however, the suggestion that employers can restrict employees' rights by creating excessively broad job descriptions. The proper inquiry is a practical one. Formal job descriptions often bear little resemblance to the duties an employee actually is expected to perform, and the listing of a given task in an employee's written job description is neither necessary nor sufficient to demonstrate that conducting the task is within the scope of the employee's professional duties for First Amendment purposes.

Justice Souter suggests today's decision may have important ramifications for academic freedom, at least as a constitutional value. There is argument that expression related to academic scholarship or classroom instruction implicates additional constitutional interests that are not fully accounted for by this Court's customary employee-speech jurisprudence. We need not, and for that reason do not, decide whether the analysis we conduct today would apply in the same manner to a case involving speech related to scholarship or teaching.

Exposing governmental inefficiency and misconduct is a matter of considerable significance. As the Court noted in *Connick*, public employers should, "as a matter of good judgment," be "receptive to constructive criticism offered by their employees." 461 U. S., at 149. The dictates of sound judgment are reinforced by the powerful network of legislative enactments—such as whistleblower protection laws and labor codes—available to those who seek to expose wrongdoing. Cases involving government attorneys implicate additional safeguards in the form of, for example, rules of conduct and constitutional obligations apart from the First Amendment. These imperatives, as well as obligations arising from any other applicable constitutional provisions and mandates of the criminal and civil laws, protect employees and provide checks on supervisors who would order unlawful or otherwise inappropriate actions. * * *

[STEVENS, J., dissenting, omitted.]

SOUTER, J., joined by STEVENS and GINSBURG, JJ., dissenting:

The Court holds that "when public employees make statements pursuant to their official duties, the employees are not speaking as citizens for First Amendment purposes, and the Constitution does not insulate their communications from employer discipline." I respectfully dissent. I agree with the majority that a government employer has substantial interests in effectuating its chosen policy and objectives, and in demanding competence, honesty, and judgment from employees who speak for it in doing their work. But I would hold that private and public interests in addressing official wrongdoing and threats to health and safety can outweigh the government's stake in the efficient implementation of policy, and when they do public employees who speak on these matters in the course of their duties should be eligible to claim First Amendment protection.

* * *

This significant, albeit qualified, protection of public employees who irritate the government is understood to flow from the First Amendment, in part, because a government paycheck does nothing to eliminate the value to an individual of speaking on public matters, and there is no good reason for categorically discounting a speaker's interest in commenting on a matter of public concern just because the government employs him. Still, the First Amendment safeguard rests on something more, being the value to the public of receiving the opinions and information that a public employee may disclose. "Government employees are often in the best position to know what ails the agencies for which they work." *Waters v. Churchill*, 511 U. S. 661, 674 (1994).

The reason that protection of employee speech is qualified is that it can distract co-workers and supervisors from their tasks at hand and thwart the implementation of legitimate policy, the risks of which grow greater the closer the employee's speech gets to commenting on his own workplace and responsibilities. * * * Even so, we have regarded eligibility for protection by *Pickering* balancing as the proper approach when an employee speaks critically about the administration of his own government employer. * * * [A] public employee can wear a citizen's hat when speaking on subjects closely tied to the employee's own job. * * *

As all agree, the qualified speech protection embodied in *Pickering* balancing resolves the tension between individual and public interests in the speech, on the one hand, and the government's interest in operating efficiently without distraction or embarrassment by talkative or headline grabbing employees. The need for a balance hardly disappears when an employee speaks on matters his job requires him to address; rather, it seems obvious that the individual and public value of such speech is no less, and may well be greater, when the employee speaks pursuant to his duties in addressing a subject he knows intimately for the very reason that it falls within his duties.[2]

* * *

Indeed, the very idea of categorically separating the citizen's interest from the employee's interest ignores the fact that the ranks of public service include those who share the poet's "object * * * to unite [m]y avocation and my vocation;"[3] these citizen servants are the ones whose civic interest rises highest when they speak pursuant to their duties, and these are exactly the ones government employers most want to attract.

* * *

Nothing, then, accountable on the individual and public side of the *Pickering* balance changes when an employee speaks "pursuant" to public duties. On the side of the government employer, however, something is different, and to this extent, I agree with the majority of the Court. The majority is rightly concerned that the employee who speaks out on matters subject to comment in doing his own work has the greater leverage to create office uproars and fracture the government's authority

---

2. I do not say the value of speech "pursuant to * * * duties" will always be greater, because I am pessimistic enough to expect that one response to the Court's holding will be moves by government employers to expand stated job descriptions to include more official duties and so exclude even some currently protectable speech from First Amendment purview. Now that the government can freely penalize the school personnel officer for criticizing the principal because speech on the subject falls within the personnel officer's job responsibilities, the government may well try to limit the English teacher's options by the simple expedient of defining teachers' job responsibilities expansively, investing them with a general obligation to ensure sound administration of the school. Hence today's rule presents the regrettable prospect that protection under *Pickering* may be diminished by expansive statements of employment duties. The majority's response, that the enquiry to determine duties is a "practical one," does not alleviate this concern. It sets out a standard that will not discourage government employers from setting duties expansively, but will engender litigation to decide which stated duties were actual and which were merely formal.

3. R. Frost, Two Tramps in Mud Time, Collected Poems, Prose & Plays 251, 252 (R. Poirier & M. Richardson eds. 1995).

to set policy to be carried out coherently through the ranks. "Official communications have official consequences, creating a need for substantive consistency and clarity. Supervisors must ensure that their employees' official communications are accurate, demonstrate sound judgment, and promote the employer's mission." Up to a point, then, the majority makes good points: government needs civility in the workplace, consistency in policy, and honesty and competence in public service.

But why do the majority's concerns, which we all share, require categorical exclusion of First Amendment protection against any official retaliation for things said on the job? Is it not possible to respect the unchallenged individual and public interests in the speech through a *Pickering* balance without drawing the strange line * * *?

Two reasons in particular make me think an adjustment using the basic *Pickering* balancing scheme is perfectly feasible here. First, the extent of the government's legitimate authority over subjects of speech required by a public job can be recognized in advance by setting in effect a minimum heft for comments with any claim to outweigh it. Thus, the risks to the government are great enough for us to hold from the outset that an employee commenting on subjects in the course of duties should not prevail on balance unless he speaks on a matter of unusual importance and satisfies high standards of responsibility in the way he does it. The examples I have already given indicate the eligible subject matter, and it is fair to say that only comment on official dishonesty, deliberately unconstitutional action, other serious wrongdoing, or threats to health and safety can weigh out in an employee's favor. If promulgation of this standard should fail to discourage meritless actions * * *, the standard itself would sift them out at the summary-judgment stage.

My second reason for adapting *Pickering* to the circumstances at hand is the experience in Circuits that have recognized claims like Ceballos's here. First Amendment protection less circumscribed than what I would recognize has been available in the Ninth Circuit for over 17 years, and neither there nor in other Circuits that accept claims like this one has there been a debilitating flood of litigation. * * *

For that matter, the majority's position comes with no guarantee against factbound litigation over whether a public employee's statements were made "pursuant to * * * official duties". In fact, the majority invites such litigation by describing the enquiry as a "practical one," apparently based on the totality of employment circumstances. Are prosecutors' discretionary statements about cases addressed to the press on the courthouse steps made "pursuant to their official duties"? Are government nuclear scientists' complaints to their supervisors about a colleague's improper handling of radioactive materials made "pursuant" to duties?

* * *

This ostensible domain beyond the pale of the First Amendment is spacious enough to include even the teaching of a public university professor, and I have to hope that today's majority does not mean to imperil First Amendment protection of academic freedom in pub[l]leges and universities, whose teachers necessarily speak and write "[pursu]ant to * * * official duties."

* * *

BREYER, J., dissenting:

* * * Like the majority, I understand the need to "affor[d] government employers sufficient discretion to manage their operations." And I agree that the Constitution does not seek to "displac[e] * * * managerial discretion by judicial supervision." Nonetheless, there may well be circumstances with special demand for constitutional protection of the speech at issue, where governmental justifications may be limited, and where administrable standards seem readily available—to the point where the majority's fears of department management by lawsuit are misplaced. In such an instance, I believe that courts should apply the Pickering standard, even though the government employee speaks upon matters of public concern in the course of his ordinary duties.

This is such a case. The respondent, a government lawyer, complained of retaliation, in part, on the basis of speech contained in his disposition memorandum that he says fell within the scope of his obligations under *Brady v. Maryland*. The facts present two special circumstances that together justify First Amendment review.

First, the speech at issue is professional speech—the speech of a lawyer. Such speech is subject to independent regulation by canons of the profession. Those canons provide an obligation to speak in certain instances. And where that is so, the government's own interest in forbidding that speech is diminished. * * * The objective specificity and public availability of the profession's canons also help to diminish the risk that the courts will improperly interfere with the government's necessary authority to manage its work.

Second, the Constitution itself here imposes speech obligations upon the government's professional employee. A prosecutor has a constitutional obligation to learn of, to preserve, and to communicate with the defense about exculpatory and impeachment evidence in the government's possession. * * *

Where professional and special constitutional obligations are both present, the need to protect the employee's speech is augmented, the need for broad government authority to control that speech is likely diminished, and administrable standards are quite likely available. Hence, I would find that the Constitution mandates special protection of employee speech in such circumstances. Thus I would apply the *Pickering* balancing test here.

While I agree with much of Justice Souter's analysis, I believe that the constitutional standard he enunciates fails to give sufficient weight to the serious managerial and administrative concerns that the majority describes. The standard would instruct courts to apply *Pickering* balancing in all cases, but says that the government should prevail unless the employee (1) "speaks on a matter of unusual importance," and (2) "satisfies high standards of responsibility in the way he does it." Justice Souter adds that "only comment on official dishonesty, deliberately unconstitutional action, other serious wrongdoing, or threats to health and safety can weigh out in an employee's favor."

There are, however, far too many issues of public concern, even if defined as "matters of unusual importance," for the screen to screen out very much. Government administration typically involves matters of public concern. * * *

Moreover, the speech of vast numbers of public employees deals with wrongdoing, health, safety, and honesty: for example, police officers, firefighters, environmental protection agents, building inspectors, hospital workers, bank regulators, and so on. Indeed, this categorization could encompass speech by an employee performing almost any public function, except perhaps setting electricity rates. * * *

The underlying problem with this breadth of coverage is that the standard (despite predictions that the government is likely to prevail in the balance unless the speech concerns "official dishonesty, deliberately unconstitutional action, other serious wrongdoing, or threats to health and safety,") does not avoid the judicial need to undertake the balance in the first place. And this form of judicial activity—the ability of a dissatisfied employee to file a complaint, engage in discovery, and insist that the court undertake a balancing of interests—itself may interfere unreasonably with both the managerial function (the ability of the employer to control the way in which an employee performs his basic job) and with the use of other grievance-resolution mechanisms, such as arbitration, civil service review boards, and whistle-blower remedies, for which employees and employers may have bargained or which legislatures may have enacted. * * *

I conclude that the First Amendment sometimes does authorize judicial actions based upon a government employee's speech that both (1) involves a matter of public concern and also (2) takes place in the course of ordinary job-related duties. But it does so only in the presence of augmented need for constitutional protection and diminished risk of undue judicial interference with governmental management of the public's affairs. In my view, these conditions are met in this case and *Pickering* balancing is consequently appropriate.

With respect, I dissent.

NOTES

1. The majority described the Court's previous decisions as seeking "to promote the individual and societal interests that are served when employees speak as citizens on matters of public concern and to respect the needs of government employers attempting to perform their important public functions." How does the *Garcetti* decision balance these twin objectives?

2. What is the purpose of constitutional protection for citizen speech? Does protecting the speech of citizens who are public servants serve the same purposes? Are there societal interests in protecting the speech of public servants? Should such interests be protected by the constitution or some other vehicle?

3. Both the majority and Justice Breyer suggest that the public interest in exposure of government wrongdoing and inefficiency is protected by whistleblower laws. Is this conclusion correct? Consider the following assessment of the effectiveness of federal whistleblower laws:

> The House committee also found that the statistical record indicated that the [Merit Systems Protection Board] and the Federal Circuit of Appeals "have not been favorable to Federal whistleblowers." In the first two years after enactment of the [Whistleblower Protection Act], whistleblowers won approximately 20% of MSPB decisions on the merits. From FY1991 to FY1994, that rate dropped to 5%; instead of providing a balance, the Federal Circuit "has been more hostile than the Board. Since its 1982 creation, in reported decisions employees have prevailed only twice on the merits with the whistleblower defense." The committee said it had received "extensive testimony at hearings that the MSPB and the Federal Circuit have lost credibility with the practicing bar for civil service cases." In November 1993, GAO released a report indicating that 81 percent of federal employees who sought whistleblower reprisal protection from [Office of Special Counsel] gave the office a generally low to very low rating for overall effectiveness.
>
> A more recent study indicates that whistleblowers continue to fare poorly in the MSPB and Federal Circuit. According to the Government Accountability Project, a nonprofit, whistleblower advocacy group, only two out of 30 whistleblowers prevailed on the merits before the MSPB from 1999 to 2005, and only one whistleblower claim out of 96 prevailed on the merits before the Federal Circuit from 1995 to 2005. (Citations omitted).

Louis Fisher, *National Security Whistleblowers* 21, Congressional Research Service Report for Congress, December 2005. For further discussion of whistleblower protection laws, see Chapter 3, § C.

4. How do the dissents differ from one another?

5. Is the speech of a police officer who reports misconduct by fellow officers protected by the First Amendment after *Garcetti*? What incentives does *Garcetti* create for police officers who observe misconduct by other officers? Consider the following cases: In *Williams v. Riley*, 275 Fed. App'x 385 (5th Cir. 2008), the court found a genuine issue of material fact regarding the question of whether the employees' job duties as jailers required reporting inmate abuse, although there was a written policy which the employer claimed required such reporting. The Fifth Circuit noted that *Garcetti* did not consider written job duties as dispositive. In *Skrutski v. Marut*, 288 Fed. App'x 803 (3d Cir. 2008) the court reversed a jury verdict in favor of police supervisor who reported misconduct of other police officers, because he was acting as their supervisor and reporting to his own supervisors, thereby bringing his reports within his official duties. In *Huppert v. City of Pittsburg*,

574 F.3d 696 (9th Cir. 2009), the court found that a police officer's duties include reporting illegal activity so that activities relating to police department corruption including cooperating with the FBI, working with the District Attorney, and testifying before a grand jury were all unprotected employee speech. Compare *Reilly v. Atlantic City*, 532 F.3d 216 (3d Cir. 2008) where the court found that testimony by a police officer in support of the prosecution of a fellow officer was citizen speech, although his knowledge came from his work as a police investigator, because all citizens have a duty to testify truthfully to assist law enforcement.

6. What is the relevance of the forum in which the speech occurred to the determination of whether it is "pursuant to the employee's official duties"? Consider the following cases. In *Haynes v. City of Circleville*, 474 F.3d 357 (6th Cir. 2007) the court relied on the fact that the employee's complaint was made solely to his supervisor, and not in a public forum to determine that he was speaking as an employee. In *Andrew v. Clark*, 561 F.3d 261 (4th Cir. 2009), the court reversed the district court's *Garcetti*-based dismissal of case where a police officer sent an internal memorandum of complaint to a newspaper, which published an article regarding his concerns about the actions of other officers in an incident that resulted in the death of an elderly man. The district court had held that the officer could not convert an employee complaint made pursuant to official duties to a citizen complaint by sending the complaint to a newspaper, but the court of appeals found that there was a genuine dispute about whether the internal memo was pursuant to official duties. In *Rohr v. Nehls*, No. 04–C477, 2006 WL 2927657 (E.D. Wis., October 11, 2006), the court concluded that because the deputy sheriff bypassed the official complaint channels, his complaints were protected as they were not made pursuant to official duties. In *Ranck v. Rundle*, No. 08–22235–CIV, 2009 WL 1684645 (S.D. Fla. June 16, 2009) the court found that an assistant state's attorney engaged in citizen speech when he posted on his blog a memo he wrote about a police-involved shooting that he was assigned to investigate. While the court found that the original memo was employee speech, it was posted on the blog four years later, albeit while the investigation was still open, after the attorney obtained a copy of the memo he wrote through a freedom of information act request. Does *Garcetti* encourage employees to go public with complaints that might otherwise be resolved internally? Similar incentives exist in the private sector where laws that bar retaliation by employers against employees who report violations of law to government agencies often exclude protection for internal complaints.

7. Suppose an FBI agent, criticized by her boss for failing to pursue a lead on a suspected terrorist, holds a press conference and criticizes her boss for the way in which investigations are handled. Can she be fired? See Jamie Sasser, Silenced Citizens: The Post–*Garcetti* Landscape for Public Sector Employees Working in National Security, 41 *University of Richmond Law Review* 759 (2007). For a description of the unsuccessful efforts of FBI agents to investigate terrorist suspects that later committed the 9/11 bombings and the subsequent letter written to the FBI Director and obtained by the media outlining problems within the FBI that stymied the investigation, see Michael Weisskopf, *Why Didn't the FBI Fully Investigate Moussaoui?*, TIME, May 23, 2002, http://www.time.com/time/nation/article/0,8599,249500,00.html. The let-

ter writer, FBI Agent Colleen Rowley, was later named one of the perso they year by Time, along with other whistleblowers. Richard Lacayo Amanda Ripley, *Persons of The Year 2002: The Whistleblowers*, TIME, Dec. 30, 2002, http://www.time.com/time/magazine/article/0,9171,1003998,00.html.

8. Under the official duties test, the same speech can be both protected and unprotected depending on the circumstances. In *Morales v. Jones*, 494 F.3d 590 (7th Cir. 2007), the Seventh Circuit Court of Appeals remanded for a new trial a case in which the jury was presented with evidence of both protected and unprotected speech. The plaintiff police officer had reported allegations against his superior officers to the Assistant District Attorney in the discussion of an arrest, which the court found unprotected under *Garcetti*, but he repeated the same allegations in a deposition in an unrelated civil suit, which the court found outside his official duties and therefore protected. On remand, how should the court determine whether the transfer of the officer to night shift patrol duty constituted unlawful retaliation? See *Mt. Healthy City School District Board of Education v. Doyle*, 429 U.S. 274, 97 S.Ct. 568, 50 L.Ed.2d 471 (1977). *Mt. Healthy* applied a burden shifting framework for cases with dual motives for adverse actions taken against employees, one lawful and one unlawful. The employee must show that she engaged in constitutionally protected conduct which was a motivating factor in the employer's action. The employer can then escape liability by establishing that it would have taken the same action in the absence of the improper motive.

9. Most union contracts are enforceable by utilizing a grievance procedure which is negotiated as a part of the contract. Is the filing of a grievance to enforce the collective bargaining agreement protected speech under the First Amendment? See *Weintraub v. Board of Education of City School District of New York*, 593 F.3d 196 (2d Cir. 2010) (Held: no). What arguments would you make on behalf of the employee? On behalf of the employer? Would the subject matter of the grievance be a relevant consideration? See also *Bivens v. Trent*, 591 F.3d 555 (7th Cir. 2010). In *Bivens,* the district court granted summary judgment to the employer based on *Garcetti* on a police officer's claim that he was retaliated against for filing a grievance complaining about the high lead levels at the gun range he managed. The district court found that the safety of the range was part of his job responsibility, and hence the speech was unprotected. The Seventh Circuit affirmed on different grounds, however, using the fact that he filed a grievance to support its finding that the complaint was personal to the officer, not based on public safety, and hence the speech was not a matter of public concern. Note that filing a grievance is typically protected activity under labor statutes. See Chapter 5, § E. Why might an employee choose to file a constitutional claim instead of a statutory claim? Would the remedy be a factor? The effectiveness of the union? Other considerations?

10. The Supreme Court has recognized that academic freedom is "a special concern of the first amendment." *Keyishian v. Board of Regents*, 385 U.S. 589, 603, 87 S.Ct. 675, 683, 17 L.Ed.2d 629, 640 (1967). In *Keyishian*, the Court struck down New York's law which authorized refusal to hire or discharge of any teacher who supported violent overthrow of the government and made membership in any of a list of organizations prima facie evidence of such support. The *Garcetti* Court disclaimed any intent to decide whether the

analysis in the case applied in the context of academic freedom, while the dissent expressed concern that the case threatened academic freedom. Why is academic freedom of special concern? What is encompassed by academic freedom and who is protected? Is the First Amendment protection intended for individual faculty or for the educational institution or both? Is the protection for teaching, scholarship, curricular decisions and/or governance of the institution? Does *Garcetti* threaten academic freedom? Consider *Hong v. Grant*, 516 F.Supp.2d 1158 (C.D. Cal. 2007) where the court concluded that a professor's criticism of the university's hiring and staffing practices was not protected speech because it was pursuant to his official duties and of little interest to the public. See also *Capeheart v. Northeastern Ill. Univ.*, No. 08 CV 1423, 2008 WL 4671771 (N.D. Ill. Oct. 21, 2008) (dismissing on other grounds a case alleging that a professor was unconstitutionally denied a promotion because of her complaints at a faculty meeting about the university's treatment of students protesting the Iraq War); *Sheldon v. Dhillon*, No. C–08–03438 RMW, 2009 WL 4282086 (N.D. Cal. Nov. 25, 2009) (refusing to apply the *Garcetti* test to a case filed by a college biology teacher alleging retaliation for her classroom remarks regarding environmental and genetic factors affecting sexual orientation, applying instead pre-*Garcetti* Ninth Circuit law regarding academic speech and denying the defendant's motion to dismiss the claim); *Kerr v. Hurd,* 694 F.Supp.2d 817 (S.D.Ohio 2010) (finding an academic freedom exception to the *Garcetti* rule, thus denying summary judgment to the employer on medical school professor's claim that he suffered retaliation for speech to his students and other faculty on obstetrical delivery techniques); Sheldon H. Nahmod, Public Employee Speech, Categorical Balancing and § 1983: A Critique of *Garcetti v. Ceballos*, 42 *University of Richmond Law Review* 561 (2008) (discussing *Garcetti*'s impact on academic freedom in addition to providing a broad-based critique of the decision); Judith Areen, Government as Educator: A New Understanding of First Amendment Protection of Academic Freedom and Governance, 97 *Georgetown Law Journal* 945 (2009) (discussing the application of *Garcetti* to academic governance speech).

C. FREEDOM OF ASSOCIATION AND POLITICAL ACTIVITY

All citizens have a right to freedom of association arising from the protection of liberty by the due process clause of the Fourteenth Amendment and from the First Amendment's protection of freedom of speech, assembly and religion as well as the right to petition the government. The former protects the right to engage in intimate human relationships while the latter protects the right to associate to exercise other constitutional freedoms, often referred to as expressive association. See *Roberts v. United States Jaycees*, 468 U.S. 609, 617–18, 104 S.Ct. 3244, 3249, 82 L.Ed.2d 462, 471 (1984). Where the government interferes with the rights of individuals to join with others in a common cause, both aspects may be affected. In cases involving the associational rights of government employees in the mid-twentieth century, the Supreme Court struck down requirements that employees swear an oath regarding their political affiliations,

Wieman v. Updegraff, 344 U.S. 183, 73 S.Ct. 215, 97 L.Ed. 216 (1952) and disclose organizational memberships as a condition of employment, *Shelton v. Tucker,* 364 U.S. 479, 81 S.Ct. 247, 5 L.Ed.2d 231 (1960). The right to freedom of association also protects public employees who want to join unions. For further discussion of this associational right in the context of union membership, see Chapter 4. For a critical exploration of the right to association in the workplace, see Paul M. Secunda, Reflections on the Technicolor Right to Association in American Labor and Employment Law, 96 *Kentucky Law Journal* 343 (2007).

Not surprisingly many cases involving freedom of association in the public workplace relate to political affiliation and activity. Particularly acute problems arise when employees are immediately supervised by political appointees advancing the interests of an elected regime. In this context, it is also relevant to note that the United States is relatively unique among developed countries in the absence of a Labor Party.

1. THE HATCH ACT CASES

Originally enacted in 1939 and amended several times since, the federal Hatch Act provides that a federal employee may not "(1) use his official authority or influence for the purpose of interfering with or affecting the result of an election;" or "(3) run for the nomination or as a candidate for election to a partisan political office." 5 U.S.C. § 7323(a). The Act also imposes limits on soliciting campaign contributions and engaging in political activity while on duty. 5 U.S.C. § 7323(a)(2); 7324. Other provisions of the Act impose similar restrictions on state and local government employees whose primary employment is involves an activity funded by the federal government. See 5 U.S.C. §§ 1501, 1502.

In *United Public Workers v. Mitchell,* 330 U.S. 75, 67 S.Ct. 556, 91 L.Ed. 754 (1947), the Supreme Court upheld the constitutionality of the Hatch Act on the basis of Congress' general power to regulate political activities of government employees in support of an "efficient public service." In *Civil Service Commission v. National Association of Letter Carriers*, 413 U.S. 548, 93 S.Ct. 2880, 37 L.Ed.2d 796 (1973) the Court reaffirmed *Mitchell.* Applying the 1968 *Pickering* balancing test, Justice White's opinion for the majority found the free speech claims of the public employees to be outweighed by three government interests: insuring that public employees "administer the law in accordance with the will of Congress, rather than [the] will of a political party," preventing the use of government workers "to build a powerful, invincible, and perhaps corrupt political machine," and insuring "that Government employees are free from pressure [to] vote in a certain way or to perform political chores in order to curry favor with their superiors rather than to act out of their own beliefs." These cases upheld an earlier and more restrictive version of the Hatch Act which barred public employees from taking "an active part in political management or in political campaigns." 413 U.S. at 550. The statute was amended in 1993 to loosen the restrictions on federal employees' political activity, with the exception of employees from certain government agencies who are still barred from active political management and campaigning. See 5 U.S.C. § 7324(b)(2). The Court has also upheld state "little Hatch Acts" to the same effect. *Broadrick v. Oklahoma*, 413 U.S. 601, 93 S.Ct. 2908, 37 L.Ed.2d 830 (1973).

2. THE PATRONAGE CASES

In *Elrod v. Burns*, 427 U.S. 347, 96 S.Ct. 2673, 49 L.Ed.2d 547 (1976), the Supreme Court considered the First Amendment constitutional issues presented when the newly elected Democratic Sheriff of Cook County, Illinois, upon taking office, discharged several employees—process servers, a bailiff, and a security guard—because they were Republicans. There was no majority opinion. Justice Brennan's plurality opinion, joined by Justices White and Marshall, reasoned that patronage practices were not justified by considerations of efficiency, or the need for preserving the two-party political system, or (except for employees who hold "policymaking" positions) by considerations of political loyalty. Justice Stewart, concurring separately, and joined by Justice Blackmun, would have described the area of permissible patronage to include "confidential" as well as "policymaking" positions. Justice Powell's dissent, joined by Justices Burger and Rehnquist, argued that patronage practices have value in stimulating political activity and strengthening political parties, especially at the local level, and in his view these interests were sufficient to outweigh the First Amendment interests in avoiding coercion of political choice. The issue came back to the Court four years later in the following case, with similar facts.

BRANTI v. FINKEL

United States Supreme Court, 1980.
445 U.S. 507, 100 S.Ct. 1287, 63 L.Ed.2d 574.

STEVENS, J. delivered the opinion of the Court.

The question presented is whether the First and Fourteenth Amendments to the Constitution protect an assistant public defender who is satisfactorily performing his job from discharge solely because of his political beliefs. Respondents, Aaron Finkel and Alan Tabakman, commenced this action in the United States District Court for the Southern District of New York in order to preserve their positions as assistant public defenders in Rockland County, New York. On January 4, 1978, on the basis of a showing that the petitioner public defender was about to discharge them solely because they were Republicans, the District Court entered a temporary restraining order preserving the status quo. After hearing evidence * * * the District Court * * * permanently enjoined petitioner from terminating or attempting to terminate respondents' employment "upon the sole grounds of their political beliefs." The Court of Appeals affirmed in an unpublished memorandum opinion.

The critical facts can be summarized briefly. The Rockland County Public Defender is appointed by the County Legislature for a term of six years. He in turn appoints nine assistants who serve at his pleasure. The two respondents have served as assistants since their respective appointments in March 1971 and September 1975; they are both Republicans. Petitioner Branti's predecessor, a Republican, was appointed in 1972 by a Republican-dominated County Legislature. By 1977, control of the legislature had shifted to the Democrats and petitioner, also a Democrat, was appointed to replace the incumbent when his term expired. As soon as petitioner was formally appointed on January 3, 1978, he began executing termination notices for six of the nine assistants then in office. Respondents were among those who were to be terminated. With one possible exception, the nine who were to be appointed or retained were all Democrats and were all selected by Democratic legislators or Democratic town chairmen on a basis that had been determined by the Democratic caucus.

* * * Having concluded that respondents had been discharged solely because of their political beliefs, the District Court held that those discharges would be permissible under this Court's decision in *Elrod v. Burns,* 427 U.S. 347, 96 S.Ct. 2673, 49 L.Ed.2d 547 (1976), only if assistant public defenders are the type of policymaking, confidential employees who may be discharged solely on the basis of their political affiliations. The court concluded that respondents clearly did not fall within that category. Although recognizing that they had broad responsibilities with respect to particular cases that were assigned to them, the court found that respondents had "very limited, if any, responsibility" with respect to the overall operation of the public defender's office. They did not "act as advisors or formulate plans for the implementation of the broad goals of the office" and, although they made decisions in the context of specific cases, "they do not make decisions about the orientation and operation of the office in which they work." The District Court also rejected the argument that the confidential character of respondents' work justified conditioning their employment on political grounds. The court found that they did not occupy any confidential relationship to the policymaking process, and did not have access to confidential documents that influenced policymaking deliberations. Rather, the only confidential information to which they had access was the product of their attorney-client relationship with the office's clients; to the extent that such information was shared with the public defender, it did not relate to the formulation of office policy. In light of these factual findings, the District Court concluded that petitioner could not terminate respondents' employment as assistant public defenders consistent with the First and Fourteenth Amendments. On appeal, a panel of the Second Circuit affirmed * * *. We granted certiorari, and now affirm.

Petitioner advances two principal arguments for reversal: First, that the holding in *Elrod v. Burns* is limited to situations in which government employees are coerced into pledging allegiance to a political party that would not voluntarily support and does not apply to a simple ement that an employee be sponsored by the party in power; and, l, that, even if party sponsorship is an unconstitutional condition of continued public employment for clerks, deputies, and janitors, it is an acceptable requirement for an assistant public defender.[6]

In *Elrod v. Burns* the Court held that the newly elected Democratic Sheriff of Cook County, Ill., had violated the constitutional rights of certain non-civil-service employees by discharging them "because they did not support and were not members of the Democratic Party and had failed to obtain the sponsorship of one of its leaders." That holding was supported by two separate opinions.

Writing for the plurality, Mr. Justice Brennan identified two separate but interrelated reasons supporting the conclusion that the discharges were prohibited by the First and Fourteenth Amendments. First, he analyzed the impact of a political patronage system on freedom of belief and association. Noting that in order to retain their jobs, the Sheriff's employees were required to pledge their allegiance to the Democratic Party, work for or contribute to the party's candidates, or obtain a Democratic sponsor, he concluded that the inevitable tendency of such a system was to coerce employees into compromising their true beliefs.[8] That conclusion, in his opinion, brought the practice within the rule of cases like *Board of Education v. Barnette,* 319 U.S. 624, 63 S.Ct. 1178, 87 L.Ed. 1628 (1943), condemning the use of governmental power to prescribe what the citizenry must accept as orthodox opinion.

Second, apart from the potential impact of patronage dismissals on the formation and expression of opinion, Mr. Justice Brennan also stated that the practice had the effect of imposing an unconstitutional condition on the receipt of a public benefit and therefore came within the rule of cases like *Perry v. Sindermann*, 408 U.S. 593, 92 S.Ct. 2694, 33 L.Ed.2d 570 (1972). In support of the holding in *Perry* that even an employee with

---

6. Petitioner also makes two other arguments. First, he contends that the action should have been dismissed because the evidence showed that he would have discharged respondents in any event due to their lack of competence as public defenders. See *Mt. Healthy City Board of Ed. v. Doyle*, 429 U.S. 274, 97 S.Ct. 568, 50 L.Ed.2d 471. The Court of Appeals correctly held this contention foreclosed by the District Court's findings of fact, which it found to be adequately supported by the record. * * * Second, relying on testimony that an assistant's term in office automatically expires when the public defender's term expires, petitioner argues that we should treat this case as involving a "failure to reappoint" rather than a dismissal and, as a result, should apply a less stringent standard. Petitioner argues that because respondents knew the system was a patronage system when they were hired, they did not have a reasonable expectation of being rehired when control of the office shifted to the Democratic Party. A similar waiver argument was rejected in *Elrod v. Burns*. After *Elrod v. Burns,* it is clear that the lack of a reasonable expectation of continued employment is not sufficient to justify a dismissal based solely on an employee's private political beliefs. Unlike Mr. Justice Powell in dissent, petitioner does not ask us to reconsider the holding in *Elrod v. Burns*.

8. * * * Mr. Justice Brennan also indicated that a patronage system may affect freedom of belief more indirectly, by distorting the electoral process. Given the increasingly pervasive character of government employment, he concluded that the power to starve political opposition by commanding partisan support, financial and otherwise, may have a significant impact on the formation and expression of political beliefs.

no contractual right to retain his job cannot be dismissed for engaging in constitutionally protected speech, the Court had stated:

> For at least a quarter-century, this Court has made clear that even though a person has no 'right' to a valuable governmental benefit and even though the government may deny him the benefit for any number of reasons, there are some reasons upon which the government may not rely. It may not deny a benefit to a person on a basis that infringes his constitutionally protected interests—especially, his interest in freedom of speech. For if the government could deny a benefit to a person because of his constitutionally protected speech or associations, his exercise of those freedoms would in effect be penalized and inhibited. This would allow the government to 'produce a result which [it] could not command directly.' *Speiser v. Randall*, 357 U.S. 513, 78 S.Ct. 1332, 2 L.Ed.2d 1460. Such interference with constitutional rights is impermissible.
>
> * * *

If the First Amendment protects a public employee from discharge based on what he has said, it must also protect him from discharge based on what he believes. Under this line of analysis, unless the government can demonstrate "an overriding interest, of vital importance," requiring that a person's private beliefs conform to those of the hiring authority, his beliefs cannot be the sole basis for depriving him of continued public employment.

* * *

Petitioner argues that *Elrod v. Burns* should be read to prohibit only dismissals resulting from an employee's failure to capitulate to political coercion. Thus, he argues that, so long as an employee is not asked to change his political affiliation or to contribute to or work for the party's candidates, he may be dismissed with impunity—even though he would not have been dismissed if he had the proper political sponsorship and even though the sole reason for dismissing him was to replace him with a person who did have such sponsorship. Such an interpretation would surely emasculate the principles set forth in *Elrod v. Burns*. While it would perhaps eliminate the more blatant forms of coercion described in *Elrod v. Burns*, it would not eliminate the coercion of belief that necessarily flows from the knowledge that one must have a sponsor in the dominant party in order to retain one's job. More importantly, petitioner's interpretation would require the Court to repudiate entirely the conclusion of both Mr. Justice Brennan and Mr. Justice Stewart that the First Amendment prohibits the dismissal of a public employee solely because of his private political beliefs.

In sum, there is no requirement that dismissed employees prove that they, or other employees, have been coerced into changing, either actually or ostensibly, their political allegiance. To prevail in this type of an action, it was sufficient, as *Elrod* holds, for respondents to prove that they were charged "solely for the reason that they were not affiliated with or sponsored by the Democratic Party."

Both opinions in *Elrod* recognize that party affiliation may be an acceptable requirement for some types of government employment. Thus, if an employee's private political beliefs would interfere with the discharge of his public duties, his First Amendment rights may be required to yield to the State's vital interest in maintaining governmental effectiveness and efficiency. In *Elrod*, it was clear that the duties of the employees—the chief deputy of the process division of the sheriff's office, a process server and another employee in that office, and a bailiff and security guard at the Juvenile Court of Cook County—were not of that character, for they were, as Mr. Justice Stewart stated, "nonpolicymaking, nonconfidential" employees.

As Mr. Justice Brennan noted in *Elrod,* it is not always easy to determine whether a position is one in which political affiliation is a legitimate factor to be considered. Under some circumstances, a position may be appropriately considered political even though it is neither confidential nor policymaking in character. As one obvious example, if a State's election laws require that precincts be supervised by two election judges of different parties, a Republican judge could be legitimately discharged solely for changing his party registration. That conclusion would not depend on any finding that the job involved participation in policy decisions or access to confidential information. Rather, it would simply rest on the fact that party membership was essential to the discharge of the employee's governmental responsibilities.

It is equally clear that party affiliation is not necessarily relevant to every policymaking or confidential position. The coach of a state university's football team formulates policy, but no one could seriously claim that Republicans make better coaches than Democrats, or vice versa, no matter which party is in control of the state government. On the other hand, it is equally clear that the Governor of a State may appropriately believe that the official duties of various assistants who help him write speeches, explain his views to the press, or communicate with the legislature cannot be performed effectively unless those persons share his political beliefs and party commitments. In sum, the ultimate inquiry is not whether the label "policymaker" or "confidential" fits a particular position; rather, the question is whether the hiring authority can demonstrate that party affiliation is an appropriate requirement for the effective performance of the public office involved.

Having thus framed the issue, it is manifest that the continued employment of an assistant public defender cannot properly be conditioned upon his allegiance to the political party in control of the county government. The primary, if not the only, responsibility of an assistant public defender is to represent individual citizens in controversy with the State. As we recently observed in commenting on the duties of counsel appointed to represent indigent defendants in federal criminal proceedings: "[T]he primary office performed by appointed counsel parallel office of privately retained counsel. Although it is true that appo counsel serves pursuant to statutory authorization and in furtherance of the federal interest in insuring effective representation of criminal defendants, his duty is not to the public at large, except in that general way. His principal responsibility is to serve the undivided interests of his client. Indeed, an indispensable element of the effective performance of his responsibilities is the ability to act independently of the government and to oppose it in adversary litigation." *Ferri v. Ackerman,* 444 U.S. 193, 100 S.Ct. 402, 62 L.Ed.2d 355 (1979). Thus, whatever policymaking occurs in the public defender's office must relate to the needs of individual clients and not to any partisan political interests. Similarly, although an assistant is bound to obtain access to confidential information arising out of various attorney-client relationships, that information has no bearing whatsoever on partisan political concerns. Under these circumstances, it would undermine, rather than promote, the effective performance of an assistant public defender's office to make his tenure dependent on his allegiance to the dominant political party.

In his brief petitioner attempts to justify the discharges in this case on the ground that he needs to have absolute confidence in the loyalty of his subordinates. In his dissenting opinion, Mr. Justice Stewart makes the same point, relying on an "analogy to a firm of lawyers in the private sector." We cannot accept the proposition, however, that there cannot be "mutual confidence and trust" between attorneys, whether public defenders or private practitioners, unless they are both of the same political party. To the extent that petitioner lacks confidence in the assistants he has inherited from the prior administration for some reason other than their political affiliations, he is, of course, free to discharge them.

Accordingly, the entry of an injunction against termination of respondents' employment on purely political grounds was appropriate and the judgment of the Court of Appeals is Affirmed. [STEWART, J. dissented, on the ground that the employees were "confidential." POWELL, J., joined by REHNQUIST, J. dissented from what he characterized as a "continue[d] evisceration of patronage practices begun in *Elrod*."]

NOTES

1. In a footnote to the opinion of the principal case, Justice Stevens contrasted the duties of the public defender to the "broader public responsibility of an official such as a prosecutor," saying "we express no opinion as to whether the deputy of such an official could be dismissed on grounds of political party affiliation or loyalty." How should the Court answer that question?

2. Courts have found political affiliation to be a relevant requirement for the following positions: Assistant Attorney for a county Department of Social Services (*Vona v. County of Niagara,* 119 F.3d 201 (2d Cir. 1997)); Assistant Director of a city Department of Social Services (*Nader v. Blair,* 549 F.3d 953

(4th Cir. 2008)); Chief Deputy to a County Clerk (*Summe v. Kenton County Clerk's Office*, 626 F.Supp.2d 680 (E.D. Ky. 2009)); Deputy Bureau Chief in a state Attorney General's office (*Butler v. New York State Department of Law*, 211 F.3d 739 (2d Cir. 2000)); and Director of Office of Federal Programs for a city (*Ortiz–Pinero v. Rivera–Arroyo*, 84 F.3d 7 (1st Cir. 1996)). Why is political affiliation "an appropriate requirement for the effective performance" of these jobs? What about a Deputy Sheriff? Compare *Heggen v. Lee*, 284 F.3d 675 (6th Cir. 2002) (finding that deputies did not perform discretionary duties on matters of political concern and therefore could not be terminated for political affiliation) with *Terry v. Cook,* 866 F.2d 373 (11th Cir. 1989) (finding loyalty to sheriff and his goals and policies essential and therefore termination of deputies based on political affiliation permissible).

3. Did the Court in *Branti* value sufficiently the need of government officials to have subordinates who are loyal and trustworthy in order to effectively accomplish the business of government? Did the Court in *Connick v. Myers, supra,* § B, which upheld the discharge of Assistant District Attorney Myers for circulating a questionnaire to her coworkers regarding office policies and morale, place too much weight on the need for loyal and trustworthy subordinates?

4. In *Rutan v. Republican Party of Illinois,* 497 U.S. 62, 110 S.Ct. 2729, 111 L.Ed.2d 52 (1990), the Court in an opinion by Justice Brennan extended *Elrod* and *Branti* to decisions about hiring, promotion, transfer, and recalls from layoff. The case arose when the Republican Governor of Illinois instituted a hiring freeze, subject to exceptions depending on permission from his office. Plaintiffs alleged the permission procedure operated as a "patronage machine," and that they were denied promotions, transfers, and recalls because they lacked Republican credentials. Justice Scalia, joined by Chief Justice Rehnquist and Justice Kennedy, and in part by Justice O'Connor, dissented, calling for *Elrod* and *Branti* to be overruled. Reiterating views expressed in those cases by Justice Powell, Justice Scalia pointed out the benefits of patronage identified by its supporters. "[P]atronage stabilizes political parties and prevents excessive political fragmentation." Party discipline leads to party success. In addition, pointing to the historical use of patronage by ethnic groups to enhance political power, he argued that patronage serves as a "powerful means of achieving the social and political integration of excluded groups." While recognizing the disadvantages of patronage, Justice Scalia concludes that patronage does not represent a "significant impairment of free speech or free association," and whatever constraint does exist is, in light of these considerations, justified as a political choice by elected representatives. Do Justices Powell and Scalia or the majorities in the patronage cases have the better argument?

5. Should employees be protected from discrimination for lack of political affiliation or is constitutional protection reserved for those who actually engage in political speech and association? See *Galli v. New Jersey Meadowlands Commission*, 490 F.3d 265 (3d Cir. 2007) (finding political silence is constitutionally protected). Is there an argument to the contrary?

D. DUE PROCESS OF LAW

The Fifth Amendment (applicable to the federal government) and the Fourteenth Amendment (applicable to the states) prohibit the taking of "life, liberty or property without due process of law." In the 1970s, the Court began to apply this prohibition to nontraditional forms of property. In *Goldberg v. Kelly*, 397 U.S. 254, 90 S.Ct. 1011, 25 L.Ed.2d 287 (1970), the Court held that a person's welfare benefits constituted "property" within the meaning of the Fifth Amendment, so as to require a pretermination hearing before welfare benefits are withdrawn. In 1972, the Supreme Court considered the application of this principle in two cases involving termination from public employment. In the first of these, *Perry v. Sindermann*, 408 U.S. 593, 92 S.Ct. 2694, 33 L.Ed.2d 570 (1972), the Court held that a college professor who lacked formal tenure nevertheless had a protected property interest in his job by reason of an informal system of tenure which prevailed at his college, and that due process required at least that he receive notice of the charges against him and an opportunity to respond before he could be terminated.

In a companion case, *Board of Regents v. Roth*, 408 U.S. 564, 92 S.Ct. 2701, 33 L.Ed.2d 548 (1972), the Court held that, in the absence of an informal tenure system such as that present in *Perry*, a college professor hired for one year at a campus of Wisconsin State University had no right to a pretermination hearing when he was informed, without explanation, that he would not be rehired the following year. Justice Stewart's opinion for the Court explained:

> [T]he 14th Amendment's procedural protection of property is a safeguard of the security of interests that a person has already acquired in specific benefits. These interests—property interests—may take many forms. [Thus,] the welfare recipients in *Goldberg v. Kelly*, 397 U.S. 254, 90 S.Ct. 1011, 25 L.Ed.2d 287 (1970), had a claim of entitlement to welfare payments that was grounded in the statute defining eligibility for them. [Similarly] respondent's 'property' interest in employment at the University was created and defined by the terms of his appointment, [which] specifically provided that the respondent's employment was to terminate on June 30. [There was] no provision for renewal whatsoever. Thus, the terms of the respondent's appointment secured absolutely no interest in re-employment for the next year. [Nor,] significantly, was there any state statute or University rule or policy that secured his interest in re-employment or that created any legitimate claim to it. In these circumstances, the respondent surely had an abstract concern in being rehired, but he did not have a *property* interest sufficient to require the University authorities to give him a hearing when they declined to renew his contract.
> [A footnote to the penultimate stated: "To be sure, the respondent does suggest that most teachers hired on a year-to-year basis are, in fact, rehired. But the District Court has not found that there is

anything approaching 'common law' of re-employment, see *Perry v. Sindermann*, 408 U.S. 593, 92 S.Ct. 2694, 33 L.Ed.2d 570 (1972) * * * so strong as to require University officials to give the respondent a statement of reasons and a hearing on their decision not to rehire him."]

When a public employee is found to have a "property interest" in employment, what kind of hearing is required?

CLEVELAND BOARD OF EDUCATION v. LOUDERMILL

Supreme Court of the United States, 1985.
470 U.S. 532, 105 S.Ct. 1487, 84 L.Ed.2d 494.

WHITE, J. delivered the opinion of the Court.

In these cases we consider what pretermination process must be accorded a public employee who can be discharged only for cause.

I.

In 1979 the Cleveland Board of Education hired respondent James Loudermill as a security guard. On his job application, Loudermill stated that he had never been convicted of a felony. Eleven months later, as part of a routine examination of his employment records, the Board discovered that in fact Loudermill had been convicted of grand larceny in 1968. By letter dated November 3, 1980, the Board's Business Manager informed Loudermill that he had been dismissed because of his dishonesty in filling out the employment application. Loudermill was not afforded an opportunity to respond to the charge of dishonesty or to challenge his dismissal. On November 13, the Board adopted a resolution officially approving the discharge.

Under Ohio law, Loudermill was a "classified civil servant." Such employees can be terminated only for cause, and may obtain administrative review if discharged. Pursuant to this provision, Loudermill filed an appeal with the Cleveland Civil Service Commission on November 12. The Commission appointed a referee, who held a hearing on January 29, 1981. Loudermill argued that he had thought that his 1968 larceny conviction was for a misdemeanor rather than a felony. The referee recommended reinstatement. On July 20, 1981, the full Commission heard argument and orally announced that it would uphold the dismissal. Proposed findings of fact and conclusions of law followed on August 10, and Loudermill's attorneys were advised of the result by mail on August 21.

Although the Commission's decision was subject to judicial review in the state courts, Loudermill instead brought the present suit in the Federal District Court for the Northern District of Ohio. The complaint alleged that Section 124.34 was unconstitutional on its face because it did not provide the employee an opportunity to respond to the charges against him prior to removal. As a result, discharged employees were deprived of liberty and property without due process. The complaint also alleged that the provision was unconstitutional as applied because discharged employees were not given sufficiently prompt postremoval hearings.

Before a responsive pleading was filed, the District Court dismissed for failure to state a claim on which relief could be granted. It held that because the very statute that created the property right in continued employment also specified the procedures for discharge, and because those procedures were followed, Loudermill was, by definition, afforded all the process due. The post-termination hearing also adequately protected Loudermill's liberty interests. Finally, the District Court concluded that, in light of the Commission's crowded docket, the delay in processing Loudermill's administrative appeal was constitutionally acceptable.

The other case before us arises on similar facts and followed a similar course. Respondent Richard Donnelly was a bus mechanic for the Parma Board of Education. In August 1977, Donnelly was fired because he had failed an eye examination. He was offered a chance to retake the examination but did not do so. Like Loudermill, Donnelly appealed to the Civil Service Commission. After a year of wrangling about the timeliness of his appeal, the Commission heard the case. It ordered Donnelly reinstated, though without backpay. In a complaint essentially identical to Loudermill's, Donnelly challenged the constitutionality of the dismissal procedures. The District Court dismissed for failure to state a claim, relying on its opinion in *Loudermill*. A divided panel of the Court of Appeals for the Sixth Circuit reversed in part and remanded. After rejecting arguments that the actions were barred by failure to exhaust administrative remedies and by res judicata—arguments that are not renewed here—the Court of Appeals found that both respondents had been deprived of due process. It disagreed with the District Court's original rationale. Instead, it concluded that the compelling private interest in retaining employment, combined with the value of presenting evidence prior to dismissal, outweighed the added administrative burden of a pretermination hearing. With regard to the alleged deprivation of liberty, and Loudermill's 9–month wait for an administrative decision, the court affirmed the District Court, finding no constitutional violation.

II.

Respondents' federal constitutional claim depends on their having had a property right in continued employment. If they did, the State could not deprive them of this property without due process. * * * The Parma Board argues, however, that the property right is defined by, and conditioned on, the legislature's choice of procedures for its deprivation. The Board stresses that in addition to specifying the grounds for termination, the statute sets out procedures by which termination may take place.[6] The

---

6. After providing for dismissal only for cause, Section 124.34 states that the dismissed employee is to be provided with a copy of the order of removal giving the reasons therefor. Within 10 days of the filing of the order with the Director of Administrative Services, the employee may file a written appeal with the State Personnel Board of Review or the Commission. "In the event such an appeal is filed, the board or commission shall forthwith notify the appointing authority and shall hear, or appoint a trial board to hear such appeal within thirty days from and after its

procedures were adhered to in these cases. According to petitioner, "[t]o require additional procedures would in effect expand the scope of the property interest itself."

This argument, which was accepted by the District Court, has its genesis in the plurality opinion in *Arnett v. Kennedy*, 416 U.S.134, 94 S.Ct. 1633, 40 L.Ed.2d 15 (1974). *Arnett* involved a challenge by a former federal employee to the procedures by which he was dismissed. The plurality reasoned that where the legislation conferring the substantive right also sets out the procedural mechanism for enforcing that right, the two cannot be separated: "The employee's statutorily defined right is not a guarantee against removal without cause in the abstract, but such a guarantee as enforced by the procedures which Congress has designated for the determination of cause. * * * Where the grant of a substantive right is inextricably intertwined with the limitations on the procedures which are to be employed in determining that right, a litigant in the position of appellee must take the bitter with the sweet."

This view garnered three votes in *Arnett*, but was specifically rejected by the other six Justices. Since then, this theory has at times seemed to gather some additional support. * * * More recently, however, the Court has clearly rejected it. * * * In light of these holdings, it is settled that the "bitter with the sweet" approach misconceives the constitutional guarantee. If a clearer holding is needed, we provide it today. The point is straightforward: the Due Process Clause provides that certain substantive rights—life, liberty, and property—cannot be deprived except pursuant to constitutionally adequate procedures. The categories of substance and procedure are distinct. Were the rule otherwise, the Clause would be reduced to a mere tautology. "Property" cannot be defined by the procedures provided for its deprivation any more than can life or liberty. The right to due process "is conferred, not by legislative grace, but by constitutional guarantee. While the legislature may elect not to confer a property interest in [public] employment, it may not constitutionally authorize the deprivation of such an interest, once conferred, without appropriate procedural safeguards." In short, once it is determined that the Due Process Clause applies, "the question remains what process is due." The answer to that question is not to be found in the Ohio statute.

III.

An essential principle of due process is that a deprivation of life, liberty, or property "be preceded by notice and opportunity for hearing appropriate to the nature of the case."[4] We have described "the root requirement" of the Due Process Clause as being "that an individual be given an opportunity for a hearing *before* he is deprived of any significant property interest." *Boddie v. Connecticut*, 401 U.S. 371, 91 S.Ct. 780, 28 L.Ed.2d 113 (1971) (emphasis in original) * * * . This principle requires

filing with the board or commission, and it may affirm, disaffirm or modify the judgment of the appointing authority." Either side may obtain review of the Commission's decision in the State Court of Common Pleas.

"some kind of a hearing" prior to the discharge of an employee who has a constitutionally protected property interest in his employment. *Board of Regents v. Roth*, 408 U.S. 564, 92 S.Ct. 2701, 33 L.Ed.2d 548; *Perry v. Sindermann*, 408 U.S. 593, 92 S.Ct. 2694, 33 L.Ed.2d 570 (1972). As we pointed out last Term, this rule has been settled for some time now. * * * Even decisions finding no constitutional violation in termination procedures have relied on the existence of some pretermination opportunity to respond. For example, in *Arnett* six Justices found constitutional minima satisfied where the employee had access to the material upon which the charge was based and could respond orally and in writing and present rebuttal affidavits. See also *Barry v. Barchi*, 443 U.S. 55, 99 S.Ct. 2642, 61 L.Ed.2d 365 (1979) (no due process violation where horse trainer whose license was suspended "was given more than one opportunity to present his side of the story").

The need for some form of pretermination hearing, recognized in these cases, is evident from a balancing of the competing interests at stake. These are the private interests in retaining employment, the governmental interest in the expeditious removal of unsatisfactory employees and the avoidance of administrative burdens, and the risk of an erroneous termination. See *Mathews v. Eldridge*, 424 U.S. 319, 96 S.Ct. 893, 47 L.Ed.2d 18 (1976). First, the significance of the private interest in retaining employment cannot be gainsaid. * * * We have frequently recognized the severity of depriving a person of the means of livelihood. * * * While a fired worker may find employment elsewhere, doing so will take some time and is likely to be burdened by the questionable circumstances under which he left his previous job. * * * Second, some opportunity for the employee to present his side of the case is recurringly of obvious value in reaching an accurate decision. Dismissals for cause will often involve factual disputes. * * * Even where the facts are clear, the appropriateness or necessity of the discharge may not be; in such cases, the only meaningful opportunity to invoke the discretion of the decisionmaker is likely to be before the termination takes effect.[8]

The cases before us illustrate these considerations. Both respondents had plausible arguments to make that might have prevented their discharge. The fact that the Commission saw fit to reinstate Donnelly suggests that an error might have been avoided had he been provided an opportunity to make his case to the Board. As for Loudermill, given the Commission's ruling we cannot say that the discharge was mistaken.

8. This is not to say that where state conduct is entirely discretionary the Due Process Clause is brought into play. See *Meachum v. Fano*, 427 U.S. 215, 96 S.Ct. 2532, 49 L.Ed.2d 451 (1976). Nor is it to say that a person can insist on a hearing in order to argue that the decisionmaker should be lenient and depart from legal requirements. See *Dixon v. Love*, 431 U.S. 105, 97 S.Ct. 1723, 52 L.Ed.2d 172 (1977). The point is that where there is an entitlement, a prior hearing facilitates the consideration of whether a permissible course of action is also an appropriate one. This is one way in which providing "effective notice and informal hearing permitting the [employee] to give his version of the events will provide a meaningful hedge against erroneous action. At least the [employer] will be alerted to the existence of disputes about facts and arguments about cause and effect * * * . [H]is discretion will be more informed and we think the risk of error substantially reduced." Goss v. Lopez, 419 U.S. 565, 95 S.Ct.729, 42 L.Ed. 725 (1975).

netheless, in light of the referee's recommendation, neither can we say ...t a fully informed decisionmaker might not have exercised its discretion and decided not to dismiss him, notwithstanding its authority to do so. In any event, the termination involved arguable issues,[9] and the right to a hearing does not depend on a demonstration of certain success. *Carey v. Piphus*, 435 U.S. 247, 98 S.Ct. 1042, 55 L.Ed.2d 252 (1978).

The governmental interest in immediate termination does not outweigh these interests. As we shall explain, affording the employee an opportunity to respond prior to termination would impose neither a significant administrative burden nor intolerable delays. Furthermore, the employer shares the employee's interest in avoiding disruption and erroneous decisions; and until the matter is settled, the employer would continue to receive the benefit of the employee's labors. It is preferable to keep a qualified employee on than to train a new one. A governmental employer also has an interest in keeping citizens usefully employed rather than taking the possibly erroneous and counterproductive step of forcing its employees onto the welfare rolls. Finally, in those situations where the employer perceives a significant hazard in keeping the employee on the job, it can avoid the problem by suspending with pay.

IV.

The foregoing considerations indicate that the pretermination "hearing," though necessary, need not be elaborate. We have pointed out that "[t]he formality and procedural requisites for the hearing can vary, depending upon the importance of the interests involved and the nature of the subsequent proceedings." *Boddie v. Connecticut*, 401 U.S., at 378, 91 S.Ct., at 786. See *Cafeteria Workers v. McElroy*, 367 U.S. 886, 81 S.Ct. 1743, 6 L.Ed.2d 1230 (1961). In general, "something less" than a full evidentiary hearing is sufficient prior to adverse administrative action. *Mathews v. Eldridge*, 424 U.S., at 343, 96 S.Ct., at 907. Under state law, respondents were later entitled to a full administrative hearing and judicial review. The only question is what steps were required before the termination took effect. In only one case, *Goldberg v. Kelly*, 397 U.S. 254, 90 S.Ct. 1011, 25 L.Ed.2d 287 (1970), has the Court required a full adversarial evidentiary hearing prior to adverse governmental action. However, as the *Goldberg* Court itself pointed out, that case presented significantly different considerations than are present in the context of public employment.

Here, the pretermination hearing need not definitively resolve the propriety of the discharge. It should be an initial check against mistaken decisions—essentially, a determination of whether there are reasonable grounds to believe that the charges against the employee are true and support the proposed action. The essential requirements of due process,

9. Loudermill's dismissal turned not on the objective fact that he was an ex-felon or the inaccuracy of his statement to the contrary, but on the subjective question whether he had lied on his application form. His explanation for the false statement is plausible in light of the fact that he received only a suspended 6-month sentence and a fine on the grand larceny conviction.

and all that respondents seek or the Court of Appeals required, are notice and an opportunity to respond. The opportunity to present reasons, either in person or in writing, why proposed action should not be taken is a fundamental due process requirement. The tenured public employee is entitled to oral or written notice of the charges against him, an explanation of the employer's evidence, and an opportunity to present his side of the story. * * * To require more than this prior to termination would intrude to an unwarranted extent on the government's interest in quickly removing an unsatisfactory employee.

V.

Our holding rests in part on the provisions in Ohio law for a full post-termination hearing. In his cross-petition Loudermill asserts, as a separate constitutional violation, that his administrative proceedings took too long.[10] The Court of Appeals held otherwise, and we agree. The Due Process Clause requires provision of a hearing "at a meaningful time." * * * At some point, a delay in the post-termination hearing would become a constitutional violation. * * * In the present case, however, the complaint merely recites the course of proceedings and concludes that the denial of a "speedy resolution" violated due process. This reveals nothing about the delay except that it stemmed in part from the thoroughness of the procedures. A 9–month adjudication is not, of course, unconstitutionally lengthy per se. Yet Loudermill offers no indication that his wait was unreasonably prolonged other than the fact that it took nine months. The chronology of the proceedings set out in the complaint, coupled with the assertion that nine months is too long to wait, does not state a claim of a constitutional deprivation.

VI.

We conclude that all the process that is due is provided by a pretermination opportunity to respond, coupled with post-termination administrative procedures as provided by the Ohio statute. Because respondents allege in their complaints that they had no chance to respond, the District Court erred in dismissing for failure to state a claim. The judgment of the Court of Appeals is affirmed, and the case is remanded for further proceedings consistent with this opinion. So ordered.

[JUSTICE REHNQUIST dissented from the rejection of his view in *Arnett*. JUSTICES MARSHALL and BRENNAN filed separate dissents, arguing for more extensive pretermination hearings and disagreeing with the court's conclusion that the hearing was timely].

10. Loudermill's hearing before the referee occurred two and one-half months after he filed his appeal. The Commission issued its written decision six and one-half months after that. Administrative proceedings in Donnelly's case, once it was determined that they could proceed at all, were swifter. A writ of mandamus requiring the Commission to hold a hearing was issued on May 9, 1978; the hearing took place on May 30; the order of reinstatement was issued on July 6. Section 124.34 provides that a hearing is to be held within 30 days of the appeal, though the Ohio courts have ruled that the time limit is not mandatory. * * * The statute does not provide a time limit for the actual decision.

NOTES

1. In *Bishop v. Wood*, 426 U.S. 341, 96 S.Ct. 2074, 48 L.Ed.2d 684 (1976), a police officer fired for "insubordination," "causing low morale" and "conduct unsuited to an officer" argued that even if he had no "property" interest requiring a hearing, he had a "liberty" interest which entitled him to a hearing in order to clear his name. The court rejected that claim because there had been no "public disclosure" of the charges. Would the situation be different if the charges were public? See *Rush v. Perryman*, 579 F.3d 908 (8th Cir. 2009). What constitutes public disclosure? Compare *Sciolino v. City of Newport News*, 480 F.3d 642 (4th Cir. 2007), *cert. denied*, 552 U.S. 1076, 128 S.Ct. 805, 169 L.Ed.2d 606 (2007) (information placed in personnel file that prospective employers or the public are likely to view) with *Johnson v. Martin*, 943 F.2d 15, 16–17 (7th Cir.1991) (information must be actually provided to a prospective employer) and *Clark v. Mann*, 562 F.2d 1104 (8th Cir. 1977) (information is in file that would be available to prospective employer). Which is the best rule for triggering a requirement of a name-clearing hearing?

2. Could an employee ever have a property interest in a promotion? See *Jones v. Hernandez*, No. 07–2042, 2007 WL 4269052 (10th Cir. Dec. 6, 2007) (Held: yes). What circumstances might warrant a finding of a property interest in a promotion?

3. In *Linton v. Frederick County Board of Commissioners,* 964 F.2d 1436 (4th Cir. 1992) the employee returned from vacation to be confronted by his manager with a two page notice of dismissal containing specifics regarding one very recent incident and more general descriptions of other incidents (for example, "improperly dumping waste material at 14+ sites") as well as a generalized charge of failing to use "Best Management Practices." The specific incident involved actions which led to a citation of the county for failing to get a permit for particular work. In the very brief meeting (five minutes according to the employee and twenty minutes according to the manager), the employee responded that he had heard about the citation, that he had been in charge of the operation, and that he did not believe that a permit was required. Upon being asked to resign or be fired, he requested the opportunity to speak with his family and was given one day to do so. He was terminated after refusing to resign and he challenged the termination using available post-termination procedures. Did he receive adequate due process prior to termination?

4. Does an applicant for employment have any constitutional rights to due process or equal protection?

E. EQUAL PROTECTION

The Fourteenth Amendment prohibits any state from "deny[ing] to any person within its jurisdiction the equal protection of the laws." A similar guarantee of equal protection applies to federal employees derived from the Fifth Amendment. See *Washington v. Davis*, 426 U.S. 229, 96 S.Ct. 2040, 48 L.Ed.2d 597 (1976). Government employees frequently have relied on the guarantee of equal protection to challenge employment decisions. The gravamen of an equal protection claim is disparate treatment. In analyzing the claims, courts apply differing levels of scrutiny to government action based on the classification involved. Classifications based on race, ethnicity, and alienage earn strict scrutiny, gender-based classifications are analyzed using intermediate scrutiny, and other classifications will be sustained if supported by a rational basis. To survive strict scrutiny, government action must be narrowly tailored and serve a compelling state interest. Under intermediate scrutiny, the action must be substantially related to an important government interest. Rational basis scrutiny requires only a rational relationship to a legitimate government purpose.

Since the enactment of the various federal statutes prohibiting employment discrimination, constitutional claims have typically been accompanied by statutory claims where applicable. Federal statutes now bar discrimination based on race, color, religion, national origin, gender, age and disability. There are differences between constitutional claims and statutory claims, however, among them that Constitutional claims require proof of discriminatory intent while many discrimination statutes allow claims based on the discriminatory impact of employer action without proof of intent. *Id.* Affirmative action in government employment also has been challenged on equal protection grounds. The same levels of scrutiny are applied to classifications that benefit groups that have been historically discriminated against. *Adarand Constructors, Inc. v. Pena*, 515 U.S. 200, 115 S.Ct. 2097, 132 L.Ed.2d 158 (1995).

Equal protection claims in government employment are more fully explored in courses on Constitutional Law and Employment Discrimination. In this section we treat a limited number of equal protection cases, giving particular attention to issues that arise most frequently in government employment.

1. CITIZENSHIP REQUIREMENTS FOR JOB ELIGIBILITY

Some governmental employers have required that their employees be citizens. In *Sugarman v. Dougall*, 413 U.S. 634, 93 S.Ct. 2842, 37 L.Ed.2d 853 (1973), the Supreme Court applied strict scrutiny to New York's law providing that only American citizens could hold permanent positions in the competitive classified civil service, and held it invalid. Justice Blackmun's opinion for the court noted that the law applied to relatively menial positions as well as high policymaking positions, and therefore had "little, if any relationship" to the State's "substantial" interest in having an employee of "undivided loyalty." At the same time, the opinion did not preclude a State from requiring citizenship "in an appropriately defined class of positions," including "persons holding elective or important non-elective executive, legislative and judicial positions, for officers who partic-

ipate directly in the formulation, execution, or review of broad public policy or perform functions that go to the heart of representative government."

After *Dougall*, the Court declined to apply strict scrutiny to New York's rule barring employment of aliens as state troopers, upholding the law as having a "rational relationship to the special demands of the particular position," which entails an "almost infinite variety of discretionary powers" requiring a "very high degree of judgment and discretion." *Foley v. Connelie*, 435 U.S. 291, 98 S.Ct. 1067, 55 L.Ed.2d 287 (1978). In *Ambach v. Norwick*, 441 U.S. 68, 99 S.Ct. 1589, 60 L.Ed.2d 49 (1979), the Court upheld a state's refusal to employ as elementary and secondary school teachers aliens who are eligible for citizenship but refuse to seek naturalization. The Court explained that the assumption of citizenship status "denotes an association with a polity which, in a democratic republic, exercises the powers of governance." The Court stressed the importance of public schools in preparing individuals for participation as citizens, and in "the preservation of values on which our society rests."

However, in *Bernal v. Fainter*, 467 U.S. 216, 104 S.Ct. 2312, 81 L.Ed.2d 175 (1984), the Court struck down a Texas requirement of citizenship to be a notary public. Justice Marshall's opinion for the Court applied strict scrutiny, emphasizing "that the political-function exception must be narrowly construed; otherwise the exception will swallow the rule and depreciate the significance that should attach to the designation of a group as a 'discrete and insular' minority for whom heightened judicial solicitude is appropriate." The opinion noted that the duties of notaries public were "essentially clerical and ministerial," and involved neither policymaking nor broad discretion.

In *Hampton v. Mow Sun Wong*, 426 U.S. 88, 96 S.Ct. 1895, 48 L.Ed.2d 495 (1976), the Court invalidated on non-constitutional grounds a federal Civil Service Commission regulation barring resident aliens from employment in the federal competitive service, but in its opinion recognized that "overriding national interests may provide a justification for a citizenship requirement in the federal service [though] an identical requirement may not be enforced by a State." May the federal government constitutionally require citizenship for the job of searching persons and luggage at airports?

2. SEXUAL ORIENTATION

Over the years, government employees have brought claims challenging discrimination based on sexual orientation on constitutional grounds. This has been a particularly important cause of action for government employee plaintiffs since, unlike race, gender, religion, national origin, age and disability, there is no federal statutory protection against discrimination based on sexual orientation. Federal legislation has been proposed repeatedly, but not yet enacted. States and local governments are increasingly incorporating such protection in statutes and local ordinances, however. Results of constitutional cases have been mixed, although as society has become more accepting of diversity in sexual orientation employee challenges have succeeded more frequently.

GLOVER v. WILLIAMSBURG LOCAL SCHOOL DISTRICT BOARD OF EDUCATION

United States District Court for the Southern District of Ohio, 1998.
20 F.Supp.2d 1160.

DLOTT, J.

I. INTRODUCTION

This is a civil rights action in which a public school teacher, Bruce Glover, claims that the decision not to renew his teaching contract at the Williamsburg Local School District was * * * based on his sexual orientation * * * [T]he defendants claim that the decision not to renew Glover was based on his inability to effectively manage student behavior.

* * *

II. BACKGROUND AND FINDINGS OF FACT

A. *The Parties*

The plaintiff Bruce Glover, is a forty-six year old white man. Glover is gay, and his partner, John Wright, is an African–American man. Glover and Wright have lived together in Mt. Orab, Ohio, for approximately three years. Glover was a first-year teacher at the Williamsburg Elementary School in the 1995–96 school year.

The Williamsburg Local School District ("the District") is located in Clermont County, Ohio. Williamsburg, Ohio is a small, rural community. The District is governed by the Williamsburg Local School District Board of Education ("the Board"), a defendant in this action. * * * [D]efendant Michael McEvoy was the Principal of Williamsburg Elementary School and defendant Barry Campbell was Superintendent of the District.

B. *Glover's Hiring at Williamsburg*

* * * Barry Campbell was serving as Principal of Williamsburg Elementary School during 1994–95, and he also served as the Superintendent of the District for the latter part of that school year. * * * Campbell was impressed with Glover's performance as a substitute teacher, describing him as "excellent." * * * When a job opening arose for the 1995–96 school year, Campbell recommended Glover for a full-time teaching position, relying upon Glover's excellent performance and his strong references. Campbell was aware of Glover's sexual orientation at the time he recommended Glover for employment. At the May 1995 School Board meeting,

the Board voted to offer Glover a one-year contract to teach at Williamsburg Elementary School for the 1995–96 school year.

C. The 1995–96 School Year

1. First Semester

* * *

Teacher Evaluation at Williamsburg

[Teacher evaluations were conducted by the principal based on classroom observations. The principal made a recommendation to the superintendent who made an independent recommendation to the Board of Education which made the final decision on contract renewal. The evaluation forms completed by the principal were available to the superintendent and the Board.]

Glover's First Evaluation

Glover received a positive evaluation from McEvoy for the first semester. * * * McEvoy's observation notes included many positive comments, and McEvoy testified that he was impressed with Glover's teaching. * * *

* * * Glover's scores were generally above average, although he received below average scores for managing student behavior and for conformity with professional standards. McEvoy testified that he gave Glover a below average rating for behavior management because he thought that Glover was too quick to use the discipline technique of sending students to the Principal's office. * * *

McEvoy's positive reviews were consistent with the impressions of other teachers at Williamsburg who taught in close proximity to Glover's classroom. * * *

The False Rumor

The lowest mark received by Glover in his first semester evaluation was in the category of conformity to professional standards. On the evaluation form, McEvoy added a comment to explain the low score: "Mr. Glover has used some indiscretions which may have had a detrimental effect on the respect he receives from students. He was warned at the beginning of the school year not to repeat such behavior." In fact, Glover had never received any warning and he had committed no indiscretion whatsoever. The low score was based on a false rumor which * * * involved Glover and his partner, John Wright, allegedly holding hands at school during a holiday party.

[The false rumor came from a woman who phoned the superintendent. There was a party which Wright and several other adults attended to help out. It was a common practice among teachers to invite family and friends to help at parties and the superintendent acknowledged that it violated no rule.]

After receiving the phone call, Campbell reported the rumor to McEvoy. * * * According to McEvoy, Campbell was upset when he reported the complaint to McEvoy, and Campbell presented it as the truth, not as a rumor. McEvoy then incorporated the alleged indiscretion into Glover's evaluation, giving him a rating of "poor" for conformity with professional standards. Neither Campbell nor McEvoy checked out the rumor or asked Glover about it.

* * *

[After protest by Glover and further investigation which revealed that the rumor was false, the evaluation was changed].

* * * Campbell and McEvoy did not merely revise the evaluation to correct their earlier mistake. They also made efforts to warn Glover about his behavior. McEvoy and Campbell cautioned Glover about how easily rumors can start in a small, conservative community like Williamsburg. Although the hand-holding rumor was untrue, Campbell and McEvoy warned Glover to be careful not to do anything which might fuel rumors and upset the community.

* * * Campbell reported the incident to School Board * * * before the rumor was found to be untrue. * * * Campbell told the Board he had received some complaints and would check it out. Despite subsequently learning that the rumor was false, Campbell never reported back to the Board about the incident.

2. Second Semester

[The principal increased his observations of Glover's classroom in part based on a complaint from a school board member with a student in the class. Despite a contractual requirement that he notify the teacher of such a complaint and offer a meeting with the complaining parent, the principal never told Glover about the complaint.]

After completing his observations, McEvoy produced a teaching evaluation for Glover for the second semester. Glover's scores dropped from the first semester evaluation * * * .

* * * McEvoy told Glover that he would recommend to Superintendent Campbell that Glover's contract be renewed. Campbell, however, decided that his recommendation to the Board would be that Glover not be renewed.

3. Theresa Whiteman

[Whiteman, a white heterosexual woman also in her probationary year, received substantially lower evaluations than Glover in the first semester and lower evaluations in the second semester. Her written scores and the principal's comments rated her worse on management of classroom behavior. In fact, a student was taken to a hospital for treatment as a result of an incident in her class. Although the principal recommended renewal with a one year probationary contract, the superintendent did not.]

4. The School Board's Decision Not to Renew Glover's Contract

* * * On April 15, 1996, the Board held a meeting at which the nonrenewal of Glover and Whiteman was on the agenda. The two teachers were invited to address the Board * * *. Whiteman chose to speak privately to the Board during executive session.

Glover chose to address the Board publicly. The meeting was unusually well-attended for a School Board meeting, and television cameras were present during the meeting. In his public statement to the Board, Glover stated that he believed that the unfounded rumor affected his evaluations and "started the trouble" which led to the steep decline in his second semester scores. When asked by Board President Croswell whether he believed his nonrenewal was a "sexual preference issue," Glover responded that he did believe it was sexual orientation discrimination.

* * * At the close of the April meeting, the Board voted not to renew the contracts of both Whiteman and Glover.

* * * Both Glover and Whiteman were given an opportunity to present an appeal to the Board. * * * On May 24, the Board's initial decision not to renew Whiteman's contract was reversed, and the Board granted Whiteman a new contract. As for Glover, the Board voted unanimously to affirm its decision not to renew his contract. Board member Russell read a statement to the press following the meeting which stated that the reason for Glover's nonrenewal was his inability to manage student behavior in the classroom.

At trial, * * * several Board members stated that their decision concerning Glover was related to the issue of student behavior management. However, Board members also gave several additional reasons for the decision. * * *

* * * Glover has not found a permanent teaching position since the nonrenewal of his contract by Williamsburg in 1996, although he has applied for teaching jobs in various nearby school districts.

III. CONCLUSIONS OF LAW

A. *The Claims*

* * *

1. Equal Protection Claims

Glover maintains that the non-renewal decision violated the Equal Protection Clause because the Board discriminated against him on the basis of his sexual orientation, his gender, and the race of his partner. The defendants deny that the decision was motivated by bias, claiming that Glover was not renewed because of a deficiency in his teaching, specifically his inability to manage student behavior.

* * * Sexual orientation classifications (and all other classifications which are not considered "suspect" or "quasi-suspect") receive the lowest

level of scrutiny: they need only be rationally related to a legitimate state purpose. Regardless of the level of scrutiny, only intentional, purposeful discrimination violates the Equal Protection Clause.

Sexual Orientation Discrimination

* * *

Homosexuals, while not a "suspect class" for equal protection analysis, are entitled to at least the same protection as any other identifiable group which is subject to disparate treatment by the state. *See Stemler,* 126 F.3d 856 at 874 ("The principle would be the same if Stemler had been arrested discriminatorily based on her hair color, her college bumper sticker * * * or her affiliation with a disfavored sorority or company."). Furthermore, a state action which discriminates against homosexuals and is motivated solely by animus towards that group necessarily violates the Equal Protection Clause, because a "desire to effectuate one's animus against homosexuals can never be a legitimate governmental purpose." *Stemler,* 126 F.3d at 874 (citing *Romer v. Evans,* 116 S.Ct. at 1629); *Romer,* 116 S.Ct. at 1628 ("If the constitutional conception of 'equal protection of the laws' means anything, it must at the very least mean that a bare * * * desire to harm a politically unpopular group cannot constitute a legitimate governmental interest.")

* * *

The Framework for Proving Intentional Discrimination

Title VII case law has established a framework for analyzing claims of intentional employment discrimination. This framework can also be used to analyze equal protection claims brought pursuant to 42 U.S.C. § 1983 * * *. Thus, Glover's discrimination claims, which are brought pursuant to both Ohio law and the Equal Protection Clause, can be analyzed under the Title VII framework. This is not surprising since the ultimate issue under Ohio law, Title VII, and the Equal Protection Clause is whether the plaintiff can prove by a preponderance of the evidence that he was the victim of intentional discrimination.

The established framework for deciding employment discrimination cases involves three stages of proof with shifting evidentiary burdens. First, the plaintiff must establish a prima facie case of discrimination. In this case, Glover has established a prima facie case by showing: 1) he is in a protected class; 2) that he was qualified for the job for which the employer was seeking applicants; 3) that he was rejected; and 4) that he was replaced by someone outside the protected class.

Once a plaintiff has established a prima facie case, the burden of production shifts to the defendant to articulate a legitimate, nondiscriminatory reason for the adverse employment action taken against the plaintiff. The defendants in this case have met this burden by claiming that Glover's nonrenewal was based upon his inability to manage student behavior. Finally, if the defendant puts forth a legitimate, nondiscriminatory reason, then the plaintiff must prove by a preponderance of the evidence that the defendant's proffered reasons were not its true reasons, but were merely pretext for illegal discrimination. Thus, the present case turns on whether Glover can prove that the defendants' proffered reason for his nonrenewal was pretextual and the true reason was his sexual orientation, his gender, or the race of his partner.

1. Sexual Orientation Discrimination

a. McEvoy and Campbell

* * * The evidence revealed that the behavior of McEvoy and Campbell was at times unprofessional, and it can be inferred that they would have acted differently if Glover were not homosexual. Their response to the hand-holding rumor is illustrative. First, Campbell received the complaint about a single incident in which Glover allegedly held hands with Mr. Wright at school. Campbell passed along the rumor to McEvoy, both of whom assumed the reported "indiscretion" to be true. Neither approached Glover to discuss the complaint, as specified in the procedures for Williamsburg schools, and in fact Campbell refused to identify the complainant when asked by Glover. If either McEvoy or Campbell had followed school procedures and discussed the allegation with Glover, it is likely that the matter would have been resolved quickly and without incident.

Instead, McEvoy accepted the rumor as true and considered it a serious enough indiscretion to incorporate it as the worst mark on Glover's formal teaching evaluation. Meanwhile, Campbell, upset about the indiscretion, reported the incident to the Board and promised he would check it out. Despite having informed the Board of a complaint serious enough to affect Glover's teaching evaluation, Campbell never reported back to the Board to explain that the rumor was unfounded.

The questionable behavior of McEvoy and Campbell did not cease once the rumor was discovered to be false. In a meeting with Glover, they agreed to revise the evaluation. They proceeded, however, to warn Glover about his behavior, despite the fact that the very purpose of the meeting was to acknowledge that Glover had never behaved improperly. In fact, it was Campbell and McEvoy who had erred when they repeated a false rumor and used the information on Glover's evaluation without informing Glover or verifying the information. Glover was also told at the meeting that Mr. Wright was not to return to the school, although it was customary at Williamsburg for adult acquaintances of teachers to visit the school. Finally, following the incident of the false rumor and redacted evaluation, the scores on Glover's teaching evaluation dropped dramatically. This decline is at least suspicious, in light of its timing and magnitude, and Glover contends that it reflects a discriminatory attitude toward Glover as a gay teacher.

b. The Board

Although the actions of McEvoy and Campbell are important to understand the context for the nonrenewal decision, it is the Board's motivation which is critical to Glover's case. After listening to the testimony of the Board members and reviewing the information available to the Board at the time of the nonrenewal decision, the Court agrees with Glover that the purported reason for his nonrenewal was pretextual. As explained below, the Court found the testimony of the Board members to be contradictory and not entirely credible. Based upon all the evidence presented at trial, the Court is convinced that the Board did in fact discriminate against Glover based upon his sexual orientation when it decided not to renew his teaching contract.

Behavior Management as Pretext

Although the Board members stated that behavior management was the reason for Glover's nonrenewal, this justification does not ring true in light of the comparison of Glover to Theresa Whiteman. The Board considered Whiteman for renewal at the same time as Glover, and the Board decided to renew Whiteman, thereby replacing Glover as a sixth grade teacher. Comparing the scores on the teaching evaluations, which Board members reviewed in making their decisions, one finds that Glover's evaluations were superior to Whiteman's in both semesters. In the first semester, Glover's evaluation was considerably better than Whiteman's.

The decision to renew Whiteman rather than Glover is particularly curious in light of the purported reason for Glover's nonrenewal: management of student behavior. There was testimony at trial that behavior management is a common problem for first-year teachers, and thus it is not surprising or unusual that both Glover and Whiteman had difficulty in this area. Both teachers were below average with respect to management of student behavior. According to the evaluations, however, Whiteman was worse, perhaps illustrated by the incident in which a student was injured in her class. Whiteman received ratings of "poor" and "below average" while Glover was rated "below average" both semesters. In addition to the evaluations, the Board had additional information concerning Glover's ability to manage classroom behavior. McEvoy's observation notes for the second semester reveal that Glover employed a variety of disciplinary approaches, in accordance with McEvoy's earlier suggestion. The Board also heard testimony at the May hearing from Ava Blair, who stated that she had never heard disruptions from Glover's classroom, which was directly across the hall from her own. * * *

Furthermore, although the Board repeatedly and publicly took the position that the sole reason for Glover's nonrenewal was management of student behavior, the rationale for the decision shifted at trial, where Board members articulated different reasons. * * * In sum, in light of the information available to the Board and the other evidence of this case, the

Court finds that the defendants have failed to establish a credible reason for renewing Whiteman over Glover.

Other Evidence to Support an Inference of Discrimination

In addition to the evidence described above, conflicting testimony from various Board members further convinced the Court that the true motivation for the Board's decision not to renew Glover was his sexual orientation. For example, the Board members contradicted each other regarding when the Board was first informed that Glover was gay and whether the Board ever discussed Glover's homosexuality. * * * It is impossible to know why the Board members' testimony was contradictory on this point. At the very least, however, this testimony calls into question the credibility of some of the Board members on an important issue: if and when the Board ever discussed the fact that Glover is homosexual. Finally, despite being aware of rumors and complaints about Glover's homosexuality, the Board never gave any credence to Glover's claim of sexual orientation discrimination. Board President Croswell testified that he received several calls in 1995–96 from people in the community who were concerned about the fact that Glover was gay. Moreover, the entire Board was informed in the May hearing of how an unfounded rumor (the same complaint reported by Campbell to the Board in January) had been used to lower Glover's first evaluation. The Board was also aware that within only a few months after this incident, Glover's teaching evaluation declined sharply from "above average" and "excellent" to mostly "below average." These facts together could reasonably have prompted the Board to at least explore why Glover felt he was being discriminated against or to raise questions about McEvoy's evaluation. Yet no Board member took any action to inquire whether Glover's contention had any merit. Although the failure to investigate Glover's charge is not by itself strong evidence of discrimination, it calls into question the credibility of various Board members' statements that they would never tolerate discrimination.

The Court finds that the evidence, taken together, demonstrates that the Board's purported reason for Glover's nonrenewal was pretextual, and in fact the Board discriminated against Glover on the basis of his sexual orientation. The Court can only speculate as to exactly why the Board acted as it did. Perhaps the Board feared that a gay teacher would act inappropriately or somehow be a trouble-maker. Or perhaps the Board was responding to perceived disapproval in the community of having a gay teacher at Williamsburg. * * *

The defendants have argued that Glover has no direct proof that the Board intended to discriminate against him for being homosexual. However, in discrimination cases, where the ultimate issue is the defendant's intent, it is rare that a decision-maker will admit to discriminating and it is impossible to get inside the decision-maker's mind. * * * Therefore, the fact that Glover lacked a "smoking gun" statement by the Board and proved his case by indirect evidence of discrimination is far from fatal to Glover's case. It is in fact the norm.

Having proven that the Board's nonrenewal decision was motivated by animus, Glover has established his equal protection claim. For purposes of a rational review analysis of the decision, the defendants did not present any evidence at trial to support a legitimate rationale for discriminating against homosexual teachers.[23] As noted above, their position was that no discrimination occurred. However, since the Board was motivated by animus towards Glover as a homosexual, Glover necessarily prevails under a rational basis review of the Board's decision. "Since governmental action 'must bear a rational relationship to a legitimate governmental purpose,' and the desire to effectuate one's animus against homosexuals can never be a legitimate governmental purpose, a state action based on that animus alone violates the Equal Protection Clause." *Stemler v. City of Florence,* 126 F.3d 856, 873–74 (6th Cir. 1997) (quoting *Romer v. Evans,* 517 U.S. 620, 116 S.Ct. 1620, 1629, 134 L.Ed.2d 855 (1996)).

* * *

Accordingly, the Court hereby ORDERS the Board of Education to provide the following relief to Glover:

1) reinstatement as full-time teacher at Williamsburg Elementary School with a two-year teaching contract, beginning in the 1998–99 school year;

2) compensatory damages in the amount of $71,492.00, which includes back pay and emotional distress;

3) attorneys fees and costs.

* * *

NOTES

1. Should the School Board have argued that it had a rational basis to discriminate against Glover based on the moral objections of members of the community? How might such an argument have fared? *See Weaver v. Nebo School District*, 29 F.Supp.2d 1279 (D. Utah 1998) where the school district refused to reassign plaintiff as school volleyball coach after a player asked her if she was a lesbian and when she answered yes, refused to play for her. The court noted that the plaintiff was an excellent volleyball coach and stated:

> The "negative reaction" some members of the community may have to homosexuals is not a proper basis for discriminating against them. So reasoned the Supreme Court in the context of race. See, e.g., *Brown v. Board of Education*, 347 U.S. 483, 495, 74 S.Ct. 686, 98 L.Ed. 873 (1954) (declaring that racial school segregation is unconstitutional despite the widespread acceptance of the practice in the community and in the

23. Although no evidence on this point was presented at trial, the defendants did include the following argument in their summary judgment and post-trial briefs: "While defendants deny that Glover's homosexuality played any role in the decision not to renew his contract, it is clear that a board of education could, consistent with the rational relationship test, conclude that homosexuality is morally objectionable to a substantial number of persons in the community, and might create such tensions and hostilities which would undermine the ability of a homosexual to be an effective teacher."

country). If the community's perception is based on nothing more than unsupported assumptions, outdated stereotypes, and animosity, it is necessarily irrational and under *Romer* and other Supreme Court precedent, it provides no legitimate support for the School District's decisions."

Id. at 1288–89.

2. What if the objections of parents or students to homosexual teachers and coaches are religiously-based? Do school administrators owe any greater duty to respect such objections? See Douglas NeJaime, Inclusion, Accommodation, and Recognition: Accounting for Differences Based on Religion and Sexual Orientation, 32 *Harvard Journal of Law & Gender* 303 (2009) (discussing these issues in the context of curriculum); Jack M. Battaglia, Religion, Sexual Orientation, and Self–Realization: First Amendment Principles and Anti–Discrimination Laws, 76 *University of Detroit Mercy Law Review* 189 (1999) (discussing intersection of laws against sexual orientation discrimination and constitutional freedom of religion). For cases involving the intersection of sexual orientation and religion see *Piggee v. Carl Sandburg College*, 464 F.3d 667 (7th Cir. 2006) (rejecting free speech, free exercise and equal protection claims of cosmetology instructor who was not retained by college after she gave religious pamphlets on the sinfulness of homosexuality to gay student); *Akridge v. Wilkinson*, 178 F.Appx. 474 (6th Cir. 2006) (rejecting First Amendment retaliation and due process claims by prison chaplain disciplined for insubordination for refusal to allow gay inmate to lead choir or praise band in religious services at the prison).

3. Should discrimination on the basis of gender identity be treated the same as discrimination based on sexual orientation under the Equal Protection Clause? See *Smith v. City of Salem*, 378 F.3d 566 (6th Cir. 2004).

4. Gay and lesbian employees have also used First Amendment arguments to challenge adverse actions by employers where they are penalized based on speech about sexual orientation. See *Rowland v. Mad River Local School District*, 730 F.2d 444 (6th Cir. 1984).

5. A few courts have suggested that discrimination against gays and lesbians should be subjected to a higher level of scrutiny than rational basis. See *Able v. United States*, 968 F.Supp. 850 (E.D.N.Y. 1997), *rev'd on other grounds*, 155 F.3d 628 (2d Cir. 1998). Is a higher level of scrutiny warranted for such classifications?

6. Some municipalities require that some or all employees reside in the community as a condition of employment. Such requirements have been challenged on equal protection grounds, though largely unsuccessfully. What government interests would justify such a requirement? What if the requirement applied only to police officers and firefighters? See, e.g., *Detroit Police Officers Association v. Detroit*, 385 Mich. 519, 190 N.W.2d 97 (1971).

3. A CLASS OF ONE

ENGQUIST v. OREGON DEPARTMENT OF AGRICULTURE

Supreme Court of the United States, 2008.
553 U.S. 591, 128 S.Ct. 2146, 170 L.Ed.2d 975.

ROBERTS, C.J., delivered the opinion of the Court.

The question in this case is whether a public employee can state a claim under the Equal Protection Clause by alleging that she was arbitrarily treated differently from other similarly situated employees, with no assertion that the different treatment was based on the employee's membership in any particular class. We hold that such a "class-of-one" theory of equal protection has no place in the public employment context.

I

Anup Engquist, the petitioner in this case, was hired in 1992 by Norma Corristan to be an international food standard specialist for the Export Service Center (ESC), a laboratory within the Oregon Department of Agriculture (ODA). During the course of her employment, Engquist experienced repeated problems with Joseph Hyatt, another ODA employee, complaining to Corristan that he had made false statements about her and otherwise made her life difficult. Corristan responded by directing Hyatt to attend diversity and anger management training.

In 2001, John Szczepanski, an assistant director of ODA, assumed responsibility over ESC, supervising Corristan, Hyatt, and Engquist. Szczepanski told a client that he could not "control" Engquist, and that Engquist and Corristan "would be gotten rid of." When Engquist and Hyatt both applied for a vacant managerial post within ESC, Szczepanski chose Hyatt despite Engquist's greater experience in the relevant field. Later that year, during a round of across-the-board budget cuts in Oregon, Szczepanski eliminated Corristan's position. Finally, on January 31, 2002, Engquist was informed that her position was being eliminated because of reorganization. Engquist's collective-bargaining agreement gave her the opportunity either to "bump" to another position at her level, or to take a demotion. She was found unqualified for the only other position at her level and declined a demotion, and was therefore effectively laid off.

Engquist subsequently brought suit in the United States District Court for the District of Oregon against ODA, Szczepanski, and Hyatt, all respondents here, alleging violations of federal antidiscrimination statutes, the Equal Protection and Due Process Clauses of the Fourteenth Amendment, and state law. As to Engquist's equal protection claim, she alleged that the defendants discriminated against her on the basis of her race, sex, and national origin. She also brought what is known as a "class-of-one" equal protection claim, alleging that she was fired not because she was a member of an identified class (unlike her race, sex, and national origin claims), but simply for "arbitrary, vindictive, and malicious reasons."

The District Court granted the respondents' motion for summary judgment as to some of Engquist's claims, but allowed others to go forward, including each of the equal protection claims. As relevant to this case, the District Court found Engquist's class-of-one equal protection claim legally viable, deciding that the class-of-one theory was fully applicable in the employment context. The court held that Engquist could succeed on that theory if she could prove "that she was singled out as a result of animosity on the part of Hyatt and Szczepanski"—*i.e.*, "that their actions were spiteful efforts to punish her for reasons unrelated to any legitimate state objective"—and if she could demonstrate, on the basis of that animosity, that "she was treated differently than others who were similarly situated."

The jury rejected Engquist's claims of discrimination for membership in a suspect class—her race, sex, and national origin claims—but found in her favor on the class-of-one claim. Specifically, the jury found that Hyatt and Szczepanski "intentionally treat[ed] [Engquist] differently than others similarly situated with respect to the denial of her promotion, termination of her employment, or denial of bumping rights without any rational basis and solely for arbitrary, vindictive or malicious reasons." The jury also found for Engquist on several of her other claims, and awarded her $175,000 in compensatory damages and $250,000 in punitive damages.

The Court of Appeals reversed in relevant part. It recognized that this Court had upheld a class-of-one equal protection challenge to state legislative and regulatory action in *Village of Willowbrook* v. *Olech,* 528 U.S. 562, 120 S.Ct. 1073, 145 L.Ed. 2d 1060 (2000) (*per curiam*). 478 F.3d 985, 992–993 (CA9 2007). The court below also acknowledged that other Circuits had applied *Olech* in the public employment context, *id.,* at 993 (citing cases), but it disagreed with those courts on the ground that our cases have routinely afforded government greater leeway when it acts as employer rather than regulator, *id.,* at 993–996. The court concluded that extending the class-of-one theory of equal protection to the public employment context would lead to undue judicial interference in state employment practices and "completely invalidate the practice of public at-will employment." The court accordingly held that the class-of-one theory is "inapplicable to decisions made by public employers with regard to their employees."

* * * We granted certiorari to resolve this disagreement in the lower courts, and now affirm.

II

Engquist argues that the Equal Protection Clause forbids public employers from irrationally treating one employee differently from others similarly situated, regardless of whether the different treatment is based on the employee's membership in a particular class. She reasons that in *Olech, supra,* we recognized in the regulatory context a similar class-of-one theory of equal protection, that the Equal Protection Clause protects individuals, not classes, that the Clause proscribes "discrimination arising not only from a legislative act but also from the conduct of an administrative official," and that the Constitution applies to the State not only when it acts as regulator, but also when it acts as employer. Thus, Engquist concludes that class-of-one claims can be brought against public employers just as against any other state actors, and that differential treatment of government employees—even when not based on membership in a class or group—violates the Equal Protection Clause unless supported by a rational basis.

We do not quarrel with the premises of Engquist's argument. It is well settled that the Equal Protection Clause "protect[s] persons, not groups," *Adarand Constructors v. Pena,* 515 U.S. 200, 227, 115 S.Ct. 2097, 132 L.Ed. 2d 158 (1995) (emphasis omitted), and that the Clause's protections apply to administrative as well as legislative acts, see, *e.g., Raymond* v. *Chicago Union Traction Co.,* 207 U.S. 20, 35–36, 28 S.Ct. 7, 52 L.Ed. 78 (1907). It is equally well settled that States do not escape the strictures of the Equal Protection Clause in their role as employers. * * * We do not, however, agree that Engquist's conclusion follows from these premises. Our traditional view of the core concern of the Equal Protection Clause as a shield against arbitrary classifications, combined with unique considerations applicable when the government acts as employer as opposed to sovereign, lead us to conclude that the class-of-one theory of equal protection does not apply in the public employment context.

A

We have long held the view that there is a crucial difference, with respect to constitutional analysis, between the government exercising "the power to regulate or license, as lawmaker," and the government acting "as proprietor, to manage [its] internal operation." *Cafeteria & Restaurant Workers* v. *McElroy,* 367 U.S. 886, 896, 81 S.Ct. 1743, 6 L.Ed. 2d 1230 (1961). This distinction has been particularly clear in our review of state action in the context of public employment. Thus, "the government as employer indeed has far broader powers than does the government as sovereign." *Waters* v. *Churchill,* 511 U.S. 661, 671, 114 S.Ct. 1878, 128 L.Ed. 2d 686 (1994) (plurality opinion). "[T]he extra power the government has in this area comes from the nature of the government's mission as employer. Government agencies are charged by law with doing particular tasks. Agencies hire employees to help do those tasks as effectively and efficiently as possible." *Id.,* at 674–675, 114 S.Ct. 1878, 128 L.Ed. 2d 686. See also *Connick* v. *Myers,* 461 U.S. 138, 150–151, 103 S.Ct. 1684, 75 L.Ed. 2d 708 (1983) (explaining that the government has a legitimate interest "in 'promot[ing] efficiency and integrity in the discharge of official duties, and [in] maintain[ing] proper discipline in the public service' " (quoting *Ex parte Curtis,* 106 U.S. 371, 373, 1 S.Ct. 381, 27 L.Ed. 232 (1882) (alterations in original))). "The government's interest in achieving its goals as effectively and efficiently as possible is elevated from a relatively subordinate interest when it acts as sovereign to a significant one when it acts as employer." Given the "common-sense realization that government offices could not function if every employment decision became a constitutional matter," *Connick, supra,* at 143, 103 S.Ct. 1684, 75 L.Ed. 2d 708, "constitutional review of government employment decisions must rest on different principles than review of * * * restraints imposed by the government as sovereign," *Waters, supra,* at 674, 114 S.Ct. 1878, 128 L.Ed. 2d 686 (plurality opinion).

In light of these basic principles, we have often recognized that government has significantly greater leeway in its dealings with citizen employees than it does when it brings its sovereign power to bear on citizens at large. Thus, for example, we have held that the Fourth Amendment does not require public employers to obtain warrants before conducting a search of an employee's office. *O'Connor* v. *Ortega,* 480 U.S. 709, 721–722, 107 S.Ct. 1492, 94 L.Ed. 2d 714 (1987) (plurality opinion). * * * Although we recognized that the "legitimate privacy interests of public employees in the private objects they bring to the workplace may be substantial," we found that "[a]gainst these privacy interests * * * must be balanced the realities of the workplace, which strongly suggest that a warrant requirement would be unworkable." *Id.,* at 721, 107 S.Ct. 1492, 94 L.Ed. 2d 714 (plurality opinion). We have also found that the Due Process Clause does not protect a public employee from discharge, even when such discharge was mistaken or unreasonable. See *Bishop* v. *Wood,* 426 U.S. 341, 350, 96 S.Ct. 2074, 48 L.Ed. 2d 684 (1976) ("The Due Process Clause of the Fourteenth Amendment is not a guarantee against incorrect or ill-advised personnel decisions").

Our public-employee speech cases are particularly instructive. In *Pickering* v. *Board of Ed. of Township High School Dist. 205, Will Cty.,* 391 U.S. 563, 568, 88 S.Ct. 1731, 20 L.Ed. 2d 811 (1968), we explained that, in analyzing a claim that a public employee was deprived of First Amendment rights by her employer, we must seek "a balance between the interests of the [employee], as a citizen, in commenting upon matters of public concern and the interest of the State, as an employer, in promoting the efficiency of the public services it performs through its employees."

We analyzed the contours of this balance more fully in *Connick* v. *Myers, supra.* We explained that the First Amendment protects public-employee speech only when it falls within the core of First Amendment protection—speech on matters of public concern. We recognized that the " 'First Amendment does not protect speech and assembly only to the extent it can be characterized as political,' " and that the government therefore could not generally prohibit or punish, in its capacity as sovereign, speech on the ground that it does not touch upon matters of public concern, *id.,* at 147, 103 S.Ct. 1684, 75 L.Ed. 2d 708 (quoting *United Mine Workers* v. *Illinois State Bar Ass'n,* 389 U.S. 217, 223, 88 S.Ct. 353, 19 L.Ed.2d 426 (1967)). But "[w]hen employee expression cannot be fairly considered as relating to any matter of political, social, or other concern to the community, government officials should enjoy wide latitude in managing their offices." *Connick,* 461 U.S., at 146, 103 S.Ct. 1684. As we explained, "absent the most unusual circumstances, a federal court is not the appropriate forum in which to review the wisdom of a personnel decision taken by a public agency allegedly in reaction to the employee's behavior." *Id.,* at 147, 103 S.Ct. 1684 (citing *Bishop, supra,* at 349–350, 96 S.Ct. 2074).

Our precedent in the public-employee context therefore establishes two main principles: First, although government employees do not lose their constitutional rights when they accept their positions, those rights must be balanced against the realities of the employment context. Second, in striking the appropriate balance, we consider whether the asserted employee right implicates the basic concerns of the relevant constitutional provision, or whether the claimed right can more readily give way to the requirements of the government as employer. With these principles in mind, we come to the question whether a class-of-one theory of equal protection is cognizable in the public employment context.

B

Our equal protection jurisprudence has typically been concerned with governmental classifications that "affect some groups of citizens differently than others." * * * Plaintiffs in such cases generally allege that they have been arbitrarily classified as members of an "identifiable group."

Engquist correctly argues, however, that we recognized in *Olech* that an equal protection claim can in some circumstances be sustained even if the plaintiff has not alleged class-based discrimination, but instead claims that she has been irrationally singled out as a so-called "class of one." In *Olech*, a property owner had asked the village of Willowbrook to connect her property to the municipal water supply. Although the village had required only a 15–foot easement from other property owners seeking access to the water supply, the village conditioned Olech's connection on a grant of a 33–foot easement. Olech sued the village, claiming that the village's requirement of an easement 18 feet longer than the norm violated the Equal Protection Clause. Although Olech had not alleged that the village had discriminated against her based on membership in an identifiable class, we held that her complaint stated a valid claim under the Equal Protection Clause because it alleged that she had "been intentionally treated differently from others similarly situated and that there is no rational basis for the difference in treatment." 528 U.S., at 564, 120 S.Ct. 1073 * * *.

Recognition of the class-of-one theory of equal protection on the facts in *Olech* was not so much a departure from the principle that the Equal Protection Clause is concerned with arbitrary government classification, as it was an application of that principle. That case involved the government's regulation of property. Similarly, the cases upon which the Court in *Olech* relied concerned property assessment and taxation schemes.

* * * We expect such legislative or regulatory classifications to apply "without respect to persons," to borrow a phrase from the judicial oath. As we explained long ago, the Fourteenth Amendment "requires that all persons subjected to * * * legislation shall be treated alike, under like circumstances and conditions, both in the privileges conferred and in the liabilities imposed." When those who appear similarly situated are nevertheless treated differently, the Equal Protection Clause requires at least a rational reason for the difference, to assure that all persons subject to legislation or regulation are indeed being "treated alike, under like circumstances and conditions." Thus, when it appears that an individual is being singled out by the government, the specter of arbitrary classification is fairly raised, and the Equal Protection Clause requires a "rational basis for the difference in treatment." *Olech,* 528 U.S., at 564, 120 S.Ct. 1073.

What seems to have been significant in *Olech* and the cases on which it relied was the existence of a clear standard against which departures, even for a single plaintiff, could be readily assessed. * * * This differential treatment raised a concern of arbitrary classification, and we therefore required that the State provide a rational basis for it. * * *

There are some forms of state action, however, which by their nature involve discretionary decisionmaking based on a vast array of subjective, individualized assessments. In such cases the rule that people should be "treated alike, under like circumstances and conditions" is not violated when one person is treated differently from others, because treating like individuals differently is an accepted consequence of the discretion granted. In such situations, allowing a challenge based on the arbitrary singling out of a particular person would undermine the very discretion that such state officials are entrusted to exercise.

Suppose, for example, that a traffic officer is stationed on a busy highway where people often drive above the speed limit, and there is no basis upon which to distinguish them. If the officer gives only one of those people a ticket, it may be good English to say that the officer has created a class of people that did not get speeding tickets, and a "class of one" that did. But assuming that it is in the nature of the particular government activity that not all speeders can be stopped and ticketed, complaining that one has been singled out for no reason does not invoke the fear of improper government classification. Such a complaint, rather, challenges the legitimacy of the underlying action itself—the decision to ticket speeders under such circumstances. Of course, an allegation that speeding tickets are given out on the basis of race or sex would state an equal protection claim, because such discriminatory classifications implicate basic equal protection concerns. But allowing an equal protection claim on the ground that a ticket was given to one person and not others, even if for no discernible or articulable reason, would be incompatible with the discretion inherent in the challenged action. It is no proper challenge to what in its nature is a subjective, individualized decision that it was subjective and individualized.

This principle applies most clearly in the employment context, for employment decisions are quite often subjective and individualized, resting on a wide array of factors that are difficult to articulate and quantify. As Engquist herself points out, "[u]nlike the zoning official, the public employer often must take into account the individual personalities and interpersonal relationships of employees in the workplace. The close relationship between the employer and employee, and the varied needs and interests involved in the employment context, mean that considerations such as concerns over personality conflicts that would be unreasonable as grounds for 'arm's-length' government decisions (*e.g.*, zoning, licensing) may well justify different treatment of a public employee." Unlike the context of arm's-length regulation, such as in *Olech,* treating seemingly similarly situated individuals differently in the employment context is par for the course.

Thus, the class-of-one theory of equal protection—which presupposes that like individuals should be treated alike, and that to treat them differently is to classify them in a way that must survive at least rationality review—is simply a poor fit in the public employment context. To treat employees differently is not to classify them in a way that raises equal protection concerns. Rather, it is simply to exercise the broad discretion that typically characterizes the employer-employee relationship. A challenge that one has been treated individually in this context, instead of like everyone else, is a challenge to the underlying nature of the government action.

Of course, that is not to say that the Equal Protection Clause, like other constitutional provisions, does not apply to public employers. Indeed, our cases make clear that the Equal Protection Clause is implicated when the government makes class-based decisions in the employment context, treating distinct groups of individuals categorically differently. See, *e.g., Beazer,* 440 U.S., at 593, 99 S.Ct. 1355 (upholding city's exclusion of methadone users from employment under rational-basis review); *Martin,* 440 U.S., at 199–201, 99 S.Ct. 1062 (classification between teachers who had complied with a continuing-education requirement and those who had not is rational and does not violate the Equal Protection Clause); *Murgia,* 427 U.S. at 314–317, 96 S.Ct. 2562 (upholding a mandatory retirement age—a classification based on age—under rational-basis review). The dissent's broad statement that we "excep[t] state employees from the Fourteenth Amendment's protection against unequal and irrational treatment at the hands of the State," is thus plainly not correct. But we have never found the Equal Protection Clause implicated in the specific circumstance where, as here, government employers are alleged to have made an individualized, subjective personnel decision in a seemingly arbitrary or irrational manner.

This is not surprising, given the historical understanding of the nature of government employment. We long ago recognized the "settled principle that government employment, in the absence of legislation, can be revoked at the will of the appointing officer." *McElroy,* 367 U.S., at

896, 81 S.Ct. 1743. The basic principle of at-will employment is that an employee may be terminated for a " 'good reason, bad reason, or no reason at all.' " * * * Thus, "[w]e have never held that it is a violation of the Constitution for a government employer to discharge an employee based on substantively incorrect information." *Waters,* 511 U.S., at 679, 114 S.Ct. 1878 (plurality opinion). * * *

State employers cannot, of course, take personnel actions that would independently violate the Constitution. But recognition of a class-of-one theory of equal protection in the public employment context—that is, a claim that the State treated an employee differently from others for a bad reason, or for no reason at all—is simply contrary to the concept of at-will employment. The Constitution does not require repudiating that familiar doctrine.

To be sure, Congress and all the States have, for the most part, replaced at-will employment with various statutory schemes protecting public employees from discharge for impermissible reasons. See, *e.g.,* 5 U.S.C. § 2302(b)(10) (2006 ed.) (supervisor of covered federal employee may not "discriminate * * * on the basis of conduct which does not adversely affect the performance of the employee or applicant or the performance of others") But a government's decision to limit the ability of public employers to fire at will is an act of legislative grace, not constitutional mandate.

Indeed, recognizing the sort of claim Engquist presses could jeopardize the delicate balance governments have struck between the rights of public employees and "the government's legitimate purpose in 'promot[ing] efficiency and integrity in the discharge of official duties, and [in] maintain[ing] proper discipline in the public service.' " *Connick, supra,* at 151, 103 S.Ct. 1684 (quoting *Ex parte Curtis,* 106 U.S., at 373, 1 S.Ct. 381; alterations in original). Thus, for example, although most federal employees are covered by the Civil Service Reform Act of 1978, Pub. L. 95–454, Congress has specifically excluded some groups of employees from its protection, see, *e.g.,* 5 U.S.C. § 2302(a)(2)(C) (2006 ed.) (excluding from coverage, *inter alia,* the Federal Bureau of Investigation, the Central Intelligence Agency, and the Defense Intelligence Agency). Were we to find that the Equal Protection subjects the Government to equal protection review for every allegedly arbitrary employment action, we will have undone Congress's (and the States') careful work.

In concluding that the class-of-one theory of equal protection has no application in the public employment context—and that is all we decide—we are guided, as in the past, by the "common-sense realization that government offices could not function if every employment decision became a constitutional matter." *Connick, supra,* at 143, 103 S. Ct. 1684. If, as Engquist suggests, plaintiffs need not claim discrimination on the basis of membership in some class or group, but rather may argue only that they were treated by their employers worse than other employees similarly situated, any personnel action in which a wronged employee can conjure up a claim of differential treatment will suddenly become the basis for a federal constitutional claim. Indeed, an allegation of arbitrary differential treatment could be made in nearly every instance of an assertedly wrongful employment action—not only hiring and firing decisions, but any personnel action, such as promotion, salary, or work assignments—on the theory that other employees were not treated wrongfully. On Engquist's view, every one of these employment decisions by a government employer would become the basis for an equal protection complaint. * * *

The judgment of the Court of Appeals is affirmed.

STEVENS, J. joined by SOUTER and GINSBURG JJ., dissenting.

Congress has provided a judicial remedy for individuals whose federal constitutional rights are violated by state action, 42 U.S.C. § 1983. * * * In *Garcetti*, the Court created a new substantive rule excepting a category of speech by state employees from the protection of the First Amendment. Today, the Court creates a new substantive rule excepting state employees from the Fourteenth Amendment's protection against unequal and irrational treatment at the hands of the State. Even if some surgery were truly necessary to prevent governments from being forced to defend a multitude of equal protection "class of one" claims, the Court should use a scalpel rather than a meat-axe.

I

* * *

* * * The jury's verdict * * * established that there was no rational basis for either treating Engquist differently from other employees or for the termination of her employment. The State does not dispute this finding. Under our reasoning in *Olech*, the absence of any justification for the discrimination sufficed to establish the constitutional violation.

The majority nonetheless concludes, based on "unique considerations applicable when the government acts as employer," that the "class of one" theory of equal protection is not applicable in the public employment context. Its conclusion is based upon speculation about inapt hypothetical cases, and an incorrect evaluation of the importance of the government's interest in preserving a regime of "at will" employment. Its reasoning is flawed on both counts.

II

The majority asserts that public-employment decisions should be carved out of our equal protection jurisprudence because employment decisions (as opposed to, for example, zoning decisions) are inherently discretionary. I agree that employers must be free to exercise discretionary authority. But there is a clear distinction between an exercise of discretion and an arbitrary decision. A discretionary decision represents a choice of one among two or more rational alternatives. * * * The choice may be mistaken or unwise without being irrational. If the arguments favoring each alternative are closely balanced, the need to make a choice may justify using a coin toss as a tie breaker. Moreover, the Equal Protection Clause proscribes arbitrary decisions—decisions unsupported by any rational basis—not unwise ones. Accordingly, a discretionary decision with any "reasonably conceivable" rational justification will not support an equal protection claim; only a truly arbitrary one will. There is therefore no need to create an exception for the public-employment context in order to prevent these discretionary decisions from giving rise equal protection claims.

The hypothetical situations posited by the majority do not prove otherwise. * * *

Instead of using a scalpel to confine so-called "class of one" claims to cases involving a complete absence of any conceivable rational basis for the adverse action and the differential treatment of the plaintiff, the Court adopts an unnecessarily broad rule that tolerates arbitrary and irrational decisions in the employment context.

* * *

IV

Presumably the concern that actually motivates today's decision is fear that governments will be forced to defend against a multitude of "class of one" claims unless the Court wields its meat-axe forthwith. Experience demonstrates, however, that these claims are brought infrequently, that the vast majority of such claims are asserted in complaints advancing other claims as well, and that all but a handful are dismissed well in advance of trial. Experience also demonstrates that there are in fact rare cases in which a petty tyrant has misused governmental power. Proof that such misuse was arbitrary because unsupported by any conceivable rational basis should suffice to establish a violation of the Equal Protection Clause without requiring its victim also to prove that the tyrant was motivated by a particular variety of class-based animus.

In sum, there is no compelling reason to carve arbitrary public-employment decisions out of the well-established category of equal protection violations when the familiar rational review standard can sufficiently limit these claims to only wholly unjustified employment actions. Accordingly, I respectfully dissent.

NOTES

1. How relevant is preservation of the employment at will doctrine in the public sector where a significant percentage of employees have some form of employment protection such as civil service or tenure, as well as constitutional protection? Is the Court resurrecting the rationale of *McAuliffe v. New Bedford*, discussed *supra* in § A?

2. Did the Court strike the appropriate balance between the protection of employees and the efficiency and effectiveness of the employer?

3. What if the Department of Agriculture had simply argued that it had just cause to dismiss Engquist? How does just cause fit with equal protection?

4. There is a developing movement to address bullying in the workplace. Research shows that 37% of workers have been bullied in the workplace, that it is far more common than discriminatory harassment, and that employers tend to ignore the problem. *See* Workplace Bullying Institute, *Results of the WBI U.S. Workplace Bullying Survey,* http://www.workplacebullying.org/research/WBI–Zogby2007Survey.html. Legal remedies for workplace bullying are limited, although it is costly to employers and employees. See David C. Yamada, Crafting a Legislative Response to Workplace Bullying, 8 *Employee Rights and Employment Policy Journal* 475 (2004). Did the dissent minimize the prevalence of the problem? Did the majority miss an opportunity to create a legal remedy for a widespread and costly problem? What sort of legal remedy would that have been?

F. PRIVACY

While the Constitution does not contain any express provision relating to the right to privacy, courts have recognized a constitutional privacy right for many years. Most cases in the public sector workplace involve the right to keep personal matters private, rather than the right to be free from governmental interference with private decisions. The Fourth Amendment has provided the basis for a number of constitutional challenges to actions undertaken by governmental employers.

NATIONAL TREASURY EMPLOYEES UNION v. VON RAAB

Supreme Court of the United States, 1989.
489 U.S. 656, 109 S.Ct. 1384, 103 L.Ed.2d 685.

KENNEDY, J., delivered the opinion of the Court.

We granted certiorari to decide whether it violates the Fourth Amendment for the United States Customs Service to require a urinalysis test from employees who seek transfer or promotion to certain positions. * * *

The United States Customs Service, a bureau of the Department of the Treasury, is the federal agency responsible for processing persons, carriers, cargo, and mail into the United States, collecting revenue from imports, and enforcing customs and related laws. * * * An important responsibility of the Service is the interdiction and seizure of contraband, including illegal drugs. In 1987 alone, Customs agents seized drugs with a retail value of nearly $9 billion. * * * In the routine discharge of their duties, many Customs employees have direct contact with those who traffic in drugs for profit. * * * [M]any Customs operatives carry and use firearms in connection with their official duties.

* * * [T]he Commissioner [of Customs] announced his intention to require drug tests of employees who applied for, or occupied, certain positions within the Service. The Commissioner stated his belief that "Customs is largely drug-free," but noted also that "unfortunately no segment of society is immune from the threat of illegal drug use." Drug

interdiction has become the agency's primary enforcement mission, and the Commissioner stressed that "there is no room in the Customs Service for those who break the laws prohibiting the possession and use of illegal drugs."

In May 1986, the Commissioner announced implementation of the drug-testing program. Drug tests were made a condition of placement or employment for positions that meet one or more of three criteria. The first is direct involvement in drug interdiction or enforcement of related laws, an activity the Commissioner deemed fraught with obvious dangers to the mission of the agency and the lives of Customs agents. The second criterion is a requirement that the incumbent carry firearms, as the Commissioner concluded that "[p]ublic safety demands that employees who carry deadly arms and are prepared to make instant life or death decisions be drug free." The third criterion is a requirement for the incumbent to handle "classified" material, which the Commissioner determined might fall into the hands of smugglers if accessible to employees who, by reason of their own illegal drug use, are susceptible to bribery or blackmail.

After an employee qualifies for a position covered by the Customs testing program, the Service advises him by letter that his final selection is contingent upon successful completion of drug screening. [A detailed description of the procedure for the urinalysis and the testing of the specimens follows.] * * *

Customs employees who test positive for drugs and who can offer no satisfactory explanation are subject to dismissal from the Service. Test results may not, however, be turned over to any other agency, including criminal prosecutors, without the employee's written consent.

Petitioners, a union of federal employees and a union official, commenced this suit in the United States District Court for the Eastern District of Louisiana on behalf of current Customs Service employees who seek covered positions. Petitioners alleged that the Custom Service drug-testing program violated, inter alia, the Fourth Amendment. The District Court agreed. * * * The court enjoined the drug-testing program, and ordered the Customs Service not to require drug tests of any applicants for covered positions. A divided panel of the United States Court of Appeals for the Fifth Circuit vacated the injunction. * * * We granted certiorari. We now affirm so much of the judgment of the Court of Appeals as upheld the testing of employees directly involved in drug interdiction or required to carry firearms. We vacate the judgment to the extent it upheld the testing of applicants for positions requiring the incumbent to handle classified materials, and remand for further proceedings.

II

In *Skinner v. Railway Labor Executives' Assn.*, 489 U.S. 602, 616–618, 109 S.Ct. 1402, 1412–1413, 103 L.Ed.2d 639, decided today, we held that federal regulations requiring employees of private railroads to produce urine samples for chemical testing implicate the Fourth Amendment, as those tests invade reasonable expectations of privacy. Our earlier cases have settled that the Fourth Amendment protects individuals from unreasonable searches conducted by the Government, even when the Government acts as an employer, *O'Connor v. Ortega,* 480 U.S. 709, 717, 107 S.Ct. 1492, 1498, 94 L.Ed.2d 714 (1987) (plurality opinion); see id., at 731, 107 S.Ct., at 1505 (SCALIA, J., concurring in judgment), and, in view of our holding in *Railway Labor Executives* that urine tests are searches, it follows that the Customs Service's drug-testing program must meet the reasonableness requirement of the Fourth Amendment.

While we have often emphasized, and reiterate today, that a search must be supported, as a general matter, by a warrant issued upon probable cause, our decision in *Railway Labor Executives* reaffirms the longstanding principle that neither a warrant nor probable cause, nor, indeed, any measure of individualized suspicion, is an indispensable component of reasonableness in every circumstance. As we note in *Railway Labor Executives,* our cases establish that where a Fourth Amendment intrusion serves special governmental needs, beyond the normal need for law enforcement, it is necessary to balance the individual's privacy expectations against the Government's interests to determine whether it is impractical to require a warrant or some level of individualized suspicion in the particular context.

It is clear that the Customs Service's drug-testing program is not designed to serve the ordinary needs of law enforcement. Test results may not be used in a criminal prosecution of the employee without the employee's consent. The purposes of the program are to deter drug use among those eligible for promotion to sensitive positions within the Service and to prevent the promotion of drug users to those positions. These substantial interests, no less than the Government's concern for safe rail transportation at issue in *Railway Labor Executives,* present a special need that may justify departure from the ordinary warrant and probable-cause requirements.

A

Petitioners do not contend that a warrant is required by the balance of privacy and governmental interests in this context, nor could any such contention withstand scrutiny. We have recognized before that requiring the Government to procure a warrant for every work-related intrusion "would conflict with 'the common-sense realization that government offices could not function if every employment decision became a constitutional matter.' " * * *

Furthermore, a warrant would provide little or nothing in the way of additional protection of personal privacy. * * * Under the Customs program, every employee who seeks a transfer to a covered position knows that he must take a drug test, and is likewise aware of the procedures the Service must follow in administering the test. * * *

B

Even where it is reasonable to dispense with the warrant requirement in the particular circumstances, a search ordinarily must be based on probable cause. Our cases teach, however, that the probable-cause standard " 'is peculiarly related to criminal investigations.' " In particular, the traditional probable-cause standard may be unhelpful in analyzing the reasonableness of routine administrative functions * * *. Our precedents have settled that, in certain limited circumstances, the Government's need to discover such latent or hidden conditions, or to prevent their development, is sufficiently compelling to justify the intrusion on privacy entailed by conducting such searches without any measure of individualized suspicion. We think the Government's need to conduct the suspicionless searches required by the Customs program outweighs the privacy interests of employees engaged directly in drug interdiction, and of those who otherwise are required to carry firearms.

The Customs Service is our Nation's first line of defense against one of the greatest problems affecting the health and welfare of our population. We have adverted before to "the veritable national crisis in law enforcement caused by smuggling of illicit narcotics." * * *

Many of the Service's employees are often exposed to this criminal element and to the controlled substances it seeks to smuggle into the country. The physical safety of these employees may be threatened, and many may be tempted not only by bribes from the traffickers with whom they deal, but also by their own access to vast sources of valuable contraband seized and controlled by the Service. The Commissioner indicated below that "Customs [o]fficers have been shot, stabbed, run over, dragged by automobiles, and assaulted with blunt objects while performing their duties." At least nine officers have died in the line of duty since 1974. He also noted that Customs officers have been the targets of bribery by drug smugglers on numerous occasions, and several have been removed from the Service for accepting bribes and for other integrity violations. * * *

It is readily apparent that the Government has a compelling interest in ensuring that front-line interdiction personnel are physically fit, and have unimpeachable integrity and judgment. * * * A drug user's indifference to the Service's basic mission or, even worse, his active complicity with the malefactors, can facilitate importation of sizable drug shipments or block apprehension of dangerous criminals. The public interest demands effective measures to bar drug users from positions directly involving the interdiction of illegal drugs.

The public interest likewise demands effective measures to prevent the promotion of drug users to positions that require the incumbent to carry a firearm, even if the incumbent is not engaged directly in the interdiction of drugs. Customs employees who may use deadly force plainly "discharge duties fraught with such risks of injury to others that even a momentary lapse of attention can have disastrous consequences." * * *

Against these valid public interests we must weigh the interference with individual liberty that results from requiring these classes of employees to undergo a urine test. The interference with individual privacy that results from the collection of a urine sample for subsequent chemical analysis could be substantial in some circumstances. We have recognized, however, that the "operational realities of the workplace" may render entirely reasonable certain work-related intrusions by supervisors and co-workers that might be viewed as unreasonable in other contexts. While these operational realities will rarely affect an employee's expectations of privacy with respect to searches of his person, or of personal effects that the employee may bring to the workplace, it is plain that certain forms of public employment may diminish privacy expectations even with respect to such personal searches. * * *

We think Customs employees who are directly involved in the interdiction of illegal drugs or who are required to carry firearms in the line of duty likewise have a diminished expectation of privacy in respect to the intrusions occasioned by a urine test. Unlike most private citizens or government employees in general, employees involved in drug interdiction reasonably should expect effective inquiry into their fitness and probity. Much the same is true of employees who are required to carry firearms. Because successful performance of their duties depends uniquely on their judgment and dexterity, these employees cannot reasonably expect to keep from the Service personal information that bears directly on their fitness. * * *

* * * [P]etitioners nevertheless contend that the Service's drug-testing program is unreasonable in two particulars. First, petitioners argue that the program is unjustified because it is not based on a belief that testing will reveal any drug use by covered employees. * * * Second, petitioners contend that the Service's scheme is not a "sufficiently productive mechanism to justify [its] intrusion upon Fourth Amendment interests," because illegal drug users can avoid detection with ease by temporary abstinence or by surreptitious adulteration of their urine specimens. These contentions are unpersuasive.

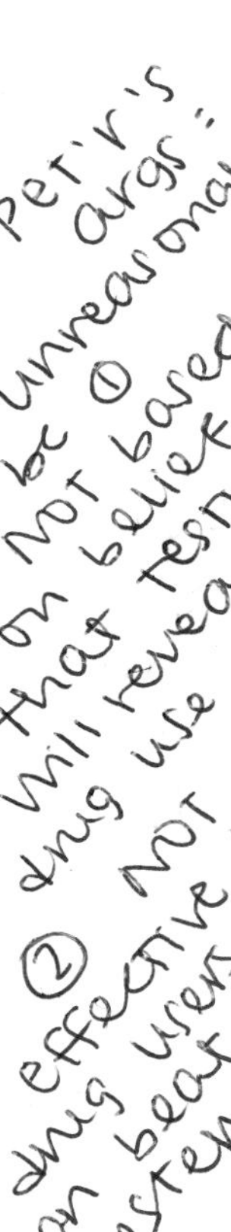

* * * In light of the extraordinary safety and national security hazards that would attend the promotion of drug users to positions that require the carrying of firearms or the interdiction of controlled substances, the Service's policy of deterring drug users from seeking such promotions cannot be deemed unreasonable. The mere circumstance that all but a few of the employees tested are entirely innocent of wrongdoing does not impugn the program's validity. * * *

We think petitioners' second argument—that the Service's testing program is ineffective because employees may attempt to deceive the test by a brief abstention before the test date, or by adulterating their urine specimens—overstates the case. As the Court of Appeals noted, addicts may be unable to abstain even for a limited period of time, or may be unaware of the "fade-away effect" of certain drugs. More importantly, the avoidance techniques suggested by petitioners are fraught with uncertainty and risks for those employees who venture to attempt them. * * * In all the circumstances, we are persuaded that the program bears a close and substantial relation to the Service's goal of deterring drug users from seeking promotion to sensitive positions.

In sum, we believe the Government has demonstrated that its compelling interests in safeguarding our borders and the public safety outweigh the privacy expectations of employees who seek to be promoted to positions that directly involve the interdiction of illegal drugs or that require the incumbent to carry a firearm. * * *

[The Court went on to state that testing of employees with access to sensitive materials was reasonable but found the record insufficient to determine whether the employees in the job categories identified for testing in fact had access to such materials and therefore remanded the case.]

[MARSHALL, J., joined by BRENNAN, J., dissented on grounds that probable cause was required for drug testing by employers but also indicated that if the balancing test applied by the Court was appropriate, he would agree with Justice Scalia that the testing was not reasonable.]

SCALIA, J. joined by STEVENS, J., dissenting.

The issue in this case is not whether Customs Service employees can constitutionally be denied promotion, or even dismissed, for a single instance of unlawful drug use, at home or at work. They assuredly can. The issue here is what steps can constitutionally be taken to detect such drug use. The Government asserts it can demand that employees perform "an excretory function traditionally shielded by great privacy," while "a monitor of the same sex * * * remains close at hand to listen for the normal sounds," and that the excretion thus produced be turned over to the Government for chemical analysis. The Court agrees that this constitutes a search for purposes of the Fourth Amendment—and I think it obvious that it is a type of search particularly destructive of privacy and offensive to personal dignity.

Until today this Court had upheld a bodily search separate from arrest and without individualized suspicion of wrongdoing only with respect to prison inmates, relying upon the uniquely dangerous nature of that environment. Today, in *Skinner*, we allow a less intrusive bodily search of railroad employees involved in train accidents. I joined the Court's opinion there because the demonstrated frequency of drug and alcohol use by the targeted class of employees, and the demonstrated connection between such use and grave harm, rendered the search a reasonable means of protecting society. I decline to join the Court's opinion in the present case because neither frequency of use nor connection to harm is demonstrated or even likely. In my view the Customs

Service rules are a kind of immolation of privacy and human dignity in symbolic opposition to drug use.

* * *

The Court's opinion in the present case, however, will be searched in vain for real evidence of a real problem that will be solved by urine testing of Customs Service employees. * * * The only pertinent points, it seems to me, are supported by nothing but speculation, and not very plausible speculation at that. * * *

What is absent in the Government's justifications—notably absent, revealingly absent, and as far as I am concerned dispositively absent—is the recitation of even a single instance in which any of the speculated horribles actually occurred: an instance, that is, in which the cause of bribe-taking, or of poor aim, or of unsympathetic law enforcement, or of compromise of classified information, was drug use. * * *

The Court's response to this lack of evidence is that "[t]here is little reason to believe that American workplaces are immune from [the] pervasive social problem" of drug abuse. Perhaps such a generalization would suffice if the workplace at issue could produce such catastrophic social harm that no risk whatever is tolerable—the secured areas of a nuclear power plant, for example * * *. But if such a generalization suffices to justify demeaning bodily searches, without particularized suspicion, to guard against the bribing or blackmailing of a law enforcement agent, or the careless use of a firearm, then the Fourth Amendment has become frail protection indeed. In *Skinner*, *Bell*, *T.L.O.*, and *Martinez-Fuerte,* we took pains to establish the existence of special need for the search or seizure—a need based not upon the existence of a "pervasive social problem" combined with speculation as to the effect of that problem in the field at issue, but rather upon well-known or well-demonstrated evils in that field, with well-known or well-demonstrated consequences. In *Skinner*, for example, we pointed to a long history of alcohol abuse in the railroad industry, and noted that in an 8–year period 45 train accidents and incidents had occurred because of alcohol- and drug-impaired railroad employees, killing 34 people, injuring 66, and causing more than $28 million in property damage. * * *

Today's decision would be wrong, but at least of more limited effect, if its approval of drug testing were confined to that category of employees assigned specifically to drug interdiction duties. Relatively few public employees fit that description. But in extending approval of drug testing to that category consisting of employees who carry firearms, the Court exposes vast numbers of public employees to this needless indignity. Logically, of course, if those who carry guns can be treated in this fashion, so can all others whose work, if performed under the influence of drugs, may endanger others—automobile drivers, operators of other potentially dangerous equipment, construction workers, school crossing guards. A similarly broad scope attaches to the Court's approval of drug testing for those with access to "sensitive information."[24] Since this category is not limited to Service employees with drug interdiction duties, nor to "sensitive information" specifically relating to drug traffic, today's holding apparently approves drug testing for all federal employees with security clearances—or, indeed, for all federal employees with valuable confidential information to impart.

There is only one apparent basis that sets the testing at issue here apart from all these other situations—but it is not a basis upon which the Court is willing to rely. I do not believe for a minute that the driving force behind these drug-testing rules was any of the feeble justifications put forward by counsel here and accepted by the Court. The only plausible explanation, in my view, is what the Commissioner himself offered in the concluding sentence of his memorandum to Customs Service employees announcing the program: "Implementation of the drug screening program would set an important example in our country's struggle with this most serious threat to our national health and security." * * * What better way to show that the Government is serious about its "war on drugs" than to subject its employees on the front line of that war to this invasion of their privacy and affront to their dignity? * * * I think it obvious that this justification is unacceptable; that the impairment of individual liberties cannot be the means of making a point; that symbolism, even symbolism for so worthy a cause as the abolition of unlawful drugs, cannot validate an otherwise unreasonable search.

* * *

NOTES

1. The Supreme Court first addressed the constitutionality of a workplace search two years before *Skinner* and *Von Raab* in *O'Connor v. Ortega*, 480 U.S. 709, 107 S.Ct. 1492, 94 L.Ed.2d 714 (1987). A majority of the Court concluded that the employee, Dr. Ortega, had a reasonable expectation of privacy in his office. Five justices agreed that the case should be remanded for a determination of whether the search of his office was reasonable and also agreed that a search to investigate possible workplace misconduct or for purposes such as retrieving workplace materials would be reasonable. The Court did not decide whether some level of individualized suspicion of engagement in misconduct was required prior to a search for evidence of misconduct.

2. In *Skinner v. Railway Labor Executives' Association*, 489 U.S. 602, 109 S.Ct. 1402, 103 L.Ed.2d 639 (1989), referred to frequently in the *Von Raab* opinions, the Court upheld the validity of regulations adopted by the Federal Railroad Administration mandating blood and urine tests for drugs in the case of employees involved in certain train accidents, and authorizing such tests in the case of employees who violate certain safety rules. The Court, in

24. The Court apparently approves application of the urine tests to personnel receiving access to "sensitive information." Ante, at 1396. Since, however, it is unsure whether "classified material" is "sensitive information," it remands with instructions that the Court of Appeals "examine the criteria used by the Service in determining what materials are classified and in deciding whom to test under this rubric."

an opinion by Justice Kennedy, reasoned that requiring a warrant would serve no useful purpose in such a context, and would likely frustrate the governmental purpose behind these searches. The Court also concluded that while probable cause based on individualized suspicion is generally required in searches that may be performed without a warrant, "[i]n limited circumstances, where the privacy interests implicated by the search are minimal, and where an important government interest furthered by the intrusion would be placed in jeopardy by a requirement of individualized suspicion, a search may be reasonable despite the absence of such suspicion. We believe this true of the intrusions in question here."

The Court acknowledged that the testing procedures, especially the urine tests, implicated privacy interests protected by the Fourth Amendment, but concluded that:

> [E]xpectations of privacy of covered employees are diminished by reason of their participation in an industry that is regulated pervasively to ensure safety, a goal dependent, in substantial part, on the health and fitness of covered employees. * * * By contrast, the government interest in testing without a showing of individualized suspicion is compelling. Employees subject to the tests discharge duties fraught with such risks of injury to others that even a momentary lapse of attention can have disastrous consequences. * * * By ensuring that employees in safety-sensitive positions know they will be tested upon the occurrence of a triggering event, the timing of which no employee can predict with certainty, the regulations significantly increase the deterrent effect of the administrative penalties associated with the prohibited conduct, concomitantly increasing the likelihood that employees will forgo using drugs or alcohol while subject to being called for duty. The testing procedures * * * also help railroads obtain invaluable information about the cases of major accidents and to take appropriate measures to safeguard the general public.

The Court concluded that the regulations are "reasonable within the meaning of the Fourth Amendment."

Justice Marshall, joined by Justice Brennan, observed that "grave threats to liberty often come in times of urgency," and accused the majority of "trivializing" both the intrusiveness of the searches and their utility, thereby succumbing to "society's obsession with stopping the scourge of illegal drugs." He cautioned that while "[t]he immediate victims of the majority's constitutional timorousness will be those railroad workers whose bodily fluids the Government may now forcibly collect and analyze * * * [,] today's decision will reduce the privacy all citizens may enjoy * * * ."

3. Note that some courts have distinguished between suspicionless testing, which occurs based on certain events such as hiring, promotion, accidents or on a periodic basis with prior notice to the employee as to when it will occur (e.g., annually), and random testing which can occur at any time without notice. Considering the rationales of *Skinner* and *Von Raab*, would the following drug testing survive constitutional challenge?

a. Suspicionless testing of public school teachers, secretaries, bus drivers and/or janitors?

b. Random testing of firefighters?

c. Suspicionless testing of prison guards?

d. Suspicionless testing of prosecutors handling criminal cases?

4. Could a requirement that all candidates for elective office certify that they have tested negative for drugs within 30 days of nomination or election withstand constitutional scrutiny? See *Chandler v. Miller*, 520 U.S. 305, 117 S.Ct. 1295, 137 L.Ed.2d 513 (1997).

5. State constitutions, some of which contain explicit protection for a right of "privacy," may provide greater protection than the federal constitution for the privacy of public employees. See *Loder v. City of Glendale*, 14 Cal.4th 846, 59 Cal.Rptr.2d 696, 927 P.2d 1200 (1997) (holding unconstitutional the City's program of drug testing all applicants for promotion).

6. How should a court treat searches of public employees' (a) lockers; (b) persons; and (c) computers?

BROWN–CRISCUOLO v. WOLFE

United States District Court, District of Connecticut, 2009.
601 F.Supp.2d 441.

SQUATRITO, J.

The plaintiff, Robin Brown–Criscuolo ("the Plaintiff") brings this action against the defendant, Robert K. Wolfe ("the Defendant"), alleging that the Defendant violated the First, Fourth, and Fourteenth Amendments to the United States Constitution, the Stored Communications Act, 18 U.S.C. §§ 2701–2707, the Wiretap Act, 18 U.S.C. §§ 2510–2511, and the Rehabilitation Act of 1973, 29 U.S.C. §§ 794 *et seq.* The Plaintiff also alleges that the Defendant intentionally or recklessly subjected her to emotional distress and invaded her privacy. The Defendant now moves for summary judgment pursuant to Rule 56 of the Federal Rules of Civil Procedure. For the reasons that hereafter follow, the Defendant's motion for summary judgment is granted in part and denied in part.

I. FACTS

The Plaintiff is an educator with over 37 years of service. * * *

In 1998, the Plaintiff became the principal of the Jerome Harrison School in North Branford, Connecticut. Her responsibilities included not only the day-to-day duties of a principal, but also the supervision of the special education program. It was the Plaintiff's responsibility to ensure that special education laws and procedures were implemented and followed, and if she saw any violations of a student's rights or failure to follow proper procedure, she was obligated to bring such problems to the attention of the Superintendent of Schools in North Branford. In addition, the Plaintiff helped identify problem students in the regular classroom and provided in-service training for teachers. This training included research-based reading instruction, classroom modification, and behavior management plans.

* * *

The Defendant became the Superintendent of Schools in North Branford in March of 2001, and is currently working in that capacity. As North Branford's Superintendent of Schools, the Defendant was the Plaintiff's supervisor. After becoming the Superintendent of Schools, the Defendant hired Suzanne Wright ("Wright") to be the new Director of Special Education. In this position, Wright implemented new policies that, according to the Plaintiff, were in direct violation of state and federal special education laws. * * *

The Plaintiff believed that, because of the policies implemented by Wright, [Planning and Placement Team (PPT)] members were afraid, intimidated or discouraged from obtaining the proper evaluations and/or services for students. Therefore, the Plaintiff concluded that students were being denied access to programs to which they were legally entitled. On February 22, 2004, the Plaintiff wrote a letter to the Defendant regarding her problems in working with Wright and her inability to effectively do her job in light of the restraints now placed upon her.

[A series of disputes between the plaintiff and defendant over the application of special education policies followed. The plaintiff and defendant agreed that there were disputes but disagreed about some of the facts relating to the disputes.]

The Plaintiff went out on an extended medical leave on January 31, 2005. * * *

* * *

* * * On June 10, 2005, the Plaintiff called the Defendant and indicated that she wanted to return to work. The Defendant agreed, and the Plaintiff returned to work on June 13, 2005.

* * * Beginning on April 1, 2005, the Defendant assumed the role of acting principal, and remained in that position until the Plaintiff returned to work. The parties dispute the Defendant's conduct during his time as acting principal, specifically his conduct with regard to the Plaintiff's emails. The Plaintiff alleges that the Defendant used the Plaintiff's work computer and looked at her emails without her permission. The Plaintiff further alleges that the Defendant forwarded to his own email account an email containing a letter, dated January 25, 2005, the Plaintiff had sent to her attorney * * *[in which] the Plaintiff described certain work-related problems she was having with the Defendant.

The Defendant, for his part, maintains that he accessed the Plaintiff's email account to review school-related messages, and he did not view any emails that were clearly identifiable as personal. The Defendant further maintains that he thought the email to Attorney Klebanoff was school-related because it was his belief that Attorney Klebanoff was a special education lawyer. The parties agree that on April 11, 2005, the email (with the letter attachment) was forwarded to the Defendant's email account, and opened and saved on the Defendant's computer.

The Plaintiff filed this action on September 22, 2005, alleging that the Defendant's conduct violated her rights in several respects. * * *

II. DISCUSSION

The Defendant now moves for summary judgment, arguing that the Plaintiff's claims fail as a matter of law. The Plaintiff argues that there are genuine issues of material fact precluding summary judgment. The Court shall discuss the parties' arguments seriatim.

* * *

C. FOURTH AMENDMENT

The Fourth Amendment to the United States Constitution reads as follows: "The right of the people to be secure in their persons, houses, papers, and effects, against unreasonable searches and seizures, shall not be violated, and no Warrants shall issue, but upon probable cause, supported by Oath or affirmation, and particularly describing the place to be searched, and the persons or things to be seized." "The touchstone of Fourth Amendment analysis is whether a person has a 'constitutionally protected reasonable expectation of privacy.'" *California v. Ciraolo*, 476 U.S. 207, 211 (1986) (quoting *Katz v. United States*, 389 U.S. 347, 360, 88 S.Ct. 507, 19 L.Ed.2d 576 (1967) (Harlan, J., concurring)). "[I]n order to claim the protection of the Fourth Amendment, a [claimant] must demonstrate that [s]he personally has an expectation of privacy in the place searched, and that h[er] expectation is reasonable; i.e., one that has a source outside of the Fourth Amendment, either by reference to concepts of real or personal property law or to understandings that are recognized and permitted by society." *Minnesota v. Carter*, 525 U.S. 83, 88 (1998).

"[T]he Fourth Amendment protects individuals from unreasonable searches conducted by the Government, even when the Government acts as an employer." *Leventhal v. Knapek*, 266 F.3d 64, 73–73 (2d Cir. 2001) "The 'special needs' of public employers may, however, allow them to dispense with the probable cause and warrant requirements when conducting workplace searches related to investigations of work-related misconduct." *Id.* at 73. * * * "In these situations, the Fourth Amendment's protection against unreasonable searches is enforced by a careful balancing of governmental and private interests." *Id.* "A public employer's search of an area in which an employee had a reasonable expectation of privacy is 'reasonable' when 'the measures adopted are reasonably related to the objectives of the search and not excessively intrusive in light of' its purpose." *Id.* * * *

1. Reasonable Expectation of Privacy

The Court must first look at whether the Defendant's conduct infringed an expectation of privacy that society would consider reasonable because "[w]ithout a reasonable expectation of privacy, a workplace search by a public employer will not violate the Fourth Amendment, regardless of the search's nature and scope. *Id.* With regard to email communications in general, the Court notes that, "[al]though e-mail communication, like any other form of communication, carries the risk of unauthorized disclosure, the prevailing view is that * * * confidential information [may be communicated] through unencrypted e-mail with a reasonable expectation of confidentiality and privacy." *In re Asia Global Crossing, LTD.*, 322 B.R. 247, 256 (Bankr. S.D.N.Y. 2005) (collecting authorities). In determining whether an employee had an expectation of privacy in emails sent or received on her employer's computer or email system, the Court should consider the following four factors:

> (1) does the corporation maintain a policy banning personal or other objectionable use, (2) does the company monitor the use of the employee's computer or e-mail, (3) do third parties have a right of access to the computer or e-mails, and (4) did the corporation notify the employee, or was the employee aware, of the use and monitoring policies?
>
> *Id.* at 257–58 * * *.

For the time period relevant to this case, the North Branford School District had an Acceptable Use Policy ("AUP"), which controlled the use of the North Branford School District's computer system. Under the AUP, the Plaintiff, as an employee, was provided with her own individual email account. It is undisputed that the Plaintiff had a password to her account, and that this password was not widely known, as apparently only the Plaintiff and the computer system's administrator had it. In addition, the terms of the AUP do not grant total privacy to users, nor do they abrogate all privacy. Instead, the AUP states that "[s]ystem users have a limited privacy expectation in the contents of their personal files on the District system." Thus, "[r]outine maintenance and monitoring of the system may lead to discovery that the user has or is violating the District [AUP], the district disciplinary code, or the law." In addition, "[a]n individual search will be conducted if there is reasonable suspicion that a user has violated the law or the district disciplinary code." Furthermore, the AUP puts employees on notice that "their personal files may be discoverable under CT State public records laws." Nonetheless, the AUP prohibits users from "attempt[ing] to gain unauthorized access to the [system] or * * * go[ing] beyond their authorized access[,] * * * includ[ing] attempting to log in through another person's account or using an open account (not logged off) to access a computer or access another person's files."

In the Court's view, the Plaintiff did have a reasonable expectation of privacy in her emails at work, and the Court is not convinced by the Defendant's arguments to the contrary. The Defendant argues that the computer system was to be used for educational and professional or career development activities. This is a correct reading of the AUP. The email and letter attachment in question, however, appear to relate to these types of activities, as they constitute communications to her lawyer expressing the Plaintiff's concerns and worries about certain aspects of her job.

The Defendant also argues that, because the AUP allows for "routine maintenance and monitoring" of the system, the Plaintiff, who was aware of this policy, could not have had a reasonable expectation of privacy in her email account. The Court is not persuaded by this argument, though, because the record does not indicate that it was actually the practice of the North Branford School District to routinely monitor system users' email accounts. The Court also does not see any evidence showing that it would be the duty of the superintendent (i.e., the Defendant), rather than the computer system's administrator, to conduct such routine maintenance and monitoring. Moreover, the Defendant does not claim that he accessed the Plaintiff's email account pursuant to his normal routine of maintaining and monitoring the computer system. The Defendant instead alleges that he accessed the email account because of a specific, particular circumstance, namely, the Plaintiff's medical leave. Indeed, from what the Court can discern in the record, it appears that the Defendant had some difficulty in accessing the Plaintiff's email account because it was protected by a password and not generally accessible to people other than the Plaintiff. In light of this, the Court fails to see how the Defendant's conduct was part of a routine of maintenance and monitoring the computer system.[4] The Defendant further argues that because the AUP advised employees that their personal files were potentially discoverable under public records laws, the Plaintiff could not have had a reasonable expectation of privacy in her email account. This argument does not persuade the Court for the simple reason that the Defendant's did not act pursuant to any such law. There is nothing in the record indicating that a request was made under any public records law to search the Plaintiff's personal files, let alone that the Defendant was acting pursuant to such a request. Therefore, given these circumstances, the Court concludes that the Plaintiff did have a reasonable expectation of privacy in her email account.

2. The Nature and Scope of the Search

Even if a plaintiff has a reasonable expectation of privacy in the workplace, "[a]n investigatory search for evidence of suspected work-related employee misfeasance will be constitutionally 'reasonable' if it is 'justified at its inception' and of appropriate scope.' " *Leventhal*, 266 F.3d at 75 (quoting *O'Connor*, 480 U.S. at 726). "The initial consideration of the search's justification examines whether 'there are reasonable grounds for suspecting that the search will turn up evidence that the employee is guilty of work-related misconduct.' " *Id.* (quoting *O'Connor*, 480 U.S. at 726). Then the Court must look at the scope of the search, which "will be appropriate if 'reasonably related to the objectives of the search and not excessively intrusive in light of the nature of the misconduct.' " *Id.* (quoting *O'Connor*, 480 U.S. at 726).

4. There is no assertion from the Defendant that he searched the Plaintiff's email account because he held a reasonable suspicion that she had violated the law or the school district's disciplinary code. In addition, there is no indication that the Defendant, in accessing the Plaintiff's email account, discovered anything that would constitute such a violation.

With regard to the initial consideration, namely, whether there were reasonable grounds for conducting the search, the Court notes that the Defendant did not conduct the search because he thought he would find evidence of wrongdoing. This makes the Court doubtful of whether the search could be considered reasonable at all. The Defendant does argue, however, that the search was necessary because he wanted to ensure that no important emails sent to the Plaintiff were overlooked on account of her medical leave.

Assuming, for the sake of argument, that the Defendant's alleged motive for conducting the search of the Plaintiff's email account could constitute a reasonable ground for doing so, the Court is not convinced that the scope of that search was appropriate. The Defendant admits that he read the email with the attached letter the Plaintiff had written to Attorney Klebanoff, who was the Plaintiff's private attorney. The Court believes that a reasonable finder of fact could find that the Defendant should have immediately realized that this communication was not relevant to the alleged purpose of his search of the Plaintiff's email account. The Defendant claims that he was simply making sure that no important emails sent to the Plaintiff were overlooked on account of her absence. A reasonable finder of fact could conclude that reading a communication that was not sent to the Plaintiff, but was rather sent by the Plaintiff, does not fall under the scope of the search.

Moreover, this communication was somehow forwarded to the Defendant's own email account. It is not readily apparent to the Court how the forwarding this communication to the Defendant's email account would be related to the objectives of Defendant's search. The Court believes that a reasonable finder of fact could find such conduct to be excessively intrusive. While the Defendant claims that it was not he who forwarded the communication to his email account, there is, at least, a factual question as to how it happened. Consequently, with regard to the Plaintiff's Fourth Amendment search and seizure claim, the Defendant's motion for summary judgment is denied.

* * *

NOTES

1. The plaintiff also alleged that the superintendent retaliated against her for her speech relating to the provision of special education services but the court denied the claim based on *Garcetti v. Ceballos, supra* § B, finding that she spoke as an employee because she was responsible for special education services in her school.

2. In contrast to *Brown–Criscuolo*, many cases involving computer searches founder on the reasonable expectation of privacy because of the computer policies adopted by the employer. If you were advising an employer, what would you recommend that the employer include in its computer policy? What actions would you recommend that the employer undertake to insure that no reasonable expectation of privacy attaches?

3. An employer's policy adopted to defeat a reasonable expectation of privacy may be negated by subsequent actions and representations of the employer. See *Quon v. Arch Wireless Operating Co.*, 529 F.3d 892 (9th Cir. 2008), *rev'd on other grounds*, 130 S.Ct. 2619, 177 L.Ed.2d 216 (2010). The Court in *Quon* declined to decide whether Quon had a reasonable expectation of privacy in his text messages sent on the employer's pager, instead finding that assuming he did, the employer's search was reasonable. In speaking of privacy expectations and new technologies, the Court stated:

> The Court must proceed with care when considering the whole concept of privacy expectations in communications made on electronic equipment owned by a government employer. The judiciary risks error by elaborating too fully on the Fourth Amendment implications of emerging technology before its role in society has become clear. See, e.g., *Olmstead v. United States*, 277 U.S. 438, 48 S.Ct. 564, 72 L.Ed. 944 (1928), overruled by *Katz v. United States*, 389 U.S. 347, 353, 88 S.Ct. 507, 19 L.Ed.2d 576 (1967). In *Katz*, the Court relied on its own knowledge and experience to conclude that there is a reasonable expectation of privacy in a telephone booth. It is not so clear that courts at present are on so sure a ground. Prudence counsels caution before the facts in the instant case are used to establish far-reaching premises that define the existence, and extent, of privacy expectations enjoyed by employees when using employer-provided communication devices.
>
> Rapid changes in the dynamics of communication and information transmission are evident not just in the technology itself but in what society accepts as proper behavior. As one amici brief notes, many employers expect or at least tolerate personal use of such equipment by employees because it often increases worker efficiency. Another amicus points out that the law is beginning to respond to these developments, as some States have recently passed statutes requiring employers to notify employees when monitoring their electronic communications. At present, it is uncertain how workplace norms, and the law's treatment of them, will evolve.
>
> Even if the Court were certain that the *O'Connor* plurality's approach were the right one, the Court would have difficulty predicting how employees' privacy expectations will be shaped by those changes or the degree to which society will be prepared to recognize those expectations as reasonable. Cell phone and text message communications are so pervasive that some persons may consider them to be essential means or necessary instruments for self-expression, even self-identification. That might strengthen the case for an expectation of privacy. On the other hand, the ubiquity of those devices has made them generally affordable, so one could counter that employees who need cell phones or similar devices for personal matters can purchase and pay for their own. And employer policies concerning communications will of course shape the reasonable expectations of their employees, especially to the extent that such policies are clearly communicated.
>
> A broad holding concerning employees' privacy expectations vis-a-vis employer-provided technological equipment might have implications for

future cases that cannot be predicted. It is preferable to dispose of this case on narrower grounds.

Id. at 226–28.

What factors should the Court consider in determining whether employees have a reasonable expectation of privacy when using employer-supplied technology or equipment? Is there a reasonable expectation of privacy when driving an employer vehicle equipped with a gps? Can the employer use that gps to monitor employee activity even when off-duty?

4. The *Quon* Court decided that the employer's review of the transcripts of two months of text messages on the employee's employer-issued pager was reasonable, stating:

> The search was justified at its inception because there were "reasonable grounds for suspecting that the search [was] necessary for a noninvestigatory work-related purpose." As a jury found, Chief Scharf ordered the search in order to determine whether the character limit on the City's contract with Arch Wireless was sufficient to meet the City's needs. * * * The City and OPD had a legitimate interest in ensuring that employees were not being forced to pay out of their own pockets for work-related expenses, or on the other hand that the City was not paying for extensive personal communications.
>
> As for the scope of the search, reviewing the transcripts was reasonable because it was an efficient and expedient way to determine whether Quon's overages were the result of work-related messaging or personal use. The review was also not " 'excessively intrusive.' " Although Quon had gone over his monthly allotment a number of times, OPD requested transcripts for only the months of August and September 2002. * * * And it is worth noting that during his internal affairs investigation, McMahon redacted all messages Quon sent while off duty, a measure which reduced the intrusiveness of any further review of the transcripts.
>
> Furthermore, the extent of an expectation [of privacy] is relevant to assessing whether the search was too intrusive. Even if he could assume some level of privacy would inhere in his messages, it would not have been reasonable for Quon to conclude that his messages were in all circumstances immune from scrutiny. Quon was told that his messages were subject to auditing. As a law enforcement officer, he would or should have known that his actions were likely to come under legal scrutiny, and that this might entail an analysis of his on-the-job communications. * * * Given that the City issued the pagers to Quon and other SWAT Team members in order to help them more quickly respond to crises—and given that Quon had received no assurances of privacy—Quon could have anticipated that it might be necessary for the City to audit pager messages to assess the SWAT Team's performance in particular emergency situations.
>
> From OPD's perspective, the fact that Quon likely had only a limited privacy expectation, with boundaries that we need not here explore, lessened the risk that the review would intrude on highly private details of Quon's life. OPD's audit of messages on Quon's employer-provided

pager was not nearly as intrusive as a search of his personal e-mail account or pager, or a wiretap on his home phone line, would have been. That the search did reveal intimate details of Quon's life does not make it unreasonable, for under the circumstances a reasonable employer would not expect that such a review would intrude on such matters. (Citations omitted).

Id. at 228–29.

In finding the search reasonable on the basis of a limited expectation of privacy, the Court seemed to ignore the fact that Quon's supervisor assured him that as long as he paid the overages, his text messages would not be reviewed. This fact was significant to the Ninth's Circuit's conclusion that Quon had a reasonable expectation of privacy. Does this suggest that the Court disagrees with Ninth Circuit although it did not decide the issue? Does the *Quon* case cast any doubt on the holding in *Brown–Criscuolo*?

5. Can evidence from a warrantless employer search be used to support criminal prosecution of an employee? See *United States v. Simons*, 206 F.3d 392 (4th Cir. 2000) (upholding denial of motion to suppress evidence of child pornography discovered on the defendant's work computer because the government employer's computer policy defeated any reasonable expectation of privacy, rejecting the argument that the employer should have stopped its investigation once it found unauthorized internet use and not pursued the warrantless investigation to find criminal misconduct).

6. Can the employer search an employee's personal computer if it is used at work? See *United States v. Barrows*, 481 F.3d 1246 (10th Cir. 2007) (upholding denial of a suppression motion because the employee had no reasonable expectation of privacy where his personal computer was connected to the employer's network, had no password protection for the files, and was used in a place accessible to the public).

7. Employee privacy in the public sector workplace may also be limited by statutes that require disclosure of government records. For a discussion of these "sunshine laws" and their effect on employee privacy, see Mitchell Rubinstein, *Privacy Legal Issues in the Public Sector* in *Workplace Privacy: Proceedings of the New York University 58th Annual Conference on Labor* 629, 645–48 (Jonathan Remy Nash, ed. 2010).

CHAPTER 3

STATUTORY EMPLOYMENT PROTECTIONS FOR PUBLIC EMPLOYEES

■ ■ ■

A large number of federal employment statutes regulate the private sector workplace. Federal statutes prohibit discrimination, govern workplace safety and health, regulate pension and welfare benefits, require notice of closings and mass layoffs, regulate wages and hours, mandate family and medical leave, bar the use of polygraphs, and prohibit retaliation for reporting certain types of employer wrong-doing. Some federal employment laws, such as the Occupational Safety and Health Act (29 U.S.C. § 652(5)) and the Employment Retirement Income and Security Act (29 U.S.C. § 1003(b)(2)) do not cover the public sector. In such areas, state laws often cover public workers. As discussed further below, parts of the Fair Labor Standards Act (FLSA) cover state and local government employees with special rules that do not apply to the private sector, and do not cover federal employees (29 U.S.C. § 207(*o*)). Title VII of the Civil Rights Act of 1964 has special procedures for enforcement when the federal government is the employer (42 U.S.C. § 2000e–16). Public employees also often enjoy statutory protections that do not apply in the private sector.

Most federal employment statutes that cover the private sector workplace also apply to public employers and employees. However, when Congress legislates in this area, its authority over state and local government employers may be constrained by the Constitution.

This chapter begins by considering the constitutional constraints on Congress' ability to regulate the public sector workplace. It then examines special rules under the Fair Labor Standards Act that apply only to public employers and employees. Finally, it focuses on special civil service, tenure and whistleblower protection available to most public employees.

A. CONSTITUTIONAL CONSTRAINTS ON EMPLOYMENT REGULATION

1. TENTH AMENDMENT IMMUNITY

Over the past several decades, government employers have claimed that they are either entirely or partially immune from suit under some employment laws pursuant to the Tenth and/or Eleventh Amendments to the Constitution. In other words, the employment statute on its face covers public workers, but government employers argue that such coverage violates the Constitution.

The most significant early challenges to extending an employment law to the public sector involved the FLSA and the Tenth Amendment. The FLSA, among other things, sets national minimum wage and overtime rules. The Tenth Amendment provides that "[t]he powers not delegated to the United States by the Constitution, nor prohibited by it to the States, are reserved to States * * * or to the people."

The Supreme Court has decided three major cases on the Tenth Amendment and the FLSA's application to public employers. First, in 1968, the Court decided *Maryland v. Wirtz*, 392 U.S. 183, 88 S.Ct. 2017, 20 L.Ed.2d 1020 (1968). *Wirtz* held that Congress had the authority under its power to regulate interstate commence to apply the FLSA to public workers, and that it did not violate the Tenth Amendment to do so.

Then in 1976, the Supreme Court reversed *Wirtz* in *National League of Cities v. Usery*, 426 U.S. 833, 96 S.Ct. 2465, 49 L.Ed.2d 245 (1976). *National League of Cities* held that the Tenth Amendment barred Congress from applying the FLSA to public workers. The Court reasoned that Congress could not regulate traditional government functions of the states, and determining the wages and hours of public employees was a traditional government function. Thus, while Congress could regulate wages and hours in the private sector pursuant to the Commerce Clause, Congress could not regulate the wages and hours of public employees because of the Tenth Amendment.

Less than a decade later, the Court reversed *National League of Cities* in *Garcia v. San Antonio Metropolitan Transit Authority*, 469 U.S. 528, 105 S.Ct. 1005, 83 L.Ed.2d 1016 (1985). *Garcia* explained that the "traditional government function" test was unworkable; it was too difficult to determine what was and was not such a function. So, the FLSA then applied in full force to public employees.

In reaction to *Garcia*, as section B discusses, Congress passed the 1985 Amendments to the FLSA, creating some special rules that apply only to public workers. Still, for about a decade, it seemed settled that the FLSA and other employment laws could be applied to employees of state and local government without any Constitutional problems.

2. ELEVENTH AMENDMENT IMMUNITY

In the second half of the 1990s, challenges under the Eleventh Amendment took center stage. The Eleventh Amendment states, "[t]he Judicial power of the United States shall not be construed to extend to any suit in law or equity, commenced or prosecuted against one of the United States by Citizens of another State or Subjects of any Foreign State."

The first major Eleventh Amendment case was *Seminole Tribe of Florida v. Florida*, 517 U.S. 44, 116 S.Ct. 1114, 134 L.Ed.2d 252 (1996). The Seminole Indian tribe had sued the state of Florida over its failure to negotiate over gambling, as required by the Indian Gaming Regulatory Act, a federal statute. *Seminole Tribe* held that Congress did not have the power under the Commerce Clause to waive a state's immunity from suit for money damages under a Federal law in federal court. "Even when the Constitution vests in Congress complete law-making authority over a particular area, the Eleventh Amendment prevents congressional authorization of suits by private parties against unconsenting States." *Id.* at 72. This conclusion came from reading the Eleventh Amendment together with a structural view of the Constitution in which state sovereignty played a strong role even beyond the text of the Constitution.

Although *Seminole Tribe* was not an employment law case, it obviously had implications for public employment. Congress had passed a number of employment laws pursuant to its power under the Commerce Clause. So, one consequence of *Seminole Tribe* was that state employers now had some form of immunity in suits by state employees in federal court under such laws. It was left to future cases to determine the precise nature and extent of that immunity.

The first major employment case on this issue was *Alden v. Maine*, 527 U.S. 706, 119 S.Ct. 2240, 144 L.Ed.2d 636 (1999). Plaintiffs were a group of probation officers alleging that their employer, the state of Maine, had violated the overtime provisions of the FLSA. Because of *Seminole Tribe*, plaintiffs sued in state court.

In a 5–4 decision with Justice Kennedy writing for the majority, the Court held that the powers delegated to Congress under Article I of the Constitution do not include the power to subject unconsenting states to private suits for damages in state courts. The majority relied not only on the Eleventh Amendment, but also on "the Constitution's structure, its history, and the authoritative interpretations by this Court." *Id.* at 715. States retain "a residuary and inviolable sovereignty" and "immunity from private suits is central to sovereign dignity." *Id.* The Court further reasoned that the Eleventh Amendment was adopted in response to *Chisholm v. Georgia,* 2 U.S. 419, 2 Dall. 419, 1 L.Ed. 440 (1793), which authorized a private citizen of another state to sue the state of Georgia without its consent; the Amendment was meant to preserve the States' traditional immunity from private suits. *Id.* at 719–22. Further, sovereign immunity derives not from the Eleventh Amendment but from the structure of the original Constitution itself. *Id.* at 728–30.

This immunity, the Court held, should apply in state, as well as federal courts: "[W]ere the rule to be different here, the National Government would wield greater power in the state courts than in its own judicial instrumentalities." *Id.* at 752.

The Court stressed policy concerns as well. "Private suits against nonconsenting States—especially suits for money damages—may threaten the financial integrity of the States." *Id.* at 750. "A general federal power to authorize private suits for money damages would place unwarranted strain on the States' ability to govern in accordance with the will of their citizens." *Id.* at 750–51.

The Court explained that the immunity described in *Alden*, often called "Eleventh Amendment immunity," is limited. First states are still covered by the laws involved; they are immune only from private suits for money damages. Private parties may still sue for injunctive relief, and in some cases may be able to sue individual state officials for money damages. Second, states do not enjoy this form of immunity from suits brought by the federal government on behalf of state employees. Thus, for example, there would be no immunity in an FLSA suit brought by the Department of Labor. Third, this immunity only applies to laws which Congress passed pursuant to its power under the Commerce Clause; it does not apply to laws Congress passed pursuant to its power under the Fourteenth Amendment (*id.* at 756, citing *City of Boerne v. Flores,* 521 U.S. 507, 117 S.Ct. 2157, 138 L.Ed.2d 624 (1997)). Finally, this immunity only limits suits against states, but not lesser entities (*e.g.* cities or counties). *Alden* at 527 U.S. at 756–57.

Justice Souter wrote a dissent, joined by Justices Stevens, Ginsburg and Breyer. Souter argued that the language of the Eleventh Amendment did not support the result in the case, and that the decision was "at odds with constitutional history and at war with the conception of divided sovereignty that is the essence of American federalism." *Id.* at 760 (Souter, dissenting). Among other things, he urged, "The State of Maine is not sovereign with respect to the national objective of the FLSA." *Id.* at 800. He dismissed the majority's concerns about state finances, stating, "So long as the citizens' will, expressed through state legislation, does not violate valid federal law, the strain will not be felt; and to the extent that state action does violate federal law, the will of the citizens of the United States already trumps that of the citizens of the State." *Id.* at 803. The dissent discounted the availability of federal agency enforcement, observing that "unless Congress plans a significant expansion of the National Government's litigating forces to provide a lawyer whenever private litigation is barred by today's decision * * * the allusion to enforcement of private rights by the National Government is probably not much more than whimsy * * * . [T]here is no reason today to suspect that enforcement by the Secretary of Labor alone would likely prove adequate to assure compliance with this federal law in the multifarious circumstances of some 4.7 million employees of the 50 States of the Union." *Id.* At 810. The dissent concluded by comparing *Alden* to "the *Lochner* era's industrial due process" jurisprudence. "I expect the Court's late essay into immunity doctrine will prove the equal of its earlier experiment in laissez-faire, the one being as unrealistic as the other, as indefensible, and probably as fleeting." *Id.* at 814.

After *Alden*, it is clear that state employers are still covered by the FLSA and other employment laws to which this immunity applies. See, *e.g.*, *Fikse v. State of Iowa Third Judicial District Department of Correctional Services*, 633 F.Supp.2d 682 (N.D. Iowa 2009). But state employees who bring private suits cannot receive money damages. As the majority noted, this immunity does not necessarily bar an employee's claims for monetary damages from individual state officers in their individual capacities. See, *e.g., Skinner v. Govorchin*, 463 F.3d 518, 524 (6th Cir. 2006). However, Eleventh Amendment immunity does extend to state officials sued in their official capacity, because in such a case the state is the real party in interest. See, *e.g.*, *Melo v. Hafer*, 912 F.2d 628, 635 (3d Cir.1990).

Thus, in a typical private suit, an employee may only be granted injunctive relief. Usually, this would mean purely prospective relief against state officials for ongoing violations of the federal law. See, *e.g.*, *State Troopers Non–Commissioned Officers Association of New Jersey v. New Jersey*, 643 F.Supp.2d 615, 623 (D.N.J. 2009) (employee allowed to sue under the "legal fiction" of *Ex Parte Young*, 209 U.S. 123, 28 S.Ct. 441, 52 L.Ed. 714 (1908) for prospective relief). While this relief is not trivial, the absence of money damages significantly undercuts the financial incentives of private parties to bring suit, and in many cases, at least arguably their ability to do so.

Alden remains good law, but also remains controversial, as the cases below illustrate. These cases also show that states have this type of immunity in suits under some employment laws other than the FLSA, but not in suits involving some other employment laws. This issue depends on the Constitutional authority Congress may validly use to pass the statute. As the materials below show, *Alden* and it progeny apply to statutes which Congress passes pursuant to its power under the Commerce Clause. The Fourteenth Amendment, however, was intended to abrogate state sovereignty and thus *Alden* immunity does not apply to statutes which Congress passed pursuant to its power under the Fourteenth Amendment. Determining which power Congress used, however, is not necessarily a simple matter.

KIMEL v. FLORIDA BOARD OF REGENTS

Supreme Court of the United States, 2000.
528 U.S. 62, 120 S.Ct. 631, 145 L.Ed.2d 522.

O'CONNOR, J. delivered the opinion of the Court.

* * * In these cases, three sets of plaintiffs filed suit under the [Age Discrimination in Employment] Act, seeking money damages for their state employers' alleged discrimination on the basis of age. In each case, the state employer moved to dismiss the suit on the basis of its Eleventh Amendment immunity. * * * Appeals in the three cases were consolidated before the Court of Appeals for the Eleventh Circuit, which held that the ADEA does not validly abrogate the States' Eleventh Amendment immunity. In these cases, we are asked to consider whether the ADEA contains a clear statement of Congress' intent to abrogate the States' Eleventh Amendment immunity and, if so, whether the ADEA is a proper exercise of Congress' constitutional authority. We conclude that the ADEA does contain a clear statement of Congress' intent to abrogate the States' immunity, but that the abrogation exceeded Congress' authority under § 5 of the Fourteenth Amendment.

I

A

The ADEA makes it unlawful for an employer "to fail or refuse to hire or to discharge any individual or otherwise discriminate against any individual with respect to his compensation, terms, conditions, or privileges of employment, because of such individual's age." 29 U.S.C. § 623(a)(1) * * * . Any person aggrieved by an employer's violation of the Act "may bring a civil action in any court of competent jurisdiction" for legal or equitable relief * * * . Section 626(b) also permits aggrieved employees to enforce the Act through certain provisions of the Fair Labor Standards Act of 1938 (FLSA), and the ADEA specifically incorporates § 16(b) of the FLSA.

* * * In 1974 * * * Congress extended application of the ADEA's substantive requirements to the States * * * . In the same 1974 Act, Congress amended 29 U.S.C. § 216(b), the FLSA enforcement provision incorporated by reference into the ADEA * * * . Section 216(b) now permits an individual to bring a civil action "against any employer (including a public agency) in any Federal or State court of competent jurisdiction." Section 203(x) defines "[p]ublic agency" to include "the Government of a State or political subdivision thereof," and "any agency of * * * a State * * * " * * * .

B

[This decision consolidated three different cases heard by District Courts, all involving private parties suing for money damages under the ADEA. In the first case, two professors claimed their employer, a state

University, had discriminated against them in violation of the ADEA. The District Court held that the ADEA did not abrogate the States' Eleventh Amendment immunity. In the second case, a group of current and former faculty and librarians at a different state university filed an ADEA disparate impact claim against their employer. The District Court in this case held that defendant had no Eleventh Amendment Immunity because, the court found, the ADEA was a proper exercise of Congress's power under the Fourteenth Amendment. In the third case, an employee claimed his employer, a state Department of Corrections, failed to promote him because of his age. The District Court in this case also found that in passing ADEA, Congress had properly used its authority to abrogate the state's Eleventh Amendment immunity under the Fourteenth Amendment. Appeals were taken in all cases.]

The Court of Appeals consolidated the appeals and, in a divided panel opinion, held that the ADEA does not abrogate the States' Eleventh Amendment immunity. Judge Edmondson, although stating that he believed "good reason exists to doubt that the ADEA was (or could have been properly) enacted pursuant to the Fourteenth Amendment," rested his opinion on the ADEA's lack of unmistakably clear language evidencing Congress' intent to abrogate the States' sovereign immunity * * * . Judge Cox concurred in Judge Edmondson's ultimate conclusion that the States are immune from ADEA suits brought by individuals in federal court. Judge Cox, however, chose not to address "the thorny issue of Congress's intent," but instead found that Congress lacks the power under § 5 of the Fourteenth Amendment to abrogate the States' Eleventh Amendment immunity under the ADEA. He concluded that "the ADEA confers rights far more extensive than those the Fourteenth Amendment provides," and that "Congress did not enact the ADEA as a proportional response to any widespread violation of the elderly's constitutional rights." Chief Judge Hatchett dissented from both grounds.

We granted certiorari to resolve a conflict among the Federal Courts of Appeals on the question whether the ADEA validly abrogates the States' Eleventh Amendment immunity * * * .

II

The Eleventh Amendment states:

> "The Judicial power of the United States shall not be construed to extend to any suit in law or equity, commenced or prosecuted against one of the United States by Citizens of another State, or by Citizens or Subjects of any Foreign State."

Although today's cases concern suits brought by citizens against their own States, this Court has long " 'understood the Eleventh Amendment to stand not so much for what it says, but for the presupposition * * * which it confirms.' " * * * . Accordingly, for over a century now, we have made clear that the Constitution does not provide for federal jurisdiction over suits against nonconsenting States * * * . Petitioners nevertheless contend that the States of Alabama and Florida must defend the present suits on the merits because Congress abrogated their Eleventh Amendment immunity in the ADEA. To determine whether petitioners are correct, we must resolve two predicate questions: first, whether Congress unequivocally expressed its intent to abrogate that immunity; and second, if it did, whether Congress acted pursuant to a valid grant of constitutional authority.

III

To determine whether a federal statute properly subjects States to suits by individuals, we apply a "simple but stringent test: 'Congress may abrogate the States' constitutionally secured immunity from suit in federal court only by making its intention unmistakably clear in the language of the statute.' " * * *. We agree with petitioners that the ADEA satisfies that test * * *. [The ADEA's enforcement provision] authorizes employees to maintain actions for backpay "against any employer (including a public agency) in any Federal or State court of competent jurisdiction...." Any doubt concerning the identity of the "public agency" defendant * * * is dispelled by looking to § 203(x), which defines the term to include "the government of a State or political subdivision thereof," * * *. In light of our conclusion that Congress unequivocally expressed its intent to abrogate the States' Eleventh Amendment immunity, we now must determine whether Congress effectuated that abrogation pursuant to a valid exercise of constitutional authority.

IV

A

This is not the first time we have considered the constitutional validity of the 1974 extension of the ADEA to state and local governments. In *EEOC v. Wyoming*, 460 U.S. 226, 103 S.Ct. 1054, 75 L.Ed.2d 18 (1983), we held that the ADEA constitutes a valid exercise of Congress' power "[t]o regulate Commerce * * * among the several States," Art. I, § 8, cl. 3, and that the Act did not transgress any external restraints imposed on the commerce power by the Tenth Amendment. Because we found the ADEA valid under Congress' Commerce Clause power, we concluded that it was unnecessary to determine whether the Act also could be supported by Congress' power under § 5 of the Fourteenth Amendment * * *. Resolution of today's cases requires us to decide that question.

In *Seminole Tribe*, we held that Congress lacks power under Article I to abrogate the States' sovereign immunity * * *. Last Term, in a series of three decisions, we reaffirmed that central holding of Seminole Tribe. *See* * * * *Alden v. Maine*, 527 U.S. 706, 119 S.Ct. 2240, 144 L.Ed.2d 636 (1999) * * *. Under our firmly established precedent then, if the ADEA rests solely on Congress' Article I commerce power, the private petitioners in today's cases cannot maintain their suits against their state employers * * *.

Section 5 of the Fourteenth Amendment, however, does grant Congress the authority to abrogate the States' sovereign immunity. In *Fitzpatrick v. Bitzer*, 427 U.S. 445, 96 S.Ct. 2666, 49 L.Ed.2d 614 (1976), we recognized that "the Eleventh Amendment, and the principle of state sovereignty which it embodies, are necessarily limited by the enforcement provisions of § 5 of the Fourteenth Amendment." * * * . Accordingly, the private petitioners in these cases may maintain their ADEA suits against the States of Alabama and Florida if, and only if, the ADEA is appropriate legislation under § 5.

B

The Fourteenth Amendment provides, in relevant part:

> "Section 1. * * * No State shall make or enforce any law which shall abridge the privileges or immunities of citizens of the United States; nor shall any State deprive any person of life, liberty, or property, without due process of law; nor deny to any person within its jurisdiction the equal protection of the laws." * * *
>
> "Section 5. The Congress shall have power to enforce, by appropriate legislation, the provisions of this article."

* * * It is for Congress in the first instance to 'determin[e] whether and what legislation is needed to secure the guarantees of the Fourteenth Amendment,' and its conclusions are entitled to much deference * * * . Congress' § 5 power is not confined to the enactment of legislation that merely parrots the precise wording of the Fourteenth Amendment. Rather, Congress' power "to enforce" the Amendment includes the authority both to remedy and to deter violation of rights guaranteed thereunder by prohibiting a somewhat broader swath of conduct, including that which is not itself forbidden by the Amendment's text.

Nevertheless, * * * Congress cannot "decree the substance of the Fourteenth Amendment's restrictions on the States * * * . It has been given the power 'to enforce,' not the power to determine what constitutes a constitutional violation." The ultimate interpretation and determination of the Fourteenth Amendment's substantive meaning remains the province of the Judicial Branch * * * .

[T]he determination whether purportedly prophylactic legislation constitutes appropriate remedial legislation, or instead effects a substantive redefinition of the Fourteenth Amendment right at issue, is often difficult. The line between the two is a fine one. Accordingly, recognizing that "Congress must have wide latitude in determining where [that line] lies," we held that "[t]here must be a congruence and proportionality between the injury to be prevented or remedied and the means adopted to that end."

In *City of Boerne [v. Flores*, 521 U.S. 507, 117 S.Ct. 2157, 138 L.Ed.2d 624 (1997)] we applied that "congruence and proportionality" test and held that the Religious Freedom Restoration Act of 1993 (RFRA) was not appropriate legislation under § 5. We first noted that the legislative record contained very little evidence of the unconstitutional conduct purportedly targeted by RFRA's substantive provisions. Rather, Congress had uncovered only "anecdotal evidence" that, standing alone, did not reveal a "widespread pattern of religious discrimination in this country." Second, we found that RFRA is "so out of proportion to a supposed remedial or preventive object that it cannot be understood as responsive to, or designed to prevent, unconstitutional behavior." * * *

C

Applying the same "congruence and proportionality" test in these cases, we conclude that the ADEA is not "appropriate legislation" under § 5 of the Fourteenth Amendment. Initially, the substantive requirements the ADEA imposes on state and local governments are disproportionate to any unconstitutional conduct that conceivably could be targeted by the Act. We have considered claims of unconstitutional age discrimination under the Equal Protection Clause three times * * *. In all three cases, we held that the age classifications at issue did not violate the Equal Protection Clause * * *.

States may discriminate on the basis of age without offending the Fourteenth Amendment if the age classification in question is rationally related to a legitimate state interest. The rationality commanded by the Equal Protection Clause does not require States to match age distinctions and the legitimate interests they serve with razorlike precision * * *. In contrast, when a State discriminates on the basis of race or gender, we require a tighter fit between the discriminatory means and the legitimate ends they serve * * *. Under the Fourteenth Amendment, a State may rely on age as a proxy for other qualities, abilities, or characteristics that are relevant to the State's legitimate interests * * *. That age proves to be an inaccurate proxy in any individual case is irrelevant. "[W]here rationality is the test, a State 'does not violate the Equal Protection Clause merely because the classifications made by its laws are imperfect.' " * * *

Judged against the backdrop of our equal protection jurisprudence, it is clear that the ADEA is "so out of proportion to a supposed remedial or preventive object that it cannot be understood as responsive to, or designed to prevent, unconstitutional behavior." * * * The Act, through its broad restriction on the use of age as a discriminating factor, prohibits substantially more state employment decisions and practices than would likely be held unconstitutional under the applicable equal protection, rational basis standard. The ADEA makes unlawful, in the employment context, all "discriminat[ion] against any individual * * * because of such individual's age." Petitioners * * * contend that the Act's prohibition, considered together with its exceptions, applies only to arbitrary age discrimination, which in the majority of cases corresponds to conduct that violates the Equal Protection Clause. We disagree * * *.

That the ADEA prohibits very little conduct likely to be held unconstitutional, while significant, does not alone provide the answer to our § 5 inquiry. Difficult and intractable problems often require powerful remedies, and we have never held that § 5 precludes Congress from enacting reasonably prophylactic legislation. Our task is to determine whether the ADEA is in fact just such an appropriate remedy or, instead, merely an attempt to substantively redefine the States' legal obligations with respect to age discrimination. One means by which we have made such a determination in the past is by examining the legislative record containing the reasons for Congress' action * * *.

Our examination of the ADEA's legislative record confirms that Congress' 1974 extension of the Act to the States was an unwarranted response to a perhaps inconsequential problem. Congress never identified any pattern of age discrimination by the States, much less any discrimination whatsoever that rose to the level of constitutional violation. The evidence compiled by petitioners to demonstrate such attention by Congress to age discrimination by the States falls well short of the mark. That evidence consists almost entirely of isolated sentences clipped from floor debates and legislative reports * * * The statements of Senator Bentsen on the floor of the Senate are indicative of the strength of the evidence relied on by petitioners. See, e.g., 118 Cong. Rec. 24397 (1972) (stating that "there is ample evidence that age discrimination is broadly practiced in government employment," but relying on newspaper articles about federal employees) * * *.

Petitioners place additional reliance on Congress' consideration of a 1966 report prepared by the State of California on age discrimination in its public agencies * * *. Like the assorted sentences petitioners cobble together from a decade's worth of congressional reports and floor debates, the California study does not indicate that the State had engaged in any unconstitutional age discrimination * * *. Even if the California report had uncovered a pattern of unconstitutional age discrimination in the State's public agencies at the time, it nevertheless would have been insufficient to support Congress' 1974 extension of the ADEA to every State of the Union. The report simply does not constitute "evidence that [unconstitutional age discrimination] had become a problem of national import."

Finally, the United States' argument that Congress found substantial age discrimination in the private sector is beside the point. Congress made no such findings with respect to the States * * *.

A review of the ADEA's legislative record as a whole, then, reveals that Congress had virtually no reason to believe that state and local governments were unconstitutionally discriminating against their employees on the basis of age * * *. In light of the indiscriminate scope of the Act's substantive requirements, and the lack of evidence of widespread and unconstitutional age discrimination by the States, we hold that the ADEA is not a valid exercise of Congress' power under § 5 of the Fourteenth Amendment. The ADEA's purported abrogation of the States' sovereign immunity is accordingly invalid * * *.

STEVENS, J., with whom SOUTER, J., GINSBURG, J., and BREYER, J., join, dissenting in part and concurring in part.

Congress' power to regulate the American economy includes the power to regulate both the public and the private sectors of the labor market. Federal rules outlawing discrimination in the workplace, like the regulation of wages and hours or health and safety standards, may be enforced against public as well as private employers. In my opinion, Congress' power to authorize federal remedies against state agencies that violate federal statutory obligations is coextensive with its power to impose those obligations on the States in the first place. Neither the Eleventh Amendment nor the doctrine of sovereign immunity places any limit on that power * * *.

The application of the ancient judge-made doctrine of sovereign immunity in cases like these is supposedly justified as a freestanding limit on congressional authority, a limit necessary to protect States' "dignity and respect" from impairment by the National Government. The Framers did not, however, select the Judicial Branch as the constitutional guardian of those state interests. Rather, the Framers designed important structural safeguards to ensure that when the National Government enacted substantive law (and provided for its enforcement), the normal operation of the legislative process itself would adequately defend state interests from undue infringement * * *.

It is the Framers' compromise giving each State equal representation in the Senate that provides the principal structural protection for the sovereignty of the several States * * *. The Framers also directed that the House be composed of Representatives selected by voters in the several States * * *.

Federalism concerns do make it appropriate for Congress to speak clearly when it regulates state action. But when it does so, as it has in these cases, we can safely presume that the burdens the statute imposes on the sovereignty of the several States were taken into account during the deliberative process leading to the enactment of the measure. Those burdens necessarily include the cost of defending against enforcement proceedings and paying whatever penalties might be incurred for violating the statute. In my judgment, the question whether those enforcement proceedings should be conducted exclusively by federal agencies, or may be brought by private parties as well, is a matter of policy for Congress to decide. In either event, once Congress has made its policy choice, the sovereignty concerns of the several States are satisfied, and the federal interest in evenhanded enforcement of federal law, explicitly endorsed in Article VI of the Constitution, does not countenance further limitations.

There is not a word in the text of the Constitution supporting the Court's conclusion that the judge-made doctrine of sovereign immunity limits Congress' power to authorize private parties, as well as federal agencies, to enforce federal law against the States. The importance of respecting the Framers' decision to assign the business of lawmaking to the Congress dictates firm resistance to the present majority's repeated substitution of its own views of federalism for those expressed in statutes enacted by the Congress and signed by the President.

The Eleventh Amendment simply does not support the Court's view. As has been stated before, the Amendment only places a textual limitation on the diversity jurisdiction of the federal courts * * *. Here, however, private petitioners did not invoke the federal courts' diversity jurisdiction; they are citizens of the same State as the defendants and they are asserting claims that arise under federal law. Thus, today's decision * * * rests entirely on a novel judicial interpretation of the doctrine of sovereign immunity, which the Court treats as though it were a constitutional precept. It is nevertheless clear to me that if Congress has the power to create the federal rights that these petitioners are asserting, it must also have the power to give the federal courts jurisdiction to remedy violations of those rights, even if it is necessary to "abrogate" the Court's "Eleventh Amendment" version of the common-law defense of sovereign immunity to do so * * *.

Despite my respect for stare decisis, I am unwilling to accept *Seminole Tribe* as controlling precedent. First and foremost, the reasoning of that opinion is so profoundly mistaken and so fundamentally inconsistent with the Framers' conception of the constitutional order that it has forsaken any claim to the usual deference or respect owed to decisions of this Court * * *. Further, *Seminole Tribe* is a case that will unquestionably have serious ramifications in future cases; indeed, it has already had such an effect, as in the Court's decision today and in the equally misguided opinion of *Alden v. Maine*, 527 U.S. 706 (1999) * * *. The kind of judicial activism manifested in cases like *Seminole Tribe*, *Alden v. Maine*, * * * represents such a radical departure from the proper role of this Court that it should be opposed whenever the opportunity arises.

Accordingly, I respectfully dissent.

[The concurring and dissenting opinion of JUSTICE THOMAS, joined by JUSTICE KENNEDY, is omitted.]

NOTES

1. The Court makes clear that Congress can validly abrogate state sovereign immunity pursuant to Congress's power under the Fourteenth Amendment (as opposed to its power under the Commerce Clause). But assertions by Congress that it passed legislation pursuant to its powers under the Fourteenth Amendment will not be sufficient to satisfy the Court that Congress actually had authority under the Fourteenth Amendment to pass the legislation. Why not?

2. In determining that Congress did not have such authority in the case, the Court dismisses evidence Congress had marshaled regarding the past history of age discrimination in employment. Perhaps most interestingly for this class, the Court dismissed evidence of a considerable history of age

discrimination in employment in the private sector, at least strongly implying that such history was not probative to the issue of age discrimination in employment in the public sector generally or state employment in particular. Is that convincing? Under this approach, what type of evidence would Congress need to produce?

3. In *Board of Trustees of the University of Alabama v. Garrett*, 531 U.S. 356, 121 S.Ct. 955, 148 L.Ed.2d 866 (2001), the Court held that states enjoyed Eleventh Amendment immunity in suits involving Title I of the Americans with Disabilities Act, 29 U.S.C. §§ 12111–12117 (ADA) for similar reasons and over a similar dissent (by Justice Breyer, joined by Justices Stevens, Souter, and Ginsberg). The Court held that: (1) the Fourteenth Amendment does not require states to make special accommodations for the disabled, so long as their actions towards such individuals are rational; (2) the legislative record of the ADA failed to show that Congress had identified a pattern of irrational discrimination by states in employment against the disabled, and thus did not support abrogation of the states' Eleventh Amendment immunity; and (3) the rights and remedies created by the ADA against states raised concerns as to its congruence and proportionality, supporting the holding that Congress did not validly abrogate the states' immunity.

In *Garrett*, the Court again stressed that most of the examples of disability discrimination that Congress cited when it passed the ADA did not specifically involve state employees. Dissenting, Justice Breyer, joined by Justices Stevens, Soutor, and Ginsberg disagreed. "The powerful evidence of discriminatory treatment throughout society in general, including discrimination by private persons and local governments, implicates state governments as well, for state agencies form part of that same larger society. There is no particular reason to believe that they are immune from the 'stereotypic assumptions' and pattern of 'purposeful unequal treatment' that Congress found prevalent. 531 U.S. at 378.

4. Could Congress try again, this time with a developed record on disability discrimination affecting state employees? If you were counsel to a relevant congressional committee, what elements would you seek to bring into such a record? How would you organize a congressional hearing on the subject?

The next case on the issue raised the question of what type of proof is sufficient to support a law passed pursuant to Congress's Fourteenth Amendment power involving a suspect classification.

NEVADA DEPARTMENT OF HUMAN RESOURCES v. HIBBS

Supreme Court of the United States, 2003.
538 U.S. 721, 123 S.Ct. 1972, 155 L.Ed.2d 953.

REHNQUIST, C.J. delivered the opinion of the Court.

The Family and Medical Leave Act of 1993 (FMLA or Act) entitles eligible employees to take up to 12 work weeks of unpaid leave annually for any of several reasons, including the onset of a "serious health condition" in an employee's spouse, child, or parent. 29 U.S.C.

§ 2612(a)(1)(C). The Act creates a private right of action to seek both equitable relief and money damages "against any employer (including a public agency) in any Federal or State court of competent jurisdiction," * * * . We hold that employees of the State of Nevada may recover money damages in the event of the State's failure to comply with the family-care provision of the Act.

* * * Respondent William Hibbs worked for the Department's Welfare Division. In April and May 1997, he sought leave under the FMLA to care for his ailing wife, who was recovering from a car accident and neck surgery. The Department granted his request for the full 12 weeks of FMLA leave and authorized him to use the leave intermittently as needed between May and December 1997. Respondent did so until August 5, 1997, after which he did not return to work. In October 1997, the Department informed respondent that he had exhausted his FMLA leave, that no further leave would be granted, and that he must report to work by November 12, 1997. Respondent failed to do so and was terminated.

Respondent sued petitioners * * * seeking damages and injunctive and declaratory relief for, *inter alia,* violations of 29 U.S.C. § 2612(a)(1)(C). The District Court awarded petitioners summary judgment on the grounds that the FMLA claim was barred by the Eleventh Amendment and that respondent's Fourteenth Amendment rights had not been violated. Respondent appealed, and the United States intervened under 28 U.S.C. § 2403 to defend the validity of the FMLA's application to the States. The Ninth Circuit reversed. 273 F.3d 844 (2001).

We granted certiorari to resolve a split among the Courts of Appeals on the question whether an individual may sue a State for money damages in federal court for violation of § 2612(a)(1)(C).

For over a century now, we have made clear that the Constitution does not provide for federal jurisdiction over suits against nonconsenting States. * * *

Congress may, however, abrogate such immunity in federal court if it makes its intention to abrogate unmistakably clear in the language of the statute and acts pursuant to a valid exercise of its power under § 5 of the Fourteenth Amendment * * * . The clarity of Congress' intent here is not fairly debatable. The Act enables employees to seek damages "against any employer (including a public agency) in any Federal or State court of competent jurisdiction," 29 U.S.C. § 2617(a)(2), and Congress has defined "public agency" to include both "the government of a State or political subdivision thereof" and "any agency of * * * a State, or a political subdivision of a State," §§ 203(x), 2611(4)(A)(iii) * * * . This case turns, then, on whether Congress acted within its constitutional authority when it sought to abrogate the States' immunity for purposes of the FMLA's family-leave provision.

In enacting the FMLA, Congress relied on two of the powers vested in it by the Constitution: its Article I commerce power and its power under § 5 of the Fourteenth Amendment to enforce that Amendment's guarantees.[1] Congress may not abrogate the States' sovereign immunity pursuant to its Article I power over commerce * * *. Congress may, however, abrogate States' sovereign immunity through a valid exercise of its § 5 power, for "the Eleventh Amendment, and the principle of state sovereignty which it embodies, are necessarily limited by the enforcement provisions of § 5 of the Fourteenth Amendment." * * *

Two provisions of the Fourteenth Amendment are relevant here: Section 5 grants Congress the power "to enforce" the substantive guarantees of § 1—among them, equal protection of the laws—by enacting "appropriate legislation." Congress may, in the exercise of its § 5 power, do more than simply proscribe conduct that we have held unconstitutional. " 'Congress' power "to enforce" the Amendment includes the authority both to remedy and to deter violation of rights guaranteed thereunder by prohibiting a somewhat broader swath of conduct, including that which is not itself forbidden by the Amendment's text.' " * * * In other words, Congress may enact so-called prophylactic legislation that proscribes facially constitutional conduct, in order to prevent and deter unconstitutional conduct.

City of Boerne also confirmed, however, that it falls to this Court, not Congress, to define the substance of constitutional guarantees * * *. Section 5 legislation reaching beyond the scope of § 1's actual guarantees must be an appropriate remedy for identified constitutional violations, not "an attempt to substantively redefine the States' legal obligations." We distinguish appropriate prophylactic legislation from "substantive redefinition of the Fourteenth Amendment right at issue," *id.,* at 81, by applying the test set forth in *City of Boerne:* Valid § 5 legislation must exhibit "congruence and proportionality between the injury to be prevented or remedied and the means adopted to that end." 521 U.S., at 520.

The FMLA aims to protect the right to be free from gender-based discrimination in the workplace.[2] We have held that statutory classifications that distinguish between males and females are subject to heightened scrutiny * * *. For a gender-based classification to withstand such scrutiny, it must "serv[e] important governmental objectives," and "the

---

1. Compare 29 U.S.C. § 2601(b)(1) ("It is the purpose of this Act * * * to balance the demands of the workplace with the needs of families, to promote the stability and economic security of families, and to promote national interests in preserving family integrity") with § 2601(b)(5) ("to promote the goal of equal employment opportunity for women and men, pursuant to [the Equal Protection C]lause") and § 2601(b)(4) ("to accomplish [the Act's other purposes] in a manner that, consistent with the Equal Protection Clause * * *, minimizes the potential for employment discrimination on the basis of sex"). See also S.Rep. No. 103–3, p. 16 (1993), U.S.Code Cong. & Admin.News 1993, pp. 3, 18 (the FMLA "is based not only on the Commerce Clause, but also on the guarantees of equal protection and due process embodied in the 14th Amendment"); H.R.Rep. No. 103–8, pt. 1, p. 29 (1993) (same).

2. The text of the Act makes this clear. Congress found that, "due to the nature of the roles of men and women in our society, the primary responsibility for family caretaking often falls on women, and such responsibility affects the working lives of women more than it affects the working lives of men." 29 U.S.C. § 2601(a)(5). In response to this finding, Congress sought "to accomplish the [Act's other] purposes * * * in a manner that * * * minimizes the potential for employment discrimination *on the basis of sex* by ensuring generally that leave is available * * * *on a gender-neutral basis*[,] and to promote the goal of equal employment opportunity for women and men 29 U.S.C. §§ 2601(b)(4) and (5) (emphasis added).

discriminatory means employed [must be] substantially related to the achievement of those objectives." * * * We now inquire whether Congress had evidence of a pattern of constitutional violations on the part of the States in this area.

The history of the many state laws limiting women's employment opportunities is chronicled in—and, until relatively recently, was sanctioned by—this Court's own opinions. For example, in *Bradwell v. State,* 83 U.S. 130, 21 L.Ed. 442 (1873) (Illinois), and *Goesaert v. Cleary,* 335 U.S. 464, 69 S.Ct. 198, 93 L.Ed. 163 (1948) (Michigan), the Court upheld state laws prohibiting women from practicing law and tending bar, respectively. State laws frequently subjected women to distinctive restrictions, terms, conditions, and benefits for those jobs they could take. In *Muller v. Oregon,* 208 U.S. 412, 28 S.Ct. 324, 52 L.Ed. 551 (1908), for example, this Court approved a state law limiting the hours that women could work for wages, and observed that 19 States had such laws at the time. Such laws were based on the related beliefs that (1) woman is, and should remain, "the center of home and family life," *Hoyt v. Florida,* 368 U.S. 57, 82 S.Ct. 159, 7 L.Ed.2d 118 (1961), and (2) "a proper discharge of [a woman's] maternal functions—having in view not merely her own health, but the well-being of the race—justif[ies] legislation to protect her from the greed as well as the passion of man," *Muller* at 208 U.S. at 422. Until our decision in *Reed v. Reed,* 404 U.S. 71, 92 S.Ct. 251, 30 L.Ed.2d 225 "it remained the prevailing doctrine that government, both federal and state, could withhold from women opportunities accorded men so long as any 'basis in reason' "—such as the above beliefs—"could be conceived for the discrimination." * * *

Congress responded to this history of discrimination by abrogating States' sovereign immunity in Title VII of the Civil Rights Act of 1964 * * * . But state gender discrimination did not cease * * * . According to evidence that was before Congress when it enacted the FMLA, States continue to rely on invalid gender stereotypes in the employment context, specifically in the administration of leave benefits. Reliance on such stereotypes cannot justify the States' gender discrimination in this area. The long and extensive history of sex discrimination prompted us to hold that measures that differentiate on the basis of gender warrant heightened scrutiny; here, as in *Fitzpatrick,* the persistence of such unconstitutional discrimination by the States justifies Congress' passage of prophylactic § 5 legislation.

As the FMLA's legislative record reflects, a 1990 Bureau of Labor Statistics (BLS) survey stated that 37 percent of surveyed private-sector employees were covered by maternity leave policies, while only 18 percent were covered by paternity leave policies * * * . The corresponding numbers from a similar BLS survey the previous year were 33 percent and 16 percent, respectively. While these data show an increase in the percentage of employees eligible for such leave, they also show a widening of the gender gap during the same period. Thus, stereotype-based beliefs about the allocation of family duties remained firmly rooted, and employers' reliance on them in establishing discriminatory leave policies remained widespread.[3]

Congress also heard testimony that "[p]arental leave for fathers * * * is rare. Even * * * [w]here child-care leave policies do exist, men, *both in the public and private sectors,* receive notoriously discriminatory treatment in their requests for such leave." * * * Many States offered women extended "maternity" leave that far exceeded the typical 4– to 8–week period of physical disability due to pregnancy and childbirth, but very few States granted men a parallel benefit: Fifteen States provided women up to one year of extended maternity leave, while only four provided men with the same * * *. This and other differential leave policies were not attributable to any differential physical needs of men and women, but rather to the pervasive sex-role stereotype that caring for family members is women's work.[5]

Finally, Congress had evidence that, even where state laws and policies were not facially discriminatory, they were applied in discriminatory ways. * * *

In spite of all of the above evidence, Justice KENNEDY argues in dissent that Congress' passage of the FMLA was unnecessary because "the States appear to have been ahead of Congress in providing gender-neutral family leave benefits,"and points to Nevada's leave policies in particular. However, it was only "[s]ince Federal family leave legislation was first introduced" that the States had even "begun to consider similar family leave initiatives" * * *.

Furthermore, the dissent's statement that some States "had adopted some form of family-care leave" before the FMLA's enactment glosses over important shortcomings of some state policies. First, seven States had childcare leave provisions that applied to women only. Indeed, Massachusetts required that notice of its leave provisions be posted only in "establishment[s] in which females are employed." These laws reinforced the very stereotypes that Congress sought to remedy through the FMLA. Second, 12 States provided their employees no family leave, beyond an initial childbirth or adoption, to care for a seriously ill child or family member. Third, many States provided no statutorily guaranteed right to

---

3. While this and other material described leave policies in the private sector, a 50–state survey also before Congress demonstrated that "[t]he proportion and construction of leave policies available to public sector employees differs little from those offered private sector employees." * * *

5. For example, state employers' collective-bargaining agreements often granted extended "maternity" leave of six months to a year to women only * * *. In addition, state leave laws often specified that catchall leave-without-pay provisions could be used for extended maternity leave, but did not authorize such leave for paternity purposes * * *. Evidence pertaining to parenting leave is relevant here because state discrimination in the provision of both types of benefits is based on the same gender stereotype: that women's family duties trump those of the workplace. Justice KENNEDY's dissent ignores this common foundation that, as Congress found, has historically produced discrimination in the hiring and promotion of women. Consideration of such evidence does not, as the dissent contends, expand our § 5 inquiry to include "*general* gender-based stereotypes in employment." To the contrary, because parenting and family leave address very similar situations in which work and family responsibilities conflict, they implicate the same stereotypes.

family leave, offering instead only voluntary or discretionary leave programs. Three States left the amount of leave time primarily in employers' hands. Congress could reasonably conclude that such discretionary family-leave programs would do little to combat the stereotypes about the roles of male and female employees that Congress sought to eliminate. Finally, four States provided leave only through administrative regulations or personnel policies, which Congress could reasonably conclude offered significantly less firm protection than a federal law. Against the above backdrop of limited state leave policies, no matter how generous petitioner's own may have been, Congress was justified in enacting the FMLA as remedial legislation.[10]

In sum, the States' record of unconstitutional participation in, and fostering of, gender-based discrimination in the administration of leave benefits is weighty enough to justify the enactment of prophylactic § 5 legislation.[11]

We reached the opposite conclusion in *Garrett* and *Kimel*. In those cases, the § 5 legislation under review responded to a purported tendency of state officials to make age- or disability-based distinctions. Under our equal protection case law, discrimination on the basis of such characteristics is not judged under a heightened review standard, and passes muster if there is "a rational basis for doing so at a class-based level, even if it 'is probably not true' that those reasons are valid in the majority of cases." * * * Thus, in order to impugn the constitutionality of state discrimination against the disabled or the elderly, Congress must identify, not just the existence of age- or disability-based state decisions, but a "widespread pattern" of irrational reliance on such criteria. We found no such showing with respect to the ADEA and Title I of the Americans with Disabilities Act of 1990 (ADA).

Here, however, Congress directed its attention to state gender discrimination, which triggers a heightened level of scrutiny. Because the standard for demonstrating the constitutionality of a gender-based classification is more difficult to meet than our rational-basis test—it must "serv[e] important governmental objectives" and be "substantially related

---

10. Contrary to the dissent's belief, we do not hold that Congress may "abrogat[e] state immunity from private suits whenever the State's social benefits program is not enshrined in the statutory code and provides employers with discretion," or when a State does not confer social benefits "as generous or extensive as Congress would later deem appropriate." The dissent misunderstands the purpose of the FMLA's family leave provision. The FMLA is not a "substantive entitlement program," Congress did not create a particular leave policy for its own sake. Rather, Congress sought to adjust family leave policies in order to eliminate their reliance on and perpetuation of invalid stereotypes, and thereby dismantle persisting gender-based barriers to the hiring, retention, and promotion of women in the workplace. In pursuing that goal, for the reasons discussed above, Congress reasonably concluded that state leave laws and practices should be brought within the Act.

11. Given the extent and specificity of the above record of unconstitutional state conduct, it is difficult to understand the dissent's accusation that we rely on "a simple recitation of a general history of employment discrimination against women." As we stated above, our holding rests on congressional findings that, at the time the FMLA was enacted, States "rel[ied] on invalid gender stereotypes in the employment context, *specifically in the administration of leave benefits.*" (emphasis added).

to the achievement of those objectives," it was easier for Congress to show a pattern of state constitutional violations. * * *

The impact of the discrimination targeted by the FMLA is significant. Congress determined:

> "Historically, denial or curtailment of women's employment opportunities has been traceable directly to the pervasive presumption that women are mothers first, and workers second. This prevailing ideology about women's roles has in turn justified discrimination against women when they are mothers or mothers-to-be." * * *

Stereotypes about women's domestic roles are reinforced by parallel stereotypes presuming a lack of domestic responsibilities for men. Because employers continued to regard the family as the woman's domain, they often denied men similar accommodations or discouraged them from taking leave. These mutually reinforcing stereotypes created a self-fulfilling cycle of discrimination that forced women to continue to assume the role of primary family caregiver, and fostered employers' stereotypical views about women's commitment to work and their value as employees. Those perceptions, in turn, Congress reasoned, lead to subtle discrimination that may be difficult to detect on a case-by-case basis.

We believe that Congress' chosen remedy, the family-care leave provision of the FMLA, is "congruent and proportional to the targeted violation." Congress had already tried unsuccessfully to address this problem through Title VII and the amendment of Title VII by the Pregnancy Discrimination Act * * *. Such problems may justify added prophylactic measures in response.

* * * By setting a minimum standard of family leave for *all* eligible employees, irrespective of gender, the FMLA attacks the formerly state-sanctioned stereotype that only women are responsible for family caregiving, thereby reducing employers' incentives to engage in discrimination by basing hiring and promotion decisions on stereotypes.

The dissent characterizes the FMLA as a "substantive entitlement program" rather than a remedial statute because it establishes a floor of 12 weeks' leave. In the dissent's view, in the face of evidence of gender-based discrimination by the States in the provision of leave benefits, Congress could do no more in exercising its § 5 power than simply proscribe such discrimination. But this position cannot be squared with our recognition that Congress "is not confined to the enactment of legislation that merely parrots the precise wording of the Fourteenth Amendment," but may prohibit "a somewhat broader swath of conduct, including that which is not itself forbidden by the Amendment's text." *Kimel, supra,* at 81. For example, this Court has upheld certain prophylactic provisions of the Voting Rights Act as valid exercises of Congress' § 5 power, including the literacy test ban and preclearance requirements for changes in States' voting procedures. * * *

Unlike the statutes at issue in *City of Boerne, Kimel*, and *Garrett,* which applied broadly to every aspect of state employers' operations, the FMLA is narrowly targeted at the fault line between work and family—precisely where sex-based overgeneralization has been and remains strongest—and affects only one aspect of the employment relationship. * * *

We also find significant the many other limitations that Congress placed on the scope of this measure * * *. The FMLA requires only unpaid leave and applies only to employees who have worked for the employer for at least one year and provided 1,250 hours of service within the last 12 months. Employees in high-ranking or sensitive positions are simply ineligible for FMLA leave; of particular importance to the States, the FMLA expressly excludes from coverage state elected officials, their staffs, and appointed policymakers. Employees must give advance notice of foreseeable leave, and employers may require certification by a health care provider of the need for leave. In choosing 12 weeks as the appropriate leave floor, Congress chose "a middle ground, a period long enough to serve 'the needs of families' but not so long that it would upset 'the legitimate interests of employers.' " * * * Moreover, the cause of action under the FMLA is a restricted one: The damages recoverable are strictly defined and measured by actual monetary losses, and the accrual period for backpay is limited by the Act's 2-year statute of limitations (extended to three years only for willful violations).

For the above reasons, we conclude that § 2612(a)(1)(C) is congruent and proportional to its remedial object, and can "be understood as responsive to, or designed to prevent, unconstitutional behavior." *City of Boerne, supra,* at 532, 117 S.Ct. 2157.

The judgment of the Court of Appeals is therefore *Affirmed.*

[JUSTICE SOUTER's concurring opinion, joined by JUSTICES GINSBURG and BREYER, is omitted.

JUSTICE STEVENS's concurring opinion is omitted.]

KENNEDY, J. with whom SCALIA and THOMAS, JJ. join, dissenting.

* * * The Court is unable to show that States have engaged in a pattern of unlawful conduct which warrants the remedy of opening state treasuries to private suits. The inability to adduce evidence of alleged discrimination, coupled with the inescapable fact that the federal scheme is not a remedy but a benefit program, demonstrate the lack of the requisite link between any problem Congress has identified and the program it mandated.

In examining whether Congress was addressing a demonstrated "pattern of unconstitutional employment discrimination by the States," the Court gives superficial treatment to the requirement that we "identify with some precision the scope of the constitutional right at issue." *Garrett* 531 U.S. at 365.

The Court suggests the issue is "the right to be free from gender-based discrimination in the workplace," and then it embarks on a survey of our precedents speaking to "[t]he history of the many state laws limiting women's employment opportunities." All would agree that women historically have been subjected to conditions in which their employment opportunities are more limited than those available to men. As the Court acknowledges, however, Congress responded to this problem by abrogating States' sovereign immunity in Title VII of the Civil Rights Act of 1964. The provision now before us has a different aim than Title VII. It seeks to ensure that eligible employees, irrespective of gender, can take a minimum amount of leave time to care for an ill relative.

The relevant question, as the Court seems to acknowledge, is whether, notwithstanding the passage of Title VII and similar state legislation, the States continued to engage in widespread discrimination on the basis of gender in the provision of family leave benefits. If such a pattern were shown, the Eleventh Amendment would not bar Congress from devising a congruent and proportional remedy. The evidence to substantiate this charge must be far more specific, however, than a simple recitation of a general history of employment discrimination against women. * * *

Respondents fail to make the requisite showing. The Act's findings of purpose are devoid of any discussion of the relevant evidence. * * *

As the Court seems to recognize, the evidence considered by Congress concerned discriminatory practices of the private sector, not those of state employers. The statistical information compiled by the Bureau of Labor Statistics which are the only factual findings the Court cites, surveyed only private employers. While the evidence of discrimination by private entities may be relevant, it does not, by itself, justify the abrogation of States' sovereign immunity. *Garrett,* 531 U.S. at 368 (Congress' § 5 authority is appropriately exercised only in response to state transgressions). * * *

The testimony on which the Court relies concerned the discrimination with respect to the parenting leave. * * * Even if this isolated testimony could support an inference that private sector's gender-based discrimination in the provision of parenting leave was parallel to the behavior by state actors in 1986, the evidence would not be probative of the States' conduct some seven years later with respect to a statutory provision conferring a different benefit. * * *

The Court's reliance on evidence suggesting States provided men and women with the parenting leave of different length suffers from the same flaw. This evidence concerns the Act's grant of parenting leave, and is too attenuated to justify the family leave provision. The Court of Appeals' conclusion to the contrary was based on an assertion that "if states discriminate along gender lines regarding the one kind of leave, then they are likely to do so regarding the other." The charge that a State has engaged in a pattern of unconstitutional discrimination against its citizens is a most serious one. It must be supported by more than conjecture. * * *

The Court next argues that "even where state laws and policies were not facially discriminatory, they were applied in discriminatory ways." * * * The study from which the Court derives this conclusion examined "the parental leave policies of Federal executive branch agencies," not those of the States. * * * A history of discrimination on the part of the Federal Government may, in some situations, support an inference of similar conduct by the States, but the Court does not explain why the inference is justified here.

Even if there were evidence that individual state employers, in the absence of clear statutory guidelines, discriminated in the administration of leave benefits, this circumstance alone would not support a finding of a state-sponsored pattern of discrimination. The evidence could perhaps support the charge of disparate impact, but not a charge that States have engaged in a pattern of intentional discrimination prohibited by the Fourteenth Amendment. * * *

Stripped of the conduct which exhibits no constitutional infirmity, the Court's "exten[sive] and specifi[c] * * * record of unconstitutional state conduct," boils down to the fact that three States, Massachusetts, Kansas, and Tennessee, provided parenting leave only to their female employees, and had no program for granting their employees (male or female) family leave. * * *

Considered in its entirety, the evidence fails to document a pattern of unconstitutional conduct sufficient to justify the abrogation of States' sovereign immunity. The few incidents identified by the Court "fall far short of even suggesting the pattern of unconstitutional discrimination on which § 5 legislation must be based." *Garrett* at 370; see also *Kimel* at 89–91.

* * * Given the insufficiency of the evidence that States discriminated in the provision of family leave, the unfortunate fact that stereotypes about women continue to be a serious and pervasive social problem would not alone support the charge that a State has engaged in a practice designed to deny its citizens the equal protection of the laws. * * *

The paucity of evidence to support the case the Court tries to make demonstrates that Congress was not responding with a congruent and proportional remedy to a perceived course of unconstitutional conduct. Instead, it enacted a substantive entitlement program of its own. If Congress had been concerned about different treatment of men and women with respect to family leave, a congruent remedy would have sought to ensure the benefits of any leave program enacted by a State are available to men and women on an equal basis. Instead, the Act imposes, across the board, a requirement that States grant a minimum of 12 weeks of leave per year. This requirement may represent Congress' considered judgment as to the optimal balance between the family obligations of workers and the interests of employers. * * * It does not follow, however, that if the States choose to enact a different benefit scheme, they should be deemed to engage in unconstitutional conduct and forced to open their treasuries to private suits for damages. * * *

* * * What is at issue is only whether the States can be subjected, without consent, to suits brought by private persons seeking to collect moneys from the state treasury. Their immunity cannot be abrogated without documentation of a pattern of unconstitutional acts by the States, and only then by a congruent and proportional remedy. There has been a complete failure by respondents to carry their burden to establish each of these necessary propositions. * * *

SCALIA, J., dissenting.

I join Justice KENNEDY's dissent, and add one further observation: The constitutional violation that is a prerequisite to "prophylactic" congressional action to "enforce" the Fourteenth Amendment is a violation *by the State against which the enforcement action is taken.* There is no guilt by association, enabling the sovereignty of one State to be abridged under § 5 of the Fourteenth Amendment because of violations by another State, or by most other States, or even by 49 other States. * * *

[T]he Court does not even attempt to demonstrate that each one of the 50 States covered by 29 U.S.C. § 2612(a)(1)(C) was in violation of the Fourteenth Amendment. It treats "the States" as some sort of collective entity which is guilty or innocent as a body. * * * This will not do. Prophylaxis in the sense of extending the remedy beyond the violation is one thing; prophylaxis in the sense of extending the remedy beyond the violator is something else. * * *

NOTES

1. The majority found sufficient evidence of discrimination specifically by states to hold that the FMLA was a valid use of Fourteenth Amendment power. Do you agree that this evidence was sufficient under *Kimel* and *Garrett*? On the other hand, do you agree with the emphasis both the majority and minority opinions place on importance of evidence of discrimination specifically by state employers?

2. What types of evidence in the Congressional record would have been sufficient to satisfy Justice Kennedy? Justice Scalia?

3. Although there is no Supreme Court case squarely deciding the issue, *Hibbs* indicates that the Court would hold that Title VII abrogates the Eleventh Amendment immunity of the states because Title VII was passed pursuant to a valid exercise of Congress's power under the Fourteenth Amendment.

4. After *Hibbs*, some lower courts have held that states nonetheless retain Eleventh Amendment immunity from FMLA suits involving leave for the employee's own sickness, as opposed to leave taken for family care. See, *e.g.*, *Toeller v. Wisconsin Dept. of Corrections*, 461 F.3d 871 (7th Cir. 2006); *Touvell v. Ohio Department of Mental Retardation*, 422 F.3d 392 (6th Cir. 2005). On what grounds could courts make this distinction?

5. As *Alden* indicated, Eleventh Amendment immunity does not apply when an agency of the Federal government brings suit against the state; it applies only to private suits by employees themselves. See, *e.g., E.E.O.C. v. Board of Supervisors for University of Louisiana System*, 559 F.3d 270 (5th Cir. 2009) (EEOC's suit under the ADEA not limited by Eleventh Amendment immunity). But as the *Alden* dissent observed, only a small fraction of FLSA cases are brought by the Secretary of Labor, and similarly, the EEOC only brings a tiny fraction of ADEA and ADA suits. Also, states can waive their immunity, although that too is uncommon. Are there other alternatives for state employees? See Melinda Herrera, Fair Labor Standards Act and Sovereign Immunity: Unlocking the Courthouse Door for Texas State Employees, 32 *Saint Mary's Law Journal* 269 (2001); Brent W. Landau, State Employees and Sovereign Immunity: Alternatives and Strategies for Enforcing Federal Employment Laws, 39 *Harvard Journal on Legislation* 169 (2002).

3. THE POTENTIAL FOR FEDERAL BARGAINING LEGISLATION

Against the backdrop above, consider the proposed "Public Safety Employer–Employee Cooperation Act of 2009," H.R. 413, introduced on January 9, 2009 (similar bills were introduced in earlier years). This Act would provide collective bargaining rights for public safety officers employed by states or local governments. It directs the Federal Labor Relations Authority (FLRA, the body that administers the federal sector bargaining statute) to determine whether state law provides specified collective bargaining rights for public safety officers. If the state had no such law or if the FLRA found the law did not meet the standards in the Act, the FLRA would prescribe regulations covering the employees.

Specifically, the Act would:

(1) grant such employees the right to form and join a labor organization which excludes management and supervisory employees;

(2) require public safety employers to recognize and agree to bargain with the employees' chosen labor organization;

(3) require the FLRA to issue regulations establishing rights and responsibilities for public safety employers and employees in states that do not substantially provide for such public safety employee rights and responsibilities.

(4) direct the Authority, in such cases, to:

(a) determine the appropriateness of units for union representation;

(b) supervise or conduct elections to determine whether a union has been selected as an exclusive representative by a voting majority of the employees in an appropriate unit;

(c) resolve issues relating to the duty to bargain in good faith;

(d) conduct hearings and resolve complaints of unfair labor practices; and

(e) resolve exceptions to arbitrators' awards.

(5) grant a public safety employer, employee, or labor organization the right to seek enforcement of Authority regulations and orders in state court;

(6) prohibit public safety employers, employees, and labor organizations from engaging in lockouts or strikes; and

(7) provide that existing collective bargaining units and agreements would not be invalidated by this Act.

Perhaps not surprisingly, police and firefighter unions are the primary lobbying forces behind this bill. What political force do they bring to its consideration? What are the prospects for similar legislation on behalf of low-paid file clerks in state government agencies? Is there a difference in principle, practices in different jobs, or just a difference in raw political power?

What type of Constitutional challenges might this bill face? Do you think the challenges would ultimately be held to be meritorious?

If the Constitutional challenges were rejected, do you think this bill represents good policy? Why or why not?

B. SPECIAL FAIR LABOR STANDARDS ACT RULES IN PUBLIC EMPLOYMENT

The Fair Labor Standards Act of 1938, 29 U.S.C. §§ 201–219, is the federal law which sets, most prominently, national overtime, minimum wage, and child labor rules. As described in section A. *supra*, the Supreme Court has decided several cases regarding the power of Congress to apply the FLSA to the public sector. Currently, the FLSA does apply to the public sector, with the caveat that state governments have Eleventh Amendment immunity as described in *Alden v. Maine*.

Unlike other employment laws which apply to the public sector, however, the FLSA contains some substantively significant special rules that apply to government employers only. Specifically, in 1985, after the *Garcia* decision, Congress passed a major amendment to the FLSA that applies only to employees of state and local governments. The special rules in the 1985 Amendments mostly involve overtime issues. The amendments were motivated by concerns that full application of all FLSA rules, especially overtime rules, would impose overly burdensome costs on state and local government employers.

1. COMPENSATORY TIME

The most important provision of the 1985 Amendments is FLSA § 207(*o*) which allows public employers, under specified circumstances, to use paid time off—compensatory time, or "comp time"—in lieu of money payment for overtime. Under the FLSA, private sector employers may not use comp time in lieu of payment in money for overtime. Thus, a private sector employee covered by the FLSA's overtime rules (a "non-exempt" employee) who works 50 hours in a week must be paid the employee's regular rate of pay for the first 40 hours of work, and then one and one half times the employee's regular hourly rate of pay for the next ten hours. In the public sector, an employer is permitted to compensate a non-exempt employee in that way, but under some circumstances, the employer may award the employee comp time instead of money for some or all of the 10 overtime hours. Comp time under § 207(*o*) is awarded at time-and-a-half rates, so, *e.g.*, the employer could credit the employee with 15 hours of paid time off for those 10 hours.

Section 207(*o*) contains a number of rules regarding the use of comp time. It provides as follows.

> (*o*) Compensatory time
>
> (1) Employees of a public agency which is a State, a political subdivision of a State, or an interstate governmental agency may receive, in accordance with this subsection and in lieu of overtime compensation, compensatory time off at a rate not less than one and one-half hours for each hour of employment for which overtime compensation is required by this section.
>
> (2) A public agency may provide compensatory time under paragraph (1) only—
>
> (A) pursuant to—
>
> applicable provisions of a collective bargaining agreement, memorandum of understanding, or any other agreement between the public agency and representatives of such employees; or
>
> (ii) in the case of employees not covered by subclause (i), an agreement or understanding arrived at between the employer and employee before the performance of the work; and (B) if the employee has not accrued compensatory time in excess of the limit applicable to the employee prescribed by paragraph (3).
>
> In the case of employees described in clause (A)(ii) hired prior to April 15, 1986, the regular practice in effect on April 15, 1986, with respect to compensatory time off for such employees in lieu of the receipt of overtime compensation, shall constitute an agreement or understanding under such clause (A)(ii). Except as provided in the previous sentence, the provision of compensatory time off to such employees for hours worked after April 14, 1986, shall be in accordance with this subsection.
>
> (3)(A) If the work of an employee for which compensatory time may be provided included work in a public safety activity, an emergency response activity, or a seasonal activity, the employee engaged in such work may accrue not more than 480 hours of compensatory time for

hours worked after April 15, 1986. If such work was any other work, the employee engaged in such work may accrue not more than 240 hours of compensatory time for hours worked after April 15, 1986. Any such employee who, after April 15, 1986, has accrued 480 or 240 hours, as the case may be, of compensatory time off shall, for additional overtime hours of work, be paid overtime compensation.

(B) If compensation is paid to an employee for accrued compensatory time off, such compensation shall be paid at the regular rate earned by the employee at the time the employee receives such payment.

(4) An employee who has accrued compensatory time off authorized to be provided under paragraph (1) shall, upon termination of employment, be paid for the unused compensatory time at a rate of compensation not less than—

(A) the average regular rate received by such employee during the last 3 years of the employee's employment, or

(B) the final regular rate received by such employee, whichever is higher

(5) An employee of a public agency which is a State, political subdivision of a State, or an interstate governmental agency—

(A) who has accrued compensatory time off authorized to be provided under paragraph (1), and

(B) who has requested the use of such compensatory time,

shall be permitted by the employee's employer to use such time within a reasonable period after making the request if the use of the compensatory time does not unduly disrupt the operations of the public agency. * * *

(7) For purposes of this subsection—

(A) the term "overtime compensation" means the compensation required by subsection (a), and

(B) the terms "compensatory time" and "compensatory time off" mean hours during which an employee is not working, which are not counted as hours worked during the applicable workweek or other work period for purposes of overtime compensation, and for which the employee is compensated at the employee's regular rate.

The Supreme Court has decided two cases involving these rules. The first involved the requirement of an "agreement" to use compensatory time described in § 207(*o*)(2)(a).

MOREAU v. KLEVENHAGEN

Supreme Court of the United States, 1993.
508 U.S. 22, 113 S.Ct. 1905, 123 L.Ed.2d 584.

STEVENS, J. delivered the opinion of the Court.

The Fair Labor Standards Act (FLSA or Act) generally requires employers to pay their employees for overtime work at a rate of 1 ½ times the employees' regular wages. In 1985, Congress amended the FLSA to provide a limited exception to this rule for state and local governmental agencies. Under the Fair Labor Standards Amendments of 1985 (1985 Amendments), public employers may compensate employees who work overtime with extra time off instead of overtime pay in certain circumstances.[2] The question in this case is whether a public employer in a State that prohibits public sector collective bargaining may take advantage of that exception when its employees have designated a union representative.

Because the text of the 1985 Amendments provides the framework for our entire analysis, we quote the most relevant portion at the outset. Subsection 7(*o*)(2)(A) states:

> "(2) A public agency may provide compensatory time [in lieu of overtime pay] only—
>
> (A) pursuant to—
>
> "(i) applicable provisions of a collective bargaining agreement, memorandum of understanding, or any other agreement between the public agency and representatives of such employees; or
>
> "(ii) in the case of employees not covered by subclause (I), an agreement or understanding arrived at between the employer and employee before the performance of the work * * *"

Petitioners are a group of employees who sought, unsuccessfully, to negotiate a collective FLSA compensatory time agreement by way of a designated representative. The narrow question dispositive here is whether petitioners are "employees not covered by subclause (i)" within the meaning of subclause (ii), so that their employer may provide compensatory time pursuant to individual agreements under the second subclause.

I

Congress enacted the FLSA in 1938 * * * . Amendments to the Act in 1966 and 1974 extended its coverage to most public employers, and gave rise to a series of cases questioning the power of Congress to regulate the compensation of state and local employees. Following our decision in *Garcia v. San Antonio Metropolitan Transit Authority,* 469 U.S. 528, 105 S.Ct. 1005, 83 L.Ed.2d 1016 1985), upholding that power, the Department of Labor (DOL) announced that it would hold public employers to the standards of the Act effective April 15, 1985.

In response to the *Garcia* decision and the DOL announcement, both Houses of Congress held hearings and considered legislation designed to

2. [29 U.S.C. § 207(*o*) provides]: * * * "(1) Employees of a public agency which is a State, a political subdivision of a State, or an interstate governmental agency may receive, in accordance with this subsection and in lieu of overtime compensation, compensatory time off at a rate not less than one and one-half hours for each hour of employment for which overtime compensation is required by this section. * * *

"In the case of employees described in clause (A)(ii) hired prior to April 15, 1986, the regular practice in effect on April 15, 1986, with respect to compensatory time off for such employees in lieu of the receipt of overtime compensation, shall constitute an agreement or understanding under such clause (A)(ii). * * *

ameliorate the burdens associated with necessary changes in public employment practices. The projected "financial costs of coming into compliance with the FLSA—particularly the overtime provisions"—were specifically identified as a matter of grave concern to many States and localities. The statutory provision at issue in this case is the product of those deliberations.

In its Report recommending enactment of the 1985 Amendments, the Senate Committee on Labor and Human Resources explained that the new subsection 7(*o*) would allow public employers to compensate for overtime hours with compensatory time off, or comp time, in lieu of overtime pay, so long as certain conditions were met: The provision of "comp time" must be at the premium rate of not less than 1 ½ hours per hour of overtime work, and must be pursuant to an agreement reached prior to performance of the work. With respect to the nature of the necessary agreement, the issue raised in this case, the Committee stated: "Where employees have a recognized representative, the agreement or understanding must be between that representative and the employer, either through collective bargaining or through a memorandum of understanding or other type of agreement."

The House Committee on Education and Labor was in substantial agreement with the Senate Committee as to the conditions under which comp time could be made available. On the question of subsection 7(*o*)'s agreement requirement, the House Committee expressed an understanding similar to the Senate Committee's: "Where employees have selected a representative, which need not be a formal or recognized collective bargaining agent as long as it is a representative designated by the employees, the agreement or understanding must be between the representative and the employer * * * "

Where the Senate and House Committee Reports differ is in their description of the "representative" who, once designated, would require that compensatory time be provided only pursuant to an agreement between that representative and the employer. While the Senate Report refers to a "recognized" representative, the House Report states that the representative "need not be a formal or recognized collective bargaining agent." The Conference Report does not comment on this difference * * * and the 1985 Amendments as finally enacted do not adopt the precise language of either Committee Report.

The issue is addressed, however, by the Secretary of Labor, in implementing regulations * * *. The relevant DOL regulation seems to be patterned after the House Report, providing that "the representative need not be a formal or recognized bargaining agent."[9] At the same time,

---

9. "(b) *Agreement or understanding between the public agency and a representative of the employees.* (1) Where employees have a representative, the agreement or understanding concerning the use of compensatory time must be between the representative and the public agency either through a collective bargaining agreement or through a memorandum of understanding or other type of oral or written agreement. In the absence of a collective bargaining agreement applicable to the employees, the representative need not be a formal or recognized bargaining

in response to concerns expressed by the State of Missouri about the impact of the regulation in States where employee representatives have no authority to enter into enforceable agreements, the Secretary explained:

> "The Department believes that the proposed rule accurately reflects the statutory requirement that a CBA [collective bargaining agreement], memorandum of understanding or other agreement be reached between the public agency and the representative of the employees where the employees have designated a representative. Where the employees do not have a representative, the agreement must be between the employer and the individual employees. The Department recognizes that there is a wide variety of State law that may be pertinent in this area. *It is the Department's intention that the question of whether employees have a representative for purposes of FLSA section 7(*o*) shall be determined in accordance with State or local law and practices.*" 52 Fed.Reg. 2014–2015 (1987) (emphasis added).

II

Petitioner Moreau is the president of the Harris County Deputy Sheriffs Union, representing approximately 400 deputy sheriffs in this action against the county and its sheriff, respondent Klevenhagen. For several years, the union has represented Harris County deputy sheriffs in various matters, such as processing grievances and handling workers' compensation claims, but it is prohibited by Texas law from entering into a collective-bargaining agreement with the county.[10] Accordingly, the terms and conditions of petitioners' employment are included in individual form agreements signed by each employee. These agreements incorporate by reference the county's regulations providing that deputies shall receive 1 ½ hours of compensatory time for each hour of overtime work.

Petitioners * * * alleg[e], *inter alia,* that the county violated the Act by paying for overtime work with comp time, rather than overtime pay, absent an agreement with their representative authorizing the substitution. Petitioners contended that they were "covered" by subclause (i) of subsection 7(*o*)(2)(A) by virtue of their union representation, and that the County therefore was precluded from providing comp time pursuant to individual agreements (or pre-existing practice) under subclause (ii).

The District Court disagreed and entered summary judgment for the county. The court assumed that designation of a union representative

---

agent as long as the representative is designated by the employees. Any agreement must be consistent with the provisions of section 7(*o*) of the Act." 29 CFR § 553.23(b) (1992).

10. As the Court of Appeals stated: "TEX.REV.CIV.STAT.ANN. art. 5154c prohibits any political subdivision from entering into a collective bargaining agreement with a labor organization unless the political subdivision has adopted the Fire and Police Employee Relations Act. Harris County has not adopted that Act; thus, * * * the County has no authority to bargain with the Union." The court went on to clarify that "Texas law prohibits any bilateral agreement between a city and a bargaining agent, whether the agreement is labeled a collective bargaining agreement or something else. Under Texas law, the County could not enter into *any* agreement with the Union." (emphasis in original) * * *.

normally would establish that employees are "covered" by subclause (i), and hence render subclause (ii) inapplicable, but went on to hold that subclause (i) cannot apply in States, like Texas, that prohibit collective bargaining in the public sector * * *. Reaching the same result by an alternate route, the court also reasoned that petitioners were not "covered" by subclause (i) because their union was not "recognized" by the county, a requirement it grounded in the legislative history of the 1985 Amendments. * * *

The Court of Appeals affirmed, but relied on slightly different reasoning. It seemed to agree with an Eleventh Circuit case, *Dillard v. Harris,* 885 F.2d 1549 (1989), cert. denied, 498 U.S. 878 (1990), that the words "not covered" in subclause (ii) refer to the absence of an *agreement* rather than the absence of a representative. Under that theory, the fact that Texas law prohibits agreements between petitioners' union and the employer means that petitioners can never be "covered" by subclause (i), making subclause (ii) available as an alternative vehicle for provision of comp time.

Because there is conflict among the Circuits over the scope of subclause (i)'s coverage,[14] we granted certiorari.

III

Respondents find the language of the statute perfectly clear. In their view, subclause (ii) plainly authorizes individual agreements whenever public employees have not successfully negotiated a collective-bargaining agreement under subclause (i). Petitioners, on the other hand, contend that ambiguity in the statute itself justifies resort to its legislative history and the DOL regulations, and that these secondary sources unequivocally preclude individual comp time agreements with employees who have designated a representative. * * *

At least one proposition is not in dispute. Subclause (ii) authorizes individual comp time agreements only "in the case of employees not covered by subclause (i)." Our task, therefore, is to identify the class of "employees" covered by subclause (i). This task is complicated by the fact that subclause (i) does not purport to define a category of employees, as the reference in subclause (ii) suggests it would. Instead, it describes only a category of agreements—those that (a) are bargained with an employee representative, and (b) authorize the use of comp time.

Respondents read this shift in subject from "employees" in subclause (ii) to "agreement" in subclause (i) as susceptible of just one meaning: Employees are covered by subclause (i) only if they are bound by applica-

14. See, *e.g., International Assn. of Fire Fighters, Local 2203 v. West Adams County Fire Dist.,* 877 F.2d 814 (CA10 1989) (employees covered by subclause (i) upon designation of representative); *Abbott v. Virginia Beach,* 879 F.2d 132 (CA4 1989) (employees covered by subclause (i) upon designation of recognized representative); *Dillard v. Harris,* 885 F.2d 1549 (CA11 1989) (employees covered by subclause (i) upon entry of agreement regarding compensatory time); *Nevada Highway Patrol Assn. v. Nevada,* 899 F.2d 1549 (CA9 1990) (employees covered by subclause (i) upon designation of representative unless state law prohibits public sector collective bargaining) * * *.

ble provisions of a collective-bargaining agreement. Under this narrow construction, subclause (i) would not cover employees who designate a representative if that representative is unable to reach agreement with the employer, for whatever reason; such employees would remain "uncovered" and available for individual comp time agreements under subclause (ii).

We find this reading unsatisfactory. First, while the language of subclauses (i) and (ii) will bear the interpretation advanced by respondents, we cannot say that it will bear no other. Purely as a matter of grammar, subclause (ii)'s reference to "employees" remains unmodified by subclause (i)'s focus on "agreement," and "employees * * * covered" might as easily comprehend employees with representatives as employees with agreements. * * *

Second, respondents' reading is difficult to reconcile with the general structure of subsection 7(*o*). Assuming designation of an employee representative, respondents' theory leaves it to the employer to choose whether it will proceed under subclause (i), and negotiate the terms of a collective comp time agreement with the representative, or instead proceed under subclause (ii), and deal directly with its employees on an individual basis. If the employer is free to choose the latter course (as most employers likely would), then it need only decline to negotiate with the employee representative to render subclause (i) inapplicable and authorize individual comp time agreements under subclause (ii).[15] This permissive interpretation of subsection 7(*o*), however, is at odds with the limiting phrase of subclause (ii) at issue here. Had Congress intended such an open-ended authorization of the use of comp time, it surely would have said so more simply * * *.

At the same time, however, we find equally implausible a reading of the statutory text that would deem employees "covered" by subclause (i) whenever they select a representative, whether or not the representative has the ability to enter into the kind of agreement described in that subclause. If there is no possibility of reaching an agreement under subclause (i), then that subclause cannot logically be read as applicable. In other words, "employees * * * covered by subclause (i)" must, at a minimum, be employees who conceivably could receive comp time pursuant to the agreement contemplated by that subclause.

The most plausible reading of the phrase "employees * * * covered by subclause (i)" is, in our view, neither of the extreme alternatives described above. Rather, the phrase is most sensibly read as referring to employees who have designated a representative with the authority to negotiate and

15. Indeed, even an employer who is party to a collective-bargaining agreement with its employees may be permitted to take advantage of subclause (ii) under respondents' construction. Because subclause (i) describes only those agreements that authorize the use of comp time, a collective-bargaining agreement silent on the subject, or even one prohibiting use of comp time altogether, would not constitute a subclause (i) agreement. Accordingly, employees bound by such an agreement would not be "covered by subclause (i)" under respondents' theory, and their employer would be free to provide comp time instead of overtime pay pursuant to individual employee agreements.

agree with their employer on "applicable provisions of a collective bargaining agreement" authorizing the use of comp time. This reading accords significance to both the focus on the word "agreement" in subclause (i) and the focus on "employees" in subclause (ii). * * *[16]

This intermediate reading of the statutory text is consistent also with the DOL regulations, interpreted most reasonably. It is true that 29 CFR § 553.23(b), read in isolation, would support petitioners' view that selection of a representative by employees-even a representative without lawful authority to bargain with the employer-is sufficient to bring the employees within the scope of subclause (i) and preclude use of subclause (ii) individual agreements * * *. So interpreted, however, the regulation would prohibit entirely the use of comp time in a substantial portion of the public sector. It would also be inconsistent with the Secretary's statement that "the question * * * whether employees have a representative for purposes of FLSA section 7(*o*) shall be determined in accordance with State or local law and practices." This clarification by the Secretary convinces us that when the regulations identify selection of a representative as the condition necessary for coverage under subclause (i), they refer only to those representatives with lawful authority to negotiate agreements.

Thus, under both the statute and the DOL regulations, employees are "covered" by subclause (i) when they designate a representative who lawfully may bargain collectively on their behalf—under the statute, because such authority is necessary to reach the kind of "agreement" described in subclause (i), and under the regulation, because such authority is a condition of "representative" status for subclause (i) purposes. Because we construe the statute and regulation in harmony, we need not comment further on petitioners' argument that the Secretary's interpretation of the 1985 Amendments is entitled to special deference.

Petitioners in this case did not have a representative authorized by law to enter into an agreement with their employer providing for use of comp time under subclause (i). Accordingly, they were "not covered by subclause (i)," and subclause (ii) authorized the individual agreements challenged in this litigation.

The judgment of the Court of Appeals is affirmed.

NOTES

1. In the debates leading to the passage of the 1985 FLSA Amendments, advocates for public sector unions were clearly attempting to make the use of

16. So read, we do not understand subsection 7(*o*) to impose any new burden upon a public employer to bargain collectively with its employees. Subsection 7(*o*) is, after all, an exception to the general FLSA rule mandating overtime pay for overtime work, and employers may take advantage of the benefits it offers "only" pursuant to certain conditions set forth by Congress. * * * Once its employees designate a representative authorized to engage in collective bargaining, an employer is entitled to take advantage of those benefits if it reaches a comp time agreement with the representative. It is also free, of course, to forgo collective bargaining altogether; if it so chooses, it remains in precisely the same position as any other employer subject to the overtime pay provisions of the FLSA.

comp time roughly equivalent to a mandatory subject of bargaining under federal law even for unions in states, such as Texas, that had not enacted collective bargaining rights for public sector workers. And, before *Moreau*, several Circuit Courts had accepted that interpretation. Should Congress, through federal employment law, essentially set certain terms of state public sector labor law? If so, are some areas of labor law more appropriate for standardized national rules than others? Which ones? If not, what is the distinction between labor laws and employment laws such as the FLSA which apply to the public sector? Is it any more intrusive for Congress to grant some bargaining rights to employees of state and government employees than it is for Congress to give such employees federal rights to overtime and the minimum wage, or anti-discrimination rights under Title VII? See the discussion of the Public Safety Employer–Employee Cooperation Act of 2009 in section A.3, *supra*.

2. *Moreau* rejects both the union's statutory argument and its reliance on the Department of Labor regulation. Do you find the Court's interpretation convincing? Note the specific reference in the House Report and the regulation to representatives that lack bargaining rights. The Court relied in part on parsing statutory language, but did the Court understand the role that such representatives have played throughout the history of public sector labor relations? See Chapter 4. If not, would such an understanding have led to a different result?

3. For employees not entitled or permitted to bargain collectively over the use of comp time, how much force does the requirement for an "agreement" before using comp time have? Note that 29 C.F.R. § 553.23 provides:

> The agreement or understanding to provide compensatory time off in lieu of cash overtime compensation may take the form of an express condition of employment, provided (i) the employee knowingly and voluntarily agrees to it as a condition of employment and (ii) the employee is informed that the compensatory time received may be preserved, used or cashed out consistent with the provisions of section 7(*o*) of the Act. An agreement or understanding may be evidenced by a notice to the employee that compensatory time off will be given in lieu of overtime pay. In such a case, an agreement or understanding would be presumed to exist for purposes of section 7(*o*) with respect to any employee who fails to express to the employer an unwillingness to accept compensatory time off in lieu of overtime pay. However, the employee's decision to accept compensatory time off in lieu of cash overtime payments must be made freely and without coercion or pressure.

Employers may prefer to grant their employees comp time in lieu of cash compensation because it saves cash in the short term or permits scheduling flexibility. Over the long term, however, the practice can actually cost more money than paying premium pay in cash. When employees use their comp time, they must be paid at their then current rates which are likely to be higher than the rates they were paid when they accumulated the comp time. Furthermore, when employees leave their employment, they must be paid for unused comp time at the higher of their current hourly rate or the average hourly rate they were paid in their last three years of employment, whichever is higher. As employers see comp time accounts build, they may fear that they have had too much of a good thing and may try to require employees to use their comp time, particularly during slow periods when the employer will not have to pay other employees overtime to cover for the employee who has taken off. The following case considers the employer's authority to do so.

CHRISTENSEN v. HARRIS COUNTY

Supreme Court of the United States, 2000.
529 U.S. 576, 120 S.Ct. 1655, 146 L.Ed.2d 621.

THOMAS, J. delivered the opinion of the Court.

Under the Fair Labor Standards Act of 1938 (FLSA), States and their political subdivisions may compensate their employees for overtime by granting them compensatory time or "comp time," which entitles them to take time off work with full pay. § 207(*o*). If the employees do not use their accumulated compensatory time, the employer is obligated to pay cash compensation under certain circumstances. § 207(*o*)(3)–(4). Fearing the fiscal consequences of having to pay for accrued compensatory time, Harris County adopted a policy requiring its employees to schedule time off in order to reduce the amount of accrued compensatory time. Employees of the Harris County Sheriff's Department sued, claiming that the FLSA prohibits such a policy. The Court of Appeals rejected their claim. Finding that nothing in the FLSA or its implementing regulations prohibits an employer from compelling the use of compensatory time, we affirm.

I

A

The FLSA generally provides that hourly employees who work in excess of 40 hours per week must be compensated for the excess hours at a rate not less than 1 ½ times their regular hourly wage. § 207(a)(1). Although this requirement did not initially apply to public-sector employers, Congress amended the FLSA to subject States and their political subdivisions to its constraints * * *. States and their political subdivisions, however, did not feel the full force of this latter extension until our decision in *Garcia v. San Antonio Metropolitan Transit Authority*, 469 U.S. 528 (1985) * * *.

The FLSA expressly regulates some aspects of accrual and preservation of compensatory time. For example, the FLSA provides that an employer must honor an employee's request to use compensatory time within a "reasonable period" of time following the request, so long as the use of the compensatory time would not "unduly disrupt" the employer's operations. § 207(*o*)(5); 29 CFR § 553.25 (1999). The FLSA also caps the number of compensatory time hours that an employee may accrue. After an employee reaches that maximum, the employer must pay cash compensation for additional overtime hours worked. § 207(*o*)(3)(A). In addition, the FLSA permits the employer at any time to cancel or "cash out" accrued compensatory time hours by paying the employee cash compensation for unused compensatory time. § 207(*o*)(3)(B); 29 CFR § 553.26(a) (1999). And the FLSA entitles the employee to cash payment for any accrued compensatory time remaining upon the termination of employment. § 207(*o*)(4).

B

Petitioners are 127 deputy sheriffs employed by respondents Harris County, Texas. * * * It is undisputed that each of the petitioners individually agreed to accept compensatory time, in lieu of cash, as compensation for overtime.

As petitioners accumulated compensatory time, Harris County became concerned that it lacked the resources to pay monetary compensation to employees who worked overtime after reaching the statutory cap on compensatory time accrual and to employees who left their jobs with sizable reserves of accrued time. As a result, the county began looking for a way to reduce accumulated compensatory time. It wrote to the United States Department of Labor's Wage and Hour Division, asking "whether the Sheriff may schedule non-exempt employees to use or take compensatory time." The Acting Administrator of the Division replied:

> "[I]t is our position that a public employer may schedule its nonexempt employees to use their accrued FLSA compensatory time as directed if the prior agreement specifically provides such a provision....
>
> "Absent such an agreement, it is our position that neither the statute nor the regulations permit an employer to require an employee to use accrued compensatory time."

After receiving the letter, Harris County implemented a policy under which the employees' supervisor sets a maximum number of compensatory hours that may be accumulated. When an employee's stock of hours approaches that maximum, the employee is advised of the maximum and is asked to take steps to reduce accumulated compensatory time. If the employee does not do so voluntarily, a supervisor may order the employee to use his compensatory time at specified times.

Petitioners sued, claiming that the county's policy violates the FLSA because § 207(*o*)(5)—which requires that an employer reasonably accommodate employee requests to use compensatory time—provides the exclusive means of utilizing accrued time in the absence of an agreement or understanding permitting some other method. The District Court agreed, granting summary judgment for petitioners and entering a declaratory judgment that the county's policy violated the FLSA * * * . The Court of Appeals for the Fifth Circuit reversed, holding that the FLSA did not speak to the issue and thus did not prohibit the county from implementing its compensatory time policy. * * * Judge Dennis concurred in part and dissented in part, concluding that the employer could not compel the employee to use compensatory time unless the employee agreed to such an arrangement in advance. * * * We granted certiorari because the Courts of Appeals are divided on the issue.

II

Both parties, and the United States as amicus curiae, concede that nothing in the FLSA expressly prohibits a State or subdivision thereof from compelling employees to utilize accrued compensatory time. Petitioners and the United States, however, contend that the FLSA implicitly prohibits such a practice in the absence of an agreement or understanding authorizing compelled use.[3]

Title 29 U.S.C. § 207(*o*)(5) provides:

"An employee * * *

"(A) who has accrued compensatory time off * * *, and

"(B) who has requested the use of such compensatory time,

"shall be permitted * * * to use such time within a reasonable period after making the request if the use of the compensatory time does not unduly disrupt the operations of the public agency."

Petitioners and the United States rely upon the canon expressio unius est exclusio alterius, contending that the express grant of control to employees to use compensatory time, subject to the limitation regarding undue disruptions of workplace operations, implies that all other methods of spending compensatory time are precluded. * * *

We find this reading unpersuasive. We accept the proposition that "[w]hen a statute limits a thing to be done in a particular mode, it includes a negative of any other mode." * * * But that canon does not resolve this case in petitioners' favor. The "thing to be done" as defined by § 207(*o*)(5) is not the expenditure of compensatory time, as petitioners would have it. Instead, § 207(*o*)(5) is more properly read as a minimal guarantee that an employee will be able to make some use of compensatory time when he requests to use it. As such, the proper expressio unius inference is that an employer may not, at least in the absence of an agreement, deny an employee's request to use compensatory time for a reason other than that provided in § 207(*o*)(5). The canon's application simply does not prohibit an employer from telling an employee to take the benefits of compensatory time by scheduling time off work with full pay.

In other words, viewed in the context of the overall statutory scheme, § 207(*o*)(5) is better read not as setting forth the exclusive method by which compensatory time can be used, but as setting up a safeguard to ensure that an employee will receive timely compensation for working overtime. Section 207(*o*)(5) guarantees that, at the very minimum, an employee will get to use his compensatory time (i.e., take time off work with full pay) unless doing so would disrupt the employer's operations. And it is precisely this concern over ensuring that employees can timely

---

3. * * * [W]e decide this case on the assumption that no agreement or understanding exists between the employer and employees on the issue of compelled use of compensatory time.

"liquidate" compensatory time that the Secretary of Labor identified in her own regulations governing § 207(*o*)(5):

> "Compensatory time cannot be used as a means to avoid statutory overtime compensation. An employee has the right to use compensatory time earned and must not be coerced to accept more compensatory time than an employer can realistically and in good faith expect to be able to grant within a reasonable period of his or her making a request for use of such time." 29 CFR § 553.25(b) (1999).

This reading is confirmed by nearby provisions of the FLSA that reflect a similar concern for ensuring that the employee receive some timely benefit for overtime work. For example, § 207(*o*)(3)(A) provides that workers may not accrue more than 240 or 480 hours of compensatory time, depending upon the nature of the job. See also § 207(*o*)(2)(B) (conditioning the employer's ability to provide compensatory time upon the employee not accruing compensatory time in excess of the § 207(*o*)(3)(A) limits). Section 207(*o*)(3)(A) helps guarantee that employees only accrue amounts of compensatory time that they can reasonably use. After all, an employer does not need § 207(*o*)(3)(A)'s protection; it is free at any time to reduce the number of hours accrued by exchanging them for cash payment, § 207(*o*)(3)(B), or by halting the accrual of compensatory time by paying cash compensation for overtime work, 29 CFR § 553.26(a) (1999). Thus, § 207(*o*)(3)(A), like § 207(*o*)(5), reflects a concern that employees receive some timely benefit in exchange for overtime work. Moreover, on petitioners' view, the compensatory time exception enacted by Congress in the wake of *Garcia* would become a nullity when employees who refuse to use compensatory time reach the statutory maximums on accrual. Petitioners' position would convert § 207(*o*)(3)(A)'s shield into a sword, forcing employers to pay cash compensation instead of providing compensatory time to employees who work overtime.

At bottom, we think the better reading of § 207(*o*)(5) is that it imposes a restriction upon an employer's efforts to prohibit the use of compensatory time when employees request to do so; that provision says nothing about restricting an employer's efforts to require employees to use compensatory time. Because the statute is silent on this issue and because Harris County's policy is entirely compatible with § 207(*o*)(5), petitioners cannot, as they are required to do by 29 U.S.C. § 216(b), prove that Harris County has violated § 207.

Our interpretation of § 207(*o*)(5)—one that does not prohibit employers from forcing employees to use compensatory time—finds support in two other features of the FLSA. First, employers remain free under the FLSA to decrease the number of hours that employees work. An employer may tell the employee to take off an afternoon, a day, or even an entire week. * * * Second, the FLSA explicitly permits an employer to cash out accumulated compensatory time by paying the employee his regular hourly wage for each hour accrued. § 207(*o*)(3)(B); 29 CFR § 553.27(a) (1999).

Thus, under the FLSA an employer is free to require an employee to take time off work, and an employer is also free to use the money it would have paid in wages to cash out accrued compensatory time. The compelled use of compensatory time challenged in this case merely involves doing both of these steps at once. It would make little sense to interpret § 207(*o*)(5) to make the combination of the two steps unlawful when each independently is lawful. * * *

III

In an attempt to avoid the conclusion that the FLSA does not prohibit compelled use of compensatory time, petitioners and the United States contend that we should defer to the Department of Labor's opinion letter, which takes the position that an employer may compel the use of compensatory time only if the employee has agreed in advance to such a practice. Specifically, they argue that the agency opinion letter is entitled to deference under our decision in *Chevron U.S.A. Inc. v. Natural Resources Defense Council, Inc.*, 467 U.S. 837 (1984). In *Chevron,* we held that a court must give effect to an agency's regulation containing a reasonable interpretation of an ambiguous statute.

Here, however, we confront an interpretation contained in an opinion letter, not one arrived at after, for example, a formal adjudication or notice-and-comment rulemaking. Interpretations such as those in opinion letters—like interpretations contained in policy statements, agency manuals, and enforcement guidelines, all of which lack the force of law—do not warrant *Chevron*-style deference. * * *

Of course, the framework of deference set forth in *Chevron* does apply to an agency interpretation contained in a regulation. But in this case the Department of Labor's regulation does not address the issue of compelled compensatory time. The regulation provides only that "[t]he agreement or understanding [between the employer and employee] may include other provisions governing the preservation, use, or cashing out of compensatory time so long as these provisions are consistent with [§ 207(*o*)]." 29 CFR § 553.23(a)(2) (1999). Nothing in the regulation even arguably requires that an employer's compelled use policy must be included in an agreement. The text of the regulation itself indicates that its command is permissive, not mandatory. * * *

As we have noted, no relevant statutory provision expressly or implicitly prohibits Harris County from pursuing its policy of forcing employees to utilize their compensatory time. In its opinion letter siding with the petitioners, the Department of Labor opined that "it is our position that neither the statute nor the regulations permit an employer to require an employee to use accrued compensatory time." But this view is exactly backwards. Unless the FLSA prohibits respondents from adopting its policy, petitioners cannot show that Harris County has violated the FLSA. And the FLSA contains no such prohibition. The judgment of the Court of Appeals is affirmed.

SOUTER, J. concurring.

I join the opinion of the Court on the assumption that it does not foreclose a reading of the Fair Labor Standards Act of 1938 that allows the Secretary of Labor to issue regulations limiting forced use.

SCALIA, J. concurring in part and concurring in the judgment.

* * * [T]he position that the county's action in this case was unlawful unless permitted by the terms of an agreement with the sheriff's department employees warrants *Chevron* deference if it represents the authoritative view of the Department of Labor. The fact that it appears in a single opinion letter signed by the Acting Administrator of the Wage and Hour Division might not alone persuade me that it occupies that status. But the Solicitor General of the United States, appearing as an amicus in this action, has filed a brief, cosigned by the Solicitor of Labor, which represents the position set forth in the opinion letter to be the position of the Secretary of Labor. That alone, even without existence of the opinion letter, would in my view entitle the position to *Chevron* deference. * * *

I nonetheless join the judgment of the Court because, for the reasons set forth in Part II of its opinion, the Secretary's position does not seem to me a reasonable interpretation of the statute.

STEVENS, J., with whom GINSBURG and BREYER JJ. join, dissenting.

Because the disagreement between the parties concerns the scope of an exception to a general rule, it is appropriate to begin with a correct identification of the relevant general rule. That rule gives all employees protected by the Fair Labor Standards Act a statutory right to compensation for overtime work payable in cash, whether they work in the private sector of the economy or the public sector. 29 U.S.C. § 206, 207. In 1985, Congress enacted an exception to that general rule that permits States and their political subdivisions to use compensatory time instead of cash as compensation for overtime. The exception, however, is not applicable unless the public employer first arrives at an agreement with its employees to substitute that type of compensation for cash. § 207(*o*); 29 CFR § 553.23. As I read the statute, the employer has no right to impose compensatory overtime payment upon its employees except in accordance with the terms of the agreement authorizing its use.

The Court stumbles because it treats § 207's limited and conditional exception as though it were the relevant general rule. The Court begins its opinion by correctly asserting that public employers may "compensate their employees for overtime by granting them compensatory time or 'comp time,' which entitles them to take time off work with full pay." It is not until it reaches the bottom of the second page, however, that the Court acknowledges that what appeared to be the relevant general rule is really an exception from the employees' basic right to be paid in cash.

In my judgment, the fact that no employer may lawfully make any use of "comp time" without a prior agreement with the affected employees is of critical importance in answering the question whether a particular method of using that form of noncash compensation may be imposed on those employees without their consent. Because their consent is a condition without which the employer cannot qualify for the exception from the general rule, it seems clear to me that their agreement must encompass the way in which the compensatory time may be used.

In an effort to avoid addressing this basic point, the Court mistakenly characterizes petitioners' central argument as turning upon the canon expressio unius est exclusio alterius. * * *

This description of the debate misses the primary thrust of petitioners' position. They do not, as the Court implies, contend that employers generally must afford employees essentially unlimited use of accrued comp time under the statute; the point is rather that rules regarding both the availability and the use of comp time must be contained within an agreement. The "thing to be done" under the Act is for the parties to come to terms. It is because they have not done so with respect to the use of comp time here that the county may not unilaterally force its expenditure.

The Court is thus likewise mistaken in its insistence that under petitioners' reading, the comp time exception "would become a nullity" because employees could "forc[e] employers to pay cash compensation instead of providing compensatory time" for overtime work. Quite the contrary, employers can only be "forced" either to abide by the arrangements to which they have agreed, or to comply with the basic statutory requirement that overtime compensation is payable in cash.

Moreover, as the Court points out, even absent an agreement on the way in which comp time may be used, employers may at any time require employees to "cash out" of accumulated comp time, thereby readily avoiding any forced payment of comp time employees may accrue. § 207(*o*)(3)(B); 29 CFR § 553.26(a) (1999). Neither can it be said that Congress somehow assumed that the right to force employees to use accumulated comp time was to be an implied term in all comp time agreements. Congress specifically contemplated that employees might well reach the statutory maximum of accrued comp time, by requiring, in § 207(*o*)(3)(A), that once the statutory maximum is reached, employers must compensate employees in the preferred form—cash—for every hour over the limit. * * *

The Department [of Labor], it should be emphasized, does not suggest that forced-use policies are forbidden by the statute or regulations. Rather, its judgment is simply that, in accordance with the basic rule governing compensatory time set down by the statutory and regulatory scheme, such policies may be pursued solely according to the parties' agreement. Because there is no reason to believe that the Department's opinion was anything but thoroughly considered and consistently observed, it unquestionably merits our respect.

In the end, I do not understand why it should be any more difficult for the parties to come to an agreement on this term of employment than on the antecedent question whether compensatory time may be used at all. State employers enjoy substantial bargaining power in negotiations with their employees; by regulation, agreements governing the availability and use of compensatory time can be essentially as informal as the parties wish. See 29 CFR § 553.23(c) (1999). And, as we have said, employers retain the ability to "cash out" of accrued leave at any time. That simple step is, after all, the method that the Department of Labor years ago suggested the county should pursue here, and that would achieve precisely the outcome the county has all along claimed it wants. * * *

[JUSTICE BREYER'S dissenting opinion, joined by JUSTICE GINSBURG, is omitted.]

NOTES

1. Compensatory time is *paid* time off. In other words, employees entitled to comp time under the FLSA must be given both payments *and* time off (at time-and-a-half rates). Given that the alternative is simply paying money without granting time off, why do employers often prefer to use comp time in lieu of money payments for overtime? Do the various rules and restrictions on the use of comp time in § 207(*o*) provide any clues?

2. Various proposals have been made to amend the FLSA to allow comp time in lieu of money for overtime in the *private* sector. For example, in 2009, a group of Republican lawmakers reintroduced the Family–Friendly Workplace Act, H.R. 933, in the House of Representatives. This bill would allow private sector workers to choose to take comp time in lieu of cash for overtime, up to 160 hours per year. An employer would be required to pay employees for accrued, unused compensatory time at the end of each year. Unions generally opposed this bill. What are the strongest arguments in favor of and against this legislation? If Congress were to make such an amendment, what sorts of rules governing the use of comp time should be provided? The same rules as in § 207(*o*), or different ones? Are there policy or practical reasons to have different rules for the public and private sectors on this issue?

2. SECTION 7(k) RULES FOR POLICE AND FIREFIGHTERS

FLSA § 7(k) provides an exception the general FLSA rule that overtime pay is required when a non-exempt employee works over 40 hours in one week. The rule applies only to public employees engaged in fire protection or law enforcement activities. Section 7(k) authorizes the Secretary of Labor to create different schedules that trigger overtime rights for such employees.

Pursuant to this authority, the Secretary of Labor has promulgated a regulation which sets alternative overtime trigger schedules based on work periods of up to four weeks. The employer (usually a police or fire department) may choose whether to use one of these alternate schedules.

Currently, 29 C.F.R. § 553.230 provides as follows:

(a) For those employees engaged in fire protection activities who have a work period of at least 7 but less than 28 consecutive days, no overtime compensation is required under section 7(k) until the number of hours worked exceeds the number of hours which bears the same relationship to 212 as the number of days in the work period bears to 28.

(b) For those employees engaged in law enforcement activities (including security personnel in correctional institutions) who have a work period of at least 7 but less than 28 consecutive days, no overtime compensation is required under section 7(k) until the number of hours worked exceeds the number of hours which bears the same relationship to 171 as the number of days in the work period bears to 28 * * * .

	Maximum hours standards	
Work period (days)	Fire protection	Law enforcement
28	212	171
27	204	165
26	197	159
25	189	153
24	182	147
23	174	141
22	167	134
21	159	128
20	151	122
19	144	116
18	136	110
17	129	104
16	121	98
15	114	92
14	106	86
13	98	79
12	91	73
11	83	67
10	76	61
9	68	55
8	61	49
7	53	43

This rule can make a significant difference regarding entitlement to overtime pay. For example, if a police department chooses the 171 hours in 28 days schedule, a police officer could work 65 hours one week, 45 hours the next week, and 30 hours in the next two weeks, and not reach the overtime trigger. A firefighter covered by the 212 hours in 28 days schedule could work 75 hours one week, 75 hours the next, and 30 hours in each of the next two weeks and not be entitled to overtime.

The FLSA does not require public employers to agree with employees over the use of a 7(k) schedule. See *Calvao v. Framingham*, 599 F.3d 10 (2010) (city not required to give prior notice to union of its decision to adopt a new schedule pursuant to § 7(k)). Neither § 7(k) nor its implementing regulations contain any language about agreements with employees or employee representatives, unlike the comp time rules in § 207(*o*)
.
Given that, could a state public sector bargaining law make this issue negotiable? Consider this again when studying the materials in Chapter 8.

The Department of Labor has issued regulations defining the types of employees § 7(k) covers, and the definitions of employees engaged in "law enforcement" or "fire protection" are fairly narrow. See, *e.g.*, 29 C.F.R. 553.210(a) (fire protection). Notably, § 7(k) does not include regular civilian employees of a police or fire department such as police dispatchers, secretaries, etc. 29 C.F.R. § 553.211(g). Thus, these employees are covered by the regular 40 hour/week overtime rules.

On the other hand, ambulance and rescue service employees of a public agency other than a fire protection agency may be treated as employees engaged in fire protection if their services are substantially related to firefighting, if the employees have received training in the rescue of fire, crime, and accident victims and such employees are regularly dispatched to fires, crime scenes, riots, natural disasters and accidents. 29 C.F.R. § 553.215

Courts are split as to whether the exemption applies to paramedics in a fire department. Compare *Lawrence v. City of Philadelphia, PA*, 527 F.3d 299 (3d Cir. 2008) (does not apply) *with Huff v. DeKalb County, GA*, 516 F.3d 1273 (11th Cir. 2008) (applies). Also, § 7(k) schedules may be used for at least some prison guards. 29 C.F.R. § 553.211(f). One court has held that § 7(k) applies to federal air marshals. *Federal Air Marshals v. the United States*, 84 Fed. Cl. 585 (2008). Inquiries into coverage are typically fact-intensive.

Why would Congress pass these special overtime trigger rules for these employees and these employees only? Is this good policy? What are the best arguments for and against this rule? While the general FLSA rule in the private sector uses the 40 hour/week trigger, note that there are some exceptions, primarily used for jobs where hours vary considerably week to week to week or month to month. See FLSA §§ 7(b)(1) and (b)(2), and § 7(f)). Consider the likely justifications for such rules, and whether those justifications apply to § 7(k). Note that it is common for firefighters to work schedules of twenty-four straight hours on duty followed by forty-eight hours off. Police, though, are not normally scheduled that way.

C. CIVIL SERVICE LAWS

1. OVERVIEW AND HISTORY

The Civil Service Act (Pendleton Act) passed by Congress in 1883 was the first comprehensive reform legislation affecting employees employed by the federal government. It followed the 1881 assassination of President Garfield by a disappointed office seeker. Support for civil service reform, however, had already been building and would have occurred eventually without the drama of Garfield's assassination. Aided by Garfield's death two months after he was attacked, the passage of the Act reflected a reaction to decades of politicalization or "democratization" of the federal work force which followed the 1828 election of Andrew Jackson. The Act responded to the increasing expansion and complexity of the national economy and the corresponding need for a hardworking and qualified federal work force. It also appeared to be the product of a strategy by Republican senators who feared they might lose the 1884 election and wished to make permanent the tenure of their office-holding friends. At the same time, Republican sponsors sought credit for supporting widely popular reform legislation. Regardless of the motivation of its supporters, when the Act was passed, the United States was among the last of the major industrialized nations to inaugurate a civil service for public employees based upon merit.

The 1883 Pendleton Act was intended to be a rejection of the "spoils system" in favor of a rational and apolitical merit civil service system designed to attract and retain competent employees to the federal service. This model of federal service was supported by a "scientific" management theory which argued that politics had to be separated from management if management was to be efficient. It was also supported by a group of prominent reformers, many born in the northeast, who were concerned that the rise of big business and the "robber barons" (business leaders who dominated their industries using unfair and often illegal practices, accumulating great fortunes) created a climate of corruption which extended to government. Initial reform legislation had first been introduced in 1865. Although passage of civil service reform took almost two decades, the interim period provided the opportunity for study of the British Civil

Service and the formation of numerous civil service reform groups throughout the country. Among those prominent in civil service reform organizations were businessmen, merchants, and bankers.

Thirteen of these groups formed the National Civil Service Reform League in 1881. Public sentiment, particularly as expressed in the Republican defeat in the 1882 congressional elections, forced a vote on reform legislation shortly thereafter, even though it was recognized that voting for reform would destroy incumbents' continuing control over patronage appointments to federal jobs. The business community added to the public pressure for reform as growing businesses became more dependent upon government activity such as the customs houses and the national post office.

The Pendleton Act established a Civil Service Commission, headed by three commissioners, with the responsibility of establishing merit-based rules and implementing a competitive examination system for filling vacancies in covered or "classified" positions. Federal employees in classified positions were to be protected from political pressure throughout their careers and in turn were expected to be politically neutral in their conduct at work. Although initially only about 10% of federal positions were designated as classified, by 1919 over 70% of federal employees were denoted classified and thus subject to merit requirements for appointment.

Limitations upon arbitrary removals of classified federal employees were not part of the Pendleton Act with the exception that the Act prohibited discharges for refusal by an employee to engage in political activity. Concern about this key omission led to an 1897 presidential executive order which stated that "no removal shall be made from any position subject to comprehensive examination except for just cause and upon written charges." A just cause requirement for dismissal of classified federal employees was incorporated into 1912 federal legislation with "cause" defined as relating to the "efficiency of the service."

Civil service reform also occurred at the local and state levels. While the Pendleton Act was being considered in Congress, the first state civil service law was drafted by leaders of the New York Civil Service Reform Association and was enacted by the New York State legislature in 1883. Similar legislation was adopted in Massachusetts in 1884 as a result of the work of the Massachusetts Civil Service Reform Association. By the turn of the century some legislative reform had occurred in Illinois, Wisconsin, Indiana, Louisiana, and Connecticut. Other states followed as a result of efforts by local reform groups and independent associations of government employees, although the first wave of civil service reform left a number of local governments untouched. In addition to reform legislation, a number of state constitutions were amended to provide varying types of constitutional protection for merit civil service systems.

By the early twentieth century, a number of cities (New York, Albany, Buffalo, Syracuse, Chicago, Evanston, and Seattle) and counties had also adopted civil service merit systems. During the early 1900s, additional cities such as Los Angeles, San Francisco, Pittsburgh, Cincinnati, Cleveland, St. Louis, and Baltimore joined the list of cities with civil service legislation. By the mid 1980s, over 88% of cities over 50,000 had some form of a civil service system while about 60% of all state employees were formally under merit systems.

Independent associations of government employees had been formed in the late nineteenth century primarily for "benevolent" purposes (such as sharing group insurance benefits). These organizations were slow to make the transition from primarily fraternal associations to effective lobbying groups for state or local government legislation providing employment benefits to their civil servant members. The spread of civil service laws at all levels of government, as well as the array of state constitutional provisions embodying aspects of the civil service system, assured government employee associations a major role, which they eventually played with intensity, when related legislation was considered.

State and local government civil service laws vary as to the positions which are covered, although the same vocabulary, "classified" was adopted in many jurisdictions. The legislation provides for a "probationary" or "working test period" which a covered employee must complete satisfactorily prior to the time the employee becomes a "permanent" employee with full civil service protections. Civil service laws usually include a procedure to appeal disciplinary discharge decisions by the public employer and establish a state or local agency similar to the federal Civil Service Commission to implement the legislation.

Once civil service laws were enacted, public employee organizations generally supported additional legislation, which sought to strengthen civil service systems and opposed legislative proposals devised to weaken the merit principle. The American Federation of State, County and Municipal Employees (AFSCME) was originally established in Wisconsin in 1934 to oppose legislation designed to weaken the state's civil service system. Broad political support, or at least the absence of effective opposition, assured the increasing acceptance of civil service systems throughout the country. By 1970, approximately 80% of all public employees in state and local governments were covered by statutory merit systems.

Over the years, the functions of state and municipal civil service commissions (or agencies with similar functions) typically expanded beyond assuring merit in appointments to classified positions and reviewing whether discharges of employees with permanent status were justified. Civil service rules commonly began to cover related topics such as procedures to layoff or "excess" employees when there is a reduction or reorganization of the public work force and related "bumping" rights to remaining public employee jobs. In addition, many details of the employment relationship well beyond those fundamental to implementing the merit principle became part of civil service rules and regulations. Job classifications and pay plans based upon "objective" factors or "scientific management" came into vogue, encouraged by the philosophy of the merit system. Eventually, many specifics of personnel administration such as sick leave, holidays, safety, attendance control programs, funeral leave, handling of grievances, and other similar employment policies also became part of the extended civil service "system."

As time went on, complaints became more vocal about the excessively complex nature of the civil service system and its procedural "baggage." Many public perceptions of the civil service were negative. Public managers began to view civil service commissions and their rule making authority as a branch of public management, particularly when civil service authorities functioned increasingly by promulgating unilateral rules relating to personnel policies which went far beyond the core merit principle areas of examination, hiring, and promotion. Public employees and their organizations increasingly considered such civil service commissions or agencies to be far from neutral and viewed many of the unilaterally adopted civil service rules and regulations as arbitrary. Employee organizations began to seek a greater voice in governmental decision making. Collective bargaining appeared to be a promising path to reform the civil service system and serve as a counterweight to managerial prerogatives.

When public sector bargaining laws began to be enacted by a number of states in the 1960s, many associations abandoned their traditional legislative agendas for an active role promoting public sector collective bargaining legislation and practices. To adapt to this new priority, some associations retained their independent status while others affiliated with existing labor unions. Public employee associations and unions continued their prior lobbying activities while they also actively sought bargaining rights to represent various groupings of public employees.

Following the widespread adoption of collective bargaining laws for the public sector, the question concerning the appropriate scope of civil service laws and rules has been revisited. Some commentators and policy makers have recommended that core merit principles incorporated into civil service law and rules governing examination, appointment, and promotion be identified, segregated, and preserved while the numerous and elaborately developed employment rules for personnel administration which have become part of an augmented civil service system be made subject to the collective bargaining process.

In this discussion, there appears to be serious political and policy support for continuing core merit principles at all levels of public employment even by strong proponents of the more recent institution of collective bargaining. Controversy persists, however, about what positions should be classified under civil service law, how to harmonize civil service laws with collective bargaining laws, and which set of laws, civil service or collective bargaining, should prevail when harmonization is not possible. Labor organizations themselves are not unified about how to resolve these difficult issues which vitally affect many of their members and involve public concerns. Despite explorations at all levels of government to resolve these issues in ways designed to decrease adversarial relationships, by creating labor-management partnerships, for example, there have only been limited successes.

NOTES

1. Decisions by state and local government civil service commissions involving employee discipline play an important role for covered civil servants in jurisdictions where these public employees do not have an option to choose, or have not chosen, collective bargaining. Even for covered civil servants who are members of a bargaining unit and represented by a union in collective bargaining, civil service commissions often continue to provide an important statutory route to challenge a public employer's adverse disciplinary action. State court decisions during the last several decades demonstrate that appeals from adverse disciplinary decisions by civil service commissions to the courts remain plentiful. An extensive sampling of these court appeals reveals that few civil service commission decisions involving disciplinary actions are reversed on appeal. They also reveal that one common basis for court appeals of civil service commission decisions is a claim that the "neutral" civil service commission was biased. Despite disciplined litigants' perceptions of bias, however, few cases are able to produce sufficient evidence for challenges to the fairness of the civil service commission decision-making processes. An older case, *Rinaldi v. Civil Service Commission, City of Livonia*, 69 Mich.App. 58, 244 N.W.2d 609 (1976), is fairly typical of many cases from that era as well as more recent times. A police officer challenged the decision of the Chief of Police to discharge him for violating rules prohibiting conduct unbecoming an officer when the police officer knowingly left the scene of an accident in which he was involved while off duty. He first appealed the decision to the city's civil service commission which held an extensive hearing, after which it upheld the discharge. In his subsequent judicial appeal, the discharged officer raised several issues including a contention that his discharge was based upon rules which had been invalidly adopted by the civil service commission and a contention that the civil service commission's decision was founded on prejudice or bias. After noting that the latter argument was stated in conclusory terms only with no evidence of impropriety presented and that the former argument was without merit, the court affirmed the civil service commission's decision.

2. In addition to appeals challenging discipline as without just cause, civil service commissions may also hear cases challenging classification of jobs from incumbents seeking the higher pay that comes with a different job classification. Depending on the jurisdiction, the commission may also hear challenges to an agency's decision to bypass a candidate on a civil service list to hire someone lower on the list. For example, in *City of Cambridge v. Civil Service Commission*, 43 Mass.App.Ct. 300, 682 N.E.2d 923 (1997), an applicant for the police department objected to the decision to bypass her for another candidate because she was involved in two prior criminal incidents, one in which she accepted responsibility for an action by her boyfriend to

protect him from conviction and one in which the complaint against her was mediated and dismissed. The commission found the bypass unjustified based on the excellent employment record of the candidate after the two incidents, but the court reversed on appeal, finding that the commission had substituted its judgment for the police department rather than determining whether the department had an adequate reason for the decision. The court concluded that the commission erred in finding the candidate's willingness to lie in a criminal matter to protect someone and her violent actions in a personal dispute were relevant to the decision as to whether to appoint her as a police officer, while second-guessing the weight given to these actions by the police department.

3. State statutory and constitutional provisions on civil service have been utilized to mount legal attacks on privatization of government functions, with mixed results. Opponents of privatization have argued that creation of the civil service system for government employment bars the use of private contractors not covered by the system to perform government functions performed by civil service employees. See *Konno v. County of Hawai'i,* 85 Haw. 61, 937 P.2d 397 (1997) (invalidating contract privatizing landfill operations as violative of civil service law). Cf. *Hawaii Government Employees Association, Local 152 v. Miike,* 103 Haw. 400, 83 P.3d 115 (2004) (rejecting similar argument where legislature specifically directed privatization of hospital). See also *Moore v. Department of Transportation & Public Facilities*, 875 P.2d 765 (Alaska 1994) (finding state constitutional provision mandating merit system did not bar state efforts to reduce costs by contracting out work); *California Correctional Peace Officers' Association v. Schwarzenegger*, 163 Cal.App.4th 802, 77 Cal.Rptr.3d 844 (2008) (finding that governor's declaration of emergency based on inmate overcrowding met requirements for exception to the constitutional prohibition on contracting out civil service work, since work at out of state prisons could not be performed by California civil service workers).

4. The United States Civil Service Commission, created by the passage of the 1883 Pendleton Act, was not the first such federal institution. President Ulysses S. Grant recommended civil service legislation to Congress in 1870. The following year legislation was passed which authorized the President to make rules and regulations for the civil service. Although the first Civil Service Commission appointed by President Grant was short-lived, in 1871 it developed many of the provisions that are still accepted in merit systems at all levels of government.

5. The initial role of the Civil Service Commission was policing to prevent patronage encroachments. By the early 1900s, a quest for greater efficiency began. The Commission, however, remained primarily an examination agency with other personnel functions administered elsewhere without central direction. Thereafter, personnel administration of the federal workforce underwent cycles of centralization and decentralization with tremendous expansion of the workforce during World War II. Despite criticism, the Commission continued its multiple, expanding, and at times conflicting functions as a central personnel agency which included: proposing legislation, developing and operating personnel programs and services, promulgating government wide standards and personnel policies, providing technical assistance to federal agencies, securing compliance with civil service laws and

merit principles, and adjudicating employee appeals. Ultimately, the Commission was reorganized out of existence as of January 1, 1979, by the Civil Service Reform Act of 1978. See further discussion of civil service reform in section 2 below.

2. CIVIL SERVICE REFORM

While support for the merit principle remains widespread, the civil service system has been challenged, not only by unions, who see the system as a tool of management which interferes with the bargaining rights of employees, but also by reformers who view the system as perpetuating government inefficiency and protecting incompetent workers. The cumbersome bureaucracy of civil service in many cases slows both hiring and firing of workers and limits the ability of agencies to hire those prospective employees identified by the agency as most qualified. Further, critics argue that the rigid job classification system makes it difficult to effectively deploy workers where and when they are needed. At the same time, creative politicians have found ways to evade the strictures of the systems and politicize hiring despite the existence of often unwieldy civil service systems. At the federal level, for example, political hiring has penetrated more deeply into agencies, eliminating some of the talented high level career employees with agency expertise. Continued pressures on civil service from many quarters have led to substantial changes in the systems at the federal, state and local levels.

At the federal level, President Jimmy Carter campaigned for civil service reform as part of his presidential campaign. He has been quoted as saying, "There is not enough merit in the merit system. There is inadequate motivation because we have too few rewards for excellence and too few penalties for unsatisfactory work." The impetus for reform legislation came from a combination of executive and legislative branch reformers who did not necessarily agree about what problems needed to be addressed and how they should be addressed. A House–Senate Conference Committee reconciled two bills produced by Congress. Floor debates following the Conference Committee Report provided most of the legislative history cited in subsequent litigation.

The 1978 Civil Service Reform Act replaced the Civil Service Commission with several new agencies. The Office of Personnel Management (OPM), an independent agency, was created with responsibility for human resources management, evaluations, and enforcement of federal personnel laws and regulations. In addition, the Merit Systems Protections Board (MSPB) was established to perform the prior Commission's appeals functions and provide some general oversight functions. While the Act contained many other important features (including the granting of collective bargaining rights to federal employees discussed in Chapter 4), the separation of the appeals function (MSPB) from the personnel function (OPM) is one of the key changes.

Despite these reforms, and the substantial reduction in the percentage of employees covered by and hired through the civil service system, criticisms of the system continue unabated. While thus far the criticisms have not led to another formal reform of the system, they have motivated other actions including reductions in some sectors of government employment, increases in outsourcing of government functions, increasing decentralization of hiring, and efforts to improve performance management.

At the state and local level, separation of civil service commissions' appeals functions from their personnel functions also occurred around the same time as federal civil service reform. It has been estimated that, by the mid 1970s, nearly half of large state and local governments had abandoned the commission form of government for personnel management, while retaining it for appeals of adverse employment actions. Chicago was one of the first cities in the United States to create a civil service commission in 1895; Chicago became the first major city to abolish its civil service commission in 1976. In many jurisdictions, however, civil service commissions and civil service laws remain. Enactment of collective bargaining laws and subsequent bargaining has led to substantial legal complications, which are discussed further in Chapters 8 and 11.

While most states and localities have engaged in incremental reforms, several (Texas and Georgia) have eliminated civil service altogether, and Florida has made major reforms that fundamentally alter the system. Limited reforms instituted by some states and localities parallel those implemented by the federal government, including reduction or elimination of the use of formal tests for hiring, decentralization of personnel functions, and broadening of job classifications. The state of Washington has reduced available appeals of discipline and broadened considerations for layoff of employees to include factors other than seniority.

The more comprehensive revisions in Texas, Georgia and Florida moved their personnel systems toward a typical private sector model. Hiring was decentralized to the agency level and use of standardized tests for hiring was reduced or eliminated. New employees were hired as employees at will, without statutory civil service protection from unjust termination, except in Florida which converted only management and supervisory employees to at will status.[1] However, Georgia and Texas allow agencies to set up their own disciplinary procedures and restrict appeals of discipline, allowing internal appeals only. Florida still allows nonsupervisory employees to appeal discipline to a neutral agency, but increased the length of the probationary period and added strict time limits for appeals and hearings. Seniority rights were eliminated for new employees (and in Florida for all employees) and regular, predictable "step" pay increases were no longer given. Georgia and Texas also allow agencies to create new positions and classifications, while Florida has collapsed job classifications into broad bands. These changes have resulted in more managerial flexibility, to the delight of agency management in the

1. Employees may still be covered by other exceptions to the doctrine of employment at will.

states. At least in Georgia, more terminations of employees have resulted as well. Pay disparities between agencies for the same type of work have been identified as a concern resulting from decentralization, leading to pressures on management to raise pay. Thus far, major patronage and bias issues have not been identified, at least by human resources managers. Legal challenges to Florida's changes filed by unions representing affected employees failed to reverse the changes, although a settlement involving the Department of Juvenile Justice gave employees laid off out of seniority order some preference for future vacancies. For a review and evaluation of these reforms, see Jonathan Walters, *Life After Civil Service Reform: The Texas, Georgia, and Florida Experiences* (2002), available at http://www.businessofgovernment.org/pdfs/Walters Report.pdf.

Some local governments have eliminated civil service as well. Brookline, Massachusetts, which implemented a civil service system in 1894, voted in 2009 to petition the state to eliminate civil service for all jobs other than police and fire. Brookline followed other Massachusetts localities which have become frustrated with the state's failure to offer tests for some positions and to update the system to include new jobs that have evolved in areas such as information technology. Andrae Downs, Town Bails on Civil Service Hiring System, *The Boston Globe*, June 25, 2009, http://www.boston.com/news/local/articles/2009/06/25/liberal_brookline_asks_out_of_most_civil_service_testing/?page=1.

Notes

1. In Florida, law enforcement officers, firefighters and nurses were exempted from the elimination of seniority and in Texas, law enforcement officers have a civil service system, retaining seniority as well as test-based promotions. What might explain these exemptions from reform?

2. Historically, civil service hiring systems added points to the test scores of veterans to provide them with a hiring preference for government jobs as a reward for their military service. How will the reduction or elimination of test-based hiring impact veterans?

3. Could shifting personnel functions such as creation of jobs and classifications, recruiting, hiring and discipline from a civil service commission to the agency have an adverse effect on agency performance? What might be the effect of such a decision on a small government agency?

4. How will elimination of civil service protection and seniority affect the ability of government agencies to recruit quality staff, particularly in times of labor shortages?

3. THE FEDERAL CIVIL SERVICE TODAY

Most employees of the federal government work in the executive branch. These employees are covered by the civil service provisions set forth in title 5 of the U.S. Code. Among other matters, title 5 governs the hiring, called "appointment," and termination, called "removal," of such employees. Removal is only one of several enumerated "adverse actions," which may be subject to civil service review. The other adverse actions are: suspension for more than 14 days, reduction in grade or pay, and furlough for less than 30 days. 5 U.S.C. §§ 7512, 7513.

As discussed in the prior section, the Civil Service Reform Act of 1978 abolished the U.S. Civil Service Commission and replaced it with two different agencies. The Office of Personnel Management (OPM) has jurisdiction over the appointment process and other personnel management matters. OPM is headed by a Director who is appointed by the President upon the advice and consent of the Senate and who reports to the President.

An employee who is subject to an adverse action may, under appropriate circumstances, appeal that action to the Merit Systems Protection Board (MSPB). MSPB is an independent regulatory agency consisting of three members, appointed by the President upon the advise and consent of the Senate. They serve staggered seven year terms and no more than two may be members of the same political party.

An employee files an adverse action appeal in the appropriate regional office of the MSPB. The appeal is heard initially by an MSPB Administrative Judge (AJ). The AJ's decision may be appealed to the full Board which meets in Washington, D.C. or, after 35 days when the decision becomes final, may be appealed directly to the Court of Appeals for the Federal Circuit. Decisions of the Board may be appealed to the Federal Circuit.[2]

Executive branch agency employees generally fall into one of three classifications: Competitive Service, Senior Executive Service and Excepted Service. Most employees are in the Competitive Service. OPM administers competitive examinations for entry into the Competitive Service. Individuals who demonstrate their qualifications on these exams are placed on registers. When an agency appointing official seeks to fill positions in the Competitive Service, the agency requests a certificate from OPM. OPM provides a certificate containing the top individuals on the relevant register so that there are three individuals for every position to be filled. The agency appointing official must fill the vacancies "with sole regard to merit and fitness." 5 C.F.R. § 332.404.

An individual in the Competitive Service has the right to appeal adverse actions to the MSPB if the individual "is not serving a probationary or trial period under an initial appointment or ... has completed 1 year of current continuous service under other than a temporary appointment limited to 1 year or less." 5 U.S.C. §§ 7511(1)(A)(i) & (ii). In *McCormick v. Department of the Air Force*, 307 F.3d 1339 (Fed. Cir. 2002),

2. If the employee alleges that an adverse action resulted from discrimination in violation of one of the equal employment opportunity laws, the employee may request review of the MSPB's decision by the Equal Employment Opportunity Commission (EEOC). If the EEOC and MSPB disagree on the outcome, the case is referred to a Special Panel consisting of an MSPB member appointed by the MSPB Chair, an EEOC Commissioner appointed by the EEOC Chair, and a Panel Chair appointed by the President. 5 U.S.C. § 7702.

Court of Appeals for the Federal Circuit held that an employee in the competitive service who has had at least one year of continuous service has appeal rights even though the employee is still serving a probationary period. Consequently, an employee who has at least one year of continuous service and who is promoted to or transfers to a new position and therefore is subject to a new probationary period has the right to appeal an adverse action taken in the new position even though it occurs during the probationary period. In *Chavies v. Department of Navy*, 104 M.S.P.R. 81, 2006 M.S.P.B. 336 (MSPB 2006), the MSPB suggested that an employee accepting a new position subject to a new probationary period may waive the right to appeal during the probationary period, but for such a waiver to be effective, the employee must receive consideration and must know of the specific rights being waived. In the case before it, the Board found that the waiver was not made with knowledge of the specific rights being waived and declined to enforce it. One Board member concurred, arguing that routine waivers executed in connection with offers of employment should be per se unenforceable.

Employees with appeal rights also have rights to procedural due process before an adverse action is imposed. These rights, as set forth in 5 U.S.C. § 7513(b), are:

(1) at least 30 days' advance written notice stating the specific reasons for the proposed action, unless there is reasonable cause to believe the employee has committed a crime for which a sentence of imprisonment may be imposed;

(2) a reasonable time, but not less than 7 days, to answer orally and in writing and to furnish affidavits and other documentary evidence in support of the answer;

(3) representation by an attorney or other representative; and

(4) a written decision and the specific reasons therefor at the earliest practicable date.

Adverse actions may only be undertaken "for such cause as will promote the efficiency of the service." 5 U.S.C. § 7513(a). Employees subject to adverse actions may appeal to the MSPB within 30 days after the effective date of the adverse action or within 30 days after receipt of the employing agency's decision, whichever is later.

The Senior Executive Service (SES) was created "to ensure that the executive management of the Government of the United States is responsive to the needs, policies, and goals of the Nation and otherwise is of the highest quality." 5 U.S.C. § 3131. The SES consists of employees classified above pay grade GS–15 who:

(A) direct[ ] the work of an organizational unit;

(B) [are] held accountable for the success of one or more specific programs or projects;

(C) monitor[ ] progress toward organizational goals and periodically evaluate[ ] and make[ ] appropriate adjustments to such goals;

(D) supervise[ ] the work of employees other than personal assistants; or

(E) otherwise exercise[ ] important policy-making, policy-determining, or other executive functions

5 U.S.C. § 3132(a)(2). OPM has developed the following core qualifications for SES appointments: leading change, leading people, results driven, business acumen and building coalitions. OPM administers peer Qualification Review Boards which certify new career appointees to the Senior Executive Service. Employing agencies establish Executive Resources Boards which coordinate the merit staffing process for Senior Executive appointments at the agency. When filling an SES position, an agency rating panel reviews and ranks the candidates. The agency's Executive Resources Board recommends the best qualified candidates. The selecting official then makes the selection. If the individual selected has not yet been certified by OPM for Senior Executive Service, the individual is referred to an OPM-administered Qualifications Review Board for certification.

Senior Executive Service members may be removed for unsatisfactory performance during a one-year probationary period. After completion of the probationary period, an agency may still remove a Senior Executive Service employee to a non-SES position, typically at the GS–15 level. In such cases, the employee is entitled to 30 days' notice of removal and, no later than 15 days before the proposed removal date, may request an informal hearing before an MSPB AJ. The judge conducts the hearing and refers the record to OPM, the Special Counsel and the agency. The employee is not entitled to any further review.

A Senior Executive Service employee who has completed the probationary period and whose removal from the federal service is sought by the agency is entitled to 30 days' notice, a reasonable time of at least seven days to respond and a written decision with specific reasons for removal at the earliest possible date. The employee is entitled to appeal the decision to the MSPB.

The Excepted Service consists of non-SES positions excepted from the Competitive Service by statute or statutorily-authorized regulation or presidential decision. Generally, Excepted Service positions are those for which a competitive examination is not practical. For example, most attorney positions are in the Excepted Service, as are teachers and administrators at Department of Defense Schools and patent examiners. At some agencies, such as the FBI, CIA and NSA, all positions are in the Excepted Service.

Originally, the only employees in the Excepted Service who had a right to appeal adverse actions to the MSPB were those who had completed at least one year of current continuous service in the same or similar positions and who were eligible for veterans' preference. "Preference eligible" status is a complex, technical determination but generally applies to veterans who served during times of active combat. The Civil Service Due Process Amendments of 1990 extended MSPB appeal rights to non-preference eligible employees not serving probationary periods or who have completed at least two years of current continuous service in the same or similar positions. However, excepted service personnel who are appointed by the President or who serve in a position that is of a confidential, policy-making, policy-determining or policy-advocating character do not have appeal rights.

In an MSPB appeal, the ultimate issue is whether the adverse action promotes the efficiency of the service. The agency has the burden of proving that the employee did what the employee was charged with, that a nexus existed between what the employee did and discipline to promote the efficiency of the service and that the discipline imposed was reasonable. As the following case illustrates, however, there are limitations on the MSPB's authority.

DEPARTMENT OF THE NAVY v. EGAN

Supreme Court of the United States, 1988.
484 U.S. 518, 108 S.Ct. 818, 98 L.Ed.2d 918.

BLACKMUN, J. delivered the opinion of the Court.

Respondent Thomas M. Egan lost his laborer's job at the Trident Naval Refit Facility in Bremerton, Wash., when he was denied a required security clearance. The narrow question presented by this case is whether the Merit Systems Protection Board (Board) has authority by statute to review the substance of an underlying decision to deny or revoke a security clearance in the course of reviewing an adverse action. The Board ruled that it had no such authority. The Court of Appeals for the Federal Circuit, by a divided vote, reversed. * * *

I

Respondent Egan was a new hire and began his work at the facility on November 29, 1981. He served as a veteran's-preference-eligible civilian employee of the Navy subject to the provisions of the Civil Service Reform Act of 1978 (Act). The mission of the Refit Facility is to provide quick-turn-around repair, replenishment, and systems check-out of the Trident submarine over its extended operating cycle. * * * As a consequence, *all* employee positions at the Refit Facility are classified as sensitive. Thus, * * * a condition precedent to Egan's retention of his employment was satisfactory completion of security and medical reports

In April 1982, respondent gained the noncritical-sensitive position of laborer leader. Pending the outcome of his security investigation, however, he performed only limited duties and was not permitted to board any submarine.

On February 16, 1983, the Director of the Naval Civilian Personnel Command issued a letter of intent to deny respondent a security clearance. This was based upon California and Washington state criminal records reflecting respondent's convictions for assault and for being a felon in possession of a gun, and further based upon his failure to disclose on his application for federal employment two earlier convictions for carrying a loaded firearm. The Navy also referred to respondent's own statements that he had had drinking problems in the past and had served the final 28 days of a sentence in an alcohol rehabilitation program.

Respondent was informed that he had a right to respond to the proposed security-clearance denial. On May 6, he answered the Navy's letter of intent, asserting that he had paid his debt to society for his convictions, that he had not listed convictions older than seven years because he did not interpret the employment form as requiring that information, and that alcohol had not been a problem for him for three years preceding the clearance determination. He also provided favorable material from supervisors as to his background and character.

The Director, after reviewing this response, concluded that the information provided did not sufficiently explain, mitigate, or refute the reasons on which the proposed denial was based. Accordingly, respondent's security clearance was denied.

Respondent took an appeal to the Personnel Security Appeals Board, but his removal was effected before that Board acted (which it eventually did by affirming the denial of clearance).

Without a security clearance, respondent was not eligible for the job for which he had been hired. Reassignment to a nonsensitive position at the facility was not possible because there was no nonsensitive position there. Accordingly, the Navy issued a notice of proposed removal, and respondent was placed on administrative leave pending final decision. Respondent did not reply to the notice. On July 15, 1983, he was informed that his removal was effective July 22.

Respondent, pursuant to 5 U.S.C. § 7513(d), sought review by the Merit Systems Protection Board. Under § 7513(a), an agency may remove an employee "only for such cause as will promote the efficiency of the service." The statute, together with § 7701 to which § 7513(d) specifically refers, provides the employee with a number of procedural protections, including notice, an opportunity to respond and be represented by counsel, and a decision in writing. The employee * * * may appeal the agency's decision to the Board, as respondent did, which is to sustain the action if it is "supported by a preponderance of the evidence." § 7701(c)(1)(B). The stated "cause" for respondent's removal was his failure to meet the requirements for his position due to the denial of security clearance. Before the Board, the Government argued that the Board's review power was limited to determining whether the required removal procedures had been followed and whether a security clearance was a condition for respondent's position. It contended that the Board did not have the authority to judge the merits of the underlying security-clearance determination.

The Board's presiding official reversed the agency's decision, ruling that the Board did have authority to review the merits. She further ruled that the agency must specify the precise criteria used in its security-clearance decision and must show that those criteria are rationally related to national security. The agency then must show, by a preponderance of the evidence, that the employee's acts precipitating the denial of his clearance actually occurred, and that his "alleged misconduct has an actual or potentially detrimental effect on national security interests." The official then held that the ultimate burden was upon the agency to persuade the Board of the appropriateness of its decision to deny clearance.

The official concluded that it was not possible to determine whether the Navy's denial of respondent's security clearance was justified because it had not submitted a list of the criteria it employed and because it did not present evidence that it had "conscientiously weighed the circumstances surrounding [respondent's] alleged misconduct and reasonably balanced it against the interests of national security." She accordingly concluded that the Navy had "failed to show it reached a reasonable and warranted decision concerning the propriety of the revocation of [respondent's] security clearance." The decision to remove respondent, therefore, could not stand.

The Navy petitioned for full Board review of the presiding official's ruling. In a unanimous decision, the Board reversed the presiding official's ruling and sustained the agency's removal action. It observed that §§ 7512 and 7513 "do not specifically address the extent of the Board's review of the underlying determinations." 28 M.S.P.R. at 514. Neither did the legislative history of the Act address the extent of the authority Congress intended the Board to exercise in reviewing revocations or denials of security clearances which result in Chapter 75 actions * * *

Respondent, pursuant to § 7703, appealed to the Court of Appeals for the Federal Circuit. By a divided vote, that court reversed the Board's decision that it had no authority to review the merits of a security-clearance determination underlying a removal. It agreed with the Board that § 7532 is not the sole authority for a removal based upon national security concerns. It noted, however, that the agency had chosen to remove respondent under § 7512 rather than § 7532 and thus that it chose the procedure "that carrie[d] Board review under section 7513," including review of the merits of the underlying agency determination to deny a security clearance. The court then remanded the case to the Board for such review, stating that the question of an appropriate remedy, should the Board now rule that a security clearance was improperly denied, was not yet ripe.

* * *

II

We turn first to the statutory structure. Chapter 75 of Title 5 of the United States Code is entitled "Adverse Actions." Its subchapter II (§§ 7511–7514) relates to removals for "cause." Subchapter IV (§§ 7531–7533) relates to removals based upon national security concerns. An employee removed for "cause" has the right, under § 7513(d), to appeal to the Board. In contrast, an employee suspended under § 7532(a) is not entitled to appeal to the Board. That employee, however, is entitled to specified preremoval procedural rights, including a hearing by an agency authority. § 7532(c)(3).

Chapter 77 of Title 5 (§§ 7701–7703) is entitled "Appeals," and Chapter 12 (§§ 1201–1209) relates to the "Merit Systems Protection Board and Special Counsel." Section 1205(a) provides that the Board shall "hear, adjudicate, or provide for the hearing or adjudication of all matters within the jurisdiction of the Board" and shall "order any Federal agency or employee to comply with any order or decision issued by the Board." In the present litigation, there is no claim that the Board did not have jurisdiction to hear and adjudicate respondent's appeal.

It is apparent that the statutes provide a "two-track" system. A removal for "cause" embraces a right of appeal to the Board and a hearing of the type prescribed in detail in § 7701. Suspension and removal under § 7532, however, entail no such right of appeal. Respondent takes the straightforward position that, inasmuch as this case proceeded under § 7513, a hearing before the Board was required. The Government agrees. What is disputed is the subject matter of that hearing and the extent to which the Board may exercise reviewing authority. In particular, may the Board, when § 7513 is pursued, examine the merits of the security-clearance denial, or does its authority stop short of that point, that is, upon review of the fact of denial, of the position's requirement of security clearance, and of the satisfactory provision of the requisite procedural protections?

III

The Court of Appeals' majority stated: "The absence of any statutory provision precluding appellate review of security clearance denials in section 7512 removals creates a strong presumption in favor of appellate review," * * * One perhaps may accept this as a general proposition of administrative law, but the proposition is not without limit, and it runs aground when it encounters concerns of national security, as in this case, where the grant of security clearance to a particular employee, a sensitive and inherently discretionary judgment call, is committed by law to the appropriate agency of the Executive Branch.

The President, after all, is the "Commander in Chief of the Army and Navy of the United States." U.S. Const., Art. II, § 2. His authority to classify and control access to information bearing on national security and to determine whether an individual is sufficiently trustworthy to occupy a position in the Executive Branch that will give that person access to such information flows primarily from this constitutional investment of power in the President and exists quite apart from any explicit congressional grant. This Court has recognized the Government's "compelling interest" in withholding national security information from unauthorized persons in the course of executive business. The authority to protect such information falls on the President as head of the Executive Branch and as Commander in Chief.

Since World War I, the Executive Branch has engaged in efforts to protect national security information by means of a classification system graded according to sensitivity. After World War II, certain civilian agencies, including the Central Intelligence Agency, the National Security Agency, and the Atomic Energy Commission, were entrusted with gathering, protecting, or creating information bearing on national security. Presidents, in a series of Executive Orders, have sought to protect sensitive information and to ensure its proper classification throughout the Executive Branch by delegating this responsibility to the heads of agencies. Pursuant to these directives, departments and agencies of the Government classify jobs in three categories: critical sensitive, noncritical sensitive, and nonsensitive. Different types and levels of clearance are required, depending upon the position sought. A Government appointment is expressly made subject to a background investigation that varies according to the degree of adverse effect the applicant could have on the national security.

It should be obvious that no one has a "right" to a security clearance. The grant of a clearance requires an affirmative act of discretion on the part of the granting official. The general standard is that a clearance may be granted only when "clearly consistent with the interests of the national security." A clearance does not equate with passing judgment upon an individual's character. Instead, it is only an attempt to predict his possible future behavior and to assess whether, under compulsion of circumstances or for other reasons, he might compromise sensitive information. It may be based, to be sure, upon past or present conduct, but it also may be based upon concerns completely unrelated to conduct, such as having close relatives residing in a country hostile to the United States. * * *. The attempt to define not only the individual's future actions, but those of outside and unknown influences renders the "grant or denial of security clearances ... an inexact science at best."

Predictive judgment of this kind must be made by those with the necessary expertise in protecting classified information. * * * Certainly, it is not reasonably possible for an outside nonexpert body to review the substance of such a judgment and to decide whether the agency should have been able to make the necessary affirmative prediction with confidence. Nor can such a body determine what constitutes an acceptable margin of error in assessing the potential risk. The Court accordingly has acknowledged that with respect to employees in sensitive positions "there is a reasonable basis for the view that an agency head who must bear the responsibility for the protection of classified information committed to his custody should have the final say in deciding whether to repose his trust in an employee who has access to such information." *Cole v. Young,* 351 U.S. 536, 546, 76 S.Ct. 861, 868, 100 L.Ed. 1396 (1956). * * * [U]nless Congress specifically has provided otherwise, courts traditionally have been reluctant to intrude upon the authority of the Executive in military and national security affairs.

We feel that the contrary conclusion of the Court of Appeals' majority is not in line with this authority.

IV

* * *

The Act by its terms does not confer broad authority on the Board to review a security-clearance determination. As noted above, the Board does have jurisdiction to review "adverse actions," a term, however, limited to a removal, a suspension for more than 14 days, a reduction in grade or pay, and a furlough of 30 days or less. §§ 7513(d), 7512. A denial of a security clearance is not such an "adverse action," and by its own force is not subject to Board review. An employee who is removed for "cause" under § 7513 when his required clearance is denied, is entitled to the several procedural protections specified in that statute. The Board then may determine whether such cause existed, whether in fact clearance was denied, and whether transfer to a nonsensitive position was feasible. Nothing in the Act, however, directs or empowers the Board to go further.

As noted above, security clearance normally will be granted only if it is "clearly consistent with the interests of the national security." The Board, however, reviews adverse actions under a preponderance of the evidence standard. § 7701(c)(1)(B). These two standards seem inconsistent. It is difficult to see how the Board would be able to review security-clearance determinations under a preponderance of the evidence standard without departing from the "clearly consistent with the interests of the national security" test. The clearly consistent standard indicates that security-clearance determinations should err, if they must, on the side of denials. Placing the burden on the Government to support the denial by a preponderance of the evidence would inevitably shift this emphasis and involve the Board in second-guessing the agency's national security determinations. We consider it extremely unlikely that Congress intended such a result when it passed the Act and created the Board.

* * *

The judgment of the Court of Appeals is reversed.

[The dissenting opinion of JUSTICE WHITE, joined by JUSTICES BRENNAN and MARSHALL, is omitted.]

NOTES

1. There was no dispute that Egan was entitled to appeal his removal to the MSPB. If the MSPB could not review the basis for the denial of his security clearance, what, if anything, is left for the MSPB to review?

2. In response to reports that an employee had used cocaine, the Department of the Navy gave the employee notice proposing to suspend him indefinitely pending the outcome of an investigation into whether his security clearance should be maintained or revoked. The notice afforded the employee an opportunity to respond. The employee submitted a response, after which, the agency suspended the employee indefinitely. Fourteen months later, the agency concluded the investigation, reinstated the employee's security clearance and returned him to duty. May the employee obtain redress for the wages and benefits lost during the period he was suspended? See *Jones v. Department of the Navy*, 978 F.2d 1223 (Fed. Cir. 1992). Would it make a difference if the agency failed to give the employee notice of the basis for the proposed suspension or an opportunity to respond? See *King v. Alston*, 75 F.3d 657 (Fed. Cir. 1996).

3. Under 5 C.F.R. § 732.201, an agency head may designate positions as "super sensitive," "critical sensitive" or "noncritical sensitive" where the occupant of the position "could bring about, by virtue of the nature of the position, a material adverse effect on the national security." The Air Force designated the position of commissary store clerk as noncritical sensitive, even though the position did not involve access to classified information. It removed an employee from the position due to the employee having been denied continued eligibility for employment in a sensitive position. To what extent, if at all, should the MSPB review the removal?

4. As developed *infra* section E, the Whistleblower Protection Act allows employees and applicants for employment to bring an individual right of action before the MSPB alleging that actions which may not be the basis for an adverse action appeal were undertaken in retaliation for the employee or applicant's protected whistleblowing. May the MSPB adjudicate a claim that an employee's security clearance was revoked or denied in retaliation for the employee's protected whistleblowing? See *Hesse v. Department of State*, 217 F.3d 1372 (Fed. Cir. 2000).

5. You are counsel to the Defense Commissary Agency (DCA) which operates a world-wide chain of commissaries providing groceries to military personnel, their families and military retirees. DCA leases space at many military bases. At one army base, the military police issued a report accusing a meat cutter at the commissary of stealing meat. The base commander issued a letter barring the meat cutter from entering the base for six years and admonishing him that if he attempted to enter the base he would be subject to arrest. The letter advised the meat cutter that he could request reconsideration by sending supporting evidence within 15 days to the Staff Judge Advocate. The meat cutter sent a response to the Commissary Officer denying that he stole meat. How would you advise the DCA to proceed? Should it request the commander to issue a limited bar that would allow the meat

cutter access to the base solely to come to work? Should it consider the meat cutter AWOL when he does not report for work because of the bar order? See *Hollingsworth v. Defense Commissary Agency*, 82 M.S.P.R. 444 (MSPB 1999).

In addition to proving that the employee did what the agency charged the employee with doing, the agency must also prove a nexus between the proven misconduct and the efficiency of the service. Although proof of nexus is required regardless of when or where the misconduct occurred, nexus is most frequently an issue in cases involving off-duty misconduct. The leading case dealing with nexus is *Merritt v. Department of Justice*, 6 M.S.P.R. 585 (MSPB 1981). There, the Board opined:

> [A] nexus determination must be based on evidence linking the employee's off-duty misconduct with the efficiency of the service or, in "certain egregious circumstances," on a presumption of nexus which may arise from the nature and gravity of the misconduct. In the latter situation, the presumption may be overcome by evidence showing an absence of adverse effect on service efficiency, in which case the agency may no longer rely solely on the presumption but must present evidence to carry its burden of proving nexus. The quantity and quality of the evidence which the agency need present in that circumstance would clearly then depend upon the nature and gravity of the particular misconduct as well as upon the strength of the showing made by the appellant in overcoming the otherwise applicable presumption.

Id. at 605.

In *Merritt*, the MSPB reversed the Bureau of Prisons' removal of a correctional officer for possession and use of a small quantity of marijuana in his home and sharing it on one occasion with two coworkers when all were off-duty. The Board reasoned:

> The agency argues that appellant's conduct evidenced a disregard for the law which destroyed the trust that the agency must have in his vigorous enforcement of the contraband regulations. However, the agency offered no evidence to show that appellant is more likely to violate those regulations, or to enforce them with less vigor, than any other Correctional Officer. Certainly, appellant's conduct in his home gives rise to no logical inference of inclination on his part to violate the contraband regulations in the future, or to enforce them with laxity, any more than his baking a cake or drinking a beer at home would support an inference of likelihood that he would introduce unauthorized food or alcoholic beverages into the penitentiary or permit others to do so.
>
> Appellant's misconduct in his home was not of an egregious character or gravity from which impairment of service efficiency can be presumed. It was, therefore, the agency's burden to present evidence tending to prove that appellant's off-duty conduct affected the efficiency of the service. This the agency failed to do. The fact that appellant's conduct may have been unlawful did not relieve the agency of its burden to establish the requisite nexus, particularly in view of limitations upon the power of the Government to intrude unnecessarily upon the discreet conduct of citizens, including federal employees, in the privacy of their homes.

Id. at 607–98.

Although the MSPB has continued to adhere to the general *Merritt* formulation of the nexus requirement, it has backed off the specific holding in the case concerning drug possession. In *Kruger v. Department of Justice*, 32 M.S.P.R. 71 (MSPB 1987), the Board found that the Bureau of Prisons had established the requisite nexus between several corrections officers' off-duty smoking of marijuana outside a tavern and the efficiency of the service. The Board expanded its analysis in *Merritt*, cataloguing three ways to establish nexus:

> (1) a rebuttable presumption of nexus that may arise in "certain egregious circumstances" based on the nature and gravity of the misconduct; (2) a showing by preponderant evidence that the misconduct affects the employee's or his co-workers' job performance, or management's trust and confidence in the employee's job performance; and (3) a showing by preponderant evidence that the misconduct interfered with or adversely affected the agency's mission.

Id. at 74. Relying on the position description and an affidavit from the warden, evidence that was not present in *Merritt*, the Board concluded that the agency had established that the conduct adversely affected the agency's mission. The Board reasoned that public awareness of correctional officers' off-duty drug use could detract from public confidence in the agency and that the officers' off-duty drug use was "antithetical to the agency's law enforcement and rehabilitative programs they are responsible for monitoring." *Id.* at 75. The MSPB, however, mitigated the employees' removals to 60–day suspensions.

Whereas nexus is often at issue with respect to off-duty activity, the most common issue arising in cases concerning on-duty activity is mitigation, that is whether an adjudicating authority may impose a lesser penalty on an employee than the penalty imposed by management. The following case remains the MSPB's lead decision concerning mitigation.

DOUGLAS v. VETERANS ADMINISTRATION

Merit Systems Protection Board, 1981.
5 M.S.P.R. 280, 5 MSPB 313.

Under 5 U.S.C. § 1205(a)(1), as enacted by the Civil Service Reform Act of 1978 ("the Reform Act"), this Board is authorized and directed to "take final action" on any matter within its jurisdiction. These cases present the question of whether that statutory power includes authority to modify or reduce a penalty imposed on an employee by an agency's adverse action, and if so, by what standards that authority should be exercised. For the reasons set out hereafter, we conclude that the Board does have authority to mitigate penalties when the Board determines that the agency-imposed penalty is clearly excessive, disproportionate to the sustained charges, or arbitrary, capricious, or unreasonable. We also conclude that this authority may be exercised by the Board's presiding officials, subject to our review under 5 U.S.C. § 7701(e)(1).

* * *

I. THE BOARD'S AUTHORITY TO MITIGATE PENALTIES

The Office of Personnel Management (OPM), most of the agencies, and AFGE [American Federation of Government Employees] urge that the Board lacks authority to mitigate an agency-selected penalty. They acknowledge that an agency's choice of penalty may be so disproportionate to an offense or otherwise improper as to constitute an abuse of discretion warranting reversal by the Board. However, they assert that in such cases the Board may not itself reduce or modify the penalty but must instead remand the appeal to the employing agency for selection and imposition by the agency of a substitute penalty, subject to further appeal to the Board from the agency's substituted penalty. For the Board itself to modify or reduce a penalty, they contend, would intrude upon the employing agency's managerial functions. The proponents of this position cite various federal court decisions referring to selection of penalties as a matter within "agency" discretion; OPM also emphasizes the purpose of the Reform Act to separate managerial from adjudicatory functions in the civil service system.

The other federal employee unions and the Acting Special Counsel, on the other hand, point to the authority previously reposed in the former Civil Service Commission to mitigate or lessen agency-imposed penalties. * * *

* * *

It cannot be doubted, and no one disputes, that the Civil Service Commission was vested with and exercised authority to mitigate penalties imposed by employing agencies. * * *

* * *

OPM argues broadly that the former Commission's mitigation authority reflected its "management responsibilities" in the Commission's dual capacity as government-wide personnel manager and appeals adjudicator, and that the separation of such "managerial decision-making" functions from the Board's adjudicatory function was one of the fundamental principles of the Reform Act.

[The Board concluded that the mitigation of penalties was part of the former Civil Service Commission's adjudicatory, rather than its management, functions.]

Beyond legal analysis, there are also practical considerations which, although not mandating our construction of the Board's authority, assure us that this construction is consistent with the Reform Act's purposes and efficient performance of the agencies' responsibilities. If we were to conclude that the Board must remand cases involving excessive penalties to the employing agency for selection and imposition of a new penalty by that agency, then a renewed appeal to the Board to review the new penalty must be allowed, as OPM, the agencies, and AFGE concede. Such successive appeals would prolong ultimate resolution of these cases, a result clearly contrary to Congress's desire for expedition in concluding adverse action appeals.

One agency suggests that if the Board has mitigation authority, managers might tend to impose unwarranted removal sanctions in reliance upon Board modification of such penalties, instead of carefully considering the most appropriate penalty at the outset. We doubt this is a substantial risk in many cases, given the care with which most agency managers properly approach the exercise of their disciplinary responsibilities, as shown in thousands of cases already reviewed by this Board and in innumerable cases before the former Civil Service Commission which was vested with that same mitigation authority. The question is not whether excessive penalties will sometimes be imposed by agencies, which is probably inevitable regardless of the scope of the Board's authority, but whether in such cases the Board must be powerless to prescribe a suitable remedy.

* * *

II. STANDARDS GOVERNING EXERCISE OF THE BOARD'S MITIGATION AUTHORITY

A. *Scope of Review*

Since the agency actions in these cases were taken under Chapter 75 of Title 5, the respective agency decisions to take those actions may be sustained only if supported by a preponderance of the evidence before the Board. 5 U.S.C. § 7701(c)(1)(B). We must therefore consider whether the preponderance standard applies only to an agency's burden in proving the actual occurrence of the alleged employee conduct or "cause" (5 U.S.C. § 7513) which led the agency to take disciplinary action, or whether that standard applies as well to an agency's selection of the particular disciplinary sanction.

We have no doubt that insofar as an agency's decision to impose the particular sanction rests upon considerations of fact, those facts must be established under the preponderance standard and the burden is on the agency to so establish them. This is so whether the facts relate to aggravating circumstances in the individual case, the employee's past work record, nature of the employee's responsibilities, specific effects of the employee's conduct on the agency's mission or reputation, consistency with other agency actions and with agency rules, or similar factual considerations which may be deemed relevant by the agency to justify the particular punishment. Section 7701(c)(1) admits of no ambiguity in this regard, since an agency's adverse action "decision" necessarily includes selection of the particular penalty as well as the determination that some sanction was warranted. The statute clearly requires that all facts on which such agency decision rests must be supported by the standard of proof set out therein.

It is also clear, however, that the appropriateness of a penalty, while depending upon resolution of questions of fact, is by no means a mere factual determination. Such a decision "involves not only an ascertainment of the factual circumstances surrounding the violations but also the application of administrative judgment and discretion." *Kulkin v. Bergland*, 626 F.2d 181, 185 (1st Cir. 1980). * * *

The evidentiary standards of 5 U.S.C. § 7701(c) specify the quantity of evidence required to establish a controverted fact. As procedural devices for allocating the risk of erroneous factual findings, those standards are inapposite to evaluating the rationality of non-factual determinations reached through the exercise of judgment and discretion. * * *

* * *

[I]n mitigating penalties we are not construing an authority newly conferred upon us but are exercising only inherited authority. Our authority in this regard is the same as that previously vested in the former Civil Service Commission. In enacting Section 7701(c), Congress understood that it was codifying the standard of proof previously used by the Commission for misconduct cases, and that for both misconduct and performance cases the evidentiary standards of Section 7701(c) apply to resolution of factual issues. There is no suggestion in the Reform Act or its legislative history that Congress sought to alter the scope of the authority previously exercised by the Commission in reviewing agency-imposed penalties * * *

By that standard, the Commission reviewed agency penalties to determine whether they were "clearly excessive" or were "arbitrary, capricious, or unreasonable." Other formulations of the standard commonly recited by the Commission were whether the penalty was "too harsh and unreasonable under the circumstances, or was "unduly harsh, arbitrary, and unreasonable," or reflected "an abuse of agency discretion, or * * * an inherent disproportion between the offense and the personnel action, or disparity in treatment" in violation of the "principle of like penalties for like offense." * * *

* * *

At all events the Board must exercise a scope of review adequate to produce results which will not be found "arbitrary, capricious, an abuse of discretion, or otherwise not in accordance with law" when reviewed by appellate courts under Section 7703(C). This is the identical standard prescribed by Section 706(2)(A) of the Administrative Procedure Act, 5 U.S.C. § 706(2)(A) (1964 ed., Supp. V). To assure that its decisions meet that standard under Section 7703(c), the Board must, in addition to determining that procedural requirements have been observed, review the agency's penalty selection to be satisfied (1) that on the charges sustained by the Board the agency's penalty is within the range allowed by law, regulation, and any applicable table of penalties, and (2) that the penalty "was based on a consideration of the relevant factors and [that] * * * there has [not] been a clear error of judgment." *Citizens to Preserve Overton Park, Inc. v. Volpe*, 401 U.S. 402, 417, 91 S.Ct. 814, 824, 28 L.Ed.2d 136 (1971). We take the expression "clear error of judgment" in the sense of "clearly erroneous," i.e., a determination "is 'clearly erroneous' when although there is evidence to support it, the [Board] * * * is left with the definite and firm conviction that a mistake has been committed."

Therefore, in reviewing an agency-imposed penalty, the Board must at a minimum assure that the *Overton Park* criteria for measuring arbitrariness or capriciousness have been satisfied. In addition, with greater latitude than the appellate courts are free to exercise, the Board like its predecessor Commission will consider whether a penalty is clearly excessive in proportion to the sustained charges, violates the principle of like penalties for like offenses, or is otherwise unreasonable under all the relevant circumstances. In making such determination the Board must give due weight to the agency's primary discretion in exercising the managerial function of maintaining employee discipline and efficiency, recognizing that the Board's function is not to displace management's responsibility but to assure that managerial judgment has been properly exercised within tolerable limits of reasonableness.

* * *

B. Relevant Factors in Assessing Penalties

* * *

Section 7513(b)(4) of Title 5 requires that written agency decisions taking adverse actions must include "the specific reasons therefor." While neither this provision nor OPM's implementing regulation, 5 C.F.R. § 752.404(f), requires the decision notice to contain information demonstrating that the agency has considered all mitigating factors and has reached a responsible judgment that a lesser penalty is inadequate, a decision notice which does demonstrate such reasoned consideration may be entitled to greater deference from the Board as well as from the courts. Moreover, aggravating factors on which the agency intends to rely for imposition of an enhanced penalty, such as a prior disciplinary record, should be included in the advance notice of charges so that the employee will have a fair opportunity to respond to those alleged factors before the agency's deciding official, and the decision notice should explain what weight was given to those factors in reaching the agency's final decision.

Court decisions and OPM and Civil Service Commission issuances have recognized a number of factors that are relevant for consideration in determining the appropriateness of a penalty. Without purporting to be exhaustive, those generally recognized as relevant include the following:

(1) The nature and seriousness of the offense, and its relation to the employee's duties, position, and responsibilities, including whether the offense was intentional or technical or inadvertent, or was committed maliciously or for gain, or was frequently repeated;

(2) the employee's job level and type of employment, including supervisory or fiduciary role, contacts with the public, and prominence of the position;

(3) the employee's past disciplinary record;

(4) the employee's past work record, including length of service, performance on the job, ability to get along with fellow workers, and dependability;

(5) the effect of the offense upon the employee's ability to perform at a satisfactory level and its effect upon supervisors' confidence in the employee's ability to perform assigned duties;

(6) consistency of the penalty with those imposed upon other employees for the same or similar offenses;

(7) consistency of the penalty with any applicable agency table of penalties;

(8) the notoriety of the offense or its impact upon the reputation of the agency;

(9) the clarity with which the employee was on notice of any rules that where violated in committing the offense, or had been warned about the conduct in question;

(10) potential for the employee's rehabilitation;

(11) mitigating circumstances surrounding the offense such as unusual job tensions, personality problems, mental impairment, harassment, or bad faith, malice or provocation on the part of others involved in the matter; and

(12) the adequacy and effectiveness of alternative sanctions to deter such conduct in the future by the employee or others.

Not all of these factors will be pertinent in every case, and frequently in the individual case some of the pertinent factors will weigh in the appellant's favor while others may not or may even constitute aggravating circumstances. Selection of an appropriate penalty must thus involve a responsible balancing of the relevant factors in the individual case. The Board's role in this process is not to insist that the balance be struck precisely where the Board would choose to strike it if the Board were in the agency's shoes in the first instance; such an approach would fail to accord proper deference to the agency's primary discretion in managing its workforce. Rather, the Board's review of an agency-imposed penalty is essentially to assure that the agency did conscientiously consider the relevant factors and did strike a responsible balance within tolerable limits of reasonableness. Only if the Board finds that the agency failed to weigh the relevant factors, or that the agency's judgment clearly exceeded the limits of reasonableness, is it appropriate for the Board then to specify how the agency's decision should be corrected to bring the penalty within the parameters of reasonableness.

* * *

III. APPLICATION TO APPELLANTS

We turn now to the application of these standards to the cases of the individual appellants. In doing so, we shall discuss the relevant facts of each case and the arguments of the parties.

A. *Curtis Douglas v. Veterans Administration*

Appellant Douglas was employed by the Veterans Administration as a Supply Clerk Dispatcher, GS–4. He was removed from the agency for being absent without leave for thirty minutes, for being away from his assigned duty station without permission, and for selling his employment services to a physically handicapped employee. These charges all arose out of events occurring on January 14, 1979. In selecting the penalty, the agency considered four past disciplinary actions: (1) a February 25, 1977 admonishment for eight hours of being AWOL; (2) a June 3, 1977 reprimand for failure to report for duty on May 28, 1977 and four hours of being AWOL on June 2, 1977; (3) a five-day suspension of June 28, 1977 for a 45–minute period of AWOL; and (4) a 20–day suspension of October 2, 1978 for another period of AWOL.

Upon appeal to the Board, the appellant declined a hearing and the presiding official sustained the action based on the evidence in the record. In his initial decision the presiding official described the facts surrounding the conduct which resulted in appellant's removal, stating:

> Here, the record reveals that on January 14, 1979 the appellant was assigned the job of SPD Dispatcher with a tour of duty from 8:00 a.m. to 4:30 p.m. and that at approximately 9:10 a.m. the telephone at the appellant's dispatch station rang several times and in his absence was finally answered by the SPD Preparation Area Supervisor, Mr. Edward L. Regan, who, after taking a request for supplies and arranging for their deliverance became aware that the appellant was absent from his work station without permission. In the meantime, the Ward Supply Clerk Supervisor, Ms. Margaret B. Thomas, was trying to contact the appellant on several occasions at his work site, the Dispatch Office, between 9:00 a.m. and 9:35 a.m. from the wards by use of the executone without success. Consequently, at 9:35 a.m., she asked Mr. Regan of the appellant's whereabouts only to learn that Mr. Regan did not know since the appellant had not requested permission to leave the work station. Thereafter, Ms. Thomas found the appellant on the sixth floor stocking nurservers for physically handicapped Supply Clerk Richard B. Eckert from whom, according to Mr. Eckert, the appellant has solicited $5.00 in payment for helping him do his work and to which the appellant offered that he needed the money.

The presiding official found, after carefully considering appellant's argument to the contrary, that the agency had proven the above facts by a preponderance of the evidence. The record does not contain any evidence which would cause us to change those factual determinations.

Appellant contended that the penalty was too severe. However, he did not explain why he believed the penalty to be too severe, nor did he introduce any evidence to support this contention. In the absence of any specific explanation of this contention from the appellant, we will consider whether, after relevant factors are considered, the penalty of removal was disproportionate to the seriousness of the offense.

The offense in this case was serious. It had a direct impact on the agency's ability to accomplish its mission. According to the agency, appellant's position was "critical to the process of furnishing vital supplies and equipment for emergency as well as routine patient care to all areas of the Medical Center." By being absent from his post, appellant created a situation which could have resulted in serious consequences to a patient who needed equipment or supplies immediately. The seriousness of the offense is compounded by the fact that appellant's absence was intentional and was occasioned by his desire for personal gain.

The record also shows that appellant has been disciplined for unauthorized absence on four previous occasions. This record of progressive discipline demonstrates that appellant was clearly on notice that unauthorized absence from his duty station was a serious offense. It also demonstrates that sanctions less severe than removal have not been successful in curbing appellant's misconduct. On the basis of the above findings, we conclude that the removal penalty was not arbitrary or unreasonable in light of all the circumstances and constituted an appropriate penalty. Accordingly, the removal action is AFFIRMED.

B. *Joseph E. Cicero v. Veterans Administration*

Appellant Cicero was removed from his position as a Housekeeping Aide, effective July 13, 1979, at the Franklin Delano Roosevelt Hospital, Montrose, New York, for failure to comply with the instructions of his supervisor to remove boxes from a hallway which were considered to be hazardous to elderly patients. Appellant's prior disciplinary record, consisting of four similar incidents involving failure to perform his work in a timely fashion, was considered by the agency. On appeal, appellant testified that although his supervisor had ordered him to remove several large boxes, the boxes had already been removed by another Housekeeping Aide. The presiding official found the appellant's testimony less credible than the supervisor's and concluded that the preponderance of evidence supported the reasons for the action. The presiding official also found that removal for failure to carry out instructions relating to the well-being of the patients "constitutes such cause as will promote the efficiency of the service."

* * *

The instant charge, standing alone, although significant, would not warrant removal because the agency failed to establish the likelihood of injury of patients as a result of appellant's failure to timely comply with his orders. However, the agency has demonstrated that its imposition of lesser penalties in the past has failed to correct appellant's insubordination. Namely, between June 1978 and January 1979 appellant was (1) suspended for 10 working days for deliberate failure or unreasonable delay in carrying out instructions; (2) issued a letter of reprimand for disobeying a direct order; (3) issued a letter of reprimand for failing to complete a work assignment; and, (4) admonished for willful idleness. This record of progressive discipline also demonstrates that appellant was on notice regarding the consequences of his failure to follow the instructions of his supervisor.

Appellant's argument that he had not been disciplined for a number of months is relevant in considering the appropriateness of the penalty. However, in this instance appellant's argument is not persuasive due to the fact that this was appellant's fourth offense involving failure to follow instructions in two years, with the suspension occurring only three months prior to notice of the proposed removal. Thus in the absence of any other relevant argument from the appellant, the question turns on the presence of other mitigating circumstances in the record. The record shows that appellant's performance was otherwise satisfactory and that he had completed five and a half years of service. However these factors are outweighed by the appellant's continued insubordination, and the fact that such continued insubordination indicates little likelihood of potential rehabilitation. An agency need not exercise forbearance indefinitely.

On the basis of the above findings, we conclude that the removal penalty was not arbitrary or unreasonable in light of all the circumstances.

* * *

NOTES

1. What was the basis for OPM's and others' arguments that the MSPB lacked authority to mitigate penalties? Why did the Board reject these arguments?

2. Compare the application of the factors to the offenses of Douglas and Cicero. Might either case have been decided differently if the employee's prior record had been stronger?

3. If the Board finds that the agency failed to consider the relevant factors or that the penalty the agency imposed was clearly unreasonable, the Board generally will reduce the penalty to the maximum reasonable penalty that could be imposed. See, e.g., *Cantu v. Department of the Treasury*, 88 M.S.P.R. 253 (MSPB 2001).

4. Should an agency be able to justify a penalty as setting an example for other employees and deterring similar misconduct? *Compare Perez v. United States Postal Service*, 48 M.S.P.R. 354 (MSPB 1991) *with Harper v. Department of the Air Force,* 61 M.S.P.R. 446 (MSPB 1994).

5. What process should be used when not all charges are sustained? Should the Board determine the maximum reasonable penalty for the charges that were sustained or should it remand to the agency for a new penalty determination? Compare *Modrowski v. Department of Veterans Affairs*, 252 F.3d 1344 (Fed. Cir. 2001) with *Coleman v. Department of Defense*, 100 M.S.P.R. 574 (MSPB 2005).

D. TEACHER TENURE LAWS

1. OVERVIEW AND HISTORY

Job security protections, similar to those covering public employees who are classified civil service workers, have also been provided by state legislation for many public school teachers and faculty in some public institutions of higher education. While civil service laws enacted to protect state and local government employees followed the federal model, the basics of teacher tenure laws enacted in a number of states followed state civil service reform legislation. As far back as 1887, a committee of the National Education Association (NEA) published a report urging that the subject of teachers' tenure be given publicity in the belief that necessary state legislation would result. For many years, the NEA's permanent platform contained the following statement:

> Teachers, regardless of position or title, are professional workers in a common cause, and, as such, have certain responsibilities and rights. The interests of the child and of the profession require: * * * Teachers who are protected from unjust discharge by effective [state] tenure laws.

The first teacher tenure act became law in New Jersey in 1908. Similar legislation followed in Montana in 1913, Massachusetts in 1914, Illinois and New York in 1917. By 1950, approximately three quarters of the states had some form of tenure law, although not all provided statewide coverage and they differed significantly in format and content.

Advocates for state teacher tenure laws had a number of arguments to support their position. The daunting effects of the "spoils system" were evident in school districts, as they had been elsewhere in public employment prior to the enactment of civil service reform legislation. Supporters pointed to the many benefits of employing experienced, professionally prepared, and career oriented teachers for both rural and urban school districts. Some commentators noted that tenure laws would attract an increasing number of males to careers in public school teaching; others noted that lobbying for teacher tenure laws paralleled the success of the women's suffrage campaign. Proponents contended that public school teachers' increased professionalism (including newly established accreditation requirements), mobility, and economic opportunities required protections for teachers so that they would not be discharged for political, religious, personal, or other "unjust" reasons. As stated by the Illinois Supreme Court:

> The Teacher Tenure Law was enacted primarily for the protection of Illinois teachers who, prior to its enactment in 1941, served at the pleasure of the boards of directors or education. Its object was to improve the Illinois school system by assuring teachers of experience and ability a continuous service and a rehiring based upon merit

rather than failure to rehire upon reasons that are political, partisan or capricious.[3]

The argument that academic freedom would also be protected by enactment of teacher tenure laws was advanced primarily on behalf of faculty at public institutions of higher education, where a growing tradition recognized the value of faculty speaking freely without fear of administrative reprisal. For elementary and secondary levels of public education, no strong tradition of academic freedom evolved comparable to that which developed in colleges and universities since the function of public schools, particularly at the elementary level, was typically viewed as transmission of knowledge rather than the discovery of knowledge.

Credit for state mandated teacher tenure, and other statutory teacher benefits, is often given to efforts by the various state teacher organizations affiliated with the NEA. State organizations became a prominent component of the NEA in the 1920s. The national NEA provided research and supportive advice to groups seeking passage of tenure laws and, once enacted, provided assistance to teachers who believed they were unfairly discharged, but it did not play a lead role in the enactment of state legislation. During much of this period, state teacher organizations often reflected interests of school administrators and academics who formed the leadership at all levels of the NEA, instead of the interests of classroom teachers who were the majority of NEA members. Therefore, state NEA organizations' legislative goals were not always clearly in favor of teacher tenure laws.

Until more recent times, the history of the other major teacher organization, the American Federation of Teachers (AFT), was almost exclusively a history of its locals. While AFT locals supported the passage of state teacher tenure laws, their primary energies were concentrated upon local issues and not lobbying for any type of protective state legislation.

Although teacher tenure laws vary widely from state to state (and a few states do not have any legislation regarding teacher tenure), these laws often incorporate both substantive and procedural protections. Teacher job security statutes either provide for tenure with protective continuing contract provisions thereafter or provide for contracts with notification before the end of the contract term (usually in the spring) if they are to be cancelled effective at the end of the school year. (Both types of legislation are usually referred to as teacher tenure laws, although only the former group strictly speaking contains provisions for "tenure.") Some laws are statewide in effect while others have a variety of provisions for different classes or sizes of school districts within the same state or for special types of schools. Rural teachers were less likely to be covered by tenure type laws than urban teachers.

In broad outline, the "pure" teacher tenure statutes are similar to civil service laws. Usually a teacher is required to go through a probation-

3. *Dunahoo v. Board of Education*, 413 Ill. 422, 425, 109 N.E.2d 787, 789 (1952).

ary period (commonly two to four years) followed by the award of job security known as tenure. Reemployment after completion of the probationary period automatically confers tenure. Tenured teachers cannot be discharged except for "cause" or "just cause." Some statutes specify causes which typically include some or all of the following: insubordination, incompetence, immorality, personal misconduct, unprofessional conduct, physical or mental incapacity and neglect of duty. Similarly, where teachers are employed under term contracts, a teacher cannot be dismissed during the term of the contract unless lawful reasons are given and an opportunity for a "hearing" provided. In some states "financial exigency" is explicitly listed as a justification for termination. Where it is not, courts have generally upheld the right of school districts to dismiss teachers for economic reasons. Some statutes contain specific requirements for these dismissals (known as "rifs", an abbreviation for reduction in force), commonly requiring dismissal of probationary teachers before tenured teachers. Tenure is a right to employment but not a right to a particular position or assignment. Thus, a school district can assign tenured teachers to particular schools, classes, and subjects as dictated by the needs of the district.

Detailed procedural requirements relating to notice and hearings are also included in many teacher tenure laws. A right to appeal a decision terminating a tenured teacher to a state official or agency and/or judicial review is sometimes expressly provided. Where no appeal provisions were included, courts have assumed jurisdiction in cases where the school board's decision is challenged as arbitrary or illegal. In jurisdictions authorizing continuing contracts unless notified of dismissal before the specified statutory date (to give the teacher the opportunity to seek employment elsewhere for the next school year), failure to re-employ a teacher at the end of a contract period is not the equivalent of a dismissal, assuming timely notification is given, and does not provide any statutory protections to a teacher not re-employed beyond the period of the contract.

In more recent decades, teacher tenure laws have been criticized as shielding mediocre and bad teachers, and school board members complain publicly from time to time that it is almost impossible to bring charges against an incompetent tenured teacher because the required burden of proof is so onerous and the termination process so time-consuming. Although coming from very different points of view, critiques by teachers and their organizations as well as school board members and their organizations have seldom succeeded in any direct modifications of teacher tenure laws, with the important exceptions of public charter schools and urban school district reorganizations. For some examples of related changes to the scope of bargaining, see Chapter 8 § C. Continuing criticism of state teacher tenure laws, however, has provided an important rationale for the movement to contract out the management of some public schools, particularly those serving large numbers of students with low achievement levels.

In general, both major teacher organizations, NEA and AFT, and state and local affiliates, have favored the retention of statutory tenure and other related teacher protections although they also have supported public sector collective bargaining legislation incorporating a broad scope of mandatory bargaining. In particular, they have endorsed public sector collective bargaining legislation which authorizes negotiation of a contractual "just cause" requirement together with a grievance arbitration hearing before an arbitrator as the preferred forum to challenge adverse school board disciplinary actions against teachers. They have also supported statutory clarification to permit collective bargaining of contractual benefits which would serve to substitute or supplement, but not decrease, other state statutory protections for teachers. Finally, teacher organizations continue to advocate for state legislation to provide schools or teachers with services or benefits they are unable to secure through collective bargaining, such as duty free lunch periods, pupil personnel services, pupil transportation, and kindergarten and early childhood programs.

NOTE

Teachers are among the most unionized groups of employees in the public sector. In providing a key service to teachers in the face of school administrator or school board attempts to impose discipline, teacher organizations favor procedures which permit them to challenge an adverse disciplinary determination in a grievance arbitration proceeding based upon a "just cause" standard. When the grievance arbitration route is not available, however, teacher organizations typically provide representation for disciplined teachers, particularly those with tenure, in connection with school board hearings, state tenure commission or similar forum hearings, and court appeals. This may account for the significant volume of litigation involving the disciplining of tenured teachers. In addition, an informal survey of approximately 100 court decisions involving discharges of tenured teachers for the use of corporal punishment against pupils reveals that, although a majority of the discharges were upheld, a number of the challenges succeeded because of judicial findings of procedural and/or substantive defects by the original decision-maker.

2. CAUSE FOR TERMINATION

WHALEY v. ANOKA-HENNEPIN INDEPENDENT SCHOOL DISTRICT NO. 11

Supreme Court of Minnesota, 1982.
325 N.W.2d 128.

AMDAHL, C.J.

This is an appeal by defendant Anoka-Hennepin Independent School District No. 11 (School Board) from an order of Judge Richard J. Kantorowicz of the Hennepin County District Court, dated October 22, 1981, which set aside the School Board's termination of the teaching contract of

Respondent Gerald Whaley. The District Court found that the evidence before the School Board did not rise to the level necessary to demonstrate Whaley's unfitness to teach under Minn. Stat. § 125.12, subd. 6 (1980), and that the termination was erroneous as a matter of law. We reverse.

Prior to his termination, respondent had served for nineteen consecutive years as a teacher and principal in the Anoka–Hennepin School District, the last three of these years as a reading teacher for grades 4, 5 and 6 at the Sandberg Elementary School. On May 5, 1980, respondent received a notice of deficiency, pursuant to Minn. Stat. § 125.12, subd. 6 (1980).[4] This notice supplemented a similar notice issued in 1978 under which no action had been taken to change respondent's teaching status. The May, 1980 notice alleged the following deficiencies: (1) poor rapport with students; (2) insufficient communications with parents and fellow staff members; (3) inappropriate use of class time; (4) failure to be punctual or appear at appointments; (5) failure to follow the school board's adopted reading program; (6) irrational grading of students; and (7) lack of student progress. Following this notice, respondent conferred with several school administrators and was advised that termination of his contract would be recommended if these deficiencies were not corrected during the upcoming school year. When school resumed for the 1980–81 school year, school administrators evaluated Whaley's teaching methods and behavior by observing his classroom on six separate occasions between September and January. Whaley participated in this evaluation by meeting with the staff members appraising his teaching performance.

On February 10, 1981, some nine months after having received the May 5, 1980, notice of deficiency, Whaley was given a notice of proposed termination. In its statement of the reasons for the proposed termination, the School Board listed the grounds specified in Minn. Stat. § 125.12, subd. 6(a), (b) and (c) (1980), and also asserted the following: (1) lack of rapport with students; (2) lack of student progress; and (3) lack of appropriate disciplinary techniques.

Upon Whaley's request, a hearing was conducted before an independent hearing officer on March 10, 11, and 12, 1981, to determine whether there was sufficient cause for Whaley's termination. * * *

On March 30, 1981, after consideration of the evidence at the hearing before the hearing officer, the School Board passed a resolution terminating Whaley's contract at the end of the 1980–81 school year. The resolu-

4. The full text of subdivision 6 reads as follows:

Subd. 6. Grounds for termination. A continuing contract may be terminated, effective at the close of the school year, upon any of the following grounds:

(a) Inefficiency;

(b) Neglect of duty, or persistent violation of school laws, rules, regulations, or directives;

(c) Conduct unbecoming a teacher which materially impairs his educational effectiveness;

(d) Other good and sufficient grounds rendering the teacher unfit to perform his duties.

A contract shall not be terminated upon one of the grounds specified in clauses (a), (b), (c), or (d), unless the teacher shall have failed to correct the deficiency after being given written notice of the specific items of complaint and reasonable time within which to remedy them.

tion includes forty-four factual findings directly related to Whaley's conduct as a teacher. From these findings the School Board concluded * * * that Whaley: (1) was inefficient; (2) neglected his duties; (3) failed to follow his principal's directions; and (4) was unfit to perform his duties. * * *

When deciding whether to hire or to terminate a teacher, a board of education is acting in an administrative capacity. On appeal to this court, a school board's decision to terminate a teacher will be set aside only if the decision is "fraudulent, arbitrary, unreasonable, not supported by substantial evidence on the record, not within the school board's jurisdiction, or is based on an erroneous theory of law." *Ganyo v. Independent School District No. 832,* 311 N.W.2d 497, 500 (Minn. 1981) * * *

This court views the record in its entirety to determine whether the board's findings are supported by substantial evidence. * * * In so reviewing the probative force of the evidence, "it is not the role of this court to try the matter de novo and to substitute its findings for those of the school board." *Lucas v. Board of Education,* 277 N.W.2d 524, 526 (Minn. 1979). * * *

Applying these standards in our review of this matter, we find that there is substantial evidence in the record to support the School Board's decision to terminate Whaley's teaching contract. The School Board based its decision on forty-four findings of fact regarding Whaley's teaching performance. These findings generally concerned four major deficiencies: (a) excessive use of worksheets; (b) lack of rapport with students; (c) lack of appropriate student discipline; and (d) lack of student progress. Although there is evidence in the record from which conflicting inferences can be drawn with regard to each deficiency, in this action's present posture the critical inquiry is whether the inferences drawn by the School Board in the course of their decision to terminate Whaley's contract are supported by substantial evidence in the record considered as a whole. We find that they are so supported.

For example, the evidence in the record regarding Whaley's use of worksheets demonstrates that Whaley used worksheets more often and more extensively than other instructors at Sandberg, and that students complained of confusion and frustration as a result of such use. The school principal, who observed Whaley's use of worksheets and assessed the effect of such use on students, testified that Whaley used worksheets to such an extent that it frustrated students and inhibited their progress. Similarly, an instruction consultant who visited Whaley's classroom testified that Whaley's undue emphasis on the use of worksheets produced a poor learning environment. Considering the probative force of this evidence, and of related evidence throughout the record, we find that the School Board's determination that Whaley used worksheets improperly and to such excess that it justified the termination of his contract is supported by substantial evidence.

Of the remaining three deficiencies relied upon by the School Board in terminating Whaley's contract, the Board's findings regarding a lack of progress by Whaley's students are the most closely related to the statutory grounds for discharge and the most clearly supported by substantial evidence in the record. Evidence in the record supporting the School Board's determination that Whaley's students did not make satisfactory progress consists of testimony by staff and faculty members who observed his students in class and who measured their progress by the speed at which they moved through the skills tests and worksheets used in the district. For example, the school district's reading curriculum consultant observed Whaley's classroom and his students' written work, and then examined the records of similar students in the district's reading program. On this basis, she concluded that Whaley's students did not make satisfactory progress. A fellow teacher responsible for keeping records in the reading program also conducted a comparative review of student records and testified that the records indicated that Whaley's students progressed more slowly than other students in the reading program. Two other teachers who commonly worked with Whaley's students also testified that Whaley's students progressed more slowly than did their own students. No teachers testified on Whaley's behalf. The only countervailing evidence on this point in the record consists of testimony offered by a few of Whaley's students to the effect that they were satisfied with their progress in Whaley's class. In so reviewing the entire record, we conclude that substantial evidence supports the School Board's findings that Whaley's students made unsatisfactory progress due to his poor teaching performance. When so established, lack of student progress is sufficient to trigger the grounds for discharge under Minn. Stat. § 125.12, subd. 6.

Reversed.

NOTES

1. Should the failure of students to progress be considered as evidence of a teacher's incompetence? See Christine Ver Ploeg, Terminating Public School Teachers for Cause Under Minnesota Law, 31 *William Mitchell Law Review* 303, 337–38 (2004), quoting *Peter W. v. San Francisco Unified School District*, 60 Cal.App.3d 814, 824, 131 Cal.Rptr. 854, 861 (1976) ("Substantial professional authority attests that the achievement of literacy in the schools, or its failure, are influenced by a host of factors which affect the pupil subjectively, from outside the formal teaching process and beyond the control of its ministers.") Several states have laws barring use of student test scores in teacher evaluations but a 2009 federal program that would deny some education funding to states with this restriction is prompting states to reconsider their laws. See Steven Brill, The Rubber Room, *The New Yorker*, Aug. 31, 2009 (discussing New York law and the federal program as well as the power of the teachers' union in New York City and the difficulty and cost of terminating incompetent teachers). Wisconsin changed its law to allow use of student test scores for teacher evaluation in 2009, specifying requirements for any evaluation plan. The law still bars use of test scores to discharge,

discipline or nonrenew teachers, however, and makes the evaluation plans mandatory subjects of bargaining for teachers represented by unions. See WISC.STAT.ANN. §§ 118.225, 118.30(2)(c), 1111.70(4)(o), 11.70(4)(o).

2. What factors might suggest that a school board's decision is not entitled to the level of deference given in *Whaley*? See *Ganyo v. Independent School District No. 832*, 311 N.W.2d 497 (Minn. 1981) where the same court applying the same standard set aside the school board's decision to terminate a tenured teacher with 25 years of experience based on several factors including lack of reasonable time to correct the deficiencies after notice (5 weeks), the use of only one classroom observer, and insufficient evidence to support other charges. In South Dakota, the test is "whether the board complied with all of the procedural requirements of the continuing contract law * * *; and second, whether the school board's decision was arbitrary, capricious, or an abuse of discretion." *Nordhagen v. Hot Springs School District No. 23–2*, 474 N.W.2d 510 (S.D. 1991).

3. While due process requires a hearing before termination of a tenured teacher, it does not require that the hearing be conducted by an independent decisionmaker. See *Hortonville Joint School District v. Hortonville Education Association*, 426 U.S. 482, 96 S.Ct. 2308, 49 L.Ed.2d 1 (1976). Some states provide for a hearing before the school board or other school official. See, e.g., VA. CODE ANN. § 22.1–308; S.C. CODE ANN. §§ 59–25–460, 470 (2009). Other states, however, use a neutral hearing officer or arbitrator for the teacher's appeal from dismissal. See, e.g., KAN.STAT.ANN. § 72–5438; MASS. GEN. LAWS ANN. Ch. 71, § 42. Some states allow unions to bargain collectively for arbitration or other alternatives to statutory procedures to challenge teacher dismissals. See, e.g., 24 PA.STAT. § 11–1133, N.Y.EDUC.LAW § 3020 (Consol. 2010). What are the benefits of using a neutral decisionmaker at the hearing level? Of having the school board decide?

4. Tenure statutes require clear notice of the charges against the teacher and without such notice a dismissal may be set aside. Why is such notice required?

5. Minnesota law, like the law of many states, requires notice of deficient performance and an opportunity to improve. In some states, the question of whether the conduct supporting termination is remediable is a crucial question in challenges to termination. See Paul W. Thurston, Dismissal of Tenured Teachers in Illinois: Evolution of a Viable System, 1990 *University of Illinois Law Review* 1. Remediable conduct requires notice and chance to correct the problem prior to termination. Even where a statute does not require remediation, hearing officers or courts may look for notice and efforts to correct a teacher's shortcomings when deciding whether to uphold a termination. Irremediable conduct, however, justifies immediate termination. What conduct is irremediable? The Illinois Supreme Court described the test as "whether damage has been done to the students, faculty or school, and whether the conduct resulting in that damage could have been corrected had the teacher's superiors warned her. Uncorrected causes for dismissal which originally were remediable in nature can become irremediable if continued over a long period of time" *Gilliland v. Board of Education.*, 67 Ill.2d 143,

153, 8 Ill.Dec. 84, 365 N.E.2d 322, 326 (1977). Consider whether the following are remediable.

a. Excessive homework, unclear instructions, keeping pupils from recess and physical education to complete work, yelling at students, physical discipline including spanking, pulling hair, shaking and hitting students with books, and throwing away assignments not in proper form, leading to parent complaints and students who feigned illness to avoid school, continuing over a four year period despite counseling. See *Gilliland, supra.* irremediable

b. Inability to maintain discipline in class leading to students fighting, playing dominoes and pennyrolling, and leaving debris in the classroom, and the teacher slapping a student who cursed, tapping students with a pointer, and holding a student around the neck. Finally, the teacher was removed from the classroom. See *Grissom v. Board of Education*, 75 Ill.2d 314, 26 Ill.Dec. 683, 388 N.E.2d 398 (1979). irremediable

c. Forcibly moving several students engaged in misconduct from one place to another during a six week period, causing scratches on one student and a bump on the head of another in a district that allowed corporal punishment. See *Board of Education v. State Board of Education*, 99 Ill.2d 111, 75 Ill.Dec. 441, 457 N.E.2d 435 (1983). remediable

d. Failure to control classroom leading to ineffective instruction and students leaving without permission. Additionally the primary assignments were copying material. These actions continued through the course of the school year with little improvement, despite suggestions for improvement and recommendations of materials to assist in correcting deficiencies. See *Board of Education v. Wolff*, 139 Mich.App. 148, 361 N.W.2d 750 (1984). remediable

e. Sexual repartee with students and staff, use of coarse language and inappropriate stories with students, and breaching confidentiality of students by junior high school guidance counselor. See *Downie v. Independent School District No. 141,* 367 N.W.2d 913 (Minn. App. 1985). irremediable

6. Many states have implemented statutory requirements for regular evaluation of teachers, both tenured and untenured. Should failure to follow the program of evaluation invalidate dismissal of a teacher? See OREGON REV.STAT. § 342.850 (stating that an error or unfair application in the program of assistance required as a part of the evaluation procedure does not invalidate dismissal or nonrenewal of a contract unless it causes a substantial and prejudicial inability to comply with the requirements of the school district); *Schaub v. Chamberlain Board of Education,* 339 N.W.2d 307, 310 (S.D. 1983) (finding that a probationary teacher was not entitled to reinstatement even if the Board violated the mandatory evaluation procedures because she was aware of her teaching deficiencies and therefore any violation did not "did not substantially or directly impair her ability to improve her teaching performance." Cf. *Cox v. York County School District No. 083*, 252 Neb. 12, 560 N.W.2d 138 (1997) reinstating probationary teacher whose contract was not renewed because she was not evaluated each semester in accordance with statutory requirements.

7. To whom should tenure protections apply? Some states limit tenure to classroom teachers, while others provide tenure to various other education-

al personnel including counselors, tutors, psychologists, librarians, nurses, social workers, superintendents, principals, and teacher's assistants. What is the rationale for providing tenure to personnel who are not classroom teachers? If a teacher is also a coach, does the teacher have tenure in the coaching position as well? Again, states vary. Some states treat the two positions as separate, while in others they may be combined as one. Even where the positions are divided, the requirements for termination differ from state to state. Compare *Tate v. Westerville City Board of Education,* 4 Ohio St.3d 206, 448 N.E.2d 144 (1983) (supplemental coaching contracts of tenured teachers can be terminated by the school board so long as the board complies with statutory notice periods) with *Reid v. Huron Board of Education*, 449 N.W.2d 240 (S.D. 1989) (finding that to be a head coach, a person must be certified as a teacher and a teacher is entitled to the full protections of the tenure law. The court also found that coaching is teaching and that the skills developed by the coach are educationally important) and *Munger v. Jesup Community School District*, 325 N.W.2d 377 (Iowa 1982) (finding that teacher was hired to teach and coach and the duties were inseparable; therefore, he could not resign as coach and retain his teaching position to resolve complaints about coaching where the district was satisfied with his teaching. The court went on to find that the school district did not establish cause to terminate the teacher/coach.) Even in the same state, application of tenure provisions to supplemental positions may vary depending on whether the teaching and coaching positions are sufficiently intertwined. See *Coles v. Glenburn Public School District 26,* 436 N.W.2d 262 (N.D. 1989) (holding that athletic director's position so intertwined with teaching position that it was covered by continuing contract law while coaching positions were not).

8. Generally the school district has the burden of proving that dismissal of a tenured employee is warranted? Why should this be so?

Whaley involved conduct that occurred on the job and thus was unquestionably related to his performance as a teacher. Under what circumstances would termination of a tenured teacher for activity occurring off the job be appropriate?

CHICAGO BOARD OF EDUCATION v. PAYNE

Illinois Appellate Court, 1981.
102 Ill.App.3d 741, 58 Ill.Dec. 368, 430 N.E.2d 310.

DOWNING, J.

On August 30, 1978, the general superintendent of schools instituted proceedings with the Board against Payne, charging him with conduct unbecoming a teacher in the Chicago Public Schools. This charge contained four itemized specifications, paraphrased as follows: (1) on or about February 6, 1976, Payne knowingly had in his possession a quantity of marijuana; (2) on or about January 19, 1978, Payne knowingly had in his possession a quantity of marijuana; (3) on or about the same date, Payne knowingly had in his possession a controlled substance; and (4) such conduct was irremediable. * * *

* * * Chicago policeman Thomas Skol stopped Payne for a traffic violation at about 5 p.m. on February 6, 1976. * * * As Payne was searching his pockets for the license, he pulled out a clear plastic bag containing a relatively small amount of a crushed green substance. * * * Payne admitted that the substance was marijuana and was arrested. * * * Payne pleaded guilty to possession of marijuana in return for a sentence of probation.

* * *

The hearing officer eventually ruled * * * that although Payne had pleaded guilty to the 1976 possession of marijuana charge, there was no evidence to show how this conviction had any effect upon Payne's duties as a teacher, upon the students, or upon his fellow teachers (a finding of legal insufficiency in the Board's case). * * * Consequently, he held Payne's dismissal improper. [The Circuit Court reversed the hearing officer's decision and Payne appealed.]

* * *

A.

We first note that there is no real factual dispute in this case regarding the 1976 possession of marijuana charge against Payne. He admitted his guilt of this crime in court by pleading guilty, and he received a sentence of probation therefor. On appeal, Payne's attorney attempted to lessen the impact of that guilty plea by arguing, in what amounts to a collateral attack on the judgment, that Payne was not represented by an attorney at the time of the plea, and that Payne had only entered the plea in order to receive the sentence of probation.

We reject this reasoning. There is no question in our minds that Payne did in fact plead guilty to the 1976 possession charge or that he made this plea of his free will. Therefore, we have no alternative but to find that the Board has proved by a preponderance of the evidence, as was required * * *, that Payne did indeed possess a small quantity of marijuana in February 1976. It remains for our determination whether this fact alone constitutes a sufficient basis for Payne's dismissal by the Board.

B.

No tenured school teacher may be removed from employment except for cause. The School Code is generally vague as to what constitutes cause for removal, although it does provide that the Board may dismiss a teacher for "incompetency, cruelty, negligence, immorality or other sufficient cause and * * * whenever, in its opinion, the interests of the schools require it * * *." (Emphasis added.) (Ill. Rev. Stat. 1977, ch. 122, par. 10—22.4.) The right to determine what constitutes sufficient cause lies in the first instance with the Board, with the best interests of the schools as the "guiding star." * * * "Cause" has been described as some substantial shortcoming which renders continuance in employment in some way detrimental to discipline and effectiveness of service; something which the law and sound public opinion recognizes as a good reason for the individual to no longer occupy his position. *Jepsen v. Board of Education* (1958), 19 Ill.App. 2d 204, 207, 153 N.E.2d 417. There must be present a logical nexus between the actions alleged as cause for dismissal and the individual's fitness to perform as a teacher. See *Board of Trustees v. Judge* (1975), 50 Cal.App. 3d 920, 123 Cal.Rptr. 830.

We have found no Illinois cases addressing the question of whether a teacher's possession of a small quantity of marijuana outside of the school environment is sufficient cause to warrant his dismissal. Thus, we are faced with a question of first impression. We note that the California courts have established a test to facilitate the determination of whether a logical nexus exists between a teacher's alleged activity and his fitness to teach. In *Morrison v. State Board of Education* (1969), 1 Cal.3d 214, 229, 461 P.2d 375, 386, 82 Cal.Rptr. 175, 186, the California Supreme Court set forth the following list of factors to be weighed in making this decision: (1) the likelihood of an adverse effect from the conduct upon students and other teachers, (2) the degree of adverse effect expected, (3) the type of teaching certificate held by the teacher, (4) the probability that the conduct will recur, (5) the proximity in time of the conduct to the commencement of dismissal proceedings, and (6) the presence or absence of any factors in mitigation. We will apply these factors to the evidence of this case to assist us in deciding whether Payne's 1976 conduct constitutes cause for his dismissal.

There is evidence in this case that a teacher's possession of even a small quantity of marijuana would, once it became a matter of general knowledge, have a major adverse impact upon that teacher's students and fellow teachers. Dr. Nina Jones, who qualified as an expert by virtue of her 30 years service to the Board, testified to the Board's perception of the role of a teacher in the Chicago school system. Dr. Jones stated that a teacher serves as the leader of the instructional program in his classroom, as a role model for his students who often emulate his behavior, and as a person who instills basic values of American society and good citizenship in his students. Dr. Jones further stated that publication of information that a teacher engaged in illegal conduct would have a deleterious effect on the school system as a whole, as well as on the particular school.

We are aware of the special position occupied by a teacher in our society. As a consequence of that elevated stature, a teacher's actions are subject to much greater scrutiny than that given to the activities of the average person. We do not doubt that knowledge of a teacher's involvement in illegalities such as possession of marijuana would have a major deleterious effect upon the school system and would greatly impede that individual's ability to adequately fulfill his role as perceived by the Board. This conclusion is especially true where, as here, the teacher holds a certificate to educate children ages 10 to 13 who are, according to testimony in this case, very impressionable. We can only find that general awareness of possession of marijuana by a teacher in Payne's position directly and adversely affects that individual's ability to effectively perform as a teacher.

As well, the record shows that Payne's conduct in 1976 was not an isolated occurrence. There is evidence that Payne also possessed marijuana as well as cocaine in January 1978. While we do not focus upon that incident in resolving this appeal, we find that it does demonstrate the likelihood that Payne's illegal actions could recur.

Additionally, we note that the Board commenced informal proceedings against Payne upon the newspapers' publication of the fact of Payne's 1976 conduct in January 1978. Consequently, we do not find any attenuation of the impact of that action by the mere passage of a nearly two-year period between the initial occurrence and the general awareness of that incident. Further, we find an aggravating circumstance in this case which gives weight to the Board's position. Payne testified that he was assigned to the "problem kids," those children who have already shown a degree of disrespect for authority. It is beyond argument that Payne's involvement with illegal drugs would hinder the ability of the schools to enlighten these children as to proper behavior in our society. In sum, we believe that a clear nexus has been shown in this record between Payne's conduct and his fitness to teach. We must conclude that Payne's possession of marijuana, coupled with the circumstances in which he functioned, constitutes sufficient cause for the Board to remove Payne from his position as a teacher. We cannot accept Payne's contention that his conduct was not unbecoming his status and position.

C.

Despite this conclusion, it remains necessary to determine whether the Board has also demonstrated that Payne's conduct was irremediable before this court may affirm the circuit court's decision. Payne asserts that the Board has not made this showing, and that the Board's failure to give him the statutorily required warning rendered the circuit court's decision erroneous regardless of the validity of the Board's determination that there existed cause for Payne's dismissal.

Where conduct which forms the basis of charges seeking dismissal is deemed remediable, the Board must give the teacher a written warning which informs him of the consequences of failing to take corrective measures. (Ill. Rev. Stat. 1977, ch. 122, par. 34–85.) Where no warning is given, the Board's evidence must prove that the teacher's conduct is irremediable. If the Board fails to meet this evidentiary burden, it is deprived of jurisdiction to terminate a teacher's employment. The question of remediability is for the Board in the first instance, and its decision will not be disturbed absent a showing that it is arbitrary and capricious. Conduct is irremediable where damage results therefrom which could not have been corrected regardless of whether the teacher received an adequate timely warning.

Application of simple logic to the facts of this case shows that Payne's possession of marijuana in 1976 was irremediable conduct. The damage to the students, faculty, and school which flowed from that incident and which constituted cause for dismissal occurred immediately upon revelation of it. A warning to Payne could not have remedied this damage or in any way served to lessen its impact. Thus, the case is distinguishable from those cited by Payne, * * * where the charges involved conduct such as tardiness for work, lack of discipline of students, and the like. Here, no warning was required by the Board. Payne's conduct in 1976 was clearly irremediable. The hearing officer erred in finding to the contrary.

For these reasons, we find that the circuit court correctly reversed the hearing officer's decision and ordered Payne's dismissal based upon his 1976 possession of marijuana. * * *

Affirmed.

NOTES

1. States generally require a nexus between off-duty conduct and teaching to sustain a discharge. Up until at least the 1960s, teachers were quickly terminated for violations of moral standards, even in their private lives. Consider this excerpt from an early 20th century teacher's contract. "I promise to abstain from all dancing, immodest dressing and any other conduct unbecoming a teacher and a lady. I promise not to go out with any young men except in so far as it may be necessary to stimulate Sunday school work. I promise not to fall in love, to become engaged or secretly married. I promise to sleep at least eight hours a night [and] to eat carefully * * * in order that I may be better able to render efficient service to my pupils." Louis Fischer, et al., *Teachers and the Law* (7th ed. 2007) quoting T. Minehan, The Teacher Goes Job–Hunting, 124 *The Nation* 606 (1927). In recent years, as community standards have evolved and changed and the right to privacy has become more salient, the nexus requirement has emerged to limit terminations for off-duty conduct. High standards of behavior are still employed, however, because of the responsibility of teachers for the well-being of children.

2. Consider whether the following conduct justifies termination.

a. Touching an undercover police officer in a sexually suggestive way. See *McNeill v. Pinellas County School Board,* 678 So.2d 476 (Fla.App. 1996).

b. Participating in a fight at a night club, resisting arrest and lying under oath. See *Purvis v. Marion County School Board,* 766 So.2d 492 (Fla.App. 2000).

c. Shoplifting. *See* Christine Ver Ploeg, Terminating Public School Teachers for Cause Under Minnesota Law, 31 *William Mitchell Law Review* 303, 361–62 (2004).

d. Calling in sick and going on a drinking binge, urinating in public, nearly causing a car accident and being arrested. *Id.* at 363–67. Compare *Clark v. School Board*, 596 So.2d 735 (Fla.App. 1992) (three day summer alcohol binge resulting in arrest and conviction, followed by rehabilitation).

e. Driver's education teacher with two DUI arrests in 13 months resulting in cancellation of auto insurance. See *Alabama State Tenure Commission v. Lee County Board of Education*, 595 So.2d 476 (Ala.App. 1991)

f. Having a 14 year old student in the teacher's apartment at midnight against her parents' wishes and lying about her presence when police arrived searching for the student. See *Hamm v. Poplar Bluff R–1 School District*, 955 S.W.2d 27 (Mo.App. 1997).

g. Cohabitation. See *Sherburne v. School Board Of Suwannee County*, 455 So.2d 1057 (Fla.App. 1984).

3. Should what constitutes immorality or unprofessional conduct change as social norms change? In *Gaylord v. Tacoma School District* 88 Wash.2d 286, 559 P.2d 1340 (1977) the court upheld the termination of a teacher for admitted homosexuality. Would this case be decided the same way today?

4. The *Payne* court applied the remediability test to off duty criminal conduct. Is such conduct ever remediable? In a series of cases, Illinois courts have found that the question of whether conduct could be corrected with warning is inapplicable in cases involving criminal or immoral conduct. See *Younge v. Board of Education of City of Chicago*, 788 N.E.2d 1153, 1161–2, 338 Ill.App.3d 522, 532–3, 273 Ill.Dec. 277, 285–6 (2003).

5. In *In the Matter of the Proposed Discharge of Donald Lee Shelton*, a teacher stole corporate funds from a business that he started with two other teachers. He pled guilty and his theft was common knowledge in the community. The court upheld his termination, stating the following:

> while relator may be genuinely sorry for, and may be unlikely to repeat, his conduct, the record does support the school board's conclusion that relator's continues presence in this small school district will result in faculty disorder and an unsatisfactory learning environment. Relator still has his teaching license and can continue in his profession. Faculty members testified relator is well qualified to teach in any other district. Had this matter arisen in a larger school district, it is likely reassignment of relator to another school within the district would suffice as a remedy. But given the small size of the Blooming Prairie school district and the high school which houses grades 7–12, it is not error to conclude relator's "conduct can only be remedied by his removal as a teacher in the Blooming Prairie Schools." 408 N.W.2d 594, 598 (Minn.App. 1987).

Should the application of the statutory cause for termination vary depending on the size of the school district?

3. TENURE REFORMS IN ELEMENTARY AND SECONDARY EDUCATION

Criticisms of tenure are not new but have been growing in recent years with the focus on educational reform. The most common criticism is that tenure protects incompetent teachers by making it difficult for school districts to terminate them. Additionally tenure statutes have been criticized for interfering with full integration of previously discriminatory teaching work forces. A number of states have undertaken reform of tenure laws to address the criticisms. For summaries of some statutory changes, see David J. Strom & Stephanie S. Baxter, From the Statehouse to the Schoolhouse: How Legislatures and Courts Shaped Labor Relations for Public Education Employees During the Last Decade, 30 *Journal of Law & Education* 275, 297 (2001); *Tenure Reform: Has Anything Really Changed in Termination of School Employees: Legal Issues and Techniques* (1997). Some of the changes are substantive while others are primarily cosmetic. Not surprisingly, given the lobbying power of the NEA and AFT, as part of the reforms some states made changes favorable to teachers as well. Some state statutes, including South Dakota, Florida and Colorado, eliminated the word tenure but kept the major protections of a tenure system, using terminology such as "continuing contract" in lieu of tenure. Some states, such as Texas, Massachusetts, Oregon, Michigan and New York, modified the appeal process for terminated teachers, specifying timelines for hearings and decisions or eliminating some of the multiple required hearings, in order to reduce the time required to reach a final determination. Other states made more drastic modifications. Wisconsin eliminated its tenure system as a matter of law, but allows collectively bargained tenure systems as well as retention of tenure by those who earned it prior to the change in the law. Oregon also eliminated the tenure system, substituting two year renewable contracts, but still keeping many of the protections of the tenure law. However, Oregon also limited the ability of unions to negotiate a waiver of the school district's right to consider competence in deciding which teachers to layoff and recall in the event of the need to reduce the workforce. Prior to the change in the law, unions and districts could, and did, limit layoff criteria to license and seniority. See David W. Turner & Ronald E. Wilson, The Promise of a New Day: Senate Bill 880 and its Impact on Teacher and Administrator Employment and Accountability, 34 *Willamette Law Review* 269 (1998).

As for changes favorable to teachers, Oregon's statutory revision requires teachers designated for nonrenewal to be provided with a program of assistance for improvement for one year, at which time the board must reconsider its decision not to renew the contract based on any improvement in teaching performance. Florida added similar requirements for teachers whose contract is not to be renewed for unsatisfactory performance. Oregon also added front pay and compensatory damages to the remedies available to teachers arbitrating their dismissals. In Michigan, neutral hearing officers, rather than school boards, now make decisions as to whether a teacher should receive any punishment based on school board charges and, if so what. The hearing officer's decision may be appealed to the State Tenure Commission by either party. New York's revision added a requirement for remediation of deficiencies. Nebraska has required notice and a hearing, if requested, for nonrenewal of the contracts of probationary teachers.

The results of these changes measured against the professed intent to ease the task of terminating incompetent teachers have been mixed. In some states, the changes have made little difference in the dismissal rates

of teachers, while others have seen an increase in dismissal cases and voluntary resignations. It is certainly possible, however, that the addition of more specific evaluation requirements and improvement plans has improved the quality of teachers and limited the need for termination.

NOTE

Some states have changed their tenure laws to remove specific causes for dismissal and substitute instead dismissal for just cause or good cause. What is the purpose of such a change? Will the change make it easier or more difficult to dismiss teachers? easier

4. HIGHER EDUCATION

As noted previously, the justification for tenure in higher education focuses on the need for academic freedom in addition to the reasons supporting tenure in elementary and secondary education. The 1940 Statement of Principles on Academic Freedom and Tenure, which was developed by the Association of American Colleges and the American Association of University Professors contains both a rationale for tenure and a set of principles which have guided the adoption of tenure plans in many colleges and universities. The statement begins with the following introduction:

> The purpose of this statement is to promote public understanding and support of academic freedom and tenure and agreement upon procedures to ensure them in colleges and universities. Institutions of higher education are conducted for the common good and not to further the interest of either the individual teacher or the institution as a whole. The common good depends upon the free search for truth and its free exposition.
>
> Academic freedom is essential to these purposes and applies to both teaching and research. Freedom in research is fundamental to the advancement of truth. Academic freedom in its teaching aspect is fundamental for the protection of the rights of the teacher in teaching and of the student to freedom in learning. It carries with it duties correlative with rights.
>
> Tenure is a means to certain ends; specifically: (1) freedom of teaching and research and of extramural activities, and (2) a sufficient degree of economic security to make the profession attractive to men and women of ability. Freedom and economic security, hence, tenure, are indispensable to the success of an institution in fulfilling its obligations to its students and to society.

The statement continues with a set of principles recommended for tenure, including a probationary period of no more than seven years, followed by tenure with termination only for adequate cause except for "extraordinary circumstances because of [bona fide] financial exigencies." In the event of termination for cause, there should be notice, a hearing with an opportunity for the teacher to defend the charges with a representative chosen by the teacher, a full transcript of the hearing, consideration by both a faculty committee and the governing board, testimony of teachers and scholars if the charge is incompetence, and a terminal year of employment after notification of dismissal unless the discharge is for moral turpitude. The full statement can be accessed at the AAUP's website, http://www.aaup.org/AAUP/pubsres/policydocs/contents/1940statement.htm. While this statement guides many institutions in establishing tenure policies and procedures, like those in public schools, tenure systems in higher education vary widely and some schools have no provision for tenure. Almost all public four-year colleges and universities maintain tenure provisions for full-time faculty, however.[5] In addition, and contrary to elementary and secondary education, most colleges and universities have many teaching positions where tenure is not available including adjunct faculty, part-time faculty, visiting faculty, lecturers, and graduate assistants. Some of these faculty members may have contracts which provide some protection from termination at will.

NOTES

1. Cause for termination for higher education faculty is defined by the institution or state law. Commonly included would be incompetence, neglect of duty, intellectual dishonesty, research misconduct, insubordination, and moral turpitude. How similar are these causes to those for teachers elementary and secondary education? Are there issues that should be treated differently based on the level of the educational program? For example, a sexual relationship with a student would almost always constitute cause for termination of a teacher in secondary school and certainly in elementary school. Would the same apply to a teacher of graduate or professional students?

2. A substantial controversy has arisen over whether Professor John Yoo should retain his tenure at Boalt Hall School of Law at the University of California at Berkeley. Professor Yoo took leave from his tenured position to work in the Bush administration and authored a number of legal memos that were used to justify treatment of prisoners that may have constituted torture in violation of the Geneva Convention. He has now returned to the law school, where some have demanded his termination, an action that has been resisted by the dean. The debate raises a range of questions. Would firing Professor Yoo for his memos violate his right to academic freedom? Does academic freedom apply to actions while on leave and serving in another position? As some have suggested, do his memos go beyond academic freedom and constitute advice to a client to violate the law, which resulted in illegal torture of prisoners? Are the memos so devoid of legal support that they cast doubt on Professor Yoo's competence as a teacher of professional students? Could the university try to terminate Professor Woo for criminal conduct? Only if he is convicted? The standard for criminal conviction is beyond a reasonable doubt. Could the university terminate Woo for criminal conduct, sustaining the

5. William T. Mallon, *Tenure on Trial* 16 (2001) citing survey by the National Center on Education Statistics.

charges using a less demanding standard of proof? For a series of commentaries on the subject, see Torture and Academic Freedom, *N. Y. Times*, August 20, 2009, http://roomfordebate.blogs.nytimes.com/2009/08/20/torture-and-academic-freedom/.

In another high profile case, Professor Ward Churchill was terminated by the University of Colorado–Boulder for academic misconduct. The university began an investigation into his writings after a spate of publicity initiated by protests against Hamilton College which had invited Churchill, an ethnic studies professor, to speak in 2005. The controversy surrounded an essay written after the 9/11 attacks on the World Trade Center, which suggested that U.S. policy had provoked the attacks and referred to those working in the World Trade Center as "Little Eichmanns", a reference to a Nazi war criminal. The 2005 protests led to the University of Colorado investigation and subsequently to Churchill's termination, based on findings of plagiarism and falsification of research. Churchill was victorious in a jury trial challenging his termination, although the award of damages was limited to $1, but the judge set aside the verdict. Was Churchill's termination a violation of his academic freedom? For contemporary media accounts, see T.R. Reid, Professor Under Fire for 9/11 Comments, *Washington Post*, Feb. 5, 2005, at C1, http://www.washingtonpost.com/wp-dyn/articles/A76–2005Feb4.html; Kirk Johnson & Katharine Q. Seelye, Jury Says Professor Was Wrongly Fired, *N.Y. Times*, April 2, 2009, http://www.nytimes.com/2009/04/03/us/03churchill.html?_r=1&hp.

3. Courts are very deferential to the decisions of universities to terminate faculty so long as due process has been provided to the faculty member and there is no clear violation of constitutional rights. This is true even where the teacher alleges that the termination violated a discrimination statute. Among the reasons offered for this deference are the following: 1. The expertise needed to evaluate the teaching, research and service of the faculty member; 2. A desire to avoid second guessing personnel decisions of the university; 3. The fact that a public educational institution is a governmental agency with expertise in academic decision-making; 4. A presumption that the school acted legally and reasonably; 5. The economic and institutional implications of a decision to award tenure; 6. A desire to avoid interfering with the institution's academic freedom. Which of these rationales is persuasive? For discussions of these rationales, see Terry L. Leap, *Tenure, Discrimination and the Courts* 46–60 (1993); Arval A. Morris, *Dismissal of Tenured Higher Education Faculty: Legal Implications of the Elimination of Mandatory Retirement* 23–30 (1992).

4. Why should an institution be required to demonstrate bona fide financial exigency before terminating tenured faculty? See Matthew W. Finkin, *The Case for Tenure* 128–70 (1996).

5. Like tenure in primary and secondary education, tenure in higher education has been under attack. The arguments against tenure are in some ways similar and in others different. Among the most prominent criticisms are the following: 1. Tenure protects mediocrity and poor performance, as well as preventing the upgrading of faculty; 2. Tenure allows political proselytizing in the guise of education, and irresponsible scholarship; 3. Tenure is unneces-

sary to protect academic freedom in light of other protections such as the First Amendment and the desire of Boards of Trustees to protect such freedom; 4. The up or out tenure rules cause loss of talented faculty who do not produce quickly enough or who do not have a tenured position available at the right time (a particular problem at large universities that must hire many young faculty because of teaching needs); 5. Tenure freezes the status quo, limiting the ability of traditionally excluded groups such as women and faculty of color to break into the ranks of tenured faculty. Are these arguments persuasive? Despite some drawbacks does the system nevertheless make sense in the university environment? Consider this argument of Fritz Machlup.

> "All of the disadvantages of a strict tenure system * * * are outweighed by one important advantage, accruing chiefly to society at large. * * * The largest part of the benefits derived from the scholars' exercise of their freedom to inquire, speak, teach and publish accrues not to them, but to millions of their contemporaries and millions again in posterity. * * * It happens that some of the greatest agents of progress in human affairs and scientific knowledge about nature or society have been 'troublemakers.' * * * The case for tenure would be sufficiently supported by showing that a few men once in a while might feel insecure and suppress or postpone the communication of views which, true or false, wise or foolish, could inspire or provoke others to embark on or continue along lines of reasoning which may eventually lead to new insights, new judgments, or new appraisals regarding nature or society." See *In Defense of Academic Tenure* in Finkin, *supra* note 4, at 9, 22–26.

It has also been argued that the system of probation followed by a decision on tenure makes economic sense in the specialized labor market of academia where the faculty are committed to and trained for specific occupations (e.g., a professor of English specializing in Shakespeare) not institutions, where new faculty are hired and promoted by existing faculty (who without tenure might refuse to hire candidates better than themselves) and where the evaluation process is resource intensive and must be undertaken by other faculty with multiple responsibilities to the institution. *See* Finkin, *supra*, at 98–127.

E. WHISTLEBLOWER PROTECTIONS

When Congress enacted the Civil Service Reform Act of 1978, it recognized the importance of protecting government employees who disclose wrongdoing from reprisals. The Report of the Senate Governmental Affairs Committee explained the rationale:

> Protecting employees who disclose government illegality, waste and corruption is a major step toward a more effective civil service. In the vast Federal bureaucracy, it is not difficult to conceal wrongdoing provided that no one summons the courage to disclose the truth. Whenever misdeeds take place in a Federal agency, there are employees who know that it has occurred, and who are outraged by it. What is needed is a means to assure them that they will not suffer if they help uncover and correct administrative abuses.

S. Rep. No. 95–969, at 8 (1978).

The Civil Service Reform Act of 1978 was the first statute providing general protection for federal employee whistleblowers. The statute has been amended several times since, generally to strengthen the protections. Meanwhile, the states have taken varying approaches to whistleblower protection, ranging from broad protection of public and private sector employees against retaliation for whistleblowing to protection limited to employees of state government. The scope of protection and the procedures for effectuating that protection represent policy judgments about how best to balance the benefits from the disclosure of wrongdoing by those in the best position to discover it against the potential harm to the governmental entity's mission from inaccurate disclosures, the potential that a broad scope of protection could lead to undue administrative and judicial intervention in matters of personnel management and the potential for abuse by, for example, employees who have performed poorly and fear discipline or dismissal.

1. FEDERAL EMPLOYEE WHISTLEBLOWER PROTECTION

The federal statute provides protection for employees in three ways. It provides a "safe" way for employees to report wrongdoing, provides them with protection against reprisals and provides for action to be taken against managers and others who take reprisals against employees who make protected disclosures.

Two agencies play critical roles in the federal regime: the Merit System Protection Board (MSPB) and the Office of Special Counsel (OSC). Originally housed within the MSPB, the OSC became a separate agency in 1989. OSC is headed by the Special Counsel who is appointed by the President with the advice and consent of the Senate for a term of five years, during which he or she may be removed only for "inefficiency, neglect of duty or malfeasance in office." 5 U.S.C. § 1211(b).

The statute, 5 U.S.C. § 2302(b)(8), declares it to be a prohibited personnel practice to:

> take or fail to take a personnel action with respect to any employee or applicant for employment because of
>
> (A) any disclosure of information by an employee or applicant which the employee or applicant reasonably believes evidences
>
> (i) a violation of any law, rule or regulation, or
>
> (ii) gross mismanagement, a gross waste of funds, an abuse of authority, or a substantial and specific danger to public health or safety,
>
> if such disclosure is not specifically prohibited by law and if such information is not specifically required by Executive

order to be kept secret in the interest of national defense or the conduct of foreign affairs; or

(B) any disclosure to the Special Counsel, or to the Inspector General of an agency or another employee designated by the head of the agency to receive such disclosures of information which the employee or applicant reasonably believes evidences

(i) a violation of any law, rule or regulation, or

(ii) gross mismanagement, a gross waste of funds, an abuse of authority, or a substantial and specific danger to public health or safety . . .

In many respects, the statute sweeps broadly. It protects applicants as well as incumbent employees. It does not appear to place limits on the class of parties to whom a protected disclosure may be made. Protection is not limited to disclosures of illegal conduct but encompasses disclosures of, for example, gross mismanagement, gross waste of funds and abuse of authority. It balances the benefits to be obtained from employee exposure of governmental misdeeds against the potential harm of inaccurate disclosures to the governmental entity's mission by requiring that the party making the disclosure have a reasonable belief that it evidences one of the specified misdeeds. However, the statute does not expressly define "disclosure." That task has been left to the MSPB and the Court of Appeals for the Federal Circuit.

HUFFMAN v. OFFICE OF PERSONNEL MANAGEMENT

United States Court of Appeals for the Federal Circuit, 2001.
263 F.3d 1341.

DYK, C.J.

BACKGROUND

On July 17, 1998, Kenneth D. Huffman ("petitioner") filed a complaint with the Office of Special Counsel ("OSC") alleging that he had been removed from his position as Assistant Inspector General by his employer, the Office of the Inspector General ("OIG") for the Office of Personnel Management ("agency"), for making disclosures protected by the WPA. Petitioner alleged that he made "protected disclosures" to his supervisor—Patrick McFarland, the Inspector General of the agency * * * in four memoranda * * * [:]

[A] July 22, 1997, memorandum to McFarland which included allegations that McFarland improperly preselected an agency employee for a senior executive service ("SES") position. Petitioner further asserted that the July 22, 1997, memorandum made other protected disclosures when he reminded McFarland "that he had confronted [McFarland] in the past concerning instances of abuse of authority and gross mismanagement by various OIG managers."

* * * [A] May 22, 1998, memorandum to McFarland in which petitioner urged that the OIG "had circumvented merit system principles when it hired certain auditors * * * as 'program analysts' under direct hire authority, without competition." Petitioner alleged that hiring these people without competition was "a violation of law, rule, or regulation."

* * * [A] May 29, 1998, memorandum to McFarland * * * express[ing] his disagreement with a services contract between the OIG and an organization known as All Star Personnel, to perform an organizational study, urging "that it would be a gross waste of taxpayer money to continue to pay All–Star Personnel for their contracting services to provide an organizational assessment of the OIG."

* * * [A] June 18, 1998, memorandum to McFarland regarding the workplace behavior of other OIG employees. Among other things, petitioner alleged that the Deputy Assistant Inspector General for Audits directed three auditors who were hired under the special hiring authority of the agency's Outstanding Scholar Program to falsify their government employment applications (SF–171s).

On October 16, 1998, the OSC closed its inquiry, finding that petitioner did not make any disclosures protected under the WPA, and informed petitioner of his right to seek corrective action from the Board.

On December 21, 1998, petitioner filed an Individual Right of Action ("IRA") appeal with the Board. * * * Relying on *Willis v. Department of Agriculture,* 141 F.3d 1139, 1143 (Fed.Cir.1998), and *Horton v. Department of Navy,* 66 F.3d 279, 282 (Fed.Cir.1995), the administrative judge held that petitioner's "reports to McFarland, his supervisor, are not disclosures of the type the WPA was designed to encourage and protect. The administrative judge reasoned:

> In complaining to McFarland, the [petitioner] merely was expressing disagreement with McFarland's responses (or lack thereof) to the [petitioner's] suggestions and advice and McFarland's interpretation and implementation of certain OIG policies and procedures. The [petitioner] took no action to bring an issue to the attention of authorities in a position to correct fraudulent or illegal activity.
>
> * * *

The administrative judge further * * * found that in relating his views on various matters to his supervisor, petitioner "did no more than carry out his required everyday job responsibilities and held that under *Willis,* a disclosure cannot be protected by the WPA if an employee is merely performing his required duties. * * *

Petitioner petitioned for review to the full Board, but the Board denied his petition. * * *

DISCUSSION

* * *

To maintain an IRA under the WPA, a petitioner must establish Board jurisdiction by exhausting administrative remedies before the OSC and making non-frivolous allegations that "(1) he engaged in whistleblowing activity by making a protected disclosure under 5 U.S.C. § 2302(b)(8), and (2) the disclosure was a contributing factor in the agency's decision to take or fail to take a personnel action as defined by 5 U.S.C. § 2302(a)." In the absence of a protected disclosure, the Board is without jurisdiction to entertain an IRA appeal under the WPA. Whether the Board possessed jurisdiction is a question of law which we review without deference.
* * *

At the outset, this case requires us to interpret the WPA in two separate contexts: first, where complaints are made by an employee to a supervisor about the conduct of the supervisor, and, second, where complaints are made to a supervisor about the conduct of other government employees or about other matters within the scope of the WPA.

The WPA makes it a prohibited personnel action to take or fail to take a personnel action because of "*any* disclosure of information by an employee or applicant which the employee or applicant reasonably believes evidences—(i) a violation of any law, rule, or regulation, or (ii) gross mismanagement, a gross waste of funds, an abuse of authority, or a substantial and specific danger to public health or safety." 5 U.S.C. § 2302(b)(8)(A) (1994) (emphasis added). Petitioner correctly points out that this language—"any disclosure"—was deliberately broad. The predecessor version of the current statute, enacted by the Civil Service Reform Act of 1978, Pub.L. No. 95–454, 92 Stat. 1111, was narrower, reciting that it was only a prohibited personnel action to take or fail to take a personnel action because of "*a* disclosure of information by an employee." 5 U.S.C. § 2302(b)(8)(A) (Supp. III 1979) (emphasis added). The Whistleblower Protection Act of 1989 amended this language to broaden the scope of disclosures covered by the WPA from "*a* disclosure" to "*any* disclosure." Pub.L. No. 101–12, § 4(a)(3), 103 Stat. 32 (emphases added). The Senate Committee on Governmental Affairs, explained the change as follows:

> The Committee intends that disclosures be encouraged. The OSC, the Board and the courts should not erect barriers to disclosures which will limit the necessary flow of information from employees who have knowledge of government wrongdoing. For example, it is inappropriate for disclosures to be protected only if they are made for certain purposes or to certain employees or only if the employee is the first to raise the issue. [The Senate bill] emphasizes this point by changing the phrase "a disclosure" to "any disclosure" in the statutory definition. This is simply to stress that any disclosure is protected (if it meets the requisite reasonable belief test and is not required to be kept confidential).

S.Rep. No. 100–413, at 13 (1988) (italics in original).

Congress later amended section 2302 and other sections of the WPA in 1994. Among other things, the 1994 amendment expanded whistleblower protection by adding "a decision to order psychiatric testing or examination," and "any other significant change in duties, responsibilities, or working conditions" to the list of prohibited personnel actions in 5 U.S.C. § 2302(a)(2)(A). Pub.L. No. 103–424, § 5(a)(2), 108 Stat. 4361, 4363 (1994). The disclosure language of 5 U.S.C. § 2302(b)(8)(A)(i) was not itself amended in 1994 * * * . However, we note that the committees in 1994 criticized the Board for continuing to take a narrow view of what constitutes a protected disclosure. For example, the House report for the 1994 amendment stated:

> Perhaps the most troubling precedents involve the Board's inability to understand that "any" means "any." The WPA protects "any" disclosure evidencing a reasonable belief of specified misconduct, a cornerstone to which the MSPB remains blind. The only restrictions are for classified information or material the release of which is specifically prohibited by statute. Employees must disclose that type of information through confidential channels to maintain protection; otherwise there are no exceptions.

H.R. Rep. 103–769, at 18 (1994). * * *

A. *Complaints to a Supervisor About the Supervisor's Conduct*

In our decisions in *Willis* and *Horton,* we held that the WPA does not apply where an employee makes complaints to the employee's supervisor about the supervisor's own conduct. In *Willis,* the aggrieved employee—William Willis—sent letters to his supervisor in which Willis was critical of the supervisor. The agency thereafter ordered Willis to be reassigned, but he refused to accept the assignment and eventually retired. This court held that Willis's letters to his supervisor did not qualify as protected disclosures. In so holding, this court stated:

> Discussion and even disagreement with supervisors over job-related activities is a normal part of most occupations. It is entirely ordinary for an employee to fairly and reasonably disagree with a supervisor who overturns the employee's decision. In complaining to his supervisors, Willis has done no more than voice his dissatisfaction with his superiors' decision.
>
> * * *

In *Horton,* the appellant—John Horton—had previously criticized the behavior of several fellow library staff members, including his supervisor, to the staff members themselves as well as to his supervisor. Mr. Horton's supervisor issued several warnings, at least one of which in writing, to Mr. Horton based on what the supervisor perceived as a confrontational attitude. After an incident in which Mr. Horton allegedly had a "tantrum" regarding a fellow library staff member, the supervisor initiated a removal action. This court held that Mr. Horton's verbal and written criticisms "were not the 'disclosure' contemplated by statute, for these criticisms were made directly to the persons about whose behavior Mr. Horton complained." We further noted that an allegation "directed to the wrongdoers themselves is not normally viewable as whistleblowing" under the WPA and that criticism directed directly at the wrongdoers does not further the purpose of the WPA "to encourage disclosure of wrongdoing to persons who may be in a position to act to remedy it, either directly by management authority, or indirectly as in disclosure to the press."

Petitioner urges that these cases were incorrectly decided in light of the language of the statute and the legislative history described above, and points out that those decisions did not explicitly attempt to reconcile the statutory interpretation with the language of the WPA. We are, of course, bound by *Willis* and *Horton,* but even if we were not, we could not agree with petitioner. The WPA by its terms requires that the employee have made a "disclosure" to trigger the protection of the Act. While that term is not explicitly defined in the statute, it is a basic principle of statutory interpretation that undefined terms in a statute are deemed to have their ordinarily understood meaning

The term "disclosure" is defined in *Webster's Dictionary* as "the act or an instance of disclosing: the act or an instance of opening up to view, knowledge, or comprehension." *Webster's Third New International Dictionary* 645 (1968). That dictionary further defines "disclose" as: "2a: to expose to view . . .: lay open or uncover (something hidden from view) <excavations disclosed many artifacts> b: to make known: open up to general knowledge." *Id.* * * *. *See also Black's Law Dictionary* 477 (7th ed.1999) (defining "disclosure" as: "The act or process of making known something that was previously unknown; a revelation of facts"); *Random House Webster's Unabridged Dictionary* 562 (2d ed.1998) (defining "disclose" as: "1. to make known; reveal or uncover: to disclose a secret. 2. to cause to appear; allow to be seen; lay open to view." * * *). In other words, the term "disclosure" means to reveal something that was hidden and not known. It is also quite significant that Congress in the WPA did not use a word with a broader connotation such as "report" or "state."

When an employee reports or states that there has been misconduct by a wrongdoer to the wrongdoer, the employee is not making a "disclosure" of misconduct. If the misconduct occurred, the wrongdoer necessarily knew of the conduct already because he is the one that engaged in the misconduct. The policies of the WPA hardly require a different result. The purpose of the statute is to encourage disclosures that are likely to remedy the wrong. The wrongdoer is not such a person. Extending the WPA to cover reports to a supervisor of the supervisor's own misconduct would also have drastic adverse consequences. As we stated in *Willis,* "[d]iscussion and even disagreement with supervisors over job-related duties is a normal part of most occupations. If every complaint made to a supervisor concerning an employee's disagreement with the supervisor's actions were considered to be a disclosure protected under the WPA, virtually every employee who was disciplined could claim the protection of the Act. Although Congress intended that the WPA's coverage be broad, we think it unlikely that Congress intended the Act to extend that far, and we hold that it did not.

B. *Complaints to a Supervisor About Other Employees' Conduct or Other Matters*

Both parties agree that two of the reports involved complaints to McFarland about persons other than McFarland himself. First, the May 22, 1998, memorandum alleged that OIG employees had impermissibly hired certain auditors under the agency's Outstanding Scholars Program, rather than filling the positions through open competition. Second, the June 18, 1998, memorandum alleged that the Deputy Assistant Inspector General for Audits directed three OIG auditors who were "impermissibly" hired under the Outstanding Scholars Program to "falsify" their government employment applications.

The administrative judge below and the government's brief both suggest that reports of wrongdoing are not protected if they are not made to persons in a position to correct the alleged wrongdoing. The administrative judge apparently concluded that petitioner's supervisor here somehow lacked the authority to correct wrongdoing by the other employees. In holding that complaints to a supervisor about the supervisor's own wrongdoing are not protected under the WPA, this court in *Willis* and *Horton* stated that reports must be made to persons in a position to act to remedy the alleged wrongdoing. * * *

Willis and *Horton* do not require that the reports must be made to a person with actual authority to correct the wrong. Indeed, *Horton* itself and the legislative history of the WPA recognize that disclosures to the press are protected. * * * No requirement of actual authority is found in the language of the statute, and we think it is quite clear that reports do not need to be made to those with authority to correct the alleged wrongdoing in order to be protected by the WPA. Any government employee, in a supervisory position, other than the wrongdoer himself, is in a position to "correct" or "remedy" the abuse by bringing the matter to the attention of a higher authority. To be consistent with the statute and its purposes, complaints to supervisors concerning wrongdoing by other employees or other matters within the scope of the WPA should be encouraged and not discouraged, even if the supervisor himself lacks authority to directly correct the wrongdoing. Such complaints constitute disclosures under the WPA, if, of course, they also meet the other requirements of the statute.

Alternatively, with respect to the May 22, 1998, and June 18, 1998, disclosures, the government argues that reports of misconduct are not covered by the WPA if the disclosures are part of the employee's normal duties. The government argues that reports of misconduct by petitioner here were part of his normal duties. The government relies principally on *Willis,* where we held that Willis's mere performance of his "required everyday job responsibilities" was not a protected disclosure under the WPA, because Willis "cannot be said to have risked his personal job security by merely performing his required duties." We noted that all government employees are expected to perform their required everyday job responsibilities "pursuant to the fiduciary obligation which every employee owes to his employer."

* * *

It is important, however, to distinguish three quite different situations. *First,* there is the situation in which the employee has, as part of his normal duties, been assigned the task of investigating and reporting wrongdoing by government employees and, in fact, reports that wrongdoing through normal channels. A law enforcement officer whose duties include the investigation of crime by government employees and reporting the results of an assigned investigation to his immediate supervisor is a quintessential example. Employees of an inspector general's office may be in a similar position. *Willis* holds that reporting in connection with assigned normal duties is not a protected disclosure covered by the Act. While the language of the Act is ambiguous as to whether normal duties reports are covered, the core purposes of the WPA are simply not implicated by such reporting. Extending the WPA's protections to such situations would be inconsistent with the WPA's recognition of the importance of fostering the performance of normal work obligations and subjecting employees to normal, non-retaliatory discipline.

* * *

The WPA was established to protect employees who go above and beyond the call of duty and report infractions of law that are hidden. The situations which Congress specifically covered in 1978 and 1989 were disclosures to the press or to Congress itself. As we previously stated in *Willis,* "the WPA is intended to protect government employees who risk their own personal job security for the advancement of the public good by disclosing abuses by government personnel."

* * *

Second, there is the situation in which an employee with such assigned investigatory responsibilities reports the wrongdoing outside of normal channels. An example is a law enforcement officer who is responsible for investigating crime by government employees who, feeling that the normal chain of command is unresponsive, reports wrongdoing outside of normal channels. This is clearly a disclosure protected by the Act, and the Act's core purposes are served by such a disclosure.

Third, there is the situation in which the employee is obligated to report the wrongdoing, but such a report is not part of the employee's normal duties or the employee has not been assigned those duties. The government argues here that the petitioner was obliged here to report all wrongdoing, without regard to his responsibility to investigate it, and that his reports of wrongdoing are not protected disclosures. We cannot accept the government's contention. A report may be a disclosure protected by the Act, though the employee can also be disciplined for failure to make the report. * * *

It is unclear from the Board's decision whether the reports of May 22, 1998, and June 18, 1998, concerning the conduct of other employees fall into the first, second, or third categories. We remand to the Board for consideration of this issue under the appropriate standard, which we have articulated above.

NOTES

1. The court offers two rationales for its conclusion that employees' reports to their supervisors of the supervisors' wrongdoing are not protected disclosures: reliance on dictionary definitions of "disclosure," and policy concerns underlying the Whistleblower Protection Act. As discussed earlier, determining the scope of whistleblower protection requires balancing the benefits of disclosure by those in the best position to know of wrongdoing against the potential harms to the government entity from inaccurate disclosures, undue interference in personnel management and employee abuse. How did the court strike the balance on the issue of what constitutes a "disclosure"? Could the court's decision have the ironic result of encouraging employees to by-pass their supervisors who they believe to be engaged in misconduct and report them to higher authorities or the media?

2. Consider the court's approach to disclosures that arise out of an employee's job duties. Are there any similarities between the policy concerns considered by the court under the WPA and those concerns considered by the Court in defining the scope of First Amendment protection in *Garcetti v. Ceballos*, presented in Chapter 2 at page 19?

3. Consider the four memoranda that Huffman wrote. Did they report violations of law, rule or regulation, gross mismanagement, gross waste of funds or abuse of authority?

The federal Whistleblower Protection Act utilizes the OSC to provide a safe conduit for whistleblowers to report misdeeds. Under 5 U.S.C. § 1213, employees, former employees and applicants for employment may disclose to OSC in writing evidence that they reasonably believe evidences violations of law, rule or regulation, gross mismanagement, gross waste of government funds, abuse of authority or a substantial and specific danger to public health or safety. The Special Counsel must, within 15 days, determine whether there is a substantial likelihood that the information disclosed evidences such misdeeds. Upon such a finding, the Special Counsel transmits the information to the agency head who is required to file a report with the Special Counsel within 60 days, unless the time is extended for good cause. The report must be signed by the agency head and must describe the information disclosed, the agency's investigation and any evidence obtained in the investigation, whether there were apparent violations of laws or regulations, and any action taken or planned as a result of the investigation. OSC transmits the report to the whistleblower who has 15 days to submit comments. OSC transmits the report and the comments, along with any OSC comments or recommendations, to the President and the congressional committees with jurisdiction over the agency.

Disclosure to OSC has two advantages for the whistleblower. First, the statute mandates that the Special Counsel keep the whistleblower's identity confidential unless the whistleblower consents to its release or disclosure of the identity "is necessary because of an imminent danger to public health or safety or imminent violation of any criminal law." 5 U.S.C. § 1213(h). Second, disclosures to OSC are not subject to the exception for disclosures "specifically prohibited by law [or] * * * specifically required by Executive order to be kept secret in the interest of national defense or the conduct of foreign affairs." Generally disclosures made to others are protected but if they fall into the exception they are not protected. The scope of this exception has been the subject of considerable debate.

MacLEAN v. DEPARTMENT OF HOMELAND SECURITY

United State Merit Systems Protection Board, 2009.
112 M.S.P.R. 4.

Prior to his removal, the appellant was employed by the agency's Transportation Security Agency (TSA) in the SV–I position of Federal Air Marshal (FAM). The relevant facts are undisputed. In July of 2003, the appellant received a text message on his government-issued mobile phone stating that all RON (Remain Overnight) missions up to August 9th would be cancelled. The appellant alleged that he believed that the cancellation of these missions was detrimental to public safety. He raised this concern with his supervisor. He then attempted to raise it with the Office of the Inspector General. On July 29, 2003, he disclosed the text message to the media. The agency conducted an investigation. Thereafter, by letter dated September 13, 2005, the agency proposed to remove the appellant based on three charges: (1) Unauthorized Media Appearance; (2) Unauthorized Release of Information to the Media; and (3) Unauthorized Disclosure of SSI [Sensitive Security Information]. In the notice of removal, however, the deciding official determined that charges (1) and (2) of the proposal were not sustained by the evidence of record. He sustained charge (3), Unauthorized Disclosure of SSI. In that charge, the agency alleged that on July 29, 2003, the appellant disclosed to the media that all Las Vegas Field Office FAMs were sent a text message to their government-issued mobile phones that all RON missions would be cancelled, or words to that effect, in violation of 49 C.F.R. § 1520.5(b)(8)(ii). Effective April 11, 2006, the agency removed the appellant based upon its decision to sustain charge (3) * * *

[The MSPB then recounted the procedural history of the case. MacClean filed an appeal with the MSPB of his removal. Subsequently, on August 31, 2006, the agency found the disclosure to be Safety Sensitive Information. Such decisions' findings are considered to be final orders reviewable by the courts of appeals. MacClean then requested and was granted a dismissal of his appeal of his removal without prejudice so that he could appeal the finding that his disclosure was SSI. The Ninth Circuit affirmed the agency's finding that the disclosure was of SSI, *MacLean v.*

Department of Homeland Security, 543 F.3d 1145 (9th Cir.2008), and MacClean refiled the appeal of his removal with the MSPB.]

* * *

The initial statutory provision at issue in this matter provides, in pertinent part, the following:

> **(s) Nondisclosure of Security Activities.—**
>
> **(1) In general.**—Notwithstanding section 552 of title 5, the Under Secretary shall prescribe regulations prohibiting the disclosure of information obtained or developed in carrying out security under authority of the Aviation and Transportation Security Act (Public Law 107–71) or under chapter 449 of this title if the Under Secretary decides that disclosing the information would—
>
> **(A)** be an unwarranted invasion of personal privacy;
>
> **(B)** reveal a trade secret or privileged or confidential commercial or financial information; or
>
> **(C)** *be detrimental to the security of transportation.*

49 U.S.C. § 114(s)(1) (emphasis added).

* * *

Congress initially required the federal agency responsible for civil aviation security to issue regulations prohibiting the disclosure of certain information in the interest of protecting air transportation. Federal Aviation Act of 1958, Pub.L. No. 93–366, §§ 202, 316(D), 72 Stat. 7449 (codified at 49 U.S.C. §§ 1341–1355). At that time, the Federal Aviation Administration (FAA) was the agency responsible for enforcing the requirement. *Id.* Later, Congress placed this responsibility in TSA. Aviation and Transportation Security Act of 2001 (ATSA), Pub.L. No. 107–71, § 101(e), 115 Stat. 597. Under this authority, the Under Secretary of TSA is required to "prescribe regulations prohibiting the disclosure of information obtained or developed in carrying out security * * * if the Under Secretary decides that disclosing the information would * * * be detrimental to the security of transportation." 49 U.S.C. § 114(s)(1)(C). Based upon this mandate, the Under Secretary has defined certain types of information as SSI and has limited the disclosure of that information to certain circumstances. 49 C.F.R. part 1520.

Sensitive Security Information is defined in the regulations as, among other things, "[s]pecific details of aviation security measures that are applied directly by the TSA and which includes, but is not limited to, information concerning specific numbers of Federal Air Marshals, deployments or missions, and the methods involved in such operations." 49 C.F.R. § 1520.7(j) (2003). Information of this kind, as well as records containing such information, constitutes SSI unless the Under Secretary provides in writing to the contrary. 49 C.F.R. § 1520.7. * * *

* * *

Under 49 U.S.C. §§ 114(s), 46110(a), when the Under Secretary determines by final order that particular material qualifies as SSI, that determination constitutes final agency action subject to judicial review. 49 U.S.C. § 46110. The statute authorizes review of such orders in the D.C. Circuit or the court of appeals for the circuit in which a complaining party resides or has its principal place of business. Congress provided the D.C. Circuit or U.S. Courts of Appeals with the exclusive jurisdiction to review the agency's SSI determination. * * *

* * *

In a Board appeal from an adverse action—

> an employee puts the agency in the position of plaintiff bearing the burden of first coming forward with evidence to establish the fact of misconduct, the burden of proof, and the ultimate burden of persuasion, with respect to the basis for the charge or charges. The employee (while denominated appellant) has the advantageous evidentiary position of a defendant with respect to that aspect of the case.

Jackson v. Veterans Administration, 768 F.2d 1325, 1329 (Fed.Cir.1985).

We find that the agency can meet its burden of proof on the charge because where, as here, a federal court has determined that information relevant to a Board appeal constituted SSI, that determination is binding in the Board proceeding. * * *

The fact that the agency did not issue its order finding the information the appellant disclosed to be SSI until after it had removed him does not alter our conclusion * * * because Congress provided individuals with an opportunity to challenge TSA's SSI determination before the United States Court of Appeals, and the appellant actually availed himself of that opportunity. Pursuant to 49 U.S.C. § 46110(c), the U.S. Court of Appeals for the Ninth Circuit gained "exclusive jurisdiction" over the appellant's petition challenging TSA's SSI determination "when [his] petition [was] sent [to the appropriate TSA official]." Because this grant of "exclusive jurisdiction" in federal court was triggered in this case, the Board lacks authority to review TSA's determination. * * *

* * *

The agency argues that a disclosure of information that is SSI, except to "persons with a need to know," is prohibited by statute and regulation, and as such, the appellant cannot seek the protection of the WPA to cover his alleged misconduct. The appellant contends that only agency regulations prohibit disclosure of information that is SSI, and that the Board has interpreted the exclusion from whistleblower protection for disclosures that are "prohibited by law or Executive Order" to apply only to those disclosures not allowed by "statutes and court interpretations of statutes."

Title 5 U.S.C. § 2302(b)(8)(A) excludes from coverage disclosures "specifically prohibited by law" or Executive order. The agency does not argue that any Executive order prohibited disclosure of the information the appellant allegedly disclosed. The question then is whether any "law" prohibited the alleged disclosure. The Board has held that "prohibited by law," as that term is used in section 2302(b)(8), means prohibited by statutory law as opposed to regulation. *Kent v. General Services Administration,* 56 M.S.P.R. 536 (1993). In *Kent,* the Board addressed the question of whether the General Services Administration (GSA) regulations fell within the parameters of the "prohibited by law" language set forth in 5 U.S.C. § 2302(b)(8)(A). The Board ruled that regulations promulgated by a federal agency do not fall within the term "law" as it is used in the Civil Service Reform Act of 1978 (CSRA), as amended by the WPA, after reviewing the construction of the statute and the legislative history.

Here, Congress required in the ATSA that the agency "prescribe regulations prohibiting the disclosure of information obtained or developed in carrying out security * * * if the Under Secretary decides that disclosing the information would * * * be detrimental to the security of transportation. 49 U.S.C. § 114(s)(1)(C). For the reasons set forth below, we find that disclosures that are prohibited by the regulations promulgated pursuant to 49 U.S.C. § 114(s) are "prohibited by law" within the meaning of 5 U.S.C. § 2302(b)(8)(A).

The starting point for the Board's analysis of the "prohibited by law" language is *Chrysler Corp. v. Brown,* 441 U.S. 281, 99 S.Ct. 1705, 60 L.Ed.2d 208 (1979). In *Chrysler,* the Court undertook the analogous task of interpreting a statute that contained a special exception for activities "authorized by law." In considering whether an agency regulation that authorized the activity satisfied the condition, the Court explained:

> It has been established in a variety of contexts that properly promulgated, substantive agency regulations have the force and effect of law. This doctrine is so well established that agency regulations implementing federal statutes have been held to pre-empt state law under the Supremacy Clause. It would therefore take a clear showing of contrary legislative intent before the phrase "authorized by law" in [the statutory section at issue] could be held to have a narrower ambit than the traditional understanding.

441 U.S. at 295–96.

Chrysler thus sets up a default rule, and a specific exception. That is, agency regulations that are (1) properly promulgated, and (2) substantive, must be accorded the force and effect of law absent a clear showing of contrary legislative intent. * * *

* * *

Consequently, "absent a clear showing of contrary legislative intent" the phrase "prohibited by law" in 5 U.S.C. § 2302(b)(8)(A) must be read to include disclosures prohibited by 49 C.F.R. § 1520.7 (2003). In *Kent,* the Board examined the language and legislative history of 5 U.S.C. § 2302(b)(8)(A) and discovered "a clear legislative intent to limit the term 'specifically prohibited by law' * * * to statutes and court interpretations of statutes." 56 M.S.P.R. at 542.

With regard to the statutory language, the Board concluded that inclusion of the phrase "specifically prohibited by law" following other statutory language referring to "a violation of any law, rule, or regulation," "indicated that the term 'law' was not intended to encompass rules and regulations." 56 M.S.P.R. at 542 We do not find that this distinction evidences a clear showing of legislative intent. The differing grammatical structures of the phrases are not compatible. Indeed, drawing a distinction between the phrases "of any law, rule, or regulation" and "by law" based simply on the latter's failure to include rule, or regulation begs the question at issue: whether the default construction of by law to include regulations has been overcome by clear legislative intent. Given the traditional default rule, Congress would have no reason to use the broader (and redundant) phrase "by law, rule, or regulation" when "by law" suffices. * * *

The Board in *Kent* also relied upon legislative history to support its conclusion that disclosures prohibited by regulation are not prohibited "by law" under the CSRA. The Board opined that "Congress' concern with internal agency rules and regulations impeding the disclosure of government wrongdoing is consistent with this restrictive reading of the statutory language." The Board also cited a passage from the House Conference Report explaining that "prohibited by law" refers to "statutory law and court interpretations of those statutes * * * not * * * to agency rules and regulations."

A closer examination of the legislative history indicates that Congress' intent is at best ambiguous, and therefore does not meet the standard of clarity required by *Chrysler*. The original version of the bill as introduced in both the House and the Senate protected disclosures that were "not prohibited by law, rule, or regulation." The Senate version was amended by the Senate Committee on Governmental Affairs to substitute the phrase "not prohibited by statute." The House version was amended by the House Committee on Post Office and Civil Service to substitute the phrase "not prohibited by law." The full House and Senate each passed their respective versions of the bill, both as S. 2640. In conference, the House language "not prohibited by law" was selected in lieu of the Senate language "not prohibited by statute." The selection of the broader phrase "by law" evidences Congressional intent to expand the scope of the exemption beyond mere statutes to include all "law." Under the general rules of statutory construction, Congress can be presumed to have known that its selection of the broader phrase "by law," in the absence of any limiting language, could expand the scope of the exemption to include all "law."

Moreover, the legislative history also shows that even the Senate's adoption of the narrower phrase "by statute" was not intended to exclude substantive regulations mandated by Congress, such as those promulgated pursuant to 49 U.S.C. § 114(s). The Senate Committee on Governmental Affairs modified the original bill to limit the exemption to disclosures prohibited "by statute," out of "concern that the limitation of protection in S. 2640 to those disclosures 'not prohibited by law, rule, or regulation,' would encourage the adoption of *internal procedural regulations against disclosure,* and thereby enable an agency to discourage an employee from coming forward with allegations of wrongdoing." S.Rep. No. 95–969, 95th Cong., 2d Sess. 12 (1978), *reprinted in* 1978 U.S.C.C.A.N. 2723, 2743–44 (emphasis added). "Rules of agency organization, procedure, or practice" are recognized as distinct from the "substantive rules" that are authorized by Congress and can have the force of law. Thus, by expressly excluding "internal procedural regulations," the Senate Committee implicitly included substantive agency regulations.

The House Conference Report explanation that "prohibited by law" refers to "statutory law and court interpretations of those statutes * * * not * * * to agency rules and regulations," could be construed in isolation to suggest an intent to the contrary to protect disclosures prohibited by a substantive regulation. However, in light of the contrary indicia of Congressional intent, this language alone cannot establish the "*clear showing* of contrary legislative intent" required before the phrase "prohibited by law" "could be held to have a narrower ambit than the traditional understanding." * * *

Although the AJ in this case did not undertake a detailed *Chrysler* analysis, his rationale for distinguishing *Kent* was based upon the standards addressed in *Chrysler.* He observed that the statute under which the regulation at issue in *Kent* was promulgated did not "require [the agency] to include in its regulations categories of information that may not be disclosed to a third party, as the GSA alleged Mr. Kent did in a charge underlying its action against him. Therefore, at most, Mr. Kent's disclosure(s) violated the regulations, but not the law that mandated them." The same point made under the *Chrysler* framework would be that * * * Congress did not grant the GSA authority to promulgate a regulation that prohibited the disclosure of information. In other words, the Board in *Kent* went too far by holding that a regulation could *never* be a law prohibiting disclosure within the meaning of 5 U.S.C. § 2302(b)(8). The same outcome could have been reached by holding simply that the GSA regulation at issue was not entitled to the force and effect of law under the governing standards. In contrast, those standards mandate that 49 C.F.R. § 1520.7 (2003) be given the force and effect of law in the context of 5 U.S.C. § 2302(b)(8)(A). Based upon the foregoing, we find that a disclosure in violation of the regulations governing SSI, which were promulgated pursuant to 49 U.S.C. § 114(s), is "prohibited by law" within the meaning of 5 U.S.C. § 2302(b)(8)(A) and thus cannot give rise to whistleblower protection.

NOTES

1. Consider the following additional information as reported by the Government Accountability Project which represented MacClean. See http://www.whistleblower.org/doc/2008/MacLean%20Fact%20Sheet.pdf. In July 2003, the Department of Homeland Security warned of an imminent suicide terrorist threat. The text message advising that all overnight assignments were cancelled meant that many long distance flights from Las Vegas would have no air marshal coverage because such coverage would require overnight accommodations. MacClean reasonably believed that the message would result in no coverage for some flights that were most at risk of terrorist attack. After he disclosed the text message to the media, congressional protests led the agency to cancel the ban on overnight assignments and to explain that it had been a mistake. Was MacClean's disclosure the type of whistleblower action that Congress intended to protect? On the other hand, if the disclosure had not led to cancellation of the ban on overnight assignments, would its public release have itself endangered public safety by alerting terrorists that long distance flights were operating without air marshal protection? How should the balance between protecting the government entity's mission and gaining the benefits of exposure of government misdeeds be struck in a case such as this one?

2. If MacClean's disclosure had not been prohibited by law, would it have qualified for protection? If so, under which category of protected disclosure would it have qualified?

3. Note the timing of the events. The disclosure was made in July 2003, but the agency did not declare that the information was SSI until three years later. Should this have made a difference? Why did the MSPB discount the three year gap?

The *MacClean* and *Huffman* cases came to the MSPB by different routes. Together, they illustrate the two avenues that may be available to whistleblowers to seek redress against retaliation they have suffered. As *MacClean* illustrates, civil service protected employees may assert violations of the Whistleblower Protection Act as part of their defense in appealing adverse actions that may be appealed to the MSPB.

The protections against reprisals, however, encompass personnel actions that are not appealable to the MSPB and protect individuals, such as job applicants, who are not otherwise civil service protected. As *Huffman* illustrates, whistleblowers alleging illegal retaliation may file a complaint of a prohibited personnel practice with OSC. The Special Counsel may seek corrective action from the MSPB or may terminate the investigation. If the Special Counsel terminates the investigation, the complainant may, within 60 days, file an individual right of action with the MSPB. If the Special Counsel has had the complaint for 120 days and has not notified the complainant that the Special Counsel will seek corrective actions, the complainant may file an individual right of action.

Under either route, the whistleblower may establish a prima facie case by proving by preponderance of the evidence that he or she made a protected disclosure and that the disclosure was a contributing factor in the personnel decision at issue. The agency may then establish an affirmative defense by proving by clear and convincing evidence that it would have taken the same action even in the absence of the protected disclosure. 5 U.S.C. § 1221(e). See, e.g., *Fellhoelter v. Department of Agriculture*, 568 F.3d 965 (Fed.Cir. 2009).

The Whistleblower Protection Act also provides for disciplining federal employees who retaliate against whistleblowers. When the Special Counsel determines that an employee has committed a prohibited personnel practice by retaliating against a whistleblower, the Special Counsel may prosecute the employee before the MSPB. The employee has the right to respond and the right to a hearing before an MSPB administrative judge. If the MSPB ultimately finds that the employee committed a prohibited personnel practice, it may discipline the employee by removal, reduction in grade, debarment from federal employment for up to five years, suspension, reprimand or assessment of a civil penalty of up to $1,000.

2. STATE WHISTLEBLOWER PROTECTION

A Statutory Sampler

CALIFORNIA

California Whistleblowing Protection Act, CAL. GOV'T CODE §§ 8547–8547.12

§ 8547.1 Declaration of Findings

The Legislature finds and declares that state employees should be free to report waste, fraud, abuse of authority, violation of law, or threat to public health without fear of retribution. The Legislature further finds and declares that public servants best serve the citizenry when they can be candid and honest without reservation in conducting the people's business.

§ 8547.2 Definitions

* * *

(b) "Improper governmental activity" means any activity by a state agency or by an employee that is undertaken in the performance of the employee's official duties, whether or not that action is within the scope of his or her employment, and that (1) is in violation of any state or federal law or regulation, including, but not limited to, corruption, malfeasance, bribery, theft of government property, fraudulent claims, fraud, coercion, conversion, malicious prosecution, misuse of government property, or willful omission to perform duty, or (2) is economically wasteful, or involves gross misconduct, incompetency, or inefficiency. * * *

* * *

(d) "Protected disclosure" means any good faith communication that discloses or demonstrates an intention to disclose information that may evidence (1) an improper governmental activity or (2) any condition that may significantly threaten the health or safety of employees or the public if the disclosure or intention to disclose was made for the purpose of remedying that condition.

* * *

§ 8547.3. Use or attempt to use official authority or influence to interfere with disclosure of information; prohibition; civil liability

(a) An employee may not directly or indirectly use or attempt to use the official authority or influence of the employee for the purpose of intimidating, threatening, coercing, commanding, or attempting to intimidate, threaten, coerce, or command any person for the purpose of interfering with the rights conferred pursuant to this article.

(b) For the purpose of subdivision (a), use of official authority or influence'' includes promising to confer, or conferring, any benefit; effecting, or threatening to effect, any reprisal; or taking, or directing others to take, or recommending, processing, or approving, any personnel action, including, but not limited to, appointment, promotion, transfer, assignment, performance evaluation, suspension, or other disciplinary action

(c) Any employee who violates subdivision (a) may be liable in an action for civil damages brought against the employee by the offended party.

(d) Nothing in this section shall be construed to authorize an individual to disclose information otherwise prohibited by or under law.

§ 8547.4. Administrative authority; employee engaging in improper governmental activities; procedure

The State Auditor shall administer the provisions of this article and shall investigate and report on improper governmental activities. If, after investigating, the State Auditor finds that an employee may have engaged or participated in improper governmental activities, the State Auditor shall send a copy of the investigative report to the employee's appointing power. Within 60 days after receiving a copy of the State Auditor's investigative report, the appointing power shall either serve a notice of adverse action upon the employee who is the subject of the investigative report or set forth in writing its reasons for not taking adverse action. The appointing power shall file a copy of the notice of adverse action with the State Personnel Board * * *, and shall submit a copy to the State Auditor. If the appointing power does not take adverse action, it shall submit its written reasons for not doing so to the State Auditor and the State Personnel Board, and adverse action may be taken * * * Any employee who is served with a notice of adverse action may appeal to the State Personnel Board * * *

§ 8547.5 Investigative Audits

Upon receiving specific information that any employee or state agency has engaged in an improper governmental activity, the State Auditor may conduct an investigative audit of the matter. The identity of the person providing the information that initiated the investigative audit shall not be disclosed without the written permission of the person providing the information unless the disclosure is to a law enforcement agency that is conducting a criminal investigation.

* * *

§ 8547.8 Reprisals or other improper acts * * *

(a) A state employee or applicant for state employment who files a written complaint with his or her supervisor, manager, or the appointing power alleging actual or attempted acts of reprisal, retaliation, threats, coercion, or similar improper acts prohibited by Section 8547.3, may also file a copy of the written complaint with the State Personnel Board, together with a sworn statement that the contents of the written complaint are true, or are believed by the affiant to be true, under penalty of perjury. The complaint filed with the board, shall be filed within 12 months of the most recent act of reprisal complained about.

(b) Any person who intentionally engages in acts of reprisal, retaliation, threats, coercion, or similar acts against a state employee or applicant for state employment for having made a protected disclosure, is subject to a fine not to exceed ten thousand dollars ($10,000) and imprisonment in the county jail for a period not to exceed one year. Pursuant to Section 19683, any state civil service employee who intentionally engages in that conduct shall be disciplined by adverse action * * * In addition to all other penalties provided by law, any person who intentionally engages in acts of reprisal, retaliation, threats, coercion, or similar acts against a state employee or applicant for state employment for having made a protected disclosure shall be liable in an action for damages brought against him or her by the injured party. Punitive damages may be awarded by the court where the acts of the offending party are proven to be malicious. Where liability has been established, the injured party shall also be entitled to reasonable attorney's fees as provided by law. However, any action for damages shall not be available to the injured party unless the injured party has first filed a complaint with the State Personnel Board pursuant to subdivision (a), and the board has issued, or failed to issue, findings pursuant to Section 19683(d). This section is not intended to prevent an appointing power, manager, or supervisor from taking, directing others to take, recommending, or approving any personnel action or from taking or failing to take a personnel action with respect to any state employee or applicant for state employment if the appointing power, manager, or supervisor reasonably believes any action or inaction is justified on the basis of evidence separate and apart from the fact that the person has made a protected disclosure as defined in subdivision (b) of Section 8547.2.(e). In any civil action or administrative proceeding, once it has been demonstrated by a preponderance of evidence that an activity protected by this article was a contributing factor in the alleged retaliation against a former, current, or prospective employee, the burden of proof shall be on the supervisor, manager, or appointing power to demonstrate by clear and convincing evidence that the alleged action would have occurred for legitimate, independent reasons even if the employee had not engaged in protected disclosures or refused an illegal order. If the supervisor, manager, or appointing power fails to meet this burden of proof in an adverse action against the employee in any administrative review, challenge, or adjudication in which retaliation has been demonstrated to be a contributing factor, the employee shall have a complete affirmative defense in the adverse action.

* * *

IDAHO

Idaho Protection of Public Employees Act, IDAHO CODE §§ 6–2101 to 6–2109

§ 6–2101 Legislative Intent

The legislature hereby finds, determines and declares that government constitutes a large proportion of the Idaho work force and that it is beneficial to the citizens of this state to protect the integrity of government by providing a legal cause of action for public employees who experience adverse action from their employer as a result of reporting waste and violations of a law, rule or regulation.

* * *

§ 6–2103 Definitions

* * *

(4)(a) "Employer" means the state of Idaho, or any political subdivision or governmental entity eligible to participate in the public employees retirement system, chapter 13, title 59, Idaho Code

* * *

§ 6–2104 Reporting of governmental waste or violations of law—Employer action

(1)(a) An employer may not take adverse action against an employee because the employee, or a person authorized to act on behalf of the employee, communicates in good faith the existence of any waste of public funds, property or manpower, or a violation or suspected violation of a law, rule or regulation adopted under the law of this state, a political subdivision of this state or the United States. Such communication shall be made at a time and in a manner which gives the employer reasonable opportunity to correct the waste or violation.

* * *

§ 6–2105 Remedies for employee bringing action—Proof required

* * *

(2) An employee who alleges a violation of this chapter may bring a civil action for appropriate injunctive relief or actual damages, or both, within one hundred eighty (180) days after the occurrence of the alleged violation of this chapter.

* * *

(4) To prevail in an action brought under the authority of this section, the employee shall establish, by a preponderance of the evidence, that the employee has suffered an adverse action because the employee, or a person acting on his behalf engaged or intended to engage in an activity protected under section 62104, Idaho Code

* * *

MAINE

Maine Whistleblower Protection Act, 26 M.R.S.A. §§ 831–840

* * *

§ 832 Definitions

* * *

2. Employer. "Employer" means a person who has one or more employees. "Employer" includes an agent of an employer and the State, or a political subdivision of the State. "Employer" also means all schools and local education agencies.

* * *

§ 833 Discrimination against certain employees prohibited

1. Discrimination prohibited. No employer may discharge, threaten or otherwise discriminate against an employee regarding the employee's compensation, terms, conditions, location or privileges of employment because:

A. The employee, acting in good faith, or a person acting on behalf of the employee, reports orally or in writing to the employer or a public body what the employee has reasonable cause to believe is a violation of a law or rule adopted under the laws of this State, a political subdivision of this State or the United States;

B. The employee, acting in good faith, or a person acting on behalf of the employee, reports to the employer or a public body, orally or in writing, what the employee has reasonable cause to believe is a condition or practice that would put at risk the health or safety of that employee or any other individual. The protection from discrimination provided in this section specifically includes school personnel who report safety concerns to school officials with regard to a violent or disruptive student;

* * *

2. Initial report to employer required; exception. Subsection 1 does not apply to an employee who has reported or caused to be reported a violation, or unsafe condition or practice to a public body, unless the employee has first brought the alleged violation, condition or practice to the attention of a person having supervisory authority with the employer and has allowed the employer a reasonable opportunity to correct that violation, condition or practice.

Prior notice to an employer is not required if the employee has specific reason to believe that reports to the employer will not result in promptly correcting the violation, condition or practice.

* * *

§ 834–A Arbitration before the Maine Human Rights Commission

An employee who alleges a violation of that employee's rights under section 833, and who has complied with the requirements of section 833, subsection 2, may bring a complaint before the Maine Human Rights Commission * * *

* * *

NEW JERSEY

Conscientious Employee Protection Act, N.J.S.A. §§ 34:10–1 to 34:19–8

* * *

§ 34:19–2 Definitions

As used in this act:

a. "Employer" means any individual, partnership, association, corporation or any person or group of persons acting directly or indirectly on behalf of or in the interest of an employer with the employer's consent and shall include all branches of State Government, or the several counties and municipalities thereof, or any other political subdivision of the State, or a school district, or any special district, or any authority, commission, or board or any other agency or instrumentality thereof.

* * *

§ 34:19–3 Retaliatory action prohibited

An employer shall not take any retaliatory action against an employee because the employee does any of the following:

a. Discloses, or threatens to disclose to a supervisor or to a public body an activity, policy or practice of the employer, or another employer, with whom there is a business relationship, that the employee reasonably believes:

(1) is in violation of a law, or a rule or regulation promulgated pursuant to law, including any violation involving deception of, or misrepresentation to, any shareholder, investor, client, patient, customer, employee, former employee, retiree or pensioner of the employer or any governmental entity, or, in the case of an employee who is a licensed or certified health care professional, reasonably believes constitutes improper quality of patient care; or

(2) is fraudulent or criminal, including any activity, policy or practice of deception or misrepresentation which the employee reasonably believes may defraud any shareholder, investor, client, patient, customer, employ-

ee, former employee, retiree or pensioner of the employer or any governmental entity;

* * *

c. Objects to, or refuses to participate in any activity, policy or practice which the employee reasonably believes:

* * *

(3) is incompatible with a clear mandate of public policy concerning the public health, safety or welfare or protection of the environment.

§ 34:19–4 Written notice required

The protection against retaliatory action provided by this act pertaining to disclosure to a public body shall not apply to an employee who makes a disclosure to a public body unless the employee has brought the activity, policy or practice in violation of a law, or a rule or regulation promulgated pursuant to law to the attention of a supervisor of the employee by written notice and has afforded the employer a reasonable opportunity to correct the activity, policy or practice. Disclosure shall not be required where the employee is reasonably certain that the activity, policy or practice is known to one or more supervisors of the employer or where the employee reasonably fears physical harm as a result of the disclosure provided, however, that the situation is emergency in nature.

§ 34:19–5 Civil action, jury trial, remedies

Upon a violation of any of the provisions of this act, an aggrieved employee or former employee may, within one year, institute a civil action in a court of competent jurisdiction. Upon the application of any party, a jury trial shall be directed to try the validity of any claim under this act specified in the suit. All remedies available in common law tort actions shall be available to prevailing plaintiffs. * * *

In addition, the court or jury may order: the assessment of a civil fine of not more than $10,000 for the first violation of the act and not more than $20,000 for each subsequent violation, which shall be paid to the State Treasurer for deposit in the General Fund; punitive damages; or both a civil fine and punitive damages. * * *

* * *

NOTES

1. State statutes tend to be of three types. Some provide protection broadly to private, as well as public, sector employees. Others apply only to employees of state government. A third group apply to state and local government employees. Do you see any relationship between the class of employees protected and the scope of protected disclosures? What are the advantages and disadvantages of each approach?

2. Some statutes require internal reporting before a report to a public authority will be protected. Others provide express protection only for reports

to public authorities. What are the advantages and disadvantages of these approaches?

3. Under broad statutes that protect private as well as public sector employees who report violations to public authorities, are public sector employees who report the violations to their own employers protected? Recall the *Huffman* case under the federal statute. The Michigan Whistleblowers' Protection Act protects private and public sector employees who report or are about to report a violation of law "to a public body." MICH. COMP. L. ANN. § 15.362. At one time, Michigan courts suggested that a public employee's report of wrongdoing must be made to a higher authority than the employee's employer for it to be protected by the statute. However, the Michigan Supreme Court disavowed that suggestion and held that a public employee's own employer is a public body and the employee's internal reporting is protected, even though a private employee's internal reporting would not be protected. *Brown v. Mayor of Detroit*, 478 Mich. 589, 734 N.W.2d 514 (2007). Note that the Maine statute reproduced above expressly protects internal and external reporting, and requires internal reporting prior to reporting to public authorities unless the whistleblower has specific reason to believe that internal reporting will not promptly correct the violation.

4. Some statutes simply require that the employee act in good faith to be protected. Others require that the employee's reports be based on a reasonable belief of wrongdoing. Still others place an affirmative obligation on the employee to take reasonable steps to ensure the accuracy of the reports. What are the policy advantages and disadvantages of these diverse approaches?

5. As the sample above shows, states employ a diversity of methods for redress of retaliation against whistleblowers. The options include making such retaliation actionable before administrative agencies, providing whistleblowers with private causes of action against the retaliating employer, providing whistleblowers with private causes of action against the retaliating manager, and providing a range of penalties that may be assessed against the retaliating manager. What are the advantages and disadvantages of each? What is the optimal mix of remedies?

6. For a comprehensive survey of state approaches to whistleblower protection see Elletta Sangrey Callahan & Terry Morehead Dworkin, The State of State Whistleblower Protection, 38 *Am. Bus. L.J.* 99 (2000).

MAIMONE v. CITY OF ATLANTIC CITY

Supreme Court of New Jersey, 2006.
188 N.J. 221, 903 A.2d 1055.

SKILLMAN, J.

* * *

In May 2000, defendant Arthur C. Snellbaker was appointed Chief of the Atlantic City Police Department. According to plaintiff, around eight months after Snellbaker's appointment, Captain William Glass told him at a staff meeting that he could not initiate any new promotion of prostitution investigations unless they "directly impacted the citizens of Atlantic City." Shortly thereafter, plaintiff's immediate supervisor, Sergeant Glenn Abrams, directed him to terminate all pending investigations into the promotion of prostitution and to conduct only narcotics investigations. Plaintiff alleges that Abrams told him that "they," referring to prostitution investigations, "don't exist." Plaintiff, who at that point was the only detective still actively involved in promotion of prostitution investigations, understood this directive to apply not only to him but also to all other officers in the Special Investigations Unit.

Around the same time Abrams gave plaintiff this directive, the files plaintiff had maintained regarding persons involved in the promotion of prostitution were removed from a filing cabinet under his control, and thereafter, plaintiff's access to those files was restricted. When plaintiff complained to Abrams about his loss of access to these files, Abrams allegedly told him: "You're never going to see the files again."

* * *

In 2001, Maimone also complained about Atlantic City's failure to enforce *N.J.S.A.* 2C:34–7, which makes it a fourth-degree offense for a sexually-oriented business to operate within 1,000 feet of a church or school. After the county prosecutor decided that *N.J.S.A.* 2C:34–7 should be enforced by the revocation of the mercantile licenses of offenders rather than by criminal prosecution, plaintiff wrote letters to the municipal solicitor requesting the initiation of proceedings to revoke the licenses of sexually-oriented businesses that were operating in violation of this prohibition. When the city solicitor failed to take any action, plaintiff sent a memorandum to Abrams, dated May 26, 2001, which stated in part:

> I am respectfully asking, that this Office request that the mercantile license of AC News and Video be revoked, due to the fact that this location is clearly in violation of 2C:34–7. This location is clearly a detriment to the neighborhood. There is a Covenant House for juveniles on the same block as well as an elementary school and Synagogue being nearby. As you are aware, it has been and continues to be the practice of the Atlantic County Prosecutor's Office, not to prosecute this statute. It is their contention that civil remedies (IE: Removal of Mercantile license) would be sufficient and thus relieving the Prosecutors Office from utilizing their limited resources in prosecution.
>
> If the city chooses not to enforce this statute in this matter, all future prosecutions will be jeopardized.

Within days after he sent this memorandum, Captain Glass said to plaintiff: "You're out of here, you're going to patrol." Effective June 10, 2001, plaintiff was transferred from his detective position in the Special Investigations Unit to patrol officer. Plaintiff was told that the reason for his transfer was an April 17, 2001 newspaper story that disclosed he had attended the wedding of a daughter of a suspected organized crime figure.

Plaintiff subsequently brought this CEPA action against Atlantic City and Chief Snellbaker. After the completion of discovery, defendants moved for summary judgment. The trial court * * * concluded that plaintiff had not presented evidence that could support a jury finding in his favor * * * that he "reasonably believed" Atlantic City's alleged decision to cease enforcing the provisions of the Code relating to promotion of prostitution and restricting the location of sexually-oriented businesses "violat[ed] * * * a clear mandate of public policy." *Ibid.* The court ruled that plaintiff's complaint about the municipality's failure to enforce these laws was simply a disagreement with a discretionary decision of supervisory police officials regarding the allocation of police personnel and resources. Consequently, the court concluded that plaintiff could not be found to have reasonably believed those discretionary policy decisions violated a clear mandate of public policy. Accordingly, the court granted defendants' motion for summary judgment.

The Appellate Division reversed in an unreported opinion. It concluded that the evidence, viewed in a light most favorable to plaintiff, could support a finding that he had an "objectively reasonable belief" that defendants had not simply reduced the police resources allocated to promotion of prostitution investigations, but had made a policy decision "to ignore violations of the prostitution laws within the City." * * *

* * *

Plaintiff rests his claim solely on subsection (3) of *N.J.S.A.* 34:19–3c. At the outset, it is appropriate to compare the elements of a claim under this subsection with a claim under c(1). While an employee who proceeds under c(1) must show that he or she reasonably believed that the employer's activity, policy or practice "violat[ed]" a law, rule, or regulation, an employee who proceeds under c(3) is only required to show that the employer's activity, policy, or practice is "incompatible" with a clear mandate of public policy. To "violate" a law, a person must commit "[a]n infraction or breach of the law," but a person's conduct may be found "incompatible" with a law based solely on a showing that the conduct is "irreconcilable" with that law. Moreover, since the recognized sources of public policy within the intent of c(3) include state laws, rules and regulations, a plaintiff who pursues a CEPA claim under this subsection may rely upon the same laws, rules and regulations that may be the subject of a claim under c(1). Consequently, it is easier for an employee who proceeds under c(3) to prove that he or she reasonably believed the employer's conduct was "incompatible" with a clear mandate of public policy expressed in a law, rule or regulation than to show, as required by c(1), a reasonable belief that the employer's conduct "violated" a law, rule or regulation.

However, an employee who proceeds under c(3) must establish an additional element that is not required to prove a claim under c(1). Although an employee may pursue an action under c(1) based on objections to employer conduct that he or she reasonably believes violated any law, rule or regulation, an employee who proceeds under c(3) must make the additional showing that the "clear mandate of public policy" he or she reasonably believes the employer's policy to be incompatible with is one that "concern[s] the public health, safety or welfare or protection of the environment."

* * *

[T]he provisions of the Code of Criminal Justice that prohibit promotion of prostitution and restrict the location of sexually-oriented businesses constitute "a clear mandate of public policy concerning the public health, safety or welfare[.]" The Code makes promotion of prostitution either a third or fourth-degree offense, depending on the circumstances, and it makes the operation of a sexually-oriented business within 1,000 feet of a school or church a fourth-degree offense. These provisions reflect a legislative recognition that the promotion of prostitution and other commercial sexual activities are a source of "venereal disease, * * * profit and power for criminal groups who commonly combine it with illicit trade in drugs and liquor, illegal gambling and even robbery and extortion[,] * * * [and] corrupt influence on government and law enforcement machinery." II *The New Jersey Penal Code, Final Report of the N.J. Criminal Law Revision Commission,* 301–02, cmt. 1 on *N.J.S.A.* 2C:34–2 (1971);

To prevail on a CEPA claim under 3c(3), plaintiff is not required to show that defendants' alleged policy decision to cease enforcement of the provisions of the Code prohibiting the promotion of prostitution and restricting the location of sexually-oriented businesses actually violated or was incompatible with a statute, rule or other clear mandate of public policy. Plaintiff only has to show that he had an "objectively reasonable belief" in the existence of such a violation or incompatibility. Plaintiff may carry this burden by demonstrating that "there is a substantial nexus between the complained—of conduct"—the cessation of investigations of promotion of prostitution and failure to enforce laws relating to the location of sexually-oriented businesses—and "[the] law or public policy identified by * * * plaintiff"—in this case the provisions of the Code proscribing such criminal conduct. *Ibid.*

We conclude that plaintiff's proofs met this burden. Viewing the evidence in the light most favorable to plaintiff, as required on a motion for summary judgment, it could support a finding that he had an objectively reasonable belief that defendants made a policy decision to cease all investigation and enforcement of the Code provisions prohibiting the promotion of prostitution and restricting the location of sexually-oriented businesses. Plaintiff testified that Captain Glass told him at a staff meeting in January 2001 not to initiate any new prostitution investigations unless they directly impacted the citizens of Atlantic City, and shortly thereafter, Sergeant Abrams issued a directive to terminate all pending promotion of prostitution investigations. Around the same time Sergeant Abrams issued this directive, the files plaintiff had maintained regarding persons involved in the promotion of prostitution were removed from a filing cabinet under his control, and thereafter, his access to those files was severely restricted. Since plaintiff was the only detective still actively involved in promotion of prostitution investigations at that time, he could reasonably have believed that the intent of Sergeant Abrams' directive and the removal of his investigation files was to terminate all such investigations in Atlantic City.

In addition, when plaintiff sent a memorandum requesting his superiors' assistance in persuading the municipal solicitor to initiate proceedings to revoke the mercantile licenses of sexually-oriented businesses operating in violation of *N.J.S.A.* 2C:34–7, the only response he received was Captain Glass' comment: "You're out of here, you're going to patrol." Plaintiff further testified that the City never took any action to revoke the licenses of sexually-oriented businesses that were operating in violation of *N.J.S.A.* 2C:34–7. Therefore, a trier of fact could find that plaintiff had an objectively reasonable belief that Atlantic City had made a policy decision not to enforce this statutory prohibition.

* * *

[P]laintiff's claim is not simply that defendants decided to assign a "lower degree of priority" to investigations of violations of the Code provisions prohibiting promotion of prostitution and restricting the location of sexually-oriented businesses, but rather that they made a policy decision to terminate all enforcement of these criminal laws. Plaintiff was not told, and had no other reason to believe, that this alleged policy decision was due to budgetary constraints or an administrative determination that there was a need to assign additional officers to the investigation of more serious crimes. Therefore, a trier of fact could find that plaintiff had an objectively reasonable belief that defendants made a policy decision that was incompatible with a clear mandate of public policy concerning the public health, safety and welfare.

Accordingly, the judgment of the Appellate Division is affirmed.

RIVERA-SOTO, J. dissenting.

As the majority notes, "[t]his appeal involves a claim under the Conscientious Employee Protection Act (CEPA), by a police officer who alleges he was transferred from detective to patrolman in retaliation for his objections to the Chief of Police's decision to terminate enforcement of provisions of the Code of Criminal Justice prohibiting promotion of prostitution and restricting the location of sexually-oriented businesses." The Law Division dismissed plaintiff's complaint, the Appellate Division reinstated that complaint, and the majority affirms. Because I concur with the well-reasoned judgment of the trial court in dismissing plaintiff's complaint, and because the majority appears to graft a new limitation on the discretionary governance prerogatives of an employer, I respectfully dissent.

In this case, a police officer alleges that his reassignment was precipitated by his complaints that the Atlantic City Police Department was not enforcing the laws against prostitution and related offenses to a degree that was personally satisfactory to that police officer. * * * [T]he trial court correctly framed the issue as follows: "did [plaintiff] *reasonably* believe that [defendants'] actions or inactions constituted 'misconduct' and 'illegal' or 'wrongful' activities that were incompatible with a 'clear mandate of public policy?' " Highlighting the patent absurdity that results from allowing a rank-and-file police officer to determine law enforcement policy for an entire department, the trial court narrowed the inquiry to the decision-making discretion vested in the police officer on patrol and made the common sense observation that "[i]t is self-evident that no police officer can, without prioritizing, effectively prosecute every violation of the law that comes to his or her attention." The trial court further noted that "[o]ne may reasonably conclude that a police officer should have the discretion to determine that there are legitimate priorities that would preclude the investment of the same level of resources in the enforcement of every provision of law."

Extrapolating from the discretion necessarily vested in a single police officer to that which must reside in the decision-makers responsible for law enforcement policy judgments, the trial court observed:

> The same discretionary judgment should apply to the decisions by supervising police personnel to prioritize, as they deem appropriate, the allocation of time, attention, personnel, and other resources to the investigation and prosecution of offenses such as those at issue here. It would be an unsupportable extension of the purposes and application of the [CEPA] statute, as interpreted by any reported decision, to afford to every police officer the ability, under the authority of a CEPA claim, to hold his or her department accountable to the officer for any discretionary determinations of resource allocation and law enforcement priorities solely because those determinations differed from the officer's views.
>
> Moreover, [plaintiff's] position raises as many problems as it "solves." If he is correct, then any police officer could seek to hold a police department accountable pursuant to CEPA not only for [the] investigations or prosecutions it does not undertake, as is [plaintiff's] concern here, but also for complaints about how aggressively and with what resources the battle is fought in those instances where the department does determine to act. CEPA should not, and I believe does not, have this reach.

The trial court thus concluded that

> [t]he alleged "misallocation" of resources and priorities by [defendants] and their "failure to enforce" the law, even if indeed that is what it was, did not violate any "clear mandate of public policy" because there is no such mandate that precludes this type of discretionary judgment * * * It would be manifestly inappropriate to substitute, for the City's judgment, [plaintiff's] view or that of a court or

jury with regard to the appropriate priorities for applying the law enforcement resources available to the City.

Inasmuch as the City had the discretionary authority to make the determinations that it made in the absence of a clear mandate of public policy to the contrary, and in view of the fact that [defendants'] actions were not "illegal" or "wrongful" in and of themselves, [plaintiff's] belief that [defendants'] actions constituted "misconduct" and were incompatible with a clear mandate of public policy was not "objectively reasonable" as a matter of law * * *

I cannot improve on the clear, logical and compelling thoughts expressed by the trial judge. Therefore, I would reverse the judgment of the Appellate Division and reinstate the trial court's dismissal of plaintiff's complaint. * * *

There is a further notion in the majority's reasoning that is particularly troublesome. * * *

* * *

Under the majority's view, a municipality now must be governed by its lowest common denominator or risk the imposition of liability. Stripped to its essence, the majority rules that plaintiff's claim survives summary judgment not because of any wrongful municipal action, but because "[p]laintiff was not told, and had no other reason to believe, that this alleged policy decision [to limit the resources assigned to combat the promotion of prostitution or sexually-oriented businesses] was due to budgetary constraints or an administrative determination that there was a need to assign additional officers to the investigation of more serious crimes." That turns the basis of the employer/employee relationship on its head, requiring that, in order to avoid a potential CEPA lawsuit, an employer must explain every discretionary decision to the satisfaction of every line employee. That was never CEPA's purpose or intendment.

I, therefore, respectfully dissent.

NOTES

1. Under the court's decision, was the Atlantic City Police Department obligated to enforce the ordinances against prostitution? If not, what was the basis for the city's liability to Maimone?

2. If Maimone had been an employee of the federal government, how would his claim have fared under the federal Whistleblower Protection Act? Is the policy view of the majority or the dissent more in line with the views expressed in *Huffman*?

3. Although most courts have interpreted whistleblower protection statutes broadly to effectuate their remedial purposes, there are limits. For example, in *Van v. Portneuf Medical Center*, 147 Idaho 552, 212 P.3d 982 (2009), the Idaho Supreme Court held that an employee's complaints that a contract entered into by a public hospital would lead to a waste of funds in

the future was not protected, because the Idaho Whistleblower Act protects only complaints of actual waste of funds, not the potential for future waste. In *Mallonee v. State*, 139 Idaho 615, 84 P.3d 551 (2004), the same court held that a complaint of a violation of department policy was not a complaint of a violation of law, rule or regulation protected by the statute because the department policy had not been promulgated as a rule pursuant to the state's Administrative Procedures Act.

CHAPTER 4

COLLECTIVE REPRESENTATION IN THE PUBLIC SECTOR

■ ■ ■

Unions and collective bargaining are a central feature in the landscape of public employment. Union density rates in the public sector are quite high (more than quadruple the rate in the private sector). The majority of states provide statutory collective bargaining rights to at least some and often to most public employees. Even in the minority of jurisdictions without such statutes, unions are often still active, using various tactics to represent their members. Unlike private sector labor law, public sector labor law varies dramatically among jurisdictions. Even within the majority of states that provide bargaining rights for public workers, there is a wide diversity in approaches on some central issues.

This chapter begins with a brief history of labor relations and labor law in the public sector. It then discusses the political nature of public sector bargaining. Following that are two examples of modern disputes in public sector labor law which raise broad questions about the area. The chapter then turns to a description of formal legal rights: the right to form unions and the rights to bargain. It then discusses union activities where there is no statutory right to bargain collectively. Finally, it addresses the diversity of statutory protections in the public sector.

A. A BRIEF HISTORY OF PUBLIC SECTOR COLLECTIVE BARGAINING

In the past half-century, public sector unions have been the success story of the American labor movement. From the early 1960s to today, public sector union density rose from less than 12% to around 40%; meanwhile, from the mid–1950s to today, private sector union density declined from more than 33% to less than 8%. As a result, by the year 2010, just over half of all union members in the U.S. were public workers.

As the following materials show, public workers did not begin to get the formal legal right to bargain collectively or in most cases even the right to form unions until the 1960s. Not surprisingly, union density in the public sector was significantly lower before then. Yet, just as private sector workers organized unions and took collective action before the National Labor Relations Act (NLRA) was passed, so did public workers in the decades before any law authorized them to bargain collectively. This history is important because, despite their successes, public sector unions have still not won collective bargaining rights on a national scale. A minority of states still do not grant any public employees the right to bargain, and many states only provide such rights to a few discrete categories of employees (*e.g.*, police, fire, and/or teachers). Thus, for many public employees, the present legal regime is similar to that of the early twentieth century.

Throughout American history, policymakers have treated public sector labor relations as something quite different from private sector labor relations. In 1920, Senator Charles Thomas (D–Col.) stated that the "fundamental idea lying at the foundation of organized labor * * * has been the assumption * * * of an antagonism of interest and of purpose between employer and employee. * * * That situation cannot be applied to public employment." Union supporters had a different vision. Public workers had "grievances just the same as men in other walks of life," insisted Boston's labor newspaper in 1919. "Government workers who are unorganized can be and are exploited as cruelly as unorganized workers in private industry," echoed the newspaper of Transportation Workers Union in 1942.[1]

Similar debates continue today. Government employees continue to organize unions to protect their rights as workers. On the other hand, public sector unions impact public budgets and raise issues of democratic control (how certain policies in government should be determined). In contrast to the private sector, in the public sector arguments over what types of rights to bargain collectively workers should have—and in some places, whether such rights should exist at all—inform a changing legal landscape, in which statutory and related rights are created, withdrawn, and significantly amended with some regularity.

1. PUBLIC SECTOR UNIONISM PRIOR TO 1960

Combinations of government workers have been active throughout the history of the United States. In early times, organized public employees were typically members of mostly private sector unions, *e.g.* skilled workers in naval yards. During the 1830s, skilled craft workers employed at naval shipyards organized. In 1836, a strike by shipyard workers in Washington, D.C. lasted several weeks. President Andrew Jackson intervened personally, and ultimately he agreed to the strikers' demand for a work day limited to ten hours.

During the latter part of the nineteenth century and early twentieth century, postal workers organized in many cities. In 1912, customs inspec-

1. Joseph Slater, *Public Workers: Government Employees Unions, The Law, and The State 1900–1962* 1, 27, 193 (2004).

tors organized on a national level, and in 1917, the American Federation of Labor chartered the National Federation of Federal Employees as a union for bringing federal government workers under the AFL's umbrella.

Organizing was not confined to the federal government. The Chicago Teachers Federation, the forerunner of the Chicago Teachers Union, was organized on April 9, 1898, and affiliated with the Chicago Federation of Labor in 1902 and with the American Federation of Labor in 1914. In 1917, it was reported that more than half of the 7,000 teachers in the Chicago Public Schools were members of the union. In that year, however, the Illinois Supreme Court held it lawful for the Chicago Board of Education to prohibit membership in the union on pain of discharge. *People ex. rel. Fursman v. City of Chicago*, 278 Ill. 318, 116 N.E. 158 (1917).

In 1916, the AFL chartered the American Federation of Teachers (AFT). In 1917, the AFL chartered the International Association of Fire Fighters (IAFF). Not only did firefighters organize in a number of cities, but so did police officers. The most infamous instance of police organizing in the early twentieth century occurred in Boston.

Despite a high rate of inflation induced by World War I, the wages of Boston police officers stagnated. Boston police officers also complained of intolerably long shifts and of having to stay overnight in police stations marked by unhealthy, decrepit conditions. Most Boston police officers belonged to the Boston Social Club, a fraternal organization founded by the former Boston police commissioner. Police officers used the organization to voice their concerns without success. Consequently, the Social Club applied to the AFL for a charter. The AFL chartered the Boston Policeman's Union on August 15, 1919. The Boston police commissioner responded by prohibiting membership in the organization, claiming that police officers could not have "divided loyalty." The commissioner suspended nineteen officers for membership in the union. At 5:45 p.m. on September 19, 1919, three-fourths of the force walked out on strike in protest. The commissioner responded by firing all of the strikers.

Law and order broke down with considerable looting and rioting in downtown Boston and South Boston. The breakdown lasted for two days. Massachusetts Governor Calvin Coolidge responded by mobilizing the entire State Guard to restore order. The State Guard continued to patrol the streets of Boston while the city recruited a force of replacements, obtained primarily from World War I veterans. None of the strikers ever returned to their jobs.

The Boston Police strike launched the national political career of Calvin Coolidge, leading ultimately to his election as president of the United States. It also became synonymous with the evils of public sector unionism. Following the strike, many jurisdictions barred police officers from organizing unions. All AFL-chartered police local unions and many IAFF-chartered firefighter locals soon gave up their charters. Further, local authorities issued bans on many other types of public sector unions, from teachers to street cleaners.

The effects of the Boston police strike on public sector unions lingered for decades. President Ronald Reagan cited the Boston strike as precedent for firing striking members of the Professional Air Traffic Controllers Union in 1981. Public employers frequently prohibited employees from joining unions often citing concerns about strikes, even though after the Boston strike both AFL and later CIO public sector unions renounced the strike weapon. Another lingering effect was that public employees, faced with bans on unions affiliated with the AFL, often sought to form "independent" unions the bans did not cover. Even today, some major public sector unions remain outside the AFL–CIO (*e.g.*, the Fraternal Order of Police and the National Education Association).

Also, from the New Deal into the 1960s, the U.S. had very different legal rules for public and private sector labor relations. Before 1959, no statute in the U.S. authorized collective bargaining for public employees. Thus, before the 1960s, state courts effectively made public sector labor law, typically endorsing whatever rules public employers imposed. Federal workers were marginally better off, as the Lloyd–LaFollette Act of 1912 gave federal employees the right to form unions, albeit not to bargain. This "pre-collective bargaining era" for public workers lasted decades longer in the U.S. than in many other industrialized countries. For example, in Britain and France in the first part of the twentieth century, public workers won bargaining and related rights quite similar to those of private sector workers in those countries.

Still, public workers continued to organize unions in this era. For example, the American Federation of State, County, & Municipal Employees (AFSCME) was formed in the 1930s. From the 1930s to the 1960s, public sector union density ranged from 9 to 13%. In this era, public sector unions used various tactics to represent their members. First, they engaged in politics, supporting sympathetic candidates and lobbying for laws and regulations. Second, they represented workers in civil service hearings and under other laws. Third, they provided training, information, and other resources for their members. Fourth, some participated in "informal" bargaining, which sometimes led to agreements with employers. Although no laws specifically required or even necessarily authorized such agreements, a 1946 study found that ninety-seven cities had written agreements with employee organizations. Such agreements were, however, far short of modern, binding, collective bargaining, both in their narrow scope and their dubious enforceability. Union efforts in these decades were creative and sometimes effective, but because they lacked institutional rights, they achieved at best mixed success.

Moreover, courts in this era routinely held that public employers in the U.S. were free to forbid their employees even from joining unions. This was often done by requiring employees to sign "yellow dog" contracts: contracts in which the employee promised not to be a member of a union (or, in some cases, a union affiliated with the AFL or CIO) while employed. The following case is typical of the judicial response when employees challenged these contracts.

AFSCME LOCAL 201 v. CITY OF MUSKEGON

Michigan Supreme Court, 1963.
369 Mich. 384, 120 N.W.2d 197.

CARR, C.J.

The question at issue in this litigation concerns the validity of a rule adopted by the chief of police of the city of Muskegon on March 16, 1961. Such action was taken pursuant to Sections 2–103 and 2–104 of the municipal code of ordinances which, insofar as material here, read as follows:

> Section 2–103 Rules, regulations. The following rules and regulations shall govern the police department:
>
> Section 2–104 Chief of police; powers and duties. (1) He shall be the director of the police department subject to these rules and regulations, and shall devote his full time and attention to the management of this department.
>
> (2) He shall be responsible for the government, efficiency and general good conduct of the police department, and shall supervise the instruction of the members of the department in their duties.
>
> (3) He shall have the power to prescribe, promulgate and enforce rules and regulations for the government of the members and employees of the department, which shall be approved by the city manager and filed with the city clerk, the city manager and the civil service commission. Each member of the department then shall be assumed to have knowledge of and shall become subject to such rules.

The rule in question was duly approved by the city manager and was filed as required by the code provisions. It reads as follows:

> Section 101: No police officer of the city of Muskegon police department shall hereafter be, or become a member of any organization in any manner identified with any federation or labor union which admits to membership persons who are not members of the Muskegon police department, or which would in any way exact prior consideration and prevent such officer from performing full and complete police duty at any time. Any police officer now a member of such unions shall disassociate himself within 30 days from this date. Failure to comply will constitute reason for immediate dismissal.

The situation to which the rule was intended to apply obviously had been under consideration by municipal officers prior to the adoption of the rule. Under date of March 14, 1961, the Muskegon city commission took the action indicated by the following statement and resolution:

61–165. Resolution on banning of union affiliation by police officers adopted.

Certain of the police officers of the city of Muskegon police department are dues paying members of Local No. 201, Muskegon County and Municipal Employees Union affiliated with the American Federation of State, County and Municipal Employees, AFL–CIO. This commission, as well as past commissions, have seriously questioned whether a police officer can be a member of such a union and still enforce, impartially and without prejudice the laws of our city, county and State of Michigan.

Every police officer who joins the Muskegon police department must take an oath of office to support the Constitution and bear allegiance to his city and State and its Constitution and laws and to the best of ability, skill and judgment, diligently and faithfully, without partiality or prejudice, execute his office. Police officers are invested with broad powers, few of which are given to any other government employee. They have the legal right to carry a weapon, their powers of restraint, arrest, and control of moral and physical behaviour of others are grave and serious. A police officer is required by law and invariably becomes a neutralizer in controversies involving the right of public assemblage, neighborhood disputes, domestic difficulties and strikes, between labor and management. Again, his actions in these instances must be governed by his oath of office. He must recognize certain rights of people among which is the right of collective bargaining on the part of labor. Yet, at the same time, he must protect the rights and the property of management. In this instance, again, his neutrality must be the watchword of his every activity in the effort to protect the life and property of all those involved and to preserve peace and order during periods of such difficulty.

This commission subscribes to this statement of responsibility and, as such, cannot further condone police officers of the city of Muskegon to continue to be members of a union.

In the belief that we are acting in the best interest of all of the citizens of the city of Muskegon, the following resolution is presented.

Commissioner Carlson offered the following resolution and moved its adoption:

No police officer of the city of Muskegon police department shall hereafter be, or become, a member of any organization in any manner identified with any federation or labor union which admits to membership persons who are not members of the Muskegon police department, or which would in any way exact prior consideration and prevent such officer from performing full and complete police duty at any time. Any police officer now a member of such unions shall disassociate himself within 30 days from this date. Failure to comply will constitute reason for immediate dismissal.

It is apparent that the rule promulgated by the chief of police was designed to carry out the purpose expressed by the resolution of the legislative body of the city. Plaintiffs in the instant litigation objected to the action taken and under date of April 7, 1961, filed a petition for a writ of mandamus to compel the city commission to reconsider its action or to submit the matter to a referendum vote under charter provisions applicable to ordinances. The trial court concluded that the resolution of the commission was not an ordinance and was, in consequence, not subject to a referendum.

On the same date that the mandamus proceeding was instituted plaintiffs filed suit in equity seeking injunctive relief against the enforcement of the commission's action and of the rule or regulation adopted by the chief of police. On the filing of the suit a temporary injunction was issued and proofs were taken in the case in April, 1961. On behalf of plaintiffs it was contended in the trial court that the regulation in question was uncertain in its provisions in that the word "federation" created an ambiguity, that the municipal action was arbitrary and unreasonable, and that it operated to deprive plaintiffs, and members of the police force of the city of Muskegon who were also members of the plaintiff union, of rights protected by State and Federal Constitutions. The trial court agreed with the contentions of the plaintiffs and entered a decree accordingly. Defendants have appealed.

We are unable to agree with the contention that the rule as adopted by the chief of police of defendant city is ambiguous because of the inclusion of the word "federation" therein. A reading of the entire rule leaves no question as to its purpose and intent. The reference therein to "such unions" indicates clearly the meaning to be ascribed to the expression "federation or labor union." A reading of the record suggests the absence of any question as to the application of the rule, if otherwise valid, to the plaintiffs herein.

The basic question at issue is whether the defendant city may through its duly constituted authorities prescribe a regulation of the character here involved for the members of its police department. It may be assumed that in taking the action in question due consideration was given to local conditions and to the protection of the public interest generally. That a municipality maintaining a police department may adopt reasonable rules in connection therewith is not open to question. Opinions may perhaps differ as to what may be regarded as reasonable, or as the converse thereof. In the instant case the presumption of validity attaches to the regulation adopted by the chief of police pursuant to the code of ordinances of the city, and the burden rests on those assailing it to establish that there is an unwarranted, and therefore arbitrary, interference with rights protected by constitutional guaranties. If the municipality has acted within the scope of its powers, the regulation must be sustained.

Basically the question at issue is whether the city may exercise over the members of its police department the right of control asserted by the rule in question, rather than the effect of such rule on those employees who are within its scope. The restriction imposed is not directed at a class as such but, rather, solely at those who have sought and obtained employment in the police department of the defendant city. Decisions cited by counsel for plaintiffs relating to racial discrimination are not in point. * * *

In *Fraternal Order of Police v. Lansing Board of Police & Fire Com'rs*, 306 Mich. 68, 10 N.W.2d 310 (1943), this Court had before it a suit brought by the plaintiff to restrain the defendant board from enforcing a resolution designed to prevent members of the police department from becoming members of the plaintiff organization. Plaintiff accepted as associate members private citizens who paid small fees for joining and were given identification tags that might be attached to their automobiles. It was held that defendant had acted within the scope of its authority and that neither plaintiff organization nor any of its members had been deprived of constitutional rights. In reaching such conclusion it was said, in part:

> The constitution and bylaws of plaintiff's national, state and local organizations which were received in evidence provide in effect that citizens may become associate members upon payment of dues of not less than $5 per year, and such associate members will be furnished 'a membership card' and car 'emblem.' One would be naive, indeed, to assume that such automobile emblem did not carry with it the intimation of special privileges to associate members. This of itself is enough to require the determination that the existence of plaintiff organization within the law-enforcement body of a municipality is contrary to public policy.
>
> Defendant board is necessarily vested with a large measure of discretion and the burden of showing arbitrary action is upon those who charge it.

The above decision was followed in *State Lodge of Michigan, Fraternal Order of Police v. City of Detroit*, 318 Mich. 182, 27 N.W.2d 612 (1947), which involved a regulation of the police commissioner of defendant city forbidding members of the police force from being members of a fraternal order allowing other citizens to become associate members. The Court quoted with approval from the opinion in *Carter v. Thompson*, 164 Va. 312, 180 S.E. 410 (1935), as follows:

> Police and fire departments are in a class apart. Both are at times charged with the preservation of public order, and for manifold reasons they owe to the public their undivided allegiance. The power in the city of complete control is imperatively necessary if discipline is to be maintained.

In accord with prior holdings of this Court is the decision in *Perez v. Board of Police Commissioners of the City of Los Angeles*, 78 Cal.App.2d 638, 178 P.2d 537 (1947). At issue there was a resolution of the board of police commissioners of Los Angeles forbidding police officers of the city to become members of any organization identified with "any trade association, federation or labor union which admits to membership persons who are not members of the Los Angeles police department, or whose membership is not exclusively made up of employees of the city of Los Angeles." The action of the trial court in sustaining the resolution was upheld. It was specifically held that there was no violation of the 14th amendment to the Federal Constitution, and that the order of the defendant board was not arbitrary or unreasonable. In reaching the determination indicated, it was said in part:

> Whether a rational connection exists between union membership and lack of competency as a police officer, obviously, is a matter of opinion. And the question was solely one for the board of police commissioners to determine. Regardless of what the constitution and bylaw of any organization might provide for or against, it is idle to argue that such constitution and bylaw cannot be changed by amendment. Moreover, it was for the board of police commissioners, as the representatives, agents and servants of the people, to determine what the first duties, indeed, all of the duties, of a police officer should be. It should be noted also, that the board of police commissioners probably took into account the fact that labor unions are active politically, whereas civil service employees are prevented by law and as a condition of employment, from taking an active part in politics while on official duty or during working hours and, that means would be thus provided for doing indirectly and with impunity, that which the law specifically prohibits.
>
> The Court also quoted from the opinion of the trial judge as follows:
>
> In *Hayman v. City of Los Angeles*, 17 Cal.App.2d 674, 62 P.2d 1047 (1936), in considering a question whether the discharge of a civil service employee was in violation of his rights to freedom of speech and of the press, and arbitrary, the court said:
>
> The right which is involved here is not that which petitioner thinks has been denied him, but is the right of respondents to exercise a reasonable supervision over city employees, to the end that proper discipline may be maintained and that activities among employees be not allowed to disrupt or impair the public service. Such is not only the right but the duty of the city and its several departments. In the exercise of this duty they must be allowed a wide discretion and their acts are not subject to review by the courts until they have reached the point of illegality.
>
> The rule adopted by the resolution here in question does not on its face appear unreasonable or arbitrary in the light of the foregoing authorities. Nor is it in violation of any constitutional right of police officers. If the rule is necessary and reasonable it cannot be charged with wrongfully depriving the police members of any constitutional right. All such rights are relative. Nor does the rule amount to a bill of attainder, nor does it produce or inflict any of the incidents of such

> a legislative act. It was the result of a decision by the board in the exercise of that wide discretion which is accorded to them. Neither this court nor any judge thereof has the power to substitute its or his contrary views as to the propriety, necessity, desirability or reasonableness of the rule. The rule having been created by the board under and within its charter powers, and no appearance of unreasonableness or arbitrariness or unconstitutionality manifesting itself therein, it must be concluded that such rule cannot have reached the point of illegality and subject to review and annulment by the courts either by direct action or by means of injunction against enforcement thereof.

The regulation involved in the instant case is limited in its application to members of the police department of the city of Muskegon and it applies to them solely in their capacity as such members. As this Court pointed out in *City of Detroit v. Division 26 of the Amalgamated Association of Street, Electric Railway & Motor Coach Employees of America*, 332 Mich. 237, 51 N.W.2d 228 (1952), there is no provision of either State or Federal Constitution which gives to individuals the right to be employed in government service or the right to continue therein. In said case the constitutionality of the so-called Hutchinson Act was upheld as applied to the Detroit transportation system and the employees thereof. In disposing of the issues raised it was said, in part:

> There is ample authority to the effect that public employment does not vest in such employees any fixed or permanent rights of employment. As individuals or in groups public employees may discontinue their employment, but, having done so, such public employees have no vested right to insist upon their re-employment on terms or conditions agreeable to the employees, or even without compliance with such conditions. To hold otherwise would result in public agencies being powerless to render public service and to effectively administer public affairs; and the public would thereby be deprived of its right to efficient government. For example, if the members of a fire department or of a police department collectively refuse to continue to serve except upon conditions insisted upon by them, unless their employer supinely yielded, the public, which by taxation pays therefor, would be deprived of fire or of police protection; and the right or power to exercise essential governmental affairs nullified. There seems to be ample reason and authority for holding that the right of public employees to collectively refuse to render the service for which they are employed differs in legal point of view from the right of private employees to strike, and hence the classification of 'public employees' for the purpose of applicable legislation is valid.

Plaintiffs herein have not borne the burden of proof of showing that members of the police department of Muskegon are deprived by the enforcement of the regulation in question of any constitutional rights to which they are entitled. As before suggested, they cannot claim a constitutional right to be appointed as members of said department, or to continue therein. They are subject to the authority of the municipality, granted by the Constitution and laws of the State, to manage its local affairs and to regulate the departments of municipal government. The duly constituted authorities of the city have concluded that the regulation here under attack is reasonably required in the interests of a fair and impartial administration of the law by those entrusted with its enforcement, without discrimination or partiality. The basic principles recognized in the prior decisions of this Court and by courts in other States as well are applicable here. On the record before us it may not be said that the rule is unreasonable or arbitrary in its application.

* * *

The decree of the circuit court of Muskegon county is reversed and the case is remanded with directions to dismiss plaintiffs' bill of complaint. * * *

NOTES

1. Private sector employees were guaranteed the right to form and join unions by the NLRA in 1935. By 1963, unions were well established in the private sector. Nevertheless, the court upheld the authority of the Muskegon Police Chief to prohibit police officers from joining a labor union. Why?

2. What rationale did the City give for prohibiting its police officers from joining labor unions? To what extent did the court scrutinize this rationale?

3. Would the rationale supporting the prohibition on police officers joining unions support a similar prohibition for other public employees? If so, what groups of employees? Are there any public employees for whom a prohibition on union membership could not be justified in light of the *Muskegon* case?

4. Judges in the "pre-collective bargaining era" for public workers not only generally rejected the idea of labor rights in the public sector, but sometimes used surprisingly vitriolic language in so doing. Two separate court decisions in the 1940s, from Texas and New York, used the following quote: "To tolerate or recognize any combination of * * * employees of the government as a labor organization or union is not only incompatible with the spirit of democracy but inconsistent with every principle upon which our Government is founded." *CIO v. City of Dallas*, 198 S.W.2d 143, 145 (Tex. Civ. App. 1946), *quoting Railway Mail Ass'n v. Murphy*, 180 Misc. 868, 44 N.Y.S.2d 601, 607 (1943), *rev'd on other grounds sub nom. Railway Mail Ass'n v. Corsi*, 267 App. Div. 470, 47 N.Y.S.2d 404 (1944).

Why did public sector labor law develop relatively late and unevenly in the U.S.? First, the Boston strike was a major blow. Second, judges that made the law until at least the early 1960s endorsed rules regarding state structure and sovereignty which led to considerable judicial deference to local public government bodies. Thus, local government employers often had the effective power to set the rules of public sector labor relations. Third, the federalist structure of the American state and the constitutional doctrines of the mid–20th century prevented any realistic hopes of a federal law.

In the following excerpt, Professor Slater explores another reason behind judicial support for yellow dog contracts.

THE COURT DOES NOT KNOW "WHAT A LABOR UNION IS": HOW STATE STRUCTURES AND JUDICIAL (MIS)CONSTRUCTIONS DEFORMED PUBLIC SECTOR LABOR LAW

Joseph E. Slater
79 Oregon Law Review 981 (2000).

* * * Public sector labor cases can be explained only by adding a third factor to the considerations of bias and state structure: judges falsely constructed the term "union." * * * [J]udges in public sector labor cases misconstrued the concept of "union" to exclude organizations of workers performing waged labor for the government. Critical scholars would note that courts rejected a competing construction of these terms offered by labor in word and deed: even though public sector unions had all formally renounced strikes and most were willing to forego traditional collective bargaining, at least over wages, courts insisted on seeing unions as institutions that inevitably bargained and struck. Especially in the aftermath of the infamous Boston police strike of 1919, judges could not imagine giving public workers such rights. Nor could judges believe that statutes that granted rights to "labor organizations" or "unions" could possibly cover public sector unions, even in the face of legislative history that suggested they should. Judicial construction, in turn, had a dispositive effect on the outcome of cases and, therefore, ultimately on the reality of public sector labor relations. * * *

In forming their construction of unions, judges seemed, at best, blind to relevant events outside their courtrooms. First, public sector unions in this era, while not as large or prominent as in recent decades, did exist in significant numbers: union density in the public sector began to hold steady at around 10–13% by the late thirties. In 1934, public sector unions represented 9% of the nearly 3,300,000 government workers in the United States, who in turn constituted 12.7% of all non-agricultural workers in the country. Second, these unions took actions on behalf of their members, from representing employees in civil service proceedings, to lobbying government officials for better laws or working conditions, to electing more sympathetic employers, to providing information to their members and the public. Third, these unions almost never struck. After the Boston police strike of 1919, AFL and later CIO public sector unions renounced the strike weapon, and in fact strikes by public sector unions from 1919 to 1945 were rare, small in scale, and short. But in the courtroom, unionists lacked the power to make this image of unionism real.

Instead, judges clung exclusively to the private sector image of unions, ignoring the ongoing presence of active public sector unions that did not formally bargain or strike and rejecting the sworn statements and binding documents that unions proffered as evidence of their different nature. In

1947, *King v. Priest* upheld a rule banning an AFSCME local that more than eight hundred police officers had joined. The union's charter barred striking and bargaining and stated that the oath that police officers took regarding their duties came before any obligation to the union. Instead of tactics used in the private sector, the charter continued, the local would, "by publicity, direct public attention to conditions that need correcting, * * * seek legislative action, * * * represent individuals in administrative procedure, and prevent discriminatory and arbitrary practices."

The Missouri Supreme Court would have none of it: "[T]he court, of course, knows what a labor union is. * * * " Defining the institution, the court took judicial notice of the "common knowledge" that "some of the most common methods used by labor unions * * * are strikes, threats to strike, [and] collective bargaining agreements. * * * " Refusing to accept an alternate model of "union," but without claiming that any AFSCME local had ever attempted to strike or bargain, the court asserted that "all of the rights and powers ordinarily inherent in a labor union would exist actually or potentially" in the local, "regardless of the form of its charter and the present admissions of appellants."

* * *

One lone dissent credited the claims of public sector unions that they would behave differently than private sector unions. In *City of Jackson v. McLeod*, Justice McGehee of the Mississippi Supreme Court would have held that membership in AFSCME was not sufficient cause to discharge police officers under a civil service law. Among other things, the "jury was entitled to find * * * that there is a fundamental difference between [AFSCME] and the labor unions in general." McGehee noted that the union's charter denied policemen the right to strike and that no AFSCME local had ever struck a police department. Further, the union did not advocate negotiating contracts by collective bargaining or the closed shop. McGehee even quoted a statement from former AFL president Samuel Gompers, issued in 1919 in response to the Boston turmoil, that it was the position of the AFL that police would neither strike nor assume any obligation that conflicted with their duty. Yet beyond this single voice, which itself did not come until 1946, judges uniformly refused to accept that an organization of workers could be a "union" without striking or bargaining. In taking this stance, judges not only rejected what unions said they would do, but critically they ignored what public sector unions were actually doing.

* * *

NOTES

1. On January 7, 2002, President George W. Bush issued Executive Order 13252, which, on national security grounds, prohibited collective bargaining by employees in five subdivisions of the Department of Justice: U.S. Attorney's offices, Criminal Division, INTERPOL—U.S. National Central

Bureau, National Drug Intelligence Center, and Office of Intelligence Policy and Review. *See* Section 3–A, *infra*. White House spokesman Ari Fleischer was quoted as saying, "There is a long tradition that presidents of both parties have honored about protecting the public by not allowing certain law enforcement or intelligence officials to strike." A federal statute makes a strike by a federal government employee a felony. Federal employees who strike may be discharged and federal employee unions that strike may be decertified as bargaining representatives. Compare Mr. Fleischer's justification for the Executive Order with the justifications courts gave in the first half of the twentieth century for allowing yellow dog contracts.

2. Although the Norris–LaGuardia Act had outlawed yellow dog contracts in the private sector in 1932 and the National Labor Relations Act had proclaimed the right of private sector employees to form and join unions and bargain collectively with their employers in 1935, the legal system treated unionization of public employees with tremendous hostility for decades to come. An unfavorable legal environment was not the sole factor inhibiting public sector unionization. The major industrial and craft unions were busy organizing the private sector, where union membership and collective bargaining were growing. In contrast to the private sector, organized labor did not view government workers as a particularly inviting target. There weren't as many government workers as private sector employees. The absence of institutional rights for public sector unions, including the rights to bargain and organize, were seen as a huge obstacle. Furthermore, at least in elementary education, demographics led unions to regard government workers as unorganizable. Most elementary teachers were women and many quit when they got married or were fired when they became pregnant. Consequently, many unions believed that teachers and other government workers lacked the long term commitment to their jobs that motivated interest in organizing.

2. PUBLIC SECTOR UNIONISM AFTER 1960

During the late 1950s, the legal environment regarding public sector collective bargaining began to change; however, it was during the 1960s that public sector collective bargaining made a major debut within federal and state legislation. The expansion of public sector employment as a result of the war against poverty at home, the Vietnam war, changing population demographics, and a new working class generally distrustful of the government generated pressure on governments to rethink their approaches to collective bargaining.

In 1957, the Metropolitan Transit Authority Act organized the Los Angeles Metropolitan Transit Authority and gave employees of the new unit of local government rights to form unions and bargain collectively. Two years later, California enacted the Firefighter Act, which gave firefighters limited rights to organize and present grievances and recommendations concerning wages and working conditions.

The end of the old era began with the passage of the first state statute permitting public sector collective bargaining in Wisconsin in 1959. The Municipal Employee Relations Act gave employees of local governments rights to organize and bargain collectively and prohibited employer and union interference with those rights. As amended in 1962, the law provided that if bargaining reached an impasse, a state agency could conduct mediation at the request of both parties and fact-finding at the request of either party. Later, the law was amended to provide, among other things, for binding arbitration (and later, the right to strike).

Federal government employees gained the right to bargain collectively soon after in 1962 when President Kennedy issued Executive Order 10988. That same year, Wisconsin placed administration of its public employee bargaining law in the hands of the Wisconsin Employment Relations Board (WERB). WERB, now known as the Wisconsin Employment Relations Commission, had been administering the Wisconsin Employment Peace Act, which governed the private sector, since 1938. It naturally placed a private sector imprimatur on public sector labor law.

Action by the federal government further fostered public sector collective bargaining. Local government employee collective bargaining was aided by the Urban Mass Transit Act (UMTA) of 1964. UMTA provided funds for local governments to take over previously private mass transit systems. Section 13(c) of UMTA required that the collective bargaining rights of transit employees be preserved in the process of converting their employment from the private to the public sector. The need to comply with UMTA led many states to enact legislation granting public employees collective bargaining rights.

Other factors led to the development of public sector employee organization. During the 1960s, public sector employment expanded greatly. Federal government employment expanded because of the escalation of the war in Vietnam. State and local government employment expanded even more. Several factors accounted for this expansion.

First, the demographics of the population changed. Baby boomers became old enough for school and then for college, resulting in the expansion of public school districts, community college systems and state universities. Increases in life expectancy resulted in an increased population over age 65. Children and the elderly are the two demographic groups that claim the largest percentage of government services. Since both age groups were expanding, so too were government services.

The growth of state and local government employment was also fueled by the war on poverty declared by the administration of President Lyndon Johnson and its great society programs. In addition to federal funding for a public takeover of mass transit through UMTA, discussed above, federal funding increased public services in health, education and social services. Consequently, compared to the private sector workforce which increased 89% from 1951 to 1980, the state and local government workforce increased 227%.

As the public workforce increased in size, public employers became more bureaucratized. The increase in bureaucracy led to feelings of alienation among many public employees. Furthermore, the Johnson

Administration's determination that the country could afford both guns (the war in Vietnam) and butter (expansion of social programs), led to increased rates of inflation. While private sector unions negotiated substantial pay increases and cost of living provisions in their contracts, public sector employees fell further and further behind.

Also, the 1960s was a decade of social change. Many of the new public sector employees were young people, women and minorities who were distrustful of public authority. They were open to organizing and were interested not only in improving their wages and working conditions, but also in organizing to gain a voice in the setting of governmental policies.

Growth was not instantaneous. As late as 1966, in the entire State of New York, out of 8,600 governmental employing entities, Governor Rockefeller's Committee on Public Employee Relations (the Taylor Committee) was able to find only eleven formal collective bargaining agreements. See *New York Governor's Committee on Public Employee Relations, Final Report* (1966).

Beginning in the mid 1960s, public sector unionization expanded steadily. For example, AFSCME grew from 99,000 members in 1955 to more than 250,000 members in 1969, and then to more than a million members by 1978. In 1955 public sector unions had a total of about 400,000 members; by the 1970s the total was more than 4,000,000.[2] Thus, in analyzing the history of collective bargaining in the public sector, 1960 provides a useful dividing line. It was during the 1960s that the legal, economic and political environments changed, leading to an explosion of growth in public sector unionism.

Ironically, reaction to the social changes in the 1960s and early 1970s also contributed to the increase of police employee unionism. Police officers felt themselves the targets of student and minority protestors. Many also felt besieged by judicial decisions such as *Miranda v. Arizona*, 384 U.S. 436, 86 S.Ct. 1602, 16 L.Ed.2d 694 (1966), which they felt increased the difficulty of performing their jobs. Tired of being called, "pigs," and believing they were not getting the respect to which they were entitled, many police officers organized.

These changes attracted the attention of private sector unions. Unions such as the International Brotherhood of Teamsters and the Service Employees International Union aggressively organized public employees. Public employee unions affiliated with the AFL–CIO such as the AFT made great strides in organizing employees and increasing membership. Many public employees belonged to professional and fraternal organizations. Many of these organizations reacted to the competition from traditional labor unions by embracing collective bargaining. Consequently, some of the more active public sector unions, such as the American Association of University Professors, American Nurses Association, Fra-

2. Slater, *Public Workers*, at 193; *History of AFSCME*, http://www.afscme.org/about/1028.cfm (Last visited May 27, 2010).

ternal Order of Police, and National Education Association, have evolved from professional and fraternal organizations.

Along with these changes, in the 1960s states began passing laws that allowed public sector bargaining and created specific mechanisms to resolve bargaining impasses that did not involve striking. By 1966 sixteen states had enacted laws extending some bargaining rights to at least some public workers. In 1978 the Federal Service Labor Management Relations Act of 1978 was adopted for most federal employees; it provides bargaining rights and binding arbitration at impasse.

In the late 1960s courts finally accepted an argument that public sector unionists had made for decades: the First Amendment of the Constitution prevented a public employer from firing or otherwise discriminating against a public employee because of membership in or support of a union. Thus, while some public employees are still without a legal right to bargain collectively, all have a Constitutional right to form unions. See Chapter 4, section C, *supra*.

There was also a brief period of relative militance in the public sector. In the later 1960s and 1970s, teachers, sanitation workers, and even police and firefighters, among others, engaged in job actions and (often illegal) strikes. This was after a long period (starting with the end of the Boston police strike), in which public sector strikes were rare and short when they did occur. In this new era, in some cases unions won rights with those tactics, but in some cases the actions caused a backlash. Perhaps part and parcel of the general tenor of protesting social movements, illegal strike actions decreased considerably in the 1980s and beyond. The air traffic controllers strike of 1981 was famous, but it was an exceptional event.

The public sector laws that have developed since the mid–1960s vary tremendously. At the turn of the twenty-first century, there were more than 110 separate state public sector labor law statutes, augmented by many local ordinances, executive orders, and other authority. Twenty-nine states and the District of Columbia allowed collective bargaining for all major groups of public employees; thirteen states allowed only one to four types of public workers to bargain (most commonly teachers and firefighters); and eight did not allow any public workers to bargain. While only twelve states allowed any public workers to strike, thirty-eight states provided some impasse procedures for unionized public workers. Thirty-six states used mandatory or optional mediation; thirty-four used fact-finding; and thirty had arbitration as the final step, with twenty-one states using binding arbitration. Still, a significant minority of states banned bargaining as well as striking, and a few (*e.g.*, Virginia) barred any official recognition of a public sector union.

Political fights over the rights of public workers continue. In 2004, the governors of Indiana and Missouri unilaterally withdrew executive orders permitting state employees to bargain collectively (the situation in Missouri was then changed with the *Independence* decision, *infra* Chapter 4

Section B). After the 9/11 attacks, the Bush administration would not approve a bill creating the Department of Homeland Security (DHS) unless administration officials were empowered to design a new personnel system that could eliminate labor law and civil service protections for DHS workers. Even where collective bargaining is allowed for public workers, state legislatures have sometimes narrowed existing laws to restrict the topics over which some public workers can bargain. For example, in the 1990s, Michigan restricted the topics over which teachers' unions could bargain.

3. PUBLIC SECTOR EMPLOYEES TODAY

As noted previously, union density in the public sector today greatly exceeds union density in the private sector. In the following paper, Harvard economist Richard Freeman examines results of the Public Sector Worker Survey (PSWS) conducted in the winter of 1995 and the Workplace Representation and Participation Survey (WRPS) conducted on private sector employees in 1994 and 1995 for possible explanations of the disparity.

THROUGH PUBLIC SECTOR EYES: EMPLOYEE ATTITUDES TOWARD PUBLIC SECTOR LABOR RELATIONS IN THE UNITED STATES

Richard B. Freeman
Public Sector Employment in a Time of Transition (Dale Belman et al., eds. IRRA 1996), pp. 59–83.

In 1993, 11% of workers in the private sector of the United States were organized into trade unions compared to nearly 40% of workers unionized in the public sector. * * * Some forty years earlier in 1954, union density also differed greatly by sector, but in the opposite way: More than 40% of private sector workers were unionized compared to perhaps 5% of public sector workers.

* * *

A natural starting point for any explanation of the difference in unionization between public and private sector employees is the demographic and occupational composition of workers in the sectors. Perhaps the public sector employs relatively larger proportions of workers with characteristics associated with union membership than does the private sector.

* * * To the contrary, public sector workers have characteristics that make them less likely to be union members than private sector workers. Specifically, relative to private sector workers, public sector workers are more likely to be women, nonwhite, older, more educated, white collar or professional. * * * Occupation by occupation, unionization is higher among public sector workers. The greater unionization of public sector workers is not due to the demographic or skill characteristics of those

workers compared to private sector employees. It is due to something about the public sector per se.

* * *

The PWS asked nonunion workers whether or not they would vote for a union if an election were held today. * * * The public sector respondents expressed a greater desire for unionization than did their private sector counterparts. One interpretation of this result is that there is indeed a greater preference for unionization in the public sector, which presumably contributes to its higher degree of unionization, but that the higher unionization in the public sector is not sufficient to reduce the desire for organization to the same levels among nonorganized in the private sector. The difference in preferences could also, however, reflect employee perceptions of likely management reactions to union drives. Private sector employees may be less likely to vote for a union because they feel their employers are more likely to resist unionization and to react negatively to collective bargaining. Why support a union if it will produce management hostility?

* * *

The key question regarding employee perceptions of management attitudes toward union organization is, "How might your company or organization respond to a union drive?" The responses for union and nonunion employees in the public sector were almost identical * * * Most employees expect management to oppose the union, in some cases with (illegal) threats or harassment. But a sizeable minority—17%—believe that management would welcome a union, and many felt that management would do nothing. In contrast, in the private sector, only a small minority believed that management would welcome a union, and they were largely in unionized firms. Only minuscule numbers of workers who had experienced an actual organizing drive or of nonunion workers expected their employer to welcome the union. And, while 12% of union workers in the private sector expected management to welcome a union, 28% of them expected threats or harassments, the highest proportion in the [data]. The bottom line is that public employees view their managements as less opposed to unionization than do private sector employees.

* * *

* * * There is some evidence that workers in the public sector have preferences that favor employee organizations compared to private sector employees: public sector workers report moderately greater desires for more influence or voice on the job and believe that management is less committed to employee involvement programs. These factors could lead public sector workers to seek influence through an organization. There is stronger evidence that management behavior is critical in affecting employee attitudes. Public sector employees give their management higher grades in willingness to share authority and believe management is more likely to welcome a union. These factors should make independent organizations more successful. There is also evidence that public sector workers

believe that an organization has a greater chance of succeeding without management cooperation than do private sector workers. Without gainsaying a role for differences in attitudes toward collective action between public sector and private sector workers due solely to differences in their work, I place greater weight on differences in labor-management interactions between the sectors that make management less resistant to unionization in the public sector. An explanation that stresses the incentives and activity of management is, at the minimum, consistent with the differences in responses on the Public Sector Worker Survey and on the equivalent WRPS for private sector workers. But more analysis is needed, particularly of management attitudes and behavior directly to "prove" that this is the major reason why unionization is higher in the public sector.

NOTES

1. Do you agree with Professor Freeman that employee perception of management reaction, rather than employee characteristics, explains the difference in public and private sector unionization rates? Are there other factors that the surveys might not have uncovered?

2. What are the implications of Professor Freeman's findings for management in the public and private sectors?

3. What are the implications of Professor Freeman's findings for the law in the public and private sectors?

4. Most public sector workers covered under collective bargaining laws are also covered by civil service laws that provide some form of just-cause requirement for discipline and discharge. In contrast, most private sector workers covered under the NLRA are at-will employees. How does this difference fit with Professor Freeman's findings?

B. THE POLITICAL NATURE OF PUBLIC SECTOR COLLECTIVE BARGAINING

As discussed previously, public sector employees provide services that have been deemed sufficiently important to be provided by government, rather than left to the free play of market forces. The decision to have government provide the service is itself a policy choice. Decisions concerning the level of services, how those services are to be provided and what level of resources to expend on them also involve choices of public policies.

A wide variety of issues that clearly affect public employees' working conditions also involve choices of public policy. Consider, for example, how police officers will patrol a municipality—in cars, on foot, or on a bicycle, and singularly or in pairs. Consider class size, the length of the school day and the calendar for the school year. All are teacher working conditions and all raise issues of public policy. Minimum staffing levels for fire stations, whether social workers will meet their clients in their offices or make house calls, and residency requirements for public employees are other examples. Even basic issues, such as wages and fringe benefits, involve the allocation of scarce public resources and can affect tax rates and user fees.

Some have argued that public sector collective bargaining is inherently anti-democratic because it provides one interest group, the employees' union, with an avenue of access to the public decision making process that all other interest groups lack. In the following article, Professor Summers confronts these concerns and provides one rationale for public sector collective bargaining in spite of them.

BARGAINING IN THE GOVERNMENT'S BUSINESS: PRINCIPLES AND POLITICS

Clyde Summers
18 University of Toledo Law Review 265 (1987).

I. Introduction

Public employee bargaining chronically suffers from cognitive dissonance. There is repeated acknowledgment that collective bargaining in the public sector is different from collective bargaining in the private sector. At the same time, the statutes enacted for public sector bargaining, and the administrative rules and decisions announced under those statutes are modeled on the statutory rules and decisions of the private sector. Often the same paragraph or even the same sentence affirms both of these perspectives with equal confidence and no overt recognition of the dissonance. This dissonance confuses our discussion and obscures our understanding of many of the problems in public employee bargaining.

II. The Political Character of Public Bargaining

From the union perspective, the public and private sectors have much in common. Both sectors involve the same kind of work; jobs in the public sector are matched by jobs in the private sector—truck drivers, building maintenance, typists, record keepers, teachers, guards, safety personnel, and firefighters. The employees' goals are the same—wages, medical insurance, pensions, holidays, working conditions, job security, and protection against arbitrary supervision. Workers in both sectors seek to protect these interests by the same means—collective representation and collective agreements which secure those rights and make them enforceable through a reasonably prompt and reliable procedure.

From the public employer's side, the perspective is quite different because bargaining is framed by legal and political considerations. Pension benefits may be statutorily defined, public services may be legally required, and personnel matters may be governed by civil service rules. More importantly, employer representatives at the bargaining table have limited authority to make binding agreements because wage increases or benefits are dependent on the budget, which is dependent on taxes, and these are matters for the legislative body, not the negotiators.

The crucial difference is that in the public sector the collective agreement is not a private decision, but a governmental decision; it is not so much a contract as a legislative act. Labor costs may be 70% of a city's budget. Bargaining on wages and other economic items, therefore, inevitably involves the level of taxes and the level of services. An agreement to increase wages requires either an increase in taxes or a decrease in services. Negotiated holidays close city services for the day. Other contractual provisions may affect the kind or quality of public services provided.

In the public sector the ultimate employer is not the mayor or the council but the voters. They are the ones who pay the taxes and receive the services. They are the ones to whom those who make the collective agreement are answerable. From the employer's side, the collective agreement is not an economic decision but a political decision; it shapes policy choices which rightfully belong to the voters to be made through the political processes. Collective bargaining in the public sector is properly and inevitably political; to try to make it otherwise denies democratic principles.

I would suggest that the main source of cognitive dissonance in public sector bargaining is that the participants on both sides are reluctant to confront the implications which follow from recognizing the inherently political character of the process. They feel much more comfortable following the familiar market model of the private sector, giving little more than lip service to the existence of a difference. But, there is a suppressed or subconscious awareness that the difference is fundamental and has implications which require examination.

A. Bargaining and the Political Process

It may be helpful to compare how certain decisions are made with and without collective bargaining. Consider, for example, the question of whether the salaries of teachers should be raised. In the absence of bargaining, individual teachers or teacher organizations will try to persuade the superintendent by petition, discussion or otherwise to provide for an increase in the next school budget. When the budget comes before a public hearing, the teachers, perhaps reinforced by parents or the PTA, will argue for the fairness and need for an increase. Taxpayers, individualized and organized, will argue against the increases and protest the level of taxes the budget will require. The school board or finance committee will retire to executive session and reach a decision. Consider a second question of class size. The process will be much the same, with perhaps more vigorous advocacy by the PTA, but less vigorous advocacy by the taxpayers who may not recognize the relation to taxes. Consider third the question of the teacher's authority to discipline students. Here the teachers will not speak with one voice; some will ask for authority to paddle, and some will ask that paddling be prohibited. The parents will also be divided, and the PTA's may be paralyzed. In both cases, the school board will listen, go into executive session and decide.

Collective bargaining significantly changes the political process. The union, as an exclusive bargaining representative, formulates its demands, and on each of these issues, proceeds to negotiate with the school board's representative behind closed doors. The board is required to respond by giving reasons for its positions, meeting arguments with arguments, and having those arguments examined. Parent organizations and taxpayer organizations are not present. Individual teachers with different views are not present. When an agreement is reached, it is then presented as part of a package decision including many other issues. The taxpayer, the parents and the dissenting teachers do not know the background information, the competing considerations, or the compromises which led to the decision. They have no active voice until the next election when they may by vote change the composition of the school board.

It becomes immediately evident that collective bargaining gives the teachers' collective representative a much more effective voice in the decision-making. The union has more direct access in the decision-making than the taxpayers, the parents or any other voters, and they purport to represent the viewpoint of all teachers although many may disagree. The union is able to deal with public decision-makers behind closed doors without other interests being heard, and to arrive at agreements which are politically difficult, if not legally impossible to change.

Giving employees and their collective representatives this special role in government decision-making is a significant departure from our traditional political processes. This is the discomfort of our cognitive dissonance; how do we reconcile this process with our democratic principles? I do not raise this question to argue against public employee bargaining. On the contrary, my purpose is to try to understand more exactly why we have public employee bargaining. With that understanding we may better shape the structure and scope of the system.

B. The Need for Bargaining on Public Decisions

The first, and for me, compelling reason for public employee bargaining is that our political system has a built-in bias which requires it. The ultimate public employer is the electorate, the taxpayer and the users of public service. Much like other employers they want from their employees high production and low labor costs. In political terms, they want more public service with lower taxes. With labor costs making up 70% or more of the public employer's budget, the political pressure of the whole electorate—taxpayers and service users—is to hold down wages and other economic benefits. No matter how well organized public employees are and what strategic positions they occupy, they are massively outnumbered in votes. The voter is not as compelled by self-interest as a private employer confronting non-union competition, but may be more resistant to wage demands than an employer whose competitors are also unionized and subject to standardized wage terms. Public employees are always at risk that the political demands for low taxes and more service will be placated at their expense.

The collective bargaining process which gives public employees more direct access and ability to persuade the political decision-makers helps offset this built-in political disadvantage.

* * *

NOTES

1. Is Professor Summers right in his assertion that one important justification for allowing public employee collective bargaining is that our political system has a built-in bias against public employee demands that could increase taxes?

2. For a more recent description and analysis of the argument that collective bargaining in the public sector has some anti-democratic effects, see Martin H. Malin, The Paradox of Public Sector Labor Law, 84 *Indiana Law Journal* 1369 (2009).

3. Is it true that bargaining units (voting precincts) defined by employee community of interest, winner-take-all elections, majoritarianism and the principle of exclusivity, formal negotiations monitored by a public agency, and enforceable labor agreements of fixed duration are the best way to protect the standard of living of public employees? Compare civil service and other rules, discussed *infra*, many of which existed in some form long before the 1960s. What advantages and disadvantages do these laws have, compared to laws permitting collective bargaining?

4. Consider, as you go through the following materials, whether the justifications for public sector collective bargaining or the objections to it are strengthened or weakened by some of the significant variations among public sector labor laws. What if the scope of bargaining is severely limited? What if the strike—the motivational force at the bargaining table in the private sector—is either unavailable or ineffective? What if the employer asserts its power to reject consistently the recommendations of factfinders or to frustrate the creation of a binding interest arbitration system as an alternative to strike action?

C. MODERN DEBATES OVER COLLECTIVE BARGAINING IN THE PUBLIC SECTOR

Debates over what types of rights to bargain collectively public workers should have, and indeed whether public workers should have any such rights, continue in the twenty-first century. In this sense, public sector labor law is quite unlike private sector law. The NLRA, passed in 1935, has not been significantly amended since 1959. There is no significant movement to repeal it, and attempts to expand its protections (*e.g.*, the Employee Free Choice Act), have foundered. In contrast, even well into the twenty-first century, legislatures and governors expand and contract the rights of public sector unions with some regularity, through new statutory language and executive orders. Thus, fundamental principles of public sector labor law are, in a significant number of jurisdictions across the country, hotly contested and subject to change. This is generally not true of public sector labor laws in other industrialized democracies, where public sector labor law tracks private sector law much more closely. Throughout these materials, consider when and if the public sector context justifies legal rules quite different from those used in the private sector.

This section discusses two recent examples of changes in the public sector. First, it describes the push to remove or at least substantially limit collective bargaining rights for a large number of federal employees in the Department of Homeland Security and elsewhere. Second, it describes litigation in the state of Missouri on the basic question of what the term "collective bargaining" means. Students may wish to return to these issues for reconsideration after studying the materials on public sector collective bargaining in the rest of this book.

1. ELIMINATING AND RESTRICTING RIGHTS IN THE DEPARTMENT OF HOMELAND SECURITY AND ELSEWHERE IN THE FEDERAL GOVERNMENT

The tragic attacks on September 11, 2001 prompted the reorganization of a significant sector of the federal government into a single agency, the Department of Homeland Security (DHS). From its inception through today, there have been fierce debates over the advisability of covering DHS employees with the standard, pre-existing civil service and labor laws that covered such employees in their predecessor agencies. Notably, however, well before 9/11 and the creation of the DHS, some were already arguing that the labor and civil service laws which govern most federal employees provided too many rights to employees.

These debates have broad implications about labor policy in the entire federal government and arguably beyond. Do certain rights under labor laws and related employment law statutes inhibit the provision of effective government services? Do they facilitate the provision of such services? Do they have any demonstrable impact at all on agency effectiveness? How could we test or evaluate such claims? The debates on the DHS focus on government agencies responsible for national security, but are there reasons to distinguish such agencies from other agencies in this regard? Heated arguments on these topics in federal employment have been going on for over a decade, and they show no sign of abating.

TAKING CHARGE OF FEDERAL PERSONNEL

George Nesterczuk, with Donald J. Devine and Robert E. Moffit
Heritage Foundation Backgrounder #1404
www.heritage.org/Research/GovernmentReform/BG1404.cfm (Jan. 10, 2001).

All too often, people who come to Washington with the goal of reforming government have little appreciation for the immense power and political sophistication of the federal employee network and its allies and the intensity of its resistance to serious change. They also lack a clear conception of federal management approaches and the best model of government administration that would make the federal government work better. * * *

THE POWER OF THE WASHINGTON NETWORK

Washington's notorious Iron Triangle—the alliance of the federal bureaucracy, congressional staff, and interest groups based inside the Beltway—is perhaps at its strongest in resisting civil service reform. Members of Congress and their staffs are self-interested judges in their own cause; public employee associations are generally staffed with former big-government liberals from Capitol Hill who took their generous benefits with them when they left; and federal unions are committed to strengthening their political clout. Although business groups may identify with improved government management, most are concerned with buying access to Capitol Hill and often hire well-connected, senior-level liberal congressional staffers to represent them. And conservative advocacy organizations, which often talk about the need to get "government off our backs," find the social and economic issues far more attractive than mastering the boring details of civil service laws and regulations governing the functioning of the bureaucratic system they dislike. * * *

TAKING CHARGE

* * * For the new President [George W. Bush], succumbing to temptations to rely on the career civil service to begin implementing his political and policy agenda would be a profound mistake. Career civil servants should not be tasked with formulating and executing the details of an agenda for major policy change. Political appointees, personally loyal to the President and fully committed to his policy agenda, are essential to his success * * *. The President needs a full cadre of personnel committed to him and his agenda in the federal agencies that execute the details of national policy.

* * * Political appointees should make key management decisions; such decisions should not be delegated to the career bureaucracy.

The new Administration should provide a clear rationale for continued reductions in the size of the federal workforce and for management changes; workforce reductions should be well planned and systematically implemented.

The new Administration should use the Civil Service Reform Act to improve accountability to the public and improve management of the workforce.

The new Administration should use good management and contracting-out of government services to save the taxpayers billions of dollars. * * *

STRATEGIES FOR THE NEW ADMINISTRATION

President Clinton's effort to "reinvent government" resulted in significant changes. Their net effect, however, has been to undermine strong political management and cabinet government. In order to make the sizable reductions in staffing levels he promised, he formed an alliance with federal unions. He issued an executive order (E.O. 12871) that established "labor-management partnerships"—federal councils which were new entities that elevated the status of federal unions to a level of equality with agency management. Federal unions, as political entities accountable only to their members, had thus become a counterweight to the political management appointed by the President.

The new President will need to revoke President Clinton's executive order and demonstrate from the outset that his approach to reforming the federal bureaucracy will emphasize political responsibility and accountability to the taxpayers. * * *

COMPETING THEORIES OF MANAGEMENT

It would be a profound mistake to view the recurring struggle between reformers and the permanent government as merely a contest over pay or power. Like most political struggles, this conflict exists on a higher level. It is a battle between proponents of very different theories of public administration and styles of management.

The Public Administration Model

Apologists for the permanent government, regardless of their partisan affiliation, are animated by a well-established theory of government administration known as the public administration or scientific management model. * * * It emphasizes the Progressive ideal—a value-free "scientific" program of government administration, based on objective management and policy principles, which is technically administered by neutral career public officials. In such a system, the career officials lead the political appointees, including the President, teaching them the "scientific" solutions residing within the wisdom of the expert civil service and then engineering the solution into a program of action. In other words, theory determines practice. * * *

The Political Administration Model

Policymakers today should be guided in their efforts to downsize the government and improve management practices by an alternative model of government management: the cabinet government or political administration model * * *. It emphasizes political responsibility—providing presidential leadership to committed top political officials and then holding them and their subordinates personally accountable for achievement of the President's election-endorsed and value-defined program. These Cabinet and sub-Cabinet officials then suffuse this program throughout the labyrinth of a bureaucracy that is often resistant to change.

The Pitfalls of the Clinton Approach

President Clinton followed neither approach, opting for what appears to have been a model based on power sharing among constituent interests. As a result, his Administration has at times lurched from a "high-spoils" approach (a crude version of the political management model epitomized by the firing of long-time employees in the White House Travel Office, * * *) to turning the Administration over to federal labor unions, as in the President's October 1993 executive order creating "partnership councils" (a bizarre distortion of "public administration" giving de facto daily management and policymaking authority in federal agencies to labor-management councils).

Although the size of the federal workforce was reduced substantially during Clinton's tenure, nearly three-fourths of that number is attributable to downsizing the Department of Defense, reflecting the end of the Cold War rather than a government "reinvention" initiative. * * *

Political appointees must be in charge of policy.

This * * * means that the Office of Presidential Personnel (OPP) must make appointment decisions based on loyalty first and expertise second, and that the whole governmental apparatus must be managed from this perspective. Picking appointees who are "best for the job" merely in terms of expert qualifications can be disastrous for an Administration genuinely committed to change, because the best qualified are already in the career positions and part of the status quo—the permanent government. Yet sound cabinet government is not simply a spoils system either, so expertise cannot be ignored. * * * It is the political appointees, in the end, who can and must be held accountable for how the bureaucracy functions. It is expecting too much of subordinate career executives and union officials to make difficult and politically sensitive decisions about such issues as pay, hiring, firing, and performance ratings. * * *

Turning control of management decisions over to unions makes even less sense. Unions exist entirely to get more for their members in an environment within which the public demands less. To the extent that President Clinton's plan shifted power to the labor-dominated councils, "reinventing government" proved simply to be a political gift to federal unions. In a perverse way, however, the Clinton Administration plan acknowledged that responsibility should lie with the agency head. Its plan gave decision-making power to the labor-management councils but also recommended that recourse for abuses committed on employees should be taken against the political agency head. * * *

Clinton's initial difficulty in driving the personnel reductions stemmed from his alliance with federal labor unions. The unions politically would not support policies that decimated their ranks, and Clinton promised them that reductions would come from management. His strategy was to flatten the management hierarchy and increase the supervisor-to-employee ratio from 1:7 to 1:15. This goal, however, proved to be unrealistic; the federal workforce simply did not have enough managers to meet the congressionally mandated reduction targets. * * *

In order to achieve these goals, the Administration determined that it needed the support of its political allies, the federal unions. As part of the bargain, President Clinton in October 1993 issued Executive Order 12871 creating a National Partnership Council, which he tasked with advising the Administration on a wide range of federal personnel management issues. The executive order promoted the creation of "labor-management partnerships" in every federal agency to enable the federal unions to act as "full partners with management." The order encouraged agencies to bargain voluntarily with the unions over previously non-bargainable issues reserved under statute as management rights. * * *

The inevitable result of such a course is to make government itself unaccountable. Unions are, at best, responsible to their members. At worst, they represent the permanent government acting on its own self-interest rather than on the desires of the electorate. * * *

The entire "partnership" issue threatened to get totally out of control when federal employee organizations turned to the courts for enforcement of the bargaining provisions in Executive Order 12871. This was a veiled attempt at piercing management's statutorily protected rights. The D.C. Circuit Court found that the basic statutory language of section 7106, Title 5 U.S.C. (so-called (b)(1) permissive bargaining) was not superseded by the language of E.O. 12871. The court left it to the President to force his agency heads to give up their statutory discretion. The FLRA cited this decision in its finding, in a subsequent case, that Sect. 2d of E.O. 12871 could not serve as a basis for filing an unfair labor practice. These losses, together with continued agency resistance, infuriated the Administration's labor allies and prompted President Clinton in 1999 to issue an Executive Memorandum strongly recommending that his Cabinet officers be more cooperative in bargaining with their "partners."

Placing decision-making in the hands of self-interested "partners" puts the interests of the permanent government first. Democratic government is supposed to put the interests of the people first, as those interests are expressed through the electoral process. The people direct the government and its bureaucracy through the Congress and the President. The President especially is expected to press his program through the lowest levels of the executive branch to enact his popular mandate. His subordinates should be tasked with enacting his program, not bargaining with labor unions over what should be done. It is, after all, the President who will be held accountable for the actions or inaction of his Administration—not the unions.

In the area of management of government, as noted, the new President's first act should be to revoke Executive Order 12871. * * *

NOTES

1. What are the implications of the above arguments for labor law and civil service rules in federal employment?

2. President Bush did indeed repeal the Clinton Executive Order authorizing labor-management partnerships. But he and his administration also went considerably further in altering the legal rules of federal employment.

HOMELAND SECURITY VS. WORKERS RIGHTS? WHAT THE FEDERAL GOVERNMENT SHOULD LEARN FROM HISTORY AND EXPERIENCE, AND WHY

Joseph Slater

6 University of Pennsylvania Journal of Labor and Employment Law 295 (2004).

"The Congress finds that experience in both private and public employment indicates that the * * * right of employees to organize [and] bargain collectively * * * safeguards the public interest [and] contributes to the effective conduct of public business."

— Federal Service Labor Management Relations Act (1978)

"Do we really want some work rule negotiated prior to 9/11 to prevent us from finding somebody who is carrying a bomb on a plane with your momma?"

— Senator Phil Gramm (R–Tex.) (2002)

In the aftermath of the horrific attacks of September 11, 2001, outside observers might have been puzzled as to why a push to remove workers' rights delayed the creation of the Department of Homeland Security (DHS) for several months. Specifically, the Bush administration and its Congressional allies would not approve a bill creating the DHS unless the President and administration officials were empowered to design a new personnel system that allowed them to eliminate collective bargaining rights and civil service protections for the approximately 170,000 workers coming into the DHS. Notably, about 48,000 of these workers had previously enjoyed bargaining rights in predecessor agencies.

This issue has wide implications. The administration has already implemented or proposed similar rules to remove collective bargaining and related rights in other parts of the federal government, such as the Transportation Security Administration (TSA), the vast Department of Defense (DOD), and, still in the name of national security, some workers at the Social Security Administration (SSA). * * * Most fundamentally, the DHS debate showed a deep division in how unions are generally viewed: either as useful protectors of worker rights or as obstacles to effective management. For decades, the statutory pronouncements of Congress and most state legislatures have favored collective bargaining in private and public employment. Now this principle is under attack.

During these unprecedented attempts to undo established rights, the debates were compartmentalized and ahistorical. * * * The debate was compartmentalized in that it ignored the experiences of unions outside the federal government: both unions in the private sector and the diverse experiments in public sector labor relations at the state and local level in the past forty years. Policymakers also ignored the literature demonstrating that unions often improve productivity. * * *

The discussions were ahistorical in that they rehashed—with no apparent awareness—stale arguments about the role of unions in government that date from the first half of the twentieth century. Astonishingly, policymakers ignored how the theory and practice of public sector labor relations in the second half of the century have addressed outmoded concerns that worker rights are incompatible with efficient public service and accountability. Thus, the debate was not informed by a tremendous amount of available, relevant evidence from history and experience: evidence of actual experiences under a variety of legal regimes that allow collective bargaining, and evidence of how public sector employment functioned where civil service and bargaining rules were weak or nonexistent.

Because of this, policies crucial to the future of worker rights and the provision of government services—including those relating to public safety—risk retreating into a past that legislatures and the public have largely rejected. Since 1959, no group of workers in the United States has lost the right to bargain collectively under the National Labor Relations Act (NLRA), the law governing private workers. Moreover, public workers at all levels of government have enjoyed greatly expanded collective bargaining rights, albeit under diverse state and local rules. Those arguing for an unprecedented reversal of this trend for a significant part of the federal sector should have the burden of showing why this trend has been in error or is inapplicable in this case. The history and experiences of other unionized workers shows that the opposite is true. For example, assertions that bargaining is inappropriate where public safety is involved should be tested against the reality that collective bargaining is common in police and fire departments.

More broadly, public sector labor law is an excellent example of states acting as "laboratories of democracy." The United States has more than forty years of experience with various public sector bargaining laws at the federal, state and local government level, including laws covering public safety workers. Federalist conservatives and liberals should agree that, in crafting a federal sector law, we should learn from the best practices of labor relations developed in the states. * * *

Federal workers received limited collective bargaining rights for the first time in 1962, when President John F. Kennedy signed Executive Order 10,988. * * *

The rights were limited in that even exclusive representatives could only bargain over a relatively small range of topics. Notably, compensation and hours were not negotiable, as they were set by statute; and the order had a strong management rights clause. Further, there was no mechanism to resolve bargaining impasses on subjects that were negotiable, and certainly no right to strike. Management made all final decisions. Still, federal employees, desiring some voice in their working conditions, embraced their new rights. Within two years, 730,000 federal workers were covered by collective bargaining agreements.

In 1969, President Richard Nixon issued Executive Order 11,491. * * * It added a crucial feature. * * * [I]ndependent government agencies would resolve impasses; the Federal Mediation and Conciliation Service (FMCS) would mediate, and the Federal Services Impasse Panel (FSIP) was created to settle impasses by binding arbitration. * * *

Today, the main federal sector labor law is the Federal Service Labor Management Relations Act (FSLMRA) of 1978. * * *

The FSLMRA retained significant limits on union rights, restrictions that often were understated or ignored in the DHS debates. First, federal sector unions still cannot bargain over a number of subjects that private sector unions are allowed to negotiate. For example, wages, benefits, and hours of work are still set by statute and/or regulation and are not negotiable. * * * Also, the statute has a broad management rights clause. * * *

Indeed, of all labor laws, the FSLMRA contains some of the tightest restrictions on what is legally negotiable. Federal sector unions are often reduced to bargaining over the "effects" or "impact" of management decisions, without any power to bargain over the decision itself. * * *

Second, federal sector unions cannot legally strike in any circumstance. Instead, bargaining impasses are referred first to the FMCS for mediation and then the FSIP for binding arbitration.

Still, * * * federal employees continue to join unions in great numbers. In 2001, 42% of local government workers were in union bargaining units. Unions are able to negotiate, for example, about such topics as health and safety, training, antidiscrimination rules, and grievance/arbitration procedures for discipline. Also significant for employees, in both bargaining impasses and arbitrations over contractual grievances, the FSLMRA provides for hearings by outside neutrals, instead of giving agency managers final authority. * * *

Also relevant to the DHS debate, the FSLMRA excluded or permitted the exclusion of a few agencies and employees whose work was intimately related to national security. There are three sources of such exclusions: sections 7103(a)(3); 7103(b)(1); and 7112(b)(6). The legislative history does not explain the purpose or potential scope of these exclusions, and at least until recently, all were used rarely and applied narrowly. For example, as Senator Dianne Feinstein (D–Cal.) noted during the DHS debates, "Department of Defense civilians with top secret clearances have long been union members." Indeed, employees in all of the major agencies that became part of the DHS were covered by the FSLMRA.

First, the FSLMRA specifically excludes certain agencies, including those dedicated to sensitive and secretive security matters. Section 7103(a)(3) of Title 5 excludes the FBI, CIA, National Security Agency, Secret Service, and Secret Service Uniformed Division.

Second, § 7103(b)(1) grants the President the power to exclude any agency or agency subdivision from coverage "if the President determines that (A) the agency or subdivision has as a primary function intelligence, counterintelligence, investigative, or national security work, and (B) the provisions of this chapter cannot be applied to that agency or subdivision in a manner consistent with national security requirements and considerations." This provision has been invoked fewer than a dozen times since its adoption in 1978 and usually in narrow areas like the Defense Intelligence Agency. * * * [T]he Bush administration created a controversy by applying this exception to workers less obviously enmeshed in national security, employees of U.S. Attorneys' offices around the country.

Third, § 7112(b)(6) allows agencies to exclude individual workers from union bargaining units on national security grounds. It provides that bargaining units under the FSLMRA cannot include "any employee engaged in intelligence, counterintelligence, investigative, or security work which directly affects national security." The FSLMRA does not define "security work," "directly affects," or "national security." In the first major case on this section, the [Federal Labor Relations Authority (FLRA), the agency that administers the FSLRMA] defined "national security" to "include only those sensitive activities of the government that are directly related to the protection and preservation of the military, economic, and productive strength of the United States." The exclusion did not apply to work involving mere access to and use of sensitive information. The FLRA added that this exclusion should be read narrowly because it deprived employees of unionization and bargaining rights, and Congress had determined that unions and collective bargaining in the federal sector are "in the public interest." In 1997, the FLRA slightly broadened the reach of § 7112(b)(6) by excluding certain employees in the Justice Department's Criminal Division and holding that this section can cover workers in civilian as well as military agencies. Beyond this, prior to very recent events, § 7112(b)(6) was rarely used. Indeed, there was never any attempt to apply this exception to workers in the Customs Service, Border Patrol, Immigration and Naturalization Service (INS), or other agencies that would become part of the DHS. * * *

Civil service protections are also at issue in the DHS and other agencies. Federal civil service rules originated in the Pendleton Act of 1883. * * *

The Civil Service Reform Act of 1978 sets the current civil service rules for federal employees. For example, 5 U.S.C. § 2301(b) requires that "selection and advancement" are to be determined "solely" on the basis of "relative ability, knowledge, and skills," and that "employees should be retained on the basis of the adequacy of their performance." The purpose of the law is still to protect merit principles and to avoid patronage and cronyism. * * *

The creation of the DHS was * * * delayed for several months, almost entirely because of disagreements over the amount of authority the President and the newly-created position of Secretary of Homeland Security would have to waive civil service and collective bargaining rights for workers in the new agency. Republicans argued for broader authority and Democrats resisted. * * *

Under the statute, the DHS was to fold in 170,000 employees from twenty-two predecessor agencies, over one-quarter of whom were covered by union contracts. The largest of these agencies were the TSA, the INS, the Customs Service, the FEMA, the Coast Guard, and the Animal and Plant Inspection Service. For example, the DHS includes about 22,000 former Customs workers. * * * * By September, the DHS employed one of every twelve workers in the federal government.

The DHS staff also included workers from seventeen different unions that had negotiated seventy-seven collective bargaining agreements that covered around 48,000 workers. * * *

As to the power to design a personnel system waiving bargaining and civil service rights, the final statutory language has been labeled "an interesting compromise" that creates a presumption of continued bargaining and related rights, while also creating strong authority to revoke those rights. Section 9701 of Title 5 empowers the Homeland Security Secretary to create, through joint regulations with the Director of the Office of Personnel Management (OPM), a new personnel system for the DHS. Such a system must conform with certain existing federal laws, such as antidiscrimination statutes, but it need not follow existing law in other important areas, including FSLMRA rules on collective bargaining. * * *

A few months after the DHS bill was signed into law, the administration again signaled its seriousness about this issue by banning collective bargaining at the TSA. The TSA was created on November 19, 2001 by the Aviation and Transportation Security Act. * * * The TSA soon hired nearly 56,000 screeners to work at more than 480 airports. On March 1, 2003, the TSA was transferred into the DHS.

Prior to the transfer, James Loy, the head of the TSA * * * issued an Order stating that TSA employees, "in light of their critical national security responsibilities, shall not * * * be entitled to engage in collective bargaining or be represented for the purpose of engaging in such bargaining by any representative or organization." Loy explained, "Mandatory collective bargaining is not compatible with the flexibility required to wage the war on terrorism." He added, "Fighting terrorism demands a flexible workforce that can rapidly respond to threats. That can mean changes in work assignments and other conditions of employment that are not compatible with the duty to bargain with labor unions." He also stated that the Order was a response to [the union American Federation of Government Employee's] organization of TSA employees. * * *

Furthering the trend of restricting bargaining rights in the name of national security, the Bush administration has made broad use of the existing national security exemptions in the FSLMRA. First, on January 7, 2002, President Bush issued Executive Order 13252, pursuant to his authority under FSLMRA § 7103(b). This Order excluded from collective bargaining employees in five sections of the Department of Justice, most significantly in U.S. Attorneys' Offices (affecting around 1,000 workers) and the Criminal Division of the Justice Department.

The administration has also taken a more aggressive approach with FSLMRA § 7112(b)(6), the provision allowing agencies to exclude individual workers from union bargaining units on national security grounds. In 2002, Social Security Administration [SSA] officials argued that certain SSA employees should be excluded from a bargaining unit because their work "directly affects national security." The jobs at issue—"electronics technician" and "physical security specialist"—did not even require a security clearance. But the SSA insisted that this exemption applied, arguing that there would be a "significant effect on the national economy" if information in SSA facilities were to be lost. For example, the agency maintained that if its computers were disrupted, "40 million people would be delayed in receiving their social security checks." * * *

[The FLRA's regional director rejected this position, but] in September 2003, the FLRA agreed with the SSA and reversed the decision of the regional director. The regional director had noted that none of the individuals at issue were involved in the investigation of security clearances, none maintained classified materials, none communicated top secret information, and again, none of the jobs required a security clearance. The FLRA held that the employees were excluded nonetheless. The "directly affects national security" test was met if the employees' job tasks included: "(1) the designing, analyzing, or monitoring of security systems or procedures; or (2) the regular use of, or access to, classified information." The FLRA cited the Homeland Security Act's finding that the government protects both classified and "sensitive but un-classified" materials, and the FLRA determined that an employee could be covered by § 7112(b)(6) even if the employee's job did not require a security clearance. It held for the first time that threats to "economic security" alone were covered by § 7112(b)(6). Under this standard, given that the workers at issue had some responsibility for designing or implementing security systems for SSA databases and facilities, they could be excluded from union bargaining units. * * *

Further, on January 28, 2003, James Clapper, Director of the National Imagery and Mapping Agency (NIMA) announced that NIMA employees would no longer have collective bargaining rights due to national security concerns. Clapper's memo also voided existing collective bargaining agreements among NIMA and two AFGE locals representing more than 1,000 employees. Among the employees affected were cartographers, digital imaging specialists, data management specialists, and security guards. * * *

The trend described above became even broader with new proposals for workers in the DOD. * * * . On November 24, 2004, President Bush signed legislation authorizing the DOD to create its own personnel system. Similar to the process at the DHS, the new DOD system will be created through regulations issued jointly by the Secretary of Defense and the Director of the OPM. Among other things, the new law will * * * replace Merit Systems Protection Board hearings with an internal process (with eventual appeal rights to the full Board); and, most ambiguously and potentially problematic, to replace the FLRA with another third-party to review labor disputes.

These provisions could be even more significant than the DHS law. The DOD, with roughly 700,000 employees, is the second-largest federal employer of civilian workers in the nation, after the Postal Service. Given its size, changes to the DOD's personnel system would almost surely affect other federal employees, and quite possibly affect workers outside the federal government. "We're concerned about the 'domino effect,'" said Jeff Friday, counsel for [the National Treasury Employees Union, another union representing federal employees].

NOTES

1. As Professor Slater notes in the article, the federal sector statute provides various exemptions for employees engaged in certain types of national security work. The legislative history of the statute gives little guidance as to the purpose of these exemptions. What might be the purpose be? How should the proper scope of these exemptions be determined?

2. In deciding whether certain groups of employees involved in work involving security, defense, or public safety should have no rights or sharply limited rights under general collective bargaining or civil service statutes, what sort of empirical evidence should be considered? In other words, how would one try to determine what the effects of having or not having such rights would actually be?

3. After the law authorizing the DHS was passed, the Bush administration spent a considerable amount of time in devising a new personnel system for the DHS, a system which greatly reduced employee rights. That system was then challenged as going beyond what the authorizing statute allowed.

NATIONAL TREASURY EMPLOYEES UNION v. CHERTOFF

United States Court of Appeals for the D.C. Circuit, 2006.
452 F.3d 839.

EDWARDS, J.

When Congress enacted the Homeland Security Act of 2002 ("HSA" or the "Act") and established the Department of Homeland Security ("DHS" or the "Department"), it provided that "the Secretary of Homeland Security may, in regulations prescribed jointly with the Director of the Office of Personnel Management, establish, and from time to time adjust, a human resources management system." 5 U.S.C. § 9701(a). Congress made it clear, however, that any such system "shall—(1) be flexible; (2) be contemporary; (3) not waive, modify, or otherwise affect [certain existing statutory provisions relating to, *inter alia,* merit hiring, equal pay, whistleblowing, and prohibited personnel practices, and] (4) ensure that employees may organize, bargain collectively, and participate through labor organizations of their own choosing in decisions which affect them, subject to any exclusion from coverage or limitation on negotiability established by law." *Id.* § 9701(b)(1)–(4). The Act also mandated that DHS employees receive "fair treatment in any appeals that they bring in decisions relating to their employment." Section 9701 does not mention "Chapter 71," which codifies the Federal Services Labor–Management Statute ("FSLMS"), * * *, and delineates the framework for collective bargaining for most federal sector employees.

In February 2005, the Department and Office of Personnel Management ("OPM") issued regulations establishing a human resources management system * * * ("Final Rule" or "HR system"). The Final Rule, *inter alia,* defines the scope and process of collective bargaining for affected DHS employees, channels certain disputes through the Federal Labor Relations Authority ("FLRA" or the "Authority"), creates an in-house Homeland Security Labor Relations Board ("HSLRB"), and assigns an appellate role to the Merit Systems Protection Board ("MSPB") in cases involving penalties imposed on DHS employees.

Unions representing many DHS employees (the "Unions") [challenged] aspects of the Final Rule. In a detailed and thoughtful opinion, * * * the District Court found that the regulations would not ensure collective bargaining, would fundamentally and impermissibly alter FLRA jurisdiction, and would create an appeal process at MSPB that is not fair. * * * However, the District Court rejected the Unions' claims that the regulations impermissibly restricted the scope of bargaining and that DHS lacked authority to give MSPB an intermediate appellate function in cases involving mandatory removal offenses. * * * We affirm in part and reverse in part.

We hold that the regulations fail in two important respects to "ensure that employees may * * * bargain collectively," as the HSA requires. First, we agree with the District Court that the Department's attempt to reserve to itself the right to unilaterally abrogate lawfully negotiated and executed agreements is plainly unlawful. If the Department could unilaterally abrogate lawful contracts, this would nullify the Act's specific guarantee of collective bargaining rights, because the agency cannot "ensure" collective bargaining without affording employees the right to negotiate binding agreements.

Second, we hold that the Final Rule violates the Act insofar as it limits the scope of bargaining to employee-specific personnel matters. The regulations effectively eliminate all meaningful bargaining over fundamental working conditions (including even negotiations over procedural protections), thereby committing the bulk of decisions concerning conditions of employment to the Department's exclusive discretion. In no sense can such a limited scope of bargaining be viewed as consistent with the Act's mandate that DHS "ensure" collective bargaining rights for its employees. The Government argues that the HSA does not require the Department to adhere to the terms of Chapter 71 and points out that the Act states that the HR system must be "flexible," and from this concludes that a drastically limited scope of bargaining is fully justified. This contention is specious. Although the HSA does not compel the Government to adopt the terms of Chapter 71 as such, Congress did not say that Chapter 71 is irrelevant to an understanding of how DHS is to comply with its obligations under the Act. "Collective bargaining" is a term of art and Chapter 71 gives guidance to its meaning. It is also noteworthy that the HSA requires that the HR system be "contemporary" as well as flexible. We know of no contemporary system of *collective bargaining* that limits the scope of bargaining to employee-specific personnel matters, as does the HR system, and the Government cites to none. We therefore reverse the District Court on this point.

We affirm the District Court's judgment that the Department exceeded its authority in attempting to conscript FLRA into the HR system. The Authority is an independent administrative agency, operating pursuant to its own organic statute and long-established procedures. Although the Department was free to avoid FLRA altogether, it chose instead to impose upon the Authority a completely novel appellate function, defining FLRA's jurisdiction and dictating standards of review to be applied by the Authority. In essence, the Final Rule attempts to co-opt FLRA's administrative machinery, prescribing new practices in an exercise of putative authority that only Congress possesses. Nothing in the HSA allows DHS to disturb the operations of FLRA.

Finally, we reverse without prejudice the District Court's finding that DHS was without authority to change the standard by which the MSPB might mitigate a penalty for employee misconduct. This matter is not ripe for review. * * *

BACKGROUND

The Homeland Security Act

The Homeland Security Act was enacted in November 2002. It established the Department, a cabinet-level agency whose mission is to "prevent and deter terrorist attacks[,] protect against and respond to threats and hazards to the nation[,] * * * ensure safe and secure borders, welcome lawful immigrants and visitors, and promote the free-flow of commerce." The Act merged 22 existing agencies from across the federal government, integrating 170,000 employees, 17 unions, 7 payroll systems, 77 collective bargaining units, and 80 personnel systems.

As noted above, HSA authorizes the Secretary of Homeland Security, with the Director of the Office of Personnel Management, to promulgate regulations establishing a HR system. The Act reads in pertinent part as follows:

> IN GENERAL.—* * * the Secretary of Homeland Security may, in regulations prescribed jointly with the Director of the Office of Personnel Management, establish, and from time to time adjust, a human resources management system for some or all of the organizational units of the Department of Homeland Security.
>
> SYSTEM REQUIREMENTS.—Any system established under subsection (a) shall—(1) be flexible;
>
> (2) be contemporary; * * *
>
> (4) ensure that employees may organize, bargain collectively, and participate through labor organizations of their own choosing in decisions which affect them, subject to any exclusion from coverage or limitation on negotiability established by law; * * * .

As may be seen from the text of the Act, § 9701 says little about the substantive terms of the HR system. Notably, however, the Act mandates that any HR system "ensure that employees may organize, bargain collectively, and participate through labor organizations of their own choosing in decisions which affect them." * * *

On February 1, 2005, DHS and OPM promulgated the Final Rule establishing the new HR system. * * *

Collective Bargaining

As the District Court noted, the Final Rule "contain[s] an expansive management rights provision and severely restrict[s] collective bargaining to issues that affect individual employees." Collective bargaining under the new HR system is defined to mean "the performance of the mutual obligation of a management representative of the Department and an exclusive representative of employees * * * to meet at reasonable times and to consult and bargain in a good faith effort to reach agreement with respect to the conditions of employment affecting such employees." Most "conditions of employment," however, are placed off-limits for bargaining. Thus, the Final Rule states:

> nothing in this subpart may affect the authority of any management official or supervisor of the Department—
>
> (1) To determine the mission, budget, organization, number of employees, and internal security practices of the Department;
>
> (2) To hire, assign, and direct employees in the Department; to assign work, make determinations with respect to contracting out, and to determine the personnel by which Departmental operations may be conducted; to determine the numbers, types, grades, or occupational clusters and bands of employees or positions assigned to any organizational subdivision, work project or tour of duty, and the technology,

methods, and means of performing work; to assign and deploy employees to meet any operational demand; and to take whatever other actions may be necessary to carry out the Department's mission; and

(3) To lay off and retain employees, or to suspend, remove, reduce in grade, band, or pay, or take other disciplinary action against such employees or, with respect to filling positions, to make selections for appointments from properly ranked and certified candidates for promotion or from any other appropriate source.

In addition, management "is prohibited from bargaining over the exercise of any authority under paragraph (a) of this section or the procedures that it will observe in exercising the authorities set forth in paragraphs (a)(1) and (2) of this section."

The Final Rule states that management must bargain over

(1) Appropriate arrangements for employees adversely affected by the exercise of any authority under paragraph (a)(3) of this section and procedures which management officials and supervisors will observe in exercising any authority under paragraph (a)(3) of this section; and

(2)(i) Appropriate arrangements for employees adversely affected by the exercise of any authority under paragraph (a)(1) or (2) of this section, provided that the effects of such exercise have a significant and substantial impact on the bargaining unit, or on those employees in that part of the bargaining unit affected by the action or event, and are expected to exceed or have exceeded 60 days. Appropriate arrangements within the duty to bargain include proposals on matters such as—

(A) Personal hardships and safety measures; and

(B) Reimbursement for out-of-pocket expenses incurred by employees as the direct result of the exercise of authorities under this section.

However, "[a]ppropriate arrangements within the duty to bargain do not include proposals on such matters as—(A) [t]he routine assignment to specific duties, shifts, or work on a regular or overtime basis; and (B) [c]ompensation for expenses not actually incurred, or pay or credit for work not actually performed."

In analyzing the provisions of 5 C.F.R. § 9701.511, the District Court wryly commented:

"Translated into English, this Regulation would give management full discretion over all aspects of the Department except those that might be seen as personal employee grievances."

The new HR system also authorizes the Department to unilaterally abrogate lawfully negotiated and executed collective bargaining agreements. In addition to securing DHS's authority to override agreements that are in existence when the HR system takes effect, the Final Rule purports to authorize the Department to unilaterally set aside provisions in agreements that are negotiated and executed under the new HR system. An agreement may be invalidated by DHS's Secretary (or a designee) within 30 days of being executed if found to be inconsistent with Departmental rules or regulations. Even if not explicitly disapproved, an agreement takes effect "only if consistent with law, the regulations in this part, Governmentwide rules and regulations, Departmental implementing directives and other policies and regulations, and Executive orders."

The Final Rule also gives DHS ongoing authority to abrogate agreements after they take effect:

> Provisions in existing collective bargaining agreements are unenforceable if an authorized agency official determines that they are contrary to law, the regulations in this part, Governmentwide rules and regulations, Departmental implementing directives * * * and other policies and regulations, or Executive orders.

Moreover, as noted above, the "management rights" provision in the Final Rule authorizes the Department "to take whatever other actions may be necessary to carry out the Department's mission." Taken together, these regulations subordinate all collective bargaining agreements to the prerogatives of management. * * *

2. *The Roles of the Homeland Security Labor Relations Board and the Federal Labor Relations Authority*

The Federal Labor Relations Authority is an independent administrative federal agency that was created by Title VII of the Civil Service Reform Act of 1978, also known as the Federal Service Labor–Management Relations Statute and "FSLMRS." The FSLMRS allows certain non-postal federal employees to organize, bargain collectively, and participate through labor organizations of their choice in decisions affecting their working lives. The primary statutory responsibilities of FLRA include: (1) resolving complaints of unfair labor practices, (2) determining the appropriateness of units for labor organization representation, (3) adjudicating exceptions to arbitrator's awards, (4) adjudicating legal issues relating to duty to bargain/negotiability, and (5) resolving impasses during negotiations.

The HSA does not specify a role for FLRA under the HR system. * * * DHS and many of its employees are within the purview of the Authority's jurisdiction. * * * The Authority's jurisdiction to hear matters affecting DHS employees is limited, however, to the extent that the Final Rule supplants the substantive provisions of the FSLMRS pursuant to § 9701 of the HSA.

The Final Rule establishes the Homeland Security Labor Relations Board, composed of a rotating board of members—appointed by the Secretary of Homeland Security. * * * The regulations empower HSLRB to, *inter alia,* (1) resolve issues relating to the scope of bargaining under the regulations and the duty to bargain in good faith, (2) conduct hearings and resolve complaints of unfair labor practices, (3) resolve exceptions to arbitration awards involving the exercise of management rights and the duty to bargain, (4) resolve negotiation impasses, (5) conduct *de novo* review of legal conclusions involving all matters within its jurisdiction, and (6) assume jurisdiction over any matter concerning DHS employees that has been submitted to FLRA "if the HSLRB determines that the matter affects homeland security." The regulations also authorize HSLRB to "issue binding Department-wide opinions" * * * There is no doubt that the HSLRB was created to supplant FLRA with respect to many matters that would otherwise be within the Authority's jurisdiction.

Although the Final Rule obviously was adopted to replace many of the substantive provisions of the FSLMRS, the regulations nonetheless purport to create a limited role for FLRA *under the HR system*. The Final Rule provides that any party who wishes to obtain judicial review of a HSLRB decision must first seek FLRA review. But the Authority's role is tightly circumscribed:

> The Authority must defer to findings of fact and interpretations of this part made by the HSLRB and sustain the HSLRB's decision unless the requesting party shows that the HSLRB's decision was—
>
> (i) Arbitrary, capricious, an abuse of discretion, or otherwise not in accordance with law;
>
> (ii) Based on error in applying the HSLRB's procedures that resulted in substantial prejudice to a party affecting the outcome; or
>
> (iii) Unsupported by substantial evidence.

The Final Rule also purports to give FLRA limited authority to determine the appropriateness of bargaining units within DHS, supervise or conduct elections, adjudicate some unfair labor practice disputes, and resolve some exceptions to arbitral awards. However, HSLRB "[a]ssume[s] jurisdiction over any matter concerning Department employees that has been submitted to FLRA * * * if the HSLRB determines that the matter affects homeland security." And the Final Rule confers sole authority on HSLRB to determine whether a particular matter "affects homeland security" or otherwise belongs on HSLRB's docket.

3. *The Role of the Merit Systems Protection Board*

Normally, Chapter 77 allows federal employees to appeal adverse actions to the MSPB. As noted above, the HSA states that DHS employees must receive due process in pursuing their appeals, and that * * * regulations " * * * shall modify procedures under chapter 77 only insofar as such modifications are designed to further the fair, efficient, and expeditious resolution of matters involving the employees of the Department."

MSPB's role under the HR system is sharply limited. The regulations significantly diminish MSPB's ability to mitigate penalties imposed on employees. As DHS acknowledges, normally, when MSPB reviews an agency's penalty decision under Chapter 77, it seeks to determine "not only whether [the penalties] were too harsh or otherwise arbitrary but also whether they were unreasonable under all the circumstances.'' *See Douglas v. Veterans Admin.*, 5 MSPB 313, 5 M.S.P.R. 280 (1981). The Final Rule imposes a narrower role for MSPB, stating that ''MSPB may not modify the penalty imposed by the Department unless such penalty is so disproportionate to the basis for the action as to be wholly without justification.''

The Final Rule also defines a new class of ''mandatory removal offenses'' for DHS employees. A mandatory removal offense is ''an offense that the Secretary determines in his or her sole, exclusive, and unreviewable discretion has a direct and substantial adverse impact on the Department's homeland security mission.'' Appeals of mandatory removal actions are heard by DHS's Mandatory Removal Panel (''MRP''). An employee may only obtain judicial review of a mandatory removal action after first seeking review before the MRP. When MSPB reviews an MRP decision, it ''must accept the findings of fact and interpretations of this part made by the MRP and sustain the MRP's decision unless the employee shows'' that the underlying decision was:

> (i) Arbitrary, capricious, an abuse of discretion, or otherwise not in accordance with law;
>
> (ii) Caused by harmful error in the application of the MRP's procedures in arriving at such decision; or
>
> (iii) Unsupported by substantial evidence.

* * *

C. Litigation Before the District Court

The District Court [held] that the ''*sine qua non* of good-faith collective bargaining is an enforceable contract once the parties reach an agreement.'' The court found that the Final Rule flouted this standard by allowing DHS to unilaterally abrogate agreements. The District Court tellingly noted:

> A contract that is not mutually binding is not a contract. Negotiations that lead to a contract that is not mutually binding are not true negotiations. A system of ''collective bargaining'' that permits the unilateral repudiation of agreements by one party is not collective bargaining at all. The court thus concluded that the Department was owed no deference under *Chevron* * * * on this point.

The District Court declined to accept the Unions' argument that the Final Rule impermissibly restricted the scope of bargaining, however. Although the court agreed that the regulations' ''eradication of virtually all bargaining over 'operational' issues will have a dramatic effect upon the work lives of the employees the [Unions] represent,'' it nonetheless found that ''Congress gave the [Department] the authority to ignore the provisions of Chapter 71 and to establish new metes and bounds for collective bargaining at DHS.'' * * *

The District Court sustained the Unions' objections to the role assigned to FLRA by the Final Rule. On this point, the court held that DHS could not "commandeer the resources of an independent agency and thereby fundamentally transform its functions, absent a clearer indication of congressional intent."

The District Court also found that the Final Rule violated § 9701(f)(2) of the HSA, because the restrictions on MSPB review "result[ ] in a system that is not fair." The court found that, because the Final Rule specified that MSPB could modify penalties only when they are "so disproportionate as to be wholly without justification," review would become "almost a nullity." * * *

II. ANALYSIS

* * * The question here is whether the disputed portions of the HR system adhere to the limitations imposed by § 9701. In particular, we must determine whether, in promulgating the Final Rule, DHS reasonably interpreted the controlling provisions of the HSA. In reviewing the Department's interpretations of the Act, we apply the familiar standards enunciated by the Supreme Court in *Chevron*. * * *

[T]he Unions do not question DHS's authority to promulgate regulations defining collective bargaining; they contend instead that the specific regulatory standards selected by the Department to narrow the scope of bargaining and allow for the unilateral abrogation of agreements do not give effect to the HSA's command to "ensure that employees may organize, bargain collectively, and participate through labor organizations of their own choosing in decisions which affect them." Likewise, the Unions do not doubt that the Department could have opted to have disputes arising under the HR system be resolved by FLRA pursuant to the terms of the Federal Services Labor–Management Statute (Chapter 71); rather, they contend that DHS had no authority to conscript the Authority to function under the HR system on terms defined by the Department.

C. The Duty to Ensure Collective Bargaining

* * * When § 9701 is read in its entirely, it is absolutely clear that DHS does not have a free hand to construct a HR system entirely as it prefers. * * * Most importantly, at least with respect to the issues in this case, when Congress added the substantive requirement in the HSA guaranteeing DHS employees the right to bargain collectively, it obviously intended for this requirement to be construed reasonably and applied fully.

Although the HSA requires the Department to "ensure" that their employees may bargain collectively, the Act does not define collective bargaining. Fortunately, this is not a term without meaning. Indeed, "collective bargaining" is a term of art in the federal sector that has been defined by Congress in the FSLMS:

> "[C]ollective bargaining" means the performance of the mutual obligation of the representative of an agency and the exclusive representative of employees in an appropriate unit in the agency to meet at reasonable times and to consult and bargain in a good-faith effort to reach agreement with respect to the conditions of employment affecting such employees and to execute, if requested by either party, a written document incorporating any collective bargaining agreement reached, but the obligation referred to in this paragraph does not compel either party to agree to a proposal or to make a concession. 5 U.S.C. § 7103(a)(12) (2000).

The Government's incantation of the truism that collective bargaining "is not a static concept with a fixed meaning in all circumstances," is thus beside the point. In the context of federal sector labor-relations, collective bargaining is a term of art with a well-established statutory meaning. * * *

There is a presumption that Congress uses the same term consistently in different statutes. Given the parallel provisions in the FSLMS, [and] the HSA * * * it is clear that "collective bargaining" under the HSA gains meaning from the application of that same term under Chapter 71. * * *

[T]he HSA states explicitly that, in establishing a new HR system, the Department "shall" ensure that employees may organize, bargain collectively, and participate through labor organizations of their own choosing in decisions which affect them, subject to any exclusion from coverage or limitation on negotiability established by law. This statutory obligation is mandatory, not optional. And if, as shown above, "collective bargaining" means the same thing under both the HSA and the FSLMS, then application of the term under the latter statute cannot possibly be irrelevant to an understanding of how the term applies under the former.

* * * The obvious problem with the HR system is that very few "conditions of employment" are subject to meaningful bargaining, and the few conditions over which the parties can negotiate may be unilaterally abrogated by management. A system of this sort does not even give an illusion of collective bargaining.

1. DHS's Asserted Power to Unilaterally Abrogate Collective Bargaining Agreements

The most extraordinary feature of the Final Rule is that it reserves to the Department the right to unilaterally abrogate lawfully negotiated and executed agreements. This is plainly impermissible under the HSA. If the Department could unilaterally abrogate lawful contracts, this would nullify the statute's specific guarantee of collective bargaining rights, because DHS cannot "ensure" collective bargaining without affording employees the right to negotiate binding agreements. The District Court's decision on this point is exactly right:

> The Regulations fail because any collective bargaining negotiations pursuant to its terms are illusory: the Secretary retains numerous

> avenues by which s/he can unilaterally declare contract terms null and void, without prior notice to the Unions or employees and without bargaining or recourse. * * *

In the Government's view, the provisions at issue represent a reasonable, and therefore permissible, understanding of "collective bargaining." Congress required DHS to craft a HR system that is "flexible" and "contemporary," and the Government insists that DHS deserves deference in weighing those objectives in its efforts to ensure collective bargaining. The Government's arguments on this point are completely unconvincing, because they ignore Congress' explicit command that any HR system "ensure that employees may * * * bargain collectively." A system that gives the Department a free hand to selectively vitiate collectively bargained agreements does not obey that command.

As noted above, "collective bargaining" is a term of art, defined in other statutory schemes, and DHS was not free to treat it as an empty linguistic vessel. None of the major statutory frameworks for collective bargaining allows a party to unilaterally abrogate a lawfully executed agreement. *See, e.g.,* 5 U.S.C. §§ 7102(2), 7103(a)(12) (2000) (federal sector bargaining); 29 U.S.C. § 158(a)(5), (b)(3) & (d) (2000) (private sector bargaining); 39 U.S.C. § 1206 (2000) (U.S. Postal Service); 45 U.S.C. § 152 (Fourth) (2000) (common carriers). Indeed, no statutorily mandated *collective bargaining* system that we are aware of dispenses with the premise that negotiated agreements bind both parties. * * * [W]hen pressed at oral argument, the Government could provide no counterexample.

The HR system embodied in the Final Rule has no antecedent, because it undermines the very idea of collective bargaining. Structuring collective bargaining so that labor and management meet to negotiate terms until they reach an accord or an impasse only makes sense on the assumption that each side's evolving bargaining position will reflect a series of tradeoffs that move the parties toward a mutually satisfactory end point. It is therefore dispositive that the HSA refers to *collective bargaining*—not merely "consultation" or "notification". * * * When Congress intended to *deny* collective bargaining rights and provide only advisory roles to employee representatives, it used different language. *Compare* 5 U.S.C. § 9701(b)(4) ("bargain collectively"), *with id.* § 9701(e) ("collaboration" or "consultation" through "meet and confer" process), *and* 5 U.S.C. § 7113 (2000) ("national consultation rights").

Finally, the Government's position not only defies the well-understood meaning of collective bargaining, it also defies common sense. As noted above, collective bargaining is a method of structuring the formation of labor contracts, and the notion of mutual obligation is inherent in contract law. *See Restatement (Second) of Contracts* § 3 (1979) ("* * *A bargain is an agreement to exchange promises or to exchange a promise for a performance or to exchange performances."). To imagine that a system might "ensure collective bargaining" without imposing mutual obligations is simply bizarre. * * *

2. *The Scope of Bargaining*

The right to negotiate collective bargaining agreements that are equally binding on both parties is of little moment if the parties have virtually nothing to negotiate over. That is the result of the Final Rule adopted by DHS. The scope of bargaining under the HR system is virtually nil, especially when measured against the meaning of collective bargaining under Chapter 71. And this is saying a lot, because the scope of bargaining under Chapter 71 is extraordinarily narrow. * * *

Having reviewed the Final Rule with care, we find that the limited scope of bargaining under the proposed HR system violates the Act, and on this point we reverse the District Court. * * *

We cannot assume that Congress deployed a term of art, with a long history of legal usage, while contemplating that DHS could completely drain that term of significance.

* * * As the District Court found, "[t]he HR System essentially reduces collective bargaining to employee-specific terms affecting discipline, discharge and promotion." This is so far short of the meaning of collective bargaining under Chapter 71 that we are constrained to hold that the Final Rule does not meet the HSA's requirement of bargaining in good faith over conditions of employment for purposes of reaching an agreement.

It is readily apparent that the Final Rule reflects a flagrant departure from the norms of "collective bargaining" underlying Chapter 71. * * * For example, "permissive" areas of bargaining under Chapter 71 are off limits for negotiation at DHS. This distinction is critical. Procedures for exercising rights affecting issues like work assignments and deployments are negotiable under Chapter 71, but not under the HR system. And, under the HR system, when management exercises one of its rights, it need not provide notice to labor representatives in advance. Moreover, the proposed HR system gives DHS broad new authority "to take whatever other actions may be necessary to carry out the Department's mission." Presumably, this provision empowers DHS to take any matter off the bargaining table at any time, regardless of what concessions have already been made by union representatives. No analogous power exists anywhere in Chapter 71. Most strikingly, DHS management is prohibited from negotiating over the "procedures it will observe in exercising" the authority laid out in subsections (a)(1) and (a)(2) of the management rights provision. Instead, management must merely "confer" with labor representatives about the procedures it will use. These provisions stand in sharp contrast to Chapter 71's obligation to bargain over the procedures used to exercise management rights.

Finally, Chapter 71 requires agencies to bargain over "appropriate arrangements" for employees adversely affected by the exercise of a management right. The HR system shrinks such bargaining considerably. For the "operational matters" committed to management discretion * * * DHS must negotiate appropriate arrangements only when "the effects of [management's exercise of a right] have a significant and substantial impact on the bargaining unit, or on those employees in that part of the bargaining unit affected by the action or event, and are expected to exceed or have exceeded 60 days." Even under these narrow circumstances, appropriate arrangement proposals must be limited to such matters as personal hardships and safety measures, or reimbursements for out-of-pocket expenses. The Final Rule thus effectively strips the term "collective bargaining" of any real meaning in limiting the scope of bargaining. * * *

Furthermore, it must be recalled that the duty to bargain does not require agreement, only a good faith effort by the parties to reach agreement. Additionally, employees in the federal sector are forbidden from striking, so they can add no economic leverage to their bargaining demands as can employees in the private sector. And, most importantly, employees covered by DHS's HR system will not have the advantage of an impasses panel—which can *impose* conditions of employment if the parties' negotiations reach an impasse as do employees who are covered by Chapter 71. * * *

3. *The Final Rule Fails to Ensure Collective Bargaining for DHS Employees in Two Critical Respects—Therefore No Deference is Due the Department's Interpretation of the HSA*

* * * An agency construction of a statute cannot survive judicial review * * * if a contested regulation reflects an action that is inconsistent with the agency's authority. * * *

In this case, as we have shown, DHS's Final Rule defies the plain language of the Act, because it renders "collective bargaining" meaningless; and it is utterly unreasonable and thus impermissible, because it makes no sense on its own terms. * * *

D. The Role of the HSLRB

The Unions also argue that DHS's HR system impermissibly shrinks the collective bargaining requirement in a third way: by funneling bargaining disputes to HSLRB. The Unions object to HSLRB, because, in their view, the new board lacks sufficient independence to provide the neutral adjudication required of a collective bargaining regime. * * *

Our holding in Part E below, relating to the role of FLRA under the HR system, renders this issue unripe for resolution. The Final Rule is flawed insofar as it allows DHS to encroach on FLRA's operations without the statutory authority to do so. * * *

E. DHS's Attempt to Regulate FLRA

* * * The District Court was "convinced that [DHS] cannot commandeer the resources of an independent agency and thereby fundamentally

transform its functions, absent a clearer indication of congressional intent.'' We agree.

As explained above, the Final Rule quite clearly intends to impose a novel procedural scheme on FLRA, even though nothing in the HSA authorizes DHS to regulate the work of the Authority or alter its statutory jurisdiction. The Authority is an independent agency operating pursuant to its organic statute under Chapter 71. Chapter 71 prescribes FLRA's functions and authority. * * * DHS's Final Rule attempts to conscript FLRA into reviewing a narrowly defined area of cases under an intensely deferential standard of review. Whereas FLRA's statutory function involves the exercise of judgment and significant authority, the Final Rule shrinks the Authority's role, using it only to guard against substantial adjudicative failures by HSLRB. Indeed, under the Final Rule, FLRA's role with respect to any matter relating to a DHS employee would evaporate if HSLRB ''determines that the matter affects homeland security.'' The role of FLRA under the HR system bears no resemblance to its normal statutory role, and conforming to the regulations would therefore require FLRA to substantially change its operating functions.

The Government fruitlessly searches 5 U.S.C. § 9701 for the authority necessary to rearrange FLRA's operations. * * *

III. CONCLUSION

The allowance of unilateral contract abrogation and the limited scope of bargaining under DHS's Final Rule plainly violate the statutory command in the HSA that the Department ''ensure'' collective bargaining for its employees. We therefore vacate any provisions of the Final Rule that betray this command. DHS's attempt to co-opt FLRA's administrative machinery constitutes an exercise of power far outside the Department's statutory authority. We therefore affirm the District Court's decision to vacate the provisions of the Final Rule that encroach on the Authority. We reverse the District Court's holding that MSPB's standard of review in penalty modification cases represents a failure to provide ''fair'' appellate procedures, because that issue is not yet ripe for review. And we express no view on the role of the HSLRB, because the matter cannot be addressed until DHS revises the Final Rule.

NOTES

1. The District Court for the District of Columbia came to a similar conclusion about a somewhat similar statute authorizing a new personnel system for the even larger Department of Defense (DoD). However, on appeal, the D.C. Circuit reversed, in *American Federation of Government Employees v. Gates*, 486 F.3d 1316 (D.C. Cir. 2007). The court found the statute governing the DoD, the National Defense Authorization Act (NDAA), differed in at least one significant respect from the statute governing the DHS. While certain parts of the NDAA stated that collective bargaining would be generally available to DoD employees, the Court found that other sections of the NDAA

temporarily overrode those provisions. Specifically, the NDAA provided for collective bargaining after November 2009, but it set up an experimental period before then during which the DoD had broad discretion to fashion its labor relations system. Thus, the provisions of the NDAA that permit collective bargaining for civilian workers of the DoD applied after November 2009.

2. Currently, President Obama has indicated that he would return collective bargaining rights to employees at the DHS and TSA, but some Congressional Republicans are sharply opposed to this. The disagreement helped cause long delays in appointing a new TSA director.

3. The Court held that challenges to the revised civil service rules were unripe. Nonetheless, after this case, the Bush administration did not attempt to impose the revised civil service rules, and the Obama administration has shown no interest in doing so. Thus, DHS employees remain covered by the pre-existing civil service and MSPB rules described in Chapter 3, § C. In your opinion, would any of the revisions described in *Chertoff* have been an improvement? Why or why not?

4. Judge Harry Edwards, who wrote the opinion in this case, is an expert in labor law. Also the judge who wrote the District Court opinion in this case, Rosemary Collyer, had previous served as General Counsel to the National Labor Relations Board under President Reagan. In what ways might the experience these judges had in labor law have informed their decisions?

5. Is "collective bargaining" a term of art, as *Chertoff* says? If so, what does it mean? Consider this question when you read the following materials.

2. WHAT DOES "COLLECTIVE BARGAINING "MEAN"? LITIGATION UNDER THE MISSOURI STATE CONSTITUTION

In 1945, Missouri added to its state Constitution the following clause: employees shall have the right to organize and to bargain collectively through representatives of their own choosing." In 1947, the Missouri Supreme Court held that this clause did not apply to public employees. *City of Springfield v. Clouse,* 356 Mo. 1239, 206 S.W.2d 539, 542 (1947). In 2007, the Missouri Supreme Court reconsidered *Clouse*. In so doing, it set up a fascinating and important debate over what the term "collective bargaining through representatives of their own choosing" meant.

INDEPENDENCE–NATIONAL EDUCATION ASSOCIATION v. INDEPENDENCE SCHOOL DISTRICT

Supreme Court of Missouri, 2007.
223 S.W.3d 131.

WOLFF, C.J.

Introduction

The Missouri Constitution's bill of rights contains the following guarantee: "employees shall have the right to organize and to bargain collectively through representatives of their own choosing." Missouri Constitution article I, section 29.

This case raises two issues:

1. Does the "right to organize and to bargain collectively" apply to public employees as well as private-sector employees?

2. If the public employer, in this case the school district, negotiates an agreement with its employee groups, may the public employer unilaterally impose a new employment agreement that contradicts the terms of the agreements then in effect?

The answer to the first question, which follows the plain words of the constitution, is yes.

The answer to the second question—with the understanding that the law does not require the school district as public employer to reach agreements with its employee associations—is no.

Unquestionably, public employees are differently situated from private employees and are treated differently under the law. The law, for instance, forbids strikes by public employees. *St. Louis Teachers Ass'n. v. Board of Education,* 544 S.W.2d 573, 575 (Mo. banc 1976). There are two basic reasons for the no-strike laws. The first is that many public employees-especially police and firefighters—are deemed essential to the preservation of public safety, health, and order. The second is that the economic forces of the marketplace—that limit, at least in theory, the extent to which employers can meet employee groups' demands—do not constrain the public sector. In the public sector, meeting the demands of employee groups is thought to infringe on the constitutional prerogative of the public entity's legislative powers by forcing the entity to raise taxes or distribute public services in a manner inconsistent with the best judgment of the entity's governing board.

The trial court held that the Independence School District was not required to bargain collectively with its employees and was not bound by any agreements that it had entered with groups representing its employees.

The rights guaranteed by article I, section 29 apply to "employees." Under the express words of the constitution, this provision is not limited to private-sector employees. All employees, including those represented by the employee associations in this case, have the "right to bargain collectively." Although the employer is not required to reach an agreement with employees as to working conditions, once an employer has done so, it is bound by the terms of that agreement.

The judgment of the trial court is reversed, and the case is remanded.

Facts and Procedural History

* * * Three employee associations sued the Independence School District, a public school district governed by a board of education. The Independence–Transportation Employees Association represents the dis-

trict's transportation employees. The Independence–Educational Support Personnel represents the district's custodial employees. These associations are certified as the exclusive bargaining representatives for their respective employees pursuant to Missouri's public sector labor law; section 105.500, *et seq.* The Independence–National Education Association represents the district's teachers and paraprofessionals.

Before the events at issue in this litigation, it was customary for representatives of the transportation and custodial employee associations to meet and confer separately with representatives of the board about proposals relating to the salaries and working conditions of their represented employees. The results of these discussions were reduced to writing in the form of memoranda of understanding, in accordance with the public sector labor law. Each memorandum of understanding was approved by the board's authorized representatives.

Though teachers are not included in the public sector labor law, it was customary for the district to hold discussions with representatives of the Independence National Educational Association relating to teachers' working conditions, pursuant to a "discussion procedure" that was adopted by the board.

In April 2002, the board and the employee groups had in effect memoranda of understanding and, in the case of the teachers, a "discussion procedure" agreement that the board had previously approved.

The board, however, unilaterally adopted a new "Collaborative Team Policy" in April 2002 that changed the terms of employment of the employees represented by these associations. The district did not meet and confer with the employee associations or obtain their consent before imposing the "Collaborative Team Policy."

The new policy conflicted with the memoranda of understanding then in effect for both the transportation employees and the custodial workers. The memorandum of understanding for the transportation employees contained substantive provisions, including those relating to grievances, payroll deductions, discipline, and dismissal, that were rescinded by the board's unilateral adoption of the new policy. The adoption of the policy also resulted in the unilateral rescission of the discussion procedure governing the teachers and paraprofessionals represented by the Independence National Educational Association.

The school district acknowledges that its unilateral adoption of the new policy constituted a refusal to bargain collectively with these employee associations.

The employee associations filed this suit in March 2003 challenging the district's refusal to bargain with them and the district's rescission of agreements that already had been established.

* * * The trial court agreed that the district had refused to bargain collectively with the unions and had unilaterally rescinded its agreement, but concluded that Missouri law allowed such actions. * * *

III. The District's Refusal to Bargain Collectively

A. Is legislative power being delegated?

Appellants' first claim is that the district violated article I, section 29 of Missouri's Constitution by refusing to bargain collectively with the representatives of the employee associations. There is no dispute that the district refused to bargain collectively with its employees.

Despite the plain language of the constitutional provision, which states that "employees shall have the right to bargain collectively," this Court held in *City of Springfield v. Clouse,* 356 Mo. 1239, 206 S.W.2d 539, 542 (1947), that article I, section 29 does not apply to public employees. If the guarantee applies to public employees, this Court said, the legislative powers of the public entity would be unconstitutionally delegated to nongovernmental entities through the collective bargaining process

Clouse recognizes that all employees have the right to join unions and to bring "their views and desires to any public officer or legislative body," but distinguishes this from the right to bargain collectively. This distinction is based on the now largely defunct nondelegation doctrine, which holds that it is unconstitutional for the legislature to delegate its rulemaking authority to another body. *Clouse* cites *A.L.A. Schechter Poultry Corp. v. United States,* 295 U.S. 495 (1935), which has been abandoned in subsequent decisions. *Schechter Poultry* has been called "aberrational" because it is one of very few cases that were "departure[s] from a generous recognition of congressional power to delegate rulemaking authority[.]" Since 1935, the United States Supreme Court has generally upheld delegations of congressional authority. * * *

Similarly, the nondelegation doctrine has been largely abandoned in Missouri. * * * The nondelegation *dictum* in *Clouse* and public employee cases that follow *Clouse* has rightly been called an "anachronism." James E. Westbrook, *The Use of the Nondelegation Doctrine in Public Sector Labor Law: Lessons From Cases That Have Perpetuated an Anachronism,* 30 St. Louis Univ. L.J. 331 (1986).

Clouse disapproves of including public employees in the "right to bargain collectively" because decisions relating to public employment are "legislative." As applied to the municipal employees in *Clouse,* "qualifications, tenure, compensation and working conditions of public officers and employees are wholly matters of lawmaking and cannot be the subject of bargaining or contract." For this reason, *Clouse* found that article I, section 29 did not apply to public employees because "the right to bargain collectively" in the public sector "could amount to no more than giving expression to desires for the lawmaker's consideration and guidance."

In 1965, the legislature passed the public sector labor law, which authorized most public employees "to form and join labor organizations and to present proposals to any public body relative to salaries and other conditions of employment through the representatives of their own choosing. * * * " Section 105.510. The public sector labor law excludes "all teachers of all Missouri schools." *Id.* After the law went into effect, many public employees—including the custodial, transportation, and paraprofessional employees represented by the associations in this case—had a recognized right to bargain collectively, despite this Court's language in *Clouse* that public employment can never be the subject of bargaining or contract. To be consistent with article I, section 29, the statute's exclusion of teachers cannot be read to preclude teachers from bargaining collectively. Rather, the public sector labor law is read to provide procedures for the exercise of this right for those occupations included, but not to preclude omitted occupational groups from the exercise of the right to bargain collectively, because all employees have that right under article I, section 29. Instead of invalidating the public sector labor law to the extent that it excludes teachers, this Court's reading of the statute recognizes the role of the general assembly, or in this case, the school district—in the absence of a statute covering teachers—to set the framework for these public employees to bargain collectively through representatives of their own choosing. In this regard, it is noteworthy that prior to this controversy, the district in effect recognized the teachers' right to bargain collectively through its "discussion procedure."

There is nothing in the law, as it has developed, that requires a public entity to agree to a proposal by its employee unions or organizations. In fact, this Court has repeatedly recognized that the public sector labor law allows employers to reject all employee proposals, as long as the employer has met and conferred with employee representatives.

Under this interpretation, what legislative power or prerogative is being delegated? The answer today, of course, is none. If the public employer is free to reject any proposals of employee organizations, and thus to use its governing authority to prescribe wages and working conditions, none of the public entity's legislative or governing authority is being delegated.

B. Applying the plain meaning of article I, section 29

Both sides of this controversy cite the debates of the constitutional convention to support their respective positions as to whether the constitutional convention delegates did or did not intend that public employees be included in article I, section 29.

Section 29 is part of Missouri's current Constitution, which was the product of a constitutional convention in 1943 and 1944 and was adopted by the voters in 1945. While the debates of the convention are interesting, they neither add to nor subtract from the plain meaning of the constitution's words. Missouri's voters did not vote on the words used in the deliberations of the constitutional convention. The voters voted on the words in the Constitution, which says "employees shall have the right to organize and to bargain collectively. * * * "

"Employees" plainly means employees. There is no adjective; there are no words that limit "employees" to private sector employees. The meaning of section 29 is clear and there is, accordingly, no authority for this Court to read into the Constitution words that are not there.

* * * *Clouse* contradicts the plain meaning of article I, section 29, which states simply that *employees,* without qualification, have the right to collective bargaining. Deviations from clear constitutional commands—although longstanding—do not promote respect for the rule of law. * * * *Clouse* is overruled.

* * * [T]his decision does not violate the nondelegation doctrine, to whatever extent the doctrine still exists. To allow employees to bargain collectively does not require the employer to agree to any terms with the represented groups. The employer is free to reject any and all proposals made by the employees. The employer is therefore not delegating or bargaining away any of its legislative power.

The Extent of the Constitutional Right

This Court in *Sumpter v. City of Moberly,* 645 S.W.2d 359 (Mo. 1982), held—following *Clouse*—that a city was free to disregard agreements made with employee associations or unions. The starting point was this Court's statement in *Clouse* that the "qualifications, tenure, compensation and working conditions of public officers and employees are wholly matters of lawmaking and *cannot be the subject of bargaining or contract.*" (Emphasis added.) If that statement is true—that such matters cannot be the subject of bargaining—then the public sector labor law must be held to be invalid. The title of section 105.510 states "certain employees may join labor unions and *bargain collectively.*" (Emphasis added). This law, however, was upheld in *Missey,* 441 S.W.2d at 41. * * *

The public sector labor law upheld in *Missey* does not define what is meant by the right to "bargain collectively,"[6] but describes the actions allowed under the statute: employees are granted the right to present proposals, through their representatives, to the employer; the employer is required to "meet, confer, and discuss" such proposals; and the results of this discussion are to be put in writing and "presented to the appropriate administrative, legislative or other governing body in the form of an ordinance, resolution, bill or other form required for adoption, modification or rejection." The law makes clear that a public employer is not required to agree to anything. Section 105.520.

The point of bargaining, of course, is to reach agreement. Public employers routinely engage in bargaining for employees. A school district

6. What, by common understanding, is "the right to bargain collectively?" The dictionary definition says "collective bargaining" is "negotiation for the settlement of the terms of a collective agreement between an employer or group of employers on one side and a union or number of unions on the other." Webster's Third New International Dictionary (1993). Similarly, Black's Law Dictionary (8th Ed.2004) says "collective bargaining" means "negotiations between an employer and the representatives of organized employees to determine the conditions of employment, such as wages, hours, discipline, and fringe benefits."

that wishes to hire a superintendent may negotiate and reach an agreement that then becomes the subject of a contract. Nothing obligates the school district to agree to the superintendent's proposal—the school district can set the salary and other terms of employment and the superintendent can take them or leave them.

How does individual negotiation differ from bargaining that occurs with groups of employees? Conceptually it would appear to be the same process: proposals are made and either accepted or rejected. There hardly is any need, of course, to spell out that individuals have the right to negotiate and enter agreements as a simple matter of the right of contract.

By contrast, it has been necessary to give legal recognition to the right of employees to "bargain collectively through representatives of their own choosing." Before the right to "bargain collectively" was statutorily authorized, such collective or concerted action would be considered unlawful.

Federal law, through the National Labor Relations Act, regulates labor relations between employers and employees. That law, however, does not apply to employees of "any State or political subdivision thereof." The federal statute protects the right of the employees it covers to engage in "collective bargaining." This provision was part of the federal statute when article I, section 29 was drafted and adopted as part of Missouri's Constitution in 1945. The question, then, is why is article I, section 29 in the Missouri Constitution if private employees already had that right to bargain collectively under federal law? One reason is that Article I, section 29, which has no exclusions, is broader than the federal statute, which does have exclusions-most notably for employees of the state or its subdivisions. Another reason is that the Missouri Constitution protects the right to bargain collectively regardless of whether protections under federal law continue to exist.

In any event, article I, section 29 applies to "employees," regardless of whether they are in the private or public sector, and nothing in this constitutional provision requires public employers to reach agreements with their employee associations.

Repudiation of Existing Agreements

Having determined that the law does not require the public employer to reach an agreement with its employees, what remains is the issue of whether the public employer can repudiate agreements that it has chosen to enter into.

Despite the contractual nature of the agreements in this case, the district relies upon *Sumpter* for the proposition that the district—having accepted the proposals and entered into written agreements (contracts) with the employee groups regarding their represented employees—had the right unilaterally to rescind those agreements once it had agreed to them and put them into effect.

The city in *Sumpter* reached an agreement with a union representing firefighters as to the firefighters' working conditions. This agreement was made into a written memorandum of understanding. The city council enacted an ordinance adopting the terms of the memorandum as the "working conditions" for the two years covered by the document. A few months later, while the agreement was still in effect, the city imposed a new work schedule that conflicted with the terms of the memorandum. The union attempted to enjoin the city from proceeding with these changes. The union argued that the public sector labor law "authorizes a binding agreement between the public body and its employees when it authorizes adoption of the proposal by 'ordinance, resolution, bill or other form required for adoption.' " This Court disagreed, noting that *Clouse* held that the employer could not enter into the agreement in the first place without violating the constitutional mandate of separation of powers. Even if the employer adopted the agreed-upon proposal, it was not a binding contract, but rather an ordinance, administrative rule, or regulation that could be changed by the public body at any time. This Court in *Sumpter* held that the city was not bound by the agreement it had signed with the union and that the terms could be changed unilaterally by the city even during the effective period of the agreement.

There is no such principle—that is, that a contract's terms can be changed unilaterally—that applies to contracts between individual employees and governmental bodies. * * *

Labor contracts with groups of public employees have been treated as the only contracts—entered into within the authority of the governmental entity—that have been considered unenforceable. *Sumpter's* treatment of collective bargaining agreements is inconsistent with article I, section 29, and, accordingly, *Sumpter* is overruled.

School districts execute binding contracts with school superintendents, creditors who hold the districts' bonded indebtedness, contractors that build and repair school buildings, textbook publishers, private cleaning services, and so forth. These agreements are the subject of legislative action by the school district, but that does not mean the district can repudiate its agreements at will. No contractor or supplier could do business with an entity that repudiates its agreements. * * *

The judgment of the circuit court is reversed, and the case is remanded.

PRICE, J., joined by LIMBAUGH, J. concur concurring in part and dissenting in part.

* * * The majority overrules two longstanding cases, *City of Springfield v. Clouse*, and *Sumpter v. City of Moberly*. *Clouse* should not be overruled, but *Sumpter* should. The status of either case, however, makes little difference to the outcome of this matter in light of other case and statutory law that otherwise controls. * * *

IV. Should *Clouse* be Overruled and Does it Make a Difference

A. Should *Clouse* be Overruled

Article I, section 29 does not expressly differentiate between public and private employees. As noted by the majority, when read in isolation, art. I, sec. 29 might appear to apply to public employees. But the section must be read in historical context with the understanding of collective bargaining in relation to public employees that existed at the time of its adoption in 1945.

The sponsors of art. I, sec. 29 recognized that wages and hours of public employees must be established by statute or ordinance and cannot be the subject of bargaining. The Honorable R.T. Wood, president of the State Federation of Labor and sponsor of section 29 at the convention stated: "I don't believe there is anyone in the organization that would insist upon having a collective bargaining agreement with a municipality setting forth wages, hours, and working conditions." *Clouse,* 206 S.W.2d at 543. The idea that collective bargaining was unacceptable in the public sector was also illustrated in a letter by Franklin D. Roosevelt, read at the convention:

> All Government employees should realize that the process of collective bargaining, as usually understood, cannot be transplanted into the public service. It has its distinct and insurmountable limitations when applied to public personnel management. The very nature and purposes of Government make it impossible for administrative officials to represent fully or to bind the employer in mutual discussions with Government employee organizations. The employer is the whole people, who speak by means of laws enacted by their representatives in Congress. Accordingly, administrative officials and employees alike are governed and guided, and in many instances restricted, by laws which establish policies, procedures, or rules in personnel matters.

The decision in *Clouse,* that public employees do not enjoy the right to collective bargaining under the constitution, was handed down only two years following the convention. There is no doubt the Court then knew the intent of the framers and the mood of the 1945 electorate better than the Court does now. Essentially it determined that the term "collective bargaining" simply had no relation, by definition, to public employment. The holding has been relied upon as the correct interpretation of that section in Missouri for 60 years. I would not overrule *Clouse.*

B. Does it Make a Difference

While the majority spends great effort in overruling *Clouse* and in giving "all employees, including those represented by the employee associations in this case * * * the 'right to bargain collectively,'" it does not outline what differences from existing law would result by doing so. *Missey* and the public sector labor law have already marginalized *Clouse* by allowing "meet and confer rights" and giving public employees the right to "form and join labor organizations and to present proposals to any public body * * * through the representative of their own choosing."

The majority does not expressly define the right to "collective bargaining" in the public sector as opposed to the procedure already in place. The majority limits the right of the public employees to bargain collectively by expressly acknowledging that "nothing in this constitutional provision requires public employers to reach agreements with their employee associations" and stating that "the employer is not required to reach an agreement with employees as to working conditions." As for the right to strike, the majority further limits traditional ideas of collective bargaining by stating that the law "forbids strikes by public employees". * * * The majority does not appear to have given public employees anything more than the rights public employees already enjoy to meet and confer and to choose their own representative. * * *

NOTES

1. After *Independence National Education Association*, litigation ensued over exactly what satisfied the constitutionally-mandated right to collective bargaining. In *Springfield Nat'l Educ. Ass'n v. Springfield Bd. of Educ.*, Case No. 0931–CV08322 (Cir.Ct. Greene Cty., MO., Sept. 10, 2009), a school board in Missouri set up a system for union recognition that included the following provisions. Employees in a bargaining unit of teachers could, in an initial ballot, choose to be represented by one union, multiple unions, or no union. Under the multiple union option, more than one union would represent the same group of teachers, *i.e.*, teachers in one bargaining unit would be simultaneously represented by more than one labor organization. There was no requirement that the labor organizations consent to this arrangement or have consistent goals.

A union challenged this system, claiming it did not satisfy the constitutional requirement of collective bargaining, arguing (among other things) that "collective bargaining" was a term of art that included the concept of exclusive representation, meaning that one labor organization represented one bargaining unit. *Springfield*, however, held that this system did meet the constitutional standard for collective bargaining. The court relied on the dictionary definition of "collective bargaining" cited in *Independence National Education Association*: "negotiation * * * between an employer or group of employers on one side and a union or number of unions on the other."

As a matter of practice, how do you think such a system would work? Can you think of any potential advantages or disadvantages to the employees, unions, and employer?

2. On the other hand, in *Bayless Education Association v. Bayless School District*, Case No. 09SL–CC01481 (Cir.Ct. St. Louis, Feb. 10, 2010), a union successfully challenged a different system created by another employer. In this system, the employer required employees in each school in the District to select two individual representatives and two alternates; these representatives, plus one representative designated by the union with the largest employee membership, would then be allowed, as a group, to bargain with the

employer. *Bayless* held this did not satisfy the constitutional right to bargain collectively. The court first distinguished *Springfield* in that under the system in that case, employees were at least permitted to choose a traditional exclusive representative. The *Bayless* decision then explained that the system at issue in *Bayless* "mandates collaborative bargaining, not collective bargaining through a union representative."

3. Are the cases *Springfield* and *Bayless* cases sufficiently distinguishable on the facts such that the first system is not collective bargaining through representatives of the employee's choosing, and the second system is? If so, why? If not, should both cases have found a constitutional violation, or neither? More broadly, what guidelines should Missouri courts use to determine whether a given system constitutes "collective bargaining" under the Missouri constitution?

4. In this regard, compare the discussions of what "collective bargaining" means for government employees in *Independence National Education Association*, and *NTEU v. Chertoff*, *supra*, along with the various collective bargaining systems described in the casebook. Does "collective bargaining" have a particular meaning, or prescribed range of meanings, in the public sector? Recall that *Chertoff* referred to "collective bargaining" as a "term of art."

5. *Independence Education Association* reversed *City of Springfield v. Clouse*, which had been good law in Missouri for forty years. *Clouse* refused to permit city street cleaning and sewage disposal workers to bargain collectively. "Under our form of government, public office or employment * * * cannot become a matter of bargaining and contract," the Court explained. 206 S.W.2d 539, 545. Wages and working conditions involved "the exercise of legislative powers" which local officials could not bargain away. *Id.* R. T. Wood, the president of the Missouri Federation of Labor and the man who had originally proposed section 29, presented the *Clouse* court with an alternative model of bargaining for the public sector. Wood stipulated that wages and hours were not negotiable because they were controlled by city officials and statute. Still, he contended, collective bargaining was applicable to "classifications, working conditions of all kinds, night work, day work, and a multiplicity of items aside from wages and hours." Wood urged that "collective bargaining means a good many things"; there were "many types of collective bargaining." When a "representative of the employees of the city sits down at a table and discusses * * * relations between an employee and the city, that is collective bargaining." *Id.* at 543. *Clouse* rejected this argument: "This is confusing collective bargaining with the rights of petition, peaceable assembly and free speech." *Id.* Section 29 was "intended to safeguard collective bargaining as that term was usually understood in * * * private industry." *Id.* Thus, it could not be applied to public workers. *See* Joseph Slater, *Public Workers: Government Employee Unions, the Law, and the State 1900–62* (2004), 78, 83–84.

Should Courts look to these words by Wood in determining what "collective bargaining" under the Missouri Constitution means? If so, do his words offer any specific guidance? Note that under the NLRA and all public sector collective bargaining laws, not all subjects are mandatory topics of bargaining.

Indeed, under the statute that governs most federal employees, wages and hours are not even legal subjects of bargaining, although employees may bargain over a number of other topics. See *Chertoff*.

6. On the other hand, in fleshing out what "collective bargaining" means under the Missouri state constitution, *Independence National Education Association* relied at least in part on a Missouri statute passed in 1965 that covers some but not all public employees in the state (notably it excludes police and teachers). While this statute is more specific than the constitution, when interpreting a constitutional provision added in 1945, should courts look to a statute passed twenty years later?

D. THE RIGHT TO FORM AND JOIN UNIONS

1. FIRST AMENDMENT

ATKINS v. CITY OF CHARLOTTE

United States District Court for the Western District of North Carolina, 1969.
296 F.Supp. 1068.

CRAVEN, CIRCUIT JUDGE, joined by JONES and WARLICK, DISTRICT JUDGES.[a]

This is a civil action brought to obtain a declaratory judgment and injunctive relief declaring unconstitutional and preventing enforcement of Sections 95–97, 95–98 and 95–99 of the General Statutes of North Carolina. We hold G.S. 95–97 unconstitutional on its face. We hold G.S. § 95–98 a valid and constitutional exercise of the legislative authority of the General Assembly of North Carolina. As for G.S. § 95–99, we hold it to be so related to G.S. § 95–97 that it cannot survive the invalidation of that section. * * *

Facts

The statutes sought to be invalidated are these:

> N.C.G.S. § 95–97: Employees of units of government prohibited from becoming members of trade unions or labor unions.—No employee of the State of North Carolina, or of any agency, office, institution or instrumentality thereof, or any employee of a city, town, county, or other municipality or agency thereof, or any public employee or employees of an entity or instrumentality of government shall be, become, or remain a member of any trade union, labor union, or labor organization which is, or may become, a part of or affiliated in any way with any national or international labor union, federation, or organization, and which has as its purpose or one of its purposes, collective bargaining with any employer mentioned in this article with respect to grievances, labor disputes, wages or salary, rates of pay, hours of employment, or the conditions of work of such

a. [Author's note: This case was decided under a now-repealed procedure which provided for three-judge courts, composed of two district court judges and one circuit court judge, to hear constitutional cases, with direct appeal to the Supreme Court. See Charles Alan Wright, *The Law of Federal Courts* 295–299 (4th ed. 1983).]

employees. Nor shall such an employee organize or aid, assist or promote the organization of any such trade union, labor union, or labor organization, or affiliate with any such organization in any capacity whatsoever. The terms "employee," "public employee" or "employees" whenever used in this section shall mean any regular and full-time employee engaged exclusively in law enforcement or fire protection activity.

N.C.G.S. § 95–98: Contracts between units of government and labor unions, trade unions or labor organizations concerning public employees declared to be illegal.—Any agreement, or contract between the governing authority of any city, town, county, or other municipality, or between any agency, unit, or instrumentality thereof, or between any agency, instrumentality, or institution of the State of North Carolina, and any labor union, trade union, or labor organization, as bargaining agent for any public employees of such city, town, county or other municipality, or agency or instrumentality of government, is hereby declared to be against the public policy of the State, illegal, unlawful, void and of no effect.

N.C.G.S. § 95–99: Penalty for violation of article.—Any violation of the provisions of this article is hereby declared to be a misdemeanor, and upon conviction, plea of guilty or plea of nolo contendere shall be punishable in the discretion of the court.

All of the plaintiffs are members of the Charlotte Fire Department, and the gist of the complaint is that the statutes are overbroad and prohibit constitutionally guaranteed rights of the plaintiffs in violation of the First Amendment and the Due Process and Equal Protection Clauses of the Fourteenth Amendment to the Constitution of the United States. Specifically, plaintiffs want to become dues paying members of a Local which would become affiliated with International Association of Fire Fighters, the intervenor. * * *

The City of Charlotte is a municipal corporation which operates and maintains the Charlotte Fire Department pursuant to the City Charter. * * *

The Department has approximately 438 employees, consisting of the Chief, two assistant chiefs, 14 deputy chiefs, 60 fire captains, and 56 fire lieutenants, with the remainder being fire fighters, inspectors, fire alarm personnel and office personnel. The plaintiffs consist of deputy chiefs, captains, lieutenants and fire fighters and range in service with the department from two to 40 years.

For many years prior to the enactment in 1959 of the North Carolina General Statutes complained of, the International Association of Fire Fighters operated or maintained a union made up of Charlotte Fire Department members and designated as Local 660, an affiliate of the International Association of Fire Fighters. A number of Fire Department members paid dues to that organization which was engaged in collective bargaining activity. Further, the City checked off dues for union membership.

During 1959, the North Carolina Legislature enacted General Statutes §§ 95–97 through 95–99. Following the enactment of these statutes, Local 660 terminated its affiliation with the International Association of Fire Fighters and became, or took the name, Charlotte Fire Fighters Association. This organization continued the activities and representations very much as had been the practice with Local 660. The Fire Fighters Association continued to negotiate with the City and to represent the Charlotte firemen with respect to wages, grievances, and other conditions of employment, and the City continued its recognition of the association and permitted dues check-off. This practice continued from 1959 until 1962. On January 29, 1962, the City Council received and approved a report compiled by the City Manager. One of the recommendations of this report as it was approved established as a condition of continued employment in the Fire Department non-membership in the Fire Fighters Association or in any successor thereto. The City Council approved this report after having been advised by the City Attorney that the Fire Fighters Association was not illegal per se under the statutes complained of, but that the association and its recognition by the City was in violation of public policies of the State. Sometime after this action on the part of the City Council, the Fire Fighters Association terminated its activities and the City discontinued its recognition and dues check-off. A grievance procedure was established to allow individual employees to process grievances, but no provisions were made for group grievance procedure or for collective bargaining with respect to grievances, wages, and conditions of employment.

During March of 1967, members of the Charlotte Fire Department, the plaintiffs herein, organized the Charlotte Firemen's Assembly. This organization has as its purpose collective bargaining with the City of Charlotte with respect to wages, grievances, hours of employment and other conditions of employment. It would like to become a local affiliate of intervenor but is prevented by the statutes. The Firemen's Assembly has not been recognized by the City as a representative of firemen.

* * *

The Constitutional Question and The Remedy

We think N.C.G.S. § 95–97 is void on its face as an abridgment of freedom of association protected by the First and Fourteenth Amendments of the Constitution of the United States. The flaw in it is an intolerable "overbreadth" unnecessary to the protection of valid state interests. The Supreme Court of the United States has accorded "freedom of association" full status as an aspect of liberty protected by the Due Process Clause of the Fourteenth Amendment and by the rights of free speech and peaceful assembly explicitly set out in the First Amendment. In *NAACP v. Alabama ex rel. Patterson*, the Court said:

"It is beyond debate that freedom to engage in association for the advancement of beliefs and ideas is an inseparable aspect of the 'liberty' assured by the Due Process Clause of the Fourteenth Amendment, which embraces freedom of speech. [Citations omitted.] Of course, it is immaterial whether the beliefs sought to be advanced by association pertain to political, economic, religious or cultural matters, and state action which may have the effect of curtailing the freedom to associate is subject to the closest scrutiny." 357 U.S. 449, 460–61, 2 L.Ed. 2d 1488, 1498–99, 78 S.Ct. 1163 (1958).

The Court had previously noted the close connection between the freedoms of speech and assembly. In *De Jonge v. Oregon*, 299 U.S. 353, 364, 81 L.Ed. 278, 283–84, 57 S.Ct. 255 (1937), the Court held that the right of peaceable assembly is a right cognate to those of free speech and free press and equally fundamental. It was said that the right is one that cannot be denied without violating fundamental principles of liberty and justice which lie at the base of all civil and political institutions. The Court made a careful distinction between the proper exercise of legislative power to protect against abuse of the right of assembly and legislative infringement per se of that right, holding that the latter is not permissible. Especially pertinent to the problem confronting us is the following:

"[Consistently] with the Federal Constitution, peaceable assembly for lawful discussion cannot be made a crime. The holding of meetings for peaceable political action cannot be proscribed. Those who assist in the conduct of such meetings cannot be branded as criminals on that score. The question, if the rights of free speech and peaceable assembly are to be preserved, is not as to the auspices under which the meeting is held but as to its purpose * * * ." *De Jonge v. Oregon*, 299 U.S. 353, 365, 81 L.Ed. 278, 284, 57 S.Ct. 255 (1937).

We would make the same distinction here. It matters not, we think, whether the firemen of the City of Charlotte meet under the auspices of the intervenor, a national labor union, but whether their proposed concerted action, if any, endangers valid state interests. We think there is no valid state interest in denying firemen the right to organize a labor union—whether local or national in scope. It is beyond argument that a single individual cannot negotiate on an equal basis with an employer who hires hundreds of people. Recognition of this fact of life is the basis of labor-management relations in this country. Charlotte concedes in its brief that the right of public employees to join labor unions is becoming increasingly recognized (with the exception of firemen and policemen) and even admits that collective bargaining might be beneficial in many situations in the case of municipal firemen. But Charlotte insists that the State has a valid interest in forbidding membership in a labor union to firemen. It is said that fire departments are quasi-military in structure, and that such a structure is necessary because individual firemen must be ready to respond instantly and without question to orders of a superior, and that such military discipline may well mean the difference between saving human life and property, and failure. The extension of this argument is, of course, that affiliation with a national labor union might eventuate in a strike against the public interest which could not be tolerated, and the very existence of which would imperil lives and property in the City of Charlotte. This is the only state interest that can be validly asserted for N.C.G.S. § 95–97. The thought of fires raging out of control in Charlotte while firemen, out on strike, Neroicly watch the flames, is frightening. We do not question the power of the State to deal with such a contingency.[3] We do question the overbreadth of G.S. § 95–97, which quite unnecessarily, in our opinion, goes far beyond the valid state interest that is suggested to us, and strikes down indiscriminately the right of association in a labor union—even one whose policy is opposed to strikes.

Since the only valid state interest suggested by defendants in support of the constitutionality of G.S. § 95–97 is the quite legitimate fear that fire protection for the people of Charlotte might be disrupted by violence or by strike, it seems quite clear that the statute must be invalidated for "overbreadth."

The Supreme Court "has repeatedly held that a governmental purpose to control or prevent activities constitutionally subject to state regulation may not be achieved by means which sweep unnecessarily broadly and thereby invade the area of protected freedoms." *NAACP v. Alabama*, 377 U.S. 288, 307, 12 L.Ed. 2d 325 at 338, 84 S.Ct. 1302 (1964).

Again, "even though the governmental purpose be legitimate and substantial, that purpose cannot be pursued by means that broadly stifle fundamental personal liberties when the end can be more narrowly achieved." *Shelton v. Tucker*, 364 U.S. 479, 488, 5 L.Ed. 2d 231, 237, 81 S.Ct. 247 (1960). As previously indicated, the plaintiffs and intervenor do

3. Although the question is not before us, we note the position of plaintiffs, including intervenor, on the power of the State to prevent strikes and/or violent conduct on the part of a labor union engaged in vital public employment. The following Article 22 was recommended as of January 10, 1968, for incorporation in the intervenor's constitution:

> "The International Association of Fire Fighters is a law abiding organization. Because of the public character of the work of its members and the protection of the lives and property of citizens and communities in case of fire and other hazard, no subordinate union or its members shall withhold fire protection services where collective bargaining, conciliation, mediation, fact finding with recommendations or voluntary binding conciliation or arbitration is available for resolution of disputes involving grievances, wages, hours or conditions of work. Where such procedures for resolving disputes are not available the subordinate union shall not withhold fire protection service but shall refer the matter to the International President and the International Executive Board for such further handling as may be available or necessary to secure an acceptable settlement of the dispute."

From the plaintiffs' brief:

> The State "may quite properly prohibit employees from striking or using violence in the settlement of disputes." Milk Wagon Drivers Union v. Meadowmoor Dairies, 312 U.S. 287, 85 L. Ed. 836, 61 S. Ct. 552 (1941).

From the intervenor's brief:

> It is admitted that fire fighters' "official conduct and activities are subject to reasonable restriction by the General Assembly of North Carolina."

Our helpful and valued amicus curiae suggests that North Carolina may validly impose sanctions—even criminal ones—against strikes or other refusals to act imperiling the public safety, e.g., a statute making it a criminal offense for a fireman to refuse the call of duty; a statute providing for terminal discharge of any fireman who refuses to perform his duty.

not question the power of the State to prohibit strikes against the public interest.

What we have said thus far supports our ultimate conclusion: that the firemen of the City of Charlotte are granted the right of free association by the First and Fourteenth Amendments of the United States Constitution; that that right of association includes the right to form and join a labor union—whether local or national; that membership in such a labor organization will confer upon the firemen no immunity from proper state regulation to protect valid state interests which are, in this case, the protection of property and life from destruction by fire. We think such a conclusion flows inevitably from the enunciations of the United States Supreme Court set out above. Our decision is consistent with that of the Seventh Circuit according the same right to teachers. *McLaughlin v. Tilendis*, 398 F.2d 287 (7th Cir. 1968). * * *

Entry of a declaratory judgment decreeing G.S. § 95–97 and § 95–99 invalid because in violation of the First and Fourteenth Amendments of the United States Constitution seems to us, on the facts of this case, a fully sufficient remedy. * * *

NOTES

1. In the same year, the Eighth Circuit Court of Appeals concluded that public employees terminated for joining a union had a claim for damages and injunctive relief for violation of their constitutional rights stating:

> The First Amendment protects the right of one citizen to associate with other citizens for any lawful purpose free from government interference. The guarantee of the "right of assembly" protects more than "the right to attend a meeting; it includes the right to express one's attitudes or philosophies by membership in a group or by affiliation with it or by other lawful means." * * *

Union membership is protected by the right of association under the First and Fourteenth Amendments. *Thomas v. Collins*, 323 U.S. 516, 65 S.Ct. 315, 89 L.Ed. 430 (1945) * * *. The Court commented in *Thomas*:

> * * * Great secular causes, with small ones, are guarded. The grievances for redress of which the right of petition was insured, and with it the right of assembly, are not solely religious or political ones. And the rights of free speech and a free press are not confined to any field of human interest.
>
> The idea is not sound therefore that the First Amendment's safeguards are wholly inapplicable to business or economic activity. * * *
>
> * * * This Court has recognized that "in the circumstances of our times the dissemination of information concerning the facts of a labor dispute must be regarded as within that area of free discussion that is guaranteed by the Constitution." * * * Free discussion concerning the conditions in industry and the causes of labor disputes appears to us indispensable to the effective and intelligent use of the processes

> of popular government to shape the destiny of modern industrial society." *Thornhill v. Alabama*, 310 U.S. 88, 60 S.Ct. 736, 84 L.Ed. 1093 * * *. The right * * * to discuss, and inform people concerning, the advantages and disadvantages of unions and joining them is protected not only as part of free speech, but as part of free assembly. * * * (citations omitted).

American Federation of State, County & Municipal Employees, AFL–CIO v. Woodward, 406 F.2d 137, 139–40 (8th Cir. 1969).

2. Can a state justify barring employees from joining particular unions? In *Vicksburg Firefighters Association, Local 1686 v. City of Vicksburg*, 761 F.2d 1036 (5th Cir. 1985), the court rejected a First Amendment challenge to a municipal resolution which prohibited captains in the fire department from joining any union that had as members rank and file firefighters in the Vicksburg Fire Department. In *Brennan v. Koch*, 564 F.Supp. 322 (S.D.N.Y. 1983), the court rejected a similar challenge to a provision of the collective bargaining law which prohibited certification of a union to represent police officers if the union met one of two conditions: 1) if the union admitted to membership employees other than police officers or was affiliated with a union which admitted other employees to membership; or 2) if the union advocated the right to strike. What might justify such restrictions on the First Amendment rights of employees to join labor organizations?

3. Note the shift in views in *Atkins* from earlier cases regarding the potential for public employee strikes. The *Atkins* court refused to presume that a strike would occur if the employees were permitted to unionize, recognized the provisions of the union constitution barring strikes and held that the state could address the concern about strikes legislatively without impairing the constitutional rights of employees. Compare the rationale of *Atkins* to the case of *Local 201, AFSCME v. City of Muskegon*, 369 Mich. 384, 120 N.W.2d 197 (1963), in § 4A *supra*, where the court rejected the union's challenge to a municipal rule barring police officers from joining any union which had as members employees other than those in the Muskegon police department. The court there was willing to defer to the conclusion of the city that the ban was necessary and reasonable, indicating that there was no constitutional right to the job of police officer and invoking the specter of a strike to support its decision.

2. STATE CONSTITUTIONAL PROVISIONS

In addition to the federal constitutional right, several state constitutions have incorporated a right to join a labor union which applies to public employees. The Florida Constitution states: "The right of persons to work shall not be denied or abridged on account of membership or non-membership in any labor union or labor organization." FLA. CONST. ART. I, § 6. While Florida's provision covers public and private sector employees, Hawaii's Constitution contains a specific provision for public employees stating: "Persons in public employment shall have the right to organize for the purpose of collective bargaining as provided by law." HAW. CONST. ART. XIII, § 2. As noted *supra*, Missouri's constitutional provision protecting the right to organize and bargain, MO. CONST. ART. I, § 29 was interpreted to apply to public sector employees in 2007 by the Missouri Supreme Court in *Independence–National Education Association v. Independence School District*, 223 S.W.3d 131 (Mo. 2007).

E. THE RIGHT TO BARGAIN

1. FEDERAL CONSTITUTIONAL LIMITATIONS

While the constitutional right to join a union is well-established, the federal right is limited as evidenced in the following case and notes. For discussion of federal and state constitutional issues relating to the right to strike, see Chapter 9.

SMITH v. ARKANSAS STATE HIGHWAY EMPLOYEES, LOCAL 1315

United States Supreme Court, 1979.
441 U.S. 463, 99 S.Ct. 1826, 60 L.Ed.2d 360.

PER CURIAM.

In grievance proceedings initiated by employees of the Arkansas State Highway Department, the State Highway Commission will not consider a grievance unless the employee submits his written complaint directly to the designated employer representative. The District Court for the Eastern District of Arkansas found that this procedure denied the union representing the employees the ability to submit effective grievances on their behalf and therefore violated the First Amendment. The United States Court of Appeals for the Eighth Circuit affirmed. We disagree with these holdings; finding no constitutional violation in the actions of the Commission or its individual members, we grant certiorari and reverse the judgment of the Court of Appeals.

The First Amendment protects the right of an individual to speak freely, to advocate ideas, to associate with others, and to petition his government for redress of grievances. And it protects the right of associations to engage in advocacy on behalf of their members. *NAACP v. Button*, 371 U.S. 415, 83 S.Ct. 328, 9 L.Ed.2d 405 (1963); *Eastern Railroad Presidents Conf. v. Noerr Motor Freight, Inc.*, 365 U.S. 127, 81 S.Ct. 523, 5 L.Ed.2d 464 (1961). The government is prohibited from infringing upon these guarantees either by a general prohibition against certain forms of advocacy, *NAACP v. Button*, supra, or by imposing sanctions for the expression of particular views it opposes, e.g., *Brandenburg v. Ohio*, 395 U.S. 444, 89 S.Ct. 1827, 23 L.Ed.2d 430 (1969); *Garrison v. Louisiana*, 379 U.S. 64, 85 S.Ct. 209, 13 L.Ed.2d 125 (1964).

But the First Amendment is not a substitute for the national labor relations laws. As the Court of Appeals for the Seventh Circuit recognized in *Hanover Township Federation of Teachers v. Hanover Community School Corp.*, 457 F.2d 456 (1972), the fact that procedures followed by a public employer in bypassing the union and dealing directly with its members might well be unfair labor practices were federal statutory law applicable hardly establishes that such procedures violate the Constitution. The First Amendment right to associate and to advocate "provides no guarantee that a speech will persuade or that advocacy will be effective." The public employee surely can associate and speak freely and petition openly, and he is protected by the First Amendment from retaliation for doing so. See *Pickering v. Board of Education*, 391 U.S. 563, 88 S.Ct. 1731, 20 L.Ed.2d 811 (1968); *Shelton v. Tucker*, 364 U.S. 479, 81 S.Ct. 247, 5 L.Ed.2d 231 (1960). But the First Amendment does not impose any affirmative obligation on the government to listen, to respond or, in this context, to recognize the association and bargain with it.

In the case before us, there is no claim that the Highway Commission has prohibited its employees from joining together in a union, or from persuading others to do so, or from advocating any particular ideas. There is, in short, no claim of retaliation or discrimination proscribed by the First Amendment. Rather, the complaint of the union and its members is simply that the Commission refuses to consider or act upon grievances when filed by the union rather than by the employee directly. Were public employers such as the Commission subject to the same labor laws applicable to private employers, this refusal might well constitute an unfair labor practice. We may assume that it would and, further, that it tends to impair or undermine—if only slightly—the effectiveness of the union in representing the economic interests of its members.

But this type of "impairment" is not one that the Constitution prohibits. Far from taking steps to prohibit or discourage union membership or association, all that the Commission has done in its challenged conduct is simply to ignore the union. That it is free to do.

The judgment of the Court of Appeals is therefore reversed.

[JUSTICE POWELL took no part in the consideration or decision of the case; JUSTICE MARSHALL'S dissenting opinion is omitted].

NOTES

1. Recall the case of *Moreau v. Klevenhagen*, 508 U.S. 22, 113 S.Ct. 1905, 123 L.Ed.2d 584 (1993), Chapter 3, p. 116. In *Moreau*, the Court rejected the union's argument that the Fair Labor Standards Act required the employer to bargain with the union about comp time for employees, despite the fact that the union did not have collective bargaining rights under state law. Are there similar policy and federalism concerns underlying *Moreau* and *Smith*?

2. In upholding the constitutionality of the statute that barred the state of North Carolina and its municipalities from bargaining with labor unions, the court in *Atkins v. City of Charlotte* stated the following:

> We find nothing unconstitutional in G.S. § 95–98. It simply voids contracts between units of government within North Carolina and labor

> unions and expresses the public policy of North Carolina to be against such collective bargaining contracts. There is nothing in the United States Constitution which entitles one to have a contract with another who does not want it. It is but a step further to hold that the state may lawfully forbid such contracts with its instrumentalities. The solution, if there be one, from the viewpoint of the firemen, is that labor unions may someday persuade state government of the asserted value of collective bargaining agreements, but this is a political matter and does not yield to judicial solution. The right to a collective bargaining agreement, so firmly entrenched in American labor-management relations, rests upon national legislation and not upon the federal Constitution. The State is within the powers reserved to it to refuse to enter into such agreements and so to declare by statute. 296 F.Supp. at 1077.

3. Is there any value or purpose in protecting the right to organize while denying constitutional protection for the right to bargain? Does the failure to require bargaining impair the constitutional right to organize unions?

4. In 2007, the Canadian Supreme Court, in a reversal of prior decisions, ruled that collective bargaining is a constitutional right. *Health Services and Support Facilities Subsector Bargaining Association v. British Columbia*, [2007] 2 S.C.R. 391, 2007 SCC 27 (Can.) To support its decision, the court relied on the labor standards of the International Labor Organization finding the right to association and collective bargaining to be fundamental rights. Should these standards influence the interpretation of the U.S. Constitution? For an analysis of the decision and its impact, see Brian Etherington, The B.C. Health Services and Support Decision—The Constitutionalization of a Right to Bargain Collectively in Canada: Where Did it Come From and Where Will it Lead?, 30 *Comparative Labor Law & Policy Journal* 715 (2009).

2. STATE CONSTITUTIONS

Some state constitutions provide explicit protection, not only for the right to organize, but for the right to bargain as well. The Florida Constitution, Article I, Section 6, provides in part: "The right of employees, by and through a labor organization, to bargain collectively shall not be denied or abridged." The Florida Supreme Court has construed this provision to limit the authority of the Legislature to eliminate or curtail bargaining by public employees. *Chiles v. United Faculty of Florida*, 615 So.2d 671 (Fla. 1993). The Hawaii Constitution, in Article XIII, Section 2, provides, "Persons in public employment shall have the right to organize for the purpose of collective bargaining as provided by law." The Hawaii Supreme Court has construed this provision to entail a right to bargain similar to that in the Florida Constitution. See *United Public Workers, AFSCME Local 646 v. Yogi*, 101 Haw. 46, 62 P.3d 189 (2002). And, as discussed above, the Missouri Supreme Court held in 2007 that the constitutional right to bargain contained in Article I, § 29 applies to public employees and guarantees their right to bargain as well. *Independence–National Education Association v. Independence School District*, 223 S.W.3d 131 (Mo. 2007), *supra*.

F. UNIONIZATION IN THE ABSENCE OF STATUTORY PROTECTION

As evidenced by the *Atkins* case, in some states, there is no statutory protection of the right to unionize for some or all employees. These states fall into three categories. Some states specifically outlaw bargaining. In others, bargaining is authorized by executive order or local ordinance. In the last category, there is no legislation authorizing or prohibiting bargaining. While some states treat all employees the same in terms of their organizational and bargaining rights, in others the legal protection for public employees varies. In a unique provision affecting only transit employees with a history of collective bargaining under private ownership, the federal Urban Mass Transportation Act, in Article 13(c) guarantees no loss of collective bargaining rights if the transit system is transferred to public ownership. This requirement, a condition of receiving federal funds, has enabled transit employees to bargain with their employer even in states with limitations on bargaining for other public employees. The following sections will explore the diverse legal effects of the absence of statutory protection.

1. STATUTES PROHIBITING PUBLIC SECTOR COLLECTIVE BARGAINING

As noted above in the discussion of the North Carolina law, despite the trend to enact legislation authorizing various forms of public sector collective bargaining, a few states have statutes making public sector bargaining illegal. North Carolina's 1959 statute declares any agreement between a public employer and labor organization representing its public employees "to be against the public policy of the State, illegal, unlawfully void and of no effect." N.C.GEN.STAT. § 95–98. The legislative initiative that led to the North Carolina statute at issue in *Atkins* was prompted by an effort by the Teamsters Union, headed by the powerful Jimmy Hoffa, to organize the police officers in Charlotte, N.C. Although the Teamsters soon terminated their organizing drive, the concern generated, along with a fear of strikes by public employees, continued to fuel the push for legislation. For descriptions of the history that led to the North Carolina law, see Michael G. Okun, Public Employee Bargaining in North Carolina: From Paternalism to Confusion, 59 *North Carolina Law Review* 214, 218–28 (1980); Jason Burton & David A. Zonderman, *Where Did This Law Come From? A History of General Statute 95–98*, available at http://www.nccouncilofchurches.org/areasofwork/issues/economic_justice/GS_95–98_Summary.htm. Texas outlaws collective bargaining for government employees except for police and firefighters, by local option. TEX.GOV'T CODE ANN. § 617.002; TEX.LOC.GOV'T CODE ANN. § 174.023. Virginia enacted a statute in 1993, VA.CODE ANN. § 40.1–57.2, which codified a decision of the Virginia Supreme Court holding that subdivisions of the state were not authorized to enter into collective bargaining agreements with unions.

Commonwealth v. County Board of Arlington County, 217 Va. 558, 580–81, 232 S.E.2d 30, 44–45 (Va. 1977). The decision in that case nullified a number of existing collective bargaining agreements and caused a substantial drop in public sector union membership in Virginia. The lawsuit by the state, which challenged the spread of public sector bargaining in northern Virginia, followed a series of reports by state commissions considering, and in some cases recommending, implementation of legislation authorizing some form of collective bargaining for public employees. Fear of strikes by public employees played a role in Virginia's refusal to enact legislation authorizing bargaining. For a history of these efforts in Virginia, see Ann. C. Hodges, Lessons From the Laboratory: The Polar Opposites on the Public Sector Labor Law Spectrum, 18 *Cornell Journal of Law and Public Policy* 735, 744–48, 758–65 (2009). The political and economic culture of the south has also played a role in the limitation of public sector bargaining. *Id.* at 756–57.

Of course, as noted above employees in these jurisdictions have the right to join unions and have done so, in significant numbers in some professions. For example, in Virginia in 2008, 9.3% of public employees were members of unions. In particular firefighting and education unions maintain substantial memberships despite the legal prohibition on bargaining. Professor Ann Hodges studied public sector unionization in Virginia finding that some unions successfully organized and maintained their membership, providing services to their members and in some cases, even negotiating nonbinding memoranda of agreement.

LESSONS FROM THE LABORATORY: THE POLAR OPPOSITES ON THE PUBLIC SECTOR LABOR LAW SPECTRUM

Ann C. Hodges
18 Cornell Journal of Law and Public Policy 735, 749–55 (2009).

Unions in the public sector promote legislation that favors public employees and oppose legislation that they identify as detrimental to public employees. These unions speak before legislative commissions, county boards, city councils, school boards, and other governmental bodies to advocate for employee rights. Unions also represent employees in the existing grievance procedures established by law. Such representation may obviate the need for legal representation, which can be costly for employees. The existence of the grievance procedure, while it may have been intended to forestall unionization and substitute in part for collective bargaining, provides a vehicle for unions to prove their value to current and potential members. Unions also represent employees in other legal proceedings related to their employment. In some jurisdictions, employees have even engaged in concerted activities such as "working to the rule" or taking down from the classroom all items paid for by the teachers. In short, public sector unions in Virginia, like public sector unions * * * nationwide, serve as a voice for the workers they represent. In addition to representation in various legislative, judicial, and administrative forums, unions provide other value-added benefits to their members such as insurance, educational workshops, and support for families of members who have been killed or injured. Unions also engage in charitable endeavors to benefit their communities. These activities can generate support for the union. When the union needs political support, it may contact those who have benefited from union largesse to make calls and write letters to political leaders in support of union objectives.

The limits on Virginia unions, however, preclude them from negotiating binding collective bargaining agreements. * * * In Virginia, * * * the unions must convince employees to join the union and pay dues despite the inability to negotiate a binding agreement. * * * Union leaders in Virginia describe a continual need to organize the workforce. The organizing campaign does not end with certification, as it often does in states with collective bargaining and fair share rights.

Furthermore, because any agreements that are reached are nonbinding, unions in Virginia must also work continually to sustain relationships with employers and legislative bodies that control the terms and conditions of employment. Even in the absence of collective bargaining rights, however, several unions in Virginia have negotiated nonbinding memoranda of agreement with employers. According to the unions, employers generally comply with such agreements. Employers and unions in some areas of Virginia have reported healthy, productive relationships where they work together on a regular basis.

Given the absence of collective bargaining rights, how have unions been able to achieve such agreements? One possible explanation is that some of the union-management relationships preceded the elimination of collective bargaining in Virginia. In addition, some of the union officers have been leaders of their organizations for many years, allowing for continuity and stability within both the union and the union-employer relationship. Those unions that operate most effectively in Virginia are concentrated in firefighting and education—areas with strong national organizations and a strong history of organizational activity. Further, public sector unions have an advantage that private sector unions lack, as public sector unions can play a role in electing their employers through the exertion of political influence in campaigns for the same public offices that are responsible for negotiating with unions. Thus, they can mobilize political power to help them accomplish their goals by supporting candidates that are more sympathetic to unions' positions. * * *

All is not rosy for unions in Virginia, however. The unions that are thriving represent workers primarily in local government in large metropolitan areas. As noted, the unions in firefighting and education have been particularly successful. This success may be attributable to the existence of these unions as professional associations with substantial membership prior to widespread unionization in government. It has been more difficult for unions to organize effectively at the state level and in smaller localities. While unions that have been able to build effective, politically savvy organizations have prospered, many employees remain without any union representation. Although some employees would not choose union representation regardless of the state of the law, there are likely other employees who would prefer union representation, yet currently have none. In addition, a downside to the lack of collective bargaining and the reliance on personal relationships to uphold agreements is, in most cases, the absence of formal written documentation of agreements. When union leadership changes, institutional memory may be lost and the status of agreements may be cast into doubt.

Specific salary data for some job categories suggest that, compared to Illinois, in the less unionized environment of Virginia, average pay is lower. * * *

It is clear that there are significant difficulties for unions in states where bargaining is outlawed. Union membership in such states is significantly lower than in more favorable legal environments, and the wages for many of the same positions in those states are lower as well. Nevertheless, some unions have survived in hostile legal climates such as Virginia, and some have even prospered. For example, it is interesting that public sector union membership in Virginia is higher than national private sector union membership although federal law is less hostile to collective bargaining. Clearly then, the law is not the only factor.

NOTES

1. Professor Hodges suggests that some employers may be more willing to work cooperatively with unions where no binding collective bargaining agreement is possible. Does this suggest a downside to laws requiring collective bargaining?

2. Is there anything that unions and employers in collective bargaining states and the private sector can learn from the Virginia experience?

3. Despite the legal prohibition on collective bargaining, two successive North Carolina governors have issued executive orders expanding the rights of public sector unions in the state. Under the most recent order, unions with 2000 members, at least 500 of which are state or public school employees, are given access to state agencies to recruit, educate and communicate with members. Additionally, such unions have the right to meet annually with the governor, quarterly with the state personnel director and, where they represent 20% of the employees of any agency, quarterly with representatives of the agency. The elected representatives or delegates of the unions can take up to three days of leave, in addition to the leave they are otherwise entitled to as employees, to attend annual conventions of the union. See Executive Order No. 45, http://www.governor.state.nc.us/NewsItems/UploadedFiles/cd6fea24–a980–4ceb–9f43–b1d1f6a85adc.pdf. Why would the governor of a state that prohibits bargaining issue such an order? In 2007, the International Labor Organization (ILO), an agency of the United Nations, called on North Carolina to eliminate its bargaining prohibition because it violates international

labor standards, specifically the rights to freedom of association and bargaining. Does this action explain the actions of North Carolina governors? Does the fact that the United States is not a party to the three international conventions on collective bargaining and freedom of association relied on by the ILO affect your answer to this question? Contrast the actions of the North Carolina governors with those of Virginia politicians, who are reluctant to be allied with organized labor and have even suggested that one cannot support both unions and public sector bargaining and Virginia. See Hodges, 18 *Cornell Journal of Law and Public Policy* at 759–61.

4. Recall the history of public sector collective bargaining detailed in Section 4A. Are states like North Carolina and Virginia simply further behind other states in recognizing the rights of public employees? Why might that be the case?

2. UNIONIZATION UNDER EXECUTIVE ORDERS AND LOCAL ORDINANCES

For some public employees, collective bargaining has been authorized by executive order. Prior to the passage of the 1978 Civil Service Reform Act, federal employees engaged in limited forms of bargaining under an assortment of presidential executive orders, most prominently Executive Order 10988 (1962) issued by President John F. Kennedy and Executive Order 11491 (1969) issued by President Richard M. Nixon. Governors also have issued executive orders authorizing bargaining. For example, in 2007 Governor Ritter issued an executive order authorizing bargaining for state employees in Colorado. Executive orders have been subject to various legal challenges. In responding to such litigation, courts have examined carefully whether there is any constitutional or statutory provision which authorizes the challenged executive order either specifically or by implication. Where such authorization is found, the power of the governor to issue the order is upheld. See *McCulloch v. Glendening*, 347 Md. 272, 701 A.2d 99 (1997). In contrast, where a court fails to find any state constitutional or statutory authority for a governor to issue an executive order concerning executive branch employees and their working conditions, it will probably conclude that such an executive order (particularly if it provides for binding impasse arbitration) is an usurpation of legislative powers by the executive. Thus, in Missouri the governor may issue such an order absent constitutional or statutory authority, but such orders are not enforceable by the courts. See *Kinder v. Holden*, 92 S.W.3d 793 (Mo. 2002).

Bargaining by virtue of executive order may be temporary; a new governor who is not supportive of bargaining can repeal the order, either because of opposition to the practice in general or opposition to unions and government employees that did not support the newly elected governor's candidacy. Repeal of executive orders authorizing bargaining has occurred in Kentucky, Missouri[1] and Indiana in recent years. Arizona may

1. Both the repeal of the executive order and the *Kinder v. Holden* decision occurred before the Missouri Supreme Court held in *Independence–National Education Association v. Indepen-*

have had the shortest-lived executive order. On December 17, 2008 outgoing Governor Napolitano issued an order authorizing bargaining if state workers chose union representation. Executive Order 2008–30, http://www.governor.state.az.us/dms/upload/EO_2008–30.pdf. Her replacement repealed the order on April 2, 2009. Executive Order 2009–04, http://www.governor.state.az.us/dms/upload/EO_2009–04.pdf.

Bargaining by executive order also may be followed by statutory authorization for bargaining, which occurred in Maryland. Executive orders allow for trial of collective bargaining, which may demonstrate to the legislature the consequences of bargaining and support the enactment of legislation. Executive orders may also empower unions to lobby for legislative authorization of bargaining by enabling them to increase membership and employee support.

Where there is no express state law prohibiting or providing for organization and bargaining, localities may choose to recognize unions and bargain by enacting local legislation. In Colorado, for example, a number of cities amended their charters to provide for collective bargaining with municipal unions. The Colorado Supreme Court upheld their authority to do so, while striking down some provisions authorizing binding arbitration to establish the contract if the parties could not reach agreement. See *Greeley Police Union v. City Council of Greeley*, 191 Colo. 419, 553 P.2d 790 (1976). Where the charter's provision for arbitration gave the city the authority to establish the panel of arbitrators, however, the court found sufficient political accountability for the arbitration provision to pass muster as well. *Fraternal Order of Police, Colorado Lodge #19 v. City of Commerce City*, 996 P.2d 133 (Colo. 2000). Various Arizona communities have also enacted ordinances providing for a meet and confer process with unions representing employees of local governments. Under Arizona law these discussions may lead to a memorandum of understanding, which must be approved by the municipal body. See *City of Phoenix v. Phoenix Employment Relations Board*, 145 Ariz. 92, 95, 699 P.2d 1323, 1326 (App. 1985).

3. UNIONIZATION IN STATES WITH NO GOVERNING LEGISLATION

There is no consensus as to the legal result in jurisdictions which have no legislation dealing with public employee collective bargaining or have legislation extending collective bargaining rights only to some groups of public employees. In the absence of legislation, some state courts have held that a public employer may voluntarily choose to bargain with a union representing its employees. As early as 1966, the New Mexico Supreme Court in *International Brotherhood of Electrical Workers v. Town of Farmington,* 75 N.M. 393, 405 P.2d 233 (1965), held that collective

dence School District, 223 S.W.3d 131(Mo. 2007) that the constitutional provision protecting the right to organize and bargain applied to public employees.

bargaining was allowed in the absence of an active civil service system dealing with the matters under negotiations.

Similarly, in *Littleton Education Association v. Arapahoe County School Dist., No. 6,* 191 Colo. 411, 553 P.2d 793 (1976), the court held that although there was no express statutory authorization, voluntary collective bargaining is permissible and the contracts reached valid as long as they do not conflict with existing statutes concerning the governance of the state school system. The court noted that the school board had the authority to enter into contracts, to employ personnel, to set compensation and to determine policies relating to the welfare of employees that did not conflict with state law. More recent Colorado decisions continue Colorado's judicial acceptance of public sector collective bargaining in the absence of state enabling legislation. See, e.g., *Martin v. Montezuma–Cortez School District,* 841 P.2d 237 (Colo.1992) (holding that teachers' strike seeking recognition of their union by the school district was lawful and therefore the school district violated the Teacher Tenure Act by summarily dismissing them for striking). Courts in Illinois (which now has collective bargaining legislation), Arkansas, and Louisiana have reached similar results to Colorado, permitting bargaining in the absence of legislative authorization. See *Chicago Division v. Board of Education,* 76 Ill.App.2d 456, 222 N.E.2d 243 (Ill. App. 1966); *AFSCME, Local 2957 v. City of Benton,* 513 F.3d 874 (8th Cir. 2008); *Louisiana Teachers' Association v. Orleans Parish School Board,* 303 So.2d 564 (La.App. 1974). In states with current legislation, like Illinois and New Mexico, public sector collective bargaining often began on a voluntary basis prior to the enactment of authorizing legislation. The voluntary bargaining relationships served as an impetus for subsequent legislation which provided an enforceable legal framework for the parties.

In contrast to those states where courts have allowed voluntary bargaining in the absence of a statute, intermediate appellate courts in Tennessee have held that public employers in that state lack authority to enter into any collective bargaining arrangements unless there is clear statutory or constitutional authority to do so. In 1957, when there was no Tennessee statute dealing with public employee bargaining, the court in *Weakley County Municipal Electric System v. Vick,* 43 Tenn.App. 524, 309 S.W.2d 792 (1957) so held, finding a strike to obtain recognition and collective bargaining unlawful. More recently, even after enactment of legislation granting collective bargaining rights to educational professionals and public transit workers and a broad 1979 "sunshine" law requiring labor negotiations between public employees and state or local government to be open to the public, the court in *Local 760, International Brotherhood of Electrical Workers v. City of Harriman,* 2000 WL 1801856 (Tenn.App. 2000), rejected the argument that bargaining by other public employees was permissible in the absence of express authorization. As noted above, the Virginia Supreme Court reached the same conclusion in *Commonwealth v. County Board of Arlington County,* 217 Va. 558, 580–81, 232 S.E.2d 30, 44–45 (1977), prior to enactment of the statute banning bargaining. The Virginia court found that despite extensive collective bargaining by local governments and express authority to contract and to establish terms and conditions of employment, authorization to bargain was neither express nor fairly implied from authority given to local governments by the state. The court also noted that the legislature had rejected efforts to enact a statute to authorize bargaining.

NOTE

1. Courts that allow bargaining in the absence of legislation are willing to imply authority to bargain from more general authorizations to contract, hire and set terms and conditions of employment. Courts that refuse to do so look for more explicit authorization to bargain collectively. What might explain the difference in the courts' willingness to allow bargaining? Does history play a role? What about the existence of a right-to-work law or the extent of unionization in the private sector?

G. THE DIVERSITY OF STATUTORY PROTECTIONS

1. THE FEDERAL GOVERNMENT

The Civil Service Reform Act of 1978, as has been previously discussed, abolished the United States Civil Service Commission, established the Office of Personnel Management (OPM) and the Merit Systems Protection Board (MSPB), and separated the employee appeals functions from management's personnel functions. In addition, Title VII of the Act, also known as the Federal Services Labor Management Relations Statute, provided a statutory basis for federal employee collective bargaining, ending reliance on presidential executive orders for bargaining authorization. The Federal Service Labor Management Relations Statute essentially codified the scope of bargaining that existed under the Executive Orders with some modest extensions. Permissive subjects of bargaining were expanded and the management rights language was partially altered. A new agency to interpret and administer Title VII, the Federal Labor Relations Authority (FLRA), was established. It was patterned after the National Labor Relations Board. In addition, the office of the General Counsel was created to prosecute unfair labor practices. In 2002 President George W. Bush issued Executive Order 13252 which removed collective bargaining rights from some Department of Justice employees on national security grounds and strongly supported the creation by Congress of the new Department of Homeland Security, staffed by federal employees who could lose their collective bargaining rights by executive administrative action. As discussed in Section A, Congress enacted legislation which limited collective bargaining for Department of Homeland Security employees and Department of Defense employees which was the subject of litigation. Those employees continue to be covered by the provisions of the Homeland Security Act and the National Defense Authorization Act. In addition, since the passage of the Postal Reorganization Act (PRA) of 1970, following a national strike, postal service employees have been granted rights to organize and bargain collectively under provisions added to the National Labor Relations Act (NLRA), the law governing collective bargaining rights of private sector employees. Since July 1, 1971, covered postal employees have had the right to bargain about all NLRA's subjects of bargaining (including economic issues which were prohibited subjects of bargaining for federal employees). However, postal employees continue to be subject to the same ban against striking as are federal employees. Moreover, the PRA mandates binding arbitration of unresolved collective bargaining impasses (in contrast to the NLRA impasse provisions which provide for mediation only). Accordingly, the Federal Service Labor Management Relations Statute is irrelevant to the bargaining rights of postal service employees.

2. STATE AND LOCAL GOVERNMENT EMPLOYEES

An overwhelming number of states (approximately four-fifths plus the District of Columbia) have statutes authorizing public employee collective bargaining for at least some groups of employees. Only a minority of jurisdictions, however, have chosen to enact a single comprehensive law to govern all state and local government bargaining. In many jurisdictions, there is an array of distinctive legislation covering one or more occupational groups of public employees, such as teachers, state employees, police and firefighters, municipal employees, higher education employees, etc.

Unique state events may also add diversity in the legal framework governing public sector bargaining. In Indiana, the Public Employees Collective Bargaining Act was repealed in the early 1980s. However, public school teachers retain a statutory right to bargain. See IND. CODE. ANN. §§ 20–29–1–1 to 20–29–3–10. State employees were provided with bargaining rights by an executive order which was then revoked in 2005. See Indiana Executive Order 05–14, issued by Governor Daniels revoking Indiana Executive Order 90–6, issued by Governor Bayh, http://www.in.gov/gov/files/EO_05-14_Complaint_State_Employees.pdf. Local governments may bargain with their employees if they choose to do so, and if they have not chosen to bargain, governments of localities with more than 7000 people must meet and confer with majority representatives of their public safety employees. See IND.CODE ANN. §§ 36–8–22–1 to 36–8–22–16. The Indiana example illustrates the wide variety of approaches that exist in some states, which in part reflect political realities in the state.

There is a further element of diversity in several states which have enacted comprehensive collective bargaining statutes. Local governments may be expressly authorized to opt out of the state collective bargaining law if they enact their own local laws governing collective bargaining which conform to specified state standards. Within this framework, over thirty years ago New York City established a local labor relations agency to administer its local public sector collective bargaining law. California's Meyers–Millias–Brown Act of 1968 established collective bargaining rights for county and municipal employees but left its administration to local governments. In 2000, the California legislature transferred jurisdiction over the act to the California Public Employment Relations Board. However, Los Angeles County and the City of Los Angeles continue to administer the statute as it applies to their employees.

One final distinction should be noted. Most public sector collective bargaining enactments provide for implementation by a labor relations administrative agency (with public sector jurisdiction only or combined private and public sector jurisdiction) with explicit judicial review provided for or judicial review available by implication. Some statutes, however, make no provision for any administrative agency, relying exclusively upon judicial proceedings for implementation and enforcement.

Where legislation has been adopted, a remarkable diversity exists among the states as to key provisions of such legislation. The norm is non-uniform treatment on such critical issues as: which groups of public employees are covered; the extent of the duty to bargain once a collective bargaining relationship has been established; subjects of bargaining and how other state statutes regulating the employment relationship mesh with the statutory collective bargaining obligation; limitations governing public employee strikes and strike penalties; the variety of procedures available or mandated to resolve bargaining impasses; extent of union security fees to be paid by members of the bargaining unit to their exclusive bargaining representative; administration by a specially created administrative agency; and whether a local government is authorized to bargain with its employees.

Substantive areas reflecting divergent legislative, administrative and judicial approaches by various states are explored in detail in all the chapters which follow: Chapter 5 (Protecting the Right to Organize), Chapter 6 (Recognition of Exclusive Bargaining Representatives), Chapter 7 (Duty to Bargain), Chapter 8 (Scope of Bargaining), Chapter 9 (Strikes), Chapter 10 (Resolution of Bargaining Impasses), Chapter 11 (Administration of the Agreement), and Chapter 12 (Individuals and the Union).

NOTES

1. Is there a constitutional equal protection claim when collective bargaining rights are authorized for only some occupational groupings of public employees and not for other public employee groupings? See *Indiana State Teachers Association v. Board of School Commissioners of Indianapolis*, 918 F.Supp. 266 (S.D. Ind. 1996), *aff'd*, 101 F.3d 1179 (7th Cir. 1996) (finding no such claim). What rationale supports denial of such a claim?

2. Does the passage of enabling collective bargaining legislation affect public management in any ways that differ from the ways in which private sector managers may be affected?

3. Might there be a "spillover" effect upon the wages and working conditions of nonunion public employees when unionized public employees are successful (or unsuccessful) in using the collective bargaining process?

4. A majority of states have legislation covering state and local government employee collective bargaining rights. There are two distinct patterns, however, for such legislation. A number of states (including Alaska, Florida, Iowa, Massachusetts, Michigan, Minnesota, New Jersey, New York, Ohio, and Oregon) have adopted a single, comprehensive legislative approach to cover state and local government employees including teachers and other school district employees. Other states (including California, Maine, Rhode Island, Washington, and Wisconsin) have adopted multiple statutes over the years governing the rights of specified groups of public employees such as state employees, teachers, local government (non-teacher) employees, police, firefighters, and public college and university faculty and staff. California, Rhode Island, and Washington lead the list of jurisdictions with multiple collective bargaining statutes covering various groupings of public employees while Wisconsin has two distinct statutes, one governing state employees' collective bargaining rights and the other governing municipal (including school district) employees' collective bargaining rights. Illinois has two statutes, one governing educational employees and the other all other governmental employees. The latter statute provides for two separate panels of the administrative enforcement board, one covering Chicago and Cook County, in which Chicago sits, and the other covering the state and its employees and all other localities. What factors might account for this diversity and why has this diversity from state to state and within some states persisted without any consolidation of legislation based upon experiences with public sector collective bargaining within the state or in other states?

Chapter 5

Protecting the Right to Organize

■ ■ ■

As developed in the preceding chapters, states were slow to enact statutes protecting public employees' rights to organize. When they did enact such laws, they looked to the National Labor Relations Act (NLRA), which had governed the private sector since 1935, as a model.

The NLRA guarantees private sector employees the right to organize and protects that right with a series of prohibitions on employer and union conduct, known as unfair labor practices. A party who believes that an employer or a union has committed an unfair labor practice files a charge in a regional office of the NLRB. The staff of the regional office investigates the charge. If the Regional Director, serving as designee of the NLRB's General Counsel, finds reasonable cause to believe that an unfair labor practice occurred, the Regional Director issues a complaint. Typically, an attorney in the regional office prosecutes the complaint before an administrative law judge (ALJ). The ALJ issues a recommended decision. The losing party may file exceptions with the Board, which issues a final order. That order may be appealed to the United States Court of Appeals. NLRB orders, however, are not self-enforcing. Even if no appeal is filed, if the respondent does not comply with the Board's order, the Board must petition the Court of Appeals for an order of enforcement.

Most public sector jurisdictions follow the NLRA model of protecting the right to organize through the prohibition of unfair labor practices. Typically, however, public sector jurisdictions do not have a separate arm for labor board prosecution of unfair labor practice complaints comparable to the NLRB General Counsel. Instead, they require the charging party to prosecute the charge before the board.

This chapter explores the adaptation of the NLRA model to the public sector. It focuses on the scope of protected activity and the most common ways in which unfair labor practice prohibitions affect employees' rights to organize.

A. THE SCOPE OF PROTECTED ACTIVITY

Section 7 of the National Labor Relations Act declares that employees in the private sector "shall have the right to self-organization, to form, join, or assist labor organizations, to bargain collectively through representatives of their own choosing, and to engage in other concerted activities for mutual aid or protection, and shall also have the right to refrain from any or all such activities * * *." Section 7's protection is broader than traditional union activity. No formal organization need be involved. For example, in *NLRB v. Washington Aluminum Co.*, 370 U.S. 9, 82 S.Ct. 1099, 8 L.Ed.2d 298 (1962), a group of employees walked off the job to protest extremely cold temperatures in their workplace. The Supreme Court held their action protected even though no formal labor union was involved.

Most states that have enacted public sector collective bargaining statutes have copied the language of Section 7 of the NLRA. A few state statutes, however, define the scope of protected activity more narrowly. For example, Section 3515 of the California State Employer–Employee Relations Act provides:

> Except as otherwise provided by the Legislature, state employees shall have the right to form, join, and participate in the activities of employee organizations of their own choosing for the purpose of representation on all matters of employer-employee relations. State employees also shall have the right to refuse to join or participate in the activities of employee organizations. * * *

WEST'S ANN.CAL.GOV'T.CODE § 3515.

Similarly, Section 202 of New York's Taylor Law provides:

> Public employees shall have the right to form, join and participate in, or to refrain from forming, joining, or participating in, any employee organization of their own choosing.

NEW YORK–MCKINNEY'S CIVIL SERVICE LAW § 202.

Oregon's Public Employee Collective Bargaining Act declares:

> Public employees have the right to form, join and participate in the activities of labor organizations of their own choosing for the purpose of representation and collective bargaining with their public employers on matters concerning employment relations.

OREGON REV.STAT. § 243.662.

What is the significance of a state's adoption of a definition of employee rights that is narrower than Section 7 of the NLRA? Consider the following case.

NEW YORK CITY TRANSIT AUTHORITY v. PUBLIC EMPLOYMENT RELATIONS BOARD

New York Court of Appeals, 2007.
8 N.Y.3d 226, 832 N.Y.S.2d 132, 864 N.E.2d 56.

SMITH, J.

The National Labor Relations Act (NLRA), as interpreted in *NLRB v. J. Weingarten, Inc.*, 420 U.S. 251, 95 S.Ct. 959, 43 L.Ed.2d 171 (1975), gives to an employee of a firm subject to the NLRA the right to have a union representative present with the employee at an investigatory interview, if the employee reasonably believes that the interview might result in disciplinary action—a so-called "*Weingarten* right." We hold today that the Taylor Law does not give a *Weingarten* right to New York public employees.

Facts and Procedural History

This case arises out of the New York City Transit Authority's interview of one of its employees, Igor Komarnitskiy. The Authority was informed that Komarnitskiy, a car inspector, had become angry when asked to show a pass before entering a train yard and that, in objecting to the request, he had used a racial slur in referring to employees he thought were treated less strictly. The Authority asked Komarnitskiy for a written response to the allegation, and Komarnitskiy provided one that he had prepared with the help of a representative of the Transport Workers Union (TWU). The Authority, suspicious that the TWU representative had influenced or dictated the content of the response, ordered Komarnitskiy to come to a supervisor's office to prepare a new response, and refused to allow TWU representatives to come with him.

The TWU filed an improper practice charge against the Authority, claiming that it had violated Komarnitskiy's *Weingarten* right. The Public Employment Relations Board (PERB) upheld the charge, and the Authority brought this CPLR article 78 proceeding against PERB and the TWU, asking that PERB's decision be annulled. The Supreme Court dismissed the proceeding, and the Appellate Division affirmed. We granted leave to appeal, and now reverse.

Discussion

* * *

Civil Service Law § 202 provides: "Public employees shall have the right to form, join and participate in, or to refrain from forming, joining, or participating in, any employee organization of their own choosing."

This statutory language is in some ways similar to, but in more relevant ways different from, that of the statute interpreted in *Weingarten*, section 7 of the NLRA (29 USC § 157). Section 7 provides:

> "Employees shall have the right to self-organization, to form, join, or assist labor organizations, to bargain collectively through representa-

> tives of their own choosing, and to engage in other concerted activities for the purpose of collective bargaining or other mutual aid or protection, and shall also have the right to refrain from any or all of such activities * * * "

While some of the rights given by section 7 ("to form, join, or assist labor organizations, to bargain collectively through representatives of their own choosing") have close counterparts in section 202 ("to form, join and participate in * * * any employee organization of their own choosing"), those are not the rights that the Supreme Court relied on in *Weingarten*. Rather, *Weingarten* upheld the NLRB's decision that the right to "engage in * * * concerted activities for the purpose of * * * mutual aid or protection" included a right to have union representatives present at disciplinary interviews (420 U.S. at 260, 95 S.Ct. 959). Since the "mutual aid or protection" language is absent from section 202, *Weingarten* does not support a holding that section 202 creates a *Weingarten* right. * * *

PERB and the TWU argue that a *Weingarten* right may be inferred from section 202's provision for "the right to * * * participate in" labor unions. The right to union representation at disciplinary interviews, however, is not inherent in the right to participate in a union. Of course, employees may seek such a right of representation in collective bargaining; in doing so, they are protected by the Taylor Law's provision, in Civil Service Law § 203, that they "shall have the right * * * to negotiate collectively with their public employers in the determination of their terms and conditions of employment." But nothing in the text of the Taylor Law suggests that a *Weingarten* right is given by the statute itself.

The text and legislative history of a later-enacted statute strongly support our conclusion that the Taylor Law does not confer a *Weingarten* right. In 1993, 26 years after the Taylor Law's enactment, and 18 years after *Weingarten,* the Legislature amended Civil Service Law § 75(2)—which applies to many, though not all, of the public employees protected by the Taylor Law—to add the following language:

> An employee who at the time of questioning appears to be a potential subject of disciplinary action shall have a right to representation by his or her certified or recognized employee organization under article fourteen of this chapter and shall be notified in advance, in writing, of such right. If representation is requested a reasonable period of time shall be afforded to obtain such representation. If the employee is unable to obtain representation within a reasonable period of time the employer has the right to then question the employee. A hearing officer under this section shall have the power to find that a reasonable period of time was or was not afforded. In the event the hearing officer finds that a reasonable period of time was not afforded then any and all statements obtained from said questioning as well as any evidence or information obtained as a result of said questioning shall be excluded, provided, however, that this subdivision shall not modify

or replace any written collective agreement between a public employer and employee organization negotiated pursuant to article fourteen of this chapter." (L. 1993, ch. 279, § 1.)

Section 75(2) gives the employees to which it applies a kind of *Weingarten* right, but one different from the right that PERB and the TWU ask us to find in the Taylor Law. Under section 75(2), a violation of a *Weingarten* right results not in an improper practice proceeding before PERB, but in the exclusion from a disciplinary hearing of statements made at the interview and evidence obtained as a result. And the *Weingarten* right created by section 75(2), unlike the right given by the Taylor Law to "participate in * * * employee organization[s]," may be surrendered in collective bargaining. It would have made no sense to create the section 75(2) version of the *Weingarten* right if a more robust version of that right already existed under the Taylor Law.

The history of the 1993 legislation shows clearly that its supporters did not believe that any *Weingarten* right existed in New York law before 1993. The supporting memorandum of the Senate sponsor of the 1993 legislation says: "New York State public employees do not have the same protection enjoyed by private sector employees during interviews and discussions by their employers," and goes on to defend the idea of creating such a right with language taken from the Supreme Court's *Weingarten* decision. A letter from a supporter of the legislation, the president of a civil service union, similarly notes that, under existing law, New York public employees lack the protections enjoyed by private sector employees, and adds: "This protection has been affirmed by the United States Supreme Court in *NLRB v. Weingarten.* * * *". We see no basis for concluding that the supporters of the 1993 legislation misunderstood the existing law, and were wasting their time in changing it.

Accordingly, the order of the Appellate Division should be reversed, with costs, the petition granted, PERB's determination of October 2, 2002 annulled, and the improper practice charge dismissed.

KAYE, C.J., dissenting.

In 1967, the New York State Legislature enacted the Public Employees' Fair Employment Act (Civil Service Law, art. 14, § 200 *et seq.*, popularly known as the Taylor Law [L. 1967, ch. 392, § 2]), explicitly to promote harmonious labor relations in the public sector. Today's decision will, I fear, foster dissonance.

The Public Employment Relations Board (PERB) determined that permitting an employee to have a union representative at an interview which the employee reasonably fears may result in discipline is a right granted under the Taylor Law. Construing the statute de novo (assuming that is the proper standard), I agree with PERB that the fundamental right to participate in a union—as the Legislature intended—includes the right to a union representative's attendance at a precharge interview, and

I would affirm the orders of the trial court and the Appellate Division so holding.

* * *

In *Weingarten* the United States Supreme Court upheld a National Labor Relations Board (NLRB) determination that an employee in the private sector has a right "to refuse to submit without union representation to an interview which he reasonably fears may result in his discipline" (*id.* at 256, 95 S.Ct. 959, 43 L.Ed.2d 171). The case involved a lunch counter worker accused of stealing. When a store manager and security agent questioned her, she was denied her request to have the presence of her union representative at the interview. Bursting into tears, she explained that she had thought she was permitted to eat lunch without paying, and the manager pressed her to sign a statement; but the manager later learned that a different branch of the store where she had recently worked did have the "free lunch" policy.

The Court in *Weingarten,* upholding the finding that the employer had committed an unfair labor practice, based its determination that employees may be represented at an interview that could lead to discipline on language in National Labor Relations Act § 7 that " '[e]mployees shall have the right ... to engage in ... concerted activities for the purpose of ... mutual aid or protection.' " * * * The Court also based its rationale on the policies underlying the statute:

> Requiring a lone employee to attend an investigatory interview which he reasonably believes may result in the imposition of discipline perpetuates the inequality the [National Labor Relations] Act was designed to eliminate, and bars recourse to the safeguards the Act provided 'to redress the perceived imbalance of economic power between labor and management' (*id.* at 262, 95 S.Ct. 959 [citation omitted]).

The Supreme Court emphasized the benefits to employers as well as employees: "A single employee confronted by an employer investigating whether certain conduct deserves discipline may be too fearful or inarticulate to relate accurately the incident being investigated, or too ignorant to raise extenuating factors. A knowledgeable union representative could assist the employer by eliciting favorable facts, and save the employer production time by getting to the bottom of the incident occasioning the interview."

A court must give effect to the intention of the Legislature by considering, first, the language in "its natural and most obvious sense," then "the general spirit and purpose underlying its enactment" and, later, extrinsic evidence, such as legislative history. The majority today reverses PERB's determination essentially because the words, "concerted activities for the purpose of * * * mutual aid or protection" are not found in the Taylor Law. That section 202 of the Taylor Law omits these words, however, does not contravene an interpretation that the word "participate" in its "natural signification" in the Taylor Law manifests a legislative intent to allow public employees the right to union representation a[illegible] an investigatory interview when the employee seeks that representation.

Section 200 of the Taylor Law states its underlying purpose:

> The legislature of the state of New York declares that it is the public policy of the state and the purpose of this act to promote harmonious and cooperative relationships between government and its employees and to protect the public by assuring, at all times, the orderly and uninterrupted operations and functions of government. These policies are best effectuated by (a) granting to public employees the right of organization and representation * * *

Issues concerning union representation on disciplinary matters for bargaining unit members are part of the employment relationship in the public sector. Thus, a proper interpretation of the Taylor Law is that it incorporates the right to have representation relating to informal investigations of employee conduct—a construction that is not negated by the existence of a statute that addresses formal disciplinary actions in Civil Service Law § 75. To "participate" means to take part in something, usually in common with others. Seeking advice from a union representative when a bargaining unit member is most vulnerable certainly is encompassed in the plain language of "participate."

As noted above, the underlying purposes of the Taylor Law are to promote cooperation and to assure "the orderly and uninterrupted operations and functions of government"—in other words, to prevent strikes. In 1969—two years after the original law was passed and six years before *Weingarten* was decided—a panel led by George W. Taylor, after whom the law was named, issued a report (*see* New York [State] Governor's Committee on Public Employee Relations. Recommendations for current legislative action with respect to the Taylor Law [1969] [Report]). The Report emphasized the need to use impasse panels and other deterrents—such as fines and imprisonment—in order to prevent illegal strikes. Section 209–a was added in 1969 (L. 1969, ch. 24, § 7). Thus, at the same time that the Legislature added the section delineating improper practices to ensure that employers would adhere to the statute as a whole, the Legislature also included section 209–a(3) (now subd. [6]), which provides: "In applying this section, fundamental distinctions between private and public employment shall be recognized, and no body of federal or state law applicable wholly or in part to private employment, shall be regarded as binding or controlling precedent."

The thrust of this section is to reinforce the point that public employees in the state do not have the same right to strike as those employees covered by the NLRA—not that state employees do not have the same rights to participate in union activity. Indeed, it is likely that the main reason that section 202 does not include the words, "mutual aid or protection" is to bar strikes—and section 209–a (6) was meant to reinforce that point.

* * *

While the comparison between the Taylor Law and the NLRA * * * highlighted the differences between an "employee organization" as defined in section 201 of the Taylor Law and an unorganized group of individuals, here public and private employees represented by a union are in essentially the same position—seeking to participate in a protected union activity of getting advice from a union representative when discipline is an issue. I take guidance from the *Weingarten* decision that representation in the circumstances of an employee's reasonable fear that an investigatory interview may result in discipline is consistent with the "most fundamental purposes" of the Taylor Law.

* * *

Moreover, the 1993 amendments in Civil Service Law § 75 do not foreclose a finding of a *Weingarten* right in the Taylor Law. The underlying policies of the Taylor Law and section 75 address different issues. It is possible, for example, for an employee to be terminated following a section 75 hearing, but then be reinstated after PERB finds that the employer committed an improper practice—perhaps discrimination or retaliation. Section 75 sets forth procedures for imposing discipline in accordance with due process. Section 75(2) provides that an employee has a right to representation at the time of questioning and "shall be notified in advance, in writing, of such right." Section 75(2) also provides for a representative when an employee has already been charged with a disciplinary infraction. The rationale for ensuring that an employer does not "interfere" with a bargaining unit member's representation before the formal filing of charges is to attempt to balance the equities between the power of the employer and the vulnerability of the employee. Deferring representation makes it "increasingly difficult for the employee to vindicate himself, and the value of representation is correspondingly diminished." That the Legislature chose to add a right to section 75 that an employee be represented is by no means dispositive that the right to have representation upon request at an investigatory interview is excluded in the Taylor Law.

* * *

NOTES

1. In reaction to the Court of Appeals' decision, the New York legislature amended the statute. Section 209–a(1)(g) of the Taylor Law now makes it an improper practice for an employer:

> to fail to permit or refuse to afford a public employee the right, upon the employee's demand, to representation by a representative of the employee organization, or the designee of such organization, which has been certified or recognized under this article when at the time of questioning by the employer of such employee it reasonably appears that he or she may be the subject of a potential disciplinary action. If representation is requested, and the employee is a potential target of disciplinary action at

> the time of questioning, a reasonable period of time shall be afforded to the employee to obtain such representation. It shall be an affirmative defense to any improper practice charge under paragraph (g) of this subdivision that the employee has the right, pursuant to statute, interest arbitration award, collectively negotiated agreement, policy or practice, to present to a hearing officer or arbitrator evidence of the employer's failure to provide representation and to obtain exclusion of the resulting evidence upon demonstration of such failure. Nothing in this section shall grant an employee any right to representation by the representative of an employee organization in any criminal investigation.

Compare the new statutory provision to the *Weingarten* right as developed under the National Labor Relations Act. Do they differ in any significant ways?

2. In *Dutchess Community College*, 17 PERB 3093 (1984), *rev'd*, 128 Misc.2d 628, 490 N.Y.S.2d 705 (Supt. Ct. Dutchess Cnty.), *rev'd sub nom Rosen v. PERB*, 125 A.D.2d 657, 510 N.Y.S.2d 180 (2d Dep't 1986), *aff'd*, 72 N.Y.2d 42, 530 N.Y.S.2d 534, 526 N.E.2d 25 (1988), the New York PERB, affirmed by the New York courts, held that a group of teachers were not protected when they voiced concerns to management over salaries, classroom size and course load. PERB reasoned that although their conduct was concerted and for mutual aid and protection, it did not constitute participation in an employee organization. Why might a state limit protection to participation in union-related activity, rather than concerted activity generally?

3. Unlike the private sector, most public sector employees are protected by civil service and tenure statutes that contain procedures governing lengthy suspensions and dismissals. Should the presence of such procedures mitigate against applying *Weingarten* in the public sector? The Pennsylvania Labor Relations Board rejected such an argument and applied *Weingarten* in *Township of Shaler*, 11 Pa.P.E.R. ¶ 11347 (Pa.LRB. 1980).

4. In *Commonwealth v. Pennsylvania Labor Relations Board*, 591 Pa. 176, 916 A.2d 541 (2007), the Pennsylvania Supreme Court affirmed the holding in *Shaler*, and also held that the right to union representation in an investigatory interview belongs to the employee rather than the union. Consequently, the court held, the employee is entitled to the union representative of his or her choice, provided that the chosen representative is available.

5. If *Weingarten* applies in the public sector, may a union waive the right in a collective bargaining agreement? If so, what language is necessary to waive the right? See *Ehlers v. Jackson County Sheriff's Merit Commission*, 183 Ill.2d 83, 231 Ill.Dec. 932, 697 N.E.2d 717 (1998).

6. In the private sector, the NLRB has frequently changed its position over whether employees in non-unionized workplaces have a rights under section 7 of the NLRA to have a coworker present for an interview that they reasonably believe could lead to discipline against them. See *IBM Corp.*, 341 N.L.R.B. 1288 (2004) (holding no and overruling *Epilepsy Foundation of Northeast Ohio*, 331 N.L.R.B. 676 (2000), which overruled *Sears, Roebuck & Co.*, 289 N.L.R.B. 627 (1988), which overruled *Materials Research Corp.*, 262 N.L.R.B. 1010 (1982)). If a public sector labor board is inclined to follow

private sector precedent, what should it do when private sector case law is continuously changing.

Some activities are literally concerted and for mutual aid and protection but, nevertheless, for policy reasons the law does not protect them. For example, employees who assault an abusive supervisor would be acting in concert and for mutual aid and protection but would not be protected against employer discipline or discharge. The National Labor Relations Board and the courts have developed standards governing when concerted activity for mutual aid and protection loses its protection for policy reasons. Should the private sector standards apply in the public sector?

OMAHA POLICE UNION LOCAL 101, IUPA v. CITY OF OMAHA

Supreme Court of Nebraska, 2007.
274 Neb. 70, 736 N.W.2d 375.

STEPHAN J.

This appeal presents the issue of whether a public employer engages in a prohibited practice under the Industrial Relations Act (the Act) by taking disciplinary action against public employees belonging to a labor organization for statements made and published by those employees. In this action commenced by Omaha Police Union Local 101 (Union) against the City of Omaha and Omaha chief of police Thomas Warren (collectively the appellants), the Commission of Industrial Relations (CIR) concluded that disciplinary action taken against a police officer who authored an article in a Union publication constituted a prohibited practice. In reaching this conclusion, the CIR used a legal standard applied in private sector labor relations cases. We conclude that the CIR should have applied a different standard utilized by courts and administrative agencies to resolve protected speech issues in public sector employment cases.

I. BACKGROUND

1. ANDERSEN INVESTIGATION

On December 14, 2004, a Union meeting was held for the member police officers of the Omaha Police Department (OPD). During the meeting, OPD Sgt. Timothy Andersen, then president of the Union, was asked a question concerning how OPD calculated 911 emergency dispatch service response times. Andersen opined that the method by which OPD calculated response times was misleading. In expressing his view, Andersen provided a hypothetical example on how police officers were trained by OPD to respond to certain high priority 911 calls that required response by two officers.

Several days after the meeting, reports of Andersen's statements were relayed to Warren. On December 20, 2004, Warren initiated an Internal Affairs (IA) investigation of Andersen in which he sought to determine exactly what Andersen said at the December 14 meeting and whether

Andersen had advised officers to disregard departmental standard operating procedures.

In June 2005, IA determined that Andersen had not violated departmental procedures and had not acted unprofessionally. Warren adopted those findings and took no disciplinary action against Andersen.

2. HOUSH INVESTIGATION AND DISCIPLINE

In response to the events involving Andersen, OPD Sgt. Kevin Housh wrote an article in the February 2005 issue of the Union newspaper, "The Shield," which is distributed to members of the Union as well as to members of the community. Housh's article was generally critical of the standard operating procedures for two-officer 911 calls and the manner in which the city and OPD calculated response time. Housh characterized city officials as "[a] bunch of grown men and women, supposedly leaders, acting like petty criminals trying to conceal some kind of crime." He also stated that "[t]hey refuse to do it, they know they've screwed up, and rather than admitting guilt, they (whoever they are) will make history and try to control what is said/revealed during union meetings regarding response time."

On February 7, 2005, Warren initiated an IA investigation of Housh based on his article in The Shield. Describing the language from the article as derogatory and inflammatory, Warren alleged that Housh's conduct constituted gross disrespect and insubordination and was unbecoming an officer, in violation of OPD rules of conduct.

After conducting its investigation, IA determined that the unprofessional conduct allegation against Housh should be sustained. On February 24, 2005, Warren adopted that finding. However, contrary to other recommendations for discipline, Warren terminated Housh's employment. The Union subsequently appealed Housh's termination to the city personnel board. Thereafter, the city and the Union reached an agreement whereby Housh was reinstated to OPD but was required to, among other things, serve a 20-day suspension without pay and discontinue working on the emergency response unit.

3. MEETING WITH WARREN

On August 22, 2005, two Union representatives met privately with Warren in an attempt to discuss the appropriate methods of handling future Union speech issues as well as OPD's handling of Andersen's case. The Union claims that it sought assurances from Warren that he would not interfere with, investigate, or discipline off-duty officers for their conduct at Union meetings or in Union publications. Warren refused to discuss Andersen's case, as it was still an ongoing controversy. Warren also purportedly stated that he retained the right "to initiate an internal investigation on off duty union activities if he determines they involve either insubordination or gross disrespect of himself or his administration or false comments [or] slander." But, Warren also commented that he was not trying to censor anyone and that he would only initiate an IA investigation of an officer if he believed there was merit to such investigation.

4. CIR PROCEEDINGS

On September 2, 2005, the Union filed a petition with the CIR against the appellants. The Union claimed that the appellants' investigations of Andersen and Housh and termination of Housh's employment had "chilled" other Union members' expression of opinions at Union meetings and in the Union publication. As a result, the Union alleged that the appellants had engaged in prohibited labor practices under § 48–824(2)(a) by interfering with, restraining, and coercing Union members in their exercise of rights granted under § 48–837. * * *

After conducting a trial in which testimony was heard and evidence was received, the CIR issued a written order granting a portion of the relief sought by the Union. The CIR found that numerous employees had indicated that Warren's actions had limited their involvement with the Union, including decreased meeting attendance and fewer articles submitted for publication. However, the CIR concluded that the IA investigation of Andersen did not constitute an interference, restraint, or coercion in the exercise of the right to participate in Union activities.

As to Housh, the CIR reasoned that his article was a protected union activity if it was "concerted activity" falling under the protection of § 48–824(2)(a). Looking to federal labor cases for guidance, the CIR noted that employee speech was a protected concerted activity if it related to working conditions. It then determined that Housh's article pertained to officer safety, which was a working condition and a mandatory subject of bargaining. The CIR also found, based on federal labor case law, that an employee only loses protection for speech that is deliberately or recklessly untrue. The CIR concluded that "Housh's statements, while certainly constituting intemperate, abusive and insulting rhetorical hyperbole, fall short of deliberate or reckless untruth. The comments were made in a union publication in the context of a management/union disagreement, and they were therefore protected from interference, restraint or coercion by management."

As a remedy, the CIR ordered the appellants "not to interfere in any way" with statements made by employees in the Union publication which did not violate the standard of deliberate or reckless untruth. The appellants were also ordered to place a statement in the Union newsletter indicating that they would recognize the Union members' rights to protected activity. The appellants perfected this timely appeal, which we moved to our docket pursuant to our statutory authority to regulate the caseloads of the appellate courts of this state.

The appellants assign, restated, that the CIR erred in finding that (1) the calculation of response times was a mandatory bargaining issue and

(2) all speech by employees in the Union newspaper is protected unless deliberately or recklessly untrue.

* * *

III. STANDARD OF REVIEW

Any order or decision of the CIR may be modified, reversed, or set aside by the appellate court on one or more of the following grounds and no other: (1) if the CIR acts without or in excess of its powers, (2) if the order was procured by fraud or is contrary to law, (3) if the facts found by the CIR do not support the order, and (4) if the order is not supported by a preponderance of the competent evidence on the record considered as a whole.

* * *

IV. ANALYSIS

1. CITY'S APPEAL

(a) Mandatory Subject of Collective Bargaining

* * *

In their first assignment of error, the appellants assert that the CIR erred in finding that "[t]he calculation of response times is a working condition which affects safety and is a mandatory subject of bargaining." The appellants contend that the calculation of response time is not a working condition, but, rather, a mechanism for measuring departmental effectiveness. They argue that such calculation is merely a statistical tool that OPD management uses to evaluate OPD's ability to respond to 911 emergency calls. The appellants argue that changing the method of calculation would not affect OPD's service to the public or officer safety, but would impair the ability of OPD to compare future response times with past response times. The appellants thus contend that as an evaluative tool, the response time calculation is solely within management's prerogative.

The Union, on the other hand, argues that calculation of response time has broader implications which affect departmental staffing. The Union contends that if response time is calculated in the manner it claims is proper, the calculations would reveal longer 911 response times, which may indicate that OPD staffing is deficient. The Union contends that these staffing issues have an effect on officer safety, a condition of employment.

A matter which is of fundamental, basic, or essential concern to an employee's financial and personal concern may be considered as involving working conditions and is mandatorily bargainable even though there may be some minor influence on management prerogative. Company rules relating to employee safety and work practices involve conditions of employment. Conversely, management prerogatives include the right to hire, to maintain order and efficiency, to schedule work, and to control transfers and assignments. Based on our review of the record we conclude that the CIR's finding that the calculation of response times implicates officer safety is supported by the evidence. On the surface, both parties are arguing in terms of the calculation of response times. But the essential nature of their arguments is whether an OPD response to a two-officer 911 call is completed when the first officer arrives at the call location or when the second officer arrives at the call location. Thus, the real issue can be understood to involve how officers should respond to two-officer 911 calls, not merely how OPD calculates their response time. Under this broader reading of the issue, which the CIR deemed appropriate, it can be fairly said that response time does relate to officer safety and, thus, the manner in which it is determined affects a condition of employment.

(b) Protected Union Speech

Section 48–824(2) of the Act states: "It is a prohibited practice for any employer or the employer's negotiator to: (a) Interfere with, restrain, or coerce employees in the exercise of rights granted by the Industrial Relations Act." Section 48–837 provides that "[p]ublic employees shall have the right to form, join, and participate in * * * any employee organization of their own choosing [and] shall have the right to be represented by employee organizations to negotiate collectively with their public employers in the determination of their terms and conditions of employment * * *." As framed by the parties, the prohibited practice issue before the CIR was whether the actions taken by Warren against Andersen and Housh and the comments made by Warren to Union leadership interfered with, restrained, or coerced employees from exercising their right to participate in the Union.

(i) NLRA Speech Standard

The CIR determined that § 48–824(2)(a) is "almost identical" to § 8(a)(1) of the National Labor Relations Act (NLRA). Recognizing that decisions under the NLRA can be helpful in interpreting the Act, but are not binding, the CIR looked to decisions by the National Labor Relations Board for guidance.

Under the NLRA, employees have the right to engage in "concerted activities for the purpose of * * * mutual aid or protection." The National Labor Relations Board construes this right to extend protection to employee speech which relates to working conditions. While not condoned by the board, employees may use " 'intemperate, abusive, or insulting language without fear of restraint or penalty if the speaker believes such rhetoric to be an effective means to make a point.' " But protection of speech under the NLRA is not unrestricted; it is lost when work-related speech constitutes a "deliberate or reckless untruth."

Importantly, the scope of NLRA coverage is limited. By its own terms, the NLRA does not apply to the federal government or any state or municipal governments in their capacities as employers. Instead, it applies only to private sector employment.

(ii) Public Sector Employees

In this case, the CIR applied the NLRA "deliberate and reckless untruth" standard in determining whether Housh's speech exceeded the protections granted under the Act. But, public sector employees, like OPD police officers, are not guaranteed the rights and protections of the NLRA. Thus, we are presented with the legal question of whether the Act guarantees similar rights and protections to public sector employees in Nebraska. While the language of the Act is broad enough to encompass the rights granted under the NLRA, we are not persuaded that the "deliberate or reckless untruth" standard is the appropriate method to analyze the speech of public sector employees.

The Act has a somewhat different focus than the NLRA. Although couched in broad Commerce Clause language, the NLRA attempts to rectify the "inequality of bargaining power between employees * * * and employers" by providing certain rights to employees. The Act, on the other hand, focuses almost exclusively on protecting the public.

> The continuous, uninterrupted and proper functioning and operation of the governmental service * * * to the people of Nebraska are hereby declared to be essential to their welfare, health and safety. It is contrary to the public policy of the state to permit any substantial impairment or suspension of the operation of governmental service * * * by reason of industrial disputes therein. It is the duty of the State of Nebraska to exercise all available means and every power at its command to prevent the same so as to protect its citizens from any dangers, perils, calamities, or catastrophes which would result therefrom. It is therefore further declared that governmental service * * * are clothed with a vital public interest and to protect same it is necessary that the relations between the employers and employees in such industries be regulated by the State of Nebraska to the extent and in the manner hereinafter provided.

§ 48–802(1).

While the Act does provide public employees some of the same rights granted under the NLRA, it also explicitly removes other rights utilized by private sector employees, most notably the right to strike. Therefore, we view the Act not only as an attempt to level the employment playing field, but also as a mechanism designed to protect the citizens of Nebraska from the effects and consequences of labor strife in public sector employment. As a result, we believe the NLRA's "deliberate and reckless untruth" standard is inappropriate in the context of public sector employment.

We are also cognizant of the fact that the labor conflict in this case involves parties serving a special purpose to the public. As a police department, OPD operates as a paramilitary organization charged with maintaining public safety and order. Federal courts have recognized this special purpose, finding that these employers should be given "more latitude in their decisions regarding discipline and personnel regulations than an ordinary government employer."

* * *

(iii) Appellants' Proposed Speech Standard

In their second assignment of error, the appellants argue that this is actually a First Amendment free speech case and that the proper standard is the balancing test espoused by the U.S. Supreme Court in *Pickering v. Board of Education*. As the basis for this argument, the appellants contend that both the U.S. Constitution and the Nebraska Constitution already provide protection to public employees for engaging in work-related speech. Under the appellants' theory, the Union members would be required to assert their First Amendment rights by means of claims against the appellants pursuant to 42 U.S.C. § 1983 (2000). But, the CIR has no authority to vindicate constitutional rights. Therefore, the CIR would have no jurisdiction to hear a case of this nature.

While we agree with the appellants that public employees do have First Amendment speech rights, we are not persuaded that the *Pickering* balancing test is the appropriate method to determine whether union speech is protected under the Act. The CIR is not a court and is in fact an administrative body performing a legislative function. It has only those powers delineated by statute, and should exercise that jurisdiction in as narrow a manner as may be necessary. Allowing the CIR to decide cases based on constitutional jurisprudence would blur the jurisdictional boundaries between that administrative body and the courts of law. Therefore, we reject the appellants' overture to apply the *Pickering* balancing test to prohibited practice cases under the Act.

(iv) Federal Employee Speech Standard

Although by its terms, the NLRA does not apply to public sector employment, federal employees are afforded labor protections under the Federal Service Labor–Management Relations Act. In 5 U.S.C. § 7116(a) of those statutes, it provides that "it shall be an unfair labor practice for an agency * * * (1) to interfere with, restrain, or coerce any employee in the exercise by the employee of any right" under these statutes. Likewise, 5 U.S.C. § 7102 states:

> Each employee shall have the right to form, join, or assist any labor organization * * * freely and without fear of penalty or reprisal, and each employee shall be protected in the exercise of such right. Except as otherwise provided under this chapter, such right includes the right-
>
> (1) to act for a labor organization in the capacity of a representative and the right, in that capacity, to present the views of the labor organization to heads of agencies and other officials of the executive branch of the Government, the Congress, or other appropriate authorities, and

(2) to engage in collective bargaining with respect to conditions of employment through representatives chosen by employees under this chapter.

While these statutes are not identical to the comparable provisions of the Act in Nebraska, the language is substantively similar. Because of this similarity to the federal act, we find it helpful to consider Federal Labor Relations Authority (FLRA) cases interpreting § 7102.

In *U.S. Dept. of Veterans Affairs Med. Ctr. Jamaica Plain, Mass.*, 50 F.L.R.A. 583 (1995), a police officer was suspended for insubordination for making threatening remarks in a letter to the chief of police. The FLRA noted that under § 7102, employees had the right to present labor organization views to management. It further recognized that "employee action to publicize labor disputes or issues that have a direct bearing on conditions of employment is protected activity" and that such protection "extends to the publicizing of such disputes or issues through the media." However, it acknowledged that "an agency has the right to discipline an employee who is engaged in otherwise protected activities for actions that 'exceed the boundaries of protected activity such as flagrant misconduct.'" Such flagrant misconduct includes remarks or actions that are of an " 'outrageous and insubordinate nature' " and which "compromise an agency's ability to accomplish its mission, disrupt discipline or are disloyal."

We conclude that a similar legal standard should apply to the determination of whether speech is protected under the Act. Under this new standard, public employees belonging to a labor organization have the protected right to engage in conduct and make remarks, including publishing statements through the media, concerning wages, hours, or terms and conditions of employment. However, employees lose the statutory protection of the Act if the conduct or speech constitutes "flagrant misconduct." Flagrant misconduct includes, but is not limited to, statements or actions that (1) are of an outrageous and insubordinate nature, (2) compromise the public employer's ability to accomplish its mission, or (3) disrupt discipline. It would also include conduct that is clearly outside the bounds of any protection, including, for example, assault and battery or racial discrimination. Importantly, the CIR must balance the employee's right to engage in protected activity, which permits some leeway for impulsive behavior, against the employer's right to maintain order and respect for its supervisory staff. Factors that the CIR may consider, but would not necessarily be determinative, include: (1) the place and subject matter of the conduct or speech, (2) whether the employee's conduct or speech was impulsive or designed, (3) whether the conduct or speech was provoked by the employer's conduct, and (4) the nature of the intemperate language or conduct.

(v) Conclusion

Because we have prescribed a new standard for determining when union speech is protected under the Act, we deem it appropriate that the

CIR should apply the standard in the first instance to the facts pertaining to the Housh article. Accordingly, we reverse, and remand to the CIR with directions to make that determination.

* * *

NOTES

1. On remand, the Commission on Industrial Relations found Housh's speech protected. As described by the Nebraska Supreme Court:

> The CIR noted that the newsletter in which Housh's article was published was primarily a Union newsletter, although it is not distributed exclusively to Union members. Housh's article was "designed, rather than impulsive," and the CIR could not say it was provoked by the employer's words or actions. Housh's conduct was, as previously determined, "intemperate, abusive and insulting." However, the CIR found that the remarks did not reach the level of flagrant misconduct. "They were in fact rhetorical hyperbole, which would not be reasonably believed by any reader as accusing of any crime or wrongdoing. They were intemperate, immature hyperbole, but they were nonetheless protected union speech in the context of the newsletter." The CIR found no evidence of any loss of discipline, respect, or ability to accomplish the police department's mission that could be attributed to the publication of the article, and the CIR doubted that the remarks would reflect poorly on anyone other than Housh and the newsletter's editor. The CIR concluded that Housh's remarks were protected speech.

The City of Omaha again appealed to the Nebraska Supreme Court. This time the court observed that, had it conducted its own review of Housh's speech, it might have reached a different result. The court, nevertheless, deferred to the CIR's conclusion because it was supported by the facts as found by the Commission. *Omaha Police Union Local 101, IUPA v. City of Omaha*, 276 Neb. 983, 759 N.W.2d 82 (2009).

2. What differences did the court discern between the purposes behind the NLRA and the purposes behind the Nebraska Industrial Relations Act? How did those differences translate into different standards for finding concerted activity unprotected?

3. The court declined to read a constitutional standard into the Nebraska statute. Would the case have been decided differently if a constitutional standard had been used? Is it appropriate to read a constitutional standard into a public employee collective bargaining statute? See *Service Employees International Union Local 73 and Palatine Community Consolidated School District No. 15*, *infra* at page 314.

4. The first issue that the court decided was whether the calculation of response time was a working condition and, therefore, a mandatory subject of bargaining. The scope of bargaining and the definition of mandatory subjects of bargaining are considered in greater detail in chapter 8. For present purposes, it is sufficient to note that statutes protect concerted activity as it relates to the employees' working conditions. Thus, if the court had concluded

that response time did not relate to working conditions, it would have found the statements unprotected. Assume that a group of teachers send a letter to all of the parents of children attending their school, criticizing the administration and the school's governing council for alleged mismanagement and fiscal irresponsibility. Is the letter protected activity? Should it matter if the teachers work at a public charter school which emphasizes a "collaborative structure of governance involving teachers, parents and management"? See *California Teachers Association v. PERB*, 169 Cal.App.4th 1076, 87 Cal. Rptr.3d 350 (2009).

5. A full-time equipment operator for Clay County also worked during his off hours for the Clay County Fair Board, a private not-for-profit corporation, as did two other county employees. The Fair Board paid them considerably less than the county. The equipment operator on behalf of himself and his two colleagues negotiated wage increases with the Fair Board's manager. Subsequently, the manager told the county engineer that the equipment operator had represented that the engineer would not allow the Fair Board to use county equipment unless it paid the equipment operator the same wage rate that the county paid him. Based on this allegation, the county engineer fired the equipment operator whose union then filed unfair labor practice charges. The labor board credited the equipment operator's testimony that he never made such a representation and concluded that the county had discharged him for engaging in the protected activity of negotiating wage increases with the Fair Board. You represent the county. What arguments will you make on appeal? See *Clay County v. Public Employment Relations Board*, No. 08–1208, 784 N.W.2d 1 (Iowa 2010).

6. In the private sector, certain acts of disloyalty, such as disparagement of the employer's products or services, are not protected, even where undertaken to pressure the employer during collective bargaining. See *NLRB v. Electrical Workers Local 1229 (Jefferson Standard Broadcasting Co.)*, 346 U.S. 464, 74 S.Ct. 172, 98 L.Ed. 195 (1953). Should similar disloyal conduct be unprotected in the public sector?

B. ACCESS TO EMPLOYEES

In the private sector, the National Labor Relations Act protects employees' rights by prohibiting five unfair labor practices. Most states have similar provisions in their public employee bargaining statutes. The unfair labor practices that protect employee organizing rights prohibit employers from interfering with, restraining or coercing employees in their exercise of their statutory rights; dominating and/or interfering with the administration of or unlawfully supporting a labor organization; and discriminating to encourage or discourage membership in a labor organization.

In the private sector, restrictions placed by employers on solicitation of employees for union organization are analyzed under the prohibition of employer interference, restraint and coercion. In *Republic Aviation Corp. v. NLRB*, 324 U.S. 793, 65 S.Ct. 982, 89 L.Ed. 1372 (1945), the Supreme Court held that employers may prohibit employees from soliciting their coworkers on company property during working time but not during nonworking time, such as breaks and wash-up time, unless the employer is able to show special circumstances that justify the broader prohibition to avoid disruptions to the business. However, in *NLRB v. Babcock & Wilcox Co.*, 351 U.S. 105, 76 S.Ct. 679, 100 L.Ed. 975 (1956), and *Lechmere, Inc. v. NLRB*, 502 U.S. 527, 112 S.Ct. 841, 117 L.Ed.2d 79 (1992), the Court held that employers may bar non-employees from soliciting employees on company property, except where the employees are so inaccessible as to be beyond the reach of reasonable alternative means of communication. The crucial distinction between employees and non-employees is that the former are lawfully on the employer's property when the solicitation takes place but the latter are seeking to trespass. Therefore, the employer's property rights are much stronger in cases of non-employee solicitation. Should this approach be followed in the public sector workplace?

SERVICE EMPLOYEES INTERNATIONAL UNION LOCAL 73 AND PALATINE COMMUNITY CONSOLIDATED SCHOOL DISTRICT NO. 15

Illinois Educational Labor Relations Board, 2002.
18 P.E.R.I. ¶ 1043.

This case arises out of the Union's attempt to organize the District's bus drivers. The District's bus drivers begin work at approximately 5:30 a.m. when they conduct a safety inspection of the bus, make their first run and then return to the bus garage at approximately 9:30 a.m. Upon returning to the bus garage, the drivers punch out for their break and remain on break until their next run.

Drivers routinely discuss work and non-work related issues while both on and off the clock. The District has no written policy regarding what the drivers are allowed to discuss when they are either on or off the clock.  However, bus drivers routinely engage in various types of solicitation while both on and off the clock, including Tupperware sales, craft item sales, wrapping paper and candy sales and other fund-raising sales.

In spring 1999, two bus drivers, Sue Hernandez and Marge Hunn, contacted the Union because they were dissatisfied with the District's treatment of the bus drivers. On October 31, 1999, the Union began organizing the bus drivers at the District's bus garage. Cathy Nicosia, union business representative, and Joseph Richert, a union representative, talked to bus drivers about the Union and handed out literature and doughnuts to the drivers as they came in to work. Later, in fall 1999, Nicosia, Richert and Bill Silver, a union representative, went to a District school to speak with bus drivers as they waited in their empty busses for children to be released from school. The bus drivers told the Union representatives that, when they stepped on District property, the drivers were instructed to call dispatch, and someone from the District would come and ask them to leave.

On December 7, 1999, Assistant Superintendent for Personnel and Human Services Linda Vass issued a memorandum to the bus drivers in response to complaints she received about the Union organizing campaign.

The memorandum informed drivers that they did not have to talk to the Union representatives and that the Union had no right to interfere with the driver's work time. Vass also sent a copy of the memorandum to Nicosia with a letter stating that the Union was not to conduct business on school property during work time.

Nicosia responded in writing to Vass's memo stating that the Union was not interfering with the bus driver's work time and that the Union was willing to reach a compromise with the District regarding the organizing campaign. Subsequently, on January 5, 2000, Nicosia and Vass met informally and agreed that Union representatives would not enter school grounds to distribute leaflets, but would be allowed to distribute information and talk to the bus drivers at the bus garage during non-work periods. However, shortly thereafter, the District informed the Union representatives that they were only allowed to hand out leaflets on the public sidewalk across the street from the area where the drivers came in to work or while standing in the road.

* * *

On March 9, 2000, Union organizer Joseph Richert stood on the sidewalk next to the driveway leading into the school grounds and talked to the drivers as they came down the driveway on the way to their cars. Vass told Richert that he must leave the sidewalk because he was intimidating drivers. Richert responded that he was standing on a public sidewalk and that he had a right to be there. Vass said that if Richert did not leave, she would call the police, and then left. Vass and Director of Transportation Bill Willetts then went to the parking lot behind the school and asked another union official, Bill Silver, to leave District property.

* * *

Under Section 14(a)(1) of the Act, an employer is prohibited from "interfering, restraining or coercing employees in the exercise of the rights guaranteed under this Act." ILL.-SMITH-HURD ANN. 115 ILCS 5/14(a)(1). The right to organize and choose a collective bargaining representative is a fundamental right under the Act.

* * *

In *Lechmere, Inc. v. NLRB*, 502 U.S. 527, 112 S.Ct. 841, 117 L.Ed.2d 79 (1992) the Supreme Court addressed whether private employers could bar non-employee union organizers from their premises. The Court held that Section 7 of the National Labor Relations Act confers rights on employees, not unions or their non-employee organizers. The Court reaffirmed the general rule of *NLRB v. Babcock & Wilcox Co.*, 351 U.S. 105, 76 S.Ct. 679, 100 L.Ed. 975 (1956) that an employer may validly prohibit non-employee distribution of union literature on its property. According to the Court, it is only where access to employees outside of the employer's property is not feasible that employers' private property rights are balanced against employees' rights under Section 7 of the National Labor

Relations Act. Thus, except under extremely limited circumstances, a private employer may prohibit non-employee access to its premises for the purposes of union organizing. In *Lechmere*, where the employer owned a store within a shopping plaza, the Court determined that the employees were accessible through other means and the employer did not commit an unfair labor practice by excluding non-employee organizers from its property.

Lechmere, however, only applies to private employers. In the case of a public employer, the public owns the property. Non-employee union organizers, like other individuals, are members of the public. The adverse private ownership interest that was present in *Lechmere* is absent. Thus, *Lechmere* does not apply to situations involving public property.

In *Perry Education Ass'n v. Perry Local Educators' Ass'n*, 460 U.S. 37, 103 S.Ct. 948, 74 L.Ed.2d 794 (1983), the Supreme Court held that public property can be identified as either a public forum or non-public forum. In a non-public forum, distinctions in access may be drawn if "they are reasonable in light of the purpose which the forum at issue serves," and are not an attempt to suppress expression merely because public officials disagree with it. In *Perry*, the Court determined that a school's internal mail system was not a public forum. Thus, school property that has not been opened to public communication is a non-public forum, as opposed to streets and parks, which are considered public forums. Because school property is generally a non-public forum, schools may reasonably regulate certain types of speech and restrict access to their premises. For example, a school may allow access to organizations "that engage in activities of interest and educational relevance to students," without being required to permit access to organizations concerned with terms and conditions of employment.

Here, the District banned all non-employee union organizers from access to school property. Under *Perry*, a school may restrict access to its premises because the school is a non-public forum. In this case, the District did not open its doors to the public, as it would have for a school play or basketball game. If the District had opened its doors to the public, then arguably it could be considered a public forum at those times. However, the District was conducting its normal operations and did not open its doors to the public. Thus, it was reasonable for the District to prohibit the expression of views which would interfere with the District's normal operations in a non-public forum.

Union representatives stood in the parking lot in front of the bus garage and on school grounds at busses waiting to pick up children. These locations were reserved for the District's transportation functions and were not devoted to the public expression of views. Similarly, although union organizer Richert was standing on a sidewalk, he was speaking to employees who were on a driveway devoted to the District's transportation functions.

Because the District's schools and the specific locations where non-employee organizing activity occurred were non-public forums, the District acted lawfully by restricting non-employee union access to its premises. Accordingly, based on the above analysis, the District did not violate Section 14(a)(1) of the Act by prohibiting all non-employee union organizer access to school property that was not a public forum.

NOTES

1. Recall the *Omaha Police Association* case, found at page 304 *supra*, where the Nebraska Supreme Court declined to read First Amendment standards into the labor relations act. Do the two decisions represent different philosophical approaches to reliance on constitutional standards in interpreting public employee labor relations acts or can an argument be made in support of both decisions? In *United Transportation Union and Southeastern Pennsylvania Transportation Authority*, 40 Penn. Pub. Emp. Rpr. ¶ 87 (Pa. LRB 2009), organizers from an incumbent union were barred from soliciting employees to vote for the union in an upcoming representation election in which a different union was seeking to oust the incumbent. The organizers sought to solicit employees at a driver's room and at bus and trolley platforms where the riding public was allowed. The Hearing Examiner dismissed the union's unfair labor practice charges, relying on *Lechmere*. On appeal, the union argued that *Lechmere* should not apply because the employer was a public entity and the property involved was public property. The Pennsylvania Labor Relations Board affirmed the Hearing Examiner without further discussion of *Lechmere*. The Board held that because the organizer was seeking to access employees during working time, the employer could prohibit such access.

2. How does the labor board's public forum test in *Palatine* differ from the private sector approach under *Babcock & Wilcox* and *Lechmere*? Does the public forum test appropriately capture the public employer's interests that are comparable to the private employer's property rights?

3. A community college has a policy that allows outside organizations to rent rooms "provided the use does not interfere or conflict with the normal operations or external programs of the college; the use is consistent with the philosophy, goals and mission of the college; and the use conforms to federal, state, local laws and ordinances." The college also prohibits "solicitation including but not limited to commercial, charitable and political, using college buildings, equipment, services or grounds." When deciding whether to grant requests to rent college facilities, the college considers the day and time of the proposed use, the impact on campus parking and the class schedule. It has allowed a variety of community, educational and fraternal groups to rent rooms, generally in the evenings. It has rejected requests from commercial establishments, such as banks and cellular phone providers, who sought to solicit college employees and students. It has generally allowed college organizations to reserve rooms for use during weekday hours. The college's faculty and its maintenance employees are organized and the college has routinely allowed the exclusive bargaining representatives to use rooms during weekday hours. College support staff, however, are not organized. A small group of

support staff have formed an organizing committee. Their committee has no charter, by-laws or constitution. They, and the union with which they are working to organize support staff, sought to rent a room on a weekday from 10:00 a.m. to 6:00 p.m. for an open house and pizza luncheon. Their intent was to invite employees during non-working time to come by and learn about the benefits of union representation and to ask them to sign cards authorizing the union to serve as their exclusive representative. The college denied the request. Was the denial an unfair labor practice? See *Staff Association of Waubonsee Community College and Waubonsee Community College*, 24 Pub. Emp. Rpr. Ill. 63 (Ill. Educ. Lab. Rel. Bd. 2008).

4. In *The Guard Publishing Co. d/b/a The Register–Guard*, 351 N.L.R.B. 1110 (2007), *rev'd*, 571 F.3d 53 (D.C. Cir. 2009), the NLRB held that under the NLRA, an employer has a property right to completely prohibit employees from using the employer's e-mail system to solicit coworkers. The NLRB further held that an employer that allows some employee e-mail solicitations but not others commits an unfair labor practice only when it bases its determination of what to allow on protected concerted activity. The D.C. Circuit reversed the NLRB on the ground that the Board's findings that the employer did not discriminate on the basis of concerted activity were not supported by substantial evidence. The court declined to rule on the Board's other holdings in the case.

Public sector labor boards have taken varying approaches to employer prohibitions on employee use of e-mail for concerted activity. In *University of Wisconsin Hospitals*, Dec. No. 30203–C (Wis. Emp. Rel. Comm'n Apr. 12, 2004), the Wisconsin Employment Relations Commission (WERC), applying the Wisconsin Employment Peace Act (WEPA), balanced the interests of the union and employees in having access to the hospital's e-mail system against the hospital's interest in precluding such access. The WERC concluded that the hospitals had violated WEPA by blocking all union access to the hospital's e-mail system. In *Oakland County*, 15 Mich. Pub. Emp. Rptr. (LRP) ¶ 33018 (Mich. Emp. Rel. Comm'n 2001), the Michigan Employment Relations Commission (MERC) held that the county did not violate the Michigan Public Employment Relations Act when it denied the request of the grievance chair of one bargaining unit to use the e-mail system to poll unit members concerning a request that the union support a different union concerning an issue in the second union's bargaining unit. The record reflected that the employer had and enforced a policy prohibiting all non-business use of e-mail. MERC analogized the e-mail system to bulletin boards and telephones and held that an employer may deny all access but may not discriminate against access for union-related purposes when it allows other non-business access. In the case before it, MERC found no evidence that the employer had allowed other non-business access.

In *State of California*, 22 Pub. Emp. Rptr. Cal. (LRP) ¶ 29148 (Cal. Pub. Emp. Rel. Bd. 1998), the California Public Employment Relations Board held that by prohibiting the use of the e-mail system for employee organization matters while allowing its use for personal e-mails, several state agencies had unlawfully interfered with employees' rights to participate in the activities of employee organizations and with the right of their union to communicate with its members in violation of the Dills Act. See also *AFSCME Local 575 v. Los*

Angeles County Superior Court, 32 P.E.R.C. (LRP) 151 (Cal. PERB 2008) (finding a violation of Myers Millias Brown Act to prohibit sending e-mail to 55 court clerks at one courthouse announcing a lunchtime union meeting because it misapplied a policy that prohibited use of court's e-mail system in a manner or to a degree that was detrimental to the court or to employee performance). Similarly, in *City of Clearwater*, 32 Fla. Pub. Emp. Rptr. (LRP) ¶ 210 (Fla. Pub. Emp. Rel. Comm'n 2006), the Florida Public Employment Relations Commission (PERC) held that the city violated the Florida public employee relations statute by banning the use of the city's computers to promote charitable activities, volunteer organizations and special interest groups without approval and by banning employee use of internal e-mail distribution lists for non-business purposes but allowing a wide variety of non-business related e-mail communications while prohibiting union communications. The Florida PERC opined that the city "has absolute control over its e-mail and computer systems and is free to operate those systems as it chooses. However, when an employer discriminatorily bans its employees from using its computer and e-mail systems because the City disapproves of the union-related messages, then its interference is unlawful * * *" Are the relevant considerations for regulating employer bans on the use of e-mail for concerted activities the same in the public and private sectors?

5. In *Republic Aviation*, *supra*, the Supreme Court also upheld the NLRB's ruling that the employer's prohibition on employees wearing buttons violated section 8(a)(1) when applied to employees wearing pro-union buttons. The Court indicated that the Board must balance the employees' rights to wear the buttons against the employer's managerial interests in preventing it. Consider the following situations: A school district prohibits teachers from wearing any signs, buttons or other objects favoring or opposing matters that are the subjects of negotiations between the district and the union when in the classroom or other instructional areas in the presence of students. See *East Whittier Education Association v. East Whittier School District*, 29 P.E.R.C. (LRP) 40 (Cal. PERB 2004). A Department of Corrections prohibits correctional employees from wearing pins saying "No Scabs" in solidarity with employees on strike against a private contractor at the prison. See *AFSCME Council 31 v. Illinois Department of Central Management Services*, 25 P.E.R.I. (LRP) 12 (IL. LRB 2009).

6. In *Excelsior Underwear, Inc.*, 156 N.L.R.B. 1236 (1966), the National Labor Relations Board ruled that after it directs that a representation election be held to determine whether a majority of the employees wish to be represented by a labor organization, the employer must provide the NLRB's regional director with a list of the names and home addresses of the employees in the bargaining unit within which the election will take place. The regional director then furnishes that list to the labor organization(s) on the ballot. Most public sector labor boards have followed a similar procedure. Occasionally, a state codifies the procedure in its statute. See, e.g., Ill.-Smith-Hurd Ann. 5 ILCS 315/9.

7. For further discussion of access rules in representation election campaigns, see Chapter 6 § D.

C. EMPLOYER COERCION

1. THREATS OF REPRISALS

In the private sector, employers commonly run very active campaigns to persuade their employees to reject the union's organizing drive. The NLRB and the courts have had to draw fine lines between lawful predictions and expressions of opinion, on the one hand, and unlawful threats of reprisals or other coercion on the other. Such vigorous anti-union campaigns are much less common in the public sector. Political concerns, including the desire for union support in future elections and bad publicity with the broader electorate that may result from running aggressive opposition campaigns, often constrain public employer opposition to unions. Additionally, public sector managers are frequently less motivated than private sector managers to oppose unionization because of the absence of a profit motive, and the perception that union-negotiated improvements in compensation and benefits may be extended to them. Nevertheless, such campaigns do occur, calling on labor boards and courts to draw similar lines of demarcation between lawful and unlawful speech.

Special concerns may arise in the context of a representation election, in which employees vote whether to be represented by a union. In addition to protecting employee rights through unfair labor practice proceedings, the NLRB has held that representation elections must be conducted under conditions that approximate those of a laboratory to ensure that the election represents the employees' free and fair choices. See *General Shoe Corp.*, 77 N.L.R.B. 124 (1948). Conduct which is not an unfair labor practice can breach laboratory conditions and result in an election being set aside and the holding of a rerun election.

MOUNT PLEASANT COMMUNITY SCHOOL DISTRICT v. PERB

Iowa Supreme Court, 1984.
343 N.W.2d 472.

UHLENHOPP, J.

In June 1981, several nonteaching employees of the Mount Pleasant Community School District (district) who were members of the Para-Professionals, Aides, Secretaries Organization (organization) petitioned PERB [Public Employment Relations Board] to conduct a representation election. On October 6, 1981, PERB conducted the election, which the organization lost by a vote of ten to twelve.

The organization challenged the result. It claimed that a notice posted on October 5, 1981, some thirty hours before the election, misrepresented material facts and threatened organization members with loss of employment if the union won the election. The notice was posted by Superintendent Richard Goodwin of the district in each of the school buildings where members of the organization were likely to see it. The notice was the only campaign statement made by the district. It read:

NOTICE

Secretaries, Aides, Para–Professionals

FACTS TO BE CONSIDERED

BEFORE YOU VOTE

1. *If the union wins, what happens?* Many think that if the union wins the election it is an automatic contract. The law says that the School District must negotiate with the union in good faith. Good faith bargaining (includes rejecting) a demand we feel in any way would put the school district in a bad position. That's what good faith means. The only things required by law exist. Everything is "horse trading," you might gain some things that you don't presently have, but you also might lose some things that you presently have because bargaining starts with a bare table not at where you are today.

2. *How about job security?* Certainly, unions are in no position to talk about job security. In short, unionized employers throughout the nation, when layoffs become necessary, have been forced to take layoff action. It is quite obvious that a collective bargaining agreement cannot guarantee against staff reduction—nor, for that matter, does it protect against discharge for cause. Bringing it closer to home, anyone who knows us must agree that we do not enjoy staff reduction, but it must be recognized that it is an occasional but real fact of life in the school business when our enrollment is declining.

3. *How about fringe benefits?* How do your fringe benefits compare to other like job classifications in the private sector? Would they be better if you pay union dues?

4. *What does it mean if I signed an authorization card?* It means only that you are willing to have a union vote. It does not mean that you must vote for the employee organization.

5. *How have the non-certified employees salary increases compared to the certified staff over the last several years?* FACT: As a group, percentage of dollar increase has been at least as much or more every year.

6. *Importance of voting!* Under the Public Employment Relations Board procedures, you should vote if you are for the union or against the union representing you in collective bargaining. The winner of the election will be whichever received the majority of the votes cast, not of those eligible to vote.

REMEMBER YOUR VOTE IS A SECRET BALLOT

THANK YOU FOR TAKING TIME TO READ THIS NOTICE.

[Signed] Mr. Goodwin

The organization asserted that paragraphs 1 and 2 of the notice violated rules 660–5.4(3)(b) and (g) of the Iowa Administrative Code. Those rules read as follows:

5.4(3) *Objectionable conduct during election campaigns.* The following types of activity, if conducted during the period beginning with the filing of an election petition with the board and ending at the conclusion of the election, and if determined by the board that such activity could have affected the results of the election, shall be considered to be objectionable conduct sufficient to invalidate the results of an election:

* * *

b. Misstatements of material facts by any party to the election or their representative without sufficient time for the adversely affected party to adequately respond;

* * *

g. Any other misconduct or other circumstance which prevents employees from freely expressing their preferences in the election.

* * *

The organization claims that paragraphs 1 and 2 of the notice contain the following "substantial departure[s] from the truth" as set forth by the hearing officer, and had a significant impact on the election:

> 1) The notice gives the employees the mistaken impression that if they select the Organization as their bargaining representative, the employees would not be guaranteed a contract regardless of the fact that the Act provides for impasse procedures ending with arbitration and a binding collective bargaining agreement. 2) An employee, unsophisticated in labor relations matters, could reasonably conclude from reading the notice that the District could unilaterally reject without further negotiations any union proposal which the District considered to be detrimental to the District. 3) The District's statement "The only things required by law exist" would lead the employees to question the need for an exclusive bargaining representative if, in fact, negotiations only included mandatory subjects of bargaining. And 4) Although the Organization cannot guarantee job security, Section 9 of the Act requires the District to negotiate on several mandatory items affecting job security such as seniority, transfer procedures and staff reduction procedures. Additionally, the Organization contends that it did not have adequate time the day before the scheduled election to respond to the District's notice by either seeking legal advice or drafting a response.

The organization thus concludes that invalidation is required. * * * The hearing officer reached a different conclusion, with which the board agreed:

> It is my considered opinion however that the statements at issue do not contain any substantial misrepresentations of fact or law. Rather, the statements can best be described as being inartistically or vaguely worded. Clearly, the statements are subject to different interpretations. Although the District's definition of good faith bargaining does

> not technically meet the established legal definition I cannot conclude, as the Organization contends, that this statement or the other statements in the notice substantially distort the essential elements of the truth. Indeed, the notice clearly emphasizes the District's position that the District will bargain over only mandatory subjects of bargaining. The notice does not state that the District will refuse to negotiate with the Organization. These statements constitute the District's bargaining position and as such do not violate Board Rule 5.4(3)b.

We think this interpretation of paragraphs 1 and 2 is plausible and we thus uphold the determination of the hearing officer and the board. We need not decide whether a contrary holding by them would have had substantial evidentiary support.

B. As to PERB's holding that the district's notice contained "a veiled threat [in violation of rule 5.4(3)(g)] that [employees] would be laid off if they voted for the organization," rule 5.4(3)(g) proscribes conduct which "prevents employees from freely expressing their preferences in the election."

* * *

[We] conclude in this case that substantial evidence does not exist in support of PERB's conclusion the notice posted by the superintendent constituted proscribed conduct. The notice contained no express or implied threat of job elimination. It merely set forth conditions, which neither the district nor the union could control, under which staff reductions become necessary. The district made no reference to adverse consequences that it would inflict on its own volition if the union won, nor did the district fabricate "hobgoblin" consequences outside its control having no basis in objective fact. The notice was no more than a statement, based on well-known fact, that the union could not guarantee the existence of jobs; it was not a threat.

Although the notice was not threatening, we nonetheless consider the question of whether it prevented the employees "from freely expressing their preferences in the election." This second part of the test under rule 5.4(3)(g) involves an evaluation of the impact of the notice. In considering impact, "factors to be considered include the rank of the individual who engaged in the conduct, whether the employer or the employee initiated the communication, the total background of all pre-election conduct and of course any evidence directly suggesting that the conduct had either an isolated or pervasive impact." Other factors include "the number of threats, the severity of the threats and whether those threatened were put in fear, the number of workers threatened, whether the threats were made close to the election and whether they persisted in the minds of the employees at the time of the election, whether the reports of threats were widely circulated, whether the effect of pro-union threats were cancelled out by pro-management threats, the closeness of the vote * * * and whether the threats can be attributed to the union or management." Also to be weighed is the impact of an employer's economic control over an employee.

* * *

The notice was nothing more than an isolated, non-threatening statement of the district's opinion as to what the union would be able to provide in the way of job security. Such a statement cannot be "transformed or transmuted by the magic of semantic labels" into a threat which had a significant impact on the election. * * * Here, the record does not support an inference that the notice was such as would have affected the ability of the employees to make a free choice, contrary to rule 5.4(3)(g).

NOTES

1. Should the labor board police the factual accuracy of the parties' representation campaign propaganda? The NLRB has vacillated on this question. See *Midland National Life Insurance Co.*, 263 N.L.R.B. 127 (1982). If a public sector labor board follows the NLRB's approach and the NLRB reverses itself, should the public sector labor board follow suit?

2. In the private sector, most employees are terminable at will. In the public sector, most employees are protected against arbitrary discharge by civil service or tenure statutes. Should the different environments concerning job security affect the analysis of employer anti-union propaganda?

3. The Illinois Public Labor Relations Act makes it an unfair labor practice for an employer:

> To expend or cause the expenditure of public funds to any external agent, individual, firm, agency, partnership, or association in any attempt to influence the outcome of representational elections held pursuant to * * * this Act; provided, that nothing in this subsection shall be construed to limit an employer's right to internally communicate with its employees as provided in subsection (c) of this Section, to be represented on any matter pertaining to unit determinations, unfair labor practice charges, or pre-election conferences in any formal or informal proceeding before the board, or to seek or obtain advice from legal counsel. Nothing in this paragraph shall be construed to prohibit an employer from expending or causing the expenditure of public funds on, or seeking or obtaining services or advice from, any organization, group, or association established by and including public or educational employers, whether covered by this Act, the Illinois Educational Labor Relations Act or the public employment labor relations law of any other state or the federal government, provided that such services or advice are generally available to the membership of the organization, group, or association, and are not offered solely in an attempt to influence the outcome of a particular representational election.

ILL.-SMITH-HURD ANN. 5 ILCS 315/10(a)(6). What public policies support such a restriction on employer opposition to union campaigns? What public policies argue against such a restriction?

2. INTERROGATION

In the private sector, the NLRB and the courts have reviewed the questioning of employees concerning their union sympathies in light of the power imbalance in the employment relationship. Such interrogation is not considered per se illegal. Factors considered in determining whether such questioning is coercive include the time, place, personnel involved, information sought, the employer's known preferences and other indicia of the surrounding atmosphere. See *Blue Flash Express*, 109 N.L.R.B. 591 (1954) (holding that employer interrogation of employees regarding their union sentiments is not illegal unless, "under all the circumstances, the interrogation reasonably tends to restrain or interfere with the employees in the exercise of rights guaranteed by the [National Labor Relations] Act"). Should a similar approach be used in the public sector? Might the availability of civil service or tenure system protection make interrogation less threatening in the public sector than the private sector?

3. GRANTING OR WITHHOLDING BENEFITS

DISTRICT 2A TRANSPORTATION, TECHNICAL, WAREHOUSE & SERVICE EMPLOYEES UNION v. CANAVERAL PORT AUTHORITY

Florida Public Employee Relations Commission, 1998.
24 F.P.E.R. ¶ 29,228.

On November 17, 1997, the Canaveral Port Authority (Authority) filed a petition pursuant to Section 447.207(7), Florida Statutes, and Florida Administrative Code Rule 38D–22.002. The petition requests that the Commission issue a declaratory statement as to whether it may continue a practice of providing discretionary pay increases in light of representation-certification petitions filed by two employee organizations which seek to represent affected Authority employees.

* * *

Each year, during December, Authority employees are interviewed individually to determine whether each will receive a pay raise and, if awarded, the amount of the raise. The Authority does this each year for employees who are both in the proposed bargaining unit, as well as for its employees who are unaffected by the pendency of the representation petitions. A decision as to which employee will receive a raise, as well as how much, is subject to discretion by Authority officials to the extent that no particular employee could reasonably expect to receive a wage increase each year. However, each Authority employee nonetheless has a reasonable expectation that the underlying process of awarding wage increases will continue uninterrupted and each employee will be interviewed and eligible for an increase in January 1998. The Authority has budgeted a pay raise for employees for 1998, consistent with its actions in prior years, even though the December 1997 interviews to determine individual raises have not taken place because of the pending representation petitions. Based upon the foregoing undisputed facts, the Authority requests that the Commission decide whether the Authority may lawfully interview its employees and then exercise its discretion and decide whether particular employees should be paid wage increases pursuant to those interviews, despite the pendency of representation petitions.

Implicit in the statutory mandate to order representation elections is the understanding that Commission elections will be conducted in an atmosphere which does not inhibit employees' freedom of choice. Accordingly, the Commission has long held that a public employer's act, after the filing of a representation petition, of withholding benefits which the employees have a reasonable expectation of receiving, constitutes an unfair labor practice in violation of Section 447.501(1)(a), Florida Statutes, because this reasonably interferes with employees' free choice during the subsequent Commission election. Conversely, Section 447.501(1)(a) is also violated when unexpected economic benefits are paid after the filing of a representation petition because this too reasonably interferes with employees' free choice during a subsequent election. "The evil to be avoided regarding changes in the status quo during the period immediately prior to a representation election is the creation of a reasonable belief on the part of the employees that any change in economic benefits was motivated by the representation petition."

The danger inherent in well-timed increases in benefits is a suggestion of a fist inside the velvet glove. Employees are not likely to miss the inference that the source of benefits now conferred is also the source from which future benefits must flow and which may dry up if it is not obliged. *NLRB v. Exchange Parts Co.*, 375 U.S. 405, 84 S.Ct. 457, 11 L.Ed.2d 435 (1964).

The Commission has previously given the following general guidance for all public employers during the pendency of representation petitions:

> To be sure, an employer acts at his peril when he grants or withholds economic benefits during the pendency of an organizational campaign. However, each case must turn on its own particular facts and circumstances. Thus, as a general rule, increases granted on the basis of previously announced plans in accordance with established practice or business necessity will not be found in violation of the Public Employees Relations Act, and an unfair labor practice. Similarly, the withholding of new or increased benefits, the mechanics and resolution of which have not been finally formalized, where the record contains no credible evidence of anti-union animus, will also not constitute discrimination, coercion, restraint or interference in violation of the Public Employees Relations Act, and an unfair labor practice. In the latter cases, full explanation of the reasons for the withholding, along with the assurance of future consideration of the withheld benefits notwithstanding the outcome of the employee organization's election campaign, will serve to dissipate the assumption that the employees

may or may not have that the organization's presence is the sole obstacle to the ultimate realization of the promised benefits.

To determine the propriety of granting pay raises during the pendency of a representation case, the Commission must decide whether the Authority's pay raises constitute an established practice which, as the status quo, must not be changed. An established practice is unequivocal, has existed substantially unchanged for a significant period of time, and bargaining unit employees would therefore reasonably expect it to continue. It is the objective expectations of employees which is the most important factor in determining the status quo. The reasonable expectation of bargaining unit members that they will receive a pay increase is not vitiated by the fluctuations in the amount of the increase from year to year.

The Authority has a past practice of wage increase payments to all of its employees as a whole, although the decisions as to the amounts and which individual employees will receive the payments are discretional. The money for the payments has been appropriated for the current year. Under these circumstances, affected employees may believe that the pendency of the representation petitions has unlawfully caused the status quo to be disrupted if Authority employees as a whole are not interviewed and considered for pay raises, even though individual employees may or may not receive pay increases. Under these circumstances, the Commission grants the Authority's petition for a declaratory statement and holds that it may lawfully interview and then grant discretional pay raises to affected employees which are consistent with its past practice.

NOTES

1. In *NLRB v. Exchange Parts Co.*, cited in the principal case, the Supreme Court held that a private sector employer violates the National Labor Relations Act if it grants a benefit with the intent to influence the outcome of a representation election. Generally, intent to influence is inferred from the grant of benefits while an election is pending unless the employer can show objective evidence that the benefit was unrelated to the election. Similarly, an employer commits a violation if, with an election pending, it withholds a benefit increase that it otherwise would have given. Should these private sector rules be imported into the public sector where benefits are more closely regulated by statute? As developed in Chapters 9 and 10, states have different approaches to resolving impasses in collective bargaining. Some recognize a right to strike for public employees. Some provide for issues at impasses to be submitted to arbitration for resolution. Some provide for non-binding factfinding and factfinder recommendations. Should the method of impasse resolution in a particular jurisdiction make a difference in whether that jurisdiction follows the private sector model with respect to changes in compensation or working conditions while a representation election is pending?

2. Is the court's decision in the principal case favorable to the employer? What risks does the Canaveral Port Authority face if it follows its usual pay

raise procedure? What is likely to occur if the most vocal union supporters receive lower raises than the other employees?

3. Suppose with an organizing drive underway, the employer distributed the following notice:

> Any wage increase while the organizing is going on could be called an unfair labor practice intended to buy your support and discourage union activity; or the union could take credit for the raise as evidence of what they can accomplish in a short time. If enough cards are signed and an election is scheduled, any increase could be called unlawful, intended to influence your vote.
>
> If an election is held and the union wins, wages and all other conditions of your employment will be subjects of negotiations between the City and the union. That means NOTHING, including wage rates, will increase or decrease until the negotiations result in a contract, or, if no agreement is reached, impasse procedures are exhausted. (Emphasis in original.)
>
> If the organizing attempt terminates and the union gives up; or if an election is held and the union loses, the City will be free to legally make changes in the terms and conditions of your employment.

Is the notice lawful? For an analysis under the National Labor Relations Act, see *Nevada Security Innovations, Ltd.*, No. 31–CA–25173 (NLRB Adv.Div. 2001).

D. EMPLOYER DOMINATION OF A LABOR ORGANIZATION

Section 8(a)(2) of the NLRA prohibits employer domination, interference in the administration of, or unlawful support of a labor organization. The term labor organization is defined broadly as "any organization of any kind, or any agency or employee representation committee or plan, in which employees participate and which exists for the purpose, in whole or in part, of dealing with employers concerning grievances, labor disputes, wages, rates of pay, hours of employment, or conditions of work." Most state public sector labor relations acts contain comparable provisions.

OAK GROVE EDUCATORS ASS'N, CTA/NEA v. OAK GROVE SCHOOL DISTRICT

California Public Employment Relations Board, 1986.
10 P.E.R.C. ¶ 17,134.

BURT, MEMBER

When Dr. Robert Lindstrom was hired as superintendent at Oak Grove School District in 1979, one of his primary responsibilities was to improve communications with teachers. In order to do so, Lindstrom first granted one extra leave day a month to the leaders of the various unions in the District, with the condition that at least part of each of these days would be spent discussing District problems with the superintendent. Lindstrom also visited the schools in the District to meet with teachers. During these meetings, it was suggested that the superintendent revive a practice of a previous superintendent called the "superintendent's roundtable." Lindstrom hoped that the roundtable would provide an opportunity for teachers to deal face-to-face with the superintendent. He testified that he never intended that the roundtable take the place of negotiations with the [Oak Grove Educators] Association [the teachers' exclusive bargaining representative].

One of the teachers who suggested the resurrection of the roundtable was Claudelle Bonaccinie, an Association member. Lindstrom testified that he expressed concern to Bonaccinie both as to the amount of time the roundtable would require and whether the Association might be concerned that the roundtable was an attempt to infringe on the Association's authority. Although Bonaccinie did not recall precisely this statement, she did remember Lindstrom wondering what the Association would think. She said she told him she could not speak for the Association, but that she personally thought the roundtable was a good idea.

Lindstrom issued a bulletin on August 27, 1981, outlining his plans for increasing communication, including the reinstitution of the roundtable. The memo read in part:

> I am also establishing a certificated staff roundtable which will consist of a member from each of the schools. This group will meet monthly, and it will be an opportunity to discuss issues and provide some creative solutions to problems facing education. I hope that through this forum we will be able to discuss creative approaches. Perhaps even the air-conditioning systems can be made well; who knows?

The group became known as the Teachers Forum, composed of one staff representative from each school. Selection of the school representative was left up to each principal; some asked for volunteers, some allowed teachers to select a representative, and some selected their school's representative themselves. OGEA was not invited to send a representative; Lindstrom testified that he wanted to keep the group as "nonpolitical" as possible and wanted to avoid having a "watchdog" in the group. OGEA members were not precluded from attending, however, and several of the Forum's representatives were also OGEA members.

Meetings were held once a month. Representatives with questions or issues to raise would telephone the superintendent's secretary in advance, and she would include those items on the agenda. The superintendent did not choose agenda items except in response to questions raised. Various representatives would raise the issues of interest to them; there would be general discussion, and some questions and answers. The superintendent's secretary took minutes, and the representatives reported back to their respective schools at the regular mandatory faculty meetings.

On one District committee, the budget study committee, a Forum representative was appointed to participate along with the OGEA representative.

At the hearing, OGEA introduced minutes of the meetings and meeting agendas to show that some of the topics discussed at forum meetings were within the scope of negotiations and/or were actually subjects of negotiations at the time. For example, as well as items of educational concern, the following subjects were discussed: overloaded classrooms and class size, teachers' working five hours without a break or preparation period, differences in lunch prices among schools, shared contracts, whether Martin Luther King Day was a holiday, a staff incentive award program and the status of laid-off teachers now working as substitutes.

The District introduced testimony to show that no actual negotiations took place over the matters which were within the scope of representation; the conversation was repeatedly described as informational. The superintendent often concluded such discussions by remarking that the issue was the subject of ongoing negotiations and was inappropriate for further discussion.

Both Lindstrom and the subsequent superintendent, Anthony Russo, testified that they did not want the Forum to disrupt the District's relationship with OGEA and went out of their way to avoid discussing negotiable items. No proposals or counterproposals were made, and the ALJ concluded that there was no credible evidence that any complaints were resolved as a result of Forum discussions.

Nevertheless, it is clear from the record that various teachers came to view the Teachers Forum as a more successful route to solving problems than the Association. One OGEA representative testified:

> On going back to our building and discussing this with our building superintendent, it was the feeling that there would be quicker service if the teacher Forum representative were to deal with this problem because he had direct communication with the superintendent and he met with the superintendent every two weeks. Whereas, if the concerns were expressed through the teachers' Association, it would have to go through channels and it would be a long time before anything happened. So, using that as an example, it appeared that the teachers' Forum would provide better, faster services for the health and safety of teachers than would expressing those same concerns through Association channels.

An OGEA building representative at Herman Junior High School, who was also a Forum member, suggested at an OGEA meeting that it would be better to handle the suggested elimination of a prep period through the Forum rather than OGEA. Thomas Richardson, the OGEA representative at Dickinson School, testified that teachers at his school felt that the Forum was a more effective way to get things done and that attendance at OGEA meetings fell off by about one-half during the term of the Forum meetings. Richardson voiced opposition to faculty participation in the Forum and he believed this position contributed to the fact that he was voted out as building representative.

* * *

Section 3543.5(d) of the Educational Employment Relations Act [EERA] provides that it shall be unlawful for a public school employer to:

> (d) dominate or interfere with the formation or administration of any employee organization, or contribute financial or other support to it, or in any way encourage employees to join any organization in preference to another.

Initially, the District argues that it was not in violation of Section 3543.5(d) by its formation of the Teachers Forum since the Forum is not an "employee organization."

In Section 3540.1(d), EERA provides the following definition:

> (d) 'Employee organization' means any organization which includes employees of a public school employer and which has as one of its primary purposes representing those employees in their relations with that public school employer. 'Employee organization' shall also include any person such an organization authorizes to act on its behalf.

Here, there is no question that the Teachers Forum includes employees of the employer. The central question is whether it has as one of its primary purposes representing employees in their relationship with the employer.

In seeking to define "employee organization," the Board has previously determined that an organization need not have formal structure, seek exclusivity, or be concerned with all aspects of the employment relationship in order to constitute a statutory labor organization. The Board adopted the National Labor Relations Board's (NLRB) approach in inquiring whether the group has as a central focus the representation of employees on employment-related matters.

* * *

Here the record shows that the Forum was established and used to improve communications and solve problems. It functioned as a representative body, with one teacher representing each school and raising at the meetings problems suggested by teachers from that school. Many of those problems touched on matters of employment relations and working conditions—the air conditioner, prep periods, etc. Thus, although no actual negotiations took place, negotiable items were indeed discussed.

The record also shows that, although various teachers suggested topics to be discussed at the Forum meetings, the agenda was finalized at the superintendent's office. Although the record indicates the superintendent would end discussions of certain topics by saying they concerned negotiable items and were therefore not appropriate for discussion at the Forum, he apparently did not take steps to prevent such items from being raised and addressed in the first place. Moreover, it is clear that, whatever the original intent, the Forum came to be perceived by employees as a better way to solve problems involving working conditions than through OGEA.

Under the circumstances here, we find the Teachers Forum to be an employee organization within the meaning of 3543.5(d). Having so found, there is no question that the organization was dominated by the District in violation of Section 3543.5(d). It was established by the superintendent, who directed the principal of each school to provide a representative, appointing one if necessary. Meetings were scheduled during working hours for which employees were paid, and a report was made of these meetings at mandatory faculty meetings of the individual schools. None of these privileges was accorded to the Association. At some schools, the Forum meetings were noticed in the principal's letter, while Association meetings were not.

This is not to say that all faculty councils or groups are per se unlawful, or that individual employees cannot speak to their employers about working conditions, including those within the scope of representation. But when the District sets up an organized group of teachers to meet at regular intervals on school time to discuss topics of mutual interest, it permits discussion of negotiable subjects at its own risk.

* * *

HESSE, CHAIRPERSON, dissenting.

I cannot concur with my colleagues in their conclusion that the Superintendent's Forum constituted an employee organization under the EERA, nor that the District in any way sought to bypass the exclusive representative.

As I read the statutory requirements the Forum would constitute an employee organization if the following elements were present: (1) it was an organization, (2) having as a primary purpose (3) the representation of employees (4) in their relations with the employer on matters within the scope of representation. * * * In this case, the proof falls far short of showing that these elements were present.

As noted by the majority, the easiest element to prove is the existence of "an organization." Long-settled case law points to as few as two employees constituting an organization, even if the employees themselves were unaware of their collective status and did not intend to act as an organization. Here, there was a group of a continuing nature, made up of employees. Thus, I can agree that the Forum was "an organization."

Further, given that the purpose of the Forum was to disseminate and receive information from representatives of rank and file teachers, I can also concur that the panel members were to represent the employees at their various schools. Although the meetings were in theory open to anyone, and the panel members themselves were given their jobs by a number of different methods (election, appointment, volunteering), the purpose behind the structure reasonably is seen to be to have the members of the Forum report back to their own schools with information, and to bring discussion items from their faculties to the Forum. Thus, two of the four elements of the statutory requirements were met in this case. In truth, the same two elements are met every time a school holds a faculty or department head meeting, or a district sponsors a districtwide staff meeting. But the two remaining elements were not proven on this record.

The EERA requires that the employee organization must have as a "primary purpose" the representation of employees on matters within scope. Certainly it can have other purposes: providing professional group support, making available low cost supplemental insurance plans, giving opportunities for training and professional growth, etc. But in order to fit the definition of Section 3540.1(d), the purpose of representation on matters within scope must be the primary goal. Here, the purpose of the Forum is less than that. Rather, its primary purpose was to give the rank and file employees access to the new superintendent, as a morale booster. The instigation for the Forum came from the teachers, not vice versa. The teachers' feeling, evidently shared by the board of education, was that the lines of communication between the staff and the superintendent were in need of repair. To that end, the teachers suggested reinstituting the Forum. The District agreed, noting that morale was low due to the perception that the teachers had no voice that was listened to. Formation of the Forum served a twofold purpose: it provided a vehicle for the superintendent and the teachers to exchange information, and by doing so it raised employees' morale.

There is no indication that the primary purpose of the Forum was to represent employees on matters within scope.

Entwined with the question of the group's primary purpose is the question of whether matters within scope were discussed, and whether those discussions led to impermissible action by the District. The record is devoid of any instance when subjects within scope were discussed. Indeed, the record is replete with examples of subjects that teachers wanted to discuss, but where the District instead referred the Forum representatives to the Association as the appropriate place to raise those issues. In another instance, the teachers were curious as to the District's plan for Martin Luther King Day. The District did not bargain over the holiday. Instead, it gave the teachers an update on the legislation authorizing the holiday, and noted how various districts were implementing the holiday. I find it difficult to believe that EERA was intended to preclude an employer from informing the employees on the status of a legal holiday. There may have been other instances when items discussed encroached on a subject within scope. But that is inevitable and, as long as no negotiations occurred, then I cannot find an exchange of information between employer and employee harmful. To so limit exchanges is not the purpose of the Act, and is based on a naive understanding of employer/employee communication.

Furthermore, not only is there no evidence of either negotiation or of a unilateral change made in response to any of the discussions, there is no evidence that the superintendent made any changes as a result of the Forum discussions. Thus, I find it impossible to believe that the Association was bypassed in any way, or that its authority as the exclusive representative was undermined in the least.

NOTES

1. How does the majority's analysis of the issue differ from the dissent's? Which opinion has the better of the argument?

2. What could the school superintendent have done to have achieved his goal of improving communications without running afoul of the Labor Relations Act?

3. Employee committees and other representative employee bodies are much more common in the public sector than in the private sector. This is particularly so in education. Indeed, in the private sector, the existence of university committees as instruments of faculty governance has led the Supreme Court to hold that university faculty members are management and, thus are excluded from coverage under the NLRA. *NLRB v. Yeshiva University*, 444 U.S. 672, 100 S.Ct. 856, 63 L.Ed.2d 115 (1980). Are such committees and faculty senates compatible with a system of collective bargaining in the public sector? In an early case, a union petitioning to represent faculty members at the State University of New York sought to disqualify the SUNY faculty senate from the ballot in the representation election, arguing that it was employer-dominated. The New York PERB hearing officer deferred the issue, finding that it could only be appropriately raised in an unfair labor practice proceeding. Consider the hearing officer's observations:

> A university is an historically unique employer in that faculty members, although they are technically "rank-and-file" employees, share authority for managing the university with management personnel. At SUNY, the vehicle for faculty participation in management has been the Senate, a representative body, which has functioned as a structural component of SUNY since the early 1950's. * * * The chancellor of SUNY and two of his designated representatives are constitutionally ordained members of the Senate, with one representative entitled under the Senate's constitution to sit on its executive committee.
>
> The Senate charges no dues and relies upon SUNY for funding. Thus, each year, the Senate presents its budget request to SUNY which, after review, is incorporated into SUNY's budget request which is submitted to the State Legislature for adoption. Once the Legislature has approved the executive budget and appropriated funds for the Senate, the Senate is free to spend such funds in any way it chooses.
>
> * * *

> Despite the outward indicia of employer control, the record, at least to some extent, supports a conclusion that the Senate has operated in fact as an independent organization inasmuch as it has adopted positions which were opposed by management. * * * [R]egarding its financial arrangements, the Senate has placed on the record assurances that it will in the future adhere to whatever standards of financing [PERB] may establish for employee organizations. As a beginning, it has pledged to finance its election campaign at SUNY and its negotiating activities through voluntary contributions and educational foundation grants. * * * Furthermore, the Senate intends to exclude all senators not included in a negotiating unit which it may represent from involvement in senate consideration of matters relevant to its status as a negotiating representative.

State University of New York, 2 N.Y.P.E.R.B. ¶ 4010 (1969).

E. EMPLOYER DISCRIMINATION

Section 8(a)(3) of the NLRA prohibits employer discrimination to discourage or encourage membership in a labor organization. Virtually every public sector labor relations act has a comparable provision. The most common 8(a)(3) complaint involves the alleged discharge of a union supporter in retaliation for engaging in protected activity. Such discharges are less common in the public sector, but, as the following case illustrates, they do arise.

WISCONSIN DEPARTMENT OF EMPLOYMENT RELATIONS v. WERC

Wisconsin Supreme Court, 1985.
122 Wis.2d 132, 361 N.W.2d 660.

CECI, J.

This case involves an unfair labor practice complaint brought on behalf of Karen Hartberg by her labor union, District 1199W/United Professionals for Quality Health Care (Union). The following facts are undisputed.

Hartberg was employed by the Wisconsin Department of Health and Social Services (Department) from January, 1978, to November, 1980. On September 25, 1980, Hartberg received a letter from the acting administrator of the Department's division of health, informing her of an intent to terminate her trainee position as a Public Health Educator (PHE). The reasons set out in the letter for her termination were failure to follow established procedures, absence from her station during scheduled hours, and ignoring instructions from her supervisor. The letter also advised Hartberg of an opportunity to request a hearing to respond to the reasons for her termination. On October 7, 1980, a meeting was conducted, and on October 23, 1980, Hartberg received a letter stating that she had failed to refute the allegations against her.

Hartberg's position was terminated effective October 26, 1980. The effect of this discharge was that she returned to the position she held with the Department prior to her appointment as a PHE. Since this prior position had been eliminated due to reorganization, Hartberg was eventually laid off.

On or about October 1, 1980, Hartberg filed a complaint with the Wisconsin State Personnel Commission, alleging that she was terminated because she had previously filed complaints with the personnel commission and had supported a co-employee's charge of sexual harassment. We are unaware of the outcome of this charge. Subsequently, on January 6, 1981, the Union filed an unfair labor practice charge with the WERC [Wisconsin Employment Relations Commission] * * * alleging that the State violated the State Employee Labor Relations Act (SELRA) by terminating Hartberg because of her union activities.

[A hearing examiner] found that the recommendation of two Department employees to terminate Hartberg's appointment was based, in part, upon hostility toward Hartberg for having engaged in protected concerted activity, and, as a matter of law, the State, through these two employees, committed unfair labor practices. * * *

The examiner ordered the State to reinstate Hartberg to her trainee position as a PHE with back pay, but declined to credit the time she was laid off toward the remaining training period, because there was evidence that she had violated work procedures. * * * WERC adopted the examiner's findings of fact, conclusions of law and order on May 17, 1982.

The final order of the WERC was appealed by the State to the circuit court for Dane County. * * * The circuit court upheld the WERC's order and held that the WERC's conclusion that the Department's decision to terminate Hartberg was based in part on anti-union animus was supported by substantial evidence in the record. The second issue on appeal was whether the WERC erred in this case in applying our decision in *Muskego–Norway C.S.J.S.D. No. 9 v. WERB*, 35 Wis. 2d 540, 151 N.W.2d 617 (1967), to Hartberg's unfair labor practice charge under the provisions of SELRA. The standard adopted by this court in *Muskego–Norway* was applied to an unfair labor practice charge under the Municipal Employment Relations Act (MERA). The trial court reasoned that "no rational basis exists on which to distinguish MERA from SELRA" and held that the WERC correctly applied the holding of *Muskego–Norway* to the facts in this case.

The circuit court's judgment was subsequently affirmed by the court of appeals, [which] * * * held that there was substantial evidence that Hartberg was unlawfully terminated in part for anti-union reasons under SELRA. Second, the court of appeals concluded that our decision in *Muskego–Norway* was correctly applied to this case, even though the action arose under SELRA and not under MERA.

The State does not appeal the finding of the court of appeals that there was substantial evidence that Hartberg was terminated in part because of anti-union animus. The sole issue presented for review is on law, simply, whether this court, with respect to SELRA, should apply long-standing "in part" test espoused in *Muskego–Norway*, or the federal test applied by the National Labor Relations Board in *Wright Line, a Division of Wright Line, Inc.*, 251 N.L.R.B. 1083 (1980). This is a question of first impression for this court.

* * *

Resolution of the issue at hand necessarily begins with a discussion of our holding in *Muskego–Norway*. One issue on appeal in *Muskego–Norway* was whether a school board's refusal to renew an employment contract with one of its teachers because of the teacher's activities in the school district's labor association violated MERA. MERA guarantees municipal employees the right to self-organize, to affiliate with labor organizations, and to be represented by labor organizations. Section 111.70(3)(a)1, Stats., prohibits municipal employers from interfering with, restraining, or coercing municipal employees in the exercise of these rights.

The trial court in *Muskego–Norway* reversed the finding of the WERB (now WERC) that the school board had violated MERA, the trial court holding that if a valid reason for discharging an employee exists, there is a sufficient basis for holding that the employee was not dismissed for union activities. We rejected this premise, holding, "* * * an employee may not be fired when one of the motivating factors is his union activities, no matter how many other valid reasons exist for firing him."

This standard has been coined the "in part" test. Under *Muskego–Norway*, a municipal employee cannot be terminated if the employer was motivated in part by antiunion animus, even though valid reasons exist for the discharge.

The WERC in this case applied the "in part" test to SELRA, requiring the Union to establish, by a clear and satisfactory preponderance of the evidence, that (1) Hartberg had engaged in protected concerted activity, (2) that the employer was aware of said activity and hostile thereto, and (3) that the employer's action was based at least in part upon said hostility. The examiner's inquiry ceased upon a finding of these three elements, and he concluded that the employer's action constituted an unfair labor practice. * * *

The State criticizes this approach and advocates adoption of the test advanced by the NLRB in *Wright Line*. Under the *Wright Line* standard, the employee has the burden of proving that anti-union animus contributed to the employer's decision to discharge the employee. If the employer fails to rebut this prima facie showing, he or she can avoid the finding that the action violated the National Labor Relations Act (NLRA) by demonstrating as an affirmative defense that the employee would have been fired even if he or she had not engaged in union activity. * * *

We recognize that the *Wright Line* test is obviously more advantageous to the employer than to the employee. Application of this standard permits an employer to voice his or her hostility toward union activists and even fire employees engaging in union activity, as long as he or she can provide a legitimate reason for terminating employment. Conduct of this nature will not be encouraged or tolerated by this court, and we, therefore, refuse to join the NLRB in the use of the *Wright Line* test. In reaching this conclusion, we generally recognize the delicate balance that exists between management and labor. On one hand, the state of Wisconsin should be a paragon of fairness toward labor unions. Indeed, Wisconsin has had an admirable history of fostering a favorable climate for labor unions. However, the laws of this state must also be flexible enough to allow for efficiency and productivity in the marketplace. We believe that the *Wright Line* test would disrupt the relative balance between management and labor that this state strives for. For the reasons listed below, we reaffirm the validity of the "in part" test of *Muskego–Norway*.

First, the "in part" test recognizes the practical difficulty that a discharged employee may have in proving a violation of SELRA and refuting an allegation of misconduct. The discharged employee and the employer do not stand on equal footing in cases alleging unfair labor practice, because of the employer's advantage of being able to monitor the employee's work performance and document any bona fide basis for discipline. * * *

Second, the State is concerned that use of the "in part" test necessarily excludes an employer's affirmative proof that the employee was fired for legitimate reasons. This is not true. A violation of SELRA is not established by merely proving the presence of protected concerted activity. The employee must show that the employer was motivated, at least in part, by anti-union hostility. Therefore, proof that the employee was discharged for legitimate reasons is relevant in determining the employer's motive. The WERC in this case explains, "As the key element of proof involves the motivation of [the employer] and as, absent an admission, motive cannot be definitively demonstrated given the impossibility of placing oneself inside the mind of the decisionmaker, [the employee] must of necessity rely in part upon the inferences which can reasonably be drawn from facts or testimony. On the other hand, it is worth noting that [the employer] need not demonstrate 'just cause' for its action. However, to the extent that [the employer] can establish reasons for its action which do not relate to hostility toward an employee's protected concerted activity, it weakens the strength of the inferences which [the employee] asks the [WERC] to draw."

Additionally, in dual-motive cases, evidence that legitimate reasons contributed to the employer's decision to discharge the employee can be considered by the WERC in fashioning an appropriate remedy. For example, to remedy the violation of SELRA in this case, the examiner ordered the State to reinstate Hartberg but, because there was evidence that Hartberg failed to comply with work procedures, declined to credit the time Hartberg was laid off toward the remaining training period.

* * *

In conclusion, we hold that an employer who terminates a state employee in part because of his or her participation in union activities violates Section 111.84(1)(a), Stats., by interfering with, restraining, or coercing state employees in the exercise of their rights to engage in lawful, concerted activity, and Section 111.84(1)(c), by discouraging membership in labor organizations by discrimination in regard to hiring, tenure, or other terms or conditions of employment. When anti-union hostility enters into the state's decision to terminate an employee, not only are the rights of that individual employee violated, but also, in effect, the rights of co-employees are violated, because union participation is stifled in the work place. This result is deemed undesirable by this court.

NOTES

1. The United States Supreme Court approved the NLRB's *Wright Line* test in *NLRB v. Transportation Management Corp.*, 462 U.S. 393, 103 S.Ct. 2469, 76 L.Ed.2d 667 (1983). The test originated in *Mt. Healthy City School Board of Education v. Doyle*, 429 U.S. 274, 97 S.Ct. 568, 50 L.Ed.2d 471 (1977), a case brought under 42 U.S.C. § 1983.

2. Many other jurisdictions have followed *Wright Line* in the public sector. See, e.g., *McPherson v. PERB*, 189 Cal.App.3d 293, 234 Cal.Rptr. 428 (1987); *Hardin County Education Association v. IELRB*, 174 Ill.App.3d 168, 124 Ill.Dec. 49, 528 N.E.2d 737 (1988); *Maine State Employees Association v. State Development Office*, 499 A.2d 165 (Me.1985); *Michigan Educational Support Personnel Association v. Evart Public Schools*, 125 Mich.App. 71, 336 N.W.2d 235 (1983); *In re Bridgewater*, 95 N.J. 235, 471 A.2d 1 (1984); *Upland Borough*, 25 Pa.P.E.R. ¶ 25,195 (Pa. L.R.B. 1994); but see *SERB v. Adena Local School District*, 66 Ohio St.3d 485, 613 N.E.2d 605 (1993) (holding that the in part test is mandated by the Ohio statute).

3. Does the "in part" test used in Wisconsin or the *Wright Line* approach adequately safeguard the public's interest? In the private sector, if an incompetent or malfeasant employee is reinstated because of the employer's anti-union animus, the damage is borne by the employer and its shareholders. In the public sector, should the labor boards and courts be concerned that the damage will be borne ultimately by the public?

4. Filing grievances is generally considered to be protected activity under public sector labor relations statutes. What test should apply to an allegation that an employer terminated an employee for filing grievances? Compare the protection given under labor relations statutes to that given under the First Amendment discussed in Note 7 following *Garcetti v. Ceballos* in Chapter 2.

Chapter 6

Recognition of Exclusive Bargaining Representatives

■ ■ ■

A union's goal in any organizing campaign is to become the exclusive bargaining representative for all employees in a defined segment of the employer's workforce, known as a "bargaining unit." In the private sector, both the National Labor Relations Act and the Railway Labor Act provide that the labor organization designated or selected by a majority of the employees is the exclusive bargaining representative. Consequently, even those employees opposed to union representation are bound by the contract negotiated by the exclusive representative. Moreover, the employer may not bypass the exclusive representative to deal directly with individual employees.

The system of exclusive representation which prevails in the private sector was not uniformly accepted in the early days of public sector bargaining. California's first comprehensive public sector statute, for example, adopted in 1961, provided that the public employer was to meet and confer with representatives of an employee organization "on behalf of its members." Thus, two or more employee organizations could be recognized simultaneously, each on behalf of its members only, within the same grouping of employees.

Minnesota and California experimented with a second system of recognition based on proportional representation, a system that is common in Europe. Organizations representing teachers were allowed representation on a negotiating council in proportion to their membership within the bargaining unit. Both states have since abandoned that system in favor of exclusive representation. This chapter explores the consequences of exclusive representation and the numerous substantive and procedural issues that commonly arise with respect to the recognition of exclusive bargaining representatives.

A. CONSEQUENCES OF EXCLUSIVE REPRESENTATION

BARGAINING IN THE GOVERNMENT'S BUSINESS: PRINCIPLES AND POLITICS

Clyde Summers
18 University of Toledo Law Review 265 (1987).

* * *

The principle of exclusive representation is considered fundamental in our labor law. It approaches being the First Commandment with the deification of the majority union. "I am the Lord thy God, Thou shalt have no other gods before me." But it is not written on stone from Sinai; it has more practical origins. The historical purpose of exclusive representation was to prevent an employer from playing one union against another to divide and conquer, and its practical purpose was to establish a single contract with standardized terms.

The principle has been carried over from the private sector to the public sector with little recognition that in the public sector it is at most only half viable. The need for standardized terms is even greater in the public than the private sector, for traditions of classified service and insistence on equal treatment generates nearly irresistible demands of equal pay for equal work, and an increase for one group must be matched by equal increases for other groups. But exclusive representation in bargaining units carved out according to the private sector pattern denies the political reality.

If city officials negotiate first with the union representing employees in the public works department, that agreement will provide the benchmark for other bargaining units represented by other unions, from the parks department to the city clerk's office. The contract made with the police will be the blueprint for the contract with the firefighters. The increases won by the teachers union will determine the increases for the administrators. The public works union, the police union and the teachers union become, for purposes of negotiating wages and other economic benefits, the effective representatives of employees who have selected different exclusive representatives.

City officials, in negotiating economic terms of one contract, must calculate its impact on other employees, for all of the money comes out of the same budget and is reflected in a single tax millage. In this respect, exclusive representation is a misleading myth. It is not the instrument for standardizing terms—that is done by the employer, and it does not produce unity on the employee side, but insures fragmentation and provides opportunity for manipulation by the public employer.

Multiple bargaining units do, of course, serve the purpose of enabling special groups to deal with special problems, to make variations to fit particular preferences, and at times to make adjustments in the general wage structure. Perhaps most important, multiple units give employees greater control over selection of those who represent them daily in handling their grievances. What is plainly needed in the public sector is some form of two-level bargaining [one level in issues which are special to each bargaining unit and a second level where standardized terms for all units are needed]. But the idolizing of principles from the private sector has obstructed serious consideration of such needed solutions.

Exclusive representation is only half, or less than half, viable in the public sector in another respect. One accepted corollary of exclusive representation in the private sector is that the employer cannot consult or discuss terms and conditions of employment with an individual employee or any other employee representative. In the public sector such a rule curbing open communication has serious implications for the political process.

* * *

NOTES

1. Do you agree or disagree with Professor Summers' viewpoint on the appropriateness of exclusivity in the public sector? Why has exclusive union representation become the dominant United States public sector labor law pattern with so little debate, particularly when no other country except Canada has adopted it?

2. The Federal Service Labor Management Relations Statute, which governs employees of the federal government, provides, "If, in connection with any agency, no labor organization has been accorded exclusive recognition on an agency basis, a labor organization which is the exclusive representative of a substantial number of the employees of the agency, as determined in accordance with criteria prescribed by the Authority, shall be granted national consultation rights by the agency." 5 U.S.C. § 7113(a). An agency must inform a union with national consultation rights of any proposed substantive changes in conditions of employment and must afford that union an opportunity to present its views and recommendations concerning the proposed changes. The agency need not bargain with the union but must consider its views and recommendations before taking action and must provide the union with a statement of its reasons for the actions it takes. *Id.* § 7113(b).

3. The exclusive bargaining representative has a duty of fair representation to each member of the bargaining unit. If a public employee who is a member of a bargaining unit has exercised a statutory right not to join the union which has exclusive bargaining rights, may the union refuse to represent that bargaining unit member in a grievance arbitration case unless that member pays a share of arbitration costs or is this an unfair labor practice? These issues are also explored in Chapter 12.

MINNESOTA STATE BOARD FOR COMMUNITY COLLEGES v. KNIGHT

United States Supreme Court, 1984.
465 U.S. 271, 104 S.Ct. 1058, 79 L.Ed.2d 299.

O'CONNOR, J. delivered the opinion of the Court.

The State of Minnesota authorizes its public employees to bargain collectively over terms and conditions of employment. It also requires public employers to engage in official exchanges of views with their professional employees on policy questions relating to employment but outside the scope of mandatory bargaining. If professional employees forming an appropriate bargaining unit have selected an exclusive representative for mandatory bargaining, their employer may exchange views on nonmandatory subjects only with the exclusive representative. The question presented in these cases is whether this restriction on participation in the nonmandatory-subject exchange process violates the constitutional rights of professional employees within the bargaining unit who are not members of the exclusive representative and who may disagree with its views. We hold that it does not.

* * *

Appellees do not and could not claim that they have been unconstitutionally denied access to a public forum. A "meet and confer" session is obviously not a public forum. It is a fundamental principle of First Amendment doctrine, articulated most recently in *Perry Education Assn. v. Perry Local Educators' Assn.*, 460 U.S. 37, 103 S.Ct. 948, 74 L.Ed.2d 794 (1983), that for government property to be a public forum, it must by long tradition or by government designation be open to the public at large for assembly and speech. Minnesota college administration meetings convened to obtain faculty advice on policy questions have neither by long tradition nor by government designation been open for general public participation. The District Court did not so find and appellees do not contend otherwise.

* * *

The Constitution does not grant to members of the public generally a right to be heard by public bodies making decisions of policy. In *Bi–Metallic Investment Co. v. State Board of Equalization*, 239 U.S. 441, 36 S.Ct. 141, 60 L.Ed. 372 (1915), this Court rejected a claim to such a right founded on the Due Process Clause of the Fourteenth Amendment. Speaking for the Court, Justice Holmes explained:

> Where a rule of conduct applies to more than a few people it is impracticable that every one should have a direct voice in its adoption. The Constitution does not require all public acts to be done in town meeting or an assembly of the whole. General statutes within the state power are passed that affect the person or property of individuals, sometimes to the point of ruin, without giving them a

chance to be heard. Their rights are protected in the only way that they can be in a complex society, by their power, immediate or remote, over those who make the rule.

In *Madison Joint School District No. 8 v. Wisconsin Employment Relations Comm'n*, 429 U.S. 167, 97 S.Ct. 421, 50 L.Ed.2d 376 (1976) which sustained a First Amendment challenge to a restriction on access to a public forum, the Court recognized the soundness of Justice Holmes' reasoning outside the due process context. The Court stated: "Plainly, public bodies may confine their meetings to specified subject matter and may hold nonpublic sessions to transact business."

Policymaking organs in our system of government have never operated under a constitutional constraint requiring them to afford every interested member of the public an opportunity to present testimony before any policy is adopted. Legislatures throughout the Nation, including Congress, frequently enact bills on which no hearings have been held or on which testimony has been received from only a select group. Executive agencies likewise make policy decisions of widespread application without permitting unrestricted public testimony. Public officials at all levels of government daily make policy decisions based only on the advice they decide they need and choose to hear. To recognize a constitutional right to participate directly in government policymaking would work a revolution in existing government practices.

* * *

The academic setting of the policymaking at issue in these cases does not alter this conclusion. To be sure, there is a strong, if not universal or uniform, tradition of faculty participation in school governance, and there are numerous policy arguments to support such participation. But this Court has never recognized a constitutional right of faculty to participate in policymaking in academic institutions.

* * *

Although there is no constitutional right to participate in academic governance, the First Amendment guarantees the right both to speak and to associate. Appellees' speech and associational rights, however, have not been infringed by Minnesota's restriction of participation in "meet and confer" sessions to the faculty's exclusive representative. The State has in no way restrained appellees' freedom to speak on any education-related issue or their freedom to associate or not to associate with whom they please, including the exclusive representative. Nor has the State attempted to suppress any ideas.

It is doubtless true that the unique status of the exclusive representative in the "meet and confer" process amplifies its voice in the policymaking process. But that amplification no more impairs individual instructors' constitutional freedom to speak than the amplification of individual voices impaired the union's freedom to speak in *Smith v. Arkansas State Highway Employees*, 441 U.S. 463, 99 S.Ct. 1826, 60 L.Ed.2d 360 (1979).

Moreover, the exclusive representative's unique role in "meet and negotiate" sessions amplifies its voice as much as its unique role in "meet and confer" sessions, yet the Court summarily affirmed the District Court's approval of that role in these cases. Amplification of the sort claimed is inherent in government's freedom to choose its advisers. A person's right to speak is not infringed when government simply ignores that person while listening to others.

* * *

The District Court erred in holding that appellees had been unconstitutionally denied an opportunity to participate in their public employer's making of policy. Whatever the wisdom of Minnesota's statutory scheme for professional employee consultation on employment-related policy, in academic or other settings, the scheme violates no provision of the Constitution. The judgment of the District Court is therefore reversed.

[JUSTICE MARSHALL'S concurring opinion, JUSTICE BRENNAN'S dissenting opinion, and JUSTICE STEVENS' opinion (in which JUSTICE POWELL joined in part) are omitted.]

NOTES

1. The legislation challenged in *Knight* states the following:

MINN.STAT.ANN. § 179A.03. Definitions:

Subdivision 10. Meet and confer. "Meet and confer" means the exchange of views and concerns between the employer and their employees.

MINN.STAT.ANN. § 179A.08. Policy consultants.

Subdivision 1. Professional employees. The legislature recognizes that professional employees possess knowledge, expertise, and dedication which is helpful and necessary to the operation and quality of public services and which may assist public employers in developing their policies. It is, therefore, the policy of this state to encourage close cooperation between public employers and professional employees by providing for discussions and the mutual exchange of ideas regarding all matters that are not terms and conditions of employment.

Subdivision 2. Meet and confer. The professional employees shall select a representative to meet and confer with a representative or committee of the public employer on matters not specified under Section 179A.03, subdivision 19, relating to the services being provided to the public. The public employer shall provide the facilities and set the time for these conferences to take place. The parties shall meet at least once every four months.

Why would the state extend the concept of exclusive representation to encompass discussion of subjects over which the employer was not required to bargain?

2. Does this case highlight Professor Summers' concern that curbing employer consultation with employee representatives other than the exclusive representative "has serious implications for the political process?"

B. DETERMINING THE BARGAINING UNIT

Bargaining unit determinations serve a dual function in both the public and private sectors: They determine the constituency for purposes of selecting the majority representative, and they mold the structure of collective bargaining which takes place after a representative, if any, is selected. Unions, particularly where two or more unions are competing for representation of overlapping groups, are likely to be more interested in the first function. For example, if Union A traditionally represents counselors and psychologists employed by school districts, Union A's survival may be at stake in a case where Union B seeks a unit consisting of counselors, psychologists, and classroom teachers. Union A may not be able to win an election in the larger unit. This aspect of unit determination is present in both private and public sectors, but it tends to be intensified in the public sector where one of the competing organizations is an association which preexisted collective bargaining, and whose membership consisted of a group of employees (e.g., all civil service employees) on a basis which had nothing to do with a collective bargaining relationship.

A statewide civil service association, for example, is likely to have a vital stake in seeing that bargaining units are drawn broadly; indeed, the best of all possible worlds for such an association is likely to be one in which only a single statewide civil service unit of state employees is permitted. In sum, unit determination contests with more than one union tend to be manifestations of interunion as well as union-employer conflict. Interunion tensions in the public sector are illustrated by the competition for representation that is sometimes provided by an employee association which existed long before collective bargaining became authorized and necessarily operated in a manner entirely out of character with the conventional relationship between an employer and a union.

The following excerpt from a 1969 article remains a classic description of unit determination issues posed in the public sector. The author was the labor relations advisor to the City of Philadelphia between 1952 and 1962 where, as he notes, there is a single bargaining unit for City employees (excluding police and firefighters).

THE APPROPRIATE UNIT QUESTION IN THE PUBLIC SERVICE: THE PROBLEM OF PROLIFERATION

Eli Rock
67 Michigan Law Review 1001 (1969).

I. Introduction

It is becoming increasingly clear that of the numerous problems which complicate the practice of collective bargaining in the public sector, none is more important than the appropriate unit question. In the public sector as well as in private industry, determination of the size and composition of the bargaining unit at the initial stages of organization and recognition can be decisive of the question of which employee organization will achieve majority recognition, or whether any organization will win recognition. Save for the employee organization which limits its jurisdiction along narrow lines, such as the craft practiced by its members, the normal tendency may be to request initially a unit whose boundaries coincide with the spread of the organization's membership or estimated strength. The public employer, on the other hand, may seek to recognize a unit in which the no-union votes will be in the majority, or a favored employee organization will have predominant strength; or the employer may simply seek to avoid undue proliferation of bargaining units.

The problem in the public sector, however, is of far greater depth than the initial victory-or-defeat aspect of recognition. In the private sector, it is clear that the scope and nature of the unit found to be appropriate for bargaining has acted as an important determinant of the union's basic economic strength—that is, its bargaining over bread-and-butter economic issues. In the public sector, it seems clear that the scope and nature of the unit found to be appropriate will also affect the range of subjects which can be negotiated meaningfully, the role played in the process by the separate branches of government, the likelihood of peaceful resolution of disputes, order versus chaos in bargaining, and ultimately, perhaps, the success of the whole idea of collective bargaining for public employees.

* * *

Traditionally, the public employer and union have given little thought to the appropriateness of a unit that requested recognition. More often than not, in the years prior to the enactment of definitive rules for recognition of public employees, a union requesting and receiving some form of recognition was considered the spokesman for its members—in whatever job classifications, functional departments, or physical locations they happened to be. This lenient approach was facilitated by (and perhaps had its start in) the fact that "recognition" frequently carried no legal consequences beyond the ability to appear before legislative or executive bodies hearing budgetary requests or the power to lobby with key political figures. Even when recognition was followed by a procedure similar to bargaining—including in some instances an embodiment of the bargain in a written agreement or memorandum—little if any consideration was given to the appropriateness of the unit being dealt with. Apart from the obvious problems stemming from the failure to grant "exclusive bargaining rights" to these early public employee units and from the inattention to the matter of excluding supervisors from the units representing those whom they supervise, a groundwork was laid for the creation of illogical unit lines. All too frequently the result was a proliferation of bargaining units.

* * *

At the state and local levels, virtually all of the significant legislation passed since 1960 has spelled out standards of some type of unit determination. In many instances these state enactments made possible further proliferation by adding to the existing illogical patterns of recognition new units made possible through espousal of the federal "community of interest" standard and its converse, separate units for groups having "conflicting interests;" * * * [and in some states] by permitting the government agency to rely on the extent of employee organization. Notwithstanding the fact that some of the state laws embody specific standards used by the National Labor Relations Board for the private sector, observers familiar with bargaining conditions in both sectors have contended that the degree of fragmentation in some of the states exceeds that of the private sector.

Clearly, at both state and federal levels the standards place a high premium on the subjective judgment of the decision-making body or individual, and results are also shaped to a high degree by the happenstance of the petitioning organization's requested unit at the time of the petition. Particularly when there is no rival organizational claim for a larger unit—which is often the case—the over-all effect has been to encourage recognition of the smaller unit. Even if a union succeeds in winning recognition in a large unit, employees in that unit are generally not required to become members of the union. The relative lack of union security clauses in the collective bargaining agreements of the public service assures that, to a degree unparalleled in the private sector, dissident small-unit groups are able to maintain their separate identities and to prolong the battle for break-off from the larger group's exclusive bargaining agent.

The Case for and Against the Small Unit

It cannot be assumed automatically that the pattern of many small units is wrong. A single craft, classification, department, or installation which would otherwise constitute a small minority if included in a larger unit can argue with some justification that its specialized interests and needs may be subordinated to the wishes of the larger unit's majority. Moreover, the smaller unit which performs a particularly essential function may also be capable of striking a better bargain for itself when left to do its own negotiating.

"Community of interest" is more than a catch phrase. It not only points up that like-situated employees will better understand their own problems and press their unique needs, but it also recognizes the instinct of exclusiveness which causes employees to *want* to form their own organization rather than become part of a larger organization in which they may feel themselves strangers. The desire to possess such "freedom of choice" or "self-determination" should, it can be argued, receive greater weight for public employees, because they are "public," than for those in the private sector.

There is nothing inherently wrong in permitting an employee organization to gain a foothold in a smaller unit, if the employees in that unit select it; and, if the union is effective in the small unit, it may grow and achieve recognition in other separate units or in a single large unit. This consideration may be particularly significant in the early period after the promulgation of legislation or executive orders encompassing a vast group of employees whose right to representation had not previously been formally legitimized. It is frequently easier for unions to secure employees' allegiance in smaller, distinctive groups than in larger, heterogeneous ones.

At the same time, there are important considerations which, it seems, point toward a unique, long-range need for larger units in the public sector. The special problems of unit determination in the public sector were most clearly recognized legislatively in 1967 in New York's Taylor Law, which included, in addition to the common standards of community of interest and necessity to promote the public welfare, the further requirement that in defining an appropriate unit the following standard should be taken into consideration: "the officials of government at the level of the unit shall have the power to agree, or to make effective recommendations to other administrative authority or the legislative body with respect to, the terms and conditions of employment upon which the employees desire to negotiate. * * *." The latter clause clearly reflects awareness of the fact that the employer-negotiator in the public service frequently has only limited authority, and that this condition will affect the scope of bargaining. As pointed out by the New York Governor's Committee on Public Employee Relations, the picture in the public sector is fundamentally different from that in the private sector. In private business, the authority to bargain on all of the normally bargainable matters is present or can be delegated, no matter what the size or make-up of the bargaining unit. By contrast, in the public service the necessary authority may not be delegable to lower-level functional units; legal requirements and tradition often call for uniformity of certain working conditions for like categories of employees throughout the governmental entity, regardless of bargaining unit categorization; and, even at the top of the particular level of government involved, authority is normally divided at least three ways—among the executive branch, the legislative branch, and a civil service commission.

Inherent in the previously quoted section of the Taylor Law, therefore, is the necessity that some consideration be given to the nature of the subject matter sought to be bargained upon in seeking to arrive at the appropriateness of a unit. This provision of the Taylor Law also recognizes that the subject matter of bargaining must normally be limited by the scope of the "employer's" authority to make agreements or effective recommendations, and a likely consequence is that the smaller the unit decided upon, the more restricted the scope of the bargaining by that unit will be.

Apart from this inhibiting effect on the bargaining experience, an approach which permits or favors small units makes it very difficult to resolve other institutional complications which arise in bargaining in the public service. The New York Governor's Committee, in both its 1966 Report and its 1968 Report, pointed out the unique importance of completing a negotiation with public employees in time to incorporate the agreement's financial essence in the budget of the governmental unit—which, by law, generally must be submitted to the legislature by a specified date. However, many of the annual bargaining sessions in the public sector today are extraordinarily prolonged, starting with direct negotiation, followed by resort to mediation and the frequently used machinery of factfinding or impasse panels. After all of this, there may be further extensive dealings with upper-echelon individuals or groups in the executive and legislative branches. Thus, the sheer weight of the process may lead to its breakdown if the trend toward proliferation of bargaining units in numerous jurisdictions continues unabated. It is noteworthy that in the City of Philadelphia—which is frequently cited as an example of well-established, peaceful, and effective bargaining at the municipal level—all employees except policemen and firemen have been represented by a single unit for most of the last two decades. Even with only a single unit and without use of impasse resolution machinery, however, the experience in Philadelphia has been marked by many instances of abnormally prolonged annual negotiations. The Philadelphia experience also demonstrates the need to establish detailed liaison between the executive branch, the legislative branch, and the civil service commission during the course of an annual bargaining program in order to minimize the chaotic effects of overlapping authority on the government side.

While it is possible that a city the size of Philadelphia might also have had a history of successful labor relations in the public sector under a pattern which broke down the public employee bargaining group into a small number of separate units, there is little question that the success could not have been achieved under the patterns of excessive fragmentation found elsewhere. In any event, the existence of the single large unit clearly contributed significantly to that city's ability to surmount effectively the institutional obstacles complicating public sector bargaining. Moreover, proliferation can and does breed excessive competition among rival organizations. One consequence of this may be a high incidence of breakdowns in peaceful bargaining. To be sure, competition in bargaining is to some extent unavoidable; this condition is not necessarily undesirable socially, and will continue to characterize the experience in private and public sector alike, regardless of the size of units involved. Nevertheless, there is hardly a permanent justification for permitting what appears to be a greater proliferation of bargaining units in the public sector than that now prevailing in the private sector. The institutional factors discussed above add a unique dimension to the task of achieving peaceful and successful bargaining in the public sector. Because of this, and because of the likelihood that proliferation will result in an increased number of breakdowns in the bargaining process, larger units must become the accepted norm in the public sector.

* * *

Another interesting development [took] place in New York City. With the creation of the Office of Collective Bargaining, New York City began to consolidate its bargaining units through techniques such as recognition by citywide job classifications. This transition was followed, in the spring of 1968, by the truly basic step of recognizing one exclusive bargaining agent for *all* the employees of the mayoral agencies for purposes of those citywide working conditions which are required to be uniform for such employees. Separate representation in smaller units continues for purposes of other issues, and this condition is no doubt prolonging the same problems that are found elsewhere; but the basic trend appears to be a salutary one.

A third experience of interest involve[d] the employees of the State of New York. Prior to the enactment of the Taylor Law, which defined the first set of rules for bargaining by both state and local government personnel, the majority of the state's 124,000 employees had belonged to the statewide Civil Service Employees Association (CSEA)—an organization which, at least in its earlier years, had shunned the concept of formalized collective bargaining. Following enactment of the Taylor Law, the state, as employer, recognized the CSEA as the bargaining agent for a "general unit" of all the employees. After nearly a year of bargaining by this unit, the Public Employment Relations Board (PERB), the state agency charged with administering the Taylor Law, received petitions challenging the appropriateness of the general unit. In opposition to the CSEA, twelve separate employee organizations requested recognition in twenty-five different bargaining units. The proposed units were drawn along highly diverse occupational, departmental, or installation lines.

Shunning the extremes of either one general unit or twenty-five separate units, the PERB ruled in favor of five separate statewide negotiating units and directed elections to determine the majority agent in each of those units. The units were not constituted along lines cutting across departments; instead, the employees were grouped into families of occupations primarily on the basis of function and training. In denying the requested continuance of the general unit, the PERB adopted an earlier finding of its Director of Representation regarding the unit's inconsistency with the "community of interest" standard of the law and, noting that the employees were divided among ninety occupational groupings, encompassing more than 3,700 separate job classifications, held: "The enormity of this diversity of occupations and the great range in the qualifications requisite for employment in these occupations would preclude effective and meaningful representation in collective negotiations if all such employees were included in a single unit." On the other hand, the PERB concluded that accepting the opposite extreme of twenty-five separate units would foster a proliferation of small groups and would cause "un-

goal of effective + meaningful representation

warranted and unnecessary administrative difficulties" which "might well lead to the disintegration of the State's current labor relations structure." In addition to these policy considerations, the PERB relied upon the provision of the Taylor Law requiring that the bargaining unit be "compatible with the joint responsibilities of the public employer and public employees to serve the public." This standard, the PERB determined, "requires the designation of as small a number of units as possible consistent with the overriding requirement that the employees be permitted to form organizations of their own choosing" in order to achieve meaningful representation.

The PERB did not make specific reference to the statutory standard requiring consideration of a requested unit in terms of the employer-agency's existing authority to deal effectively with possible bargaining subject matter within such a unit. There seems to be little question, however, that the size and nature of the five designated statewide units insure adequate authority, on the side of the state's negotiating representatives, to make meaningful agreements or recommendations with respect to a large portion of the substantial issues normally deserving of consideration in an effective collective bargaining relationship. Moreover, since the employees were geographically dispersed and because the general unit presented serious problems of providing direct representation, the PERB's breakdown of the employees into five large families of jobs probably maximizes the possibilities for self-determination and adequate union responsiveness in representing the various segments within each family.

The New York experience is also noteworthy because the direct confrontation between the two opposite extremes presented by the requested patterns at the inception of newly formalized public sector collective bargaining afforded an opportunity to weigh the basic implications of excessive fragmentation. In contrast to policy makers in cities like New York and Detroit * * *, the New York State PERB was able to adopt a coherent policy at a time when the damage had not yet been done. At the same time, the Board's decision rejected a monolithic bargaining unit which would have been neither proper nor realistic for public employees at this stage of history.

* * *

NOTES

1. As Mr. Rock observed, unions and employees frequently seek bargaining units in which they believe they can win the election. Should a labor relations board be limited to selecting a unit proposed by one of the parties or may it define a unit that no party requested?

2. In the private sector, the NLRB presumes that a single location is an appropriate bargaining unit even though the employer operates at multiple locations. A party opposing a single location unit has the burden of showing that it is not appropriate. Should such a single location presumption apply in

the public sector? Consider, for example, a representation petition filed by employees of one correctional facility in a state-wide corrections system; by the teachers at the one high school in a school district that also has two middle schools and six elementary schools; by the clerical and technical staff at one campus of a state university that has four campuses scattered at various locations across the state.

A STATUTORY SAMPLER

The following reflects the diversity in statutory provisions relating to unit determinations:

HAWAII

HAWAII REV.STAT. § 89–6

Appropriate bargaining units. (a) All employees throughout the State within any of the following categories shall constitute an appropriate bargaining unit:

(1) Nonsupervisory employees in blue collar positions;

(2) Supervisory employees in blue collar positions;

(3) Nonsupervisory employees in white collar positions;

(4) Supervisory employees in white collar positions;

(5) Teachers and other personnel of the department of education under the same pay schedule, including part-time employees working less than twenty hours a week who are equal to one-half of a full-time equivalent;

(6) Educational officers and other personnel of the department of education under the same pay schedule;

(7) Faculty of the University of Hawaii and the community college system;

(8) Personnel of the University of Hawaii and the community college system, other than faculty;

(9) Registered professional nurses;

(10) Institutional health and correctional workers;

(11) Firefighters;

(12) Police officers; and

(13) Professional and scientific employees, who cannot be included in any of the other bargaining units.

(b) Because of the nature of work involved and the essentiality of certain occupations which require specialized training, supervisory employees who are eligible for inclusion in units (9) through (13) shall be included in units (9) through (13), respectively, instead of unit (2) or (4).

ILLINOIS

Illinois Public Labor Relations Act, § 9(b), ILL.-SMITH-HURD ANN. 5 ILCS 315/9(b)

(b) The Board shall decide in each case, in order to assure public employees the fullest freedom in exercising the rights guaranteed by this Act, a unit appropriate for the purpose of collective bargaining, based upon but not limited to such factors as: historical pattern of recognition; community of interest including employee skills and functions; degree of functional integration; interchangeability and contact among employees; fragmentation of employee groups; common supervision, wages, hours and other working conditions of the employees involved; and the desires of the employees. For purposes of this subsection, fragmentation shall not be the sole or predominant factor used by the Board in determining an appropriate bargaining unit.

NEW YORK

NEW YORK–MCKINNEY'S N.Y. CIVIL SERVICE LAW § 207.

Determination of Representation Status—For purposes of resolving disputes concerning representation status, pursuant to Section two hundred five or two hundred six of this article, the board or government, as the case may be, shall

1. define the appropriate employer-employee negotiating unit, taking into account the following standards:

(a) the definition of the unit shall correspond to a community of interest among the employees to be included in the unit;

(b) the officials of government at the level of the unit shall have the power to agree, or to make effective recommendations to other administrative authority or the legislative body with respect to, the terms and conditions of employment upon which the employees desire to negotiate; and

(c) the unit shall be compatible with the joint responsibilities of the public employer and public employees to serve the public.

OHIO

OHIO REV. CODE § 4117.06

Appropriate bargaining unit

(A) The state employment relations board shall decide in each case the unit appropriate for the purposes of collective bargaining. The determination is final and conclusive and not appealable to the court.

(B) The board shall determine the appropriateness of each bargaining unit and shall consider among other relevant factors: the desires of the employees; the community of interest; wages, hours, and other working conditions of the public employees; the effect of over-fragmentation; the efficiency of operations of the public employer; the administrative structure of the public employer; and the history of collective bargaining.

(C) The board may determine a unit to be the appropriate unit in a particular case, even though some other unit might also be appropriate.

* * *

WISCONSIN

Municipal Employment Relations Act, WISCONSIN STAT.ANN. 111.70(d)

* * *

2. a.The commission shall determine the appropriate bargaining unit for the purpose of collective bargaining and shall whenever possible, unless otherwise required by this subchapter, avoid fragmentation by maintaining as few units as practicable in keeping with the size of the total municipal work force. In making such a determination, the commission may decide whether, in a particular case, the employees in the same or several departments, divisions, institutions, crafts, professions or other occupational groupings constitute a collective bargaining unit. * * *

NOTES

1. Note that all of the statutes sampled direct that fragmentation of employees is a factor in bargaining unit determination, but only Illinois expressly declares that "fragmentation shall not be the sole or predominant factor used by the Board in determining an appropriate bargaining unit." Why is there special concern about proliferation of bargaining units in the public sector (in contrast to the private sector)?

2. Why would a state legislature (such as Hawaii) mandate statutory bargaining units while other state legislatures follow the private sector and delegate the responsibility for unit determinations to an administrative agency with few specific guidelines? Note that several other states mandate statutory bargaining units for state employees but not for employees of units of local government.

MICHIGAN EDUCATION ASSOCIATION v. ALPENA COMMUNITY COLLEGE

Supreme Court of Michigan, 1998.
457 Mich. 300, 577 N.W.2d 457.

PER CURIUM

The Michigan Education Association is the collective bargaining representative for a unit of nonsupervisory office personnel at Alpena Community College. Building service employees, including custodians and maintenance workers, are represented by a separate union. It appears from the record that a third bargaining unit exists for Alpena Community College faculty.

As of September 1993, approximately thirty employees remained outside the three bargaining units. This residual group was a diverse collection of unrepresented nonsupervisory support staff. In the course of its decision on this matter, the MERC [Michigan Employment Relations Commission] provided a roster of the positions held by these persons:

> The petition, as supplemented by the record, identified the following positions, some of which are part-time or combined positions, or held

by more than one employee, as being part of the proposed residual group: health fitness/activities technician; evening college technician; bookstore manager; developmental studies technician; library technician; volunteer coordinator; admission/activities technician; administrative assistant; mail processing/distribution technician; volunteer center coordinator; youth corps program coordinator, and service learning coordinator; volunteer center coordinator; data processing laboratory technician; senior parking attendant; tutor coordinator/technician; biology lab assistant; toolcrib person-automotive or machine tool; assistant bookstore manager; learning resource center (LRC) media technician; director of public information; consultant-resource/foundation development; administrative technician, upward-bound student advocate; developmental studies technician; financial aid and student services technician; switchboard operator; art technician; and placement coordinator. The petition also includes the added positions of administrative technician-Huron Shores TLC; administrative technicians, economic development (Iosco County); job development specialist; and student coordinator.

In a September 1993 petition, the MEA asked the MERC to "accrete" the residual unit to the existing MEA unit of clerical employees. That is, the petition sought an election among the residual group to determine whether those persons wanted to join the existing unit and be represented by the MEA.

After an evidentiary hearing, the MERC ruled in favor of the MEA, directing that the election be conducted. The Court of Appeals stayed the election and denied the MEA's motion to affirm. The Court then reversed the decision of the MERC.

* * *

Where the bulk of an organization's employees are formed into several collective bargaining units, leaving behind a handful of unrepresented employees, it is quite foreseeable that the residual group will be a scattering of persons with miscellaneous duties. So it is in this case.

In such a situation, the MERC faces a tension between two competing considerations as it fulfills its statutory obligation to determine a proper bargaining unit. One is the principle of "community of interest," which calls for employees to have shared interests with others in their bargaining unit. The opposing consideration is that collective bargaining units should be reasonably large to avoid a proliferation of fragmented bargaining units.

In *Hotel Olds v. State Labor Mediation Bd.*, 333 Mich. 382, 53 N.W.2d 302 (1952), we adopted this concise statement from an earlier Massachusetts case:

> In designating bargaining units as appropriate, a primary objective of the commission is to constitute the largest unit which, in the circumstances of the particular case is most compatible with the effectuation

of the purposes of the law and to include in a single unit all common interests.

Elaborating on the analysis to be employed by the MERC, the Court of Appeals said this in 1990:

> In designating appropriate bargaining units, the commission's primary objective is to constitute the largest unit which, under the circumstances of the case, is most compatible with the effectuation of the purposes of the law and includes in a single unit all common interests. Consistent with this objective, the commission's policy is to avoid fractionalization or multiplicity of bargaining units. The touchstone of an appropriate bargaining unit is a common interest of all its members in the terms and conditions of their employment that warrants inclusion in a single bargaining unit and the choosing of a bargaining agent. This Court abides by the commission's policy to constitute the largest bargaining unit compatible with the effectuation of the PERA.

Muskegon Co. Professional Command Ass'n v. Muskegon Co., 186 Mich. App. 365, 464 N.W.2d 908 (1990).

In the present case, the MERC determined that the proposed residual unit was appropriate, and directed that the election be held * * * concluding:

> Although not all employees in the proposed unit have similar duties, skills, or educational qualifications, there are similarities in these areas among individual positions. The fact that salaries and benefits vary among the positions sought is not sufficient to destroy their community of interest. The employees all work on the Employer's main or auxiliary campuses, and the Employer's organization chart demonstrates a centralized management system. Under *Hotel Olds*, we are required to find appropriate the single largest group of employees who share a community of interest. This rule is for the benefit of employers, since it minimizes the fragmentation of units, prevents units based on extent of organization, and eliminates problems associated with multiple bargaining obligations. We find that the unit sought by Petitioner satisfies this requirement. We conclude, therefore, that the residual group in this case, all nonsupervisory, nonfaculty employees excluded from existing units, may be accreted to the existing clerical unit to form a single all-college unit.

In its majority opinion, the Court of Appeals agreed with Alpena Community College that the employees "do not enjoy a community of interest." The majority explained:

> Respondent notes that the employees have different duties, educational requirements, pay and benefits. While we recognize the MERC policy towards achieving the largest compatible bargaining units, we must agree with respondent that the employees sought to be accreted are simply too diverse to be considered to have a community of

interest. A mere reading of the job titles demonstrates this. They work in a variety of different areas of the college in numerous different tasks. Some are technicians, while others are managers and directors. There are administrative support employees, student activities employees, bookstore employees, and even parking lot employees. The only commonality we see among these employees is that they have the same employer. Accordingly, we conclude that the trial court erred in its conclusion.

Writing in dissent, Judge White quoted at length from the MERC opinion, noting that Alpena Community College had variously argued below that the proposed unit was both too narrow and too broad, though the college had not proposed an alternative unit. Accepting the conclusions reached by the MERC, Judge White wrote that the "MERC's determination prevented further fragmentation and the leaving behind of even smaller groups of unrepresented employees, and was appropriate under the circumstances."

* * *

We agree with Judge White that the decision of the MERC was sound. While the residual group contains persons with varying responsibilities and compensation levels, we see no sign that the statutory purposes or the goals of collective bargaining would be frustrated by formation of the unit approved by the MERC. On review of this matter, we are satisfied that its findings were supported by competent, material, and substantial evidence.

For these reasons, we reverse the judgment of the Court of Appeals and reinstate the decision of the Michigan Employment Relations Commission.

NOTES

1. The court observes that the approach in the Michigan public sector is to select the largest possible unit of employees who share a community of interest. This typifies the approach in many jurisdictions to define the most appropriate unit of public sector employees. In contrast, the Ohio statute declares, "The board may determine a unit to be the appropriate unit in a particular case, even though some other unit might also be appropriate." OHIO REV. CODE § 4117.06(C). What policies support this legislative choice? What policies support a requirement in the public sector that a unit be the "most appropriate unit?" On the general subject of "an" versus "most" appropriate unit, see Andrea S. Knapp, Anatomy of a Public Sector Bargaining Unit, 35 *Case Western Reserve Law Review* 395, 404–05 (1985); Joseph R. Crowley, The Resolution of Representation Status Disputes Under the Taylor Law, 37 *Fordham Law Review* 517, 518–20 (1969).

2. Would the principal case be decided differently in Illinois, whose statute directs that "fragmentation shall not be the sole or predominant factor" in unit determination?

3. When it was created, the state Liquor Control Board enforced state liquor laws and administered liquor licensing procedures. Sixteen years later,

the legislature transferred liquor law enforcement to the State Police and the Liquor Control Board employees were allowed to choose which agency to join. Those who transferred to the State Police became liquor enforcement officers, while those who remained with the Liquor Control Board became licensing analysts. Liquor enforcement officers received firearms training, were issued firearms and were subject to the same physical and educational standards as State Troopers. Licensing analysts did not participate in criminal investigations or raids, did not carry firearms, were not subject to State Police physical requirements and tended to work from their homes. The union that represented both groups of employees in a single bargaining unit filed a petition to divide the employees into two separate units. Should the petition be granted? See *Fraternal Order of Police v. Pennsylvania Labor Relations Board*, 557 Pa. 586, 735 A.2d 96 (1999).

C. SPECIAL ISSUES CONCERNING CERTAIN TYPES OF EMPLOYEES

1. SUPERVISORS

Since 1947, private sector supervisors have been expressly excluded from National Labor Relations Act coverage; they are not eligible for inclusion in bargaining units of employees that an employer is obligated to recognize. The NLRA defines supervisor as "any individual having authority, in the interest of the employer, to hire, transfer, suspend, lay off, recall, promote, discharge, assign, reward, or discipline other employees, or responsibly to direct them, or to adjust their grievances, or effectively to recommend such action, if in connection with the foregoing the exercise of such authority is not of a merely routine or clerical nature, but requires the use of independent judgment." 29 U.S.C. § 152(11).

Some public sector jurisdictions, such as Iowa, Ohio and the federal government (under the Federal Service Labor Management Relations Statute regulating collective bargaining among federal government employees) follow the NLRA model. However, because historically many public sector labor unions evolved from professional and fraternal organizations that prior to the advent of collective bargaining lobbied on behalf of their members, the lines of fracture between supervisory and rank-and-file employees are not as clear as in the private sector. Consequently, one finds a variety of approaches to the subject of collective bargaining rights for supervisors in the public sector.

CITY OF FREEPORT v. ILLINOIS STATE LABOR RELATIONS BOARD

Supreme Court of Illinois, 1990.
135 Ill.2d 499, 143 Ill.Dec. 220, 554 N.E.2d 155.

[The City of Freeport Police Department patrol division consisted of three lieutenants, three sergeants, three corporals and 21 patrol officers. The lieutenants served as full time shift commanders, while the sergeants served as shift commanders in the lieutenants' absence, approximately ten times per month. When not acting as shift commanders, sergeants and lieutenants (collectively known as ranking officers) performed patrol functions. They generally patrolled for 6 ½ hours in an eight hour shift. As shift commanders, they led roll call, reviewing the latest reports and assigning officers to beats; approved overtime and vacation requests; approved officer requests to trade days off; evaluated officers; and counseled and administered verbal reprimands to officers. The Illinois State Labor Relations Board held that the ranking officers were not supervisors.

The Village of Wheeling Fire Department employed six lieutenants. They worked as shift commanders, responsible for the condition of the station, equipment and personnel assigned to their shifts. They ensured that their stations met the department's minimum staffing requirements and administered verbal warnings for unexcused tardiness. The Illinois State Labor Relations Board held that the lieutenants were not supervisors.]

WARD, J.

These consolidated actions are before this court on administrative review of certain orders of the Illinois State Labor Relations Board (Board). We must consider whether the Board erred in determining that certain employees of the Village of Wheeling fire department and of the City of Freeport police department were not supervisors within the meaning of Section 3(r) of the Illinois Public Labor Relations Act (Act).

* * *

Section 3(r) of the Act defines a "supervisor" as follows:

> "Supervisor" is an employee whose principal work is substantially different from that of his subordinates and who has authority, in the interest of the employer, to hire, transfer, suspend, lay off, recall, promote, discharge, direct, reward, or discipline employees, or to adjust their grievances, or to effectively recommend such action, if the exercise of such authority is not of a merely routine or clerical nature, but requires the consistent use of independent judgment. Except with respect to police employment, the term 'supervisor' includes only those individuals who devote a preponderance of their employment time to exercising such authority State supervisors notwithstanding.

This definition is similar to that in the National Labor Relations Act (NLRA), which also excludes supervisors from collective-bargaining units. The exclusion of supervisors in the NLRA was thought necessary to redress a perceived imbalance in labor-management relationships that arose when supervisors were put in the position of serving two masters with opposing interests. The exclusion of supervisory employees from bargaining units ensures employers that pro-union bias will not impair the supervisor's ability to apply the employer's policies to subordinates according to the employer's best interests.

This same philosophy is reflected in our Act. The definition of "supervisor" in our statute, however, is narrower than that in the NLRA. Under the NLRA, an individual who has authority to perform supervisory functions with independent judgment is considered a supervisor and excluded from bargaining units. Our Act, however, adds two requirements which are not included in the NLRA's definition. First, the individual's principal work must be substantially different from that of his subordinates. Second, except with respect to police employment, only those individuals who spend the preponderance of their employment time exercising the enumerated supervisory functions may be considered supervisors. * * *

* * *

[P]olice employees qualify as supervisors within the meaning of the Act only if they: (1) perform principal work substantially different than their subordinates; (2) have authority in the interest of the employer to perform one or more of 11 enumerated supervisory functions, or to effectively recommend such action; and (3) consistently use independent judgment in performing or recommending the enumerated actions.

* * *

Both parties agree with the Board's conclusion that the lieutenants and sergeants in the patrol and detective divisions satisfy the second prong of the supervisory definition. The Board determined that these ranking officers, as shift commanders, have authority to perform at least four supervisory functions. First, they have authority to direct their subordinate officers, in that they approve overtime and personal holiday requests, review police incident reports, assign partners, beats and squads, and occasionally take command of a call. Second, they have authority to discipline subordinate officers with written reprimands. Third, the ranking officers may suspend an officer for tardiness and may recommend disciplinary suspension to the chief. Finally, they have authority to adjust minor grievances of patrol officers.

* * *

1. Principal Work

As stated, an employee may be considered a supervisor only if his principal work is substantially different from that of his subordinates. In applying this prong to police employment, the Board has stated:

> For an employee to be a supervisor, the employee's main undertaking must differ from the main undertakings of his subordinates. He may, at times, engage in similar work as his subordinates and still be determined a supervisor. However, his foremost activity must not be similar. This is not necessarily a quantitative test. An employee may engage in the same work as his subordinates the majority of his time, but if the essence of his work differs from that of his subordinates, a supervisory determination may result if other indicia are present.

* * * Where the alleged police supervisor performs functions facially similar to those of the rank and file, * * * the Board will look at what the alleged supervisor actually does, to determine whether the 'nature and essence' of his work is substantially different. In doing so, the Board considers three factors.

First, it considers whether the alleged supervisor patrols in a different manner than the rank and file. The Board attempts to determine whether the alleged supervisor patrols to provide a police officer presence on the streets and to personally provide police services to the community, or whether the nature and essence of his patrol function is substantially different. Second, the Board considers rank and the supervisory hierarchy. Finally, the Board considers the extent to which the alleged supervisor exercises supervisory authority over his subordinates. If the alleged supervisor frequently exercises supervisory authority, the Board concludes that the nature and essence of his work is substantially different from that of his subordinates.

The Board considers these factors in an attempt to determine whether the alleged supervisor's employment is more similar to, than dissimilar from, that of the rank and file. Where the 'community of interest' lines up with the rank and file, the alleged supervisor will be included in the collective-bargaining unit notwithstanding the exercise of supervisory functions.

Applying this standard to the facts in this case, the hearing officer concluded that the ranking officers in the patrol division did not perform "substantially different principal work" than their subordinates. The hearing officer found that the ranking officers patrolled in the same manner as their subordinates, and exercised their supervisory authority so routinely or sporadically that their principal work was not substantially different from that of their subordinates. The Board adopted the hearing officer's conclusions.

* * *

We conclude that the Board's interpretation of the principal-work prong of the supervisory definition with respect to police employment was erroneous. * * *

The Board improperly gave dispositive weight to the amount of time the ranking officers spend exercising their supervisory authority. The Board essentially requires that the ranking officers be principally involved in exercising supervisory functions before it will find that their work is substantially different from that of their subordinates. The Act expressly states, however, that the fourth prong of the supervisory test need not be satisfied with respect to police employment. Thus, a police employee may be deemed a supervisor under the Act even if he does not devote a preponderance of his work time to exercising supervisory authority.

The legislature may have eliminated the preponderance prong with respect to police employment because it believed that supervisory performance in smaller police departments does not require much time, or because it believed that there is less need for supervision given the paramilitary organization of police departments. Whatever the reason for exempting police supervisory employees from the preponderance prong of the supervisory definition, we conclude that the Board's rigid counting of the number of times the ranking officers exercised supervisory authority in an attempt to determine whether their principal work was substantially different from that of the patrol officers was improper.

Supervisors are excluded from bargaining units under the Act to avoid the conflict of interest which arises when supervisors, who must apply the employer's policies to subordinates, are subject to control by the same union representing those subordinates. In determining the status of supervisory employees whose duties closely parallel those of their subordinates, the Board must identify the point at which an employee's supervisory obligation to the employer conflicts with his participation in union activity with the employees he supervises. The Board's analysis in this case fails to identify the point at which such a conflict of interest arises.

The potential for a conflict of interest lies in the supervisor's authority to influence or control personnel decisions in areas most likely to affect the employment of subordinates and, thus, most likely to fall within the scope of union representation. The Board's reliance upon the number of times such authority was exercised was improper. * * *

In this case, the ranking officers in the patrol division exercise supervisory authority in several areas likely to fall within the scope of union representation. For example, ranking officers have authority to discipline patrol officers through verbal and written reprimands. Ranking officers also have authority to recommend more severe discipline, including disciplinary suspension for up to five days. A record of such disciplinary measures may be placed in a patrol officer's personnel file, which is submitted to the police and fire commission for consideration. Including the ranking officers in a bargaining unit with those they supervise might adversely affect the ranking officers' willingness to discipline patrol officers.

In addition to their authority to discipline, the ranking officers are also solely responsible for managing and directing the operation of the Freeport police department during their shifts. The chief and the assistant chief are not involved in the daily supervision of patrol officers. * * * The chief relies upon the ranking officers to observe, direct, evaluate and discipline their subordinates and to ensure that the patrol officers are properly performing their jobs. In this capacity, the ranking officers represent the interests of the chief vis-a-vis the patrol officers and are not simply the members of the team who give routine instructions.

Their responsibility for directing the officers and for managing the operation of the department clearly aligns the ranking officers more closely with the chief than with the patrol officers. The authority to direct subordinate officers and to adversely impact those officers through discipline or other measures falling within the scope of union representation makes the nature and essence of the ranking officers' principal work substantially different from that of the patrol officers. It is this authority which creates a possibility of conflicting loyalties, and which requires the exclusion of ranking officers from the bargaining unit.

2. Independent Judgment

We next consider whether the ranking officers satisfy the third prong of the supervisory definition, which specifies that the exercise of supervisory authority must not be routine and clerical in nature, but must involve the consistent use of independent judgment. * * *

We need only consider the hearing officer's analysis of the ranking officers' authority to discipline. The hearing officer determined that the ranking officers did not satisfy the third prong of the supervisory definition with respect to discipline because they did not impose discipline frequently. Again, the hearing officer improperly gave controlling weight to the number of times ranking officers exercised their authority to discipline. In requiring the "consistent use of independent judgment," the legislature clearly was not referring to the number of times the alleged supervisor actually exercised his supervisory authority. Rather, the legislature was referring to the number of times in which independent judgment might be required in performing a particular supervisory function.

Certain supervisory functions are routine or ministerial in nature and do not generally require the use of independent judgment. The fact that performance of such functions may occasionally require the ranking officer to use discretion or independent judgment is not sufficient to satisfy the third prong of the supervisory definition. For example, the ranking officers do not consistently use independent judgment when exercising their authority to suspend patrol officers for tardiness exceeding 30 minutes, because such suspensions are required by orders of the chief. On the other hand, when the ranking officers exercise their authority to issue written reprimands and to recommend disciplinary suspension, they ordinarily must choose between two or more significant courses of action. Accordingly, the ranking officers consistently use independent judgment when exercising their authority to discipline patrol officers.

It is the authority to use independent judgment in imposing discipline, rather than how often such discipline is imposed, which is important. It would be absurd to require a supervisor to continuously discipline subordinates who do not deserve discipline. The supervisor's authority to discipline is what distinguishes him from his subordinates. The fact that the ranking officers exercise this authority infrequently is proof that the patrol officers do not warrant discipline rather than that their supervisors do not use independent judgment when they impose discipline. The ranking officers clearly satisfy the third prong of the supervisory definition with respect to discipline.

* * *

[The court then considered the supervisory status of the lieutenants in the Wheeling Fire Department.]

Section 3(r) of the Act specifies that in determining the supervisory status of firefighters in new bargaining units, firefighters of the rank of company officer and below are employees under the Act, unless the company officer otherwise meets the Act's four-part supervisory definition. The lieutenants in question here are company officers. Thus, unless they meet the definition of supervisor within the Act, they must be found to be employees with the right to engage in collective bargaining activities.

1. Principal Work

In analyzing the "principal-work" requirement, the Board concluded that the principal work of the lieutenants was facially similar to that of the firefighters. In reaching this conclusion, the Board noted that the housekeeping tasks performed by firefighters and the administrative tasks performed by lieutenants were "facially similar" because both served a similar purpose; that is, to keep the personnel active and alert and to maintain optimal preparation for emergencies. The Board thus concluded that because the firefighters and the lieutenants both performed tasks to maintain their readiness to respond to emergencies, their principal work was facially similar.

The Board then stated that it would consider whether the amount of supervisory authority exercised by the lieutenants rendered the nature and essence of their work substantially different from that of the firefighters. Instead, however, the Board simply noted that the lieutenants and firefighters shared a "strong camaraderie which is unique among firefighters." Relying upon this strong community of interest, the Board concluded that the lieutenants at issue were more aligned with the firefighters than with management. The Board therefore held that the lieutenants' principal work was not substantially different from the firefighters and that they were not supervisors within the meaning of the Act.

The Board's strained analysis of the principal-work prong was clearly improper. Even assuming that the principal work of all firefighting personnel is to maintain their readiness to respond to fire emergencies, the lieutenants and the firefighters perform completely different functions in their efforts to maintain such readiness. The administrative tasks which lieutenants perform are certainly not "facially similar" to the household and inspection tasks which the firefighters perform. In addition to performing tasks which are "obviously and visibly different" from those of their subordinates, the lieutenants also have significant supervisory authority which makes the nature and essence of their duties substantially different from those of the firefighters.

* * *

Like the ranking officers in the Freeport police department, the lieutenants here exercise supervisory authority in several of the areas most likely to fall within the scope of union representation. The existence of this authority and the power to adversely affect the employment of the firefighters at any time make the "nature and essence" of the lieutenants' principal work substantially different from that of the firefighters. The fact that a strong camaraderie exists among the firefighters and lieutenants does not change the fact that the daily activities and responsibilities of the lieutenants are very dissimilar from those of the firefighters. We must conclude that the Board's finding that the lieutenants' principal work was not substantially different from that of their subordinates was erroneous.

2. Supervisory Authority

The second prong of the supervisory definition specifies that an employee must have authority, in the interest of the employer, to perform one or more of 11 enumerated functions or to effectively recommend such action. The hearing officer found that the lieutenants satisfied this second prong because they had the authority to direct and discipline firefighters. The officer held that lieutenants have authority to direct firefighters at the fire stations, in that they transfer firefighters between stations, approve duty trades, assign tasks and conduct training exercises. She also concluded that the lieutenants have authority to direct firefighters at the scene of a fire. In addition, the hearing officer determined that lieutenants have authority to discipline firefighters with oral reprimands and to recommend written reprimands to the chief. The Board adopted the hearing officer's findings.

* * *

3. Independent Judgment

The third prong of the supervisory definition specifies that the exercise of supervisory authority must not be routine or clerical in nature, but must involve the consistent use of independent judgment. The hearing officer concluded that the lieutenants satisfied this prong only with respect to their authority to discipline.

The Village argues that the hearing officer erred in concluding that the lieutenants do not use independent judgment when exercising their authority to direct the firefighters at the fire station and in emergency situations. The evidence in the record, however, supports the Board's conclusion that the lieutenants do not use independent judgment when directing the firefighters at the fire station. Tasks are assigned according to a system agreed upon by the firefighters and must be performed in accordance with standards set forth in the chief's manual. The lieutenants' authority to transfer firefighters between stations is also routine, in that such transfers are made to meet minimum staffing standards established by the chief. Similarly, the lieutenants' authority to call in off-duty firefighters from a list based on seniority to meet the chief's minimum staffing requirements is routine in nature.

The hearing officer's conclusion that the lieutenants do not use independent judgment in the interest of the employer when directing firefighters at the scene of a fire, however, is less convincing. She concluded that the firefighters were trained to respond automatically and with little direction in emergency situations, and that the lieutenants therefore were not required to use independent judgment when directing the firefighters at fires. Although the fire department's operational procedures are standardized so far as possible, written protocol cannot possibly fit every conceivable situation which arises. The hearing officer's conclusion rests upon the unrealistic view that all fires are routine, present no unanticipated or unique characteristics and are controlled by the mechanistic application of set procedures. This view conflicts with common knowledge of such disasters. We agree, however, with the hearing officer's conclusion that any direction which the lieutenants give to firefighters at the fire scene is derived from their superior skill, experience and technical expertise and therefore does not require the use of independent judgment "in the interest of the employer" as required by the statute.

* * *

4. Preponderance of Employment Time Performing Supervisory Functions

The fourth prong of the supervisory definition specifies that the alleged supervisor must spend the preponderance of his employment time exercising supervisory authority. The Board has interpreted the term "preponderance" to mean that the most significant allotment of the employee's time must be spent exercising supervisory functions. In other words, the employee must spend more time on supervisory functions than on any one nonsupervisory function. In this case, the evidence demonstrates that the lieutenants rarely exercise their authority to suspend or discipline firefighters. It is therefore clear that the lieutenants do not spend more time exercising this authority than they devote to any other function. The lieutenants therefore do not satisfy the fourth prong of the supervisory definition.

Because the lieutenants of the Wheeling fire department do not satisfy all four prongs of the statutory definition, we must conclude that they are not supervisors within the meaning of the Act. Accordingly, they were appropriately included in the bargaining unit.

NOTES

1. As the court noted, the Illinois statute requires that employees spend a preponderance of their time on supervisory functions to be considered supervisors. This requirement is not found in the NLRA. Thus, under the NLRA, it is the possession of supervisory authority that makes an employee a supervisor but under the Illinois statute it is the actual exercise of that authority. However, the preponderance of time requirement under he Illinois statute does not apply to police officers. Why might the Illinois legislature have excluded police officers from this requirement?

2. Even though the preponderance of the time requirement did not apply to police officers, the labor board still found that police sergeants and lieutenants in the City of Freeport were not supervisors. On what basis? Why did the court reject this finding?

3. Although the Federal Service Labor Management Relations Statute generally follows the NLRA model for determining supervisory status, it provides that in any bargaining unit which includes nurses or firefighters, employees are supervisors only if they devote a preponderance of their employment time to exercising supervisory authority. 5 U.S.C. § 7103(a)(10). What are the advantages of the preponderance of the time requirement? What are the disadvantages? As a consequence of the preponderance of the time requirement, the Wheeling Fire Department lieutenants were included in the same bargaining unit as the firefighters that they supervised. Is this good labor relations policy?

Many states grant supervisors collective bargaining rights but require, either by statute or labor board or court decision, that they be placed in a separate bargaining unit from the employees they supervise. Placement in a separate bargaining unit is thought to mitigate the potential conflict of interests between supervisors and their subordinates. How far should separation of supervisors and subordinates go to avoid conflicts of interest? Consider the following case.

APPEAL OF MANCHESTER BOARD OF SCHOOL COMMITTEE

Supreme Court of New Hampshire, 1987.
129 N.H. 151, 523 A.2d 114.

BROCK, C.J.

The underlying issue in this case is whether a group of school principals, certified as a bargaining unit under NEW HAMPSHIRE REV.STAT. ANN. (RSA) 273–A:8, II by the New Hampshire Public Employee Labor Relations Board (the PELRB), may be represented by the same union representative as the teachers whom they supervise. The PELRB ruled that they could, and after a representative election held on September 26, 1985, the PELRB formally certified the Manchester Education Association (the Association), also the teachers' representative, as the representative of the school principals.

The Manchester Board of School Committee (the School Committee) appeals from the PELRB's certification decision, claiming *inter alia* that it is erroneous as a matter of law because of the inherent conflicts of interest that exist in such an arrangement. Specifically, the School Committee argues that the Association's status as exclusive representative for both supervisory and non-supervisory personnel is contrary to RSA 273–A:8, II and would lead to actual and potential conflicts of interest and/or a division of loyalties between the Association and the principals and teachers.

* * *

RSA 273–A:8, II explicitly prohibits "[p]ersons exercising supervisory authority involving the significant exercise of discretion [from belonging] to the *same bargaining unit* as the employees they supervise." (Emphasis added.) In *City of Concord v. PELRB,* 119 N.H. 725, 407 A.2d 363 (1979), we further interpreted RSA chapter 273–A as a whole, and Section 8, II in particular, as requiring that supervisory personnel be kept separate from the employees they supervise, not only by maintaining separate bargaining units, but also by refraining from commingling in the *same negotiating teams.* In the present appeal, the School Committee urges us to further interpret RSA 273–A:8 as prohibiting supervisors from being represented by the same union that is already representing the rank-and-file employees whom they supervise.

In adopting RSA chapter 273–A, the legislature declared that "it is the policy of the state to foster harmonious and cooperative relations between public employers and their employees and to protect the public by encouraging the orderly and uninterrupted operation of government." Laws 1975, 490:1 (statement of policy). With this purpose in mind and because we agree with the statement of the Nebraska Supreme Court that "[t]o permit supervisory personnel to retain the same bargaining agent as the employees' union would be tantamount to permitting them to enter the same bargaining unit," *Nebraska Ass'n of Pub. Emp. v. Nebraska Game & Parks Commission*, 197 Neb. 178, 247 N.W.2d 449 (1976), we hold that supervisory personnel may not retain the same exclusive representative as the rank-and-file employees they supervise.

In *City of Concord v. PELRB*, we recognized that the basis of the requirement of RSA 273–A:8, II, that supervisory personnel not be in the same unit with the rank-and-file, was "to avoid conflicts between the two groups because of the differing duties and relationships which characterize each group." Giving logical effect to the "inten[t] to keep supervisory personnel separate from the rank and file," we held that supervisory and non-supervisory personnel should "not be allowed to commingle on each other's negotiating teams." In the present case, we see the same potential for conflicts of interest arising due to the differing duties and relationships of the groups.

At oral argument, counsel for the Association conceded that there was the theoretical potential for conflicts of interest under such an arrangement, but argued that the absence of conflicts of interest in actual practice should be controlling. We reject this argument. Even if it is true that the Manchester school system has generally functioned well and has experienced good relations between its principals and teachers, it is not necessary for us to sit by and "allow events to unfold to the extent that the disruption of the [school] and the destruction of working relationships is manifest before taking action." To the contrary, "[a]n identity of interests on the part of supervisors with the rank and file poses a significant threat that the loyalties of the supervisors will be divided and that consequently the discipline and effectiveness of [the school system] will be impaired."

Vicksburg Firefighters Etc. v. City of Vicksburg, Miss., 761 F.2d 1036 (5th Cir.1985), thus warranting preventive action.

* * *

The Association further alleges that if joint representation is prohibited in this case, we will be impinging upon the right of the principals to join the labor union of their choice. In effect, however, our decision precludes principals from choosing a particular representative, the one already chosen by the teachers. The principals are free to choose any other bargaining representative. We conclude that this limitation on their ability to choose a representative is reasonable in view of the purpose and mandates of RSA chapter 273–A.

The PELRB's certification order is vacated and the case remanded for further proceedings consistent with this opinion.

NOTES

1. For a contrary result see *City of Highland Park*, 6 Mi.P.E.R. ¶ 24062 (Mi.E.R.C. 1993); *Hillsdale Community Schools*, 1968 MERC Lab. Op. 859 (Mi.E.R.C. 1968), *aff'd*, 24 Mich.App. 36, 179 N.W.2d 661 (1970). Why have there been difficulties in coming to a consensus about public sector supervisors' statutory bargaining rights?

2. Why do some statutes which generally prohibit the placement of supervisors in the same bargaining unit as nonsupervisory employees nevertheless authorize placement of protective services (police and firefighters) supervisors, such as sergeants, lieutenants, and captains, in the same bargaining unit as rank-and-file employees?

2. MANAGERIAL AND CONFIDENTIAL EMPLOYEES

Unlike supervisors, with their qualified right to participate in the collective bargaining process, as provided in many public sector statutes, managers are excluded from the definition of employee in virtually all public sector enactments. The definition of management employee most commonly found in public sector legislation is derived from decisions interpreting the National Labor Relations Act, which does not contain a definition of management employee nor a statutory exclusion for such employee. See *NLRB v. Bell Aerospace Co.,* 416 U.S. 267, 94 S.Ct. 1757, 40 L.Ed.2d 134 (1974), which approves the definition of management employee fashioned by the National Labor Relations Board: "[persons] who are in a position to formulate, determine, and effectuate management policies."

Sometimes, a public sector jurisdiction equates managerial employees with executive employees. In many jurisdictions, the exclusion of manager/executives from statutory coverage is read narrowly. For example, the New Jersey statute excludes "managerial executives," which it defines as persons who "formulate management policies and practices" or who "are charged with the responsibility of *directing and effectuating* such policies and practices." NEW JERSEY STAT. ANN. 34:13A3(f) (emphasis added). The New Jersey Supreme Court has elaborated:

> A person formulates policies when he develops a particular set of objectives designed to further the mission of [a segment of] the governmental unit and when he selects a course of action from among available alternatives. A person directs the effectuation of policy when he is charged with developing the methods, means and extent of reaching a policy objective and thus oversees or coordinates policy implementation by line supervisors. * * * Whether or not an employee possesses this level of authority may generally be determined by * * * three factors: (1) the relative position of that employee in his employer's hierarchy; (2) his functions and responsibilities; and (3) the extent of discretion he exercises.

New Jersey Turnpike Authority. v. AFSCME Council 73, 150 N.J. 331, 696 A.2d 585 (1997). The court distinguished a manager who directs and effectuates management policies and practices from one who makes operative such policies and practices. To the court, directing and effectuating indicates a higher level of responsibility than making operative policies and practices.

In the bargaining unit context, confidential employees are only those who are involved in the employer's labor-management relations activities and thus have access to confidential information about the employer's labor relations as part of the employee's regular job duties. They are excluded from the definition of employee by decisional law in the private sector and often by express statutory terms in the public sector. Should information technology specialists who have access to all user names and passwords and all files stored on the employer's network be excluded as confidential employees? See *Niles Township High School District 219 v. Illinois Educational Labor Relations Board*, 387 Ill.App.3d 58, 900 N.E.2d 336, 326 Ill.Dec. 700 (2008).

3. HOME HEALTH CARE AIDS AND IN–HOME DAY CARE PROVIDERS

THE PUBLICIZATION OF HOME–BASED CARE WORK IN STATE LABOR LAW

Peggie R. Smith
92 Minnesota Law Review 1390 (2008).

Home-based care workers have experienced a labor metamorphism of sorts over the last decade. The workers, most of whom are women, care for children and the elderly from within the private sphere of the home in exchange for compensation. Once invisible and ignored, they have become darlings of the labor movement. While they have not halted the persistent decline in union density, they have helped to reinvigorate organized labor. The transformation first attracted national attention in 1999 when the

Service Employees International Union (SEIU) won the right to represent 74,000 home care workers in Los Angeles, California. The victory marked the largest increase since 1941 in new union membership resulting from a single union election. Six years later, SEIU charted new territory once again when more than 49,000 family child care providers in Illinois voted overwhelmingly to join the union. The vote netted labor its second largest membership election since 1941.

* * *

In both the family child care and home care settings, the state pays workers to provide care, yet the compensation rates are too low to ensure a decent wage. In addition, most states insist that home-based care workers are not government employees, but rather independent contractors to whom states owe no obligation under applicable labor and employment laws. This dynamic has set the stage for union efforts to gain collective bargaining rights on behalf of publicly subsidized home-based care workers in order to provide such workers with a voice in negotiating with government agencies over the terms of their labor arrangements.

I. BACKGROUND: THE SHARED CHARACTERISTICS OF HOME–BASED CARE WORK

This Article uses the phrase "home-based care work" to refer to two types of paid caregiving that occur within the home: home care and family child care. Home care refers to in-home services provided to elderly and/or disabled individuals who require assistance with personal care tasks such as grooming, dressing, and bathing, and household activities such as shopping, cleaning, and meal preparation. Most home care consumers are elderly individuals with long-term-care needs. Family child care refers to child care services that a worker provides for compensation in her own residence to two or more unrelated children.

* * *

The demographic profile of home-based care workers combined with their economic status and poor working conditions help explain the difficulty in maintaining a stable workforce. Women account for the overwhelming majority—at least ninety percent—of home care workers and family child care providers. As with paid care work generally, race and ethnicity heavily mediate these occupations, resulting in overrepresentation of women of color, especially African Americans and Latinas. Many of the workers are also immigrants, especially in the home care context.

As a group, home-based care workers are disproportionately poor and low-income women whose earnings place them near the bottom of the economic ladder. In 2006, they earned less per hour than workers employed as locker room and coatroom attendants, gaming-booth cashiers, meter readers, and bicycle repairers. In addition, most home-based care workers do not receive job-related benefits such as health insurance, medical leave, or retirement plans.

* * *

II. CHALLENGES TO EMPOWERING HOME–BASED CARE WORKERS

* * *

A. Mobilizing the Workers

The invisibility of home-based care workers presents a first-order obstacle to organizing them. How does one effectively organize workers whose jobs seem completely antithetical to any notion of collective action? Before workers can be organized, they must be identified and mobilized. In the traditional arena of manufacturing jobs, this first-order step was relatively straightforward—union organizers could stand at the factory gate and both identify and recruit workers as they entered or departed. This approach, however, has no utility when applied to home-based care workers. Not only are workers hidden in individual homes, but they are also fragmented throughout neighborhoods, towns, and cities. Instead of laboring together in central locations, home-based care workers most commonly work alone in private homes. Even more problematic for organization purposes, a home care worker frequently cares for several clients, and thus works at several different "worksites."

Labor has responded to this challenge by employing strategies to mobilize nontraditional workforces like home care workers and family child care providers. These strategies include reaching out to workers by forging ties with groups and organizations in their communities, using the media to reach workers, and holding rallies to vocalize issues of concern to workers. In addition, union organizers commonly go door-to-door to contact workers at their homes. Although extremely resource intensive, these strategies have allowed labor to effectively mobilize home-based care workers.

B. Following the Money: Identifying Commonality for Bargaining Purposes

Together with figuring out how to mobilize home-based care workers, unions must solve the dilemma posed by the fact that many home-based care workers lack a traditional employment relationship with a common employer for bargaining purposes. * * *

In the family child care industry, providers usually enter into individual contracts with the parents for whom they provide child care. If the law were to recognize an employment relationship in this context, it would be between the provider and each parent, and the relationship would appear to fall within the NLRA's coverage. Because providers exercise considerable control over how they perform their jobs, however, it is extremely unlikely that a provider-parent employment relationship exists. Instead, family child care providers generally operate as independent contractors and, as a result, they are outside the NLRA's purview. Yet even if the law did regard the provider-parent relationship as an employment relationship covered by the NLRA, considerable hurdles to unionization would remain.

As an initial matter, a provider could not engage in collective bargaining unless she joined forces with other providers, which would be no easy task given that providers typically work alone. Assuming, however, that a group of providers did join forces, a fatal problem would still remain because the providers, as a group, lack an identifiable parent-employer with whom to bargain, since each provider works for many different parents.

The difficulties in gaining employee status and in determining the employer for purposes of bargaining are absent in a center-based child care setting. In this context, where parents contract with the center to provide care and the center employs the workers, a union can readily identify both the bargaining unit (employees of the center), as well as the employer (the center).

The structure of home care lends itself to a comparable analysis. Most home care workers are employed by home care agencies and, similar to center-based child care workers in the family child care context, if employed by a private agency, they most likely possess rights under the NLRA. In this scenario, the identification of a bargaining unit and the employer with whom to bargain does not pose any particular hurdles.

Obstacles, however, surface in the context of home care workers who are hired directly by individual clients and/or their family members. At first glance, because these independent workers likely can establish an employment relationship with clients, it appears that they may fare better than family child care providers in terms of securing protection under the NLRA. Unlike family child care providers, who clearly lack an employment relationship with the parents of the children for whom they care, independent home care workers may well qualify as employees of their clients (and/or family members of the clients) given that the clients may exert considerable control over the manner in which the workers perform their jobs.

Yet even if such an employment relationship exists, it does not afford the worker protection under the NLRA. Like many labor and employment law statutes, the NLRA contains a domestic-service provision that exempts from coverage anyone employed "in the domestic service of any family or person at his home" including home care workers. According to the National Labor Relations Board, this exemption applies where the "employment [is] on an individual and personal basis." As a result, home care workers in the employ of individual homeowners lack coverage under the NLRA. Even assuming workers could overcome this exception, they, like family child care providers, lack an identifiable entity with which to bargain, as each worker may have several employers, and the workers would seldom have employers in common.

Home-based care workers who provide publicly subsidized care have also tried to secure collective bargaining rights by claiming that they are employees of the government agencies that fund such care. Unfortunately, courts have rejected these claims and have ruled that publicly subsidized, home-based care workers have an independent contractor relationship with government funding agencies, not an employment relationship. * * *

III. THE PROMISES AND PITFALLS OF LABOR CAMPAIGNS

* * * To date, the labor movement has campaigned successfully to extend labor law protections to publicly subsidized home care workers in at least nine states, including California, Illinois, Iowa, Massachusetts, Michigan, Ohio, Oregon, Washington, and Wisconsin. Family child care has experienced an even greater flurry of organizing activity. In the last two years, the labor movement has secured labor rights for publicly subsidized family child care providers in ten states: Illinois, Iowa, Kansas, Michigan, New Jersey, New York, Oregon, Pennsylvania, Washington, and Wisconsin.

This extension of labor rights to independent home-based care workers often stems from state legislation, executive orders issued by state governors, and the acts of municipalities. Antitrust law, however, could interfere with such rights, as it generally prohibits independent contractors from engaging in collective bargaining. Yet despite this general rule, under the state action doctrine, state regulation can immunize labor activity from antitrust review. While the state action doctrine applies most clearly to state regulation, including legislation, it may also apply to regulation undertaken by governors in their executive capacity and by municipalities.

A. Home Care

The home care campaign first achieved national attention in California, where SEIU, in its early attempts to procure labor rights for publicly funded home care workers, focused on the judiciary as a means for reform. Specifically, the union tried to persuade the California courts to recognize publicly funded home care workers—who cared for elderly and disabled clients in the Los Angeles County—as employees of the county under the Meyers–Milias–Brown Act, the California law governing labor relations for local government employees. SEIU argued that the county, as the workers' employer, was obligated to negotiate with it as a representative of the county's home care workers.

The court disagreed with this theory, holding that the workers were employed not by the county, but by the individual recipients of the workers' services. In response to this judicial defeat, SEIU redirected its efforts to the legislative process, where it met success. In 1992, the California legislature passed a law that authorized, and later required, each county in the state to create "public authorities," agencies that would serve as the legal employer for home care workers for purposes of local collective bargaining laws. Los Angeles County established a public authority in 1997, and two years later SEIU won the right to represent the county's 74,000 home care workers.

Hoping to follow in California's footsteps, the Oregon Public Employees Union (OPEU), an SEIU affiliate, supported a bill introduced in the Oregon legislature in 1999 that would have provided for the establishment of a statewide home care commission, and that would have given publicly funded home care workers in the state the ability to unionize. When the bill died in the legislature, OPEU switched tactics and successfully placed Measure 99 on the 2000 ballot. The measure, which garnered the approval of sixty-three percent of the voters, amended the Oregon Constitution to create a Home Care Commission. It serves as the workers' employer of record for purposes of collective bargaining and enables the workers to unionize. In addition, the workers are regarded as public employees of the state and thus subject to Oregon's Public Employee Collective Bargaining Act. In 2001, the workers voted to have SEIU represent them.

The approach to unionization of publicly funded home care workers in Washington followed a trajectory similar to that in Oregon. In 2001, legislators considered a bill that would have provided labor rights to home-based care workers through a public authority model comparable to those established in California and Oregon. When the bill languished in committee, its proponents turned to a ballot initiative, known as the Homecare Quality Initiative. Approximately sixty-two percent of Washington voters approved the initiative, which established a Home Care Quality Authority and granted collective bargaining rights to publicly subsidized home care workers. During the 2002 legislative session, the legislature codified the text of the initiative. The law names the authority as the employer of record for the workers for purposes of collective bargaining.

Both Michigan and Wisconsin also use a public-authority model to recognize union representatives of publicly funded home care workers. These states' public authorities, however, were created not by legislation or executive order, but by intergovernmental cooperation agreements. Such agreements enable local governments to join together to address shared problems or to provide coordinated services. In the home care context, the agreements allow local governments to work together to improve the delivery and the quality of subsidized home care on behalf of consumers. In addition, the agreements enable local governments to jointly facilitate the workplace interests of workers by designating an employer of record on behalf of the workers for bargaining purposes.

In Michigan, an intergovernmental agreement signed by the Michigan Department of Community Health and the Tri–County Aging Consortium established the Michigan Quality Community Care Council in 2004. The agreement tasks the council with facilitating the provision of "employer-related functions" for publicly subsidized home care providers and promoting an effective home care system on behalf of consumers. Under the agreement, the council also has "the right to bargain collectively and enter into agreements with labor organizations." In 2005, more than 41,000 publicly subsidized home care workers in the state took the first step toward collective bargaining when they voted to elect SEIU as their representative in negotiations with the council.

In Wisconsin, an intergovernmental cooperation agreement was used to establish a public authority known as the Quality Home Care Commission (QHCC), which has the power to bargain collectively with labor organizations that represent publicly subsidized home care workers. Whereas the council in Michigan is statewide, Wisconsin has adopted a county approach similar to that utilized in California. The Wisconsin agreement allows the state to contract with individual counties regarding the provision of publicly funded home care services. While each county will continue to finance home care within its boundaries, the QHCC will serve as an employer of record for home care workers in the counties.

* * *

In a few states, including Illinois and Iowa, the labor movement was successful in persuading state governors to take action to extend labor law protections to publicly funded home care workers. In Illinois, * * * in 2003, * * * Governor Blagojevich signed an executive order that requires the state to "recognize a representative designated by a majority of [the workers] as the[ir] exclusive representative" and to "engage in collective negotiations with said representative concerning all terms and conditions" of the workers' employment. In 2005, the Illinois legislature codified the provisions of the executive order in the Illinois Public Labor Relations Act.

The then-Governor of Iowa, Tom Vilsack, followed the lead of Governor Blagojevich when, in 2005, he signed an executive order that required a state agency to "meet and confer with the authorized representative of the individual [home care] providers, as designated by the majority of the individual providers." Iowa's * * * meet-and-confer provisions * * * possess less bite than collective bargaining provisions. * * *

B. Family Child Care

* * * [I]n the context of home care, states have responded to labor advocates in a variety of ways. In contrast, states have taken a much more uniform approach in the family child care context: they have relied overwhelmingly on executive orders to grant labor law rights to family child care providers. Of the ten states that presently have a process in place to recognize family child care unions, the governors in nine of those states signed executive orders mandating the process. Illinois was the first state to bring publicly subsidized family child care providers into the scope of its labor laws, doing so in 2005 pursuant to an executive order. The order, which mirrors an earlier order signed on behalf of home care workers in Illinois, requires the state to "recognize a representative designated by a majority of [the providers] * * * * as the[ir] exclusive representative." It also grants the "representative the same rights and duties granted to employee representatives by the Illinois Public Labor Relations Act." Later that year, the Illinois legislature codified the order, providing the workers with even stronger rights than those expressed in the order. Notably, the law states in clear terms that the providers are deemed state employees for the purpose of the Illinois Public Labor

Relations Act, and adds that the state "shall engage in collective bargaining" with their representative.

Washington followed closely behind Illinois in granting authority for the state's publicly subsidized family child care providers to engage in collective bargaining with the state. In September 2005, Governor Christine Gregoire sent an executive directive to the Secretary of the State Department of Social and Health Services (DSHS), directing DSHS "to define a process for family child care providers * * * to have a strong, ongoing voice" in matters related to their working conditions. The letter also specified that the providers should have a chance to "select a representative for negotiations on their behalf with DSHS," and that DSHS should meet with the representative to discuss matters such as "reimbursement rates, regulation, and licensing procedures." Shortly thereafter, the workers selected SEIU as their representative. In 2006, the legislature codified the directive and strengthened its essential points. Under the law, providers are state employees who are entitled to representation for the purpose of "collective bargaining." The law also designates the governor or a designee as the providers' employer of record.

In 2005, AFSCME Council 75 presented union authorization cards to the Oregon Employment Relations Board (OERB) requesting permission to represent certified and registered family child care providers in Oregon. The following year, SEIU Local 503 submitted union authorization cards to the OERB requesting to represent subsidized, license-exempt family child care providers in the state. In both instances, OERB certified the cards, following which Oregon's governor, Theodore Kulongoski, issued executive orders directing state agencies to meet and confer with the relevant union officials on behalf of the providers "regarding issues of mutual concern." In 2007, the Oregon legislature codified the provisions of both executive orders, but replaced the executive orders' "meet-and-confer" approach with a much stronger "collective bargaining" process. The legislation provides that the state will serve as the public employer of record for the providers, and treats the providers as public employees for the sole purpose of "collective bargaining."

The executive orders and subsequent statutes in Illinois, Washington, and Oregon comprise an approach that emphatically extends to publicly subsidized family child care providers state labor law protection in the form of collective bargaining rights. Iowa and Wisconsin, by comparison, permit the unionization of providers, but are far more restrictive in terms of the actual rights given to the providers. In 2006, Iowa's governor signed executive orders regarding both registered family child care providers and license-exempt providers of subsidized child care. The orders provide that state agencies "shall meet and confer with the authorized representative" of the providers, and that in doing so, the agencies "shall discuss issues of mutual concern, including training requirements, reimbursement rates, payment procedures, [and] health and safety conditions." Although AFSCME has since won a union election, giving it the right to represent registered providers in Iowa, the executive orders suffer from the same limitations discussed earlier in the context of the Iowa executive order for independent home care workers: the orders grant the providers only meet-and-confer rights and do not treat the providers as state employees for any purpose. Finally, because the legislature has not codified the orders' provisions, any subsequent governor or legislature can eliminate these rights with the stroke of a pen.

The union status of family child care providers in Wisconsin is somewhat comparable to that of Iowa. In 2006, Wisconsin Governor Jim Doyle signed an executive order that takes the form of a meet-and-confer requirement. The order requires the Department of Health and Family Services "to meet and confer with a recognized exclusive majority representative of family child care providers in Wisconsin" for the purpose of discussing various issues including "reimbursement and payment procedures," as well as training. The providers have since voted to have AFSCME as their representative. However, as is true of the Iowa order, the Wisconsin order has not been codified by the legislature, and the order does not regard the workers as state employees for any purpose.

NOTES

1. Note the common approach of the states in providing collective bargaining rights for home health care workers and in-home childcare providers is to designate the state as employer of record for purposes of negotiating a collective bargaining agreement. This is necessary because at common law, home health care workers and in-home day care providers are probably employees of their clients or independent contractors. What challenges might the parties encounter in negotiating the collective bargaining agreement resulting from the bargaining unit members not being common law employees of the state?

2. If the state wishes to improve the compensation and working conditions of home health care workers and in-home day care providers, why do so via collective bargaining? Why not simply raise the compensation levels and otherwise improve working conditions unilaterally as a condition of the provision of state subsidies?

4. ATTORNEYS

CITY OF NEWARK v. ASSOCIATION OF GOVERNMENT ATTORNEYS

Superior Court of New Jersey, Appellate Division, 2002.
346 N.J.Super. 460, 788 A.2d 776.

BAIME, P.J.A.D.

The novel question presented by this appeal is whether non-supervisory attorneys employed by the City of Newark in its office of corporation counsel may organize and join a union. Following an election ordered by the Public Employment Relations Commission, the Association of Government Attorneys was certified as the employees' representative. The City appeals. * * *

* * *

We turn to the City's argument that the Rules of Professional Conduct [RPC] preclude its lawyers from unionizing for the purpose of collective negotiations. The City contends that the interjection of a union will seriously impair the attorney-client relationship by creating dual loyalties. The City further claims that unionization of municipal attorneys creates an appearance of impropriety. In advancing these contentions, the City heavily relies on RPC 1.7(b) and (c)(2). These rules bar an attorney from representing a client if such representation may be "materially limited by the lawyer's responsibilities to another client or to a third person, or by the lawyer's own interests," or if such "multiple representation" might create a perception of impropriety in an "ordinary knowledgeable citizen acquainted with the facts." *Ibid.*

We find no merit in this contention. There is nothing fundamentally incompatible between the constitutional right of government employees to organize for the purpose of collective negotiations, *N.J. Const.*, art. I, ¶ 19., and the duty of loyalty owed by a municipal attorney to his client. In earlier days, the legal profession harbored a strong bias against governmental attorneys joining unions or other employee organizations. See, e.g., *ABA Informal Ethics Opns.*, No. 917 (Jan. 25, 1966) (a government lawyer owes undivided loyalty to the agency for which he or she works and may not join a labor union). However, the American Bar Association subsequently discarded that position and recognized the right of government attorneys and corporate lawyers to organize "for the purpose of negotiating wages, hours, and working conditions" so long as they perform their duties in accordance with * * * the Canons of Ethics." 2 *ABA Informal Ethics Opns.*, No. 986 (July 3, 1967). The American Bar Association's *Model Code of Professional Responsibility*, EC 5–13 states in pertinent part that "although it is not necessarily improper for a lawyer employed by a corporation or similar entity to be a member of an organization of employees, he should be vigilant to safeguard his fidelity as a lawyer to his employer, free from outside influences." Although in 1983, the American Bar Association replaced the Model Code of Professional Responsibility with the Model Rules of Professional Conduct, which is silent on the question, the bar association's current position appears to be that unionization is permitted as long as the attorney conducts himself in accordance with ethical rules.

We adopt this pragmatic approach. The number of lawyers who represent single employer clients, such as governmental agencies, has increased substantially in recent years. The relationship between a government lawyer and his client in terms of compensation and working conditions is different from that of the attorney who represents a number of different clients in his daily practice. Government lawyers have only one client, do not charge fees for their individual work, and their compensation generally is not related to a particular assignment but instead is related to the overall duties they perform. This does not diminish their duty of loyalty owed to their client or their obligation to conduct themselves in accordance with accepted ethical standards. However, the impersonality of the relationship might well weigh heavily in the need to organize for the purpose of collective negotiations.

We perceive no blanket, *per se* violation of the duty of loyalty owed by a lawyer to his client when government attorneys exercise their constitutional and statutory rights to organize for the purpose of collective negotiations. The growing phenomenon of single client lawyers requires a realistic accommodation between an attorney's professional obligation and the rights he or she may have as an employee.

There is an inherent tension in the attorney-client relationship, just as there is an inherent tension in the employer-employee relationship. In that context, it is important to note that an attorney's personal interests in securing equitable compensation and benefits are the same whether they are advanced by the attorney individually or by a union. In both cases, the attorney's stringent ethical obligations trump his personal interests. That cardinal principle must prevail in determining whether an attorney, in pursuit of an employee organization's objectives, oversteps ethical boundaries. That determination must rest on the application of specific ethical and disciplinary rules, most particularly the principles adopted by our Supreme Court, to insure the attorney's unfettered duty to represent the client faithfully, competently, and fairly.

* * *

Candor requires us to add that not all of the concerns expressed by the City are fanciful. We recognize that the course we have taken is not free of obstacles. Public employees may not engage in a strike, and so we need not concern ourselves with that issue. But difficult questions will undoubtedly be raised in the future, such as whether a union representing municipal attorneys may sue the City or seek redress for labor law violations in other forums. So too, difficult questions may arise as to whether the City could punish an attorney-employee because of his union activities. We are also mindful of the possibility that unionization may put a strain on the attorney-client relationship, and may tend to diminish the client's confidence in the attorney's loyalty. Moreover, the action of the union or that of the municipality may create lasting antagonism. Such antagonism in the labor relations context is unfortunately commonplace. We do not underestimate the difficulty of providing solutions to these problems. But the constitutional and statutory rights to organize for the purpose of collective negotiations were not established for the ease and comfort of the judiciary. We are confident in the capacity of the parties, and ultimately the ability of judges, to resolve these and other questions.

* * *

We also disagree with the City's contention that unionization of the City's attorneys creates a perception of impropriety. RPC 1.7(c)(2). We acknowledge that "the 'appearance' doctrine is intended not to prevent any actual conflicts of interest but to bolster the public's confidence in the integrity of the legal profession." "Thus, it is that sometimes an attorney, guiltless in any actual sense, nevertheless is required to stand aside for the sake of public confidence in the probity of the administration of justice." * * * Undoubtedly, the need to dispel all appearances of impropriety becomes even more compelling and acute when the attorney is a government lawyer. When representation of public bodies is involved, our Supreme Court has recognized that the appearance of impropriety assumes an added dimension because "government attorneys * * * are more visible to the public." * * *

The Court has also said that "the 'appearance' of impropriety must be something more than a fanciful possibility." "It must have some reasonable basis." * * * Applying that principle, we are satisfied that ordinary, knowledgeable citizens acquainted with the facts would see nothing amiss in extending the organizational rights and benefits afforded by our Constitution and statutes to the City's attorneys.

For the sake of completeness, we add that our holding is supported by other jurisdictions that have considered the question. See *Santa Clara County Counsel Attorneys Ass'n v. Woodside*, 7 Cal.4th 525, 869 P.2d 1142 (1994) (en banc) (attorneys in the public sector may organize and sue employer for labor law violations); *Chiles v. State Employees Attorneys Guild*, 734 So.2d 1030 (Fla.1999) (government lawyer "does not violate ethical standards simply by being a member of a union"); *Chiles v. Public Employees Relations Comm'n*, 630 So.2d 1093 (Fla.1994) (Commission statutory certification process does not infringe upon [Supreme Court's] jurisdiction over attorneys); *City of Philadelphia v. Pennsylvania Labor Relations Bd.*, 163 Pa. Cmwlth. 628, 641 A.2d 709 (1994) ("There is nothing in the Rules of Professional Conduct which prohibits an attorney from being a member of a union"). These decisions stand for the proposition that government lawyers have an interest in dealing with their employer concerning compensation, benefits and other core working conditions, but this interest is inherent in every employment relationship, that all attorneys have an interest in addressing these issues whether or not they organize for the purpose of collective negotiations, and that interjection of a union does not alter this interest, but instead changes the method of communicating it to the employer. We agree with these observations.

We next consider the City's argument that the Commission infringed upon the power of the Supreme Court over the practice of law. * * *

"The intent of the 1947 Constitutional Convention was to vest the Supreme Court with the broadest possible administrative authority.'" * * * Resolution of the ethical propriety of an attorney's conduct is thus "within the exclusive province of the Supreme Court. It is safe to say that generally, almost without exception, no branch of government has the power to authorize either explicitly or implicitly, conduct by attorneys that violates the ethical standards imposed by the judiciary. Neither the Legislature nor the Executive has any power to overrule attorney ethical standards promulgated by [the] Court." Clearly, the Commission has no authority to override the Supreme Court's constitutional power.

This much conceded, the Commission's decision did not authorize any conduct barred by an ethical standard adopted by the Court. The Commission's determination did not insulate the City's attorneys from the Court's authority. The pivotal issue is whether the Commission's statutory certification process intrudes upon the court's jurisdiction over attorneys. We find that collective negotiations by the City's attorneys does not encroach upon the Court's authority in the absence of any action by the Court to the contrary. As a matter of comity and respect for the other branches of government, we accord deference to the Commission's decision. * * *

NEW JERSEY STAT.ANN. 40A:9–139 requires every municipality to adopt an ordinance providing for the appointment of a municipal attorney. The City implemented that statute by enacting Newark Ordinance § 2.6–7(a), which provides that the corporation counsel may appoint legal assistants, and that "all said persons [are to] serve at the pleasure of the corporation counsel." The City argues that unionization of its attorneys unlawfully burdens the corporation counsel's power.

* * *

Undoubtedly, there are issues and areas that cannot be the subject of negotiations because they are preempted by statute or otherwise inconsistent with corporation counsel's statutory power. We have no occasion here to set the exact boundaries of permissible collective negotiations. We are concerned here with the much broader question concerning the right of the City's attorneys to organize and join a union. That right is not forbidden by statute or ordinance.

The City's final argument is that its attorneys are supervisors, managerial executives or confidential employees and are thus barred from organizing or joining a union under NEW JERSEY STAT.ANN. 34:13A–5.3. * * *

At the outset, we reject the City's argument that its attorneys are forbidden from organizing because they act as supervisors to support staff such as paralegals, administrative assistants or interns. Whether or not the attorneys are supervisors is essentially irrelevant. The statutory language bars supervisors from being represented in collective negotiations by an employee organization that admits nonsupervisory personnel. The statute provides no blanket prohibition against supervisors joining a union.

We also find no sound basis to disturb the Director's finding that the City's attorneys are not "managerial executives." The term "managerial executives" refers to persons who formulate management policies and practices, and persons who are charged with the responsibility of directing the effectuation of such management policies and practices." NEW JERSEY STAT.ANN. 34:13A3(f). * * *

Within this analytical framework, we emphasize that all of the attorneys represented by the Association are lower level employees in the office of corporation counsel. It is undisputed that they report to a section chief who reports to one of the two first assistants who, in turn, reports to corporation counsel. While the lower level attorneys may occasionally make recommendations concerning the formulation of policy, they are not policy makers. They do not develop objectives to further the City's mission. They, instead, render advice on legal questions and represent the City in litigation. As attorneys, they develop legal strategies to advance legislative and administrative policies, but this function is not the equivalent of "oversee[ing] or coordinat[ing] policy implementation by line supervisors." While the attorneys are vested with some degree of discretion, it is plain from the record that they are closely supervised and that their power and authority are narrowly circumscribed.

We do not regard the City's attorneys as "confidential employees." The term "confidential employees" refers to "employees whose functional responsibilities or knowledge in connection with the issues involved in the collective negotiations process would make their membership in any appropriate negotiating unit incompatible with their official duties." NEW JERSEY STAT.ANN. 34:13A–3(g).

* * *

[T]here is no evidence that the information to which the attorneys have access is significant in the context of their work responsibilities and the collective negotiations process. It is to be recalled that those having such information—the attorneys assigned to labor law tasks, section chiefs, and first assistants—were excluded from the negotiating unit.

* * *

Despite the vagaries inherent in the statutory definition of "confidential employees," we are thoroughly satisfied that the City's lower level attorneys do not so qualify. If the Legislature intended to prohibit all municipal attorneys from joining a union, it would have said so, as it did in the case of deputy attorneys general under NEW JERSEY STAT.ANN. 52:17A–7. We see no valid basis for vitiating the Commission's determination.

NOTES

1. As the court notes in its opinion, most jurisdictions that have considered the issue have held that attorneys are not per se excluded from collective bargaining in the public sector. Indeed, even attorneys employed by the National Labor Relations Board have their own union which negotiates pursuant to Title VII of the Civil Service Reform Act of 1978 (Federal Service Labor Management Relations Statute).

2. This view, however, is not universal. Section 201(7)(b) of New York's Taylor Law expressly provides that "assistant attorneys general, assistant

district attorneys, and law school graduates employed in titles which promote to assistant district attorneys upon admission to the bar of the state of New York shall be designated managerial employees * * *." The Illinois courts have held that public sector attorneys are not employees entitled to collectively bargain under the Illinois Public Labor Relations Act. *Chief Judge v. Illinois State Labor Relations Board*, 178 Ill.2d 333, 227 Ill.Dec. 313, 687 N.E.2d 795 (1997) (assistant public defenders); *Cook County State's Attorney v. Illinois Local Labor Relations Board*, 166 Ill.2d 296, 209 Ill.Dec. 761, 652 N.E.2d 301 (1995) (assistant state's attorneys); *Chief Judge v. AFSCME Council 31*, 229 Ill.App.3d 180, 171 Ill.Dec. 102, 593 N.E.2d 922 (1992) (guardians ad litem); *Salaried Employees of North America v. Illinois Local Labor Relations Board*, 202 Ill.App.3d 1013, 148 Ill.Dec. 329, 560 N.E.2d 926 (1990) (attorneys employed by the City of Chicago Law Department). The Illinois cases reason that the attorneys serve as surrogates of the heads of the entities for whom they work. For example, assistant state's attorneys act as surrogates for the state's attorney and assistant public defenders act as surrogates for the public defender. Consequently, the Illinois courts regard them as managerial employees. But see *Illinois Department of Central Management Services v. Illinois Labor Relations Board*, 388 Ill.App.3d 319, 902 N.E.2d 1122, 327 Ill.Dec. 736 (2009) (holding that staff attorneys in the Department of Healthcare and Family Services, Office of Inspector General, Bureau of Administrative Litigation, who prosecute respondents in license revocation and similar administrative hearings are not managerial employees because they do not act as surrogates for the Inspector General and do not have authority to take action independently in the Inspector General's absence or without the Inspector General's approval); *AFSCME Council 31 and State of Illinois, Department of Central Management Services (Illinois Commerce Commission)*, 26 P.E.R.Ill. ¶ 40 (Ill. L.R.B. 2010) (holding that administrative law judges in the Illinois Commerce Commission are not managerial employees because they do not act as surrogates for the commissioners but hold hearings and draft recommended decisions which are subject to further review).

3. What conflicts can arise between public sector attorneys' roles as counsel for their employer and as an employee represented by a labor organization? What is the appropriate body to resolve such role conflicts?

5. GRADUATE ASSISTANTS

GRADUATE EMPLOYEES ORGANIZATION v. ILLINOIS EDUCATIONAL LABOR RELATIONS BOARD

Illinois Appellate Court, 2000.
315 Ill.App.3d 278, 248 Ill.Dec. 84, 733 N.E.2d 759.

THEIS, P.J.

Petitioner Graduate Employees Organization, IFT/AFT, AFL–CIO, petitions for direct review from an opinion and order of respondent Illinois Educational Labor Relations Board (IELRB), which dismissed petitioner's petition requesting certification and recognition as the collective bargaining representative for all teaching assistants, graduate assistants and research assistants at the University of Illinois at Urbana–Champaign. On direct review, petitioner contends that the opinion and order of the IELRB were in error. At issue is whether teaching assistants, graduate assistants and research assistants, who are seeking to organize, are "educational employees" who are authorized to organize or "students" who are precluded from organizing. For the reasons that follow, we reverse and remand for further proceedings.

The Illinois Educational Labor Relations Act (Act) was enacted by our General Assembly in 1983. The Act, together with the Illinois Public Labor Relations Act, represents "the first comprehensive statutory regulation of public sector collective bargaining in Illinois history." Martin H. Malin, Implementing the Illinois Educational Labor Relations Act, 61 *Chi.–Kent L. Rev.* 101, 101 (1985). Indeed, prior to the Act's passage, Illinois collective bargaining law was "chaotic." 61 *Chi.–Kent L. Rev.* at 123. To be sure, public education employees had a constitutional right to unionize. Employers, however, were under no legal obligation to recognize any such union. 61 *Chi.–Kent L. Rev.* at 121. Moreover, even if a union was recognized, an employer was still free to rescind such recognition at its discretion. 61 *Chi.–Kent L. Rev.* at 121. Employers were also free to discriminate between unions and determine which issues would be the subject of collective bargaining and which would not. 61 *Chi.–Kent L. Rev.* at 121–22. Despite this rather unfavorable state of the law, unions grew quickly in Illinois. 61 *Chi.–Kent L. Rev.* at 123. So, too, however, did the number of strikes. In fact, strikes became routine. 61 *Chi–Kent L. Rev.* at 123.

As a result, the Illinois Educational Labor Relations Act was enacted to alleviate such disputes and "to promote orderly and constructive relationships between all educational employees and their employers." Indeed, the Act sprang from our General Assembly's conclusion that "unresolved disputes between the educational employees and their employers are injurious to the public * * * and * * * that adequate means must be established for minimizing them and providing for their resolution." In order to best accomplish the purpose of the Act, "educational employers" were required "to negotiate and bargain with employee organizations representing educational employees and to enter into written agreements evidencing the result of such bargaining." "Procedures to provide for the protection of the rights of the educational employee, the educational employers and the public" were also enacted. Our General Assembly further codified the right of employees to "organize, form, join, or assist in employee organizations or engage in lawful concerted activities for the purpose of collective bargaining."

However, our General Assembly did not intend for all employees to enjoy such rights. Only "educational employees," as that term is defined within Section 2(b) of the Act, were entitled to organize. Certain employees, although employed by "educational employers," were expressly denied the right to organize. Those employees were defined within Section 2(b) of the Act to include "supervisors, managerial, confidential, short term employees, student[s], and part-time academic employees of community colleges employed full or part time by an educational employer."

* * *

[T]he IELRB made the following findings of fact.

> The University of Illinois enrolls approximately 9,000 graduate students at its Urbana–Champaign campus. Of those 9,000 graduate students, about 6,000, or two-thirds, hold one or more teaching, graduate or research assistantships. As compensation, assistants receive a monthly stipend and their tuition and fees are waived. With some exceptions, to be eligible for an assistantship, an individual must be admitted and enrolled as a student. Generally, graduate students obtain assistantships by applying and being accepted into particular programs at the University. An admissions committee then attempts to match the interests and qualifications of graduate students with available positions. However, the procedure is not uniform and for some positions students are required to interview or submit a resume.
>
> There is no uniformity between assistantship positions. Some assistantships are for a period of one semester, while others may be for a period of up to one year. Some assistants are required to work 10 hours per week, while others are required to work more. Moreover, there is no uniformity in the level of responsibility, independence, supervision, and training associated with an assistantship.
>
> Generally, teaching assistants either teach classes to undergraduate students or assist faculty with discussion groups, laboratory exercises and student assignments. Although some teaching assistants work in areas related to their field of study, others do not.
>
> The duties of graduate assistants range from answering telephones to arranging research symposia. At times, their work is related to their studies; at other times, it is not.
>
> Research assistants conduct experiments, analyze data and present findings in publications or dissertations. Additionally, research assistants assist faculty in conducting studies. Usually the work of a research assistant is related to his or her field of study, although that is not always the case.

After considering the parties' arguments, the IELRB rejected the interpretation of the term "student[s]" employed by the administrative law judge, which equated enrollment with student status. The IELRB disagreed, finding the administrative law judge's analysis too simplistic. A majority of the IELRB employed what may be termed the "significant connection" test, concluding that, if an assistantship held by a graduate student is significantly connected to his or her status as a student, then he or she is a "student" within the meaning of Section 2(b) of the Act and, thus, precluded from organizing. Applying this test, the IELRB reasoned that, because all assistantships are a form of financial aid and because financial aid is given only to students, there is a significant connection between employment as a teaching assistant, graduate assistant or research assistant and the student status of the graduate students holding those assistantships. Accordingly, the IELRB held that all teaching assistants, graduate assistants and research assistants at the University of Illinois at Urbana–Champaign were "student[s]" as that term is used within Section 2(b) of the Act and, therefore, precluded from organizing.

A dissent was filed, contending the significant connection test was too broad and that teaching assistants, graduate assistants and research assistants should be considered "student[s]" within the meaning of Section 2(b) of the Act only if the primary purpose of such assistantships, as established through objective evidence, was the furtherance of their educations.

* * *

[T]he IELRB's determination is best characterized as involving a mixed question of fact and law. The IELRB's finding is in part factual, because it involved assessing the characteristics of various assistantship positions and determining whether the assistantships were significantly connected to the assistants' status as students such that they should be characterized as "student[s]" under Section 2(b) of the Act, as opposed to "educational employees." However, the IELRB's finding also concerns a question of law, because "student" is a legal term that requires interpretation. As this case involves an analysis of the legal effect of a given set of facts, it involves a mixed question of fact and law, which is reviewed under the clearly erroneous standard.

Pursuant to Section 2(b) of the Act, "student[s]" are excluded from the definition of "educational employees" and are, therefore, precluded from organizing. ILL.-SMITH-HURD ANN. 115 ILCS 5/2(b). In determining whether assistants should be characterized as students, the administrative law judge reasoned that the term "students" is commonly understood to mean those persons who are enrolled for study at a school, college or university. *Webster's Third New International Dictionary* 2268 (1993). Thus, based on the plain meaning of the term "students," the administrative law judge concluded that the assistants were properly characterized as "students" and, therefore, were not entitled to organize.

The IELRB rejected the plain meaning approach, concluding that its application conflicted with the purpose of the statute and would lead to absurd results. The IELRB reasoned that when an individual must be enrolled as a student to hold a position but the position has no relationship to the individual's status as a student, the connection between the position and the status as a student is a mere formality. Apart from this formality, the individual is indistinguishable from other employees and, in his or her role as an employee, is not, in any meaningful sense, a student.

Furthermore, the IELRB found that the adoption of a broad definition of "student" would lead to absurd results. For example, it is not uncommon for an educational employer to offer reduced tuition for employees who wish to continue their educations. Under the interpretation employed by the administrative law judge, an employee who enrolled in a class pursuant to such an offer would be deemed a "student" as that term is used within Section 2(b) of the Act and, therefore, precluded from organizing. Such a result clearly defeats the manifest purpose of the Act. For these reasons, we agree with the IELRB that the interpretation of the term "student" as one who is enrolled at a school is too broad. See 61 *Chi.-Kent L. Rev.* at 110–11.

In contrast to the administrative law judge, the majority of the IELRB interpreted the term "student[s]" within Section 2(b) of the Act to mean those graduate students whose assistantships were significantly connected to their status as students. Accordingly, the IELRB reasoned that "the term 'student' must be interpreted in relation to [an] individual's employment * * * and not to his [or] her role in any other context." Thus, mere designation of an individual as a student does not transform that individual into a student for purposes of Section 2(b) of the Act. To be characterized as a student for purposes of Section 2(b), an individual's work must be more than incidental to his or her academic duties.

The dissent contended the significant connection test was still too broad to serve the purposes of the statute and argued in favor of the primary purpose test. Under that test, only teaching assistants who are teaching to meet a degree requirement and research assistants whose work is related to their dissertation are students and, therefore, excluded from collective bargaining.

We believe the primary purpose test is too narrow and that the significant connection test, as articulated by the majority of the IELRB, avoids the distinct problems associated with an overly broad definition of the term "student." When properly applied, the significant connection test reconciles the statutory policy of creating harmonious labor relations in education with the potential risk that collective bargaining could undermine student-teacher relationships. Bargaining over issues such as job security, discipline or evaluations for positions that are peripheral to academic duties would not interfere with the educational relationship. Accordingly, the test adopted by the majority is not unreasonable or erroneous.

However, the IELRB failed to properly apply the significant connection test. To say, as the IELRB did, that an assistantship is significantly connected to the student status of an individual because it is a form of financial aid is merely a reformulation of the overly simplistic interpretation advanced by the administrative law judge and rejected by the IELRB. There is simply no difference between the administrative law judge defining students as all those who are enrolled in a school, college or university and the IELRB defining students as those receiving financial aid.

In support of its decision that receipt of payments constituting financial aid should be equated with student status, the IELRB relied on *Leland Stanford Junior University*, 214 N.L.R.B. 621 (1974) (decision and order). However, when that case is contrasted with the case at bar, the flaws in the IELRB's decision become clearly apparent. In *Leland Stanford*, the National Labor Relations Board found that all of the research assistants seeking to organize were required to engage in research as part of their course of instruction. Thus, financial aid provided graduate students a stipend for doing what was required of them to earn their degrees and, therefore, they were primarily students.

In contrast to the Stanford assistants, those assistants at the University of Illinois who are seeking to organize constitute a diverse group without universally shared characteristics. While all assistants share a desire to pursue an education and the corresponding need for financial support, the degree to which their work is related to their academic duties varies greatly. For example, research assistants usually perform work related to their dissertations or theses. However, graduate students who receive a stipend to answer phones are indistinguishable from other office workers. Therefore, we hold that the IELRB's conclusion that the receipt of financial aid is the determinative indicia of a significant connection between assistants' employment and their role as students is clearly erroneous.

Accordingly, this matter is remanded to the IELRB with directions to apply the significant connection test to the facts presented at the evidentiary hearings in a fair and thorough manner. Proper application of the test will exclude from organizing those graduate students whose work is so related to their academic roles that collective bargaining would be detrimental to the educational process. However, those individuals whose assistantships are not significantly connected to their status as students must be allowed the same statutory right to organize as other educational employees.

NOTES

1. What tests did the IELRB administrative law judge, the IELRB majority and the IERLB dissent apply to determine whether the graduate assistants were students excluded from the act's coverage? How did these tests differ?

2. How did the court and the labor board differ over application of the substantial connection test?

3. Collective bargaining rights for graduate assistants raise issues of role conflicts. How do the role conflict issues differ from those raised for attorneys? How are they the same?

4. The *Leland Stanford Jr. University* case discussed in the opinion was reversed by the NLRB. In *New York University*, 332 N.L.R.B. 1205 (2000), the Board held that graduate assistants are employees under the NLRA. However, in *Brown University*, 342 N.L.R.B. 483 (2004), the NLRB overruled *New York University* and again excluded graduate assistants from statutory coverage "[b]ecause they are first and foremost students and their status as a graduate student assistant is contingent on their continued enrollment as students

* * * '' The California Public Employee Relations Board at one time held that graduate assistants were not employees. *Association of Graduate Student Employees v. Regents of the University of California,* 13 PERC ¶ 20087 (1989). However, the PERB reversed itself in *Regents of the University of California,* 22 PERC ¶ 29,084 (1998). For further discussion of the issues see Grant M. Hayden, The University Works Because We Do: Collective Bargaining Rights for Graduate Assistants, 69 *Fordham Law Review* 1233 (2001).

6. PROFESSIONAL EMPLOYEES

Many state statutes follow the lead of the National Labor Relations Act in defining professional employees. The Illinois Public Employee Relations Act, 5 ILCS 315/3(m), definition is typical:

> "Professional employee" means any employee engaged in work predominantly intellectual and varied in character rather than routine mental, manual, mechanical or physical work; involving the consistent exercise of discretion and adjustment in its performance; of such a character that the output produced or the result accomplished cannot be standardized in relation to a given period of time; and requiring advanced knowledge in a field of science or learning customarily acquired by a prolonged course of specialized intellectual instruction and study in an institution of higher learning or a hospital, as distinguished from a general academic education or from apprenticeship or from training in the performance of routine mental, manual, or physical processes; or any employee who has completed the courses of specialized intellectual instruction and study prescribed in this subsection (m) and is performing related work under the supervision of a professional person to qualify to become a professional employee as defined in this subsection (m).

In the private sector, professional employees may not be placed in the same bargaining unit with employees who are not professionals unless a majority of the professional employees vote for such a mixed unit. Some public sector collective bargaining statutes include a similar rule, while others require a vote for the mixed unit by both the professional employees and the nonprofessional employees.

What arguments support the private sector rule? Are there any special features of the public sector that support a rule requiring a majority of *each* group to vote affirmatively for inclusion in a mixed unit? Would this rule be equally sound for the private sector?

D. THE REPRESENTATION ELECTION PROCESS

Most states follow the NLRA model and provide for the holding of representation elections and certification of a union as exclusive bargaining representative if it receives a majority of the votes in the election. There is some variation, however. For example, in Oregon, college and university professors vote separately (a) for or against representation, and (b) for the particular labor organization, if any, they wish to have represent them. If a majority votes against representation, the ballots for particular organizations are not counted. OREGON REV.STAT. § 243.686(6).

The representation process begins with the filing of a petition with the relevant labor board. Under the NLRA, a labor organization may file a representation petition if it can show substantial interest among the employees in representation by that union. The NLRB administratively interprets substantial interest to mean 30% of the employees in the bargaining unit. Unions typically make this showing with cards signed by employees authorizing the union to serve as their exclusive bargaining representative. Because the 30% showing of interest is an administrative rule of thumb, it is not subject to collateral attack by the employer. Most public sector statutes expressly require a 30% showing of interest in support of a representation petition. It could be argued in those jurisdictions that the 30% showing of interest is a statutory standard and a party may contest the petitioning union's showing. However, most states that have addressed the issue have held that the showing of interest is not subject to collateral attack. See, e.g., *Detroit Public Schools*, 1994 M.E.R.C. Lab. Op. 1047 (Mi.E.R.C. 1994). The New Jersey intermediate appellate court explained the rationale:

> Any error made in determining a "showing of interest" will be remedied by the election itself. In this case, for example, the election result—certification of the Association—discloses a strong likelihood that there was sufficient support for the union at the time the petition was filed. We acknowledge, of course, that this is not inevitably true and that employees who cast their ballots in favor of the Association may have been against the union when first confronted by the question. But measured by the election result, any error in the preliminary proceedings would be considered harmless.

City of Newark v. Association of Government Attorneys, 346 N.J.Super. 460, 788 A.2d 776 (2002).

Most jurisdictions' statutes also provide that an employer may file a representation petition when a union has demanded recognition and the employer has reason to doubt the union's claim of majority support. When a representation petition is filed, most jurisdictions allow other unions to intervene in the proceeding with a 10 or 15% showing of interest. Most jurisdictions also allow employees to file a petition to decertify an incumbent exclusive representative with a showing that at least 30% of the employees in the bargaining unit no longer wish to be represented by the union.

The NLRB has developed certain bars to the filing of a representation or decertifcation petition. The NLRB bars the filing of such a petition within one year following a valid election and within one year following certification of an exclusive bargaining representative. The Board also bars the filing of a petition when a written collective bargaining agreement of up to three years' duration is in effect, except for a window period ninety to sixty days before the contract's scheduled expiration date. When the contract expires, it may no longer bar the filing of a petition unless a new contract has taken effect.

APPEAL OF STATE EMPLOYEES' ASSOCIATION OF NEW HAMPSHIRE, INC., SEIU LOCAL 1984

Supreme Court of New Hampshire, 2009.
158 N.H. 258, 965 A.2d 1103.

DALIANIS, J.

The petitioner, the State Employees' Association of New Hampshire, Inc., SEIU, Local 1984 (SEA), appeals an order of the New Hampshire Public Employee Labor Relations Board (PELRB) denying SEA's motion to dismiss the certification petitions filed by the respondent, the New England Police Benevolent Association (NEPBA), in which NEPBA sought to represent a bargaining unit of certain officers employed by the New Hampshire Department of Corrections (DOC). In denying the motion to dismiss, the PELRB ruled that the 2007–2009 collective bargaining agreement between the State and SEA did not bar the certification petitions. *See* RSA 273–A:11, I(b) (1999). We reverse and remand.

* * * SEA has negotiated with the State on behalf of DOC employees since 1976 * * * The most recent collective bargaining agreement (CBA) between the State and SEA was executed on July 19, 2007. * * *

The State and SEA began negotiating the 2007–2009 CBA in January 2007. After more than thirty bargaining sessions, they reached a tentative oral agreement on June 14, 2007, which was reduced to a writing the following day, and finalized on or before June 20, 2007. This tentative agreement was submitted to the joint committee on employee relations for approval, *see* RSA 273–A:9 (Supp.2008), and, on June 27, 2007, its cost items were funded by the legislature, *see* RSA 273–A:3, II (1999). The tentative agreement was submitted to union members on June 22, 2007; voting on ratification closed on July 5, 2007. On July 9, 2007, NEPBA filed the instant petitions. Later that evening, SEA officials counted union member votes and certified that the tentative agreement was ratified by a vote of 1607 to 1405. On July 19, 2007, the Governor and SEA President signed the 2007–2009 CBA.

* * *

RSA 273–A:11, I(b), which governs the timing of representation elections, states:

> Public employers shall extend * * * to the exclusive representative of a bargaining unit * * * [t]he right to represent the bargaining unit exclusively and without challenge during the term of the collective bargaining agreement. Notwithstanding the foregoing, an election may be held not more than 180 nor less than 120 days prior to the

budget submission date in the year such collective bargaining agreement shall expire.

Under this provision, referred to as the "contract bar rule," a CBA bars an election for a new representative unless the election occurs "not more than 180 nor less than 120 days prior to the budget submission date in the year such collective bargaining agreement shall expire." RSA 273–A:11, I(b).

While the statutory contract bar rule concerns actual elections, the PELRB has promulgated *New Hampshire Administrative Rules,* Pub. 301.01 (Rule 301.01), which applies to certification petitions * * *

Under this rule, where, as here, an exclusive bargaining representative is in place, a certification petition may not be filed sooner than 210 days nor later than 150 days before the employer's budget submission date in the year that the agreement expires. "The purpose for creating such a window is to allow for the conduct of an orderly election and still leave sufficient time, deemed 120 days prior to the budget submission date, for the parties to negotiate a CBA. * * *

The parties' dispute centers upon the first sentence of RSA 273–A:11, I(b), which insulates a certified representative from challenge "during the term of the collective bargaining agreement." NEPBA contends that its petitions were not filed "during the term of the collective bargaining agreement," because by July 9, 2007, the 2005–2007 CBA had expired and the 2007–2009 CBA had not yet been executed. Relying upon decisions by the National Labor Relations Board (NLRB) interpreting its contract bar rule, NEPBA asserts that, for a contract to act as a bar to a certification petition, it must be signed by the parties. *See Appalachian Shale Products Co.,* 121 N.L.R.B. 1160, 1162 (1958). Because the 2007–2009 CBA was not signed until after NEPBA filed its petitions, it did not bar them.

SEA counters that, even if we assume, without deciding, that the 2005–2007 CBA expired on June 30, 2007, the 2007–2009 CBA barred the petitions because before NEPBA filed them, this CBA had been reduced to a writing, the legislature had approved legislation to fund all of its cost items, and voting on ratification had closed. Under these circumstances, SEA urges, the 2007–2009 CBA barred NEPBA's petitions.

Based upon our review of the relevant statutory scheme, construed as a whole, we hold that SEA's position best comports with the legislature's intent as expressed in the plain meaning of the pertinent statutes. We conclude, therefore, that the PELRB erred when it ruled that the 2007–2009 CBA could not act as a bar to NEPBA's petitions because the CBA had not been executed when those petitions were filed.

RSA chapter 273–A governs collective bargaining for state employees. This chapter obligates the State to negotiate with the certified representative of its employees regarding all cost items and "terms and conditions of employment affecting state employees in the classified system." RSA 273–A:9; *see* RSA 273–A:3 (1999). A cost item, as defined by RSA 273–A:1, IV

(1999), is "any benefit acquired through collective bargaining whose implementation requires an appropriation by the legislative body of the public employer with which negotiations are being conducted." Any party seeking to bargain must serve written notice of this intent at least 120 days before the State's budget submission date. *See* RSA 273–A:3, II(a). Bargaining must begin "not later than 120 days before the deadline for submission of the governor's proposed operating budget." *Id.*

Assuming that the parties reach agreement, they must then submit the cost items contained therein to the proper legislative body. RSA 273–A:3, II(b). CBAs negotiated between a public employer and the union representing its employees are unenforceable until the proper legislative body ratifies the agreement's cost items. A public employer commits an unfair labor practice by refusing to negotiate in good faith with the exclusive representative of its employees as well as by failing to submit to the legislative body any negotiated cost item. RSA 273–A:5, I(e) (1999).

The New Hampshire legislature is the legislative body that approves the cost items in CBAs affecting state employees. *See* RSA 273–A:9, V(d). The joint committee on employee relations reviews the items first and then submits recommendations to the legislature. *See* RSA 273–A:9, V. If the legislature rejects any part of the submission or takes any action that would result in modifying the terms of the cost items submitted to it, "either party may reopen negotiations on all or part of the entire agreement." RSA 273–A:3, II(b).

* * *

Nothing in this legislative scheme suggests that a CBA remains unenforceable until it is executed. While the scheme contemplates that such agreements will be signed, *see* RSA 273–A:16, it does not require that execution take place before they are enforceable. There is no requirement, for instance, that the legislature act only upon signed CBAs. *Compare* RSA 273–A:3 *with* Mass. Gen. Laws ch. 150E, § 7 (West Supp.2008). Execution, under these circumstances, is merely a ministerial act.

Given this legislative scheme, we conclude that the PELRB erred when it ruled that the 2007–2009 CBA could not bar NEPBA's petitions because it was unsigned when NEPBA filed them. The record shows that when NEPBA filed its petitions, not only was the CBA reduced to a writing, as required by RSA 273–A:4, but its cost items had been approved by the legislature, *see* RSA 273–A:3, II(b), and union members had completed voting on whether to ratify it. Under these circumstances, we hold that NEPBA's petitions were filed "during the term" of the 2007–2009 CBA, and, thus, that the 2007–2009 CBA could bar them despite the fact that it was unsigned.

NEPBA argues that the PELRB's decision is correct, in part, because it is consistent with decisions of the NLRB. * * *

Under the NLRB's contract bar rule, a contract of definite duration that is reduced to a writing and executed by the parties "will act as a bar for up to 3 years of its term to an election petition filed by an employee or rival union after the contract is executed." *City Markets,* 273 N.L.R.B. 469, 469 (1984). The NLRB, however, has established a thirty-day period during which petitions may be filed, notwithstanding the existence of a valid CBA. *See N.L.R.B. v. F & A Food Sales, Inc.,* 202 F.3d 1258, 1260 n. 1 (10th Cir.2000). Accordingly, "a valid contract not exceeding three years in duration will bar a representation election unless a petition is filed more than 60 and less than 90 days before the end of the contract." *N.L.R.B. v. Dominick's Finer Foods, Inc.,* 28 F.3d 678, 683 (7th Cir.1994). At the conclusion of this window period, "the final 60 days of [an] existing collective bargaining agreement is an 'insulated period' during which the contract bars petitions for elections." *Crompton Company, Inc.,* 260 N.L.R.B. 417, 418 (1982).

The contract bar doctrine is designed to promote stability in the collective bargaining relationship and, at the same time, afford employees a reasonable opportunity to change or eliminate their bargaining representative. *East Manufacturing Corporation,* 242 N.L.R.B. 5, 6 (1979). "Basic to the whole * * * contract-bar policy is the proposition that the delay of the right to select representatives can be justified only where stability is deemed paramount." *Paragon Products Corporation,* 134 N.L.R.B. 662, 663 (1961).

Because the NLRB's contract bar "prevents employees from freely choosing representation over a specified period" not to exceed three years, *N.L.R.B. v. Arthur Sarnow Candy Co., Inc.,* 40 F.3d 552, 557 (2d Cir. 1994), the NLRB has required that, to serve as a bar, the agreement "must contain substantial terms and conditions of employment deemed sufficient to stabilize the bargaining relationship," and be signed by the parties before a petition is filed, "even though the parties consider it properly concluded and put into effect some or all of its provisions." *Appalachian Shale Products, Co.,* 121 N.L.R.B. at 1162–63. To satisfy the signature requirement, however, "the document signed need not be a formal collective-bargaining agreement, nor must the signatures appear on the same document." *Waste Management of Maryland, Inc.,* 338 N.L.R.B. 1002, 1002 (2003). "Recognizing that parties do not always ceremonially sit down to sign a formal, final, document upon the successful conclusion of negotiations, the [NLRB] has held that informal documents laying out substantial terms and conditions of employment can serve as a bar, so long as those informal documents are signed." *Id.* at 1002–03.

The rule of *Appalachian Shale,* that only a written agreement will bar the processing of an election petition, is essentially an effort to avert the danger that unions and employers may collude to defeat employees' representational wishes on the basis of illusory or fabricated agreements." *YWCA of Western Massachusetts,* 349 N.L.R.B. 762, 764 (2007). "Requiring evidence of an executed, written agreement is designed to assure that employee rights are protected from such deception." *Id.*

Under the NLRB's contract bar rule, if a petition is filed before the execution date of a contract that is effective either immediately or retroactively and is otherwise timely, the contract subsequently entered into will not bar the processing of the petition and the holding of an election. *City Markets,* 273 N.L.R.B. at 469. If the incumbent union prevails in the election, any contract executed with the employer is valid and binding. *Id.* If, however, the incumbent union loses, the contract is null and void. *Id.* at 469–70.

Significantly, the NLRB's contract bar rule, unlike New Hampshire's contract bar rule, is not mandated by statute. Rather, it "is an administrative device early adopted by the [NLRB] in the exercise of its discretion as a means of maintaining stability of collective bargaining relationships." *Direct Press Modern Litho, Inc.,* 328 N.L.R.B. 860, 860–61 (1999) (quotation omitted). Because it is an administrative device, "[t]he [NLRB] has discretion to apply a contract bar or waive its application consistent with the facts of a given case, guided by [its] interest in stability and fairness in collective-bargaining agreements." *Id.* at 861. By contrast, the New Hampshire contract bar rule is a creature of statute, and the PELRB has no discretion to waive it. *See Appeal of State Employees' Assoc. of N.H.,* 156 N.H. at 511, 939 A.2d 209.

Given the NLRB's broad discretion to waive its own contract bar rule, including its self-imposed requirement that to act as a bar, a contract must be signed, we have no way of knowing whether, if faced with identical facts involving a private sector employer, the NLRB would have ruled as the PELRB did. We, therefore, are not persuaded that the PELRB's decision is consistent with the NLRB's jurisprudence. Had the NLRB been faced with these facts—a statutory mandate that bargaining take place within a certain time frame and that all cost items be approved by a legislative body, approval by the legislature of the legislation necessary to fund the agreement's cost items, and a written CBA which union members had already voted to ratify—it may well have waived its own contract bar rule. Under these circumstances, the interest in stability in labor relations appears to outweigh the employees' interest in a change of bargaining representative. Collusion is not an issue under these circumstances, and, thus, "the policy considerations justifying the *Appalachian Shale* rule do not arise in this case." *YWCA,* 349 N.L.R.B. at 764.

NEPBA argues as well that the PELRB's decision is correct because it is consistent with the decisions of other jurisdictions. NEPBA, however, has not directed us to any jurisdiction with a statutory scheme similar to New Hampshire's that has adopted the NLRB's requirement that a CBA be signed before it may bar a petition. To the contrary, the three jurisdictions to which NEPBA points, Maine, Massachusetts and Vermont, have statutory schemes that differ from ours.

Maine's contract bar rule, set forth by statute, *see* 26 Me.Rev.Stat. Ann. § 967(2) (West 2007), is expressly based upon the NLRB's rule. *See MSAD 16 Support Staff Assoc./MEA/NEA,* No. 00–UD–04 (M.L.R.B. Apr.

26, 2000), *at* http://janus.state.me.us/mlrb/decisions/rep/00–ud–04.htm. Thus, the fact that Maine has adopted the NLRB's signature requirement is consistent with its overall intent to mirror the NLRB's contract bar rule. *See id.*

By contrast, the Vermont contract bar rule is merely an administrative rule that the Vermont Labor Relations Board may apply or waive as the facts of a given case may demand. *See* Vt. Labor Relations Board, *Case Law Summary of Labor Relations Decisions, at* http://www.state.vt.us/vlrb/NCaseLaw_II.htm#A.

Similarly, the Massachusetts rule is an administrative rule that the Massachusetts Division of Labor Relations may waive for good cause shown. *See* 456 Code Mass. Rules § 14.06(1)(a), *available at* http:// www.lawlib.state.ma.us/456CMR14.pdf. Moreover, the statutory scheme in Massachusetts expressly requires that a public sector CBA be executed before it is submitted to the Massachusetts Labor Commission for review and to the legislature for approval of its cost items. *See* Mass. Gen. Laws ch. 150E, §§ 1, 7 (Supp.2008). Accordingly, that Massachusetts requires a collective bargaining agreement to be signed before it may act as a bar is consistent with the statutory scheme there.

Because we conclude that the PELRB erred when it ruled that the 2007–2009 CBA could not bar NEPBA's petitions because it was not signed before they were filed, we reverse its ruling and remand for further proceedings consistent with this opinion. * * *

NOTES

1. The contract bar rule results from a balancing of interests in labor relations stability against interests in protecting employee fee choice. Are there concerns that counsel for striking the balance differently in the public sector than in the private sector?

2. On what basis did the New Hampshire Supreme Court reject NEPBA's arguments based on NLRB authority? On what basis did the court reject the arguments based on other New England states' authorities?

3. Consider that collective bargaining in the public sector tends to take longer than in the private sector and that tentative agreements in the public sector often must be submitted to the employer's governing body for approval. Do these differences counsel against applying the private sector's contract bar rule? If so, in what ways?

When a representation petition is filed, the labor board investigates and if it determines that a question concerning representation exists and if the parties do not agree to such election details as the appropriate bargaining unit, conducts a hearing to resolve those issues. Once those issues are resolved, if a question concerning representation continues to exist, the labor board conducts a secret ballot election. The petitioning union, the incumbent union (if there is one), and intervening unions and the choice of "no representative" are on the ballot. If a union receives the votes of a majority of employees voting, it is certified as exclusive bargaining representative. If no representative receives a majority of the votes, that result is certified. If none of the choices garners majority support, a runoff is held between the top two vote getters.

Following the election, any interested party may file objections seeking to overturn the election outcome and obtain a new election. As mentioned in Chapter 5 § C.1, the NLRB has held that representation elections should be conducted under conditions that approximate those of a laboratory to ensure employee free choice. One of the requirements of the laboratory conditions doctrine is that the employer provide a list of employee names and home addresses for the union(s) to use in their campaign(s). This list is commonly known as the "Excelsior List," after the case in which the NLRB first adopted the requirement. *Excelsior Underwear, Inc.*, 156 N.L.R.B. 1236 (1966).

CHIEF JUDGE OF THE 11TH JUDICIAL CIRCUIT v. ILLINOIS FRATERNAL ORDER OF POLICE LABOR COUNCIL

Illinois Labor Relations Board–State Panel.
18 P.E.R.Ill. ¶ 2074 (2002).

[The Fraternal Order of Police filed a petition seeking to represent probation officers employed by the Chief Judge's Department of Court Services. On November 9, 2000, the Board's executive director notified the employer that the election was scheduled for December 7, 2000, and advised the employer to furnish a list of names and addresses of all employees eligible to vote to the Board and the union within seven days. On November 20, 2000, the employer furnished the list to the Board but not to the union. On December 4, 2000, the union's attorney notified the Board and the employer that it had not received the list of eligible voters. On December 6, the employer's attorney provided the list and offered to reschedule the election by one week to give the union additional time to campaign. The union rejected the offer. The election was held as scheduled on December 7, and the employees voted 15 to 13 against representation. The union filed objections to the election. The Administrative Law Judge held that, by its failure to seek the list sooner, the union manifested indifference to the list and that the union was not prejudiced by the employer's tardiness in providing the list.]

* * *

The sole issue in this case is whether the Employer's failure to provide the Union with a timely copy of the list of employees eligible to vote in the representation election constitutes objectionable conduct requiring the setting aside of the election results. This is an issue of first impression for the Board.

Section 9(d) of the Act is explicit in its specification of the requirements imposed upon public employers in this regard:

> Within 7 days after the Board issues its bargaining unit determination and direction of election, the public employer shall submit to the labor organization the complete names and addresses of those employ-

ees who are determined by the Board to be eligible to participate in the election.

It is clear in this case that the Employer has not fulfilled this duty. There is no question that the Employer did not provide the Union with a copy of the *Excelsior* list in a timely manner. Thus, the question here is not whether the Employer has complied with the Board's requirements, but whether its non-conformance warrants setting aside the election results.

We find the NLRB's handling of these cases instructive. The NLRB has dealt with numerous cases involving an employer's failure to submit a timely *Excelsior* list to the petitioning union and has devised a test for determining whether an employer has substantially complied with the requirements of the *Excelsior* rule. In making this determination, it considers three factors: (1) the number of days the list was overdue; (2) the number of days the union has had the list prior to the election; and (3) the number of employees eligible to vote in the election.

In applying these factors, the NLRB has come to varying results. The analysis of each case is fact-specific. Nevertheless, it appears that if the unit involved consists of more than merely a few employees, and the Union had the list only a short period of time prior to the election, the election will be overturned.

The NLRB's test serves an important policy function. It is designed to preserve the "laboratory conditions" standard for elections, as enunciated in *General Shoe Corp.*, 77 NLRB 124 (1948). That standard holds that it is the NLRB's function to provide a laboratory in which an experiment may be conducted, under conditions as nearly ideal as possible, to determine the uninhibited desires of employees. Specifically, the NLRB, in *Excelsior Underwear, Inc.*, stated:

> [W]e regard it as the Board's function to conduct elections in which employees have the opportunity to cast their ballots for or against representation under circumstances that are free not only from interference, restraint, or coercion violative of the [National Labor Relations Act, 29 U.S.C. §§ 151–169 (2000)], but also from other elements that prevent or impede a free and reasoned choice. Among the factors that undoubtedly tend to impede such a choice is lack of information with respect to one of the choices available. In other words, an employee who has had an effective opportunity to hear the arguments concerning representation is in a better position to make a more fully informed and reasonable choice. Accordingly, we think that it is appropriate for us to remove the impediment to communication to which our new rule is directed.
>
> * * *

Here, it is undisputed that the Employer provided the list to the Union approximately 20 days late, that the Union received the list only one day prior to the election and that the unit consisted of approximately

30 employees. Given that the policy behind the *Excelsior* rule is to afford unions sufficient opportunity to communicate with employees prior to an election so that all of the voters are exposed to arguments for and against unionization, an employer's actions must be sufficient to effectuate that policy. Allowing the Union in this case only one day to communicate with approximately 30 employees—on the eve of the election—is insufficient. This is particularly true because, without the list of employees' addresses, the Union had inadequate opportunity to mail any information to the employees; any mailing would have been received after the election took place and therefore would have been rendered useless. Additionally, since the election results in this case were very close, we cannot presume that the Union's attempts to communicate with employees would not have made a difference. As the Union was not afforded a reasonable opportunity to communicate with the employees prior to the election, and as the employees were not accorded the opportunity to make a free and reasoned decision, the election must be overturned due to the Employer's noncompliance with the *Excelsior* list requirement.

This result is not changed by the Employer's arguments that its failure to submit the list to the Union was inadvertent and that the Union was not, in fact, actually prejudiced by its failure. The NLRB has found that it is appropriate to presume that an employer's failure to substantially comply with the *Excelsior* requirement has a prejudicial effect on the election. Thus, the NLRB will not consider the extent to which voters actually were aware of the election, nor will it consider whether the union actually had access to the employees.

Further, the question of whether the employer's failure to substantially comply was the result of bad faith or mere inadvertence is not at issue. As the NLRB stated in a case involving an employer's omission of voters' names from the *Excelsior* list:

> Evidence of bad faith and actual prejudice is unnecessary because the rule is essentially prophylactic, i.e., the potential harm from list omissions is deemed sufficiently great to warrant a strict rule that encourages conscientious efforts to comply.

Thrifty Auto Parts, Inc., 295 NLRB 1118 (1989). Ultimately, to look beyond substantial compliance of the rule into the issue of whether employees were actually sufficiently informed about election issues would "spawn an administrative monstrosity." *Mod Interiors, Inc.*, 324 NLRB 164 (1997), *citing, Sonfarrel, Inc.*, 188 NLRB 969, 970 (1971). Therefore, even if there had been evidence in this case that the Union had an opportunity to communicate with unit employees prior to the election, that would not be a basis for dismissing the Union's objection.

Moreover, any arguments that the Union had an affirmative duty to request the list at an earlier date or to agree to postpone the election when given the opportunity by the Employer must fail. Such requirements do not exist in the Act or in the Board's Rules; rather, both place the duty to conform to the *Excelsior* list requirements squarely in the hands of employers. The NLRB has also rejected such defenses, finding that unions bear no duty to procure a list or to postpone an election after a list has not been timely provided. Specifically, regarding an employer's offer to postpone the election, the NLRB has stated, "We see no reason to require the petitioner to choose between a prompt election and an accurate *Excelsior* list when the employer's compliance with the rule would have avoided the problem in the first place." *Mod Interiors, Inc.*, 324 NLRB 164 (1997). Similarly, there is no reason here to require the Union to postpone the election after it has been the victim of the Employer's objectionable conduct. We thus conclude that the Administrative Law Judge erred in determining, first, that the Union's failure to inquire about the list earlier demonstrated that it was not prejudiced by not receiving the list, and second, that the supposed lack of prejudice was determinative of this issue. We instead conclude that the Employer's failure to provide the Union with a timely *Excelsior* list constitutes objectionable conduct that necessitates setting aside the results of the parties' December 7, 2000 representation election.

NOTES

1. What differences exist between the public and private sectors with respect to access to employees and the likelihood of aggressive employer anti-union campaigns? In light of these differences, should public sector labor boards simply adopt NLRB precedent concerning the *Excelsior* list?

2. In *Peerless Plywood Co.*, 107 N.L.R.B. 427 (1953), the NLRB held that an employer may not hold a "captive audience" meeting to encourage employees to reject union representation within 24 hours of a representation election. If it does and the union loses the election, the election is set aside and rerun. Should a similar rule apply in the public sector? See *Clovis Unified School District*, 8 P.E.R. Cal. ¶ 15,119 (Cal. P.E.R.B. 1984) (refusing to follow NLRB's per se approach and holding that effects of a captive audience presentation are to be evaluated on a case-by-case basis); *School Board of Alice County*, 10 F.P.E.R. ¶ 15216 (Fla. P.E.R.C. 1984) (same).

E. RECOGNITION WITHOUT AN ELECTION

In the private sector, the NLRA does not expressly regulate an employer's voluntary recognition of an exclusive bargaining representative. The Supreme Court has held that an employer that recognizes a labor organization as the exclusive bargaining representative at a time that the union does not enjoy the support of a majority of the employees in the bargaining unit provides unlawful support to that labor organization in violation of Section 8(a)(2) of the NLRA, 29 U.S.C. § 158(a)(2). *International Ladies' Garment Workers Union v. NLRB (Bernhard–Altmann Texas Corp.)*, 366 U.S. 731, 81 S.Ct. 1603, 6 L.Ed.2d 762 (1961). Otherwise, an employer generally is free to recognize voluntarily a labor organization that has the uncoerced, unassisted support of a majority of the employees unless and until another labor organization files a valid petition with the NLRB seeking a representation election. See *Abraham Grossman d.b.a. Bruckner Nursing Home*, 262 N.L.R.B. 955 (1982).

Many public sector jurisdictions' statutes are similarly silent concerning voluntary recognition. The Alaska Public Employment Relations Act expressly provides, "Nothing in this Chapter prohibits recognition of an organization as the exclusive representative by a public agency by mutual consent." ALASKA STAT. 23.40.100(d). On the other hand, Kansas requires a secret ballot election for a public employer to recognize a union as exclusive bargaining representative. See KAN. STAT. ANN. § 75–4327(d). Ohio (by statute) and Pennsylvania (by labor board rule) require an employer that intends to voluntarily recognize a labor organization to post notice of the proposed voluntary recognition and allow other unions to intervene and oppose the voluntary recognition. They further require the employer to submit evidence of the union's majority support to the labor board.

In the private sector, an employer may refuse or even ignore a union demand for recognition even if the union has the support of a majority of the employees in the bargaining unit. This approach essentially places the burden of filing a petition for an election on the union. See *Linden Lumber Division v. NLRB*, 419 U.S. 301, 95 S.Ct. 429, 42 L.Ed.2d 465 (1974). In Ohio, however, the burden is reversed. If a union requests recognition from an employer and supports that request with substantial evidence that a majority of employees in the bargaining unit wish to be represented by the union, the employer must either file a petition for an election with the labor board or post notice of voluntary recognition in accordance with the statutory procedure. OHIO REV. CODE § 4117.05(A)(2).

A number of states mandate recognition based on evidence of union majority support without an election. New York's Taylor Law, since its enactment in 1967, has provided for the New York PERB to:

> ascertain the public employees' choice of employee organization as their representative choice (in cases where the parties to a dispute have not agreed on the means to ascertain the choice, if any, of the employees in the unit) on the basis of dues deduction authorization and other evidences, or, if necessary, by conducting an election.

N.Y. Civil Service Law § 207(2). The New York PERB has long held that certification based on dues deduction authorization and other evidence, rather than election, is the preferred method for ascertaining employee choice. See *Town of Islip*, 8 N.Y.P.E.R.B. ¶ 3049 (N.Y.P.E.R.B. 1975). For a comprehensive discussion of the history of recognition without elections in New York see William A. Herbert, The Development and Administration of Non–Electoral Certifications in New York, 74 *Albany Law Review* ___ (forthcoming 2010).

In 2003, Illinois amended its public sector collective bargaining laws in a manner based on the New York approach. The meaning of this language came before the Illinois Supreme Court in the following case.

COUNTY OF DU PAGE v. ILLINOIS LABOR RELATIONS BOARD

Supreme Court of Illinois, 2008.
231 Ill.2d 593, 900 N.E.2d 1095, 326 Ill.Dec. 848.

FITZGERALD, C.J.

* * *

BACKGROUND

The Illinois Public Labor Relations Act (the Act) grants public employees "full freedom of association, self-organization, and designation of representatives of their own choosing for the purposes of negotiating wages, hours and other conditions of employment." 5 ILCS 315/2 (West 2004). Prior to the adoption of section 9(a–5) of the Act (see Pub. Act 93–444, eff. August 5, 2003), unless a public employee was a member of a historically recognized bargaining unit, or the public employer voluntarily recognized a labor organization as the exclusive bargaining representative for a unit of employees, the only means available for public employees to exercise their collective-bargaining rights was through a secret ballot election. See 5 ILCS 315/3(f), 9(d), (f) (West 2002). When the legislature enacted section 9(a–5), it provided public employees and labor organizations an alternative to the election process. Section 9(a–5) states:

> "The [Illinois Labor Relations] Board shall designate an exclusive representative for purposes of collective bargaining when the representative demonstrates a showing of majority interest by employees in the unit. If the parties to a dispute are without agreement on the means to ascertain the choice, if any, of employee organization as their representative, the Board shall ascertain the employees' choice of employee organization, on the basis of *dues deduction authorization and other evidence*, or, if necessary, by conducting an election. If either party provides to the Board, before the designation of a representative, clear and convincing evidence that the dues deduction authorizations, and other evidence upon which the Board would otherwise rely to ascertain the employees' choice of representative, are fraudulent or were obtained through coercion, the Board shall promptly thereafter conduct an election. The Board shall also investigate and consider a party's allegations that the dues deduction authorizations and other evidence submitted in support of a designation of representative without an election were subsequently changed, altered, withdrawn, or withheld as result of employer fraud, coercion, or any other unfair labor practice by the employer. If the Board determines that a labor organization would have had a majority interest but for an employer's fraud, coercion, or unfair labor practice, it shall designate the labor organization as an exclusive representative without conducting an election." (Emphasis added.) 5 ILCS 315/9(a–5) (West 2004).

A union seeking to be certified under section 9(a–5) must file with the Board a "majority interest petition," *i.e.*, a representation petition "accompanied by a showing of interest evidencing that a majority of the employees in the petitioned-for bargaining unit wish to be represented by the labor organization." 80 Ill. Adm.Code § 1210.80(b) (as amended at 28 Ill. Reg. 4172, eff. February 19, 2004). Under the Board's rules, the showing of interest in support of such a petition "may consist of *authorization cards, petitions, or any other evidence* that demonstrates that a majority of the employees wish to be represented by the union for the purposes of collective bargaining." (Emphasis added.) 80 Ill. Adm.Code § 1210.80(d)(2)(A) (as amended at 28 Ill. Reg. 4172, eff. February 19, 2004). The evidence of majority support must contain original, legible, signatures, which do not predate the filing of the petition by more than six months. 80 Ill. Adm.Code §§ 1210.80(d)(2)(B), (d)(2)(C), (d)(2)(D) (as amended at 28 Ill. Reg. 4172, eff. February 19, 2004). In addition, the showing of interest "shall state that by signing the card the employee acknowledges that if a majority of his/her coworkers in an appropriate unit sign evidence of majority support, the card can be used by the petitioner to obtain certification as the employees' exclusive representative without an election." 80 Ill. Adm.Code § 1210.80(d)(2)(E) (as amended at 28 Ill. Reg. 4172, eff. February 19, 2004). Evidence of majority support is not furnished to any of the parties. 80 Ill. Adm.Code § 1210.80(e)(1) (as amended at 28 Ill. Reg. 4172, eff. February 19, 2004).

The employer is required to submit signature exemplars for the employees in the proposed bargaining unit and is permitted an opportunity to respond to the petition. 80 Ill. Adm.Code §§ 1210.100(b)(2), (b)(3) (as amended at 28 Ill. Reg. 4172, eff. February 19, 2004). In addition to providing "clear and convincing evidence of any alleged fraud or coercion in obtaining majority support," the employer must set forth its "position with respect to the matters asserted in the petition, including, but not limited to, the appropriateness of the bargaining unit and, to the extent known, whether any employees sought by petitioner to be included should be excluded from the unit." 80 Ill. Adm.Code § 1210.100(b)(3) (as amended at 28 Ill. Reg. 4172, eff. February 19, 2004). "Any person aggrieved" by an order of the Board certifying a labor organization "may apply for and obtain judicial review in accordance with provisions of the Administrative Review Law directly in the Appellate Court for the district in which the aggrieved party resides or transacts business." 5 ILCS 315/9(i) (West 2004).

The present legal dispute arose out of a majority interest petition filed by [Metropolitan Alliance of Police] MAP on June 15, 2005, in case number S–RC–05–153, in which MAP sought to be certified as the exclusive representative for a unit of Du Page County deputy sheriffs. The Employer objected to the petition on several grounds. * * * The Employer argued that section 9(a–5) required the Union to submit both dues deduction authorization evidence and some other evidence of majority support, and that the Board's rules to the contrary were invalid. The

Employer also argued that it was entitled to copies of the Union's evidence and that the requested bargaining unit was inappropriate.

The Board rejected the Employer's arguments and, on March 23, 2006, certified MAP as the exclusive bargaining representative for the requested employee unit. The Board's tally indicated that 189 employees were in the unit; 111 valid cards were signed in support of MAP; no cards were found, or even alleged, to have been obtained through the use of fraud or coercion; and 14 cards were found invalid for other reasons (*e.g.*, the employee was not included in the unit, or the card was not signed or dated).

The Employer sought administrative review of the Board's decision, arguing that the word "and," as used in the statutory phrase "dues deduction authorization and other evidence" (5 ILCS 315/9(a–5) (West 2004)), should be read in its conjunctive sense, and that the Board's rules contradict the statute and are therefore invalid. The Employer also argued that the Board likely applied the invalid regulations and did not require the Union to supply both dues deduction authorization and other evidence in support of its petition. The Employer also renewed its challenge to the makeup of the bargaining unit.

* * *

The appellate court vacated the Board's decision and remanded the matter to the Board for further proceedings. 375 Ill.App.3d 765, 314 Ill.Dec. 409, 874 N.E.2d 319. The appellate court determined that both constructions of section 9(a–5) advanced by the parties were reasonable and that the statute was therefore ambiguous. 375 Ill.App.3d at 773–74, 314 Ill.Dec. 409, 874 N.E.2d 319. Ultimately, however, the appellate court agreed with the Employer: "[T]he majority interest provision requires that both dues deduction authorization and other evidence be submitted demonstrating that a majority of the employees support representation by the named organization." 375 Ill.App.3d at 776, 314 Ill.Dec. 409, 874 N.E.2d 319. The appellate court also held that because the Board's regulations only require one form of evidence to support a majority interest showing, and do not require dues deduction authorization evidence, the Board's regulations conflict with the requirements of section 9(a–5) and, therefore, are invalid. 375 Ill.App.3d at 777, 314 Ill.Dec. 409, 874 N.E.2d 319. The appellate court further held that the Board's decision on a majority interest petition is a final order, expressly subject to administrative review, and that meaningful review requires, at a minimum, that the reviewing court be able to ascertain that the evidence submitted to the Board was "the type and amount" sufficient to demonstrate a showing of interest by a majority of the eligible employees. 375 Ill.App.3d at 777–78, 314 Ill.Dec. 409, 874 N.E.2d 319. The appellate court noted that there was no evidence of record to support the Board's decision, and inferred that MAP submitted evidence in conformance with the Board's invalid regulations, rather than the requirements of section 9(a–5). Accordingly, the appellate court held that the Board's decision certifying MAP was against the manifest weight of the evidence. 375 Ill.App.3d at 778–79, 314 Ill.Dec. 409, 874 N.E.2d 319.

The appellate court also concluded that no reason existed to prohibit the Employer from reviewing the Union's evidence of majority interest, where the employees' identities are redacted. "Further, because the majority interest petition stands in lieu of an election, and to allow the meaningful review of the Board's decision, the Board must adopt some sort of regulation that provides for the submission of the evidence it relied upon to the reviewing court." 375 Ill.App.3d at 779, 314 Ill.Dec. 409, 874 N.E.2d 319. The appellate court found it unnecessary to address the Employer's contention regarding the makeup of the bargaining unit. 375 Ill.App.3d at 779, 314 Ill.Dec. 409, 874 N.E.2d 319.

* * *

ANALYSIS

* * *

I. "Dues deduction authorization and other evidence"

* * *

The Board argues that the word "and," as used in the phrase "dues deduction authorization and other evidence," when considered in the context of section 9(a–5) as a whole, should be read in the disjunctive. Under this reading, "dues deduction authorization and other evidence" establishes a range or category of evidence which will support a majority interest petition, but it does not require that the petition be supported by all such evidence. Rather, dues deduction authorization *or* other evidence, similar in kind to dues deduction authorizations, is sufficient. This interpretation is reflected in the Board's rules, which state in relevant part: "The showing of interest in support of a majority interest petition may consist of authorization cards, petitions, *or* any other evidence that demonstrates that a majority of the employees wish to be represented by the union for the purposes of collective bargaining." (Emphasis added.) 80 Ill. Adm.Code § 1210.80(d)(2)(A) (as amended at 28 Ill. Reg. 4172, eff. February 19, 2004).

* * *

The Employer argues that "and" typically "signifies and expresses the relation of addition," and thus is generally read in the conjunctive. * * *

* * *

We conclude that the basic premise underlying the Board's reading of the statute-that "and" does not necessarily mean "and"-and the basic premise underlying the Employer's reading of the statute-that "and" typically means "and"-both appear, at first blush, to be on solid ground. We conclude also that both interpretations can be harmonized, to a greater or lesser degree, with section 9(a–5) as a whole, including the "otherwise" clause. Accordingly, because section 9(a–5) is " 'capable of being understood by reasonably well-informed persons in two or more different senses,' " we deem the statute ambiguous.

To resolve this ambiguity, we turn to the legislative history of section 9(a–5), which began its life as House Bill 3396. We find instructive the statements of Senator Martin Sandoval, who spoke in support of this bill:

> Under current law, workers must go through a difficult process to form a union. Workers must first sign union authorization cards stating that they want a union. Then, even though they've already said they want a union, they must file for a Labor Board-run election. The election process can be lengthy and cumbersome, as we all know, during which time the employer has control of the employers [*sic*] and can interfere with the employees' decision. And, in fact, employers routinely use this time to scare workers into voting against a union even if the workers want a union. Solution to this problem for public employees is to allow them to vote for a union through a process called card check." 93d Ill. Gen. Assem., Senate Proceedings, May 21, 2003, at 12 (statements of Senator Sandoval).

The senator's statements indicate that the legislature intended, through its adoption of House Bill 3396, to provide an alternative to the "lengthy and cumbersome" statutory election procedure, namely, a simple "card check" procedure. We therefore cannot agree with the Employer that the legislature would have complicated the card check procedure by requiring two forms of evidence: a dues checkoff card and some other unspecified form of evidence.

Support for this conclusion is also found in the statements of Representative Larry McKeon: "House Bill 3396 is modeled after a piece of legislation in New York that simplifies the manner in which elections may be held to certify a collective bargaining agent." 93d Ill. Gen. Assem., House Proceedings, March 31, 2003, at 50 (statements of Representative McKeon).

The New York legislation to which Representative McKeon referred is section 207 of New York's Public Employees' Fair Employment Act. The New York statute requires that for purposes of resolving disputes concerning representation status, the public employees' choice of representative shall be ascertained "on the basis of dues deduction authorization *and* other evidences." (Emphasis added.) N.Y. Civ. Serv. § 207 (Consol.2008). To implement the statute, New York's labor board adopted rules requiring a majority of the employees to indicate their choice of representative "by the execution of dues deduction authorization cards which are current *or* individual designation cards." (Emphasis added.) N.Y. Comp.Codes R. & Regs. tit. 4, § 201.9(g)(1) (2008). We presume that our legislature, having modeled House Bill 3396 on the New York statute, was also aware of the corresponding administrative regulations, which were then in effect. Having adopted language that mirrors in pertinent part the language of the New York statute, we also presume that the legislature intended a similar result. The Board's reading of section 9(a–5), as reflected in its regulations, achieves that result.

* * *

We hold that the word and, as used in the phrase dues deduction authorization and other evidence, was intended by the legislature to mean or. The appellate court therefore erred in holding section 1210.80(d)(2)(A) of the Board's regulations, which do not require dues deduction authorization evidence, invalid.

* * *

II. Employer Review of Majority Interest Evidence

* * *

The Board's rules state that "[t]he Board shall maintain the confidentiality of the showing of interest," and that such evidence "shall not be furnished to any of the parties." 80 Ill. Adm.Code § 1210.80(e)(1) (as amended at 28 Ill. Reg. 4172, eff. February 19, 2004). The Board argues that if the confidentiality of the evidence of majority support is not preserved, the basic purposes of the Act will be undermined. Relying upon federal case law analyzing the National Labor Relations Act (29 U.S.C. § 151 *et seq.*), the Board contends that "employees have a strong privacy interest in their personal sentiments regarding union representation, and that this right to privacy is a right necessary to full and free exercise of the[ir] organizational rights" under the Act. *Pacific Molasses Co. v. National Labor Relations Board Regional Office #15,* 577 F.2d 1172, 1182 (5th Cir.1978). According to the Board, disclosure of authorization cards, which identify the signers, would chill the right of employees to express their union sentiments. *Pacific Molasses,* 577 F.2d at 1182; *Committee on Masonic Homes of R.W. Grand Lodge v. National Labor Relations Board,* 556 F.2d 214, 221 (3d Cir.1977). The Board notes that even the attempted discovery of union authorization cards by an employer has been deemed an "illegal objective" by the federal court of appeals. *Wright Electric, Inc. v. National Labor Relations Board,* 200 F.3d 1162, 1167 (8th Cir.2000).

* * *

[H]owever, the appellate court attempted to address the Board's confidentiality concerns. The appellate court stated:

> "We note that respondents [the Board and the Union] raise concerns over breaching the anonymity protections of the employees who might be seeking to organize union representation, and the chilling effect on unionization that review of the majority interest petition might entail. We note further, however, that petitioners [the Employer] appear to be sensitive to such concerns and have requested only that they be allowed to review such redacted evidence that demonstrates majority interest on the part of the eligible deputies while maintaining the anonymity of the deputies. We certainly see no problems in providing for some sort of review of the redacted evidence in support of a

majority interest petition. Further, because the majority interest petition stands in lieu of an election, and to allow the meaningful review of the Board's decision, the Board must adopt some sort of regulation that provides for the submission of the evidence it relied upon to the reviewing court and follows the mandates of section 9(a–5). We imagine that the submission of redacted dues authorization cards and other evidence will both preserve the employees' anonymity and allow the employer to have the same rights of review as provided in section 9(a) regarding the secret ballot election of a representative."

The Board questions the value of submitting redacted authorization cards. The Board notes that if all of the identifying information is redacted (name, signature, address, social security number, work unit), only the original preprinted card remains. Whatever the benefits, or burdens, in submitting redacted copies of the evidence of majority support, the submission of redacted evidence at least appears to address the confidentiality concerns raised by the Board.

The Board's disagreement with the appellate court opinion, however, goes beyond issues of confidentiality. The Board also disagrees with the appellate court's rationale for allowing an employer access to the evidence of majority support. The appellate court reasoned as follows. The Board's certification order is a final administrative decision and therefore subject to review by the appellate court under section 9(i) of the Act (5 ILCS 315/9(i) (West 2004)). Review must be meaningful, *i.e.,* the court must be able to ascertain that the union's evidence was the type and amount sufficient to demonstrate majority support. Therefore, the evidence of support must be submitted to the reviewing court and to the employer.

The Board argues that the appellate court's reasoning overlooks that the Act limits an employer's role in the determination of majority interest, and that except in narrow circumstances not present here, the Board's majority interest determination is not litigable. See 80 Ill. Adm.Code § 1210.80(e)(3) (as amended at 28 Ill. Reg. 4172, eff. February 19, 2004) (providing that the showing of interest shall be determined administratively by the Board and is not subject to litigation, except for cases of fraud or coercion). We understand the Board's argument to be this. If, under the Act, an employer may not challenge the Board's determination of majority status, then this is not an issue that could be raised before the Board and not an issue that could be raised on administrative review. Therefore, no need exists to submit copies of the evidence of majority support (redacted or otherwise) to the employer. In evaluating this argument, we return to the language of the Act.

Section 9(a–5) mandates that "[t]he Board shall designate an exclusive representative for purposes of collective bargaining when the representative demonstrates a showing of majority interest by employees in the unit." 5 ILCS 315/9(a–5) (West 2004). Significantly, the legislature provided for minimal involvement by the employer in this procedure. Section

9(a–5) states: "If either party provides to the Board, before the designation of a representative, clear and convincing evidence that the dues deduction authorizations, and other evidence are fraudulent or were obtained through coercion, the Board shall promptly thereafter conduct an election." 5 ILCS 315/9(a–5) (West 2004). The legislature made no other provision for the employer to involve itself in the process by which the union seeks certification under section 9(a–5), or the process by which the Board determines whether a union has established majority support under section 9(a–5). We will not assume that the legislature intended a larger role for the employer than the language of section 9(a–5) allows. We thus agree with the Board that its determination of whether a union enjoys majority support may not be litigated.

This conclusion finds support in the fact that, at the time the legislature adopted section 9(a–5), the Board's rules provided that the showing of interest under section 9(a) would be determined administratively by the Board and would not be subject to litigation. 80 Ill. Adm.Code § 1210.80(d)(3) (as amended at 27 Ill. Reg. 7393, eff. May 1, 2003). If the legislature desired a different result when it adopted section 9(a–5), it could have included appropriate language in the statute. It did not do so.

To the extent section 9(a–5) could be considered ambiguous and the legislature's intent in doubt, we would defer to the Board's reasonable construction of the statute. The Board's construction, which limits the employer's ability to challenge a finding of majority support, is consistent with the legislative history, set forth in section I *supra,* demonstrating that the General Assembly intended section 9(a–5) to limit an employer's ability to delay or interfere in the process of union recognition. See 93d Ill. Gen. Assem., Senate Proceedings, May 21, 2003, at 12 (statements of Senator Sandoval). The legislature would not have provided a streamlined "card check" procedure for union recognition on the one hand, but on the other hand provide an employer the ability to delay a certification order by allowing a fishing expedition in the union's evidence of support.

* * *

In sum, we hold that section 9(a–5) precludes an employer from litigating the Board's determination that a union enjoys majority status and, consequently, that an employer is not entitled to review the evidence of majority support. The appellate court erred in requiring the Board to make this evidence available to the employer.

* * *

NOTES

1. The court cites legislative history to the effect that the majority interest petition procedure was designed to streamline the recognition procedure and insulate it from employer interference. One study found that the union win rate in labor board elections in the public sector in Illinois approached 90%. See Martin H. Malin, *Public Sector Collective Bargaining:*

The Illinois Experience, 2 Policy Profiles No. 2 (NIU Center for Government Studies, Jan. 2002). What might this suggest about the rationale behind the legislative change?

2. How does the court view the employer's role in the certification process? Is such a limited role for the employer appropriate? Why or why not?

3. The Illinois statutes allow the certification petition to be attacked only with clear and convincing evidence of fraud or coercion in obtaining the evidence of majority support. If fraud or coercion are established, the remedy is to conduct an election. Similar provisions are commonly found in other state statutes providing for certification without an election. Do they provide sufficient protection for employee free choice? What justifications support such a limited grounds for attacking the certification petition?

4. The New York PERB rules require that a union seeking certification without an election submit a sworn declaration of authenticity attesting on personal knowledge or inquiries that the affiant has made that the cards were signed by the individuals whose names appear on them on the dates specified, that they are in fact current members of the union, and that inquiry was made as to whether they were included in any existing negotiation unit. *N.Y.P.E.R.B. Rules* § 201.4(d). During the Illinois boards' rulemaking implementing the 2003 amendments, employer representatives proposed a similar rule but the Illinois boards rejected it. What arguments can you make for and against such a rule?

5. In addition to Illinois and New York, California, New Jersey, New Hampshire, Massachusetts and Oregon have provided for certification without elections. Most states by regulation provide language that must appear on authorization cards if they are to serve as evidence of majority support, the duration for which cards will be valid (typically six months but varying from 90 days in Oregon to one year in Massachusetts) and provisions for posting a notice of a petition for certification without an election and a procedure for objections to be filed to the petition.

6. A study of majority interest petitions filed between 2003 and 2009 in Illinois, New Jersey, New York and Oregon found 1,073 orders of certification and over 1,300 petitions. The authors found only five allegations of union misconduct raised with the labor boards, none of which were sustained. Robert Bruno et al., *Majority Authorizations and Union Organizing in the Public Sector: A Four State Perspective* (May 14, 2009).

Chapter 7

Duty to Bargain

■ ■ ■

In the private sector, under the National Labor Relations Act (NLRA), it is an unfair labor practice for an employer or a union to refuse to "bargain collectively" with the other. The NLRA defines "bargain collectively" as:

> The performance of the mutual obligation * * * to meet at reasonable times and confer in good faith with respect to wages, hours, and other terms and conditions of employment, or the negotiation of an agreement, or any question arising thereunder, and the execution of a written contract incorporating any agreement reached if requested by either party, but such obligation does not compel either party to agree to a proposal or require the making of a concession.

29 U.S.C. § 158(d).

Early in the development of public sector labor law, there was considerable resistance—on the part of some public employers and lawmakers—to characterize the union-employer relationship as "collective bargaining," as that term was thought to convey an inappropriate sense of bilateralism. Some statutes used the term "consult" to convey the idea that the public entity, while open to suggestions it might hear from its employees, nevertheless retained ultimate authority to act unilaterally. Other statutes avoided the term "bargaining" but nevertheless imposed a duty to "meet and confer"—the equivalent of bargaining as defined in federal law.

Some modern statutes use the terms "meet and confer" or "consult" to refer to an obligation on the part of the public employer to listen to employee representatives with respect to the formulation of policies that lie outside the scope of mandatory bargaining. In a few states, courts have held that these terms mean something less than the traditional duty to bargain in good faith. But most statutes adopt, or have been interpreted by courts to adopt, the NLRA definition of the bargaining duty with respect to those subjects which are within the scope of mandatory bargaining. Some statutes include, within the bargaining obligation, a duty to utilize available dispute resolution procedures, such as factfinding, mediation, or advisory arbitration. This duty adds a dimension to the duty to bargain which does not exist in the private sector.

This chapter begins by explaining the difference between employer obligations under "meet and confer" rules and the traditional duty to bargain in good faith. It then explains the attempt by agencies and courts to distinguish between "surface bargaining" and "hard bargaining." Thereafter, it considers principles that have been developed to try to define more objectively what the requirement of "good faith" bargaining requires or prohibits: the ban on unilateral action prior to impasse, the duty to supply information, and other "per se" rules. Finally, it considers the effect of a collective bargaining agreement on the duty to bargain, and remedies for violation of the duty.

A. THE DUTY TO "MEET AND CONFER"

Some states impose a duty on employers (and unions) merely to "meet and confer." For example, the Missouri statute, V.A.M.S. 105.520 provides:

> Whenever * * * proposals are presented by the exclusive bargaining representative to a public body, the public body or its designated representative or representatives shall meet, confer and discuss such proposals relative to salaries and other conditions of employment of the employees of the public body with the labor organization which is the exclusive bargaining representative of its employees * * *. Upon the completion of discussions, the results shall be reduced to writing and be presented to the appropriate administrative, legislative or other governing body in the form of an ordinance, resolution, bill or other form required for adoption, modification or rejection."

In *Sumpter v. City of Moberly*, 645 S.W.2d 359, 363 (Mo. 1982), the court explained this obligation as follows: "The public employer is not required to agree but is required only to 'meet, confer and discuss' * * *. The act provides only a procedure for communication between the organization selected by public employees and their employer without requiring adoption of any agreement reached." Quoting *Curators of the University of Missouri v. Public Service Employees Local No. 45*, 520 S.W.2d 54 (Mo. banc 1975), the *Sumpter* decision explained that, "[t]he Law gives public employees the vehicle for petitioning their employer through a designated representative." When a union submits proposals, the public employer "must acknowledge such proposals and grievances and must discuss them" with the union. "[T]he public body's representative acts essentially as a hearer and a receptor of the employees' petitions and remonstrances. His duty is to discuss them with the bargaining representative * * *. The public body must then give them its consideration 'in the form of an ordinance, resolution, bill or other form required for adoption, modification or rejection.'" In sum, the law's requirements "merely provide a procedural vehicle for assertion by [a union and its members] of their constitutional rights to peaceably assemble and to petition for redress of grievances." 645 S.W.2d at 362. While *Independence National Education Association v. Independence School District*, *supra* Chapter 4, overturned part of *Sumpter*, it did not explicitly change this definition of "meet and confer" for the purposes of the Missouri statute.

In *City and Borough of Sitka v. International Brotherhood of Electrical Workers Local 1547*, 653 P.2d 332 (Alaska, 1982), the Alaska Supreme Court found a similar duty in a city charter that provided for recognizing unions and signed labor contracts, but was ambiguous as to the duty to negotiate. The court first held that "collective bargaining" was a "term of art" with significant consequences, and that such obligations should not be imposed without explicit use of that term in the statute. 653 P.2d 332, 336. Since the term was not used, the court held that the city's obligation was only to "meet and confer," an obligation which "imposes only the duty to meet at reasonable times and to discuss recommendations or proposals submitted by the employee organization." 653 P.2d at 337, n.13.

A Minnesota statute requires public employers to "meet and confer" with public employees who are "professionals." Employers must discuss matters relating to employment that are outside the scope of mandatory bargaining, but there is no further duty to bargain in good faith. MINN. STAT. ANN. §§ 179.63, 179.65, 179.73. See *Minnesota State Bd. for Community Colleges v. Knight*, 465 U.S. 271, 104 S.Ct. 1058, 79 L.Ed.2d 299 (1984) (upholding the Constitutionality of this statute), *supra* Chapter 5.

This area can be confusing, because courts are not always precise in distinguishing the terms "collective bargaining," with its accompanying duty to bargain in good faith, from the term "meet and confer," with its lesser duty. For example, in *Independence National Education Association v. Independence School District*, *supra* Chapter 4, the Court referred to the process under the Missouri "meet and confer" statute as "collective bargaining." On the other hand, some jurisdictions use the term "meet and confer" in their statutes, but require something essentially similar to the traditional duty to bargain in good faith discussed below. See, *e.g.*, *City of Phoenix v. Phoenix Employment Relations Board ex rel. AFSCME Local 2384*, 145 Ariz. 92, 699 P.2d 1323 (Ariz.App. 1985).

What policy reasons support "meet and confer" rules? What actual benefits might the parties or the public get from a such a rule? For unions, is such a provision better than nothing?

B. "SURFACE BARGAINING" v. "HARD BARGAINING"

The majority of public sector jurisdictions adopt the duty to bargain in good faith as used in the private sector, including the duty to bargain to agreement or impasse over mandatory topics of negotiation. See, *e.g.*, *In the Matter of County of Morris v. Morris Council No. 6, NJCSA, IFPTE, AFL–CIO*, 371 N.J.Super. 246, 255–56, 852 A.2d 1126, 1131–32 (N.J. Super 2004) ("[NLRA] precedents should guide our interpretation" of duty to bargain in good faith issues); *Pasco County School Board v. Florida Public Employees Relations Commission*, 353 So.2d 108, 122–26 (Fla.App. 1977) (citing private-sector precedents as good law for the duty to bargain in good faith under the Florida statute).

In such jurisdictions, one often hears employer or union representatives complain that the other party is not bargaining "in good faith." Typically what they mean is that the other party is being, in their view, unreasonably stubborn at the bargaining table. But in the face of the principle, generally recognized in the public as well as in the private sector, that the duty to bargain does not require agreement or concessions, when, if ever, can stubbornness constitute "bad faith"?

When, if ever, can a party's substantive proposals be evidence of "bad faith"? Consider the following case.

OAKLAND COMMUNITY COLLEGE AND TEAMSTERS LOCAL 241

Michigan Employment Relations Commission, 2001.
15 Mi.P.E.R. ¶ 33006.

[Teamsters Local 214 was certified in February, 1996 as the exclusive representative in a bargaining unit of approximately 1124 full-time administrative and management employees of Oakland Community College (OCC). Two years later, despite 13 sessions with a mediator, the parties had reached tentative agreement only on a few issues such as recognition, non-discrimination, work schedules, and holidays. Among other points of disagreement, the Union objected to a proposed "management rights clause" stating:

> The College also retains the sole right to manage its affairs, including but not limited to the right to plan, direct and control its operations; to determine and redetermine the location of its facilities; to decide and redecide the hours of its programs; to decide and redecide the types of services it shall provide, including the scheduling and means of providing such services, to study and/or introduce new or improved methods or facilities; to maintain order and efficiency in its departments and operations; to promulgate and repromulgate rules unilaterally or in conjunction with and consent of the Union; to hire, lay off, assign, transfer and promote employees; and to determine and redetermine the starting and quitting time, work schedules and the number of hours to be worked, the number and composition of the work force, and to determine and redetermine the qualifications of its employees, and all other rights and prerogatives including those exercised unilaterally in the past, subject only to clear and express restrictions on the exercise of these rights as provided in this Agreement.

OCC's initial proposal would have excluded all these matters from the grievance procedure. Later, it modified the proposal to allow such matters to be grieved up to the Chancellor, but not to binding arbitration. There were other areas of disagreement as well. In April 1998, the parties jointly petitioned MERC to appoint a factfinder as provided in the applicable statute calling for factfinding with recommendations. Meetings prior to formal factfinding produced agreement on additional issues, including leaves of absence, short term disability, performance evaluation, union representation, and a just cause provision. In its presentation to the factfinder, OCC stressed its need for flexibility, and maintained that because the bargaining unit was comprised of management employees, traditional union benefits and rights (such as seniority, recall or bumping rights, or dues checkoff) would not be appropriate. The factfinder's report found in favor of the Union's position on certain issues, in favor of the Employer on certain issues, and recommended further negotiations on others, including wages.

The Union indicated it was prepared to accept the recommendations of the factfinder on all issues, and submitted a package proposal. OCC, however, indicated that while it was generally pleased with the report it had objections to certain recommendations, and, after some delays, submitted to the Union a proposal on May 7, 1999, that included several items not previously presented. These included a provision mandating a minimum of 40 hours of staff development training, a provision that adjustments to individual members' wage would be made only by the Chancellor and not subject to the grievance procedure, and language providing that in the event of arbitration the parties would utilize the Commission's list of arbitrators, with the Commission choosing an arbitrator if the parties were unable to agree. Although in factfinding the Employer had proposed continuation of the policy of granting sabbatical leave to administrators and management employees, it now proposed limiting such leave to administrators. Additionally, it proposed for the first time linking the salary schedule to student enrollment.

A face-to-face meeting to discuss the two proposals was held on June 14, 1999. At that meeting, OCC declared its proposal to be its "last best offer." No agreement was reached, and two days later OCC communicated to the Union its opinion that impasse had been reached and it intended to implement its proposal unilaterally, with the exception of certain provisions favorable to the Union. Exceptions included provisions relating to probationary periods and reductions in force.

The Union, disagreeing with OCC that negotiations had reached an impasse, filed charges with the Commission, accusing OCC of bargaining in bad faith by "surface bargaining," and by acting unilaterally prior to impasse. The Administrative Law Judge (ALJ) found in favor of the Union on both counts, and the Commission affirmed. Following are excerpts from the ALJ's opinion.]

* * * In response to the Union's charge of surface bargaining, the Employer maintains that even if its proposals were "harsh," the law does not prevent either party from proposing severe language. It is true that the parties may engage in hard bargaining, and a party does not violate

PERA [Public Employee Relations Act] simply by making a proposal that the union finds undesirable. However, it has been found that under certain circumstances, the content of bargaining proposals may be a factor in determining bad faith. In *Reichhold Chemicals*, 288 N.L.R.B. 69, *aff'd in pertinent part sub nom*, *Teamsters Local 515 v. NLRB*, 906 F.2d 719 (D.C.Cir.1990), the NLRB clarified that this does not mean a determination that particular proposals are "acceptable" or "unacceptable" but whether a demand is clearly designed to frustrate agreement on a collective bargaining contract. The Board has sustained a charge of surface bargaining in circumstances where employer proposals reflect an insistence on unilateral control over virtually all significant terms and conditions of employment, in effect stripping the union of any effective method of representing its members.

The Employer justifies its stringent proposals by its asserted need for flexibility to remain competitive as an institution and maintain professionalism, seeming to imply that the scope of bargaining under PERA is limited in an institution of higher learning. Such an argument has been rejected by the Michigan Supreme Court.

Admittedly, a determination of when a party exceeds lawful hard bargaining and instead demonstrates bad faith is difficult; however, I conclude that the Employer's proposals, considered in totality, do not evidence a mind set open to compromise or a desire to reach an agreement. An examination of the Employer's proposals here, as they interrelate, demonstrates that the Employer was seeking to deny the union any effective voice in representing employees and sought to retain almost total control over working conditions. There was no recognition of traditional bargainable matters such as seniority, recall rights after a layoff, or dues checkoff. The management rights clause, combined with the Employer's vague and indefinite proposal on "realignment" and its provision on reorganization, gave the Employer complete control over all personnel actions including reorganization, reclassifications, and reassignments with no right to grieve these matters. In addition, the Employer's proposals included the unrestricted right to subcontract, layoff employees, and determine merit increases. Under the Employer's proposals, the ability to grieve employer action was severely limited, and for actions subject to the grievance procedure, only discharges or suspensions without pay could advance to arbitration. Promoted or transferred employees were required to serve a new probationary period which left them totally unprotected, subject to termination for any reason with no ability to grieve or return to their previous position. I find that the combination of all these proposals demonstrates bad faith by undermining the Union's role in representing employees and denying the Union any effective voice in jointly determining terms and conditions of employment.

In summary, I find that the record as a whole [establishes] the Employer's desire to avoid its statutory duty to bargain in good faith. The Employer failed to engage in meaningful bargaining over the factfinder's report; declared impasse when the parties were clearly not at impasse;

bypassed the bargaining agent with its wage proposal; and engaged in surface bargaining. * * * When all of these factors are considered, along with the Employer's refusal to make any meaningful concessions after the Union had repeatedly done so, I find that [the Employer's] actions were inconsistent with a sincere desire to reach an agreement and violated [its statutory duty to bargain].

NOTES

1. What does it mean to say that, under the circumstances described by the ALJ, the OCC's actions were "inconsistent with a sincere desire to reach an agreement"? Do you think the OCC was trying to avoid reaching any agreement at all? Or was it willing to reach an agreement so long as it was on OCC's terms? Should the law interfere if an economically powerful employer can achieve an agreement highly favorable to its own interest? Is the case for intervention in the bargaining process stronger or weaker in the public than in the private sector?

2. Note that the ALJ, after finding that OCC had engaged in surface bargaining, based her conclusion that OCC's actions were unlawful upon other conduct as well, including unilateral action prior to impasse. It is rare, in either the private or public sectors, for an agency or court to find a violation in surface bargaining alone.

3. As a remedy for the surface bargaining violation, the ALJ recommended an order requiring OCC to "cease and desist" from refusing to bargain in good faith, and extending the initial year of the Union's certification as bargaining representative to the date on which OCC commenced bargaining in good faith. The Commission rendered its opinion adopting the OCC's order on October 24, 2001, five and one-half years after the Union was initially certified. Who won?

While public sector law often tracks NLRA law on this issue, the context and practices of government employment can sometimes raise difficult issues, especially in tough economic times.

ASSOCIATION OF OREGON CORRECTIONS EMPLOYEES v. STATE OF OREGON, DEPARTMENT OF CORRECTIONS

Oregon Court of Appeals, 2007.
213 Or.App. 648, 164 P.3d 291.

WOLLHEIM, J.

Following the dot-com boom years of the late 1990s and the early 2000s, this state faced a serious recession. As a result of that recession, revenue to the state fell far short of previous revenue forecasts. This case arose from state employee salary freezes during the 2003–2005 biennium and involves a dispute between two labor organizations and two state agencies under the Public Employees Collective Bargaining Act (PECBA), ORS 243.650 to 243.782. The Association of Oregon Corrections Employees (AOCE) filed an unfair labor practice complaint against the Oregon Department of Corrections (DOC), and the Oregon State Police Officers' Association (OSPOA) filed an unfair labor practice complaint against the Oregon State Police (OSP). Both complaints alleged that the state agencies committed unfair labor practices during the course of negotiating new contracts. * * * The [State Labor board] dismissed the complaints, and both unions (collectively, petitioners) seek judicial review. For the reasons explained below, we affirm.

* * * When the new Governor took office in January 2003, the state was in the midst of a recession; forecasted revenues for the 2003–2005 biennium showed a budgetary shortfall of more than $1 billion. [As a result, the Governor proposed and the legislature passed a 2003–2005 budget providing that no state employee would receive either a cost-of living increase or a "step" increase based on merit or longevity.]

* * * In February 2003, the state began negotiations with the Service Employees International Union Local 503, Oregon Public Employees Association (SEIU), which represents about 65 percent of the state's employees * * * . After months of bargaining, the state and SEIU reached tentative agreement on a 2003–2005 CBA. Under the agreement, wages for bargaining unit members would be frozen for the 2003–2005 biennium. There would be no COLAs or step increases. However, each employee who worked for the state from July 1, 2003 through January 2005 would receive a one-time "workload adjustment" payment of $350.

Gary Weeks, then administrator of the Department of Administrative Services * * * spoke with Leslie Frane, the head of the SEIU bargaining unit. Frane noted that SEIU was the first union to reach agreement with the state, and she expressed concern that other unions might receive more favorable contract terms. * * * Weeks told Frane that the state would take the same position with all other unions as it had taken with SEIU and that other unions also would receive wage freezes because there was no money for COLAs or step increases. * * *

AOCE is the exclusive representative of a mixed bargaining unit of DOC employees. In January 2003, AOCE and DOC began negotiations for a new CBA * * * .

AOCE and DOC did not reach voluntary agreement, and the matter proceeded to mediation and then arbitration. * * *

Ultimately, the arbitrator selected DOC's last best offer. With respect to the parties' negotiations over the 2003–2005 CBA, the board found:

> * * * AOCE and DOC offered concessions on a variety of proposals and exchanged counterproposals on a number of subjects. As part of this process, DOC proposed increases in health insurance, an adjustment to the pay differential received by certain non-security employees, and a choice for each employee between accepting a one-time 'workload adjustment' payment of $350 or accepting additional leave. During the negotiations process, the parties reached agreement on a

number of contract articles and proposals and signed off on these agreements.

OSPOA is the exclusive representative of a mixed bargaining unit of OSP employees. Its bargaining history regarding the 2003–2005 CBA with OSP largely paralleled AOCE's experience with DOC. * * *

On judicial review, petitioners argue that * * * the board erred in concluding that the state did not engage in so-called surface bargaining in violation of the duty to bargain in good faith imposed by ORS 243.672(1)(e). * * *

Under ORS 243.672(1)(e), it is an unlawful labor practice for a public employer to "[r]efuse to bargain collectively in good faith with the exclusive representative." Surface bargaining has been described as "going through the motions of negotiating, without any real intent to reach an agreement. It violates the [NLRA]'s requirement that parties negotiate in good faith." *K–Mart Corp. v. NLRB*, 626 F.2d 704, 706 (9th Cir. 1980).[2]

According to petitioners, "[a]ny time an employer makes a deal with a bargaining unit that no other bargaining unit will receive a better economic package it commits a *per se* violation of its duty to bargain in good faith with the other units." In petitioners' view, once the state promised SEIU that no other bargaining unit would get a better deal than it had gotten, the state's negotiations with petitioners were—as a matter of law—not conducted in good faith. Petitioners go on to argue that, even if the state's behavior did not constitute a *per se* violation of the duty to bargain in good faith, under the "totality-of-conduct" standard applied by the board, the state did not bargain in good faith.

The state responds that it was budget constraints, not the promise to SEIU, that dictated the state's position in bargaining with petitioners. In light of the state constitutional requirement of a balanced budget and the economic conditions at the time, the state asserts, the legislature could not have intended that the duty to bargain in good faith precluded the state from taking the positions that it did. "[I]n enacting ORS 243.672(1)(e)," the state contends, "the legislature could not have intended that the state's decision during collective bargaining to remain within the funds available would constitute a *per se* violation of the duty to bargain in good faith." Finally, the state argues, under the board's "totality-of-conduct" standard, the state's actions did not amount to a failure to bargain in good faith. As did the board, we agree with the state.

* * * In *Olney School Dist. 11 v. Olney Education Assn.*, 145 Or.App. 578, 582–83, 931 P.2d 804 (1997), we described our standard of review: "By using the phrase 'bargain collectively in good faith with the exclusive

---

2. In *Portland Assn. Teachers v. Mult. Sch. Dist. No. 1*, 171 Or.App. 616, 631 n. 6, 16 P.3d 1189 (2000), we explained:

> Oregon's Public Employees Collective Bargaining Act (PECBA), including ORS 243.672, was adopted to model the National Labor Relations Act * * *. We therefore may look to cases decided under the federal act-and particularly to cases decided before 1973, the year in which PECBA was adopted-for guidance in interpreting PECBA.

representative,' in ORS 243.672(1)(e), the legislature expressed a general legislative policy and delegated to [the board] the responsibility to complete that policy by specifying what constitutes bargaining collectively in good faith.'' * * * In this case, we defer—as we consistently have—to the board's methodology for determining whether parties have bargained in good faith. * * *

The board's case law interpreting that provision posits two categories of violations of the duty to bargain in good faith. The first is a *per se* violation, premised on the idea that some conduct is "so inimical to the bargaining process that it amounts to a *per se* violation of the duty to bargain in good faith." Examples of conduct that the board has concluded amounts to a *per se* violation include (1) an employer's unilateral implementation of a change in a mandatory subject of bargaining; (2) submitting a new proposal at the mediation stage; and (3) submitting a new proposal in a final offer.

The second way in which any party may violate its duty to bargain in good faith is where "the totality of that party's conduct during the period of negotiations * * * indicates an unwillingness on the part of the charged party to reach a negotiated agreement." *School Employees Local Union 140 v. School District No. 1, Multnomah County,* 20 PECBR 420, 431 (2003). In its order in this case, the board explained how it applies that test:

> In applying this 'totality-of-conduct' standard, this Board analyzes the following factors to determine whether an employer's conduct indicates an unwillingness to reach agreement: (1) dilatory tactics—whether the employer used tactics that unreasonably impeded negotiation; (2) contents of the proposals—whether the employer made unduly harsh or unreasonable proposals; (3) behavior of the spokesperson—whether the negotiator's behavior was extremely discourteous; (4) concessions—whether the employer made some 'reasonable effort' to settle differences with the union; (5) failure to explain bargaining positions—whether the employer adequately explained its proposals; and (6) course of negotiations—whether the employer 'rushes through the negotiation process mandated by the PECBA,' demonstrating a lack of serious intention to reach agreement.

Petitioners argued to the board that the state's conduct—in promising SEIU that no other union would receive a better contract offer than SEIU received—was a *per se* violation of the duty to bargain in good faith. The board, describing the state's promise to SEIU as a kind of "reverse parity clause," rejected petitioners' argument. On appeal, petitioners reiterate their argument, asserting that the state's "actions should be seen as similar to a refusal to meet and confer and should be found a *per se* violation of the duty to bargain in good faith." In response, the state argues:

In light of the constitutional balanced-budget requirement, and the intent stated in ORS 291.232(1),[5] the legislature could not have intended that where it deliberately includes no money in the budget for cost-of-living or step increases, a state agency's decision to stand firm in collective bargaining and not grant such increases constitutes a *per se* violation of the duty to bargain in good faith. Such a construction would mean that, by complying with ORS 291.232(1)—electing to spend moneys appropriated in accordance with the legislatively adopted budget and the agency's enabling statutes—an agency would, **as a matter of law,** violate ORS 243.672(1)(e).

We agree with that analysis and reject petitioners' argument that the state's conduct was a *per se* violation of the good faith bargaining requirement. We turn, accordingly, to petitioners' alternative argument that the state's actions constituted a failure to bargain in good faith under the board's totality-of-conduct test.

Applying the three relevant factors from its six-factor test—contents of the proposals, concessions, and course of the negotiations—the board concluded that the state had not violated the good faith bargaining requirement by refusing to budge on the salary freeze issue. The board reasoned that, although the state's wage freeze proposals were "obviously unacceptable" to petitioners, those salary freeze proposals must be viewed in the totality of the circumstances surrounding the negotiations—specifically, the budget constraints under which the state was operating. And viewing the content of the salary freeze proposals, the board concluded that the state's harsh position was not a refusal to bargain in good faith. We agree. Given the economic hand it was dealt, the state's wage freeze proposals cannot be said to have been "unduly harsh or unreasonable."

Regarding the second relevant factor—any concessions—the board found, as set out above, that all parties offered concessions on a variety of proposals and exchanged counterproposals on a number of subjects. And some concessions ultimately were made. For example, DOC agreed to provide fully paid health insurance benefits for 2004 and agreed to provide each employee with a choice of a $350 "workload adjustment" payment or paid leave. OSP made similar concessions regarding the workload adjustment and health insurance. In short, although the state never wavered in its position that it could not afford to provide COLAs and step increases, the state made concessions where it could. That factor, like the first, does

5. ORS 291.232(1) provides:

It is declared to be the policy and intent of the Legislative Assembly that:

(a) The legislatively adopted or approved budget for a state agency constitutes a determination by the Legislative Assembly of the amount needed by the agency for the biennium to meet the responsibilities imposed on the agency through the budget and through statutes governing the agency; and

(b) Except as provided in subsections (2) and (3) of this section, appropriations from the General Fund to a state agency constitute a direction to the agency to spend the amount of moneys appropriated in order to meet the responsibilities imposed on the agency through the budget and through statutes governing the agency.

not support petitioners' argument that the state refused to bargain in good faith.

Finally, examination of the course of the negotiations between the state and petitioners establishes that the state did not rush through the negotiation process mandated by PECBA, "demonstrating a lack of a serious intention to reach agreement." The board found that AOCE and DOC "participated in seven collective bargaining sessions between January 22 and June 24, 2003" and at least four mediation sessions, findings that AOCE does not challenge on review. Similarly, OSPOA and OSP participated in a number of collective bargaining and mediation sessions. As noted above, the last best offers by the state differed from its initial proposals. PECBA's definition of "collective bargaining" notes: "The obligation to meet and negotiate does not compel either party to agree to a proposal or require the making of a concession." ORS 243.650(4). The state met regularly with petitioners, made concessions, and agreed to some of petitioners' proposals. * * *

Looking at the course of negotiations, the nature of the state's proposals (in light of the strict budgetary constraints under which it was operating), and the concessions made by the state, we conclude that the state did not violate its duty under ORS 243.672(1)(e) to bargain in good faith by insisting on a salary freeze like that agreed to by SEIU.[6]

In summary, the board did not err in concluding that the state's hard-line bargaining position regarding the 2003–2005 CBAs was dictated, not by a promise made to SEIU, but by the real budgetary constraints facing the state in difficult economic times * * * . Affirmed.

NOTES

1. Here the state legislature passed a statute barring certain forms of pay increases. Is this a reasonable but probably unusual act designed to help address difficult economic times? Or should unions be concerned that this could be a precedent for other acts by state governors that will greatly vitiate the ability of unions to negotiate wages?

2. *Association of Oregon Corrections Employees* refers to "parity clauses," a practice which has raised duty to bargain issues. A "parity" clause requires an employer and a union to enter into the same or similar terms to which the employer and a different union have agreed. For example, a contract between a city and its firefighters union would provide that wage increases for firefighters will be the same percentage as the percentage wage increase the city negotiates with its police union. One advantage to such clauses is that it limits jealousy and competition among different categories of city employees in different bargaining units. Also, smaller bargaining units

6. Regarding the other factors, the parties stipulated that no party engaged in dilatory tactics; that, during the course of the negotiations, the parties "behaved appropriately and professionally towards each other"; and that the parties "engaged in a reasonable period of negotiations, a reasonable number of mediation sessions * * * and following mediation continued to negotiate up to interest arbitration."

that negotiate parity clauses with larger units may benefit from the greater bargaining power of the larger unit. But these clauses raise a legal issue: is the union used to set the parity (*e.g.*, the police union in the above example) unfairly burdened in its bargaining? Note that if the employer gives a raise to the police union in the preceding example, it would also be obligated to give a similar raise to the firefighters.

In some jurisdictions, parity agreements constitute a *per se* violation of the duty to bargain in good faith. *Local 1650, IAFF v. City of Augusta*, No. 04–14 (Me.L.R.B. Aug. 10, 2004) held that "parity agreements are inherently destructive of collective bargaining rights and are therefore a *per se* violation of [the public sector labor statute]." The Maine Board reasoned that parity clauses subvert the bargaining process by burdening the bargaining agent and making it unable to fully avail itself of the opportunities granted by the state statute.

Other jurisdictions take a case-by-case approach. In *Whatcom County Deputy Sheriff's Guild v. Whatcom County*, Decision 8512–A (PECB 2005), the Washington Public Employment Relations Commission held that parity clauses are not *per se* violations of the duty to bargain in good faith. Instead, in any given case, the charging party has the burden of proving that the parity clause did in fact burden its negotiations. And in the instant case, the party did not meet that burden. For a similar holding, see *TWU Local 106 and New York City Transit Auth.*, 39 NY PERB ¶ 3021 (2006).

C. THE BAN ON UNILATERAL ACTION PRIOR TO IMPASSE

One aspect of the duty to bargain under the NLRA is that an employer may not unilaterally institute changes regarding matters which are subjects of mandatory bargaining without first consulting the recognized union. While discussions are still underway, and prior to an "impasse" in negotiations, implementing a unilateral change is an unfair labor practice. In *NLRB v. Katz*, 369 U.S. 736, 82 S.Ct. 1107, 8 L.Ed.2d 230 (1962), the Supreme Court explained the reason for that rule:

> Clearly the duty [to bargain] may be violated without a general failure of subjective good faith; for there is no occasion to consider the issue of good faith if a party has refused even to negotiate *in fact*—'to meet * * * and confer'—about any of the mandatory subjects. * * * We hold that an employer's unilateral change in conditions of employment under negotiation is similarly a violation of Section 8(a)(5), for it is circumvention of the duty to negotiate which frustrates the objectives of Section 8(a)(5) much as does a flat refusal.

In principle, the ban on unilateral action applies to unions as well, though it is rare that a union will be in a position to institute a unilateral change in working conditions.

The *Katz* principle has been adopted in the public sector by courts in most jurisdictions. See, *e.g.*, *Detroit Transportation Corporation and Teamsters Local 214*, 20 MPER ¶ 112 (Mich. Emp. Rel. Comm. 2007) (neither side may take a unilateral action on a mandatory topic absent impasse, citing *Katz*); *Union of American Physicians & Dentists v. State of California*, 30 PERC ¶ 142 (Cal. PERB ALJ 2006) (same); *Rockford Education Association and Rockford School District 205*, 21 PERI ¶ 179 (Ill. ELRB ALJ 2005) (same).

But the application of this rule raises certain problems. One of these is the definition of "impasse." Impasse does not occur simply because one party repeatedly rejects the position of the other. Neither does it require a complete cessation of negotiations, since the parties remain under a continuing duty to bargain. It occurs when, despite good faith bargaining on both sides, there is a deadlock such that, for the time being at least, further bargaining seems futile. It is an imprecise concept at best, requiring fact-specific judgments on the part of the agency or court. In the public sector, the problem is complicated by the existence of mandated dispute resolution procedures—factfinding, mediation, and sometimes arbitration. How do these procedures figure into the definition of "impasse"?

MOUNTAIN VALLEY EDUCATION ASSOCIATION v. MAINE SCHOOL ADMINISTRATIVE DISTRICT NO. 43

Maine Supreme Judicial Court, 1995.
655 A.2d 348.

WATHEN, C.J.

The [Education] Association and the Maine School Administrative District No. 43 (SAD 43) began negotiations in June 1990 for an initial contract for the benefit of a combined unit of teacher aides and assistants. The negotiations were long and arduous, with the parties participating in three mediation sessions and in factfinding. Thereafter, the parties submitted several issues including wages, health insurance, and duration of the contract to arbitration. Following a hearing, the arbitration panel issued a report on July 9, 1992 making nonbinding recommendations on wages, retirement payment, and health insurance, but imposing a two-year duration of contract for the school years 1991–92 and 1992–93.

In September of 1992, SAD 43 sent a proposal on wages and insurance to the Association. The terms were an improvement over those previously proposed by SAD 43 but not in complete accord with the arbitrators' recommendations. The parties met, but the Association rejected the offer and made counterproposals. In November of 1992, SAD 43 notified the Association of its last best offer on wages and insurance. The Association immediately filed for mediation. SAD 43 thereafter implemented its wage and insurance proposals.

The Association filed a prohibited practice complaint with the Board alleging that SAD 43 had violated the Act [Municipal Public Employees Labor Relations Law, 26 MAINE REV.STAT.ANN. §§ 961–974] by unilaterally implementing its proposal on wages and insurance and by failing to observe the arbitrators' binding determination on the duration of the agreement. The Board ruled that SAD 43 committed no violation of the Act by unilaterally imposing its wage and insurance proposals. It held that SAD 43 did violate the Act by refusing to implement the binding arbitration award on the duration of the agreement. The Association * * * filed a petition for review of final agency action. The Superior Court affirmed the Board's order. The Association now appeals.

I. Unilateral Implementation of Last Best Offer Following Impasse

* * * In order to support the bargaining process and prevent it from being circumvented or disparaged, federal law has long been interpreted to prevent either party from unilaterally changing wages, hours, or working conditions. * * * Thus, while bargaining, and before impasse, a private employer is prevented from "going over the head" of the bargaining agent by unilaterally increasing or decreasing wages. The parties are required to maintain the *status quo* while bargaining, and this principle applies both to negotiations before an initial contract and to post-expiration negotiations for a new contract. Here, in Maine, the Board adopted the rule against unilateral changes with respect to public sector bargaining, and we have upheld the Board's use of this rule.

In 1978, the Board adopted from federal labor law the impasse exception to the rule against unilateral change. The exception allows a party to unilaterally implement its last best offer when negotiations have reached a *bona fide* impasse. Once the parties have in good faith exhausted the prospects of reaching an agreement, unilateral change that is reasonably comprehended within the pre-impasse proposals no longer violates the Act. After impasse, however, the duty to bargain is not extinguished. Rather it is temporarily suspended until changed circumstances indicated that the parties are no longer deadlocked.

Notwithstanding the similarities with federal law, Maine law differs in at least one respect—impasse cannot occur until specified forms of intervention have been exhausted. Public employees in Maine, unlike employees in the private sector, do not have the right to strike or engage in work stoppages. Having eliminated the most common form of impasse resolution procedure, Maine law adds to the definition of good-faith bargaining the obligation to participate in mediating, factfinding, and arbitration procedures. 26 MAINE REV.STAT.ANN. § 965(1)(E). These "peaceful" third party intervention procedures are intended as substitutes for strikes and work stoppages and are designed to provide escalating pressure on both parties to produce a voluntary settlement. * * * The final step, arbitration, is binding on all issues except the important subjects of wages, insurance, and pensions, for which it is advisory only. This diluted form of arbitration brings pressure to bear on the employer, while preserving for public officials the prerogatives of public management, fiscal control, and lawmaking. * * * In recognition of Maine's unique scheme of statutory procedures, the Board ruled in 1989 that, absent extraordinary circumstances, it would thereafter find that an employer's implementation of a last best offer prior to completion of requested impasse resolution procedures to constitute a *per se* violation of the obligation to bargain in good faith. * * * The issue in the present case is whether, following completion of these procedures, and after impasse, the Act permits an employer to unilaterally impose its last best offer. We find no error in the Board's construction of the statutory duty to bargain in good faith.

[The Association argued that in light of the availability of binding arbitration through mutual consent, parties rejecting that option should be obliged to continue to maintain the *status quo* pending agreement. The Court rejected that argument, observing that the statute precludes binding arbitration for wages, salaries, and insurance.]

The Association next argues that a unilateral change, even if made after exhaustion of the statutory procedures, frustrates the Act's policy that "neither side should be compelled to agree to a proposal or be required to make a concession." Along the same lines, the Association contends that if the Board cannot impose wage terms on parties under its remedial authority, *Caribou Sch. Dep't v. Caribou Teachers Ass'n*, 402 A.2d 1279 (Me.1979), neither can SAD 43 impose concessions on its employees without their agreement. In *Caribou,* we found that the Board, by ordering retroactive payment of wage and benefit increases, was making a contract for the parties, something that it did not have the authority to do. The Association confuses the making of a contract with the unilateral implementation of a last best offer during a period in which no contract exists. * * * The Association has neither been compelled to agree to SAD 43's proposal, nor, by receiving less of an increase than it sought, has it been required to make concessions within the meaning of the Act. Rather, the effect of the unilateral increase after impasse is to create a new *status quo* from which the parties must bargain once the duty to bargain is no longer dormant. Although labor relations in the public sector differ from those in the private sector, there is nothing to suggest that the Legislature intended to reject the impasse doctrine as a *quid pro quo* for the denial of the right to strike. The Board's longstanding reliance on the rule against unilateral change, and the impasse exception to that rule, constitutes a rational adaption of private sector labor law and serves the goals set forth in the Act.

[Portions of the Court's opinion dealing with other issues and the dissenting opinion of LIPEZ, J. are omitted.]

NOTES

1. The Association seemed to argue that, in the absence of a right to strike, there should be no impasse exception to the ban on unilateral action. As a matter of policy, does that argument have any merit?

2. In jurisdictions with mandatory impasse procedures, the general rule is that the employer may not implement proposals on mandatory topics at impasse until completing the impasse procedures. In *Moreno Valley Unified*

School District v. Public Employment Relations Board, 142 Cal.App.3d 191, 191 Cal.Rptr. 60 (Cal.App. 1983), the court rejected the employer's argument that this approach "failed to distinguish between pre-impasse bargaining and statutory impasse procedures" available under the state public sector statute, the EERA. 142 Cal.App.3d at 198. Quoting the state labor board's decision with approval, the court explained:

> 'The assumption of unilateral control over the employment relationship prior to exhaustion of the impasse procedures frustrates the EERA's purpose of achieving mutual agreement in exactly the same ways that such conduct frustrates that purpose when it occurs at an earlier point. * * * The impasse procedures of EERA contemplate a continuation of the bilateral negotiations process. Mediation remains fundamentally a bargaining process, albeit with the assistance of a neutral third party.' (*Moreno Valley Educators Assn.* v. Moreno Valley Unified School Dist., *supra*, PERB Dec. No. 206, pp. 4–5.)
>
> The Board's conclusion that impasse under the EERA is, unlike NLRA impasse, a continuation of mutual dispute resolution efforts and not a signal that economic pressure tactics may begin, is a reasonable interpretation of the statutory scheme. * * *

3. What if a jurisdiction using this approach—that an employer cannot unilaterally implement a change in a mandatory term of bargaining until completing statutory impasse procedures—also had a statutory impasse procedure that required certain unions and employers to engage in mandatory, binding arbitration if agreement could not otherwise be reached? Could the employer *ever* unilaterally impose the change in a mandatory term?

4. Most states that allow public employees to strike follow the NLRA model, allowing the employer to implement proposals unilaterally at impasse. The Pennsylvania courts have adopted a different rule, unique to the public sector: an employer may not make a unilateral change in a mandatory subject even if the parties are at an impasse, so long as the union does not strike. *Philadelphia Housing Authority v. Pennsylvania Labor Relations Board*, 153 Pa.Cmwlth. 20, 620 A.2d 594 (1993). What are the arguments for and against this solution?

5. To the extent that a public employer is obliged to maintain the "status quo" pending impasse, how should that state of affairs be defined? The next case addresses that question.

BOARD OF TRUSTEES OF THE UNIVERSITY OF MAINE SYSTEM v. ASSOCIATED COLT STAFF

Maine Supreme Judicial Court, 1995.
659 A.2d 842.

CLIFFORD, J.

The Associated COLT Staff of the University of Maine System (ACSUM) and the Maine Labor Relations Board (Board) appeal from a judgment of the Superior Court vacating the Board's decision that the

University of Maine System (University) breached its duty to bargain in good faith by discontinuing the annual step increase in wages included as a wage provision in the collective bargaining agreement that had expired. The requirement to bargain and negotiate in good faith includes the obligation to maintain the status quo following the expiration of a contract. Applying a "dynamic" status quo rule that it had adopted after the contract had been entered into, the Board imposed on the University a duty to continue paying to its employees the annual step increases in wages included in the expired agreement. The Board concluded that the failure of the University to do so constituted a unilateral change in the status quo prohibited under the law. Beyond the particular unfairness of the application of the dynamic status quo rule retroactively to the facts of this case, such application requires the University to pay wage increases not collectively bargained for and not approved by the University, and thus violates the letter and spirit of the Public Employee Labor Relations Law. Accordingly, we affirm the Superior Court.

The University and ACSUM had a collective bargaining agreement of three years' duration, commencing in 1989, and expiring on June 30, 1992. The agreement contained separate wage scales with an across-the-board increase for each year of the contract. The wage schedule for each year was divided into wage bands for different levels of employment, and each band included six to eight steps based on seniority. The agreement provided that on each of the anniversary dates of the agreement, employees would advance from one lettered step to the next and receive the specified increase in wages. When the agreement expired, the University adhered to the last wage schedule, and discontinued the annual step increases, except as they applied to promotions.

In December 1992, ACSUM filed a prohibited practice complaint with the Board, alleging that the University violated the University of Maine System Labor Relations Act, 26 MAINE REV.STAT.ANN. §§ 1021–1035 (1988 & Supp. 1994). After a hearing, the Board ruled that the discontinuance of the payment of salary step increases after the expiration of the collective bargaining agreement constituted a unilateral change in the conditions of employment in violation of the University's duty to bargain pursuant to 26 MAINE REV.STAT.ANN. § 1027(1)(A) and (E). The Board ordered the University to continue to advance each employee one step higher on the existing wage scale annually, until the parties agree otherwise or bargain in good faith to impasse. In addition, the Board ordered the University to reimburse employees for the wages and interest lost as a result of the delay in granting the first increase following the expiration of the contract. The University filed a petition for review of final agency action with the Superior Court pursuant to 26 MAINE REV.STAT.ANN. § 1029(7) and M.R. CIV.P. § 80C. The Superior Court concluded that the Board's decision was "an improper imposition into the substance of collective bargaining processes" and vacated the Board's decision. This appeal by the Board and ACSUM followed.

Pursuant to the University of Maine System Labor Relations Act, the University is required to bargain and negotiate in good faith. That requirement includes the obligation to maintain the status quo following the expiration of a contract. See *Lane v. Board of Directors of M.S.A.D. No. 8*, 447 A.2d 806 (Me.1982) (employer may not unilaterally alter terms and conditions of employment after expiration of collective bargaining agreement).

The definition of status quo at the expiration of the collective bargaining agreement is at the crux of this case. Until 1991, the Board had construed status quo to mean that wages existent at the expiration of a collective bargaining agreement were frozen. In doing so, the Board rejected the notion that increases in wages scheduled in the expired contract should be extended beyond the expiration of that contract. *M.S.A.D. No. 43 Teachers' Ass'n v. M.S.A.D. No. 43 Bd. of Directors*, 432 A.2d 395 (Me.1981). In *M.S.A.D. No. 43*, we agreed that the application of a static status quo rule to collective bargaining was appropriate. "To say that the status quo must be maintained during negotiations is one thing; to say that the status quo includes a change and means automatic increases in salary is another. * * * The matter of increments can be negotiated and, if it is agreed that such increments can and should be paid, provision can be made for payment retroactively." Quoting *Board of Coop. Educ. Servs. v. New York State Pub. Employment Relations Bd.*, 41 N.Y.2d 753, 395 N.Y.S.2d 439, 363 N.E.2d 1174 (1977).

In 1991, the Board reversed its previous position and adopted what is known as the dynamic status quo rule, thereby requiring public employers to pay their employees any annual step increases in wages included in an agreement that expired. * * * To apply the dynamic status quo rule to the circumstances of this case, and require the University to pay increases in wages in an expired collective bargaining agreement that was negotiated at a time when the Board was applying a different status quo rule is particularly unfair. The parties negotiated this contract with the understanding that during any interim period following the expiration of the contract, wages would be frozen and maintained at the level existing on the date of expiration. The Board's subsequent departure from many years of precedent disregards the parties' reliance on the prior rule, and places on the University the burden of funding wage increases not budgeted for. * * *

Beyond the unfairness of the dynamic status quo rule's application in this case, however, is its contravention of the statutory language and the legislative history of Maine's public employment labor relations law. The very section imposing the duty to negotiate in good faith, and thus to maintain the status quo when a contract expires, provides "except that by such obligation [to negotiate] neither party shall be compelled to agree to a proposal or be required to make a concession." 26 MAINE REV.STAT.ANN. § 1026(1)(C). The payment of wages can have an "enormous impact" on the University's budget, * * * and constitutes a substantial concession by the University in direct contravention of the prohibition contained in

Section 1026(1)(C). *Caribou Sch. Dep't v. Caribou Teachers Ass'n*, 402 A.2d 1279 (Me.1979) (Board has no authority to impose duty on public employer to pay wage increases not agreed to); see also *Appeal of Milton Sch. Dist.*, 137 N.H. 240, 625 A.2d 1056 (1993) (Board has no authority to require district to pay "cost items" not approved by town).

Other provisions in the statute make clear that the Legislature was careful to protect the public fisc from wage increases that were neither bargained for nor approved by the public employer. Although the law provides for binding arbitration as the preferred method of settling disputes when negotiation fails, the Legislature specifically excluded salaries, pensions, and insurance from binding arbitration. Arbitrators may only recommend, and not bind the parties, as to salaries and pensions in Maine. * * * Contrary to this proposition, however, the Board effectively has constrained the University to accept an increase in salaries.

The static status quo rule is consistent with the Legislature's clearly expressed intent to protect municipal and state agency budgets from increases in wages imposed without agreement by the governing body. The recently adopted dynamic status quo rule, on the other hand, obligates the University to pay substantial increases in wages not approved by its trustees, and dramatically alters the status and bargaining positions of the parties. It changes, rather than maintains, the status quo.

Although the dynamic status quo rule may be utilized in private sector labor law, and in some public sector labor law, its adoption by the Board is contrary to the intent of Maine's public employer labor statute as expressed in its plain language and history. Accordingly, deference to the Board's newfound construction is not warranted.

Judgment affirmed.

WATHEN, C.J., joined by GLASSMAN and LIPEZ, JJ., dissenting:

* * * I reject the Court's conclusion that the Board's adoption of the "dynamic rule" is inconsistent with the intent, plain language, and history of Maine's public sector labor law. I respectfully dissent.

I. Authority of the Board

The initial question before us relates to the Board's statutory authority to find that a change in the conditions of employment occurred when the University unilaterally discontinued the existing schedule of annual step increases. The Board has consistently tracked private sector labor law in ruling that the duty to confer and negotiate in good faith imposes an ancillary duty to maintain the status quo during negotiations until a new agreement is reached, or impasse occurs.

In 1979, in *Easton Teachers Ass'n v. Easton Sch. Comm.*, No. 79–14, at 7 (Me. L.R.B. Mar. 13, 1979) the Board first applied the "static status quo" rule to post-expiration wages. Under this rule, the status quo is maintained after contract expiration by freezing wages at the level they were when the contract expired. The Board expressly noted in *Easton* that it preferred a static view of the status quo as opposed to the dynamic view. Shortly thereafter, however, in a case involving the University, the Board refused to apply the "static" rule to a wage dispute during negotiations for an initial contract, instead adopting the "dynamic" rule for this situation. *Teamsters Local Union No. 48 v. University of Me.*, No. 79–08 (Me. L.R.B. June 29, 1979), *appeal dismissed for lack of prosecution*, No. CV–79–406 (Me.Super.Ct., Ken.Cty., Dec. 30, 1981). The Board explained the reasons for this different treatment. First, in the pre-contract period, there "could be no understanding or agreement on a termination date at which point wage levels might be frozen in the future." Second, the Board pointed out that it can take years to negotiate an initial contract, and employers could enjoy a windfall if automatic wage escalator provisions could be terminated on certification of a bargaining agent.

In 1991, two years before the decision in this case, the Board reversed itself completely and adopted the "dynamic" rule for post-expiration wages. The Board offered the following explanation: "Why should the terms and conditions in a contract provision, however it is drafted, be frozen upon contract expiration for health insurance and other terms and conditions of employment, but not when that contract provision contains a wage escalator? After careful consideration, we conclude that *Easton* must be overturned, to the extent that it treats wage escalator provisions of an expired contract differently than it treats other provisions. We find the following principle, stated in *Easton* itself, to be a sound approach to the issue of maintaining the status quo, which principles should be applied consistently. In essence, there is no difference between collective bargaining for an initial agreement, during which all existing terms and conditions of employment are frozen until proposed changes have been fully negotiated, and collective bargaining for subsequent agreements, during which existing terms and conditions of employment (as embodied in a prior agreement) are again frozen until proposed changes have been fully negotiated. *Auburn Sch. Adm'rs Ass'n v. Auburn Sch. Comm.*, No. 91–19, at 20–21 (Me.L.R.B. Oct. 8, 1991), *consolidated appeals dismissed per stipulation*, No. CV–91–459 and –464 (Me.Super.Ct., And.Cty., Apr. 24, 1992)."

The new "dynamic" rule is in accord with pre-contract wage treatment and also with the Board's treatment of health insurance. Consistent with the "dynamic" rule applied in *Teamsters* and *Auburn*, the Board noted in the present case that "it is the wage provision that is frozen, not wages themselves."

The University challenges the Board's decision and argues that the parties agreed to freeze wages at the expiration of the agreement pending a successor agreement, "because that was the law [in 1989] when the Agreement was executed." Although, for purposes of constitutional analysis, we have held that contracts are subject to statutes in effect when the contracts are entered into, there is no authority for the proposition that a contract silently incorporates all existing administrative decisions on matters that could have been dealt with expressly. When it executed the agreement, the University may have assumed that the "static" rule would prevail on expiration, but that assumption was dispelled before the agreement expired, and is secured neither in contract nor law. Moreover, the unfairness that the Court finds compelling in this case could have been addressed in the original agreement or could have been the subject of bargaining before the expiration of the agreement.

I reject the University's contention that the Board's order compels the University to implement a wage increase that it never agreed to, in violation of 26 MAINE REV.STAT.ANN. § 1026(1)(C) ("neither party is compelled to agree to a proposal or required to make a concession") and our holding in *Caribou Sch. Dep't v. Caribou Teachers' Ass'n*, 402 A.2d 1279 (Me.1979) (finding that the Board, by ordering retroactive payment of wage and benefit increases, was making a contract for the parties, which the Board did not have the authority to do). In a similar vein, the University argues that requiring it to pay higher wages after the agreement expired effectively extends the contract term beyond the three-year limit provided in 26 MAINE REV.STAT.ANN. § 1026(1)(D). The Act limits the term of a collective bargaining agreement to three years, but it places no specific time limit on the duty to bargain. The preservation of the status quo is an attribute of bargaining in good faith, and it results in neither an agreement nor a concession. As is well stated by the Associated COLT Staff, the Board has no authority to determine what the parties should be bargaining toward (the final terms of an agreement) but it is empowered to determine what the parties should be bargaining from (the existing terms and conditions of employment).

I disagree with the opinion of the Court that the Board's adoption of the "dynamic" rule is plainly inconsistent with the provisions of the Act. The rule is fashioned from a comparable rule in private sector labor law, see Robert A. Gorman, *Basic Text on Labor Law, Unionization and Collective Bargaining* (1976), and refines the prohibition against unilateral change that is universally recognized in both the private and public sector. The specific application of the "dynamic" rule in public employment to wage provisions in an expired contract is supported by court and agency decisions in other states.[6] In my view, the Board acted well within its statutory authority.

---

6. See *Vienna Sch. Dist. No. 55 v. Illinois Educ. Labor Relations Bd.*, 162 Ill.App.3d 503, 113 Ill.Dec. 667, 515 N.E.2d 476 (1987); *Board of Educ. of Springfield Pub. Sch. v. Springfield Educ. Ass'n*, 47 Ill.App.3d 193, 5 Ill.Dec. 374, 361 N.E.2d 697 (1977); *Indiana Educ. Employment Relations Bd. v. Mill Creek Classroom Teachers Ass'n*, 456 N.E.2d 709 (Ind.1983); *Wayne County Gov't Bar Ass'n v. County of Wayne*, 169 Mich.App. 480, 426 N.W.2d 750 (1988); *Local 1467, Int'l Ass'n of Firefighters v. City of Portage*, 134 Mich.App. 466, 352 N.W.2d 284 (1984); *West Cent. Educ. Ass'n v. WERC*, No. 87CV257 (Cir.Ct.Wis. Apr. 22, 1988); *California Sch. Employees Ass'n v. Davis Unified Sch. Dist.*, 4 Pub. Employee Rep. (Cal ed.) (Lab. Rel. Press) ¶ 11031 (Cal.Pub. Empl. Rel. Bd. Feb. 22, 1980); *International Ass'n* of *Firefighters Local 2416 v. City of Cocoa*, No. CA–88–014, 11 Nat'l Pub. Empl. Rep. (Lab.Rel.Press) FL–19311 (Fla.Pub. Employees Rel. Comm'n Oct. 17, 1988).

The New Hampshire Supreme Court, however, has applied the "static" rule to wage step increases in public employment. See *Appeal of Milton Sch. Dist.*, 137 N.H. 240, 625 A.2d 1056 (1993). Interestingly, the dissent in that opinion would have found the step increases to be part of the status quo to be maintained. The Pennsylvania Supreme Court also has applied the "static"

II. Fiscal Concerns

Underlying the Court's opinion and running throughout the argument of the University and the brief filed by the Maine School Boards Association as amicus curiae is the policy argument articulated by the Superior Court—the Board should not be permitted to require a public employer "caught in difficult economic times to continue to increase wages at rates agreed to when times were better." * * * Implicit within the Superior Court's ruling is the argument that the Board is improperly infringing on "governmental authority and the accountability of public employers to the taxpayer and citizenry." * * * It is true that the Legislature carefully preserved the power of the public employer not to agree. *Mountain Valley Educ. Ass'n v. Maine School Administrative Dist. No. 43*, 655 A.2d 348 (1995). But it is equally true that the same Legislature imposed the duty to bargain, and it is that duty that the Board has interpreted to require the preservation of existing practices until impasse. * * *

Unquestionably there are significant fiscal implications involved when a public employer is required to continue a past practice set forth in an expired wage provision or health care plan while bargaining for a new contract. There is a meaningful legal difference, however, between compelling an agreement, and preserving the status quo while the parties are bargaining. * * * It is this distinction that the Act compels.

In an effort to balance the bargaining relationship, the Legislature replaced the right to strike and engage in work stoppages with mediation, factfinding, and arbitration. See 26 MAINE REV.STAT. ANN. § 1026. In public sector employment, impasse cannot occur until those procedures have been exhausted. *Mountain Valley*, 655 A.2d at 352. If impasse occurs, however, either party is free to institute unilateral change. It is conceivable that, in a particular case, before reaching impasse the parties may face a delay that exceeds the length of any contract that might be considered. The impasse procedures mandated by the Legislature necessarily involve delay. Obviously, the financial consequences resulting from the combination of delay and the requirement of preserving the status quo, whether dynamic or static, are most pronounced in time of financial crisis. In my view, however, such policy concerns are properly matters for legislative consideration rather than a judicially-crafted hardship exception to the duty to bargain. See Stephen F. Befort, *Public Sector Bargaining:Fiscal Crisis and Unilateral Change*, 69 Minn.L.Rev. 1221 (1985) (Public sector bargaining is not "an aberration that need be tolerated only when convenient or when its results are not too painful.").

I would vacate the judgment and remand with instructions to enter an order affirming the decision of the Board.

---

rule to public employment wage increases. However, that case arose in the context of unemployment compensation claims, not a prohibited practice complaint. *Fairview Sch. Dist. v. Commonwealth of Pennsylvania Unemployment Compensation Bd. of Review*, 499 Pa. 539, 454 A.2d 517 (1982).

NOTES

1. Who has the better of this debate? The "dynamic status quo" rule is adopted by most state courts, as the citations in the footnote to the dissenting opinion indicate. Does the rule alter the dynamics of bargaining in favor of public employees? Does the opposite ("static status quo" rule) adopted by some jurisdictions tip the balance in favor of public employers?

2. Does the public sector context provide additional reasons for the "static" rule, as opposed to the "dynamic" rule used in the private sector? A more recent case adopting the (minority) static rule stressed that "there are fundamental distinctions between public and private employers * * * public employers conduct their operations using public money and so face unique budgetary pressures." *Pennsylvania State Park Officers Association v. Pennsylvania Labor Relations Board*, 854 A.2d 674, 684 (Pa. Commw. 2004). Is that convincing in general (private employers face financial difficulties of their own), and is it a good reason to use a different rule defining "status quo" than that used in the private sector? For further thoughts on this issue, see STEVEN J. SCOTT, *The Status Quo Doctrine: An Application to Salary Step Increases for Teachers*, Note, 83 CORNELL L. REV. 194 (1997).

3. The dynamic status quo rule is sometimes referred to as the *Triborough* doctrine, after a 1977 New York State Public Employment Relations Board case involving the Triborough Bridge and Tunnel Authority, 5 N.Y.P.E.R.B. ¶ 4505, *aff'd*, 5 N.Y.P.E.R.B. 3037 (1972). The New York State Legislature later codified the Board's decision into law. NEW YORK-MCKINNEY'S. CIVIL SERVICE LAW § 209–a.1(e), but with this difference: while the PERB's rule applied only to *mandatory* subjects of bargaining, the statute requires continuance of *all* the terms of an expired agreement until a new agreement is reached. The failure of the codification to distinguish between permissive and mandatory subjects may create problems when it comes to the resolution of impasses through interest arbitration.

4. In a state which has the "dynamic status quo" rule, how could a public employer avoid its application? See *Suffolk County and Faculty Association of Suffolk County Community College*, 18 N.Y.P.E.R.B. ¶ 3030 (1985) (enforcing terms of agreement to that effect).

5. Suppose a public employer has a long-standing practice, accepted by the Union representing its employees, of giving merit increases each year to certain employees the employer considers to have done an outstanding job. At the conclusion of the current contract, and while negotiations are in progress, would it be an unfair labor practice for the employer to continue that practice? To discontinue it?

D. THE DUTY TO SUPPLY INFORMATION AND OTHER "PER SE" RULES

In addition to the general obligation to bargain in "good faith," and the obligation to refrain from unilateral change without bargaining, the duty to bargain typically is interpreted to impose certain specific obligations upon the public entity and the union. For example, while breach of the agreement is ordinarily not an unfair labor practice, and is therefore subject to remediation through arbitration or court action, the Illinois Local Labor Relations Board has held that a "public employer violates the statutory duty to bargain in good faith when it repudiates a clear and undisputed grievance settlement agreement." *AFSCME Council 31 and County of Cook*, 13 P.E.R. Ill. ¶ 3005 (Ill.Loc.L.R.B.1997). Similarly, while acknowledging that contract ratification procedures are exclusively an internal union matter, the Michigan Employment Relations Commission has held that a union violates its duty to bargain by failing to schedule a ratification vote until more than six weeks after reaching a tentative agreement with the public employer. *Teamsters Local 214 and City of Portage*, 11 Mi.P.E.R. ¶ 29034 (1998).

The most important specific obligation, however, is the employer's duty to supply information the union requires to fulfill its bargaining obligation. In *California Faculty Association v. Trustees of the California State University*, 28 Pub. Emp. Rptr. for Cal. ¶ 75 (Cal. PERC 2004), the California Commission noted that "the failure to provide necessary and relevant information is a *per se* violation of the duty to bargain in good faith." This duty to provide information is statutory and not dependent on a labor contract. *Id.*; *Town of Evans*, 37 NY PERB ¶ 3016 (NY PERB 2004). Also, this obligation extends beyond the negotiation of the agreement to the handling of grievances, as discussed in the following case.

INTERNATIONAL UNION OF OPERATING ENGINEERS LOCAL 49 v. CITY OF MINNEAPOLIS

Minnesota Supreme Court, 1975.
305 Minn. 364, 233 N.W.2d 748.

MACLAUGHLIN, J.

This dispute arises out of the administration of a civil service examination for the position of foreman of equipment repair for the Department of Public Works of the city of Minneapolis. Applicants for the position were judged on the basis of oral and written examinations and on the basis of an efficiency rating and a seniority rating. After the results of the examination were released, several complaints were received regarding the content of the written examination. On July 2, 1973, respondent, upon appeal to the Minneapolis Civil Service Commission, raised several questions concerning the examination, including allegations that some of the designated answers to the examination questions were incorrect and that many of the employees who took the examination had been rated by supervisors under whom they had either not worked or had not worked for a substantial period. Respondent appeared at an October 11, 1973, meeting of the Civil Service Commission, at which it requested copies of all questions and answers to the examination and a list of the supervisors who had rated the applicants, together with information detailing when and for how long each applicant had worked for the supervisor making the rating. At a meeting on October 23, 1973, the Civil Service Commission admitted that they had credited incorrect answers for some questions and that there was more than one correct answer for other questions. At that meeting it was agreed that respondent would be supplied with copies of 11 examination questions protested by individual employees who had taken the examination, together with the correct answers. The city also identified the supervisors who rated the employees.

On November 8, 1973, the Civil Service Commission refused to supply respondent with (1) the remaining examination questions and the answers to those questions; and (2) information as to when and for how long each employee had worked for the supervisor who had rated his performance. Respondent sought a writ of mandamus requiring appellant to supply the requested information. The district court issued an order granting respondent's request, and appellant has appealed to this court. We affirm.

* * *

In interpreting provisions of the PELRA [Public Employee Labor Relations Act], it is often instructive to refer to decisions interpreting the National Labor Relations Act (NLRA). Under the NLRA, the duty to bargain collectively is defined as "the performance of the mutual obligation of the employer and the representative of the employees to meet at reasonable times and confer in good faith with respect to wages, hours, and other terms and conditions of employment." The obligation to meet and confer in good faith includes the obligation to honor a good-faith request by a union to furnish the union with the information necessary to the union's intelligent functioning as a collective bargaining agent. If the employer refuses to supply requested information and that refusal materially hampers the union, the employer is guilty of an unfair labor practice. See, e.g., *NLRB v. Acme Industrial Co.*, 385 U.S. 432, 87 S.Ct. 565, 17 L.Ed.2d 495 (1967); *NLRB v. Truitt Mfg. Co.*, 351 U.S. 149, 76 S.Ct. 753, 100 L.Ed. 1027 (1956). The scope of the duty extends to information peculiarly accessible to the employer and peculiarly inaccessible to the union. And this duty extends beyond the negotiation stages and applies to grievances and labor management relations during the term of the agreement. *NLRB v. C & C Plywood Corp.*, 385 U.S. 421, 87 S.Ct. 559, 17 L.Ed.2d 486 (1967); Annotation, 2 A.L.R.3d 880. Promotions are considered mandatory subjects of bargaining under the NLRA, and thus information regarding promotions must be furnished to unions under the NLRA. See, e.g., *U.S. Gypsum Co.,* 94 N.L.R.B. 112 (1951). The same rationale has been applied to collective bargaining regarding aptitude testing in NLRA cases. See, e.g., *American Gilsonite Co.*, 122 N.L.R.B. 1006 (1959).

We are, of course, not bound by these decisions. The NLRA governs private sector employment while the PELRA governs public sector employment. * * * In enacting the PELRA, the legislature declared that "(i)t is the public policy of this state and the purpose of (the PELRA) to promote orderly and constructive relationships between all public employers and their employees * * * ." § 179.61. This policy can only be fulfilled if the duty to meet and negotiate is meaningful. We therefore conclude that it was the intent of the legislature that the duty to meet and negotiate in good faith includes the obligation to provide that information which is necessary to intelligent functioning in the bargaining process. But this right is not unqualified. The legislature has directed that the purpose of promoting orderly and constructive relationships between all public employers and their employees is "subject * * * to the paramount right of the citizens of this state to keep inviolate the guarantees for their health, education, safety and welfare." § 179.61.

With these principles in mind, we now turn to the question of whether or not the particular information requested by respondent must be divulged by appellant. Respondent's first request is for the questions and the answer key to the civil service examination. Respondent is challenging the validity of this examination; and for that purpose a review of the entire examination, including the questions and answer key, is essential if respondent is to effectively and intelligently represent the interests of the involved employees. On the other hand, civil service examinations are intended to be used more than once so that the cost of administering the civil service system can be kept at a minimum. Appellant argues that if respondent is allowed access to the questions and answer key the examination can then only be used effectively once, causing an increase in cost to the Civil Service Commission. While this is a legitimate concern, we feel that the public interest in protecting the confidentiality of civil service examinations can be adequately served if respondent is directed to refrain from disclosing the requested information to applicants who will take this examination in the future. Upon oral argument, respondent agreed that it would comply with such a direction. Therefore, we affirm the trial court's decision ordering appellant to divulge the questions and answer key, but direct that respondent respect the need for the confidentiality of this information.

Respondent's second request is for information indicating when and for how long each employee had worked for the supervisor who had rated his performance. This information is clearly relevant to the dispute in so far as it challenges the validity of the efficiency rating given to each applicant; and without the information it will be difficult, if not impossible, for respondent to intelligently challenge individual efficiency ratings. We are aware of no public interest to be served by keeping this information confidential, and we therefore hold that the trial court acted correctly in ordering appellant to divulge this information.

Appellant argues that any provision of a contract required by the PELRA which conflicts with the rules of the Civil Commission must be made consistent with those rules. Appellant claims that since it has already distributed to respondent all the information that is required to be distributed under the rules, it cannot be required to turn over any more information. Appellant argues [on the basis of language in the PERLA deferring to city charters] that rules of the Minneapolis Civil Service Commission are enacted pursuant to authority vested in the Civil Service

Commission by the charter of the city of Minneapolis, and that these rules have the force and effect of statutory law and, therefore, have priority over the provisions of the PELRA. If we accept this argument, any contract provision contrary to a civil service rule would be void and of no effect. We cannot agree that the legislature intended such a result, and we therefore reject appellant's arguments. The rules of the Civil Service Commission are not statutes and, at least for the purpose of our interpretation of the meaning of the terms as used in Section 179.66, subd. 5, are not rules or regulations promulgated pursuant to statute, or ordinances or resolutions adopted pursuant to a home rule charter. As a result, the issue of whether or not appellant is required to turn over the questions and answer key is unaffected by Section 179.66, subd. 5.

Appellant also argues that all matters relating to selection of personnel for promotion are exempt from the scope of the PELRA, basing the argument on Section 179.66, subd. 1, which excepts from mandatory negotiation "matters of inherent managerial policy." This argument does not apply to the issue in this case, however. Appellant is correct in stating that the decision to administer competitive examinations is not subject to negotiation. However, this dispute does not concern the question of the propriety of using competitive examinations. Rather it relates to the fairness of a specific given examination, and as such it is a dispute involving terms and conditions of employment and subject to negotiation under the PELRA and not a matter of inherent managerial policy. Therefore, the duty to supply information clearly applies.

Appellant contends that the Minneapolis Civil Service Commission is not a public employer within the meaning of the PELRA. We disagree. Section 179.63, subd. 4, in so far as it is relevant, defines a public employer as the State of Minnesota and its political subdivisions and any agency or instrumentality of either. The appellant Civil Service Board is clearly an agency or instrumentality of appellant city. [The remainder of the court's opinion, discussing other issues, is omitted].

NOTES

1. In *Detroit Edison Co. v. NLRB,* 440 U.S. 301, 99 S.Ct. 1123, 59 L.Ed.2d 333 (1979), the Supreme Court held (1) that an employer should *not* be required to furnish directly to a union tests and answer sheets used for promotion because of the risk of disclosure, the Board's order barring the Union from disclosing them being judged inadequate; and (2) that the employer should not be required to disclose individual test scores, absent consent from the examinees, when to do so would breach the company's promise of confidentiality. Is that case distinguishable from *Operating Engineers Local 49*?

2. Compare *Department of Defense v. FLRA*, 510 U.S. 487, 114 S.Ct. 1006, 127 L.Ed.2d 325 (1994) (holding that disclosure of home addresses of federal civil service employees pursuant to a request by their collective bargaining representative would constitute a "clearly unwarranted invasion"

of the employees' personal privacy within the meaning of the Freedom of Information Act, 5 U.S.C. § 552). Also, *Michigan Federation of Teachers v. University of Michigan*, 481 Mich. 657, 753 N.W.2d 28 (Mich. 2008), citing *Department of Defense v. FLRA*, held that the home addresses and telephone numbers of the employees of a state university are not subject to disclosure under the Michigan Freedom of Information Act.

3. Most public-sector jurisdictions, however, follow the private-sector rule that home addresses are subject to the duty to provide information. See, *e.g.*, *Morris County v. Morris Council No. 6*, 30 NJPER 93 (N.J. Sup.Ct. App. Div. 2004) (employer violated the New Jersey statute by refusing to disclose employee home addresses to unions); *California School Employees Association v. Bakersfield City School District*, 22 PERC ¶ 29089 (Cal. PERB 1998) (employer violated its bargaining obligation by refusing to provide a union with an updated list of employee home addresses and phone numbers). Which is the better rule? Is the public sector context a sufficient reason to use a different rule than that used in the private sector?

E. THE DUTY TO BARGAIN DURING THE LIFE OF THE AGREEMENT

In the private sector, the duty to bargain over mandatory subjects does not end with the formation of the collective bargaining agreement. The duty continues during the life of the agreement, but its contours are shaped by negotiating history, the language of the agreement, and the manner in which the issue arises. The duty to bargain may be waived, for example, through discussion in negotiations, or by contractual language, but a distinction is made between union-instituted negotiations over new matters and unilateral action by an employer: the NLRB and the courts are more likely to find a waiver of the right to bargain when the issue is whether the employer must bargain over some new union proposal advanced during the term of the agreement than when the issue is whether the employer must bargain before making a unilateral change in working conditions. Often, for example, contracts will contain "zipper clauses," declaring that each side waives the right to bargain with respect to any subject matter not specifically referred to or covered by the agreement, and such clauses may be sufficient to constitute a defense to a demand by a union that the employer bargains over some new proposal, but are likely to be insufficient as a defense to unilateral action, absent some more specific language. In the following case, the Supreme Court grappled with the issue of midterm modification under the federal public employment statute.

NATIONAL FEDERATION OF FEDERAL EMPLOYEES v. DEPARTMENT OF INTERIOR

United States Supreme Court, 1999.
526 U.S. 86, 119 S.Ct. 1003, 143 L.Ed.2d 171.

BREYER, J. delivered the opinion of the Court.

The Federal Service Labor–Management Relations Statute requires federal agencies and the unions that represent their employees to "meet and negotiate in good faith for the purposes of arriving at a collective bargaining agreement." 5 U.S.C. § 7114(a)(4). We here consider whether that duty to bargain extends to a clause proposed by a union that would bind the parties to bargain midterm—that is, while the basic comprehensive labor contract is in effect—about subjects not included in that basic contract. We vacate a lower court holding that the statutory duty to bargain does not encompass midterm bargaining (or bargaining about midterm bargaining). We conclude that the Statute delegates to the Federal Labor Relations Authority the legal power to determine whether the parties must engage in midterm bargaining (or bargaining about that matter). We remand these cases so that the Authority may exercise that power.

I.

Congress enacted the Federal Service Labor–Management Relations Statute (Statute or FSLMRS) in 1978 [also known as Title VII of the Civil Service Reform Act of 1987]. See 5 U.S.C. § 7101 et seq. Declaring that "labor organizations and collective bargaining in the civil service are in the public interest," § 7101(a), the Statute grants federal agency employees the right to organize, provides for collective bargaining, and defines various unfair labor practices. See §§ 7114(a)(1), 7116. It creates the Federal Labor Relations Authority, which it makes responsible for implementing the Statute through the exercise of broad adjudicatory, policymaking, and rulemaking powers. §§ 7104, 7105. And it establishes within the Authority a Federal Service Impasses Panel, to which it grants the power to resolve negotiation impasses through compulsory arbitration, § 7119, hence without the strikes that the law forbids to federal employees, § 7116(b)(7).

Of particular relevance here, the Statute requires a federal agency employer to "meet" with the employees' collective-bargaining representative and to "negotiate in good faith for the purposes of arriving at a collective bargaining agreement." § 7114(a)(4). The Courts of Appeals disagree about whether, or the extent to which, this good-faith-bargaining requirement extends to midterm bargaining. Suppose, for example, that the federal agency and the union negotiate a basic 5–year contract. In the third year a matter arises that the contract does not address. If the union seeks negotiations about the matter, does the Statute require the agency to bargain then and there, or can the agency wait for basic contract renewal negotiations? Does it matter whether the basic contract itself contains a "zipper clause" expressly forbidding such bargaining? Does it matter whether the basic contract itself contains a clause expressly permitting midterm bargaining? Can the parties insist upon bargaining endterm (that is, during the negotiations over adopting or renewing a basic labor contract) about whether to include one or the other such clauses in the basic contract itself?

In 1985 the Authority began to answer some of these questions. It considered a union's effort to force midterm negotiations about a matter the basic labor contract did not address, and it held that the Statute did not require the agency to bargain. *Internal Revenue Service*, 17 F.L.R.A. 731 (1985) (*IRS I*). The Court of Appeals for the District of Columbia Circuit, however, set aside the Authority's ruling. The court held that in light of the intent and purpose of the Statute, it must be read to require midterm bargaining, inasmuch as it did not create any distinction between bargaining at the end of a labor contract's term and bargaining during that term. *National Treasury Employees Union v. FLRA*, 810 F.2d 295 (1987) (*NTEU*). On remand the Authority reversed its earlier position. *Internal Revenue Service*, 29 F.L.R.A. 162 (1987) (*IRS II*). Accepting the D.C. Circuit's analysis, the Authority held: "[T]he duty to bargain in good faith imposed by the Statute requires an agency to bargain during the term of a collective bargaining agreement on negotiable union-initiated proposals concerning matters which are not addressed in the [basic] agreement and were not clearly and unmistakably waived by the union during negotiation of the agreement."

The Fourth Circuit has taken a different view of the matter. It has held that "union-initiated midterm bargaining is not required by the statute and would undermine the congressional policies underlying the statute." *Social Security Administration v. FLRA*, 956 F.2d 1280 (4th Cir.1992) *(SSA)*. Nor, in its view, may the basic labor contract itself impose a midterm bargaining duty upon the parties. *Department of Energy v. FLRA*, 106 F.3d 1158 (4th Cir.1997) (holding unlawful a midterm bargaining clause that the Federal Service Impasses Panel had imposed upon the parties' basic labor contract).

In the present suit, the National Federation of Federal Employees, Local 1309 (Union), representing employees of the United States Geological Survey, a subagency of the Department of the Interior (Agency), proposed including in the basic labor contract a midterm bargaining provision that said: "The Union may request and the Employer will be obliged to negotiate [midterm] on any negotiable matters not covered by the provisions of this [basic] agreement." The Agency, relying on the Fourth Circuit's view that the Statute prohibits such a provision, refused to accept, or to bargain about, the proposed clause. The Authority, reiterating its own (and the D.C. Circuit's) contrary view, held that the Agency's refusal to bargain amounted to an unfair labor practice. The Statute itself, said the Authority, imposes an obligation to engage in midterm bargaining-an obligation that the proposed clause only reiterates.

And even if such an obligation did not exist under the Statute, the Authority added, a proposal to create a contractual obligation to bargain midterm is a fit subject for endterm negotiation. Consequently, the Authority ordered the Agency to bargain over the proposed clause.

The Fourth Circuit set aside the Authority's order. *United States Dept. of Interior v. Federal Labor Relations Authority*, 132 F.3d 157 (4th Cir.1997). The court reiterated its own view that the Statute itself does not impose any midterm bargaining duty. That being so, it concluded, the parties should not be required to bargain endterm about including a clause that would require bargaining midterm. The court reasoned that once bargaining over such a clause began, the employer would have no choice but to accept the clause. Were the employer not to do so (by bargaining to impasse over the proposed clause), the Federal Service Impasses Panel would then inevitably insert the clause over the employer's objection, as the Impasses Panel (like the D.C. Circuit) believes that a midterm bargaining clause would merely reiterate the duty to bargain midterm that the Statute itself imposes. We granted certiorari to consider the conflicting views of the Circuits.

II.

We shall focus primarily upon the basic question that divided the Circuits: Does the Statute itself impose a duty to bargain during the term of an existing labor contract? The Fourth Circuit thought that the Statute did not impose a duty to bargain midterm and that the matter was sufficiently clear to warrant judicial rejection of the contrary view of the agency charged with the Statute's administration. We do not agree with the Fourth Circuit, for we find the Statute's language sufficiently ambiguous or open on the point as to require judicial deference to reasonable interpretation or elaboration by the agency charged with its execution.

The D.C. Circuit, the Fourth Circuit, and the Authority all agree that the Statute itself does not expressly address union-initiated midterm bargaining. The Statute's relevant language simply says that federal agency employer and union representative "shall meet and negotiate in good faith for the purposes of arriving at a collective bargaining agreement." 5 U.S.C. § 7114(a)(4). It defines the key term "collective bargaining agreement" as an "agreement entered into as a result of collective bargaining." § 7103(a)(8). And it goes on to define "collective bargaining" as involving the meeting of employer and employee representatives "at reasonable times" to "consult" and to "bargain in a good-faith effort to reach agreement with respect to the conditions of employment," incorporating "any collective bargaining agreement reached" as a result of these negotiations in "a written document." § 7103(a)(12). This language, taken literally, may or may not include a duty to bargain collectively midterm. The Agency, here represented by the Solicitor General, argues that in context, this language must exclude midterm bargaining. We shall explain why we do not agree with each of the Agency's basic arguments.

First, the Agency makes a variety of linguistic arguments. As an initial matter, it emphasizes the words "arriving at" in the Statute's general statement that the parties must bargain "for the purposes of arriving at a collective bargaining agreement." This statement tends to exclude midterm bargaining, the Agency contends, because parties engage in midterm bargaining, not for the purpose of arriving at, but for the purpose of supplementing, their basic, comprehensive labor contract. In other words, the basic collective-bargaining agreement is the only appropriate destination at which negotiations might "arriv[e]." The Agency adds that "collective bargaining agreement" is a term of art, which only and always refers to basic labor contracts, not to midterm agreements.

Further, while the Agency acknowledges that there is a duty to bargain midterm in the private sector, see *NLRB v. Jacobs Manufacturing Co.*, 196 F.2d 680 (2d Cir.1952), it argues that this private-sector duty is based upon language in the National Labor Relations Act (NLRA) that is different in significant respects from the language in the Statute here. The Agency explains that the NLRA defines private-sector collective bargaining to include (1) negotiation "with respect to wages, hours, and other terms and conditions of employment, or [(2)] the negotiation of an agreement, *or* any question arising thereunder." 29 U.S.C. § 158(d) (emphasis added). The "or," under this view, indicates that private-sector employers have a comprehensive duty to "bargain collectively" whether or not such bargaining is part of "the negotiation of an agreement" leading to "written contract."

In our view, these linguistic arguments, while logical, make too much of too little. One can easily read "arriving at a collective bargaining agreement" as including an agreement reached at the conclusion of midterm bargaining, particularly because the Statute itself does no more than define the relevant term "collective bargaining agreement" in a circular way—as "an agreement entered into as a result of collective bargaining." 5 U.S.C. § 7103(a)(8). Nor have we found any statute, judicial opinion, agency document, or treatise that says whether the words "collective bargaining agreement" are words of art that must necessarily exclude midterm agreements. Finally, the linguistic differences between the NLRA and the FSLMRS tell us little, particularly given the fact that the two labor statutes, like collective bargaining itself, are not otherwise identical in the two sectors. For all these reasons, we find in the relevant statutory language ambiguity, not certainty.

Second, the Agency—like the Fourth Circuit—contends that the Statute's policies demand a reading of the statutory language that would exclude midterm bargaining from its definition of "collective bargaining." The availability of midterm bargaining, the Agency argues, might lead unions to withhold certain subjects from ordinary endterm negotiations and then to raise them during the term, under more favorable bargaining conditions. A union might conclude, for example, that it is more likely to get what it wants by presenting a proposal during the term (when no other issues are on the table and a compromise is less likely) and then negotiating to impasse, thus leaving the matter for the Federal Service Impasses Panel to resolve. The Agency also points out that public-sector and private-sector bargaining differ in this respect. Private-sector unions enforce their views through strikes, and because they hesitate to strike midterm, they also have no particular incentive to bargain midterm. But public-sector unions enforce their views through compulsory arbitration, not strikes. Hence, the argument goes, public-sector unions have a unique incentive to bargain midterm on a piecemeal basis, thereby threatening to undermine the basic collective-bargaining process.

Other policy concerns, however, argue for a different reading of the Statute. Without midterm bargaining, for example, will it prove possible to find a collective solution to a workplace problem, say, a health or safety hazard, that first appeared midterm? The Statute's emphasis upon collective bargaining as "contribut[ing] to the effective conduct of public business," 5 U.S.C. § 7101(a)(1)(B), suggests that it would favor joint, not unilateral, solutions to such midterm problems. The Authority would seem better suited than a court to make the workplace-related empirical judgments that would help properly balance these, and other, policy-related considerations. The Statute does not indicate that Congress itself decided to make these specific policy judgments. Hence the Agency's policy arguments illustrate the need for the Authority's elaboration or refinement of the basic statutory collective-bargaining obligation; they illustrate the appropriateness of judicial deference to considered Authority views on the matter; and, most importantly, they do not narrow the scope of a statutory provision the language of which is consistent with a variety of interpretations.

Third, the Agency argues that the Statute's history and prior administrative practice support its view that federal agencies have no duty to bargain midterm. The Statute grew out of an Executive Order that previously had governed federal-sector labor relations. See Executive Order No. 11491, 3 C.F.R. § 861 (1966–1970 Comp.), as amended by Executive Order Nos. 11616, 11636, and 11838, 3 C.F.R. §§ 605, 634, 957 (1971–1975 Comp.). In support, the Agency cites a case in which an Assistant Secretary of Labor, applying that Executive Order, dismissed an unfair labor practice complaint on the ground, among others, that a federal agency need not bargain over midterm union proposals. * * * A single alternative ground, however—in a single, unreviewed decision from before the Statute was enacted—does not demonstrate the kind of historical practice that one might assume would be reflected in the Statute, particularly when at least one treatise suggested at the time that federal labor relations practice was to the contrary. See H. Robinson, *Negotiability in the Federal Sector* 10–11, and n. 9 (1981) (stating that under the Executive Order both unions and agencies had a continuing duty to bargain through the term of a basic labor contract).

The Agency also points to a Senate Report in support of its interpretation of the Statute. That Report speaks of the parties' "mutual duty to bargain" with respect to (1) "changes in established personnel policies proposed by management," and (2) "negotiable proposals initiated by either the agency or [the union] * * * in the context of negotiations leading to a basic collective bargaining agreement." S.Rep. No. 95–969, p. 104 (1978). This Report, however, concerns a bill that contains language similar to the language before us but was not enacted into law. According to the D.C. Circuit, at least, any distinction between basic and midterm bargaining that is indicated by this passage "did not survive the rejection by Congress of the Senate's restrictive view of the rights of labor and the importance of collective bargaining." *NTEU*, 810 F.2d, at 298. In any event, the Report's list of possible occasions for collective bargaining does not purport to be an exclusive list; it does not say that the Statute was understood to exclude midterm bargaining; and any such implication is simply too distant to control our reading of the Statute.

Fourth, the Agency and the Fourth Circuit contend that the "management rights" provision of the Statute, 5 U.S.C. § 7106, does authorize limited midterm bargaining in respect to certain matters (not here at issue), and that by negative implication it denies permission to bargain midterm in respect to any others. See, e.g., *SSA, supra*, at 1284 ("The inclusion of a specific duty of midterm effects bargaining * * * suggests the inadvisability of reading a more general duty into the statute"). Our examination of that provision, however, finds little support for such a strong negative implication. Subsection (a) of the management rights provision withdraws from collective bargaining certain subjects that it reserves exclusively for decision by management. It specifies, for example, that federal agency "management official[s]" will retain their authority to hire, fire, promote, and assign work, and also to determine the agency's "mission, budget, organization, number of employees, and internal security practices." Section 7106(a).

Subsection (b), however, permits a certain amount of collective bargaining in respect to the very subjects that subsection (a) withdrew. Subsection (b) states:

> "*Nothing in this section shall preclude* any agency and any labor organization from negotiating—
>
> "(1) at the election of the agency, on the numbers, types, and grades of employees or positions assigned to any organizational subdivision, work project, or tour of duty, or on the technology, methods, and means of performing work;
>
> "(2) procedures which management officials * * * will observe in exercising any authority under this section; or
>
> "(3) appropriate arrangements for employees adversely affected by the exercise of any authority under this section by such management officials." Section 7106(b) (emphasis added).

The two subsections of the management rights provision, taken together, do not help the Agency. While the provision contemplates that bargaining over the impact and implementation of management changes may take place during the term of the basic labor contract, subsection (b) need not be read to actually impose a duty to bargain midterm. The italicized clause, "[n]othing in this section shall preclude," indicates only that the delegation of certain rights to management (e.g., promotions) shall not preclude negotiations about certain related matters (e.g., promotion procedures). By its terms, then, subsection (b) does nothing more than create an exception to subsection (a), preserving the duty to bargain with respect to certain matters otherwise committed to the discretion of management. Because Section 7106(b) chiefly addresses the subject matter of bargaining and not the timing, one could reasonably conclude that while that subsection contemplates midterm bargaining in the circumstances there specified, the duty to bargain midterm finds its source elsewhere in the Statute. Hence, the management rights provision seems to hurt, as much as to help, the Agency's basic argument.

The upshot of this analysis is that where the Agency and the Fourth Circuit find a clear statutory denial of any midterm bargaining obligation, we find ambiguity created by the Statute's use of general language that might, or might not, encompass various forms of midterm bargaining. That kind of statutory ambiguity is inconsistent both with the Fourth Circuit's absolute reading of the Statute and also with the D.C. Circuit's similarly absolute, but opposite, reading * * * .

The statutory ambiguity is perfectly consistent, however, with the conclusion that Congress delegated to the Authority the power to determine—within appropriate legal bounds. See, e.g., 5 U.S.C. § 706 (Administrative Procedure Act); *Chevron U.S.A. Inc. v. Natural Resources Defense Council, Inc.*, 467 U.S. 837, 104 S.Ct. 2778, 81 L.Ed.2d 694 (1984)—whether, when, where, and what sort of midterm bargaining is required. The Statute's delegation of rulemaking, adjudicatory, and policymaking powers to the Authority supports this conclusion. * * * This conclusion is also supported by precedent recognizing the similarity of the Authority's public-sector and the National Labor Relations Board's private-sector roles. As we have recognized, the Authority's function is "to develop specialized expertise in its field of labor relations and to use that expertise to give content to the principles and goals set forth in the Act," and it "is entitled to considerable deference when it exercises its 'special function of applying the general provisions of the Act to the complexities' of federal labor relations." *Bureau of Alcohol, Tobacco and Firearms v. FLRA*, 464 U.S. 89, 104 S.Ct. 439, 78 L.Ed.2d 195 (1983) (quoting *NLRB v. Erie Resistor Corp.*, 373 U.S. 221, 83 S.Ct. 1139, 10 L.Ed.2d 308 (1963)).

We conclude that Congress "left" the matters of whether, when, and where midterm bargaining is required "to be resolved by the agency charged with the administration of the statute in light of everyday realities." *Chevron*, *supra*.

III.

The specific question before us is whether an agency must bargain endterm about including in the basic labor contract a clause that would require certain forms of midterm bargaining. As is true of midterm bargaining itself, and for similar reasons, the Statute grants the Authority leeway (within ordinary legal limits) in answering that question as well.

The Authority says that it has determined, as a matter of its own judgment, that the parties must bargain over such a provision. Our reading of its relevant administrative determinations, however, leads us to conclude that its judgment on the matter was occasioned by the D.C. Circuit's holding that the Statute must be read to impose on agencies a duty to bargain midterm. * * * In light of our determination that the Statute does not resolve the question of midterm bargaining, nor the related question of bargaining about midterm bargaining, we believe the Authority should have the opportunity to consider these questions aware that the Statute permits, but does not compel, the conclusions it reached. The judgment of the Fourth Circuit is vacated, and the cases are remanded for further proceedings consistent with this opinion.

[The dissenting opinion of JUSTICE O'CONNOR, joined by the CHIEF JUSTICE and in part by JUSTICES SCALIA and THOMAS, is omitted.]

NOTES

1. On remand, the FLRA adhered to its original position that the agency was required to bargain with the union over its proposal obligating the agency to engage in midterm bargaining "over matters not contained in or covered by the terms," as the proposal merely restated the agency's statutory obligation. *Department of Interior*, 56 FLRA 45 (2000). The FLRA reasoned:

> [M]atters appropriate for resolution through collective bargaining are sometimes unforeseen and unforeseeable at the time of term negotiations. These matters include not only problems that might arise because of a change in workplace environment, but also new areas of agency discretion occasioned by changes in law or regulations. * * * Such bargaining furthers the Statute's goal of enabling employees 'through labor organizations of their own choosing' to more timely participate in 'decisions which affect them' and in cooperatively resolving disputes. 5 U.S.C. § 7101(a)(1). Moreover, the negotiation of such workplace issues is preferable to addressing them through the more adversarial grievance/arbitration process. * * * [T]he ability to bargain over such issues in a timely manner is preferable to the alternative of leaving potentially important concerns unaddressed for perhaps a period of years until term negotiations on the basic contract commences again. Moreover, requiring unions to raise matters that do not currently present problems, but might do so in the future, could unnecessarily and inefficiently broaden and prolong term negotiations.
>
> * * *
>
> [W]e find that the evidence in the record before us supports the conclusion that requiring agencies to bargain over union-initiated midterm proposals will not result in significant costs or disruptions that would outweigh the benefits of such bargaining. * * * In addition, constraints

on union-initiated midterm bargaining make it unlikely that it will lead to continuous issue-by-issue bargaining. First, an agency is not required to bargain during the term of a collective bargaining agreement on matters that are 'contained in or covered by' an agreement. * * * Second, an agency is not required to bargain midterm where the union has waived its right to bargain over the subject matter involved. Waivers of bargaining rights may be established by express agreement or by bargaining history. The test to analyze whether there has been waiver by bargaining history is set out in *Selfridge National Guard Base*, 46 FLRA at 585 (examining whether matter has been 'fully discussed and consciously explored during negotiations' and whether union has 'consciously yielded or otherwise clearly and unmistakably waived its interest in the matter').

2. The FLRA says that waiver of the duty to bargain may be found in "express agreement." Should a general "zipper clause" be accepted as waiver of the duty to bargain? Should it make a difference whether the matter on which the union seeks to bargain was or was not reasonably foreseeable at the time the agreement was entered into?

3. While the public sector generally adopts the private sector rule that a unilateral change in a contract term is a violation of the duty to bargain in good faith, some variations exist. In *SERB v. Toledo District Board of Education*, 18 OPER ¶ 1645 (OH SERB 2001), the Ohio SERB explained that in the public sector, the "parties must be able to respond to emergency situations that arise during the term of the collective bargaining agreement, especially in situations where they cannot reach agreement after engaging in good-faith negotiations." SERB thus added two exceptions to the rule: "a party cannot modify an existing collective bargaining agreement without the negotiation by and agreement of both parties unless immediate action is required due to (1) exigent circumstances that were unforeseen at the time of negotiations or (2) legislative action taken by a higher-level legislative body after the agreement became effective that requires a change to conform to the statute." SERB did not explain what would count as "exigent circumstances." What should?

4. In *SERB v. Toledo District Board of Education, supra*, the Ohio SERB also held that in Ohio, the parties should not use statutory impasse procedures for mid-term bargaining. Rather, SERB encouraged unions and employers to specify their own procedures for mid-term bargaining in their contracts. Absent such procedures, SERB held, the employer may implement its last best offer at impasse. Contrast *Teamsters Local 764 v. Snyder County*, 36 PPER ¶ 96 (PA Labor Rel. Bd. 2005), holding that the statutory impasse procedure did apply to mid-term bargaining. The Pennsylvania Board reasoned that the impasse procedures were the *quid pro quo* for the bar on strikes and that this principle applied to mid-term negotiations. While the latter approach is more common, can you think of some arguments supporting the position that statutory impasse procedures are less appropriate for mid-term bargaining?

5. When a union files an unfair labor practice charge with a labor relations agency alleging that the employer has violated its duty to bargain by instituting a unilateral change in working conditions during the term of an

agreement, the common practice in the public sector, as in the private, is for the agency to defer the matter pending arbitration. For further discussion of deferral, see Chapter 11, § D.2.

F. REMEDIES FOR VIOLATION OF THE DUTY TO BARGAIN

If an employer violates its duty to bargain by changing working conditions unilaterally without bargaining, it can be ordered to reinstate the *status quo* and compensate workers who suffered injury as a result of the unlawful act. And if the violation consists of a failure to do something specific, such as supplying information, a board or a court can order the information to be supplied. Otherwise, the generally available remedy for violation of the duty to bargain is a cease and desist order (from an agency) or an injunction (from a court). How effective is such a remedy likely to be, in the case of an employer whose goal is to avoid reaching agreement? Should a labor relations agency have authority to bring additional remedies to bear? Consider the following case.

SEATTLE v. PUBLIC EMPLOYMENT RELATIONS COMMISSION

Washington Supreme Court, 1992.
118 Wash.2d 621, 826 P.2d 158.

ANDERSON, J.

The question raised by this appeal is whether the Public Employment Relations Commission (PERC) has authority to order "interest" arbitration as part of an unfair labor practice remedy. We hold that, in limited circumstances, it does.

The PERC order challenged in this action requires the employer, Municipality of Metropolitan Seattle (Metro), to participate in interest arbitration if collective bargaining between Metro and the International Federation of Professional and Technical Engineers, Local 17, AFL–CIO (Local 17) does not result in a collective bargaining agreement. "Interest" (or contract) arbitration differs from the more familiar "grievance" arbitration. Grievance arbitration requires the employer and union to submit unresolved disputes regarding the interpretation or application of an existing collective bargaining contract to an objective arbitrator. Interest arbitration, on the other hand, occurs only at a point where an impasse has been reached in new contract negotiations. At that point, the unresolved items of the new collective bargaining agreement are submitted to an arbitrator who then decides the terms of the future collective bargaining contract.

This case concerns five employees who, until April 1984, worked as clerical employees for the City of Seattle's commuter pool. The city employees were represented by their exclusive bargaining agent, Local 17. In 1982 or 1983, Metro, a public transit authority serving the greater

Seattle area, began negotiating with the City of Seattle for a transfer of the City's commuter pool program to Metro. The plan involved the transfer of approximately 29 employees, including the five clerical employees who were members of Local 17. The statute authorizing such transfers places certain obligations, including the duty to collectively bargain with existing unions, upon any metropolitan corporation which acquires an existing transportation system.

The five commuter pool employees were transferred to Metro in early April 1984. In the years from the date of that transfer to the present time, Metro has refused to recognize Local 17 as the appropriate bargaining unit for the transferred employees. During those years, Metro has also refused to bargain with the union, despite court and PERC orders to do so. [Portions of the court's opinion detailing the history of Metro's attempts to avoid bargaining through legal actions, including a petition for "unit clarification" are omitted.]

In February 1985 Local 17 filed the unfair labor practice complaint that resulted in the appeal before us. Local 17's complaint alleged a refusal to bargain on the part of Metro. Although the hearing on the unfair labor practice complaint was held in early November 1986, the decision was not issued until January 1988. The delay was due to PERC's decision to hold the matter in abeyance until a decision was reached by the King County Superior Court in Metro's unit clarification action. In the unfair labor practice case, Metro argued that it had changed its operations to such an extent that the commuter pool which was transferred from the City was no longer intact and thus no longer existed as a separate bargaining unit. The PERC hearing examiner found this argument to be "frivolous" in light of settled law requiring that the "effects" of such significant changes in working conditions must be bargained before being implemented. The hearing examiner noted that during the pendency of the action, and after the previous unit clarification petition had been dismissed, Metro had filed yet another petition with PERC asking that its bargaining obligations toward Local 17 be terminated. The hearing examiner found:

> METRO has attempted at every turn to evade its bargaining obligations. It is evident that METRO has not given up the fight, and that it is still not prepared to fulfill its bargaining obligations towards Local 17. * * * METRO will likely continue to put up one defense after another in an ongoing attempt to defeat having a bargaining relationship with Local 17. * * * METRO has asserted, and continues to assert, inherently frivolous defenses in an ongoing effort to subvert and avoid its bargaining obligations towards Local 17.

The hearing examiner then crafted the order which is now before us on Metro's challenge. The order requires Metro to restore the status quo with respect to the five commuter pool employees and to make those employees whole. Based on a finding of bad faith on the part of Metro, it requires Metro to pay the union's reasonable attorneys' fees and costs. It orders

Metro to post notices with respect to the unfair labor practice and orders that Metro [bargain with the Union in good faith] and, if no agreement is reached through bilateral negotiations within sixty (60) days after Local 17 has requested to bargain, either party may request the Public Employment Commission Relations [sic] to provide the services of a mediator to assist the parties. If no agreement is reached by using the mediation process, and the Executive Director, on the request of either of the parties and the recommendation of the assigned mediator, concludes that the parties are at impasse following a reasonable period of negotiations, shall submit the remaining issues to interest arbitration using the procedures of 41.56.450, et seq., and the standards for * * * firefighters. The decision of the neutral arbitration panel shall be final and binding upon both the parties.

* * *

Metro appealed the PERC decision to the Superior Court for King County which affirmed. The case was then appealed to the Court of Appeals. On appeal, Metro challenged the PERC order on the grounds that (1) PERC did not have the authority to order Metro to return its employees to the status quo that existed in August 1984 (6 months before the unfair labor practice complaint was filed) and (2) PERC did not have authority to order interest arbitration as an unfair labor practice remedy. The Court of Appeals affirmed the order requiring restoration of the status quo but reversed that portion of the order directing interest arbitration in the event of bargaining impasse.

PERC and Local 17 petitioned this court for review of the interest arbitration issue; we granted the petition, [and conclude that] PERC does have the authority, in limited and extraordinary circumstances, to order interest arbitration as part of an unfair labor practice remedy. Such a remedy must be cautiously and sparingly used, however, and used only in those cases where there is a clear history of bad faith refusal to bargain and where there is a very strong likelihood that such refusal will continue despite PERC's order to bargain in good faith.

This case presents a conflict between the need to preserve the integrity of the collective bargaining process on the one hand, and, on the other, the genuine need to remedy flagrant abuses of that process in situations where employees are unable, through legal means or by use of traditional economic weapons, to remedy the situation themselves. The Public Employees' Collective Bargaining Act, WEST'S REV.CODE WASH.ANN. 41.56, was enacted in 1967, in order to promote the continued improvement of the relationship between public employers and their employees by providing a uniform basis for implementing the right of public employees to join labor organizations of their own choosing and to be represented by such organizations in matters concerning their employment relations with public employers. The Act requires public employers, including municipal corporations such as Metro, to participate in collective bargaining with the exclusive bargaining representatives of its employees. Collective bargaining is defined by the Act as the performance of the mutual obligations of the public employer and the exclusive bargaining representative to meet at reasonable times, to confer and negotiate in good faith, and to execute a written agreement with respect to grievance procedures and collective negotiations on personnel matters, including wages, hours and working conditions, which may be peculiar to an appropriate bargaining unit of such public employer, except that by such obligation neither party shall be compelled to agree to a proposal or be required to make a concession unless otherwise provided in this chapter. WEST'S REV.CODE WASH.ANN. 41.56.030(4).

Employers have traditionally not been compelled to agree or to accept the terms of a collective bargaining contract to which they do not agree. Resolution of bargaining impasses has thus depended on the economic pressures that the employer and employees could bring to bear upon one another. Where those economic pressures can be limited or prohibited or where their usefulness is questionable, other—more peaceful—methods of resolving contract impasses may be advantageous. While interest arbitration is generally a voluntary process both this court and the Legislature have given limited approval to the use of compulsory interest arbitration to resolve collective bargaining impasses in the public employment arena. WEST'S REV.CODE WASH.ANN. 41.56.450 requires interest arbitration between law enforcement and firefighter unions and their employers when contract negotiations and mediation have failed to produce a contract. In *Green River Comm'ty College v. Higher Educ. Personnel Bd.*, 95 Wash.2d 108, 622 P.2d 826 (1980), *modified on reconsideration*, 95 Wash.2d 962, 633 P.2d 1324 (1981), this court approved a regulation promulgated by the Higher Education Personnel Board (HEP Board) that permitted either a college or its employee union to submit unresolved collective bargaining issues to the HEP Board for compulsory resolution through interest arbitration. Heretofore we have not determined whether PERC has the power to order interest arbitration as a remedy for an unfair labor practice.

An agency has only those powers which are expressly granted or which are necessarily implied from statutory grants of authority. PERC derives its power from WEST'S REV.CODE WASH.ANN. 41.58, the statute that creates the Commission, and from WEST'S REV.CODE WASH.ANN. 41.56, the Public Employees' Collective Bargaining Act. The creation of the Commission was intended to achieve more efficient and expert administration of public labor relations administration and to thereby ensure the public of quality public services. WEST'S REV.CODE WASH.ANN. 41.58.005. In addition to other duties, PERC is empowered and directed to prevent any unfair labor practice and to issue appropriate remedial orders. RCW 41.56.160.

When interpreting the Public Employees' Collective Bargaining Act, we will liberally construe the Act in order to accomplish its purpose. The purpose of the Act "is to provide public employees with the right to join and be represented by labor organizations of their own choosing, and to provide for a uniform basis for implementing that right." With that purpose in mind, we interpret the statutory phrase "appropriate remedial orders" to be those necessary to effectuate the purposes of the collective bargaining statute and to make PERC's lawful orders effective. The authority granted PERC by the remedial provision of the statute has been interpreted to be broad enough to authorize an award of attorney fees when such an award "is necessary to make the order effective and if the defense to the unfair labor practice is frivolous or meritless. In *State ex rel. Wash. Fed'n of State Employees v. Board of Trustees*, 93 Wash.2d 60, 605 P.2d 1252 (1980), this court stated that the HEP Board's determination as to remedies under the Public Employees' Collective Bargaining Act should be accorded considerable judicial deference, and noted that the "relation of remedy to policy is peculiarly a matter of administrative competence." PERC's expertise in resolving labor disputes also has been judicially recognized and accorded deference. * * * PERC thus has authority to issue appropriate orders that it, in its expertise, believes are consistent with the purposes of the Act, and that are necessary to make its orders effective unless such orders are otherwise unlawful.

* * *

Metro argues that because the Legislature did not include transit workers within the interest arbitration provisions of the statute, it intended that those workers not participate in interest arbitration. This argument ignores the impact of *Green River Comm'ty College v. Higher Educ. Personnel Bd.*, 95 Wash.2d 108, 622 P.2d 826 (1980), *modified on reconsideration*, 95 Wash.2d 962, 633 P.2d 1324 (1981). Many of the arguments here presented by Metro were considered in *Green River*, where this court rejected those arguments and ruled that the HEP Board, through its regulatory powers, could require all public colleges and their employees to participate in interest arbitration, if collective bargaining and contract mediation failed. This court found such a regulation to be consistent with the intent and purpose of the law governing collective bargaining between public colleges and their employees.

The *Green River* court distinguished significant federal precedent that is now relied on by Metro. In *Green River*, this court declined to follow *H.K. Porter Co. v. NLRB*, 397 U.S. 99, 90 S.Ct. 821, 25 L.Ed.2d 146 (1970), a United States Supreme Court case that held the NLRB did not have authority to require a particular provision be included in a collective bargaining agreement.

This court, in distinguishing *H.K. Porter Co.*, stated that reliance on NLRA precedents in the present context is inappropriate. The NLRA regulates labor relations only in the private sector. The Act specifically guarantees employees the right to strike. Private sector bargaining and public sector bargaining are radically different, as both parties agree. *Green River* supports the union's and PERC's position that interest arbitration need not be specifically permitted or required by statute in order for it to be lawful.

Metro also argues that compelled interest arbitration is contrary to traditional collective bargaining principles and to the philosophy behind collective bargaining. When faced with a situation such as that which exists here, there is little that a union can legally do to enforce the collective bargaining rights of its members. For 7 years Metro has been involved in litigation over the representation rights of these five employees. Court orders and financial sanctions have had no effect on Metro. The employer's delays and legal maneuvering have, in fact, resulted in a prolonged period in which the employees have not had an opportunity to negotiate the terms and conditions of their employment. During this time Metro accomplished the disbursement of the employees represented by Local 17 so that the bargaining unit became unidentifiable. This disbursement of employees throughout other bargaining units was the reason for PERC's order requiring a return to the status quo. The conflict here thus arises because the employer in this case has been able to use the law to avoid its clear obligation to collectively bargain with the union and now, when ordered to participate in interest arbitration, claims that such an order is violative of the philosophy behind collective bargaining. In this case PERC specifically found that the remedy of interest arbitration, upon impasse, was necessary to make its order to bargain effective. In the very limited circumstances presented by the facts of this case, such an order is not contrary to collective bargaining principles. Instead, it serves as an impetus to successfully negotiate an agreement.

NOTES

1. How would you define the "limited circumstances" which justified the imposition of interest arbitration as a remedy in this case? Under what other circumstances, if any, would such a remedy be justified? Would it be appropriate under a system which calls for non-binding factfinding?

2. The rationale of *H.K. Porter* is that since the duty to bargain does not require acceptance of any particular proposal, to order an employer to agree to anything it has not already agreed to is beyond the scope of appropriate remedy. Is that rationale equally applicable to the public sector?

3. Why would an agency use interest arbitration as a remedy rather than having the agency itself directly mandate a remedy? Should the union have to wait even longer for a final resolution? Or can the arbitration process offer benefits the agency process cannot?

Chapter 8

Scope of Bargaining

■ ■ ■

Once a collective bargaining relationship has been established, determining what subjects must be negotiated (mandatory subjects), may be negotiated (permissive subjects), and are prohibited from being negotiated (prohibited subjects) is crucial for the two parties and for the public as well. The substance and breadth of public sector bargaining often directly impacts taxpayers' pocketbook interests. The scope of public sector bargaining may also collide with citizens' policy concerns, particularly with respect to bargaining by the large number of public sector professionals who have elected to do so.

Moreover, the labeling of subjects of bargaining as mandatory, permissive, or prohibited directly affects the parties during three critical periods of their relationship. First, the label is important in actual negotiations. The discussion of issues at the bargaining table is restricted to mandatory subjects, unless both parties agree to expand their talks to include non-mandatory subjects. If one party insists that the other party bargain a non-mandatory subject, it has committed an unfair labor practice (sometimes called a prohibited or improper practice in the public sector) and typically subjects itself to an administrative labor relations agency remedial order. Second, the label is important if parties reach impasse. A jurisdiction's procedures to resolve impasses are restricted to mandatory subjects of bargaining, unless one party fails to raise a timely objection to the inclusion of a non-mandatory subject during compulsory impasse procedures. In jurisdictions which permit public employee strikes, it is an unfair labor practice to strike to support adoption of the union's position on a permissive subject of bargaining or for the employer to lockout its employees to support adoption of the employer's position on a permissive subject of bargaining.

Finally, the label is important if a party unilaterally implements its position. A public employer (or union) may unilaterally implement a permissive subject under its control, at any time, unless it is restricted from doing so by the terms of a collective bargaining agreement. (Since few permissive subjects are under a union's control, the rule primarily affects public employers). Regarding mandatory subjects of bargaining, however, prior to reaching agreement on an initial collective bargaining agreement as well as after the expiration of a collective bargaining agreement, the public employer is required to maintain the "status quo" until all impasse procedures are completed.

The statutory framework governing the subjects of bargaining plays a critical role in the dynamics of public sector collective bargaining in each jurisdiction. Rulings interpreting scope legislation by various administrative labor relations agencies and/or courts are also of great importance in understanding the legal framework governing the parties' behavior during the collective bargaining process. Regardless of litigation outcomes, however, one notable aspect of scope litigation is that it probably will result in long delays and thus will have consequences to the parties' relationship in the labor relations context. This chapter explores the diversity that has resulted from decisions by legislatures, administrative labor relations agencies, and courts relating to the scope of bargaining in the public sector. Scope of bargaining is an area of public sector law that in many states differs significantly from private sector law. In addition, there is wide variation among the states. The chapter begins with a summary of how private sector law relating to scope of bargaining has developed under the National Labor Relations Act. The private sector's history and terminology has directly affected the development of public sector law, even in jurisdictions rejecting private sector scope of bargaining doctrine. The chapter continues with a sampling of legislative language relating to subjects of bargaining. It then explores judicial and administrative rulings covering a variety of scope issues. The chapter ends with a discussion of the interrelationship between labor-management partnerships which have been developing in the public sector and the judgments about what constitutes the appropriate scope of bargaining in the public sector, noting a trend to narrow the mandatory scope of bargaining in the public sector.

A. HISTORY AND TERMINOLOGY

THE APPROPRIATE SCOPE OF BARGAINING IN THE PUBLIC SECTOR: THE CONTINUING CONTROVERSY AND THE WISCONSIN EXPERIENCE

June Miller Weisberger
1977 Wisconsin Law Review 685.

Deciding what issues should be resolved by labor-management negotiations has been controversial from the time collective bargaining was first proposed for public employees. Much of the heated debate which has surrounded the beginnings of public sector bargaining during the past decade has centered upon this problem of public policy.[2] Not only has this

2. *See* Paul Prasow, *Scope of Bargaining in the Public Sector—Concepts and Problems* (U.S. Department of Labor 1972); Harry Wellington & Ralph Winter, Jr., *The Unions and The Cities* (1971); Patricia N. Blair, *State Legislative Control Over the Conditions of Public Employment: Defining the Scope of Collective Bargaining for State and Municipal Employees,* 26 Vand.L.Rev. 1 (1973); Harry T. Edwards, *The Emerging Duty to Bargain in the Public Sector,* 71 Mich.L.Rev.

key aspect of the collective bargaining process evoked intense interest in state legislatures whenever public sector collective bargaining legislation is first introduced, but the controversy will continue unabated before administrative agencies and state courts in an increasing number of jurisdictions when parties litigating cases raise conflicting policy arguments in their efforts to secure favorable administrative or judicial rulings on the appropriate scope of bargaining in a wide variety of situations facing public employees and employers. No consensus is yet evident.

* * *

Basically, the issue of the scope of bargaining deals with conditions of employment which may (or may not) be appropriately resolved by labor and management utilizing the negotiations process. In the private sector, the National Labor Relations Act established a duty to bargain for covered employers, but did not enumerate the specific subjects over which bargaining must take place. Despite congressional attempts to legislate an explicit list of bargainable subjects,[5] the role of defining the required subjects has been assumed by the National Labor Relations Board, the agency established in 1935 to administer federal labor policies for the private sector. From its early years on, the Board issued a number of decisions, in the context of adjudicatory administrative proceedings, interpreting what elements of the employment relationship were covered by the requirement in the National Labor Relations Act that there be bargaining over "wages, hours, or other working conditions."

In *NLRB v. Wooster Division of the Borg–Warner Corp.*, 356 U.S. 342, 78 S.Ct. 718, 2 L.Ed.2d 823 (1958),[8] the United States Supreme Court affirmed and adopted the approach of the Board and the circuit courts of appeals in classifying subjects of bargaining as mandatory (the subjects over which labor and management *must* bargain), permissive (the subjects over which labor and management *may* bargain), and illegal or prohibited (the subjects over which labor and management *cannot* bargain). The analysis of scope in terms of mandatory, permissive, and prohibited subjects of bargaining has been criticized but it continues to be applied by the Board and the courts. Decisions subsequent to *Borg–Warner* have attempted to clarify and apply the very general guidelines adopted by the

885 (1973); Donald H. Wollett, *The Bargaining Process in the Public Sector: What is Bargainable?*, 51 Ore.L.Rev. 177 (1971).

Public sector employees, from the very beginning of public sector bargaining, have pushed hard to obtain a wide scope of bargaining, unlike their private sector counterparts.

5. In 1947, a majority of the House Committee on Labor and Education and of the full House supported a bill listing definitively the subjects of bargaining. *See* Nathan P. Feinsinger, *The National Labor Relations Act and Collective Bargaining*, 57 Mich.L.Rev. 807 (1959) for a history of § 8(d).

8. The employer had insisted that the collective bargaining agreement include (1) a recognition clause solely with the local union as bargaining representative and not with the parent international although only the latter had received Board certification, and (2) a ballot clause which required a secret ballot vote of all members of the bargaining unit on the employer's last offer. If rejected, the employer would have 72 hours to modify its position followed by a repetition of the voting process. Only after these procedures were exhausted would the union be free to strike.

majority in *Borg–Warner*. Litigation before the Board and the courts continues to raise novel scope issues which test the meaning of *Borg–Warner*. Recent split decisions among decisionmakers in both administrative and judicial forums indicate a lack of consensus in this area of private sector labor law although the *Borg–Warner* terminology clearly controls both the majorities and the dissenters.

Meanwhile, in the public sector, there is a recurring question as to whether it is appropriate to utilize the *Borg–Warner* analysis, particularly in the permissive category for bargainable subjects. The main public sector justification for excluding a legal topic from the mandated bargaining process is that the demand involves a significant public policy question which should not be determined in the isolation of the bargaining process in which other vital public interests are not directly represented. If a topic is "too significant" to be classified as a mandatory subject of bargaining, does it make any sense to say it may be bargained about if labor and management agree? * * * [T]his argument has exerted some influence on legislation and decisional law covering public employees although few legislatures, administrative agencies, or courts have chosen to eliminate the permissive category from public sector bargaining and adopt instead a system of classifying bargaining demands as mandatory or illegal only.

When a bargaining demand is labeled mandatory, permissive, or prohibited, certain well-established legal consequences result under interpretations of the National Labor Relations Act. First, during negotiations for a labor agreement, one party has a legal right to refuse to bargain over the opposing party's demand if that demand is permissive. No party may refuse to bargain over a mandatory demand. Second, if a party insists upon a permissive demand to the point of impasse or utilizes a primary economic strike or lock-out to support a permissive bargaining demand in the face of the opposing party's lack of consent to negotiate, the Board will find a violation of the statutory duty to bargain. A mandatory demand, however, may be pushed to impasse and may be supported by a primary economic strike or lock-out. Third, either party at any time may implement unilaterally any matter which is labeled permissive, in the absence of a contract provision restricting that right. A mandatory matter may not be implemented unilaterally unless a contract provision explicitly gives a party the right to take unilateral action or the opposing party has by some other act waived his right to insist upon bargaining over the mandatory matter. In the public sector where public employees are prohibited from striking and the negotiation processes are subjected to mandated impasse procedures when there is a breakdown in negotiations, must not the legal consequences flowing from the labeling of bargaining demands be modified?

In addition to devising guidelines for labeling bargaining demands and attaching consequences to the classification, other legal doctrines have been developed under the National Labor Relations Act to delineate the scope of the bargaining duty. For example, managerial decisions to subcontract, to automate, to relocate, or to close down a business operation in whole or in part have been subjected to special scrutiny by the Board and the courts to determine whether or not such decisions should be subjected to a bargaining requirement. In *Fibreboard Paper Products Corp. v. NLRB,* 379 U.S. 203, 85 S.Ct. 398, 13 L.Ed.2d 233 (1964), a majority of the United States Supreme Court pragmatically stressed the suitability of the negotiations process to resolve one employer's economic problems if the employer wished to substitute a subcontractor's employees for the regular maintenance workers. Particularly since there was extensive industrial experience negotiating subcontracting clauses with unions and a likelihood that bargaining discussions on the problem could be fruitful, the majority did not hesitate to impose a bargaining duty. The concurring opinion emphasized that the majority's holding was limited to situations where "larger entrepreneurial questions" were not involved. There has been much post-*Fibreboard* litigation testing its meaning and application to a wide range of managerial decisions. In general, the approach of the concurring opinion has been adopted by the circuit courts of appeals and, more recently, by the Board.

* * *

Although, under *Fibreboard* and subsequent cases, a "basic" managerial decision will not be held to be a mandatory subject of bargaining if it is made for an economic reason, in all instances the effects or impact of a "basic" managerial decision upon the affected employees' terms and conditions of employment will be subjected to a bargaining requirement. Effects bargaining, bargaining over the rights of employees whose employment status will be altered by the managerial decision, may include such questions as severance pay, order of layoffs, recall or preferential employment rights, and layoff or termination notification procedures. If work is to be shifted to other workers, mandated effects bargaining will also include the impact of these changes upon the retained employees' terms and conditions of employment.

* * *

Some prominent practitioners and researchers have suggested that the legal doctrines relating to scope of bargaining described briefly above have been unduly emphasized. They point to many instances where the legal doctrine rarely determined what was actually bargained. For these pragmatists, there is little practical difference between a mandatory and a permissive demand because bargaining outcomes depend upon bargaining power and pressures and not upon technical legal distinctions. Thus, if a public employee union is strong enough to exert effective pressure, often political, then it will be successful in securing desired concessions regardless of the labels attached to bargaining demands. Similarly, weak unions will be unable to secure agreement at the bargaining table upon admittedly mandatory demands despite the presence of a duty to bargain. Indeed, even prohibited demands may be secured by effective union bargaining since legislation may be enacted to modify existing statutory constraints.

Any person knowledgeable about the dynamics of collective bargaining must acknowledge that there is much truth in the above-stated position that, in many instances, bargaining results are not primarily determined by the legal rules related to the scope of bargaining. This does not mean, however, that the law which defines scope is irrelevant to the bargaining process. At the very least, legal scope doctrines may be used tactically by one or both parties during the bargaining process to manipulate timing and secure delays. The large volume of public sector scope litigation is one clear-cut indication that legal scope determinations must indeed play some role in the bargaining process. At times, legal doctrines relating to scope may be used as a sword by a weak union or weak management to provide additional bargaining leverage or as a shield to provide some protection against granting undesired bargaining concessions. Moreover, in the "real" bargaining world, parties usually seek to arrange workable tradeoffs. These may be easier to arrange when there is a broad scope of bargaining which gives the parties greater flexibility. For a variety of reasons, therefore, it appears reasonable to assume that the "legalities" do play some role in most bargaining relationships although it is not clear what specific effects the legal rules on scope may have on the actual bargaining process.

* * *

When collective bargaining was first contemplated and introduced into the public sector, the differences between the private and public sectors tended to be emphasized. Special features of the public sector were often stressed and policy arguments relating to its uniqueness were particularly popular in debates over the appropriate scope of bargaining.

* * *

During the initial phase of considering public sector collective bargaining legislation, policy arguments concerning uniqueness produced an array of legislative solutions which usually rejected the National Labor Relations Act formulation in favor of some experiments with substantive scope restrictions. Statutory formulations of management rights became an integral part of some enabling legislation to protect public officials from being required to bargain on specified subjects or to prohibit officials from bargaining on these enumerated subjects. In other instances, the public sector collective bargaining statutes were drafted to include different explicit restrictions on scope or they set forth an exclusive list of items subject to the bargaining requirement. Several statutes were drawn to include explicit guarantees that if a conflict arose between the collective bargaining obligation and other legislated obligations, the latter would prevail. Private sector terminology was usually rejected or combined with new language to form hybrid variations.

* * *

During the period following legislative enactment, significant scope litigation has been initiated in virtually every jurisdiction. In contrast, in the private sector, scope litigation was rarely engaged in either during the period immediately following enactment of the National Labor Relation Act or during the initial stage of a bargaining relationship. During the second phase of defining the scope of public sector bargaining, administrative agency or court rulings have been sought to clarify the limitations of the statutory language adopted. This is true regardless of whether scope has been described using National Labor Relations Act terminology, statutory management rights provisions, listings of specified mandatory subjects of bargaining and exclusions from bargaining, or hybrid provisions which have been fashioned which combine features of each.

NOTES

1. In *First National Maintenance Corp. v. NLRB,* 452 U.S. 666, 101 S.Ct. 2573, 69 L.Ed.2d 318 (1981), the Court held that an employer could terminate a contract with a customer without first bargaining with the union representing the discharged employees about this decision. The Court articulated a balancing test to determine the appropriate scope of mandatory bargaining required by the NLRA: the benefits for labor-management relations by requiring bargaining must be greater than the burden placed upon an employer being subjected to the bargaining requirement. In the required balancing, special weight was given to the employer interests to be free from bargaining constraints "for the running of a profitable business" but, in order for an employee interest to be considered in the balancing, it must be found to "vitally affect wages, hours, and other terms and conditions of employment." The Court's majority expressed its concern for the employer's need for speed, flexibility, and secrecy which, in its view, outweighed the possible advantage to be gained from the bargaining process in this case.

The NLRB and reviewing courts have applied *First National Maintenance* in cases involving management decisions such as plant relocations, sales, and partial plant closings. Even where bargaining over the decision to take such actions is not required, the effects or impact remain mandatory subjects of bargaining to the extent that they affect "wages, hours, and other terms and conditions of employment." This area of law remains unstable and the decisions are difficult to predict. As you review the cases *infra* involving scope of bargaining in the public sector, consider whether managerial rights in the public sector are analogous to entrepreneurial decisions in the private sector and whether a similar bargaining test should apply?

2. In the public sector, the judicial response to scope litigation is also difficult to predict. Diverse statutory language covering scope of bargaining in the public sector accounts for some of the significant differences in results. However, even after public sector bargaining has been in place for several decades, there are few discernible stable trends in legislation or judicial interpretation. Some legislatures and courts continue to use and apply private sector terminology and concepts (such as mandatory, permissive, and prohibited subjects) while others have fashioned unique doctrines for the public sector. (For an example of the latter, see Section C for New Jersey's judicial approach to scope of bargaining in the public sector.)

3. Is there any rationale that supports a scope of bargaining for public employees broader than the scope of bargaining for private sector employees? What reasons support a scope of bargaining for public employees narrower than the scope of bargaining for private sector employees?

4. Can parties realistically separate a requirement that they must only bargain over the effects of a management decision from a requirement that they bargain about the decision itself? If the employer proposes to subcontract work because of the labor costs, is a proposal by the union to reduce labor costs a request to bargain over the decision or the effects? Does a proposal to require the subcontractor to hire the employer's employees relate to the decision or the effects? What about a proposal to allow employees to transfer to other jobs, bumping less senior employees who hold those jobs currently? Could a union's proposals for severance pay, continued health insurance, pension payments and other benefits for employees who lose their jobs be so expensive that the costs outweigh the savings? If so is that a request to bargain about the effects or the decision?

5. A knowledgeable practitioner and academic with broad experience as an advocate in the private sector (on the management side) and public sector (first on the union side and subsequently on the management side) has provocatively argued:

> My thesis is that the vast literature concerning the scope of bargaining is much ado about nothing and that the preoccupation with this subject is mischievous as well as mistaken.
>
> * * *
>
> The case for my thesis lies in the attitude which one brings to the bargaining table. If the negotiator conceives his function to be one of establishing immutable principles, winning points and outscoring the adversary, massaging his client's ego, or building a reputation as a protagonist of ordered government and managerial sovereignty, the issue of what is bargainable is fertile ground. If, on the other hand, he approaches the table in a spirit of meeting problems rather than avoiding them, and of trying to find ways to reach agreement rather than identifying obstacles which make a negotiated settlement impossible, I submit that the question of scope of bargaining becomes of little significance.

Donald H. Wollett, The Bargaining Process in the Public Sector: What is Bargainable?, 51 *Oregon Law Review* 177 (1971).

Evaluate the above argument, particularly in terms of whether the public interest in what happens at the bargaining table is adequately reflected.

6. In the private sector a unilateral change in a permissive subject that is embodied in a collective bargaining agreement may breach the contract but it is not an unfair labor practice. *Allied Chemical Workers v. Pittsburgh Plate Glass Co.*, 404 U.S. 157, 92 S.Ct. 383, 30 L.Ed.2d 341 (1971). In the public sector, however, some jurisdictions have found unilateral modification of contractual provisions relating to permissive subjects of bargaining to violate the statute as well as the contract. See *County of Kalamazoo*, 22 Mich. Pub. Employee Rep. ¶ 94 (Mich. ERC 2009). The Michigan Employment Relations Commission in this case was particularly concerned that the permissive

subject was intertwined with a mandatory subject and the employer had obtained benefits in exchange for the agreement it attempted to repudiate. Which is the preferable approach for dealing with unilateral changes in permissive subjects of bargaining?

The next two sections provide a sampling of the variety of statutory language governing scope of bargaining in the public sector and the various administrative agency and judicial responses which have been made. As you read the statutes and cases, try to account for the notable diversity in statutory language and case analysis which these examples reflect.

B. STATUTORY DIVERSITY

ILLINOIS PUBLIC LABOR RELATIONS ACT

ILL.-SMITH-HURD ANN. 5 ILCS 315/4. Management rights

Employers shall not be required to bargain over matters of inherent managerial policy, which shall include such areas of discretion or policy as the functions of the employer, standards of services, its overall budget, the organizational structure and selection of new employees, examination techniques and direction of employees. Employers, however, shall be required to bargain collectively with regard to policy matters directly affecting wages, hours and terms and conditions of employment as well as the impact thereon upon request by employee representatives.

* * *

ILL.-SMITH-HURD ANN. 5 ILCS 315/7. Duty to bargain

A public employer and the exclusive representative have the authority and the duty to bargain collectively set forth in this Section.

For the purposes of this Act, "to bargain collectively" means the performance of the mutual obligation of the public employer or his designated representative and the representative of the public employees to meet at reasonable times, including meetings in advance of the budget-making process, and to negotiate in good faith with respect to wages, hours, and other conditions of employment, not excluded by Section 4 of this Act, or the negotiation of an agreement, or any question arising thereunder and the execution of a written contract incorporating any agreement reached if requested by either party, but such obligation does not compel either party to agree to a proposal or require the making of a concession.

IOWA PUBLIC EMPLOYMENT RELATIONS ACT

IOWA CODE ANN. § 20.9. Scope of negotiations

The public employer and the employee organization shall meet at reasonable times, including meetings reasonably in advance of the public employer's budget-making process, to negotiate in good faith with respect to wages, hours, vacations, insurance, holidays, leaves of absence, shift differentials, overtime compensation, supplemental pay, seniority, transfer procedures, job classifications, health and safety matters, evaluation procedures, procedures for staff reduction, in-service training and other matters mutually agreed upon. * * *

Nothing in this section shall diminish the authority and power of the merit employment department, board of regents' merit system, educational radio and television facility board's merit system, or any civil service commission established by constitutional provision, statute, charter or special act to recruit employees, prepare, conduct, and grade examinations, rate candidates in order of their relative scores for certification for appointment or promotion or for other matters of classification, reclassification or appeal rights in the classified service of the public employer served.

All retirement systems shall be excluded from the scope of negotiations.

MICHIGAN PUBLIC EMPLOYMENT RELATIONS ACT

MICH.COMP. LAWS ANN. § 423.215. Collective Bargaining

Section 15 (1) A public employer shall bargain collectively with the representatives of its employees * * * and is authorized to make and enter into collective bargaining agreements with such representatives. Except as otherwise provided in this section, to bargain collectively is the performance of the mutual obligation of the employer and the representative of the employees to meet at reasonable times and confer in good faith with respect to wages, hours, and other terms and conditions of employment * * *.

(2) A public school employer has the responsibility, authority, and right to manage and direct on behalf of the public the operation and activities of the public schools under its control.

(3) Collective bargaining between a public school employer and a bargaining representative of its employees shall not include any of the following subjects:

(a) Who is or will be the policyholder of an employee group insurance benefit. This subdivision does not affect the duty to bargain with respect to types and levels of benefits and coverages for employee group insurance. A change or proposed change in a type or to a level of benefit, policy specification, or coverage for employee group insurance shall be bargained by the public school employer and the bargaining representative before the change may take effect.

(b) Establishment of the starting day for the school year and the amount of pupil contact time required to receive full state school aid * * *.

* * *

(d) The decision of whether or not to provide or allow interdistrict or intradistrict open enrollment opportunity in a school or of which grade levels or schools in which to allow such an open enrollment opportunity.

(e) The decision of whether or not to act as an authorizing body to grant a contract to organize one or more public school academies under the revised school code * * * .

(f) The decision of whether or not to contract with a third party for one or more noninstructional support services; or the procedures for obtaining the contract for noninstructional support services other than bidding described in this subdivision; or the identity of the third party; or the impact of the contract for noninstructional support services on individual employees or the bargaining unit. However, this subdivision applies only if the bargaining unit that is providing the noninstructional support services is given an opportunity to bid on the contract for the noninstructional support services on an equal basis as other bidders.

(g) The use of volunteers in providing services at its schools.

(h) Decisions concerning use of experimental or pilot programs and staffing of experimental or pilot programs and decisions concerning use of technology to deliver educational programs and services and staffing to provide the technology, or the impact of these decisions on individual employees or the bargaining unit.

(i) Any compensation or additional work assignment intended to reimburse an employee for or allow an employee to recover any monetary penalty imposed under this act.

(4) Except as otherwise provided in subsection (3)(f), the matters described in subsection (3) are prohibited subjects of bargaining between a public school employer and a bargaining representative of its employees, and, for the purposes of this act, are within the sole authority of the public school employer to decide.

NEW YORK PUBLIC EMPLOYEES' FAIR EMPLOYMENT ACT

NEW YORK MCKINNEY'S CIVIL SERVICE LAW § 201. Definitions

As used in this Article:

* * *

4. The term "terms and conditions of employment" means salaries, wages, hours and other terms and conditions of employment provided, however, that such term shall not include any benefits provided by or to be provided by a public retirement system, or payments to a fund or insurer to provide an income for retirees, or payment to retirees or their beneficiaries. No such retirement benefits shall be negotiated pursuant to this Article, and any benefits so negotiated shall be void.

PENNSYLVANIA PUBLIC EMPLOYEE RELATIONS ACT

43 PA.STAT. § 1101.701. Matters Subject to Bargaining

Collective bargaining is the performance of the mutual obligation of the public employer and the representative of the public employees to meet at reasonable times and confer in good faith with respect to wages, hours and other terms and conditions of employment, or the negotiation of an agreement or any question arising thereunder and the execution of a written contract incorporating any agreement reached but such obligation does not compel either party to agree to a proposal or require the making of a concession.

PENNSYLVANIA PUBLIC EMPLOYEE RELATIONS ACT

43 PA.STAT. § 1101.702. Matters Not Subject to Bargaining

Public employers shall not be required to bargain over matters of inherent managerial policy, which shall include but shall not be limited to such areas of discretion or policy as the functions and programs of the public employer, standards of services, its overall budget, utilization of technology, the organizational structure and selection and direction of personnel. Public employers, however, shall be required to meet and discuss on policy matters affecting wages, hours and terms and conditions of employment as well as the impact thereon upon request by public employee representatives.

NOTES

1. Generally, what are the advantages and disadvantages of each of the following:

(a) a "laundry list" approach (statute contains listing of subjects of bargaining);

(b) a "pure" NLRA approach (statute requires bargaining on "wages, hours, and terms and conditions of employment" and gives an administrative agency the duty to interpret the general statutory language);

(c) a "modified" NLRA approach (statute contains general NLRA language and some express prohibited subjects of bargaining or some specific examples of required subjects of bargaining)?

2. Wisconsin's two bargaining statutes differ in their approach to scope of bargaining. The statute covering state employees uses a "laundry list" approach while the statute covering municipal employees such as cities and school districts utilizes broad language similar to the NLRA to describe the required scope of bargaining? What might explain this choice? Is there a principled explanation for the difference or are practical factors the more likely explanation?

3. Some statutory provisions relating to management rights in the public sector make the described management rights prohibited subjects of bargaining while other statutes make their management rights provisions a permissive subject of bargaining. What arguments support (or oppose) each approach?

4. Statutes in Michigan and Wisconsin were extensively amended in the 1990s. The original scope language in Michigan's Public Employment Relations Act followed closely the private sector language; the amended version is

set forth above. Wisconsin's State Employment Labor Relations Act already contained an extensive "laundry list" of prohibited subjects of bargaining. The amendments in both states added many new prohibited subjects. What accounts for these amendments in Michigan, Wisconsin, and elsewhere—and why have other jurisdictions which retain their original scope language been immune to these pressures?

5. Recall the discussion of bargaining rights under the federal statute in Chapter 4, § C. The scope of bargaining provisions governing the collective bargaining rights of federal employees covered under the Federal Services Labor Management Relations Statute are exceedingly intricate. Negotiations over compensation and fringe benefits are generally prohibited and any proposals that conflict with other federal law or government-wide rules or regulations are also prohibited. The Act contains a management rights provision which serves as an additional limitation on the scope of mandatory bargaining. For a discussion of the scope of federal employee collective bargaining rights, see Michael R. McMillion, Collective Bargaining in the Federal Sector: Has the Congressional Intent Been Fulfilled?, 127 *Military Law Review* 169 (1990). Why is the scope of bargaining for federal employees so narrow? This issue is discussed further in § C.5 below.

C. DIVERSE JUDICIAL RESPONSES

1. INTERPRETING THE STATUTORY BARGAINING LANGUAGE: GENERAL v. SPECIFIC DESCRIPTIONS OF BARGAINING SUBJECTS AND MANAGEMENT'S RIGHTS

As noted above some states have followed the NLRA approach of generally describing bargaining subjects while others have taken the "laundry list" approach of specifying subjects of bargaining. The following case discusses the interpretation of the statutory language by the courts where the law specifies bargaining subjects, contrasting it with the interpretation of more general language. In this case, as in many public sector bargaining cases, the issue is differentiating between bargainable subjects and those issues that are inherently managerial and thus, not subject to negotiation.

whatever is not included is excluded vs. w/e is not specifically excluded is included if it touches on wages, hours, conditions of employment

WATERLOO EDUCATION ASSOCIATION v. IOWA PUBLIC EMPLOYMENT RELATIONS BOARD

Supreme Court of Iowa, 2007.
740 N.W.2d 418.

APPEL, J.

In this case, we must decide whether an overload pay proposal submitted by the Waterloo Education Association (Association) to the Waterloo Community School District (District) is a mandatory or permissive subject of collective bargaining under section 20.9 of the Iowa Public Employment Relations Act (PERA). The Public Employment Relations

Board (PERB) ruled that the proposal was a permissive subject of bargaining. The district court affirmed. We find the specific proposal in this case to be a mandatory subject of collective bargaining. We therefore reverse the district court and remand the matter for further proceedings.

I. Prior Proceedings.

The Association filed a petition with PERB seeking an expedited determination on whether the overload pay proposal it presented to the District was a mandatory subject of bargaining under section 20.9 of PERA. The overload pay proposal provided that elementary teachers who teach more than three hundred minutes per day as part of regular work assignments "shall receive additional compensation." "Secondary and middle school teachers who are assigned to teach six (6) classes per day" were also entitled to additional compensation. The overload pay proposal provided that additional teaching assignments would be compensated at "the employee's hourly proportionate per diem rate."

PERB issued a preliminary ruling finding that the proposal constituted a permissive subject of bargaining and followed the preliminary ruling with a lengthy final order containing the Board's reasoning. In its final order, PERB stated that it believed that the precedents of this court required the result. PERB, however, stated that this court's precedents suffer from an error that PERB itself may have precipitated through its own poorly reasoned decisions. The Board stated that if it did not feel constrained by our precedents, it would hold that the proposal was a mandatory subject of collective bargaining.

The Association appealed the decision to district court, which affirmed the PERB decision. The Association then filed a timely notice of appeal with this court.

II. Standard of Review.

As a threshold matter, we must determine whether the Board's interpretation of section 20.9 is entitled to deference. Under Iowa Code section 17A.19(10)(*c*), (*l*) (2005), deference is warranted where interpretation of the statute is "clearly * * * vested by a provision of law in the discretion of the agency." "If the interpretation is so vested, then the court may reverse only upon a finding the agency's interpretation was 'irrational, illogical, or wholly unjustifiable.' " *Birchansky Real Estate, L.C. v. Iowa Dep't of Pub. Health, State Health Facilities Council*, 737 N.W.2d 134, 138 (Iowa 2007) (quoting Iowa Code § 17A.19(10)(*c*), (*l*)). Alternatively, if interpretation has not been explicitly vested in the agency, our review is for errors at law. *Id.* Whether a proposal is a mandatory subject of collective bargaining, as defined by Iowa Code § 20.9, has not been explicitly vested in PERB's discretion. * * * Therefore, our review is for correction of errors at law.

III. Discussion.

A. Introduction to Scope of Bargaining Issues.

With the enactment at the height of the Great Depression of the National Labor Relations Act (NLRA), 29 U.S.C. sections 151–69 (2005), the prevailing view was that mandatory collective bargaining was an appropriate mechanism to adjust the conflicting relationship between economically powerful employers and comparatively weak employees. While the power of employees would obviously be strengthened by collective bargaining, it was generally believed that market forces would prevent employees from gaining too much at the expense of an employer. If wages became too high, the price of goods or services offered by the employer could become uncompetitive, thereby forcing moderation in employee demands.

In contrast, it was almost unanimously assumed that the collective bargaining model had no application to the public sector. Even President Franklin D. Roosevelt advised public employee leaders that "the process of collective bargaining, as usually understood, cannot be translated into the public service" because the employer was "the whole people" speaking through their public representatives. Letter from Franklin D. Roosevelt to Luther Steward (August 31, 1937) * * *. In short, it was feared that collective bargaining would intrude too deeply upon public policy matters that should be decided by responsible public officials.

Over time, the presumption that the collective bargaining model had no application to the public sector came under challenge. As noted by Professor Merton Bernstein, after the enactment of the NLRA and the growth in the number and power of private sector unions, a large number of semiskilled and skilled workers entered the middle class, while public employees such as teachers did not experience similar gains. This apparent disparity increasingly caused government employees to demand reforms designed to improve their economic standing. Merton C. Bernstein, *Alternatives to the Strike in Public Labor Relations*, 85 Harv. L. Rev. 459, 460 (1971). Across the country, various commissions and studies were conducted to determine if and how collective bargaining concepts could be applied to the public sector.

Beginning with Wisconsin in 1959, state legislatures began to enact legislation authorizing collective bargaining in the public sector. * * * By 1974, forty states had adopted some kind of collective bargaining for public employees, while twenty-eight states enacted comprehensive statutes of general applicability. *Id.*

Most of these state public collective bargaining statutes adopted language similar to the NLRA model, which expansively authorized mandatory collective bargaining over wages, hours, and "other terms and conditions of employment." Many state public collective bargaining statutes, however, also included management rights provisions designed to reserve certain managerial and policy decisions. The goal seems to have been to allow public employees to collectively bargain to improve their economic well-being without unduly sacrificing the ability of politically responsible officials to manage public bodies and establish the broad contours of public policy.

Iowa lagged behind in the enactment of public employment collective bargaining legislation. At first, public employees pursued collective bargaining through exclusive employee representatives without express legislative authorization. In *State Board of Regents v. United Packing House & Allied Workers, Local No. 1258*, 175 N.W.2d 110 (Iowa 1970), this court held that public agencies did not have the power to agree to exclusive representation by an employee organization for collective bargaining without legislative authorization. 175 N.W.2d at 113–14. Four years later in 1974, the Iowa legislature enacted PERA.

In PERA, the legislature declined to adopt the NLRA model on the question of what subject matters are mandatory subjects of collective bargaining. Instead of incorporating the expansive NLRA language mandating collective bargaining over wages, hours and "other terms and conditions of employment," the Iowa legislature instead specifically enumerated seventeen topics subject to collective bargaining. Iowa Code § 20.9.

These seventeen topics are sometimes referred to as the "laundry list" of mandatory subjects of collective bargaining. Specifically, section 20.9 provides that the public employer and the employee organization "shall" negotiate in good faith with respect to "wages, hours, vacations, insurance, holidays, leaves of absence, shift differentials, overtime compensation, supplemental pay, seniority, transfer procedures, job classifications, health and safety matters, evaluation procedures, procedures for staff reduction, in-service training, and other matters mutually agreed upon." *Id.*

Like many other states, the Iowa legislature also included a management rights provision in the statute. Section 20.7 of PERA states that public employers shall have "the exclusive power, duty, and right to," among other things, "[d]irect the work of its public employees," "[m]aintain the efficiency of governmental operations," and "[d]etermine and implement methods, means, assignments and personnel by which the public employer's operations are to be conducted." *Id.* § 20.7. Thus, Iowa's PERA contains both a provision establishing mandatory collective bargaining on specified matters and a contrapuntal management rights clause preserving exclusive, public management powers in traditional areas.

This court has recognized that section 20.9 establishes two classes of collective bargaining proposals: mandatory and permissive. * * * Mandatory subjects are those matters upon which the public employer is required to engage in bargaining. Permissive subjects are those that the legislature did not specifically list in section 20.9, but are matters upon which both the public employer and the employee organization simply agree to bargain.

Whether a proposal is a mandatory or permissive subject of bargaining under section 20.9 is a critical issue. If a subject is within the scope of mandatory bargaining, the parties are required to bargain over the issue, and if agreement is not reached, the statutory impasse procedures, which ultimately lead to binding arbitration, are available. * * * If, on the other hand, the proposal is a permissive subject of bargaining under section 20.9, the public employer may reserve the right to decide the issue unilaterally by declining to participate in bargaining. When the employer declines to bargain over a permissive subject, the impasse procedures in PERA are not available and decisions related to the subject remain within the exclusive power of the public employer.

The central issue presented in this case is whether the Association's overload wage proposal is a mandatory or permissive subject of collective bargaining.

B. Methods of Resolving Scope of Bargaining Disputes.

1. *Scope of bargaining in the state and federal courts.* From the beginning of collective bargaining, the question of what subject matters are mandatory subjects of collective bargaining sparked considerable litigation as employers and employee organizations jockeyed for position. In general, the United States Supreme Court has construed the NLRA to provide a relatively broad scope of mandatory bargaining under the phrase "wages, hours, and other terms and conditions of employment."

The United States Supreme Court has, however, held that even the expansive NLRA scope-of-bargaining provision has limits. For example, in *Fibreboard Paper Products Corporation v. National Labor Relations Board*, 379 U.S. 203, 85 S.Ct. 398, 13 L.Ed. 2d 233 (1964), the high court observed that the phrase "other terms and conditions of employment" was a flexible term which would expand to conform with prevailing industry practices. *Id.* at 210, 85 S.Ct. at 402–03, 13 L.Ed.2d at 238.

In an important concurring opinion in *Fibreboard*, Justice Potter Stewart advanced the concept that there were certain core entrepreneurial activities that were not subject to collective bargaining. *Id.* at 223, 85 S.Ct. at 409–10, 13 L.Ed.2d at 245–46 (STEWART, J., concurring). This line drawing, however, between bargainable "terms and conditions" and core entrepreneurial activities was to be done on a case-by-case basis. *Id.* Ultimately, the Supreme Court articulated a balancing test for scope-of-bargaining issues in which the benefits for labor-management relations must be greater than the burdens placed on an employer subject to bargaining. *First Nat'l Maintenance Corp. v. Nat'l Labor Relations Bd.*, 452 U.S. 666, 679, 101 S.Ct. 2573, 2581, 69 L.Ed.2d 318, 331 (1981).

In the context of state public bargaining statutes that use the expansive NLRA phrase "other terms and conditions of employment" to describe mandatory bargaining subjects, the analysis becomes even more complicated with the inclusion of a management rights provision. Employment terms and conditions are often intertwined or entangled with public policy issues that have traditionally been within the purview of public employers. In order to accommodate the special needs of public employers, state courts with NLRA-type scope-of-bargaining provisions have developed a wide variety of "balancing tests" to be applied at the threshold stage of the scope-of-bargaining analysis. *See, e.g.*, *Central City Educ. Ass'n, IEA/NEA v. Illinois Educ. Labor Relation Bd.*, 149 Ill. 2d 496, 599 N.E.2d 892, 904–05, 174 Ill. Dec. 808 (Ill. 1992) (holding that test includes whether benefits of bargaining for employee outweighs burden on employer); *City of Biddeford by Board of Educ. v. Biddeford Teachers Ass'n*, 304 A.2d 387, 420 (Me. 1973) (Wernick, J., concurring in part, dissenting in part) (noting quantitative and qualitative importance of invasion of managerial functions may override prima facie eligibility for collective bargaining as working condition); *Local 195, IFPTE, AFL–CIO v. State*, 88 N.J. 393, 443 A.2d 187, 192–93 (N.J. 1982), *superseded by statute*, N.J. Stat. Ann. § 34.13A–23 (1990), *as recognized in Jackson Twp. Bd. of Educ. v. Jackson Educ. Ass'n ex rel. Scelba*, 334 N.J. Super. 162, 757 A.2d 311, 314 (N.J. Sup. Ct. 2000) (stating proper approach is to balance degree to which a proposal intimately and directly affects the work and welfare of employees against the degree to which the proposal significantly interferes with management prerogatives related to government policy); *Pennsylvania Labor Relations Bd. v. State College Area Sch. Dist.*, 461 Pa. 494, 337 A.2d 262, 268 (Pa. 1975) (discussing whether impact of issue on interest of employee in wages, hours, and other terms and conditions of employment outweighs its probable effect on basic policy of school system).

The rationale of state courts adopting the threshold balancing approach is that the "terms and conditions of employment" that constitute mandatory subjects of collective bargaining are also invariably connected with some functions arguably within the purview of management, either through a management rights provision or through traditional analysis. *City of Biddeford*, 304 A.2d at 419 (Wernick, J., concurring in part, dissenting in part) (noting as a practical matter, working conditions are invariably connected with some managerial function). Conversely, almost every management decision traditionally thought to be within the purview of a public employer has some impact on an employee's terms and conditions of employment. *Rapid City Educ. Ass'n v. Rapid City Area Sch. Dist. No.51–4*, 376 N.W.2d 562, 566 (S.D. 1985) (Henderson, J., concurring) (stating that almost every decision of public employer affects "terms and conditions of employment") * * * .

Thus, in cases involving statutes with expansive NLRA-type scope-of-bargaining provisions, there is a conflict between the expansive concepts of employee rights and traditional public employer prerogatives. These are two highly territorial pikes at large in the legal pond of collective bargaining, each with the capacity of devouring the other. In order to avoid the predominance of either management or employee rights, state courts have concluded that they have no other choice but to engage in balancing of some kind. *Joint Bargaining Comm. of Pennsylvania Soc. Serv. Union v. Pennsylvania Labor Relations Bd.*, 503 Pa. 236, 469 A.2d 150, 153 (Pa.

1983) (noting "[w]ithout a proper balance the two sections [scope of bargaining including "terms and conditions" and management rights provision] might negate each other"); *Rapid City*, 376 N.W.2d at 566 (Henderson, J., concurring) (stating that the court is required to walk "legal tightwire" between employer and employee rights).

The judgment of these courts that they must somehow accommodate employee and management rights through a balancing process is certainly understandable. Without clear legislative standards as to the scope of bargaining, the courts in these states have been left to their own devices to fill in the statutory gap. * * *

While a judicially created balancing test has the potential of preserving the rough contours of the grand legislative compromise between management and employee rights over time, any balancing test is extraordinarily difficult to apply in individual cases. This difficulty is not surprising in light of the fact that it is impossible to objectively measure or quantify the weight of employer and employee interests. Further, even if there was some kind of objective measurement of each interest, the balancing test requires courts to balance the apples of employee rights against the oranges of employer rights. No court has been able to successfully advance a convincing formula for determining how many employee rights apples it takes to equal an employer rights orange. Finally, the ill-defined nature of balancing tests in general gives rise to the possibility that invisible, unconscious, but perhaps inevitable judicial bias could creep into the decision-making process. * * * As noted by Harry H. Wellington and Ralph K. Winter in their classic essay, courts are badly suited to make judgments about which issues should be bargainable. Harry H. Wellington & Ralph K. Winter, *The Limits of Collective Bargaining*, 78 Yale L.J. 1107, 1126 (1968).

In light of these challenges, it is not surprising that the state court application of threshold balancing tests in the scope-of-bargaining context has yielded a riot of fact-specific results that defy orderly characterization. For instance, a lengthy annotation presents in excruciating detail the conflicting results on a myriad of issues. *See generally* James D. Lawlor, *Validity and Construction of Statutes or Ordinances Providing for Arbitration of Labor Disputes Involving Public Employees,* 68 A.L.R.3d 885 (2007), comparing, for example, *West Hartford Educ. Ass'n v. DeCourcy*, 162 Conn. 566, 295 A.2d 526 (Conn. 1972) (class size subject to mandatory bargaining), with *West Irondequoit Teachers Ass'n v. Helsby*, 35 N.Y.2d 46, 315 N.E.2d 775, 358 N.Y.S.2d 720 (N.Y. 1974) (class size not bargainable), *Clark County Sch. Dist. v. Local Gov't Employee Management Relations Bd.*, 90 Nev. 442, 530 P.2d 114 (Nev. 1974) (school calendar issues negotiable), with *Burlington County College Faculty Ass'n v. Bd. of Trustees, Burlington County College*, 64 N.J. 10, 311 A.2d 733 (N.J. 1973) (college calendar not negotiable), and *Local 195*, 443 A.2d at 187 (subcontracting of work not subject to mandatory negotiation), with *Unified Sch. Dist. No. 1 of Racine County v. Wisconsin Employment Relations Comm'n*, 81 Wis. 2d 89, 259 N.W.2d 724 (Wisc. 1977) (issue of subcontracting subject to mandatory bargaining). While a balancing test for determining scope-of-bargaining issues may be necessary when legislatures have delegated open-ended authority to the courts, it is an imperfect approach for courts that favor principled decision-making over ill-defined discretionary exercises. Balancing tests are a product of raw legal necessity, not judicial preference.

Where a legislature elects not to use the expansive NLRA phrase "other terms and conditions of employment" and chooses instead to list a finite number of enumerated topics, the case for a balancing test becomes even less compelling. For example, in Kansas, the legislature originally adopted an NLRA-type mandatory bargaining provision in a statute regarding public teacher collective bargaining. In response, the Kansas Supreme Court developed an impact test that involved balancing the impact of an issue on the well-being of the individual against the overall effect on the operation of the school system. *Nat'l Educ. Ass'n of Shawnee Mission, Inc. v. Bd. of Educ. of Shawnee Mission Unified Sch. No. 512*, 212 Kan. 741, 512 P.2d 426, 435 (Kan. 1973) * * * .

While the Kansas legislature at first embraced the approach of *Shawnee Mission*, it later amended its statute to delete the NLRA-type scope-of-bargaining language. *Unified Sch. Dist. No. 501 v. Sec'y of Kansas Dep't of Human Resources*, 235 Kan. 968, 685 P.2d 874, 876–77 (Kan. 1984). Instead the legislature provided a closed, finite list of topics that would be mandatory subjects of collective bargaining for teaching professionals. *Id.* In light of the legislative action, the Kansas Supreme Court, following the lead of the responsible administrative agency, sanctioned the adoption of a topics test to replace its prior impact balancing test to determine scope-of-bargaining issues. *Id.*

Under the topics test, the scope of bargaining is determined by whether the topic of a proposal is within the scope of one of the specifically enumerated subjects of collective bargaining. If a proposal was definitionally within the scope of one of the enumerated topics, it is a mandatory subject of collective bargaining. If it fell outside the definition of any mandatory topic, the proposal was not negotiable. *Id.* at 877. A threshold balancing determination is not required under the topic test because the legislature has already performed the balancing by including each specific topic as a subject of mandatory bargaining.

Thus, instead of dealing with two pikes in a pond, legislatures that have adopted a "laundry list" have gone to dry land and established a legal shooting range with a series of legislatively established targets of mandatory bargaining. Proponents of mandatory bargaining must hit one of the targets, or come close enough to one, in order to avoid characterization of the proposal as permissive. The role of the courts in this setting is not to balance the pikes, but to judge the accuracy of the proponent's legal shot.

2. *Iowa approach to scope of bargaining issues.* In determining whether a proposal is within the scope of section 20.9, this court noted

early on that the Iowa House of Representatives approved an amendment to the original bill deleting the expansive NLRA phrase "or other terms and conditions of employment" from the list of mandatory subjects. * * * The final version of the bill did not contain the expansive NLRA language. Instead, the final version of the Iowa PERA contained a finite, or laundry list, of mandatory subjective of collective bargaining. 1974 Iowa Acts ch. 1095, § 9. Because the Iowa PERA does not include the phrase "other terms and conditions of employment," this court has held that if a proposal does not fall within one of the laundry list of terms contained in section 20.9, it is not a subject of mandatory bargaining. *Charles City I*, 275 N.W.2d at 771–73; *Fort Dodge*, 275 N.W.2d at 397–98. In other words, this court has held that the legislature's laundry list in section 20.9 is exclusive and not merely descriptive or suggestive. * * *

C. Application of Scope-of-Bargaining Principles.

1. *Introduction.* In this case, the parties in *Waterloo I* [an earlier case involving the question of whether a proposal regarding overload assignments was negotiable] are back before us. This time, however, the posture of the case is different in two respects. First, the proposal now advanced by the Association does not allow teachers to opt out of overload assignments. As a result, unlike in *Waterloo I*, management retains the unfettered right to assign overload work to any teacher of its choosing. In addition, PERB has taken the unusual posture of participating actively in this litigation. As noted previously, the Board's decision explicitly questioned both the wisdom and consistency of its and this court's prior mandatory bargaining opinions. In its brief filed in this case, PERB urged this court to clarify the confusion.

2. *Proper test of negotiability.* At the outset, we must determine the proper test for determining whether a proposal is subject to mandatory bargaining under section 20.9. The determination of whether a proposal is a mandatory subject of collective bargaining is an issue of law based upon a facial review of the proposal.

In resolving scope-of-bargaining issues, we reject the approach that any proposal which "infringes" upon management rights is not subject to mandatory bargaining. As was stated in *State*, all mandatory subjects of bargaining infringe in some way on management rights. If the test of negotiability were truly a simple infringement test, literally nothing would be subject to mandatory collective bargaining. Certainly any wage proposal "infringes" on management rights by allocating resources that might be otherwise available for programming or other educational expenditures.

We also reject the notion that the issue of negotiability should ordinarily be resolved at the outset by balancing the employer's interest in management rights against the interest of employees in mandatory bargaining. As noted above, while many states adopt such threshold balancing tests, the states which employ this method are generally operating under NLRA-type statutes which couple the expansive "other terms and conditions of employment" language with management rights provisions. The balancing test is necessary, in these jurisdictions, to prevent management rights from being totally eviscerated by unfettered collective bargaining.

Because Iowa's PERA does not contain this expansive language, the subjects of mandatory bargaining delineated in section 20.9 should be viewed as exceptions to management rights reserved in section 20.7. By creating the section 20.9 laundry list of exceptions to management prerogatives, the legislature has already done the balancing. There is no occasion for this court to judicially rebalance what the legislature has already balanced.

As a result, we reject the "infringement" or threshold balancing test approach and instead reaffirm the two-pronged approach to negotiability * * *. The first prong for determining whether a proposal is subject to collective bargaining, the threshold topics test, is ordinarily a definitional exercise, namely, a determination of whether a proposal fits within the scope of a specific term or terms listed by the legislature in section 20.9. Once that threshold test has been met, the next inquiry is whether the proposal is preempted or inconsistent with any provision of law. Ordinarily, this two-step process is the end of the matter. Only in unusual cases where the predominant topic of a proposal cannot be determined should a balancing-type analysis be employed to resolve the negotiability issue. *See Clinton Police Dep't Bargaining Unit v. Iowa Pub. Employment Relations Bd.*, 397 N.W.2d 764 (Iowa 1986) (hybrid proposal involving both safety and staffing subjects held to primarily relate to staffing and thus not subject to mandatory collective bargaining).

3. *Application of topics test to overload pay proposal.* Having determined that the two-pronged approach of *State* and *Northeast* is the proper test of negotiability, we now must apply the test to the overload pay proposal presented here. In order to apply the threshold topics test, however, we must first determine the meaning of the term "wages" in section 20.9. Then, we must determine if the proposal falls within the scope of that definition.

In determining the meaning of the term "wages," our prior cases embrace several guides to interpretation. These cases hold that because the legislature has listed the term "wages" in section 20.9 as a topic separate and apart from other tangible employee benefits, such as vacation and insurance, the term "wages" is subject to a relatively narrow construction in order to avoid an interpretation that renders subsequent items in the laundry list redundant and meaningless. Under these cases, the term "wages" cannot be interpreted to include a broad package of fringe benefits because the legislature has specifically included some fringe benefits in this section's laundry list. We see no reason to depart from the approach of these prior cases.

On the other hand, the legislature's use of a laundry list of negotiable subjects does not mean that the listed terms are subject to the narrowest possible interpretation, but only that the listed terms cannot be interpreted in a fashion so expansive that the other specifically identified subjects of mandatory bargaining become redundant. The approach most consistent with legislative intent thus is to give the term "wages" its common and ordinary meaning within the structural parameters imposed by section 20.9.

In order to determine the common or ordinary meaning of words, we have often consulted widely used dictionaries. *Black's Law Dictionary* defines "wages" as "[p]ayment for labor or services, usually based on time worked or quantity produced." *Merriam–Webster's Collegiate Dictionary* defines wages as payment for labor or services on an "hourly, daily, piecework basis."

Applying the threshold topics test in *State*, we conclude that the proposal falls within the definition of the term "wages." At its core, the proposal simply seeks to introduce an element of piecework pay into the school district's wage structure. The proposal, moreover, calls for the payment of money and not some other kind of fringe benefit. The proposal if implemented would provide an economic reward based upon services rendered. As noted by one state public employee relations board when considering the bargainability of an overload pay proposal, "It is only possible to rationally bargain for 'an honest day's pay' if one can also negotiate the boundaries and the contents of 'an honest day's work.' " *Oregon Pub. Employees Union, Local 503 v. State of Oregon*, 10 PECBR 51 (July 1987); *see also Rapid City*, 376 N.W.2d at 565 (proposal for twenty percent increase in annual compensation for each fifty-five-minute period in excess of five at junior or senior high level subject to mandatory collective bargaining)

The employee's economic interest in more pay for more work is precisely the kind of employee interest that leading commentators for decades have suggested should be subject to collective bargaining. Clyde Summers, *Bargaining in the Government's Business: Principles and Politics*, 18 U. Tol. L. Rev. 265, 271 (1987); Clyde W. Summers, *Public Employee Bargaining: A Political Perspective*, 83 Yale L.J. 1156, 1192–95 (1974). The interest of the employees in more pay for less work is generally opposed by the majority of voters and taxpayers who are interested in obtaining more services at less cost. Summers, 18 U. Tol. L. Rev. at 271. The inclusion of the term "wages" in the laundry list is designed to provide employees with a degree of protection on economic issues from potentially powerful low-wage political influences.

The overload pay proposal in this case is distinct from the proposal involved in *Waterloo I*. In *Waterloo I*, the proposal sought to prohibit management from assigning overload work to an employee who did not wish to undertake it. As a result, in *Waterloo I* the proposal involved a hybrid of "wages" and "management rights." *Waterloo I*, 650 N.W.2d at 634. Although not articulated in this fashion, there was at least an issue as to which topic dominated the proposal. In contrast, the proposal here does not seek to limit management's discretion to assign work, but relates solely to payment for an amount of services rendered by an individual teacher. The proposal does not handcuff management prerogatives in any way other than to require increased payment for certain services.

Of course, whenever management is required to pay more for teacher services, the resultant increase in costs impinges on other management choices by diverting available resources from other potential uses. This impingement happens, in all cases involving wages and simply cannot be the basis for excluding a proposal from mandatory collective bargaining. Otherwise, the term "wages" would be entirely written out of the statute.

We recognize the possibility that artful negotiators may attempt to craft proposals that incidentally involve payment of increased wages to teachers, but which are really designed to influence educational policy or limit management discretion. The *State* test, however, requires that a proposal relate predominantly to a bargainable issue. It further allows a balancing of interests in those unusual hybrid cases where mandatory and permissive elements are inextricably intertwined in a proposal.

[The court then found that bargaining over the proposal was not illegal.]

In closing, we note that, as was consistently emphasized in our prior cases, we do not pass in any way on the merits of the overload pay proposal. We hold only that the question of whether the overload pay proposal made in this case should be adopted in whole or in part by the district must be determined, if possible, by the parties themselves through good faith negotiations and in the event of impasse, through binding arbitration as provided in PERA. The finding of this court that the overload pay proposal is subject to mandatory bargaining is an endorsement only of the legislature's chosen process of resolving employer-employee disputes involving "wages," not the merits of the proposal.

IV. CONCLUSION.

We hold that the overload wage proposal in this case presents a mandatory subject of collective bargaining under section 20.9 of PERA. As a result, the decision of the district court is reversed and the case remanded for further proceedings.

NOTES

1. The Iowa court critiques the balancing approach used in many states with more general statutes as difficult to apply, unpredictable and susceptible to bias. Is the court correct? How else might the courts determine whether a subject is negotiable as a term or condition of employment or protected from bargaining as a management right?

2. Is the legislature a better body than the court to make specific decisions about what subjects are negotiable? Why or why not? What is likely to inform the legislature's decision?

3. Does the legislative specification of bargaining subjects make the court's job easier? Is the result more predictable and less susceptible to bias?

4. The court suggests that policy judgments are inherently managerial. Is there an argument that employees, represented by the union, should have input into these policy decisions?

5. How important was the management rights provision in the statute to the court in reaching its decision? Does a management rights provision serve the same role or a different role when the statute contains a more general description of bargaining subjects? Consider the following case.

BONNER SCHOOL DISTRICT NO. 14 v. BONNER EDUCATION ASSOCIATION

Supreme Court of Montana, 2008.
341 Mont. 97, 176 P.3d 262.

MORRIS, J.

The Bonner Education Association (BEA) appeals from an order of the First Judicial District, Lewis and Clark County, granting the Bonner School District No. 14's (District) motion for summary judgment. We reverse.

BEA presents the following issues for review:

Whether the District Court properly determined that teacher transfers and assignments are not mandatory subjects of bargaining under Montana's Collective Bargaining for Public Employees Act.

* * *

PROCEDURAL AND FACTUAL BACKGROUND

* * * The District involuntarily transferred and reassigned several teachers at [new superintendent] Ardiana's direction during the 2003–2004 school year.

The transfers and reassignments affected the subjects taught and the teachers' areas of expertise. The District had not involuntarily transferred or reassigned teachers within the previous ten years. BEA responded * * * by filing an unfair labor practice claim * * * alleg[ing] that the District improperly had refused to bargain for the transfers and reassignments. BEA alleged that the District violated §§ 39–31–401 and 39–31–305(2) MCA, by refusing to bargain in good faith with respect to a condition of employment.

BEA and the District were parties to a collective bargaining agreement (CBA) * * * [that] did not specifically provide procedures for teacher transfers and reassignments. The CBA did include a management rights clause that recognized the School Board's prerogative to manage the school district, "except as limited by explicit terms of [the CBA]."

The Board conducted a hearing to determine whether Montana law or the terms of the CBA required the District to bargain in good faith for the transfers. The Board considered both the explicit statutory management right to "hire, promote, transfer, assign, and retain employees * * *," provided in § 39–31–303(2), MCA, and the statutory duty to bargain in good faith for conditions of employment, provided in § 39–31–305(2), MCA. The Board determined that involuntary teacher transfers constituted mandatory subjects of bargaining as conditions of employment and as conditions that "can have a great impact on the well-being of an individual teacher," citing its own decision in *Florence–Carlton Unit v. Board of Trustees of School District No. 15–6* (1979), ULP 5–77.

* * *

The Board finally determined that the CBA's integration clause and the management rights clause did not constitute a waiver of BEA's right to bargain for transfers and reassignments. The Board applied a federal interpretative scheme that considered the parties' past bargaining history and the absence of an express waiver of BEA's right in the CBA. The Board determined that the parties past bargaining practice of not addressing transfers and reassignments and the absence of an express waiver preserved BEA's right to bargain for transfers and reassignments in the CBA. The Board therefore concluded that the District committed an unfair labor practice when it transferred or reassigned teachers without bargaining with BEA.

The District petitioned the District Court for judicial review. Both parties moved for summary judgment. The District Court determined that the statutory management right contained in § 39–31–303, MCA, expressly reserved to the District the right to transfer or assign involuntarily as evidenced by management's "prerogative[ ] * * * [to] hire, promote, transfer, assign, and retain employees * * *." The District Court concluded that only "other working" conditions not expressly listed under § 39–31–303, MCA, represented mandatory subjects of collective bargaining.

* * *

DISCUSSION

Whether the District Court properly determined that teacher transfers and assignments are not mandatory subjects of bargaining under Montana's Collective Bargaining for Public Employees Act.

Section 39–31–305(2), MCA, obligates a public employer to bargain "in good faith with respect to wages, hours, fringe benefits, and other conditions of employment. * * *" This mandate is virtually identical to the collective bargaining mandate in title 29, section 158(d) of the United States Code, a section of the federal National Labor Relations Act (NLRA). Section 158(d) provides that the parties must negotiate "in good faith with respect to wages, hours, and other terms and conditions of employment. * * *" 29 U.S.C. § 158(d). An employer commits an unfair labor practice under § 39–31–401(5), MCA, if it refuses to negotiate in good faith on any of these subjects. Neither the Montana Collective Bargaining for Public Employees Act, nor the NLRA defines "other conditions of employment." We have not had the opportunity yet to examine the scope of "other conditions of employment."

This Court has looked previously to federal courts' construction of the NLRA as an aid to interpretation of the Montana Public Employees Collective Bargaining Act. The similarity between § 39–31–305(2), MCA, and 29 U.S.C. § 158(d), and the fact that we have not yet explored the scope of "other conditions of employment," leads us to look to these federal decisions for instruction.

The U.S. Supreme Court and the National Labor Relations Board (NLRB) have construed conditions of employment broadly for purposes of the collective bargaining mandate. For example, the Court in *Fibreboard Corp. v. NLRB,* 379 U.S. 203, 209–16, 85 S.Ct. 398, 402–05, 13 L.Ed.2d 233 (1964), stated that the policy of fostering "industrial peace" represents a primary consideration when classifying a bargaining subject as a condition of employment under the NLRA. * * * In *Ford Motor Co.,* where the U.S. Supreme Court held that the setting of food prices for in-plant meals for employees constituted a condition of employment, it described conditions of employment as matters "plainly germane to the working environment," and "not among those managerial decisions which lie at the core of entrepreneurial control." *Ford Motor Co.,* 441 U.S. at 498, 99 S.Ct. at 1850 (citing *Fibreboard Corp.,* 379 U.S. at 222–23, 85 S.Ct. at 409) (internal quotation marks omitted). Managerial decisions that "lie at the core of entrepreneurial control," as distinguished from conditions of employment, include those things related to the "basic scope of the enterprise. * * *" *Fibreboard Corp.,* 379 U.S. at 223, 85 S.Ct. at 409 (Stewart, J. concurring).

The federal courts and the NLRB have determined that a diverse range of issues qualify as conditions of employment, and thus constitute mandatory bargaining subjects. * * *

The federal courts and the NLRB, in early cases interpreting the scope of the NLRA, specifically have held that employee transfers constitute conditions of employment that must be bargained under the NLRA. * * *

We agree with those early federal NLRA decisions that employee transfers and reassignments, like those at issue in this case, constitute conditions of employment. The teacher transfers in Bonner were "plainly germane to the working environment," perhaps more plainly so than the in-plant meal prices for employees in *Ford Motor Co.,* 441 U.S. at 498, 99 S.Ct. at 1850. The involuntarily transferred Bonner teachers experienced changes in the subjects they were expected to teach, the number of subjects they were expected to teach, and the abilities and special needs of the students they were expected to teach. The Board recognized the importance of a teacher's particular assignment. The Board noted the expertise that teachers acquire over years of teaching the same subject, the supplies and materials pertinent to each subject (sometimes purchased with their own funds), and the value of the continuing education unique to their particular subject or grade level.

The teacher transfers did not concern the "basic scope of the enterprise," and thus did not lie "at the core of entrepreneurial control." *Fibreboard Corp.,* 379 U.S. at 223, 85 S.Ct. at 409. The transfers did not concern the subjects being taught at the school. The transfers concerned who would teach those subjects. The transfers did not concern which grades were taught at the school. The transfers concerned who would teach those grades. The scope of the school's enterprise remained the same—educating students in grades kindergarten through eight. The conditions changed under which its employees were expected to work.

We hold that teacher transfers and reassignments constitute "other conditions of employment" as contemplated by § 39–31–305(2), MCA. This interpretation comports with the policy goals pronounced by the legislature in enacting the collective bargaining statutes. Section 39–31–101, MCA, articulates that the overarching policy behind the Collective Bargaining for Public Employees Act encourages "the practice and procedure of collective bargaining to arrive at friendly adjustment of all disputes between public employers and the employees." This policy mirrors the U.S. Supreme Court's decision in *Fibreboard,* in which it held that fostering "industrial peace" must be a primary consideration in determining whether an issue constitutes a condition of employment under the NLRA.

The District points out that the NLRA lacks a management rights provision that corresponds to § 39–31–303, MCA. The District argues that this omission precludes us from analogizing to federal law concerning topics deemed to be conditions of employment and therefore subject to mandatory collective bargaining. The Montana management rights provision recognizes, in pertinent part, the "prerogatives of public employers to operate and manage their affairs in such areas as, but not limited to * * * hire, promote, transfer, assign, and retain employees." BEA acknowledges this distinction between Montana and federal law, but asserts nevertheless that federal court and NLRB decisions should guide our decision in light of the fact the U.S. Supreme Court has recognized an implicit and inherent right to manage existing in the NLRA.

* * *

A comparison of the implicit federal management right recognized by the federal courts with the explicit management right provided in § 39–31–303(2), MCA, reveals the undefined federal right to be more expansive. The federal management right contains no defined scope or outer limit. The federal courts nevertheless have determined that employers have a duty to bargain for employee transfers under the NLRA. The Montana management rights provision, on the other hand, discusses a "prerogative" rather than a "right," and defines the particular subjects to which it applies.

* * *

Moreover, as a matter of statutory construction, the statutory management rights provision does not absolve public employers from their duty to bargain for employee transfers. The management rights provision refers to management's "prerogative[ ]" to "hire, promote, transfer, assign, and retain employees." Section 39–31–303(2), MCA. Both BEA and the District urge that we interpret "prerogative" according to the plain dictionary meaning of the term. Both rely on substantially similar definitions of prerogative as "an exclusive or special right, power or privilege."

The District contends that an exclusive right, power, or privilege means an unlimited right with regard to the subjects listed in the management rights provision regardless of the duty to bargain under § 39–31–305, MCA. The District argues that the provision absolves it of a duty to bargain for all subjects listed. BEA counters that the prerogative means the exclusive right to make a final decision in the matter. BEA points out that this right to decide remains intact whether the statute requires the employer to bargain. BEA asserts that a bargaining mandate only obligates the employer to meet with the employees' representative and negotiate in good faith. The statute mandates the process. It requires management to concede nothing. We agree.

Such an interpretation avoids unnecessary conflict between the two statutes. * * * In light of our determination that § 39–31–305(2), MCA, requires the District to bargain regarding teacher transfers, we hold that the District Court improperly determined that the District was not required to bargain for teacher transfers and reassignments under the Montana Collective Bargaining for Public Employees Act.

* * *

Reversed.

NOTES

1. Montana's language regarding bargaining subjects was broad and its management's rights provision specific. Why did the court find transfers negotiable? Does the "prerogative of transfers" not limit the definition of conditions of employment? As will be evident from the cases that follow, the Montana court's broad reading of the scope of bargaining, particularly in the face of the management rights clause specifically referring to transfers, is unusual.

2. How did the court view the value collective bargaining in the *Bonner* case? Did the court in *Waterloo Education Association v. Iowa PERB* have the same view?

3. In the private sector, matters of entrepreneurial control are reserved to the employer. The court finds that the transfers here are not matters of entrepreneurial control as they do not relate to what subjects are taught but who teaches them. Is the court correct? Are entrepreneurial decisions in the private sector analogous to managerial policy decisions in the public sector?

4. Is the court correct in stating that the final decision on transfers is still up to the employer so long as it bargains? Most employees in Montana have the right to strike. Would the case have come out differently if the law

provided for impasse arbitration allowing an arbitrator to make the final decision? See Martin H. Malin, The Paradox of Public Sector Labor Law, 84 *Indiana Law Journal* 1369, 1397 (2009).

2. DISTINCTIVE EDUCATION ISSUES: YEAR-LONG SCHOOL PROGRAM AND CLASS SIZE

As evidenced by the previous cases, there are many issues in the educational setting that involve aspects of educational policy yet also significantly affect working conditions. Courts have struggled to determine what is negotiable in such cases. In the *Waterloo* case *supra*, the court dealt with a statute containing a list of bargainable subjects and a statutory management rights clause. In the case below the statute was more like the statute in *Bonner,* containing a more general description of bargaining subjects and a statutory reservation of management rights which are not negotiable except as they affect terms and conditions of employment.

RACINE EDUCATION ASSOCIATION v. RACINE UNIFIED SCHOOL DISTRICT

Wisconsin Employment Relations Commission, 1996.
Decision No. 27972–C., available at http://www.wisbar.org/res/wercd/1996/27972–c.htm.

[The WERC hearing examiner dismissed a complaint filed by the Racine Education Association (REA) that alleged that the school district violated its duty to bargain as to a year-round education program which it planned to implement. The Association appealed to the WERC to review the Hearing Examiner's Findings of Fact, Conclusions of Law and Order.]

At the outset of our consideration of the issues in this case, it is important to make several general observations. To some extent, the Complainant Association concedes that it may be appropriate for Respondent District to unilaterally determine as a matter of educational policy that it wishes to have some students attend school on a year-round basis. Complainant then argues that it only wishes to bargain about how year-round school will be implemented, vis-a-vis employee work schedules, etc. Another way of framing this analytical perspective would be to say that the Respondent District can unilaterally decide which days students will be present but Respondent District must bargain over which days teachers will be present to teach those students. Because of the obvious and essential need to have students and teachers present at the same time if any education is to occur, this approach to the issues before us is not a valid one.

Instead, any analysis of school calendar issues must acknowledge the reality that determinations of when students will be in school also determine when teachers will work. Acknowledging this reality, we proceed to decide whether the change in student schedule/employee work schedule unilaterally implemented herein did or did not violate the Respondent District's duty to bargain with Complaint Association.

It is well settled that during a contractual hiatus, a municipal employer is obligated to maintain the *status quo* to all mandatory subjects of bargaining and that, absent a valid defense, a unilateral change in said *status quo* violates the municipal employer's duty to bargain under the Municipal Employment Relations Act.

Here, the unilateral implementation occurred during a contractual hiatus. Thus, the initial question becomes one of determining whether the change in employe[e] work schedule constituted a change in a mandatory subject of bargaining.

The general legal framework within which we determine whether a matter is a mandatory subject of bargaining matter begins with the text of Sec. 111.70(1)(a), Stats. * * *

In *West Bend Education Ass'n v. WERC*, 121 Wis.2d 1, 357 N.W.2d 534 (1984), the Wisconsin Supreme Court concluded the following as to how Section 111.70(1)(a), Stats., (then Section 111.70(1)(d), Stats.) should be interpreted when determining whether a subject of bargaining is mandatory:

> Section 111.70(1)(d) sets forth the legislative delineation between mandatory and nonmandatory subjects of bargaining. It requires municipal employers, a term defined as including school districts, Section 111.70(1)(a), to bargain "with respect to wages, hours and conditions of employment." At the same time it provides that a municipal employer "shall not be required to bargain on subjects reserved to management and direction of the governmental unit except insofar as the manner of exercise of such functions affects the wages, hours and conditions of employment of the employees." Furthermore, Section 111.70(1)(d) recognizes the municipal employer's duty to act for the government, good order and commercial benefit of the municipality and for the health, safety and welfare of the public, subject to the constitutional statutory rights of the public employees.
>
> Section 111.70(1)(d) thus recognizes that the municipal employer has a dual role. It is both an employer in charge of personnel and operations and a governmental unit, which is a political entity responsible for determining public policy and implementing the will of the people. Since the integrity of managerial decision-making and of the political process requires that certain issues not be mandatory subjects of collective bargaining, *Unified School District No. 1 of Racine County v. WERC*, 81 Wis.2d 89, 259 N.W.2d 724 (1977), Section 111.70(1)(d) provides an accommodation between the bargaining rights of public employees and the rights of the public through its elected representatives.
>
> In recognizing the interests of the employees and the interests of the municipal employer as manager and political entity, the statute

necessarily presents certain tensions and difficulties in its application. Such tensions arise principally when a proposal touches simultaneously upon wages, hours, and conditions of employment and upon managerial decision-making or public policy. To resolve these conflict situations, this court has interpreted Section 111.70(1)(d) as setting for[th] a "primarily related" standard. Applied to the case at bar, the standard requires WERC in the first instance (and a court on review thereafter) to determine whether the proposals are "primarily related" to "wages, hours and conditions of employment," to "educational policy and school management and operation," to " 'management and direction' of the school system" or to "formulation or management of public policy." *Unified School District No. 1 of Racine County v. WERC.* This court has construed "primarily" to mean "fundamentally," "basically," or "essentially," *Beloit Education Ass'n v. WERC*, 73 Wis.2d 43, 242 N.W.2d 231 (1976).

As applied on a case-by-case basis, this primarily related standard is a balancing test which recognizes that the municipal employer, the employees, and the public have significant interests at stake and that their competing interests should be weighed to determine whether a proposed subject for bargaining should be characterized as mandatory. If the employees' legitimate interest in wages, hours, and conditions of employment outweighs the employer's concerns about the restriction on managerial prerogatives or public policy, the proposal is a mandatory subject of bargaining. In contrast, where the management and direction of the school system or the formulation of public policy predominates, the matter is not a mandatory subject of bargaining. In such cases, the professional association may be heard at the bargaining table if the parties agree to bargain or may be heard along with other concerned groups and individuals in the public forum. *Unified School District No. 1 of Racine Co. v. WERC*; *Beloit Education Association.* Stating the balancing test, as we have just done, is easier than isolating the applicable competing interests in a specific situation and evaluating them.

* * * [T]he precise details of the implementation [of year-round school] are not definitively established in the record. However, it appears reasonably well established from the record that the year-round program did not increase the number of teacher work days but did change the distribution pattern of those work days. Thus, although the number of school/work days did not change, there was a change in the length of the school year and the timing and length of vacation periods. Put another way, the amount of scheduled work time and non-work time did not change but the timing of work time/time off during the calendar year did change.

Complainant correctly argues that in *School District of Janesville*, Dec. No. 21466 (WERC, 3/84), the Commission * * * concluded that there was a duty to bargain over: (1) the length of the school year; (2) the number of teaching days; (3) in-service days; (4) convention days; and (5) vacation periods. However, Commission duty to bargain decisions are always based upon the record presented by the parties. Thus in *Janesville*, the Commission majority commented: "We see no basis in this record for overturning those prior determinations."

Here, we are presented with the record these parties have created. We proceed to decide this case based on this record.

As recited by the Examiner * * * the redistribution of work time/time off was based upon educational policy judgments by the District that learning opportunities would improve. Thus, the year-round school program had a direct and substantial relationship to educational policy. As also recited by the Examiner, the change to a year-round school calendar had a direct and substantial impact on the timing of employee vacations and thus on employee hours and conditions of employment. When the Examiner balanced these impacts and relationships, he concluded the relationship of the year-round school program to educational policy predominated over the relationship to employee wages, hours and conditions of employment. In the context of this record, we agree with the Examiner. Thus, we affirm his conclusion that the District alteration of the timing of the pre-existing work/vacation schedule for teachers who would staff the newly created year-round schools did not alter the *status quo* as to a mandatory subject of bargaining and thus did not constitute a violation of the District's duty to bargain with Complainant.

Complainant argues that because all school calendars presumably reflect some educational policy judgments, the result reached by the Examiner (and now affirmed by the Commission) has the effect of making all school calendar issues permissive subjects of bargaining and overturning prior Commission precedent. We disagree. The Commission has not previously had occasion to consider duty to bargain issues surrounding a shift from a traditional school calendar to a year-round calendar. As we are always obligated to do, we decided this case based upon the facts and argument presented. Respondent persuasively established that the redistribution of an existing schedule of work/time off created by a year-round school program primarily related to educational policy. Our decision stands for no more than that.

As previously noted, the record does not definitively tell us the extent to which the year-round calendar implemented by the Respondent altered the schedule of in-service days, convention days, holidays, pay days, snow makeup days, etc. Suffice it to say that these aspects of "school calendar" have historically been found to be mandatory subjects of bargaining and that any change by Respondent in these areas would be subject to the same "primarily related" analysis we have applied to the redistribution of work/vacation time. If the "educational policy" dimensions of when paychecks are distributed, when snow days are made up, when in-service is conducted, whether employees can attend union conventions, or whether employees would have to work "holidays" predominated over the impact on employee wages, hours and conditions of employment, then the Respondent would not be obligated to bargain over such matter(s). If the wage, hour and condition of employment relationship predominated, then these matters would be mandatory subjects of bargaining.

* * *

[Turning to the issue of impact bargaining, the WERC concurred with the Examiner that the School District satisfied its obligation to bargain impact before implementation. Accordingly, the WERC affirmed the Examiner's dismissal of the REA's complaint.]

NOTES

1. The subsequent history of this administrative agency decision illustrates the importance of prevailing before an administrative agency. On appeal, the WERC's decision was affirmed by the circuit court and the court of appeals. In *Racine Education Association v. WERC*, 214 Wis.2d 353, 571 N.W.2d 887 (Wis. Ct. App. 1997), the Wisconsin Court of Appeals first discussed the appropriate standard for its review of the WERC's decision:

> On appeal, we review WERC's decision, not the decision of the circuit court. There are three levels of deference afforded conclusions of law and statutory interpretation in agency decisions. 'Great weight' is the first and highest amount of deference given to agency interpretations. Under this standard, a reviewing court will defer to an agency interpretation unless '[it] is an irrational one.' This standard is the one generally applied in review of agency determinations and has been described as follows:
>
> > [I]f the administrative agency's experience, technical competence, and specialized knowledge aid the agency in its interpretation and application of the statute, the agency's conclusions are entitled to deference by the court. Where a legal question is intertwined with factual determinations or with value or policy determinations or where the agency's interpretation and application of the law is of long standing, a court should defer to the agency which has primary responsibility for determination of fact and policy.
>
> A second level of review is a midlevel standard, the "due weight" or "great bearing" standard. This is used if the agency's decision is "very nearly" one of first impression. Finally, for questions that are "clearly one of first impression" in which the agency has "no special expertise or experience" a de novo standard of review is applied. This is the least deferential standard.
>
> We initially consider the question of whether this court's review of WERC's decision should be the highly deferential standard urged by the District or whether either of the lower standards is applicable because, as WERC acknowledged, it "has not previously had occasion to consider duty to bargain issues surrounding a shift from a traditional school calendar to a year-round calendar."
>
> Although WERC has not previously considered a duty to bargain within this particular context, determinations of questions of mandatory

versus permissive bargaining are frequently considered by WERC. In each instance, WERC's determination hinges on the specific facts of the case. As the supreme court noted in *School District of Drummond v. WERC*, 121 Wis.2d 126, 133, 358 N.W.2d 285, 289 (1984):

> The district alleges the commission has no experience on the subject of anti-nepotism rules and their effect on labor relations. *Though this may be true, that allegation ignores the experience of the commission in determining subjects of mandatory or permissible bargaining which is the issue in this action.* In any case where the commission is asked to determine whether a subject matter is mandatorily or permissibly bargainable, this court will apply the great weight—any rational basis standard to its "primary relation" conclusion.

Whether implementation of a year-round educational program is a subject for mandatory or permissive bargaining is a question of law that intertwines facts, values and policy. Our case law recognizes that "WERC * * * has special competence in the area of collective bargaining and has developed significant experience in deciding cases involving the issue of mandatory bargaining." These factors argue in favor of giving "great weight" to WERC's rulings on the bargaining nature of the year-round educational proposals.

We conclude that the highly deferential "great weight" standard is applicable to this case. The issue presented is whether a particular proposal, year-round schooling, is a matter for mandatory or permissive bargaining. WERC has extensive experience in determining whether an issue is subject to mandatory or permissive bargaining. We note, however, that even without this beneficial standard of review, the balancing analysis performed by WERC passes muster. Therefore, while our analysis proceeds as highly deferential to WERC, we could, and would, affirm even if we were to conclude that either the "due weight" or de novo standard of review was appropriate.

* * *

The "primary related" test does not lend itself to "broad and sweeping rules that are to be applied across the board to all situations." Instead, it is intended to be applied on a case-by-case approach to specific situations. In this case, WERC weighed the evidence and testimony presented by both sides and concluded that the implementation of a year-round program was primarily related to educational policy. A different set of facts could result in a different decision. In this case, we conclude that there is a rational basis for the conclusion of WERC, and consequently affirm.

2. The appellate court decision in the *Racine Education Association* case applied a limited standard of review. That view is fairly typical of the "second wave" of judicial decisions reviewing administrative labor relations agency decisions on public sector scope of bargaining disputes. In contrast, earlier decisions by courts reviewing administrative labor relations agency decisions were likely to discuss in depth the merits of the scope dispute when dealing with cases of first impression, regardless of whether the court agreed or

disagreed with the administrative labor relations agency conclusion. In more recent years, however, the losing party before an administrative agency has had a heavy burden to persuade a reviewing court to overturn an administrative agency decision. Accordingly, administrative agency decisions play an increasingly important role in shaping the law defining mandatory subjects of bargaining.

Courts often talk about deferring to an administrative labor relations agency's "expertise," particularly in cases affirming an agency's decision. What type of expertise does the agency have or are courts relying upon? Also, why would a court give "great weight" to an administrative agency decision, affirm the agency decision, and then proceed to discuss why it would reach the same conclusion as the agency did?

3. Would other aspects of the school calendar be mandatorily negotiable? What about the scheduling of teachers' work days and days off? See *School District of Clear Lake*, No. 31627–B (Wisc. ERC 2006), available at http://werc.wi.gov/decisions/31627–B.pdf.

4. Consider the decisions in *Waterloo Education Association v. Iowa PERB* and *Racine Education Association v. Racine Unified School District*. Did the differences in the statute affect the outcome of the cases?

5. There has been much litigation concerning another educational issue: whether teacher union proposals which limit class sizes are mandatory or permissive subjects of bargaining. In *Tualatin Valley Bargaining Council v. Tigard School District,* 106 Or.App. 381, 808 P.2d 101 (1991), the Oregon Court of Appeals affirmed the Employment Relations Board (ERB) decision that the union's proposal specifying grade-by-grade class size limits was a mandatory subject of bargaining. The court held that the ERB had correctly applied a balancing test to determine that the class size proposal was an "other condition of employment." Oregon legislation required bargaining "with respect to employment relations" and "employment relations" was defined as including but not limited to "matters concerning direct or indirect monetary benefits, hours, vacations, sick leave, grievance procedures and other conditions of employment." An earlier precedent had mandated a balancing test only to determine whether the challenged proposal was of like kind to the enumerated conditions of employment and also met the requirement of general applicability. The *Tigard School District* decision is decidedly a minority approach. Indeed, the decision was reversed by the Oregon Supreme Court, on grounds, inter alia, that the ERB had incorrectly failed to apply the balancing test to the proposal, instead holding that it had already applied a balancing test to find that proposals regarding workload were mandatory subjects of bargaining and this proposal concerned workload; therefore it was a mandatory bargaining subject. *Tualatin Valley Bargaining Council v. Tigard School District 23J*, 314 Ore. 274, 840 P.2d 657 (1992). The court remanded to the ERB, expressing no opinion on whether the proposal was mandatorily negotiable, however.

Effective 1995, Oregon legislation excluded class size from the mandatory bargaining subjects. A new section expressly excludes the following from the statutory definition of "employment relations":

> class size, the school or educational calendar, standards of performance or criteria for evaluations of teachers, the school curriculum, reasonable dress, grooming and at-work personal conduct respecting smoking, gum chewing and similar matters of personal conduct, the standards and procedures for student discipline, the time between student classes, the selection, agendas and decisions of 21st Century Schools Councils * * *, and any other subject proposed that is permissive under [related Sections].

OREGON REV.STAT. § 243.650(e).

Related sections state that "employment relations" does not include the following: subjects determined to be permissive, nonmandatory subjects of bargaining by the ERB prior to the effective date of the legislation; subjects which the ERB determines after the effective date to have a greater impact on management prerogatives than on employee wages, hours, or other terms and conditions of employment; and subjects that have an insubstantial or de minimus effect on public employee wages, hours, and other terms and conditions of employment. *Id.* §§ 243.650(b), (c), (d). Nevada amended its statute to specify bargainable subjects which did not include class size after its administrative agency, affirmed by the state supreme court, found class size negotiable. The decision also found the school calendar and student discipline negotiable. Neither subject was included on the list of negotiable subjects in the amended statute, although the number of workdays in a work year is negotiable. See *Washoe County Teachers Association v. Washoe County School District*, 90 Nev. 442, 530 P.2d 114 (1974); NEV.REV.STAT. § 288.150. What accounts for these legislative responses?

6. The majority approach is reflected in *West Irondequoit Teachers Association v. Helsby,* 35 N.Y.2d 46, 49–52, 358 N.Y.S.2d 720, 721–23, 315 N.E.2d 775, 776–78 (1974) where the court stated:

> The PERB majority recognized, as the board of education conceded, that class size bore on teacher load and that as a consequence of class size this impact on the teachers would be subject to mandatory negotiation; but it was held that the fixing of class size initially was purely the subject of educational policy made in light of the employers' resources and the needs of its constituency. The dissenting member could not make the division between the original designation of class size and the resulting impact on working conditions and stated that the causal chain was so direct as not to admit of the distinction imposed by the majority.
>
> The Appellate Division unanimously upheld the PERB majority stating that the distinction was well taken and provided a reasonable basis for the majority's decision. We agree. * * *
>
> As a reviewing court in an Article 78 proceeding where the question is whether the administrative agency made a correct legal interpretation, our task is merely to see whether the determination "was affected by an error of law or was arbitrary and capricious or an abuse of discretion." So long as PERB's interpretation is legally permissible and so long as there is no breach of constitutional rights and protections, the courts have no power to substitute another interpretation on the strength of what the NLRB or the Federal courts might do in the same or a similar situation.

The Legislature, in Article 14 of the Civil Service Law, has provided that terms and conditions of employment are subject to mandatory negotiation (§ 204, subd. 2; *Board of Educ. v. Associated Teachers of Huntington,* 30 N.Y.2d 122, 127, 331 N.Y.S.2d 17, 282 N.E.2d 109 (1972)), defined "terms and conditions of employment" [to mean] salaries, wages, hours and "other terms and conditions of employment" (Section 201, subd. 4), created PERB (Section 205), and lodged with PERB the power to resolve disputes arising out of negotiations (Section 209). Inherent in this delegation is the power to interpret and construe the statutory scheme. Such construction given by the agency charged with administering the statute is to be accepted if not unreasonable. * * *

It is to be noted that PERB has held only that determination of class size is not negotiable. It has not been held that the impact of class size on the teachers is not negotiable. As stated in PERB's majority opinion: "Nevertheless, impact is a matter for negotiations. Thus, it is not the thrust of this decision that an employer is not required to negotiate on subjects which affect the allocation of resources because salaries clearly have such an effect; rather, the thrust of this decision * * * is that basic policy decisions as to the implementation of a mission of an agency of government are not mandatory subjects of negotiations." PERB's rationale could, we believe, be crystallized with this example: The decision whether, say, sections of the fourth grade should contain 25, 28 or 32 pupils is a policy decision and not negotiable; whereas whether the teachers responsible for the sections are to receive varying consideration and benefits depending on the ultimate size of each section as so determined is mandatorily negotiable as a condition of the employment.

7. There is a significant difference between the issue of a year round school calendar in *Racine* and the class size issue in *Tigard* and *West Irondequoit.* The economic cost to implement a year round school calendar may be minimal (it may even save money for a school district) in contrast to reducing class sizes which has serious economic consequences. Proposals to decrease class size are often very expensive because they require a significant increase in the number of teachers, support staff, capital expenditures, and operating costs. Nevertheless, both issues are usually found to be nonmandatory subjects of bargaining. Is this result consistent or inconsistent?

8. Should a school district that wishes to discourage student smoking by establishing a strict no-smoking policy for employees be required to bargain about its no-smoking policy with the unions representing its employees? (In answering this question, should the outcome differ depending upon whether the employees represented by the union are teachers or white collar or blue collar workers?)

9. These cases, and the laws on which they are based, view bargaining subjects as dichotomous. Either the subject is negotiable, requiring negotiation and allowing the parties to bargain to impasse and use economic weapons or submit to impasse resolution procedures, or it is solely within the authority of management. Is there another way? Professors Malin and Kerchner suggest that the law channels employers and unions to an industrial bargaining model. Martin H. Malin & Charles Taylor Kerchner, Charter Schools and

Collective Bargaining: Compatible Marriage or Illegitimate Relationship? 30 *Harvard Journal of Law & Public Policy* 885 (2007). Because the law restricts bargaining to subjects like wages, hours and benefits, and limits bargaining on educational policy issues, teachers focus on the negotiable subjects to obtain benefits and protection and the employer may have no incentive, and certainly no obligation, to seek teacher input on policy issues as they are outside the scope of mandatory bargaining. The authors provides examples, however, of more cooperative relationships where unions and employers have worked jointly on issues such as peer review, professional development and training, and merit pay. Professional or reform unionism, the authors suggest, can be an effective method of using joint-labor management teams to focus on educational problems utilizing the expertise of both management and unions. How might you draft a law responding to this suggestion?

3. DISTINCTIVE LAW ENFORCEMENT ISSUES: USE OF WEAPONS

As in education, issues involving law enforcement employees may implicate public policy questions. The case below involves a statute with a general description of both bargaining subjects and exclusions from bargaining.

SAN JOSE PEACE OFFICERS v. CITY OF SAN JOSE

California Court of Appeal, 1978.
78 Cal.App.3d 935, 144 Cal.Rptr. 638.

BROWN, J.

Defendants City of San Jose, a chartered city, its city manager and its chief of police (hereinafter appellants) appeal from a judgment declaring that they must meet and confer with the San Jose Police Officer's Association (hereinafter respondent) before changing the portion of their use of force policy governing when a peace officer may discharge his firearm. Respondent has cross-appealed from the portion of the judgment refusing to award it attorney's fees. For the reasons hereinafter stated, we reverse the judgment of the trial court, except for the portion refusing to award respondent attorney's fees, as to which we affirm.

Respondent is a recognized employee organization within the meaning of the Meyers–Milias–Brown Act (hereinafter the MMBA), [WEST'S ANN. CAL.]Gov.Code §§ 3500–3510, representing peace officers of the San Jose Police Department below the level of assistant chief.

Prior to the incidents involved herein, San Jose's police department adopted a regulation effective May 1, 1972, governing the circumstances under which a policeman would be permitted to discharge a firearm. As conceded by counsel for respondent during argument, this regulation was adopted unilaterally by the police department, and no request was made that the police department meet and confer with respondent with respect to its adoption. Said regulation provided as follows:

Part XI—Use of Firearms

311.1. *Firearm Regulations.*

a. *When Firearms May be Discharged.* Firearms may be discharged in the performance of a police duty only under the circumstances listed below.

If, in the opinion of the officer involved, he can safely accomplish the ends described in (3), (4) and (5) by firing a warning shot or shots, he may do so.

(1) At an approved range.

(2) When killing seriously wounded or dangerous animals when other disposition is impractical.

(3) When necessary in the defense of his own life when all other reasonable means have failed.

(4) When necessary in the defense of another person's life when all other reasonable means have failed.

(5) When necessary to effect the capture of, or prevent the escape or rescue of a person whom the member has reasonable cause to believe has committed a felony involving the use or a threat to use deadly force, when all other reasonable means have failed.

b. *When Firearms Will Not be Discharged.* Firearms will not be discharged under the following circumstances:

(1) At misdemeanants.

(2) To effect the capture or prevent the escape or rescue of a person whom the member has reasonable cause to believe has committed a felony which did not involve the use or a threat to use deadly force.

(3) At moving or fleeing vehicles involved in violations of the Vehicle Code (including felony violations such as 20001, 10851, 23105) unless necessary to defend the life of the officer or another person.

Representatives of San Jose and respondent entered into a memorandum of understanding pursuant to the MMBA, covering the period July 1, 1972 through June 30, 1975. This memorandum of understanding was later adopted by San Jose's city council. On January 23, 1975, the chief of police issued a new policy governing the use of firearms. Appellants did not meet and confer with respondent before doing so. The policy of January 23, 1975 provided in part as follows:

BACKGROUND AND PURPOSE.

* * * Thus, it is seen that our new policy is not a radical departure from the evolving standards, but rather it reflects some generally accepted values of our modern society and the criminal justice system; to wit, the use of deadly force is justifiable only as a means of preserving life. The discharge of firearms is never justifiable solely for the purpose of apprehension. It should be emphasized that

there is nothing in this policy that prohibits police officers from protecting themselves or another person from a danger of death or of great bodily injury.

3111.1. *Definition of Deadly Force.*

* * *

e. *An honest and reasonable belief* is a judgment based on a set of circumstances that would cause a person of ordinary caution and prudence to reasonably entertain (have in mind) a strong suspicion amounting to a belief that a certain condition exists that requires the use of deadly force. In determining reasonableness, the officer should honestly believe (in fact entertain) certain conditions exist that require the use of deadly force. The judgment is not reasonable if the officer is negligent in surveying the facts or is negligent in acquiring any knowledge needed to understand the set of circumstances, the applicable laws, or the policies of his Department.

The San Jose Police Department qualifies its members by periodic training as stated elsewhere in this policy and each officer must demonstrate the ability to understand laws and policies, analyze combat situations, and defend himself and others.

P. *Force necessary to protect* is that force required to protect against a manifest peril to life or great bodily injury. Manifest peril occurs when there is a combination of time, space and reason to believe a perilous action will occur. There are three general situations of manifest peril involving these combinations which justify the use of deadly force:

(1) Instant Peril—At this moment and this place the officer has reason to believe that this person has the ability to kill or do great bodily injury and will do so.

(2) Near Peril—At the next moment and in this place, the officer has reason to believe that this person will have the ability to kill or do great bodily injury and will do so.

This place, as used in (1) and (2), is defined as that area in proximity to the officer in which he can, at this time, personally observe the activity of the person.

(3) Foreboding Peril—At another time and in an unknown place, the officer has reason to believe that this person will have the capacity to kill or do great bodily harm and will do so because he has demonstrated a wanton disregard for human life.

3111.2. *When deadly force may be used.* A police officer may use deadly force when all other reasonable means have failed and the officer honestly and reasonably believes that such force is necessary to protect himself or another person from death or great bodily injury.

3111.3. *When firearms may be discharged.* A police officer may discharge a firearm:

a. As provided in Section 3111.2.

b. At a firing range pursuant to all safety rules and instructions.

c. To kill seriously injured or dangerous animals when no other disposition is practical and the public safety is not jeopardized by the discharge.

On February 25, 1975, respondent's counsel sent a letter to the city manager alleging that respondent had not received a copy of the new policy until February 10, 1975, and requesting that San Jose meet and confer concerning the policy. On February 26, 1975, counsel wrote another letter stating that, having read the memorandum of understanding between San Jose and respondent, he was of the opinion that San Jose could only change the use of force policy if respondent was willing to meet and confer on the issue.

Thereafter respondent filed an action in superior court seeking a temporary restraining order and a preliminary and permanent injunction restraining appellants from giving effect to the new use of force policy until they met and conferred with respondent. Respondent also sought a judgment declaring that the use of force policy was a "meet and confer" item under the MMBA and the memorandum of understanding and that San Jose's unilateral action violated both the MMBA and the memorandum of understanding.

On March 7, 1975, the trial court issued a temporary restraining order granting the injunctive relief prayed for. On April 2, 1975 appellants answered the complaint and the chief of police withdrew the new use of force policy and reinstated the former policy. Following a trial to the court, the trial court rendered judgment for respondent and issued a permanent injunction which enjoined appellant from altering the 1972 use of force policy without meeting and conferring with respondent and from changing the 1972 use of force policy prior to June 30, 1975, without permission from respondent. The trial court further declared that the use of force policy regarding firearms was a mandatory subject of the meet and confer process under the MMBA. Finally the trial court denied respondent attorney's fees.

The principal issue presented by this appeal is whether appellants were required, under the MMBA, to notify respondent of the proposed change in the use of force policy and to meet and confer with respondent before changing that policy. Counsel have cited no controlling authority, and our own research has disclosed none. The issue appears to be one of first impression.

The MMBA applies to all local government employees in California. It provides for negotiation ("meet and confer") and mediation but not for factfinding or arbitration. (Sections 3505 and 3505.2.) "Meet and confer in good faith" is defined in Section 3505 as exchanging information, opinions and proposals, and endeavoring "to reach an agreement on matters within the scope of representation. * * * " Section 3504 defines the scope of representation as follows:

> The scope of representation shall include all matters relating to employment conditions and employer-employee relations, including, but not limited to, wages, hours, and other terms and conditions of employment, except, however, that the scope of representation shall not include consideration of the merits, necessity or organization of any service or activity provided by law or executive order.

Respondent argues that the use of force policy relates to "terms and conditions of employment" and thus is within "the scope of representation." Appellants argue that the use of force policy relates to the "merits, necessity or organization of any service or activity provided by law or executive order" and thus is without "the scope of representation."

The issue thus presented is a most delicate one requiring the resolution of significant competing considerations. Respondent argues that the 1975 use of force policy issued by appellants curtailed the situations under which an officer may pull his firearm and fire. Respondent further argues that the 1975 use of force policy subjected peace officers, and the citizenry in general, to greater danger because it limits the situations in which a firearm may be discharged to the firing range, to the killing of a seriously injured or dangerous animal, and to situations where deadly force is involved. The trial court so found in its findings of fact. Appellants argue that it is contrary to the MMBA and to public policy for the conditions under which a police officer may kill a person to be placed on the bargaining table, to be traded off against increases or decreases in wages, hours, and fringe benefits. Appellants further argue that the conditions under which a police officer may kill are a fundamental governmental prerogative, a management decision, the formulation of which should be left to the appropriate elected representatives of the people whose lives and safety are directly affected by such decisions.

In *Fire Fighters Union v. City of Vallejo*, 12 Cal.3d 608, 116 Cal.Rptr. 507, 526 P.2d 971 (1974), the leading case on the meaning and interpretation of the MMBA, the court examined the problem of "reconciling the two vague, seemingly overlapping phrases of the statute: 'wages, hours and working conditions,' which, broadly read could encompass practically any conceivable bargaining proposal; and 'merits, necessity or organization of any service' which, expansively interpreted, could swallow the whole provision for collective negotiation and relegate determination of all labor issues to the city's discretion."

The court pointed out that because of the similarities in language between the MMBA and the National Labor Relations Act (hereinafter the NLRA) (29 U.S.C. § 158(d)) federal precedents provide useful analogies in determining the parameters of the phrase "wages, hours and other terms and conditions of employment." However, the court also explained:

> The origin and meaning of the second phrase—excepting 'merits, necessity or organization' from the scope of bargaining—cannot claim

> so rich a background. Apparently the Legislature included the limiting language not to restrict bargaining on matters directly affecting employees' legitimate interests in wages, hours and working conditions but rather to forestall any expansion of the language of 'wages, hours and working conditions' to include more general managerial policy decisions.

The court further concluded, however, that:

> Although the NLRA does not contain specific wording comparable to the 'merits, necessity or organization' terminology in the city charter and the state act, the underlying fear that generated this language—that is, that wages, hours and working conditions would be expanded beyond reasonable boundaries to deprive an employer of his legitimate management prerogatives—lies imbedded in the federal precedents under the NLRA. As a review of federal case law in this field demonstrates, the trepidation that the union would extend its province into matters that should properly remain in the hands of employers has been incorporated into the interpretation of the scope of 'wages, hours and terms and conditions of employment.' Thus, because the federal decisions effectively reflect the same interests as those that prompted the inclusion of the 'merits, necessity or organization' bargaining limitation in the charter provision and state act, the federal precedents provide reliable if analogous authority on the issue.

One of the most often cited analyses of the federal standard is the concurring opinion of Mr. Justice Stewart in *Fibreboard Corp. v. NLRB*, 379 U.S. 203, 85 S.Ct. 398, 13 L.Ed.2d 233 (1964), which contains a careful and detailed discussion of the history of the NLRA and the limitations and exceptions in the term "working conditions" as that term applies in the private sector to employment security vis-a-vis entrepreneurial decisions. Mr. Justice Stewart said:

> While employment security has thus properly been recognized in various circumstances as a condition of employment, it surely does not follow that every decision which may affect job security is a subject of compulsory collective bargaining. Many decisions made by management affect the job security of employees. Decisions concerning the volume and kind of advertising expenditures, product design, the manner of financing and sales, all may bear upon the security of the worker's jobs. Yet it is hardly conceivable that such decisions so involve 'conditions of employment' that they must be negotiated with the employees' bargaining representative.
>
> In many of these areas the impact of a particular management decision upon job security may be extremely indirect and uncertain, and this alone may be sufficient reason to conclude that such decisions are not 'with respect to * * * conditions of employment.' Yet there are other areas where decisions by management may quite clearly imperil job security or indeed terminate employment entirely.

An enterprise may decide to invest in labor-saving machinery. Another may resolve to liquidate its assets and go out of business. Nothing the Court holds today should be understood as imposing a duty to bargain collectively regarding such managerial decisions, which lie at the core of the entrepreneurial control. Decisions concerning the commitment of investment capital and the basic scope of the enterprise are not in themselves primarily about conditions of employment, though the effect of the decision may be necessarily to terminate employment. If, as I think clear, the purpose of § 8(d) is to describe a limited area subject to the duty of collective bargaining, those management decisions which are fundamental to the basic direction of a corporate enterprise or which impinge only indirectly upon employment security should be excluded from that area.

In *Fire Fighters,* in its discussion of the union's proposal that more firefighters be added, our Supreme Court shed some light on the considerations which govern the resolution of the issue in this case. The City of Vallejo argued that the level of manpower in the fire department was inevitably a matter of fire prevention policy, and thus not within the scope of representation under the MMBA. The court commented that if the union's manpower proposal was aimed at maintaining a particular level of fire protection in the community the city's argument would be well taken. The union argued, however, that the more firemen the city employed, the less the workload of each would be and that because of the hazardous nature of the job, the number of men available to fight a fire directly affected the safety of the firemen. The court pointed out that under federal decisions, questions of employee workload and safety are recognized as mandatory subjects of bargaining. The court disposed of the issue by sending the case to an arbitrator, pursuant to provision of the City of Vallejo Charter similar to the MMBA, to decide in the first instance whether the manpower question "*primarily* involves the workload and safety of the men ('wages, hours and working conditions') or the policy of fire prevention of the City ('merits, necessity or organization of any governmental service').

A similar test has been applied to cases arising under the NLRA by the Court of Appeals for the Ninth Circuit.

* * *

It is undoubtedly true, as the trial court found, that a change in the use of force policy, particularly when such a change inhibits the ability of a police officer to fire at a suspected criminal, has some effect on the safety of the police officer—clearly a term or condition of employment. It is equally true, however, that the use of force policy is as closely akin to a managerial decision as any decision can be in running a police department, surpassed only by the decision as to whether force will be used at all. While private managerial concepts do not translate easily to the public sector, we can imagine few decisions more "managerial" in nature than the one which involves the conditions under which an entity of the state will permit a human life to be taken. In a different context, involving issues of due process and equal protection rather than the MMBA, the Court of Appeal for the second district in *Long Beach Police Officers Assn. v. City of Long Beach*, 61 Cal.App.3d 364, 132 Cal.Rptr. 348 (1976), stated the following with respect to the adoption of a use of force policy:

> The formulation of a policy governing use of deadly force by police officers is a heavy responsibility involving the delicate balancing of different interests: the protection of society from criminals, the protection of police officers' safety, and the preservation of all human life if possible. This delicate judgment is best exercised by the appropriate legislative and executive officers. The effort of the appropriate officials of the City of Long Beach to make that determination in the interests of its citizens and its police officers should be upheld if it is consistent with state law and constitutional standards.

It is, unfortunately, true that the job of a police officer is a dangerous one. The danger, however, is inherent in the calling: a police officer's situation is unique, and in today's world, oftentimes unenviable. Unlike the normal job in the private sector, or indeed, the job of a fire fighter, police work presents danger from third parties, rather than from dangerous working conditions. Thus the employer cannot eliminate safety problems merely by purchasing better equipment or by increasing the work force, as in *Fire Fighters*. The danger posed to a police officer by a suspected criminal must be balanced against difficult considerations of when an escaping criminal should pay the price of death for ignoring a peace officer's command to stop. Viewed in this context, the safety of the policeman, as important as it is, is so inextricably interwoven with important policy considerations relating to basic concepts of the entire system of criminal justice that we cannot say that the use of force policy concerns "primarily" a matter of wages, hours or working conditions.

It is important to note that San Jose's 1975 use of force policy does not restrict a police officer's right to defend himself from the threat of great bodily harm. The danger presented is an indirect one, in that a suspect who is able to escape because the police officer is not permitted to discharge his firearm in capturing the suspect, may later harm the police officer. While expressing no opinion as to the wisdom of such a decision by appellants, we observe that any such danger obviously extends equally as much to the public at large as it does to the individual police officer. Such an effect on public safety lends further support to our conclusion that the use of force policy is primarily a matter of public safety and therefore not a subject of meeting and conferring under the MMBA. While the policy may impinge on a condition of employment, it impinges only indirectly.

The power of a city to enact and enforce regulations relating to the use of firearms by police officers is in the exercise of the police power granted by Article XI, Section 7 of the California Constitution (*Long Beach Police Officers Assn. v. City of Long Beach*). A governmental agency may not suspend, bargain or contract away its police power. * * *

Respondent argues correctly that appellants are not required to come to an agreement with respondent on the use of force policy, but only to negotiate the policy. WEST'S ANN.CAL. GOV.CODE § 3505; *Los Angeles County Employees Association, Local 660 v. County of Los Angeles*, 33 Cal. App.3d 1, 108 Cal.Rptr. 625 (1973). However, the MMBA does require the parties to meet and confer in good faith and "endeavor to reach an agreement" (Section 3505) on matters which are within the scope of representation.

* * *

The real vice in respondent's position is demonstrated by its argument in its post trial brief to the trial court. There, in arguing that the trial court should grant declaratory relief as a guide for the parties' future conduct, respondent said: "Here both parties should know while they're carrying on meet and confer sessions whether or not they are bound to negotiate the gun policy if same is brought up, *whether or not they should bring it up as a possible exchange for favor or concession by the other side,* and the like. That is, the parties will more effectively be able to carry on negotiations if they have a judicial determination of the negotiability of a gun policy; *they should not, at least in part, have to base negotiating strategies and postures on the possible outcome of a suit* to be brought when and if the City refuses to negotiate on a gun policy and/or attempts unilaterally to change the policy again." [Emphasis supplied.] The forum of the bargaining table with its postures, strategies, trade-offs, modifications and compromises * * *, is no place for the "delicate balancing of different interests; the protection of society from criminals, the protection of police officers' safety, and the preservation of all human life, if possible." *Long Beach Police Officers Assn. v. City of Long Beach, supra.*

We conclude that San Jose's use of force policy falls within the exception delineated in Section 3504. Respondent in fact challenged the merits or necessity of a "service or activity provided by law or executive order" (Section 3504), i.e., the policy of when and under what circumstances San Jose will permit a human life to be taken. This policy clearly constitutes a managerial decision which is not properly within the scope of union representation and collective bargaining. As our Supreme Court has pointed out, the analogous federal precedents have established substantive limitations upon the extent to which "working conditions" may be defined under the NLRA, so that decisions which are plainly within the realm of managerial discretion are excluded from the meet and confer requirements of the MMBA. See *Fire Fighters Union v. City of Vallejo, supra.* As stated in *NLRB v. Transmarine Navig. Corp.*, 380 F.2d 933 (9th Cir.1967): "A decision of such fundamental importance as to the basic direction of the corporate enterprise is not included within the area of mandatory collective bargaining." This is consistent with the language in *Long Beach Police Officers Assn. v. City of Long Beach, supra*, that the heavy responsibility and delicate balancing of the different interests referred to above, involved in a use of force policy, are best exercised by the appropriate legislative and executive officers, who are then directly responsible to the people for such decisions.

* * *

The judgment of the trial court is reversed.

NOTES

1. In the *San Jose Peace Officers* case, the court relied heavily upon the decision of the California Supreme Court in *Fire Fighters, Local 1186 v. City of Vallejo,* 12 Cal.3d 608, 116 Cal.Rptr. 507, 526 P.2d 971 (1974). The *Fire Fighters* case involved a number of scope issues which arose when the employer refused to proceed to impasse arbitration under the city charter because it believed that four of the twenty-eight unresolved issues were not within the mandatory scope of bargaining and, therefore, not arbitrable. The disputed issues were: schedule of hours, vacancies and promotions, maintaining the existing manning schedule, and personnel reduction procedures. The case required interpretation of the Vallejo City Charter's scope of bargaining provisions which were similar to those contained in California's Meyers–Milias–Brown Act (MMBA). The court concluded that all of the issues should be submitted to arbitration with some qualifications:

> (1) The Schedule of Hours proposal must be submitted to arbitration in full.
>
> (2) The proposal as to Vacancies and Promotions is arbitrable. The arbitrators shall additionally hear the facts to determine whether the position of deputy fire chief is a supervisory one and thus excluded from the bargaining unit. If so, the Vacancies and Promotions proposal cannot apply to the deputy fire chief position.
>
> (3) The proposal that the manning schedule presently in effect be continued without change during the term of the new agreement is arbitrable to the extent that it affects the working conditions and safety of the employees.
>
> (4) As to Personnel Reduction, the proposal to reduce personnel is arbitrable only insofar as it affects the working conditions and safety of the remaining employees. Matters of seniority and reinstatement included in the Personnel Reduction proposal are arbitrable.

Some of these scope issues are discussed later in this Section. In determining what issues must be bargained or submitted to impasse arbitration procedures, is it relevant that the parties' scope dispute in the *Fire Fighters* case arose after the parties had reached a bargaining impasse and the issue became one of arbitrability? In the public sector, unlike the private sector, litigation concerning scope of bargaining may arise in a variety of procedural settings in addition to unfair labor practice proceedings. (One unintended consequence of this public sector phenomenon is to make locating scope rulings a more complex task!) Why have administrative agencies and courts been amenable to legal challenges concerning the appropriate scope of public sector bargaining through a variety of proceedings in addition to the traditional challenge alleging refusal to bargain in good faith?

2. Consider whether the following should be mandatory, permissive or illegal subjects of bargaining.

Should a city which wishes to improve its community relations by requiring all police officers to reside within the city be legally bound to bargain on this decision with the police officers' union?

Should a public employer be required to bargain over whether employees may drive employer-owned vehicles to and from work? Is your answer different if such a practice is already in effect and then the employer unilaterally abolishes the practice?

Should a city that wants to require police officers to complete a form regarding the perceived or known race or ethnicity of drivers whose vehicles are stopped by the police be required to bargain?

Should a city's requirement that police officers wear a uniform three inch by one inch metal identifying nameplate at all times be negotiable?

3. Whether employee drug testing is a mandatory or permissive subject of bargaining has been a controversial issue, particularly because it is an emotional and sensitive subject. Various decisions have established that drug testing of applicants for employment is not a mandatory subject of bargaining. Drug testing of current employees, however, is less settled with some jurisdictions holding that it is a mandatory subject while others concluding that it is a permissive subject. Since drug testing implicates an employee's constitutional right of privacy, this constitutional dimension relating to drug testing raises additional policy concerns and litigation. See *Anchorage Police Department Employees Association v. Municipality of Anchorage*, 24 P.3d 547 (Alaska 2001) (city's policy subjecting police and fire department employees to random drug testing was unconstitutional). Another difficult related issue is whether a union can bargain away the right of bargaining unit members to be free from unconstitutional drug testing. Cases have reached mixed results on the question of whether unions can waive employees' Fourth Amendment rights. See *Bolden v. SEPTA*, 953 F.2d 807, 826–29 (3d Cir. 1991) (indicating that union may consent to drug testing that implicates employees' Fourth Amendment rights so long as union does not breach its duty of fair representation); *Geffre v. Metropolitan Council*, 174 F.Supp.2d 962 (D. Minn. 2001) (same); *Anonymous Fireman v. Willoughby*, 779 F.Supp. 402, 415 (N.D. Ohio 1991) (allowing HIV testing under Fourth Amendment but finding union cannot waive employee's constitutional right through collective bargaining). Courts have split on whether unions can waive other constitutional rights as well. See, e.g., *Romano v. Canuteson*, 11 F.3d 1140, 1141 (2d Cir. 1993) (stating unions can waive employees' due process rights in collective bargaining agreement); *Florio v. City of Ontario*, 130 Cal.App.4th 1462, 1467, 30 Cal. Rptr.3d 841, 844 (2005) (holding union cannot waive employees' due process rights).

In deciding whether a public employer should be required to bargain about a drug testing program which it wishes to implement, is it relevant whether the employees in the bargaining unit are police officers, teachers, or clerical employees? Should the outcome depend upon whether the public employer wishes to impose a random or reasonable suspicion drug testing program? These factors appear to influence the determination of many courts. How should these factors affect the determination?

For a sampling of drug testing cases, see *City of New York v. Patrolmen's Benevolent Association,* 14 N.Y.3d 46, 924 N.E.2d 336, 897 N.Y.S.2d 382 (2009) (finding that employer's change in method and triggers for drug testing was not negotiable because it was part of the police commissioner's discretionary authority for police discipline provided by statute and therefore excluded from bargaining); *Law Enforcement Labor Services v. Sherburne County,* 695 N.W.2d 630 (Minn. App. 2005) (finding establishment of random drug testing policy and designation of which employees are safety sensitive, and thus subject to testing, to be managerial prerogative and not subject to bargaining, but implementation of the policy was subject to bargaining to the extent that it could be separated from establishment); *County of Cook v. Licensed Practical Nurses Association,* 284 Ill.App.3d 145, 219 Ill.Dec. 620, 671 N.E.2d 787 (1996) (county's unilateral implementation of drug testing policy without collective bargaining was an unfair labor practice and violated Illinois' Public Labor Relations Act); *Fraternal Order of Police, Miami Lodge 20 v. City of Miami*, 609 So.2d 31 (Fla. 1992) (absent express legislation, random drug testing of police officers is a mandatory subject of bargaining but where there is evidence of drug involvement by specific officers, drug testing is a managerial prerogative); *Holliday v. City of Modesto,* 229 Cal.App.3d 528, 280 Cal.Rptr. 206 (1991) (fire chief's order that firefighters submit to drug testing was a condition of employment and subject to negotiations with the union, rather than a general managerial policy decision beyond the scope of mandatory bargaining).

4. LAYOFFS, CONTRACTING, AND SUBCONTRACTING

Layoffs, contracting and subcontracting have a substantial effect on the economics of government. Like many of the other topics in this section, they have elements of managerial policy but also have a significant impact on the jobs of government employees. As a result of these factors, there are many cases on the topic. Additionally, as noted in Section A, in the private sector the Supreme Court has created a specific standard to determine whether negotiations are required over employer decisions such as subcontracting, partial business closings, and relocations. The cases below show how different jurisdictions have responded to the issue of negotiability of these subjects.

CITY OF BROOKFIELD v. WISCONSIN EMPLOYMENT RELATIONS COMMISSION

Supreme Court of Wisconsin, 1978.
87 Wis.2d 819, 275 N.W.2d 723.

COFFEY, J.

[The WERC ordered the City of Brookfield to reinstate and reimburse five city firefighters laid off due to a decrease in funds allocated by the city to the fire department during a tight budget period. The WERC's remedial order was based upon its finding that the city had violated its duty to bargain collectively when it refused to negotiate the decision to lay off the firefighters or the effects of the lay off decision. The circuit court reversed the WERC order, finding that Brookfield was not required to negotiate the lay off decision; the WERC conclusion in regard to the duty to bargain the effects of the lay off decision was affirmed and is not at issue in this appeal. The facts of the case are not disputed. The parties' agreement did not contain a minimum daily manpower clause nor a specific waiver of bargaining clause, a management's rights clause or a provision restricting the employer's right to lay off unit employees.]

On November 14, 1972 the Brookfield City Council reduced the fire department's 1973 budget allocation by $80,000. The budgets of other city departments were also reduced. The city council requested department heads to submit proposals on how these budget reductions could be met. The fire chief suggested personnel lay offs and also expressed concern over the reduction in the quality of services provided. Members of Local 2051 were aware of the anticipated lay offs resulting from the $80,000 budget cut and, in the words of Mike Sueflohn [a department firefighter and member of the union bargaining team], "tried very hard through the news media and other avenues (distribution of fliers and newsletters) open to us to educate citizens of the city what was going to happen to their fire service." The fliers that were distributed were designed to encourage Brookfield residents to attend and voice an opinion at a city council meeting on November 28, 1972 at which time the $80,000 budget cut would be discussed and implemented by lay offs or other appropriate action. The fliers read in part:

> BROOKFIELD LIVES AND PROPERTY IN JEOPARDY * * * UNLESS YOU SAY NO!
>
> The proposal to cut firefighters from the department means placing your family life in danger, higher homeowners and business insurance rates.
>
> Learn the facts about what this proposal really means by attending a public meeting.
>
> PLEASE ATTEND * * * for your FAMILY'S SAKE.
>
> Citizens Committee to Protect Brookfield. Dr. R.A. Toepfer, Mr. & Mrs. David Ninstil and Brookfield Fire Fighters Association.

Local 2051 efforts to prevent the lay off of firemen were unsuccessful, despite the appearance at the November 28th city council meeting of 17 people who spoke on behalf of Local 2051. Speaking against the cut in manpower was John Pavlik, a former fire chief.

The city council's action on November 28th was described in a Local 2051 newsletter in the following language:

> CITY OF BROOKFIELD VOTES TO LAY OFF FIREFIGHTERS: Despite strong efforts of Local 2051, with the help of the IAFF and

their neighboring locals, the Aldermen voted 8 to 5 to cut 6 men from the Fire Department. This means the 6 men hired just 2 1/2 years ago to man a new Aerial will be put out of a job as will the Aerial as a first line rig.

All department heads have been told to cut their budgets, but only the Fire Chief submitted a proposal on how it could be done. He later pointed out that this was not good for the fire protection, but the Finance Committee had by then taken a public stand and we all know how politicians hate to admit they may have been wrong.

At the contract bargaining session on December 5th Local 2051 asked for the discussion of severance pay for the five firefighters who were about to be laid off. The Brookfield representative stated that the matter would have to be considered by the city finance committee. A committee member had previously stated during the negotiation sessions that because of the city's financial crunch, he was going to propose a return to an all volunteer fire department. On December 8, 1972 Brookfield notified the five firefighters of lowest seniority that they would be laid off effective December 31, 1972. At the December 13, 1972 bargaining conference, a city representative stated that no unemployment benefits would be accorded and that the matter was not negotiable as it was a management prerogative. The five firefighters were laid off on December 31, 1972 without any collective bargaining discussion as to the decision or the implementation of the lay offs. On that date, the number of employees on a twenty-four hour shift was reduced from 15 employees to 13.

[Local 2051 filed unfair labor practice complaints with the WERC alleging that Brookfield refused to negotiate the lay off decision and refused to bargain the impact of the decision.]

* * *

We hold that economically motivated lay offs of public employees resulting from budgetary restraints is a matter primarily related to the exercise of municipal powers and responsibilities and the integrity of the political processes of municipal government. The citizens of a community have a vital interest in the continued fiscally responsible operation of its municipal services. Thus, it is imperative that we strike a balance between public employees' bargaining rights and protecting the public health and safety of our citizens within the framework of the political and legislative process.

* * *

In municipal employment relations the bargaining table is not the appropriate forum for the formulation or management of public policy. Where a decision is essentially concerned with public policy choices, no group should act as an exclusive representative; discussions should be open; and public policy should be shaped through the regular political process. Essential control over the management of the school district's affairs must be left with the school board, the body elected to be responsible for those affairs under state law.

The court recognizes that unions, such as Local 2051, are not powerless in their ability to formulate and influence the direction of public policy decisions. As demonstrated in this case, unions can and do attend public budget meetings and can and do lobby with legislative bodies and organize and motivate the general public regarding the union's position. The distribution of informational fliers, newsletters and media releases as well as the solicitation of prominent and influential speakers are but a few of the ways in which unions can and do have a significant impact on the political processes. Local 2051 exerted acceptable political pressures upon the Brookfield City Council to halt the lay offs resulting from the budget cut. To decide the issue to be a mandatory subject of bargaining would destroy the equal balance of power that insures the collective bargaining rights of the union and protects the rights of the general public to determine the quality and level of municipal services they consider vital. The legislature has made it clear that a budgetary lay off decision is not a subject of mandatory bargaining. If it were, the right of the public to voice its opinion would be restricted as to matters fundamentally relating to the community's safety, general welfare and budgetary management. * * *

NOTES

1. If courts are so concerned about the integrity of the political process and continued fiscally responsible operation of municipal services, why are wages and economic benefits such as health insurance generally regarded as mandatory subjects of bargaining, particularly since these expenses typically constitute a large portion of governmental operating budgets?

2. Does requiring bargaining over a subject necessarily limit the input of the public? How might the government obtain the input of citizens on a matter subject to collective bargaining?

3. In contrast to the conclusion in *Brookfield* and similar public sector cases, other courts have held that economically motivated layoffs are a mandatory subject of bargaining. One such case is *Central City Education Association v. Illinois Educational Labor Relations Board*, 149 Ill.2d 496, 174 Ill.Dec. 808, 599 N.E.2d 892 (1992) (affirming appellate court holding that a reduction of the workforce due to economic reasons was a mandatory subject of bargaining).

4. Recall from Chapter 4, §B, Professor Summers' argument that although public sector bargaining is anti-democratic it is necessary to protect public employees outnumbered by citizens who desire low taxes but high levels of government service, an objective most easily achieved by reducing labor costs which are the largest part of the public employer's budget. Were the firefighters in Brookfield in a disadvantageous position vis-a-vis the general public with regard to the proposed reductions in force? Why or why not? Should the determination of negotiability be determined by whether the employees interests are at odds with those of the general public as they are,

for example, when employees want a wage or benefit increase and citizens want increased service with lower taxes?

5. *Detroit Fire Fighters Association IAFF Local 344 v. City of Detroit*, 482 Mich. 18, 753 N.W.2d 579 (2008) provides an example of a scope of bargaining case arising in a different context. The employer and union were in the process of compulsory interest arbitration after failing to reach an agreement when the employer implemented a restructuring plan due to financial difficulties which required substantial layoffs of both rank and file firefighters and battalion chiefs and a reduction in the number of battalions and engine and ladder companies. The union sought an injunction on the basis that the employer was required to maintain the status quo during the arbitration process, arguing that while layoffs were not a mandatory subject of bargaining, the restructuring altered mandatory subjects including minimum staffing, job duties, seniority and firefighter safety. The circuit court, affirmed by the court of appeals, issued the injunction, but the Michigan Supreme Court reversed and remanded. The court held that "whether a layoff and restructuring plan jeopardizes employee safety requires a careful examination of the plan details and a finding that the plan is 'inextricably intertwined with safety' such that it would have a 'significant impact' on safety." *Id.* at 33, 579 N.W.2d at 587. The court remanded with a requirement that the circuit court determine whether the union satisfied the traditional requirements for injunctive relief. When determining the likelihood of success on the merits, the court was directed to apply the test articulated above, lest it intrude on the employer's right to make staffing decisions unilaterally. If the injunction were granted, the court must follow with a final determination on the merits, again applying the test of whether the layoffs were "inextricably intertwined with safety" to determine whether there was an improper alteration of the status quo relating to a mandatory bargaining subject. How might the court on remand determine if layoffs or restructuring of operations are inextricably intertwined with safety? What factors would you advise the court to consider?

LOCAL 195, IFPTE v. STATE OF NEW JERSEY

Supreme Court of New Jersey, 1982.
88 N.J. 393, 443 A.2d 187.

PASHMAN, J.

[During contract negotiations between the state and two unions, Local 195, International Federation of Professionals and Technical Engineers and the State Supervisory Employees Association, disputes arose as to the negotiability of several union proposals. The disputed provisions included one limiting contracting and subcontracting and another relating to the establishment of a workweek. The New Jersey Public Employment Relations Commission (PERC) held that the disputed provisions were mandatory subjects of bargaining. On appeal, the Appellate Division affirmed PERC's determination regarding the workweek, but reversed PERC's decision regarding contracting and subcontracting. A majority held that the determination to contract or subcontract was an inherent managerial prerogative.]

* * *

Scope of Negotiability

Public employees in New Jersey have a constitutional right to organize and present "grievances and proposals" to public employers through representatives of their own choosing. The parameters of collective negotiations about such proposals were established in 1968 by the New Jersey Employer–Employee Relations Act and later by judicial decisions.

The central issue in a scope of negotiations determination is whether or not a particular subject matter is negotiable. This depends on careful consideration of the legitimate interests of the public employer and the public employees. The process of balancing those competing interests is constrained by the policy goals underlying relevant statutes and by the Constitution.

The Legislature has recognized that, like private employees, public employees have a legitimate interest in engaging in collective negotiations about issues that affect "terms and conditions of employment." However, the scope of negotiations in the public sector is more limited than in the private sector.[7] This is so because the employer in the public sector is government, which has special responsibilities to the public not shared by private employers.[8] What distinguishes the State from private employers is the unique responsibility to make and implement public policy.

Matters of public policy are properly decided, not by negotiation and arbitration, but by the political process. This involves the panoply of democratic institutions and practices, including public debate, lobbying, voting, legislation and administration. We have stated that the very foundation of representative democracy would be endangered if decisions on significant matters of governmental policy were left to the process of collective negotiations * * *. Our democratic system demands that governmental bodies retain their accountability to the citizenry. *Ridgefield Park Ed. Ass'n v. Ridgefield Park Bd. of Ed.*, 78 N.J. 144, 393 A.2d 278 (1978). We have therefore divided subjects of public employment negotiation into two categories: "mandatorily negotiable terms and conditions of employment and non-negotiable matters of governmental policy."

7. For example, there are generally no permissive subjects of negotiation in New Jersey public employment. *Board of Education of Woodstown–Pilesgrove Regional School District v. Woodstown–Pilesgrove Regional Education Association,* 81 N.J. 582, 410 A.2d 1131 (1980); *Ridgefield Park Education Association v. Ridgefield Park Board of Education*, 78 N.J. 144, 393 A.2d 278 (1978).

8. Thus, we have consistently held that federal precedents concerning the scope of collective bargaining in the private sector are of little value in determining the permissible scope of negotiability in the public sphere. *In the Matter of Paterson Police PBA Local No. 1 v. Paterson,* 87 *N.J.* 78, 432 *A.*2d 847 (1981); *Ridgefield Park.* For this reason, the United States Supreme Court decision holding subcontracting to be a negotiable subject in the context of a private employer is not persuasive authority in this case. *See Fibreboard Paper Products Corp. v. NLRB,* 379 U.S. 203, 85 S.Ct. 398 233, 13 L.Ed.2d 233 (1964).

The role of the courts in a scope of negotiations case is to determine, in light of the competing interests of the State and its employees, whether an issue is appropriately decided by the political process or by collective negotiations. In making this sensitive determination, the mere invocation of abstract categories like "terms and conditions of employment" and "managerial prerogatives" is not helpful. To determine whether a subject is negotiable, the Court must balance the competing interests by considering the extent to which collective negotiations will impair the determination of governmental policy.

Our opinions on public employment have established a three-part test for scope of negotiations determinations. First, a subject is negotiable only if it "intimately and directly affect[s] the work and welfare of public employees * * *." The prime examples of subjects that fall within this category are rates of pay and working hours. Any subject which does not satisfy this part of the test is not negotiable.

Second, an item is not negotiable if it has been preempted by statute or regulation. If the Legislature establishes a specific term or condition of employment that leaves no room for discretionary action, then negotiation on that term is fully preempted. If the statute sets a minimum or maximum term or condition, then negotiation may be confined within the parameters established by these limits. However, the mere existence of a statute or regulation relating to a given term or condition of employment does not automatically preclude negotiations. Negotiation is preempted only if the "statutory or regulatory provisions * * * speak in the imperative and leave nothing to the discretion of the public employer."

Third, a topic that affects the work and welfare of public employees is negotiable only if it is a matter "on which negotiated agreement would not *significantly* interfere with the exercise of inherent management prerogatives pertaining to the determination of governmental policy." This principle rests on the assumption that most decisions of the public employer affect the work and welfare of public employees to some extent and that negotiation will always impinge to some extent on the determination of governmental policy. The requirement that the interference be "significant" is designed to effect a balance between the interests of public employees and the requirements of democratic decision-making. As Justice Schreiber wrote in *Woodstown–Pilesgrove,*

> The nature of the terms and conditions of employment must be considered in relation to the extent of their interference with managerial prerogatives. A weighing or balancing must be made. When the dominant issue is [a governmental] goal, there is no obligation to negotiate and subject the matter, including its impact, to binding arbitration. Thus these matters may not be included in the negotiations and in the binding arbitration process even though they may affect or impact upon the employees' terms and conditions of employment.

Thus negotiation will be allowed on a subject that intimately and directly affects the work and welfare of public employees unless such negotiated agreement would significantly interfere with the determination of governmental policy.

To summarize, a subject is negotiable between public employers and employees when (1) the item intimately and directly affects the work and welfare of public employees; (2) the subject has not been fully or partially preempted by statute or regulation; and (3) a negotiated agreement would not significantly interfere with the determination of governmental policy. To decide whether a negotiated agreement would significantly interfere with the determination of governmental policy, it is necessary to balance the interests of the public employees and the public employer. When the dominant concern is the government's managerial prerogative to determine policy, a subject may not be included in collective negotiations even though it may intimately affect employees' working conditions.

Contracting and Subcontracting

The proposed contract provisions at issue state:

> The State shall meet with the Association to *negotiate* all incidents of contracting or subcontracting whenever it becomes apparent that a layoff or job displacement might result.

and:

> The State agrees to meet with the Union to *discuss* all incidences of contracting or subcontracting whenever it becomes apparent that a layoff or job displacement will result.

These provisions would require negotiation or discussion only if subcontracting might result in layoffs or displacement. "Nothing more directly and intimately affects a worker than the fact of whether or not he [or she] has a job." The clause clearly meets the requirements of the first part of the test for negotiability.

We next decide whether negotiation about subcontracting has been preempted by statute. * * * [and hold that] the regulation does not preempt subcontracting as a negotiable subject.

Finally, we consider whether negotiation on the substantive decision to contract or subcontract would significantly interfere with the determination of governmental policy. The issue of subcontracting does not merely concern the proper technical means for implementing social and political goals. The choice of how policies are implemented, and by whom, can be as important a feature of governmental choice as the selection of ultimate goals. It is a matter of general public concern whether governmental services are provided by government employees or by contractual arrangements with private organizations. This type of policy determination does not necessarily concern solely fiscal considerations. It requires basic judgments about how the work or services should be provided to best satisfy the concerns and responsibilities of government. Deciding whether or not to contract out a given government service may implicate important tradeoffs.

Allowing such decisions to be subject to mandatory negotiation would significantly impair the ability of public employers to resort to subcontracting. We have previously held that decisions to reduce the work force for economy or efficiency are non-negotiable subjects. The decision to contract out work or to subcontract is similarly an area where managerial interests are dominant. This is highlighted by the fact that allowing subcontracting to be negotiable may open the road to grievance arbitration. Imposing a legal duty on the state to negotiate all proposed instances of subcontracting would transfer the focus of the decision from the political process to the negotiating table, to arbitrators, and ultimately to the courts. The result of such a course would significantly interfere with the determination of governmental policy and would be inimical to the democratic process.

We therefore hold that to the extent the contractual provision at issue includes negotiation on the ultimate substantive decision to subcontract, it is a non-negotiable matter of managerial prerogative. We recognize that our ruling on subcontracting is at odds with decisions in other jurisdictions. These decisions rest on the assumption that subcontracting "does not represent a choice among alternative social or political goals or values." As we have stated, we do not agree that the decision to contract out work necessarily concerns merely the technical means of implementing policy. The decision can be an important policy choice in its own right.

These out-of-state decisions also emphasize the wisdom of pursuing discussion between public employers and employees. We fully agree that such discussions are valuable and should be fostered. They would undoubtedly promote labor peace and harmony, a major goal of the New Jersey Employer–Employee Relations Act. Moreover, they may even result in greater efficiency or economy. If a public employer is considering subcontracting as a means to achieve these goals, employees may be motivated to suggest changes in working conditions that could accomplish the same or better results.

For these reasons, we fully expect that discussion between public employers and employees will be undertaken by the State. It is clearly in the interest of the State to do so. At oral argument, the representatives of the State voiced a commitment to pursue discussion with public employees before resorting to subcontracting. This is altogether appropriate. We do not mean to stifle discussion. We encourage it. State officials would be derelict in their public responsibilities if they did not pursue such discussions.

To this end, we hold that a public employment contract may include a provision reciting an agreement by the State to *discuss* decisions to contract or subcontract whenever it becomes apparent that a layoff or job displacement will result, if the proposed subcontracting is based on solely fiscal considerations. In such situations, the public would clearly benefit from suggestions by public employees directed toward improving economy or efficiency. While the public employees have no right to negotiate on the ultimate decision to subcontract, they may have a procedural right to present their position on the economic issue. Thus, for example, they could seek to show the employer that the employees are willing to perform the same job at a price competitive with the private replacements.

Discussion of subcontracting which is contemplated for purely fiscal reasons does not implicate governmental policy to the extent that it would if the decision were based on non-fiscal reasons. Replacing public employees with private employees solely to save money does entail a choice about the level of government spending, a matter of great public concern. However, discussion about such a replacement would not significantly interfere with the determination of public goals. In fact, as we have explained, such discussions would be in the public interest, since employees could demonstrate that they would do the same work more efficiently than a private contractor.

In *Local 195,* the contract provision would be acceptable if it limited discussion to occasions of subcontracting or contracting likely to result in job layoffs only when the subcontracting is done solely for fiscal or economic reasons. However, as written, the provision is overly broad. Placing a legal duty on the State to discuss subcontracting when proposed for broader policy purposes would place too great a burden on the determination of governmental policy. Only when the contracting out is proposed for purely economic reasons does the employee interest in discussion of alternative solutions become dominant.

Both contract provisions appear to allow negotiation or discussion not only on the ultimate issue of subcontracting but on the effects of subcontracting on public employees. To the extent the provisions impose a duty on the State to negotiate procedural aspects of the subcontracting decision as they affect employees, the clauses are negotiable. For example, negotiation could occur on the issue of adequate notice to employees that they are going to be laid off. We have held that, although substantive policy decisions may be non-negotiable matters, procedural aspects of the decision are negotiable. Negotiation about the procedures for laying off employees will not significantly interfere with the underlying policy determination. They are therefore negotiable terms and conditions of employment.

We emphasize that our holding today does not grant the public employer limitless freedom to subcontract for any reason. The State could not subcontract in bad faith for the sole purpose of laying off public employees or substituting private workers for public workers. State action must be rationally related to a legitimate governmental purpose. Our decision today does not leave public employees vulnerable to arbitrary or capricious substitutions of private workers for public employees.

We conclude that, as written, both proposed contractual provisions relating to contracting and subcontracting are non-negotiable matters of managerial prerogative.

Workweek Provisions

The workweek provision in dispute states:

Where practicable: the normal workweek shall consist of five (5) consecutive workdays.

We find that this provision intimately and directly affects the work and welfare of public employees.

We further find that the clause is not preempted by statute. The disputed provision does not constrain the right of the State to determine the number or classification of employees on duty at any time. It merely governs negotiations concerning which employees within a given classification will work at any particular time. No statutes set the workweek for individual employees. [They] merely provide that the basic workweek shall be 40 hours, where practicable, and that any employee working longer than this shall receive overtime. These provisions leave considerable discretion to the public employer in deciding who shall work when. Likewise, [another statute] empowers certain administrative officials of the Civil Service to prepare regulations concerning work hours, holidays, attendance and leaves of absence. This statute again leaves considerable discretion to public authorities.

We have previously held that, while the establishment of a school calendar, *In re Burlington Cty. College Faculty Ass'n v. Bd. of Trustees*, 64 N.J. 10, 311 A.2d 733 (1973), or the hours of instruction in a school day, *Woodstown–Pilesgrove, supra,* are non-negotiable subjects, the days and hours worked by individual employees are negotiable. The contract provision in this case concerns the negotiable subject of individual work schedules rather than the formation of an overall calendar. The provision does not interfere with the State's power to determine the number of classification of employees working at any given time. Nor does it interfere with the determination of the hours or days during which a service will be operated. The Association wishes only to negotiate the hours of employment of individual employees within the system established by the State. Negotiation on this issue will not significantly interfere with the determination of governmental policy, particularly since the term applies only "[w]here practicable." It is true that negotiation on the issue of practicability would impinge on the State's power to deviate from the provision. Nonetheless, the interests of the employees predominate and negotiation on the subject would not significantly interfere with determination of governmental policy.[13]

---

13. We do not hold that the decision as to which employees are working at a given time would never significantly interfere with the determination of governmental policy. In certain instances, such a decision may impinge on the ability of the governmental entity to determine policy.

We therefore conclude that the workweek provision in dispute is a negotiable term and condition of employment.

* * *

Conclusion

We hold that in public employment law, the substantive decision to subcontract or to contract out work is a non-negotiable subject of managerial prerogative. However, a public employment contract could contain a provision requiring the State to discuss the economic aspects of subcontracting contemplated for purely fiscal reasons when a job layoff may result. Moreover, negotiation may take place on the procedural aspects of subcontracting as they affect public employees. The provision relating to the workweek is negotiable. * * *

Affirmed in part and reversed in part.

[JUSTICES HANDLER and O'HERN concurred in part and dissented in part.]

NOTES

1. The New Jersey Supreme Court takes a different approach than most jurisdictions regarding classification of bargaining subjects. What are the advantages and disadvantages of New Jersey's determination that all non-mandatory subjects of bargaining are prohibited subjects of bargaining?

2. Unlike New Jersey, decisions in other states have classified contracting out or subcontracting as a mandatory or permissive subject of bargaining. See, e.g., *Rialto Police Benefit Association v. City of Rialto*, 155 Cal.App.4th 1295, 66 Cal.Rptr.3d 714 (2007) (requiring bargaining about decision to contract law enforcement services to the county sheriff, eliminating the police department). Where decisions require bargaining in the public sector, they often rely upon the rationale of *Fibreboard* and *First National Maintenance*, the major private sector precedent (discussed in Section A). In these cases, the employer often argues that its decision to contract out is for economic and/or managerial reasons while the union points to actual or potential loss of bargaining unit positions. A variation of these arguments occurred in *International Association of Firefighters, Local 672 v. City of Boise City*, 136 Idaho 162, 30 P.3d 940 (2001). The City decided to subcontract air rescue firefighting services at the municipal airport to the Idaho National Guard in an effort to continue its prior cooperation with the Guard and to maximize the resources of both entities. City firefighters whose positions were eliminated were reassigned and the number of bargaining unit employees did not decrease. The Idaho Supreme Court considered federal case law, particularly *Fibreboard*, to be persuasive and held that the contracting out was a mandatory subject of bargaining under Idaho's public sector collective bargaining statute and that the firefighters' union was entitled to bargain with the City in anticipation of the replacement of bargaining unit members under the proposed cooperative agreement with the Guard.

3. Should a county nursing home employer be required to bargain over a decision to sell its nursing home facility and go out of the business of

providing public nursing home services because the cost of operating the facility is a "drain" on a "tight" county budget?

4. In discussing whether a particular subject should be labeled mandatory, some jurisdictions require that the subject must be "primarily" or "materially" or "significantly" or "fundamentally" related to or "vitally" or "directly" affect "wages, hours, and other terms and conditions of employment." In predicting the outcome of scope litigation, are any of these phrases helpful to understand how various factors are being weighed by the decision-making body, administrative or judicial? When a balancing test is applied, what factors do you think should be considered and how much weight should be assigned to each factor? Why aren't the decisions more helpful in explaining how the decision makers reach their conclusions?

5. Many of the scope of bargaining cases in the public sector have been initiated by organizations representing police, firefighters, and teachers. What explains this phenomenon?

6. Is it at all relevant to a dispute over the scope of bargaining whether there is evidence that some other public sector collective bargaining agreements have included the disputed provision?

7. Should a statutory right to strike or mandatory impasse procedures affect legislative or judicial decisions governing what subjects are within the appropriate scope of mandatory bargaining in that jurisdiction? The interrelationship between the impasse procedures adopted by a state and its scope of bargaining legislation is explored further in Section D below and in Chapter 10 (Resolution of Bargaining Impasses).

5. THE FEDERAL SYSTEM AND MANAGEMENT'S RIGHTS

As noted previously, the scope of bargaining in the federal sector is quite limited. The statute contains a broad management rights clause, but allows negotiation over some subjects related to management rights. The provision states as follows:

§ 7106. Management rights

(a) Subject to subsection (b) of this section, nothing in this chapter shall affect the authority of any management official of any agency—

(1) to determine the mission, budget, organization, number of employees, and internal security practices of the agency; and

(2) in accordance with applicable laws—

(A) to hire, assign, direct, layoff, and retain employees in the agency, or to suspend, remove, reduce in grade or pay, or take other disciplinary action against such employees;

(B) to assign work, to make determinations with respect to contracting out, and to determine the personnel by which agency operations shall be conducted;

(C) with respect to filling positions, to make selections for appointments from—

(i) among properly ranked and certified candidates for promotion; or

(ii) any other appropriate source; and

(D) to take whatever actions may be necessary to carry out the agency mission during emergencies.

(b) Nothing in this section shall preclude any agency and any labor organization from negotiating—

(1) at the election of the agency, on the numbers, types, and grades of employees or positions assigned to any organizational subdivision, work project, or tour of duty, or on the technology, methods, and means of performing work;

(2) procedures which management officials of the agency will observe in exercising any authority under this section; or

(3) appropriate arrangements for employees adversely affected by the exercise of any authority under this section by such management officials.

The following case considers the application of this provision and its exceptions.

AMERICAN FEDERATION OF GOVERNMENT EMPLOYEES LOCAL 171 AND UNITED STATES DEPARTMENT OF JUSTICE FEDERAL BUREAU OF PRISONS

Federal Labor Relations Authority, 2009.
64 F.L.R.A. 275.

POPE, CHAIRMAN, AND BECK AND DUBESTER, MEMBERS

DECISION AND ORDER ON A NEGOTIABLITY ISSUE

I. Statement of the Case

This case is before the Authority on a negotiability appeal filed by the Union under § 7105(a)(2)(E) of the Federal Service Labor–Management Relations Statute (the Statute). * * * The dispute involves a single proposal related to searches of employees' personal property located within their assigned work stations.

For the reasons that follow, we find that the proposal is within the duty to bargain.

II. Proposal

> Where a reasonable expectation of privacy exist[s] and there is reasonable suspicion, searches of employee[s'] personal property within their assigned/work stations by management or a representative of the employer will have a union representative present, absent an overriding exigency. The Union representative will be designated by the Union President or his designee.

III. Meaning of the Proposal

The Union contends that the proposal requires the Agency to permit Union representation at Agency searches of employees' personal property located within their work stations when: (1) there is a reasonable expectation of privacy; (2) there is reasonable suspicion; and (3) no overriding exigency exists. The Agency argues that the intent of the proposal is to establish an expectation of privacy, but concedes that the proposal could be interpreted as the Union contends.

When a union's explanation of a proposal is consistent with the plain wording of the proposal, the Authority adopts the explanation. *AFSCME Local 2830*, 60 FLRA 671 (2005). As the Union's explanation is consistent with the plain wording of the proposal, we adopt it.

IV. Positions of the Parties

A. Agency

The Agency contends that the proposal is contrary to its right to determine the policies and practices that are part of its internal security plan. In this connection, the Agency argues that the Supreme Court has held that the prison environment presents significant security concerns, and has concluded that prison administrators are entitled to deference on security issues.

The Agency asserts that it has published rules related to searches at its facilities, and that there is no expectation of privacy within the secure areas of those facilities. The Agency also asserts that, under the proposal, before the Agency could search an employee's personal property within the work space, the Agency would be required "to wait, no matter how many hours or days it may take, for a Union representative to arrive * * *, unless there is an overriding exigency." In addition, the Agency argues that the proposal would preclude random searches and would require the Agency "to always have a Union representative present unless the extremely high overriding exigency standard is met." Finally, the Agency contends that the proposal is not sufficiently tailored to constitute an appropriate arrangement and that any Union argument to the contrary should be rejected as a bare assertion.

B. Union

The Union contends that the proposal requires Union representation at searches of employees' personal property within their work spaces for reasons similar to those that permit union representation at investigatory interviews under § 7114(a)(2)(B) of the Statute.[3] The Union argues that the proposal would "not affect internal security in any way or conflict with any investigative techniques that the [A]gency may choose to pur-

3. Section 7114(a)(2)(B) of the Statute provides, in pertinent part, that in certain circumstances an exclusive representative of bargaining-unit employees shall be given the opportunity to be represented at "any examination of an employee in the unit by a representative of the agency in connection with an investigation[.]"

sue." The Union asserts that any concern over delay, disruption or denial of a search by virtue of any Union representative's unavailability or refusal to participate is negated by: (a) ready access to representatives on all shifts; and (b) the overriding-exigency wording in the proposal. *Id.* at 4. Finally, the Union contends that the proposal is "a procedure and/or appropriate arrangement[.]"

V. Analysis and Conclusions

A. The proposal does not establish an expectation of privacy that does not already exist at the Agency's facilities.

The Agency contends that the proposal assumes that employees have an expectation of privacy that does not exist under the Agency's current rules. However, the Agency's own rules regarding searches at its facilities refute its contention.

In particular, 28 C.F.R. § 511.10 makes it clear that the rules regarding searches of non-inmates apply to all persons, and the Agency acknowledges that the rules apply to non-visitors as well as non-inmates. Thus, the rules apply to employees. Further, § 511.15(a)(2) and § 511.17 indicate that non-inmates have the right to refuse a search by leaving Agency grounds instead of submitting to a search. Therefore, a non-inmate does not automatically surrender his or her expectation of privacy when entering the prison, and even if a non-inmate is selected for a random search, he or she can preserve his or her privacy rights by electing to vacate the premises. Of course, if an employee makes such an election, then other personnel issues—including those related to absence without leave—may arise. Nevertheless, the Agency's rule provides employees with a reasonable expectation of privacy, even if that expectation must be balanced against the consequences of acting on it. Although § 511.15(a) addresses random searches, the ability to refuse a reasonable-suspicion search by electing non-entry or departure from the Agency facility is set forth in § 511.17 of the rules. Put simply, under the Agency's own published rules, all non-inmates, including employees, have a reasonable expectation of privacy by virtue of their ability to leave the facility rather than submit to a search.

In addition, the proposal applies only to reasonable-suspicion searches. In other words, under the proposal, the presence of a Union representative is not required at every search of an employee's personal property; only reasonable-suspicion searches are covered. Section 511.15(b) of the Agency's rules addresses reasonable-suspicion searches and provides that reasonable suspicion exists if a staff member knows of facts and circumstances that warrant rational inferences that a non-inmate may be engaged in, attempting, or about to engage in, criminal or other prohibited activity. That is, such searches necessitate facts and circumstances warranting rational inferences of illegal activity by someone in the bargaining unit. There is no basis for finding that the proposal is inconsistent with these rules.

For the foregoing reasons, the proposal does not establish an expectation of privacy that the Agency does not already recognize, and the Agency's privacy-related arguments do not provide a basis for finding the proposal outside the duty to bargain.

B. The proposal is not contrary to management's right to determine internal security.

The right to determine internal security practices includes the authority to determine the policies and practices that are part of an agency's plan to secure or safeguard its personnel, physical property or operations against internal and external risks. When management shows a link or reasonable connection between its objective of safeguarding its personnel, property, or operations and the investigative technique designed to implement that objective, a proposal that conflicts with the technique affects management's right. In deciding whether a proposal affects management's right to determine its internal security practices, the Authority does not examine the merit of the practices adopted by an agency.

The Authority has recognized that Federal correctional facilities are different from other types of facilities and that, at a correctional facility, internal security practices are of paramount importance and there is a critical need to prevent the introduction of unauthorized weapons and contraband into the facility. Accordingly, the Authority has held that proposals that address how an agency is to conduct reasonable-suspicion searches of employees' personal property within the workplace affect management's right to determine internal security.

However, even if a proposal affects a management right under § 7106(a) of the Statute the proposal is within the duty to bargain if it constitutes an appropriate arrangement under § 7106(b)(3) of the Statute. To determine whether a proposal constitutes an appropriate arrangement, the Authority applies the test set forth in *NAGE, Local R14–87*, 21 FLRA 24, 31–33 (1986) (*KANG*). Under this test, the Authority initially determines whether the proposal is intended to be an "arrangement" for employees adversely affected by the exercise of a management right. If the proposal is an arrangement, then the Authority determines whether the arrangement is appropriate or whether it is inappropriate because it excessively interferes with management's rights. *See KANG*, 21 FLRA at 31. In making this determination, the Authority balances the proposal's benefits to employees against its burdens on management.

The proposal would permit employees to have Union representation, under certain circumstances, when they are searched by management pursuant to management's exercise of its right to determine internal security practices. As such, it is tailored to benefit only employees who are adversely affected by the exercise of that management right, and we find that it is an arrangement.

As to whether the arrangement is "appropriate," or whether it is inappropriate because it excessively interferes with management's rights, the Union cites *El Reno*, 59 FLRA 536. In *El Reno*, the Authority found that an award enforcing a provision similar to the proposal here did not excessively interfere with management's right to determine its internal security practices. *Id.* at 538. Specifically, the Authority found that by ensuring both the "integrity" of searches and the "authenticity of any findings," the provision at issue afforded "significant" benefits to employees. *Id.* Moreover, noting that the provision permitted searches without representation in an "overriding exigency" and that there was no indication how this wording would be applied in future cases, the Authority rejected the agency's contention that, on its face, the provision was not enforceable under § 7106(b)(3) of the Statute. *Id.* at 539.

Like the provision in *El Reno*, the proposal here permits reasonable-suspicion searches without Union representation when there is an overriding exigency. Also like the provision in *El Reno*, the proposal would afford employees significant benefits. Although the Agency claims that the proposal is nonnegotiable on its face, the effect and benefits of this proposal are indistinguishable from the effects and benefits of the provision at issue in *El Reno*. Thus, *El Reno* supports a conclusion that the proposal is within the duty to bargain.

We reject the Agency's argument that application of this proposal would obligate it "to wait, no matter how many hours or days it may take, for a Union representative to arrive prior to a search, unless there is an overriding exigency." As the Union states, there are approximately twenty union representatives employed at the facility, some of whom are present on every shift. Further, other than the Agency's unsupported assertion of undue delay, the Agency does not explain why a Union representative's attendance at searches where overriding exigencies do not exist would excessively interfere with management's right to determine internal security practices.

For the foregoing reasons, we find that the proposal does not excessively interfere with management's right to determine internal security practices and, thus, constitutes an appropriate arrangement within the meaning of § 7106(b)(3) of the Statute. Accordingly, it is within the duty to bargain.

VI. Order

The proposal is within the duty to bargain, and the Agency shall, upon request, or as otherwise agreed to by the parties, negotiate with the Union over that proposal.

NOTES

1. The Federal Service Labor–Management Relations Statute contains a provision that allows labor organizations to file an expedited appeal of an agency's claim that a particular bargaining subject is not negotiable. The appeal is made directly to FLRA, with short timelines for filing the appeal and the agency response. FLRA has discretion to hold a hearing on the issue and

is directed by the statute to expedite the decision in order to avoid bargaining delays. See 5 U.S.C. § 7117(c).

2. Recall the discussion of federal sector bargaining in § A, *supra*. Does this decision provide any insight as to why the scope of bargaining for federal employees is so narrow? Review the statutory management rights provision quoted above. It provides significant restrictions on the scope of bargaining and then some exceptions. Does the decision provide a useful and workable test for determining whether a proposal is within management's rights or one of the exceptions to management's rights? Is it surprising that there are a large number of negotiability appeals? That despite the provision for expedited appeals of negotiability, there are long delays in deciding the cases? That negotiations in the federal sector are prolonged?

3. When refusing to bargain about some union demands, public officials commonly rely upon management rights set forth in collective bargaining statutes or concepts of implied management prerogatives borrowed from the private sector. Do these management rights theories hide the issue of whether certain public decisions should not be made by means of the collective bargaining process where the public's participation is typically restricted?

4. Are the different outcomes in the cases in this chapter solely or primarily explainable in terms of different statutory language covering scope of bargaining?

5. On the one hand, it has been argued that restricting the scope of bargaining for public employees will prevent responsiveness to changing conditions and new problems, make collective bargaining a frustrating and dysfunctional experience, and encourage lobbying by unions for legislated public employee benefits when they are outside the restricted scope of bargaining. On the other hand, it has been argued that the price paid by public employees for lesser bargaining rights than their private sector counterparts have is more than compensated for by the many advantages of public employment such as statutory benefits and the right to participate as citizens in employment-related decision-making. Which side of this debate has the stronger arguments?

6. It has already been noted that it is difficult, if not impossible, to discern general trends relating to public sector scope of bargaining provisions. What accounts for this notable lack of rethinking or developing a consensus on scope of bargaining issues in the public sector? Why aren't jurisdictions "learning" and "borrowing" from each other in the area of legal scope of bargaining, particularly since decisions from other jurisdictions are so readily available?

Many of the concerns articulated regarding scope of bargaining relate to the concern about government's retention of the right to decide matters of policy and a fear that collective bargaining will restrict public participation in such decisions. Consider the following assessment of that concern.

THE PARADOX OF PUBLIC SECTOR LABOR LAW

Martin H. Malin
84 Indiana Law Journal 1369 (2009).

* * *

Two of the most powerful arguments against public employee collective bargaining are that it is antidemocratic and that it impedes effective government. At one time these arguments were invoked to justify prohibiting public employees from joining unions. Today, the arguments are invoked in some jurisdictions to preclude collective bargaining by public employees. However, even in jurisdictions that recognize public employees' rights to bargain collectively, these concerns are used to narrow the scope of what must be and, in some cases, what may be negotiated. The argument that collective bargaining is antidemocratic is invoked most often by courts in narrowing the scope of what is negotiable. Although the argument that collective bargaining impedes effective government is sometimes advanced by courts when refusing to enforce collective bargaining agreements, the effective government argument is more often used by the legislative and executive branches as a backlash against public employee unions and as justification for further narrowing the scope of negotiability.

In this Article, I contend that the narrowness of what is negotiable which results from concerns with the antidemocratic tendencies of collective bargaining leads to collective bargaining impeding effective government. Specifically, I argue that the law governing negotiability channels unions away from participation in, and hence responsibility for, decisions affecting the risks of the public sector enterprise and restricts the unions to negotiating contract provisions that protect employees from those risks. Unions perform their narrow role very effectively—so effectively that the results can impede effective government. * * *

The view that public sector collective bargaining is antidemocratic is not confined to those who advocate prohibiting unionization of public employees. Wellington and Winter, for example, cite their concerns with the antidemocratic nature of public sector collective bargaining as grounds for prohibiting public employee strikes, and for limiting the scope of issues subject to negotiation. Similarly, Clyde Summers, a staunch supporter of public sector collective bargaining, urges that its antidemocratic nature drives the determination of which subjects are mandatorily bargainable.

These views have not been lost on the courts. Courts have cited the antidemocratic nature of public sector collective bargaining as a primary justification for limiting the subjects over which public employers are required to negotiate. * * *

Jurisdictions have adopted a variety of approaches to curbing the antidemocratic nature of public sector collective bargaining. A few specify in the statute what subjects must be negotiated. Most follow the National

Labor Relations Act model and require bargaining on wages, hours, and other terms and conditions of employment, but temper that mandate with broadly worded management rights clauses. States such as New Jersey and South Dakota go so far as to prohibit bargaining on subjects not deemed mandatorily negotiable. * * *

Most jurisdictions follow the private sector model of dividing subjects of bargaining into mandatory, permissive, and prohibited. The problem that labor boards and courts have had to confront is how to deal with two potentially extremely broad concepts. At some level, every decision affects conditions of employment, and, at some level, every decision affects public policy or managerial authority. Even bargaining about such basic matters as wages affects the allocation of scarce public resources and thereby affects the determination of public policy. * * *

The most common response to this problem has been to balance the interests of employees in bargaining an issue against the impact of the issue on managerial prerogatives and public policy. * * *

A survey of the results of such ad hoc balancing across jurisdictions makes it clear that whether a subject primarily affects working conditions or managerial policy is in the eyes of whoever is reading the scale. * * *

Concern that public employee collective bargaining is antidemocratic excludes unions from negotiation over any issue that a labor board or court deems a matter of public policy. It channels unions to negotiate only over those issues where the direct effects on wages and working conditions (i.e. traditional bread and butter issues) outweigh the effects on public policy. Where unions gain the right to negotiate issues that significantly affect public policy, they do so by stressing the bread and butter nature of the issue, even though the union's motivation may be to serve as a voice for the employees in the making of the policy. For example, a police union gains the right to negotiate over drug testing by emphasizing drug testing as an issue of employee discipline. Yet the union may be seeking a voice for police officers in the setting of policy on drug testing in light of the effects of drug testing on officer morale, the ability of citizens to exploit the policy to harass innocent officers with fraudulent complaints, and the need to effectively root out impaired officers whose presence endangers not only public safety but the safety of fellow officers. Similarly, a teacher's union gains the right to negotiate class size by portraying it as an issue of employee workload, even though its motive may be to serve as a vehicle for teacher voice in the educational policy concerns involved in setting class size.

* * *

The paradox of public sector labor law is that to avoid antidemocratic aspects of public sector collective bargaining, the law has channeled public employee unions away from investing in the risks of the public enterprise and toward insulating their members from those risks. Unions have done such an effective job in their channeled role that their collective bargaining agreements can impede effective government.

There is good reason to believe that giving employees, through their unions, an institutional voice in the initial decision making will increase the likelihood that they will become agents of, instead of obstructions to, effective change. Studies in the private sector show that when unions are strong and have a cooperative relationship with management, they provide independent employee voice that plays a crucial role in the successful development and sustenance of high performance workplace practices. These findings are consistent with the general social-psychology procedural justice literature which finds positive outcomes associated generally with employee voice, that is, having an opportunity to be heard concerning decisions that affect them, even when the outcomes are not what the employees desired.

Experiences in the public sector suggest similar positive results from an institutionalized employee collective voice in the decision-making process. Consider the complaint that unions impede reform in public education by clinging to the salary grid, which bases teachers' pay exclusively on education level and years of service. When movement away from the salary grid is imposed unilaterally, union resistance is almost reflexive. For example, when the New York public schools announced a pilot program to estimate the value added to student test performance by teachers in schools, union president Randi Weingarten responded that the union would "fight this on all grounds—educational, legal and moral."

Contrast the reaction in New York to the union's engagement in Denver, Colorado. In 2004, the membership of the Denver Classroom Teachers Association (DCTA) voted to approve a union-school district incentive pay plan known as the Professional Compensation System for Teachers (Pro Comp). A design team consisting of five teachers, five administrators, and two citizens devised the plan. * * *

Public sector collective bargaining is said to impede effective government by making it difficult, if not impossible, to terminate ineffective employees. Where management controls the evaluation and discipline of employees, the union is channeled into a role of protecting its members from management-imposed discipline. It protects its members collectively by negotiating controls over the implementation of management's unilaterally promulgated performance standards. * * * It protects its members individually by challenging management to justify disciplinary measures in an adversarial proceeding, such as an arbitration or statutory tenure or civil service proceeding.

When the union serves as a vehicle for collective employee voice in the evaluation and discipline of employees, the union can be transformed from an impediment to effective government into a contributor. Such has been the case with teacher peer review. * * *

Peer review has been successful in large part because of teacher involvement through their unions in developing the evaluation standards. Teachers are forced to reflect on what constitutes good teaching and express those standards in terms that are accessible and acceptable to their peers. Having actively participated in developing the standards, the union is more likely to view its role as protecting the standards of teaching instead of protecting individual teachers from evaluations unilaterally imposed from above. * * *

* * * Contracting out is often put forth as a panacea for remedying public employee collective bargaining's impediments to effective government. Some jurisdictions further this alternative by holding that the decision to subcontract is not a mandatory subject of bargaining. However, although the decision may not be mandatorily negotiable, the employer generally remains obligated to bargain the impact of the decision on the employees. In such impact bargaining, the union may seek to raise the transaction costs of contracting to such a level as will induce the employer to abandon the option.

An alternative to public employers avoiding collectively represented employees by contracting their jobs to the private sector is to empower those workers to compete against private contractors for the work. One example of such empowerment, highlighted by the Secretary of Labor's Task Force, occurred in the Massachusetts Highway Department. When the state decided to subcontract highway maintenance, the unions who represented the employees who had been performing those duties formed a coalition and bid against the contractors. They were awarded the job and assumed responsibility for organizing and managing it. The resulting improvements included a sixty percent reduction in workers' compensation claims, a seventy percent reduction in overtime and a 49.5% reduction in sick time. Improved efficiency saved the state more than $7.8 million. Road sweeping and cleaning of gutters became more regular. Worker suggestions for improved maintenance of equipment enabled the purchase and lease of new equipment. As with teacher peer review, the role of the union changed dramatically. The Secretary of Labor's Task Force quoted one union official involved, "My job used to be to go around and ask people what grievances they had. My job is now to go around asking people what ideas they have to improve this job."

* * *

There are numerous approaches that jurisdictions might consider for enhancing collective employee voice in an institutionalized way. Jurisdictions might experiment with broadening the scope of traditional bargaining. * * *

They might make such decisions mandatory subjects of bargaining for purposes of negotiations but permissive subjects for purposes of strikes, in right to strike jurisdictions, and interest arbitration in jurisdictions that mandate arbitration as their impasse resolution procedure. * * *

Alternative models for consideration exist. These include the labor-management partnerships established under the Clinton Administration. The structure of those partnerships evolved during President Clinton's two terms in office. Initially, they consisted of representatives of the employer and the union, but they evolved to include representatives of middle-level managers.

Another model has emerged for some employees in Minnesota. Minnesota requires that employers meet and confer with representatives of their professional employees to discuss policies and other matters relating to employment that are not mandatory subjects of bargaining. * * *

The experiences of employers such as the City of Indianapolis and the Massachusetts Highway Department suggest that jurisdictions consider requiring public employers to afford unions the opportunity to bid and provide them with the information necessary to make informed bids, before contracting out bargaining unit work. * * *

A common characteristic of all of the above models is that they mandate collective employee voice without mandating all of the elements of formal collective bargaining. * * * Once jurisdictions break with the NLRA bipolar model that provides that every matter is either mandatorily negotiable or left to unilateral management control, they can experiment with vehicles of enhanced employee voice which may solve the paradox in public sector labor law by preserving democratic processes while transforming the roles of exclusive bargaining representatives.

NOTES

1. Is Professor Malin onto something? Why haven't more states followed the lead of the success stories he cites?

2. If Professor Malin's recommendations were followed what subjects should remain mandatory bargaining subjects with the full range of impasse procedures available to the parties? What subjects are more appropriate for meet and confer or bargaining without the availability of strikes or other impasse procedures like interest arbitration? Would any subjects be off limits altogether?

3. What impact might such a system have on litigation over the scope of negotiations?

4. How might unions respond to such a system?

6. CIVIL SERVICE, TEACHER TENURE, AND OTHER LAWS: POTENTIAL CONFLICTS WITH COLLECTIVE BARGAINING

As discussed in Chapter 3, long before the advent of collective bargaining and the increasing regulation in the private sector, the public workplace was governed to a considerable extent by a network of constitutional provisions, laws, and charters. In some instances, laws even provided for very specific workplace rules (for example, workers are entitled to certain designated holidays or vacation leave, teachers are to be paid in accordance with a statutory salary schedule, or city police officers must reside within city limits). In other instances, the law provided a general standard (for example, a requirement that public employees' salaries be set on the basis of wages prevailing in other private or public employment for comparable work). In still others, laws allocated decision-making authority over certain employment conditions to a particular individual or body, such as a police chief, sheriff, or school board, often in connection with a generalized system of civil service or teacher tenure regulations.

When public sector collective bargaining legislation was introduced, questions arose as to the relationship between that process and these pre-existing forms of workplace governance. Except for constitutional provisions, such questions were subject to being answered by the state legislatures although only some legislatures accepted that responsibility. Legislative answers varied substantially from state to state and in some cases the answers varied from one collective bargaining statute to another within the same state.

In Illinois, for example, the statute applicable to state and local government employees provides that any collective bargaining agreement negotiated pursuant to the statute supersedes conflicting laws (ILL.-SMITH-HURD ANN. 5 ILCS 315/15), while the statute applicable to educational employees provides that the parties shall not effect or implement contract provisions in violation of or inconsistent with other statutes (ILL.-SMITH-HURD ANN. 115 ILCS 5/10(b)).

California's statute pertaining to state employees adopts a middle course: it lists the statutory provisions which may be preempted by a collective agreement, and those that may not be preempted if the State Personnel Board finds the collective agreement to be inconsistent with the merit principle. WEST'S ANN.CAL.GOV.CODE §§ 3517.6, 3517.61. The law also specifies that if any contract provision requires statutory amendment or expenditure of funds, legislative action must occur before the provision is effective. *Id.*

A Florida statute provides that if a collective agreement conflicts with a law, ordinance, rule, or regulation that the negotiating employer has no power to amend, the negotiating employer is under an obligation to propose an amendment to the appropriate body; meanwhile, the conflicting contract provision is inoperative. WEST'S FLA.STAT.ANN. § 447.309(3).

Legislative attempts to address some of the foreseeable complications which arise when a new collective bargaining system is superimposed upon a broad array of existing regulation of the public sector workplace were not widespread. They often failed to provide a clear answer in a particular case or provided no answer at all. Resolutions for these thorny questions remained to be decided by administrative labor relations agencies and the courts.

Such questions may arise in a variety of procedural contexts: a generalized attack on the collective bargaining statute, a dispute over the scope of bargaining, a dispute over the arbitrability of a particular issue, or a dispute over the enforceability of an arbitrator's award. The case examples which follow concern the two most pervasive systems of workplace governance that preceded collective bargaining in the public sector: civil service and teacher tenure.

NOTES

1. What considerations would you expect (a) a public employer and/or (b) a union to take into account in deciding what position to take with respect to the relationship between collective bargaining and various external regulations and systems? Of what relative importance are the outcome of the current case, and the long term effects on employee rights, management rights and collective bargaining?

2. If you were advising a legislative body with respect to an appropriate public policy concerning such relationships, what would you recommend? Should collective bargaining contracts predominate over other laws or should other laws take precedence? Should the parties be allowed to negotiate provisions that conflict with other laws subject to legislative approval? Should a legislature try to address specifically each law that might potentially conflict or construct a general provision applicable to all conflicts? Should the legislature leave the matter to courts and administrative agencies to address on a case by case basis? What are the advantages and disadvantages to these various approaches?

3. What factors might determine whether such a challenge would arise as a broad-based challenge to a collective bargaining system, a scope of negotiability case, or a challenge to arbitrability either before or after an arbitrator's decision? Would it depend on the particular statute, the parties' awareness of the applicability of the statute, the involvement of attorneys in the case or other factors?

PACIFIC LEGAL FOUNDATION v. BROWN

Supreme Court of California, 1981.
29 Cal.3d 168, 172 Cal.Rptr. 487, 624 P.2d 1215.

TOBRINER, J.

Over the past 20 years, the California Legislature has enacted a series of legislative measures granting public employees, at both the state and local level, a variety of organizational and negotiating rights somewhat analogous to the rights long afforded most employees in the private sector by the federal labor relation laws of the 1930's. In the instant mandate proceeding, petitioners have mounted a sweeping constitutional challenge to one of the most recent of these public labor relations measures, the State Employer–Employee Relations Act (SEERA), enacted in 1977 to regulate the state's labor relations with state employees (codified in [WEST'S ANN.CAL.]GOV.CODE, § 3512 et seq.). Petitioners principally contend that SEERA is unconstitutional on its face because it allegedly conflicts with the "merit system" of employment embodied in the civil service provisions of Article VII of the California Constitution, and, in particular, with the powers that Article VII assertedly assigns exclusively to the jurisdiction of the State Personnel Board. On the basis of these constitutional contentions, petitioners seek a writ of mandate striking down the 1977 statute and compelling the various respondent public officers and agencies to conduct their operations without regard to the provisions of SEERA.

* * *

1. *Background and description of the provisions of SEERA.*

Prior to 1961, public employees in California enjoyed no formal rights to participate in the decision-making processes which determined the terms and conditions of their employment. In 1961, the evolution of public employee rights in this state began with the enactment of the George Brown Act (codified in §§ 3525–3536). As originally enacted, the act applied to employees of the state, cities, counties, school districts and institutions of higher education, granting such employees the right to join employee organizations of their choosing, and requiring public employers to "meet and confer" with employee organizations prior to undertaking action on "all matters relating to employment conditions and employer-employee relations."

Although it represented a significant first step, the George Brown Act omitted a number of key elements that have proven to be important factors in formulating peaceful labor relations in the private sector. Thus the act did not provide any mechanism for recognizing an employee organization as the exclusive representative of a group of employees, and placed no obligation on either the employer or employees to attempt to reach an agreement on terms and conditions of employment, i.e., to negotiate in good faith. Moreover, the act afforded the parties no explicit authority to reach binding agreements and did not establish an expert labor relations agency with authority to oversee the process and devise appropriate remedies for improper conduct by employees or employers.

Subsequent legislative and gubernatorial actions over the past decade and a half have been aimed, in large part, in overcoming these deficiencies and in tailoring the labor relations process to the special conditions of different segments of the public labor force. In 1965, the Winton Act expanded the "meet and confer" rights of public school employees, and in 1968, the Legislature enacted the Meyers–Milias–Brown Act (MMBA) (codified at § 3500 et seq.) to provide a more structured collective bargaining process for most local government employees. See *Glendale City Employees' Association, Inc. v. City of Glendale*, 15 Cal.3d 328, 124 Cal.Rptr. 513, 540 P.2d 609 (1975).

The early 1970's brought an increasing demand among state employees for a formal system of collective bargaining that would provide them with a more meaningful role in establishing the terms and conditions of their employment. See King, *Deliver Us From Evil: A Public History of California's Civil Service System* (1979). In response, Governor Reagan in March 1971 issued an executive order centralizing the "meet and confer" process by designating one state official, chosen by the Governor, to be responsible for meeting and conferring with employee organizations for the purpose of reaching an agreement on salary and employee benefits (Executive Order Number. R–25–71.) [These duties were transferred in 1975 by executive order to a newly created Office of Employee Relations.]

In 1972, following the first major state employee strike, the Legislature created the Assembly Advisory Council on Public Employee Relations, chaired by UCLA Professor Benjamin Aaron, to formulate recommendations "for establishing an appropriate framework within which disputes can be settled between public jurisdictions and their employees." In its 1973 report the Advisory Council recommended the enactment of a comprehensive state law, modeled on the National Labor Relations Act, which would afford formal collective bargaining rights to all public employees.

The Legislature, however, was unable to agree on a comprehensive bill covering all public employees and decided instead to draft separate collective bargaining statutes directed to the specific needs and problems of different categories of public entities. In line with this approach, the Legislature in 1975 first enacted the Educational Employment Relations Act (EERA) (codified in Section 3540 et seq.); EERA repealed the Winton Act, established formal negotiating rights for public school employees, and created the Educational Employment Relations Board, an expert, quasi-judicial administrative agency modeled after the National Labor Relations Board, to enforce the act. In 1977, the Legislature adopted SEERA, the legislation challenged in the instant proceeding, to provide formal collective bargaining rights to state employees. Finally, the legislative sequence was completed in 1978 with the adoption of the Higher Education Employer–Employee Relations Act (HEERA) (codified in Section 3560 et seq.), granting similar rights to employees in the state university and University of California systems. As this brief historical overview demonstrates, SEERA constitutes one significant component in a network of recent statutes affording collective bargaining rights to California public employees.

Although a detailed discussion of all of SEERA's provisions is not necessary for the purposes of this decision, it may be helpful to highlight the major features of the statute. To begin with, the act modifies the George Brown Act in a number of respects in order to strengthen the role of employees and to increase the efficiency of the employer-employee negotiation process. First, the act establishes the principle of exclusive representation on matters of employment relations by employee organizations chosen by a majority of employees in administratively designated bargaining units. Sections 3520.5, 3521. Second, the act requires the Governor and the exclusive employee representatives to meet and confer in good faith for the purpose of reaching agreement on wages, hours and other terms and conditions of state employment. Section 3517. Finally, the act specifically directs that any such agreement that the parties do reach be set forth in a written memorandum of understanding. Section 3517.5.

Although the act thus affords state employees significant new rights, the Legislature at the same time placed definite limits on the scope of representation and retained substantial control over state employee compensation and many other terms and conditions of state employment. SEERA specifically precludes bargaining over "the merits, necessity, or organization of any service or activity provided by law or executive order." Section 3516. The act also provides that as to matters within the scope of representation, a memorandum of understanding requiring the expenditure of funds does not become effective unless it is approved by the Legislature in the annual Budget Act, Section 3517.6; under this provision, virtually all salary agreements are subject to prior legislative approval.

The act further provides that, except with respect to a number of specific statutes which the Legislature has expressly determined may be superseded by a memorandum of understanding, any provision of a memorandum of understanding in conflict with a statutory mandate shall not be effective unless approved by the Legislature. *Ibid.* In addition, the act provides that any terms of a memorandum of understanding in conflict with specified statutes relating to layoffs or demotions shall not be controlling if the State Personnel Board finds those terms to be inconsistent with the merit employment principles of Article VII of the California Constitution. *Ibid.*

Finally, to protect the rights and enforce the obligations of employees, employee organizations and the state, SEERA expanded the jurisdiction and changed the name of the Educational Employment Relations Board to the Public Employment Relations Board (PERB). Under SEERA, PERB's principal responsibilities and duties include: (1) determining appropriate units of employees, (2) determining whether a particular item is within the scope of representation, (3) arranging for and supervising representation elections and resolving disputes relating to certification or decertification, (4) establishing a list of available mediators, arbitrators and factfinders, and (5) investigating unfair practice charges relating to alleged violations of SEERA, and taking such actions with respect to such charges as are necessary to effectuate the purposes of the Act. Sections 3513, subd. (g), 3541.3, 3514.5.

* * *

3. *SEERA does not conflict with the general "merit principle" of civil service employment embodied in Article VII of the California Constitution.*

In challenging the constitutionality of SEERA, petitioners rely primarily on the asserted conflict between the act and several Sections of Article VII of the California Constitution, the Article pertaining to the state civil service.[5] Although, as we discuss below, the principal thrust of

---

5. Article VII, Sections 1, 2 and 3, the constitutional Sections most relevant to the present case, provide in pertinent part:

petitioners' challenge relates to the legislation's alleged conflict with the duties and powers afforded the State Personnel Board by Article VII, Section 3, subdivision (a), petitioners apparently also assert more broadly that the entire collective bargaining process adopted by SEERA conflicts with the "general system" of merit appointment and promotion mandated by Article VII, Section 1, subdivision (b). Because a review of the origins of the constitutional civil service provisions sheds considerable light on all of petitioners' contentions with respect to Article VII, we turn directly to the history of the constitutional provision.

In 1913, the California Legislature enacted a statute creating California's first civil service system in an attempt to combat the "spoils system" of political patronage in state employment. (Stats.1913, ch. 590, p. 1035.) By the early 1930's, however, the existing statutory civil service system was obviously failing in its primary task. The deficiencies in the system stemmed from several principal sources. First, acceding to political pressure, both the Legislature and the statutory civil service commission itself had over the years exempted numerous departments and positions from the civil service restrictions: indeed, by 1932 the exemptions had become so widespread that "[o]f the 23,222 full-time state employees, only 11,917 held permanent civil service positions." (King, *Deliver Us from Evil: A Public History of California's Civil Service System* (1979), p. 26). Thus, fully one-half of the permanent state employees were exempt from the civil service law.

"A second abuse of the Civil Service Act was the gross misuse of authorizations for temporary employment [which was not subject to the civil service act]. * * * Officially, temporary appointments followed the three month rule, but this had never been followed. By August 1931, temporary employees constituted more than a third of the entire state service." *Id.* Finally, in the early 1930's considerable public attention was focused on the problem by widespread newspaper accounts of the allegedly numerous politically motivated appointments made by the incumbent Governor.

It was in this milieu and in response to the specific problems of the times that in 1934 the people adopted Article XXIV of the state Constitu-

---

Section 1. (a) The civil service includes every officer and employee of the state except as otherwise provided in this Constitution.

(b) In the civil service permanent appointment and promotion shall be made under a general system based on merit ascertained by competitive examination.

Section 2. (a) There is a Personnel Board of 5 members appointed by the Governor and approved by the Senate, a majority of the membership concurring, for 10–year terms and until their successors are appointed and qualified. * * *

Section 2. * * *

(c) The Board shall appoint and prescribe compensation for an executive officer who shall be a member of the civil service but not a member of the board.

Section 3. (a) The board shall enforce the civil service statutes and, by majority vote of all its members, shall prescribe probationary periods and classifications, adopt other rules authorized by statute, and review disciplinary actions.

(b) The executive officer shall administer the civil service statutes under rules of the board.

tion. The ballot argument accompanying the 1934 initiative measure sets forth in clear terms both the objectives and the limits of the proposed constitutional provision.

The ballot argument stated: "The purpose of this constitutional amendment is to promote efficiency and economy in State government. *The sole aim of the act is to prohibit appointments and promotion in State service except on the basis of merit, efficiency and fitness ascertained by competitive examination.* Appointments of inefficient employees for political reasons are thereby prohibited, thus eliminating the 'spoils system' from State employment. * * * [T]his constitutional amendment provides: (1) Employment in the classified service based solely on merit and efficiency; (2) a nonpartisan Personnel Board; (3) prohibition against exemptions from the merit system of employment; (4) correction of the temporary political appointment evil. *Having by constitutional mandate prohibited employment on any basis except merit and efficiency, thereby eliminating as far as possible the 'spoils system' of employment, the Legislature is given a free hand in setting up laws relating to personnel administration for the best interests of the State,* including the setting up of causes for dismissal such as inefficiency, misconduct or lack of funds."

As this ballot argument demonstrates, the "sole aim" of the amendment was to establish, as a constitutional mandate, the principle that appointments and promotions in state service be made solely on the basis of merit. Having established this "merit principle" as a matter of constitutional law, and having established a nonpartisan Personnel Board to administer this merit principle, the constitutional provision left the Legislature with a "free hand" to fashion "laws relating to personnel administration for the best interests of the State."

From this description, we conclude that the collective bargaining process established by SEERA does not on its face conflict with the basic constitutional principles of Article VII, Section 1, subdivision (b). As we have seen, nothing in the history of the amendment suggests that the establishment of a general system of appointment and promotion based on merit proposed to prohibit the Legislature from adopting a labor relations policy affording employees a meaningful voice in determining the terms and conditions of their employment; instead, the amendment simply sought to eliminate the "spoils system" of public employment.

We recognize, of course, that theoretically the *product* of the collective bargaining process may possibly in specific instances conflict with the merit principle of employment embodied in Article VII. Such a conflict would be most evident, for example, if the Governor and an exclusive bargaining representative agreed to a memorandum of understanding purporting to authorize hiring or promotion on a politically partisan basis. The provisions of SEERA, however, neither explicitly nor implicitly authorize any such encroachment on the merit principle of Article VII through the collective bargaining process. On the contrary, in drafting SEERA the Legislature explicitly reaffirmed the primacy of the merit principle of employment and crafted the statute carefully so as to minimize any potential conflict with such principle.

* * *

Moreover, in designating the statutes that may be superseded by a memorandum of understanding without legislative approval, the Legislature excluded those statutes relating to classification, examination, appointment, or promotion, areas in which a potential conflict with the merit principle of employment would be most likely to occur. Finally, the Legislature's sensitivity to the preservation of the merit principle is additionally evident in the numerous legislative modifications contained in the 1978 "clean-up" legislation to SEERA, changes which were made largely upon the recommendation of the State Personnel Board to avoid any potential clash with the merit principle.[9]

These numerous provisions demonstrate beyond question that the Legislature drafted SEERA with the merit principle of Article VII firmly in mind, fashioning the statute specifically to avoid any conflict with that constitutional mandate. As noted earlier, under familiar principles the legislative judgment in this regard is entitled to great weight, and in light of our own review of the history of Article VII, we find no conflict between the general collective bargaining process authorized by SEERA and the merit principle of civil service employment guaranteed by the California Constitution. Cf. *Los Angeles County Civil Service Com. v. Superior Court*, 23 Cal.3d 55, 151 Cal.Rptr. 547, 588 P.2d 249 1978 (local civil service charter provision does not conflict with county's statutory "meet and confer" obligation).

4. *SEERA does not contravene article VII in authorizing the ultimate setting of civil service salaries by the Governor and the Legislature rather than by the State Personnel Board.*

Petitioners additionally claim that even if the collective bargaining process established by SEERA does not conflict with the merit principle of civil service employment, SEERA nonetheless is unconstitutional because it assigns the task of setting the salaries of civil service employees to the Governor and the Legislature rather than to the State Personnel Board. In this regard, petitioners rely on Section 3, subdivision (a) of Article VII, the constitutional provision describing the powers and duties of the State Personnel Board, which provides: "The [State Personnel Board] shall enforce the civil service statutes and, by majority vote of all of its members, shall prescribe probationary periods and classifications, adopt

9. In the 1978 amendments to SEERA, the Legislature (1) deleted several statutes from the list of statutes subject to supersession which the State Personnel Board indicated might pose a conflict with the merit principle, (2) provided that nine additional statutes, relating to layoffs and demotions, which had been originally subject to supersession, would not be superseded by a memorandum of understanding if the State Personnel Board finds the terms of the memorandum to be inconsistent "with merit employment principles as provided for by Article VII of the California Constitution" and (3) modified two additional statutes which had originally been subject to supersession, transferring the potentially merit-related portions of the statutes into different statutes not subject to supersession, and leaving the nonmerit related subjects in the statutes that remained subject to supersession.

other rules authorized by statute, and review disciplinary actions." Although neither Section 3, subdivision (a), nor its constitutional antecedent, explicitly endows the State Personnel Board with the authority to set salaries, petitioners argue nonetheless that the State Personnel Board's constitutional salary setting authority flows both from the Board's authority to "prescribe * * * classifications" and from its duty to "enforce the civil service statutes." We address each of these contentions in turn.

(a) *The State Personnel Board's constitutional authority to prescribe classifications does not encompass the power to set the particular salary for such classifications.*

On its face, SEERA clearly does not conflict with the State Personnel Board's constitutional authority to prescribe classifications for the state civil service. No provision of the act purports to authorize any other agency to classify positions in the civil service, and the act excludes the numerous statutory provisions relating to the State Personnel Board's classification power (Sections 18800–18806, 18523) from the list of statutes that may be superseded by the terms of a memorandum of understanding. (§ 3517.6.) Furthermore, the act provides that the State Personnel Board's existing classification structure is one of the specific criteria PERB must consider in determining the appropriate units for the selection of an exclusive representative. Section 3521, subd. (b)(2).

Petitioners argue, however, that an integral part of the State Personnel Board's authority to prescribe classifications is the power to establish salaries for the classifications so set. An almost identical contention came before the Colorado Supreme Court in *Vivian v. Bloom* (1947) 115 Colo. 579, 177 P.2d 541 (1947). * * *

In *Vivian,* the Colorado Supreme Court rejected the plaintiffs' contention, stating: "It is insistently urged that the power to classify carries with it by necessary implication the power to fix compensation. In this contention we cannot concur. Elsewhere, systems are set up with like divisions of authority. * * * We are constrained to conclude that the power to fix compensation within the classified service still abides in the [Legislature]. The [Legislature] has the burden of determining and providing for the amount of revenue to be made available for payment of salaries and is immediately responsible to the people's will therein, so it seems not improper that it should retain ultimate control of its ancient prerogative."

As the *Vivian* decision suggests, although the power to classify positions has frequently been lodged in civil service commissions or personnel boards, the actual authority to set salaries has traditionally been viewed as a legislative function, with ultimate authority residing in the legislative body. A host of California decisions demonstrate that this fundamental principle has long been followed in this state in jurisdictions operating under civil service provisions.

Petitioners assert, however, that the classification authority granted the State Personnel Board by Article VII, Section 3, subdivision (a) should be interpreted to include the power to set salaries because under the civil service statutory schemes in force in California since 1913, the State Personnel Board or its predecessor, the Civil Service Commission, has continually been accorded the task of both classifying positions and also establishing salary ranges for the classifications it establishes. Petitioners insist that this long-standing practice demonstrates that the power to set salaries is part of the State Personnel Board's constitutional power under Article VII.

With the exception of one decision discussed below, however, judicial authorities have uniformly indicated that the State Personnel Board's authority to establish salary ranges rests simply on a delegation of legislative authority under the relevant statutes, and does not reside in the board by virtue of any constitutional mandate. * * *

This view of both the source and the extent of the salary setting power exercised by the State Personnel Board in the past is directly confirmed by an examination of the actual legislative practice that has been followed in this state since the inception of the civil service system.

* * *

Petitioners argue, however, that while these actions by the Legislature and Governor may demonstrate that the State Personnel Board does not have unlimited power to set salaries in excess of authorized appropriations, such actions do not conflict with a recognition of the board's constitutional authority over the setting of salaries and distribution of funds within appropriated limits. Although the actions noted above may not be inconsistent with such a view, a host of other legislative actions over the years clearly conflicts with even this more limited version of the State Personnel Board's constitutional authority.

* * *

These numerous legislative actions, reaching back more than 40 years, demonstrate an unvarying legislative view that the salary setting authority for civil service employees has not been ceded to the State Personnel Board by Article VII or its constitutional predecessors, but rather has been left with the Legislature. This consistent legislative interpretation is, of course, entitled to great weight, particularly since the constitutional civil service provision was revised and updated in 1970 without any indication that the drafters intended to alter this established interpretation.

Moreover, the State Personnel Board itself has consistently concurred in the view that its constitutional authority to prescribe classifications does not encompass the ultimate authority to set civil service salaries.

* * *

Although we have determined that SEERA's salary setting provisions are not inconsistent with the State Personnel Board's authority to prescribe classifications, we do not intend to suggest that the board's classification decisions will have no effect whatsoever on the salary measures to which the parties may properly agree under SEERA. Because we face no specific salary measures which assertedly conflict with the personnel board's classification scheme, we do not believe that we should at this stage attempt to determine precisely what constraints the board's classification decisions will place on permissible salary agreements.[16] As with other aspects of the "merit principle" of civil service employment, however, the parties are not free to adopt salary measures that interfere with any fundamental "merit principle" element that the classification system serves. This caveat, of course, in no sense renders SEERA unconstitutional on its face; if any improper salary measure should be agreed to by the Governor and approved by the Legislature in the future, petitioners or other interested parties will be free to challenge such measures at that time.[17]

* * *

(b) *SEERA does not conflict with the State Personnel Board's authority to "enforce the civil service statutes."*

As noted above, in addition to contending that the salary setting provisions of SEERA conflict with the State Personnel Board's authority to "prescribe classifications," petitioners claim that the act's delegation to the Governor of the power to negotiate and agree to salaries conflicts with the portion of Article VII, Section 3, subdivision (a) which provides that "[t]he [State Personnel Board] shall enforce the civil service statutes." Recognizing that the language of the present constitutional provision affords little support to their argument, since SEERA would not normally be thought of as a "civil service statute," petitioners rely instead on the language of former article XXIV, Section 3, subdivision (a), the provision from which the current Section 3, subdivision (a) derives. As we shall explain, however, the provision's history and its consistent interpretation belie petitioners' suggested interpretation. * * *

4. *PERB's jurisdiction to investigate and devise remedies for unfair practices is not unconstitutional on its face.*

Petitioners contend that the provisions of SEERA granting PERB jurisdiction to investigate and devise remedies for unfair practices are irreconcilably in conflict with the State Personnel Board's jurisdiction to "review disciplinary actions" under article VII, Section 3, subdivision

16. For similar reasons, we have no occasion in this case to determine whether the "like-pay-for-like-work" concept is a constitutionally based doctrine embedded in either the merit principle of article VII, Section 1, subdivision (b) or the State Personnel Board's classification power under Section 3, subdivision (a), or alternatively is solely of statutory origin. (See, e.g., §§ 18500, subd. (c)(1); 18850.)

17. In its brief, the State Personnel Board indicates that it intends to promulgate "guidelines" identifying those areas of salary setting that may potentially conflict with the board's classification authority and with the merit principle. The board requests that this court "make clear that the Governor must observe the limits established" by such guidelines.

In our view, any ruling on such guidelines is premature. As of this time, the board has not even formally promulgated the guidelines and there is no indication that the Governor will not voluntarily agree to be guided by the board's advice. Until a concrete controversy arises, it would not be appropriate to express an opinion either upon the authority of the board to promulgate such guidelines or on the substantive validity of any particular guideline.

(a).[18] Although petitioners do not complain of any specific issue that has arisen to date, they urge our court to invalidate PERB's authority to act in this area because of an alleged inevitable conflict with the State Personnel Board's powers. We conclude that petitioners' challenge to the facial validity of PERB's jurisdiction fails on several grounds.

First, as the State Personnel Board itself recognizes, many areas of PERB's unfair practice jurisdiction do not overlap with the State Personnel Board's "disciplinary action" jurisdiction at all. In these areas, obviously, no constitutional problems arise. Thus, for example, if the state denies rights which SEERA grants to employee organizations, or the state fails to meet and confer in good faith, PERB could clearly adjudicate unfair practice charges against the state without any danger of conflict with the personnel board's disciplinary action jurisdiction. Moreover, even in the case of employer reprisals against an employee for protected activity, PERB's unfair practice jurisdiction would clearly pose no conflict with the State Personnel Board's jurisdiction if the reprisal took a form that did not constitute a "disciplinary action" reviewable by the board. Because there is thus a substantial area in which PERB's unfair practice jurisdiction can unquestionably operate without damage to the State Personnel Board's jurisdiction, the provisions in question are not unconstitutional on their face.

Second, even in those areas in which the jurisdiction of the State Personnel Board and PERB do overlap, familiar rules of construction counsel our court to attempt to harmonize the disparate procedures, rather than simply to invalidate one or the other on broad constitutional grounds.[19] As a New Jersey court recently observed in reviewing a conflict between quasi-judicial rulings of a civil service commission and the Public Employee Relations Board in that state: "The inquiry is properly not so much which statutory scheme prevails [over the other], but rather how each can be harmonized to give them reasonable and full effect. Each agency operates under different statutory schemes, but not to defeat each

---

18. The State Personnel Board, asserting that its jurisdiction in the areas of examination, selection, probation, promotion and discipline is "exclusive," joins with petitioners in arguing that PERB's unfair practice jurisdiction is unconstitutional insofar as it authorizes PERB to act with reference to discriminatory or retaliatory actions in any of these areas.

In taking this position in the instant case, the State Personnel Board has modified the views it expressed in its 1974 position paper on collective bargaining. In that document, the State Personnel Board expressly advocated the creation of a Public Employment Relations Commission which would, inter alia, "hear unfair practice complaints." (A Perspective on Collective Bargaining in the State Civil Service). The document also stated that the State Personnel Board had considered whether it would be advisable for it to assume the duties of such a commission but had ultimately decided against the board's assumption of such a role because "we believe that the administering agency would be more acceptable to both management and employees if it were an entity with no other involvement in the personnel management process."

19. The parties have advanced differing views as to whether, under article XIV, Section 1 of the California Constitution, PERB's adjudicatory jurisdiction, like that of the State Personnel Board, flows from the Constitution itself. Although it may well be that PERB should be considered a constitutional agency by virtue of article XIV, Section 1 (cf. *Perry Farms Inc. v. Agricultural Labor Relations Bd.*, 86 Cal.App.3d 448, 150 Cal.Rptr. 495 (1978)), we need not definitively decide that issue in this case because even if PERB's authority derives only from statute the accommodation of the two agencies' respective jurisdictions would still be appropriate.

other's authority." *City of Hackensack v. Winner* 162 N.J.Super. 1, 392 A.2d 187 (1978), *aff'd*, 82 N.J. 1, 410 A.2d 1146 (1980).

As the *Hackensack* decision suggests, PERB and the State Personnel Board are not in competition with each other; rather, each agency was established to serve a different, but not inconsistent, public purpose. The State Personnel Board was granted jurisdiction to review disciplinary actions of civil service employees in order to protect civil service employees from politically partisan mistreatment or other arbitrary action inconsistent with the merit principle embodied in article VII. As we noted in *Skelly v. State Personnel Bd.*, 15 Cal.3d 194,124 Cal.Rptr. 14, 539 P.2d 774 (1975): "To help insure that the goals of civil service are not thwarted by those in power, the statutory provisions implementing the constitutional mandate of article XXIV [now article VII] * * * invest employees with substantive and procedural protections against punitive actions by their superiors."

PERB, on the other hand, has been given a somewhat more specialized and more focused task: to protect both employees and the state employer from violations of the organizational and collective bargaining rights guaranteed by SEERA. Although disciplinary actions taken in violation of SEERA would transgress the merit principle as well, the Legislature evidently thought it important to assign the task of investigating potential violations of SEERA to an agency which possesses and can further develop specialized expertise in the labor relations field. Thus, insofar as possible, we should construe the relevant provisions to permit an accommodation of the respective tasks of both the State Personnel Board and PERB.

* * *

Because no actual jurisdictional conflict between PERB and the State Personnel Board confronts us in this proceeding, we have no occasion to speculate on how some hypothetical dispute that might be presented for decision in the future should properly be resolved. As numerous authorities in other jurisdictions make clear, however, any conflicts which may arise in this area can be resolved either by administrative accommodation between the two agencies themselves[21] or, failing that, by sensitive application of evolving judicial principles.

Accordingly, we conclude that the fact that PERB's jurisdiction over unfair practices may in some cases overlap with the State Personnel Board's jurisdiction to review disciplinary actions provides no basis for finding the applicable provisions of SEERA unconstitutional on their face.

4. *SEERA is not an unlawful delegation of legislative authority nor does it infringe on the gubernatorial veto power.*

---

21. In Los Angeles County, a jurisdictional conflict between a charter-established civil service commission and a local employment relations commission created by a county ordinance was ultimately resolved by an agreement of each agency to adopt corresponding regulations "which in effect, establish a policy of not hearing any part of a complaint that is within the jurisdiction of, and has been heard by, either an arbitrator or the other commission."

Finally, petitioners contend that even if SEERA does not fatally conflict with any of the provisions of article VII of the California Constitution, our court should strike down the collective bargaining statute on its face as either an unlawful delegation of legislative authority or as an unconstitutional infringement on the gubernatorial veto power. Both of these contentions are plainly without merit.

* * *

[JUDGE RICHARDSON'S dissent is omitted.]

NOTES

1. Civil service systems typically provide for a right of appeal by disciplined employees to an "independent" public agency called a civil service board, or personnel board. Public sector unions are often distrustful of such procedures, over which they have no control, and seek to negotiate independent review of discipline or other employment decisions through bilateral grievance and arbitration procedures. Thus, questions arise as to the relationship between these two regimes: Are civil service procedures exclusive, so that the parties are not free to negotiate a bilateral alternative? Or, if civil service and bilateral procedures may co-exist, what is their relationship to one another? May an employee pursue either (or both) at his option? If so, what is the effect of a determination under one or the other?

In some states, statutes address such questions specifically, though their answers vary. The Wisconsin statute pertaining to state employees stipulates that the disciplinary standards and procedures in collective bargaining agreements displace civil service standards and procedures. WIS.STAT.ANN. § 230.34(1)(ar). In New Jersey, on the other hand, negotiated grievance procedures are mandatory but cannot replace and nor be inconsistent with civil service or tenure laws and the parties can negotiate binding arbitration for minor discipline only for employees with statutory protection under tenure or civil service law. NEW JERSEY STAT. § 34:13A–5.3. In some states statutes are silent on the subject, and the questions are open for litigation with inconsistent results. See *Pontiac Police Officers Association v. City of Pontiac,* 397 Mich. 674, 246 N.W.2d 831 (1976) (collective bargaining law, as a later enactment, takes priority over civil service law for local government employees, so that an agreement providing for binding arbitration of suspension and discharge of police officer is enforceable); *AFSCME v. County of Lancaster,* 200 Neb. 301, 263 N.W.2d 471 (1978) (civil service statute, enacted subsequent to collective bargaining law, controls).

2. Administrative agencies and courts usually work diligently to harmonize statutory provisions when they appear to conflict. When harmonization is not possible and there is no statutory guidance, decision makers must face the difficult problem of selecting what set of laws will prevail over another set. As already noted, an "easy way" out of this difficulty is to hold that the most recent enactment prevails based upon the reasoning that the more recent legislative enactment was intended to repeal by implication all prior conflicting legislative provisions. The effect of this approach sometimes favors collective bargaining and sometimes favors other legislation, depending

upon which is passed more recently. Most courts have not opted for this simple mechanical rule. Why?

3. Consider the following analysis:

> States can resolve the perceived conflict between civil service law and bargaining over employee discipline without interfering with the goals of either statute. Although statutory provisions may appear to conflict, permitting negotiation over disciplinary procedures and standards does not hinder and may, in fact, promote merit employment. Accordingly, states should allow unions and employers to negotiate over these issues and to determine the appropriate disciplinary procedures and standards for the relevant employment setting.

Ann C. Hodges, The Interplay of Civil Service Law and Collective Bargaining in Public Sector Employee Discipline Cases, 32 *Boston College Law Review* 95, 166 (1990).

Do you agree or disagree?

4. As indicated in note 1, unions have often been suspicious of civil service systems but on occasion, creative unions have tried to use civil service law to the benefit of employees. In *California Attorneys v. Schwarzenegger*, 174 Cal.App.4th 424, 94 Cal.Rptr.3d 275 (2009), the union representing certain attorneys and administrative judges employed by the state sought a writ of mandamus ordering the state to adjust the employees' pay based on a survey or formula, after failing to reach agreement with the state on a collective bargaining contract. The union argued that the Governor and Department of Personnel Administration were violating the constitutional merit principle by failing to pay the union represented attorneys comparable pay with other government attorneys, interfering with the civil service classification system and the incorporated principle of like pay for like work. In support of its position, the union cited the dissent in the principal case, *Pacific Legal Foundation*. The union also obtained the support of the state Attorney General who cited the difficulty in recruiting attorneys and as an illustrative example, pointed out that corrections officers, who needed only a high school diploma, frequently earned more than the attorneys who convicted the prison inmates. The court agreed with the majority in the principal case that the merit principle was focused on eliminating patronage employment, and refused to issue the writ, finding no constitutional violation. Was the union trying to have its cake and eat it too? The concurrence pointed out an additional irony in the case. The Attorney General supporting the union's case was Edmund G. Brown, Jr., who campaigned for governor on the promise of obtaining collective bargaining legislation for state employees, winning the election and succeeding in his objective with the passage of SEERA, which he signed in 1977.

5. In *State of Connecticut, Office of Policy and Management*, Dec. No. 4096 (Conn. St. Lab. Rel. Bd. 2005), the Board concluded that a union proposal seeking information about the process for ranking and evaluating candidates for civil service positions was not a mandatory bargaining subject and could not be submitted to interest arbitration. The process of conducting merit exams and rating candidates was exempted from negotiation by statute

and the union could not bargain for information about the process which was exempt from bargaining.

ASSOCIATION OF NEW JERSEY STATE COLLEGE FACULTIES, INC. v. DUNGAN

Supreme Court of New Jersey, 1974.
64 N.J. 338, 316 A.2d 425.

JACOBS, J.

[On September 15, 1972, the defendant Board of Higher Education adopted a resolution which set forth general guidelines for the granting of tenure to faculty members in the State Colleges and for the periodic evaluation of tenured faculty members. The resolution followed recommendations made by the Office of the Chancellor, Department of Higher Education. On October 20, 1972, the Board adopted a similar resolution with respect to County Colleges. The State College resolution embodied the following principles:

> 1) Each college Board of Trustees shall prepare a ten-year plan for its institution indicating the steps it plans to take to achieve a future balance of faculty in which no more than a reasonable proportion are ultimately tenured. The purpose of limiting the proportion of tenured faculty on each campus is to retain flexibility to enable the institution to respond to changing educational needs in the future. The plan established by each board shall include the proportion of tenured faculty projected each year during the ten-year period. The college trustees shall report their plan to the Board of Higher Education and shall inform the Board each year of the progress being made in achieving their goals.
>
> 2) Each State College Board of Trustees shall establish internal policies which indicate either that it will impose specific restrictions or more intensive and rigorous review procedures for any reappointment conferring tenure which brings the proportion of individuals in a department (or other major academic sub-unit) or in the college as a whole above its present level. Reappointments conferring tenure which raise the tenure rate above that level shall be made only as an unusual action when judged by the college Board of Trustees as being in the best interests of the college.
>
> 3) A reappointment conferring tenure may be offered only to faculty members who possess an appropriate terminal degree or its equivalent, except under unusual circumstances when the granting of tenure to an individual not having these qualifications is judged by a college Board of Trustees as being in the best interests of the institution.
>
> 4) Tenure should be awarded only to individuals whose performance during their probationary period gives clear evidence of the

ability and willingness to make a significant and continuing contribution to the growth and development of the institution.

5) Tenure should be awarded after presentation of positive evidence of excellence in teaching, scholarly achievement, contribution to college and community, and fulfillment of professional responsibilities, and not solely because negative evidence to the contrary is not presented.

6) Each college Board of Trustees should establish a procedure which the college will employ to regularly evaluate the performance of tenured faculty members. Such evaluations should occur not less frequently than every five years. These evaluations, which should include student input, should comprehend such factors as continued teaching competence, professional preparation and attainments which are directly related to teaching or administrative assignments, contributions to campus life beyond formal, assigned instructional activity and significant research, scholarly or community activity.

Plaintiff association attacked the resolutions on the ground, among others, that they were adopted without benefit of bargaining.]

* * *

In their third and final point the plaintiffs contend that "the unilateral adoption of the Tenure Rules violated the New Jersey Employer–Employee Relations Act." That Act provides in Section 7 that a majority representative of public employees in an appropriate unit may act for all employees in the unit and that the majority representative and designated representatives of the public employer shall meet at reasonable times and "negotiate in good faith" with respect to grievances and "terms and conditions of employment." It also provides that proposed new rules or modifications of existing rules governing "working conditions" shall be negotiated with the majority representative before they are established. The Act is unclear in failing to define "working conditions" or "terms and conditions of employment" as used in Section 7 and in failing to specify what subjects are mandatorily negotiable and what subjects are exclusively within management's prerogatives. But it makes clear that its statutory terms may not be viewed so expansively as to negate the Board of Higher Education's overall supervisory responsibilities as set forth in New Jersey's Education Law (Title 18A). See, E.g., Section 10 (NEW JERSEY STAT. ANN. 34:13A–8.1 [hereinafter N.J.S.A.]) which explicitly provides that no provision in the Act shall "annul or modify any statute or statutes of this State."

In *Dunellen Board of Education v. Dunellen Education Association,* 64 N.J. 17, 311 A.2d 737 (1973), we were recently called upon to decide whether the local board of education's determination to consolidate the chairmanships of the Social Studies Department and the English Department was a proper subject of mandatory negotiation or arbitration under the Employer–Employee Relations Act. We held that it was not, pointing out that the determination to consolidate was predominantly a matter of educational policy within the exclusive management prerogatives of the local board. Similarly in *Burlington County College Faculty Association v. Board of Trustees, Burlington County College,* 64 N.J. 10, 311 A.2d 723 (1973), we held that the fixing of the college calendar involved a major educational determination within the exclusive responsibility of those entrusted with administering the college.

In the aforecited cases we noted that it was "our clear judicial responsibility to give continuing effect to the provisions in our Education Law (Title 18A) without, however, frustrating the goals or terms of the Employer–Employee Relations Act (N.J.S.A. 34:13A–1 et seq.)." *Dunellen, supra.* As pointed out earlier in this opinion, the tenure resolutions of the Board of Higher Education were adopted well within the statutory powers and duties set forth in [various New Jersey statutes]. They represent major educational policy pronouncements entrusted by the Legislature to the Board's educational expertise and objective judgment. While the guidelines towards institutional excellence and greater administrative care in the granting of tenure undoubtedly entail individual consequences, they embody only matters not mandatorily negotiable under the principles expressed in *Dunellen* and *Englewood.* Cf. Faculty Tenure report (Jossey–Bass Series): "The commission recommends that collective bargaining in colleges and universities not extend to academic freedom and tenure and related faculty personnel matters and that grievances involving issues of freedom and tenure be referred to academic procedures outside the collective bargaining process."

The legislature has not indicated any disagreement with the *Dunellen* principles or their application to date. Nor has it expressed itself on tenure in relation to negotiation except in Section 4 of Chapter 163 of the Laws of 1973. That Section provides in effect that, notwithstanding the prescribed five-year probationary period, the board of trustees of the college may "as an exceptional action," and by a two-thirds majority of all of its members, grant tenure to "an individual faculty member" after employment for two consecutive academic years. Section 4 then concludes with the following: "The provisions of this Section shall not be negotiable as a term and condition of employment under the 'New Jersey Employer–Employee Relations Act.' " It is noteworthy that in this single statutory mention of tenure in relation to negotiation, mandatory negotiation is specifically excluded. It appears evident to us, particularly in the light of the continuing effect of Section 10 of the Employer–Employee Relations Act that the legislative silence elsewhere may not fairly or sensibly be construed as impairing the Board of Higher Education's exclusive statutory power under the Education Law to promulgate tenure guidelines which are reasonable in nature and which are not in conflict with any specific statutory provision dealing with tenure.

Although our present decision supports the Board of Higher Education's position that its tenure guidelines were not mandatorily negotiable, it is not to be taken as support for any notion that such guidelines or alterations therein should be promulgated without full and timely prior consultation with accredited faculty representatives and others interested. On the contrary, we take this occasion to reiterate the views expressed in the following concluding paragraph in *Dunellen* which may be taken to have general application:

> The holding that the consolidation was predominantly a matter of educational policy not mandatorily negotiable does not indicate that the Board would not have been well advised to have voluntarily discussed it in timely fashion with the representatives of the teachers. Peaceful relations between the school administration and its teachers is an ever present goal and though the teachers may not be permitted to take over the educational policies entrusted by the statutes to the Board they, as trained professionals, may have much to contribute towards the Board's adoption of sound and suitable educational policies. Before the passage of New Jersey's Employer–Employee Relations Act it was recognized that public employees had the right to be heard through their representatives on their proposals and grievances. The Act significantly broadened that right and, with the goal of peaceful labor relations in mind, created fields of mandatory negotiation. It would seem evident that, when dealing in fields with which the teachers are significantly concerned though outside the fields of mandatory negotiation, the end of peaceful labor relations will generally be furthered by some measure of timely voluntary discussion between the school administration and the representatives of its teachers even though the ultimate decisions are to be made by the Board in the exercise of its exclusive education prerogatives.

Affirmed.

NOTES

1. What assumptions underlie the New Jersey court's conclusions in *Dungan?* Are they different from the assumptions underlying the California court's conclusion in the preceding case? Are there differences between a civil service system and a tenure system which are relevant to the scope of bargaining in the public sector?

2. In addition to questions relating to the bargainability of tenure rules considered in *Dungan,* there are questions relating to the arbitrability of tenure decisions. Such questions are considered in Chapter 11 (Administration of the Contract).

3. The New Jersey Supreme Court recommends that employers discuss matters of educational policy with teachers, although negotiation is not required. What incentives exist to encourage such discussion? Are there disincentives? If you were representing a school board would you recommend such discussion? Why or why not?

4. A further example of the impact of external law upon public employer-union relationships is New York's statute permitting a Board of Cooperative Educational Services (BOCES) to offer academic summer programs, providing a procedure for two or more local school districts to request the

services of BOCES, and providing that when BOCES takes over a program formerly operated by a school district, teachers whose positions are abolished as a result have certain rights to employment with BOCES. NEW YORK-MCKINNEY'S EDUCATION LAW § 1950(4)(bb). When a union attempted to bargain over a school district's decision to subcontract summer teaching to BOCES, the New York Court of Appeal held that these provisions evidence the legislature's intent that such a decision not be subject to bargaining. *Webster Central School District v. PERB,* 75 N.Y.2d 619, 555 N.Y.S.2d 245, 554 N.E.2d 886 (1990).

5. In HEERA, the Act covering higher education employees, the California legislature attempted to guarantee that academic or faculty senates would survive the advent of collective bargaining and have an independent sphere of operation by (1) declaring its desire to preserve and encourage the tradition of joint decision-making between administration and faculty or academic employees through shared governance mechanisms or practices, including the academic senates of the University of California and the California State University and Colleges and other faculty councils, WEST'S ANN.CAL.GOV'T CODE § 3561(b); (2) specifying that senates are not labor organizations, WEST'S ANN. CAL.GOV'T CODE § 3562(f)(2); (3) permitting academic management to consult with senates apparently on any and all matters, WEST'S ANN.CAL.GOV'T CODE § 3571(f); and (4) excluding from the scope of representation many of the subjects typically dealt with by governance systems: the merits, necessity, or organization of any service, activity or program; student fees; admission requirements; standards for awarding degrees; content and conduct of courses, curricula, and research programs, WEST'S ANN.CAL.GOV'T CODE §§ 3562(q)(1)(A)–(C) and 3562(r)(1)(A)–(C); and (for CSUC) "criteria and standards" used for appointment, promotion, evaluation and tenure of academic employees, WEST'S ANN.CAL.GOV'T CODE § 3562(r)(1)(D), or (for U.C.) "procedures and policies" used for appointment, promotion, and tenure as well as procedures used for evaluation and the processing of grievances. WEST'S ANN.CAL.GOV'T CODE § 3562(q)(1)(D).

These Sections of the statute accomplish two significant things. First, they legitimize governance and senate structures. Second, they keep the subjects of governance off the bargaining table unless the regents or the trustees withdraw a matter covered by §§ 3562(q)(1)(D) or (r)(1)(D), respectively, from the senates in U.C. or CSUC, in which case it becomes bargainable or (in U.C. only) the academic senate (without relinquishing any of its own jurisdiction) decides that one or all of the subjects is bargainable. The power of a U.C. academic senate to do this is constrained by § 3579(e) which limits the scope of bargaining by a union representing a single campus unit to "matters which have customarily been determined on a division [campus] basis."

Why have special efforts been made to preserve academic or faculty senate structures in higher education while infrequent efforts have been made to clarify the relationship between collective bargaining and various other external regulations and systems?

6. While tenure and civil service laws may impact the scope of bargaining in almost every jurisdiction, there are a wide variety of other laws in the

public sector that are frequently used to argue that bargaining is precluded. For example, in *County of Erie v. New York PERB*, the operation of the jail was transferred to the county sheriff. 12 N.Y.3d 72, 903 N.E.2d 1163, 875 N.Y.S.2d 842 (2009). New York Corrections Law required the sheriff to establish a classification system for inmates and specified particular factors to be considered in maintaining that system. The sheriff changed the classification system used when the county executive operated the jail, resulting in changes in the work of employees in the two bargaining units which had previously divided the guard duties by sentencing status of the inmates. The unions charged that the employer made an unlawful unilateral change, but the court found that bargaining was not required because the statute mandated the factors for classification and neither the sentencing status of the inmates nor the duties of the bargaining unit employees were among the factors listed in the statute. The employer did have to bargain about the impact of the change on the employees, however.

On the other hand, in *Johnston School Committee v. Rhode Island State Labor Relations Board*, the court rejected the employer's argument that the Children's Online Protection Act, which required an internet safety policy to protect children from accessing harmful materials, permitted the employer to avoid bargaining about its new internet policy prohibiting employees from personal use of the internet, since the policy went far beyond what the law required and impacted the employees' terms and conditions of employment. No. Civ. A. PC 03–0141, 2004 WL 877619 (R.I. Super. Apr. 5, 2004). Similarly, in *Pennsylvania State System of Higher Education*, the Pennsylvania Labor Relations Board held that the state's Clean Air Act did not privilege the employer's unilateral imposition of a smoking ban on all college campuses as it prohibited only indoor smoking, allowing bargaining over smoking in other campus locations. 40 Pa. Pub. Employee Rep. ¶ 43 (2009). The determination of negotiability often requires parsing of the allegedly conflicting law and determining the legislative intent to decide whether it precludes or allows bargaining. The determination may also depend on the particular bargaining proposal.

7. Recall from Chapter 3, § B.2 that Congress authorized the Secretary of Labor to create special overtime pay triggers for law enforcement and fire protection personnel in order to minimize the cost of overtime payments. The Secretary issued a regulation which provides alternative overtime triggers that employers in these sectors may choose based on work periods of up to four weeks. The effect of adopting one of these alternatives is to reduce the likelihood of overtime pay. Does a municipality have to bargain over the decision to adopt an alternative overtime pay system pursuant to this regulation? See *City of Boston v. Commonwealth Employment Relations Board,* 453 Mass. 389, 902 N.E.2d 410 (2009) (upholding the decision of the Labor Relations Commission that the city was required to bargain about the decision to adopt a longer work period for purposes of overtime pay pursuant to the Department of Labor regulations).

D. SCOPE OF BARGAINING AND PUBLIC SECTOR LABOR–MANAGEMENT COOPERATION

In the mid 1980s, the U.S. Department of Labor authorized studies to assess whether the existing legal framework impeded or barred many cooperative labor-management efforts. As part of this effort, labor laws and collective bargaining practices in state and local government were reviewed since public employers and unions were increasingly interested in cooperative approaches to labor-management relations.

Professor Robert B. Moberly in his 1989 report to the United States Department of Labor identified legal impediments to labor-management cooperation by state and local governments. He included the narrow scope of bargaining in the public sector as one such barrier.

> It appears that labor-management cooperation programs are more extensive in those states which have a broader definition of subjects of bargaining, such as New York and Massachusetts. It seems likely that undue restrictions on the scope of bargaining discourage labor-management cooperation [e.g., by necessarily limiting the subjects on which the parties can cooperate] and reduce the effectiveness of the entire statute as a dispute settlement mechanism designed to encourage cooperation.

Robert B. Moberly, *Legal Impediments to Labor–Management Cooperation in State and Local Government, in U.S. Labor Law and the Future of Labor–Management Cooperation: Final Report* (U.S. Dept. of Labor, Bureau of Labor Management Relations and Cooperative Programs, BLMR 134, June 1989). In addition, Professor Moberly pointed to overly broad civil service laws as a further impediment to labor-management cooperation, particularly in jurisdictions where civil service provisions prevail over collective bargaining.

The Secretary of Labor's Task Force on Excellence in State and Local Government through Labor–Management Cooperation, chaired by Governor James J. Florio and Mayor Jerry Abramson, pointedly commented in its 1996 Report that:

> In instances where the parties emphasized legalisms and formalities, vital issues can go undiscussed because governing bodies may fear losing a non-negotiable managerial prerogative or unions may fear the dilution of a statutory or contractual benefit. Fear of setting a precedent often seems to interfere with developing a solution to a significant problem. These attitudes can be obstacles to making the commitments necessary to resolving personnel, labor relations and service-related issues.
>
> * * *
>
> [T]o improve service, the clearest need is for workers, managers and union leaders to be able to discuss the full range of issues affecting

the service they are working to improve. * * * [Successful cooperative] parties find a way to talk about what must be addressed either within the existing contract framework or by modifying that framework to accommodate the mutual interest and responsibilities for service excellence.

Recall that Professor Malin argued in *The Paradox of Public Sector Labor Law*, *supra,* that a narrow scope of bargaining channels unions into negotiating protections for employees against the risks of the public enterprise rather than encouraging them to be a part of the process of reform and change. He suggests a number of possible solutions including cooperative partnerships between management and labor and encouraging discussion of issues that may not be appropriate for collective bargaining.

NOTES

1. Consider Professor Malin's proposal that jurisdictions should experiment with an alternative to the present state of the law concerning permissive subjects of bargaining. He believes that "public sector labor law is ripe for the recognition of an intermediate duty to consult" and recommends consideration of Minnesota's "meet and confer" model mandating discussion, but not bargaining, about policy matters relating to the services to the public provided by represented professional public employees. Wisconsin has enacted legislation requiring chancellors of the University of Wisconsin System's colleges and universities to "meet and confer" with representatives of faculty and academic staff regarding permissive subjects of bargaining unless the issue is being actively considered by a faculty and/or academic staff governance organization. WIS.STAT.ANN. § 111.998(3). For the text of the Minnesota "meet and confer" legislation, see Chapter 6, § A.

Is a requirement to "meet and confer" on a regular basis with the bargaining representative of professional employees about policy issues excluded from the scope of mandatory bargaining an idea whose time has come? If so, should the "meet and confer" but not negotiate requirement be applied not only to professional public employees but to a broader category of public employees?

2. To implement recommendations received by his administration officials and to authorize creation of the National Partnership Council and multiple labor-management partnerships throughout the executive branch, President Clinton issued Executive Order 12871 on October 1, 1993. To encourage labor-management partnerships to handle important "non-traditional" issues, the Executive Order further required federal agencies subject to the Federal Services Labor Management Relations Statute (FSLMRS) to negotiate subjects designated as permissive in the Act. (The Executive Order purported to exercise federal agencies' discretion to elect to bargain permissive subjects of bargaining enumerated in the FSLMRS.) When several agencies refused to bargain over such subjects, the unions involved filed unfair labor practice charges with the Federal Labor Relations Authority (FLRA) against the agencies. In *United States Department of Commerce v. Patent Office Professional Association*, 54 F.L.R.A. 360 (1998), the FLRA held that

Executive Order 12871 did not constitute an agency election to bargain over permissive subjects as required by the FSLMRS and, therefore, with one exception, found that the agencies had not committed unfair labor practices when they refused to bargain. (FLRA distinguished between a presidential mandate to agencies to negotiate and an agency's election to negotiate.) FLRA's decisions were upheld in *National Association of Government Employees v. FLRA*, 179 F.3d 946 (D.C. Cir.1999).

3. Not all commentators agree that creating labor-management partnerships is a wise public policy and that a broader scope of bargaining would be of benefit to the public sector. The Heritage Foundation's research paper, *Taking Charge of Federal Personnel* (Backgrounder #1404 dated January 10, 2001) (reproduced in Chapter 4, *supra*) argued that, for the new Bush administration to succeed in implementing its agenda, it needs to stress "the importance of basing personnel management decisions on performance in carrying out the mission of the President" using lessons from the past to encourage a managerial "take charge" or "just do it" strategy.

Soon after his inauguration, President George W. Bush issued an Executive Order revoking Executive Order 12871, dissolving the National Partnership Council, and directing agency heads to move promptly to rescind any actions that had been taken to implement Executive Order 12871. After his election, President Obama reinstituted labor-management partnerships through Executive Order 13522. In addition to including many of the same provisions as the executive order issued by President Clinton, the Obama order provides for pilot projects to evaluate the effect of negotiations over permissive subjects of bargaining on agency effectiveness, employee morale and labor relations.

4. Several jurisdictions have amended their public sector collective bargaining statutes to narrow the scope of mandatory bargaining. Some examples have already been given in this chapter. As originally enacted in 1967, New York's public sector scope language was brief and followed National Labor Relations Act (NLRA) language. Subsequently, New York's law was amended to prohibit bargaining on retirement benefits. Michigan also originally adopted NLRA language in 1965 but added a "laundry list" of prohibited subjects in 1994 relating mostly to public school employers. The constitutionality of these scope restrictions was upheld in *Michigan State AFL-CIO v. Michigan Employment Relations Commission*, 212 Mich.App. 472, 538 N.W.2d 433 (1995). For another example, see 1995 amendments to Oregon's definition of "employment relations" which adds an extensive list of prohibited subjects (noted in Section C) prohibiting bargaining on a number of policy oriented school issues such as class size and standards for teacher evaluations, typical nonmandatory subjects of bargaining. The list also prohibits bargaining on "reasonable dress, grooming, and at-work personal conduct requirements respecting smoking, gum chewing and similar matters of personal conduct."

Additional school district bargaining restrictions are to be found in 1995 Illinois legislation which restricts Chicago teachers from bargaining on issues pertaining to class size, length of the school day, and use of technology in the classroom. The Illinois Legislature amended the statute in 2003 to make bargaining on these subjects permissive. ILL.-SMITH-HURD ANN. 115 ILCS 5/4.5.

Also in 1995, the Wisconsin legislature amended the teacher tenure provisions applicable to Milwaukee teachers to abolish future grants of tenure and adopted amendments to the Municipal Employment Relations Act in order to authorize the Milwaukee Board of School Directors to reassign Milwaukee teachers without regard to seniority, operate a charter school, or close schools without bargaining on those decisions or their impact. These are now prohibited subjects of bargaining. See WIS.STAT.ANN. 111.70(4)(m).

In higher education, the Ohio legislature addressed the decline in the amount of time public university professors devoted to teaching as opposed to research by requiring public universities to develop standards for instructional workloads and prohibiting bargaining on that subject. The union representing university professors challenged the constitutionality of the statute. Although the Ohio Supreme Court invalidated the statute on equal protection grounds in *AAUP v. Central State University*, 83 Ohio St.3d 229, 699 N.E.2d 463 (1998), the United States Supreme Court in *Central State University v. AAUP*, 526 U.S. 124, 119 S.Ct. 1162, 143 L.Ed.2d 227 (1999) reversed. The per curiam opinion found that Ohio's legislative classification was an entirely rational step to accomplish its objective.

Some state legislatures have attempted to meet financial crises by imposing a variety of economic restrictions upon future contracts. In *United Public Workers v. Yogi*, 101 Haw. 46, 62 P.3d 189 (2002), the Hawaii Supreme Court invalidated legislation which barred negotiations over all cost items regarding "wages, hours, health fund contributions by the employer and other terms and conditions of employment" for the 1999–2001 biennium. It held that the legislature did not have absolute discretion to change the scope of public sector bargaining in light of the state's constitutional provision which protected public employees' right to bargain collectively "as provided by law."

Wisconsin has attempted to control costs by amending the statute relating to impasse arbitration. The factors which impasse arbitrators had to consider in making their arbitration awards were changed from a statutory list without any priorities to a mandated listing of factors which must be given greatest weight, factors to be given greater weight, and other factors to be considered. See WIS.STAT.ANN. 111.70(4)(cm)(7), (7g), and (7r).

Is narrowing the scope of bargaining an effective response to the issues raised in this chapter? Will it remove the antidemocratic effects of bargaining? Lead to more cooperative relationships and greater union participation in solving the problems of government? Reduce litigation over scope of bargaining or make bargaining more effective?

5. (Re)evaluate the arguments for and against broadening the scope of public sector bargaining. Which side has the more compelling arguments?

Chapter 9

Strikes

■ ■ ■

The right to strike lies at the center of federal labor policy in the private sector. As the late George Taylor once put it, the strike provides the motive power for agreement. Although the incidence of strikes in the private sector has diminished in recent years, a credible strike threat can still force both sides to weigh alternatives carefully; both presumably would be hurt economically by a work stoppage; the question each must consider is whether strike costs are greater or lesser than the costs of reaching some kind of compromise.

Thus, the National Labor Relations Act expressly protects the right to strike. The right to strike also is encompassed in the right to engage in concerted activity for mutual aid and protection. The NLRA requires that a party wishing to terminate or modify an existing collective bargaining agreement serve on the other party a notice of the proposed termination or modification sixty days prior to the agreement's expiration date. That party must also serve a notice of the existence of a labor dispute on the Federal Mediation and Conciliation Service thirty days later. Strikes that occur during the notice period are not protected under the statute. Generally, these notice requirements are the only express regulation of private sector strikes under the NLRA.

There are exceptions to this liberal approach to strikes in the private sector. The NLRA requires that a union give ten days notice of its intent to strike or picket a health care institution. The Railway Labor Act, which governs railroads and airlines, requires a party who wishes to modify a collective bargaining agreement to serve a notice of intent on the other party. If negotiations do not produce an agreement, either party may request mediation from the National Mediation Board (NMB). The NMB must then mediate the dispute. If the NMB concludes that further mediation efforts will be futile, it must offer the parties the option of arbitrating their dispute. If either party rejects the offer of arbitration, a thirty-day cooling off period begins. It is only at the end of the cooling off period that the union may lawfully strike.

In the private sector, the union's right to strike is balanced by employer economic weapons. Although an employer may not discharge striking employees, it may permanently replace them as long as the strike has not been caused or prolonged by employer unfair labor practices. Even where a union does not strike, an employer may lock out employees to pressure the union's position in bargaining. The strength of each party's economic weapons and the credibility of each party's threat to use those weapons largely determines the party's bargaining power. The parties' mutual desire to avoid resorting to economic warfare motivates their reaching agreement.

In the private sector, the strike is an economic weapon. Unions seek to shut down, or at least disrupt substantially, employer operations, resulting in lost employer revenue. The continuing loss of revenue pressures the employer to reconsider its position in negotiations. Similarly, employees are not paid while on strike or locked out, and, as the strike progresses, their economic plight increases the pressure on the union to reconsider its bargaining position.

In the public sector, however, the strike is not primarily an economic weapon. Although some public employers, such as parks and transit systems, may experience a decrease in user fees when a strike disrupts operations, the predominant source of public employer revenue is taxes. Strikes do not excuse residents from their legal obligation to pay taxes. Thus, strikes do not directly disrupt the revenue flow for most public employers. Even public employers who collect user fees may actually save money during a strike because they will continue to collect taxes and the money saved on strikers' wages may more than offset the lost user fee revenue.

In public education, the economic effects of a strike are muted even further. Most states, as a condition of receiving state aid, mandate that school districts have a 180–day school year. If a strike closes the schools, upon settlement of the strike, the school district will probably make up the days lost to the strike to avoid losing state aid. In such cases, the school district suffers no loss of revenue and the striking employees suffer no overall loss of income because the income lost during the strike will be replaced by the wages paid to them for the make-up days.

Thus, the public sector strike is primarily a political weapon. By disrupting public services with a strike, unions seek to place political pressure on public officials to reexamine their positions in bargaining. Of course, the strike may backfire and generate political pressure on the union to give in. The crucial difference is that a public sector strike is a political war rather than an economic one.

The government provides services that, as a matter of policy, we have determined should not be left to the vagaries of the private sector marketplace. Consequently, some people regard public services as inherently essential such that they should never be interrupted by an employee work stoppage. Others have argued that some public employees' functions are less essential than those performed by some private sector employees.

Some observers have maintained that despite prohibition, strikes by public employees occur with a fair degree of frequency.

Jurisdictions have taken a wide variety of approaches to public employee strikes. Most prohibit them, but their methods of prohibition vary from criminal sanctions to standards that make it difficult to enjoin an illegal strike. Some jurisdictions have recognized a right to strike in the public sector, but they have varied in the extent to which they have restricted and regulated that right.

This chapter begins by examining the policy debate over public employee strikes. It then considers strike prohibitions, focusing on the definition of a strike, injunctions against illegal strikes, sanctions against strikers and their unions, and the availability of damage claims against striking unions. It concludes by examining the legalization of public employee strikes, focusing on the consequences of legalization, different statutory approaches to legalization, and the availability of injunctions in jurisdictions where public employee strikes are lawful.

A. THE POLICY DEBATE CONCERNING PUBLIC EMPLOYEE STRIKES

Some people regard public sector collective bargaining as anti-democratic. They regard public employees as an interest group, and public sector collective bargaining as giving that interest group an avenue of access to public officials that all other interest groups lack.

Some who support public sector collective bargaining as a matter of policy oppose allowing public employees to strike because, in their view, such job actions distort the democratic process. They agree with opponents of collective bargaining that public employees' wages and working conditions raise political issues, but do not see public employee unions' exclusive access to public officials through bargaining as anti-democratic. Nevertheless, they consider the strike as a weapon that greatly magnifies public employees' power in exploiting their exclusive avenue of access to public officials. They fear that citizens react to public employee strikes by demanding a quick settlement, causing public officials to agree to union demands regardless of the wisdom of doing so. They maintain that this danger is particularly acute where employees are performing essential services, but is also present where the loss of services due to a strike causes significant inconvenience. They conclude that the right to strike excessively empowers public employee unions in a forum from which all other interest groups have been excluded.

However, as discussed in Chapter 4, others see public sector collective bargaining as providing an exclusive forum that public employees need because they are otherwise disadvantaged vis-a-vis other interest groups on matters affecting their wages and working conditions. Most citizens would like to get the maximum public service for the minimum price and, because they outnumber the employees, the political process will drive wages and working conditions down in the absence of collective bargaining. When viewed this way, public employee strikes do not distort the political process. Instead, such strikes are aimed at the very constituents against whom public employees must compete in the political process of setting their wages and working conditions. Strikes thus force other interest groups to assess just how strongly they hold their positions.

President Franklin Delano Roosevelt, the same President who signed the National Labor Relations Act into law, once wrote, "[A] strike of public employees manifests nothing less than an intent on their part to prevent or obstruct the operations of Government until their demands are satisfied. Such action, looking toward the paralysis of Government by those who have sworn to support it, is unthinkable and intolerable." Letter from Franklin Roosevelt to the president, National Federation of Federal Employees (August 16, 1937), quoted in *Norwalk Teachers' Association v. Board of Education*, 138 Conn. 269, 83 A.2d 482 (1951). The majority of jurisdictions prohibit strikes by all public employees. The federal government makes it a felony for its employees to strike. Even those jurisdictions that recognize a public employee's right to strike prohibit police and firefighters from striking, as well as other employees they deem "essential." Consider the discussion of public sector strikes in the following case.

COUNTY SANITATION DISTRICT v. SEIU LOCAL 660

California Supreme Court, 1985.
38 Cal.3d 564, 214 Cal.Rptr. 424, 699 P.2d 835.

BROUSSARD, J.

Defendants appeal from a judgment awarding plaintiff sanitation district damages and prejudgment interest in connection with defendant union's involvement in a labor strike against plaintiff. The case squarely presents issues of great import to public sector labor-management relations, namely whether all strikes by public employees are illegal and, if so, whether the striking union is liable in tort for compensatory damages. After careful review of a long line of case law and policy arguments, we conclude that the common law prohibition against all public employee strikes is no longer supportable. Therefore, the judgment for the plaintiff finding the strike to be unlawful and awarding damages, interest and costs must be reversed.

I. Statement of the Case.

Defendants' union (Local 660 or the union) is a labor organization affiliated with the Service Employees International Union, AFL–CIO, and has been the certified bargaining representative of the blue collar employees of the Los Angeles Sanitation District since 1973. Plaintiff is one of 27 sanitation districts within Los Angeles County and is charged with providing, operating and maintaining sewage transport and treatment facilities and landfill disposal sites throughout the county. The District employs some 500 workers who are directly or indirectly responsible for the operation and maintenance of its facilities and who are members of, or represented by, Local 660. Since 1973, the District and Local 660 have bargained concerning wages, hours and working conditions pursuant to the Meyers–Milias–Brown Act (MMBA). WEST'S ANN.CAL.GOV.CODE §§ 3500–3511 [hereinafter GOV.CODE]. Each year these negotiations have resulted in a binding labor contract or memorandum of understanding (MOU).

On July 5, 1976, approximately 75% of the District's employees went out on strike after negotiations between the District and the union for a new wage and benefit agreement reached an impasse and failed to produce a new MOU. The District promptly filed a complaint for injunctive relief and damages and was granted a temporary restraining order. The strike continued for approximately 11 days, during which time the District was able to maintain its facilities and operations through the efforts of management personnel and certain union members who chose not to strike. On July 16, the employees voted to accept a tentative agreement on a new MOU, the terms of which were identical to the District's offer prior to the strike.

The District then proceeded with the instant action for tort damages. The trial court found the strike to be unlawful and in violation of the public policy of the State of California and thus awarded the District $246,904 in compensatory damages, prejudgment interest in the amount of $87,615.22 and costs of $874.65.

II. The Traditional Prohibition Against Public Employee Strikes.

Common law decisions in other jurisdictions at one time held that no employee, whether public or private, had a right to strike in concert with fellow workers. In fact, such collective action was generally viewed as a conspiracy and held subject to both civil and criminal sanctions. Over the course of the 20th century, however, courts and legislatures gradually acted to change these laws as they applied to private sector employees; today, the right to strike is generally accepted as indispensable to the system of collective bargaining and negotiation, which characterizes labor-management relations in the private sector.

By contrast, American law continues to regard public sector strikes in a substantially different manner. A strike by employees of the United States government may still be treated as a crime, and strikes by state and local employees have been explicitly allowed by courts or statute in only eleven states.

Contrary to the assertions of the plaintiff as well as various holdings of the Court of Appeal, this court has repeatedly stated that the legality of strikes by public employees in California has remained an open question. * * *

Before commencing our discussion, however, we must note that the Legislature has also chosen to reserve judgment on the general legality of strikes in the public sector. As Justice Grodin observed in his concurring opinion in *El Rancho Unified School District v. National Education Assn.*, 33 Cal.3d 946, 192 Cal.Rptr. 123, 663 P.2d 893 (1983), "the Legislature itself has steadfastly refrained from providing clearcut guidance." With the exception of firefighters (WEST'S ANN.CAL.LAB.CODE § 1962 [hereinafter LAB.CODE]), no statutory prohibition against strikes by public employees in this state exists. The MMBA, the statute under which the present controversy arose, does not directly address the question of strikes.

The MMBA sets forth the rights of municipal and county employees in California. GOV.CODE §§ 3500–3511. The MMBA protects the right of such employees "to form, join, and participate in the activities of employee organizations * * * for the purpose of representation on all matters of employer-employee relations." It also requires public employers to "meet and confer" in good faith with employee representatives on all issues within the scope of representation. As explained in its preamble, one of the MMBA's main purposes is to improve communications between public employees and their employers by providing a reasonable method for resolving disputes. A further stated purpose is to promote improved personnel relations by "providing a uniform basis for recognizing the right of public employees to join organizations of their own choice."

On its face, the MMBA neither denies nor grants local employees the right to strike. This omission is noteworthy since the Legislature has not hesitated to expressly prohibit strikes for certain classes of public employees. For example, the * * * prohibition against strikes by firefighters was enacted nine years before the passage of the MMBA and remains in effect today. Moreover, the MMBA includes firefighters within its provisions. Thus, the absence of any such limitation on other public employees covered by the MMBA at the very least implies a lack of legislative intent to use the MMBA to enact a general strike prohibition.

* * *

In the absence of clear legislative directive on this crucial matter, it becomes the task of the judiciary to determine whether, under the law, strikes by public employees should be viewed as a prohibited tort.

III. The Common Law Prohibition Against Public Employee Strikes.

As noted above, the Court of Appeal and various lower courts in this and other jurisdictions have repeatedly stated that, absent a specific statutory grant, all strikes by public employees are per se illegal. A variety of policy rationales and legal justifications have traditionally been advanced in support of this common law "rule," * * * . The various justifications for the common law prohibition can be summarized into four basic arguments. First—the traditional justification—that a strike by public employees is tantamount to a denial of governmental authority/sovereignty. Second, the terms of public employment are not subject to bilateral collective bargaining, as in the private sector, because they are set by the legislative body through unilateral lawmaking. Third, since legislative bodies are responsible for public employment decision making, granting public employees the right to strike would afford them excessive bargaining leverage, resulting in a distortion of the political process and an improper delegation of legislative authority. Finally, public employees provide essential public services which, if interrupted by strikes, would threaten the public welfare.

Our determination of the legality of strikes by public employees necessarily involves an analysis of the reasoning and current viability of each of these arguments. The first of these justifications, the sovereignty argument, asserts that government is the embodiment of the people, and hence those entrusted to carry out its function may not impede it. * * *

The sovereignty concept, however, has often been criticized in recent years as a vague and outdated theory based on the assumption that "the King can do no wrong." Judge Harry T. Edwards has cogently observed:

> the application of the strict sovereignty notion—that governmental power can never be opposed by employee organizations—is clearly a vestige from another era, an era of unexpanded government * * *. With the rapid growth of the government, both in sheer size as well as in terms of assuming services not traditionally associated with the 'sovereign,' government employees understandably no longer feel constrained by a notion that 'The King can do no wrong.' The distraught cries by public unions of disparate treatment merely reflect the fact that, for all intents and purposes, public employees occupy essentially the same position vis-a-vis the employer as their private counterparts.

Harry T. Edwards, The Developing Labor Relations Law in the Public Sector, 10 *Duq.L.Rev.* 357 (1972).

In recent years, courts have rejected the very same concept of sovereignty as a justification for governmental immunity from tort liability. * * * [P]erpetuation of the doctrine of sovereign immunity in tort law led to many inequities, and its application effected many incongruous results. Similarly, the use of this archaic concept to justify a per se prohibition against public employee strikes is inconsistent with modern social reality and should be hereafter laid to rest.

The second basic argument underlying the common law prohibition of public employee strikes holds that since the terms of public employment are fixed by the Legislature, public employers are virtually powerless to respond to strike pressure, or alternatively that allowing such strikes would result in "government by contract" instead of "government by law." This justification may have had some merit before the California Legislature gave extensive bargaining rights to public employees. However, at present, most terms and conditions of public employment are arrived at through collective bargaining under such statutes as the MMBA.

* * * The overall framework of the MMBA represents a nearly exact parallel to the private sector system of collective bargaining—a system which sets forth the guidelines for labor-management relations in the private sphere and which protects the right of private employees to strike. By enacting these significant and parallel protections for public employees through the MMBA, the Legislature effectively removed many of the underpinnings of the common law per se ban against public employee strikes. While the MMBA does not directly address the issue of such strikes, its implications regarding the traditional common law prohibition are significant.

This argument was eloquently explained by Justice Grodin in his concurring opinion in *El Rancho Unified Sch. Dist. v. National Education Assn.*, 33 Cal.3d 946, 192 Cal.Rptr.123, 663 P.2d 893 (1983), where he pointed out that "[t]he premise * * * that it is necessarily contrary to public policy to establish terms and conditions of employment for public employees through the bilateral process of collective bargaining rather than through unilateral lawmaking has since been rejected by the Legislature. The heart of the statute under consideration in this case [the Educational Employment Relations Act] for example, contemplates that matters relating to wages, hours and certain other terms and conditions of employment for teachers will be the subject of negotiation and agreement between a public school employer and organizations representing its employees. Thus, the original policy foundation for the 'rule' that public employee strikes are illegal in this state has been substantially undermined, if not obliterated."

The remaining two arguments have not served in this state as grounds for asserting a ban on public employee strikes but have been advanced by commentators and by courts of other states. With the traditional reasons for prohibiting such strikes debunked, these additional reasons do not convince us of the necessity of a judicial ukase prohibiting all such strikes.

The first of these arguments draws upon the different roles of market forces in the private and public spheres. This rationale suggests that because government services are essential and demand is generally inelastic, public employees would wield excessive bargaining power if allowed to strike. Proponents of this argument assume that economic constraints are not present to any meaningful degree in the public sector. Consequently, in the absence of such constraints, public employers will be forced to make abnormally large concessions to workers, which in turn will distort our political process by forcing either higher taxes or a redistribution of resources between government services.

There are, however, several fundamental problems with this "distortion of the political process" argument. For one, as will be discussed more fully below, a key assumption underlying the argument—that all government services are essential—is factually unsupportable. Modern governments engage in an enormous number and variety of functions, which clearly vary as to their degree of essentiality. As such, the absence of an unavoidable nexus between most public services and essentiality necessarily undercuts the notion that public officials will be forced to settle strikes quickly and at any cost. The recent case of the air-traffic controllers' strike is yet another example that governments have the ability to hold firm against a strike for a considerable period, even in the face of substantial inconvenience. * * *

Other factors also serve to temper the potential bargaining power of striking public employees and thus enable public officials to resist excessive demands: First, wages lost due to strikes are as important to public employees as they are to private employees. Second, the public's concern over increasing tax rates will serve to prevent the decision-making process from being dominated by political instead of economic considerations. A third and related economic constraint arises in such areas as water, sewage and, in some instances, sanitation services, where explicit prices are charged. Even if representatives of groups other than employees and the employer do not formally enter the bargaining process, both union and local government representatives are aware of the economic implications of bargaining which leads to higher prices which are clearly visible to the public. A fourth economic constraint on public employees exists in those services where subcontracting to the private sector is a realistic alternative. For example, Warren, Michigan resolved a bargaining impasse with an American Federation of State, County and Municipal Employees (AFSCME) local by subcontracting its entire sanitation service; Santa Monica, California, ended a strike of city employees by threatening to subcontract its sanitation operations; in fact, San Francisco has chosen to subcontract its entire sanitation system to *private* firms. If this subcontract option is preserved, wages in the public sector clearly need not exceed the rate at which subcontracting becomes a realistic alternative.

The proponents of a flat ban on public employee strikes not only ignore such factors as the availability of subcontracting, but also fail to adequately consider public sentiment towards most strikes and assume that the public will push blindly for an early resolution at any cost. In fact, public sentiment toward a strike often limits the pressure felt by political leaders, thereby reducing the strike's effectiveness. * * *

In sum, there is little, if any empirical evidence which demonstrates that governments generally capitulate to unreasonable demands by public employees in order to resolve strikes. The result of the strike in the instant case clearly suggests the opposite. During the 11–day strike, negotiations resumed, and the parties subsequently reached an agreement on a new MOU, the terms of which were *precisely the same* as the District's last offer prior to the commencement of the strike. Such results certainly do not illustrate a situation where public employees wielded excessive bargaining power and thereby caused a distortion of our political process.

The fourth and final justification for the common law prohibition is that interruption of government services is unacceptable because they are essential. As noted above, in our contemporary industrial society the presumption of essentially of most government services is questionable at best. In addition, we tolerate strikes by private employees in many of the same areas in which government is engaged, such as transportation, health, education, and utilities; in many employment fields, public and private activity largely overlap.

* * *

We of course recognize that there are certain "essential" public services, the disruption of which would seriously threaten the public health or safety. In fact, defendant union itself concedes that the law should still act to render illegal any strikes in truly essential services which would constitute a genuine threat to the public welfare. Therefore, to the extent that the "excessive bargaining power" and "interruption of essential services" arguments still have merit, specific health and safety limitations on the right to strike should suffice to answer the concerns underlying those arguments.

* * *

It is unrealistic to assume that disputes among public employees and their employers will not occur; in fact, strikes by public employees are relatively frequent events in California. For example, 46 strikes occurred during 1981–1983, which actually marks a significant decline when compared to the number during the 5 previous years. Although the circumstances behind each individual strike may vary somewhat, commentators repeatedly note that much of the reason for their occurrence lies in the fact that without the right to strike, or at least a credible strike threat, public employees have little negotiating strength. This, in turn, produces frustrations which exacerbate labor-management conflicts and often provoke "illegal" strikes.

* * *

It is universally recognized that in the private sector, the bilateral determination of wages and working conditions through a collective bargaining process, in which both sides possess relatively equal strength, facilitates understanding and more harmonious relations between employers and their employees. In the absence of some means of equalizing the parties' respective bargaining positions, such as a credible strike threat, both sides are less likely to bargain in good faith; this in turn leads to unsatisfactory and acrimonious labor relations and ironically to more and longer strikes. Equally as important, the possibility of a strike often provides the best impetus for parties to reach an agreement at the bargaining table, because *both* parties lose if a strike actually comes to pass. Thus by providing a clear incentive for resolving disputes, a credible strike threat may serve to avert, rather than to encourage, work stoppages.

* * *

A final policy consideration in our analysis addresses a more philosophical issue—the perception that the right to strike, in the public sector as well as in the private sector, represents a basic civil liberty. The widespread acceptance of that perception leads logically to the conclusion that the right to strike, as an important symbol of a free society, should not be denied unless such a strike would substantially injure paramount interests of the larger community.

* * *

For the reasons stated above, we conclude that the common law prohibition against public sector strikes should not be recognized in this state. Consequently, strikes by public sector employees in this state as such are neither illegal nor tortious under California common law. We must immediately caution, however, that the right of public employees to strike is by no means unlimited. Prudence and concern for the general public welfare require certain restrictions.

The Legislature has already prohibited strikes by firefighters under any circumstances. It may conclude that other categories of public employees perform such essential services that a strike would invariably result in imminent danger to public health and safety, and must therefore be prohibited.

* * *

After consideration of the various alternatives before us, we believe the following standard may properly guide courts in the resolution of future disputes in this area; strikes by public employees are not unlawful at common law unless or until it is clearly demonstrated that such a strike creates a substantial and imminent threat to the health and safety of the public. This standard allows exceptions in certain essential areas of public employment (e.g., the prohibition against firefighters and law enforcement personnel) and also requires the courts to determine on a case-by-case basis whether the public interest overrides the basic right to strike.

Although we recognize that this balancing process may impose an additional burden on the judiciary, it is neither a novel nor unmanageable task. Indeed, an examination of the strike in the instant case affords a good example of how this new standard should be applied. The 11–day strike did not involve public employees, such as firefighters or law enforcement personnel, whose absence from their duties would clearly endanger the public health and safety. Moreover, there was no showing by the District that the health and safety of the public was at any time imminently threatened. That is not to say that had the strike continued indefinitely, or had the availability of replacement personnel been insufficient to maintain a reasonable sanitation system, there could not have been at some point a clear showing of a substantial threat to the public health and welfare. However, such was not the case here, and the legality of the strike would have been upheld under our newly adopted standard.

* * *

We conclude that it is not unlawful for public employees to engage in a concerted work stoppage for the purpose of improving their wages or conditions of employment, unless it has been determined that the work stoppage poses an imminent threat to public health or safety. Since the trial court's judgment for damage in this case was predicated upon an erroneous determination that defendants' strike was unlawful, the judgment for damages cannot be sustained.

The judgment is reversed.

LUCAS, J., dissenting:

I respectfully dissent. In my view, public employees in this state neither have the right to strike, nor should they have that right. In any event, in light of the difficulty in fashioning proper exceptions to the basic "no strike" rule, and the dangers to public health and safety arising from even a *temporary* cessation of governmental services, the courts should defer to the Legislature, a body far better equipped to create such exceptions.

The majority paints a glowing picture of the public strike weapon as a means of "enhanc[ing] labor-management relations," "equalizing the parties' respective bargaining positions," assuring "good faith" collective bargaining, and "providing a clear incentive for resolving disputes." Indeed, so enamored is the majority with the concept of the public strike that it elevates this heretofore *illegal* device to a "basic civil liberty." Though wholly unnecessary to its opinion, the majority in dictum even suggests that public employees may have a *constitutional* right to strike which cannot be legislatively abridged absent some "substantial or compelling justification."

Thus, in the face of an unbroken string of Court of Appeal cases commencing nearly 35 years ago which hold that public strikes are illegal, we suddenly announce our finding that public strikes are not only lawful in most cases, but indeed they may constitute a panacea for many of the social and economic ills which have long beset the public sector. One may wonder, as I do, why we kept that revelation a secret for all these years.

Despite the majority's encomiums, the fact remains that public strikes may devastate a city within a matter of days, or even hours, depending on the circumstances. For this reason, among many others, the courts of this state (and the vast majority of courts in other states and the federal government) have declared *all* public strikes illegal. * * *

* * *

The decision to allow public employee strikes requires a delicate and complex balancing process best undertaken by the Legislature, which may formulate a comprehensive regulatory scheme designed to avoid the disruption and chaos which invariably follow a cessation or interruption of governmental services. The majority's own proposal, to withhold the strike weapon only where "truly essential" services are involved and a "substantial and imminent threat" is posed, will afford little guidance to our trial courts who must, on a "case-by-case" basis, decide such issues. Nor will representatives of labor or management be able to predict with any confidence or certainty whether a particular strike is a lawful one or, being lawful at its inception, will become unlawful by reason of its adverse effects upon the public health and safety. In short, the majority's broad holding will prove as unworkable as it is unwise.

Of the few states that permit strikes by public employees, virtually all do so by comprehensive statutory provisions. Some of the statutory schemes begin by creating classifications of employees, distinguishing, for example, workers whose services are deemed essential (e.g., police, firefighters), those who services may be interrupted for short periods of time (e.g., teachers), and those whose services may be omitted for an extended time (e.g., municipal golf course attendants). These schemes typically define various prerequisites to the exercise of the right to strike for those categories of workers permitted that option. The prerequisites include a period of mandatory mediation as well as advance notice to the employer. In addition, some statutory schemes lay out the ground rules for binding arbitration.

In contrast, the majority's new California rule is hopelessly undefined and unstructured. In addition to the breadth of the majority's "truly essential" standard, the statutes presently provide no systematic classification of employees according to the nature of their work and the degree to which the public can tolerate work stoppages. Only firefighters are expressly prohibited from striking and giving recognition to picket lines. (LAB.CODE, § 1962.) Moreover, the four principal statutory schemes regulating other public employees establish widely differing approaches to labor relations for different types and levels of employees. Compare GOV.CODE, §§ 3500–3510 [Meyers–Millias–Brown Act, covering local government employees]; 3512–3524 [State Employer–Employee Relations Act, covering state employees]; 3540–3549.3 [Ed.Employment Relations Act, covering public school employees]; 3560–3599 [governing employment in higher education]. Thus, these statutes produce inconsistent results when, as here, the right to strike is given recognition almost across the board.

The Meyers–Milias–Brown Act, for example, provides "no clear mechanism for resolving disputes" between local governments and their workers. In the absence of an administrative agency to settle charges of unfair labor practices and compel such remedies as mediation, presumably all strike-related issues will go to the courts in the first instance, but the courts are poor forums for the resolution of such issues. On the other hand, issues arising out of work stoppages by public school employees are to be resolved by the Public Employee Relations Board (PERB) on the basis of PERB's own set of remedies. Of course, this anomalous situation is in large part the product of this court's tolerance of strikes by teachers, *El Rancho Unified Sch. Dist. v. National Ed. Assn., supra*; *San Diego Teachers Assn. v. Superior Court,* 24 Cal.3d 1, 154 Cal.Rptr. 893, 593 P.2d 838 (1979), and PERB's correlative expansion of its authority so that it may compel mediation or adopt other remedies in labor disputes in public education. See WEST'S ANN.CAL.ADMIN.CODE, § 3600 et seq.

Finally, nothing in PERB's explicit statutory powers (GOV.CODE, § 3541.3) extends to mandatory arbitration, for example, so it remains to be established whether state employees, also under PERB's jurisdiction (*id.*, § 3513, subd. (g)), will be governed by the same ground rules as educational employees, or whether some of them, perhaps deemed "truly essential," will be subject to binding arbitration under rules that do not now exist.

I would affirm the judgment.

[Justice Kaus wrote an opinion concurring in the judgment (joined by Justice Reynoso) insofar as it held that a common law tort action for damages does not lie against a public sector union for a peaceful strike. The two justices reserved judgment on the question of whether such a strike is legal or illegal in an abstract sense or whether and under what circumstances an injunction might issue.

[Justice Grodin wrote a separate concurrence agreeing with Justice Broussard that the Meyer–Milias–Brown Act had removed the underpinning for the doctrine that public employee strikes are tortious and expressing his view that a blanket prohibition of all public employee strikes would raise substantial constitutional questions. Chief Justice Bird concurred on the ground that the right to withhold personal services in concert is protected by the First, Thirteenth, and Fourteenth amendments.]

NOTES

1. Some jurisdictions have reached results similar to California. In *Davis v. Henry*, 555 So.2d 457 (La.1990), the Supreme Court of Louisiana held that all public employees have the right to strike, with the exception of strikes which clearly endanger the public health and safety. To the argument that strikes by public employees are illegal under the common law, the Louisiana Court said that this argument was inoperative since Louisiana is not a common law jurisdiction.

Some state courts have interpreted state statutes as including a right to strike. For example, in *Martin v. Montezuma–Cortez School District RE–1*, 841 P.2d 237 (Colo. 1992), the Colorado Supreme Court interpreted that state's Industrial Relations Act, 38 COLO. REV. STAT. §§ 8–1–101 *et seq.*, a statute enacted in 1915 in response to violent strikes in Colorado's mining industry, to confer a limited right to strike on public employees. The statute authorized the Director of the Division of Labor to investigate labor disputes in the public and private sectors and to attempt to resolve them with mediation and voluntary arbitration. The court held that while the Director exercised jurisdiction, strikes were prohibited but upon termination of the Director's jurisdiction, employees could strike. In *International Association of Firefighters Local 1494 v. City of Coeur d'Alene,* 99 Idaho 630, 586 P.2d 1346 (1978), the court interpreted IDAHO CODE § 44–1811, which expressly prohibits strikes by firefighters during the term of a collective bargaining agreement. The court held that a firefighter strike occurring after the expiration of a collective bargaining agreement was lawful. In *State v. Public Employees Craft Council*, 165 Mont. 349, 529 P.2d 785 (1974), the Montana Supreme Court held that the state's public employee collective bargaining statute's right to engage in concerted activities for mutual aid and protection included a right to strike, except for those employees expressly prohibited from striking by statute.

2. A three judge federal district court considered the constitutionality of a prohibition on strikes by federal employees in *United Federation of Postal Clerks v. Blount*, 325 F.Supp. 879 (D.D.C.), *aff'd w/out opinion*, 404 U.S. 802, 92 S.Ct. 80, 30 L.Ed.2d 38 (1971). The majority observed:

> At common law no employee, whether public or private, had a constitutional right to strike in concert with his fellow workers. Indeed, such collective action on the part of employees was often held to be a conspiracy. When the right of private employees to strike finally received full protection, it was by statute. * * * It seems clear that public employees stand on no stronger footing in this regard than private employees and that in the absence of a statute, they too do not possess the right to strike. The Supreme Court has spoken approvingly of such a restriction, and at least one federal district court has invoked the provisions of a predecessor statute to enjoin a strike by government employees. Likewise, scores of state cases have held that state employees do not have a right to engage in concerted work stoppages, in the absence of legislative authorization. It is fair to conclude that, irrespective of the reasons given, there is a unanimity of opinion on the part of courts and legislatures that government employees do not have the right to strike.

The court conceded that public employees have a fundamental right to freely associate in labor organizations, but concluded:

> There certainly is no compelling reason to imply the existence of the right to strike from the right to associate and bargain collectively. In the private sphere, the strike is used to equalize bargaining power, but this has universally been held not to be appropriate when its object and purpose can only be to influence the essentially political decisions of Government in the allocation of its resources. Congress has an obligation to ensure that the machinery of the Federal Government continues to function at all times without interference. Prohibition of strikes by its employees is a reasonable implementation of that obligation.

Chief Judge J. Skelly Wright of the D.C. Circuit concurred. He agreed with the majority that the established case law compelled upholding the prohibitions on federal employee strikes. However, he expressed personal misgivings with that result:

> If the inherent purpose of a labor organization is to bring the workers' interests to bear on management, the right to strike is, historically and practically, an important means of effectuating that purpose. A union that never strikes, or which can make no credible threat to strike, may wither away in ineffectiveness. That fact is not irrelevant to the constitutional calculations. Indeed, in several decisions, the Supreme Court has held that the First Amendment right of association is at least concerned

with essential organizational activities which give the particular association life and promote its fundamental purposes. I do not suggest that the right to strike is co-equal with the right to form labor organizations. * * * But I do believe that the right to strike is, at least, within constitutional concern and should not be discriminatorily abridged without substantial or 'compelling' justification.

3. The Thirteenth Amendment to the Constitution prohibits "involuntary servitude." Does a strike prohibition violate the Thirteenth Amendment? Would an injunction ordering strikers back to work violate the Thirteenth Amendment?

4. The California Supreme Court's decision resolved the issue at common law. Statutes that are more specific may govern over the common law. For example, in *SouthBay Union School District v. Southwest Teachers Association*, 14 P.E.R.Cal. ¶ 21118 (Cal.PERB 1990), the California PERB held that a strike, and preparations for a strike and a threat to strike while engaging in statutory impasse procedures constituted a failure to bargain in good faith in violation of the California Education Employees Relations Act.

5. The court in *County Sanitation District* indicates that strikes may become unlawful when they create "a substantial and imminent threat to the health and safety of the public." In *City of San Jose v. Operating Engineers Local Union No. 3*, 49 Cal.4th 597, 232 P.3d 701, 110 Cal.Rptr.3d 718 (2010), the California Supreme Court held that generally the issue of whether a strike involves such a threat to health and safety falls within the primary jurisdiction of the California Public Employment Relations Board. The court held that the City of San Jose could not sue in court for an injunction unless it could clearly establish that its remedies before PERB would be inadequate. In the case, the union had agreed to give the city at least 72 hours' notice of its intent to strike. The court observed that PERB's regulations required, in the case of a work stoppage, for the PERB general counsel to investigate and recommend to the Board whether to seek an injunction within 24 hours of receiving a request for injunction. If the Board did not act on the recommendation within 24 hours of receiving it, the general counsel had authority to apply to the appropriate court for a preliminary injunction. The court concluded that because of the union's agreement to give 72 hours' notice of its intent to strike, the city could not establish that its remedies before PERB would be inadequate. For discussion of enjoining otherwise lawful strikes on these and related grounds, see Section C.3.

B. STRIKE PROHIBITIONS

1. THE SCOPE OF THE STRIKE PROHIBITION

Many statutes go beyond expressly prohibiting traditional strikes to prohibit concerted refusals to work, work stoppages, job actions or withholding of services. These statutes are designed to encompass such concerted activities as the "blue flu," where employees concertedly call in sick. The breadth of such provisions has been litigated on numerous occasions. Consider the following case.

APPEAL OF CITY OF MANCHESTER

New Hampshire Supreme Court, 1999.
144 N.H. 320, 741 A.2d 70.

BROCK, C.J.

The petitioner, the City of Manchester (city), appeals a decision of the public employee labor relations board (PELRB) dismissing the city's unfair labor practice petition filed against the respondent, the Manchester Police Patrolman's Association (union). We affirm.

The city is a public employer of police officers and other employees within the meaning of [NEW HAMPSHIRE REV.STAT.ANN.] 273–A:1, X [hereinafter RSA]. The union is the certified bargaining agent for the approximately 150 regular full-time police officers employed by the city. The city and the union are parties to a collective bargaining agreement (CBA) for the period commencing July 1, 1991, and running through June 30, 1994. At the time of the underlying events in August and September 1996, negotiations toward a new CBA were stalled, and the parties' relationship remained in status quo.

The annual Riverfest festival, sponsored by Riverfest, Inc., was scheduled to be held in Manchester on September 5–8, 1996. In 1994 and 1995, police officers had volunteered for extra-duty details at Riverfest, but officers did not volunteer in 1996. In August 1996, the union encouraged its members not to volunteer because it had scheduled an informational picket at Riverfest to inform the public of the lack of an agreement between the union and the city for the previous two years, and that negotiations on a new contract were stalled.

By August 27, police supervisors became aware that officers were not signing up for extra-duty Riverfest details. On August 30, the city filed a petition for an ex parte temporary injunction, which the Superior Court (*Perkins*, J.) denied. On September 4, the Superior Court (*Lynn*, J.) denied the city's petition for temporary injunctive relief.

The superior court reasoned that "it is clear, both from the text of article 12 [of the CBA, providing for extra details by off-duty officers] and from two prior arbitration decisions dealing with the issue, that extra detail work is entirely voluntary and that no officer can be compelled to perform such duties." The court also found that, "notwithstanding the refusal of [union] members to volunteer for extra detail work at Riverfest, the city unquestionably has the authority under article 9 of the CBA to compel overtime work from a sufficient number of officers to meet the policing and security needs occasioned by that event." * * *

In a letter from the union to its membership following the superior court's order, the union summarized its position regarding Riverfest:

> It is to be the directive of the Manchester Police Patrolman's Association that *NO MEMBER* is to *voluntarily* work the Riverfest detail. We have met with the Chief of Police and the department will ORDER

officers to work overtime per Article 9 of our collective bargaining agreement. Do not circumvent our accomplishments by trying to be a *"nice guy"* and volunteer to work for those officers who may be ordered to work. *You will be crossing a picket line manned by members of your OWN union.*

The officers who are ordered to work will have no choice and must work the detail. * * * If you are *NOT ORDERED* to work, *YOU HAVE A CHOICE. DO NOT VOLUNTEER AND DO NOT CROSS THE LINE.*

* * *

As a preliminary matter, we review the applicable provisions of the CBA. Article 12 provides a procedure for off-duty officers to volunteer for extra details. Article 12 defines an extra detail as "duty performed by an off-duty police officer for an employer other than the Manchester Police Department." Officers desiring extra details under article 12 "shall submit their names in writing to the Chief of Police or his designee." Officers may also withdraw their names from the extra-duty roster. Officers volunteering for article 12 details are generally compensated at one and one-half times a single designated pay rate from the pay-scale table. Participating officers compensate the city for administering the article 12 extra-details program.

In contrast, article 9 provides a procedure for the city to require off-duty officers to accept extra work assignments as necessary. Article 9 provides that "all officers shall be required to work emergency or unscheduled overtime when requested." It further provides that "[p]lanned overtime * * * shall be assigned to officers on a voluntary basis. If insufficient officers volunteer within five (5) calendar days of the scheduled event then assignments shall be made to regular officers first, in inverse order of seniority, and auxiliary officers second, as needed." Officers ordered to work under article 9 are paid at one and one-half times their regular hourly rate.

Article 26.1 provides that "[n]o employee covered by this [CBA] shall engage in, induce or encourage any strike, work stoppage, 'sick-in,' 'sick-out,' slowdown or withholding of services to the City of Manchester." Article 26.2 provides: "The [union] agrees that neither it, nor any of its officers or agents, national or local, will call, institute, authorize, participate in, sanction or ratify any such strike, work stoppage, slowdown or withholding of service of [*sic*] the City of Manchester." Finally, article 26.3 provides that any employees participating in any identified misconduct "shall be subject to disciplinary action, including immediate dismissal."

We first consider whether the union's actions violated RSA 273–A:13, which provides:

> Strikes and *other forms of job action* by public employees are hereby declared to be unlawful. A public employer shall be entitled to petition the superior court for a temporary restraining order, pending a final

order of the [PELRB] under RSA 273–A:6 for a strike or other form of job action in violation of the provisions of this chapter, and may be awarded costs and reasonable legal fees at the discretion of the court. (Emphasis added.)

A "job action" generally involves union activities such as strikes, or sickouts, in which a public employer is unable to perform its essential governmental functions. * * *

Although the union encouraged its members not to volunteer under article 12 for Riverfest details, the city exercised its right to compel officers to work overtime under article 9. The PELRB found that "police services, security and public safety—the essential functions of the police department—were maintained without interruption or deprivation." Accordingly, because the city could and did compel the officers to work overtime, the city's ability to perform its essential functions was not frustrated by the union's directive not to volunteer. Because the union did not undertake actions that frustrated the city's ability to perform its governmental functions, its action did not constitute a "job action" in violation of RSA 273–A:13.

Similarly, we conclude that there was no breach of articles 12 and 26 [of the CBA]. * * * In its directive not to volunteer for extra-detail work at Riverfest, the union recognized its obligations under article 9. Although the union sanctioned the officers' refusal to volunteer, its express acknowledgment that "officers who are ordered to work will have no choice and must work the detail" demonstrates that it did not sanction a "withholding of services." [U]nder these facts, there was neither a "withholding of services," nor any action by the union to "call, institute, authorize, participate in, sanction or ratify" a withholding of services as proscribed by article 26.2.

NOTES

1. What factors led the court to conclude that the concerted refusal to volunteer for Riverfest was not a job action or a withholding of services?

2. Following destruction by fire of the building in which they normally worked, employees of the New York State Unemployment Insurance Department refused to work in a temporary location (for which no Certificate of Occupancy had been issued) because working conditions were hazardous and uncomfortable. The building was unheated because the boiler was not operating. The wires from the space heaters lying along the floor made walking hazardous, the electricity was deficient, the exits were limited, and one toilet was clogged. Did this action violate New York's Taylor Law's blanket prohibition against strikes which it defines as "any strike or other concerted stoppage of work or slowdown by public employees"? See *Acosta v. Wollett*, 55 N.Y.2d 761, 447 N.Y.S.2d 241, 431 N.E.2d 966 (1981).

3. Sometimes employees will engage in a "work to rule" campaign. In such an action, employees insist on obeying all rules and regulations to the letter. The result is to slow down the work and drastically reduce productivi-

ty. Does such a campaign amount to an illegal work stoppage? See *Local 252, Transport Workers Union of America v. New York State Public Employment Relations Board*, 58 N.Y.2d 354, 461 N.Y.S.2d 262, 448 N.E.2d 116 (1983) (bus drivers concerted refusal to operate buses which violated the requirements of the Vehicle and Traffic Law). Would a concerted ticket writing blitz, where police officers greatly increase the numbers of traffic and parking tickets that they give, proclaiming that such increased revenues are necessary because the city claims it cannot afford to pay its employees decent wages, violate a state's strike prohibition?

4. While negotiations over a new agreement were in progress, the Union urged its members to refrain from (1) completing student progress reports and grades, (2) attending after-school meetings and activities, (3) supervising students except in the classroom, (4) completing attendance registers, (5) administering standardized tests, (6) providing coverage for other employees, and (7) submitting any records to school officials. Is this conduct a strike? See *Los Angeles Unified School District v. United Teachers of Los Angeles*, 14 P.E.R.Cal. ¶ 21082 (Cal. PERB 1990). What if the teachers decide they will not arrive early or stay after their assigned quitting time? They meet in the parking lot each morning and enter the building as a group at precisely the time they are required to report. Is such activity an illegal strike?

5. If an employee, dissatisfied with working conditions, chooses to resign from his job, is he striking? What if a number of employees tender their resignations at the same time; is that a "strike"? What if the resignations are executed collectively by the signing of petitions, are delivered to and held by the union for submission to the employer only if a satisfactory contract is not reached, and are set in a context of plans for picketing and other activities commonly associated with strikes? See *Board of Education v. Shanker*, 54 Misc.2d 641, 283 N.Y.S.2d 432 (1967), *aff'd without opinion*, 29 A.D.2d 634, 286 N.Y.S.2d 453 (1967). On the other hand, if the mass resignations are bona fide and do not therefore constitute a strike or a threat to strike, may they nevertheless constitute unlawful "collective action"? See *Board of Education v. New Jersey Education Association*, 53 N.J. 29, 247 A.2d 867 (1968).

At times during negotiations, a union may threaten to strike, take a strike authorization vote and even engage in strike preparations, even though the strike would be illegal. The usual purpose of such actions is to pressure the employer to change its position in collective bargaining. Are such threats lawful, even though carrying them out would be illegal? Consider the following case.

COMMONWEALTH EMPLOYMENT RELATIONS BOARD v. BOSTON TEACHERS UNION, LOCAL 66, AFT

Appeal Court of Massachusetts, 2009.
74 Mass. App. Ct. 500, 908 N.E.2d 772.

GRAHAM, J.

The Boston Teachers Union, Local 66, AFT, AFL–CIO (union) appeals from a judgment ordering it to pay $30,000 to the general fund of the Commonwealth, following an adjudication that the union was in contempt of an order of the Superior Court. In the order, the union was found to have violated the provisions of G.L. c. 150E, § 9A, which prohibits public employees and their unions from inducing, encouraging, or condoning a strike. The union contends that the judge's order, issued after the union set a date for a strike vote, but prior to the actual strike vote, violated the union members' rights under the First Amendment to the United States Constitution by imposing a prior restraint upon the union's right to free speech and assembly. We affirm.

Background. The union represents teachers and aides employed in Boston's public school system by the Boston School Committee (school committee). As the certified bargaining representative for public employees, the union's collective bargaining relationship is governed by G.L. c. 150E, §§ 1 et seq. (Act). The Commonwealth Employment Relations Board (board) is charged with administering and enforcing the Act.

General Laws c. 150E, § 9A(*a*), added by St.1973, c. 1078, § 2, prohibits public employees and their organizations from engaging in a strike, and further provides that "no public employee or employee organization shall induce, encourage or condone any strike, work stoppage, slowdown or withholding of services by such public employees." General Laws c. 150E, § 9A(*b*), directs the board to prevent or correct violations of § 9A(*a*) as follows: "Whenever a strike occurs or is about to occur, the employer shall petition the [board] to make an investigation. If, after investigation, the [board] determines that any provision of paragraph (*a*) of this section has been or is about to be violated, it shall immediately set requirements that must be complied with, including, but not limited to, instituting appropriate proceedings in the superior court for the county wherein such violation has occurred or is about to occur for enforcement of such requirements.

The events leading to the Superior Court action began in December of 2006. The school committee and the union were parties to a collective bargaining agreement that expired on August 31, 2006. Since January, 2006, the parties had been involved in unsuccessful and acrimonious negotiations for a successor collective bargaining agreement. Convinced that the pressure of a pending strike vote was needed to motivate compromise by the school committee on terms of a new collective bargaining agreement, the union, on January 6, 2007, posted on its Web site an "emergency" "e-Bulletin" announcing a motion "[t]o place before the membership on February 14, 2007 for discussion, consideration, and debate by that body, in accordance with the bylaws, the question whether there should be a one-day strike on February 15, 2007 or on such other dates as may be chosen by the membership."

The e-Bulletin stated that the bargaining sessions over the previous twelve months "have not been productive" and that the parties "are still far apart on key issues;" described the school committee's proposal as "insulting to us;" and asserted that "[t]he school committee is apparently willing to foist the contract settlement on the new superintendent, using stall and crawl tactics." The e-Bulletin advised the union members that, in accordance with the motion, "over the next five weeks, we will be preparing for all exigencies that could result." It also scheduled "an emergency Area Captains meeting" for January 11, 2007, "an emergency, sign-in Building Representatives meeting" for February 1, 2007, and the strike vote meeting for February 14, 2007.

On January 7, 2007, the union president telephoned the Boston school superintendent and gave him a "heads up" about the February 14, 2007, strike vote and the February 15, 2007, strike date. Then, on January 11, 2007, the union advised its members by way of another e-Bulletin that on the previous day the membership had voted to approve the motion for "a strike vote to be taken" at the February 14, 2007, meeting. The e-Bulletin noted that the January 10, 2007, meeting "was [the] highest-attended membership meeting in over two years" and that the vote "was unanimous."

Meanwhile, the school committee, anticipating that union membership would authorize a strike, petitioned the board on January 9, 2007, to initiate an investigation pursuant to G.L. c. 150E, § 9A(*b*). The board conducted an investigation and held a hearing during which the parties had an opportunity to present evidence and examine witnesses. Following the investigation, the board concluded that although a strike vote had not yet been taken and approved by the union membership, the union's actions were "'"reasonably construed as constituting 'induce[ment], encourage[ment] or condon[ation of] any strike, work stoppage, slowdown or withholding of services by such public employees' " in violation of § 9A(*a*); and that a strike was "about to occur." Acting pursuant to § 9A(*b*), the board issued an order that required the union, its officers, and its executive board members, inter alia, to rescind and disavow their motion for a strike vote.

* * *

Superior Court proceedings. After the union failed to comply with the order, the board filed a complaint in the Superior Court seeking enforcement of its order. The school committee was allowed to intervene as a plaintiff. A judge of the Superior Court held an evidentiary hearing on February 12, 2007. The following day, the judge granted the board and the school committee a temporary restraining order. In his order, the judge found that the union had engaged in prohibited § 9A(*a*) activities, and found that a strike by the Union was "about to occur." He therefore (a) enjoined the union, its members, officers, and executive board members from engaging in or threatening a strike or work stoppage; (b) enjoined the union from inducing, encouraging, or condoning any strike or work stoppage; and (c) required the union, by 11:00 A.M. on February 14, 2007, to disavow, publicly, the motion for a strike vote, notify its members of the disavowal and the members' obligation to perform their duties and refrain from participating in a strike. The union was also required to inform the members of the provisions of §§ 9A(*a*) and (*b*) of G.L. c. 150E, and of the board's order.

* * *

No strike vote occurred on February 14, 2007, and there was no strike on February 15, 2007. Instead of providing the union membership with the notices set out in the judge's order, the union issued a "special" e-Bulletin dated February 14, 2007, in which it announced that "[t]he following motion passed the [union] membership this afternoon: To recess today's meeting" to 2/28/07 and to defer, in light of recent developments, any discussion, consideration and debate on the Executive Board's December 20, 2006 motion to that meeting. This action prompted the board to return to the Superior Court and file a complaint for contempt.

After an evidentiary hearing, the judge found the union in contempt of his earlier order, and imposed a prospective "coercive fine" against the union. The union complied with the judge's order the following day, and later filed a timely appeal to this court.

Discussion. The union argues that the board prematurely and improperly concluded that a strike was "about to occur." The union further argues that the board has long held that the trigger for a determination that an employee organization is about to strike is when "certain conditions precedent have been satisfied such that it can be said that no further union action is necessary for a strike to commence." The trigger, the union notes, has always been the actual strike vote by union membership.

The union acknowledges that, in the circumstances of this case, the board's ability to intervene before any actual strike is significantly impaired, but argues that such impairment is relatively minor, and that the board's investigation would be simplified because "it will be considerably easier for the employer-petitioner to prove its case if a strike has already commenced when a strike investigation hearing is convened." We are not persuaded. The purpose of the Act, set forth in clear and unequivocal language, is to allow the board to intervene in a labor dispute at a point where the board may set the requirements necessary to prevent an illegal strike that is about to occur.

The longstanding "actual vote" rule assumes that a public employer will have sufficient time to engage the process set forth in the Act once a strike vote has been held. That assumption is invalid in the particular circumstances of this case, and we therefore reject the interpretation of the statute suggested by the union because it would make the statute ineffective.

We conclude that the evidence before the board amply supported its conclusion that the union violated the provisions of § 9A(*a*) by encouraging and inducing a strike. That evidence included the e-Bulletins and articles from the union newspaper. A reasonable inference that the union was involved in encouraging a strike was warranted, if not compelled, by all of the evidence.

The union also alleges that the judge imposed a judicial prior restraint upon the union's exercise of protected speech and right to peaceful assembly guarantees in the First Amendment and in art. 16 of the Massachusetts Declaration of Rights by enforcing the board's alleged unconstitutional application of § 9A and issuing an injunction prohibiting the union "from gathering to discuss the merits of a strike and requiring it to disavow prior statements." We disagree. The union concedes, as it must, that there is no constitutional right of public employees to strike. In addition to barring strikes, § 9A also makes it unlawful for a public employee or union to "induce, encourage or condone" a strike.

The injunction issued by the judge imposed four requirements, namely, it enjoined the union, its executive board, and its members from engaging in or threatening a strike, and prohibited the union, its executive board, and its officers from inducing, encouraging, or condoning a strike; ordered them to disavow the executive board vote that scheduled the strike vote; required them to notify the members of their legal obligation not to engage in a strike; and required them to inform the members of the provision of § 9A and of the board's decision. The injunction placed no prior restraint upon the union to engage in public speech or debate, but rather prohibited it from engaging in actions that properly were prohibited under § 9A.

Moreover, to the extent that the conduct regulated by § 9A "includes both 'speech' and 'nonspeech' elements, the purpose of the statute is entirely unrelated to the suppression of free expression." The board has a substantial interest in preventing a strike by the union members, and "[a]ny incidental limitation of First Amendment freedoms" is justified.

Accordingly, the judgment is affirmed

NOTES

1. After the Massachusetts Supreme Court denied review, 455 Mass. 1102, 914 N.E.2d 330 (2009), the U.S. Supreme Court denied certiorari. 130 S.Ct. 1738, 176 L.Ed.2d 213 (2010).

2. Other jurisdictions have reached varying results when confronted with questions of whether votes to authorize and preparations for illegal strikes are unfair labor practices. In *Chicago Transit Authority v. Illinois Labor Relations Board*, 386 Ill.App.3d 556, 325 Ill.Dec. 443, 898 N.E.2d 176 (2008), the Illinois Appellate Court held that a strike authorization vote and strike preparations did not amount to a failure to bargain in good faith even though the strike itself would have violated the Illinois Public Labor Relations Act. The court reasoned that although the statute prohibited the strike, it did not expressly prohibit the strike authorization vote or preparations for the strike. In the court's view, the union's actions were designed to place pressure on the employer and, in so doing, further the collective bargaining process. On the other hand, in *California Nurses Association v. Regents of the University of California*, 34 P.E.R.C. 41 (Cal. PERB 2010), the California PERB held that the union committed an unfair labor practice where its strike threat and

strike preparations were sufficiently substantial to create a reasonable belief in the employer that an illegal strike would occur.

3. As will be discussed in greater detail in Chapter 12, in many jurisdictions, a union and an employer may agree that as a condition of employment employees must either join the union or pay to the union a fee representing the employee's share of the costs of representation. In a series of decisions, the Supreme Court has held that charging objecting fee payers for their share of certain expenditures, such as expenditures on political and ideological activity not directly related to collective bargaining violates the fee payers' First Amendment rights. In *Lehnert v. Ferris Faculty Association*, 500 U.S. 507, 111 S.Ct. 1950, 114 L.Ed.2d 572 (1991), the Court held that charging fee payers for expenditures on preparations for an illegal strike did not violate the fee payers' First Amendment rights. The Court recognized that charging fee payers for the costs of conducting an illegal strike would violate their rights, but reasoned with respect to strike preparations:

> Petitioners can identify no determination by the State of Michigan that mere preparation for an illegal strike is itself illegal or against public policy, and we are aware of none. Further, we accept the rationale provided by the Court of Appeals in upholding these charges that such expenditures fall "within the range of reasonable bargaining tools available to a public sector union during contract negotiations." The District Court expressly credited trial testimony by an MEA representative that outward preparations for a potential strike serve as an effective bargaining tool and that only one out of every seven or eight "job action investigations" actually culminates in a strike. The Court of Appeals properly reviewed this finding for clear error. In sum, these expenses are substantively indistinguishable from those appurtenant to collective-bargaining negotiations. The District Court and the Court of Appeals concluded, and we agree, that they aid in those negotiations and inure to the direct benefit of members of the dissenters' unit.

2. INJUNCTIONS AGAINST ILLEGAL STRIKES

ONEIDA COUNTY v. ONEIDA EDUCATION ASSOCIATION

Idaho Supreme Court, 1977.
98 Idaho 486, 567 P.2d 830.

SHEPARD, J.

[During negotiations for a collective bargaining agreement, the Oneida Education Association threatened to strike. Oneida County petitioned for an injunction against the threatened strike. The trial judge refused to receive any evidence but the Association made an offer of proof that during negotiations the County had acted in bad faith. The trial judge ruled that as a matter of the law strike would be illegal and enjoined it. The Association appealed.]

* * *

The trial court ruled as a *matter of law* that the injunction should issue and we must assume, in the absence of any evidentiary record, that he concluded that a strike by teachers is illegal in Idaho. Assuming without deciding that he was correct in this conclusion, nevertheless, mere illegality of an act does not require the automatic issuance of an injunction.

That logic has been expressly applied to situations involving teacher strikes and the automatic issuance of an injunction has been refused and condemned. *School Dist. for City of Holland v. Holland Educ. Assoc.*, 380 Mich. 314, 157 N.W.2d 206 (1968); *School Com. v. Westerly Teachers Assoc.*, 111 R.I. 96, 299 A.2d 441 (1973); *Timberlane School Dist. v. Timberlane Educ. Assoc.*, 114 N.H. 245, 317 A.2d 555 (1974).

In the private sector the right to strike is viewed as an integral and necessary part of the collective bargaining process. However, in the public sector the denial of the right to strike has the effect of weighing the scales heavily in favor of the government during the collective bargaining process. In Idaho our legislature has made the policy judgment as to the merits of *not* providing public employees with the right to strike. Rather, it has developed statutory alternative processes to resolve labor disputes between teachers and school boards. It would not be an appropriate judicial function to fault the legislature in those determinations.

We cannot ignore an *alleged* refusal to abide by and engage in those legislatively authorized procedures for resolution of impasse situations. While neither we nor the trial court should condone or approve the calling of an illegal strike by appellants (although the record does not appear to demonstrate actual engagement in strike and picketing procedures), neither should we or a trial court condone or approve the failure to abide by and utilize the statutorily prescribed procedures for possible resolution of the problem. It has long been a basic maxim of equity that one who seeks equitable relief must enter the court with clean hands.

We hold that the trial court erred in issuing the orders complained of here in what was effectively an ex parte proceeding. If testimony had been permitted and required and the trial court had accepted as correct the allegations of the appellant regarding the bad faith of the school board he might have issued the injunction, but also as a corollary thereof required the school board to engage in the statutorily mandated impasse procedure. Such order did issue but not for some months following the issuance of the preliminary injunction.

Since the dispute between the parties and the threatened strike which resulted from non-resolution of that dispute has ended we see no necessity for a remand for further proceedings. We reverse the orders of the trial court, remand the cause and order that the temporary and permanent injunctions be dissolved.

BAKES, J., concurring in the judgment and dissenting in part:

* * *

[I]t seems to me that the majority is saying that teachers' strikes are prohibited, i.e., that they are illegal, although that point is not entirely clear. But there is no Idaho statute which prohibits a strike by public school teachers. Although IDAHO CODE § 33–1271 provides for labor negotiations by public school teachers, that statute says nothing about strikes. In contrast, the statute which provides for labor negotiations by firefighters expressly prohibits strikes by firefighters. IDAHO CODE § 44–1811. In the absence of a direct statutory prohibition, what basis is there for saying that teachers' strikes are illegal?

* * *

The relationship between employers and workers is very different today from that in which the common law rule against strikes by workers developed. Today, collective bargaining between employers and employees in the private sector is protected—even mandated under most circumstances—by federal law. Similarly, our legislature has expressly provided for labor negotiations between public school teachers and the school districts. IDAHO CODE §§ 33–1271 *et seq.* It is also a practical and historical fact of life thoroughly recognized by judicial decisions, that the strike, or at least a threat to strike, is what brings the employees' interests to bear upon the employer. A labor organization that can make no credible threat to strike is simply impotent in labor negotiations.

After concluding that strikes by school teachers are prohibited and illegal the majority equivocates, it seems to me, suggesting that the trial court did not have to grant an injunction for the "illegal strike" of the school teachers if it found that the school board was acting in bad faith, citing the "basic maxim of equity that one who seeks equitable relief must enter the court with clean hands." * * *

It seems to me that the problem is compounded by this line of reasoning. Thus, now by mandate of this Court, not only can teachers not strike, but by judicial *fiat,* school boards must now negotiate in good faith or lose the availability of a court injunction. This effectively means that the final arbiters in wage negotiations between teachers and school districts are going to be the courts who must decide whether the parties are negotiating in good faith, imposing or withholding the court's injunctive powers based upon the outcome of that finding. I doubt the wisdom of placing the courts in such a position. It is not every social ill which can be resolved by the courts. It is my considered view that, in the absence of legislation holding otherwise, our society would be better served in most instances by a rule which permitted teachers to strike and school boards to negotiate within the statutory framework, whether in good or bad faith, letting economic and other social factors finally forge the conclusion of that conflict, rather than interjecting the courts into the fray where the threat of an injunction dangles over the head of teachers, but only if, in the opinion of the court, the school board has negotiated in good faith.

Our legislature, when it enacted the Professional Negotiations Act, IDAHO CODE § 33–1271 *et seq.*, which provided for negotiations between teachers' organizations and their employers, the school districts, was presumably well aware of the present state of labor relations in this country, which generally favors an economic, rather than judicial determination of wage disputes. In adopting that act the legislature might have prohibited strikes by teachers as it did in the legislation providing for labor negotiations by firefighters. IDAHO CODE § 44–1811. Having made no provision prohibiting strikes by teachers in their negotiations with school boards, it seems to me that the legislature has itself opted for an economic rather than a judicial determination of wage disputes between teachers and school boards. Therefore I cannot concur with the majority of this Court when they state, albeit by dictum, that teachers' strikes are prohibited and illegal and that courts should employ their injunctive powers to prohibit strikes by school teachers. In concluding otherwise it is not necessary to assert that the right of teachers to strike is a constitutionally protected right. It is merely enough to observe that the legislature has not prohibited strikes by teachers, and the common law strike/conspiracy rule is totally inappropriate to present day circumstances. Therefore, the right of teachers to strike is neither prohibited nor illegal.

For this reason * * * I would join in the decision of the majority reversing the orders of the trial court which granted the injunctions. * * *

NOTES

1. The *Holland, Westerly Teachers Association,* and *Timberlane Regional School District* line of cases upon which the Idaho Court relies hold that an illegal public employee strike will not automatically be enjoined. Rather, the employer must make a showing of irreparable harm and is subject to a union defense that by negotiating in bad faith, the employer is coming into court with unclean hands. These decisions express a minority view. See also *Wilson v. Pulaski Association of Classroom Teachers*, 330 Ark. 298, 954 S.W.2d 221 (1997) (upholding trial court's denial of an injunction against teacher strike for failure to prove irreparable harm). The majority position is illustrated by *Anchorage Education Association v. Anchorage School District*, 648 P.2d 993 (Alaska 1982), which holds that the illegality of a strike is itself sufficient harm to justify injunctive relief. Implicit in these cases is the recognition that by making a public sector strike illegal, the legislature has decided that it causes irreparable harm.

2. The Michigan Legislature has effectively overruled the *Holland* case. A 1994 amendment to the Michigan Public Employment Relations Act provided that a public school employer may seek an injunction against a strike by public school employees and that the circuit court shall grant such relief upon finding that a strike has occurred "without regard to the existence of other remedies, demonstration of irreparable harm, or other factors." MICH.COMP. LAWS ANN. § 423.202a(10), effectively overruling the *Holland* case. Unions representing educational employees in Michigan challenged the constitutionality of the 1994 amendment. The Wayne County Circuit Court upheld the constitutionality of most of the amendment but struck down the provision mandating strike injunctions as violative of the principle of separation of

powers. The union appealed the court's decision upholding most of the rest of the amendment but the state did not cross appeal. The Michigan Court of Appeals affirmed the trial court's decision upholding the constitutionality of portions of the amendment on which the unions appealed and the Michigan Supreme Court affirmed the Michigan Court of Appeals. However, because of the absence of a cross appeal, neither court addressed the constitutionality of the provision mandating injunctions without regard to traditional equitable factors. *Michigan State AFL–CIO v. Michigan Employment Relations Commission*, 212 Mich.App. 472, 538 N.W.2d 433 (1995), *aff'd*, 453 Mich. 362, 551 N.W.2d 165 (1996).

clean hands

3. The parties' collective bargaining agreement specified the dollar amount the employer was obligated to contribute to a trust fund which provided health insurance for the employees and their dependents. The fund's actuary notified the parties that if the contributions did not increase, the fund would become insolvent. The parties negotiated but were unable to agree on how to make up the shortfall. The fund trustees, to stave off insolvency, drastically reduced benefits. In response, the union went on strike. Assuming that strikes by public employees are illegal in this jurisdiction, what arguments may be made by the employer and the union in the employer's action for an injunction? May the court condition any injunction on the employer increasing its contributions to the fund? See *Gary Community School Corp. v. Service Employees International Union Local 73*, 839 N.E.2d 1191 (Ind.App. 2005).

4. The Supreme Court of Pennsylvania held in *Gulnac v. South Butler County School District*, 526 Pa. 483, 587 A.2d 699 (1991), that parents and students who were disadvantaged by a teachers' strike of nearly two months' duration lacked standing to seek injunctive relief against the striking teachers. Should anyone other than the employer have standing to seek an injunction against an illegal strike?

5. Despite the common availability of injunctive relief, some public employers have displayed reluctance to seek injunctions, or to enforce them after they have been obtained. Unions often defy strike injunctions. Such defiance escalates the conflict to a new level. The employer may seek contempt sanctions against the union, union officials or striking union members. Such actions usually lead to union demands for amnesty as a condition of settlement. An agreement settling the strike is not likely to be reached while union negotiators are in jail for contempt. Recognizing these possibilities, judges facing injunction requests sometimes attempt to mediate the underlying labor dispute. Considering the possible reactions to an injunction petition, how would you advise an employer facing a threat of an illegal strike? Should the employer seek an injunction before the strike begins? Continue negotiating and seek an injunction immediately after the strike begins? Continue negotiating even after the strike begins, using the threat of seeking an injunction as a tool in negotiations?

6. In some states, violation of an injunction has led to substantial contempt penalties. See, e.g., *County of Orange v. Civil Service Employees Association*, 54 A.D.2d 921, 388 N.Y.S.2d 120 (1976) (fine of $200,000 reduced to $100,000). Some statutes prescribe penalties for violation of an injunction.

In Wisconsin, for example, a union which violates a no-strike injunction is subject to a penalty of $2 per member per day, not to exceed $10,000 per day. Individuals who strike after an injunction issues are subject to a fine in the amount of $10 per day. WIS. STAT.ANN. § 111.70(7m)(c)1.b. Are fines for contempt effective and appropriate? What are the alternatives for enforcing a strike injunction?

3. SANCTIONS AGAINST STRIKING EMPLOYEES

Public employees who illegally strike are subject to a variety of sanctions which vary from jurisdiction to jurisdiction. Federal employees who strike commit a felony and numerous leaders of the 1981 air traffic controllers' strike were prosecuted criminally. A few states also criminalize public employee strikes. Employees who violate the strike ban contained in New York's Taylor Act are subject to mandatory monetary penalties equal to twice their daily rate of pay for each day in which they participate in prohibited conduct. NEW YORK–MCKINNEY'S CIV.SERV.L. § 210(2). Similarly, public school employees striking in Michigan are subject to fines by the Michigan Employment Relations Commission of one day's pay for each day of the strike. MICH.COMP.L.ANN. § 423.202a(4).

For sanctions to apply, there must be a finding that the employee participated in the strike. Many jurisdictions employ a presumption that any employee in the bargaining unit absent on the day of a strike participated in the strike. The employee has the burden to rebut the presumption. One obvious method of rebutting the presumption is to provide medical documentation that the employee was disabled from working. See *City of Pittsburgh v. Fraternal Association of Professional Paramedics*, 140 Pa.Cmwlth. 248, 592 A.2d 786 (1991) (employees on vacation at time of strike are not strikers and are entitled to their vacation pay). Assume that an employee who is absent during a strike testifies that he or she did not participate in the strike but stayed away from work out of fear of retribution for crossing the picket line. Should such testimony be held to have rebutted the presumption? See *Johnson v. Department of Transportation*, 735 F.2d 510 (Fed.Cir. 1984).

One sanction commonly threatened against striking employees is discharge. In this regard, consider the following case.

HORTONVILLE JOINT SCHOOL DISTRICT v. HORTONVILLE EDUCATION ASSOCIATION

United States Supreme Court, 1976.
426 U.S. 482, 96 S.Ct. 2308, 49 L.Ed.2d 1.

BURGER, C.J. delivered the opinion of the Court.

The petitioners are a Wisconsin school district, the seven members of its School Board, and three administrative employees of the district. Respondents are teachers suing on behalf of all teachers in the district and the Hortonville Education Association (HEA), the collective-bargaining agent for the district's teachers.

During the 1972–1973 school year Hortonville teachers worked under a master collective-bargaining agreement; negotiations were conducted for renewal of the contract, but no agreement was reached for the 1973–1974 school year. The teachers continued to work while negotiations proceeded during the year without reaching agreement. On March 18, 1974, the members of the teachers' union went on strike, in direct violation of Wisconsin law. On March 20, the district superintendent sent all teachers a letter inviting them to return to work; a few did so. On March 23, he sent another letter, asking the 86 teachers still on strike to return, and reminding them that strikes by public employees were illegal; none of these teachers returned to work. After conducting classes with substitute teachers on March 26 and 27, the Board decided to conduct disciplinary hearings for each of the teachers on strike. Individual notices were sent to each teacher setting hearings for April 1, 2, and 3.

On April 1, most of the striking teachers appeared before the Board with counsel. Their attorney indicated that the teachers did not want individual hearings, but preferred to be treated as a group. Although counsel agreed that the teachers were on strike, he raised several procedural objections to the hearings. He also argued that the Board was not sufficiently impartial to exercise discipline over the striking teachers and that the Due Process Clause of the Fourteenth Amendment required an independent, unbiased decisionmaker. An offer of proof was tendered to demonstrate that the strike had been provoked by the Board's failure to meet teachers' demands, and respondents' counsel asked to cross-examine Board members individually. The Board rejected the request, but permitted counsel to make the offer of proof, aimed at showing that the Board's contract offers were unsatisfactory, that the Board used coercive and illegal bargaining tactics, and that teachers in the district had been locked out by the Board.

On April 2, the Board voted to terminate the employment of striking teachers, and advised them by letter to that effect. However, the same letter invited all teachers on strike to reapply for teaching positions. One teacher accepted the invitation and returned to work; the Board hired replacements to fill the remaining positions.

Respondents then filed suit against petitioners in state court, alleging, among other things, that the notice and hearing provided them by the Board were inadequate to comply with due process requirements. The trial court granted the Board's motion for summary judgment on the due process claim. The court found that the teachers, although on strike, were still employees of the Board under Wisconsin law and that they retained a property interest in their positions under this Court's decisions in *Perry v. Sindermann*, 408 U.S. 593, 92 S.Ct. 2694, 33 L.Ed.2d 570 (1972), and *Board of Regents v. Roth*, 408 U.S. 564, 92 S.Ct. 2701, 33 L.Ed.2d 548 (1972). The court concluded that the only question before the Board on

April 1 and 2 was whether the teachers were on strike in violation of state law, and that no evidence in mitigation was relevant. It rejected their claim that they were denied due process, since the teachers admitted they were on strike after receiving adequate notice and a hearing, including the warning that they were in violation of Wisconsin law.

On appeal, the Wisconsin Supreme Court reversed. On the single issue now presented it held that the Due Process Clause of the Fourteenth Amendment to the Federal Constitution required that the teachers' conduct and the Board's response be evaluated by an impartial decisionmaker other than the Board. The rationale of the Wisconsin Supreme Court appears to be that although the teachers had admitted being on strike, and although the strike violated Wisconsin law, the Board had available other remedies than dismissal, including an injunction prohibiting the strike, a call for mediation, or continued bargaining. * * * [T]he Wisconsin court then held "it would seem essential, even in cases of undisputed or stipulated facts, that an impartial decisionmaker be charged with the responsibility of determining what action shall be taken on the basis of those facts." The court held that the Board was not sufficiently impartial to make this choice: "The background giving rise to the ultimate facts in this case reveals a situation not at all conducive to detachment and impartiality on the part of the school board." In reaching its conclusion, the court acknowledged that the Board's decision could be reviewed in other forums; but no reviewing body would give the teachers an opportunity to demonstrate that "another course of action such as mediation, injunction, continued collective bargaining or arbitration would have been a more reasonable response on the part of the decision maker."

* * *

The sole issue in this case is whether the Due Process Clause of the Fourteenth Amendment prohibits this School Board from making the decision to dismiss teachers admittedly engaged in a strike and persistently refusing to return to their duties. The Wisconsin Supreme Court held that state law prohibited the strike and that termination of the striking teachers' employment was within the Board's statutory authority. We are, of course, bound to accept the interpretation of Wisconsin law by the highest court of the State. The only decision remaining for the Board therefore involved the exercise of its discretion as to what should be done to carry out the duties the law placed on the Board.

* * *

Respondents' argument rests in part on doctrines that have no application to this case. They seem to argue that the Board members had some personal or official stake in the decision whether the teachers should be dismissed, comparable to the stake the Court saw in *Tumey v. Ohio*, 273 U.S. 510, 47 S.Ct. 437, 71 L.Ed. 749 (1927), or *Ward v. Village of Monroeville*, 409 U.S. 57, 93 S.Ct. 80, 34 L.Ed.2d 267 (1972); see also *Gibson v. Berryhill*, 411 U.S. 564, 93 S.Ct. 1689, 36 L.Ed.2d 488 (1973), and that the Board has manifested some personal bitterness toward the teachers, aroused by teacher criticism of the Board during the strike, see, e.g., *Taylor v. Hayes*, 418 U.S. 488, 94 S.Ct. 2697, 41 L.Ed.2d 897 (1974); *Mayberry v. Pennsylvania*, 400 U.S. 455, 91 S.Ct. 499, 27 L.Ed.2d 532 (1971). Even assuming that those cases state the governing standards when the decisionmaker is a public employer dealing with employees, the teachers did not show, and the Wisconsin courts did not find, that the Board members had the kind of personal or financial stake in the decision that might create a conflict of interest, and there is nothing in the record to support charges of personal animosity. The Wisconsin Supreme Court was careful "not to suggest * * * that the board members were anything but dedicated public servants, trying to provide the district with quality education * * * within its limited budget." That court's analysis would seem to be confirmed by the Board's repeated invitations for striking teachers to return to work, the final invitation being contained in the letter that notified them of their discharge.

* * *

Respondents' claim and the Wisconsin Supreme Court's holding reduce to the argument that the Board was biased because it negotiated with the teachers on behalf of the school district without reaching agreement and learned about the reasons for the strike in the course of negotiating. From those premises the Wisconsin court concluded that the Board lost its statutory power to determine that the strike and persistent refusal to terminate it amounted to conduct serious enough to warrant discharge of the strikers. Wisconsin statutes vest in the Board the power to discharge its employees, a power of every employer, whether it has negotiated with the employees before discharge or not. The Fourteenth Amendment permits a court to strip the Board of the otherwise unremarkable power the Wisconsin Legislature has given it only if the Board's prior involvement in negotiating with the teachers means that it cannot act consistently with due process.

Due process, as this Court has repeatedly held, is a term that "negates any concept of inflexible procedures universally applicable to every imaginable situation." *Cafeteria Workers v. McElroy*, 367 U.S. 886, 81 S.Ct. 1743, 6 L.Ed.2d 1230 (1961). Determining what process is due in a given setting requires the Court to take into account the individual's stake in the decision at issue as well as the State's interest in a particular procedure for making it. * * * Our assessment of the interests of the parties in this case leads to the conclusion that * * * the Board's prior role as negotiator does not disqualify it to decide that the public interest in maintaining uninterrupted classroom work required that teachers striking in violation of state law be discharged.

The teachers' interest in these proceedings is, of course, self-evident. They wished to avoid termination of their employment, obviously an important interest, but one that must be examined in light of several factors. Since the teachers admitted that they were engaged in a work stoppage, there was no possibility of an erroneous factual determination on this critical threshold issue. Moreover, what the teachers claim as a property right was the expectation that the jobs they had left to go and remain on strike in violation of law would remain open to them. The Wisconsin court accepted at least the essence of that claim in defining the property right under state law, and we do not quarrel with its conclusion. * * *

The governmental interests at stake in * * * the Board's decision whether to dismiss striking teachers involve broad considerations, and do not in the main turn on the Board's view of the "seriousness" of the teachers' conduct or the factors they urge mitigated their violation of state law. It was not an adjudicative decision, for the Board had an obligation to make a decision based on its own answer to an important question of policy: What choice among the alternative responses to the teachers' strike will best serve the interests of the school system, the interests of the parents and children who depend on the system, and the interests of the citizens whose taxes support it? The Board's decision was only incidentally a disciplinary decision; it had significant governmental and public policy dimensions as well.

State law vests the governmental, or policymaking, function exclusively in the School Board and the State has two interests in keeping it there. First, the Board is the body with overall responsibility for the governance of the school district; it must cope with the myriad day-to-day problems of a modern public school system including the severe consequences of a teachers' strike; by virtue of electing them the constituents have declared the Board members qualified to deal with these problems, and they are accountable to the voters for the manner in which they perform. Second, the state legislature has given to the Board the power to employ and dismiss teachers, as a part of the balance it has struck in the area of municipal labor relations; altering those statutory powers as a matter of federal due process clearly changes that balance. Permitting the Board to make the decision at issue here preserves its control over school district affairs, leaves the balance of power in labor relations where the state legislature struck it, and assures that the decision whether to dismiss the teachers will be made by the body responsible for that decision under state law.

Respondents have failed to demonstrate that the decision to terminate their employment was infected by the sort of bias that we have held to disqualify other decisionmakers as a matter of federal due process. A showing that the Board was "involved" in the events preceding this decision, in light of the important interest in leaving with the Board the power given by the state legislature, is not enough to overcome the presumption of honesty and integrity in policymakers with decisionmaking power. Accordingly, we hold that the Due Process Clause of the Fourteenth Amendment did not guarantee respondents that the decision to terminate their employment would be made or reviewed by a body other than the School Board.

[The dissenting opinion of JUSTICE STEWART, joined by JUSTICES BRENNAN and MARSHALL, has been omitted.]

NOTES

1. The teachers admitted that they engaged in an illegal strike but defended that the school board's alleged provocation of, and unreasonable response to, the strike mitigated against the penalty of discharge. Thus, the teacher's defense called for the school board members to evaluate their own conduct. How, in the Court's view, could they do so without violating the teachers' due process rights?

2. Should a public employer be required to resort to civil service or tenure dismissal procedures to terminate striking tenured employees, or should the employer be able to fire them summarily? See *Rockwell v. Board of Education*, 393 Mich. 616, 227 N.W.2d 736 (1975), *appeal dismissed*, 427 U.S. 901, 96 S.Ct. 3184, 49 L.Ed.2d 1195 (1976).

3. As counsel to a public employer facing an illegal strike, would you advise your client to discharge the strikers? What factors support such advice? What factors advise against it?

4. A regulation of the Office of Personnel Management (OPM) in effect at the time of the air traffic controllers strike in 1981 provided that OPM may, in its discretion, bar an individual from eligibility for a civil service appointment for a period of three years after the individual had been the subject of a statutory disqualification from employment. One such statutory disqualification applied to individuals engaged in a strike against the federal government. In December 1981, pursuant to a directive from President Reagan, OPM issued an interpretive bulletin declaring that all strikers would be barred indefinitely from employment with the Federal Aviation Administration (FAA). The FAA also inserted in its contracts with private companies a provision prohibiting those companies from employing any former controller who had struck. (President Clinton repealed these policies in August 1993.) Were the actions of the FAA and OPM lawful? See *Clarry v. United States*, 85 F.3d 1041 (2d Cir.1996). lawful but unjust

4. SANCTIONS AGAINST STRIKING UNIONS

Unions that strike illegally are also subject to sanctions. The mere fact that a strike occurs does not establish the union's legal responsibility for the strike. Factors considered include the extent of union member participation, whether union officers participated in the strike, and the actions of union officials in response to the strike, including whether they made reasonable efforts to get the strikers to return to work. See *Egan v. Newman*, 92 A.D.2d 1007, 461 N.Y.S.2d 464 (1983).

In many jurisdictions, an illegal strike is an unfair labor practice, subjecting the union to the labor board's remedial authority. For example, as a result of the air traffic controllers' strike, the Federal Labor Relations Authority decertified PATCO, effectively putting it out of business. See

Professional Air Traffic Controllers Organization v. FLRA, 685 F.2d 547 (D.C.Cir. 1982). The Florida statute authorizes the Florida Public Employee Relations Commission to order a striking union to cease and desist, suspend or revoke the union's status as exclusive bargaining representative, revoke the union's dues checkoff privileges, and fine the union $20,000 per day or an amount equal to the cost to the public of each day of the strike. The latter amount is not limited to $20,000. West's Fla.Stat. Ann. § 447.507(6)(a). New York's Taylor Law also provides for revocation of dues checkoff as a sanction for a union's illegal strike. That provision is explored in the following case.

UNITED FEDERATION OF TEACHERS, LOCAL 2, NYSUT, AFT, AFL–CIO

New York Public Employment Relations Board, 1982.
15 N.Y.PERB ¶ 3091.

This matter now comes to us on a motion made by the United Federation of Teachers, Local 2, NYSUT, AFT, AFL–CIO (Federation) on July 8, 1982. It moves this Board for an order reducing the duration of the dues deduction forfeiture penalty imposed upon it on October 8, 1976 (9 PERB ¶ 3071). The motion was supplemented on August 4 and 9, 1982 by an affirmation that it "does not assert the right to strike against any government, nor to assist or participate in any such strike, nor to impose an obligation to conduct, assist or participate in any strike" and that it does not adhere to a "no contract, no work" policy.

The dues deduction forfeiture was imposed as a penalty because the Federation engaged in an illegal five-day strike between September 9 and 16, 1975. The 1976 order of the Board provided that the dues deduction privileges of the Federation would be forfeited for an indefinite period of time, but that the Federation was authorized to apply for its reinstatement at any time after the passage of two years from the effective date of the forfeiture upon an affirmation that it no longer asserted the right to strike against any government and an indication that it no longer adhered to a "no contract, no work" policy. Moreover, the Federation was authorized to apply, after the expiration of only 14 months, for a suspension of the balance of the forfeiture upon the same conditions that it would apply 10 months later for the full restoration of its dues deduction privileges. By reason of court litigation in which the 1976 order of this Board was challenged, the forfeiture ordered by this Board was not effectuated until May 1, 1982.

The basis of the motion is that the loss of dues deduction privileges has impaired the Federation's ability to provide representational services to the employees in the negotiating units that it represents. In support of this proposition the Federation has submitted evidence that it has made substantial efforts to collect the dues by several, reasonably available alternatives. Notwithstanding these efforts, and for only the months of May and June, the Federation has suffered a loss of income from dues and agency shop fee payments in the amount of $870,355, or approximately 30% of its normal income from these sources. This loss has forced it to curtail services that it normally renders to unit employees. Most particularly, it refers to the temporary closing of its borough offices through which it provides such services as representation in unsatisfactory rating hearings, pension advice, workshops on contract rights, and consultation in connection with grievance and arbitration hearings. The Federation indicates that these offices, the focal point for rendering assistance may have to be closed permanently if its financial problems are not relieved. It also indicates that it has had to lay off employees and since March 1, 1982 left vacancies unfilled; thus further interfering with its ability to service the employees in the negotiating units it represents.

* * *

We find the evidence submitted by the Federation to be persuasive. Although that evidence concerns only two months, a third has now passed. As the two-month loss of income is more than $870,000, the Federation has already lost more than $1.3 million in income when the third month is considered. It is more difficult to project the Federation's expenses in trying to collect its dues through reasonably alternative means, because the evidence regarding those costs does not indicate which are one-time only, start-up costs as opposed to recurrent operational costs. It is reasonable, however, to conclude that as of this date the expenses of the Federation and its loss of income aggregate about $2,000,000.

* * *

Basically, the Taylor Law is designed to punish employee organizations that strike by putting them to the task of collecting their dues without the assistance of dues checkoff privileges. It does not impose a forfeiture of that dues income. This is readily apparent in the concern expressed in the Law that the financial resources of the employee organization be a factor in determining the extent of the penalty. It is also apparent in the Legislature's rejection of the recommendation of the Taylor Committee that a striking employee organization be denied its right to represent the negotiating unit by withdrawing its certification. The employee organization's continuing status as the certified (or recognized) negotiating representative clearly contemplates a continuing income to enable it to act in that capacity. * * * The difficult and most delicate role of this Board is to balance the statutory dictate of punishment for engaging in a strike and the need to preserve the solvency of the negotiating agent so that it may fulfill its statutory purpose of representing all unit employees in the negotiation and administration of collective bargaining agreements.

This is not the first time that the Federation has sought relief from our order of dues forfeiture. Previously its assertion that the dues forfeiture would threaten its solvency was denied as being "based upon conjecture." Now, however, its financial straits are real. The Federation has demonstrated that, despite substantial vigorous and costly efforts, it has been unable to collect necessary income; it has shown that representational services have already been impaired and that the continuation of the penalty will lead to the elimination or diminution of other necessary and material services to the public employees. This justifies reconsideration and modification of the forfeiture.

NOW, THEREFORE, WE MODIFY our order to the extent that the forfeiture of the Federation's dues deduction privilege is suspended; that such suspension is subject to revocation in the event of a strike or strike threat. The Federation may apply to this Board, on notice to the Corporation Counsel, in April 1984 for full restoration of its dues deduction privileges.

NOTES

1. The constitutionality of the suspension of dues checkoff was upheld in *Shanker v. Helsby*, 676 F.2d 31 (2d Cir.1982); *Buffalo Teachers Federation v. Helsby*, 676 F.2d 28 (2d Cir.1982).

2. What is the purpose of the suspension or revocation of dues checkoff? Was that purpose served by the Board's modification of the sanction in the United Federation of Teachers' case?

3. Under the Taylor Law, a court, as well as the PERB, may suspend a striking union's dues deductions. In 2005, the Transport Workers Union engaged in an illegal strike against the New York City Transit Authority. The trial court enjoined the union's dues checkoff. When the union petitioned the court to reinstate its dues checkoff, the court denied the petition because the union provided only an affidavit from its president stating that the union did not assert the right to violate the Taylor Law. The trial court ordered that any future petition to reinstate the dues checkoff must be accompanied by affidavits from each member of the union's executive board averring "that the Union does not assert the right to strike against any government, to assist or participate in any such strike, or to impose an obligation to conduct, assist, or participate in such a strike, and that the Union has no intention, now or in the future, of conducting, assisting, participating, or imposing an obligation to conduct, assist, or participate in any such strike, or threatening to do so, against the plaintiffs or any governmental employer." Should such an order be upheld on appeal? See *New York City Transit Authority v. Transport Workers Union of America*, 55 A.D.3d 699, 866 N.Y.S.2d 684 (2008).

5. ACTIONS FOR DAMAGES

WHITE v. INTERNATIONAL ASSOCIATION OF FIREFIGHTERS, LOCAL 42

Missouri Court of Appeals, 1987.
738 S.W.2d 933.

BERREY, J.

Plaintiffs, Loretta White and Charles A. White, brought suit against the International Association of Firefighters, AFL–CIO, Local 42 of the

International Association of Firefighters, eight named individuals who were union officers or representatives of Local 42 and "John Doe 1–8–70," for property damage sustained during a firefighters' strike or work stoppage against Kansas City, Missouri. The trial court granted the defendants' motion to dismiss for failure to state a claim on which relief could be granted. Plaintiffs contend the trial court erred in granting defendants' dismissal because a private citizen may maintain a cause of action under a theory of an intentional tort against the firefighters' union for damages occurring during an illegal strike by public employees.

The judgment of the trial court is affirmed.

Plaintiffs' petition * * * alleges in Count I that on March 17, 1980, the defendants began a strike and refused to respond to fire alarms or calls; established picket lines to hinder the City's normal operations; engaged in acts of sabotage against the City's firefighting equipment and facilities; and that these actions were in violation of Section 105.530 RSMo 1978 [VERNON'S ANN.MO.STAT. § 105.530], the prohibition against public employee strikes. It was further alleged that on March 20, 1980, a fire was discovered on plaintiffs' property located at 4003 Prospect and with the inexperienced personnel and inadequate equipment available, the fire was not brought under control and totally destroyed their real and personal property. Plaintiffs contend that had defendants "been performing the duties for which they were employed. The fire could have been brought under control with inconsequential damages to the premises and its contents." Count II of plaintiffs' petition incorporates the allegations of Count I and asserts defendants' actions established the tort of outrage.

In determining whether the trial court erred in dismissing plaintiffs' petition, this court must decide if plaintiffs' allegations invoke principles of substantive law which may entitle them to relief. Plaintiffs draw upon the principles set forth in this court's decision in *State v. Kansas City Firefighters Local 42,* 672 S.W.2d 99 (Mo.App.1984), in support of their assertion that a private citizen has a cause of action for damages intentionally inflicted by the firefighters who failed to perform their duty in providing firefighting services.

This court's decision in *Kansas City Firefighters, supra,* a lodestone for legal commentary, see Note, Illegal Public Employee Strikes: Allowing a Civil Suit for Damages, 33 *UMKC L.Rev.* 299 (1985), and Note, Prima Facie Tort—a Judicial Reaction to Public Employee Strikes in Missouri, 50 *Mo.L.Rev.* 687 (1985), held that a public employer could maintain a cause of action, implied by the state statute prohibiting public employees strikes, under the theory of an intentional tort for damages it incurred during an illegal public employee firefighter strike. There, on October 3, 1975, after long unsuccessful negotiations with the City on the issue of remuneration, the firefighters' union struck the City and union members failed to report for firefighter duty. With the City in a critical situation, the Governor of the State ordered the state militia into emergency duty. The strike ended on October 7, 1975, after the state had incurred

$128,782.72 in expenses for the militia's services during this period. The State, in its amended petition, pled for recovery in tort for reimbursement of those expenses.

The *Kansas City Firefighters* court relying on the doctrine of implied rights as set forth in Restatement (Second) Section 874(A), found the policy behind the Public Sector Law precluding public employee strikes Section 105.530, that is, to "ensure the uninterrupted delivery of services vital to the public welfare," would be furthered by allowing a civil remedy for damages sustained during an illegal strike. The court found the function of the firefighters was indispensable to public safety but confined the scope of liability to extend to only these public employees on the basis it refused to exercise its judicial power in this "delicate area of public employment." The court's decision was further restricted to those cases where it is pleaded and proven that the action intended to produce the resulting harm, or that the result was a natural and probable consequence of the intended act—requirements for the claim of an intentional tort.

The court, in its analysis of the implied cause of action, acknowledged another limitation: "the suitor must be a member of the class for whose especial benefit the statute was enacted." The *Kansas City Firefighters'* court stated that the Public Sector Law was enacted for the benefit of the public body or the public employer and found the State—who provided the essential services—succeeded to the rights and remedies of the City and was the public employer, or intended beneficiary, for the purposes of the action. In this regard, the court did not further describe other potential beneficiaries but specifically stated, ["w]e need not, and do not, decide whether the policy of the Public Sector Labor Law benefits a third party other than the public employer."

Whether a cause of action inures (beyond the public employer) to third party has been examined in only a few jurisdictions, *Boyle v. Anderson Fire Fighters Association,* 497 N.E.2d 1073 (Ind.App. 2 Dist. 1986); *Burke & Thomas, Inc. v. International Organization of Masters,* 92 Wash.2d 762, 600 P.2d 1282 (banc 1979); *Jamur Productions Corp. v. Quill,* 51 Misc.2d 501, 273 N.Y.S.2d 348 (1966); *Caso v. District Council 37,* 43 A.D.2d 159, 350 N.Y.S.2d 173 (1973); *Burns Jackson Miller, ETC v. Linder,* 59 N.Y.2d 314, 464 N.Y.S.2d 712, 451 N.E.2d 459 (1983); *Fulenwider v. Firefighters Association Local Union 1784,* 649 S.W.2d 268 (Tenn.1982). Two of the decisions have allowed private citizens to maintain damage actions, one under a nuisance theory; *Caso v. District Council 37, supra*; and the other under an intentional tort theory, *Boyle v. Anderson Fire Fighters Association Local 1262, supra.* While these two cases rest upon different theories of recovery, both decisions tend to focus upon the same policy consideration: the public's need to have uninterrupted essential governmental services which, if suspended, would have the potential of endangering the health and welfare of the people. * * *

The cases refusing to allow private causes of action present equally diverse analysis in reaching their conclusions. In *Jamur v. Quill*, *supra*, the New York Supreme Court held it would not imply an action because the legislature failed to expressly or implicitly provide for a cause of action and thus, refused to allow a damage suit against New York public transit workers who illegally struck. The *Jamur* court, citing to *Schmidt v. Merchants Despatch Transportation Co.,* 270 N.Y. 287, 200 N.E. 824 (1936), stated that "[w]hen the statute merely defines, in the interest of the general public, the degree of care which shall be exercised under specified circumstances, it does not 'create' a new liability." The Supreme Court of Washington in *Burke & Thomas, Inc. v. International Organization of Masters, supra,* similarly refused to allow a private damage action against public ferry workers who illegally struck the city under a theory of tortious inference of business relationships. The court found that the careful balancing of public employment would be disturbed and the function of the State Public Employment Relations Commission, which is to resolve labor disputes, would be effectively usurped. In *Burns Jackson Miller, etc. v. Lindner, supra,* the New York Court of Appeals found the Taylor Law, previously dealt within *Caso v. District Council 37, AFSCME, supra,* did not give rise to an *implied private cause of action* because such implication is inconsistent with one of the primary purposes of the legislation: the elimination of tensions in public employer-employee relations and the maintenance of labor peace. The court noted that the Taylor Law, undergoing many amendments, including creating a Public Employment Relations Board, from the time *Caso, supra,* was decided, revealed an intent to protect the labor union's demise. And finally, the Supreme Court in Tennessee in *Fulenwider v. Firefighters Association Local Union 1784, supra,* found a private action for damages against a firefighters union and its members could not be maintained where there was no allegation of wilful or even negligent destruction of property by direct action. The court stated the claim was based only upon " 'secondary' or incidental harm as a by-product of the work stoppage."

These cases disclose that regardless of the theories upon which the action is brought, * * * the courts weigh competing policy considerations that exist between the public's need for vital governmental services and the need for harmony in public employment relations. As noted in *Kansas City Firefighters,* one of the requirements of the doctrine of implied rights is that the purpose of the Public Sector Law be furthered by the allowance of a civil cause of action. The *Kansas City Firefighters* court determined a damage suit by a public employer would further one of the primary policies of the Public Sector Law, the uninterruption of essential governmental services, a policy consideration relied on in other jurisdictions to justify other theories of recovery against Unions who participate in illegal work stoppages. The *Kansas City Firefighters* court, however, recognized (although in a footnote) "the other cognate, primary policy of the statute is to vouch-safe to public employees a means to acquit the right conferred by the United States and Missouri Constitutions of peaceable assembly and to petition for redress of grievances."

One cannot doubt that the potential for numerous private civil actions would be an influencing factor in the firefighters' decision to strike and may effectively curtail further walkouts. As one commentator noted, however, "[a]ctions by third parties for wrongful death or destruction of valuable property * * * are more likely to threaten the existence of a union than suits for compensation for replacement labor such as *Kansas City Firefighters*. This is due to the potentially greater number and virtually unlimited monetary risk involved in the former type of suit." Toni Blackwood, Casenote, *Illegal Public Employee Strikes: Allowing Civil Suit for Damages,* 53 UMKC L.Rev. 299 (1985). The possibility of financial collapse of the union by large damage verdicts may also be antagonistic toward the City providing continued firefighting services. First, individual firefighters could be subject to unlimited liability under the doctrine of virtual representation, and although firefighters who do not assent to strike will not be held responsible, this potential for liability may prevent competent persons from pursuing careers as firefighters. Secondly, the bargaining process between the City and the Union could be stymied:

* * * It is not hard to imagine a scenario whereby a strike is prolonged, with the possibility of liability incurring, because of the union's insistence upon indemnifications from tort actions like the one sub judice.

The decision to foreclose plaintiffs' right to sue is further buttressed by the *Kansas City Firefighters* court's analysis of the implied rights doctrine in which there is a limitation that "the suitor must be a member of the class for whose especial benefit the statute was enacted." The court stated that the Public Sector law was enacted for the benefit of the *public body* or public employer, and found that the State, who provided the replacement labor, succeeded to the rights and remedies of the City, and was the public employer, the intended beneficiary, for the purposes of the action. We note that in *Burke and Thomas, Inc. v. International Organization of Masters*, *supra*, the court stated "the primary function of [a] strike * * * is usually as a tool to gain bargaining leverage during contract negotiations with the employer. The object of the work stoppage is typically not to injure any third party, but rather to apply pressure to the employer. * * * " Under § 105.500 RSMo 1986, "public body" is defined as "the state of Missouri, or any officer, agency, department, bureau, division, board or commission of the state, or any other political subdivision of or within the state." These entities listed are those likely to engage in the bargaining process with public employees and be the direct recipients of the leverage mechanism, the strike. Thus, the intended beneficiaries of the Public Sector Law are not individuals like the plaintiffs, but governmental instrumentalities.

In this same vein, we note that public officers are not liable to individuals for injuries or damages for the failure to carry out those duties which are owed to the general public. [T]his court acknowledged that a municipal fire department is fashioned for the benefit of the entire community and that no cause of action accrues to an individual based on a breach of duty for failure to perform services due to the public at large. It should be noted that plaintiffs' petition did not allege that the union (or its members) started the fire at plaintiffs' home or did any specific acts which prevented the personnel who responded to the call from combating the fire. Such acts go beyond the protection of the public duty doctrine.

For the foregoing reasons, this court affirms the trial court's order dismissing plaintiffs' petition.

NOTES

1. As the principal case makes clear, the majority view is that there is no private cause of action against a union for damages caused by an illegal strike. Which view has the better argument?

2. Does the analysis change when it is the struck employer suing the union for its damages, or suing on behalf of the public or should the struck employer be treated the same way as the private citizen? See *City and County of San Francisco v. United Association of Journeymen and Apprentices of the Plumbing and Pipefitting Industry, Local 38*, 42 Cal.3d 810, 230 Cal.Rptr. 856, 726 P.2d 538 (1986).

3. Some states have resolved the damage issue by statute. The Florida statute authorizes a public employer to sue a union for damages resulting from an illegal strike and to attach the union's dues checkoff as a method of collecting the judgment. The statute requires the court to consider any action or inaction by the employer that may have provoked the strike. WEST'S FLA.STAT.ANN. § 447.507(4).

C. LEGALIZING PUBLIC EMPLOYEE STRIKES

1. THE CONSEQUENCES OF LEGALIZING STRIKES

PUBLIC EMPLOYEES' RIGHT TO STRIKE: LAW AND EXPERIENCE

Martin H. Malin
26 University of Michigan Journal of Law Reform 313 (1993).

* * *

In 1984, public employees in Illinois and Ohio obtained the right to strike. One could expect that such action would lead to an increase in public sector strikes in those jurisdictions for several reasons. First, it seems intuitive that legalizing an activity that was previously illegal would tend to encourage that activity. Second, the strike legalization accompanied each state's first comprehensive public employee collective bargaining act. Thus, along with the right to strike came procedures to compel employer recognition of and negotiation with unions representing their workers. By increasing the number of units engaged in collective bargaining, such legislation increased the opportunities for strikes. Third, the experience in states other than Illinois and Ohio suggests that, at least initially, increased strike activity may accompany the legalization of public employee strikes. Contrary to this expectation, however, strike activity actually has declined in both states since legalization.

Ohio's legalization of public employee strikes took effect on April 1, 1984. Over the eight years beginning April 1, 1984, through April 30, 1992, there have been 110 strikes in Ohio. * * * [T]here have been far fewer strikes in Ohio since they were legalized.

* * *

Strikes outside of education are almost nonexistent in the Illinois public sector. They typically occur less than once per year. * * * [N]oneducational employees who now have the right to strike in Illinois. * * * from 1974 through 1979, * * * averaged 9.67 strikes per year, a considerably higher frequency than has occurred since strikes were legalized.

* * *

During the first year of the [Illinois Educational Labor Relations Act] IELRA, 776 K–12, school districts engaged in teacher bargaining, representing a 53% increase over the pre-Act years. The increase does not include the nonteaching staff and higher education units. During the nine years preceding the statute, K–12 teacher strikes averaged 24.56 per year. The incidence of thirty-five strikes experienced in 1984–85 is roughly comparable, given the increase in bargaining. Since the first year of the IELRA, strike activity has dropped dramatically, hitting a low of six in the 1987–88 and 1988–89 school years, even though the number of bargaining units increased substantially.

Thus, the experiences in Ohio and Illinois run counter to the expectation that enactment of comprehensive public sector bargaining laws containing a right to strike would increase the incidence of strikes. Despite an increase in bargaining activity in the first eight years under the Ohio statute, strikes averaged 13.75 per year, compared with an average of 55.71 strikes per year from 1974 to 1980. In the first eight years of the Illinois statute, strikes averaged 15.75 throughout public education, despite an increase in bargaining, compared to an average of 24.56 strikes per year among K–12 teachers prior to the IELRA.

Of course, the enactment of the new legislation was not the only factor which might have influenced the changes in strike activity over the years in Ohio and Illinois. Two economic factors which merit attention are the unemployment rate and the inflation rate. Studies in the private sector generally agree that strikes decline as the unemployment rate increases. Intuition suggests a similar result in the public sector. As unemployment increases, employees lower their expectations for a new collective bargaining agreement. Higher levels of unemployment also reduce the availability of temporary work while on strike and increase the availability of striker replacements. Studies in the public sector, however, have reached inconsistent results regarding the relationship between unemployment rates and strikes, although most find a relationship similar to that in the private sector.

As the inflation rate increases, employees' expectations in collective bargaining probably increase as they try to regain losses in real wage levels. Therefore, it is not surprising that studies generally find that the incidence of public sector strikes is positively correlated with inflation. * * *

To further evaluate the experiences in Ohio and Illinois with legalizing public employee strikes, we ran single and multivariate regression analyses of the data. * * * Each regression showed a very strong correlation between the change in the law in Ohio and the decrease in the number of strikes.

Regression analyses of the experience with strikes in Illinois public education yielded considerably weaker results. Although in the single-variate regression, the change in the law was correlated with a decrease of slightly more than ten strikes per year and was significant below the .025 confidence level, the change in the law explained only between twenty and 25% of the change in strike activity. Multivariate regressions of various combinations of the change in the law with inflation and unemployment rate independent variables produced little improvement in the explanatory ability of the model and showed the change in the law correlated with decreases in the number of annual strikes ranging from just under seven to between ten and eleven. All combinations, except for those limited to the change in the law and the unemployment rate, showed the change in the Illinois law as not statistically significant.

Interpretation of this data requires caution. Although the Ohio data showed a very strong correlation between passage of the public sector collective bargaining act and the decrease in strike activity, data was not available for five years. Although the Illinois data consistently showed a correlation between the Illinois statute and a decrease in strike activity, each model explained a very small portion of the decrease in the number of strikes, thus suggesting that the independent variables analyzed here cannot predict strike frequency.

Several caveats apply to the data from both states. First, the data in both states do not take into account the increase in bargaining activity that followed the enactment of the statutes. To this extent, the data underestimate the effects of the statutes on decreasing strike frequency.

Second, the data do not take into account other factors that may affect strike frequency. Chief among these omitted factors is the employer's fiscal climate. Experienced negotiators generally agree that tight fiscal constraints often lead to more strikes. Another factor not captured by the data is the relative experience of the negotiators.

Third, the pre-Act data in both states are not completely comparable to the post-Act data. The pre-Act Ohio data may include some strikes by employees who now have the right to go to interest arbitration, such as nurses and employees of the state schools for the blind and deaf and the state retirement system. To the extent that such strikes are included, the data overstate the number of pre-Act strikes and overestimate the effect of the statute in decreasing strike frequency. On the other hand, the Illinois pre-Act data covered only K–12 teachers and, therefore, may exclude pre-Act strikes by employees who now have the right to strike. To the extent that such strikes are not included, the Illinois data understate the number of pre-Act strikes and underestimate the effect of the statute in decreasing strike frequency.

Finally, the data may overestimate the effect of legalizing public employee strikes on decreasing strike frequency because the data do not distinguish between strikes over bargaining impasses and strikes over recognition. In addition to legalizing strikes, the Illinois and Ohio statutes provide procedures whereby a union may force recognition by petitioning for and winning a representation election conducted by the labor board. There is strong evidence that by reducing the union's need to resort to self-help to force recognition, comprehensive public employee collective bargaining statutes reduce strikes over recognition as well as strikes over the parties' first collective bargaining agreement.

Indiana, for example, has a comprehensive collective bargaining statute governing public education, but does not have a similar statute governing the remainder of the public sector. Recognition strikes in public education are virtually nonexistent, but occur frequently in the rest of the public sector. Similarly, recognition strikes in Ohio and Illinois during the 1970s occurred significantly more often than in the rest of the country.

Undoubtedly, some of the reduction in strike incidence in Illinois and Ohio resulted from taking the fight over recognition out of the streets and placing it before the labor boards. It is not likely, however, that this accounts for most of the reduction. Indeed, the IELRA replaced a 1981 amendment to the Illinois School Code that provided a procedure for recognition elections in teacher bargaining units. * * *

Reasonable theoretical grounds exist for believing that legalizing strikes may reduce the number of strikes overall. Artificial strike prohibitions distort the communication value of the union's strike threat. While at the bargaining table, unions threatening an illegal strike usually maintain that they are fully prepared to deal with the consequences of the strike's illegality. Employers may excessively discount such representations, thereby underestimating the settlement that the union is willing to accept. A lawful and credible strike threat is a great incentive for peaceful settlement. Eliminating artificial strike prohibitions may promote more realistic bargaining.

The data presented in this Article, however, do not firmly support a conclusion that the legalization of public employee strikes in Illinois and Ohio caused their frequency to decrease. On the other hand, there is no evidence that legalization caused strikes to increase in frequency. All of the evidence is to the contrary. * * * Legislators and other policymakers may take heart from the experiences in Illinois and Ohio and may grant public employees a legal right to strike without fear that doing so will lead to an increase in strike frequency.

* * *

2. STATUTORY APPROACHES TO LEGALIZING STRIKES

State statutory provisions legalizing public employee strikes vary considerably. For example, although a municipal employee right to strike is on the books in Wisconsin, it is largely illusory. The Wisconsin statute provides for arbitration to resolve bargaining impasses for municipal employees but recognizes a right to strike if both parties withdraw their final offers from the arbitrator. WISCONSIN STAT.ANN. § 111.70(4)(c)(6)(c). As of this writing no parties have ever mutually withdrawn their final offers.

Statutes authorizing public employee strikes uniformly prohibit police and firefighters from striking. Statutes deem a variety of other employees as essential and prohibit them from striking, with the specific types of employees varying greatly from state to state. Vermont limits its statutory right to strike to municipal employees. As discussed in Chapter 6.B, Hawaii's statute expressly defines the units that are appropriate for collective bargaining. It also expressly designates which units have the right to strike. Alaska divides its public employees into three classifications: those whose services may not be lost for even the shortest period of time are prohibited from striking; those whose services may be interrupted for a limited period are allowed to strike unless and until the strike has begun to threaten the public health, safety or welfare; and those whose work stoppages may be sustained for extended periods without serious effects on the public are afforded a broad right to strike.

Statutes generally require that the parties engage in mediation before a strike may occur. They also generally require the union to give the employer a specified period of notice of intent to strike. One major difference among the states is whether the parties are required to engage in factfinding before they may strike.

As will be developed more fully in the next chapter, factfinding is a process where a neutral factfinder convenes a hearing and makes written recommendations for settlement of the dispute. The recommendations are not binding on the parties. States that require pre-strike factfinding require a cooling off period between the issuance of the factfinder's recommendations and the beginning of a lawful strike. These mandatory cooling off periods range from ten to sixty days, depending on the state. Ohio requires that either the union membership or the employer's governing body, by a vote of three-fifths of all eligible voters, reject the factfinder's recommendations within seven days. Otherwise, the parties are deemed to have accepted them.

Illinois and Minnesota do not require pre-strike factfinding. Pennsylvania leaves it to the discretion of the Pennsylvania Labor Relations Board to impose such a requirement on a case-by-case basis outside of public education and requires pre-strike factfinding upon the request of either party in public education. Hawaii, Ohio, Oregon and Vermont require pre-strike factfinding, as does Alaska for public school employees. What are the advantages and disadvantages of such a requirement? See Martin H. Malin, Public Employees' Right to Strike: Law and Experience, 26 *University of Michigan Journal of Law Reform* 313, 379–95 (1993).

3. STRIKE INJUNCTIONS IN STATES THAT RECOGNIZE A RIGHT TO STRIKE

States that legalize public employee strikes generally authorize injunctions if the strike poses an imminent threat or a clear and present danger to the public. The states differ over the standard for an injunction. Some states, such as Hawaii, Illinois and Ohio require a threat or danger to public health and safety. Others, such as Alaska, Oregon, Pennsylvania and Vermont require a threat to public health, safety or welfare. The following case explores the standards for enjoining an otherwise lawful strike.

MASLOFF v. PORT AUTHORITY OF ALLEGHENY COUNTY

Pennsylvania Supreme Court, 1992.
531 Pa. 416, 613 A.2d 1186.

ZAPPALA, J.

Amalgamated Transit Union Local 85 (Local 85) and its President, Larry L. Klos, appeal from the adjudication and decree entered on April 10, 1992, by Judge Silvestri of the Commonwealth Court permanently enjoining the work stoppage by the Union and directing the authorized representatives of Local 85 and the Port Authority of Allegheny County (PAT) to engage in court-supervised negotiations until an agreement was reached.

Local 85 is the certified collective bargaining representative for approximately 2,700 individuals employed by PAT. Local 85 and PAT were parties to a collective bargaining agreement that expired by its terms on November 30, 1991. The parties' negotiations for a successor agreement were initiated in October, 1991, but were unsuccessful.

On March 16, 1992, the members of Local 85 went on strike. On March 31, 1992, Sophie Masloff, individually and as the mayor of the City of Pittsburgh, and the City of Pittsburgh filed a Complaint in Equity against PAT and Local 85 in the Court of Common Pleas of Allegheny County seeking, *inter alia*, injunctive relief enjoining the strike. The City also filed an Application for Extraordinary Relief with this Court requesting that we assume plenary jurisdiction of this matter under 42

[PENN.STAT.] § 726. On April 1, 1992, we entered an order assuming jurisdiction of this matter.

Local 85 filed an answer to the equity complaint and PAT filed preliminary objections in the nature of a petition raising the defense of lack of capacity to sue. We dismissed PAT's preliminary objections by Order of Court dated April 6, 1992, and determined that the City had standing to bring the Complaint in Equity. We remanded the matter to Commonwealth Court for expedited disposition and directed that President Judge David Craig assign the matter forthwith for disposition.

President Judge David Craig assigned the matter to Judge Silvestri. Hearings were held by Judge Silvestri on April 7–9, 1992, during which the City introduced testimony of various witnesses to demonstrate that the strike created a clear and present danger and a threat to the health, safety, and welfare of its citizens. Judge Silvestri concluded that the City had presented sufficient evidence of the far-reaching effect that the strike had upon commercial, academic, medical and social institutions and that the evidence submitted by PAT was neither of the quantity nor quality sufficient to rebut the overwhelming evidence presented by the City. Based upon the evidence, Judge Silvestri determined that a permanent injunction enjoining Local 85 from continuing the work stoppage was necessary to ensure the safety of the citizens and to prevent the immediate and irreparable harm that would result from a denial of the requested relief. An adjudication and decree was entered on April 10, 1992, enjoining the work stoppage, establishing a schedule for the representatives of Local 85 and PAT to engage in court-supervised negotiations, and directing the parties and participants to refrain from making any public statements without prior court approval.

* * *

Prior to its amendment in 1986, the Port Authority Act required PAT to submit any labor dispute concerning wages, salaries, hours, working conditions or benefits to arbitration by a board composed of three persons. * * * The employees did not have a right to strike after the term of a collective bargaining agreement had expired. The collective bargaining provisions of the Port Authority Act were substantially revamped by the legislative amendments in 1986. Section 3 of the Port Authority Act, 55 PENN.STAT. § 563.2, establishes the revised collective bargaining procedures governing PAT and its employees. Collective bargaining must begin at least one hundred days prior to the expiration of a collective bargaining agreement. In the case of any labor dispute where collective bargaining does not result in an agreement, the dispute may be submitted to final and binding interest arbitration only with the written consent of both parties. * * * When the parties have agreed to submit the labor dispute to binding arbitration, all contract provisions remain the status quo during the period of arbitration. No lock-outs, strikes, or other interference with or interruption of transit operations are permitted during the arbitration period. 55 PENN.STAT. § 563.2(f).

Within forty-five days of the termination date of the collective bargaining agreement, either party may make a written request for the appointment of a neutral factfinder by the Pennsylvania Labor Relations Board (PLRB). When factfinding has not been requested by either party prior to the expiration of the term of the collective bargaining agreement, both parties must immediately make a written request that the PLRB appoint a neutral factfinder. Collective bargaining may continue during the factfinding process. 55 PENN.STAT. § 563.2(g).

Within forty-five days of the appointment, the factfinder must submit findings of facts and recommendations to the PLRB and both parties. 55 PENN.STAT. § 563.2(i). The parties are required to notify the PLRB and each other whether or not the recommendations of the factfinder are accepted. The findings and recommendations are publicized if they are rejected. 55 PENN.STAT. § 563.2(j).

Once the recommendations have been rejected and PAT and the employees' representative have refused to mutually agree to final and binding interest arbitration, the employees shall have the right to strike in regard to that dispute. No strike is permitted, however, until the completion of a thirty-day "cooling-off" period, beginning immediately after the termination of the collective bargaining agreement. 55 PENN.STAT. § 563.2(*l*). When the employees have exercised their right to strike, the Port Authority Act provides:

> * * * such strike shall not be prohibited unless or until such a strike creates a clear and present danger or threat to the health, safety or welfare of the public: Provided that such strike shall not be prohibited on the grounds that it creates a clear and present danger or threat to the health, safety or welfare of the public unless the court's order granting relief further mandates that both parties submit the labor dispute to final and binding interest arbitration by a board of arbitration under the provisions of this Section. No party, other than the authority, shall have any standing to seek any relief in any court of this Commonwealth under this Subsection.

55 PENN.STAT. § 563.2(k).

In its equity action, the City challenges the constitutionality of this provision insofar as it denies access to the courts to any party other than PAT to seek injunctive relief to prohibit a strike when there is a clear and present danger or threat to the health, safety or welfare of the public. The City asserts that Section 563.2(k) violates Article 1, Section 11 of the Pennsylvania Constitution to the extent that the City is denied access to the courts to enjoin the strike. The City contends also that Section 563.2(k) is an impermissible delegation to PAT of its duty to protect the health, safety, and welfare of its citizens in contravention of Article 3, Section 31 of the Pennsylvania Constitution.

* * *

It is indeed troubling and at times disconcerting that parties to an agreement cannot resolve their disputes in an amicable fashion. Be that as it may, the courts cannot and will not sit idly by while others who are non-participants in the dispute essentially suffer the greatest harm. In the wisdom of the framers of the Pennsylvania Constitution, such incidents were anticipated so that the framers provided that where a legal injury is sustained, there shall and will always be access to the courts of this Commonwealth.

Article 1, Section 11 of the Pennsylvania Constitution provides:

> All courts shall be open; and every man for an injury done him in his lands, goods, person or reputation shall have remedy by due course of law, and right and justice administered without sale, denial or delay. Suits may be brought against the Commonwealth in such manner, in such courts and in such cases as the Legislature may by law direct.

"It is the constitutional right of every person who finds it necessary or desirable to repair to the courts for the protection of legally recognized interests to have justice administered without sale, denial or delay." *Commonwealth ex rel. Duff v. Keenan*, 347 Pa. 574, 33 A.2d 244 (1943). Article 1, Section 11 can be invoked only with respect to a legal injury. *Jackman v. Rosenbaum Co.*, 263 Pa. 158, 106 A. 238 (1919), *aff'd*, 260 U.S. 22, 43 S.Ct. 9, 67 L.Ed. 107 (1922).

Local 85 contends that the Legislature was acting within its authority to foreclose certain avenues of relief for aggrieved plaintiffs and that Article 1, Section 11 does not grant every individual or entity who believes that a wrong has been suffered a right of redress in the courts. Concurring in that position, PAT asserts that the City does not have a legally cognizable interest in the matter because the 1986 amendments to the Port Authority Act gave PAT the sole right to seek injunctive relief. The rationale underlying their conclusion is that the Legislature has eliminated a cause of action for all those who are injured by a transit strike, except for PAT. The Legislature has not in fact done so.

The Legislature has neither eliminated a cause of action nor foreclosed an aggrieved individual from seeking redress in the courts. Section 563.2(k) expressly recognizes that the health, safety, and welfare of the public may be endangered by a transit strike, and, also, that redress for such injury may be sought in the courts. The oddity of the statute is that while the Legislature has not extinguished a cause of action for injuries sustained by the public as a result of a transit strike, it has restricted standing to seek any relief in the courts to PAT, a party which is not representative of the public. Thus, while the public has a legally cognizable interest that may be protected by resort to the courts, by legislative design access to the courts is denied unless PAT exercises its discretion to seek relief for the injury to the public. * * * In vesting the discretion to seek redress for a legal injury in an entity other than the one who sustains the injury, the statutory provision has run afoul of Article 1, Section 11 of the Pennsylvania Constitution. While Article 1, Section 11 does not prevent the Legislature from extinguishing a cause of action in all instances, it does prevent the Legislature from denying an injured party the right to seek relief from the courts for a legal injury by vesting that right solely in a third party who has the absolute discretion to choose whether to do so. PAT may well exercise its prerogative to not seek injunctive relief in the courts. The administrative decisions made by PAT in declining to exercise that option cannot deprive an individual of the right to seek a remedy from the courts for any legal injury sustained as a result of the strike. To the extent that Section 563.2(k) restricts standing to seek relief in any court of this Commonwealth under Subsection (k) to PAT, it is hereby declared to be unconstitutional.

Local 85 contends that the City failed to establish the existence of a clear and present danger to the public that would justify the issuance of an injunction. The case law definition of "clear and present danger" which has been employed in the context of labor disputes by public employees under the Public Employee Relations Act, 43 PENN.STAT. § 1101.101 *et seq.* is applicable in this instance. In *Armstrong Education Association v. Armstrong School District*, 5 Pa.Cmwlth. 378, 291 A.2d 120 (1972), the Commonwealth Court utilized the following definition:

> The "clear" in that epigram is not limited to a threat indubitably etched in every microscopic detail. It includes that which is not speculative but real, not imagined but actual. The "present" in the epigram is not restricted to the climatically imminent. It includes that which exists as contrasted with that which does not yet exist and that which has ceased to exist.

The ordinary inconveniences resulting from a strike will not suffice to establish a clear and present danger to the health, safety, or welfare of the public. The concept of "clear and present danger" will encompass the consideration of the effects which are ordinarily incidental to a strike, however, when such matters accumulate to such an extent, have continued for so long, or are aggravated by unexpected developments that the public's health, safety, or welfare is endangered.

In his adjudication and decree, Judge Silvestri addressed the testimony that was introduced by the City, stating:

> During the parade of thirty (30) witnesses presented by the City, testimony was elicited about the impact of the mass transit strike upon families, individuals, and businesses. Blind, epileptic, professional, student, and blue-collar witnesses testified about the effect of the lack of public transportation upon their lives. While the lack of such transportation is a matter of inconvenience for some, it is devastating to others. Renal, cancer and psychiatric patients are often unable to get to appropriate medical facilities for treatment. Emergency medical services are delayed in attempts to reach citizens in need. Citizens are endangering their safety by walking along public roads to get to work because other modes of transportation are unavailable. Residents have been forced to find alternate living accommodations with friends

or family because of the inaccessibility to work, school or day care. From the testimony presented, the City has demonstrated the far-reaching effect the strike has had upon commercial, academic, medical and social institutions.

Local 85 argues that the evidence was insufficient because it reflected what one would ordinarily expect to occur in the event of a cessation of virtually all public transportation in a metropolitan area. The City's evidence did not simply establish the disruption of the witnesses' daily routines, however. The evidence established, *inter alia*, that public services, such as ambulance, fire, and police services, were severely hampered by the increased traffic congestion resulting from the strike. To the extent that Local 85's argument suggests that the adverse effect on and threat to essential public services such as fire and police protection and emergency medical services are the ordinary and anticipated consequences of a transit strike, we are unpersuaded. We conclude that reasonable grounds existed for the equitable relief ordered by Judge Silvestri.

* * *

Accordingly, the adjudication and decree of the Commonwealth Court is affirmed.

LARSEN, J., dissenting:

* * *

I strongly disagree * * * with the majority's conclusion that reasonable grounds existed for the equitable relief ordered by the Chancellor in this case. * * * Senior Judge Silvestri of the Commonwealth Court, sitting as Chancellor, granted, *inter alia*, a permanent injunction enjoining appellant, Amalgamated Transit Union Local 85 (Union) and all of its members, from continuing the work stoppage initiated on March 16, 1992. * * *

All of the consequences of the strike described by the Chancellor in his adjudication are precisely the kinds of inconveniences, disruptions and hardships which are incident to and normally expected when a transit strike occurs in a major metropolitan area. For example, it is reasonable to expect that persons who rely on public transportation to go to work or school will walk along public roads to get to work or school during a mass transit strike. Also, it is a normal expectation that business will decline at retail stores which depend upon customers who use public transportation. None of the consequences described by the witnesses in this case can be said to be unexpected or unanticipated by the Legislature when it enacted legislation permitting the Union to strike. The courts and the legislature of this Commonwealth have recognized that certain inconveniences, disruptions and hardships are inherent in any strike and such inherent inconveniences, disruptions and hardships do not constitute a clear and present danger or threat to the health, safety or welfare of the public.

> The 'clear' in that epigram is not limited to a threat indubitably etched in every microscopic detail. It includes that which is not

speculative but real, not imagined but actual. The 'present' in the epigram is not restricted to the climatically imminent. It includes that which exists as contrasted with that which does not yet exist and that which has ceased to exist." * * * In this light, the determination of whether or not a strike presents a clear and present danger to the health, safety or welfare of the public must, therefore, require the court to find that the danger or threat is real or actual and that a strong likelihood exists that it will occur. *Additionally, it seems to us that the 'danger' or 'threat' concerned must not be one which is normally incident to a strike by public employees. By enacting [legislation] which authorizes such strikes, the legislature may be understood to have indicated its willingness to accept certain inconveniences for such are inevitable, but it obviously intended to draw the line at those which pose a danger to the public health, safety or welfare.* (Emphasis supplied).

Armstrong School District v. Armstrong Education Association, 5 Pa. Cmwlth. 378, 291 A.2d 120 (1972). Thus, the Chancellor erred in enjoining the strike in the instant case.

The majority herein, in reaching to uphold the Chancellor's injunction, does not rely only upon the inconveniences and disruptions of the public's normal daily routines as being sufficient to constitute a clear and present danger to the health, safety or welfare of the public, but combines the evidence of the daily inconveniences and disruptions with an unsupported declaration that ambulance, fire and police services and protection were severely hampered in concluding that there was a clear and present danger which justified an injunction. The majority states:

> The City's evidence did not simply establish the disruption of the witnesses' daily routines, however. The evidence established, *inter alia*, that public services, such as ambulance, fire and police services, were severely hampered by the increased traffic congestion resulting from the strike. To the extent that Local 85's argument suggests that the adverse effect on and threat to essential public services such as fire and police protection and emergency medical services are the ordinary and anticipated consequences of a transit strike, we are unpersuaded.

I must respectfully disagree with the majority's characterization of the evidence and the argument of the Union. There was scant evidence of disruption of the City's ability to provide adequate fire protection, police protection and emergency medical services because of the strike. As the Union points out in its brief, no testimony was offered by the City pertaining to the City's ability or inability to provide adequate fire and police protection as a result of the strike. The only evidence offered by the City which directly pertained to the City's ability to provide emergency medical services was the testimony of Robert Kennedy, Chief of the Bureau of Emergency Medical Services for the City of Pittsburgh Department of Public Safety. Chief Kennedy testified that peak demand for emergency medical services is from 2:00 p.m. to 10:00 p.m. Monday through Saturday. Mr. Kennedy testified that his Bureau did experience some difficulty in moving units to respond to calls. He testified anecdotally to a report of a unit on the North Side of Pittsburgh dispatched to the South Side of Pittsburgh in response to a call at approximately 3:30 p.m. on March 30. Due to the volume of traffic at that time, the unit was unable to cross either the West End bridge or the Fort Duquesne bridge, even with its warning devices, and could not complete the call. He testified as to "having some problem entering downtown [Pittsburgh] from the east due to congestion on Liberty Avenue;" "we are very often forced now to go long distances down Liberty Avenue into town opposing traffic." Chief Kennedy stated that paramedics have reported to him that they were finding difficulty on secondary roads because of the presence of more traffic than usual on those roads. The traffic conditions and delays described by Chief Kennedy are not dissimilar to that which is encountered during busy traffic hours when traffic on a major thoroughfare (such as the Parkway East or Parkway West in Pittsburgh) is limited because of the resurfacing and/or repairs of such thoroughfare. The City offered no other evidence of its inability to provide adequate fire and police protection and emergency medical services. * * *

The disruptions of routine daily activities such as, traveling to and from employment, school, meetings, business appointments, personal appointments, medical appointments, social functions, etc. are indeed significant and often painful inconveniences to the public, particularly for the young and the elderly. These disruptions and inconveniences are inherent in the very nature of any mass transit strike in a metropolitan area. The majority, by elevating these disruptions and inconveniences to a clear and present danger or threat to the health, safety or welfare of the public renders the right to strike granted transit workers by the Port Authority Act illusory. I cannot conceive of a strike by transit employees which did not impact the public in the various ways described by the witnesses in this case. Surely, the disruptive effect of a mass transit strike upon the public is rightfully a matter for concern. In enacting the Port Authority Act, 55 PENN.STAT. § 551, *et seq.*, however, the General Assembly weighed the competing interests which would be affected by legislation permitting Port Authority employees to strike and enacted legislation in favor of allowing such strikes. The majority's opinion in this case which makes it inevitable that all strikes by Port Authority employees will be enjoined upon petition renders the Legislature's action useless.

* * *

NOTES

1. The struck employer was the Port Authority, but the injunction action was brought by the mayor of Pittsburgh. On what basis did the court grant the mayor standing to seek an injunction? Should parties other than the struck employer be allowed to seek injunctions?

2. Pennsylvania's standard for an injunction is a clear and present danger to the public health, safety or welfare. Would the same result have been reached in a state where the standard is clear and present danger to the public health and safety?

3. A city owns and operates an electric utility. The union which represents the city's linemen has threatened to strike. Linemen perform maintenance and repairs on the electrical power distribution facilities and equipment. Four non-bargaining unit supervisors are qualified to perform linemen's duties, but the city estimates that it will take ten times as long to restore power in the event of a major power failure utilizing supervisory personnel as it would take utilizing the full strength of the bargaining unit. Should the threatened strike be enjoined? *See City of Naperville*, 13 P.E.R.Ill ¶ 2044 (Ill.SLRB 1997); *City of Naperville*, 7 P.E.R.Ill. ¶ 2033 (Ill. SLRB 1991).

4. Should a strike or threatened strike by deputy court clerks be enjoined where the clerks' duties include processing documents in criminal cases, preparing orders of protection and processing arrest warrants? Compare *Clerk of the Court of Adams County v. International Association of Machinists Local 822*, 21 P.E.R.I. 161 (Ill. L.R.B. 2005) with *Clerk of the Court of Winnebago County v. AFSCME Council 31*, 20 P.E.R.I. 16 (Ill. L.R.B. 2003).

5. In the principal case, after enjoining the strike, the court ordered the parties to negotiate under court supervision. What other approaches might be used to resolve the impasse once a lawful strike is enjoined?

6. In the private sector, Sections 206–210 of the Taft–Hartley Act (also known as the Labor Management Relations Act), 29 U.S.C. §§ 176–80, authorize the President to appoint a board of inquiry when a strike or threatened strike will imperil national health or safety. Upon receipt of the board's report, the president may direct the attorney general to seek an injunction against the strike for 60 days, at which time the board of inquiry reports to the president on the state of the dispute, including each party's final offer. The NLRB is empowered to conduct a secret ballot election among the employees as to whether they wish to accept the employer's final offer. Section 10 of the Railway Labor Act, 45 U.S.C. § 160, authorizes the president to create a special emergency board to investigate and make recommendations when a railroad or airline strike threatens to deprive any section of the country of essential transportation service. The presidential emergency board has 30 days to make its report, after which the parties are required to maintain the status quo for an additional 30 days. How do these private sector approaches compare to those used in the public sector?

CHAPTER 10

RESOLUTION OF BARGAINING IMPASSES

■ ■ ■

As seen in Chapter 9, unlike the private sector where strikes and other economic pressures play a pivotal role in the bargaining process, in the public sector strikes are usually prohibited. As a result of the intolerance of strikes in the public sector, there has been a continuing search for substitutes for economic weapons. Consequently, unlike the private sector where third party involvement in interests disputes is usually consensual, third party involvement in the public sector is often compelled.

Interests disputes do not involve the interpretation and application of agreed-upon language. They are controversies over what the terms of the collective bargaining agreement should be. It is this type of dispute which, if unresolved, most frequently results in concerted job action of one kind or another.

Public aversion to the proposition that employees in the public sector should have the right to engage in concerted work stoppages poses a dilemma. If the ability to strike or to make a credible strike threat is the motive power which causes the bargaining parties to make maximum effort to reach agreement, how is the system to work if the rules eliminate the strike or the threat of a strike from the process?

During the past forty years, legislatures have devised a diversity of procedural arrangements designed to make the bargaining process work without resort to strike action. These range from mediation, which is the least invasive form of intervention, to arbitration, which is the most invasive. In between are factfinders who make recommendations and advisory arbitrators whose awards are not binding.

Statutory schemes often employ several of these techniques. One of the most flexible approaches to public sector impasse resolution is found in the Federal Service Labor Management Relations Statute (FSLMS). Under the FSMLS, parties must first resort to third party mediation, typically performed by the Federal Mediation and Conciliation Service. If mediation does not resolve the dispute, either party may petition the Federal Service Impasses Panel (FSIP) for assistance. The FSIP consists of seven members appointed by the President to staggered five year terms. Panel members may be removed at any time by the President. Once FSIP determines that it has jurisdiction over the dispute, the statute empowers it to "take whatever action is necessary * * * to resolve the impasse." 5 U.S.C. § 7119(c)(5)(B). The FSIP has, among other approaches, required the parties to submit their final offers and supporting evidence in writing with the Panel awarding final terms; appointed a single Panel member to mediate and, if unable to obtain a settlement, make recommendations to the entire Panel of terms to be awarded; and appointed a single Panel member to mediate and, if necessary, arbitrate the dispute and award specific terms.

This chapter focuses on the approaches to impasse resolution adopted in the public sector. Section A discusses mediation, the use of a third party mediator to assist the parties in reaching agreement. Section B examines factfinding, where a third party finds facts and makes recommendations for resolution of the bargaining impasse. Section C focuses on interest arbitration, where the dispute is submitted to a third party for binding resolution. It examines the constitutionality of interest arbitration, criteria used in interest arbitration, the different types of interest arbitration, mediation by the arbitrator, and judicial review of the arbitration award.

A. MEDIATION

Mediation is a process whereby a neutral third party assists the parties in their efforts to reach agreement. Public sector mediators frequently come from the Federal Mediation and Conciliation Service (FMCS) or from comparable state agencies. At times, the parties will hire a private mediator.

Mediation is also used with great frequency in the private sector. However, mediation of public sector collective negotiations differs from mediation in the private sector in several important respects. In the private sector, except for the railroad and airline industries which are governed by the Railway Labor Act, and hospitals which are governed by special provisions of the National Labor Relations Act, mediation is a completely consensual process. In the public sector, however, mediation is often mandated by statute. Most state statutes that set forth impasse procedures containing steps leading to factfinding, interest arbitration, or a right to strike require the parties to resort to mediation before they can move to another stage of the process. Statutes commonly provide for the appointment of a mediator upon the request of only one party. Several states empower the public labor relations board to appoint a mediator on its own motion, and in some states appointment of a mediator is automatic if agreement has not been reached within a specified time frame.

In the private sector, it is expected that the employer's bargaining team comes to the table with authority to settle. In the public sector, tentative agreements reached in collective bargaining are often subject to ratification by the employer's governing body.

In the private sector, most mediation occurs with the understanding that failure to reach agreement will lead to a strike, lockout or unilateral implementation by the employer of its final offer. In the public sector, strikes and lockouts are prohibited in most jurisdictions and strikes and lockouts for police and firefighters are universally prohibited.

Mediators serve several important roles in assisting the parties in reaching agreement. Mediators can educate the parties concerning the likelihood of achieving particular goals in the negotiations. They can engage in reality testing of particular proposals. They can assist the parties in prioritizing their demands and can communicate each party's priorities to the other. They can facilitate communication between the parties, searching for areas in which movement is possible. Mediators can meet with the parties in separate confidential caucuses and ascertain areas that will be fruitful for compromises. Sometimes a mediator may propose a compromise. Furthermore, the very presence of a neutral third party places pressure on the parties to work harder toward settlement and to "get real" in the positions they take at the bargaining table.

To what extent does the absence of a right to strike, the absence of employer-negotiator authority to bind the employer, and the absence of consent to mediation affect the mediator's approach? How does mediation under threat of interest arbitration differ from mediation under threat of strike? How does it differ from mediation in the absence of a right to interest arbitration or a right to strike?

A two-year study published in 1983 compared mediation of private sector collective bargaining conducted by FMCS mediators with mediation of public sector bargaining conducted by state agency mediators in the same state. The researcher accompanied the mediators over a two-year period. She concluded that the state mediators' approach differed markedly from the FMCS mediators' approach in the private sector. She found that FMCS mediators in the private sector cases served as orchestrators, insisting that responsibility for settlement rested with the parties, and viewing their roles as assisting the parties in narrowing the issues in accordance with the parties' priorities. She found that the state mediators in the public sector served as dealmakers who argued with each party, insisting that it convince the mediator of its position. Based on these arguments and the party's statement of priorities, the mediator and the party built a proposal that the mediator then attempted to sell to the other party. She observed that by using a "frenetic, high-pressured building strategy," the state mediators sought to compensate for the absence of a strike threat. See Deborah Kolb, *The Mediators* (MIT Press 1983).

The state mediators the researcher studied attempted to compensate for the lack of immediate consequences to the parties of a failure to settle in the mediation proceeding. Where strikes are illegal, the consequence of a failure to settle is to move on to another proceedings, such as fact-finding or interest arbitration. Do you think the study's findings are peculiar to the state agency that was studied, or may we extrapolate from the study to mediation in the public sector generally? How should a mediator deal with a threat to strike in a jurisdiction where strikes are illegal?

In the federal sector, when the FSIP delegates to an individual Panel member authority to mediate and, if necessary arbitrate an impasse, the Panel member will combine the two processes in a single proceeding. The parties are told that if they do not reach agreement in mediation, the Panel member will use the record developed in the mediation as the basis for an arbitration award imposing contract terms on the parties. This approach presents the parties with immediate consequences of a failure to settle, thereby increasing the pressure on them to reach agreement. Can you think of other advantages to this "med-arb" approach? Can you think of any disadvantages?

B. FACTFINDING

Many jurisdictions provide that if the parties are unable to reach agreement with the assistance of a mediator, they then proceed to factfinding. In this procedure, a neutral third party conducts a hearing at which the parties present their most recent offers and evidence and arguments as to why their offers and not those of the other party should be adopted. The neutral third party issues findings of fact and recommendations for settlement. If the parties are still unable to reach agreement, the recommendations may be made public. The expectation is that the persuasive force of the factfinder's recommendations and the prospect of public disclosure will motivate the parties to reach agreement. The factfinder's recommendations at times can provide a party with the political cover it needs to be able to settle the contract.

Factfinders' approaches can be situated along a continuum, ranging from an objective adjudicator model to a subjective mediation model. The objective adjudicator functions like an interest arbitrator, producing findings and recommendations based solely on the adjudicator's view of the evidence. The mediator factfinder aims to provide findings and recommendations that are most likely to be accepted by the parties, regardless of the objective merits of their positions.

Factfinding can be useful in providing the parties with the political cover they need to settle their dispute. A union bargaining team concerned over its ability to concede on an issue over which the membership feels strongly may rely on the factfinder's recommendation to justify its concession. Similarly, an employer bargaining team may use the factfinder's recommendation to sell a politically unpopular agreement to the employer's governing body or the general public.

The primary drawback to factfinding is that it is not final. The parties may simply not fear public disclosure of the factfinder's report, and there may be insufficient incentive for them to resolve their impasse. Indeed California's PERB has held that the parties, in discharge of their mutual obligation to bargain with each other and follow impasse resolution procedures in good faith, have no duty to meet and confer and discuss the recommendations of the factfinder point-by-point. The Board specifically rejected the suggestion that the employer has an obligation to enter into a face-to-face and item-by-item explanation of its reasons for rejecting the factfinder's report. See *Charter Oak Educators Association, CTA/NEA v. Charter Oak Unified School District,* 15 P.E.R.Cal. ¶ 22067 (Cal. PERB 1991). It is enough, said PERB, if the employer in good faith considers the factfinder's report and the union's offer to accept it, rejecting both; the impasse that precipitated factfinding continues and the employer may implement its last best offer—"policies reasonably comprehended within previous offers."

Where either or both parties reject the factfinder's recommendations and the parties fail to reach agreement, jurisdictions that do not recognize a right to strike and do not mandate interest arbitration take varying approaches. Some require that the impasse be submitted to the employer's governing body for resolution. Others allow the employer to impose its final offer on the employees. Some jurisdictions limit the effects of an employer-imposed contract offer. For example, in Florida, the terms are effective only until the end of the fiscal year in which they are imposed, with further negotiations required thereafter.

C. INTEREST ARBITRATION

Limitations inherent in non-final systems of dispute resolution have led to increased consideration of procedures by which settlements are imposed upon the parties. The most common procedure is arbitration, referred to in this context as "interest" arbitration to distinguish it from the arbitration of grievances under an existing agreement.

Interest arbitration hearings tend to differ from other adjudicatory hearings. Although the record in interest arbitration may be developed through witness testimony, frequently the facts are not disputed. In such cases, the evidence is provided in detailed exhibit books containing the objective facts, including characteristics of communities that a party contends are comparable to the community at issue; wages, benefits and working conditions in those communities; cost of living data; and data concerning the employer at issue, including its budget, tax base, economic trends, and wages and benefits of its other employees. Frequently, the parties supplement their exhibit books with narrative presentations. Individual testimony often is given as much for its political effect as for its probative value. For example, in a dispute over residency restrictions on employees, the mayor may testify concerning how strongly the municipality believes that employees should reside within municipal boundaries and employees may testify as to the effect the residency requirement has had on their families. Typically, only mandatory subjects of bargaining may be submitted to interest arbitration unless both parties consent to submission of a permissive subject.

1. CONSTITUTIONALITY OF INTEREST ARBITRATION

A fundamental question pertaining to interest arbitration is whether it is compatible with democratic values. An interest arbitrator may be called upon to decide issues with wide-ranging public significance, monetary and otherwise. Is it appropriate for such issues to be determined by a person not accountable to the political process in the normal ways in which public officials are accountable? George Taylor pointed out many years ago that binding interest arbitration cuts against our political grain: "[A] strike of government employees interferes with the orderly performance of the functions of the representative government. Compulsory arbitration is a greater threat—it entails a delegation to 'outsiders' of the authority assigned by the electorate to elected officials, who are subject to the checks and balances of our governmental institutions." George Taylor, Public Employment: Strikes or Procedures?, 20 *Industrial & Labor Relations Review* 617, 632 (1967).

JUDICIAL RESPONSE TO ARBITRATION

Joseph R. Grodin & Joyce M. Najita
Public Sector Bargaining (Benjamin Aaron et al., eds., 2d ed., IRRA, BNA, 1988) pp. 229–265.

Statutes mandating interest arbitration for public employees have been challenged on a variety of state constitutional grounds, most of them involving either the relationship of state to local authority, the relationship of arbitration to the legislative process, or a combination of the two. The first category of challenge—that the statute intrudes impermissibly upon the autonomy of a "home rule" city or county—has been uniformly rejected by the courts and need not concern us here. The second category, involving the relationship of arbitration to the legislative process, may take a variety of forms: that the statute constitutes an unlawful delegation of legislative power to private parties, that the statute contains insufficient standards or safeguards to guide or check arbitral discretion, that it represents an unconstitutional delegation of the taxing power, or that the method by which arbitrators are chosen violates the "one man, one vote" principle. The third category of challenge stems from the provisions, known as "ripper clauses," found in 18 state constitutions and prohibiting the legislature from delegating to a "special or private body" any power to interfere with "municipal moneys or to perform municipal functions."

Prior to 1975, Pennsylvania was the only state in which interest arbitration was held constitutionally impermissible, and that was on the basis of a ripper clause that has subsequently been amended to permit arbitration. After that amendment, the state interest-arbitration statute was sustained. The supreme court of Wyoming upheld that state's interest-arbitration statute despite a ripper clause in the state's constitution, and the courts of Rhode Island, Maine, and Nebraska (which have no ripper clauses) rejected constitutional challenges based on other grounds. The supreme court of Maine was equally divided on the question of unlawful delegation, but since the lower court had sustained the statute, the effect of the division was to affirm. Thus, by the end of 1974, the score stood 5–0 in favor of constitutionality.

Since that time, interest's arbitration's constitutional batting average has been rising. The highest courts in Connecticut, Maine, New Jersey, Minnesota, New York, Massachusetts, Washington, and Michigan have sustained the constitutionality of interest arbitration in those states; and courts in South Dakota, Colorado, Utah, and Maryland have reached the opposite conclusion. While each of the latter state constitutions contained ripper clauses, the decisions in Colorado and Utah went beyond those clauses to rely generally on unconstitutional delegation doctrine. In California, the supreme court in a footnote in one case rather summarily dispensed with a constitutional attack raised by an amicus curiae to the constitutionality of a city-charter provision calling for binding interest arbitration; however, the vitality of that footnote is dampened somewhat by the reasoning of the same court in an opinion which holds that an arrangement by a general-law city for interest arbitration would constitute an impermissible delegation of wage-fixing authority under a state statute providing that "by resolution or ordinance the city council shall fix the compensation of all appointive officers."

COUNTY OF RIVERSIDE v. SUPERIOR COURT

California Supreme Court, 2003.
30 Cal.4th 278, 132 Cal.Rptr.2d 713, 66 P.3d 718.

CHIN, J.

The Legislature recently enacted Senate Bill No. 402, which requires counties and other local agencies to submit, under certain circumstances, to binding arbitration of economic issues that arise during negotiations with unions representing firefighters or law enforcement officers. We must determine whether this legislation violates either or both of two provisions of article XI of the California Constitution. Section 1, subdivision (b), states that a county's "governing body shall provide for the * * * compensation * * * of employees." Section 11, subdivision (a), forbids the Legislature to "delegate to a private person or body power to * * * interfere with county or municipal corporation * * * money * * * or perform municipal functions."

We conclude, as did the Court of Appeal, that Senate Bill 402 violates both constitutional provisions. It deprives the county of its authority to provide for the compensation of its employees (Section 1, subd. (b)) and delegates to a private body the power to interfere with county financial affairs and to perform a municipal function (Section 11, subd. (a)).

I. FACTS AND PROCEDURAL HISTORY

Riverside County (the County) and the Riverside Sheriff's Association (Sheriff's Association) engaged in negotiations over compensation for employees of the probation department. In May 2001, they reached an impasse. The Sheriff's Association requested that the dispute be submitted to binding arbitration pursuant to Code of Civil Procedure Section 1299 et seq. The County refused, claiming that those provisions violate the California Constitution. The Sheriff's Association filed an action in the superior court to compel arbitration. The court ordered arbitration. It found the binding arbitration law constitutional, explaining, "The matters at issue, to wit, the possible disruption of law enforcement and firefighter services, are not matters of purely local concern but rather are of statewide concern. This statewide concern authorizes the Legislature to act and supports the constitutionality of this legislation."

The County filed a petition for a writ of mandate in the Court of Appeal asking that court to order the superior court to set aside its order compelling arbitration and enter a new order denying the motion to compel arbitration. The Court of Appeal granted the petition. It found that Senate Bill 402 violates both Section 1, subdivision (b), and Section 11, subdivision (a). We granted the Sheriff's Association's petition for review.

II. DISCUSSION

A. Background

Senate Bill 402, entitled "Arbitration of Firefighter and Law Enforcement Officer Labor Disputes," added Section 1299 et seq. to the Code of Civil Procedure. The Court of Appeal opinion describes the bill: "Senate Bill 402 empowers unions representing public safety employees to declare an impasse in labor negotiations and require a local agency to submit unresolved economic issues to binding arbitration. Each party chooses an arbitrator, who together choose the third arbitrator. The panel then chooses, without alteration, between each side's last best offer, based on a designated list of factors." The bill applies to any local agency or any entity acting as an agent of a local agency, but it does not apply to the State of California even acting as such an agent.

* * *

The County argues that the Legislature's compelling it to enter into binding arbitration of compensation issues violates Section 1, subdivision (b), and Section 11, subdivision (a). At the outset, we emphasize that the issue is not whether a county may voluntarily submit compensation issues to arbitration, i.e., whether the county may delegate its own authority, but whether the Legislature may compel a county to submit to arbitration involuntarily. The issue involves the division of authority between the state and the county, not what the county may itself do.

* * *

B. Section 1, subdivision (b)

Section 1, subdivision (b), provides as relevant: "The governing body [of each county] shall provide for the number, compensation, tenure, and appointment of employees." The County argues that Senate Bill 402 violates this provision by compelling it to submit to binding arbitration of compensation issues. We agree. The constitutional language is quite clear and quite specific: the county, not the state, not someone else, shall provide for the compensation of its employees. Although the language does not expressly limit the power of the Legislature, it does so by "necessary implication." An express grant of authority to the county necessarily implies the Legislature does not have that authority. But Senate Bill 402 compels the county to enter into mandatory arbitration with unions representing its employees, with the potential result that the arbitration panel determines employee compensation. Senate Bill 402 permits the union to change the county's governing board from the body that sets compensation for its employees to just another party in arbitration. It thereby deprives the county of authority Section 1, subdivision (b), specifically gives to counties.

* * *

The Sheriff's Association argues that Senate Bill 402 is valid because it involves a matter of "statewide concern." It cites the legislative findings in support of the bill, including that "strikes taken by firefighters and law enforcement officers against public employers are a matter of statewide concern," and that the "dispute resolution procedures" the bill establishes "provide the appropriate method for resolving public sector labor disputes that could otherwise lead to strikes by firefighters or law enforcement officers." These findings are entitled to great weight. But they are not controlling. A court may not simply abdicate to the Legislature, especially when the issue involves the division of power between local government and that same Legislature. The judicial branch, not the legislative, is the final arbiter of this question. * * *

The Sheriff's Association cites two cases that permitted the Legislature to regulate relations between local governmental entities and their employees. In *Baggett v. Gates*, 32 Cal.3d 128, 185 Cal.Rptr. 232, 649 P.2d 874 (1982), we held that the Public Safety Officers' Procedural Bill of Rights Act, which, as its name suggests, provides procedural protections to public safety officers, applies to chartered cities despite the home rule provisions of the current Section 5, subdivision (b). * * * [W]e said that "general laws seeking to accomplish an objective of statewide concern"—in that case, creating uniform fair labor practices—"may prevail over conflicting local regulations even if they impinge to a limited extent upon some phase of local control." We found that "the maintenance of stable employment relations between police officers and their employers is a matter of statewide concern." Similarly, in *People ex rel. Seal Beach Police Officers Assn. v. City of Seal Beach*, 36 Cal.3d 591, 205 Cal.Rptr. 794, 685 P.2d 1145 (1984), we held that a charter city is subject to the meet-and-confer requirements of the Meyers–Milias–Brown Act.

The Sheriff's Association argues, "It is well established that the Legislature may regulate labor relations in the public sector because it is a matter of statewide concern." We agree that Legislature may regulate as to matters of statewide concern even if the regulation impinges "to a limited extent" on powers the Constitution specifically reserves to counties (Section 1) or charter cities (Section 5). However, regulating labor relations is one thing; depriving the county entirely of its authority to set employee salaries is quite another.

In *Sonoma County Organization of Public Employees v. County of Sonoma*, 23 Cal.3d 296, 152 Cal.Rptr. 903, 591 P.2d 1 (1979), we noted that Section 5 expressly gives charter cities authority over their employees' compensation. Because of this constitutional mandate, as well as prior authority, we held that "the determination of the wages paid to employees of charter cities as well as charter counties is a matter of local rather than statewide concern." Accordingly, we found unconstitutional Government Code Section 16280, which prohibited the distribution of certain state funds to local public agencies that granted their employees cost-of-living increases, despite a legislative declaration that the statute was a matter of statewide concern. For similar reasons, and despite a similar legislative declaration, we later invalidated legislation requiring the University of California to pay its employees at least prevailing wages. *San Francisco Labor Council v. Regents of University of California*, 26 Cal.3d 785, 163 Cal.Rptr. 460, 608 P.2d 277 (1980).

Sonoma County Organization of Public Employees v. County of Sonoma, and *San Francisco Labor Council v. Regents of University of California* control this case. In *Baggett v. Gates*, we distinguished those two cases by noting that the Public Safety Officers' Procedural Bill of Rights Act, which was limited to providing procedural safeguards, "impinges only minimally on the specific directives of Section 5, subdivision (b)." Especially pertinent here, we stressed "that the Act does not interfere with the setting of peace officers' compensation." By contrast, Senate Bill 402 does not minimally impinge on a specific constitutional directive; it contravenes that directive entirely. Section 1, subdivision (b), specifically directs that counties have authority over the compensation of their employees; Senate Bill 402 takes that authority away from counties.

Similarly, in *People ex rel. Seal Beach Police Officers Assn. v. City of Seal Beach*, the law in question did not establish a binding process but merely imposed procedural requirements. "While the Legislature established a procedure for resolving disputes regarding wages, hours and other conditions of employment, it did not attempt to establish standards for the wages, hours and other terms and conditions themselves." We found no conflict between the city's constitutional powers and the limited state regulation. "Although the [law in issue] encourages binding agreements resulting from the parties' bargaining, the governing body of the agency * * * retains the ultimate power to refuse an agreement and to make its own decisions." Here, the county's governing body does not retain the ultimate power; Senate Bill 402 gives that power to an arbitration panel at the behest of the union.

We have "emphasized that there is a clear distinction between the substance of a public employee labor issue and the procedure by which it is resolved. Thus there is no question that 'salaries of local employees of a charter city constitute municipal affairs and are not subject to general laws.' Nevertheless, the process by which the salaries are fixed is obviously a matter of statewide concern and none could, at this late stage, argue that a charter city need not meet and confer concerning its salary structure." *People ex rel. Seal Beach Police Officers Assn. v. City of Seal Beach, supra*. Senate Bill 402 is not merely procedural; it is substantive. It permits a body other than the county's governing body to establish local salaries.

* * *

For these reasons, we agree with the Court of Appeal: "Senate Bill 402 removes from local jurisdictions, at the option of public safety unions, the authority to set the compensation of public safety employees that is expressly given to them by Section 1, subdivision (b). This clearly violates Section 1, subdivision (b)."

C. Section 11, subdivision (a)

Section 11, subdivision (a), provides: "The Legislature may not delegate to a private person or body power to make, control, appropriate, supervise, or interfere with county or municipal corporation improvements, money, or property, or to levy taxes or assessments, or perform municipal functions." The county argues that in enacting Senate Bill 402, the Legislature has impermissibly delegated to a private body—the arbitration panel—the power to interfere with county money (by potentially requiring the county to pay higher salaries than it chooses) and to perform municipal functions (determining compensation for county employees). Again, we agree. This constitutional provision expressly denies the Legislature the power to act in this way.

The Sheriff's Association primarily argues that this delegation of authority to the arbitration panel is permissible because the delegation does not involve a purely municipal function but a matter of statewide concern. * * *

The Sheriff's Association argues that because of "the threat to the public safety caused by work stoppages," all matters concerning firefighters and peace officers are of statewide concern that the state may delegate as it thinks best. We disagree. * * *

* * *

As with Section 1, subdivision (b), the Sheriff's Association argues that the Legislature's power to regulate labor relations as to matters of statewide concern permits it to delegate this regulatory authority to an arbitration panel. The argument fails for the same reasons: Senate Bill 402 does not just permit the arbitration panel to impinge minimally on the county's authority; it empowers the panel actually to set employee salaries. The Sheriff's Association also argues that binding arbitration is a "quid pro quo for the lack of a right to strike." This may (or may not) provide a policy argument in favor of binding arbitration, but it provides no reason to disregard a clear constitutional mandate. Moreover, like the Court of Appeal, we note that the state has exempted itself from this binding arbitration requirement. We are skeptical that awarding binding arbitration as a quid pro quo can be of statewide concern to everyone except the state.

The Sheriff's Association argues that the arbitration panel is a public, not private, body within the meaning of Section 11, subdivision (a). We disagree. The statute requires the two parties to select a "person" to be a member of the panel. These two then select "an impartial person with experience in labor and management dispute resolution to act as chairperson of the arbitration panel." If the two do not agree on the third person, the statute has other provisions for selecting that person, but it continually uses the word "person" or "persons" to describe who may be the chairperson. Nothing in the statute requires the arbitrators to be public officials; indeed, the statute appears to contemplate, and the parties assume, they will be private persons.

The Sheriff's Association agrees that the members of the arbitration panel may be private persons, but it argues that empowering them to render binding arbitration decisions makes them a public body. It relies on a Rhode Island case that involved a similar mandatory arbitration law. *City of Warwick v. Warwick Regular Firemen's Ass'n,* 106, R.I. 109, 256 A.2d 206 (1969). In that case, the court reasoned that the Legislature gave the arbitration panel "the power to fix the salaries of public employees * * * without control or supervision from any superior," and, therefore, each member of the panel "is a public officer and * * * collectively the three constitute a public board or agency." The Sheriff's Association seeks to apply this reasoning here. But the constitutional provision in that case was very different than the one here. The Rhode Island Constitution merely stated that the "legislative power * * * shall be vested" in the senate and house of representatives. It contained no language limiting the Legislature's delegation power like that of Section 11, subdivision (a). [I]f delegating to private persons the power to do a public act makes them a public body for purposes of Section 11, subdivision (a), then "the constitutional provision would never be violated. Anyone to whom the Legislature delegated the power to tax [or any other power specified in Section 11, subdivision (a)] would automatically cease being a 'private person or body.'" Section 11, subdivision (a), is not self-canceling. The act of delegation does not change a private body into a public body and thereby validate the very delegation the Section prohibits. The Legislature has, indeed, delegated authority to a private body.

Both parties cite decisions from other states in support of their positions. The only cases that are relevant are those that involve statutory and constitutional provisions comparable to California's. These cases generally support the County. * * * The Pennsylvania courts originally invalidated binding arbitration legislation under their constitutional provision. *Erie Firefighters Local No. 293 v. Gardner*, 406 Pa. 395, 178 A.2d 691 (1962). As the Sheriff's Association notes, the Pennsylvania Supreme Court has since upheld binding arbitration. *Harney v. Russo*, 435 Pa. 183, 255 A.2d 560 (1969). But that was after the Pennsylvania Constitution was amended specifically to permit such arbitration. * * * The California Constitution has not been amended to permit the Legislature to impose binding arbitration on counties. Thus, the Pennsylvania experience supports the County's position.

Two other states have also invalidated arbitration provisions under constitutional provisions similar to Section 11, subdivision (a). *City of Sioux Falls v. Sioux Falls, etc.*, 89 S.D. 455, 234 N.W.2d 35 (1975) (binding arbitration); *Salt Lake City v. I.A. of Firefighters, etc.*, 563 P.2d 786 (Utah 1977) (arbitration that is partially binding, but advisory only as to salary and wage matters). One court reached a contrary result, but it was unable to achieve a majority opinion. *State v. City of Laramie,* 437 P.2d 295 (Wyo.1968). We find the Wyoming case unconvincing. As recognized in *City of Sioux Falls v. Sioux Falls, etc., supra*, the Wyoming court cited Pennsylvania law but failed to note that the Pennsylvania Constitution had been amended to permit binding arbitration. In any event, California's constitutional history, including that behind Section 1, subdivision (b), distinguishes California from Wyoming. This history, and the two California constitutional provisions, read together, make clear that, in California, the county, not the state or anyone else, sets compensation for its employees.

* * *

III. CONCLUSION

John Donne wrote, "No man is an island, entire of itself." So, too, no county is an island, entire of itself. No doubt almost anything a county does, including determining employee compensation, can have consequences beyond its borders. But this circumstance does not mean this court may eviscerate clear constitutional provisions, or the Legislature may do what the Constitution expressly prohibits it from doing.

The Court of Appeal correctly held that Senate Bill 402 violates Sections 1, subdivision (b), and 11, subdivision (a). Accordingly, we affirm the judgment of the Court of Appeal.

[The concurring opinions of CHIEF JUSTICE GEORGE and JUSTICE MORENO are omitted.]

NOTES

1. In reaction to the *County of Riverside* decision, the California legislature amended the statute to empower the employer's governing body to reject the interest arbitration award by unanimous vote. In *County of Sonoma v. Superior Court*, 173 Cal.App.4th 322, 93 Cal.Rptr.3d 39 (2009), the California Court of Appeal held the amendment unconstitutional. The court reasoned

that the statute only gave the governing body power to veto the arbitration award. It did not allow the governing body to set the employees' compensation and terms of employment. All the governing body could do was prevent another body, the interest arbitration panel, from setting terms of employment. Furthermore, in the court's view, the requirement of a unanimous vote to reject the arbitration award allowed a minority of the members of the governing body to accept the award, something the court reasoned, "would be . . . deeply offensive to basic principles of democracy." 173 Cal.App.4th at 344, 93 Cal.Rptr.3d at 55. The California PERB, reasoning that it was bound by the Court of Appeal's decision, dismissed unfair labor practice charges which had challenged Sonoma County's refusal to participate in interest arbitration. *Sonoma County Law Enforcement Association v. County of Sonoma*, 34 P.E.R.Cal. ¶ 54 (Cal. PERB 2010).

2. As Professor Grodin observed, most jurisdictions that have considered the issue have upheld the constitutionality of interest arbitration. Was the California Supreme Court's decision based solely on quirks of California constitutional law, or does it have implications for the constitutionality of interest arbitration generally?

3. Consider whether the presence of the following would save an interest arbitration statute from the claim that it delegates governmental authority to a private body:

a. a list of specific factors on which the panel must base its decision?

b. provision for appointment of the arbitrator by a public agency, such as the state labor relations board?

c. the availability of judicial review of the arbitration award?

4. The Pennsylvania statute mandating interest arbitration to resolve impasses in police and firefighter negotiations provides that if the arbitration award requires legislative action for implementation, the legislation shall be enacted within one month following the award but need not take effect until the beginning of the next fiscal year. In *Lycoming County v. Pennsylvania Labor Relations Board*, 943 A.2d 333 (Pa. Cmwlth.Ct. 2008), the arbitration panel's award exceeded what the county had budgeted for detectives by $12,731.00. The court held that the county was obligated to implement the award immediately, reasoning that the award did not require legislative action to implement because the county had a $150,000 contingency fund from which it could transfer funds to cover the additional costs of the award. Should a private arbitration panel be able to, in effect, order a governmental body to reallocate funds from the original budget?

5. In *International Association of Firefighters Local 1687 v. City of Carlsbad*, 147 N.M. 6, 216 P.3d 256 (App. 2009), the New Mexico Court of Appeals interpreted a provision of the New Mexico Public Employee Bargaining Act which provided that an impasse resolution requiring an expenditure of funds "shall be contingent on the specific appropriate of funds by the legislature and the availability of funds." Although the statute also provided that interest arbitration awards were final and binding on the parties, the court held that the contingency provision took precedence over the final and binding provision. Consequently, the employer could avoid the award on

economic issues by failing to appropriate funds needed for implementation. Do such holdings ensure democratic processes? Do they undermine the role of interest arbitration in motivating settlement in negotiations and resolving impasses with finality?

6. If you were the arbitrator in an interest arbitration proceeding and you became aware that the parties, while unwilling to assume public responsibility for a particular result, would nevertheless find that result "acceptable," would you see any ethical problem in framing your award to suit their expectations? Is the situation different from the "rigged award" in a grievance arbitration situation?

2. CRITERIA USED BY INTEREST ARBITRATORS

Statutes frequently list the factors that the arbitrator is to consider in rendering an interest award. The following language appears in several statutes, including those governing interest arbitration for police and firefighters in Illinois, Michigan and Wisconsin:

> [T]he arbitration panel shall base its findings, opinions and order upon the following factors, as applicable:
>
> (a) The lawful authority of the employer.
>
> (b) Stipulations of the parties.
>
> (c) The interests and welfare of the public and the financial ability of the unit of government to meet these costs.
>
> (d) Comparison of the wages, hours and conditions of employment of the employees involved in the arbitration proceeding with the wages, hours and conditions of employment of other employees performing similar services and with other employees generally:
>
> (i) In public employment in comparable communities.
>
> (ii) In private employment in comparable communities.
>
> (e) The average consumer prices for goods and services, commonly known as the cost of living.
>
> (f) The overall compensation presently received by the employees, including direct wage compensation, vacations, holidays and other excused time, insurance and pensions, medical and hospitalization benefits, the continuity and stability of employment, and all other benefits received.
>
> (g) Changes in any of the foregoing circumstances during the pendency of the arbitration proceedings.
>
> (h) Such other factors, not confined to the foregoing, which are normally or traditionally taken into consideration in the determination of wages, hours and conditions of employment through voluntary collective bargaining, mediation, factfinding, arbitration or otherwise between the parties, in the public service or in private employment.

ILL.-SMITH-HURD ANN. 5 ILCS 315/14(h); MICH.COMP.LAWS ANN. § 423.239; WISCONSIN STAT.ANN. § 111.77(6).

Some states specify factors on which the arbitrator must place primary reliance. See WISCONSIN. STAT.ANN. § 111.70(4)(cm)(6 or 7). Where the statute gives the arbitrator discretion, arbitrators tend to rely heavily on comparability. This is because the arbitrator is called upon to craft an award that resembles the agreement the parties most likely would have reached had their bargaining process not broken down. Agreements reached in comparable communities provide powerful evidence of the agreement the parties before the arbitrator would have reached had their negotiations been successful. Consequently, parties often select their comparable communities strategically and which communities are truly comparable becomes a frequently litigated issue.

Arbitrators also tend to have a heavy presumption against "breakthroughs," or changes in provisions from prior contracts. Prior contracts contain what the parties actually agreed to and provide strong evidence of what they would have agreed to again if their negotiation process had been successful. Arbitrators are not likely to change contract language or structure merely because one party wants the change.

Arbitrators tend to discount employer claims of inability to pay, regarding it as an affirmative defense. Similarly, the mere fact that the employer has the ability to pay the union's offer does not justify awarding the union's offer.

LOCAL 1752–D AFSCME, WAUSAUKEE SCHOOL DISTRICT EMPLOYEES AND SCHOOL DISTRICT OF WAUSAUKEE

Mary Jo Schiavoni, Arbitrator 2009.
Wisconsin Employment Relations Commission Case 56 No. 66997, Dec. No. 32479–a. http://werc.wi.gov/interest_awards/int3247.pdf

SHIAVONI, ARB.

FINAL OFFERS OF THE PARTIES:
UNION'S FINAL OFFER
Wages

06–08	08–09
$0.29 per hour	$0.29 per hour

Health Insurance [Contribution]

06–08	08–09
Employer/Employee	Employer/Employee
96/4	94/6

Status quo on remainder of Agreement

DISTRICT'S FINAL OFFER

Amend Cover Page to Read: July 1, 2007 to June 30, 2009

Amend Article 3—Subcontracting to Read:

The parties agree that if and when the District contemplates subcontracting, it shall notify the Union and provide the Union with an opportunity to negotiate over the decision and impact of subcontracting.

Should a dispute arise, any impasse shall be resolved by mediation/arbitration, pursuant to Section 111.70(4)(cm), Wisconsin Statutes.

The District may subcontract its transportation services. The provisions of this Article, above, will not apply to the District's decision to subcontract transportation services, nor to the impact of that decision.

Amend Article 15–Health, Life and Disability Insurance to Read:

A. The School District shall make payment of health and dental insurance premiums for twelve (12) Months. The fringe benefits year shall be from July through June. For individuals employed by the District on July 1, 2008, and for individuals that, on July 1, 2008 are on layoff status, have remaining recall rights, and are recalled, the health and dental insurance premiums will be paid on the following basis:

Ninety percent (90%) of such premiums for employees working thirty-five (35) to forty (40) hours per week for at least nine (9) months;

Sixty-three percent (63%) of such premiums for employees working thirty (30) to thirty-five (35) hours per week for at least nine (9) months;

Fifty percent (50%) of such premiums for employees working fifteen (15) to thirty (30) hours per week for at least nine (9) months;

None of such premium for employees working less than fifteen (15) hours per week; Until such time as the District subcontracts its busing services, the school District shall pay fifty percent (50%) of such premiums for bus drivers who have had one (1) consecutive prior year of employment with the School District.

(new Section B) and Re–Letter Current Section B and C to Read C and D as follows:

B. For individuals hired by the District after July 1, 2008, the District will pay health and dental insurance premiums on the following basis:

Eighty percent (80%) of such premiums for employees working thirty-five (35) to forty (40) hours per week for at least nine (9) months;

Fifty-six percent (56%) of such premiums for employees working thirty (30) to thirty-five (35) hours per week for at least nine (9) months;

Fifty percent (50%) of such premiums for employees working twenty (20) to thirty (30) hours per week for at least nine (9) months.

None of such premium for employees working less than twenty (20) hours per week;

* * *

Amend Exhibits A & B—Wage Schedules as follows:

Modify any date references to correspond to the current term of this contract

For the 2007–2008 school year, increase wage schedules by zero (0%)

For the 2008–2009 school year, increase wage schedules by zero (0%)

2007–2008 Compensation: The District will compensate individuals employed during the 2007–2008 school year with a bonus of up to $1,000 per employee. Bonus payments will be prorated based on 2080 hours.

2008–2009 Compensation: The District will compensate individuals employed during the 2008–2009 school year with a bonus of up to $1,000 per employee. Bonus payments will be prorated based on 2080 hours.

Bus Driver Severance Benefits: In addition to benefits available under Article 13, Section D.2., Bus Drivers who will no longer be District employees pursuant to the above modifications to Article 3, will receive a severance payment of up to $1000. Severance payments will be prorated based on 900 hours.

* * *

STATUTORY CRITERIA:

The criteria to be utilized by the Arbitrator in rendering the award are set forth in Section 111.70(4)(cm), Wis. Stats., as follows:

7. 'Factor given greatest weight.' In making any decision under the arbitration procedures authorized by this paragraph, the arbitrator or arbitration panel shall consider and shall give the greatest weight to any state law or directive lawfully issued by a state legislative or administrative officer, body or agency which places limitations on expenditures that may be made or revenues that may be collected by a municipal employer.

7g. 'Factor given greater weight.' In making any decision under the arbitration procedures authorized by this paragraph, the arbitrator or arbitration panel shall consider and shall give greater weight to economic conditions in the jurisdiction of the municipal employer than to any of the factors specified under subd. 7r.

7r. 'Other factors considered.' In making any decision under the arbitration procedures authorized in this paragraph, the arbitrator or arbitration panel shall also give weight to the following factors:

1. The lawful authority of the municipal employer.
2. Stipulations of the parties.
3. The interests and welfare of the public and the financial ability of the unit of government to meet the costs of any proposed settlement.
4. Comparison of wages, hours and conditions of employment of the municipal employees involved in the arbitration proceedings with the wages, hours and conditions of employment of employees performing similar services.

5. Comparison of the wages, hours and conditions of employment of the municipal employees involved in the arbitration proceedings with the wages, hours and conditions of employment of other employees generally in public employment in the same community and in comparable communities.
6. Comparison of the wages, hours and conditions of employment of the municipal employees involved in the arbitration proceedings with the wages, hours and conditions of employment of other employees in private employment in the same community and in comparable communities.
7. The average consumer prices for goods and services, commonly known as the cost of living.
8. The overall compensation presently received by the municipal employees, including direct wage compensation, vacation, holidays and excused time, insurance and pensions, medical and hospitalization benefits, the continuity and stability of employment, and all other benefits received.
9. Changes in any of the foregoing circumstances during the pendency of the arbitration.
10. Such other factors, not confined to the foregoing, which are normally or traditionally taken in consideration in the determination of wages, hours and conditions of employment through voluntary collective bargaining, mediation, fact-finding, arbitration or otherwise between the parties, in the public service or in private employment.

POSITION OF THE PARTIES:

* * *

The District * * * argues that its unique financial situation is untenable and requires significant and meaningful union concessions, noting in particular that the District was the only district in Wisconsin to have a deficit in its general fund at the end of the 2007–2008 school year. Noting the drastic decline in student enrollment which led to an actual decrease in revenue limit funds available for District use during an eight year period beginning in 2000–2001, the District points out that its financial shortcomings forced it to spend down its fund balances and that enrollments will continue to decrease or stagnate resulting in decreasing revenue limit funds in the foreseeable future.

The District has regularly levied the maximum amount of property taxes possible under state-imposed revenue caps, yet has been forced to make deep cuts in personnel, programming and student services. The District's offer provides bargaining unit employees with the same frozen salary schedule offered and agreed to by the teachers, administrators, and other non-union personnel. Notwithstanding the frozen salary schedule, the compensation bonuses equate to 3.48% of the compensation received in 2006–2007 and the District's offer on health insurance provides the same contribution levels as agreed to by the teachers and other non-Union employees. Furthermore, the District's offer provides bus drivers with severance benefits, increased wages and increased benefit possibilities in exchange for working for a subcontractor rather than as a District employee.

According to the District, the Union's final offer ignores the significant concessions made by the teachers and other non-union personnel. It ignores the freeze in teacher salary schedules for two years, as well as the fact that administrative employees' wages were also frozen for the same period. Instead the Union's salary offer increases the salary schedules for non-bus drivers by nearly 5% over the two-year contract term, although there is a salary schedule/wage freeze for bus drivers during the same period.

* * *

The District lags behind its comparables with regard to revenue limit per member, being $208 less than the average of the comparables. Because of the statutory revenue limits, the District has little hope of catching up with the districts in the comparable group. The District is also incredibly low with regard to its receipt of State aid as compared to its external comparables. It has gone from receiving 51% funding in 1999–2000 to 10% funding seven years later, resulting in a drop of 41% while districts in the athletic conference have decreased only 11% and contiguous districts decreased by 24%. The declining enrollment problem has forced it to deficit spend every year since 2000–2001. It has been forced to spend down its fund balance to a negative balance of $129,401 at the end of the 2007–2008 school year. The District's fund balance to revenue ratio as contrasted to comparable districts is in the negative and has caused it to incur significant additional interest on its annual short-term borrowing needs. If the District could raise its fund balance to revenue ratio to the 15% to 20% range it could avoid the annual interest payments on its short-term borrowing. As the situation stands now, the District's financial problems have seriously hampered its ability to short-term borrow during the summer prior to the 2008–2009 school year. Had two local banks been unwilling to provide the assistance, the District would not have been able to make payroll or pay its real estate taxes.

These financial problems forced the District to go to a referendum three separate times and to begin the process of dissolving the District. According to the District, the public defeated the referendum the first two times because it wanted to see sacrifices and concessions from the school district employees. Noting that employee compensation costs for teachers and support staff comprise 80% of the District's annual operating expenses, the District points to cuts and concessions made by the teachers' bargaining unit and administrators. The District consolidated the positions of full-time principal, dean of students, and District Administrator in one person, rather than employing two or three employees, saving approximately $105,000 per year. The District has cut back on expenditures, such as textbooks, and has not replaced buses since 2003. The District reduced the teaching staff by 6.2 FTE. Prior to 2008–2009, it eliminated a ½ time art position, all of its business education programming, its family and consumer education program and reduced its technology education program down to 62.5%. It also reduced its English FTE's and library media specialist position from 100% to 75%. It made numerous reductions in its extra-curricular offerings; and during 2007–2008, it eliminated 3.5 FTE support staff positions. It redesigned teacher schedules to maximize the efficiency of the remaining teachers.

The District notes that as part of the teacher settlement, the teachers voluntarily agreed to freeze their salary schedule for two years, receiving step and lane movement during the 2007–2008 school year capped at a $1000 increase over their 2006–2007 wage. Those not receiving a step or lane increase received a $1,000 bonus. For 2008–2009, all teachers received a $1000 bonus. In addition to frozen salary schedules and step and lane advancement, the current teachers agreed to pay 10% of their health insurance premiums with new hires to pay 20% of the premium, with prorata amounts for part-time teachers.

Administrative staff wages were frozen and they did not receive a $1000 bonus. Currently administrative staff contributes 10% of the health insurance premium with new hires paying 20%. The Union cannot argue that the District has singled out the support staff to shoulder a larger portion of the sacrifices than other employees.

Acknowledging that a 10–year, $675,000 per year referendum passed on the third attempt, the District maintains that it was necessary to stabilize the District over the long term. Despite the passage, the District argues that it remains in dire financial straits. Regardless of which final offer the arbitrator selects, the District projects that it will be forced to deficit spend at some point in the future. The Union's offer would accelerate the rate at which the District spending outstrips its meager resources. Selection of the Union's offer will result in a greater budget imbalance than already exists and necessitate significant additional budget cuts the District could avoid with selection of its offer. The District is currently having financial difficulties and it is taxing at the maximum possible rate. It regularly levies the maximum amount of property taxes allowable under Wisconsin's revenue limit law. The severe decline in student enrollments have led to devastating decreases in revenue limit funds. Selection of the Union's offer will force the District to hire a transportation director and to purchase or build a structure, to repair the bus fleet, or spend thousands to replace its fleet. The projected four-year cost difference of between $688,348 and $840,742 is a significant sum of money. Because of these added expenses, the costing difference between the two offers far exceeds $54,622. By subcontracting its bus services in 2009–2010, the District stands to save between $123,091 and $175,927.

* * *

To the extent that the Union might argue that the District should utilize the funds received through the passage of its third referendum attempt to fund the Union offer, the District makes three arguments. First, this is an implicit admission that the greatest weight factor heavily favors the District. Second, a primary reason why the District was able to succeed in the passage of its third referendum attempt in 6 months was the cost savings and concessions achieved through the settlement with the teachers. Third, another reason that the District was able to succeed in the passage was the School Board's vote to dissolve the District effective July 1, 2010. Community sentiment demanded employee concessions on wages and benefits. It would be a violation of public trust to provide the Union with significant salary increases and health insurance contribution benefits after all other employees made deep cuts.

The District offer maintains its internal settlement pattern and this should be granted paramount consideration. The Union's offer would disrupt the District's internal settlement pattern, increase the District's administrative burden and create "lone holdout"/fairness issues among District employees. * * *

* * *

The Union insists that there is no evidence that any claim by the District supports its offer under the "greatest weight" factor in this dispute. Because the voters agreed to a referendum which offered $675,000 per year for 10 years from 2008–2009 through 2017–2018, which is approximately 9% of the District annual budget, the ability to rely upon this additional funding places the District in a unique or at least quite unusual situation. Citing the District's own exhibits, the Union notes that the District Fund 10 balance prior to the passage of the referendum was-$55,280 in 2007–2008, which would grow to $182,239 in 2008–2009. Furthermore, as the Fund 10 balance had declined at slightly more than $210,000 per year on average since 2004–2005, the projected $182,000 deficit for 2008–2009 has been eliminated and the District has $490,000 additional funds available for its business needs. The Union notes that District Administrator Dooley admitted that the District is on secure financial footing as a result of the passage of the referendum. This representation was made one month prior to the arbitration hearing in this dispute.

The District has fixated on its admittedly difficult financial status prior to the successful referendum. It has failed to recognize the substantial effects of the additional revenue. Rather the District is forcing a very aggressive offer by refusing to acknowledge that things have changed since the passage of the referendum.

* * *

The District's offer contains three elements which are unusually aggressive and therefore extraordinary in Wisconsin interest arbitration. It proposes a wage freeze. It also proposes a very significant alteration for employee contributions for health insurance premiums, including a provision requiring new employees hired after July 1 2008 to pay 20% of the premium, and adjusting pro-rations for less than full time to significantly lower levels of employer contributions. Finally, the District seeks to eliminate by the selection of its offer, almost 45% of the remaining Union positions.

Any one of these proposals would require that the District meet a fairly heavy burden of proof. All three demands are unprecedented. The interests of the public are best served by the selection of the Union's offer because there could hardly be a job where a reliable, prudent, experienced individual would serve the society's interest more than those to whom we entrust out children. The continuity and long-term relationship between the District and the Union, through the collective bargaining agreement foster just such employment. The elimination of these positions will not serve the public.

* * *

DISCUSSION:

The Current Contract Language and the Offers of the Parties

Under the expired agreement, the District agreed to pay 100% of the premiums for employees working 35 to 40 hours per week for at least nine months, 70% for employees working 30–35 hours per week for at least nine months, 50% for employees working 15–30 hours per week for at least nine months, and none of the premium for those working under 15 hours. It also agreed to pay 55% of such premiums for bus drivers who have one year of prior employment with the District.

With regard to wages, the expired agreement provided Wage Schedules attached as Exhibits A, B, and C, which provided steps of 1–2 years, 3–4 years and 5+ years in all positions. Also of particular note is the compensation for bus drivers set forth as follows in Exhibit C:

Bus Driver*	1–2 years	3–4 years	5+ yrs
Monthly:	236.86	265.79	294.72
Mileage:	.37	.40	.44
Hourly:	8.37	9.4	10.42
Mileage:	.37	.40	.44

* 2. Minimum trip payment shall be the greater between the mileage rate and the hourly rates.

One time payment of $100 per employee, July 1, 2006.

* * *

Comparables

The parties agreed to external comparables from a previous arbitration. These districts are the following: Beecher–Dunbar–Pembine, Coleman, Crivitz, Gillett, Goodman–Armstrong, Lena, Marinette, Niagara, Peshtigo, Suring, and Wabeno.

Background

As with all of these cases, both parties introduced substantial evidence regarding the financial state of the District. There is no question that the District was in extraordinary, dire straits prior to the passing of the third referendum in August of 2008. The Annual Financial Report of June 30, 2007 sets forth the poor financial condition of the District at that time. As the District Administrator succinctly summed it up for the community in October of 2007, the overall tax levy would be dropping by 3.44% or 3.12% in spite of a drop in state aid by 2.66% over the previous year. Declining enrollment and significant increases in equalized value had resulted in a massive loss of state aid since 1996–1997, decreasing from 58.6% to 14.98% in 2007–2008. Property values were rising, student enrollment decreasing and state aid funding dependent upon property value per student was decreasing. As of June 30, 2007, the general fund had a fund deficit of $55,280. Certain portions of the governmental fund balances are reserved and not available for appropriation or are legally restricted for use for a specific purpose. As of June 30, 2007, various fund balances were reserved as follows: (1) General Fund Prepaids—$25,227, (2) Debt Service—$158,664, and (3) Community Service—$31,886 totaling $215,777.

As of October 2007, the District could not balance its budget as total revenue had dropped by $66,685 while expenses dropped by $2,030 over the previous year's revenue and expenditures.

In March of 2008, the teachers' bargaining unit tentatively agreed to the concessions. By June of 2008, the District had commenced dissolution proceedings, concluding that, absent the voters passing a referendum, the District must enter into some form of bankruptcy. According to Exhibit 23 and the testimony of the District Administrator, the District currently owes $743,600 as of March 27, 2008 in principal in unfunded pension liability which must be retired by March of 2023. The District has been paying approximately $77,000 a year in interest on this amount. If there is no pay down on this amount, interest costs from 2009 to 2023 will be $392,213. The Board's Treasurer testified that the District wanted to pay approximately half of the principal remaining, $330,000, in 2008–2009 and the second half of the principal in the next year, thus saving the District the interest payments in future years.

Furthermore, at the end of the 2007–2008 school year, the District ended up with a negative Fund 10 balance of $129,401, which affected the interest costs on short-term borrowing. The Business Manager confirmed that the projected deficit before the referendum passed was approximately $230,000. Finally on the third try, on August 19, 2008, a referendum was approved to exceed the revenue caps on a non-recurring basis in the amount of $675,000 for ten (10) years. The District's Business Manager testified that as a result for the 2008–2009 year, the District projected a surplus in the fund of $129,000 so that after this year, the net fund balance would be at zero.

The District took out short-term loans of $2,400,000 for the 2009–2010 year with interest costs of about $103,000.

However, with the passage of the third referendum, the representations of both parties as to the District's current and future financial status must be thoroughly examined. Furthermore, in light of the dramatic negative impact that the District's proposal will have on the bargaining unit as a whole, but especially the bus drivers, it is appropriate to view the District's financial status vis-à-vis its proposal with especially strict scrutiny.

Wages

With the exception of Lena, a District where the support staff is not represented by a Union, all of the comparables have settled for hourly amounts in excess of the $.29 per hour requested by the Union for both 2007–2008 and 2008–2009. Only Lena took a wage freeze for both years. For 2007–2008, Niagara and Peshtigo agreed to $.30 per hour with Marinette, Coleman, and Crivitz agreeing to ranges depending on job classification from $.30 to $.50. Wabeno agreed to $.50, Gillett, $.55, Beecher–Dunbar–Pembine, $.35, and Suring $.70. For 2008–2009, based upon Union Exhibit 12 A, Lena and Peshtigo are either unknown or at $.00, while all other settled support staffs have agreed to increases between $.30 and $.70. The undersigned has reviewed the tables set forth by the District and considered its argument that its wages are regularly at or above the average wages found in comparable districts. Accepting the District's offer will result in erosion of Wausaukee's ranking among the comparables for various job classifications, especially at the base rates, e.g., base wages for building custodians, building secretaries, teacher's aids and cooks. Notwithstanding the District's contention, there is no question that the external comparables with regard to wages favor the Union's offer.

Internal comparables with respect to wages, however, strongly favor the District. There are only two represented bargaining units in the District, the teachers,' or professional unit, and this support staff unit. Recognizing that the District intended to dissolve, the teachers agreed to a wage freeze for both years along with the $1000 per year bonus. It may have been a "poor bargain," as the Union here argues, but nevertheless, it was and is the agreement that the teachers ratified based upon the circumstances at the time they settled, i.e., no referendum had passed and the District was taking steps towards dissolution.

The average teacher's salary for 2007–2008 was $49,981. For 2008–2009, it was $46,914. Under the teachers' settlement, the average bonus per teacher for 2007–2008 was $653 and for 2008–2009, it was $878. For the teachers' bargaining unit, the bonus compared to salary was 1.13% for 2007–2008 and 1.87% for 2008–2009.

In contrast, the average salary per employee of the support staff for 2007–2008 was $14,844. In 2008–2009, it was $15,317. The average bonus under the District's offer per employee was $510 for 2007–2008 and $527 for 2008–2009. For the support staff, the bonus compared to salary was 3.43% for 2007–2008 and 3.44% for 2008–2009. The District offer provides each employee with $.48 per hour in 2007–2008 and $.48 per hour in 2008–2009.

* * *

Health Insurance

The same analysis generally applies to health insurance. * * *

Under the District's offer for current support staff working in excess of 1820 hours (full-time employees) who elect the single premium, the District will pay 90%. For new support staff hired after July 1, 2008, the District will pay 80%. Three of the comparable districts pay 100% and two pay 90%. The remainder range from 92.5% to 95%. For those opting for the single premium, the comparable average is 93.8%. Looking at those working 1260 hours, the District would pay 90% (80% for new employees) while the comparable average is 89.44%. At 1080 hours, the District's contribution would be 63% (56% for new employees) while the comparable average is 68.34%. For family premiums, a similar analysis finds that for 1820 hours, three districts pay 100%, two pay 90% with the remainder ranging from 95% to 92%. The comparable average is 93.88%. For those employees working 1260 hours, one district pays 100%, one pays, 92.5%, six pay 90% and the remainder range from 64% to 87.5%. The comparable average is 88.67%. The District would pay 90% or 80%. At 1080 hours, one district pays 100%, one pays 95%, two pay nothing, four pay 90%, and the remainder range from 52% to 79%. The comparable average is 67.68% as contrasted to Wausaukee's 63% or 56%. The District's offer is especially troubling with respect to the percentage that it is willing to pay for new employees in this bargaining unit. New employees will have to contribute much more than employees employed by comparable districts. Based on the above information and considering that Wausaukee's premiums are much lower than those of the comparables, it is concluded that the external comparables support the Union's offer.

The internal comparables, however, support the District's offer. The teacher's bargaining unit agreed to the 90% contribution for current teachers and 80% contribution for new teachers. Notwithstanding the health insurance benefit for retirees, this is a significant concession by the professional bargaining unit and strongly weighs in favor of the District's offer to the support staff.

Total Costs of Wage and Health Insurance Proposals

The District costed its offer and the Union's offer. The Union did not provide independent costing information. Relying upon the District's costing (without considering its representations as to costs associated with abolishing pro rata contributions for health insurance and considering a $.29 hourly raise for bus drivers each year), the total package costs of the

District's offer for 2007–2008 will be $606,132 versus the cost of the Union's offer at $609,243. The difference for 2007–2008 is $3,111. For 2008–2009, the cost of the District's offer will be $522,585 versus the Union offer's cost of $574,096, the difference being $51,511. For the two years, the difference in total package costs is $54,622.

Sub–Contracting Proposals

The District strongly asserts that the cost of the wage and health proposals is not the real cost of the Union's offer because, should the Union's final offer be selected, the District will be forced to spend substantial sums of money to update it buses, transportation facility, and to hire management personnel. In fact, it concludes its brief by arguing that accepting the Union's final offer will cost the District between $688,348 and $840,742 more than the Board's offer over the next four years. A substantial amount of this sum is premised upon assumed savings from subcontracting the bus operation to a private contractor or, in the alternative, having to update transportation facilities and the buses themselves.

Four points should be made with respect to the District's proposal to subcontract. Much of the evidence that it presented at hearing is speculative, based upon forecast models with attendant costs. It is also based upon anticipated savings in the future from subcontracting. This will be addressed below. Second, approximately 73% of the comparable districts do not have in-house bus drivers and do not have to maintain buses, and facilities for their care and upkeep. The record is unclear as to whether or not they have transportation managers or directors but they clearly do not have to employ mechanics for the upkeep of buses. Third, there is no external comparable which possesses the subcontracting language that the District proposes and it is clearly a departure from the *status quo*. Finally, the right to subcontract the bus driving, in this instance, eliminates forty-five percent of the positions within this bargaining unit and is not likely to be a proposal to which a union could agree at the bargaining table even if it were offered a very substantial *quid pro quo*.

The Union would have the undersigned accept some version of the following: Although the District was in bad financial shape, voters have now passed a referendum funding it for the duration of this agreement. Because the District is now solvent, the Union's modest wage offer, along with its concession on health insurance, should be found more reasonable and the arbitrator should reject the District's subcontracting proposal under a traditional failure to meet its burden to change the *status quo* and insufficient *quid pro quo* analysis.

The District, on the other hand, insists that this unit involuntarily accept the same sacrifices made by the teachers, the only other represented unit employed by the employer. It asks the undersigned to project much farther than the term of the collective bargaining agreement both expenses and savings to be incurred with regard to its transportation operations. To support these concessions, the District argues that it is uniquely situated among its comparables with respect to its poor economic future. In its view, this unique situation justifies and makes its offer the more reasonable.

Hyperbole and simplicity aside, both the subcontracting proposal and determinations about the reasonableness of both offers rest in ultimate conclusions and analysis about the financial state of this District as compared to other comparable districts in the past, at present, and as best as can be anticipated, in the near future.

Both parties agree that prior to the passage of the third referendum, the District's financial picture until August of 2008 was bleak and, in fact, bleaker than its comparables. The * * * District has made a persuasive case that it lags behind its comparables because its revenue limit per member is $229 less than the average of the comparables for 2006–2007. It has shown that its enrollment is declining and is projected to continue to decline as a result of open enrollment and other factors, which affects the state aid formula now and into the future. The formula is based upon $6,300 in state aid for every student. In 2006–2007, the gap between the District and its comparables in revenue limit funds increased from $136,240 in 2005–2006 to $144,957 in 2006–2007. Because of the declining enrollment, the District has been forced to deficit spend for each year since 2000–2001, spending down its fund to a negative balance of $55,280 at the beginning of 2007–2008 with a negative fund balance of $129,401 at the end of the 2007–2008 school year. The negative fund balance and other District financial problems affected its ability to short-term borrow during the summer prior to 2008–2009. This difficulty in securing short-term loans has been heightened due to the status of the economy and financial markets as a whole. Not as clear, and certainly subject to dispute by the Union, is the present financial status of the District after the passage of the third referendum. One clear measure of current financial status of the District as compared to its comparables is the extent to which all of the districts continue to have unfunded pension liability obligations. * * * Six of the ten comparables were sufficiently stable financially to pay off their unfunded pension liability entirely. While Marinette's status is unknown, Coleman and Goodman–Armstrong have made significant payments in paying off some of the principal. Because Wausaukee was in such bad financial shape during the period in which these other districts were beginning to address their unfunded pension liability, it was not able to reduce the principal. Should the District continue to make minimal payments on this debt, it will incur over $400,000 in interest costs. Furthermore, the District does not have 15 to 20 percent of its expenditures in its general fund balance which has affected its ability to engage in short-term borrowing. When Wausaukee's desire to retire its principal on the unfunded pension principal within two years with the referendum monies, and to maintain a larger general fund balance ratio to debt, so as to save on the interest payments, is viewed in this context, it is reasonable.

Transportation costs and transportation aid must also be considered. Union Exhibit 9e makes it clear that Wausaukee, from 2001–2002 to 2006–2007, has consistently ranked 2nd or 3rd (with the exception of 2002–2003 when it ranked 4th) in receipt of transportation aid. Wausaukee possesses the largest area in square miles of all the comparables at 420.66 square miles, the second largest being Wabeno at 327.45. Due to the large distances that it must cover in the transportation of pupils, its transportation costs including fuel alone will be larger than those of comparable districts. For 2006–2007, the District had total transportation costs of $337,504. The District spent no monies since 2003 in upgrading its fleet of buses. The District has a signed contract with the subcontractor for $323,162 in 2009–2010, for $334,472 for 2010–2011, for $346,179 in 2011–2012, and $358,295 in 2012–2013, capped at 3.5% increases for the next three school years. Even assuming the undersigned permits the District to subcontract its transportation service, Exhibit 31 projects a Fund 10 Deficit of $221,386 by 2012–2013. This projection also includes an unfunded pension liability payment of $343,677 in 2009–2010. Under various other scenarios with the same pension liability payment, were the District to purchase two buses at $83,000 each and to outsource bus repair (Exhibit 30), the projected deficit for 2012–2013 will be much higher, $323,260. With the purchase of two buses at $50,000 each, in-house bus repair and the purchase of extra space for a bus garage, the deficit would be $333,450 (Exhibit 31B). With two buses purchased at $65,000 each and the outsourcing of repairs, the deficit would be $287,260 (Exhibit 31A).

The District has introduced evidence that suggests that comparable districts with "in-house" transportation systems have experienced an average annual cost increase of 10.76% per year as compared to 3.44% average annual increases from those who subcontract their services.

It should be noted that all of these scenarios extend out four years and that they are simply projections, it being well nigh impossible to forecast exactly what will occur in a four-year period of time. It should also be noted that under all of these projections the District remains solvent until 2012–2013.

Greatest Weight

From an accounting standpoint, it is obvious that now that the referendum has passed, the District has the funds to meet the Union's offer but feels the need to pay off the unfunded pension liability, to maintain a better general fund to borrowing ratio, and to deal with known transportation costs offered in the contract with the subcontractor. The District wishes to spend the referendum money to get its financial house in order so as to have a more favorable general fund balance of 15 to 20 percent. What appears to be equally evident is that, if the District's projections are accurate, it will have a Fund 10 deficit by 2012–2013 no matter which scenario or offer is selected. The only difference will be the amount of the deficit by the end of 2012–2013. Although the referendum was passed granting $675,000 per year which allows the District to remain solvent, this sum does not permit a great degree of discretionary spending given the unfunded pension liability which the majority of comparable districts have paid off, the expectation of continuing loss of state aid because of continuing loss of enrollment, the small ratio of general funds to expenditures making borrowing difficult, and the need to purchase essentials such as textbooks and other indispensable educational materials which the District had deferred based upon its poor financial condition in the past.

The voters passed the referendum after the third try in large measure as a result of "shared sacrifices" on the part of the teachers and the administration. The "greatest weight" standard, under these circumstances, requires the undersigned to consider the delicate balance between all of these interests. Should the Union offer be selected, it is highly likely that the teachers unit, which sacrificed during this bargaining cycle, will come back seeking to be treated as favorably as the support staff in the next cycle. Moreover, there is a good possibility that the Union's having reaped the benefit of holding out will interfere with the trust the voters had in approving the referendum on the assumption that everyone would "share the pain." Looking at the totality of the situation, the District's offer is preferred over that of the Union under the greatest weight criterion.

Greater Weight

The "greater weight" criterion also favors the District because it has shown that its situation substantially differs from that of the other comparable districts especially with regard to its previous financial state, its large geographic area, and its projected declining enrollments. It is a poor district in one of the poorest geographical areas with declining enrollments and continuing declining state aids based upon those enrollments. In the absence of a change in the state aid formula or new-found prosperity in the counties in which the district is located, the state of the local economy also favors the District's offer.

Other Factors

Section 7r., (a) and (b) are not the subject of any arguments of the parties. Under (c) the "interests and welfare of the public" factor weighs in favor of the District's offer as it contains future costs, especially transportation costs, much better than does the Union's. Furthermore, given that the same individuals will be driving the same buses, but for the private contractor, at least in the near future, the interests and welfare of the public with respect to the quality of transportation services provided will not be adversely affected by acceptance of the District's offer.

Subsection 7r., (d) favors the Union's proposal on both wages and health insurance. Neither offer is favored with respect to the subcontracting issue inasmuch as it appears that over 75% of the comparable districts do not have in-house busing but utilize subcontractors, although the language proposed by the District is definitely a departure from the status quo. Subsection 7r., (e) strongly favors the District's offer with respect to both wages and the health insurance proposal. The fact that the professional bargaining unit accepted the wage freeze and the District's health insurance proposals weighs heavily for the District's offer. Subsection 7r., (f) is not determinative.

Subsection 7r., (g) does slightly favor the Union's offer as the Consumer Price Index for Midwest Size D as of June 7, 2008 and June 8, 2009 is considered.

It is subsections 7r., (h), (i), and (j) which are determinative in the instant dispute. They will be dealt with below.

Subsection 7r., (h) requires the arbitrator to consider "the overall compensation presently received by the municipal employees, including direct wage compensation, vacation, holidays and excused time, insurance and pensions, medical and hospitalization benefits, the continuity and stability of employment, and all other benefits received." With the wage freeze, bonus, and health insurance concessions contained in the District's offer, bargaining unit employees will lose ground in comparisons with the comparable bargaining unit employees. But it is the District's subcontracting proposal which impacts the continuity and stability of employment, at least for the bus drivers in this bargaining unit. The Union urges that a traditional departure from the *status quo* analysis be employed, correctly noting that the District has failed to offer a meaningful *quid pro quo* in the form of the severance bonuses. While a traditional analysis may be appropriate in normal financial times, these are not normal financial times.

Since the hearing in this case, the general economy has gone into a serious recession. There are foreclosures, job losses, and shrinking sources of revenue within the state of Wisconsin. Credit has all but dried up. This unanticipated turn in the general economy is a factor to be considered under subsections 7r., (j) and (i). No one anticipated the severity of the recession even as of the date of the arbitral hearing in this matter. The District has established that throughout the 2007–2008 school year it was experiencing significant budgetary pressures that affected its ability to pay before the referendum and way before the turn of the general economy. Although there has been an intervening subsection 7r., (i) factor, the voters passage of the third referendum, the general economy has "tanked."

Although the referendum has passed, the District has convincingly established that its position remains precarious, more precarious than that of comparable districts, for the future under either offer. The District's offer attempts to pay down debt to save interest costs and to ensure future borrowing at the lowest rates to keep the District financially viable. Under Subsections 7r., (j) and (i) it is preferred.

The undersigned is mindful that this decision removes forty-five per cent of the employees in the bargaining unit from public employment with the auxiliary benefits arising therefrom. They will be assured of employment for the time being under the District's contract with the subcontractor, but the loss of job security and other benefits that they have enjoyed as a result of Union representation will be lost. But for the current economic environment and the compelling case presented by the District of its need to cut or at least assure known, predictable "transportation costs," such a subcontracting proposal without a substantial *quid pro quo* would doom such an offer.

In light of the economic climate as it currently exists, the District has demonstrated that it has taken measures, other than simply failing to provide the average percentage wage increases offered by the other comparable districts, to address its financial difficulties. It has laid off employees, deferred necessary expenditures for textbooks, borrowed short-term and delayed making capital expenditures such as buying new text-books and buses, and delayed paying the principal on its unfunded pension liability. Given the state of the current economic climate, the District has shown the necessity for its proposed departure from the *status quo* with respect to the subcontracting language that it seeks. It has succeeded in persuading the only other bargaining unit in its employ to "share the pain." Given these factors, but in particular the teachers' bargain, the unfunded pension liability, and the future financial projections under both offers, the City's conservative offer in conjunction with its proposed economic strategy is found to be more reasonable.

CONCLUSION

The District's offer with respect to wages and health insurance and total compensation under the greatest weight and great weight criteria is favored. The Union's offer with respect to wages and health insurance as compared to the external comparables is favored as more reasonable. The District's offer with respect to wages and health insurances in so far as the internal comparables is favored. The District's subcontracting proposal is reasonable in view of the financial condition of the District. Because the undersigned is satisfied that the District has shown how the revenue limits, the state aids, and its current situation after the passage of the referendum have affected its budgetary choices and desire to act with economic prudence in the current economic climate, the District's offer on balance is preferred.

NOTES

1. As detailed in the arbitrator's opinion, the Wisconsin statute categorizes factors as, "greatest weight," "greater weight," and "other factors." Do you think the arbitrator would have reached the same decision if the statute did not rank the factors in such a manner?

2. The arbitrator found that the external comparables favored the union's final offer. Nevertheless, she awarded the employer's final offer. Why? Under what circumstances, if any, should an arbitrator issue an award that is contrary to the wages and working conditions in comparable communities?

3. The award allowed the employer to subcontract its transportation services, eliminating the bus drivers who comprised a substantial portion of the bargaining unit. A major reason was the cost to the employer of purchasing new buses and other costs associated with continuing to provide transportation in house. Many of these costs were the result of decisions made by the employer over the years, such as decisions to defer maintenance on its fleet of buses. Should an employer be able to create the conditions that result in higher costs in subsequent years and then rely on those higher costs to justify its proposal to contract out bargaining unit work?

4. Recall the discussion in chapter 8 concerning whether the decision to subcontract should be a mandatory subject of bargaining. Revisit that discussion in light of the instant case.

5. To what extent should an arbitrator take into account extraordinary economic events such as the crash of the housing market that occur during the course of the proceeding?

3. TYPES OF INTEREST ARBITRATION

Three types of interest arbitration have developed: conventional, final offer package and final offer issue-by-issue. In conventional arbitration, the arbitrator may issue an award anywhere between the parties' final offers. Conventional arbitration maximizes arbitrator flexibility and enables the arbitrator to craft the most reasonable and equitable award under the circumstances. However, conventional arbitration has been criticized as having a "chilling effect" on the bargaining process. Parties lack incentive to reduce the number of issues proceeding to arbitration. Parties, concerned that the arbitrator will "split the difference," tend to present positions that are not truly their final offers. The parties' concerns turn into a self-fulfilling prophecy as the arbitrator, facing two unreasonable offers, issues an award in between them. In subsequent years, with their concerns reinforced, the parties continue to hold something back for the arbitrator, thereby inhibiting their reaching agreement and sending them back to arbitration. In this manner, conventional arbitration has a "narcotic effect," that is it becomes a habit that the parties seem unable to break.

As an antidote to the chilling and narcotic effects, a number of states have instituted final offer package arbitration. In such proceedings, the arbitrator is required to award either the union's or the employer's final offer as a whole; that is the arbitrator may not "split the difference." The expectation is that each party will avoid unreasonable offers and will avoid holding something back out of fear that the arbitrator will award the other party's final offer. The *Wausaukee School District* award excerpted above is an example of final offer package arbitration.

Some states attempt to preserve arbitrator flexibility while mitigating the chilling and narcotic effects of conventional arbitration by requiring final offer issue-by-issue arbitration, where the arbitrator must award the final offer of one of the parties on each issue but may award one party's final offer on one issue and the other party's final offer on a different issue. As the following case illustrates, this approach also raises issues.

WEST DES MOINES EDUCATION ASSOCIATION v. PUBLIC EMPLOYMENT RELATIONS BOARD

Iowa Supreme Court, 1978.
266 N.W.2d 118.

MASON, J.

The Public Employment Relations Board (PERB) appeals from the judgment of the Polk District Court reversing a declaratory ruling issued by PERB upon petition submitted to it by the West Des Moines Education Association (Association). In its ruling PERB held the phrase "impasse item" as used in Sections 20.22(3) and 20.22(11) of the Public Employment Relations Act (Act) as it existed in the Code of 1973 meant subject category and, consequently it held the parties must submit their final offers of a subject category to the arbitrator. The court in its judicial review of the PERB ruling reversed the PERB and determined the phrase "impasse item" referred to any word, clause, phrase, sentence or paragraph upon which the parties were in disagreement.

At this point it is necessary to explain certain matters about arbitration and to explain how the Public Employment Relations Act works. In its brief to this court the PERB set out explanations of both matters which are particularly succinct. It stated:

* * *

> In conventional arbitration, the arbitrator tailors a resolution which resolves the bargaining impasse. The arbitrator can, and many times does, fashion a remedy somewhere between the last offers of the parties.
>
> * * *
>
> "However, a problem commonly perceived concerning a conventional arbitration is its 'narcotic effect.' This problem is believed to stem from the arbitrator's real or imagined tendency to 'split the difference' between the parties' positions. Management argues that because the employee organization is primarily the demanding party in negotiations, with conventional arbitration as an end result, true collective bargaining will not occur if the employee representative feels ultimate victory lies in the hands of the arbitrator rather than at the bargaining table. In other words, the availability of conventional arbitration will have a 'chilling' effect on the parties' incentives to bargain in good faith."
>
> "In order to limit this chilling or narcotic effect, Legislatures have developed a form of arbitration which circumscribed the arbitrator's discretionary power—final-offer arbitration. Final-offer arbitration limits the arbitrator to choosing between the last and the best offer of one party or the other on an entire package basis or on an

issue-by-issue basis based upon a rule of reasonableness generally spelled out in the enabling legislation. The virtue of this type of arbitration is that it is final and binding on the parties based upon their proposed last and best offers without granting the arbitrator an undue amount of discretion. Thus, there is an element of coercion which encourages mutual agreement because a third party will select one of the offers as binding without compromise between them. In other words, 'final offer arbitration should not have a chilling effect because it will function as a "strikelike" mechanism by posing potentially severe costs of disagreement in a manner that conventional arbitration does not.' If the parties are sensitive to what will be perceived as reasonable by the arbitrator, they will tend to tailor their final offer in that manner."

Rynicki and Gausden, Current Trends in Public Sector Impasse Resolution, *State Government*, Autumn 1976 at 274–76.

* * *

Arbitration under the Public Employment Relations Act is but the last of three steps in the statutory procedure. The first step in this process is mediation. Section 20 of the Public Employment Relations Act provides for the appointment of a mediator at the request of either party to the dispute. The mediator's function is to guide the parties toward a resolution of the dispute by persuasion, by analysis, and by seeking modifications in each side's position. Mediation is not an adjudicative or quasi-adjudicative process. The number of issues which are unresolved going into mediation is reduced substantially during this process and typically, where complete settlement is not achieved, only a handful of issues remain for the next step in the process.

Failing a settlement of the dispute in mediation, Section 21 of the Public Employment Relations Act requires the appellant Board to appoint a *factfinder*. The factfinder is required to conduct a hearing, take evidence and issue written findings of fact and a recommendation for the resolution of the dispute. The factfinder is not limited to the final offers of the parties when making his recommendation but is permitted to recommend any solution. We submit that the definition of impasse item sought by the appellee is more appropriately restricted to a proceeding in front of a factfinder who does not function under a statutory mandate wherein he must choose one of two offers submitted to him.

* * *

The parties are not compelled, however, to accept the factfinder's report and either party may request, under Section 22 of the Public Employment Relations Act, the appointment of a panel of three arbitrators or a single arbitrator.

* * *

The Iowa "final offer" scheme contains a wrinkle not found elsewhere and not at issue here wherein the arbitrator may choose among not only the offers of the parties, but also may choose the position taken by the factfinder on the issue.

Thus, in a contract negotiation, the parties would ordinarily commence with all items at issue and unresolved and would proceed through few or many negotiation sessions to seek and reach agreements on numbers of issues.

Then if they require the help of neutral third parties, the Public Employment Relations Act provides a system which clearly contemplates a continued narrowing or reduction of the unresolved issues. This process continues to the last point, final offer arbitration, known also as last offer arbitration, or forced-choice arbitration, which is designed to encourage hard bargaining by the parties before they resort to arbitration. Final offer interest arbitration enables "the parties to retain maximum participation all the way up to finalization of a decision with minimum exercise of power by a third party."

[In a declaratory ruling, the state PERB opined that, if the parties had reached agreement on all elements of a grievance procedure except the question whether a grievance could be filed by the association (as distinguished from an employee), that question would be an "impasse item" within the meaning of the statute. If there were disagreements over that question and a number of other questions relating to the grievance procedure as well (e.g., whether the procedure should apply to claimed violations of school board policy as well as contract violations, the time limits applicable to the filing of grievances, whether group grievances should be permitted, and whether arbitration should be binding or advisory), then all the points in dispute relating to the grievance procedure would collectively constitute an "impasse item," and the arbitrator would choose between the positions of the parties on a "package" basis. The association, contending that each point in dispute constituted a separate "impasse item," sought review of PERB's decision in court, and was successful at the trial level. Portions of the Supreme Court opinion discussing the applicable procedure and standard for review are omitted.]

The phrase "impasse item" is not defined in Chapter 20, The Code [IOWA CODE ANN. § 20]. The parties here do not dispute the meaning given the word in the Act: "'Impasse' means the failure of a public employer and the employee organization to reach agreement in the course of negotiations." IOWA CODE ANN. § 20.3(10). Their disagreement centers around the word "item." The Association contends the word refers to any word, clause, phrase, sentence or paragraph while the other parties here argue it refers to a subject category of negotiable items.

* * *

Our research indicates the majority of researchers and writers on the topic of final offer arbitration agree that where subject category or package final offers, rather than issue by issue final offers, must be submitted to the arbitrators, the goals of final offer arbitration are more nearly fulfilled.

In *Final Offer Selection–Panacea or Pandora's Box?,* 19 N.Y.L.F. 567, 578–79 (No. 3, 1974), appeared the following pertinent comments by Arnold M. Zack:

> The choice in final offer selection should be between total packages rather than issue by issue. Although it is true that a more equitable resolution might be achieved if the decisions were made on an issue by issue basis, and certainly the arbitrators would be more comfortable with this arrangement, it must be borne in mind that the sense of reasonableness on the part of the arbitrator and the achievement of the most equitable or desirable agreement, are not the primary purposes of final offer selection. Rather, the objective is independent settlement by the parties. The greater the risk to each party of submitting a final offer, the greater the likelihood of settlement. Each party must run the risk of its whole package being thrown out because of the unreasonableness or unacceptability of even one element therein. Only in that way can the greatest pressure be exerted on the parties for direct settlement. Indeed, to the extent that a whole package may be thrown out because of one element which is deemed objectionable by the arbitrator, * * * the prospect is improved for future voluntary settlements.
>
> Issue by issue arbitration encourages leaving political and low priority demands on the table, wasting the time and money of both parties and cluttering the procedure. Forcing the parties to drop such demands or place them in the final offer, is likely to dispose of most, if not all, such items. There are, of course, situations where it is not politically feasible for a party to voluntarily withdraw such items. To provide for situations where the negotiators on both sides of the bargaining table recognize the need for saving face, there should be a mechanism permitting them to 'get off the hook.' A factfinding or an ancillary 'informed award' [occurs when the negotiators privately work out a settlement of the impasse and the arbitrator adopts the results thereof as his award] arbitration procedure would serve such end.
>
> It should be noted that the final offer selection procedure does not easily lend itself to issue by issue determination. Multiple proposals are too often intertwined and dependent upon one another. For example, whether certain fringe benefits should be granted, or more para-professional aides hired, depends upon the total amount of money allocated to the entire package. Twin issues such as whether or not an additional step should be added to the increment schedule, or longevity increases granted, cannot practically be separated in an

issue by issue final offer selection. Such related items are best handled on the package basis.

If the objectives of final offer arbitration are to be carried out it is plain they will best be carried out through a system whereby the parties must make final offers on subject categories.

Chapter 20 contains provisions which indicate to us the legislature intended to carry out the objectives of final offer arbitration through a system mandating subject category final offers.

Section 20.9 delineates the scope of negotiations between the parties. It provides in pertinent part as follows:

> The public employer and the employee organization shall meet at reasonable times, including meetings reasonably in advance of the public employer's budget-making process, to negotiate in good faith with respect to '*wages, hours, vacations, insurance, holidays, leaves of absence, shift differentials, overtime compensation, supplemental pay, seniority, transfer procedures, job classifications, health and safety matters, evaluation procedures, procedure for staff reduction, in-service training* and other matters mutually agreed upon.' " (Emphasis supplied.)

As the IASB correctly points out the emphasized portion of this provision deals with subjects of negotiation, not with the individual words, phrases, clauses, sentences or paragraphs of these subjects. This provides strong evidence the legislature intended subject categories to be submitted to the arbitrator.

Sections 20.21 and 20.22(11) also provide indications the legislature intended to achieve the objectives of final offer arbitration through establishment of a system of subject category final offers. Section 20.21 provides for a factfinder who is to make recommendations for resolution of the impasse reached between the public employer and public employee organization. Section 20.22(11) makes clear the arbitrator may choose only one of three positions, that of either party or that of the factfinder.

In our system the factfinder is a neutral who would be expected to recommend to the arbitrator the most reasonable offer. The arbitrator, mindful of the factfinder's neutrality, will often be prone to choosing the factfinder's position in making his award. This propensity will force the parties to make more reasonable offers because the party who wins over the factfinder will enter arbitration with a powerful ally. The party which fails to have the factfinder recommend its position will be forced to think long and hard before it continues onto arbitration.

In addition, Section 20.22(4)(d) makes the "losing" party at factfinding level even less likely to continue on to arbitration. This Section requires the parties to pay the costs of arbitration. A losing party who continues on to arbitration and loses will have a difficult time explaining to its constituents why it incurred the expense of arbitration when the probability of losing was so great.

In our opinion these Sections are an attempt to carry out the objectives of final offer arbitration. Together they make it imperative that the parties present reasonable offers at the factfinding stage, which in itself promotes settlement. They encourage settlement after factfinding and prior to arbitration.

* * *

In order to carry out this legislative intent we interpret the phrase "impasse item" means subject categories which requires the parties to submit to an arbitrator their final offer on a subject category basis. Each subject category submitted shall constitute an impasse item.

The PERB was correct in its interpretation of the phrase and in its answers to the questions presented by the Association. The trial court was incorrect in its interpretation and in its answers.

NOTES

1. Iowa's use of the factfinder's recommendation in its final offer, issue-by-issue arbitration is a unique form of final offer arbitration which has attracted much interest because parties typically settle after factfinding since experience has shown that arbitrators often favor the factfinder's recommendations.

2. In 1991, Iowa amended its Public Employment Relations Act to exempt bargaining units of teachers from the requirement to go to factfinding. Since 1991, teachers may proceed directly to interest arbitration. IOWA CODE § 20.21. Why might the legislature have done this?

3. Iowa uses a "laundry list" approach to determining what are mandatory subjects of bargaining. Would the case have been decided the same way in a state which generally requires bargaining on "wages, hours and terms and conditions of employment"?

As Arnold Zack (quoted with approbation by the court in the *West Des Moines* case) stated, issue-by-issue final-offer arbitration may produce decisions with which the arbitrator is comfortable, but it is not as likely as final-offer package arbitration to produce overall settlement by the parties. In final offer issue-by-issue arbitration, parties may add unimportant issues to the impasse list because they feel they must give the arbitrator something to award the other side. Furthermore, some proposals are intertwined and dependent upon others. Realistically they cannot be separated. The reverse is also sometimes true; that is, a matter may be characterized as presenting one issue when in reality there are two issues. To deal with these concerns, a number of states require the arbitrator to select the entire final offer of one side. Such final offer package arbitration may maximize the likelihood that the parties will settle but it too presents concerns.

OREGON STATE POLICE OFFICERS ASSOCIATION AND OREGON DEPARTMENT OF STATE POLICE

Unpublished Award of Arbitrator Howell K. Lankford, 2000.

LANKFORD, ARB.

This is a statutory interest arbitration proceeding under the Oregon Public Employees Collective Bargaining Act, OREGON REV.STAT. 243.650 et. sec. The bargaining unit consists of about 148 FTE non-sworn employees, and a bit less than 600 sworn employees, of the Department of State Police. * * *

The parties have reached agreement on the majority of their new, 1999–2001 contract; and the present case addresses their dispute primarily over education/certification incentives—which is far the most costly issue—and over several selective wage rate incentives.

* * *

FACTORS

The statutory list of factors to be considered in interest arbitration was changed substantially under SB–750. Much of the body of accumulated interest arbitration decision and case law arose under the prior version of OREGON REV.STAT. 243.742. Although the current version of the interest arbitration statute has been in place for some years now, it is useful in this case to begin by comparing it with its predecessor. (The current statute appears in proper order, and the pre SB–750 version is rearranged to make the equivalent provision appear beside the current language.)

Pre SB–750	CURRENT LANGUAGE
(4) Where there is no agreement between the parties * * * and wage rates or other conditions of employment under the proposed new or amended agreement are in dispute, the arbitration panel shall base its findings, opinions and order on the following factors, as applicable:	(4) Where there is no agreement between the parties * * * **unresolved mandatory subjects submitted to the arbitrator in the parties' last best offer packages shall be decided by the arbitrator. Arbitrators shall base their findings and opinions on these criteria giving first priority to paragraph (a) of this subsection and secondary priority to subsections (b) to (h) of this subsection as follows:**
(a) The lawful authority of the employer.	[There is no express equivalent in the current language of the statute.]
(b) Stipulations of the parties.	[This element in now designated "(g)."]
(c) The interest and welfare of the public *and the financial ability of the unit of government to meet those costs.* [The italicized language was expanded into subsection (b).]	(a) The interest and welfare of the public. **(b) The reasonable financial ability of the unit of government to meet the costs of the proposed contract**

Pre SB–750	CURRENT LANGUAGE
	giving due consideration and weight to the other services, provided by, and other priorities of, the unit of government as determined by the governing body. A reasonable operating reserve against future contingencies, which does not include funds in contemplation of settlement of the labor dispute, shall not be considered as available toward a settlement.
[There was no express equivalent in the prior language of the statute.]	(c) **The ability of the unit of government to attract and retain qualified personnel at the wage and benefit levels provided.**
(f) The overall compensation presently received by the employees, including direct wage compensation, vacations, holidays and other excused time, insurance and pensions, medical and hospitalization benefits, the continuity and stability of employment, and all other benefits received.	(d) The overall compensation presently received by the employees, including direct wage compensation, vacations, holidays and other excused time, insurance and pensions, medical and hospitalization benefits, the continuity and stability of employment, and all other benefits received.
(d) Comparison of the wages, hours and conditions of employment of other employees performing similar services and with other employees generally: (A) In public employment in comparable communities. (B) In private employment in comparable communities.	(e) Comparison of the **overall compensation** of other employees performing similar services ~~and with other employees generally~~ **with the same or other employees in comparable communities. As used in this paragraph, "comparable" is limited to communities of the same or nearest population range within Oregon. Notwithstanding the provisions of this paragraph, the following additional definitions of "comparable" apply in the situations described as follows:** **(A) For any city with a population of more than 325,000, "comparable" includes comparison to out-of-state cities of the same or similar size;** **(B) For counties with a population of more than 400,000, "comparable" includes comparison to out-of-state counties of the same or similar size; and** **(C) For the State of Oregon, "comparable" includes comparison to other states.**
(g) Changes in any of the foregoing circumstances during the pendency of the arbitration proceedings.	[There is no equivalent provision in the current language of the statute.]

Pre SB–750	CURRENT LANGUAGE
(e) The average consumer prices for goods and services commonly known as the cost of living.	(f) **The CPI–All Cities Index**, commonly known as the cost of living.
[This factor was numbered "(b)" in the prior version of the statute.]	(g) Stipulations of the parties.
(h) Such other factors, not confined to the foregoing, which are normally or traditionally taken into consideration in the determination of wages, hours and conditions of employment through voluntary collective bargaining, mediation, factfinding, arbitration or otherwise between the parties, in the public service or in private service.	(h) Such other factors, ~~not confined to the foregoing, which~~ **consistent with Sections (a) to (g) of this subsection as** are normally or traditionally taken into consideration in the determination of wages, hours and conditions of employment. ~~through voluntary collective bargaining, mediation, factfinding, arbitration or otherwise between the parties, in the public service or in private service.~~ **However, the arbitrator shall not use such other factors, if in the judgment of the arbitrator, the factors in paragraphs (a) to (g) of this subsection provide sufficient evidence for an award.**

The single most substantial change wrought by SB–750, of course, is that the Legislature ended the interest arbitrator's responsibility for crafting the best possible solution—within his or her ability—to each of the several issues in the case and replaced it with a simple duty to choose one package or the other on the basis of the listed factors.

The "package" approach to interest disputes inherently means that more expensive proposals will usually be the "dog" in these cases, and low cost or cost-free issues will more often be the "tail." This unavoidable tendency is also reinforced by the fact that all of the major, specifically listed "secondary" issues are monetary. It is possible to dream up hypothetical situations to the contrary, in which, for example, a cost-free language proposal could be so clearly repugnant to the welfare and interest of the public that an arbitrator would feel obliged to reject that package regardless of the merits of the economic dispute. But this is not such a case, and there are so very many fundamental issues presented here that I will not further expand this written discussion by examining each of the less-expensive portions of the "package" dispute in the same detail that is appropriate for the major—i.e. most expensive—divisions between the two packages.

The change from issue-by-issue to package-based interest arbitration sets a pattern for the other changes which produced the current language of the Section: The overall theme is the Legislature's apparent determination to simplify—or restrict—the factors and issues in these cases. That theme also appears in the specification of a single federal consumer price index for the prior general reference to "the average consumer prices for goods and services"; in the general "limitation" of salary comparators to "communities of the same or nearest population range within Oregon"; and in the specific directive on dealing with contingency funds. But the most sweeping statement of the theme appears at the end of subsection (h), which controls the arbitrator's consideration of "other factors." In the prior version of the statute the "other factors" provision was straightforward *enabling* language. Its general thrust was to allow the interest arbitration process to be a continuation and replication of collective bargaining: whatever sorts of arguments and evidence were traditionally a part of the collective bargaining process for determining wages, etc., those arguments and evidence were proper factors for the consideration of an interest arbitrator.

Although the current "other factors" provision begins much as its predecessor did, the final sentence transposes the subsection from language of enablement to language of restriction: "[T]he arbitrator *shall not use* such *other factors, if* in the judgment of the arbitrator, the factors in paragraphs (a) to (g) of this subsection provide *sufficient evidence* for *an* award." I can find no justification in the overall statutory scheme for not applying this very narrow restriction just as it stands. * * *

* * *

I must conclude that consideration of factors other than those explicitly listed in the statute is permissible only if the interest arbitrator determines that the issue before him or her cannot be decided at all without such consideration. In the case at hand, with respect to the economic and costable portions of the dispute, at least, I cannot conclude in good faith that the specifically listed factors do not provide sufficient evidence for an award, and I am therefore forbidden to consider any additional factors.

There remains one final puzzle in interpreting and applying the current language of subsection (h): Given that the "primary" factor is the "interest and welfare of the public," may an arbitrator analyze *that* primary factor in terms of considerations beyond the listed "secondary" factors? The overall answer, it seems to me, is that the Legislature clearly intended arbitrators to understand that they are generally to restrict their considerations to the factors specifically set out in the statute. Reading the statute in a fashion that allowed interest arbitrators to consider whatever factors and evidence they want as long as it is done under the guise of analyzing the welfare and interest of the public would create a hole in that rule the size of Alaska. I respectfully decline to adopt such an interpretation.

A striking result seems to follow inevitably from the determination to apply the current language of the statute as it appears on its face: In general, the interest arbitrator's award is no longer to be determined by all the factors traditionally considered in the determining wages, hours and conditions of employment "through voluntary collective bargaining, mediation, factfinding, arbitration or otherwise between the parties." It seems to me inescapable that the current statute does not allow my consideration of at least the following such alternative, "traditional" factors.

First, bargaining and contract history does not fall within any of the listed "secondary" factors. In the case at hand, for example, OSP argues that the parties' contract once included substantial incentive pay provisions, which the Association intentionally traded for longevity, and that the reintroduction of incentives would run counter to that trade. Of course, there is nothing to suggest that the parties ever expressly agreed that the contract would never again include an education or certification incentive; but the State is certainly correct in offering this consideration as the sort of "course of dealing" or "bargaining history" evidence that interest arbitrators commonly pay at least some attention to in such disputes. But this is certainly an "other factor," and is therefore barred, in the case at hand, by the unscalable barrier of the threshold finding required in subsection (h).

Second, recent settlement data does not fall within any of the listed "secondary" factors. It is common for one party or the other to support its bargaining position by pointing out that other employers and unions in the same industry and in the same region have settled for the proposed deal. Of course, a pattern of increases may be relevant to comparability; but the traditional argument "there is a wave of 3% settlements, so this unit should accept/get 3%, too" is no longer a proper consideration in interest arbitration.

Third * * *, the current language of the statute limits consideration of cost of living factors to a single Bureau of Labor Statistics CPI index; and an interest arbitrator may not go around that express limitation under the guise of an "other factor."

* * *

Comparability: This is the factor that most often provides the driving force behind wage disputes, so it makes sense to begin the analysis here. The case at hand presents six preliminary issues of comparability which must be addressed before I can deal with the compensation numbers in the record.

First, by far the most costly provision at issue here is the Association's incentive proposal for 3% for an AA degree or Intermediate DPSST certificate and 6% for a BA degree or Advanced certificate. The Department proposes 2% for an AA or 4% for a BA, with no DPSST equivalency.

Virtually every other police employer in the State uses the DPSST training program for new recruits; but OSP trains its own. DPSST gives credit for 680 hours for OSP recruit school and gives credit for the Department's 20 hours per year of required patrol inservice training. Thus, without any formal college *degree* at all, OSP required recruit and inservice training will make an employee eligible for an intermediate certificate after five years of experience (with the addition of 38 education "points") and eligible for an advanced certificate after ten years (with 40 education "points"). The Department therefore characterizes the Association's proposal as a "thinly disguised" pay rate increase, and I will essentially treat it as such for purposes of comparability analysis. * * *

Second, the statute clearly and expressly requires a comparability analysis in terms of "the overall compensation" received by the employees being compared, rather than an analysis in terms of the costs to the employers. "Overall compensation" is defined in the prior subsection; and the Legislature changed the language of the comparability provision to *echo* that term exactly, lest there be room for doubt. Suppose, for example, that an employer pays $10 per hour and is subject to a 20% payroll tax which does not inure to the benefit of the employees. Regardless of whether those employees were the ones at issue in an interest arbitration proceeding or were proposed as comparables, their "overall compensation" would be $10 per hour and not $12. In the real world, of course, it is unusual to find a cost to the employer which indisputably "does not inure to the benefit of the employees"; but not all employer costs automatically translate dollar for dollar as compensation received by the employees. (This case presents a classic example, because both parties propose to include in the primary comparables some states which are FICA participants and some states which are not.) Both the current and the prior versions of the statute clearly require the comparison analysis to reflect "vacations, holidays and other excused time" as part of the "overall compensation" of the employees being compared. Moreover, on the face of the current statutory language the comparison is expressly required to be conducted *in terms of* overall compensation reflecting all such leave time.

Third, the statute requires comparison of the compensation "of *other employees* performing similar services," but of course it does not tell the arbitrator where OSP compensation should be in relation to such a comparison. At the "average"? Above it? At some particular rank? Both parties here propose the four contiguous states as "primary comparables"; but they disagree substantially on how OSP compensation should stand in comparison to that paid in the four contiguous states.

This issue has come up in every one of the parties' prior resorts to interest arbitration. * * * OSP again proposes to compare trooper salaries to what it calls the "average" of the four contiguous states. Of course, the statute does not use the term "average"; and not a single one of the interest arbitrators who have dealt with this unit in prior years has been sold on the "average" of the four comparator states. * * * As far as this record shows, none of the comparable employees of other public employers have the breadth of training and responsibilities of an Oregon State Patrol Trooper or Senior Trooper. It is largely for that reason that every single interest arbitrator who has considered this issue in the past has found, in effect, that OSP compensation should be above the four state "average" and should fall just behind that of similar employees in California, and ahead of similar employees in the other three comparator states. Nothing in the record before me justifies a departure from that conclusion.

The fourth preliminary issue is whether OSP pay should be compared with the rates of pay offered by the largest cities and counties for the same services. * * * This simply recognizes that large police employers are inherently the primary competitors for the limited human resource of skilled police officers. Considering the role that recruitment and retention play in the current version of the Oregon interest arbitration statute, it makes no sense to refuse to compare OSP compensation with that offered by the actual local competitors for these employees' services.

* * *

On the merits: The State's attempt to produce "overall compensation" numbers reflecting "vacations, holidays and other excused time" ran into some mathematical problems. As the Association's Post Hearing Brief points out, the State's analysis essentially backed out the leave numbers it had added in an attempt to reflect these factors. The State's numbers are still useful, however. It makes sense to adjust for differences in total hours of leave—as the statute expressly requires—by subtracting all such leave hours from annual hours of work: Because the employee does not have to work during his or her leave hours, the annual salary actually results from work during a period determined by the annual hours less the total hours of leave. Using the State's numbers, skipping over all the other remaining issues (e.g., how to properly factor in insurance benefit costs, etc.) and calculating all compensation on the basis of the adjusted annual hours (i.e., annual hours less total annual leave hours) produces the results shown in Table 1.

State	Adjusted Pay	% +/− of OR	% +/− of OR
	Trooper at 5 years:		
California	38.92	21.6	14.7
Washington	34.4	7.5	1.4
Oregon	**32.01**		
+ **6%**	**33.93**		
Nevada	29.28	−8.5	−13.7
Idaho	25.96	−18.9	−23.5
	Trooper at 10 years:		
California	39.44	12.5	6.1
Washington	35.36	0.8	−4.9
Nevada	35.18	0.3	−5.4
Oregon	**35.07**		
+ 6%	**37.17**		
Idaho	31.3	−10.7	−15.8

Table 1

These numbers are actually *less* bleak than those of the State's own exhibit (which attempts unsuccessfully to factor in hours of leave). On that exhibit, at the five-year point OSP "adjusted" wages are over 25% behind California and over 7% behind Washington; and at ten years they are almost 16% behind California, 0.4% behind Washington, and a virtual tie with Nevada. The picture gets no brighter when we turn to the Association's "secondary," local comparators. Using the Association's numbers (which are based on 1999–2000 top wage scales, adjusted only for PERS pick-up rate), all of the following local jurisdictions are more than 10% ahead of OSP: Portland, Beaverton, Gresham, Salem, Eugene, and Clackamas, and Washington Counties. Among local jurisdictions, OSP provided numbers only for the counties. According to those numbers—regardless of whether or not they are corrected to actually reflect leave time—only Clackamas County is 10% ahead of OSP at the ten-year point, but all three of the Portland metropolitan counties are over 10% ahead at five years.

The Department did not provide data for major Oregon cities; but its own county data—offered in response to the Association's proposal to compare with the largest Oregon counties—continues the same theme. At the five-year point (using figures corrected for hours of leave as above) the Department is 18% behind Multnomah and Clackamas Counties, 14% behind Washington County, over 9% behind Marion County and 7% behind Lane County. Once again, the ten-year picture is a bit better: 10% behind both Multnomah and Clackamas County, 7.6% behind Washington County, and nearly tied with Marion and Lane Counties.

In short, for what the parties agree to be the "primary comparators," the State's figures set out in Table 1 are as rosy as the picture gets from OSP's point of view. I therefore skip over many subsidiary comparability issues (e.g., the proper treatment of employer and employee insurance costs and of employer retirement contributions), simply because, on the most optimistic picture the record provides, and treating the Association's incentive proposal simply as a disguised wage increase as OSP characterizes it, the maximum 6% education and certification incentive would still leave a Trooper behind Washington—and, of course, quite far behind California—at the ten-year point. At the five-year point, where the total compensation lag is the greatest, an employee with a minimum of 38 education "points" would automatically receive at least the 3% intermediate certification incentive. (On the Department's proposal, such an employee would receive no incentive increase unless he or she had actually been awarded an AA degree.) As far as this record shows, no interest arbitrator who has ever considered the issue has found such a rate of overall compensation to serve the interest and welfare of the public.

Recruitment and Retention: * * *

There is not much dispute that Troopers have not often voluntarily departed from the Department in the past. In the 1997–1999 biennium there were only five resignations (three of which occurred in the course of personnel investigations). The Association argues, and I must agree, that those figures should not be automatically projected into the future, because the seniority composition of the unit is changing substantially. Police officers seldom move in the later part of their careers; but the seniority composition of this unit grows shorter and shorter due to the increase in the sworn workforce coupled with the unusual volume of retirements.

There is no dispute in the record that State Police Officers are extremely expensive to train. A Trooper spends sixteen weeks in the academy and three months with a coach before even being allowed the opportunity to be minimally productive on the road. The unusually long, 18–month trial service period for these employees shows how long it takes—and how much initial wage and training costs must be invested—before OSP can even make an informed judgment about whether or not an applicant will make a good Trooper.

The OSP hires at the bottom. As far as this record shows, the agency makes no particular systematic attempt to lure employees from other police agencies in mid career. That means that the evidence of the agency's "ability * * * to *attract* * * * qualified personnel" is inherently limited: there could be crowds of potential mid-career applicants, or none. OSP has no opportunity to argue that crowds of trained and experienced mid-career police officers are beating on the door; because that door is notoriously closed to lateral transfers. On the other hand, that same policy answers the Association's argument that police officers are not transferring *into* what should be "the premier law enforcement agency in the state" from any other major local police forces.

OSP's applicant pool numbers are not encouraging. In 1995, OSP invited over 4,200 minimally qualified applicants to take the admission test, and 1,157 (about 25%) accepted. At the beginning of 1996, OSP invited 2,279 such applicants, and 761 (33%) accepted. At the beginning of 2000, OSP invited almost 1,500; 587 (39%) tested; and 277 (18% of those invited and 47% of those tested) passed the written and physical tests. After the subsequent interviews, the Department determined that 84 of the applicants were qualified for the 40 vacancies. If those numbers are not untypical, then it takes about 18 minimally qualified applicants to generate one qualified potential OSP trainee. (The record provides no adequate explanation for the apparent steady decline in the numbers of minimally qualified applicants for Trooper positions.)

There were 90 retirements and a total of 14 other departures from the Department's Trooper/Senior Trooper ranks during the 1997–1999 biennium. As long ago as 1996, OSP accurately projected its retirements during the current, 1999–2001 biennium at 110, with an additional 82 during the 2001–2003 biennium. In addition, the Legislature authorized 100 new patrol officers. Filling those 292 vacancies, at the rate of 18 minimally qualified applicants per each qualified potential trainee, would take a pool of over 5,200 minimally qualified applicants; and nothing in this record suggests that such a pool is available at current pay levels. In fact, the OSP recruiting officer told the Association President that OSP, like many other police employers, was having trouble finding adequate qualified applicants.

The record shows no *retention* problem to date. Police officers are among the most employer-stable of public employees. The Association argues that stability is generally less in the early years of a law enforcement career. If that general claim is correct, then the high percentage of recent hires may justify some concern over retention in the near future, given the compensation differential between OSP and large local police agencies. In mid–1999 52% of the force was Senior Trooper; and by January 2000 that percentage had declined to 47. The Association's figures show that a young Trooper with a BA degree could make almost $1,000 more per month by transferring out to the City of Portland. Moreover, as the Association points out, "virtually every mid to large police agency in the Willamette Valley and the State of Oregon offers an incentive based on DPSST certificates [so] a trooper with an intermediate or advanced DPSST can turn that certificate into cash simply by taking a position with another Oregon jurisdiction."

The CPI Index: The Department argues that "compensation for a typical Trooper/Senior Trooper has significantly outpaced the CPI since the inception of the unit." The Department calculates the wage increase since 1992 at 18.9%, compared with an 18.1% increase in the All Cities CPI–W index. Neither party finds any greater support than that in considerations of the CPI index factor.

Ability to pay: The parties agree that they do not have very good data about how many employees would be eligible for the education and certification incentives which account for most of the difference in the costs of the two packages. With that caveat, OSP calculates the 1999–2001 cost difference in the two packages at approximately $200,000.

* * *

There is not much dispute that neither the Department nor the State is carrying more than "a reasonable operating reserve against future contingencies." There is not much dispute that the OSP has substantially reduced capital outlay expenditures (by about $1.3M, or 18% of that item budget). The Department's current budget also reduced costs by almost $1M by delaying three planned recruit schools for periods varying from one to five months. Of course, that delay also retards the appearance of those new Troopers on the street. In addition, OSP cut another $0.7M in costs by holding vacant 11 management, four non-sworn, two sworn fish and wildlife, and one sworn investigative positions. Once again, of course, the consequences of that action is that those employees are not on the street. The Association argues that the relatively modest difference in the costs of the proposals here has actually already been more than covered by additional vacancies maintained since the last visit to the Emergency Board.

The Department proposes to include consideration of the projected cost difference between the two proposals in the next biennium. The Association objects, and I must agree that the primary focus of the ability to pay inquiry must be on *current* ability. There are imaginable situations in which a forthcoming revenue shortfall or economic downturn would have to be addressed as a train already on the track and coming up fast. This is not such a case. * * *

Issues other than the education/certification incentive: As I indicated at the beginning, none of these issues comes close to the overall cost or general public interest significance of the main dispute, and I will therefore recite the issues and underlying facts only briefly.

Bomb Squad differential: Both parties propose increasing the compensation of these employees, but the Association proposes a 10% differential (on the base) and OSP proposes to double the current $5 per hour and to expand the time during which that differential will be paid to include work on "actual or suspected explosive devices" and the destruction of high explosives (adding a definition of that term). OSP employs one of four specialized bomb squads in Oregon, in three teams, in Salem, Medford and Pendleton. The others are part of the Eugene, Salem and Portland police departments. There are six Bomb Technicians in this unit. For most of the Bomb Technicians, those duties account for only a small part of their working time.

As far as the record shows, OSP has consistently filled these positions with internal postings, and there have been no recent voluntary departures from the bomb squad.

Pilot differential: The Department proposes to double the existing differential, from $5 to $10 per hour for actual flying time. The Association proposes 15% of base pay for the first three years in the assignment and 20% thereafter.

OSP uses both single and twin engine planes. Although the larger planes require more skill, training and experience, the current system of paying for pilot differential by the hour does not reflect that difference; and the pilots of the smaller planes actually make more in differential payments. There has been only one opening in the last three years, when the incumbent voluntarily returned to patrol; and there are now several Troopers with some flight time who would like a pilot slot if one were to open in the near future. Flying hours appear to run between about 300 and 500 per year (out of 2080).

Questioned Document Examiner differential: According to the Association's numbers, at the five-year point OSP is just about 60% behind the total compensation of similar employees in California and over 7% behind those in Washington.

Communications System Analyst and CSA 2 differential: The Association proposes a 7% January 1, 2000, and again January 1, 2001. Within the State's workforce, CSAs are employed in OSP, ODOT, Forestry and Corrections. There is no serious dispute that the selective increase proposed for these employees in the case at hand is the direct result of ODOT's setting very significantly higher pay rates for the ODOT employees performing substantially the same work (there titled Information

System Specialists). Although the State attempts to maintain a coherent pay rate system, some large individual agencies have the authority to set their own pay rates. The record does not show whether ODOT's rates were set through inadvertence or were calculated to raid other agencies for the short supply of such skills. At least two such employees left OSP for the higher pay doing fundamentally the same work at ODOT. There are ten such employees at OSP. The Department costs the Association's proposed selective wage rate increase at just over $26,000.

The Department's Post Hearing Brief argues that "one agency's aberrant classification cannot serve as a benchmark for a salary increase * * * for properly classified OSP employees * * *." But of course an underlying axiom for the arbitration of most classification and pay rate disputes is that it does not matter what the employer *calls* any of the employees being compared; what matters is *the work* they do. In this case, there is no substantial dispute that no difference in the character of the work performed by the OSP and by the ODOT employees justifies a substantial pay rate differential between them.

Telecommunicators: The Department proposes two 3% increases (as of July 1, 2000, and January 1, 2001) for these employees to address a chronic recruitment and retention problem. The Association opposes the increase. It agrees that there is a chronic turnover problem, but argues that the record does not suggest that problem is based on compensation. The Association's 1995–97 proposal in interest arbitration included a special increase for these employees; the OSP prevailed in that case. The parties then agreed to a 10% special increase for them in the 1997–1999 contract.

There are about 22 FTE budgeted Telecommunicator 1 positions, and 62 FTE Telecommunicator 2 positions. More than a dozen of those positions are now vacant—including 12 at the Western Regional office in Salem—and have been for a considerable time, despite OSP's attempts to recruit for them. On the other hand, OSP's own numbers seem to show that Telecommunicator 2s are now at 115% of the four contiguous state "average" at the ten-year point. They are 6.5% over California and about 7.25% over Washington (without correcting for the slightly higher total paid leave hours of the OSP employees). Of the 26 departures from these positions in calendar 1998 and 1999, as far as OSP's records show, only three could possibly be characterized as wage-rate-driven, and the employees frequently mention dissatisfaction with mandatory overtime, inflexible scheduling, and conflicts with supervisors. On the other hand, there is no reason at all to doubt the Division Director's testimony that there is an open and competitive market for such call-takers in dispatch centers around the state.

Trades Maintenance Worker 2 & Coordinator differential: The Department proposes a 3% differential for these employees, and the Association proposes instead to add a step at the top of their pay range. The record on this issue is very sketchy; but what record there is shows that employees in the same classification—and performing the same work—in the State's general employee bargaining unit represented by OPEU top out one step higher than the corresponding OSP employees.

Vacation Accrual: The Association proposes to increase the maximum vacation accrual from 250 to 350 hours while not increasing the amount of vacation accrual that an employee may cash out upon termination. The Department argues that there is no comparability data justifying that proposal (California combines vacation and sick leave hours and those numbers are therefore uninstructive); but the limit proposed by the Association is exactly that now applicable to executive service, management service and unclassified unrepresented State employees.

Other language issues: The parties agree that the other minor language changes they propose are not of substantial significance, except that the Association opposes the Department's proposal to incorporate various MOUs into the language of the contract itself. As far as the record shows, that proposal, too, is not of substantial significance.

CONCLUSION:

THE INTEREST AND WELFARE OF THE PUBLIC

The bottom line in this case is pretty simple: Even using the Department's comparability figures, and even without addressing the many disputes about various aspects of those figures, the overall compensation numbers now show that the Department has fallen out of its proper place with respect to the agreed four comparable states, particularly at the five-year point. The substantial number of new hires over the course of this contract makes that decline particularly untimely. The Association's education/certification incentive program amounts to an almost automatic 3% increase at the five-year point. Considering the education/certification proposal as a "thinly disguised" pay rate increase, that increase remedies a comparability picture which no arbitrator who has ever considered this unit has found to be acceptable. Considering the very long start-up time and substantial initial training costs of a Trooper, the loss of only a very few troopers through lateral transfer would ultimately be more expensive than the modest cost of the Association's proposal. Moreover, the addition of the new incentives will make the Department more competitive in the market for the short supply of truly qualified applicants, and particularly for the part of that pool with AA and BA degrees.

There are two unfortunate consequences of the overall superiority of the Association's package: First, if this were an issue-by-issue proceeding, I would certainly award the Telecommunicators the increase proposed by the Department. * * * Second, considered in isolation, nothing in this record begins to justify the Association's proposed 20% differential for pilots of more than three year's tenure. In package-based interest arbitration there is an inevitable hazard that the prevailing package will include one or two quite disreputable minor proposals. This is such a case.

None of the other disputes here weigh very strongly toward one package or the other, so the final answer must be that the Association's education/certification proposal will put the key classifications into nearly their proper relationship to their agreed comparables, particularly at the five-year point which should be most attractive for recruitment purposes. None of the other secondary factors outweighs this consideration, and the interest and welfare of the public will better be served by the Association's package.

NOTES

1. Arbitrator Lankford observes that under final offer package arbitration, the most costly economic issues will drive the decision. Is this appropriate? Does this suggest a disadvantage of final offer package arbitration?

2. Recall the *Wausaukee School District* interest arbitration award excerpted at pages 626–642. Wisconsin, like Oregon, uses final offer package arbitration. Do you think the case would have been decided the same way under final offer issue-by-issue or conventional arbitration? What, if anything, does the *Wauseekee* case add to your evaluation of the advantages and disadvantages of final offer package arbitration?

3. A small municipality and its police union have never had a formal pay plan. The municipality has hired officers "at the going rate," meaning at whatever salary the officer negotiated. The municipality and the union have negotiated across the board percentage increases. Over the years, this has resulted in an irrational salary system. Officers separated by less than two years' experience make widely different salaries while officers separated by more than five years' experience make very similar salaries. The parties agreed to negotiate a formal salary system but reached impasse. The union's final offer provides for uniform step increases at two and one-half year intervals. However, it also provides average pay increases that greatly exceed increases agreed to or awarded in comparable municipalities and are, for some officers, four times the increases in the cost of living. The employer's final offer provides for reasonable average salary increases but leaves the overall salary structure almost as irrational as the status quo. As arbitrator, whose offer will you award?

4. MEDIATION BY THE ARBITRATOR

For many years, Wisconsin experimented with a system known as "med-arb." Med-arb has four essential characteristics. First, the parties have agreed to forego resorting to a work stoppage. Second, the intervention by the neutral is continuous throughout the negotiations process from the moment it enters the med-arb stage. Third, the neutral initially directs his or her energies toward achieving a mediated settlement—one to which the parties themselves agree. Finally, failing that, he or she imposes a settlement which the parties have agreed in advance to accept as binding.

In the mediation phase of med-arb, the neutral is a mediator who can alter the parties' bargaining power by controlling the alternative to a negotiated settlement. Through that modification of bargaining power, the neutral has considerable leverage in pressing the parties to "accept" a settlement. In the arbitration phase, the format is adversarial, that is, the evidence is developed and positions are taken "on the record" in a hearing.

Most jurisdictions have not adopted the med-arb approach. Instead, they provide that, upon exhausting the earlier stages of the statutory impasse procedure, such as mediation and in some states factfinding, either party may demand that unresolved issues be submitted to arbitration. Nevertheless, interest arbitrators frequently mediate and most cases in which arbitration has been demanded ultimately settle. But, consider the following case.

TOWNSHIP OF ABERDEEN v. PATROLMEN'S BENEVOLENT ASSOCIATION, LOCAL 163

New Jersey Superior Court, Appellate Division, 1996.
286 N.J.Super. 372, 669 A.2d 291.

BAIME, J.

This appeal presents a novel question under the Compulsory Interest Arbitration Act. The Act and its implementing regulations permit a mediator in a public employment dispute to serve as the arbitrator in the event that mediation efforts are not successful. We hold that information learned by an arbitrator during the mediation process but not presented at the arbitration hearing may not be considered by the arbitrator in rendering the final decision.

I.

* * * This case arises from a dispute between the Township of Aberdeen and the union representing its police officers. For several years, the Township and the union were parties to a series of collective bargaining agreements. Near the expiration of the 1992–1993 contract, the parties entered into negotiations for a successor agreement. When the negotiations reached an impasse, the union petitioned the Public Employment Relations Commission (PERC) to initiate interest arbitration. Prior to commencement of the formal arbitration hearings, the parties agreed at the suggestion of the arbitrator to engage in mediation. Acting as a mediator, the arbitrator met with the parties jointly and individually on six separate occasions over the course of four months.

* * *

During mediation, both parties agreed upon the need for additional police officers to be hired at an entry level salary below the current salary guidelines. In addition, the Township proposed that the workweek for all police officers be increased from an average of thirty-five hours to forty hours in order to reduce overtime costs and provide greater protection to the public. The additional hours would result in an increase to the base salaries of existing police officers in order to compensate them for the loss of overtime.

On July 14, 1994, the parties entered into a written stipulation permitting the Township to hire additional police officers at a reduced starting salary. The purpose of the stipulation was to allow the Township to hire these individuals immediately so that they could commence training at the police academy rather than waiting six months for the new collective bargaining agreement to be signed. According to the union, the parties also reached an oral understanding that the Township would adopt a forty-hour workweek with a corresponding increase in the base salary of existing police officers. The Township's version is markedly different. It claims that it reserved agreement on the proposed revision of the work schedule and the increase in base salaries pending the approval of its Mayor and Council. Immediately prior to the next scheduled mediation session, the Township announced that it was no longer seeking a forty-hour schedule but preferred to remain with the current thirty-five hour work week. Retaining the thirty-five hour week meant that existing officers would lose overtime pay due to the addition of the newly hired officers without receiving the increase to their base pay resulting from a longer work week. The Township also rejected the union's proposed annual increase in base salaries of 4.5%. The Township's decision was perceived by the union as an act of bad faith, and mediation efforts terminated at that point.

Following protracted arbitration hearings, the arbitrator issued his report in which he adopted the union's final offer on the outstanding economic issues. Although the arbitrator reviewed each of the statutory factors required to be considered by NEW JERSEY STAT.ANN. 34–13A–16g, he additionally made repeated references to information received and statements made during the mediation process. None of these references was grounded in the evidence presented at the arbitration hearings. The arbitrator also described in great detail the Township's shifting positions during the mediation process. * * * The arbitrator repeatedly returned to these subjects in his discussion of the statutory factors, virtually all of which he found to favor the union's proposal.

The Township filed a complaint in the Chancery Division seeking an order vacating the award, and the union counterclaimed. * * * The Chancery Division vacated the award on the ground that the arbitrator had impermissibly relied upon information presented only in the mediation proceedings. In reaching this conclusion, the court found that the arbitrator had been improperly influenced by the manner in which the Township had conducted negotiations during the mediation process. The union appeals. We affirm.

II.

* * *

[W]e conclude that the arbitrator in the present case violated his obligations to act fairly and impartially and to decide the issues solely on the evidence adduced before him at the arbitration hearings. The arbitrator improperly held against the Township the negotiating tactics it had employed during the mediation process. * * * The arbitrator obviously believed that the Township had taken unfair advantage of the union during mediation. Perhaps, there was some justification for this belief, although that is an issue we need not decide. The point to be stressed is that the arbitrator did not have the right to penalize the Township for its negotiating tactics during mediation in the course of applying the statutory factors and rendering his arbitration award.

We know of no reported decision dealing with this precise issue. However, the conclusion we have reached is compelled by important public policy considerations and by regulations promulgated by PERC. Although mandating arbitration, the Compulsory Interest Arbitration Act "was not intended to * * * discourage public employers and their police and fire-fighting employees from voluntarily resolving their differences." Indeed, its provisions do not become operative unless and until negotiations have reached an impasse. Even at this stage, PERC is encouraged to "take such steps including the assignment of a mediator * * * [in order] to effect a voluntary resolution of the impasse." Although the Act does not expressly provide for revision of offers during the process of arbitration, our Supreme Court, and PERC, have recognized that the parties may revise their last offers and enhance their factual support at any time before the conclusion of the arbitration hearings. The importance of mediation is further evidenced by N.J.S.A. 34:13A–16f(3), which provides that "throughout formal arbitration proceedings the chosen arbitrator * * * may mediate or assist the parties in reaching a mutually agreeable settlement." Compulsory arbitration "was thus intended to constitute a 'last resort' measure for the resolution of impasses. * * *"

Mediation would be a hollow practice if the parties' negotiating tactics could be used against them by the arbitrator in rendering the final decision. The parties should feel free to negotiate without fear that what they say and do will later be used against them. While perhaps the analogy is imperfect, it would be unthinkable for a trial court to base its decision on information disclosed in pretrial settlement negotiations. Indeed, evidence of settlement negotiations, including offers of compromise, is generally inadmissible to prove a party's liability for a claim. Such evidence is excluded because it is not relevant to the question of liability and because its admissibility would discourage parties from attempting to settle claims out of court. Negotiations during the mediation process should be subject to similar protection. * * *

We conclude that the arbitrator improperly relied upon information he learned during the failed mediation process when rendering his arbitration decision. Accordingly, the judgment of the Chancery Division vacating the arbitrator's award is affirmed.

NOTES

1. If the success of med-arb in obtaining settlements is based, in part, on the neutral's leverage resulting from the parties' knowledge that if they do not settle, the neutral will decide the issue, does the court's decision undermine that leverage? Alternatively, does the court's decision protect the mediation process by ensuring its confidentiality?

2. Is it feasible to expect an arbitrator to ignore what occurred when the arbitrator was functioning as a mediator? Does the court's decision merely encourage arbitrators to not reveal in their awards the impact of the mediation session on their decisions?

3. Sometimes interest disputes are arbitrated before a three-person panel, with one member of the panel appointed by each party and a neutral chair mutually selected. The use of a three-member panel facilitates the neutral chair's ability to mediate a resolution that becomes the panel's award. Assume that a party-appointed arbitrator tells the neutral, in the presence of the other party-appointed arbitrator, "We can live with the other side's final offer on this issue. Draft the award adopting it, but, for political reasons, I will have to dissent." If the losing party appeals the award, what should be the result?

5. JUDICIAL REVIEW OF INTEREST AWARDS

HILLSDALE PBA LOCAL 207 v. BOROUGH OF HILLSDALE

New Jersey Supreme Court, 1994.
137 N.J. 71, 644 A.2d 564.

POLLOCK, J.

This case * * * involves the sufficiency of a compulsory-interest-arbitration award. Petitioner, Hillsdale PBA Local 207 (Local 207 or the PBA), and respondent, Borough of Hillsdale (the Borough or Hillsdale), could not agree on the terms of a collective-negotiation agreement for the Borough police force for the years 1991, 1992, and 1993. Pursuant to * * * the Compulsory Interest Arbitration Act (the Act), Local 207 petitioned the Public Employment Relations Commission (PERC) to initiate interest arbitration. NEW JERSEY STAT.ANN. 34:13A–16 (Section 16) requires the arbitrator to choose between the parties' final offers. The arbitrator chose Local 207's offer, and the Chancery Division confirmed the award. The Appellate Division reversed, vacating the award and remanding the matter for a new hearing before a new arbitrator. We granted Local 207's petition for certification and now reverse. Although we agree substantially with the Appellate Division that the arbitrator's award did not comply with the requirements of Section 16g, under the circumstances we believe that we should not disturb the award.

I.

* * *

In their negotiations, Hillsdale and Local 207 resolved all non-economic issues for the 1991–93 collective contract, but not two economic issues concerning salary increases and the "banking" of compensatory time beyond a calendar year. In response to Local 207's petition, PERC appointed an arbitrator to conduct compulsory interest arbitration to resolve the two issues.

Hillsdale's last offer proposed banking up to eighty hours of compensatory time and annual salary increases:

1991, 7%; 1992, 6.5%; 1993, 6.2%.

By comparison, Local 207's last offer proposed banking up to 100 hours of compensatory time and semi-annual salary increases. Such increases, which are peculiar to police and firefighter contracts, compound annual salary increases. Local 207 proposed increases:

January 1, 1991, 5%; July 1, 1991, 3%; January 1, 1992, 4%; July 1, 1992, 4%; January 1, 1993, 3%; July 1, 1993, 4%.

Section 16g mandates that interest arbitrators, when choosing between two final offers, shall consider eight factors. The factors include the public welfare, comparisons of salaries and conditions of employment to certain other public and private employees, overall compensation, stipulations of the parties, the lawful authority of the municipality, financial effect on the community, the cost of living, and the continuity and stability of police and fire-department employment.

Before the arbitrator, the dispute centered on a comparison of the parties' final offers with salaries and non-wage benefits paid to police officers in similar communities. * * *

* * * Hillsdale also contended that the police enjoyed more stable and secure employment than other Borough employees and that police salaries were higher than the salaries of those other employees. The Borough pointed out that it had a high tax rate with low assessed valuation per capita, that it depended heavily on the taxation of residential real estate, and that it had limited land available for development. Finally, it also demonstrated that over the preceding nine years Hillsdale police had received a 66% salary increase, which far exceeded the 46% increase in the Consumer Price Index over the same period.

The arbitrator quoted Section 16g, recited the parties' final offers, and selected Local 207's offer, stating:

> Initially it should be noted that the statutory criteria usually dissolves [sic] into a determination of the more reasonable offer. Rarely is a determination reached under any single criteria [sic] which proves dispositive of the issue in and of itself. In this case the expert testimony established to my satisfaction the Borough's ability to pay. Dr. Werner's [Local 207's expert witness'] credentials were impressive and his testimony was convincing. Undoubtedly any award of wages will have an impact on the Borough but no substantially detrimental result was proven by the Borough.

> Analyzing the numerous exhibits, particularly those relating to comparability leads me to the inevitable conclusion that the increases sought by the PBA are reasonable. The only issue remaining is whether it is the more reasonable of the two.
>
> The Association has met that burden also—i.e., proving that its offer is more reasonable. A review of the comparables shows that the Association's request is modest. Although one can certainly question the level of increase in light of the current economic times, nevertheless, this is the neighborhood out there. Clearly the PBA's offer is midstream. * * * Had circumstances been demonstrated that would have created financial difficulties, or operational problems or any difficulty created or worsened by the award of the PBA Last Offer, then Hillsdale's offer may well have been deemed the more reasonable.

Although the Chancery Division confirmed the award, the Appellate Division reversed, finding that the arbitrator's decision was flawed and not supported by substantial credible evidence. The court determined that the parties' failure to adduce evidence on each of the Section 16g factors did not excuse the arbitrator from obtaining such evidence. Reasoning that under Section 16g each factor was presumptively relevant, the court required arbitrators to compel the parties to produce evidence on each factor and to provide a factor-by-factor analysis of their final offers. The Appellate Division explained:

> A presumption that all of the statutory factors are relevant requires parties to submit evidence on each subject, either to negate or reinforce a given factor's relevance. This would afford a proper basis for public interest arbitrators to make an informed decision as to relevance. As a corollary, the interest arbitrators must detail in their opinions the specific reasons why an enumerated factor is not "judged relevant" in arriving at a final determination. This would also facilitate judicial review of public sector interest arbitration awards. See NEW JERSEY STAT.ANN. 34:13A–16f(5). We do not hold that each factor be accorded equal weight. We merely require that the arbitrator's award indicate what factors are deemed relevant, satisfactorily explain why a certain factor (or factors) is not relevant, and provide an analysis of the evidence on each relevant factor.

The court found "from a review of the statutory factors, neither the parties nor arbitrators sufficiently considered the statutory factors set forth in NEW JERSEY STAT.ANN. 34:13A–16g." It then detailed the deficiencies of the arbitrator's award in a factor-by-factor analysis.

II.

In general, compulsory interest arbitration is a statutory method of resolving collective-negotiation disputes between police and fire departments and their employees. * * *

If the parties reach an impasse in negotiations, either party may initiate compulsory interest arbitration by filing a petition with PERC. PERC and the parties then select an arbitrator from a panel of arbitrators maintained by PERC. The parties may also select which terminal procedure the arbitrator will use to resolve the issues in dispute. * * * If the parties cannot agree on a terminal procedure, the parties are confined to the last-offer procedure. Economic disputes, those that involve salaries, insurance, vacations, holidays, and other items having a direct relationship to employee income and can be readily calculated, are resolved as a single package; non-economic issues are resolved on an issue-by-issue basis.

* * *

In reaching a decision, the arbitrator must choose between the parties' final offers. As stated above, Section 16g lists eight factors that arbitrators must consider in making that choice. In general, the relevance of a factor depends on the disputed issues and the evidence presented. The arbitrator should determine which factors are relevant, weigh them, and explain the award in writing. In brief, the arbitrator's opinion should be a reasoned explanation for the decision.

Either party may institute judicial proceedings to enforce the award. Generally speaking, the standard that governs judicial review of interest arbitration is whether the award is supported by substantial credible evidence in the record as a whole. Judicial scrutiny in public interest arbitration is more stringent than in general arbitration. The reason for more intensive review of public interest arbitration is that such arbitration is statutorily-mandated and public funds are at stake. Accordingly, a reviewing court may vacate an award when the decision fails to give "due weight" to the Section 16g factors, when the award has been procured by corruption, fraud, or undue means, when arbitrators have refused to hear relevant evidence or committed other prejudicial errors, or when arbitrators have so imperfectly executed their powers that they have not made a final award.

Although compulsory interest arbitration is essentially adversarial, the public is a silent party to the process. Compulsory interest arbitration of police and firefighters' salaries affects the public in many ways, most notably in the cost and adequacy of police and fire-protection services. Indeed, Section 16g expressly requires the arbitrator to consider the effect of an award on the general public. Hence, an award runs the risk of being found deficient if it does not expressly consider "the interests and welfare of the public."

Our concern in the present case is with the adequacy of the arbitrator's award, a concern that involves both the sufficiency of the evidence and the relevance of the various Section 16g factors. * * *

As the statute states, an arbitrator need rely not on all factors, but only on those that the arbitrator deems relevant. An arbitrator should not deem a factor irrelevant, however, without first considering the relevant evidence. An arbitrator who requires additional evidence may request the parties to supplement their presentations. Contrary to the Appellate Division, however, the arbitrator need not require the production of evidence on each factor. * * * Such a requirement might unduly prolong a process that the Legislature designed to expedite collective negotiations with police and fire departments.

Whether or not the parties adduce evidence on a particular factor, the arbitrator's opinion should explain why the arbitrator finds that factor irrelevant. Without such an explanation, the opinion and award may not be a "reasonable determination of the issues." Neither the parties, the public, nor a reviewing court can ascertain if the determination is reasonable or if the arbitrator has given "due weight" to the relevant factors.

In concluding that an arbitrator must consider all eight factors, we need not go so far as the Appellate Division, which presumed each factor to be relevant to every dispute. A requirement that an arbitrator find facts on each factor, even those deemed irrelevant, would undermine the purpose of arbitration as an expeditious means of resolving contract negotiations. We believe we come closer to satisfying the legislative intent by requiring arbitrators to identify and weigh the relevant factors and to explain why the remaining factors are irrelevant. A reasoned explanation along those lines should satisfy the requirement for a decision based on "those factors" that are "judged relevant." Also, such an explanation should satisfy the requirement that the arbitrator "give due weight" to each factor. Anything less could contravene the Act's provision for vacating an award "for failure to apply the factors specified in subsection g." In sum, an arbitrator's award should identify the relevant factors, analyze the evidence pertaining to those factors, and explain why other factors are irrelevant.

One of the problems in this case results from the arbitrator's emphasis on a comparison of salaries and benefits of police and fire departments in similar communities. * * * Section 16g(2) expressly requires:

> Comparison of the wages, salaries, hours, and conditions of employment of the employees involved in the arbitration proceedings with the wages, hours, and conditions of employment of other employees performing the same or similar services and with other employees generally:
>
> (a) In public employment in the same or similar comparable jurisdictions.
>
> (b) In comparable private employment.
>
> (c) In public and private employment in general.

The terms of Section 16g require more than a comparison of police salaries in other communities. Section 16g(2) invites comparison with other jobs in both the public and private sectors. The arbitrator should also consider the relationship between any such increases and increases in comparable areas of private employment. Having considered such additional information, an arbitrator may still conclude that police and firefighters' salaries in similar municipalities provide the most relevant comparables. If so, the arbitrator should set forth the reasons supporting that conclusion. Missing from the subject award is a reasoned explanation for accepting the PBA's submission of the salary increases from other municipalities. Also missing is an explanation for rejecting other bases for comparison.

Another problem concerns the meaning of the factor pertaining to "the financial impact on the governing unit, its residents and taxpayers." The terms of that factor do not equate with the municipality's ability to pay. As the Appellate Division noted, "it is not enough to simply assert that the public entity involved should merely raise taxes to cover the costs of a public interest arbitration award."

Here, the arbitrator placed on Hillsdale the burden of proving a substantial detriment from the arbitrator's selection of the PBA's final offer. Section 16g(6), however, does not require a municipality to prove its financial inability to meet the other party's final offer. The statutory direction to consider the financial impact on the municipality demands more than answering the question whether the municipality can raise the money to pay the salary increase. Given the existence of financial constraints and budget caps, an award to police or fire departments necessarily affects other municipal employees and the entire municipal budget.

III.

In the present case, the arbitrator's award did not discuss all the Section 16g factors. Instead, it unduly emphasized the comparison with police salaries in other communities and inappropriately relied on the Borough's perceived "ability to pay." * * * Missing from the award is the reasoned explanation required by the Act.

The Chancery Division confirmed the award on December 18, 1991. On May 4, 1992, the court denied Hillsdale's application for a stay, and on May 15, 1992, it granted the PBA's application for an order to enforce litigant's rights. Hillsdale did not seek a stay from the Appellate Division. Instead, it implemented the award by paying five of the six semi-annual payments authorized by the award. Based on the March 17, 1993, judgment of the Appellate Division vacating the award, however, Hillsdale did not implement the sixth and final payment, which was scheduled to take effect on the basis of the increments that took effect from January 1, 1991, through January 1, 1993. Moreover, two police officers retired in reliance on the award before the date of the Appellate Division decision. Under the circumstances, we believe that the appropriate decision is not to disturb the payments that Hillsdale has made to its police officers. Because Hillsdale never implemented the sixth payment, which was scheduled to take effect on July 1, 1993, we remand the matter to the arbitrator for a hearing limited to the officers' entitlement to that payment. We disagree with the Appellate Division, particularly in light of the limited nature of the remand, that the matter should proceed before a different arbitrator.

* * *

The judgment of the Appellate Division is affirmed in part and reversed in part, and the matter is remanded for arbitration limited to choosing between the last offers of the parties for the second half of 1993.

NOTES

1. Intermediate appellate courts in New York have disagreed over whether the arbitrator must expressly address every statutory factor, even those the arbitrator considers irrelevant. Compare *City of Yonkers v. International Association of Fire Fighters Local 628*, 80 A.D.2d 597, 436 N.Y.S.2d 1009 (N.Y.Sup.Ct.App. Div. 2d Dept. 1981) (holding that arbitrator must expressly address each statutory factor) *with Buffalo Professional Firefighters Association v. Masiello*, 50 A.D.3d 106, 850 N.Y.S.2d 744 (N.Y.Sup.Ct.App.Div. 4th Dept. 2008) (holding that arbitrator need not expressly address every statutory factor), *aff'd in part, rev'd in part on other grounds*, 13 N.Y.3d 803, 890 N.Y.S.2d 375, 918 N.E.2d 887 (2009). Why might a court require the arbitrator to expressly address every statutory factor? Does a court's approach reflect that the court regards interest arbitration as primarily a tool of collective bargaining or as an adjudicative process?

2. Interest arbitration often is a time-consuming process. It is common for arbitration awards to be issued long after the prior collective bargaining agreement has expired and sometimes even after the award itself will have expired. Will close judicial scrutiny of interest arbitration awards promote or undermine the primary purpose of interest arbitration statutes of encouraging settlement at the bargaining table?

3. Is close judicial scrutiny necessary for resolving the tension between interest arbitration and democratic values?

4. Courts generally have enforced interest arbitration awards when the awards fell within the authority of the arbitrator(s) and have refused to enforce awards that infringed on managerial prerogatives or otherwise required violations of positive law. Compare *Local 2071, International Association of Firefighters v. Town of Bellingham*, 67 Mass.App.Ct. 502, 854 N.E.2d 1005 (2006), *aff'd*, 450 Mass. 1014, 877 N.E.2d 552 (2007) (enforcing award requiring change from 10 and 14 hour shifts to 24 hour shifts as involving a mandatory subject of bargaining and within the arbitrators' authority) and *Washington County v. Washington Court Association of Professional Employees*, 948 A.2d 271 (Pa.Cmwlth. 2008) (enforcing award increasing county probation officers' workday from 7 ½ to 8 hours because it did not infringe on the judiciary's right to hire fire and supervise its personnel) with *City of Scranton v. E.B. Jermyn Lodge No. 2 Fraternal Order of Police*, 965 A.2d 359 (Pa.Cmwlth. 2009) (modifying award to conform to requirements of financial recovery plan imposed on City under the Municipalities Financial Recovery Act); *City of Scranton v. Fire Fighters Local 60*, 964 A.2d 464 (Pa.Cmwlth. 2009) (same); *Schuylkill Haven Borough v. Schuylkill Haven Police Officers Association*, 914 A.2d 936 (Pa.Cmwlth. 2006) (vacating portion of award

ordering employer to match employee contributions to tax deferred compensation plan because employer lacked statutory authority to match such contributions); *Northampton Township v. Northampton Police Benevolent Association*, 885 A.2d 81 (Pa.Cmwlth. 2005) (vacating award that reduced employee contributions to defined benefit pension plan because arbitrators lacked statutorily required estimate of costs of the reduction prepared by an actuary).

5. When a court finds that part of an award exceeds the arbitrator's authority, should it remand the matter to the arbitrator to reconsider the award or modify the award itself? See *City of Scranton v. E.B. Jermyn Lodge No. 2 Fraternal Order of Police*, 965 A.2d 359 (Pa.Cmwlth. 2009); *City of Scranton v. Fire Fighters Local 60*, 964 A.2d 464 (Pa.Cmwlth. 2009).

6. The New Jersey legislature subsequently enacted the Police and Fire Public Interest Arbitration Reform Act, which took effect on January 10, 1996. The Reform Act provides for conventional interest arbitration unless the parties agree to a different procedure. It also provides for PERC to appoint the arbitrator by lot from a panel of PERC accredited arbitrators, unless the parties agree to a specific arbitrator. Arbitration awards may be appealed to PERC, rather than to the Superior Court, although PERC's decision may be appealed to the Superior Court, Appellate Division. The Reform Act requires the arbitrator to "indicate which of the [statutory] factors are deemed relevant, satisfactorily explain why the others are not relevant, and provide an analysis of the evidence on each relevant factor." NEW JERSEY STAT.ANN. 34:13A–16(g). It elaborates on the financial impact factor as follows:

> The financial impact on the governing unit, its residents, and taxpayers. When considering this factor in a dispute in which the public employer is a county or a municipality, the arbitrator or panel of arbitrators shall take into account, to the extent that evidence is introduced, how the award will affect the municipal or county purposes element, as the case may be, of the local property tax; a comparison of the percentage of the municipal purposes element or, in the case of a county, the county purposes element, required to fund the employee's contract in the preceding local budget year; the impact of the award for each income sector of the property taxpayers of the local unit; the impact of the award on the ability of the governing body to (a) maintain existing local programs and services, (b) expand existing local programs and services for which public moneys have been designated by the governing body in a proposed local budget, or (c) initiate any new programs and services for which public moneys have been designated by the governing body in a proposed local budget.

Id. 34:13A–16(g)(6).

CHAPTER 11

ADMINISTRATION OF THE AGREEMENT

■ ■ ■

It is generally recognized that the collective bargaining agreement, once entered into, is binding upon both parties. The California Supreme Court stated in *Glendale City Employees' Association v. City of Glendale*, 15 Cal.3d 328, 336, 540 P.2d 609, 615, 124 Cal.Rptr. 513, 519 (1975), that "[s]uccessful bargaining rests upon the sanctity and legal viability of the given word." And in *National Treasury Employees Union v. Chertoff*, 452 F.3d 839, 844 (D.C. Cir. 2006), *supra* Chapter 4 at page 269, the court, in striking down the regulations under the Homeland Security Act, concluded that "[i]f the Department could unilaterally abrogate lawful contracts, this would nullify the Act's specific guarantee of collective bargaining rights, because the agency cannot 'ensure' collective bargaining without affording employees the right to negotiate binding agreements."

In difficult economic times, governments often attempt to reduce labor costs, a measure which may violate existing collective bargaining agreements. In efforts to protect their agreements, labor unions have urged that governmental abrogation of collective bargaining agreements violates the constitutional limitation on impairment of contracts. These efforts have achieved mixed success. In *Opinion of the Justices (Furlough),* 135 N.H. 625, 609 A.2d 1204 (1992), the New Hampshire Supreme Court expressed its views, at the request of the state legislature, on a bill that would have forced public employees to take unpaid leave. Finding that proposal to be in violation of the applicable collective bargaining agreement, the Court opined that, if enacted into law, the bill would constitute a "substantial" impairment of contract in violation of the federal Constitution, Article 1, Section 10 and a similar provision of the state Constitution. Also, on behalf of the state legislature it was argued that any impairment was justified by the "public interest in achieving fiscal stability and a desire on the part of the Legislature to do so at the least cost to the operation of state government and its employees." The court rejected that argument, reasoning that "[a] state * * * 'cannot refuse to meet its legitimate financial obligations simply because it would prefer to spend the money to promote the public good rather than the private welfare of its creditors.' " (quoting *United States Trust Co. v. New Jersey*, 431 U.S. 975, 97 S.Ct. 2942, 53 L.Ed.2d 1073 (1977)). The Fourth Circuit reached a different result in *Baltimore Teachers Union v. Mayor and City Council of Baltimore*, 6 F.3d 1012, 1015 (4th Cir. 1993), upholding employee furloughs as reasonable and necessary to address a budget crisis, although they constituted a substantial impairment of the labor agreements covering the employees. The key is whether the court finds the contract abrogation reasonable and necessary for an important public purpose.

Far more common, however, is a claim that the employer has violated the terms of an agreement. Where there is a dispute ("grievance") concerning the meaning or application of the contract terms, how is the grievance to be resolved? Consider the following possibilities:

(1) The dispute can be resolved in court, as with most other contracts in the absence of arbitration.

(2) Violation of the agreement can be made an unfair labor practice, subject to the jurisdiction of the labor relations agency.

(3) The dispute, if it concerns discharge or discipline, can be resolved within the public authority through a civil service commission or board.

(4) The dispute can be submitted to various levels within the public authority ("grievance steps"), or to mediation, or to "advisory arbitration," with the public authority having the last word if the parties fail to reach agreement or to adopt the an arbitrator's recommendations.

(5) The dispute can be submitted to final and binding decision by a neutral arbitrator ("grievance arbitration").

Which of these alternatives is preferable from the perspective of (a) the public authority; (b) the union; (c) the individual employee?

All of these alternatives exist, in one form or another, and occasionally in combination, in states and in the federal government, making generalization difficult. In the private sector, binding arbitration is the norm. While public entities initially resisted the practice, it has become the norm in the public sector as well. But that does not mean that it necessarily takes the same form as in the private sector. Differences may arise out of public policy considerations, or the coexistence of arbitration with other forms of dispute resolution peculiar to the public sector, such as civil service systems. This chapter examines both the similarities and the differences.

In the famous *Steelworkers Trilogy* cases of 1960, the U.S. Supreme Court found in the federal Labor Management Relations Act a strong policy favoring arbitration of grievances, and established a legal framework for its effectuation. When the question is whether a court should order a resisting party to arbitrate, the Court declared, courts are not to pass upon the merits of the underlying dispute, but only to determine whether the party seeking arbitration is making a claim which "on its face is governed by the contract." *United Steelworkers of America v. American Manufacturing Co.,* 363 U.S. 564, 568, 80 S.Ct. 1343, 1346, 4 L.Ed.2d 1403, 1407 (1960). Courts are not to deny arbitration "unless it may be said with positive assurance that the arbitration clause is not susceptible to an interpretation that covers the asserted dispute." *United Steelworkers of America v. Warrior & Gulf Navigation Co.*, 363 U.S. 574, 582–83, 80 S.Ct. 1347, 1353, 4 L.Ed.2d 1409, 1417 (1960). When the question is whether a court should order enforcement of an arbitrator's award, the court should decline to review the merits of the award "so long as it draws its essence from the collective bargaining agreement." *United Steelworkers of America v. Enterprise Wheel & Car Corp.*, 363 U.S. 593, 597, 80 S.Ct. 1358, 1361, 4 L.Ed.2d 1424, 1428 (1960).

Apart from the "essence" test, which results in affirmance of the arbitration award in all but a very few cases, the principle of arbitral finality is limited in the private sector only by a narrow exception for awards which offend "public policy" and for situations in which the union is found to have breached its duty of fair representation. The application of these exceptions in the public sector is explored below.

The *Trilogy* cases identified the policies underlying judicial deference to arbitration, and to the arbitrator's judgment. One was avoidance of labor disputes, the Court's premise being that in the labor arena, unlike the commercial arena, arbitration substitutes for "industrial strife," not litigation. A second was a preference for industrial self-governance, *i.e.* a private system of ordering the workplace. Since the *Trilogy* cases, however, the Court has come to apply nearly identical principles of deference to commercial and employment arbitration, where the policy is aimed more at the avoidance of litigation. And in both labor and commercial contexts, the Court has justified deference policies in terms of giving effect to the presumed desire of the parties to resolve their disputes through a mutually selected arbitrator with minimal interference by the courts. Are these same policy considerations applicable to the public sector? If not, are there other policy considerations that support similar rules of judicial deference?

Professor Hodges has identified, and criticized, from the cases and commentaries four arguments for a less deferential approach to arbitration in the public sector: (1) that the limited history of arbitration in the public sector precludes an inference that the parties intended a broad arbitration clause; (2) that arbitration in the public sector must be narrowly circumscribed to protect the public interest; (3) that the standard of review should be broader because of the statutory responsibilities imposed on public employers to provide public services; and (4) that the standard of review should be broader because issues presented to arbitration in the public sector frequently are intertwined with statutory issues. Ann C. Hodges, The Steelworkers Trilogy in the Public Sector, 66 *Chicago–Kent Law Review* 631 (1992). To what extent do you find merit in any of these arguments?

A. GRIEVANCE ARBITRATION IN THE PUBLIC SECTOR: OVERVIEW

In the early years of organizing and collective bargaining in the public sector, some jurisdictions resisted the very idea of grievance arbitration, contending that it involved an impermissible delegation of public responsibility. That is still true in some jurisdictions, insofar as a statute may be interpreted to preclude arbitration of a particular issue. As state legislatures came to give their blessing to collective bargaining, however, courts began to accept grievance arbitration, even in the absence of express statutory authority, as an appropriate means of giving effect to an otherwise valid contract. See, e.g., *AFSCME Local 1226 v. City of Rhinelander*, 35 Wis.2d 209, 151 N.W.2d 30 (1967) (a statute which authorized binding agreements, permitted, by implication, binding agreements to arbitrate grievances). Over time, most state courts came to accept *Trilogy* principles as being applicable to determinations of arbitrability and finality in the public sector, at least in theory. Still, the legal landscape in the public sector, if one looks carefully, may not be quite the same.

New York provides an interesting case study. In an early case, *Board of Education v. Associated Teachers of Huntington*, 30 N.Y.2d 122, 331 N.Y.S.2d 17, 282 N.E.2d 109 (1972), the New York Court of Appeals spoke glowingly of arbitration as "part and parcel of the administration of grievances," and of arbitrators who, being "selected because of their impartiality and their intimate knowledge of school board matters" are fully qualified to decide whether a teacher should be dismissed for incompetence or misconduct. Five years later, the same court backtracked. In *Acting Superintendent v. United Liverpool Faculty Association*, 42 N.Y.2d 509, 399 N.Y.S.2d 189, 369 N.E.2d 746 (1977). it reversed the *Trilogy* presumption of arbitrability, holding that in making determinations of arbitrability under the Taylor Act "courts are to be guided by the principle that the agreement to arbitrate must be express, direct and unequivocal as to the issues or disputes to be submitted to arbitration." The reason, the court explained, was that:

> In the field of public employment, as distinguished from labor relations in the private sector, the public policy favoring arbitration—of recent origin—does not carry the same historical or general acceptance, nor, as evidenced in part by some of the litigation in our Court, has there so far been a similar demonstration of the efficacy of arbitration as a means for resolving controversies in government employment. Accordingly, it cannot be inferred as a practical matter that the parties in collective bargaining agreements always intend to adopt the broadest permissible arbitration clauses. Indeed, inasmuch as the responsibilities of the elected representatives of the tax-paying public are overarching and fundamentally nondelegable, it must be taken, in the absence of clear, unequivocal agreement to the contrary, that the board of education did *not* intend to refer differences which might arise to the arbitration forum.

Liverpool was an aberration, and even in New York its holding suffered from progressive erosion until a 1999 decision laid it to rest. Or did it?

BOARD OF EDUCATION OF WATERTOWN CITY SCHOOL DISTRICT v. WATERTOWN EDUCATION ASSOCIATION

New York Court of Appeals, 1999.
93 N.Y.2d 132, 710 N.E.2d 1064, 688 N.Y.S.2d 463.

ROSENBLATT, J.

The questions of law common to the two appeals before us involve public sector arbitration under the Taylor Law. In each appeal the ultimate question is whether the claimed grievance is arbitrable, but the cases raise broader concerns that involve presumptions relating to arbitrability in the public sector, the respective roles of courts and arbitrators, and an examination of this Court's decision in *Matter of Acting Supt. of Schools of Liverpool Cent. School Dist. [United Liverpool Faculty Assn.]*, 42 N.Y.2d 509, 399 N.Y.S.2d 189, 369 N.E.2d 746 (1977).

The Watertown Dispute. In this litigation, the Watertown City School District and the Watertown Education Association are opponents. The Association is the collective bargaining representative of teachers and other employees in the District. The parties entered into a collective bargaining agreement (CBA) that defined various terms and conditions of employment. It contained provisions relating to health insurance benefits that included the District's choice of insurance carriers and the percentage breakdown of premium costs allocable to the parties.

Shortly before the CBA went into effect, the District, along with other school districts (including Indian River, the district involved in the companion appeal), entered into a Municipal Cooperation Agreement to provide health insurance benefits for employees of participating districts. The insurance was provided through the Jefferson–Lewis Health Plan, an entity managed by a Board of Trustees comprised of the chief executive officers of the Plan participants, including the Watertown City School District and the Indian River Central School District. Subsequently, owing to financial considerations, the Plan raised the employees' co-payment cap. The Association filed a grievance alleging, in essence, that this change constituted an impermissible, unilateral reduction in employee benefits and a violation of the District's obligations under the CBA. After the District denied the grievance, the Association made a demand for arbitration, which the District then sought to stay, claiming that the dispute was not covered by the CBA. The Association cross-moved to compel arbitration.

The CBA contained a broad arbitration clause which provided that "any alleged violation of this Agreement, or any dispute with respect to its meaning or application" was arbitrable. Notwithstanding this language, Supreme Court ruled in favor of the District, granted its application for a stay, and denied the Association's cross-application to compel arbitration, holding that the parties had not agreed to arbitrate the dispute at issue.

The Appellate Division affirmed, for reasons stated in the decision at Supreme Court.

The Indian River Dispute. This dispute is identical to *Watertown.* The parties are the School District and the Indian River Education Association (by its President). They entered into a CBA which contained a broad arbitration clause identical to the one in *Watertown.* The Indian River School District acquired health insurance coverage for its members under the same Municipal Cooperation Agreement as in *Watertown.* The Indian River CBA also contained a clause setting the percentage breakdown for health insurance premiums allocable to the parties. The case followed a procedural history similar to *Watertown.* * * * The Supreme Court noted that in light of its decision it need not consider whether the Association failed to comply with a condition precedent to arbitration. The Appellate Division affirmed, without opinion, citing *Watertown.* We reverse both Appellate Division orders and direct that both cases proceed to arbitration.

The Taylor Law. Based on their status as employee organizations and public employers, both parties couch their arguments in the context of the Taylor Law, NEW YORK–MCKINNEY'S CIVIL SERVICE LAW art. 14. In 1967 the State Legislature enacted the Taylor Law, which governs labor relations in the public sector. It deals with rights and relationships involved in public employment, such as organizing, collective bargaining, the prohibition of strikes by public employees, and the creation of the Public Employment Relations Board. The Taylor Law contemplates two types of arbitration: compulsory and permissive. The former is found in Civil Service Law § 209 and involves what has been termed "interest arbitration." This deals, in essence, with terms and conditions of employment not previously agreed upon. Normally those disputed issues are settled by negotiation, but the Legislature provided that if an impasse occurs in collective negotiations involving public employees, the compulsory arbitration provisions of Civil Service Law § 209 come into play.

In addition to imposing these obligations, the Taylor Law permits public sector parties to submit CBA grievances to arbitration (Civil Service Law § 204). This species of arbitration—grievance arbitration—is at issue in this case. The question whether a particular grievance is arbitrable under the Taylor Law has occupied the courts of this State in scores of cases over the last three decades. * * *

The Liverpool Two–Step Format. In 1977 this Court decided *Liverpool, supra,* which established criteria for determining whether and when a particular public sector grievance is subject to arbitration. The *Liverpool* protocol entails a two-step inquiry. Initially the Court must determine whether arbitration claims with respect to the particular subject matter are authorized by the terms of the Taylor Law. The second step involves "a determination of whether such authority was in fact exercised and whether the parties did agree by the terms of their particular arbitration clause to refer their differences in this specific area to arbitration." Succinctly, the test centers on two distinct inquiries as to the public parties' purported entry into the arbitral forum: may they do so and, if yes, did they do so.

Liverpool's First Step. The first ("may-they-do-so") step calls for an examination, by the court, of the subject matter of the dispute. Drawing on earlier decisions that discussed the lawfully permissible scope of arbitrability the Court in *Liverpool* pointed out that owing to public policy or to statutory or constitutional restrictions there are certain matters that are off-limits for arbitration. Although this inquiry deals with whether the parties may arbitrate, it typically involves an assertion by the public employer that it may not or should not lawfully submit itself to a particular grievance arbitration. The inquiry is less concerned with the wording of the parties' intent to arbitrate than with the lawfulness of that intent. Commentators have described this concern as having been born of a number of factors, including a reluctance to deprive the government of what has been its ultimate decision-making prerogatives.

In the 22 years following *Liverpool*, however, this Court has overwhelmingly rejected contentions by public employers that particular issues fall outside the scope of permissible grievance arbitration. E.g., *Matter of Committee of Interns & Residents [Dinkins]*, 86 N.Y.2d 478, 634 N.Y.S.2d 32, 657 N.E.2d 1315 (1995) [City's malpractice insurance coverage obligation]; *Matter of Board of Educ. [Connetquot Teachers Assn.]*, 60 N.Y.2d 840, 470 N.Y.S.2d 132, 458 N.E.2d 373 (1983) [right of teachers' association to use of the office space in school building]; *Board of Educ. v. Glaubman*, 53 N.Y.2d 781, 439 N.Y.S.2d 907, 422 N.E.2d 567 (1981) [employee's right to be rehired on basis of seniority]; *Matter of United Liverpool Faculty Assn. v. Board of Educ.*, 52 N.Y.2d 1038, 438 N.Y.S.2d 505, 420 N.E.2d 386 (1981) [evaluation of teacher]; *Matter of Franklin Cent. School [Franklin Teachers Assn.]*, 51 N.Y.2d 348, 434 N.Y.S.2d 185, 414 N.E.2d 685 (1980) [grievance of nonteaching employee under teachers' collective bargaining agreement]; *Board of Educ. v. Barni*, 49 N.Y.2d 311, 425 N.Y.S.2d 554, 401 N.E.2d 912 (1980) [violation of disciplinary provisions as to probationary teacher]; *Board of Educ. v. Patchogue–Medford Congress of Teachers*, 48 N.Y.2d 812, 424 N.Y.S.2d 122, 399 N.E.2d 1143 (1979) [denial of sabbatical leave or summer study grants]; *Matter of Wyandanch Union Free School Dist. v. Wyandanch Teachers Assn.*, 48 N.Y.2d 669, 421 N.Y.S.2d 873, 397 N.E.2d 384 (1979) [school board's failure to submit change in educational policy to advisory professional council; and whether certain duties were properly imposed upon teachers]; *Matter of Triborough Bridge & Tunnel Auth. [Bridge and Tunnel Officers Ben. Ass'n]*, 44 N.Y.2d 676, 405 N.Y.S.2d 39, 376 N.E.2d 199 (1978) [compensation for peace officer relating to off-duty arrest]; *Matter of South Colonie Cent. School Dist. v. Longo,* 43 N.Y.2d 136, 400 N.Y.S.2d 798, 371 N.E.2d 516 (1977) [dispute involving no-reprisal clause in agreement].

This is not to say that the concept of public policy (or statutory or constitutional) restrictions on public sector arbitration are extinct. To be sure, there are instances in which arbitration has been prohibited. E.g.,

Matter of Blackburne (Governor's Off. of Empl. Relations), 87 N.Y.2d 660, 642 N.Y.S.2d 160, 664 N.E.2d 1222 (1996) (termination of state agency employee for violation of Hatch Act); *Honeoye Falls–Lima Cent. School Dist. v. Honeoye Falls–Lima Educ. Assn.*, 49 N.Y.2d 732, 426 N.Y.S.2d 263, 402 N.E.2d 1165 (1980) (seniority dispute involving adequate academic standards); *Board of Educ. v. Areman*, 41 N.Y.2d 527, 394 N.Y.S.2d 143, 362 N.E.2d 943 (1977) (Board accessibility to teachers' personnel files); *Cohoes City School Dist. v. Cohoes Teachers Assoc.*, 40 N.Y.2d 774, 390 N.Y.S.2d 53, 358 N.E.2d 878 (1976) (tenure decisions); see also, *Matter of Sprinzen (Nomberg)*, 46 N.Y.2d 623, 630, 415 N.Y.S.2d 974, 389 N.E.2d 456 (1979) (cataloging non-arbitrable issues as a matter of public policy, including punitive damage awards, claims concerning insolvent insurance companies, usury determinations, and antitrust issues). Moreover, our courts have vacated arbitral awards or portions thereof as having been against public policy. *See, Matter of Cohoes City School District v. Teachers Assn., supra*. In all, however, the decisional law reflects the reality of greatly increased public sector arbitration, and its acceptance, compatible with the government's public policy concerns.

Liverpool's Second Step. If the first step is scaled, and the subject matter declared lawfully fit for arbitration, the *Liverpool* protocol next calls for a determination as to whether the parties agreed to arbitrate the grievance. The second ("did-they-do-so") step invokes the sort of conventional judicial analysis that is influenced by the wording of the CBA. Descending from the higher reaches of public policy, this step typically turns on drafting skills and language entirely within the control of the parties.

Here, too, in the vast majority of post-*Liverpool* cases, this Court has determined that the public sector parties had, by the broad arbitration clause language of the collective bargaining contracts, agreed to arbitrate the particular grievances involved. * * * This case catalog is revealing. It not only speaks to the litigational aftermath of the two *Liverpool* steps, but also sheds light on an additional theme in *Liverpool*, notably, the approach in evaluating the intention of the parties with regard to public sector arbitration.

Liverpool and Presumptions Regarding Arbitrability. In 1960, 17 years before *Liverpool*, the United States Supreme Court decided *United Steelworkers of Am. v. Warrior & Gulf Nav. Co.*, 363 U.S. 574, 80 S.Ct. 1347, 4 L.Ed.2d 1409 (1960)—a case that involved private sector parties and a Federal statute—in which it adopted a "presumption of arbitrability." The Supreme Court observed that the Federal Labor Management Relations Act, 29 USC § 141 et seq., was imbued with a congressional policy in favor of arbitration to resolve labor disputes and that courts should interpret arbitration clauses accordingly, "unless it may be said with positive assurance that the arbitration clause is not susceptible of an interpretation that covers the asserted dispute. Doubts should be resolved in favor of coverage." This has been a consistent theme in Federal labor law cases.

In pre-*Liverpool* cases that involved the application of Federal law, this Court applied the *Steelworkers* "presumption of arbitrability." Emphasizing, however, the relatively brief acquaintance that the State had with Taylor Law grievance arbitration, and lacking an adequate, reassuring experience, the Court, in *Liverpool*, expressed hesitancy over the prospect of prematurely expanding the arbitral portals in public sector cases. In *Liverpool* the Court emphasized that arbitration did "not yet carry the same historical or general appearance" or "demonstration of efficacy" in the public sector as it did in the private sector. In the absence of unequivocal agreement to the contrary, it was to be taken that a public employer, being charged with nondelegable responsibilities, did not intend to arbitrate grievances.

That was 1977, and it epitomized a wait-and-see attitude. We have waited, and we have seen. Arbitration in the public arena is no longer unfamiliar or unaccepted. It is a reality, and it is widespread. The enormous growth in the use of collective bargaining agreements has generated vast experience in drafting arbitration clauses. Public sector parties may now use phrases that have been litigated into familiarity. They are free to negotiate language that will define disputes in areas of the broadest permissible scope. Parties are likewise free to negotiate exclusions, and to word arbitration clauses with sufficient clarity for a court to be able to tell, on a threshold determination, whether they intended a permissible subject or type of dispute to be arbitrable or not. *Liverpool* did not expressly create a "presumption" against public sector arbitrability. To the extent, however, that one may be implied or fairly so characterized, an anti-arbitrational presumption is no longer justified either in law, or in the public sector labor environment. The lengthy chronicle of this Court's cases after *Liverpool* proclaims as much, as does the huge increase of public sector arbitration over the last quarter century.

Liverpool's approach calls for a two-step analysis necessary in public sector arbitrations which, by its nature involves concerns of public policy not at issue in *Steelworkers*. We will stay with the *Liverpool* format because it has been workable for over two decades, with results that have largely comported with the *Steelworkers* presumption with respect to CBA interpretation. We will preserve the two-step *Liverpool* analysis for judicial threshold consideration, free of any presumptions.

Merits Consideration by the Courts. It is also clear that the merits of the grievance are not the courts' concern. Even an apparent weakness of the claimed grievance is not a factor in the court's threshold determination. It is the arbitrator who weighs the merits of the claim. CPLR 7501 explicitly provides: "In determining any matter arising under this article, the court shall not consider whether the claim with respect to which arbitration is sought is tenable, or otherwise pass upon the merits of the dispute." This was added by Section 47 of chapter 532 of the Laws of 1963 for the purpose of abrogating what was left of the so-called "*Cutler–Hammer*" rule of *International Assn. of Machinists* (*Cutler–Hammer,*

Inc.), 297 N.Y. 519, 74 N.E.2d 464 (1947), in which our courts had taken a more expansive view of the merits, in determining arbitrability. While some case records contain enough information for a court to make a penetrating analysis of the scope of the substantive provisions of the CBA, an undertaking of that kind is not the function of the court. A judicial inquiry of that sort would involve an inapt flirtation with the merits, or an inappropriate use of the judicial scalpel to split the hairs that mark the perimeters of the contractual provisions. History, legislation, and experience dictate that courts not revert to the business of merits inquiries of the kind that existed under the *Cutler–Hammer* doctrine before the enactment of CPLR 7501.

The "Reasonable Relationship" Test. In the two cases before us, there is no dispute as to the first step. Both sides have recognized the subject matter as arbitrable. As for the second step, the courts below assessed the Associations' claims and ruled that they were not arbitrable. In both cases, and in the face of broad arbitration clauses, they addressed the nature of the dispute, and, acting as would an arbitrator, interpreted the scope of the substantive provision of the contract. They then found the grievances to be outside of the parties' agreement to arbitrate. This was error. A court confronted with a contest of this kind should merely determine whether there is a reasonable relationship between the subject matter of the dispute and the general subject matter of the CBA. If there is none, the issue, as a matter of law, is not arbitrable. If there is, the court should rule the matter arbitrable, and the arbitrator will then make a more exacting interpretation of the precise scope of the substantive provisions of the CBA, and whether the subject matter of the dispute fits within them. The parties in the cases before us chose to arbitrate any alleged violation of the CBA or any dispute with respect to its meaning or application. Given a clause of this breadth, and the presence of language dealing specifically with health insurance benefits, we determine that the reduction of benefits by increasing the employees' co-payments was an arbitrable issue.

We reach this conclusion even though, as the District stresses, it was the Plan, a non-party, that reduced the benefits. The Districts assert that even though the Plan is governed by a Board of Trustees comprised of District CEOs, the Districts do not control the amount or type of health insurance benefits that the Plan provides. Whether this is so, and whether the District violated the CBA with regard to maintaining a certain level of benefits, is for the arbitrator. * * *

NOTES

1. Is the "reasonable relationship" test the same as or different from the "positive assurance" established in *Warrior & Gulf*, cited in the principal case? In that case, the United States Supreme Court held that a union was entitled to proceed to arbitration on its claim that the employer's subcontracting of work was in violation of the collective agreement even though the

agreement said nothing about subcontracting, and excluded from arbitration matters which were "strictly a function of management," it being the union's contention that past practice created an implied limitation. Would the "reasonable relationship" test produce the same result?

2. In *United Steelworkers v. American Manufacturing Co.,* cited in the principal case, the United States Supreme Court rejected the *Cutler–Hammer* doctrine as a matter of federal labor law, saying that "courts * * * have no business weighing the merits of the grievance, considering whether there is equity in a particular claim, or determining whether there is particular language in the written instrument which will support the claim. * * * The processing of even frivolous claims may have therapeutic values of which those who are not a part of the plant environment may be quite unaware." Is the New York court accepting that view of arbitrability?

3. In California, an early decision appeared to follow the lead of *Liverpool* in distinguishing between arbitrability principles in the private and public sectors, *Service Employees International Union v. County of Napa,* 99 Cal.App.3d 946, 160 Cal.Rptr. 810 (1979), but other decisions have embraced *Trilogy* principles. For example, subsequently the California Court of Appeal, in *United Transportation Union v. Southern California Rapid Transit District,* 7 Cal.App.4th 804, 9 Cal.Rptr.2d 702 (1992), explicitly refused to follow *Service Employees*, stating, "while arbitration in New York may not carry the same historical or general acceptance or efficiency in the public sector as it does in the private sector, the appellate decisions of the courts of this state do not show a like experience. Further, in his dissent in *Service Employees*, Justice Grodin noted that, '[t]he applicability of *Steelworkers* trilogy principles to the public sector has been recognized by nearly all state courts which have considered the question.' "

4. The Pennsylvania Supreme Court has gone beyond *Trilogy* principles, holding that under a statute mandating arbitration of grievances, the issue of whether a particular matter is arbitrable is one for the arbitrator in the first instance, and not the court. *Pennsylvania Labor Relations Board v. Bald Eagle Area School District*, 499 Pa. 62, 451 A.2d 671 (1982) (declaring it was "folly [to allow] a full preliminary bout in the courts over the issue of an arbitrator's jurisdiction"); see also *Township of Sugarloaf v. Bowling*, 563 Pa. 237, 759 A.2d 913 (2000) (confirming that position as "even more appropriate" in the context of arbitration of grievances with police officers and firefighters). What are the advantages and disadvantages of Pennsylvania's approach to arbitrability?

5. *Procedural Arbitrability*. Under the federal Labor Management Relations Act questions of procedural arbitrability, such as whether the failure to comply with a time limit for filing the grievance or requesting arbitration bars any remedy for a contractual violation, are decided by the arbitrator, not the courts. See *John Wiley & Sons v. Livingston*, 376 U.S. 543, 84 S.Ct. 909, 11 L.Ed.2d 898 (1964). That principle has been generally accepted in the public sector as well. E.g., *City School District of Poughkeepsie v. Poughkeepsie Public School Teachers Association*, 35 N.Y.2d 599, 364 N.Y.S.2d 492, 324 N.E.2d 144 (1974).

In the following case considering the arbitrability of a grievance protesting the employer's outsourcing of bargaining unit work, also the subject of the grievance in the *Trilogy* case of *United Steelworkers v. Warrior & Gulf Navigation Co.*, 363 U.S. 574, 80 S.Ct. 1347, 4 L.Ed. 1409 (1960), both the majority and the dissent relied on the *Steelworkers Trilogy*. The *Trilogy* cases, both in determining arbitrability and in deciding whether to enforce arbitrator's awards caution courts against involvement in the substantive merits of the parties' claims as the decision on the merits is for the arbitrator. How successful is the court in the case below at avoiding consideration of the merits of the grievance?

CLASSIFIED EMPLOYEES ASSOCIATION v. MATANUSKA–SUSITNA BOROUGH SCHOOL DISTRICT

Supreme Court of Alaska, 2009.
204 P.3d 347.

MATTHEWS, J.

I. INTRODUCTION

The Matanuska–Susitna Borough School District decided to provide custodial services for its schools through an independent contractor rather than by employing custodial workers. The main question in this case is whether the District's outsourcing decision is arbitrable under its collective bargaining agreement with the Classified Employees Union. We conclude that it is not, primarily because no reasonable argument has been made that outsourcing is prohibited under the agreement. We therefore affirm the superior court's decision.

II. FACTS AND PROCEEDINGS

A. The Parties and the Collective Bargaining Agreement

The Classified Employees Association (CEA) * * * and the District are parties to a collective bargaining agreement (CBA) that defines the terms and conditions of employment applicable to the CEA's members. The agreement at issue was in effect from July 1, 2005, to June 30, 2008. * * * Article XI of the agreement outlines the procedures for dealing with grievances made by employees. * * *

Article XI sets out the stages in the grievance process. The fourth and final stage of the process allows for the parties to "submit the issue to arbitration" if the issue has not been resolved by the grievant's department director or administrator, the superintendent, or by mediation. Under the terms of Article XI the decision of the arbitrator "shall be final and binding upon both parties." The arbitrator "can add nothing to, nor subtract anything from the Agreement between the parties or any policy of the School Board."

Article XIII, the "Savings Clause," indicates that the "Labor Agreement contains the full and complete agreement between the parties on all subjects upon which the parties did bargain or could have bargained." The article continues that the "Agreement terminates all prior agreements and understandings" made between the parties. The agreement contains no clause describing specific powers that are reserved to management.

B. Bargaining History

In 1993 the District attempted to add a provision to the collective bargaining agreement which stated that "[t]he parties expressly agree that nothing in this Agreement shall be construed as prohibiting the District from contracting with independent contractors for activity drivers." The CEA did not agree to this language and the clause was not included in the contract; however, the CEA consented to a change to the 1993 agreement that allowed for outsourcing bus drivers if "an activity bus driver resigns, transfers, or takes a long term leave of absence."

The 2005–2008 agreement does not have any provision dealing with the outsourcing of activity drivers (or any specific provisions for outsourcing) because, according to the CEA, "the outsourcing of activity bus drivers was not successful." But apparently the question of outsourcing was a much-discussed subject during the negotiations for the 2005–2008 agreement. Robert Johnson, who was a member of the District's bargaining team and the school board in 2004, stated that "[o]utsourcing was [a] * * * key issue[ ]" for both the District and the CEA in the negotiations. He said that the District "wanted to be able to outsource" CEA work in the new agreement but the "CEA members didn't want to change the way things had been done in the past" and "asked for the District's assurances that bargaining unit work would not be outsourced." Johnson claimed that the District gave assurances that work would not be outsourced,[1] although "[t]he parties did not come up with contract language to commemorate their agreement."

C. The District's Decision to Outsource and Initial Court Proceedings

[The District entered into a contract outsourcing custodial services and maintenance, replacing union custodial workers, and the union filed a grievance which the District refused to arbitrate. The union sued to compel arbitration, also arguing that state law prohibited outsourcing. The District counterclaimed arguing that there was no agreement to arbitrate outsourcing decisions and that outsourcing is a managerial decision not subject to mandatory bargaining.]

* * *

On October 24, 2006, Superior Court Judge Beverly W. Cutler decided in favor of the District as a matter of law * * * .

* * *

1. The District disputes this assertion.

V. DISCUSSION

A. The Superior Court's Grant of Summary Judgment

* * *

In this opinion we too deal solely with the "purely legal question" of whether the District's decision to outsource is arbitrable as a matter of law.

B. The Presumption in Favor of Arbitrability

The CEA stresses the presumption in favor of arbitrability in its briefs. The CEA writes that this presumption means that the "burden of proof is on the party seeking to avoid arbitration" and that the superior court erred in not resolving its doubts about whether the issue was arbitrable in favor of arbitration. However, the District replies that the CEA has misread the presumption: it is not merely a blanket presumption in favor of arbitration come what may, but a presumption that only applies when the contract that provides for arbitration is ambiguous. The District avers that the contract in question in this case leaves no doubt that outsourcing is not a matter for arbitration.

We have ruled that there is a presumption in favor of arbitrability. In *University of Alaska v. Modern Construction, Inc.*, we noted that the common law and statutes of Alaska evince "a strong public policy in favor of arbitration." [522 P.2d 1132, 1138 (Alaska 1974)]. * * * We have also endorsed the United States Supreme Court's standard that "[a]n order to arbitrate the particular grievance should not be denied unless it may be said with positive assurance that the arbitration clause is not susceptible to an interpretation that covers the dispute. Doubts should be resolved in favor of coverage."[10] As we summed up the presumption in *Ahtna, Inc. v. Ebasco Constructors, Inc.*, "[a]ny ambiguity with regard to arbitrability is to be construed in favor of arbitration." [894 P.2d at 662.]

But the presumption in favor of arbitration is limited. Arbitration is a creature of contract, and if there are terms in a contract that either exclude arbitration or indicate that an issue should not be subject to arbitration, then requiring that the matter be sent to arbitration would be inappropriate. As this court put it in *Lexington Marketing Group v. Goldbelt Eagle, LLC*, "[b]ecause arbitration is a matter of contract, parties can only be compelled to arbitrate a matter where they have agreed to do so." [157 P.3d 470, 477 (Alaska 2007).] Accordingly, if a dispute is not, under a plausible interpretation, covered under the arbitration clause of a collective bargaining agreement, it should not be arbitrated because "a party cannot be required to submit to arbitration any dispute which he had not agreed so to submit."

---

10. *Ahtna, Inc. v. Ebasco Constructors, Inc.*, 894 P.2d 657, 662 n. 7 (Alaska 1995) (quoting *United Steelworkers v. Warrior & Gulf Navigation Co.*, 363 U.S. 574, 582–83, 80 S.Ct. 1347, 4 L.Ed.2d 1409 (1960)).

As this discussion implies, arbitrability is a threshold question for the court, not the arbitrator.[14] One reason for this division of authority is "[b]ecause arbitrators have such broad discretion, it is often problematic for them to decide their own jurisdiction, for if they are wrong, there may be essentially no review. This is so because the superior court reviews an arbitrator's decision under a standard giving extreme deference to the arbitrator." A court should determine that a claim is arbitrable, if, as stated above, a plausible or reasonably arguable case for arbitrability has been made. Conversely, if there are no plausible or reasonably arguable grounds supporting arbitrability, it is the duty of a court to decline to order arbitration.

C. Interpreting the Grievance Clause

1. Outsourcing may be "an event or condition which affects the conditions or circumstances under which an employee works."

Under the CBA only grievances may be arbitrated. The grievance clause defines "grievance" as

> a claim by an employee based upon an event or condition which affects the conditions or circumstances under which an employee works caused by misinterpretation or inequitable application of District policies or procedures on personnel matters directly pertaining to these conditions or circumstances, and/or the terms of this Agreement and amendments thereof.

The superior court determined that the CEA's claim was not arbitrable because outsourcing could not plausibly be characterized as an "event or condition" which affects the " 'condition' and 'circumstance' *under* which an employee works." In the court's words, "[t]he plain language of the clause indicates that the parties designed it to address grievances by employees related to unfair treatment by the District relating to the wages, hours and conditions of employment."

We are not so sure that this reading is correct. Outsourcing, which in this case involved laying off custodial workers in order to replace them with services provided by a contractor, is plausibly an "event" that affects the "circumstances" under which employees work. When a custodial employee's job is outsourced, the conditions and circumstances under which he works are affected because the worker is no longer employed. Something may *affect* the conditions or circumstances under which an employee works without itself being a condition or circumstance under which the employee works.

---

14. *See State v. Pub. Safety Employees Ass'n,* 798 P.2d 1281, 1285 (Alaska 1990). An exception to this rule applies when the contract clearly provides that the determination of arbitrability is for the arbitrator. *Id.* The CBA in this case does not so provide. Where a petition to enforce a CBA is filed with the Alaska Labor Relations Agency, the agency has jurisdiction to decide arbitrability, subject to judicial review. *See Fairbanks Fire Fighters Ass'n, Local 1324 v. City of Fairbanks,* 48 P.3d 1165, 1169–70 (Alaska 2002).

We therefore decline to rule that the District's decision to outsource is not arbitrable because it does not affect the conditions or circumstances "under which" employees work.

2. The District's decision to outsource was not a misinterpretation or inequitable application of a term of the agreement.

The question presented is whether the arbitration clause in the CBA between the District and the CEA can reasonably be interpreted in such a way that allows the District's decision to be arbitrated. The grievance clause permits the arbitration of claims based on an "event or condition" affecting the "conditions or circumstances under which an employee" works in two situations: first, where those events or conditions are caused by a "misinterpretation or inequitable application" of District "policies and procedures on personnel matters," and second, where they are caused by a "misinterpretation or inequitable application" of the terms of the CBA. We conclude that the CEA's alleged grievance does not fit either of these situations.

We address first the possibility that the CEA's claim is based on the District's misinterpretation or inequitable application of the terms of the agreement. The CEA points to no term in the contract that the District has misinterpreted or inequitably applied. And indeed it is hard to see how it could. There is no clause in the CBA discussing outsourcing, nor is there a clause which specifies the rights of management, both of which would be plausible candidates for "misinterpretation" or "inequitable application."

The CEA's argument about a possible oral side contract between the CEA and the District regarding outsourcing is unavailing. Alaska Statute 23.40.210(a), a subsection of the Public Employment Relations Act (PERA), requires that collective bargaining agreements be in writing.[18] We think the subsection acts as a kind of specialized statute of frauds, under which oral agreements are not permitted. Thus, if there was an oral agreement between the parties it would be invalid under subsection .210(a).

To the extent subsection .210(a) may be seen instead as a sort of statutory parol evidence rule, it could be argued that evidence of an oral agreement regarding outsourcing could be used to interpret ambiguous terms of the CBA that are reasonably susceptible to an interpretation that outsourcing is prohibited. Oral agreements can be so used with respect to integrated written contracts that are subject to the parol evidence rule. But no benefit to the CEA is gained from this possibility, because there are no clauses in the CBA that even hint at a ban on outsourcing.

The District has referred us to a case which in some respects resembles the present one. In *Local Union No. 483, International Brotherhood of Boilermakers v. Shell Oil Co.*, the district court refused to require arbitra-

18. AS 23.40.210(a) provides in part: "Upon the completion of negotiations between an organization and a public employer, if a settlement is reached, the employer shall reduce it to writing in the form of an agreement."

tion of complaints that arose when an employer decided to contract out work on a refinery renovation project. Under the collective bargaining agreement arbitration was limited to complaints arising out of the interpretation or application of the agreement. The district court found that the agreement did not prohibit or limit the practice of contracting out. On appeal the circuit court affirmed, stating with reference both to a prior case and the case before it:

> [F]undamentally the question decided there, and here, is that where arbitration is limited in the bargaining agreement to questions involving the application and interpretation of the agreement, and the agreement does not limit the freedom of the employer to contract out work, a court should not compel arbitration. [*Local Union No. 483,* 369 F.2d at 528–29.]

As did the court in *Local Union No. 483,* we conclude that arbitration may not be compelled here under the portion of the grievance clause that permits arbitration of claims caused by the misinterpretation or misapplication of the CBA because the CBA does not forbid or limit outsourcing. The dissent offers several other federal circuit opinions that are said to reach contrary results. We believe that these cases mainly represent differences in how settled principles should be applied because most of them advert to the need for a threshold finding as to whether a particular grievance raises a question concerning the interpretation of the collective bargaining agreement. This is not to say that all federal labor law cases decided by the circuit courts are necessarily consistent either in principle or in spirit with our opinion in the present case. But our opinion is consistent with the United States Supreme Court case relied on by the dissent, *AT & T Technologies, Inc. v. Communications Workers of America,* [475 U.S. 643, 106 S.Ct. 1415, 89 L.Ed.2d 648 (1986).] * * *

The Supreme Court began with familiar general principles: arbitration is a matter of contract and only disputes that the parties have agreed to submit to arbitration should be arbitrated; questions of arbitrability are for the courts; in deciding arbitrability courts should not rule on the merits of the underlying controversy; and there is a presumption in favor of arbitrability. The Court then turned to the policy reasons underlying the need for courts to determine arbitrability:

> The willingness of parties to enter into agreements that provide for arbitration of specified disputes would be "drastically reduced," however, if a labor arbitrator had the "power to determine his own jurisdiction * * * ." Were this the applicable rule, an arbitrator would not be constrained to resolve only those disputes that the parties have agreed in advance to settle by arbitration, but, instead, would be empowered "to impose obligations outside the contract limited only by his understanding and conscience."
>
> [*Id.* at 651, 106 S.Ct. 1415 (quoting Archibald Cox, *Reflecting Upon Labor Arbitration,* 72 HARV. L.REV. 1482, 1509 (1959)).]

Based on these policy reasons the Court found that the lower courts had erred in ordering the parties to arbitrate without first determining arbitrability:

> It is the court's duty to interpret the agreement and to determine whether the parties intended to arbitrate grievances concerning layoffs predicated on a "lack of work" determination by the Company. If the court determines that the agreement so provides, then it is for the arbitrator to determine the relative merits of the parties' substantive interpretations of the agreement. It was for the court, not the arbitrator, to decide in the first instance whether the dispute was to be resolved through arbitration. [*Id.*]

The Court stated that the issue on remand

> is whether, because of express exclusion or other forceful evidence, the dispute over the interpretation of Article 20 of the contract, the layoff provision, is not subject to the arbitration clause. That issue should have been decided by the District Court and reviewed by the Court of Appeals; it should not have been referred to the arbitrator. [*Id.* at 652, 106 S.Ct. 1415.]

As in *AT & T*, it is the duty of the judiciary in the present case to interpret the CBA to determine whether the parties intended to arbitrate the issue of outsourcing. We have concluded that they did not, for the reasons already expressed. In addition, PERA's limited provision for binding "interest" arbitration—arbitration that resolves impasses in contract formation—provides further forceful evidence that requiring arbitration here would be improper.

PERA governs collective bargaining between units of state and local government and their employees. Subsection .200(a) of the act defines three classes of employees: (1) those whose services are indispensable, (2) those whose services may be briefly suspended, and (3) those whose services may be suspended for long periods of time without adverse effects. The CEA represents employees of the third class, (a)(3). * * * Employees in classes (a)(2) and (a)(3) may strike. In *Alaska Public Employees Ass'n v. City of Fairbanks* we explained that (a)(2) and (a)(3) employees lack the ability to compel binding interest arbitration:

> So although the legislature has taken from the (a)(1) employees their right to strike, it has given, as a *quid pro quo,* the statutory right to compulsory binding arbitration. Since the class (a)(2) and (a)(3) employees have the right to strike, they do not have this arbitration right.

Since interest arbitration for (a)(3) employees is distinctly not state policy, care must be taken to distinguish cases where grievances are sought to be arbitrated from cases where the arbitration objective is to amend a collective bargaining contract by adding a provision that it cannot fairly be said to contain. Because the CBA simply does not speak to the subject of outsourcing, the CEA's complaint is of the latter type.

In summary, there are a number of forceful indicators pointing to the conclusion that the question whether outsourcing is prohibited by the CBA should not be arbitrated. One is, as indicated above, because interest arbitration for (a)(3) employees is not provided by PERA. Two others are contained in the collective bargaining agreement itself. Clause (4)(b) of the arbitration clause provides that the arbitrator "can add nothing to, nor subtract anything from, the agreement between the parties or any policy of the school board." The agreement goes on to state that the written collective bargaining agreement is the whole of the parties' agreement, bargaining on new terms may not be compelled during the term of the agreement, and no side agreements survive. Article XIII.B provides:

> It is agreed that this Labor Agreement contains the full and complete agreement between the parties on all subjects upon which the parties did bargain or could have bargained. Neither party shall be required, during the term of this Agreement, to negotiate or bargain upon any other issue. This Agreement terminates all prior agreements and understandings, and concludes collective bargaining for this Agreement.

Finally, PERA itself makes clear that collective bargaining agreements must be in writing, meaning that when we address the question whether a dispute plausibly involves the interpretation or application of a term of an agreement, we look to the written agreement. Here, the written agreement is silent on the subject of outsourcing.

3. The District's decision to outsource was not a "misinterpretation" or "inequitable application" of a District policy or procedure.

* * * Under the CBA a claim based on an event or condition affecting conditions of employment "caused by misinterpretation or inequitable application of District policies or procedures on personnel matters" is grievable and arbitrable. The CEA argues * * * that the District's decision to outsource is a policy that is being inequitably applied to the workers who have lost their bargaining unit jobs as a result of outsourcing. The CEA's argument is * * * that outsourcing is inherently inequitable. But this amounts to an attack on the policy itself. The CBA makes clear that the merits of any policy of the school board may not be altered by the arbitrator. Clause IV(B) of the grievance procedure of the CBA provides: "The arbitrator shall limit himself to the issue submitted to him and shall consider nothing else. He can add nothing to, nor subtract anything from the Agreement between the parties or any policy of the School Board." The same conclusion is inherent in the grievance clause itself. Only misinterpretations or inequitable applications of policies may be grieved, not the policies themselves. Thus the CEA's challenge to the outsourcing policy is not subject to arbitration.

* * *

For the above reasons we conclude that the outsourcing question presented by the CEA is not arbitrable. To use the language employed by the United States Supreme Court in *AT & T*, to leave that question to the arbitrator under the facts and circumstances of this case would be to empower the arbitrator "to impose obligations outside the contract limited only by his understanding and conscience."

[The court also ruled that the law did not bar outsourcing of custodial work.]

* * *

FABE, C. J., with whom CARPENETI, J., joins, dissenting.

The court's decision today rests entirely on its determination that, contrary to the contentions of the Classified Employees Association (CEA), the parties' collective bargaining agreement (CBA) cannot plausibly be read to prohibit or limit outsourcing by the Matanuska–Susitna Borough School District. Because I believe that the determination whether CEA's interpretation of the CBA is plausible should be made by the arbitrator, not by the court, I disagree with the court and would reverse the superior court's decision not to compel arbitration.

CEA claims that the District's outsourcing decision violated the parties' CBA. Under the CBA's grievance arbitration clause, employee grievances alleging "misinterpretation or inequitable application" of the terms of the CBA are arbitrable. CEA's claim that outsourcing violates the terms of the CBA, whether meritorious or wildly improbable, is a grievance regarding the proper interpretation of the CBA and is thus the type of grievance that the parties have agreed to arbitrate.

The court concludes otherwise first by determining that the CBA cannot reasonably be interpreted to prohibit outsourcing, then by reasoning that therefore CEA's complaint about outsourcing does not actually involve interpretation of the CBA, and finally by concluding that CEA's complaint is thus not actually encompassed by the arbitration clause. But in doing so the court directly hinges its decision regarding the *arbitrability* of CEA's claim on its own view of the *merits* of CEA's claim—something that is not generally appropriate in the context of labor arbitration.

The court is correct that the threshold question of whether a claim is arbitrable is one for the courts, not for the arbitrator. A court confronting this question must determine, keeping in mind the presumption in favor of arbitrability, whether there is a plausible interpretation *of the CBA's arbitration clause* (taking into account any exclusionary clauses) that covers the type of claim presented. But in doing so the court should not examine the plausibility *of the claim itself.*

Where, as here, the CBA's arbitration clause explicitly covers all claims alleging "misinterpretation or inequitable application" of the terms of the CBA, and there is no exclusionary clause, the court's role is limited to deciding whether the claim, on its face, concerns the proper interpretation of the CBA. The court concludes here that CEA's grievance "does not concern the proper interpretation of" the CBA. But CEA contends that the CBA prohibits outsourcing—asserting, among other things, that the CBA's silence regarding outsourcing means that outsourcing is not permitted. While perhaps practically or legally incorrect, this claim inescapably involves interpretation of the CBA. Though the court finds CEA's interpretation of the CBA untenable, it is nonetheless an interpretation of the CBA. And choosing between competing interpretations of the CBA is precisely the task the parties have agreed to put in the hands of the arbitrator.

Because the instant case does not fall under the National Labor Relations Act, we need not necessarily adopt the reasoning of federal labor law cases; however, as the court seemingly acknowledges, such cases are nonetheless instructive. In *AT & T Technologies, Inc. v. Communications Workers of America,* the United States Supreme Court reviewed and reaffirmed various basic legal principles pertaining to the arbitrability of labor disputes, including that "in deciding whether the parties have agreed to submit a particular grievance to arbitration, a court is not to rule on the potential merits of the underlying claims" and that "[w]hether 'arguable' or not, indeed even if it appears to the court to be frivolous, the union's claim that the employer has violated the collective-bargaining agreement is to be decided, not by the court asked to order arbitration, but as the parties have agreed, by the arbitrator."[8]

The court notes that "CEA points to no term in the contract" to support its position and that furthermore there is "no clause in the CBA discussing outsourcing." But the fact that CEA's claim that outsourcing violates the CBA may not be plausible and is not necessarily supported by any specific language in the CBA does not mean that it is not arbitrable. In *Building Materials & Construction Teamsters Local No. 216 v. Granite Rock Co.,*[851 F.2d 1190, 1193–95 (9th Cir.1988),] a case that we have recently cited, the Ninth Circuit found that a union's claim that an employer violated an *implied* term of a CBA was arbitrable under an arbitration clause that covered only disputes "arising under" the CBA, regardless of whether the union's claim was plausible or supported by any language in the CBA. Though the employer argued that the CBA could not be reasonably interpreted to contain the implied term that provided the basis for the union's claim, the Ninth Circuit reasoned that "[t]he district court was not required to determine whether the union's claim rested on a 'plausible' reading of the agreement" and that "once the court determines

8. 475 U.S. 643, 649–50, 106 S.Ct. 1415, 89 L.Ed.2d 648 (1986). *AT & T*, though it eloquently summarizes these important basic principles, is factually distinguishable from the instant case in that *AT & T* involved competing interpretations of an exclusionary clause in the CBA asserted by the employer to preclude arbitration of a particular dispute. *Id.* at 644–46, 106 S.Ct. 1415. Because the threshold question of arbitrability must be decided by the court, the *AT & T* Court held that it was improper for the trial court to submit to the arbitrator the issue of the proper interpretation of the CBA's arbitration and exclusionary clauses. *Id.* at 651, 106 S.Ct. 1415. In this case, by contrast, it is not competing interpretations of the CBA's arbitration clause or of an exclusionary clause that are at issue, but competing substantive interpretations of the CBA. Indeed, the *AT & T* Court acknowledged that if the arbitration provisions were interpreted to cover the type of dispute at issue it would be "for the arbitrator to determine the relative merits of the parties' substantive interpretations of the agreement." *Id.*

that the parties' dispute concerns the proper interpretation of the agreement, it has 'no business weighing the merits of the grievance, considering whether there is equity in a particular claim, or determining whether there is particular language in the written instrument which will support the claim.' "

Similarly, in *International Brotherhood of Electrical Workers, Local 1228 v. WNEV–TV, New England Television Corp.,* the First Circuit concluded that a union's claim—maintaining that an employer had violated the parties' CBA by eliminating an employee lounge—was arbitrable under an arbitration clause that encompassed "all complaints, disputes or questions as to the interpretation, application or performance of" the CBA. The First Circuit came to this conclusion despite the fact that the trial court found that there was no language in the CBA creating a duty to provide or maintain such a lounge. The court in *WNEV–TV* recognized that

> [w]hat one man considers frivolous another may find meritorious, and it is common knowledge in industrial relations circles that grievance arbitration often serves as a safety valve for troublesome complaints. Under these circumstances it seems proper to read the typical arbitration clause as a promise to arbitrate every claim, meritorious or frivolous, which the complainant bases upon the contract. The objection that equity will not order a party to do a useless act is outweighed by the cathartic value of arbitrating even a frivolous grievance and by the dangers of excessive judicial intervention. [778 F.2d 46, 46–48 (1st Cir.1985).]

The Second Circuit in *Procter & Gamble Independent Union of Port Ivory, N.Y. v. Procter & Gamble Manufacturing Co.*[, 298 F.2d 644, 645 (2d Cir.1962),] rejected a company's contention, similar to the District's contention in this case, that arbitration should be refused because "none of the alleged grievances were specifically covered by any particular provision of the agreement" and the arbitration clause bound it only to the arbitration of grievances "having to do with the interpretation or application of any provision of" the CBA. The Second Circuit held that the union's grievances, which included a complaint about outsourcing, were arbitrable, reasoning that "the interpretation or construction of the agreement by the Board of Arbitration is the very thing the parties bargained for." The *Procter & Gamble Manufacturing* court did not examine whether or not the union's claims had merit or were grounded in any specific language in the CBA.

Similarly, in *International Union of Electrical, Radio & Machine Workers v. General Electric Co.,* the Second Circuit held that a union's complaint about an employer's subcontracting of work was arbitrable under an arbitration clause encompassing disputes about "the interpretation or application of a provision of" the CBA, despite the employer's argument that the CBA contained no express provisions regarding subcontracting and the fact that the union had unsuccessfully attempted to negotiate for provisions limiting subcontracting. The Second Circuit remarked:

> What the company has done * * * is to attempt to persuade us to decide that the grievance is not arbitrable because the grievance is groundless inasmuch as [no] substantive provision of the collective bargaining agreement, according to the company, forbids or restricts subcontracting. But whether a certain brand of company conduct is prohibited by a provision of a collective bargaining agreement will always be the ultimate question which the grievance itself will present * * *. For us to yield to the urgings of the company and decide it ourselves would be to ignore the admonition contained in the *Warrior & Gulf* case that courts should not become "entangled in the construction of the substantive provisions of a labor agreement."
>
> [332 F.2d 485, 489–90 (2d Cir.1964) (quoting *United Steelworkers of Am. v. Warrior & Gulf Nav. Co.,* 363 U.S. 574, 585, 80 S.Ct. 1347, 4 L.Ed.2d 1409 (1960)).]

As the court points out, the above-cited cases do indeed "advert to the need for a threshold finding as to whether a particular grievance raises a question concerning the interpretation of the collective bargaining agreement." But the court here goes beyond simply making a threshold determination as to whether CEA's claim involves interpretation of the CBA—the court examines the merits of CEA's interpretation and then concludes that because CEA's interpretation is not reasonable, *it is not actually an interpretation.* Such reasoning puts the cart before the horse and thus is not in line with the predominant federal approach.

The court cites two Seventh Circuit cases in support of its decision: *Local Union No. 483, International Brotherhood of Boilermakers v. Shell Oil Co.* and *Independent Petroleum Workers of America, Inc. v. American Oil Co.,* on which *Local Union No. 483* relies. Each of these cases held that where a CBA was silent with regard to outsourcing, arbitration of an outsourcing dispute could not be compelled under an arbitration clause that limited arbitration to questions arising from CBA interpretation. However, *Local Union No. 483* and *Independent Petroleum Workers* appear to be outliers, and the continued validity of their approach has been questioned. * * *

Additionally, in both *Local Union No. 483* and *Independent Petroleum Workers* the Seventh Circuit actually considered the bargaining history between the parties in the course of concluding that the CBAs did not prohibit outsourcing (and thus that outsourcing disputes were not arbitrable)—something the court here seems unwilling to do despite CEA's entreaties. And in both of these cases the bargaining history between the parties was the *opposite* of the bargaining history in the instant case—that is, in both of these cases the unions repeatedly tried and failed to negotiate for CBA provisions specifically *prohibiting* outsourcing, whereas in the instant case there is evidence that the employer tried and failed to negotiate for CBA provisions specifically *permitting* outsourcing. Accordingly, to the extent that these two cases relied on bargaining history to interpret the CBA's silence regarding outsourcing, they are importantly distinguishable from the instant case.

Coupled with the strong presumption in favor of arbitrability, which is accurately set forth in the court's opinion, the many cases admonishing against delving into the merits of a union's claim in order to determine its arbitrability suggest that the court has chosen to take a distinctly minority approach by resting its decision on a preliminary determination that CEA's interpretation of the CBA is implausible.

The court attempts to bolster its decision to take this minority approach by pointing out that the Public Employment Relations Act (PERA) does not give CEA's employees the power to compel binding interest arbitration. But this is irrelevant. CEA seeks only grievance arbitration, which the parties have specifically contracted for, not interest arbitration. CEA claims that the District's outsourcing violates the parties' *existing* CBA—it does not seek to compel arbitration for the purpose of renegotiating the terms of the CBA. The court thinks that CEA's interpretation of the CBA is implausible and thus characterizes CEA's claim not as a dispute about the interpretation of the CBA but as an effort "to amend a collective bargaining contract by adding a provision that it cannot fairly be said to contain." But the fact that CEA's grievance involves a potentially implausible interpretation of a CBA does not mean that its request for grievance arbitration under the CBA's arbitration clause should be viewed as if it is a request for interest arbitration under PERA. * * *

As the court points out, under the CBA's arbitration clause the arbitrator "can add nothing to, nor subtract anything from" the CBA. Accordingly, an arbitrator evaluating CEA's outsourcing grievance would be limited to examination and interpretation of the parties' existing CBA and would not have the power to modify the CBA. Thus limited, an arbitrator might well conclude, as the court has concluded, that CEA's interpretation of the CBA is implausible and that "the CBA simply does not speak to the subject of outsourcing." But that determination would be one for the arbitrator to make because "the interpretation or construction of the [CBA] by the [arbitrator] is the very thing the parties bargained for."

Therefore, I respectfully dissent.

NOTES

1. Both the majority and the dissent cite the *Steelworkers Trilogy*, and in addition the Supreme Court's decision in *AT & T Technologies, Inc. v. Communications Workers of America,* 475 U.S. 643, 106 S.Ct. 1415, 89 L.Ed.2d 648 (1986). Which justice has the better of the argument as to the application of the principles from these cases to the case at bar?

2. The collective bargaining agreement contained no language regarding outsourcing. Does that doom the union's attempt to arbitrate? Should the

union have cited to other provisions of the agreement in support of its claim that outsourcing was prohibited? What other provisions might be relevant? Wages? Benefits? The description of the employees in the bargaining unit, e.g, custodial employees? In one of the *Trilogy* cases, *United Steelworkers v. Warrior & Gulf Navigation Co.*, 363 U.S. 574, 80 S.Ct. 1347, 4 L.Ed.2d 1409 (1960), the grievance also involved contracting out. The court said "[t]he labor arbitrator's source of law is not confined to the express provisions of the contract, as the industrial common law—the practices of the industry and the shop—is equally a part of the collective bargaining agreement although not expressed in it." Is this statement equally applicable in the public sector? The majority rejected the union's argument that the bargaining history indicated the claim was arbitrable. Was the majority correct?

3. The majority and dissent also disagreed about the relevance of the fact that the employees did not have access to interest arbitration but instead retained the right to strike. Which was more persuasive? Does the presence of the right to strike suggest that grievance arbitration is more important? In the *Trilogy* the court distinguished labor arbitration from commercial arbitration because it was a substitute for the strike rather than for litigation, thus justifying a presumption of arbitrability. At the time of the *Trilogy*, commercial arbitration was disfavored by the courts.

4. The contract at issue did not contain a management's rights clause. Which party do you think viewed the absence of such a clause favorably before this decision? After the decision? Would you advise the union to support inclusion of such a clause in the next set of contract negotiations? Would you advise the employer to do so?

5. As the dissent noted, the Court in the *Trilogy* pointed out the value of arbitrating even frivolous grievances. Is arbitrating frivolous grievances of equal value in the public sector? Arbitration costs each side thousands of dollars. For the employer these costs come from public funds. Should public funds be spent to arbitrate frivolous grievances? On the other hand, why would a union spend thousands of dollars to arbitrate a frivolous grievance?

B. NON-DELEGABILITY OBJECTIONS TO ARBITRABILITY

As the court observed in *Watertown*, a public entity will sometimes resist arbitration on the ground that it had no authority to agree to arbitrate the type of controversy asserted in the union's grievance. Such arguments were more successful in the early years of public sector bargaining but, again as observed in *Watertown*, the issue is not extinct. Indeed, a subsequent decision of the New York Court of Appeals demonstrates its continuing, though rare, viability.

CITY OF NEW YORK v. UNIFORMED FIRE OFFICERS ASSOCIATION, LOCAL 854, IAFF, AFL–CIO

New York Court of Appeals, 2000.
95 N.Y.2d 273, 716 N.Y.S.2d 353, 739 N.E.2d 719.

WESLEY, J.

The issue we must address today is whether public policy bars arbitration of this dispute over whether the employee rights provisions of a collective bargaining agreement (CBA) can be invoked to limit or restrict the procedures of criminal investigations commenced by the New York City Department of Investigation (DOI). We conclude that it does.

In February 1996, DOI subpoenaed several firefighters as part of criminal investigations it was conducting. One investigation concerned an attempt by a firefighter to obtain higher pension benefits by fraudulently claiming that he sustained a disabling injury in the line of duty. The scheme involved one firefighter calling in a false alarm to afford the injured firefighter the opportunity to claim that his injury occurred in responding to the alarm. Among those firefighters interviewed were members of appellant Union, Uniformed Fire Officers Association, Local 854 (UFOA).

The applicable citywide CBA contains provisions for individual employee rights under Article XVII and arbitration of grievances under Articles XVIII and XXI. Article XVII relates to interrogations, interviews, trials and hearings. Those afforded by Article XVII include the requirement that the employee be given written notice of an interview, interrogation, trial or hearing. The employee must be informed of the subject matter of the proceeding and must be informed if he or she is being considered a suspect or a non-suspect. Any questioning of an employee is to be of reasonable duration and the interrogator is prohibited from using offensive or profane language, from threatening the employee for failure to answer questions and from promising anything to the employee if that employee does answer questions. Where an employee is "a suspect in a departmental investigation or trial" the employee must be advised of the right to refuse to answer questions, that the answers may not be used against him or her in criminal proceedings so long as they are truthful and that the failure to answer renders the employee subject to dismissal. The employee must also be advised of the right to counsel and of the right to union representation. If the employee invokes the right to counsel and/or union representation, the matter must be adjourned for two working days.

Article XVII further imposes restrictions on the scope of any questioning concerning personal behavior outside of work except with respect to matters related to official business, extra-departmental employment, conflict of interest, injuries or illness, residency, performance as a volunteer firefighter or loss or improper use of departmental property. Non-suspect employees are required to cooperate and their statements may not be used against them. Finally, where the City fails to comply with the provisions of

Article XVII, any questions put to an employee shall be withdrawn and the refusal to answer any such questions shall not be prejudicial to the employee.

During one of the February 1996 DOI interviews, a fire officer's union representative was excluded over objections of the union counsel. At another interview, the union counsel questioned the adequacy of the notice under Article XVII. The Union thereafter filed a request for arbitration of the grievance, claiming that the City was violating Article XVII by the failure of its agency, DOI, to abide by Article XVII. The City challenged the arbitrability of the request before appellant New York City Board of Collective Bargaining (BCB). The BCB issued a determination finding the dispute to be arbitrable.

The City thereafter commenced this special proceeding pursuant to CPLR articles 75 and 78 in Supreme Court, seeking to annul the BCB's determination and to enjoin arbitration of the dispute. According to the City, it never agreed to arbitrate the procedures employed by the DOI in conducting its criminal investigations; the CBA cannot, as a matter of public policy, supplant or impair those procedures; and the grievances are not arbitrable because to do so would violate public policy.

The Supreme Court set aside the BCB's determination and enjoined arbitration, stating that "the core function of ensuring governmental integrity is a public policy sufficiently strong as to preclude referral of this dispute to arbitration." *Matter of City of New York v. DeCosta*, 176 Misc.2d 936, 675 N.Y.S.2d 517 (2000). The Appellate Division unanimously affirmed, holding that public policy, as reflected in the New York City Charter and in decisional law, prohibits any interference with DOI's authority to question public employees in the course of an investigation. We now affirm.

Determining arbitrability requires a two-pronged inquiry. First, a court must decide whether "arbitration claims with respect to the particular subject matter of the dispute [are] authorized," i.e., that the claims are "lawfully fit for arbitration." *Matter of New York City Dept. of Sanitation v. MacDonald*, 87 N.Y.2d 650, 642 N.Y.S.2d 156, 664 N.E.2d 1218 (1996). Second, the court must ascertain whether the authority to arbitrate was in fact exercised and the parties consented by the terms of their particular agreement to refer disputes in this specific area to arbitration. * * *

Under the first prong, the subject matter of the dispute controls the analysis. The court must determine "that there is nothing in statute, decisional law or public policy which would preclude the municipality and its employee or group of employees from referring the dispute to arbitration." *Matter of Committee of Interns & Residents (Dinkins)*, 86 N.Y.2d 478, 634 N.Y.S.2d 32, 657 N.E.2d 1315 (1995). If there is some statute, decisional law or public policy that prohibits arbitration of the subject matter of dispute," then the answer to the first inquiry is no, and the claim is not arbitrable regardless of the answer to the second question." *Id.* We have recognized limited instances where arbitration is prohibited on public policy grounds alone. See e.g., *Matter of Blackburne (Governor's Off. of Empl. Relations)*, 87 N.Y.2d 660, 642 N.Y.S.2d 160, 664 N.E.2d 1222 (1996) (termination of an employee who violated the Hatch Act); *Honeoye Falls–Lima Cent. School Dist. v. Honeoye Falls–Lima Educ. Assn.*, 49 N.Y.2d 732, 426 N.Y.S.2d 263, 402 N.E.2d 1165 (1980) (school district's ability to layoff those with the least seniority to maintain academic standards); *Board of Educ. v. Areman*, 41 N.Y.2d 527, 394 N.Y.S.2d 143, 362 N.E.2d 943 (1977) (school board's right to inspect teacher personnel files); *Matter of Cohoes City School Dist. v. Cohoes Teachers Assn.*, 40 N.Y.2d 774, 390 N.Y.S.2d 53, 358 N.E.2d 878 (1976) (school board's ability to terminate probationary teachers and make tenure decisions).

The public policy at stake here is DOI's ability to conduct criminal investigations. We have recognized that "[p]ublic policy, whether derived from, and whether explicit or implicit in statute or decisional law, or in neither, may * * * restrict the freedom to arbitrate." *Matter of Susquehanna Val. Cent. School Dist. [Susquehanna Val. Teachers' Assn.]*, 37 N.Y.2d 614, 376 N.Y.S.2d 427, 339 N.E.2d 132 (1975). From our review of the statutory and decisional law concerning the DOI, its purpose and its powers, we conclude that a strong public policy enjoins the arbitration of the grievance here.

The Legislature has recognized the importance of allowing a city to conduct investigations into its internal affairs. General City Law § 20(21) empowers every city in the State to "investigate and inquire into all matters of concern to the city or its inhabitants, and to require and enforce by subpoena the attendance of witnesses at such investigations." DOI is the entity charged by the City of New York with the critical responsibility of investigating possible criminal conduct and conflicts affecting City agencies or City employees (N.Y. City Charter § 803). The power to investigate matters pertaining to corrupt or other criminal activity, conflicts of interest, gross mismanagement or abuse of authority within the City, is firmly vested with DOI. * * * To effectuate this mandate, DOI is authorized "to compel the attendance of witnesses, to administer oaths and to examine such persons as [it] may deem necessary." N.Y. Charter § 805(a).

It is evident from the Charter that DOI enjoys full latitude in conducting its investigations; Section 1128(a) of the City Charter prohibits any person from preventing, interfering with, obstructing or hindering in any way, an investigation conducted pursuant to the Charter and renders any attempt to do so cause for suspension or removal from office or employment. Moreover, Section 1128(b) of the Charter mandates full cooperation with the Commissioner of the DOI.

The courts have also recognized the important role DOI plays in facilitating the honest workings of the City of New York. As Chief Judge Cardozo noted in sustaining the broad investigatory powers of the Commissioner of Accounts (the predecessor to the Commissioner of the DOI), "[t]he powers devolved by the charter upon the Commissioner of Accounts are of great importance for the efficient administration of the huge machinery of government in the City of New York. * * * In a great city like New York, working under a charter as complex as its charter is, public policy requires that every available means of examining the administration of the various departments and offices of the city government be utilized to their fullest extent and statutes having this object in view should be liberally construed." *Matter of Edge Ho Holding Corp*, 256 N.Y. 374, 176 N.E. 537 (1931).

The City (and its residents) has a significant interest in ensuring that the inner workings of the machinery of public service are honest and free of corruption. We conclude that this public policy restricts the freedom to arbitrate under the circumstances presented here. To allow an arbitrator to grant a city employee or a union the ability to restrict the DOI's investigatory procedures by invoking the employee rights provisions of a CBA would amount to an impermissible delegation of the broad authority of the City to investigate its internal affairs. It is DOI, and not an arbitrator, that is the entity mandated by law to control all aspects of the criminal investigation; permitting an arbitrator, who may not have any background information on the nature or complexity of the DOI investigation or the severity of the offense, to dictate the procedures over who should be present at a DOI interview or to direct that notice be given to an employee concerning the subject matter of the DOI investigation would only hinder the DOI's role as a fact investigator and would contravene the City Charter's prohibition against interference with an investigation. N.Y. City Charter § 1128[a]. Moreover, subjecting DOI inquiries to the arbitration process would introduce elements that could compromise criminal investigations.

We further reject the contention of the Union and our dissenting colleague that the courts below acted too quickly in staying the arbitration in that an arbitrator could fashion an award to determine the dispute in a manner that would not offend public policy considerations. We have recognized that judicial intervention to stay arbitration on public policy grounds is not without restrictions. For example, we have noted that although a school district's statutory authority in certain areas of school operation may not be bargained away or otherwise delegated, the violations of the procedural and substantive aspects of those reserved powers must nevertheless be treated separately. While a Board of Education may not surrender its ultimate responsibility for making tenure decisions or restrict its exclusive right to terminate probationary teacher appointments, the courts may not nullify the bargained-for procedural steps preliminary to the board's final action to grant or withhold tenure.

Thus, in *Port Washington*, we acknowledged that situations may exist in which although public policy would be violated by granting the remedy requested by one or more of the parties, it may still be premature for a court to intercede because the arbitrator may be able to fashion a remedy not in violation of public policy. *Matter of Port Washington Union Free*

School Dist. v. *Port Washington Teachers Assn.*, 45 N.Y.2d 411, 408 N.Y.S.2d 453, 380 N.E.2d 280 (1978). We have also recognized other situations in which no remedy could be granted without violating public policy. See, *Matter of Blackburne [Governor's Off. of Empl. Relations]*, 87 N.Y.2d 660, 642 N.Y.S.2d 160, 664 N.E.2d 1222 (1996). In *Blackburne*, an employee, who had violated the Federal Hatch Act, claimed that he was terminated in violation of the procedural guarantees found in the CBA. This Court held that the arbitrator could not mandate compliance with the CBA's procedural guarantees concerning employee termination without subjecting the State to loss of Federal funds for the Hatch Act violation. To allow the arbitrator to make such a decision constituted an impermissible delegation of the State's sovereign authority. Thus, where a court examines an arbitration agreement or an award on its face and concludes that the granting of any relief would violate public policy without extensive factfinding or legal analysis, courts may then intervene and stay arbitration.

In this case, the procedural protections afforded a City employee under Article XVII of the CBA cannot be separated from their impact on a DOI criminal investigation. The granting of any relief under the procedural protections of the CBA would not only impinge on DOI's ability to conduct a criminal investigation, but would add another layer of process, decision-making and potential conflict. Thus, to the extent that public policy considerations preclude arbitration here, the courts below did not act precipitously and arbitration must be permanently stayed.

Finally, we conclude that, in this case, BCB's determination that the dispute is arbitrable is not entitled to due deference. The determination of the BCB, the statutorily authorized neutral adjudicative agency charged with making determinations under the New York City Collective Bargaining Law, will not be disturbed unless it is arbitrary and capricious or an abuse of discretion, or unless arbitration of the dispute offends public policy. Because we conclude that the arbitration here is prohibited by public policy, the courts did not err in overturning the BCB's determination.

Contrary to the dissent, we feel that it is clear from the record that DOI was conducting a criminal investigation; the investigations did not involve the conduct of the fire officers themselves but concerned their observations as witnesses to allegations of fraud. Moreover, the Union does not contest that the DOI investigations conducted here began as criminal investigations. Rather, the Union contends that there is no distinction between DOI's power to conduct criminal investigations and its power to conduct disciplinary investigations. * * * The Union therefore seeks arbitration of all investigation-based claims (criminal and disciplinary).

Lastly, we agree with our dissenting colleague that there is no concern in this case that arbitration could delay criminal investigations. The courts below granted the City's stay, avoiding any further possible interference with the criminal investigation through after-the-fact remedies. To the extent that the dissent contends that the Union is merely seeking a post-deprivation remedy, that belies the fact that the Union is seeking to restrict all future DOI investigations involving its members. The Union seeks the remedy of "[c]ompliance by the Department of Investigation with contractual requirements when noticing and conducting investigations involving members of the UFOA bargaining unit." UFOA Request for Arbitration. The Union is not seeking the immunization of statements already given by its member officers in this case (although an arbitrator might decide that is a remedy); rather the remedy sought is for an arbitrator to determine when and how DOI investigations involving UFOA members are to be conducted. That is a power the City cannot give. Accordingly, the order of the Appellate Division should be affirmed, with costs.

KAYE, C.J., dissenting.

In a freely-negotiated collective bargaining agreement (CBA), the City of New York agreed to give fire officers certain procedural rights—including notice, representation by counsel and a union representative, and use immunity—when interrogated by their "Employer." When interviewing several fire officers in an investigation concerning alleged pension fraud, the New York City Department of Investigation (DOI) refused to recognize those rights. After the completion of the investigation (which resulted in a firefighter—not a fire officer—pleading guilty to a crime), the Uniformed Fire Officers Association filed a grievance. The Board of Collective Bargaining (BCB) held that an arbitrator should resolve two questions: whether the procedural protections in the collective bargaining agreement apply to criminal investigations conducted by DOI, and if so, whether the officers' rights were violated in the case at hand. The Majority holds that public policy forbids these questions from even being submitted to an arbitrator. Because I believe that, under the particular circumstances here, the City's petition to stay arbitration was premature, I respectfully dissent.

Several longstanding policies of this State weigh against granting the City's petition to stay arbitration at this early stage.

First, the public policy exception to arbitrability is very narrow. "[J]udicial intervention to stay arbitration on public policy grounds is exceptional and itself limited to circumstances specifically identified or rooted in statute or case law." *Matter of New York City Dept. of Sanitation v. MacDonald*, 87 N.Y.2d 650, 642 N.Y.S.2d 156, 664 N.E.2d 1218 (1996). By and large, this Court has "overwhelmingly rejected contentions by public employers that particular issues fall outside the scope of permissible grievance arbitration." *Matter of Board of Educ. [Watertown Educ. Assoc.]*, 93 N.Y.2d 132, 688 N.Y.S.2d 463, 710 N.E.2d 1064 (1999) (collecting cases). As this Court recently reaffirmed, public policy bars arbitration only where "strong and well-defined policy considerations embodied in constitutional, statutory or common law prohibit a particular matter from being decided or certain relief from being granted by an arbitrator." *Matter of New York State Correctional Officers & Police Benevolent Assn. v. State of New York*, 94 N.Y.2d 321, 704 N.Y.S.2d 910, 726 N.E.2d 462 (1999).

Further, a petition to stay arbitration is an extreme remedy that will be granted only if there is no possibility that the arbitrator could fashion any relief consistent with public policy. Where the arbitrator has the ability to impose "adequately narrowed" relief and thus avoid violating public policy, "a stay of arbitration on policy grounds is premature and unjustified." *Matter of Port Washington Union Free School Dist.* v. *Port Washington Teachers Assn.*, 45 N.Y.2d 411, 408 N.Y.S.2d 453, 380 N.E.2d 280 (1978). Indeed, where an arbitrator "may be able to fashion a remedy not in violation of public policy, it would be improper for a court to intervene preemptively." *Matter of Committee of Interns and Residents [Dinkins]*, 86 N.Y.2d 478, 634 N.Y.S.2d 32, 657 N.E.2d 1315 (1995).

In addition, the BCB is entitled to substantial deference, and its determination as to whether a claim is arbitrable "may not be upset unless it is arbitrary and capricious or an abuse of discretion, as the Board is the neutral adjudicative agency statutorily authorized to make specified determinations." *Matter of New York City Dept. of Sanitation v. MacDonald*, 87 N.Y.2d 650, 642 N.Y.S.2d 156, 664 N.E.2d 1218 (1996).

In the case at hand, these combined factors lead me to conclude that the City's petition to stay arbitration was premature. I of course acknowledge, as the Majority skillfully recounts, the broad powers given to DOI to investigate crime and corruption in City government. And I share the Majority's concern regarding undue interference with serious criminal investigations. But a stay of arbitration should be reserved for the clearest of cases where there is no question that a strong public policy bars arbitration of a grievance, and where there is no possibility that the arbitrator could fashion an acceptable, intermediate remedy. Here, we are a long way from requiring the immediate and drastic remedy of a stay.

As an initial matter, the arbitrator could very well issue a ruling that would moot the City's public policy argument. As the Majority acknowledges, the City's argument rests on the assertion that the collective bargaining agreement impedes "DOI's ability to conduct criminal investigations." We do not yet know, however, whether the CBA applies to criminal investigations, or, for that matter, to any investigation conducted by DOI. Indeed, the Individual Rights provisions of the CBA make repeated references to interrogations by the "Employer," and to "Departmental" investigations and trials. Arguably, these provisions apply only to internal Fire Department investigations—not to DOI investigations or serious criminal investigations. Were the arbitrator to make such a finding, the CBA would not violate public policy. Alternatively, the arbitrator could find that some of the CBA provisions apply to DOI investigations but not others—for instance, that fire officers are entitled to notice of interrogations but not use immunity or union representation. I am not convinced that such a finding would necessarily contravene public policy. At the very least, it would be beneficial for the courts to have the decision of the arbitrator—including an authoritative interpretation of the CBA—before they are forced to determine whether the CBA violates public policy.

A stay would also be particularly inappropriate here because there appear to be lingering factual questions that are not made clear by the record. Significantly, contrary to the Majority, it is not clear whether DOI in this case was conducting a criminal investigation of the fire officers. The City asserts that it was; the Union, however, insists that this was merely a disciplinary investigation. The record before us contains no details concerning the investigation, except that a firefighter eventually pleaded guilty to a crime. Notably—and disturbingly—the City has not rested its argument on the particular importance of this investigation, but instead contends that all DOI investigations—whether criminal or disciplinary in nature—are immune from the CBA provisions as a matter of public policy. I, however, find the nature of the particular investigation of critical importance in determining whether the public policy exception applies. Given the lack of factual detail in the record, this is yet another matter on which the arbitrator should be permitted to make a finding before the courts invoke the broad sweep of the public policy exception.

Finally, there is no concern that arbitration would delay a criminal investigation in the case at hand. The investigation has already been completed; the Union has not sought to stay interrogations or any investigative proceedings. Rather, the Union is seeking a post-deprivation remedy for alleged violations that occurred in the past. And contrary to the Majority, the Union is not seeking to arbitrate "all future DOI investigations." Rather, it is seeking only to arbitrate the alleged violations under the particular facts of the case at hand. Thus, there is no need for an unusually expeditious resolution in the instant case. * * * I would reverse the order of the Appellate Division, vacate the stay and remit the matter for further proceedings before the arbitrator.

NOTES

1. What is the relationship between the "legal arbitrability" question and the scope of bargaining? Does it follow from the court's opinion that the union could not have insisted that the City bargain over procedures to be followed in investigations of firefighter misconduct? That the City could not have willingly agreed to such procedures?

2. New York courts have continued to apply the non-delegability doctrine in reviewing arbitration decisions. In *Matter of County of Chautauqua v. Civil Service Employees Association, Local 1000, AFSCME*, 8 N.Y.3d 513, 838 N.Y.S.2d 1, 869 N.E.2d 1 (2007), the court declined to order arbitration of a dispute regarding employee layoffs. The union asserted that employees must be laid off by overall seniority according to the collective bargaining agreement, but the court found that the civil service law required layoff by

seniority within position. Thus, prior to any layoffs the county was required to identify the positions in which layoffs were necessary, a duty that was not delegable. To allow the county to negotiate away this prerogative would have the potential of impairing public service by requiring layoff of essential qualified employees. Does the non-delegability doctrine allow employers to avoid compliance with contractual obligations? To negotiate unenforceable agreements? How should a court determine that a duty is non-delegable?

3. Courts seem especially sensitive to the claim of non-delegability when school teachers or education issues are involved. See, e.g., *Berkshire Hills Regional School District Committee v. Berkshire Hills Education Association*, 375 Mass. 522, 377 N.E.2d 940 (1978) (power to appoint a principal is a non-delegable managerial prerogative); *Marion County Board of Education v. Marion County Education Association*, 86 S.W.3d 202 (Tenn.App.2001) (accord); *School Administrative District No. 58 v. Mount Abram Teachers Association*, 704 A.2d 349 (Me.1997) (setting aside arbitration award that modified school board's policies with respect to teaching of books with sexually explicit content). But compare *School Committee of Danvers v. Tyman*, 372 Mass. 106, 360 N.E.2d 877 (1977), in which a teachers' union sought arbitration of a grievance asserting that, in evaluating an English teacher for tenure, the school committee failed to follow evaluation procedures contained in an applicable collective bargaining agreement. The trial court ordered a stay of arbitration but the Supreme Judicial Court reversed:

> Although a school committee may not surrender its authority to make tenure decisions, there is no reason why a school committee may not bind itself to follow certain procedures precedent to the making of any such decision. * * * In this case, no occasion for a stay of the arbitration arises merely from the possibility of an arbitrator's award which might purport to intrude into the school committee's inviolate authority. * * *
>
> If a violation is found by the arbitrator, he may not grant tenure to the teacher, but he may fashion a remedy which falls short of intruding into the school committee's exclusive domain. Some violations of evaluation procedures may be trivial and not justify any relief. * * * The arbitrator might direct merely that the omitted procedures be followed and the teacher's record corrected as appears appropriate. However, in other cases, the failure to follow evaluation procedures may be shown to have so prejudiced a teacher's position that more substantial relief may be in order. It would be premature in this case to announce any limits on the scope of an arbitrator's award in such a case, provided it does not award tenure to the teacher.

What might explain the receptiveness to nondelegability arguments in the cases involving public education?

C. ARBITRAL FINALITY AND JUDICIAL REVIEW

In the face of concerns over the impact of arbitration in the public sector, some jurisdictions experimented with forms of arbitration that were explicitly non-final, such as "advisory arbitration," in which the public entity remained free to reject the arbitrator's award. Advisory arbitration is now a rare phenomenon, and most jurisdictions accept the finality of arbitration awards, generally along the lines of the *Enterprise Wheel* standard, which calls for enforcement of the award so long as it draws its "essence" from the agreement. See Ann C. Hodges, The Steelworkers Trilogy in the Public Sector, 66 *Chicago-Kent Law Review* 631, 648 (1992). There remain, however, variations in application of the test, as the following case illustrates.

1. DEFERRING (OR NOT) TO THE ARBITRATOR'S INTERPRETATION OF THE AGREEMENT

A common law of contract interpretation has developed based on the decisions of arbitrators over many years. No decision of an arbitrator is binding on any other but arbitrators often follow this common law, if only because it is often in accord with the parties' expectations. Questions of interpretation of collective bargaining agreements often turn on the question of the role of past practices of the parties. The parties may argue that past practices inform as to the meaning of the contract, modify express provisions of the contract, or create binding terms and conditions of employment even in the absence of contract language. Arbitrators vary in their use of past practice for these purposes. Zipper clauses and integration clauses may also be important in contract interpretation. An integration clause typically states that the written agreement is the entire agreement between the parties and no modifications are permitted except by written agreement. A zipper clause acknowledges that the parties had a full opportunity to bargain over the terms of the agreement and waives the right to bargain over matters not covered by the agreement during the term of the contract. Finally, contract clauses reserving particular rights to management are often important provisions in contract interpretation decisions. Of course, the terms of the particular agreement are most important in the decisions of arbitrators.

COUNTY OF ALLEGHENY v. ALLEGHENY COUNTY PRISON EMPLOYEES INDEPENDENT UNION

Pennsylvania Supreme Court, 1977.
476 Pa. 27, 381 A.2d 849.

POMEROY, J.

The question presented by this appeal is whether, in an arbitration of a grievance by public employees under a collective bargaining agreement, an award sustaining the grievance may properly be based on a practice of the parties which had been obtained during a period prior to the agreement. Under the facts of this case and in light of the terms of the agreement, which contains no past practice clause nor any mention of the practice in question, but does contain an integration clause, we answer the question in the negative.

This case was initiated by the appellant, Allegheny County Prison Employees Independent Union (hereinafter "Union") when on May 10, 1972, it filed a grievance against the County of Allegheny (hereinafter "County") under the provisions of a collective bargaining agreement between the parties. The grievance concerned two aspects of mealtime conditions for guards working at the Allegheny County jail: The Union demanded that the officers' lounge where the guards took their meals be supervised at mealtime by a guard and that the guards be able to select for their meals any food available from the jail kitchen rather than being limited to the menus offered to the prisoners. The matter proceeded to arbitration and, following a hearing in which the County entered only a "special" appearance, the arbitrator issued an award which agreed with appellant's position and sustained the grievance. On appeal, the Commonwealth Court, in a unanimous opinion, set aside the arbitrator's award. This Court then granted the Union's petition for allowance of appeal. * * *.

The ultimate question before us is whether the arbitrator's interpretation of the collective bargaining agreement "can in any rational way be derived from the agreement, viewed in the light of its language, context, and any other indicia of the parties' intention. * * * " *Community College of Beaver v. Community College of Beaver County, Society of the Faculty*, 473 Pa. 576, 375 A.2d 1267 (1977). Because we conclude that the negative answer which the Commonwealth Court gave to this question was correct, we affirm its order setting aside the award. * * *

I.

The threshold question in this case is whether the subject matter of the asserted grievance was arbitrable. As this Court noted in *Board of Education of Philadelphia v. Federation of Teachers Local No. 3*, 464 Pa. 92, 346 A.2d 35 (1975), Pennsylvania labor policy not only favors but requires the submission to arbitration of public employee grievances "arising out of the interpretation of the provisions of a collective bargaining agreement." * * * From this policy is derived the corollary principle that where, as here, an arbitrator has interpreted a collective bargaining agreement in favor of the arbitrability of the grievance before him, a reviewing court should be slow indeed to disagree. * * *

After reviewing the applicable clauses of the collective bargaining agreement in question[8] we cannot say that the arbitrator was in error

8. The pertinent clauses are as follows:

Article III Grievance Procedure. 1. Grievance Procedure Definitions: A. Grievance—An alleged breach or violation of this Agreement or a dispute arising out of the interpretation or application of the provisions of this Agreement. * * * 2. Scope of Grievance Procedure: Any matter not specifically defined as a grievance in Section 1 above, as well as any matter reserved to the discretion of the County by the statutes, legal precedents and regulations of the Commonwealth of Pennsylvania, and/or by the terms of this Agreement is not a grievance and will not be construed as a grievance. * * *

Article XII Management Rights. The County retains and reserves unto itself all powers, rights, authority, duties and responsibilities including but not limited to the security of the prison

when he concluded that the dispute concerning the mealtime conditions of the employee guards arose out of the interpretation or application of the provisions of the agreement. We must, therefore, disagree with the Commonwealth Court insofar as it held that the grievance filed by the Union was not arbitrable.

II.

Turning to the substantive question of whether the arbitrator's award had a rational basis in the collective bargaining agreement, we must conclude that it did not. The agreement contains no provision whatever which deals either with the question of security arrangements for the employees' mealtimes or with what food should be available to the employees from the prison kitchen.[9] The arbitrator's decision that the union members were entitled to choose for their luncheons any food available in the prison kitchen and were not limited to the items available on the daily prison menu was based on what he found to have been the past practice of the parties over a period of time, a practice which, so the arbitrator held, had been implicitly incorporated in the collective bargaining agreement which became effective in 1972.[10]

A recognized commentator[11] in the field of labor law identifies four situations in which evidence of past practice is used in arbitrations: (1) to clarify ambiguous language; (2) to implement contract language which sets forth only a general rule; (3) to modify or amend apparently unambig-

---

conferred upon and vested in it by the Commonwealth of Pennsylvania and all matters not covered by this Agreement. * * *

9. The only clause of the agreement which refers to meals is found in Article VII, Section 4: "A lunch period of 30 minutes shall be made available to all employees before their sixth hour of work." The Union argued to the arbitrator that implicit in this clause are both a choice of foods to be served to the guards and a requirement that security be provided during mealtimes. The arbitrator did not address himself to this contention in his opinion and award, nor did he in his award purport to interpret either the 30 minute lunch clause or the integration clause, (Article XXIV, Sec. 1), discussed infra. The dissenting opinion of Mr. Justice Roberts, post, has ascribed to the arbitrator interpretations that simply are not to be found in his decision.

10. The facts shown by the record are as follows:

Before 1967, prison guards at the Allegheny County jail ate their meals in the prison kitchen, either bringing their lunches from outside or choosing from any of the food available within the prison. In May of 1967, the warden directed employees to cease bringing their own lunches. The Union protested this directive and submitted a grievance to a three member panel authorized by the predecessor statute to PERA, * * *. This panel recommended that the prohibition against lunches brought from outside be continued, but that the guards be given a choice of any food available in the prison kitchen. For some time this recommendation, although not legally binding, was followed. When later an officer's lounge was established the guards were permitted to take their luncheons from the kitchen to the lounge to be eaten. In December, 1970, the warden issued an order, which although objected to was apparently complied with, restricting the prison guard personnel to a choice of food from the daily prison menu. After the collective bargaining agreement became effective in May of 1972, the Union filed the present grievance challenging the 1970 directive of management. When, apparently in response to the filing of this grievance, the prison authorities issued further orders restricting the guards' privileges, the Union filed an unfair labor practice charge with the Pennsylvania Labor Relations Board. This charge was settled by the County's agreement to rescind the later restrictions, with the understanding that the processing of the grievance would continue. After this settlement, the old practice of allowing each employee to select any food available was, according to the arbitrator, gradually reinstated.

11. R. Mittenthal, *Past Practice and the Administration of Collective Bargaining Agreements, Proceedings of the 14th Annual Meeting of the National Academy of Arbitrators* 30 (1961).

uous language which has arguably been waived by the parties; and (4) to create or prove a separate, enforceable condition of employment which cannot be derived from the express language of the agreement. In the case at bar, the arbitrator concluded that the implementation by the County of the advisory recommendation of a panel of arbitrators in 1967 created a binding past practice, a clear example of the fourth use of past practices in the above formulation. With this implementation, the arbitrator held,

> the Guards acquired a working condition which constituted a recognizable benefit. Its constant, continual use caused the benefit to ripen into a binding practice. * * * The privilege given to each Guard to choose his meal from the available kitchen foods became one of the many day-to-day facets of the working relationship between the Prison administration and its Guards.[14]

As for the Union demand for protection of its members by a guard posted in the officers' lounge at mealtimes, the arbitrator concluded that a "slightly different" problem was involved but that the contractual reservation to the County in Article XII of all responsibility relating to security, see n.8, *supra*, "must be interpreted in a reasonable fashion. The Union is not seeking to interfere with the security of the Prison. On the contrary, it is trying to insure the physical safety of its member Guards. * * * The Prison was sufficiently concerned about the problem to provide a Guard over the residents when employees ate in the Prison kitchen. There is no reason why the same protection ought not to be afforded to employees while they are eating in the Officers' Lounge."

---

14. The arbitrator gave the following rationale in support of his conclusion that the past practice was implicitly included in the bargaining agreement:

> The Warden was, or should have been, aware that a contractual grievance procedure provided the only practicable way by which the Union could attack his December 1970 edict (restricting the employees to food on the daily menu). * * * During the negotiations leading up to the 1972 collective bargaining agreement, which first provided that type of grievance procedure, this awareness must be imputed to the County. It would obviously be impossible, in such an agreement, to incorporate all of the work practices and customs previously accepted by the mutual consent of the parties. If the County wished to bar this particular matter from the grievance procedure, the County had the duty to seek specific contract language on the subject. In this particular instance, the absence of a past practice clause does not eliminate the eating customs in effect as of December 1970. * * *

In contrast, the Commonwealth Court, in an alternative ground for its decision, concluded as follows from its review of the record:

> If there did, in fact, exist a past policy regarding luncheon procedure, it was a policy of constant change. Being aware of the ever-varying nature of appellant's practice towards guards' luncheons, to escape the application of (those provisions of the agreement dealing with management's discretion over all matters not covered by the agreement), it was incumbent upon (the Union) to have negotiated and explicitly reached an agreement upon this particular condition of employment."

In light of our disposition of this case there is no need for us to resolve the question of which, if either, party had the responsibility to take the initiative in making past practices a subject of negotiation. Similarly, we are not called upon to decide whether a practice which was legally but unilaterally terminated by employer direction a year and a half before the collective bargaining agreement was entered into, but which termination has been a subject of continuing controversy between the parties, is properly to be considered a "past practice" as a matter of law. See Mittenthal, *Past Practice and the Administration of Collective Bargaining Agreements*, 59 Mich. L.Rev. 1017, 1033–34 (1961).

The question for decision is whether the arbitrator was correct in concluding that the parties to the contract here involved implicitly incorporated into it, as separately enforceable conditions of their employment relationship, practices relative to food and security at lunch times which had prevailed for a time in the past, when those practices are neither repudiated in the agreement nor inconsistent with its terms, but when the contract includes a broad clause to the effect that the agreement as written is the complete agreement between the parties.[15] Although the non-inclusion of the practices in the bargaining agreement does not necessarily compel the conclusion that past practices are not impliedly so incorporated, the existence in a contract of a broad integration clause, if it means anything, does clearly negate the notion that the parties meant to include any terms or conditions, including those based only on past practices, not specifically incorporated in the written contract or reasonably inferable from its provisions. We think that this provision is dispositive of this case. At least one arbitrator has expressly so held, *Lone Star Brewing Co.*, 53 LA 1317 (1969) (LeRoy Autrey), and we know of no decision to the contrary. See also Cox & Dunlop, *The Duty to Bargain Collectively During the Term of an Existing Agreement*, 63 Harv.L.Rev. 1097, 1116–1117 (1950).

In deciding as we do, we hold only that where a collective bargaining agreement not only makes no mention whatever of past practices but does include a broad integration clause, an award which incorporates into the agreement, as separately enforceable conditions of the employment relationship, past practices which antedate the effective date of that agreement cannot be said to "draw its essence from the collective bargaining" agreement. *United Steelworkers v. Enterprise Wheel and Car Corp.*, 363 U.S. 593, 80 S.Ct. 1358, 4 L.Ed.2d 1424 (1960). We hasten to add that courts are not to become super-arbitrators and are bound to defer to the arbitrators' findings relative to the intent of the parties as the arbitrators perform their task of interpreting labor contracts negotiated under PERA. The able arbitrator in this case, however, was not so much interpreting the contract before him as he was declaring, no doubt out of his conviction of what was fair and reasonable, that the employer should be bound by a non-existent provision which the arbitrator then incorporates into the contract by implication. But there is here nothing to support the implication. Conceding that the past attitude of the management of the County's prison may have been petty, it is nevertheless a function of future bargaining to remedy the situation. For the arbitrator to seek to supply the remedy is on these facts not in accord with the approach of *Enterprise*,

15. The clause is contained in Article XXIV of the agreement and is as follows: Article XXIV "1. The parties mutually agree that the terms and conditions expressly set forth in this Agreement represent the full and complete agreement and commitment between the parties thereto."

Paragraph 2 of Article XXIV provides as follows: "2. All items proposed by the Union, whether agreed to or rejected, will not be subject to renegotiation until negotiations for a new contract commence * * * and items included within the scope of the bargaining which were or are not proposed by the Union shall likewise not be subject to negotiation until the period specified above."

supra, which we have adopted as the proper one for applying the Arbitration Act in public employment contracts. The award must, therefore, be set aside. What we have said, of course, is not to suggest that in another case the evidence may not justify a contrary conclusion. Nor do we intend to say that an arbitrator's reliance on past practices to clarify ambiguous language in the collective bargaining agreement, to implement general contract language or to show that a specific provision in the contract has been waived by the parties, would be improper although the agreement in question included an integration clause.

The order of the Commonwealth Court is affirmed.

ROBERTS, J. dissenting.

* * * I agree with the majority's conclusion that the grievance is arbitrable. I disagree, however, with the majority's conclusion that the arbitrator's award exceeded the bounds of the collective bargaining agreement. The majority reaches its result because it asserts that the arbitrator drew upon "past practices" in making his award, and that consideration of such practices is barred by an integration clause in the collective bargaining agreement. In so holding, however, the majority substitutes its interpretation of the integration clause for that of the arbitrator, in contravention of the contractual arbitration clause which gives the arbitrator power to interpret all parts of the collective bargaining agreement including the integration clause itself. The majority also contravenes the decisions which make the arbitrator the final interpreter of the contract both as to law and to fact. * * *

The majority's holding deprives the arbitrator of two of his most valuable tools in settling labor disputes whenever the collective bargaining agreement contains a boilerplate integration clause. These tools are the arbitrator's knowledge of the particular conditions in which labor and management operate and his knowledge of the rules the "law of the shop" which labor and management have developed to respond to these conditions. I cannot agree that the presence of an integration clause so completely alters the basic rules of the arbitration process. I therefore dissent.

The majority holds that the arbitrator failed to give proper weight to the "integration clause" in the collective bargaining agreement. In so doing, however, the majority misapplies the "essence test," the standard by which courts of this Commonwealth are to review arbitration awards. The "essence test" adopted in *Community College of Beaver County*, *supra*, was the first set forth by the Supreme Court of the United States in *United Steelworkers v. Enterprise Wheel & Car Corp.*, 363 U.S. 593, 80 S.Ct. 1358, 4 L.Ed.2d 1424 (1960):

> [T]he arbitrators under these collective agreements are indispensable agencies in a continuous collective bargaining process. They sit to settle disputes at the plant level—disputes that require for their solution knowledge of the custom and practices of a particular factory or of a particular industry as reflected in particular agreements. When

an arbitrator is commissioned to interpret and apply the collective bargaining agreement, he is to bring his informed judgment to bear in order to reach a fair solution of a problem. This is especially true when it comes to formulating remedies. There the need is for flexibility in meeting a wide variety of situations. The draftsmen may never have thought of what specific remedy should be awarded to meet a particular contingency. Nevertheless, an arbitrator is confined to interpretation and application of the collective bargaining agreement; he does not sit to dispense his own brand of industrial justice. He may of course look for guidance from many sources, yet his award is legitimate only so long as it draws its essence from the collective bargaining agreement. When the arbitrator's words manifest an infidelity to this obligation, courts have no choice but to refuse enforcement of the award.

This "essence test" reflects a judgment that arbitrators, and not courts, are best equipped to deal with the multitude of potential disputes which the parties agree to submit to them. This deferential standard also serves to solidify the integrity of the arbitration process by giving the parties the assurance that the decision of the arbitrator will, in the vast majority of cases, be final.

The majority's decision is contrary to these policies. The majority, by requiring the arbitrator to conform to the strict rules of contract law applied by the courts in non-labor contract cases deprives him of the opportunity to employ his knowledge of the customs and practices of the industry and the shop involved. As the Supreme Court of the United States stated in *United Steelworkers v. Warrior & Gulf Navigation Co.*, 363 U.S. 574, 80 S.Ct. 1347, 4 L.Ed.2d 1409 (1960):

> "the institutional characteristics and the governmental nature of the collective-bargaining process demand a common law of the shop which implements and furnishes the context of the agreement. We must assume that intelligent negotiators acknowledged so plain a need unless they stated a contrary rule in plain words." The labor arbitrator's source of law is not confined to the express provisions of the contract, as the industrial common law, the practices of the industry and the shop is equally a part of the collective bargaining agreement although not expressed in it. The labor arbitrator is usually chosen because of the parties' confidence in his knowledge of the common law of the shop and their trust in his personal judgment to bring to bear considerations which are not expressed in the contract as criteria for judgment.

In view of the fact that the guards are required to eat their meals on the premises, the award here which covers the meals for guards and the security available to the guards while eating involves important working conditions. By allowing a boilerplate integration clause to divest the arbitrator of the ability to make an award concerning these important conditions, the majority defeats the policy which encourages arbitrators to draw upon their knowledge of the particular job setting so that a "fair solution of the problem" can be reached. The majority forces the arbitrator to treat the integration clause with more deference than the parties to the collective bargaining agreement may have intended, given their particular work situation. In so holding, the majority discourages the arbitrator from performing fully the services expected from him.

Moreover today's decision destroys the stability of the arbitration process. * * * If an award of an arbitrator is upheld by the courts so long as it is rationally based, then parties can respect the decision of the arbitrator as a final resolution of the dispute between them. If, instead, the award of the arbitrator is open to unnecessary judicial modification, the arbitrator becomes only a small step in the process of resolving labor disputes; the judgment of the arbitrator which the parties bargained for is thereby replaced with the judgment of the courts.

* * *

It is part of the arbitrator's function, not part of a court's, to determine the import of an integration clause in a collective bargaining agreement, at least where the contract contains a clause submitting to arbitration any "dispute arising out of the interpretation or application of the provisions of this Agreement." We must realize that an arbitrator may draw his understanding of any clause in the contract, including an integration clause, from the particular labor setting in which the contract was signed. * * * Here, the arbitrator specifically found that the parties could not have reduced to writing all aspects of the ongoing labor-management relationship. In fact, the "lunch period" clause does not specifically mention all the conditions under which employees are to take their meal breaks. The arbitrator concluded that the contract should be interpreted so that the conditions under which the lunch break is taken are appropriate to the workplace in which these employees find themselves. These employees are prison guards. They are prohibited from leaving prison grounds during lunch. It was wholly rational for the arbitrator to use his knowledge of what work in a prison is like to conclude that when the contract specified a "30–minute lunch period" it must have meant a lunch period during which there is adequate protection for those guards who are eating. Similarly, it is not so irrational as to go beyond the essence of the agreement for the arbitrator to conclude that a "30–minute lunch period" was intended to be a period at which the guards, like most American workers, have a reasonable choice of foods. The arbitrator was aware of the impracticality of allowing the guards to enter and leave the prison grounds during lunch in order to find a choice of foods. He also considered the prison rule prohibiting guards from bringing their own lunches. He devised means of implementing the collective bargaining agreement based on the peculiar circumstances of these particular workers in this particular prison. This is the arbitrator's job.

The arbitrator reached these conclusions in light of the arbitration and integration clauses in the contract. It was his duty under the arbitration clause to interpret the "lunch" clause. He interpreted it in light of management rules and working conditions which require prison employees to remain on the premises and to eat food from the prison kitchen. In the course of interpreting the "lunch" provision of the contract, he found the integration clause did not preclude his award. I would reverse the order of the Commonwealth Court and enforce the award of the arbitrator.

[The dissenting opinion of MANDERINO, J. is omitted.]

NOTES

1. Do you agree that the arbitrator's reading of the agreement was "irrational"? Which view of the matter, the majority's or the dissent's, is likely to appeal to public employers? To unions? Which best serves the policies underlying the collective bargaining statute?

2. Both the majority and the dissent cite the private sector *Steelworkers' Trilogy* and purport to follow it. Which opinion is more faithful to the principles of the *Trilogy*? As in the case of arbitrability issues the *Trilogy* admonishes courts to avoid entanglement in the merits of the dispute when reviewing arbitration awards. Did the majority do so in this case? How can a court review a decision to determine whether it draws its essence from the agreement while avoiding consideration of the merits of the case?

3. If the court had deferred to the arbitrator's interpretation of the integration clause, would it also have had to defer to the arbitrator's finding that a contractually binding past practice existed although the practice had ceased by the employer's unilateral action months before the execution of the contract in which it was assertedly incorporated? See the facts recited at n.14 of the case.

4. Most efforts to vacate arbitration awards focus on the decision of the arbitrator regarding the merits of the grievance. Should the courts review procedural decisions of arbitrators? In *City of Philadelphia v. Fraternal Order of Police Lodge No. 5*, 985 A.2d 1259 (Pa. 2009), the court overturned an arbitrator's decision to preclude the city from using evidence which it had failed to turn over to the union in response to a subpoena. As a result of the decision, the city was unable to prove its case and lost the arbitration. Despite the extremely limited statutory grounds for review, the court concluded that review was permissible because there was an issue of constitutional due process, and appeals on constitutional grounds were permissible. The court evaluated the arbitrator's decision against the standard for discovery sanctions and found it wanting because of the limited prejudice suffered by the union and the absence of willful misconduct on the part of the city. The dissent argued that the arbitrator's decision was evidentiary and not subject to review by the court.

What impact would allowing judicial review of procedural rulings of arbitrators have on arbitral finality? Does review of procedural rulings necessarily second-guess the arbitrator's decision? The union in *City of Philadelphia* sought the sanctions, and the arbitrator awarded them, in part based on the claim of repeated discovery violations by the city in many arbitrations. Given the decision in this case, what can and should a union, at least in Pennsylvania, do about repeated employer violations of the requirement that they provide information to unions necessary to prepare for arbitration? In many cases, as in this case involving discharge of a police officer, much of the investigatory information is in the possession of the employer. Might this case have come out differently if the sanction had not barred essentially all of the employer's evidence? If the employer had not turned the information over to the union two weeks before the rescheduled arbitration? Should those factors make a difference to the court reviewing the arbitrator's decision? Subsequent to the *City of Philadelphia* case, the Commonwealth Court of Pennsylvania upheld the Court of Common Pleas' refusal to overturn an arbitrator's award because the arbitrator refused to reopen the record to accept evidence acquired after the hearing which purported to contradict the testimony of the union president. *City of Wilkes–Barre v. Wilkes–Barre Fire Fighters Association Local 104*, 992 A.2d 246 (Pa. Commw. Ct. 2010).

5. It is not uncommon for arbitrators to order reinstatement of discharged employees without back pay, effectively imposing a suspension for the length of time that it takes from discharge to the decision of the arbitrator. Private sector challenges to such decisions are neither common nor successful, although the practice has been subject to significant criticism. Some cynically suggest that it is the arbitrator's method of splitting the baby, i.e., giving something to both sides, in order to obtain future employment. See Laura J. Cooper, et al., *ADR in the Workplace* 324–27 (2005).

2. POST–ARBITRAL DETERMINATION OF INARBITRABILITY

A public entity that has participated in arbitration may be able to challenge the award on the ground that the issue was not legally subject to arbitration in the first place. An example is *Board of Education v. Round Valley Teachers Association*, 13 Cal.4th 269, 52 Cal.Rptr.2d 115, 914 P.2d 193 (1996), in which the California Supreme Court unanimously overturned an arbitration award based on procedural and "just cause" protections for probationary employees provided in the applicable collective bargaining agreement. The court found that the collectively bargained procedures were in conflict with the procedures prescribed by the California Education Code, which permitted school boards to decline reappointment of probationary employees without cause, and the statutory provisions were preemptive: "[T]he intent of [the statutory provision] was to vest *exclusive* discretion in the school district to decide whether or not to reelect probationary teachers, and the procedures set forth in the [the collective agreement] effectively supersede that discretion." When the 'legislature vests such discretion in a body, the Court observed, "the subject matter may not be the subject of either mandatory or permissive collective bargaining." To similar effect, see *Chicago School Reform Board of Trustees v. Illinois Educational Labor Relations Board*, 309 Ill.App.3d 88, 242 Ill.Dec. 397, 721 N.E.2d 676 (1999) (setting aside arbitrator's order reinstating full-time substitute teacher, on grounds that the School Board had exclusive and nondelegable power to discharge teachers under state's School Code).

Compare *In the Matter of the Arbitration Between Professional, Clerical, Technical Employees Association and Buffalo Board of Education*, 90 N.Y.2d 364, 660 N.Y.S.2d 827, 683 N.E.2d 733 (1997), in which the Board of Education challenged an arbitrator's award requiring promotion of the highest scoring person on the promotional list, on the ground that it interfered with the Board's statutory discretion. The challenge alleged violation of the rule-of-three principle, a common provision in civil service rules that requires an appointing authority to choose one of the top three candidates on the list of qualified individuals established by the civil service commission. The New York Court of Appeals acknowledged the propriety of the post-arbitral challenge procedure ("Given that the arbitrator here may have fashioned an award that did not implicate the public policy concerns now raised by the Board, a stay of arbitration on public policy grounds would have been premature"), but concluded on the merits that:

> there is nothing in our State's Constitution, the Civil Service Law or decisional law that prohibits an appointing authority from agreeing through collective negotiations on the manner in which it will select one of the top three qualified candidates from an eligible list for promotion. * * * While the Board has relied on long-settled precedent providing that restrictions upon an appointing authority's discretion afforded by the one-of-three rule may not be *imposed* by the Legislature or other external source * * * that precedent is not controlling where, as here the restrictions on the Board's discretion are self-imposed. * * * No precedent of this Court suggests that a public employer may not voluntarily bargain with respect to the exercise of such discretion.

Do you agree that the collectively-bargained restrictions are self-imposed?

3. OVERTURNING AWARDS ON THE BASIS OF PUBLIC POLICY

In the private sector the United States Supreme Court has declared that a court may overturn an arbitration award on the basis that it conflicts with public policy, but the policy must be "well defined and dominant," and ascertained "by reference to the laws and legal precedents and not from general considerations of supposed public interests," *W.R. Grace & Co. v. Local Union 759*, 461 U.S. 757, 103 S.Ct. 2177, 76 L.Ed.2d 298 (1983). The Court has never affirmed the overturning of an award on that ground. Rather, it has insisted on enforcement of awards that ordered reinstatement of an employee who operated dangerous machinery, fired for allegedly smoking marijuana in a car on company property, *United Paperworkers v. Misco*, 484 U.S. 29, 108 S.Ct. 364, 98 L.Ed.2d 286 (1987) and, more recently, that ordered reinstatement of a truck driver, discharged after he tested positive for marijuana in a random drug test required by Department of Transportation regulations for workers performing "safety sensitive" tasks. *Eastern Associated Coal Corporation v. United Mine Workers of America*, 531 U.S. 57, 121 S.Ct. 462, 148 L.Ed.2d 354 (2000). The Court has resisted the consistent invitation of unions to declare that an award must be enforced unless it requires violation of some applicable law, but as Justice Scalia observed in a concurring opinion in *Eastern Associated Coal*, it is hard to imagine how an arbitration award would ever violate a public policy as defined by the majority without actually conflicting with positive law. Before *Eastern Associated Coal*, courts periodically overturned private sector arbitration awards on public policy grounds but following that case, it is rare, and those few district courts that have overturned awards have been reversed on appeal.

In the public sector, some courts use the public policy exception to arbitral finality more freely. For example:

AFSCME v. Department of Central Management Services, 173 Ill.2d 299, 219 Ill.Dec. 501, 671 N.E.2d 668 (1996). In February 1990, Vera Dubose, a Child Welfare Specialist with the Illinois Department of Children and Family Services (DCFS), was fired after it was discovered that she had submitted a progress report stating that she had seen three children assigned to her supervision and that they were "doing fine," when in fact (it was later discovered) they had all perished in an accidental fire at their home the month before. Her union filed a grievance asserting, among other things, that the agency had failed to impose discipline in a timely manner, in violation of the collective agreement, which required that discipline "shall be imposed as soon as possible after the Employer is aware of the event or action giving rise to the discipline and has a reasonable period or time to investigate the matter," and in any event not more than 45 days after completion of the predisciplinary meeting. Ms. Dubose's false report was submitted in February 1990, and the agency learned of its falsity in August 1990. An investigator submitted a report on the matter in December 1990. The report disclosed that Ms. Dubose had failed to submit case plans for the family for the prior three years. No further action was taken until June 1991, when a predisciplinary meeting was conducted on the 24th of that month. On September 2, 1991, a predisciplinary report was issued recommending suspension, but the Agency decided instead upon discharge, and the union asked for arbitration.

The arbitrator sustained the grievance and reinstated Dubose on grounds of untimeliness of the discipline, but the Illinois Supreme Court held that the award should be set aside as contrary to public policy:

> [T]he State's interest in its children's welfare and protection must override AFSCME's concerns for timeliness. In certain cases, inter-

> preting the time provisions as the arbitrator did in this case and ordering reinstatement will not contravene the public policy enunciated above. * * * As with any limitation, the nature of the conduct at issue must be considered before arbitrary time restrictions can be imposed. * * * [The arbitrator] failed to make *any* determination that the welfare of the minors in the DCFS system will not be compromised by such a reinstatement. Rather, he avoided discussion of the charges against DuBose. He did not take any precautionary steps to ensure the misconduct at issue here will not be repeated, and he neither considered nor respected the pertinent public policy concerns that arose from them. The remedy in this case violates public policy in that it totally ignores any legitimate public policy concerns. * * * Even if the arbitrator had considered issues of public policy, we may not abdicate to him our responsibility to protect the public interest at stake. * * * DCFS, in agreeing to a time provision that does not allow for exigent disciplinary circumstances, has compromised its ability to discharge its duties as expressed by the General Assembly. * * * We believe that a bright-line test requiring that the award itself violate an *explicit* law has the potential to swallow the public policy exception. Indeed, this case illustrates why such a narrow view is unworkable. None of the acts enacted by the legislature concerning DCFS contain any statute which explicitly prohibits the agency from hiring 'dishonest' workers or workers previously disciplined for dishonesty. True, too, there is no statute which expressly prohibits DCFS workers from submitting a false case report. Such prohibitions are absent because the very essence of the act *presupposes* that only trustworthy worker will be hired.

Do you agree with the Court's analysis? Consider Justice Nickel's dissent: "I recognize that there exists a general policy favoring the diligent protection of minors. * * * However there exists no policy that mandates the discharge of every DCFS employee that files a false report, regardless of the circumstances." Is the majority saying that the Agency could not lawfully agree to a contract that would require reinstatement of an employee under the circumstances presented? Would the Agency have acted unlawfully if it had followed the recommendation of the disciplinary panel, and suspended the grievant instead of firing her?

Following *AFCSME v. Department of Central Management Services*, the Illinois Appellate Court decided *Central Community Unit School District No. 4 v. Illinois Educational Labor Relations Board*, 388 Ill. App.3d 1060, 328 Ill.Dec. 451, 904 N.E.2d 640 (2009). The employee, a high school custodian and substitute bus driver was fired after four incidents. Two of the incidents occurred in 2002 and involved the use of profanity at work, once in front of a fellow employee, referring to the school superintendent who had ordered him to do some work, and once in front of students in a confrontation with the basketball coach about players tracking mud in the gym. A three-day suspension was issued for those incidents. In 2004, he used profanity in front of students after a student spilled milk in the cafeteria. Later that same month while acting as a bus driver, he confiscated a cd player from a student on the bus and threw it into the trash, breaking the player. He was terminated for failure to control his anger and improper conduct, including use of profanity, and after a hearing challenging the termination as without just cause, the arbitrator ordered reinstatement to the custodian position subject to a 10–day suspension. The arbitrator declined to consider the bus incident because the employee had already been terminated as a bus driver. The Illinois Educational Labor Relations Board found that the employer violated the law by refusing to comply with the award but, on review, the Illinois Appellate Court disagreed, finding the award violated public policy by failing to consider the incident on the bus. While recognizing that earlier cases, including *AFSCME v. Department of Central Management Services,* had found public policy embodied in specific statutes, the court stated:

> we find support for the position there is a general policy in favor of the safety of school children in section 24–24 of the School Code. 105 ILCS 5/24–24 (West 2006). Section 24–24 places "teachers, other certificated educational employees, and any other person, whether or not a certificated employee, providing a related service for or with respect to a student" in the relation of parents and guardians to the pupils in all matters relating to discipline and conduct of the schools. 105 ILCS 5/24–24 (West 2006). They are charged with maintaining discipline in the schools. 105 ILCS 5/24–24 (West 2006). This relationship extends to all activities connected with the school and may be exercised at any time for the safety and supervision of the pupils in the absence of their parents or guardians. 105 ILCS 5/24–24 (West 2006).
>
> Schumacher's conduct as a bus driver is part of the evidence showing he has anger-management issues and that he has, on several occasions, directed his temper at school children. His anger-control issues were further displayed in other incidents at the school when Schumacher was performing his duties as a custodian, although those incidents involving students were verbal in nature. * * * Terminating Schumacher's employment as a bus driver and reassigning him to a custodian position at the elementary school does not (1) ensure he will have no contact with children or (2) eliminate the possibility he will have another incident involving his temper at or in the presence of children. All relevant evidence must be considered in this case because the safety and protection of school children is at issue. Accordingly, the decision to disregard Schumacher's conduct as a bus driver was arbitrary and capricious and this matter must be remanded for the Arbitrator to consider this evidence in reaching his decision. *Id.* at 1071–72, 904 N.E.2d at 649–50.

Consider the breadth of the public policy found by the court. Does it provide a potential avenue for challenging many other arbitration awards? What is the impact on the finality of arbitration? What incentives does this provide for parties dissatisfied with the outcome of an arbitration decision?

Cleveland Board of Education v. International Brotherhood of Firemen Local 701, 120 Ohio App.3d 63, 696 N.E.2d 658 (1997). A school bus mechanic was discharged after he tested positive for cocaine in a random drug test. An arbitrator ordered his reinstatement (subject to a one-month suspension without pay and a drug-free probation period of two years) on the grounds that nothing in the agreement permitted discharge on the basis of a positive drug test absent evidence of on-the-job use, and that the employer had not previously discharged other employees who tested positive for drug use. A trial court set the award aside, and the Ohio Court of Appeals affirmed on the ground that the award was "contrary to an explicit, well-defined and dominant public policy of state and federal law to suppress illegal drug use among transportation employees."

Other courts are more reluctant to set aside awards on public policy grounds. In *State of Minnesota v. Minnesota Association of Professional Employees*, 504 N.W.2d 751 (Minn.1993), a local government auditor, Beer, was discharged by the state auditor for falsifying expense reports and for being untruthful during an investigation into that misconduct. An arbitrator ordered his reinstatement on the ground that, while the auditor's misconduct justified discipline, discharge was too harsh because his "voluntary confession about his past misconduct, though incomplete, implies an intention to reform and thereby eliminate[s] the risk to the Employer of harm from future similar misconduct." The arbitrator reduced the discipline to suspension without back pay. A Minnesota trial court vacated the award on the ground that

> there is an explicit, well-defined, and dominant public policy favoring the proper expenditure of public funds, and the honesty and integrity of those charged with insuring that public funds are properly and honestly expended. Because Beer was one of the guardians of this system, his activities struck a blow at its very heart. His reinstatement might not adversely affect the operations of the State Auditor, but it would further damage the operation of the legislatively created system for monitoring public spending by reducing the public's confidence in that system and by demonstrating to other public employees that no serious consequences flow from a deliberate violation of the public's trust.

The Minnesota Court of Appeals reversed the trial court, and the Minnesota Supreme Court affirmed the appellate ruling:

> Under the terms of this agreement, it was the arbitrator's duty to determine whether there was "just cause" to discharge Beer, and the arbitrator's powers were limited only by the provision which stated, "The Arbitrator shall be without power to make decisions contrary to or inconsistent with or modifying or varying in any way the application of laws, rules, or regulations having the force and effect of law." * * *

> * * * [W]hile Beer's conduct would appear to violate a well-defined and dominant public policy against the embezzlement of state funds by public employees * * * courts must focus not on the grievant's conduct but on whether enforcement of the award would violate some well-defined and dominant public policy.

The court concluded it would not, and declined to decide whether a public policy exception might exist on another set of facts.

To similar effect is *City of Lynn v. Thompson*, 435 Mass. 54, 754 N.E.2d 54 (2001). A police officer with nineteen years of service was discharged for alleged use of excessive force in restraining a mentally ill woman for involuntary commitment, in the course of which he broke her arm. An arbitrator ruled there was no "just cause" for the discharge. While the officer's handling of the woman was "lacking in sensitivity," and he was therefore guilty of "conduct unbecoming an officer" warranting some discipline, the evidence did not support the charge of excessive force. And, while the same officer had previously been suspended for the use of excessive force in the application of handcuffs, after he and the city were named in a lawsuit which resulted in a judgment against both, that suspension had been reversed by another arbitrator, so that the officer had an "unblemished record." The City was ordered to reinstate the officer with back pay, subject to a two-week disciplinary suspension. Subsequently, the City settled a civil rights lawsuit based on the incident for $350,000.

A state trial court set aside the award on public policy grounds, and the Appeals Court affirmed, concluding that the officer's reinstatement violated public policy by "permit[ting] the continued presence on the police force of someone whose past and current conduct permits a strong inference that members of the public will be placed at risk of serious physical harm." The Massachusetts Supreme Judicial Court reversed. Rejecting the city's suggestion that the scope of review should be enlarged in cases involving the public sector, the court reasoned:

> Rightly or wrongly, the arbitrator found that Thompson was justified in using force to extract the cigarette lighter from [the woman's] hand, that he did not apply an excessive amount of force when he held up her arm and pried open her fingers, and that it was [the woman's] exceptionally fragile bones and her own 'thrashing about' that caused her injury. * * * One may well take issue with the arbitrator's analysis. The conclusion that an officer, whose record includes a civil rights judgment against himself and the city for excessive force (including an award of $30,000 in punitive damages), nevertheless has an unblemished record because another arbitrator determined that Thompson should not be disciplined for that incident, appears notably unsound. Similarly, the conclusion that force sufficient to break a person's arm, even the arm of a person with fragile bones, is not "excessive" when the person does not even pose a current danger to the officers is a conclusion that seems indefensible.

Finally common sense would dictate that the city would not voluntarily pay [the woman] $350,000 to settle her civil rights claim unless there were significant evidence supporting that claim. Yet, we are not free to ignore the arbitrator's conclusions merely because they appear unsound, poorly reasoned, or otherwise flawed. * * * From the arbitrator's conclusion that there was merely 'insensitive' conduct that was unbecoming an officer, one cannot conclude that Thompson poses an ongoing risk of physical injury to members of the public. It may be distasteful to keep such an officer on the force, but it does not violate public policy.

NOTES

1. How would you decide the following cases:

a. A child protective investigator received a report of alleged child abuse, investigated partially, but did not interview an apparent witness. To make up for it, she falsified her report, describing an interview which never took place. She was fired, but the arbitrator ordered her reinstated, on grounds that the employer should have engaged in progressive discipline. See *Department of Central Management Services v. AFSCME*, 245 Ill.App.3d 87, 185 Ill.Dec. 379, 614 N.E.2d 513 (1993).

b. A psychology professor was fired for smoking marijuana with his students at his condominium. An arbitrator found that discharge was too severe a penalty considering the professor's good record with the college, the fact that the students were adults, and the college's failure to promulgate rules on faculty drug use. See *Lansing Community College v. Lansing Chapter, Michigan Association for Higher Education,* 161 Mich. App. 321, 409 N.W.2d 823 (1987).

c. A state trooper was fired for his membership in the Ku Klux Klan. An arbitrator set aside the discharge finding that there was no evidence that his beliefs or membership had in the past, or were likely in the future, to affect his work, including his relationships with officers of color or the effective functioning of the agency. The membership was discovered after a tip to the agency that a patrol officer was participating in a members only online forum of the organization. See *State of Nebraska v. Henderson*, 277 Neb. 240, 762 N.W.2d 1 (2009).

d. An employee was fired for sexually harassing another employee in violation of the employer's sexual harassment policy. The arbitrator found that the employee did commit serious sexual harassment, but the employer did not show that it continued after it was reported to his supervisor, who warned the employee to cease the conduct. Also the arbitrator noted that, despite the policy, the employer tolerated sexual horseplay in the workplace. Accordingly the arbitrator reinstated the employee with full back pay. Title VII of the Civil Rights Act of 1964 prohibits sexual harassment and holds employers liable for harassment by rank-and-file employees if they knew or should have known of the harassment and failed to take appropriate remedial action. See *Philadelphia Housing Authority v. American Federation of State, County and*

Municipal Employees Local 934, 956 A.2d 477 (Pa.Commw.Ct. 2008), *appeal granted*, 601 Pa. 313, 972 A.2d 482 (May 18, 2009).

e. A city bus driver was fired after his employer found that some years before, but during his employment, he had been convicted of sexual abuse of his stepdaughter. Based largely on the testimony of his treating counselor, the arbitrator found a low risk of repetition of the conduct and ordered reinstatement conditioned on continued treatment. State law bars employment of sex offenders as school bus drivers but not as public transit drivers. See *Chicago Transit Authority v. Amalgamated Transit Union, Local 241*, 399 Ill.App.3d 689, 339 Ill.Dec. 444, 926 N.E.2d 919 (2010).

2. A further ground for denying arbitral finality may exist when it is found that the union has violated its duty of fair representation by the manner in which it handled the grievant's case. This issue is discussed in Chapter 12.

D. RELATIONSHIP OF ARBITRATION TO OTHER DISPUTE RESOLUTION FORA

As discussed in previous chapters, collective bargaining agreements in the public sector may cover matters that are also covered by other laws including, *inter alia*, civil service and tenure laws. Additionally, a claim of violation of a collective bargaining agreement might overlap with a claim of violation of the statute governing labor relations. Each of these other laws has its own enforcement mechanism, with a specified forum for resolution of disputes. This section discusses the relationship of arbitration under the collective bargaining agreement to other dispute resolution forums such as the courts, labor relations agencies, and other administrative agencies. As you read the materials in this section, consider what difficulties the overlap in available forums creates for the union, the employer and the employee. For arbitrators and statutorily-created administrative agencies such as civil service commissions and labor relations agencies. For courts.

1. ARBITRATION AND THE COURTS

In the private sector, the general rule is that an employee may not sue the employer on a claim arising under a collective bargaining agreement if the agreement contains an arbitration procedure applicable to the claim. *Republic Steel Corporation v. Maddox*, 379 U.S. 650, 85 S.Ct. 614, 13 L.Ed.2d 580 (1965). This rule of preclusion does not apply to a claim arising out of a statute or common law principle, except in a narrow category of cases in which resolution of the claim requires interpretation of the agreement. *Lingle v. Norge Division of Magic Chef, Inc.*, 486 U.S. 399, 108 S.Ct. 1877, 100 L.Ed.2d 410 (1988) (an employee claiming his discharge was tortious under state law because contrary to public policy could sue even though a claim for discharge without just cause could have been submitted to arbitration under the collective agreement). The preclusive effect of an arbitration provision is referred to as "Section 301 preemption"—Section 301 being the provision of the LMRA which governs enforcement of collective bargaining agreements.

Similar principles have been adopted in the public sector. For example, in *Coffey v. County of Plymouth*, 49 Mass.App. 193, 727 N.E.2d 856 (2000), a county correctional officer sued under a state statute providing, in Section 18A, that correctional officers who lose work as a result of injuries inflicted by violent prisoners or patients are guaranteed the difference between workers compensation benefits and their "regular salary." The issue involved the interpretation of the statutory term "regular salary," the county contending it meant the salary at the time of injury, and the deputy contending that it meant the current salary for the same position. The trial court dismissed the action on the ground that the deputy had failed to exhaust remedies available through the grievance and arbitration procedure of the applicable agreement, employee salaries being a subject within the scope of the agreement. The Court of Appeals of Massachusetts reversed:

> The legal principle which is to be applied in resolving this threshold issue is well established. "[S]ubstantive rights in the labor relations context can exist without interpreting collective-bargaining agreements." *Lingle v. Norge Div. of Magic Chef, Inc.*, 486 U.S. 399, 411 S.Ct. 1877, 100 L.Ed.2d 410 (1988). * * * The losses to which Section 18A extends are those which arise from the nature of the employment, not the collective bargaining agreement. There is nothing in the agreement that deals with the application of Section 18A which requires the employee to submit to a grievance procedure. * * * Parties to collective bargaining agreements are bound to arbitrate only disputes within the scope of the arbitration clause. * * * The arbitration clause here applies only to grievances as to "the meaning or application of the specific provisions of [the] Agreement," and thus is not relevant to Sec. 18.

In the private sector, an exception to the Section 301 exhaustion requirement exists when an employee is able to demonstrate that his failure to pursue contractual remedies was due to the union's violation of its duty of fair representation. The duty of fair representation is violated when a union's conduct toward a member of the bargaining unit is "arbitrary, discriminatory, or in bad faith." A union violates its duty of fair representation with respect to a grievance if it "arbitrarily ignore[s] a meritorious grievance or process[es] it in a perfunctory fashion." In such a case the employee may proceed in court against both the employer and the union and, if he succeeds in establishing a contact breach he may recover damages against both. *Vaca v. Sipes,* 386 U.S. 171, 87 S.Ct. 903, 17 L.Ed.2d 842 (1967). As discussed above, if arbitration has taken place, an exception to the usual rule of arbitral finality exists if an employee can demonstrate that the union violated its duty of fair representation in the manner in which it handled the grievance in arbitration, so as to "seriously undermine the integrity of the arbitral process." In such a case, as in a *Vaca* case, the employer as well as the union may be sued, with damages apportioned between them. *Hines v. Anchor Motor Freight*, 424 U.S. 554, 96 S.Ct. 1048, 47 L.Ed.2d 231 (1976).

Similar principles pertain in the public sector, but with some variations. For example, in Alaska, an employee is permitted to sue if the employee has made a good faith attempt to exhaust contractual procedures and the union has refused to take the case to arbitration, without a showing that the union breached its duty of fair representation by its refusal. This is true, the Alaska Supreme Court has explained, because in Alaska a public sector job is recognized as a property right which can be terminated only with due process of law, and a requirement that an employee demonstrate a breach of the union's duty of fair representation as a condition of obtaining a full hearing into the dismissal places too great a burden on the right to due process. *Casey v. City of Fairbanks*, 670 P.2d 1133 (Alaska 1983).

In *Vaca v. Sipes*, *supra*, the Supreme Court considered and rejected an argument that an employees should have a right to have their grievances taken to arbitration, saying:

> [In giving] the union discretion to supervise the grievance machinery and to invoke arbitration, the employer and the union contemplate that each will endeavor in good faith to settle grievances short of arbitration. Through this settlement process, frivolous grievances are ended prior to the most costly and time-consuming step in the grievance procedures. Moreover, both sides are assured that similar complaints will be treated consistently, and major problem areas in the interpretation of the collective bargaining contract can be isolated and perhaps resolved. * * * If the individual employee could compel arbitration of his grievance regardless of its merit, the settlement machinery provided by the contract would be substantially undermined, thus destroying the employer's confidence in the union's authority. * * * Moreover, under such a rule, a significantly greater number of grievances would proceed to arbitration. This would greatly increase the cost of the grievance machinery and could so overburden the arbitration process as to prevent it from functioning successfully. * * * Nor do we see substantial danger to the interests of the individual employee if his statutory agent is given the contractual power honestly and in good faith to settle grievances short of arbitration.

Is the Alaska approach less damaging to the values of the grievance-arbitration process? Is it justified by considerations peculiar to the public sector? For an argument by one Justice that *Casey* should be disapproved, see *State of Alaska v. Beard*, 960 P.2d 1 (Alaska 1998).

2. ARBITRATION AND THE LABOR RELATIONS AGENCY: DEFERRAL

Under the National Labor Relations Act, a party's conduct may give rise to an unfair labor practice charge and also be subject, in whole or in part, to arbitration under the collective agreement. For example, an employer who subcontracts work during the term of an agreement without offering to bargain in advance may be in breach of the statutory duty to bargain, and may also be in breach of some express or implied provision of the agreement. In such cases, the NLRB has established the procedure, if a charge is filed, of withholding its consideration of the charge pending completion of arbitration. *Collyer Insulated Wire*, 192 N.L.R.B. 837 (1971). This is known as "*Collyer* deferral." Similar though more controversial questions arise when a charge is filed on behalf of an individual asserting, for example, discharge for union activity. While the NLRB's policy in such cases has not been consistent, its current policy is to defer to arbitration in such cases as well. *United Technologies Corp.*, 268 N.L.R.B. 557 (1984).

In *Spielberg Manufacturing Co.*, 112 N.L.R.B. 1080 (1955), the Board held that when arbitration is completed, the Board will also defer to the award, and thus decline even to consider the merits, if the proceedings appear to have been fair and regular, all parties have agreed to be bound, and the decision is not clearly repugnant to the purposes and policies of the NLRA. This is known as "*Spielberg* deferral." In *Raytheon Co.*, 140 N.L.R.B. 883 (1963) the Board added the further requirement that the arbitrator have considered the unfair labor practice issue. The Board's current position is that an arbitrator will be deemed to have met this requirement if (1) "the contractual issue is factually parallel to the unfair labor practice issue, and (2) the arbitrator was presented generally with the facts relevant to resolving the unfair labor practice." The burden of showing these standards were not met is upon the party resisting deferral. *Olin Corp.*, 268 N.L.R.B. 573, 574 (1984).

Many jurisdictions with public sector labor agencies have adopted some version of both *Collyer* and *Spielberg* deferral policies, but applications vary. One common criticism of the NLRB's approach is that it fails to recognize the extent to which issues of contract breach and unfair labor practice may be analytically distinct even though factually parallel. When an employer makes a unilateral change in working conditions during the term of an agreement, for example, an arbitrator might decide that the change did not violate the agreement because the agreement contained no express provision that prevented the change, but the change might nevertheless be an unfair labor practice because the union did not clearly waive its right to bargain. The Illinois Education Labor Relations Board has declined to adopt the *Olin* approach, insisting instead that the party seeking post-arbitral deferral to an award bear the burden of demonstrating that the arbitrator's factual findings and contractual interpretations enabled the IELRB to resolve the statutory issues in the party's favor.

University of Illinois, 8 P.E.R.Ill. ¶ 1035 (Ill. ELRB 1992). For analysis, see Gerald E. Berendt & David A. Youngerman, The Continuing Controversy Over Labor Board Deferral to Arbitration—An Alternative Approach, 24 *Stetson Law Review* 175 (1994).

Adoption of deferral by the state agency, however, does not confer jurisdiction on an arbitrator to hear a dispute that is not legally arbitrable, although the dispute involves discrimination for union activity prohibited by the state labor relations statute. In *Sunnyvale Unified School District v. Jacobs*, 171 Cal.App.4th 168, 89 Cal.Rptr.3d 546 (2009), the union arbitrated the district's failure to reappoint a probationary teacher because of his union activity and the arbitrator ruled in favor of the union, ordering the teacher's reinstatement, which would confer permanent status or tenure. Based on *Board of Education v. Round Valley Teachers Association*, 13 Cal.4th 269, 52 Cal.Rptr.2d 115, 914 P.2d 193 (1996), discussed *supra* in § 11.C.2, the court upheld the lower court's decision to vacate the arbitrator's award because decisions about reappointment of probationary teachers are the exclusive province of the school district. The Public Employee Relations Board (PERB) could have ordered reinstatement after finding the failure to reappoint the teacher violated the labor relations statute and PERB had found deferral to arbitration permissible and appropriate in a similar case, suggesting that PERB might have deferred to the award here. Nevertheless, the court declined to enforce the award. Instead of filing a grievance, the court stated, the union should have filed a charge with PERB. Why did the union in this case arbitrate without filing with PERB?

3. ARBITRATION AND CIVIL SERVICE

Professor Hodges explains, in The Interplay of Civil Service Law and Collective Bargaining Law in Public Sector Employee Discipline Cases, 32 *Boston College Law Review* 95 (1990):

> One traditional function of a civil service commission is to provide a procedure and appellate body for appeal of disciplinary decisions. Union members, however, do not view the civil service commission as an impartial body for review of disciplinary decisions but rather view it as part of management's personnel system. For that reason, unions increasingly have attempted to negotiate both standards for employee discipline and contractual grievance procedures for challenging such adverse actions. These increasing efforts to negotiate contractual limitations on management's disciplinary decisions have posed the issue of whether civil service standards and procedures or contractual standards and procedures should govern disciplinary decisions. The issue arises not only in contract enforcement actions, but also in contract negotiations when management resists bargaining about discipline and grievance and arbitration machinery on the basis that civil service laws prohibit negotiation over such matters. * * * In some states statutory provisions address the question and resolve the

conflict. In others, the statute is silent, but courts have addressed the issue and reconciled the two statutes. These resolutions run the gamut from giving priority to the collective bargaining agreement to precluding any negotiation of the discipline issue. In many states, the issue has not been addressed directly by the legislature or the courts.

CIVIL SERVICE COMMISSION v. CITY OF KELSO

Washington Supreme Court, 1999.
137 Wash.2d 166, 969 P.2d 474.

DURHAM, C.J.

[The City of Kelso suspended Officer Stair from the Kelso Police Department for two and a half days after his alleged negligence during a high speed chase resulted in a traffic accident. Officer Stair was informed that he had 10 days to file an appeal with the city's Civil Service Commission. Stair filed a timely appeal with the Commission, but on the same day initiated a grievance under the collective bargaining agreement between the city and a union, the Kelso Police Benefit Association. The Commission held a hearing and decided that, because Stair had broken several traffic laws and violated police department regulations, his suspension should be increased to 10 days. Subsequently, an arbitrator heard the case under the CBA, and decided that while Stair had indeed broken traffic laws and department regulations, the City did not have just cause to suspend him, and ordered the City to decrease Stair's suspension to a written reprimand. The Commission then filed a complaint in court, seeking a declaration that its decision was binding.

The trial court agreed with the Commission, and its judgment was affirmed on appeal, the Court of Appeals explaining that, although Stair was entitled to pursue both remedies concurrently, the doctrine of *res judicata* precluded further proceedings after the Commission's decision.]

Employees in the Kelso Police Department are * * * covered by the Kelso civil service rules, and additionally by their bargained-for rights in the collective bargaining agreement. The collective bargaining agreement contains no election of remedies clause. Under these two sets of regulations, Kelso police officers have two available avenues through which to pursue a grievance. * * *

[Res judicata principles require a showing that the same issue was previously decided].

The Commission has not met its burden of showing that the causes of action brought before the arbitrator and the Commission are the same. On the contrary, it would appear from the record that the civil service hearing and the arbitration involved the consideration of different evidence and adjudicated the infringement of different rights. The civil service hearing evaluated Officer Stair's suspension under the Kelso civil service ordinance to determine whether his suspension was "in good faith and for cause." In contrast, the arbitrator evaluated Officer Stair's more expansive rights under the collective bargaining agreement which allowed discipline only for "just cause." These two standards are not the same. * * *

* * * Although this court has yet to give a precise definition [of the "for cause" standards] the statute has not previously been interpreted to require the Commission to consider any factors apart from the particular allegation of wrongdoing and the employer's motivation for the disciplinary action. * * *

In contrast * * * "just cause" is a term of art in labor law, and its precise meaning has been established over 30 years of case law. Whether there is just cause for discipline entails much more than a valid reason; it involves such elements as procedural fairness, the presence of mitigating circumstances, and the appropriateness of the penalty. Raymond Hogler, *Just Cause, Judicial Review, and Industrial Justice: An Arbitral Critique*, 40 Lab. L. J. 281, 286 (1989). * * *

In this case the arbitrator * * * considered Stair's strong record as a police officer, the fact that other Kelso police officers have received only written reprimands after accidents, and the mitigating factor that Officer Stair was in hot pursuit of a dangerous suspect when the accident occurred. * * *

* * * The arbitrator is the ultimate authority to decide disputes over contract interpretation. *W.R. Grace & Co. v. Local Union 759*, 461 U.S. 757, 103 S.Ct. 2177, 76 L.Ed.2d 298 (1983). The arbitrator's interpretation of the meaning of "just cause" and her conclusion that the just cause standard was not applied by the Commission may not be second guessed by this court. * * * Furthermore, Officer Stair could not have raised his contract claim before the Civil Service Commission. Article XIX, Section 2, of the collective bargaining agreement provides that all grievances be resolved through arbitration.

* * *

* * * Although this resolution allows duplicative review of disciplinary actions, such inefficiency must be resolved by the parties when they next negotiate their collective bargaining agreement. Often, where a State enacts collective bargaining laws against a backdrop of existing civil service laws, the parties will specify that only one avenue of appeal is available. Ann C. Hodges, *The Interplay of Civil Service Law and Collective Bargaining Law in Public Sector Employee Discipline Cases*, 32 B.C. L. Rev. 95, 159 (1990). Several other cities in Washington that have contracted with public employee unions have bargained for election of remedies provisions that force the employee to choose which remedy to pursue.

* * *

[The concurring opinion of TALMADGE, J. is omitted.]

NOTES

1. How should the tension between the collective bargaining agreement and the civil service system be resolved as a matter of public policy? By making the civil service system exclusive? By making the grievance and arbitration procedure exclusive? By allowing employees to take advantage of both procedures? By requiring an election of remedies? By allowing the parties, through collective bargaining, to determine the resolution?

2. Where civil service remedies are exclusive, arbitration of disputes subject to civil service procedures is, by definition, precluded. See *Kucera v. Baldazo,* 745 N.W.2d 481 (Iowa 2008) (holding that deputy sheriff covered by civil service could not arbitrate discharge under collective bargaining agreement, because statutory amendments giving employees option of civil service or grievance procedure enacted after previous case finding civil service procedures exclusive did not apply to deputy sheriffs). The debate is over what happens when both procedures are available. The principal case would allow the parties to provide for election of remedies, but the absence of such a provision permits the employee to pursue both remedies. What arguments would you make for and against such a default rule? For an example of a statute which provides explicitly for election of remedies, see WEST'S FLA.STAT. ANN. § 447.401 (1999) ("A career service employee shall have the option of utilizing the civil service appeal procedure, an unfair labor practice procedure, or a grievance procedure established under this Section, but such employee is precluded from availing himself or herself to more than one of these procedures."). See *Hallandale Professional Firefighters Local 2238 v. City of Hallandale,* 777 So.2d 435 (Fla.App. 2001) (arbitration barred after pursuit of civil service remedy). In Wisconsin, the decision of the Civil Service Commission is viewed as a preliminary determination which the employee may appeal either to court or to arbitration, but not both. *Eau Claire County v. General Teamsters Union Local No. 662*, 235 Wis.2d 385, 611 N.W.2d 744 (2000).

3. In the federal system, the Civil Service Reform Act attempted to address comprehensively the relationship between mandatory grievance procedures under collectively-bargained agreements and the civil service system. The statute, 5 U.S.C. § 7121(a), provides that the mandatory grievance procedure, which must include arbitration, is the exclusive administrative remedy for disputes within its coverage, with specified statutory exceptions. With the exception of certain minor disciplinary actions, in most disputes covered by both the contract and the civil service system, discussed in Chapter 3, § C, the employee has an option of using either the grievance procedure or civil service system appeals to the Merit Systems Protection Board, with judicial review of the Board or arbitrator's decision in the U.S. Court of Appeals for the Federal Circuit. The arbitrator is required to apply the same standards in deciding the case as would be applied by an administrative judge of the Merit Systems Protection Board. *Cornelius v. Nutt,* 472 U.S. 648, 105 S.Ct. 2882, 86 L.Ed.2d 515 (1985). In *Greenstreet v. Social Security Administration*, 543 F.3d 705 (2008), the United States Court of Appeals for the Federal Circuit considered the issue of whether to enforce an award of reinstatement without back pay, a common remedy in private sector arbitra-

tion, in a case arising under a federal collective bargaining agreement. In *Greenstreet,* the remedy resulted in a 342 day suspension. The court refused enforcement, finding that the award was arbitrary because it was based solely on the time between the discharge and reinstatement, rather than upon an analysis of the appropriate length of the suspension relative to such factors as the nature of the offense and the employee's work record. On what basis would an arbitrator issue such an award? Do you agree that the award is arbitrary? Does the decision eliminate the practice of awarding reinstatement without back pay in the federal sector? What alternative remedy should an arbitrator order?

4. As in the case of grievance arbitration and civil service procedures, questions arise as to the relationship of grievance arbitration and teacher tenure procedures. In *Neshaminy Federation of Teachers v. Neshaminy School District*, 501 Pa. 534, 462 A.2d 629 (1983), the Pennsylvania Supreme Court interpreted the state's teacher tenure statute, which provided a hearing for discharged teachers, to be the exclusive remedy. The state legislature reacted by amending the school code to provide that professional employees had a right to choose between bargaining agreement remedies and those provided in the school code. See *Wilson Area Education Association v. Wilson Area School District*, 90 Pa.Cmwlth. 151, 494 A.2d 506 (1985). New York allows the parties to negotiate an employee option to choose either the statutory tenure procedure or a collectively bargained alternative to challenge termination. N.Y. EDUC. LAW § 3020. The Rhode Island Supreme Court has added a twist: a collective bargaining agreement to arbitrate dismissals of tenured teachers is permissible, but it must be explicit if it is to be enforced. *School Committee of the Town of North Kingstown v. Crouch*, 808 A.2d 1074 (R.I. 2002).

4. ARBITRATION AND STATUTORY CLAIMS

HAMMOND v. STATE OF ALASKA, DEPARTMENT OF TRANSPORTATION & PUBLIC FACILITIES

Supreme Court of Alaska, 2005.
107 P.3d 871.

CARPENETI, J.

I. INTRODUCTION

Robert Hammond was terminated from his job with the Department of Transportation and Public Facilities. He contested his termination by pursuing the grievance-arbitration mandated by his collective bargaining agreement. While his grievance was being contested, Hammond simultaneously pursued statutory whistleblower claims in state court against the Department of Transportation and Public Facilities and fellow employees David Eberle, Richard Briggs, and Gordon Keith. His grievance was ultimately dismissed after arbitration. The superior court then gave *res judicata* effect to the arbitral decision to grant summary judgment for the defendants. Hammond appeals. We hold that Hammond is not precluded from pursuing his independent statutory claims in state court because he did not clearly and unmistakably agree to submit those claims to arbitration. We therefore reverse the superior court's grant of summary judgment.

II. FACTS AND PROCEEDINGS

A. Facts

Robert Hammond was an employee of the Alaska Department of Transportation and Public Facilities (DOTPF) for approximately twenty years. In August 1994 he was assigned to DOTPF's Homer Gravel Roads Project. While working on the project, Hammond concluded that the rock being used by the contractor violated the DOTPF contract specification that established maximum rock size. Hammond made a series of complaints to the contractor, throughout the DOTPF chain of command, and to the Federal Highway Administration (FHWA) about what he believed to be a violation of contract specifications.[2] In October Hammond complained to DOTPF's Director of Design and Construction, Dean Reddick, about the project's management and about the contractor's failure to follow contract specifications. At that meeting Hammond requested that he be transferred from the project; Reddick complied.

After being transferred from the project Hammond made repeated allegations of DOTPF mismanagement. Some of these allegations were extremely serious and charged DOTPF and its personnel with corruption, fraud, and incompetence. In June 1995 Hammond received performance evaluations from his supervisor on the Homer Gravel Roads project and from Richard Briggs, his regular supervisor, stating that his performance was "mid-level acceptable." In July 1995 Hammond filed charges with FHWA alleging criminal violations of 18 USC § 1020 by DOTPF management. As a result of these charges, Hammond was placed on paid, off-site status, which subjected him to a reduction in wages. After investigation, FHWA concluded that Hammond's charges were without merit. A separate investigation into Hammond's allegations was conducted by the state, which hired an independent investigator, Richard Kerns, to investigate the Homer Gravel Roads Project and another project. Kerns's investigation found no violations of 18 USC § 1020 or the Alaska Whistleblower Act. Kerns also concluded that Hammond had no reasonable basis to make his allegations and that the allegations were not made in good faith.

David Eberle, Director of Design and Construction for the Central Region of DOTPF, terminated Hammond's employment with DOTPF on July 31, 1996, relying primarily upon the Kerns report and the recommendations of Briggs and DOTPF Regional Construction Engineer Gordon Keith. Eberle cited Hammond's "unfounded attacks impugning the integrity and competence of department staff and Federal Highway Administration personnel, threatening behavior, and refusal to follow the directions of management" as the reasons for termination.

2. The parties dispute the nature of Hammond's complaints and the response to those complaints by DOTPF employees.

B. Proceedings

On August 7, 1996 Hammond brought a grievance under his union's collective bargaining agreement (CBA), alleging that DOTPF violated the CBA by discharging him without "just cause." The parties were unable to resolve the grievance and they submitted the dispute to arbitration as mandated by the CBA.

On December 21, 1996 Hammond also filed suit in superior court against DOTPF, Eberle, Keith, and Briggs, alleging violation of the Alaska Whistleblower Act[5] and seeking compensatory and punitive damages and reinstatement to his former position.

After a hearing, the arbitrator held that Hammond's discharge was for "just cause" and therefore did not violate the CBA. The arbitrator denied Hammond's grievance based on her finding that Hammond's accusations—that DOTPF management acted dishonestly, engaged in unethical behavior, allowed contractors to cheat, falsified documents, gave away state property, and was incompetent—"stepped over the bounds of reason" and justified termination because they were not "made in good faith; that is, with a reasonable basis for believing them to be true." The arbitrator also stated that Hammond was not entitled to protection under the Alaska Whistleblower Act because the allegations for which he was terminated were not made in good faith.

After the unfavorable arbitration decision, Hammond pursued his superior court whistleblower action. In his state court action, Hammond relied upon a report on the Homer Gravel Roads project by the Alaska Division of Legislative Audit released after the arbitrator's decision. The report found that Hammond's claims had merit and that DOTPF's selection of Kerns to investigate Hammond's allegations against DOTPF was flawed; it also called Kerns's independence into question.

In February 2001 Superior Court Judge Dan A. Hensley granted DOTPF's motion for summary judgment based on the arbitrator's decision. The superior court held that Hammond was precluded from litigating his whistleblower claim in superior court because the parties understood that the arbitrator would have to address whistleblowing issues in her decision and because the arbitrator did decide the whistleblowing claim.

---

5. AS 39.90.100(a) provides in relevant part that:

> [a] public employer may not discharge, threaten, or otherwise discriminate against an employee regarding the employee's compensation, terms, conditions, location, or privileges of employment because (1) the employee * * * reports to a public body or is about to report to a public body on a matter of public concern; or (2) the employee participates in a court action, an investigation, a hearing, or an inquiry held by a public body on a matter of public concern.

We have held that AS 39.90.100(a) " 'protects public employees who report to public bodies on matters of public concern from retaliation by their employers.' " *Lincoln v. Interior Reg'l Hous. Auth.*, 30 P.3d 582, 586 (Alaska 2001) (quoting *Alaska Hous. Fin. Corp. v. Salvucci*, 950 P.2d 1116, 1121 (Alaska 1997)). In order to bring suit under the Alaska Whistleblower Act "an employee must show that (1) she has engaged in protected activity and (2) the activity was a 'substantial' or 'motivating factor' in her termination. An employer may rebut a prima facie case by demonstrating that the employee would have been discharged even had she not engaged in the protected activity." *Id.* (internal citations omitted).

* * *

IV. DISCUSSION

A. The Arbitrator's Decision in Hammond's State Court Whistleblower Action Was Not Entitled to Preclusive Effect.

1. Hammond has a right to a fully independent judicial determination of his statutory whistleblower action unless he submitted that claim to arbitration.

* * * [Hammond] contends that the arbitrator's decision should not be granted preclusive effect because the only question the parties submitted to arbitration was whether Hammond was terminated for "just cause." Thus, Hammond argues, the arbitrator lacked the authority to decide his whistleblower claim. DOTPF responds that the arbitrator's decision should have preclusive effect because (1) Hammond submitted his whistleblower claim to arbitration and (2) Hammond's CBA-based arbitration claim that he was not terminated for just cause was so connected to his statutory whistleblower claim that "[i]t simply was not possible for the arbitrator to reach a conclusion on just cause without deciding the validity of Hammond's whistleblower claims."

Because we have not yet decided the precise issue before us today, we first look to federal law for guidance in determining whether Hammond's statutory claim was precluded by his arbitration of a similar claim under the CBA. We have previously found federal precedent to be persuasive in interpreting the preclusive effects of arbitration decisions under Alaska law. In *Alexander v. Gardner–Denver Co.,* [415 U.S. 36, 94 S.Ct. 1011, 39 L.Ed.2d 147 (1974)], the United States Supreme Court held that an arbitrator's decision pursuant to a CBA should not have preclusive effect in a subsequent lawsuit asserting rights guaranteed by statute. The Court held that an employee's submission of a claim that his termination violated his CBA's nondiscrimination clause did not foreclose his right to a trial on whether his discharge violated Title VII of the Civil Rights Act of 1964. *Gardner–Denver* recognized that Title VII demonstrated a congressional "intent to accord parallel or overlapping remedies against discrimination," suggesting "that an individual does not forfeit his private cause of action if he first pursues his grievance to final arbitration under the nondiscrimination clause of a collective-bargaining agreement." The Supreme Court went on to state that the federal policy favoring arbitration of labor disputes and the federal policy against discriminatory employment practices can best be accommodated by permitting an employee to pursue fully both his remedy under the grievance-arbitration clause of a collective-bargaining agreement and his cause of action under Title VII. The federal court should consider the employee's claim de novo. The arbitral decision may be admitted as evidence and accorded such weight as the court deems necessary. *Gardner–Denver*'s protection of an employee's right to fully and independently pursue both a grievance based upon the

CBA and a lawsuit based upon the violation of statutory rights has been qualified, but preserved, by subsequent cases.

In *Gilmer v. Interstate/Johnson Lane Corp.*, [500 U.S. 20, 111 S.Ct. 1647, 114 L.Ed.2d 26 (1991)], the United States Supreme Court held that a claim under the Age Discrimination in Employment Act of 1967 "can be subjected to compulsory arbitration pursuant to an arbitration agreement in a securities registration application." In *Gilmer* the employee had agreed to arbitrate his statutory claims and the Court held that this prior agreement required that preclusive effect be given to the arbitrator's decision on the statutory claims. *Gilmer* distinguished *Gardner–Denver* because in *Gardner–Denver* "the employees * * * had not agreed to arbitrate their statutory claims, and the labor arbitrators were not authorized to resolve such claims, [so] the arbitration * * * understandably was held not to preclude subsequent statutory actions." Significantly, *Gilmer* recognized that "because the arbitration in [the *Gardner–Denver* line of] cases occurred in the context of a collective-bargaining agreement, the claimants there were represented by their unions in the arbitration proceedings. An important concern therefore was the tension between collective representation and individual statutory rights, a concern not applicable to [Gilmer's claim]."

The United States Supreme Court recently recognized the tension between *Gardner–Denver* and *Gilmer* in *Wright v. Universal Maritime Service Corp.,* [525 U.S. 70, 119 S.Ct. 391, 142 L.Ed.2d 361 (1998)], a case in which the Court held that the CBA did not waive the employee's right to bring statutory employment discrimination claims in court. *Wright* recognized that *Gilmer* supported the proposition that "federal forum rights cannot be waived in union-negotiated CBA's even if they can be waived in individually executed contracts" while also noting that the growing acceptance of arbitration has undermined *Gardner–Denver's* prohibition on union waiver of an employee's right to a judicial forum. *Wright* eventually declined to resolve this tension, instead finding that if a union has the right to waive its members' statutory rights, "such a waiver must be clear and unmistakable" and concluding that the CBA in that case did not meet this standard.

We have previously addressed the effect of arbitration on subsequent statutorily based claims in three cases. In *Public Safety Employees Ass'n v. State,* [658 P.2d 769, 774–75 (Alaska 1983)], (*PSEA I*) we held that a union member's right to sue as a tenant under the Uniform Residential Landlord Tenant Act (URLTA) "cannot be prospectively bargained away." Though that decision was predicated in part on the URLTA's explicit non-waiver provision, we later stated in *Public Safety Employees Ass'n v. State,*[799 P.2d 315 (Alaska 1990)], (*PSEA II*) that *PSEA I* "rejected the argument that the availability of arbitration precludes statutory remedies." However, *PSEA I* and *PSEA II* did not address the question whether a party can trigger preclusion of statutory claims by submitting that claim, or a similar claim involving common issues, to arbitration. This question was also left unresolved by *Barnica v. Kenai Peninsula*

Borough School District, [46 P.3d 974 (Alaska 2002)], in which four members of this court were equally divided on the question whether a CBA that mandated arbitration of discrimination claims could prevent an employee who did not use the arbitration procedure from bringing a statutory discrimination claim in court. Two members of the court relied on *Gilmer* in concluding that "a claim subject to an agreement to arbitrate for which an independent statutory judicial remedy is also available must be arbitrated, unless the history and structure of the statute in question indicate that the legislature intended to preclude waiver of the judicial remedy in favor of the arbitral forum." Under this approach, arbitration of such a claim would have preclusive effect on a subsequent state court claim. Two other members disagreed, citing *Gardner–Denver's* unequivocal holding that "a CBA could not collectively bargain away a worker's individual right to a statutory judicial remedy" and noting that at least some of this protection survived *Gilmer.* They focused on *Wright,* which held that a CBA must incorporate a "clear and unmistakable" waiver of a statutory claim in order to preclude an employee from bringing a statutory claim in state court. Implicit in this approach is the idea that, absent a clear waiver, an employee has a right both to arbitrate a claim under a CBA and to litigate a related, independent statutory claim in state court.

We now adopt this approach and hold that an employee's exercise of the right to arbitrate under a CBA does not preclude subsequent litigation of related statutory claims in state court unless the employee clearly and unmistakably submits the statutory claims to arbitration. An employee is not required to choose between the rights provided by a CBA and the rights provided by statutes such as the Alaska Whistleblower Act; absent a clear and unmistakable waiver, the employee is entitled to both. Therefore, Hammond may pursue his statutory claims in state court unless he clearly and unmistakably waived those claims. * * *

2. Hammond did not submit his Alaska whistleblower claims to arbitration.

Hammond argues that he did not knowingly, explicitly, and voluntarily submit his whistleblower claims to arbitration. Hammond notes that the arbitrator's authority was limited by the CBA to a determination of whether Hammond was fired for just cause, and he emphasizes that the arbitrator characterized the issue before her as whether the "employer violate[d] the Collective Bargaining Agreement in its dismissal of Mr. Hammond." Hammond also contends that his union did not give him notice that he would lose his right to pursue his statutory claim and that in any case the union did not have the authority to waive his right to pursue statutory claims in court.

DOTPF responds that Hammond submitted to arbitration his statutory whistleblower claims as a necessary part of his CBA-based claim that he was not terminated for "just cause." DOTPF generally alleges that Hammond's handling of his arbitration claim amounted to a voluntary submission to arbitration of his statutory whistleblower claims because it was necessary for the arbitrator to determine whether Hammond's accusations were made in "good faith" in order to determine whether DOTPF terminated him for "just cause." DOTPF also notes Hammond's own acknowledgment that this case involves the same facts, or issues, as the previous arbitration. * * *

There are three possible ways in which Hammond could have clearly and voluntarily submitted to arbitration so as to preclude subsequent litigation of his statutory whistleblower claims in court. It is possible that (1) the CBA's mandatory arbitration procedure governing grievances concerning dismissal clearly and unmistakably submitted his statutory claims to arbitration, (2) Hammond voluntarily submitted his whistleblower claims to arbitration even though he was not bound to do so by the CBA, or (3) Hammond voluntarily submitted to arbitration the issues common to both his CBA and his statutory claims and is thus precluded from relitigating the issues. We hold that Hammond did not clearly and unmistakably submit his whistleblower claims to arbitration either through his CBA or through a separate agreement and we reject the idea that independent statutory claims can be precluded when an employee exercises his right to contest a necessary issue through CBA-mandated arbitration.

a. The CBA's arbitration provisions did not waive Hammond's right to bring independent statutory whistleblower claims in court.

We accept the principle that an employee can waive at least some of the employee's rights to an independent trial of statutory claims in a judicial forum by working under a CBA that requires those rights to be resolved through arbitration. The question before us is whether the arbitration provisions of the CBA waived Hammond's right to bring an independent statutory whistleblower claim in court. We adopt *Wright's* "clear and unmistakable" standard in making this determination.

Four federal circuits have addressed the issue of what constitutes clear waiver of statutory rights in a CBA. The Second and Fourth Circuits have held that in order to clearly and unmistakably waive an employee's statutory rights a CBA must either (1) contain an arbitration clause including "a provision whereby employees specifically agree to submit all federal causes of action arising out of their employment to arbitration" or (2) contain "an explicit incorporation of the statutory anti-discrimination requirements in addition to a broad and general arbitration clause." [*Rogers v. New York Univ.*, 220 F.3d 73, 76 (2d Cir. 2000). *See Carson v. Giant Food, Inc.*, 175 F.3d 325, 331–32 (4th Cir. 1999).] The Sixth Circuit, echoing the First Circuit, has afforded even more protection to employees, holding that "a statute must specifically be mentioned in a CBA for it to even approach *Wright's* 'clear and unmistakable' standard." [*Bratten v. SSI Services, Inc.*, 185 F.3d 625, 631 (6th Cir. 1999). *See Quint v. A.E. Staley Mfg. Co.*, 172 F.3d 1, 9 (1st Cir.1999).] We adopt the less demanding test employed by the Second and Fourth Circuits.

Hammond's CBA does not manifest a clear and unmistakable waiver of his statutory claims. Instead, it explicitly limits the grievance-arbitration procedure to "any controversy or dispute involving the application or interpretation of the terms of this Agreement arising between the Union or an employee or employees and the Employer." * * * No portion of the CBA's grievance-arbitration section provided Hammond with any indication that he would forfeit his right to pursue statutory remedies in state court. Because Hammond's CBA did not contain a clear and unmistakable waiver of his statutory claims, his unsuccessful arbitration does not preclude him from litigating these claims in state court.

We need not decide whether a union-negotiated CBA can waive an employee's right to an independent determination of claims under the Alaska Whistleblower Act in state court because DOTPF presents no evidence that the CBA at issue in this case contained language clearly and unmistakably waiving such a right.

b. Hammond did not voluntarily submit his statutory whistleblower claims to arbitration.

We next consider DOTPF's argument that Hammond voluntarily submitted his statutory whistleblower claims to arbitration by the manner in which he handled the arbitration. DOTPF relies heavily upon *Nghiem v. NEC Electronic,*[25 F.3d 1437 (9th Cir.1994)], in which the Ninth Circuit held that an employee who had submitted wrongful termination, race discrimination, and antitrust claims against his former employer to arbitration was precluded from pursuing similar statutory claims in federal court. In rejecting the employee's claim to a separate statutory action, *Nghiem* stated that "[o]nce a claimant submits to the authority of the arbitrator and pursues arbitration, he cannot suddenly change his mind and assert lack of authority." * * *

We agree with DOTPF that an employee who voluntarily submits claims to arbitration, although not required to do so by the CBA, would be precluded from bringing a subsequent statutory claim in court. This is so because an employee can voluntarily agree with his or her employer to resolve a statutory claim through arbitration, as "arbitration is 'essentially a creature of contract * * * in which the parties themselves charter a private tribunal for the resolution of their disputes.' " Moreover, voluntary submission of a statutory claim to arbitration can be inferred when employees are in full control of their representation. But a different result obtains when an employee does not voluntarily submit a claim to arbitration. When an employee is required to submit a claim to arbitration pursuant to a CBA, the employee's intent to preclude subsequent statutory claims in state court cannot be inferred from such mandatory submission alone. And when arbitration is controlled by the union as a result of the CBA, the employee's submission to arbitration must be "clear and unmistakable."[42] As a review of the facts discloses, no such "clear and

42. Given that a union's waiver of independent judicial determination of statutory rights must be explicit in a CBA, *Wright*, 525 U.S. at 80, 119 S.Ct. 391, an employee's subsequent waiver of

unmistakable'' agreement to arbitrate Hammond's statutory claims occurred in this case.

Hammond's references to the statutory protection provided by the Alaska Whistleblower Act were insufficient to submit his statutory claims to arbitration and thus preclude his right to litigate those claims in state court. To the contrary, Hammond clearly did not intend to submit his statutory whistleblower claim to arbitration. Hammond's union representative understood that he was not arbitrating Hammond's statutory claims, as he stated in his affidavit that

> the union was limited in its approach and would not be representing Mr. Hammond in bringing any whistleblower action * * *. The whistleblower issue was not tried in the arbitration * * *. At all times I made it clear that we were only arbitrating Mr. Hammond's rights arising under the Collective Bargaining Agreement * * *. It came as a complete surprise to me that the arbitrator did not limit her decision to her jurisdiction; i.e., just cause under the CBA, but that she instead attempted to make whistleblower findings.

The union representative's understanding of the scope of the arbitration is supported by the arbitrator's statement, made at the start of the proceeding, that the parties ''stipulated that the issue before the Arbitrator was ['D]id the employer violate the Collective Bargaining Agreement[?'] * * *

c. Hammond's statutory whistleblower claim[s] are not precluded by resolution of common issues in the arbitration of his termination claim under the CBA's mandatory arbitration provision.

Finally, DOTPF argues that Hammond's statutory whistleblower action is precluded because, in the words of the superior court, ''Hammond raised the whistleblower claim at the arbitration and, by framing his claim as retaliation, *required* the arbitrator to rule on the whistleblowing issue.'' DOTPF is correct that Hammond understood that the whistleblower issue would be part of the arbitration because his grievance stated that ''[t]ermination of employment was without just cause. Grievant was denied overtime in retaliation for 'blowing the whistle' and exercising rights as otherwise specified in law.'' In his briefing to this court, Hammond acknowledges that the arbitration proceedings and whistleblower action involved the same underlying facts. But while Hammond clearly and unmistakably submitted to arbitration *issues* that were essential to his statutory action, he is not precluded from relitigating these issues in a subsequent statutory action because he did not submit his statutory *claims* to arbitration.

---

those rights through union representation in CBA-mandated arbitration of contractual grievances must be equally explicit. In this case, Hammond's CBA provided that the union, rather than the employee, controls the arbitration of the employee's claim. Accordingly, in asserting preclusion, DOTPF has the burden of proving that the employee, rather than the union, made a clear and unmistakable waiver of his own statutory rights.

Hammond's arbitration was conducted pursuant to his CBA. This fact is particularly significant in light of federal precedent on this subject. *Gardner–Denver* established that the CBA determines the preclusive effects of arbitration when it noted that

> the federal policy favoring arbitration of labor disputes and the federal policy against discriminatory employment practices can best be accommodated by permitting an employee to pursue fully both his remedy under the grievance-arbitration clause of a collective-bargaining agreement and his cause of action under title VII. The federal court should consider the employee's claim de novo.
>
> [*Alexander v. Gardner–Denver Co.,* 415 U.S. 36, 60, 94 S.Ct. 1011, 39 L.Ed.2d 147 (1974).]

In distinguishing *Gardner–Denver, Gilmer* held that preclusion can only be triggered by the submission of a statutory *claim* to arbitration, and not by the submission of a CBA-based claim that merely has an issue in common with a statutory claim. In *Gilmer,* the Court stated:

> Since the employees [in the *Gardner–Denver* line of cases] had not agreed to arbitrate their statutory claims, and the labor arbitrators were not authorized to resolve such claims, the arbitration in those cases understandably was held not to preclude subsequent statutory actions. [*Gilmer v. Interstate/Johnson Lane Corp.,* 500 U.S. 20, 35, 111 S.Ct. 1647, 114 L.Ed.2d 26 (1991) (quoting *Mitsubishi Motors Corp. v. Soler Chrysler–Plymouth, Inc.,* 473 U.S. 614, 625, 105 S.Ct. 3346, 87 L.Ed.2d 444 (1985)).]

The Sixth Circuit reached a similar conclusion in *Kennedy v. Superior Printing Co.*, [215 F.3d 650 (6th Cir.2000)], holding that an employee was not precluded from bringing statutory discrimination claims in state court by an arbitrator's dismissal of his CBA-based discrimination claim. In that case the employee claimed in arbitration that the employer had violated the statutory protections of the Americans with Disabilities Act (ADA) as well as his CBA's anti-discrimination provision. The Sixth Circuit held that the employee's statutory claims were not precluded by his arbitration of common issues:

> The burden was on Superior to show that Kennedy waived his *statutory* rights, not merely that he arbitrated a discrimination claim under a collective bargaining agreement that also had a basis in federal law. Superior has not met this burden. There was no written agreement providing that Kennedy would submit his ADA statutory claims to binding arbitration. [*Kennedy*, 215 F.3d at 655.]

Just as it was "not at all unreasonable or surprising that Kennedy and the arbitrator would discuss the ADA in the context of arbitrating a dispute involving a claim that the company violated the anti-discrimination clause of the [CBA] prohibiting disability discrimination," it is not unreasonable that Hammond would refer to the protection of the Alaska Whistleblower

Act when contesting whether he was terminated for "just cause" under a CBA that did not define that phrase.

Federal protection of an employee's right to litigate statutory claims in court despite the unfavorable resolution of common issues in arbitration is a persuasive model for Alaska. While we recognize that, similar to the federal policy favoring arbitration, "[t]he common law and statutes of Alaska evince 'a strong public policy in favor of arbitration,' " this policy does not outweigh Alaska's strong public policy against allowing anyone but the employee to waive the employee's right to statutory protections. A statutory grant of rights provides an employee with the right to fully litigate claims based upon those rights. Granting preclusive effect to arbitration proceedings mandated by a CBA and negotiated by the employee's union—rather than the employee—would, in the absence of a clear and unmistakable submission of the statutory claim to arbitration, unacceptably diminish these statutory rights. Accordingly, we preserve the distinct statutory remedies to which an employee is entitled under Alaska law by denying preclusive effect to a prior CBA-based arbitration involving similar issues unless the employee clearly and unmistakably submits his or her statutory *claims* to arbitration. Because Hammond did not submit his statutory whistleblower claims to arbitration, he may litigate all aspects of those claims in state court free of any preclusive effect of the arbitrator's decision and regardless of whether his CBA-based grievance implicated whistleblower issues.

B. Summary Judgment Was Not Appropriate, Despite the Arbitration's Significant Evidentiary Value, Because Hammond Presented Sufficient Evidence that His Firing Was Retaliatory To Meet the Low Summary Judgment Threshold.

DOTPF contends that the superior court's decision "could readily have been made in reliance on the arbitrator's decision as establishing the absence of any genuine dispute as to the facts material to Hammond's termination." We agree with DOTPF that an arbitrator's decision can be admitted as evidence in a subsequent proceeding.[54] Nonetheless, even if the arbitrator's decision is accorded great weight, the presence of strong evidence is an insufficient basis upon which to grant summary judgment if the party opposing the motion has presented a genuine issue of material fact. It is well established that "the evidentiary threshold necessary to preclude an entry of summary judgment is low."

Hammond presented sufficient evidence to meet this low threshold. This burden is met by Hammond's testimony concerning his various complaints about the Homer Gravel Roads Project and Project Engineer Duane Paynter's testimony that he was livid that Hammond complained

54. See *Alexander v. Gardner–Denver,* 415 U.S. 36, 60, 94 S.Ct. 1011, 39 L.Ed.2d 147 (1974) (stating that "the federal court should consider the employee's claim de novo" despite previous unfavorable arbitral decision, but that "[t]he arbitral decision may be admitted as evidence and accorded such weight as the court deems appropriate").

outside of the chain of command. Additionally, the Division of Legislative Audit (DLA) released a report after the arbitrator's decision which may be admissible as evidence in Hammond's statutory whistleblower action. The DLA report found that Hammond's claims had merit, and it called into question the independence of Richard Kerns, who was selected by DOTPF to investigate Hammond's allegations. When taken together, this evidence presents genuine issues of material fact as to whether Hammond was fired for protected whistleblowing activities. We conclude that summary judgment should not have been granted to DOTPF.

V. CONCLUSION

* * * Accordingly, we REVERSE the superior court's decision and REMAND so that Hammond may litigate his statutory whistleblower claims.

MATTHEWS, J., with whom EASTAUGH, J., joins, dissenting.

I disagree with today's opinion insofar as it holds that Hammond may litigate twice the question whether the accusations that he made against his employer were in good faith, that is, with a reasonable basis for believing them to be true.

One of the grounds the state relied on for firing Hammond was that he made unfounded attacks on the integrity and competence of DOTPF staff that undermined the department's ability to carry out its mission. To succeed in his challenge to his firing, Hammond had to establish that he acted in good faith with a reasonable belief that his accusations were true. This question was litigated in the seven-day arbitration proceeding and it was resolved against him. The same question is critical to his claim under the Whistleblower Act because the act does not protect those whose reports are not made in good faith. Unless the arbitration proceedings were unfair in some fundamental way, I believe that Hammond should be precluded from relitigating the same question in his claim under the Whistleblower Act.

The norm in our legal system is that a litigant is entitled to litigate a question only once. The doctrines of res judicata (claim preclusion) and collateral estoppel (issue preclusion) are "founded upon the principle that parties ought not to be permitted to litigate the same issue more than once and that when a right or fact has been judicially determined by a court of competent jurisdiction or an opportunity for such trial has been given, the judgment of the court, so long as it remains unreversed, should be conclusive upon the parties * * * ." A valid arbitration award generally has the same preclusive effect as a court judgment. Today's opinion declines to apply this rule on the ground that doing so would unacceptably diminish Hammond's right to sue under the Whistleblower Act. I disagree because I see no indication in the Whistleblower Act that the legislature intended to deviate from the established norm that a litigant gets only one bite at the apple.

It is important to note that the procedures under which Hammond litigated the question whether his firing was justified are mandated by statute. Hammond was a state employee whose employment was governed by a collective bargaining agreement regulated by the Public Employment Relations Act, AS 23.40.070 et seq. Under PERA, collective bargaining agreements must include a grievance procedure "which shall have binding arbitration as its final step." [AS 23.40.210(a).] Allowing an employee to relitigate against an employer questions that have already been determined in binding arbitration destroys the finality of the PERA-mandated arbitration remedy. Further, doing so permits inconsistent results, and is costly and inefficient.

Some of the differences between my views and those of today's opinion are reflected in the two opinions in *Barnica v. Kenai Peninsula Borough School District*, [46 P.3d 974 (Alaska 2002)], a case decided by an evenly divided court.[7] The dispositional opinion, which I wrote and in which Justice Eastaugh joined, held that "a claim subject to an agreement to arbitrate for which an independent statutory judicial remedy is also available must be arbitrated, unless the history and structure of the statute in question indicate that the legislature intended to preclude waiver of the judicial remedy in favor of the arbitral forum." Justice Bryner, in an opinion joined by Justice Carpeneti, dissented, taking the view that a statutory right to a judicial forum can only be waived by a provision in a collective bargaining contract that contains a "clear and unmistakable waiver."

In *Barnica* the collective bargaining agreement explicitly barred discrimination on the basis of sex. But Barnica proceeded directly to court on his sex discrimination claim without using the grievance and arbitration procedures of the collective bargaining agreement. The dispositional opinion held that he was barred from pursuing his judicial remedy because he failed to exhaust his remedies under the collective bargaining agreement. The present case differs in two respects. Protection of whistleblowers is not explicitly built into the collective bargaining contract, and Hammond, unlike Barnica, did exhaust his contract remedies. These differences are potentially important. One might say that Hammond had no duty to grieve and arbitrate his dismissal as a precondition to suit on his whistleblower claim, reasoning along the lines of the dissent in *Barnica* that the collective bargaining agreement must contain a clear and unmistakable waiver of the right to a judicial forum on a statutory claim. That position would nonetheless be consistent with the view that when the right to arbitration is actually exercised and an issue common to the claim being arbitrated and the statutory claim is determined, the issue cannot be relitigated because of established legal norms precluding litigation of an

7. A decision by an evenly divided court results in an affirmance. The opinion agreeing with the result reached by the superior court is referred to as the dispositional opinion, but it does not have the precedential effect of an opinion of the court. *Anderson v. State ex rel. Central Bering Sea Fishermen's Ass'n,* 78 P.3d 710, 713 (Alaska 2003).

issue more than once. For this reason this case presents a stronger claim for preclusion than *Barnica.*

But most of the reasons given in the dispositional opinion in *Barnica* also apply to this case. Briefly summarized, they are as follows. The legislature mandated binding arbitration in PERA; that procedure is in no sense a second-class remedy subordinate to the judicial remedy provided under the act in question. Further, we recognized that the "common law and statutes of Alaska evince 'a strong public policy in favor of arbitration' " and that arbitration compared to litigation is a "relatively inexpensive and expeditious method of dispute resolution." The dispositional opinion rejected the *Alexander v. Gardner–Denver Co.* line of cases in favor of the more recent *Gilmer v. Interstate/Johnson Lane Corp.* approach and declined to find that "the distinction between collective bargaining contracts [as in *Gardner–Denver*] and individual contracts [as in *Gilmer*] is necessarily meaningful with respect to the treatment of arbitration clauses."[19] Finally, the dispositional opinion noted that "an employee's state constitutional right to a pretermination hearing could be waived in a collective bargaining agreement so long as the remedy substituted by the collective bargaining agreement was 'fair, reasonable and efficacious.' " "[I]f constitutionally mandated remedies may be waived by alternative grievance/arbitration procedures, statutory remedies likewise may be subject to waiver because of such procedures."

As I have suggested, the legislature has the right and power to provide that facts essential to whistleblower claims cannot be resolved in PERA-mandated arbitration. But there is no indication in the text or history of the act that this was intended, nor is there an inherent conflict between arbitration and the purposes of the Whistleblower Act. Thus there is no reason not to adhere to the norm that a party is entitled to litigate an issue only once.

One of Hammond's defenses to the state's motion for summary judgment was that the arbitration proceedings were fundamentally unfair because of discovery deficiencies, because he was poorly represented, and because he was denied the opportunity to be represented by his own attorney or to represent himself. Arbitration awards should not be given preclusive effect if they lack the essential elements of fair adjudication. The superior court did not address this issue in its decision granting summary judgment. I would remand this case for that purpose. If the issue were resolved in Hammond's favor, his suit could proceed. If it were resolved in favor of the state, the question of the good faith of Hammond's accusations could not be litigated a second time.

---

19. *Barnica,* 46 P.3d at 980. We noted that individual contracts are often contracts of adhesion offered on a take-it-or-leave-it basis, while collective bargaining contracts are usually the product of bilateral negotiations and are therefore at least as fair to employees as standard individual employment contracts. * * *

NOTES

1. As a matter of policy, which view is preferable? From the perspective of the public entity? The union? The individual worker? The public at large? One concern of employers is that employees may get "two bites of the apple," litigating their discharges in several different forums with the potential for different decisions. Does the *Hammond* decision encourage or allow this?

2. Hammond argued that the arbitration should not preclude his lawsuit because the proceeding was "fundamentally unfair," citing the limited discovery, poor representation by the union, and his inability to control the proceeding himself, using his own attorney. Should these factors affect the court's decision? For discussion of the duty of fair representation, see Chapter 12.

3. Subsequent to *Hammond*, the U.S. Supreme Court ruled in a private sector case that a union can waive an employee's right to a judicial forum for a statutory claim, binding the employee to arbitrate such claims. *14 Penn Plaza, LLC v. Pyett*, ___ U.S. ___, 129 S.Ct. 1456, 173 L.Ed.2d 398 (2009). The Court did not overrule *Alexander v. Gardner–Denver Co.*, 415 U.S. 36, 94 S.Ct. 1011, 39 L.Ed.2d 147 (1974), discussed by both the majority and the dissent in *Hammond*, but rather distinguished it as involving an arbitration on a contractual claim only where there was no agreement to arbitrate statutory claims. Public sector employers are already using the *Pyett* case to urge courts to dismiss statutory claims. See, for example, *Catrino v. Town of Ocean City*, No. WMN–09–505, 2009 WL 2151205 (D. Md. July 14, 2009) (finding no waiver of a judicial forum for Americans with Disabilities Act claim because the collective bargaining agreement mandated arbitration of contractual discrimination claims only, and not those based on discrimination statutes), *vacated*, 2009 WL 3347356 (D.Md. Oct. 14, 2009) (on other grounds); *Dunnigan v. City of Peoria*, No. 09–CV–1064, 2009 WL 2566958 (C.D.Ill. Aug. 14, 2009) (declining to dismiss race discrimination claim under Title VII on the basis of prior arbitration where neither party submitted the collective bargaining agreement and there was no evidence that the plaintiff arbitrated his Title VII claim). The Court in *Pyett* did not decide whether a waiver would be upheld if the union controlled the decision about whether to arbitrate the employee's statutory claim and refused to take the claim to arbitration. Would *Hammond* would come out differently if *Pyett* had been considered?

4. Would you recommend to a union or an employer that they negotiate a requirement that employees must arbitrate statutory claims? Consider that the union owes to all employees it represents a duty of fair representation, discussed further in Chapter 12. What demands might the duty place on the union if it negotiates a provision for arbitration of statutory claims? What strains might be placed on the union's limited resources? If arbitration is negotiated, what sort of statutory claims would be most appropriate for arbitration? Discrimination cases? Pay disputes? Disputes over pensions, health insurance or other employee benefits? If you were representing an employee in a statutory case, would you be happy with a requirement that the dispute be arbitrated? If not, on what grounds might you challenge such a requirement?

5. Should state courts considering state statutory claims filed by public employees who have collective bargaining agreements with their employers

follow *Pyett*? In considering this question, consider whether a union should be permitted to waive the statutory rights of members of the bargaining unit to seek relief otherwise available under external law? Should it depend on what rights are being waived? Is there a difference between rights under the collective bargaining law and rights under other statutes that might lead to a different conclusion about the union's authority to waive the rights?

6. The Supreme Court in *Alexander v. Gardner–Denver Co.*, 415 U.S. 36, 94 S.Ct. 1011, 39 L.Ed.2d 147 (1974), while declining to find that a contractual arbitration decision precluded a statutory claim, indicated that arbitration decisions may be admitted as evidence in subsequent cases based on statutory claims and given the weight that the court deems appropriate. Courts have applied the ruling in cases involving public sector arbitrations. See *Collins v. New York City Transit Authority*, 305 F.3d 113 (2d Cir. 2002) (granting summary judgment to the employer in a Title VII race discrimination case based on an arbitration decision finding that the employee's termination was based on just cause).

7. Under the federal system, the question of the interaction of the grievance and arbitration procedure and an employee's statutory and constitutional legal claims was before the Supreme Court in *Whitman v. Department of Transportation*, 547 U.S. 512, 126 S.Ct. 2014, 164 L.Ed.2d 771 (2006). The employee challenged the Federal Aviation Administration's substance abuse testing on constitutional and statutory grounds in federal court, rather than utilizing the collectively bargained grievance procedure. The Ninth Circuit held that based on the Civil Service Reform Act's provisions making the grievance procedure the exclusive remedy, with certain limited exceptions, the court had no jurisdiction. The Supreme Court reversed and remanded, holding that the Court of Appeals failed to determine the nature of the claim to assess whether it fit within the statutory exceptions. The Court noted that federal court jurisdiction came, not from the CSRA, but from the general jurisdictional grant to the courts for claims arising under the Constitution or federal law. Thus the Ninth Circuit should determine on remand whether the CSRA withdrew jurisdiction or otherwise precluded the plaintiff's claims. The Court also indicated that if the claim was not precluded the court below should determine whether exhaustion of administrative remedies was required prior to filing suit. Thus, the decision in *Whitman* did not resolve the question, addressing only the issue of jurisdiction, which was the subject of a circuit split. The Federal Circuit, in *Mudge v. United States*, 308 F.3d 1220 (2002), held that the Civil Service Reform Act does not deprive the courts of jurisdiction over statutory claims even where they are covered by a collective bargaining agreement. Therefore, the intersection of collective bargaining agreements and legal claims in the federal sector remains an open question. For a discussion of the issues, see Barbara A. Atkin, et al., Wedging Open the Courthouse Doors: Federal Employee Access to Judicial Review of Constitutional and Statutory Claims, 12 *Employee Rights and Employment Policy Journal* 233 (2008).

8. Where the parties do agree to submit a statutory issue to the arbitrator, should the same level of deference apply to the arbitrator's decision as in the case of contract issues? For an argument that the standard should be the same, see Ann C. Hodges, The *Steelworkers Trilogy* in the

Public Sector, 66 *Chicago Kent Law Review*, 631, 674–83 (1990). See also *United States Department of Justice, Federal Bureau of Prisons, Metropolitan Correctional Center,* 63 FLRA No. 127, 2009 WL 1617785 (2009), which set aside as contrary to law a portion of the arbitrator's award on a claim for overtime pay based on the contract, the Fair Labor Standards Act, the Federal Employees Pay Act and an agency regulation. In the federal sector, the Federal Labor Relations Authority, rather than the courts, reviews some arbitration decisions. The authority can take action it deems necessary if the award is "contrary to any law, rule, or regulation" or deficient "on other grounds similar to those applied by Federal courts in private sector labor-management relations." 5 U.S.C. § 7122. The agency applied a de novo standard to review the arbitrator's conclusions of law, while deferring to his factual conclusions.

CHAPTER 12

INDIVIDUALS AND THE UNION

■ ■ ■

The principal emphasis of labor law, in both private and public sectors, is on group rights—the right of workers to organize and bargain collectively with their employers over wages and other terms and conditions of employment. That emphasis has a number of implications, some of which we have had occasion to consider in earlier chapters:[1]

(1) The union selected by a majority of employees in an appropriate unit is the *exclusive* representative for all employees in the bargaining unit, whether or not they voted for the union, and whether or not they are members of the union.

(2) The employer is precluded from bargaining with any other union, or with employees individually except with the designated union's permission.

(3) Where the collective bargaining agreement contains an arbitration clause, any individual claims under the agreement must typically be channeled through the contractual arbitration procedure, with the union making the final decision as to whether the grievance should proceed to arbitration.

(4) In many jurisdictions, the designated union is permitted to enter into an agreement with the employer requiring that all employees in the bargaining unit contribute their fair share of the costs associated with union representation, usually not to exceed initiation fees and dues paid by members.

(5) To the extent that differences arise between individual interests and group interests, those differences are subject to resolution within the union, and in accordance with its internal procedures.

The law does, however, mediate to some extent between individuals and their unions through a variety of legal doctrines. These doctrines, some of which are unique to the public sector, are the focus of this chapter.

1. As illustrated in previous chapters, some of these doctrines may not apply in some jurisdictions or may apply differently in different jurisdictions.

A. UNION SECURITY AND ITS LIMITATIONS

The term "union security" is used, in both private and public sectors, to connote an arrangement whereby employees, as a condition of employment, are required to provide financial support to a union chosen as exclusive bargaining representative for their bargaining unit. Membership in the union as a condition of obtaining a job (the "closed shop") is not permissible in either sector, but once an employee is hired, he or she may be required to pay "agency fees" or "fair share fees" as a condition of continued employment. This is known as the "agency shop". Another union security arrangement, the "union shop," requires employees to join the union after they are hired. While union shop agreements were initially permitted under the NLRA, the Supreme Court later ruled that full membership cannot be required. Current law allows only the agency shop. Under an agency shop agreement, the employee who does not pay the required fees can be terminated lawfully. This prevents "free-riders," individuals who take the benefits of unionization without paying the cost.

In the private sector the union and employer often negotiate a dues checkoff provision whereby, pursuant to the employee's written authorization, the employer deducts the appropriate amount from each employee's paycheck and transmits the amounts deducted to the union. Most employees bound by a union security clause authorize checkoff for the sake of efficiency and simplicity. Employees who choose not to authorize checkoff will still have dues payment obligations under a union security clause, and will have to make separate arrangements for payment to the union. Some public sector bargaining statutes allow payroll deduction of union fees upon agreement of the employer and union, without authorization from the employee. This prevents employee discharge for nonpayment of dues. As will be discussed further, *infra*, some states bar enforcement of all union security clauses.

It is important to distinguish between "membership" in the union and "membership" in the bargaining unit that the union represents. It may be that all the members of the bargaining unit will in fact be members of the union, but, as noted *supra,* "membership" as such cannot be required as a condition of employment, only the payment of financial support. Employees in the bargaining unit may choose to pay financial support only, in which event they escape any obligations which may be imposed upon union members through the union's constitution and bylaws, but they lose the opportunity to attend union meetings, vote for union officers, and otherwise participate in internal union governance. As will be discussed, a union owes a duty of fair representation to all employees in the bargaining unit, whether they are members of the union or not, but it also has special obligations, through its constitution and bylaws and through laws, to those who are actually members of the organization. The concept of union security and its limitations in the public sector are discussed in the following case.

ABOOD v. DETROIT BOARD OF EDUCATION

United States Supreme Court, 1977.
431 U.S. 209, 97 S.Ct. 1782, 52 L.Ed.2d 261.

STEWART, J. delivered the opinion of the Court.

The State of Michigan has enacted legislation authorizing a system for union representation of local governmental employees. A union and a local government employer are specifically permitted to agree to an "agency shop" arrangement, whereby every employee represented by a union even though not a union member must pay to the union, as a condition of employment, a service fee equal in amount to union dues. The issue before us is whether this arrangement violates the constitutional rights of government employees who object to public-sector unions as such or to various union activities financed by the compulsory service fees.

[The court's description of the complex procedural history is omitted. Briefly, the Michigan law was challenged by teachers in the Detroit School District, who alleged that they were unwilling or had refused to pay dues as required by an agreement between the District and the Detroit Federation of Teachers ["Union"], that they opposed collective bargaining in the public sector, and that the Union "carries on various social activities for the benefit of its members which are not available to non-members as a matter of right", and engages "in a number and variety of activities and programs which are economic, political, professional, scientific and religious in nature of which Plaintiffs do not approve, and in which they will have no voice, and which are not and will not be collective bargaining activities, i.e., the negotiation and administration of contracts with Defendant Board, and that a substantial part of the sums required to be paid under said Agency Shop Clause are used and will continue to be used for the support of such activities and programs, and not solely for the purpose of defraying the cost of Defendant Federation of its activities as bargaining agent for teachers employed by Defendant Board." The complaint prayed that the agency-shop clause be declared invalid on grounds, among others, that it violated their rights under the First Amendment. The Michigan Appellate Court upheld the validity of the statute authorizing the clause. While noting that the plaintiffs' claim as to the uses of dues money raised First Amendment concerns, the Court declined to rule on that issue because plaintiffs had not asserted any specific objections to use. The Michigan Supreme Court denied review, and plaintiffs appealed. While the agreement that gave rise to plaintiffs' objections had expired, new agreements containing agency shop clauses were in effect, and Justice Stewart's opinion declined to consider the issue as moot].

* * *

Consideration of the question whether an agency-shop provision in a collective-bargaining agreement covering governmental employees is, as such, constitutionally valid must begin with two cases in this Court that on their face go far toward resolving the issue. The cases are *Railway*

Employees' Dept. v. Hanson, 351 U.S. 225, 76 S.Ct. 714, 100 L.Ed. 1112 (1956), and *Machinists v. Street*, 367 U.S. 740, 81 S.Ct. 1784, 6 L.Ed.2d 1141 (1961).

In the *Hanson* case a group of railroad employees brought an action in a Nebraska court to enjoin enforcement of a union-shop agreement. The challenged clause was authorized, and indeed shielded from any attempt by a State to prohibit it, by the Railway Labor Act, 45 U.S.C. § 152 Eleventh. The trial court granted the relief requested. The Nebraska Supreme Court upheld the injunction on the ground that employees who disagreed with the objectives promoted by union expenditures were deprived of the freedom of association protected by the First Amendment. This Court agreed that "justiciable questions under the First and Fifth Amendments were presented,"*Hanson, supra*, but reversed the judgment of the Nebraska Supreme Court on the merits. Acknowledging that "(m)uch might be said pro and con" about the union shop as a policy matter, the Court noted that it is Congress that is charged with identifying "(t)he ingredients of industrial peace and stabilized labor-management relations * * *." Congress determined that it would promote peaceful labor relations to permit a union and an employer to conclude an agreement requiring employees who obtain the benefit of union representation to share its cost, and that legislative judgment was surely an allowable one. The record in *Hanson* contained no evidence that union dues were used to force ideological conformity or otherwise to impair the free expression of employees, and the Court noted that "(i)f 'assessments' are in fact imposed for purposes not germane to collective bargaining, a different problem would be presented." But the Court squarely held that "the requirement for financial support of the collective-bargaining agency by all who receive the benefits of its work * * * does not violate * * * the First * * * Amendmen(t)."

The Court faced a similar question several years later in the *Street* case, which also involved a challenge to the constitutionality of a union shop authorized by the Railway Labor Act. In *Street*, however, the record contained findings that the union treasury to which all employees were required to contribute had been used "to finance the campaigns of candidates for federal and state offices whom (the plaintiffs) opposed, and to promote the propagation of political and economic doctrines, concepts and ideologies with which (they) disagreed." The Court recognized, that these findings presented constitutional "questions of the utmost gravity" not decided in *Hanson*, and therefore considered whether the Act could fairly be construed to avoid these constitutional issues. The Court concluded that the Act could be so construed, since only expenditures related to the union's functions in negotiating and administering the collective-bargaining agreement and adjusting grievances and disputes fell within "the reasons * * * accepted by Congress why authority to make union-shop agreements was justified." The Court ruled, therefore, that the use of compulsory union dues for political purposes violated the Act itself. Nonetheless, it found that an injunction against enforcement of the union-shop agreement as such was impermissible under *Hanson*, and remanded the case to the Supreme Court of Georgia so that a more limited remedy could be devised.

The holding in *Hanson*, as elaborated in *Street*, reflects familiar doctrines in the federal labor laws. The principle of exclusive union representation, which underlies the National Labor Relations Act as well as the Railway Labor Act, is a central element in the congressional structuring of industrial relations. * * * The designation of a single representative avoids the confusion that would result from attempting to enforce two or more agreements specifying different terms and conditions of employment. It prevents inter-union rivalries from creating dissension within the work force and eliminating the advantages to the employee of collectivization. It also frees the employer from the possibility of facing conflicting demands from different unions, and permits the employer and a single union to reach agreements and settlements that are not subject to attack from rival labor organizations.

The designation of a union as exclusive representative carries with it great responsibilities.[12] The tasks of negotiating and administering a collective-bargaining agreement and representing the interests of employees in settling disputes and processing grievances are continuing and difficult ones. They often entail expenditure of much time and money. The services of lawyers, expert negotiators, economists, and a research staff, as well as general administrative personnel, may be required. Moreover, in carrying out these duties, the union is obliged "fairly and equitably to represent all employees * * *, union and nonunion," within the relevant unit. A union-shop arrangement has been thought to distribute fairly the cost of these activities among those who benefit, and it counteracts the incentive that employees might otherwise have to become "free riders"—to refuse to contribute to the union while obtaining benefits of union representation that necessarily accrue to all employees.

To compel employees financially to support their collective-bargaining representative has an impact upon their First Amendment interests. An employee may very well have ideological objections to a wide variety of activities undertaken by the union in its role as exclusive representative.

---

12. See *Hines v. Anchor Motor Freight, Inc.*, 424 U.S. 554, 96 S.Ct. 1048, 47 L.Ed.2d 231 (1976): "Because '(t)he collective bargaining system as encouraged by Congress and administered by the NLRB of necessity subordinates the interests of an individual employee to the collective interests of all employees in a bargaining unit,' *Vaca v. Sipes*, 386 U.S. 171, 87 S.Ct. 903, 17 L.Ed.2d 842 (1967), the controlling statutes have long been interpreted as imposing upon the bargaining agent a responsibility equal in scope to its authority, 'the responsibility and duty of fair representation.' *Humphrey v. Moore*, 375 U.S. 335, 84 S.Ct. 363, 11 L.Ed.2d 370 (1964). The union as the statutory representative of the employees is 'subject always to complete good faith and honesty of purpose in the exercise of its discretion.' *Ford Motor Co. v. Huffman*, 345 U.S. 330, 73 S.Ct. 681, 97 L.Ed. 1048 (1953). Since *Steele v. Louisville & N. R. Co.*, 323 U.S. 192, 65 S.Ct. 226, 89 L.Ed. 173 (1944), with respect to the railroad industry, and *Ford Motor Co. v. Huffman*, *supra*, and *Syres v. Oil Workers*, 350 U.S. 892, 76 S.Ct. 152, 100 L.Ed. 785 (1955), with respect to those industries reached by the National Labor Relations Act, the duty of fair representation has served as a 'bulwark to prevent arbitrary union conduct against individuals stripped of traditional forms of redress by the provisions of federal labor law.' *Vaca v. Sipes, supra,* 386 U.S. at 182, 87 S.Ct. 903."

His moral or religious views about the desirability of abortion may not square with the union's policy in negotiating a medical benefits plan. One individual might disagree with a union policy of negotiating limits on the right to strike, believing that to be the road to serfdom for the working class, while another might have economic or political objections to unionism itself. An employee might object to the union's wage policy because it violates guidelines designed to limit inflation, or might object to the union's seeking a clause in the collective-bargaining agreement proscribing racial discrimination. The examples could be multiplied. To be required to help finance the union as a collective-bargaining agent might well be thought, therefore, to interfere in some way with an employee's freedom to associate for the advancement of ideas, or to refrain from doing so, as he sees fit. But the judgment clearly made in *Hanson* and *Street* is that such interference as exists is constitutionally justified by the legislative assessment of the important contribution of the union shop to the system of labor relations established by Congress. "The furtherance of the common cause leaves some leeway for the leadership of the group. As long as they act to promote the cause which justified bringing the group together, the individual cannot withdraw his financial support merely because he disagrees with the group's strategy. If that were allowed, we would be reversing the *Hanson* case, sub silentio." *Machinists v. Street, supra* (Douglas, J., concurring).

B

The National Labor Relations Act leaves regulation of the labor relations of state and local governments to the States. Michigan has chosen to establish for local government units a regulatory scheme which, although not identical in every respect to the NLRA or the Railway Labor Act, is broadly modeled after federal law. * * * Several aspects of Michigan law that mirror provisions of the Railway Labor Act are of particular importance here. A union that obtains the support of a majority of employees in the appropriate bargaining unit is designated the exclusive representative of those employees. A union so designated is under a duty of fair representation to all employees in the unit, whether or not union members. [citing Michigan case law] And in carrying out all of its various responsibilities, a recognized union may seek to have an agency-shop clause included in a collective-bargaining agreement.

The governmental interests advanced by the agency-shop provision in the Michigan statute are much the same as those promoted by similar provisions in federal labor law. The confusion and conflict that could arise if rival teachers' unions, holding quite different views as to the proper class hours, class sizes, holidays, tenure provisions, and grievance procedures, each sought to obtain the employer's agreement, are no different in kind from the evils that the exclusivity rule in the Railway Labor Act was designed to avoid. * * * The desirability of labor peace is no less important in the public sector, nor is the risk of "free riders" any smaller.

Our province is not to judge the wisdom of Michigan's decision to authorize the agency shop in public employment. Rather, it is to adjudicate the constitutionality of that decision. The same important government interests recognized in the *Hanson* and *Street* cases presumptively support the impingement upon associational freedom created by the agency shop here at issue. Thus, insofar as the service charge is used to finance expenditures by the Union for the purposes of collective bargaining, contract administration, and grievance adjustment, those two decisions of this Court appear to require validation of the agency-shop agreement before us.

While recognizing the apparent precedential weight of the *Hanson* and *Street* cases, the appellants advance two reasons why those decisions should not control decision of the present case. First, the appellants note that it is government employment that is involved here, thus directly implicating constitutional guarantees, in contrast to the private employment that was the subject of the *Hanson* and *Street* decisions. Second, the appellants say that in the public sector collective bargaining itself is inherently "political," and that to require them to give financial support to it is to require the "ideological conformity" that the Court expressly found absent in the *Hanson* case. We find neither argument persuasive.

Because it is employment by the State that is here involved, the appellants suggest that this case is governed by a long line of decisions holding that public employment cannot be conditioned upon the surrender of First Amendment rights. But, while the actions of public employers surely constitute "state action," the union shop, as authorized by the Railway Labor Act, also was found to result from governmental action in *Hanson*. The plaintiffs' claims in *Hanson* failed, not because there was no governmental action, but because there was no First Amendment violation. The appellants' reliance on the "unconstitutional conditions" doctrine is therefore misplaced.

The appellants' second argument is that in any event collective bargaining in the public sector is inherently "political" and thus requires a different result under the First and Fourteenth Amendments. This contention rests upon the important and often-noted differences in the nature of collective bargaining in the public and private sectors. A public employer, unlike his private counterpart, is not guided by the profit motive and constrained by the normal operation of the market. Municipal services are typically not priced, and where they are they tend to be regarded as in some sense "essential" and therefore are often price-inelastic. Although a public employer, like a private one, will wish to keep costs down, he lacks an important discipline against agreeing to increases in labor costs that in a market system would require price increases. A public-sector union is correspondingly less concerned that high prices due to costly wage demands will decrease output and hence employment. The government officials making decisions as the public "employer" are less likely to act as a cohesive unit than are managers in private industry, in part because different levels of public authority department managers, budgetary officials, and legislative bodies are involved, and in part because each official may respond to a distinctive political constituency. And the ease of negotiating a final agreement with the union may be severely limited by statutory restrictions, by the need for the approval of a higher executive authority or a legislative body, or by the commitment of budgetary decisions of critical importance to others. Finally, decisionmaking by a public employer is above all a political process. The officials who represent the public employer are ultimately responsible to the electorate, which for this purpose can be viewed as comprising three overlapping classes of voters—taxpayers, users of particular government services, and government employees. Through exercise of their political influence as part of the electorate, the employees have the opportunity to affect the decisions of government representatives who sit on the other side of the bargaining table. Whether these representatives accede to a union's demands will depend upon a blend of political ingredients, including community sentiment about unionism generally and the involved union in particular, the degree of taxpayer resistance, and the views of voters as to the importance of the service involved and the relation between the demands and the quality of service. It is surely arguable, however, that permitting public employees to unionize and a union to bargain as their exclusive representative gives the employees more influence in the decisionmaking process than is possessed by employees similarly organized in the private sector.

The distinctive nature of public-sector bargaining has led to widespread discussion about the extent to which the law governing labor relations in the private sector provides an appropriate model. To take but one example, there has been considerable debate about the desirability of prohibiting public employee unions from striking, a step that the State of Michigan itself has taken. But although Michigan has not adopted the federal model of labor relations in every respect, it has determined that labor stability will be served by a system of exclusive representation and the permissive use of an agency shop in public employment. As already stated, there can be no principled basis for according that decision less weight in the constitutional balance than was given in *Hanson* to the congressional judgment reflected in the Railway Labor Act. The only remaining constitutional inquiry evoked by the appellants' argument, therefore, is whether a public employee has a weightier First Amendment interest than a private employee in not being compelled to contribute to the costs of exclusive union representation. We think he does not.

Public employees are not basically different from private employees; on the whole, they have the same sort of skills, the same needs, and seek the same advantages. "The uniqueness of public employment is *not in the employees* nor in the work performed; the uniqueness is in the special character of the employer." Summers, *Public Sector Bargaining: Problems of Governmental Decisionmaking*, 44 U.Cin.L.Rev. 669, 670 (1975) (emphasis added). The very real differences between exclusive-agent collective bargaining in the public and private sectors are not such as to work any greater infringement upon the First Amendment interests of public employees. A public employee who believes that a union representing him is urging a course that is unwise as a matter of public policy is not barred from expressing his viewpoint. Besides voting in accordance with his convictions, every public employee is largely free to express his views, in public or private orally or in writing. With some exceptions not pertinent here,[27] public employees are free to participate in the full range of political activities open to other citizens. Indeed, just this Term we have held that the First and Fourteenth Amendments protect the right of a public school teacher to oppose, at a public school board meeting, a position advanced by the teachers' union. *Madison School Dist. v. Wisconsin Employment Relations Comm'n*, 429 U.S. 167, 97 S.Ct. 421, 50 L.Ed.2d 376 (1976). In so ruling we recognized that the principle of exclusivity cannot constitutionally be used to muzzle a public employee who, like any other citizen, might wish to express his view about governmental decisions concerning labor relations. There can be no quarrel with the truism that because public employee unions attempt to influence governmental policymaking, their activities and the views of members who disagree with them may be properly termed political. But that characterization does not raise the ideas and beliefs of public employees onto a higher plane than the ideas and beliefs of private employees. It is no doubt true that a central purpose of the First Amendment " 'was to protect the free discussion of governmental affairs.' " But our cases have never suggested that expression about philosophical, social, artistic, economic, literary, or ethical matters to take a nonexhaustive list of labels is not entitled to full First Amendment protection. Union members in both the public and private sectors may find that a variety of union activities conflict with their beliefs. Nothing in the First Amendment or our cases discussing its meaning makes the question whether the adjective "political" can properly be attached to those beliefs the critical constitutional inquiry.

The differences between public-and private-sector collective bargaining simply do not translate into differences in First Amendment rights. Even those commentators most acutely aware of the distinctive nature of public-sector bargaining and most seriously concerned with its policy implications agree that "(t)he union security issue in the public sector * * * is fundamentally the same issue * * * as in the private sector. * * * No special dimension results from the fact that a union represents public rather than private employees." H. Wellington & R. Winter, Jr., *The Unions and the Cities* 95–96 (1971). We conclude that the Michigan Court of Appeals was correct in viewing this Court's decisions in *Hanson* and *Street* as controlling in the present case insofar as the service charges are applied to collective-bargaining, contract administration, and grievance-adjustment purposes.

C

Because the Michigan Court of Appeals ruled that state law "sanctions the use of nonunion members' fees for purposes other than collective

27. * * * Moreover, there may be limits on the extent to which an employee in a sensitive or policymaking position may freely criticize his superiors and the policies they espouse. See *Pickering v. Board of Education*, 391 U.S. 563, 88 S.Ct. 1731, 20 L.Ed.2d 811 (1968).

bargaining," and because the complaints allege that such expenditures were made, this case presents constitutional issues not decided in *Hanson* or *Street*.

* * *

Our decisions establish with unmistakable clarity that the freedom of an individual to associate for the purpose of advancing beliefs and ideas is protected by the First and Fourteenth Amendments. Equally clear is the proposition that a government may not require an individual to relinquish rights guaranteed him by the First Amendment as a condition of public employment. E.g., *Elrod v. Burns*, 427 U.S. 347, 96 S.Ct. 2673, 49 L.Ed.2d 547 (1976); *Perry v. Sindermann*, 408 U.S. 593, 92 S.Ct. 2694, 33 L.Ed.2d 570 (1972); *Keyishian v. Board of Regents*, 385 U.S. 598, 87 S.Ct. 675, 17 L.Ed.2d 629 (1967). The appellants argue that they fall within the protection of these cases because they have been prohibited, not from actively associating, but rather from refusing to associate. They specifically argue that they may constitutionally prevent the Union's spending a part of their required service fees to contribute to political candidates and to express political views unrelated to its duties as exclusive bargaining representative.

We have concluded that this argument is a meritorious one. One of the principles underlying the Court's decision in *Buckley v. Valeo*, 424 U.S. 1, 96 S.Ct. 612, 46 L.Ed.2d 659 (1976), was that contributing to an organization for the purpose of spreading a political message is protected by the First Amendment. Because "(m)aking a contribution * * * enables like-minded persons to pool their resources in furtherance of common political goals," the Court reasoned that limitations upon the freedom to contribute "implicate fundamental First Amendment interests."[30]

The fact that the appellants are compelled to make, rather than prohibited from making, contributions for political purposes works no less an infringement of their constitutional rights. For at the heart of the First Amendment is the notion that an individual should be free to believe as he will, and that in a free society one's beliefs should be shaped by his mind and his conscience rather than coerced by the State. And the freedom of belief is no incidental or secondary aspect of the First Amendment's protections: "If there is any fixed star in our constitutional constellation, it is that no official, high or petty, can prescribe what shall be orthodox in politics, nationalism, religion, or other matters of opinion or force citizens to confess by word or act their faith therein." *West Virginia Bd. of Ed. v. Barnette*, 319 U.S. 624, 63 S.Ct. 1178, 87 L.Ed. 1628 (1943).

These principles prohibit a State from compelling any individual to affirm his belief in God, *Torcaso v. Watkins*, 367 U.S. 488, 81 S.Ct. 1680, 6 L.Ed.2d 982 (1961), or to associate with a political party, *Elrod v. Burns*,

30. See also *Shelton v. Tucker*, 364 U.S. 479, 81 S.Ct. 247, 5 L.Ed.2d 231 (1960) (state statute which required every teacher to file annually an affidavit listing every organization to which he had belonged or regularly contributed is unconstitutional because of its unlimited and indiscriminate interference with freedom of association).

supra, as a condition of retaining public employment. They are no less applicable to the case at bar, and they thus prohibit the appellees from requiring any of the appellants to contribute to the support of an ideological cause he may oppose as a condition of holding a job as a public school teacher.

We do not hold that a union cannot constitutionally spend funds for the expression of political views, on behalf of political candidates, or toward the advancement of other ideological causes not germane to its duties as collective-bargaining representative. Rather, the Constitution requires only that such expenditures be financed from charges, dues, or assessments paid by employees who do not object to advancing those ideas and who are not coerced into doing so against their will by the threat of loss of governmental employment.

There will, of course, be difficult problems in drawing lines between collective-bargaining activities, for which contributions may be compelled, and ideological activities unrelated to collective bargaining, for which such compulsion is prohibited.[33] The Court held in Street, as a matter of statutory construction, that a similar line must be drawn under the Railway Labor Act, but in the public sector the line may be somewhat hazier. The process of establishing a written collective-bargaining agreement prescribing the terms and conditions of public employment may require not merely concord at the bargaining table, but subsequent approval by other public authorities; related budgetary and appropriations decisions might be seen as an integral part of the bargaining process. We have no occasion in this case, however, to try to define such a dividing line. The case comes to us after a judgment on the pleadings, and there is no evidentiary record of any kind. The allegations in the complaints are general ones, and the parties have neither briefed nor argued the question of what specific Union activities in the present context properly fall under the definition of collective bargaining. The lack of factual concreteness and adversary presentation to aid us in approaching the difficult line-drawing questions highlights the importance of avoiding unnecessary decision of constitutional questions. All that we decide is that the general allegations in the complaints, if proved, establish a cause of action under the First and Fourteenth Amendments.

In determining what remedy will be appropriate if the appellants prove their allegations, the objective must be to devise a way of preventing compulsory subsidization of ideological activity by employees who object thereto without restricting the Union's ability to require every employee to contribute to the cost of collective-bargaining activities.[35] This task is

33. The appellants' complaints also alleged that the Union carries on various "social activities" which are not open to nonmembers. It is unclear to what extent such activities fall outside the Union's duties as exclusive representative or involve constitutionally protected rights of association. Without greater specificity in the description of such activities and the benefit of adversary argument, we leave those questions in the first instance to the Michigan courts.

35. It is plainly not an adequate remedy to limit the use of the actual dollars collected from dissenting employees to collective-bargaining purposes: "(Such a limitation) is of bookkeeping significance only rather than a matter of real substance. It must be remembered that the service

simplified by the guidance to be had from prior decisions. In *Street*, the plaintiffs had proved at trial that expenditures were being made for political purposes of various kinds, and the Court found those expenditures illegal under the Railway Labor Act. Moreover, in that case each plaintiff had "made known to the union representing his craft or class his dissent from the use of his money for political causes which he opposes." The Court found that "(i)n that circumstance, the respective unions were without power to use payments thereafter tendered by them for such political causes." Since, however, *Hanson* had established that the union-shop agreement was not unlawful as such, the Court held that to enjoin its enforcement would "(sweep) too broadly." The Court also found that an injunction prohibiting the union from expending dues for political purposes would be inappropriate, not only because of the basic policy reflected in the Norris–La Guardia Act against enjoining labor unions, but also because those union members who do wish part of their dues to be used for political purposes have a right to associate to that end "without being silenced by the dissenters."

After noting that "dissent is not to be presumed" and that only employees who have affirmatively made known to the union their opposition to political uses of their funds are entitled to relief, the Court sketched two possible remedies: First, "an injunction against expenditure for political causes opposed by each complaining employee of a sum, from those moneys to be spent by the union for political purposes, which is so much of the moneys exacted from him as is the proportion of the union's total expenditures made for such political activities to the union's total budget"; and second, restitution of a fraction of union dues paid equal to the fraction of total union expenditures that were made for political purposes opposed by the employee.

The Court again considered the remedial question in *Railway Clerks v. Allen*, 373 U.S. 113, 83 S.Ct. 1158, 10 L.Ed.2d 235 (1963). In that case employees who had refused to pay union-shop dues obtained injunctive relief in state court against enforcement of the union-shop agreement. The employees had not notified the union prior to bringing the lawsuit of their opposition to political expenditures, and at trial, their testimony was principally that they opposed such expenditures, as a general matter. The Court held that the employees had adequately established their cause of action by manifesting "opposition to any political expenditures by the union," and that the requirement in *Street* that dissent be affirmatively

---

fee is admittedly the exact equal of membership initiation fees and monthly dues * * * and that * * * dues collected from members may be used for a 'variety of purposes, in addition to meeting the union's costs of collective bargaining.' Unions 'rather typically' use their membership dues 'to do those things which the members authorize the union to do in their interest and on their behalf.' If the union's total budget is divided between collective bargaining and institutional expenses and if nonmember payments, equal to those of a member, go entirely for collective bargaining costs, the nonmember will pay more of these expenses than his pro rata share. The member will pay less and to that extent a portion of his fees and dues is available to pay institutional expenses. The union's budget is balanced. By paying a larger share of collective bargaining costs the nonmember subsidizes the union's institutional activities." *Retail Clerks v. Schermerhorn*, 373 U.S. 746, 83 S.Ct. 1461, 10 L.Ed.2d 678 (1963).

indicated was satisfied by the allegations in the complaint that was filed, Court indicated again the appropriateness of the two remedies sketched in *Street*; reversed the judgment affirming issuance of the injunction; and remanded for determination of which expenditures were properly to be characterized as political and what percentage of total union expenditures they constituted.[40]

The Court in *Allen* described a "practical decree" that could properly be entered, providing for (1) the refund of a portion of the exacted funds in the proportion that union political expenditures bear to total union expenditures, and (2) the reduction of future exactions by the same proportion. Recognizing the difficulties posed by judicial administration of such a remedy, the Court also suggested that it would be highly desirable for unions to adopt a "voluntary plan by which dissenters would be afforded an internal union remedy." This last suggestion is particularly relevant to the case at bar, for the Union has adopted such a plan since the commencement of this litigation.

Although *Street* and *Allen* were concerned with statutory rather than constitutional violations, that difference surely could not justify any lesser relief in this case. Judged by the standards of those cases, the Michigan Court of Appeals' ruling that the appellants were entitled to no relief at this juncture was unduly restrictive. * * * [I]n holding that as a prerequisite to any relief each appellant must indicate to the Union the specific expenditures to which he objects, the Court of Appeals ignored the clear holding of *Allen*. As in *Allen*, the employees here indicated in their pleadings that they opposed ideological expenditures of any sort that are unrelated to collective bargaining. To require greater specificity would confront an individual employee with the dilemma of relinquishing either his right to withhold his support of ideological causes to which he objects or his freedom to maintain his own beliefs without public disclosure. It would also place on each employee the considerable burden of monitoring all of the numerous and shifting expenditures made by the Union that are unrelated to its duties as exclusive bargaining representative.

The Court of Appeals thus erred in holding that the plaintiffs are entitled to no relief if they can prove the allegations contained in their complaints, and in depriving them of an opportunity to establish their right to appropriate relief, such, for example, as the kind of remedies described in *Street* and *Allen*. In view of the newly adopted Union internal remedy, it may be appropriate under Michigan law, even if not strictly required by any doctrine of exhaustion of remedies, to defer further

40. The Court in *Allen* went on to elaborate: "(S)ince the unions possess the facts and records from which the proportion of political to total union expenditures can reasonably be calculated, basic considerations of fairness compel that they, not the individual employees, bear the burden of proving such proportion. Absolute precision in the calculation of such proportion is not, of course, to be expected or required; we are mindful of the difficult accounting problems that may arise. And no decree would be proper which appeared likely to infringe the unions' right to expend uniform exactions under the union-shop agreement in support of activities germane to collective bargaining and, as well, to expend nondissenters' such exactions in support of political activities."

judicial proceedings pending the voluntary utilization by the parties of that internal remedy as a possible means of settling the dispute.

The judgment is vacated, and the case is remanded for further proceedings not inconsistent with this opinion.

[REHNQUIST, J. and STEVENS, J. filed concurring opinions, as did POWELL, J. joined by BURGER, C.J. and BLACKMUN, J. These opinions are omitted]

NOTES

1. Justice Powell's concurrence in *Abood* objected to placing the burden upon the dissenting employee to initiate proceedings for rebate: "I would adhere to established First Amendment principles and require the State to come forward and demonstrate, as to each union expenditure for which it would exact support from minority employees, that the compelled contribution is necessary to serve overriding governmental objectives." Was he right? What would be the likely practical effect of such a requirement? What practical difficulties does the majority opinion create for unions?

2. In *Chicago Teachers Union, Local No.1 v. Hudson,* 475 U.S. 292, 106 S.Ct. 1066, 89 L.Ed.2d 232 (1986), the Court considered a procedure by which a teachers' union determined, on the basis of its own financial analysis, that approximately 5% of union dues were used for purposes unrelated to representation of unit employees, and notified dissident teachers that if they objected to the amount (which objections could be made only after the amounts were deducted from their paychecks pursuant to a dues checkoff provision with the employer) they could appeal, first to the union's executive committee, then to the union's executive board, and finally to an arbitrator selected by the union president from a list maintained by the Illinois Board of Education. After litigation was commenced by objecting teachers, the union modified the procedure to provide that deducted amounts would be held in escrow pending determination of the proper amount. Information concerning the procedure was provided to teachers though union publications.

The Supreme Court, considering the procedure prior to the adoption of the escrow arrangement, held it was inadequate to protect the teachers' First Amendment rights for three reasons. First, taking the dissidents' money subject to future rebate did not insure against the union using their money for objectionable purposes. Second, the procedure provided nonmembers with inadequate information about the basis for the union's calculation, and failed to place the burden of proof on the union. "Instead of identifying the expenditures for collective bargaining and contract administration that had been provided for the benefit of nonmembers as well as members—and for which nonmembers as well as members can fairly be charged a fee—the Union identified the amount that it admittedly had expended for purposes that did not benefit dissenting nonmembers. An acknowledgment that nonmembers would not be required to pay any part of 5% of the Union's total annual expenditures was not an adequate disclosure of the reasons why they were required to pay their share of 95%." Third, the procedure failed to provide for "prompt decision by an impartial decisionmaker." The Court suggested, however, that "an expeditious arbitration" might satisfy that requirement "so long as the arbitrator's selection did not represent the Union's unrestricted choice." The Court signaled its approval of an escrow arrangement, and suggested that a "100% escrow" would not be constitutionally required "if, for example, the original disclosure by the Union had included a certified public accountant's verified breakdown of expenditures, including some categories that no dissenter could reasonably challenge * * *." What sort of internal procedure should the union set up to comply with the Court's requirements?

3. In *Lehnert v. Ferris Faculty Association*, 500 U.S. 507, 111 S.Ct. 1950, 114 L.Ed.2d 572 (1991), the Court, in a fractured set of opinions, set down some ground rules with respect to what expenses could properly be charged under an agency shop agreement. They must be: (1) "germane" to collective bargaining activity; (2) justified by the government's vital policy interests in labor peace and avoiding "free riders"; and (3) not significantly add to the burdening of free speech that is inherent in the allowance of an agency or union shop. Applying these criteria, the Court held that a local teachers' union could charge objecting employees for their pro rata share of the costs associated with otherwise chargeable activities of its state and national affiliates, even if those activities were not performed for the direct benefit of the objecting employees' bargaining unit, if there is some indication that the payment may ultimately inure to the benefit of the local's members by virtue of their affiliation. On that basis, bargaining unit members could be charged for "program expenditures" of the parent body (the National Education Association) destined for states other than Michigan, and the expenses of publishing "Teacher's Voice", a publication of a regional affiliate (the Michigan Education Association) containing information on collective bargaining, as well as portions of the publication that concern the teaching profession generally, since they were for the benefit of all and were neither political nor public in nature. In addition, the Court authorized inclusion of expenses in preparation for a strike, even though the strike would have been illegal under Michigan law. A majority concluded that dissenters could not be charged for lobbying, electoral, or other union political activities outside the limited context of contract ratification or implementation, or for a union program designed to secure funds for public education in Michigan, or that portion of the Teacher's Voice which reported those efforts. Finally, the majority excluded public relations efforts designed to enhance the reputation of the teaching profession. Justice Scalia, joined by Justices O'Connor, Kennedy, and Souter, concurred in most of the dispositions but argued for a unitary test: expenditures necessary to the Union's function as bargaining representative.

The question of whether the costs of litigation conducted by the national union and relating to bargaining units other than the local unit could be charged to objectors did not command a majority and reached the Court later in the case of *Locke v. Karass*, ___ U.S. ___, 129 S.Ct. 798, 172 L.Ed.2d 552 (2009). The Court in *Locke* held that national litigation expenses could be charged if they met the test articulated by *Lehnert* for the chargeability of national expenses, i.e., that the litigation relates to collective bargaining, contract administration or other chargeable matters, and the local stands to benefit from the litigation. The Court found a reciprocal benefit to the local union from extra-unit litigation, because the local could obtain litigation assistance from the national union for its own litigation, thus benefitting from fees paid by employees in other local unions.

Can fee payers in the public sector be charged for expenses of organizing private sector employees under the test in *Lehnert*? See *Scheffer v. Civil Service Employees Association*, 610 F.3d 782 (2d Cir. 2010) (holding that fee paying probation officers could not be charged expenses for organizing private sector employees that performed different types of work than they performed because, although the expenses were germane to collective bargaining, they were not justified by the policy of avoiding free riders.) Why is organizing private sector employees germane to collective bargaining for public employees? Why did the court decide that the private sector organizing expenses were not justified by the interest in avoiding free riders? The court did not reach the question of whether payment of the expenses significantly burdened speech in excess of the burden imposed by the agency shop? How would you answer that question?

4. In *Davenport v. Washington Education Association*, 551 U.S. 177, 127 S.Ct. 2372, 168 L.Ed.2d 71 (2007), the Court considered the constitutionality of a Washington statute that prohibited the use of agency shop fees for political campaign purposes without express authorization from the fee payer. The Court unanimously upheld the statute, pointing out that since the state could constitutionally eliminate agency fees, it could take the lesser step of restricting their use. The Court rejected the argument that *Abood* and *Hudson* had balanced the rights of the union and the employee objectors by approving a procedure which allowed the union to escrow and refund the nonchargeable portion of agency fees only if the fee payer filed an express objection to the use of fees for nonchargeable expenses. While *Hudson* created a "constitutional floor for unions' collection and spending of agency fees" it did not establish a "constitutional ceiling for state-imposed restrictions." The Court also dismissed the argument that the statute unconstitutionally burdened the union's First Amendment rights to speak, describing the agency fee statute as "an extraordinary and totally repealable authorization to coerce payment from government employees." What is the likely practical effect of a law like the Washington statute? Note that on May 11, 2007, Washington Governor Chris Gregoire signed into law HB 2079. The new statute allows unions in Washington to use general funds for political purposes without first obtaining consent from agency fee payers whose fees are in those funds as long as the union "has sufficient revenues from sources other than agency shop fees in its general treasury to fund such contributions or expenditures." WASH.REV.CODE § 42.17.760 (2010).

5. In *Ysursa v. Pocatello Education Association*, ___ U.S. ___, 129 S.Ct. 1093, 172 L.Ed.2d 770 (2009), the union challenged an amendment to the state's right to work law, which banned the previous practice of allowing employees to authorize payroll deduction of contributions to the union's political action fund, in addition to union dues. The lower courts upheld the ban as applied to state employees, based on the cost to the state, but struck down the ban as applied to private employees and local government employees. The Supreme Court, however, reversed the decision. The Court conclud-

ed: "The First Amendment prohibits government from 'abridging the freedom of speech'; it does not confer an affirmative right to use government payroll mechanisms for the purpose of obtaining funds for expression. Idaho's law does not restrict political speech, but rather declines to promote that speech by allowing public employee checkoffs for political activities. Such a decision is reasonable in light of the State's interest in avoiding the appearance that carrying out the public's business is tainted by partisan political activity. That interest extends to government at the local as well as state level, and nothing in the First Amendment prevents a State from determining that its political subdivisions may not provide payroll deductions for political activities." *Id.* at 1096, 172 L.Ed. at 775. Dissents by Justices Souter and Stevens suggested that the statute in actuality constituted viewpoint discrimination. What facts would support such a conclusion?

6. Union dues or agency fees are typically small amounts of money per employee and nonchargeable expenses are a small percentage of that amount. For example, the entire national affiliation fee in *Locke v. Karass* amounted to only $1.34 per month for each employee and the portion of that attributable to national litigation, the amount at issue, was "considerably less." 129 S.Ct. at 802. Additionally, challenges to dues expenditures under available procedures are utilized by small numbers of employees. What explains the extraordinary number of cases, including many litigated all the way to the Supreme Court, challenging statutory and contractual provisions relating to union dues? Has the Court in these cases appropriately balanced the First Amendment interests of the employees and the unions, along with the governmental interests in stable collective bargaining, minimizing administrative costs, and avoiding free riders?

7. Arizona has a constitutional provision that prohibits requiring membership in a labor organization as a condition of employment, as well as a statute that codifies that provision. Would it be lawful for a union and employer in Arizona to negotiate a provision requiring nonmember employees to pay the cost of contract administration and bargaining? See *AFSCME v. City of Phoenix*, 213 Ariz. 358, 142 P.3d 234 (2006) (finding such a provision unlawful and finding that the provision was not limited to union membership but barred any sort of compulsory fee for union representation). Laws that bar union security provisions are commonly known as right-to-work laws and have been enacted in twenty-two states. The National Labor Relations Act has a specific provision authorizing states to enact such laws to bar union security provisions in the private sector.

B. CONSTITUTIONAL LIMITATIONS ON EXCLUSIVITY

CITY OF MADISON, JOINT SCHOOL DISTRICT NO. 8 v. WISCONSIN EMPLOYMENT RELATIONS COMMISSION

United States Supreme Court, 1976.
429 U.S. 167, 97 S.Ct. 421, 50 L.Ed.2d 376.

BURGER, C.J. delivered the opinion of the Court.

The question presented on this appeal from the Supreme Court of Wisconsin is whether a State may constitutionally require that an elected board of education prohibit teachers, other than union representatives, to speak at open meetings, at which public participation is permitted, if such speech is addressed to the subject of pending collective-bargaining negotiations.

The Madison Board of Education and Madison Teachers, Inc. (MTI), a labor union, were parties to a collective-bargaining agreement during the calendar year of 1971. In January 1971 negotiations commenced for renewal of the agreement and MTI submitted a number of proposals. One among them called for the inclusion of a so-called "fair-share" clause, which would require all teachers, whether members of MTI or not, to pay union dues to defray the costs of collective bargaining. Wisconsin law expressly permits inclusion of "fair share" provisions in municipal employee collective-bargaining agreements. WISCONSIN STAT.ANN. § 111.70(2) (1973). Another proposal presented by the union was a provision for binding arbitration of teacher dismissals. Both of these provisions were resisted by the school board. The negotiations deadlocked in November 1971 with a number of issues still unresolved, among them "fair share" and arbitration.

During the same month, two teachers, Holmquist and Reed, who were members of the bargaining unit, but not members of the union, mailed a letter to all teachers in the district expressing opposition to the "fair share" proposal. Two hundred teachers replied, most commenting favorably on Holmquist and Reed's position. Thereupon a petition was drafted calling for a one-year delay in the implementation of "fair share" while the proposal was more closely analyzed by an impartial committee.[3] The petition was circulated to teachers in the district on December 6, 1971. Holmquist and Reed intended to present the results of their petition effort to the school board and to MTI at the school board's public meeting that same evening.

Because of the stalemate in the negotiations, MTI arranged to have pickets present at the school board meeting. In addition, 300 to 400 teachers attended in support of the union's position. During a portion of the meeting devoted to expression of opinion by the public, the president of MTI took the floor and spoke on the subject of the ongoing negotiations. He concluded his remarks by presenting to the board a petition signed by

---

3. The text of the petition was as follows:

December 6, 1971

To: Madison Board of Education

To: Madison Teachers, Incorporated

We the undersigned ask that the fair-share proposal (agency shop) being negotiated by Madison Teachers, Incorporated and the Madison Board of Education be deferred this year. We propose the following: 1) The fair-share concept being negotiated be thoroughly studied by an impartial committee composed of representatives from all concerned groups. 2) The findings of this study be made public. 3) This impartial committee will ballot (written) all persons affected by the contract agreement for their opinion on the fair-share proposal. 4) The results of this written ballot be made public.

1,300–1,400 teachers calling for the expeditious resolution of the negotiations. Holmquist was next given the floor, after John Matthews, the business representative of MTI, unsuccessfully attempted to dissuade him from speaking. Matthews had also spoken to a member of the school board before the meeting and requested that the board refuse to permit Holmquist to speak. Holmquist stated that he represented "an informal committee of 72 teachers in 49 schools" and that he desired to inform the board of education, as he had already informed the union, of the results of an informational survey concerning the "fair share" clause. He then read the petition which had been circulated to the teachers in the district that morning and stated that in the 31 schools from which reports had been received, 53% of the teachers had already signed the petition. Holmquist stated that neither side had adequately addressed the issue of "fair share" and that teachers were confused about the meaning of the proposal. He concluded by saying: "Due to this confusion, we wish to take no stand on the proposal itself, but ask only that all alternatives be presented clearly to all teachers and more importantly to the general public to whom we are all responsible. We ask simply for communication, not confrontation."

The sole response from the school board was a question by the president inquiring whether Holmquist intended to present the board with the petition. Holmquist answered that he would. Holmquist's presentation had lasted approximately 2 1/2 minutes. Later that evening, the board met in executive session and voted a proposal acceding to all of the union's demands with the exception of "fair share." During a negotiating session the following morning, MTI accepted the proposal and a contract was signed on December 14, 1971.

(1)

In January 1972, MTI filed a complaint with the Wisconsin Employment Relations Commission (WERC) claiming that the board had committed a prohibited labor practice by permitting Holmquist to speak at the December 6 meeting. MTI claimed that in so doing the board had engaged in negotiations with a member of the bargaining unit other than the exclusive collective-bargaining representative, in violation of WISCONSIN STAT.ANN. §§ 111.70(3)(a)1, 4 (1973).[4] Following a hearing the Commission concluded that the board was guilty of the prohibited labor practice and ordered that it "immediately cease and desist from permitting employees, other than representatives of Madison Teachers Inc., to appear and speak at meetings of the Board of Education, on matters subject to collective

4. The statute provides in relevant part: "(3) Prohibited practices and their prevention. (a) It is a prohibited practice for a municipal employer individually or in concert with others: "1. To interfere with, restrain or coerce municipal employees in the exercise of their rights guaranteed in sub. (2). "4. To refuse to bargain collectively with a representative of a majority of its employees in an appropriate collective bargaining unit. Such refusal shall include action by the employer to issue or seek to obtain contracts, including those provided for by statute, with individuals in the collective bargaining unit while collective bargaining, mediation or fact-finding concerning the terms and conditions of a new collective bargaining agreement is in progress, unless such individual contracts contain express language providing that the contract is subject to amendment by a subsequent collective bargaining agreement."

bargaining between it and Madison Teachers Inc." The Commission's action was affirmed by the Circuit Court of Dane County.

The Supreme Court of Wisconsin affirmed. 69 Wis.2d 200, 231 N.W.2d 206 (1975). The court recognized that both the Federal and State Constitutions protect freedom of speech and the right to petition the government, but noted that these rights may be abridged in the face of " 'a clear and present danger that (the speech) will bring about the substantive evils that (the legislature) has a right to prevent.' " The court held that abridgment of the speech in this case was justified in order "to avoid the dangers attendant upon relative chaos in labor management relations."

(2)

The Wisconsin court perceived "clear and present danger" based upon its conclusion that Holmquist's speech before the school board constituted "negotiation" with the board. Permitting such "negotiation," the court reasoned, would undermine the bargaining exclusivity guaranteed the majority union under WISCONSIN STAT.ANN. 111.70(3)(a)4 (1973). From that premise it concluded that teachers' First Amendment rights could be limited. Assuming, arguendo, that such a "danger" might in some circumstances justify some limitation of First Amendment rights, we are unable to read this record as presenting such danger as would justify curtailing speech.

The Wisconsin Supreme Court's conclusion that Holmquist's terse statement during the public meeting constituted negotiation with the board was based upon its adoption of the lower court's determination that, "(e)ven though Holmquist's statement superficially appears to be merely a 'position statement,' the court deems from the total circumstances that it constituted negotiating." This cryptic conclusion seems to ignore the ancient wisdom that calling a thing by a name does not make it so. Holmquist did not seek to bargain or offer to enter into any bargain with the board, nor does it appear that he was authorized by any other teachers to enter into any agreement on their behalf. Although his views were not consistent with those of MTI, communicating such views to the employer could not change the fact that MTI alone was authorized to negotiate and to enter into a contract with the board.

Moreover, the school board meeting at which Holmquist was permitted to speak was open to the public.[6] He addressed the school board not merely as one of its employees but also as a concerned citizen, seeking to express his views on an important decision of his government. We have held that teachers may not be "compelled to relinquish the First Amendment rights they would otherwise enjoy as citizens to comment on matters of public interest in connection with the operation of the public schools in

6. This meeting was open to the public pursuant to a Wisconsin statute which requires certain governmental decisionmaking bodies to hold open meetings. There are exceptions to the statute, and one of these has been interpreted to cover labor negotiations between a municipality and a labor organization. Thus, in contrast to the open session where the public was invited, the true bargaining sessions between the union and the board were conducted in private.

which they work.'' *Pickering v. Board of Education*, 391 U.S. 563, 88 S.Ct. 1731, 20 L.Ed.2d 811 (1968). * * * Where the State has opened a forum for direct citizen involvement, it is difficult to find justification for excluding teachers who make up the overwhelming proportion of school employees and who are most vitally concerned with the proceedings. It is conceded that any citizen could have presented precisely the same points and provided the board with the same information as did Holmquist.

Regardless of the extent to which true contract negotiations between a public body and its employees may be regulated—an issue we need not consider at this time—the participation in public business cannot be confined to one category of interested individuals. To permit one side of a debatable public question to have a monopoly in expressing its views to the government is the antithesis of constitutional guarantees.[9] Whatever its duties as an employer, when the board sits in public meetings to conduct public business and hear the view of citizens, it may not be required to discriminate between speakers on the basis of their employment, or the content of their speech. See *Police Dept. of Chicago v. Mosley*, 408 U.S. 92, 92 S.Ct. 2286, 33 L.Ed.2d 212 (1972).[10]

(3)

The Employment Relations Commission's order was not limited to a determination that a prohibited labor practice had taken place; it also restrains future conduct. By prohibiting the school board from "permitting employees * * * to appear and speak at meetings of the Board of Education" the order constitutes an indirect, but effective, prohibition on persons such as Holmquist from communicating with their government. The order would have a substantial impact upon virtually all communication between teachers and the school board. The order prohibits speech by teachers "on matters subject to collective bargaining." As the dissenting opinion below noted, however, there is virtually no subject concerning the operation of the school system that could not also be characterized as a potential subject of collective bargaining. Teachers not only constitute the overwhelming bulk of employees of the school system, but they are the very core of that system; restraining teachers' expressions to the board on matters involving the operation of the schools would seriously impair the board's ability to govern the district. * * * Reversed and remanded.

[The concurring opinion of JUSTICE STEWART is omitted.]

---

9. The WERC order does not prohibit all speech to the board on the subject of collective bargaining. Union representatives would continue to be entitled to come before the board at its public meetings and make their views known. The impact of such a rule is underscored by the fact that the union need not rely upon public meetings to make its position known to the school board; it can also do so at closed negotiating sessions. See n.6, supra.

10. Surely no one would question the absolute right of the nonunion teachers to consult among themselves, hold meetings, reduce their views to writing, and communicate those views to the public generally in pamphlets, letters, or expressions carried by the news media. It would strain First Amendment concepts extraordinarily to hold that dissident teachers could not communicate those views directly to the very decisionmaking body charged by law with making the choices raised by the contract renewal demands.

BRENNAN, J., with whom MARSHALL, J. joins, concurring in the judgment:

By stating that "the extent to which true contract negotiations * * * may be regulated (is) an issue we need not consider at this time," the Court's opinion treats as open a question the answer to which I think is abundantly clear. Wisconsin has adopted, as unquestionably the State constitutionally may adopt, a statutory policy that authorizes public bodies to accord exclusive recognition to representatives for collective bargaining chosen by the majority of an appropriate unit of employees. In that circumstance the First Amendment plainly does not prohibit Wisconsin from limiting attendance at a collective-bargaining session to school board and union bargaining representatives and denying Holmquist the right to attend and speak at the session.

NOTES

1. Compare *Emporium Capwell Co. v. Western Addition Community Organization*, 420 U.S. 50, 95 S.Ct. 977, 43 L.Ed.2d 12 (1975), decided under the NLRA. African–American employees, unhappy with the way their union was handling a grievance claiming racial discrimination in violation of a non-discrimination provision in the applicable collective bargaining agreement with their retail store employer, walked out of the grievance meeting and sought to speak directly with the employer. When they were rebuffed, they distributed handbills outside the store asking customers not to patronize the store because of its discriminatory practices. They were fired for this activity, and filed a charge with the National Labor Relations Board. The Board held their activity was not protected by the NLRA because they were seeking to bargain directly with the employer in derogation of the Union's exclusive status. The United States Supreme Court, in an opinion by Justice Marshall, affirmed the Board's ruling.

2. Under the Court's ruling in the principal case, would it be permissible for the Internal Revenue Service to discuss tax policy with representatives of a union representing internal revenue agents, to the exclusion of individuals who may have different views? Under Justice Brennan's position?

C. THE UNION'S DUTY OF FAIR REPRESENTATION

In the private sector, under both the National Labor Relations Act and the Railway Labor Act, the courts, as well as the NLRB, have implied a duty of fair representation as a corollary to the exclusive representation rights of the union. The duty applies to the union's actions in both negotiating and administering the collective bargaining agreement. A union breaches this duty if its actions are arbitrary, discriminatory or in bad faith. The following case considered whether and how to apply the duty under the Rhode Island statute.

BELANGER v. MATTESON

Rhode Island Supreme Court, 1975.
115 R.I. 332, 346 A.2d 124.

KELLEHER, J.

[An agreement between the Warwick School Committee and the Warwick Teachers Union provided, with respect to promotions, that "candidates shall be recommended on the basis of qualifications for the position," and that "where qualifications are considered equal, seniority in the Warwick School District shall prevail." In 1972, the school committee appointed Belanger to a vacant promotional position as business department head of a high school. Matteson, who had greater seniority than Belanger, requested the Union file a grievance on his behalf. The Union did so, and after proceeding through the grievance steps of the agreement, took the case to arbitration as the agreement provided. After a hearing in which both Belanger and Matteson testified, the arbitrators ruled that Matteson was entitled to the appointment. Belanger sought to set aside the arbitration award on the ground, among others, that the Union breached its duty of fair representation toward him when it decided to pursue Matteson's grievance].

The question of the duty owed by a union to its members is one of first impression in this court. It has, however, been extensively litigated in other jurisdictions, most notably in the federal courts, in cases arising under the National Labor Relations Act, the Labor Management Relations Act, and the Railway Labor Act. The first of what has become a long line of cases was *Steele v. Louisville & Nashville R.R.*, 323 U.S. 192, 65 S.Ct. 226, 89 L.Ed. 173 (1944). There, the Court held that the Railway Labor Act, in providing that an organization chosen by the majority of employees would be the exclusive representative of all the employees within its class, mandated a concomitant duty "to act for and not against those whom it represents," and "to exercise fairly the power conferred upon it in behalf of all those for whom it acts * * *." This duty has also been found in unions governed by the NLRB. *Ford Motor Co. v. Huffman*, 345 U.S. 330, 73 S.Ct. 681, 97 L.Ed. 1048 (1953). By taking away the right of individual employees to further their interests individually or to organize into numerous small units to deal with their employer, Congress has given a union power and control over the working lives of each of its members. A corollary of such power is the duty to act for the benefit of its members.

Our Legislature has created a structure of labor regulations which parallels in many significant respects the federal scheme. [A Rhode Island statute] declares it to be the public policy of this state to grant public school teachers the right to organize, to be represented, and to bargain on a collective basis with school committees relevant to "hours, salary, working conditions and other terms of professional employment." RHODE ISLAND GEN. LAWS 1956 § 28–9.3–3 mandates that the school committee recognize the labor organization chosen by the teachers to be their "sole and exclusive" bargaining agent. Thus, a labor organization representing teachers of this state has the same broad authority in the negotiation, administration, and enforcement of the collective bargaining agreement as does a union regulated by federal law. We find ourselves in agreement with the persuasive logic of the *Steele* opinion and its progeny, and, therefore hereby recognize, as implicit in our Act, a statutory duty on the part of an exclusive bargaining agent to fairly and adequately represent the interests of all of those for whom it negotiates and contracts, not only those who are members, but all those who are part of the bargaining unit.

The union and its bargaining unit are necessarily composed of many individuals with diverse views and ofttimes conflicting employment demands. The whole purpose behind the creation of the union is, however, to present a solid, unified front to the employer. "In unity there is strength," went the old organizing slogan, and it was the truth. In dealing with the employer, the union gains its negotiating power from the fact that it speaks with one voice for all the employees. That we find a duty on the part of the union does not, however, solve the controversy before us. We must define the parameters of the duty, and then apply it to the facts as found by the Superior Court.

We believe at the start that we must recognize that "(a) wide range of reasonableness must be allowed a statutory bargaining representative in serving the unit it represents * * * ." *Ford Motor Co. v. Huffman*, *supra*. Recognizing that the interests of employees are often conflicting, the Court found that the union did not breach its duty to its members by bargaining for a seniority provision in the contract which favored some employees, but caused the layoff of others because of their newly lowered position on the seniority lists. The union must be an advocate for its membership and where its members disagree, the union should not be forced into a neutral position by a court-enforced obligation not to take a stand. In *Humphrey v. Moore*, 375 U.S. 335, 84 S.Ct. 363, 11 L.Ed.2d 370 (1964), a multi-employer union found itself representing the employees of two trucking companies who were merging their businesses. The employees from the dissolved outfit had an interest in retaining their seniority within the absorbing company. That company's employees obviously did not favor such a happening. The contract signed by both employers and the union was ambiguous. The contract question was put before a joint labor-management committee. The union took the side of the absorbed employees, some of the other employees were 'bumped' and they sued their union and their employer. The Court, expanding upon the *Huffman* holding, said: "Just as a union must be free to sift out wholly frivolous grievances which would only clog the grievance process, so it must be free to take a position on the not so frivolous disputes. Nor should it be neutralized when the issue is chiefly between two sets of employees. Conflict between employees represented by the same union is a recurring fact. To remove or gag the union in these cases would surely weaken the collective bargaining and grievance processes."

Given these facts of life in the labor-management world, the duty of fair representation which is imposed on the union must not be such as to squelch union advocacy of position, nor must it weaken the union's ability to act when it does for all its members, even those whose interests may not be served but who are nonetheless bound by the majority vote. The entire scheme of federal and state labor regulations would be pointless if the minority in a union were not bound by the majority will. For example, what would be the efficacy of statutes requiring an employer to bargain exclusively with the duly elected union if the minority of employees who voted against ratification of a collective bargaining contract could then turn around and require the employer to contract with them individually. Whether or not the minority should be bound by the majority in the control of the conditions of their employment is not a matter for us to decide. The Legislature has unequivocally declared that to be the policy and we cannot say otherwise. However, concurrent with the union's power to bind the minority flows the duty which we define today.

In the negotiation process, we hold that a union must make an honest effort to serve the interest of all of its members, without hostility to any, and its power must be exercised in complete good faith and with honesty of purpose. *Ford Motor Co. v. Huffman, supra.*

Where the union and the employer have provided by contract for the internal settlement of disputes by means of grievance and arbitration procedures, and where these settlement procedures can be initiated and continued solely by the union, the union is likewise subject to a duty of fair representation in its handling of employee grievances. As in contract negotiations, the union as it deals with grievances must often take a position which is detrimental to some employees as it is helpful to others. The duty upon the Union here is to "bargain in good faith and in a nonarbitrary manner, make decisions as to the merits of particular grievances," *Vaca v. Sipes*, 386 U.S. 171, 87 S.Ct. 903, 17 L.Ed.2d 842 (1967), and, if it decides to pursue a grievance, it must not do so in a perfunctory manner.

Applying these standards of conduct to the facts of this case, we are faced with a clear breach by the Union of the duty it owed to Belanger. The testimony was undisputed, and the trial justice found that throughout the grievance procedure, the Union and its representatives acted without ever contacting Belanger or considering his qualifications for the position; the Union aligned itself with Matteson in seeking Belanger's removal; and at the arbitration hearing the union representatives attempted to demonstrate that Matteson, rather than Belanger, was entitled to the position. The Union admitted at trial that it had no knowledge of Belanger's qualifications for the contested position until he testified at the arbitration hearing, and that it never contacted Belanger to discuss the impending challenge.

We have said a union may, and often must, take sides. But we wish to make it clear that it must act, when it does, in a nonarbitrary, nonperfunctory manner. Here the Union chose sides totally on the fortuitous circumstances of who the School Committee did not hire. It is true, in a very simplistic sense, that Matteson, being the only member of the bargaining unit with "a grievance," is therefore the only individual in need of Union support. But one would require blinders to accept this view. It should have been apparent to the Union that Matteson's grievance, although theoretically against the School Committee, was in reality against Belanger. Any action the Union took on Matteson's behalf threatened Belanger's job. The Union had as much of an obligation to support Belanger as it had to support Matteson until such time as it had examined the qualifications of both candidates, and it believed that the seniority clause would control the selection process.

This was clearly a situation that was akin to the situations found in *Humphrey*, *Huffman*, and *Vaca* where a union faced with conflicting loyalties must make a choice as to which member it will support. To enforce a requirement of neutrality on the union in cases such as this would not, in our opinion, further the purposes of the statute which was designed to strengthen the power of teachers in controlling their employment situation by allowing them all to speak through a single, but strong voice. Neutrality could only weaken the power of employees to deal with their employer. Even if in any particular grievance procedure neutrality would not be harmful, the cumulative effect of such a stance taken over a period of time would undermine the position of the union as employee advocate in its dealings with the employer. Also, by remaining neutral, the union would lose the ability to control the scope and focus of the arguments made on behalf of the employees.

Professor Cox has argued that the settlement of an individual employee grievance involves more than the individual because precedent is established which will control the course of future employer-employee relations.[3] This distinguished educator also points out that any time the parties do battle over their contract, they are also engaging in a process of negotiation over its terms.

The Union must choose its side in a nonarbitrary manner, based on its good-faith judgment as to the merits of the conflicting claims. In the present case the Union never offered Belanger an opportunity to present his case to them. It never recognized its duty to independently determine whether Matteson or Belanger was entitled to the job. It seems to us that the only fair procedure in this type of a conflict is for the Union, at the earliest stages of the grievance procedure, to investigate the case for both sides, to give both contestants an opportunity to be heard, and to submit their qualifications to the Union. We are not mandating a full-blown hearing, replete with strict rules of procedure and adversary proceedings. If the Union investigates in an informal manner, this would be sufficient so long as its procedure affords the two employees the ability to place all the relevant information before the Union. See *Bures v. Houston Sympho-*

3. Cox, *Rights Under A Labor Agreement*, 69 Harv.L.Rev. 601 (1956).

ny Soc'y, 503 F.2d 842 (5th Cir.1974); *Waiters Union, Local 781 v. Hotel Ass'n*, 498 F.2d 998 (D.C. Cir.1974).

For a union to make a decision affecting its members without investigating the underlying factual situation is a clear breach of the duty of fair representation. *De Arroyo v. Sindicato De Trabajadores Packinghouse, AFL–CIO*, 425 F.2d 281 (1st Cir.1970). In an examination of the union's conduct in its discharge of its duty to the members of the bargaining unit, there are three possible foci for our analysis; the union's motives, its decision-making procedures, and the reasons for its acting as it did. A court's investigation into the first two questions is proper and necessary. We will, however, be more careful in any review of the merits of the Union's decision. An inquiry into the merits would open the way for our substituting our judgment for that of the Union, and that is not our role. It will be enough protection for an employee represented by a union if we inquire into motives and ensure that the union has fairly considered both sides before taking a stand.

In examining the record presented to us, we find no evidence of bad faith by the Union. However, the Union's decision to press on with Matteson's grievance without making any effort to assess the relative qualifications of the respective candidates was patently defective. Thus, the Union breached its duty to represent fairly the interests of one of its members, Belanger.

[In the balance of its opinion, the court declined to overturn the award, on the ground that Belanger had participated fully in the arbitration proceeding, and that the arbitrators had fully considered the respective qualifications of the two candidates. Distinguishing *Vaca,* the court observed that "the Union's breach did not foreclose a fair utilization of the contractual remedy; and the employer, who had done no wrong, should not be subjected to a relitigation of the question. * * * "]

[The opinion of JUSTICE PAOLINO, concurring in part, dissenting in part, is omitted.]

NOTES

1. The court found the union's conduct in *Belanger* to be arbitrary. Why? Unions place great weight on the importance of seniority as an objective measure of qualifications. Presumably, the union's decision to support Matteson was based on the principle of seniority. Is that decision arbitrary? If the contract provision relating to promotion had stated that the most senior *qualified* individual would be promoted (without characterizing a degree of qualification, thus presumably including minimum qualifications), would the court have reached the same result? Would the court have reached the same result if the less qualified senior candidate was chosen pursuant to this contract clause? Pursuant to the clause in *Belanger*?

2. In *Abood*, the Court refers to the "great responsibilities" of the exclusive representative, and cites (footnote 6) to the duty of fair representa-

tion cases under the NLRA and the RLA. Is the Court suggesting that in the public sector the duty of fair representation is constitutionally required? If so, under what provision of the Constitution?

3. A duty of fair representation on the part of unions representing public employees has been recognized in most states, sometimes by explicit statutory provisions, e.g., IOWA CODE § 20.1, and under the Federal Service Labor Management Relations Statute, 5 U.S.C. § 7114(a)(1).

4. *Procedure and Remedies.* Under the LMRA, an employee who claims that his union violated its duty of fair representation (DFR) by failing to take his grievance to arbitration may proceed in one of two ways. Since the NLRB regards a union's DFR violation as an unfair labor practice under Section 8(b)(1)(A), 29 U.S.C. § 158(b)(1)(A) ("restraint or coercion" of employees in the exercise of their statutory rights), the employee may file a charge with the Board against the union, and the Board may grant relief that includes an order requiring the union to arbitrate the grievance, and/or damages against the union. Typically, however, the employer would not be a party to such a proceeding, and the Board would have no jurisdiction to award relief against the employer. Alternatively, under *Vaca v. Sipes*, 386 U.S. 171, 87 S.Ct. 903, 17 L.Ed.2d 842 (1967), the employee may sue both the union and the employer in court in what is known as a "hybrid" action. First, the employee must show that the union has violated its DFR by failing to take the grievance to arbitration. If he succeeds in carrying that burden, he must then show his grievance is meritorious, *i.e.,* that the employer breached the collective bargaining agreement in some way. If he is successful, then the employee may recover damages against both the employer and the union, in proportion to the responsibility of each. While apportionment is up to the jury, the Supreme Court has approved instructions which allow the jury in a discharge case to hold the employer responsible for damages before the hypothetical date on which an arbitrator would have rendered its decision if the union had not violated its duty, and to hold the union responsible for damages thereafter. *Bowen v. United States Postal Service,* 459 U.S. 212, 103 S.Ct. 588, 74 L.Ed.2d 402 (1983).

Practices among the states and in the federal sector with respect to procedures and remedies vary. Following are some examples of the variation:

(a) Some states follow the federal model of concurrent agency/court jurisdiction. See, e.g., *Farber v. City of Paterson,* 440 F.3d 131 (3d Cir. 2006) (interpreting New Jersey law); *Labbe v. Hartford Pension Commission*, 239 Conn. 168, 682 A.2d 490 (1996); *Winslow v. State*, 2 Haw.App. 50, 625 P.2d 1046 (1981); *Demings v. Ecorse,* 423 Mich. 49, 377 N.W.2d 275 (1985).

(b) In some states and in the federal government, agency remedies are exclusive. In Maine, for example, the Supreme Court has interpreted the statutes of that state to give the Labor Relations Board exclusive jurisdiction over DFR claims, but at the same time to allow the Board to grant relief against the employer as well as the union. *Brown v. Maine State Employees Association*, 690 A.2d 956 (Me.1997). See also *Anderson v. California Faculty Association,* 25 Cal.App.4th 207, 31 Cal.Rptr.2d 406 (1994); *Board of Trustees v. Myers*, 652 A.2d 642 (D.C.App. 1995); *Browning v. Brody*, 796 So.2d 1191 (Fla.App. 2001). The United States Supreme Court has reached a similar result under the Federal Service Labor Management Relations Statute, distinguishing *Vaca* on the ground that the CSRA, unlike the NLRA, contains express provisions imposing a duty of fair representation on unions and declaring that violation of the duty is an unfair labor practice. *Karahalios v. National Federation of Federal Employees*, 489 U.S. 527, 109 S.Ct. 1282, 103 L.Ed.2d 539 (1989).

(c) In some states, the agency has been held to lack jurisdiction over DFR claims, so that the remedy in court is exclusive. See, e.g., *Ziccardi v. Commonwealth of Pennsylvania*, 500 Pa. 326, 456 A.2d 979 (1982) (holding, in addition, that in such a proceeding relief is available only against the union).

(d) In Iowa, the Supreme Court has interpreted an ambiguously worded statute to mean that the state PERB has exclusive jurisdiction over DFR claims against a union, but that a district court still retains jurisdiction over claims breach of collective bargaining agreements. *O'Hara v. State of Iowa,* 642 N.W.2d 303 (Iowa 2002). See also *Fratus v. Marion Community Schools Board of Trustees*, 749 N.E.2d 40 (Ind. 2001).

These variations are dependent upon the statutory provisions and their interpretation. As a matter of policy, what procedure is preferable?

5. In the private sector, the Supreme Court, relying on the remedial nature of federal labor policy and the need to avoid depleting the resources of unions that are needed to represent employees, has ruled that punitive damages are unavailable in duty of fair representation actions. *International Brotherhood of Electrical Workers v. Foust,* 442 U.S. 42, 99 S.Ct. 2121, 60 L.Ed.2d 698 (1979). Should public sector laws follow the private sector rule? In *Akins v. United Steel Workers of America, Local 187*, No. 31,637, 2010 WL 2606307 (N.M. June 22, 2010), the court declined to follow the federal precedent, ruling that under New Mexico law, the purpose of the duty of fair representation was not solely to effectuate the collective bargaining statute. It was also a common law action to enforce the fiduciary duties of unions toward those employees they represent. The court concluded that given the unions' substantial discretion in representation and the difficulty of proving actual damages in duty of fair representation actions, punitive damages were necessary to both punish and deter misconduct. As a matter of policy, which is the preferable approach? Could the New Mexico court have been influence by the facts? The case involved a claim by an African–American employee that he sought union assistance to remedy race-based harassment by Latino employees and supervisors and was refused because of his race. As a result, he took a demotion and ultimately quit his job to avoid the harassment.

6. In *Hines v. Anchor Motor Freight*, 424 U.S. 554, 96 S.Ct. 1048, 47 L.Ed.2d 231 (1976), the United States Supreme Court held that the normal rule of arbitral finality must give way when an employee is able to show that the arbitration process was tainted by the union's violation of its duty of fair representation. The employees in *Hines* had been discharged for seeking "reimbursement for motel expenses in excess of the actual charges sustained by them." Their union carried their grievance to arbitration, and the joint labor-management arbitration committee ruled in the employer's favor. When evidence later surfaced indicating that the motel clerk was in fact the culprit, the employees sued their union and their employer, alleging that the union

had violated its duty of fair representation by acting "arbitrarily and in bad faith." The Supreme Court concluded that the employees could proceed in their hybrid suit for damages if they could show that the union breached its duty, and that the breach tainted the arbitration decision. In the following case, the Supreme Court of Alaska considered application of the *Hines* principle:

ANCHORAGE POLICE DEPARTMENT EMPLOYEES ASSOCIATION v. FEICHTINGER

Alaska Supreme Court, 1999.
994 P.2d 376.

ESTAUGH, J.

[The collective bargaining agreement between the Police Association and the Municipality of Anchorage authorized an employee to proceed to arbitration without union representation if the union refused to accept the grievance. Feichtinger, fired from his job with the police department for alleged criminal activity, filed a grievance which the union elected not to pursue. The union adhered to its position even after Feichtinger was acquitted of all criminal charges. Arbitration commenced, but Feichtinger asked for a postponement until he was able to bring legal action against the union to obtain resources to hire an attorney. When the arbitrator declined, Feichtinger walked out, and the arbitration proceeded without him. After the hearing Feichtinger submitted a pro se brief to the arbitrator, who proceeded to uphold the discharge. Feichtinger then brought action in state court against the Municipality of Anchorage, the State of Alaska, various officials, the arbitrator, and the union. Defendants other than the union were subsequently dismissed. The union filed motions for summary judgment arguing (a) that the arbitrator's decision finding just cause for the discharge precluded further litigation of that issue, and (b) that on the record presented the union did not breach its duty of fair representation. The trial court denied both motions, and the union appealed. The Alaska Supreme Court affirmed.]

III. *Discussion*

* * *

B. *When Can an Arbitration Decision Be Deprived of Its Preclusive Effect?*

* * * [T]he federal courts have created an exception to the general rule of finality, allowing relitigation of [arbitration] decisions when the employee proves: (1) that the discharge was erroneous; and (2) that the union's breach of its duty of fair representation seriously undermined the arbitral process. If the employee satisfies these two requirements, the employee is entitled to an appropriate remedy against the employer and the union. * * * We choose to look to federal authorities because we conclude that they have appropriately resolved the conflict inherent here. * * * [T]oday's case deals not with a claim that a union was merely

negligent in representing the employee, but that a union altogether failed to represent him.

In applying this rule, we recognize at the outset that its two requirements may overlap at times. Sometimes, but not always, a union's breach may so seriously undermine the integrity of the arbitration process that an erroneous decision is made. Moreover, employees are not entitled to relitigate their terminations merely because they offer newly discovered exculpatory evidence. An erroneous decision is not necessarily proof that the union breached its duty or that the breach seriously undermined the arbitral process.

The union argues that Feichtinger cannot show that the arbitration decision was erroneous because he dismissed his case against his employer. Therefore, the union contends that it is entitled to summary judgment as a matter of law. We disagree. The federal courts do not require that the employer be joined in a lawsuit against a union for a breach of the duty of fair representation. "The employee may, if he chooses, sue one defendant and not the other; but the case he must prove is the same whether he sues one, the other or both." If Feichtinger successfully proves his allegations against the union, the absence of his employer from his suit will only affect his ability to recover damages flowing from his alleged wrongful discharge. The union is not entitled to summary judgment as a matter of law on this basis.

C. *Assuming the Union Breached Its Duty of Fair Representation, a Genuine Issue of Material Fact Exists Regarding Whether the Breach Seriously Undermined the Integrity of the Arbitration.*

The union also argues that it deserves summary judgment because Feichtinger "failed to make any showing that the breach seriously undermined the arbitral process, even assuming the Union breached its duty of fair representation." Feichtinger disputes the union's argument. Before addressing the merits of this issue, we note that we are following the lead of the federal courts by permitting resolution of this issue on summary judgment. To withstand a union's motion for summary judgment on the question of whether a union's breach seriously undermined the integrity of the arbitral process, an employee must present some evidence of the nature of the breach and how the arbitration outcome might have been different absent the breach. *Hines* provides a good example of a successful claim. The employees, who were accused of overstating the expenses they incurred at a motel, insisted that they were innocent and that their union did not investigate their case thoroughly. The employees alleged that, with minimal investigation, the union would have uncovered evidence suggesting that the motel clerk was at fault; if the arbitrator had considered that evidence, the arbitration result might well have been different.

In this case, the union argues that its failure to represent Feichtinger did not affect the outcome of the arbitration because the CBA permitted him to arbitrate alone or with his own attorney. We disagree. First, the union's argument suggests that if a CBA allows employees to go to arbitration without union representation, a union's decision not to arbitrate could never undermine the arbitral process seriously enough to sustain a hybrid suit. We decline to hold that the employee's contractual right to grieve without union assistance necessarily establishes, as a matter of law, that the union's breach did not undermine the arbitral process.

Second, to establish that the arbitral process was seriously undermined, Feichtinger does not rely only on the fact that it was difficult to arbitrate alone. He also argues that in this case the lack of union representation was fatal. His case involved special facts—e.g., publicity, resource imbalance, and access to information—that made assistance of counsel and the union crucial to preserving the integrity of the process.

Feichtinger alleges that he faced "political and personal animosity" during the arbitration process. In an affidavit supporting his opposition to summary judgment, he suggested that he stood at an immediate disadvantage because his criminal case had been widely publicized and because rumors about him were rampant. Feichtinger stated that he was financially unable to retain counsel to give him substantive assistance in the arbitration. He also claimed that his lack of legal training left him at a severe disadvantage during arbitration, because he was unfamiliar with the case law cited by the municipality. Finally, he affied that without counsel or union assistance he was unable to produce the evidence necessary to counter the municipality's case. Given the negative publicity surrounding his case, union representation might have been critical to lend credibility to the substance of his grievance. Although Feichtinger filed a pro se brief with the arbitrator, it is questionable whether he was able to present his position fully without actually participating in the hearing. He apparently thought that the hearing would "extend for another week, and he had wanted to respond to the Municipality's case during that second hearing week." Viewing the evidence in Feichtinger's favor and giving him the benefit of permissible inferences, he has at least raised a factual dispute about whether his lack of counsel, resources, time, and legal expertise kept him from presenting his case and undermined the arbitral process.

For these reasons, we conclude that there is a genuine issue of material fact regarding whether any breach of the union's duty of fair representation seriously undermined the arbitral process. Summary judgment on this issue was not appropriate.

D. How Are Damages Against the Union to Be Measured?

Assuming that Feichtinger makes the requisite showing on remand so as to deprive the arbitration decision of its preclusive effect, he will be entitled to seek damages. We briefly address this issue given the possibility that it will become ripe on remand, and given the union's implicit argument that the dismissal or settlement of Feichtinger's claims against his employer prevents him from showing what damages the union may owe.

In employee hybrid suits for wrongful discharge and breach of a union's duty of fair representation, the federal courts apportion damages between the employer and union according to the damages caused by each defendant. Federal law does not control this case. But the union urges us to look to the federal standard of assessing damages. Feichtinger, on the other hand, argues that we should follow the attorney malpractice model for damages. Under this standard, as Feichtinger describes it, a union that breaches its duty of fair representation becomes liable for all damages the employee suffers, including those flowing from the employee's wrongful discharge.

We reject the attorney malpractice model of damage assessment for unfair representation cases and hold that in hybrid suits we will follow the federal model of apportioning damages as set out in *Vaca v. Sipes* and subsequent federal cases. In *Vaca*, the Supreme Court squarely rejected the imposition of joint and several liability upon a union for its breach of its duty of fair representation. Rather, it required courts to apportion damages between an employer and union based on fault. The Supreme Court explained that an award against a union that includes damages attributable only to the employer would impose too great a hardship on the union, even if the union had a right of indemnification against the employer. Although only the employer is responsible for back-pay following a wrongful discharge, subsequent federal decisions have made it clear that the union is responsible for any increases in damages, including lost wages, caused by the union's breach.

The federal courts have not agreed upon a precise method of apportionment. Two models currently exist. One bases apportionment on the hypothetical date upon which the employee would have been reinstated had the union fulfilled its duty of fair representation. The employer is liable for losses incurred before that date; the union is liable for losses incurred after that date. The other model apportions damages on a percentage basis, similar to comparative fault. We need not decide now which of the two federal models Alaska should follow. Because the superior court has not yet had an opportunity to consider whether one is particularly appropriate to these facts and because the parties' briefs do not squarely address this question, we do not address this issue and await an appeal directly presenting it to us.

E. Even If the Arbitration Award Has Preclusive Effect, Feichtinger May Recover Damages from the Union.

The union contends that if a discharge is for just cause or if the merits of the discharge cannot be reexamined, a union cannot be liable for breach of the duty of fair representation because the employee has not been injured. The union correctly notes that some case law supports this position.[45] But contrary authority also exists; it indicates that an employee

45. See, e.g., *DiPinto v. Sperling*, 9 F.3d 2 (1st Cir.1993); *Wood v. International Broth. Of Teamsters, Local 406*, 807 F.2d 493 (6th Cir.1986); *Jordan v. Washington Metro. Area Transit Auth.*, 548 A.2d 792 (D.C.App.1988).

may recover some damages (usually attorney's fees) from the union even absent a wrongful discharge.[46] An example of this latter line of authority is *Del Casal v. Eastern Airlines, Inc.* [634 F.2d 295 (5th Cir.1981)]. A pilot there sought to set aside the arbitration decision upholding his discharge by suing his employer for wrongful discharge and the pilots' union for breach of the duty of fair representation. He claimed that the union refused to represent him because he was not a union member. Although the Fifth Circuit found no justification for setting aside the arbitration decision in favor of the employer, it held that the union breached its duty of fair representation by discriminatorily refusing to represent the pilot in arbitration. It stated that "[w]hile [the union] has the authority to decide under what conditions an attorney will be supplied to a grievant, the fact that the grievant is not a member of the union can play no part in that decision." The Fifth Circuit further reasoned that even if the arbitration award was untainted by the breach (because the pilot hired his own counsel) the pilot still "suffered loss in the form of fees to be paid to his privately retained attorney." It therefore affirmed the jury's award of $35,000 in damages (the pilot's attorney's fees) for the union's breach, despite the fact that the arbitration decision was not relitigated or set aside. Additional support for this view is found in Justice Stevens's concurring opinion in *United Parcel Service, Inc. v. Mitchell* [451 U.S. 56, 101 S.Ct. 1559, 67 L.Ed.2d 732 (1981)], where he explained that the two claims are "closely related" but "conceptually distinct":

> The fact that the underlying discharge may not have violated the collective-bargaining agreement does not necessarily absolve the union of liability for its breach, although it may limit the size of the employee's recovery against the union. Thus, while a court considering an employee's claim against a union will evaluate the validity of the employer's underlying conduct, that evaluation is not central to the resolution of the duty-of-fair-representation claim.

[451 U.S. at 73, n.4, 101 S.Ct. at 1569, n.4, 67 L.Ed.2d at 747, n.4.]

We choose to follow those federal courts that reason that, even if the arbitration decision upholding an employee's discharge has preclusive effect, it does not necessarily bar the employee's suit against the union. A union is liable to the employee for damages flowing from its breach of the duty of fair representation. In most such cases, the employee's damages will be limited to attorney's fees and costs expended in the arbitration process. Applying this rule here may result in de minimus damages because Feichtinger did not retain an attorney to represent him in the

46. See, e.g., *Czosek v. O'Mara*, 397 U.S. 25, 90 S.Ct. 770, 25 L.Ed.2d 21 (implying availability of damages independent of merits of employee's wrongful discharge claim); *Dutrisac v. Caterpillar Tractor Co.*, 749 F.2d 1270 (9th Cir.1983) (affirming damage award of attorney fees against union for breach of duty of fair representation, despite finding no wrongful discharge, because union's failure to represent employee fairly in arbitration forced him to hire lawyer); *Self v. Drivers, Chauffeurs, Warehousemen & Helpers Local Union No. 61*, 620 F.2d 439 (4th Cir.1980) (finding no wrongful discharge but holding union liable for expenses incurred by employees as result of union's failure to properly press grievance against employer).

arbitration. Nonetheless, Feichtinger should have an opportunity to seek recoverable damages.

The denial of the union's summary judgment motion is affirmed. We remand for further proceedings consistent with this opinion.

[The dissenting opinion of MATTHEWS, C.J. is omitted.]

NOTES

1. Recall from *Casey v. Fairbanks,* 670 P.2d 1133 (Alaska 1983), that Alaska, contrary to federal law, allows an employee to sue for breach of contract if the union refuses to take his case to arbitration, even though the union's refusal was not a violation of its DFR. As a result of the principal case, the rule seems to be that if the collective bargaining agreement allows the employee to proceed to arbitration on his own, and the employee does so and loses, the employee must show violation of the DFR in order to get into court against the employer. What do you think the likely effect of this decision will be upon the behavior of the parties? Compare the following case from New Hampshire. In *Dillman v. Town of Hooksett,* 153 N.H. 344, 898 A.2d 505 (2006), the New Hampshire Supreme Court considered whether a union's assignment of the right to challenge an arbitration award to an affected employee was valid, a question certified to the court by the federal district court. The union had arbitrated the employee's discharge case and lost. The employee then sued to have the award vacated, arguing that the union had assigned to him the right to challenge the award in court in exchange for his agreement not to sue the union for breach of the duty of fair representation. The court held that the assignment was invalid; only a party could challenge an arbitration award in the absence of a claim of breach of the duty of fair representation. Why would a court limit the employee's right to challenge an award upholding his termination? What is the effect of such a decision? Should such assignments be permissible as a matter of policy? See Mitchell H. Rubinstein, Assignment of Labor Arbitration, 81 *St. John's Law Review* 41 (2007).

2. Consider the case of *Belanger v. Matteson, supra.* Did Belanger suffer any damages as a result of the union's breach of the duty of fair representation? To what is he entitled as a remedy?

3. When is a union's conduct "arbitrary", as distinguished from discriminatory or in bad faith? The Supreme Court considered this question in the private sector case of *Air Line Pilots Association v. O'Neill,* 499 U.S. 65, 111 S.Ct. 1127, 113 L.Ed.2d 51 (1991). The case involved a strike settlement by the Air Line Pilots Association which gave striking Continental Airlines employees arguably less protection than they would have if there had been no settlement at all. In a suit by a group of former pilots, the Court found no violation of the Union's duty of fair representation. It held that a union's actions are "arbitrary only if, in light of the factual and legal landscape at the time of [its] actions, the union's behavior is so far outside a 'wide range of reasonableness,' *Ford Motor Co. v. Huffman,* 345 U.S. 330, 338, 73 S.Ct. 681, 97 L.Ed. 1048 (1953) as to be irrational." Note the similarity between the Court's DFR standard and the standard applicable under the Fourteenth

Amendment's Equal Protection Clause to classifications which do not implicate a suspect class or fundamental interests.

Consider whether the union's conduct in the following cases was arbitrary.

a. Luis Diaz, a long-time employee of New York State's Department of Mental Hygiene, was suspended and then fired by the State of New York (State) for allegedly abusing a patient at the Pilgrim Psychiatric Center. He was a member of the negotiating unit represented by a Union, and he sought the Union's assistance in filing a grievance. The Union's contract with the State provided for mutually exclusive alternative procedures. Ordinary grievances were to be filed with the State, and could go through several steps culminating in arbitration, but where an employee was suspended there was an option of seeking immediate arbitration. To invoke this procedure, the demand for arbitration had to be filed with the American Arbitration Association (AAA) rather than with the State. Diaz, after consultation with Bertini, the Union grievance representative, decided on immediate arbitration. However, Bertini filed the papers with the State instead of with the AAA. Bertini was advised by the State's designee for agency level hearings that he should check on the matter because no arbitration had been set up. Bertini, new to the job and without relevant training, made some inquiries as to whether he followed the correct procedure, but a local Union field representative was not sufficiently knowledgeable to correct his mistake and the Union's administrator of arbitrations was on vacation. Bertini did not discover his mistake until the time for filing with the AAA had passed. When he did file, the State objected the filing was not timely, and the arbitrator dismissed the grievance. Has the Union breached its DFR? What remedy? See *Civil Service Employees Association v. PERB*, 132 A.D.2d 430, 522 N.Y.S.2d 709 (1987).

b. A social worker failed to refer a call reporting suspected child abuse for investigation and two weeks later the child was admitted to the hospital with injuries consistent with shaken baby syndrome. A grievance was filed challenging the employee's termination. The union believed that the employer had denied a grievance at the third step but in fact, the employer had made an oral response but no written response as required by the contract. Two years after the third step grievance hearing the union discovered that the employer had never responded to the grievance as required. When prompted, the employer formally denied the grievance and the union decided not to arbitrate, so informing the employee. Did the union breach its duty of fair representation by either the two year delay in acting or the decision not to arbitrate? See *State ex rel. Hall v. State Employment Relations Board,* 122 Ohio St.3d 528, 912 N.E.2d 1120 (2009).

c. A terminated employee was incorrectly advised by the union that he could make a choice between a civil service claim and a contractual grievance later in the process, although a letter the employer sent to the employee advised of a ten day deadline for a civil service appeal. The union representative disclaimed expertise in civil service matters and advised the employee to retain an attorney, but the union representative never investigated the civil service procedures. The union pursued the employee's grievance up to arbitration, but did not file for arbitration when the employee indicated that he preferred to use the civil service appeals process. In fact, the employee had already missed the deadline for a civil service appeal and thus was left without any recourse. Did the union breach its duty of fair representation? Of what importance is the fact that the employee, but not the union, received the letter containing the filing deadline? That the union is not the employee's exclusive representative on civil service matters and advised the employee to retain counsel? See *United Steelworkers of America v. Commonwealth Employment Relations Board*, 74 Mass.App.Ct. 656, 909 N.E.2d 1177 (2009).

D. THE UNION'S INTERNAL GOVERNANCE

Workers in the bargaining unit who are members of the union have the right to participate in union governance, and thereby influence union policy. The Labor Management Reporting and Disclosure Act of 1959, 29 U.S.C. §§ 401–453, prescribes minimum standards for assuring democratic procedures within unions, as well as (in Title I) a "Bill of Rights" for union members. Title I provides, among other things, for equal rights of participation, for freedom of speech and assembly, and for due process in disciplinary proceedings. In addition, the statute imposes significant financial reporting obligations. While the Act does not apply to a union which consists solely of government employees, the protections of the statute were extended to union members in the federal government sector by the Civil Service Reform Act. 5 U.S.C. § 7120. Additionally, the LMRDA will apply to a union that represents or is seeking to represent employees of non-governmental employers in interstate commerce. 29 U.S.C. §§ 402(i), (j). The law also applies to national unions that have local affiliates that represent private sector employees. *Id.* In 2003, the Department of Labor changed its interpretation of the definition to include under the statute state level intermediate bodies composed solely of governmental employees if the national union with which they were affiliated had any private sector affiliates. As a result, these intermediate bodies were subject to extensive financial reporting obligations under the statute. Labor unions immediately filed suit challenging the interpretation and after years of litigation, in 2010 the Department proposed to withdraw the interpretation and revert to the prior interpretation which had excluded these bodies for 40 years. Litigation was stayed pending final action on the proposal. See 75 Fed. Reg. 5456 (Feb. 2, 2010).

In addition, a union's constitution and bylaws are treated by courts as establishing contractual obligations on both the union and its members, and the provisions may be enforced by appropriate proceedings. See *Labor Union Law and Regulation* (William W. Osborne, Jr., Ed.-in-Chief, 2003); Joseph R. Grodin, *Union Government and the Law* (CLA Institute of Industrial Relations 1961); Martin H. Malin, *Individual Rights within the Union* (BNA 1988).

INDEX

References are to Pages

References are to Pages

References are to Pages

References are to Pages

References are to Pages

References are to Pages

References are to Pages

References are to Pages

References are to Pages

References are to Pages

References are to Pages

References are to Pages

References are to Pages

References are to Pages

References are to Pages

References are to Pages

References are to Pages

References are to Pages

†